Presidential Also-Rans and Running Mates,
1788 through 1996, *2d ed.*

Presidential Also-Rans and Running Mates, 1788 through 1996

SECOND EDITION

compiled by LESLIE H. SOUTHWICK

McFarland & Company, Inc., Publishers

Jefferson, North Carolina, and London

Front cover: Walter Mondale and Geraldine Ferraro, 1984.

Back cover (from top): Barry Goldwater (front) and William E. Miller, 1964; Gerald Ford (left) and Robert Dole, 1976.

British Library Cataloguing-in-Publication data are available

Library of Congress Cataloguing-in-Publication Data

Southwick, Leslie H., 1950–
    Presidential also-rans and running mates, 1788 through 1996 /
compiled by Leslie H. Southwick. — 2nd ed.
      p.   cm.
    Includes bibliographical references and index.
    ISBN 0-7864-0310-1 (case binding : 50# alkaline paper) ∞
    1. Presidents — United States — Election — History.
    2. Presidential candidates — United States — Biography.
    3. Vice-Presidential candidates — United States — Biography.
    4. Vice-Presidents — United States — Election — History.
    5. United States — Politics and government.   I. Title.
E175.1.S695   1998
324.973 — dc21   97-34099
                                              CIP

Manufactured in the United States of America

McFarland & Company, Inc., Publishers
  Box 611, Jefferson, North Carolina 28640

for Ruth Tarpley Southwick Flanagan

Acknowledgments to the First Edition

There is a uniquely delightful time for an author, when years of labor have been concluded, and the once random thoughts and plans have finally evolved into a completed, corrected, indexed and mailed-to-the-publisher set of proofs. Now that the work is (almost) done, a writer reflects on all the hours and all the people who made the conclusion possible. Thanks are never sufficient. A free copy of the completed book is an awkwardly small token of the gratitude due. Money would probably be appreciated, but authors generally desire to shape their gratitude in loftier forms of expression. Thus, a public acknowledgment is made to those who are owed so much. I am eager to do the same.

The staff of the Jackson Metropolitan Library, Jackson, Mississippi, whose inter-library loan department was the *sine qua non* of the book, must receive my especial gratitude. This book simply would not exist if not for the fact you borrowed, at times begged, but I suppose never stole books, articles and microfilm from distant libraries for my use. First Allan Hauth, then Margaret Dixon, and most recently Paul Smith have been in charge of inter-library loan, and have been unfailingly generous and understanding. If this fairly frequent changing of the guard in the department is a result of my many impositions, then accept my apologies as well as my appreciation. I would like to acknowledge also the assistance in the reference department rendered by Pat Beard, Rosemary Landon and Kathy Smith.

Free room and board was eagerly accepted during two trips to Washington to use the awe-inspiring collection of the Library of Congress. Two couples, John and Julie Hamre and James Rogers and Bonnie Harkness, were gracious hosts and, despite my panhandling, remain my good friends.

Generously granting library privileges at Jackson State University was Dr. Estus Smith. Bernice Bell and Dr. Lelia Rhodes helped make use of those privileges much more productive than otherwise would have been possible.

To the staffs of so many other helpful libraries across the country with whom I corresponded, I also want to extend my thanks. I have tried to give credit by name, in the bibliographies following each sketch, to those libraries that helped me in the pursuit of information on a particular individual. Undoubtedly I have omitted some important and generous people who searched and corresponded and searched again. My appreciation is for all of you, named or not. Many of the candidates themselves or some of their relatives and descendants have provided much useful information. Previous biographers at times searched their files for additional information. The grandson, Christopher Field, of one of those biographies also lent a valuable hand. I appreciate each of your efforts, and have tried to acknowledge you by name in the appropriate bibliography.

James M. Flanagan, my stepfather, literary adviser, and good friend, with a deftness indicative of his years as an English professor, pointed out problems both in style and content and made many helpful suggestions. Larry M. Southwick, a brother and as such a life-long personal critic, also pored over part of the manuscript and gave useful, candid comments. My mother, Ruth Flanagan, was less negative but equally supportive. You all helped, and I really do appreciate your efforts.

As might be expected, a little time was devoted to the typing of this manuscript. What interest some of the typists may have started with in political history was soon drained by the tedium, but thankfully they continued to help. Pam Anderson, Joey Brough, Melissa Prewitt and Betty Wingard graciously volunteered at the peak of the typing and did an awesome amount of work. Libby Christie, Lynda McLendon and Suzanne Quidor chipped in as well. Arriving late on the project, but contributing willingly, was Betty Laseter. You were all tremendous.

Saved for last, but not because she was least, is Wyeth Luter. This is almost as much her book as it is mine. She has generously handled all facets of this project, from correspondence to libraries, to typing first and second drafts of manuscript, to proofreading, and everything in between. It was a joy to work with you on this. I shall always be grateful.

This book is dedicated to my wife and son, not for the kind of help rendered by those just now gratefully acknowledged, but because of their moral support, their patience, and their love — all of which may have fluctuated during various crises in the writing of this book. In the three years this project has taken, Philip has grown from a baby to a little boy. I regret missing some (but not all) of the opportunities for sharing in the excitement of that growth. Sharon has had extra responsibilities to shoulder because the door to the study has so often been closed, and when it opened it was usually so she could compile the index. You attitude made writing this book possible. Arriving just in time to witness the publication is little Catherine. This book is for you too.

LESLIE SOUTHWICK
Spring 1984

Acknowledgments to the Second Edition

The research for this second edition has spread over all the years from the date of the first. During that time many have helped. As was true for the first edition, my debt to my wife Sharon and our daughter Cathy is immense. You both helped in indispensable ways. Our son Philip, who in 1996 thought he was to focus on his first year architecture studies at the University of Virginia, uncomplainingly also found many materials at Virginia's impressive library and performed a laborious bibliographical update.

Of delightfully willing aid in using resources not available to me were Linda and Jim Johnson. Lauren Southwick made the acquaintance of the significant collection of Socialist Party materials at the Wisconsin State Archives. Providing friendly research assistance on Lloyd Bentsen were the staffs of the Edinburg, McAllen, and Mission, Texas, public libraries. That assistance was provided in 1989 to the best research partners I have had in this project, my mother and stepfather, Ruth and Jim Flanagan. In the years since they so ably provided the materials for me to use, Mr. Jim has himself become a memory, one worth recording.

John and Julie Hamre again displayed warm hospitality during a Washington research trip.

The Reverend R. Lester Mondale and his wife Maria provided family information on their famous relative. Jack Kemp and Lloyd Bentsen were similarly generous regarding information. Dr. Charles King, head of the Eugene Debs Foundation, greatly simplified research on Debs.

The effort to add a new layer of candidates, those whose campaigns were even less successful than those of the first edition, has led to many pleas to libraries around the country. The presenter of the petitions was Charlie Brenner, the interlibrary loan maven of the Eudora Welty Library in Jackson, Mississippi. My gratitude for his exceptionally generous spirit through it all is boundless. Many others at the library helped in numerous ways, including Michelle Hudson, Roy Wilkinson, Gordon Saucier, Eleanor McQuirter, and Claudia Brooks.

Gathering pictures was perhaps the most complicated chore of this edition. Greatly and grandly reducing the time and energy necessary were David and Janice Frent, whose fabulous collection of political memorabilia was made available for this project. The immediately appealing features of this work are more the result of their contribution than that of anyone else.

Many helped with individual pictures. The names are too numerous to mention here (a cold, but accurate short-hand for ignoring exceptionally generous people). Please know that I realize your tremendous aid. I must mention those who rescued me as to several undiscovered pictures when a publication deadline loomed. Wiley Carter and Fred Pagan on United States Senator Thad Cochran's staff, and Molly Dye on Paul Coverdell's, made the impossible possible.

The last of the 116 pictures acquired for the book is the cover of a 1948 song sheet that was principally the work of a talented but elusive woman, who died without family or obituary. My thanks to her takes the form of this memorial.

Roslyn Wells Addison, born Madeleine Stagg on October 4, 1900, was the daughter of Sylvester E. and Emmy Rudolph Stagg of New York City. She married William Malborough Addison on April 27, 1935, but they soon divorced and had no children. She began in vaudeville in 1921, using the stage name Madeleine Randolph; she had an act with another singer, then a series of solo acts as a singer, pianist, and ukulele player. By 1930 she took and then kept the name Roslyn Wells. Wells toured the United States and Europe and was on the same bill with such performers as Eddie Foy and the Little Foys, and Will Rogers; she also performed with the Ziegfeld Follies. Living in Manhattan most of her life, she performed at hotels and theaters, and for church, civic groups, and small gatherings. Wells was an ardent Republican who wrote at least eight songs that she copyrighted, including campaign songs for Wendell Willkie and Tom Dewey. Wells died March 29, 1993 [Information provided by Mrs. Ralph Wattley; also *Richmond News Leader*, May 4, 1935, p. 4].

Thanks are owed to many who helped me find and use the Wells song sheet, especially Lisa Graddy, Harriet Culver, and Joyce S. Shankman, but also Lloyd Green, Gertrude Bess Parker, Thomas E. Dewey, Jr., Karl Kabelac, families of William G. Adams and Paxton Blair, Linda Beck, Donald Orians, Margaret Vollmer, Randy the bellman, Manolo Blahnik Boutique, Fanny and Ariel Grunberg, Sonia, Lynn Kanzer, Marianne Wattley, and Larry Bird. It was quite a search.

OCTOBER 1997
Jackson, Mississippi

Table of Contents

No biography included, as this candidate served at some other time as president or vice president. Italics indicate a minor candidate who receives a more limited biographical sketch.

Introduction
to the Second Edition

Looking back over the personal stories of America's presidential candidates, one is struck by the irony of chance that pushed some nominees into high office and swept others off to remote corners of our national archives. What caliber of presidents might the country have had if the votes had gone another way? Among those even more easily forgotten nominees, those for the office of vice president, what great talents remained unused? Is it possible to distinguish who were the scoundrels, the party hacks, the time-servers or other unworthies, and who had the mark of greatness?

This book provides a framework for answering these questions by giving biographical sketches of each person nominated for president or vice president who failed to achieve that goal. The major party candidates and significant third party candidates are treated in substantial biographical articles. The career journeys these 95 people took to reach the penultimate level in American politics, a national nomination, are described. The elections themselves are examined briefly, and information is provided as to what happened to the losers thereafter.

Another group of 41 candidates who did not get the level of vote of the first group, but who still were relatively meaningful participants in the elections, are covered by shorter biographical sketches. The criteria that divide these 41 from the first group of 95, and from a lower, even more futile group of 100's who are not discussed at all, will be detailed later.

Some of the losers here achieved fame in other roles. It is not hard to imagine Adlai Stevenson, Charles Evans Hughes, or Henry Clay performing brilliantly as presidents, since their actual contributions in public life were so significant. Equally expected would be dismal performances from Horace Greeley, George McClellan, or William Jennings Bryan. Other far less renowned leaders of the past are also reviewed. Once the dust on public portraits of forgotten leaders is wiped away, surprisingly revealed are some exceptional prospects for success. William Lowndes, Alton Parker, or Jim Cox among the presidential candidates and Thomas Pinckney and Albert Gallatin, among the defeated running mates, all had the makings of outstanding chief executives.

This book is not just a compilation of data about public events, of great moments in the lives of statesmen. It is meant to reveal, in the brevity to which a book of this scope is forced, a human side to the candidates. Cold-hearted banker William English, whose supposed fondness for foreclosing on mortgaged homes was gleefully trumpeted by his opponents, is sketched here. Warm, selfless Theodore Frelinghuysen, "the Christian statesman" as he was called, is shown in a much more favorable light.

Above all, this book provides information. For the 95 major candidates, many significant details are capsulized before the narrative biography, thereby permitting the sketch itself to skim over or ignore entirely many facts that are needed for a complete picture. Family data are included. Who were the candidate's parents, his brothers and sisters, his wife and children, and did they make significant contributions of their own? Some of the information may be inconsequential, but a more rounded view of the person is thereby made possible.

There are two new categories of capsule information since the book's first edition. Though not as often as for successful nominees, even also-rans and an occasional running mate have historic sites from their life that can be visited. Henry Clay's Ashland home in Lexington, Kentucky, is one. Further, the loser's state or some other entity may have honored the politicians with a memorial — eight of them have statues in the national Capitol as part of the exhibit in Statuary Hall. Statues elsewhere, such as Stephen Douglas's on the Illinois capitol lawn, or Tom Watson's at the Georgia capitol, are mentioned so that the curious may go eye the loser, face to face as it were.

The other new category is for movies about the candidate or in which the loser has some role. American movies about national leaders, even other nation's leaders, are nothing new. *The Patriot* (1928), the last silent film made by Paramount, starred Emil Jannings as the mad or mighty strange Czar Paul I of Russia; Marlene Dietrich was Catherine the Great in *The Scarlet Empress* in 1934, the same year Elisabeth Bergner starred in *Catherine the Great* and five years before Bette Davis played the leading role of *Elisabeth the Queen*. American presidents were quickly made motion picture subjects: Walter Huston in D. W. Griffith's first "talkie," the 1930 *Abraham Lincoln*; Henry Fonda in the 1939 *Young Mr. Lincoln* and Raymond Massey in the 1940 *Abe Lincoln in Illinois*. Other Lincoln movies, and additional ones about George Washington, Thomas Jefferson, Andrew Johnson, Woodrow Wilson, FDR, Truman, JFK, LBJ and many other presidents have appeared. Surprisingly, so have some about the also-rans, but usually not about their campaigns. A fictional account about Wendell Willkie's 1940 campaign, called *State of the Union*, is one of the few. More typical are such movies as *The Devil and Daniel Webster*, based on a Stephen Vincent Benét fable about a farmer who sells his soul to the devil, but Webster defends him when the reckoning arrives. Two losing tickets had nominees who both were the subjects of movies. Ross Perot's rescue of some of his employees from Iran had been made into *On Wings of Eagles* (1986), while running mate Jim Stockdale's seven-year ordeal in a Vietnam P.O.W. camp was depicted in *In Love and War* (1987). The movie *Strategic Air Command* (1955) starred Jimmy Stewart, but in a leading role also had a cigar-chomping, tough-talking head of SAC who, except in name, was General Curtis LeMay. A movie about the other half of the 1968 American Independent Party ticket, *George Wallace*, was broadcast in 1997 for the TNT television network. It starred Gary Sinise as Wallace.

After each biography, an attempt is made to judge for each of the major nominees whether that person had indicated a capacity for serving as president. Since a vice president in principle is to be ready to step into the presidency at any moment, the losing running mates are also evaluated on the basis of likely presidential performance. These admittedly subjective evaluations are meant to be catalysts for contemplating the quality of over 200 years of defeated candidates. They are certainly not meant to be the final word.

Five categories are employed. Was a candidate superior, or almost; dismal, or nearly; or average presidential material? Admittedly, many would have risen above their mediocre past; some apparently good choices would have been disappointing in office. Among the successful nominees, Abraham Lincoln and Herbert Hoover are examples of good and bad surprises. The appraisal, though, is less of a forecast of performance than a categorization of prospects.

The "probable failure" are those who because of various shortcomings seem miscast for a high leadership role. The "unsatisfactory" are the weak but not dreadful candidates, and also those nominees whose careers simply failed to give sufficient evidence one way or the other regarding their capacity for presidential leadership. They therefore represented risks that their parties should not have thrust upon the voters. The "average" nominees are the solid but unspectacular choices. The "superior" are those truly exceptional ones who in other political roles demonstrated at least the possibility of greatness. The "above average" are simply that, better than average, not quite superior.

Each reader can judge the legitimacy of the ratings, which are summarized at the end of the book by listing each candidate on a chart. Various polls of historians rating the presidents are also included, so that a comparison of loser's potential with winner's practice can be made.

The presentation of each of these 95 life stories here is by necessity brief. Even so, it is hoped that the diversity of characters who every four years have played one of these two leading election roles will be revealed.

Arrangement of the Book

There are 55 chapters in this book, covering in detail the 53 quadrennial elections from 1788/89 through 1996, as well as summaries of the Confederate States of America's two elections in 1861 (in which there was no losing candidate, just a losing country) and the vice presidential confirmations by Congress in 1973 and 1974.

Each quadrennial election chapter contains a brief description of the election, showing the nominations made at each national convention and the election results, and then biographical sketches of the losing candidates for president or vice president. If a losing candidate in that election actually served as president or vice president at some other time, there is no biography.

Following each biographical sketch is an "Analysis of Qualifications" evaluating each losing candidate. Concluding each biographical section is a bibliography for that candidate.

Near the end of the book are appendices ranking the losing presidential and vice-presidential candidates on the basis of their adjudged qualifications and prospects for success, as well as four rankings (done in 1948, 1962, 1982, and 1995) of the presidents, for comparative purposes.

A general bibliography comes next (separate bibliographies for each candidate immediately follow the sketch of that person) and a comprehensive index concludes the book.

MAJOR CANDIDATES

Each nominee of a major political party since the first election in 1788-89 is included, even if the individual refused the nomination. Nominees withdrew from the race in the elections of 1812, 1824, 1836, 1844, 1860, 1924, and 1972.

National conventions did not become permanent for each major party until 1840, and thus for elections before that date more detailed rules for deciding which candidates merited consideration had to be devised. If there was not a single, national nominating meeting for a party, then all nominees of state legislatures and state-wide conventions are included. This nominating process was utilized in 1824, 1828, and 1836. A profusion of public meetings that nominated candidates also occurred in those years, but names that surfaced only at such local meetings do not qualify for also-ran or losing running-mate honors. There was a national congressional caucus in 1824, but it was so poorly attended or respected that the state-level nominations ended up being more significant. Both the Federalists and the Democratic-Republicans had either a party congressional caucus or a national convention from 1800 through 1812, and the Democratic-Republicans continued the practice until 1824.

When neither national nor state legislative or convention nominations occurred, the generally accepted nominees for the parties, as measured by popular and electoral college vote, are then included. In each situation in which no nominations were made—1788, 1792, 1796, and for the Federalists in 1816— the top vote getter in each party for both president and vice president had more than twice as many electoral votes as the next highest party candidate. That was deemed sufficient to exclude all other candidates. In 1840, the Democrats made no nomination for vice president at the convention that selected their presidential nominee, but since the incumbent Democratic vice president got more than four times as many electoral votes as the runner-up Democratic candidate, only he is considered a loser running mate for that year.

It was considered important to include

third party nominees when their electoral support indicated that a substantial number of Americans considered them viable candidates. A cut-off point for this is highly subjective, but the figure of 10 percent of the vote was finally settled upon. Only seven third-party tickets have ever attained that level of support, making it a rare achievement only reached by the most significant of them.

A decision had to be reached not only on which candidates to consider, but also which elections. Votes for president or vice president have been cast on three occasions other than regular quadrennial elections beginning in 1788/89. A large section of the country—11 states out of 33 then in the Union—went their own way in 1861 and selected a president and vice president of the Confederate States of America. No also-rans or losing running mates resulted from that election. Further, in 1973 and 1974, the resignation of first the vice president and then the president required that there be nominations submitted to Congress to fill these vacancies. In each case, Congress accepted the nominee and there were consequently no losing candidates to qualify for inclusion in this book. Even though no additional defeated nominees emerged after determining that these exceptional elections should be considered, the three elections themselves are summarized.

Finally, this is a book about losers. Defeated nominees who also served as president or vice president at some other time have no biographies here. One exception is made, and that is for the four men who served as vice president and then were nominated for, but failed to reach the presidency. Being able to compare them both to the winning presidential candidates as well as to the other losers was found to be a compelling reason for this exception.

MINOR CANDIDATES

In addition to the 95 major candidates, 41 others receive much shorter biographical sketches and are not ranked in the evaluations. If a candidate not otherwise included in the book received at least 2 percent of the popular vote or 5 percent of the Electoral College vote, he is described in a short biography. Sympathy was given to a ticket that struggled across the election day finish line with 1.954 percent of the vote. That pair's vote was close enough, not to win, but to qualify for the pages of this book. They were William Lemke and Thomas O'Brien, the 1936 Union Party nominees.

With so many candidates, one more hardly seemed to matter. A special effort award has been granted to the candidate who at least since the 1940s has represented perseverance in presidential politics. Harold Stassen, who actually was a major contender in 1948, appears at the end of the section on that election.

PORTRAITS

It has been a delight, if time-consuming and expensive, to pull together for the first time portraits of all the losing candidates. To the extent possible, what has been used is the campaign's own joint picture—a campaign poster, or even a button. This is the presidential ticket as they wanted to be seen and are seen again here. Surprisingly, perhaps, the first posters date from 1844. They were Currier & Ives prints, and that firm continued to depict the tickets for several decades.

Presidential Also-Rans and Running Mates, 1788 through 1996

Election of 1788-1789

NOMINATIONS

The necessary ninth state to ratify the new federal constitution did not do so until June, 1788, and thus it was after that before Congress could meet to schedule elections. Wrangling by Congress over the location of a new capital prevented prompt action on elections. George Washington was the consensus choice for president. The choice of a vice president was less unanimous, but John Adams was widely accepted. Alexander Hamilton wanted a less independent candidate, but eventually acquiesced in Adams' inevitable selection. No formal nominations were made, but mentioned in letters between political leaders prior to the election were such vice presidential possibilities as John Jay, George Clinton, Robert Harrison, and others.

GENERAL ELECTION

Many states debated at length on how presidential electors would be chosen. On September 13, 1788, Congress prescribed the timetable but not the method to follow in naming electors. On January 7, 1789, the states had to choose electors; they would meet on February 4, 1789, to vote for two men, each for president. On March 4, the votes would be counted by Congress, with the recipient of the highest total becoming president, and the runner-up vice president. In three states electors were chosen by popular vote. In five the choice was by the legislature, in some because there was too little time under the prescribed schedule to hold elections. In the three others that had by then ratified the constitution, one decided on a mixture of popular vote and legislative selection; another on strict popular vote but with a majority needed for election,

with the legislature then selecting if no majority existed; and the final one, New York, never getting any decision made and therefore casting no electoral votes.

Popular Vote
    None recorded
Electoral Vote
    George Washington 69
    John Adams 34
    John Jay 9
    Robert Harrison 6
    John Rutledge 6
    John Hancock 4
    Six others 10
Winners
    George Washington, 1st president
    John Adams, 1st vice president
Losers
    John Jay, Robert Harrison, John Rutledge, John Hancock

---

*1789 recipient of
electoral votes for vice president*

John Jay

Born December 12, 1745, in New York City; died May 17, 1829 in Bedford, New York. Married Sarah Van Brugh Livingston on April 28, 1774; they had seven children.

John Jay, if not clearly a giant in early American history, was at least a very big man. He was a lead negotiator of the peace treaty ending the American Revolution, governor of New York, and the first chief justice of the

CHIEF JUSTICE JOHN JAY
(Artist: Gregory Stapko after Gilbert Stuart; from the collection of the Supreme Court of the United States)

United States Supreme Court. Out of such stock were losing vice presidential contenders made in the first few national elections.

John's father was Peter Jay, a West Indian merchant and a wealthy and influential member of the British colony of New York; his mother was Hannah McVickar. A year after John's birth the family moved to a farm at Rye, New York. John enrolled at King's College (later Columbia University) at age 14. The future chief justice began his law practice in 1768 with a prominent New York attorney, Benjamin Kissam. Six years later he married the daughter of a future governor of New Jer-

sey, William Livingston. The Livingstons and Jays were among the most influential early American families.

The first public position Jay held was as secretary of a royal commission to settle a boundary dispute between New York and New Jersey. From 1774 to 1777, he was a member of the Continental Congress, and chief justice of New York from 1777 to 1778. He returned to the Continental Congress as its president from 1778 to 1779. He helped draft the New York state constitution in 1777. Beginning in 1779, Jay spent three years as minister plenipotentiary to Spain. His diplomatic career continued when in 1782 he went to Paris to negotiate alongside Benjamin Franklin and others to reach a peace treaty with Great Britain to end the American Revolution. The 1783 Treaty of Paris resulted, and Jay headed home.

The Congress under the Articles of Confederation named him secretary for foreign affairs — in effect, the American secretary of state. He did not attend the 1787 convention that drafted the new American constitution, but played a major role along with James Madison and Alexander Hamilton in rallying public opinion in favor of the new document. These three men wrote long essays explaining the terms of the constitution. These essays were published first in newspapers and then in book form. They would come to be known as the "Federalist Papers."

In 1789 President George Washington named Jay as the first chief justice of the new Supreme Court created by the constitution. The six-justice court convened in New York City on February 1, 1790. There were as yet no cases, and after various ceremonial functions the court adjourned for six months. A Supreme Court justice also had to serve as a trial-level federal judge, and Jay held court in New York and New England. A few cases significant in the early development of supreme court authority were decided, but the workload was light. Jay allowed himself to be run as a candidate for governor of New York in 1792, even while continuing on the Supreme Court. He did no campaigning, and lost to well-entrenched incumbent George Clinton.

Jay attended no session of the court after 1793. In 1794 he went to London to negotiate an end to American-English differences. The controversial Jay Treaty resulted. Though some boundary issues were resolved and the British agreed to withdraw troops, Jay was unable to get the British to halt their most galling practice of impressing American sailors. The treaty may well have maintained necessary peace with Great Britain, but it was unpopular. While in England, Jay had been elected New York governor — without his knowledge. He resigned from the Supreme Court and took office as governor on July 1, 1795. He served until July 1, 1801, and refused to run for another term. In December 1800 President John Adams nominated him for a second stint as

chief justice. He was confirmed by the Senate, but two weeks later on January 2, 1801, Jay declined the position. Had he accepted, the 35-year service of John Marshall as chief justice would not have begun three weeks later.

Jay held no further public office. His wife died in 1802. With his children he continued to live on a 800-acre farm in Bedford, New York. Jay was strongly religious, opposed to slavery, and helped establish the American Bible Society and became its president.

The John Jay Homestead State Historic Site is in Katonah, New York, consisting of 60 acres out of the original 900-acre farm. The college of criminal justice at the City University of New York was named for Jay.

JAY BIBLIOGRAPHY

Bemis, Samuel F. *Jay's Treaty: A Study in Commerce and Diplomacy.* New York (1923).

Casto, William R. *The Supreme Court in the Early Republic: The Chief Justiceships of John Jay and Oliver Ellsworth.* Columbia, S.C. (1995).

Dilliard, Irving. "John Jay," in Friedman, Leon & Israel, Fred L., eds. *The Justices of the United States Supreme Court 1789–1969.* New York & London (1969), volume I, pp. 3-22.

Lankevich, George J. *The Supreme Court in American Life.* New York City, et al. (1990), vol. I, pp. 233–237.

Marcus, Maeva. *The Documentary History of the Supreme Court of the United States, 1789–1800.* New York City (1985), vol. 1, pp. 3–14.

Monaghan, Frank. *John Jay.* New York (1935).

Pellew, George. *John Jay.* Boston (1890).

Smith, Donald L. *John Jay: Founder of the State and Nation.* New York (1968).

Umbreit, Kenneth Bernard. *Our Eleven Chief Justices.* Port Washington, N.Y. (1969 reprint of 1938 publication), vol. I, pp. 1–50.

1789 recipient of
electoral votes for vice president

Robert H. Harrison

Born in 1745 in Charles County, Maryland; died April 2, 1790, at his home on the Potomac, 20 miles from Port Tobacco, Maryland. Married a daughter of George Johnston, Sr., around 1770; they had two daughters. His wife died before 1777.

Robert Hanson Harrison was the eldest of

ROBERT H. HARRISON
(Reproduced from the Collections of the Library of Congress)

three sons of wealthy planter, legislator, and local official Richard Harrison and his wife Dorothy Hanson Harrison. His mother's first cousin, Robert Hanson, was the first president of the American Congress under the Articles of Confederation and has on occasion been dramatically if erroneously referred to as the first president of the United States. Robert's mother died when he was six, and his father then married a widow, Elizabeth Penn.

Robert's early years are a mystery. He began the practice of law in about 1764 in Alexandria, Virginia. He attended the same church as George Washington, and also handled some of Washington's legal business. Harrison became a frequent visitor to Mount Vernon, hunting the woods along the Potomac, and socializing with Washington, George Mason, and other prominent future leaders of a revolution. Among these was George Johnston, Sr., who seconded Patrick Henry's resolution against the Stamp Act. Socializing at Johnston's home introduced Harrison to Johnston's daughters, one of whom he married, but her name is unknown.

As tensions with England grew, Harrison was appointed to Alexandria's Committee of Correspondence that maintained the flow of information with other communities and colonies. On July 18, 1774, citizens of Fairfax County, Virginia, met and adopted the Virginia Resolves. George Washington was chairman, and Harrison was clerk of the meeting.

George Washington became commander-in-chief of the Continental Army on June 15, 1775. Harrison joined the 3rd Virginia Regiment. Washington invited him to become an aide, joining a small group that composed the General's official "family." Harrison hesitated before accepting, as his wife had died and two young girls were in need of a father. He accepted, though, and the children were left with a relative. Harrison's appointment as aide-de-camp was dated November 6, 1775. In time, Harrison would be Washington's principal secretary, whose legal skills were constantly needed for writing precise, accurate orders and correspondence. Harrison was often in ill health, which handicapped his work. Alexander Hamilton joined the "family" as another aide-de-camp, and became Harrison's good friend. Harrison saw the events at the battle of Monmouth that led to Washington's relieving General Charles Lee of command for failure to obey his orders. Harrison became a principal witness at Lee's court-martial.

After five years on Washington's staff, Harrison was appointed by the Maryland Governor's Council to be chief judge of the state's General Court, and Harrison accepted. Harrison had renewed his association with that state in 1780 when he inherited much of his father's Maryland property. Harrison resigned from Washington's staff in March 1781. Later he served on a commission to resolve a territorial dispute between Massachusetts and New York. After Washington returned to Mt. Vernon, Harrison again was among his occasional guests.

The Maryland legislature in late 1786 named Harrison as one of its delegates to what became the constitutional convention in Phila-

delphia. He did not serve. When the first elections under that constitution were held, Harrison received all of Maryland's six electoral votes for vice president. On September 24, 1789, President George Washington nominated Harrison and five others to be the first justices on the U.S. Supreme Court. He was confirmed by the Senate five days later. Harrison had also just been named chancellor of Maryland, one of the highest judicial offices in the state. On October 3 he wrote Governor John Eager Howard to decline. Harrison's ill health and family responsibilities caused him to write Washington on October 27, declining the Supreme Court seat. A few days later he told mutual friend and Maryland legislator James McHenry that he had acted too hastily and wished he had the commission of appointment back. Washington on November 25 returned the commission to Harrison and asked him to reconsider. Alexander Hamilton wrote and urged him to accept. Harrison apparently decided to accept, since he left on January 14, 1790, for New York, which was then the capital and the site for the court. He only made it part-way, and wrote Washington to say he was too ill to proceed. He again told the president that he could not accept the appointment because of "the apprehension that my indisposition may continue." Harrison's pessimism was well-placed. He died ten weeks later.

HARRISON BIBLIOGRAPHY

Carson, Hampton L. *The History of the Supreme Court of the United States....* Holmes Beach, Fla. (1991, reprint of 1904 edition), vol. 1, pp. 145–147.

Marcus, Maeva. *The Documentary History of the Supreme Court of the United States, 1789–1800.* New York (1985), vol. 1, pp. 31–43.

Ness, George T., Jr. "A Lost Man of Maryland." *Maryland Historical Magazine.* Vol. 35 (1940), pp. 315–336.

Papenfuse, Edward C., et al., eds. *A Biographical Dictionary of the Maryland Legislature, 1635–1789.* Baltimore (1979), pp. 417–420 (various family members).

Perlman, Philip B. "Some Maryland Lawyers in Supreme Court History." *Maryland Historical Magazine.* Vol. 43 (1948), pp. 180–181.

Warren, Charles. *The Supreme Court in United States History.* Boston (1922) vol. 1, pp. 42–43.

*1789 recipient of
electoral votes for vice president*

John Rutledge

Born September 1739, in Charleston, South Carolina; died June 21, 1800. Married Elizabeth Grimke on May 1, 1763, who died in 1792. They had ten children.

Doctor John and Sarah (Hext) Rutledge had seven children. John was the oldest, having been born when his mother was just 15 — she married Dr. Rutledge when she was 14. Young Sarah Hext Rutledge's family was wealthy, and unfortunately she became a wealthy widow in 1750. John was educated by various tutors, and then for a few years studied law with two Charlestown attorneys, including his uncle Andrew. At age 17 John went to England to study law at Middle Temple and was called to the English bar in 1760.

When he was only 21, John returned to Charlestown and began a highly successful law practice. He was elected to the House of Assembly three months after returning from England. Rutledge became a life-long political and judicial champion of the wealthy businessmen and landowners whom he represented. He was appointed by the royal governor as attorney general in 1764 and served 10 months. In 1765 he attended as one of three South Carolina delegates a New York meeting to protest recent British actions.

For the next nine years Rutledge practiced law. Then in 1774 and 1775 he was chairman of the South Carolina delegations to the First and Second Continental Congresses. He was initially a moderate, but gradually warmed to independence. In December 1775 he helped draft a constitution for the newly proclaimed Republic of South Carolina. The voters chose a lower house, and that house when it convened in March 1776 elected Rutledge as president of South Carolina. Boldly overriding General Charles Lee's order for his troops to evacuate a fort guarding Charleston harbor, Rutledge and the South Carolinians were both sufficiently courageous and lucky to defeat a British naval force and free the South from further British incursions for almost three years. Because of differences concerning a new constitution passed by the Assembly, Rutledge resigned as president in 1778. In February 1779 the Assembly again chose Rutledge as

JOHN RUTLEDGE
(Reproduced from the Collections of the Library of Congress)

president, this time giving him near-dictatorial powers to use in thwarting the British invasion. Charleston was captured by the British in May 1780, and the whole state succumbed. Rutledge escaped to North Carolina. The effective end of the war in 1781 allowed Rutledge to return. He served until 1782, when at the end of his term he was elected to Congress. Rutledge remained in Congress until 1784, and then was appointed chief judge of the state's new court of chancery. In 1787 he became a delegate to the constitutional convention in Philadelphia. When the first presidential election was held two years later, South Carolina gave its electoral votes for vice president to Rutledge.

Rutledge was one of the president's three final candidates for chief justice of the Supreme Court, but was named an associate justice instead. Because of illness, perhaps pique at not being chief justice, and lack of business for the court, Rutledge never attended any sessions with the full court. In February 1791 he resigned in order to become chief justice of the South Carolina Court of Common Pleas. He may have come to regret the resignation. He wrote President Washington in 1795 and said he would like to become chief justice if John Jay resigned to accept election as New York governor. Washington sent a letter to Rutledge offering the position. The letter may not have yet arrived when Rutledge attended a public meeting in Charleston on July 16, 1795. There he vehemently protested the provisions in the treaty John Jay had just finished negotiating with England. Rutledge's language was so severe that he outraged the Federalists in the Senate. Many suggested he must be deranged. President Washington still wanted him as chief justice. Since the Senate was not then in session, Rutledge legally began his service and presided over the Court while awaiting Senate action. His chief justice position ended on December 15, 1795, when the Senate refused to confirm him.

Rutledge's wife had died in 1792, and there had been some friends who thought him insane at times after that. After hearing of the Senate's rejection, Rutledge tried to drown himself in Charleston Bay on the day after Christmas, 1795. Two passing slaves rescued him. He remained a recluse for most of the next five years until he died on June 21, 1800.

The Governor John Rutledge House stands at 116 Broad Street, Charleston (private). Edward Rutledge's house is at 117 Broad St.

RUTLEDGE BIBLIOGRAPHY
Barnwell, Robert W. "Rutledge: The Dictator," *Journal of Southern History.* Vol. 7, pp. 215–224 (1941).

Barry, Richard. *Mr. Rutledge of South Carolina.* New York (1942, reprinted in 1993, Ayer Press).

Cowan, George, S., Jr. "Chief Justice John Rutledge and the Jay Treaty." *South Carolina Historical Magazine* LXII (1961), 10–23.

Friedman, Leon. "John Rutledge," in Friedman, Leon & Israel, Fred L., eds. *The Justices of the United States Supreme Court 1789–1969.* New York & London (1969), vol. 1, pp. 33–49.

Haw, James. *Founding Brothers: John and Edward Rutledge of South Carolina.* Athens, Ga. (1997).

Henderson, H. James. *Party Politics in the Continental Congress.* New York (1974).

Horne, Paul A., Jr. "Forgotten Leaders: South Carolina's Delegation to the Continental Congress, 1774–1789." Ph.D. dissertation, University of South Carolina (1988).

Lankevich, George J. *The Supreme Court in American Life.* New York City, et al. (1990), vol. 1, pp. 238–241.

Marcus, Maeva. *The Documentary History of the Supreme Court of the United States, 1789–1800.* New York City (1985), vol. 1, pp. 15–23, 94–100.

Umbreit, Kenneth Bernard. *Our Eleven Chief Justices.* Port Washington, N.Y. (1969 reprint of 1938 publication), vol. 1, pp. 51–78.

1789 recipient of
electoral votes for vice president

John Hancock

Born January 12, 1736, in Braintree, Massachusetts; died October 8, 1793, in Boston. Married Dorothy Quincy on August 28, 1775; they had two children, both of whom died young.

John's parents, the Reverend John and Mary (Hawke) Hancock, had three children. When the Reverend Hancock died in 1744, young

JOHN HANCOCK
(From Prints & Photographs Div., Library of Congress)

John was adopted by his childless uncle Thomas Hancock, who was reputed to be the wealthiest merchant in Boston. John attended the Boston Latin School and Harvard College, from which he graduated in 1754. A comfortable position awaited him at his uncle's counting house. In 1760 he went to England to learn the London part of the business. After a year he was back home and became a partner in his uncle's firm in 1763. John became sole owner in 1764 when his uncle died. He apparently was not as good a merchant as his uncle, but the firm continued to make John one of the wealthiest men in Boston. Hancock tried to monopolize the sale of whale oil to England, a venture that failed and soured him on being a merchant.

Not quite 30 years old, Hancock protested to his English business contacts about the 1765 Stamp Act. His interest in politics was magnified in 1768 when his ship *Liberty* arrived with a substantial cargo of Madeira wine. Some wine was smuggled ashore without his knowledge, according to Hancock. Hancock was prosecuted for smuggling, and was defended by John Adams. The charges were dropped after a few months, but the episode helped make Hancock a popular hero.

The year after the *Liberty* affair, Hancock was elected to the Massachusetts General Court. In March 1770, tensions between British soldiers and Boston townsmen had led to a small guard of nine soldiers firing on a much larger collection of townspeople. Three Bostonians were killed, including a black man named Crispus Attucks, and eight were wounded. Hancock and Samuel Adams were on a 15-man committee that successfully demanded the removal of the soldiers. Hancock's reputation as a popular patriot was greatly enhanced. John Adams received a far more negative, but temporary reaction when he agreed to defend the officer in charge, Captain Thomas Preston. The "Massacre" is what the event was called, and shortly thereafter Hancock was made head of the town committee.

The committee's anti–British activist Samuel Adams knew the wealthy Hancock's importance to the cause and encouraged him to take bolder steps. The General Court transformed itself into the Massachusetts Provisional Congress in 1774, and Hancock was elected its president. Hancock and Samuel Adams' prominence as anti–British conspirators caused British General Thomas Gage to try capturing them with a small detachment of troops that he dispatched on the night of April 18, 1775. The two patriots were in Lexington and received the warning carried by Paul Revere and William Dawes that the British were indeed coming. Minutemen gathered on the green at Lexington, and met the advance guard of British with musket fire. Hancock and Adams were safe, and a war was on.

Hancock was a delegate to the Continental Congress from 1775 to 1780, and was president from 1775 to 1777. As president of Congress, he was the first signer of the Declaration of Independence. He was reported to say, as he gave his bold signature to the parchment, that the large writing was so that George III could read the name without his spectacles. Hancock wanted to be named commander-in-chief and was irked when the eminently more suitable George Washington was named. Hancock got a chance to command 5000 troops in 1778 in action in Rhode Island. He did not exhibit any aptitude for military command, and that was the end of his effort to try.

Leaving the battlefield, Hancock found success in the political arena. He was a delegate to the state constitutional convention in 1780. He was then elected governor of Massachusetts and served from 1780 to 1785, but stepped aside because of a bad attack of gout. He returned as governor from 1787 to 1789. Hancock was president of the state convention that ratified the federal constitution in 1788. He apparently wanted to be elected vice president in 1789, but got only four electoral votes. Instead he was again elected governor on April 7, 1789, and remained in that office, winning majorities of over 80 percent of the vote, until he died. Illness afflicted him the last few years of his life, and he died in 1793.

HANCOCK BIBLIOGRAPHY
Allan, Herbert S. *John Hancock: Patriot in Purple.* New York (1953).

Baxter, W.T. *The House of Hancock: Business in Boston, 1724–1775.* New York (1965).

Brown, Abram English. *John Hancock: His Book.* Boston (1898)

Finklestein, Robert Zeus. "Merchant, Revolutionary, and Statesman: A Re-Appraisal of the Life and Public Services of John Hancock, 1737–1793." Unpublished Ph.D. dissertation, University of Massachusetts (1978).

Fowler, William M. *The Baron of Beacon Hill: A Biography of John Hancock.* Boston (1980).

Henderson, H. James. *Party Politics in the Continental Congress.* New York (1974).

Sears, Lorenzo. *John Hancock: The Picturesque Patriot.* Boston (1913).

Election of 1792

NOMINATIONS

George Washington was the choice of all political factions for president.

Federalist or Administration Party: the political faction dominated by Alexander Hamilton reluctantly supported Vice President John Adams' re-election. No effort to make a formal nomination was made.

Anti-Federalist faction: this inchoate party which looked to Thomas Jefferson as its leader decided to contest the election of John Adams to a second term as vice president. Ten or more leaders of this opposition party met on October 16, 1792, in Philadelphia, to select a candidate and to concentrate efforts for his election. George Clinton was named. Other men were also mentioned in letters between political leaders and received some support.

GENERAL ELECTION

Popular Vote
None recorded
Electoral Vote
George Washington 132
John Adams 77
George Clinton 50
Two others 5
Winners
George Washington, 1st president
John Adams, 1st vice president
Losers
George Clinton

*1792 vice presidential nominee—
Anti-Federalist Party*

George Clinton

No biographical sketch of Clinton is included because he served as vice president from March 4, 1805, until April 20, 1812 (4th vice president).

State Represented: New York.

Birth: July 26, 1739, Little Britain, New York.

Age on Inauguration Day (March 4, 1793): 53 years, 7½ months.

Death: April 20, 1812, Washington, D.C., age 72 years, 9 months.

GEORGE CLINTON
(Reproduced from the Collections of the Library of Congress)

Election of 1796

NOMINATIONS

Federalist Party: In late spring or early summer 1796, a meeting of party leaders was held. Prior discussions with possible candidates had occurred, resulting in a decision on nominees even before the meeting. *President and vice president*— John Adams and Thomas Pinckney. Neither was termed the candidate for president and the other the running mate. It was generally accepted that Adams would be the presidential nominee, but many of his enemies within the party felt Pinckney was the better choice and worked to make him president.

Democratic-Republican Party: In late spring, 1796, party leaders met in Philadelphia. The only purpose of the gathering was to choose a running mate for Thomas Jefferson, who was the near-unanimous choice of his party for president. *President*— Thomas Jefferson, who was not voted on since he was already the consensus choice. *Vice president*—no decision was reached. Aaron Burr, Robert Livingston, Pierce Butler and John Langdon were all discussed. In most areas of the country by late summer, however, Aaron Burr was the acknowledged choice.

GENERAL ELECTION

Popular Vote
  None recorded
Electoral Vote
    John Adams 71
    Thomas Jefferson. 68

THOMAS JEFFERSON
(From the author's collection)

    Thomas Pinckney 59
    Aaron Burr 30
    Samuel Adams. 15
    Oliver Ellsworth 11
    Seven others (including
        George Washington) 22
Winners
    John Adams, 2nd president
    Thomas Jefferson, 2nd vice president
Losers
    Thomas Jefferson (for president), Thomas Pinckney, Aaron Burr, Samuel Adams, Oliver Ellsworth

*1796 presidential nominee—
Democratic-Republican Party*

Thomas Jefferson

No biographical sketch of Jefferson is included because he served as president from March 4, 1801, until March 4, 1809 (3rd president).

State represented: Virginia.

Birth: April 13, 1743, in Albemarle County, Virginia.

Age on Inauguration Day (March 4, 1797): 53 years, 10½ months.

Death: July 4, 1826, at Monticello, Virginia, age 83 years, 2½ months.

---

*1796 nominee for vice president—
Federalist Party*

Thomas Pinckney

Full name: Thomas Pinckney.

State represented: South Carolina.

Birth: October 23, 1750, Charles Town, South Carolina.

Age on Inauguration Day (March 4, 1797): 46 years, 4½ months.

Education: English schools, including Westminster School 1764–1768; admitted to Middle Temple, Oxford, in 1768 and studied at Christ Church until 1774, when admitted to bar; French Military College, Caen, France.

Religion: Episcopalian.

Ancestry/prominent relatives: Father Charles Pinckney, a prominent colonial public official; brother Charles Cotesworth Pinckney was twice a presidential nominee (see biography at election of 1800); Charles Pinckney, first cousin, prominent South Carolina leader; Charles Pinckney, son of preceding, was governor of South Carolina, U.S. Senator, and held other offices.

Occupation: Attorney, planter.

Public offices: South Carolina House of Representatives, 1778–1780; governor of South Carolina, February 21, 1787–1789; presided over state convention that ratified the federal

constitution, 1788; appointed judge, U.S. Court for District of South Carolina, by President Washington, 1789, but declined; state House of Representatives 1791; appointed ambassador to Great Britain, January 12, 1792–July 8, 1796; envoy extraordinary and minister plenipotentiary to Spain, November 24, 1794–November 1795; U.S. Representative, November 23, 1797–March 3, 1801, declined reelection; unsuccessful Federalist nominee for vice president, 1796.

Death: November 2, 1828, Charleston, South Carolina, at age 78 years, ½ month.

Burial: St. Philips Churchyard, Charleston, South Carolina.

Home: "Fairfield," on bank near mouth of Santee River.

Personal characteristics: Tall and thin, erect, dignified, courteous, well-mannered; good health throughout life; even temperament; deaf in later years.

Father: Charles Pinckney (Aug. 13, 1699/1700–July 12, 1758), prominent South Carolina colonial official, planter, judge.

Mother: Elizabeth (Eliza) Lucas (Dec. 28, 1722–May 26, 1793), married on May 27, 1744; daughter of George Lucas, a wealthy plantation owner in South Carolina.

Siblings: Charles Cotesworth Pinckney (see sketch at election of 1800). George Lucas Pinckney (June 14–29, 1747). Harriott Pinckney (Aug. 7, 1748–Dec. 19, 1830), married Daniel Horry on Feb. 15, 1768; he was a wealthy South Carolina planter.

First Wife: Elizabeth ("Betsey") Motte (Aug. 27, 1762–Aug. 24, 1794), daughter of Jacob and Rebecca (Brewton) Motte, married on July 22, 1779.

Children: Thomas (1780–July 7, 1842), married Elizabeth Izard on Dec. 27, 1803. Charles Cotesworth (bapt. May 14, 1789–1865), married Phoebe Caroline Elliott on July 31, 1811. Elizabeth Brewton (?–July 1857), married William Lowndes (see election of 1824) on Sept. 10, 1802. Harriott Lucas (?–Dec. 25, 1824), married Francis Kinloch Huger on Jan. 14, 1802. Mary (?–?), died unmarried. Rebecca Motte (bapt. Nov. 4, 1788–Dec. 24, 1797).

Second Wife: Mrs. Frances (Motte) Middleton, sister of his first wife (bapt. Sept. 29, 1763–1843), married John Middleton on July

THOMAS PINCKNEY
(From the original in the South Caroliniana Library)

31, 1783, he died Nov. 14, 1784; married Pinckney on Oct. 19, 1797.

Children: Edward Rutledge (Feb. 22, 1800–Sept. 1, 1832), member of South Carolina Senate. Mary (1804–1822), died unmarried.

Historic sites/memorials: Pinckney's home, "Fairfield," is still standing.

Thomas Pinckney's mother was the developer of indigo as a major crop for South Car-

olina plantations. His father was for a time chief justice of the colony. His brother was three times nominated for president or vice president. Thomas' achievements were no less than theirs, and the whole Pinckney family story is a remarkable one.

Thomas' father took the family to England when Thomas was only three, as the elder Pinckney was to be South Carolina's agent in the mother country. Thomas would not return to America, except for one visit, for 21 years. His father's sudden death in 1758 did not cause Thomas or his brother Charles Cotesworth to return to the colonies, but instead their mother decided to let them remain for their schooling, far superior in London than in the primitive schools of South Carolina. Thomas performed well at his studies and in 1765 entered Westminster School. Christ Church College in Oxford then accepted him in 1768. Thomas began his legal training at the Middle Temple, one of the prestigious Inns of Court at which all British law students received their instruction. He questioned the relevance of studies when the conflict between America and England was beginning to boil. His outspoken pro–American stance earned him the title "Little Rebel" at Oxford. In 1769 he went to France and probably attended the royal military academy for a short period. He then returned to Oxford and continued his studies. His first visit home in over 18 years occurred when he was about to turn 21. His visit to Charles Town (the name was later shortened to Charleston) enabled him to take possession of Auckland Plantation and several other properties. He was home almost a year and a half, but on March 2, 1773, was en route back to the Middle Temple and the completion of his legal training. Again he disputed British measures against America, including the closing of the port of Boston because of the "Tea Party." So incensed was Thomas that he, along with another young American patriot, hired a member of the British Royal guard to drill them.

Thomas was eager to finish at Oxford and return to the country he in truth knew less of than he did England. On November 15, 1774, he was received into the English bar and left almost immediately for South Carolina. He was admitted to the bar there the following year.

War with the country Thomas had lived in for 18 of his 22 years was upon him. His sympathies were not divided, however, and he was chosen a captain along with his brother Charles Cotesworth in the regular army in June 1775. There were few other volunteers and almost no weapons or ammunition. His first assignment was to try relieving the manpower shortage by recruiting. He also engaged in erecting fortifications around Charles Town harbor.

Fort Johnson faced Fort Sullivan across Charles Town harbor. Thomas was put to work supervising the strengthening of defenses at Fort Johnson. While these efforts continued, Pinckney was ordered on another recruiting expedition, because men were needed at least as desperately as fortifications. North Carolina and Virginia yielded few recruits and he returned to the fort, now renamed Fort Moultrie, in March 1777. Defeats were occurring to the Continental forces everywhere. Thomas' ardor did not wane, however. He was promoted to major in May 1778. After a year-long military lull in the South, the British launched an invasion in Georgia at the end of 1778. Thomas joined a badly outnumbered force to challenge the invasion. The important port of Savannah fell before Carolina troops arrived. After several defeats, the American forces were required to fall back to Charles Town. Discipline problems were rampant, with volunteers and short-term militia playing havoc with military order. To quiet one particular mutiny, Thomas strode into the midst of an unruly mob, struck the ringleader with his sword, and ordered the rest of the soldiers to disperse. Fortunately, they did.

As the British advanced towards the South Carolina capital of Charles Town, they burned Thomas' Auckland Plantation, at which personally valuable records and mementoes of the Pinckney family had been stored for safe-keeping. The old family home at Belmont was likewise ravaged, though the main house was, for a time, spared. A few engagements during the maneuvering earned Thomas credit for his military prowess, but the Continental army was outmatched.

In the midst of the effort to parry the British thrust towards Charles Town and areas farther north, Pinckney married Betsey Motte on July 22, 1779. As prominent as the Pinckney family was, Thomas gained even more political and social rank by marrying into this influential and wealthy family.

Pinckney served in a variety of roles. He used his fluency in French to be an interpreter with a French naval force in September 1779. He was a courier of the bad news of Charles Town's imminent fall, going through enemy lines to reach the governor. Pinckney then wanted to continue north to join relief troops he expected were being sent by General Washington. He learned such reinforcements were already on the way. Pinckney met the oncoming forces and was made an aide to the commanding general, Horatio Gates, the hero of Saratoga. Pinckney's first duty was to find a commissary general who could keep the army supplied with food.

Some of the poorly trained American troops at the Battle of Camden, South Carolina, on August 16, 1780, began to retreat wildly when they saw the opposing army. As Pinckney and others tried to rally the men, a musket ball shattered his left leg. He had to proceed to the rear while another American defeat raged in front of him. An old schoolmate from Westminster, British officer Charles McKenzie, took him to Camden where he received treatment usually only provided to wounded British soldiers. The regimental surgeon was persuaded by McKenzie to take a look at the leg and treat it. Amputation seemed a real possibility, and would have been a necessity without the special care Pinckney received. He lingered for months in fitful fever, with threats of amputation mingled with intermittent improvement. While he was suffering dreadfully from the wound, his wife and newborn son were under the effects of smallpox.

As he strengthened, Pinckney was allowed to go to Charles Town for much improved attention from his family. He received better surgical treatment, and on several occasions had bone chips removed when they surfaced through the skin. The leg finally showed that it would heal, but it would be years before constant pain relented and some semblance of normal function returned.

Brother Charles Cotesworth and Thomas shared effective imprisonment in Charles Town until they could be exchanged for similarly ranked British officers captured by the colonial forces. The two brothers traveled together to Philadelphia to await exchange. Thomas could not continue to wait, as military etiquette required, and left for South Car-

olina in January 1782. He was captured by the British, but almost immediately was released since he was a "prisoner" who had still not been exchanged. This was an old-fashioned war. He received no new military assignments before the war ended.

Pinckney was elected to the Carolina legislature in 1781 but did not serve in the Assembly. He also tried to establish a law practice that had been barely commenced in 1774 when he first returned from England. His civic activities included membership in the Society of the Cincinnati, an organization of officers from the Revolution and their first-born descendants, with Washington as the president-general. Agriculture fascinated Pinckney, intellectually as well as financially, and he joined and was active in the major South Carolina agriculture association.

Pinckney was pleased with his civic pursuits and his plantations. There was nothing to attract him to public life other than calls upon his conscience that he ought to serve. His friend and brother's law partner, Edward Rutledge, convinced Pinckney to run for governor in the 1787 election. After Pinckney agreed, Rutledge ran his campaign. There was only token opposition and Pinckney won with 163 out of 170 votes in the legislature. When the national constitution was proposed later in the year, Governor Pinckney strongly endorsed it. The governor was chosen president of the convention elected to consider ratification in the state. Adoption was favored by a two-to-one vote. The remainder of the governor's one-year term was mainly concerned with the procedures for instituting the new federal government, electing congressmen and senators, and preparing for the other changes that a strong national government required.

Governor Pinckney desired neither a second term nor election to federal office. He retired, briefly as it turned out, to his plantations. He was offered the federal judgeship for South Carolina but refused. His old plantation house at Auckland having been burned, Pinckney established his new principal residence at another, Fairfield.

Washington's entreaties finally convinced Pinckney to take the position of ambassador to Great Britain in 1792. His wife was tearful in her reluctance to go, but the whole family embarked for England on June 25, 1792. They arrived on August 3, and met King George III on August 8. The meeting was probably mutually awkward between the old officer in the revolutionary army and the king against whom he had rebelled. Coldness characterized Pinckney's reception not only from the British but from the rest of the diplomatic corps. To many, Americans were the cause of the most dangerous crisis facing their own countries — the rising spirit of democracy that had tragically led to the atrocities in France, including the beheading of the king.

Pinckney's main duty was to try to win friendship and respect for America. He was to earn Britain's friendship by showing courtesy and culture, two characteristics little expected from the representative of a nation many saw as barbaric. The principal substantive issues concerned trade. Commercial relations with England were sorely needed by merchants and farmers who prior to the Revolution had enjoyed British markets for their goods. The impressment of American sailors into service in the British navy rankled all Americans, and that issue was to be argued energetically by every American minister to London for 20 years without effect. Impressment became a constant problem for Pinckney both in his general negotiations and in the individual cases in which he tried to secure release for a particular sailor. War between Britain and France was looming. Pinckney wished to resolve the impressment issue before war because England's demand for sailors would soar after hostilities had begun. The effort failed, and matters did worsen. During the midst of his negotiations twin tragedies buffeted the American envoy. His mother died in South Carolina in 1793. Even more of a blow was the death of his wife the following year. Pinckney nonetheless persevered.

Americans had become outraged with the British while Pinckney was in London. British promises to end their occupation of forts in the northwest had not been fulfilled; Indians were being encouraged by their English patrons to attack American settlements. Impressment continued. With great reluctance, but since Pinckney had been unable to achieve

agreement on any of these issues, President Washington convinced Supreme Court Justice John Jay to become special envoy to Britain to negotiate these matters. Pinckney was galled by the slight but remained officially silent. Regardless of any personal disappointment, Pinckney worked as closely as Jay desired to assist the new representative. The controversial Jay Treaty of 1794 resulted. The British did agree to withdraw all forces to north of the Great Lakes. Payment of pre–Revolutionary debts between American and British subjects was arranged. Some provisions were halfway measures that Jay agreed to despite his instructions, thereby reaching agreement while Pinckney had failed only because Jay was willing to concede more than had Pinckney. Indemnity for slaves taken away by British troops in massive numbers and resold into further slavery was not provided for; impressment was equally ignored; and international maritime law was not declared applicable to relations between the two countries. Part of the treaty was expunged before the Senate would ratify it.

Pinckney received instructions in February 1795 to proceed to Spain, though remaining English ambassador, to negotiate over trade and boundary differences. He was able to leave on May 11 and reached Madrid on June 28. The principal negotiating points were on Spanish-American boundaries and the navigation of the Mississippi River. Spain played cat and mouse, much more concerned with internal European matters than with Pinckney. In October the Spanish minister insisted that negotiations were finished and that the latest proposal made by Spain should be signed. Pinckney refused. A crucial gamble was soon made by Pinckney, as he did not see any other way to break Spanish intransigence. He demanded that American shipping traveling down the Mississippi have the "right of deposit" for their goods, that is, to transfer at the mouth of the river their products from river vessels to ocean-going ones. The demand was refused, and Pinckney asked for his passport and said he was leaving the next day. Instead of Pinckney's departure, the next day brought agreement on all critical points by the Spanish. A great diplomatic victory had been won by persistence as well as intelligent gambling. Reaction in America was completely favorable, much in contrast to the Jay Treaty. The United States Senate approved the Pinckney Treaty unanimously.

Pinckney returned to London but wanted to continue on to America. President Washington acceded, but Pinckney had to wait for his replacement, Rufus King, to arrive. Pinckney finally left England on October 17, 1796.

The tremendously favorable reaction to the Pinckney Treaty placed the ambassador squarely in the middle of presidential politics in 1796. The Federalists needed South Carolina, and they also needed the appeal of diplomatic success. Rufus King, who was later himself to be a vice presidential and then presidential candidate, proposed Pinckney as a running mate in John Adams' attempt to move up to the presidency. Alexander Hamilton agreed, but Hamilton went further. No friend or admirer of Adams, Hamilton desired that Adams be defeated for the presidency by secretly pushing Pinckney for the top position. Until the Twelfth Amendment was added to the U.S. Constitution in 1804, presidential electors voted for two men without distinguishing on their ballots which was for president and which for the second spot. Any success in giving Pinckney just one more vote than was given to Adams would elect the South Carolinian president. Such scheming would subsequently cause the adoption of the Twelfth Amendment. For a time the Republicans were sympathetic to a Pinckney vice presidency, but giving votes to Pinckney might thwart their own presidential candidate, Thomas Jefferson. Pinckney never acceded to such a plot, but Adams and his supporters learned of it. Votes were apparently withheld from both men, making the Federalist victory painfully narrow over Jefferson. The counterscheming to deny votes to Pinckney succeeded in dropping his total below that of Jefferson's, so Pinckney received neither office. Adams was president and Jefferson was vice president.

Pinckney's political blood was on fire. He worried for his country and his state if the Jeffersonian Republicans took over; to Pinckney they represented rule by the masses without regard for education or training. Pinckney plunged energetically into South Carolina politics, and in September 1797 succeeded in being elected to the United States Congress. The same year he married the younger sister of his first wife. She was wealthy as a result of inheritance from her deceased husband, but Pinckney's own fortune made money the least of the possible attractions.

Ill health almost immediately incapacitated Pinckney in Congress. An attack of vertigo on January 31, 1798, left him temporarily blind and unable to walk. He was able to return to Congress in February, but shortly again had to leave. He lost weight and strength. In hopes of regaining his health he took a vacation to Princeton where his son Thomas was attending school, and again tried to take his Congressional seat in March. In May he left for South Carolina, and was able to return to Congress in December.

Thomas declined to run for reelection to Congress in 1800. He had been unable to vote for the Alien and Sedition Acts when they were first proposed, but in the lame duck session after the Republican victory in 1800, he voted that they be continued. Pinckney did not trust "excessive" democracy, nor did he trust the new president, Jefferson. Yet he had no choice; the people had spoken, and all Pinckney could do was return to his plantation. The Federalists would continue to have their adherents in some Northern and New England states, but the Republicans were clearly entrenched to stay in South Carolina.

The next 12 years Pinckney spent in his agricultural pursuits. He imported beef from Europe to replace inferior breeds in America. He began marshland reclamation efforts. He developed a large library at his plantation mansion that reflected his varied scientific and political interests. He was active in the state agricultural association.

A new war with Britain caused President Madison in 1812 to offer Pinckney the position of major general and command of the southern department. He was 61 years old, but had lost little of his physical or mental vigor. His command stretched south from Virginia and took in all of the southern territories and states. He never saw action, but he did help organize the troops, increase fortifications, and otherwise administer the military in his region. He became an admirer and friend of Andrew

Jackson after seeing his success in the war. The important New Orleans victory by Jackson saved American self-respect after an otherwise dismal and confusing war.

His political and military life over, Pinckney continued his other interests for the remaining 13 years of his life. He excelled in innovative farming techniques, showing that farming was perhaps at least the equal of politics as the occupation to which he was most suited. He voiced his opposition in the 1820s to the abolition of slavery, joining with his brother Charles Cotesworth in his defense of the institution. When his brother died in 1826, Thomas succeeded to the position of president general of the Society of the Cincinnati. He had outlived the start of the Revolution by 50 years, had outlived the end of his political successes by almost 30. His life was nonetheless, in so many varied ways, a tremendous victory.

Analysis of Qualifications

A Thomas Pinckney presidency almost came to pass because of the deviousness of Alexander Hamilton and Pinckney's popularity among the Jeffersonian Republicans. That the scheme was thwarted probably denied the United States the talents of an exceptionally able and public spirited man as chief executive, one who would have been remembered today as a competent, humble, but firm leader.

In 1796 Federalists and Jeffersonians alike were attracted to Thomas Pinckney because of his moderate political views, views that transcended the growing division between the parties. Not clearly a Federalist of the Hamilton variety, Pinckney was nonetheless closely enough identified with that party to be counted among its national leaders. Many saw in Pinckney the strength to avoid domination by Alexander Hamilton at the same time as he was pursuing a basically Federalist course. Thomas Jefferson himself spoke highly of this opposition leader and his brother Charles, calling them in December 1796, "honest and honorable men ... men who will not bend their politics to their purses." As many believed ardently that America should avoid party politics, Pinckney seemed to stand as an agreeable compromise between John Adams and Thomas

Jefferson — a "safe man" who had talent for high office without the rancorous personality of an Adams or the extreme democratic views of a Jefferson.

As governor of South Carolina Pinckney had been a firm executive. As a military man he had demonstrated courage, dedication and patriotism. Throughout the South, but particularly in his native state, Pinckney was highly respected for his selfless devotion to the revolution and then to the new nation. Noblesse oblige was epitomized in this wealthy planter, who loved agriculture and architecture far more than the acrimony of politics. He was a Cincinnatus, in the same manner as his mentor George Washington. Pinckney would respond to his nation's call, but it was preferable to him that the call never come. Though never placed in a position requiring comparable skills, Pinckney was frequently compared to the first president — cool judgment, self-control, dedication to duty. The combination of talents is too rare to expect that Pinckney could have matched Washington in success as president, but it is a tribute of considerable significance for the comparison to have been made by his contemporaries.

Pinckney's greatest achievement, the one that made him prime election material for both parties in 1796, was the treaty he negotiated with Spain the previous year. That treaty was extremely popular the more so because of unsatisfactory compromises that frequently had been made previously by other negotiators. By alternate tact and firmness, even to the point of threatening to break off negotiations during a critical moment, Pinckney achieved more than his nation had expected. This favorable settlement of Spanish-American differences was a signal diplomatic triumph for the young republic. Pinckney reaped considerable political credit for it. There was luck, perhaps unnecessary concessions by the Spanish, but success was also due to Pinckney's talents as a negotiator.

Thomas Pinckney, a young and vigorous man of only 46, could have been expected as president to exercise the same calm judgment, patience, and strength he had in Spain or on the American battlefields of the Revolution. He was a mild-mannered, amiable man, not given to the personality eccentricities of his running mate Adams. His principles were high, his tolerance for political chicanery low. During his short period of service in public office, whatever leadership deficiencies he might have had never had occasion to reveal themselves. Certainly the presidency would have tested his mettle far more than his truncated public career ever did in actuality. But as presidential material, Pinckney must be ranked high.

PINCKNEY BIBLIOGRAPHY

Bemis, Samuel F. *Pinckney's Treaty: America's Advantage from Europe's Distress, 1783–1800.* Westport, Conn. (1973), reprint of 1960 edition.

Cross, Jack L. *London Mission: The First Critical Years.* East Lansing, Mich. (1969).

Pinckney, The Rev. Charles Cotesworth. *Life of General Thomas Pinckney.* Boston and New York (1895).

Ravenel, Harriott Horry. *Eliza Pinckney.* New York City (1896), rev. ed., 1925.

Rogers, George C., Jr. *Charleston in the Age of the Pinckneys.* Columbia, S.C. (1980).

Salley, Alexander, Jr. "Miles Brewton and Some of His Descendants." *South Carolina Historical and Genealogical Magazine* II (1901), 23–26, 128–143.

Scherr, Arthur. "Significance of Thomas Pinckney's Candidacy in the Election of 1796." *South Carolina Historical Magazine.* Vol. 76 (1975), pp. 51–59.

Simms, William Gilmore. "Memoir of the Pinckney Family." *Dawson's Historical Magazine,* 2d series, vol. I (1867), pp. 134–38.

Webber, Mabel L. "The Thomas Pinckney Family of South Carolina." *South Carolina Historical and Genealogical Magazine* XXXIX (1938), pp. 15–35.

Williams, Frances Leigh, *A Founding Family: The Pinckneys of South Carolina.* New York City and London (1978).

---

*1796 vice presidential nominee —
Democratic-Republican Party*

Aaron Burr

No biographical sketch of Burr is included because he served as vice president from March 4, 1801, until March 4, 1805 (3rd vice president).

State Represented: New York

Birth: February 6, 1756, in Newark, New Jersey.

Age on Inauguration Day (March 4, 1797): 41 years, 1 month

Death: September 14, 1836, at Staten Island, New York, at age 80 years, 7½ months.

---

*1796 recipient of electoral votes
for vice president—
Democratic-Republican Party*

Samuel Adams

Born September 27, 1722, in Boston, Massachusetts; died October 2, 1803, in Boston. Married Elizabeth Checkley on October 7, 1749, who died in 1757; they had three children. On December 6, 1764, married Elizabeth Wells; they had two children.

Samuel Adams was one of 12 children of Samuel and Mary Fifield Adams. The family lived in Boston, where the elder Samuel owned an impressive home as well as a successful brewery. After tutoring and other schools, young Samuel entered Harvard College when he was 14. He graduated in four years, and later returned to receive a Master of Arts degree. For a short time he studied law, but did not complete his studies. With a loan from his father, Samuel started a business. After it failed, he joined his father at the brewery. When his father died in 1748, and soon thereafter his mother, Samuel became a one-third owner of the brewery. Within a few years that business too was failing. He also fell behind in his obligations as a tax collector, a post he held from 1756 to 1764, and owed a substantial sum to the city of Boston.

His failures in business were being balanced by successes in politics. He organized a political club and participated in others. By 1764 he was sufficiently in the forefront of Boston political life that he was given the task of writing Boston's resolutions opposing the Stamp Act. He was elected the next year to the Massachusetts General Court, and served from 1765 to 1774. Adams became a leader of those opposed to the entrenched, conservative

AARON BURR
(Library of Congress)

published in Boston news-papers, and his polemics helped shape public opposition to the mother country. In the early 1770s when public discontent seemed to be easing, Adams' writings continued to attack British policies. He wrote a declaration of rights that became widely circulated. One British official doubted "there is a greater incendiary in the King's dominion or a man of greater malignity of heart" than Adams.

Adams had combustible material to use with the 1773 passage in parliament of the Tea Act. In November Adams made a motion at a Boston meeting that the tea on ships in Boston Harbor "shall be returned to the place from which it came at all events." The next day the same group named Adams to the committee that would direct the continuing attempts to block the unloading of the tea. After the royal governor refused to allow the ships to leave the harbor without unloading, Adams at a December 16 meeting said, "This meeting can do nothing more to save the country." It was a signal for the rebels, dressed as Indians, to proceed in the middle of the night to throw the tea into the harbor.

On May 13, 1774, he spoke at a Boston meeting in favor of complete cut-off of trade with England, and in favor of a continental congress. He was named on June 17 by the Massachusetts General Court to be one of the delegates to the Congress. He also served in the second Continental Congress in 1775. By then he was in favor of complete and immediate independence.

With the stage set for the rebellion for which Samuel Adams had proselytized and polemicized, his influence greatly waned. His role as agitator was no longer needed. He continued in Congress until 1782. He was a member of the

merchants and businessmen who dominated Boston politics. Many of these merchants wished to continue working with the British to the greatest extent possible, but the radicals portrayed them as "enemies of liberty." Adams may not have favored the violence that arose against some of these wealthy Bostonians, but he actively played on the anger. Radicals such as Adams took control of the Massachusetts House in 1766. Adams was elected House clerk. From that post he was able to draft many of the official papers of the House, a task that allowed his sharp-edged rhetorical skills full expression. When there was discontent with the royal governor or the British parliament and king, Adams frequently was the most vocal critic. A less strident voice in Boston politics was John Adams, who would in 1797 become the country's second president. He and Samuel were distant cousins, as they had the same great-great-grandfather.

Samuel's criticisms of the British were often

SAMUEL ADAMS
(From Prints & Photographs Div., Library of Congress)

Massachusetts constitutional convention in 1779 and later in 1788. He ran for Congress in 1788 and was defeated. He served as Massachusetts lieutenant governor from 1789 to 1794, and became governor when the incumbent, John Hancock, died on October 8, 1793. He was elected to three full one-year terms, and retired on June 2, 1797. He died six years later.

Adams' statue was placed in Statuary Hall, in the national capitol, as one of the two from Massachusetts.

ADAMS BIBLIOGRAPHY

Cushing, Harry Alonzo, ed. *The Writings of Samuel Adams.* New York (4 vols. 1904–1908).
Fowler, Lillian M. *Samuel Adams: Radical Puritan.* New York (1997).

Henderson, H. James. *Party Politics in the Continental Congress.* New York (1974).

Hosmer, James K. *Life of Samuel Adams.* Boston (1885).

Lewis, Paul (Gerson, Noel B.). *The Grand Incendiary: A Biography of Samuel Adams.* New York (1973).

Rakove, Jack N. *The Beginnings of National Politics: An Interpretive History of the Continental Congress.* New York (1979).

Seccombe, Matthew. "From Revolution to Republic: The Later Political Career of Samuel Adams, 1774–1803." Unpublished Ph.D. dissertation, Yale University (1978).

Wells, William P. *The Life and Public Services of Samuel Adams.* Boston (3 vols., 1865).

*1796 recipient of votes for
vice president— Federalist Party*

Oliver Ellsworth

Born April 29, 1745, in Windsor, Connecticut; died November 26, 1807, in Windsor. Married Abigail Wolcott in 1772. They had at least three sons and one daughter.

Oliver was the son of Captain David and Jemima Leavitt Ellsworth. They lived on a Connecticut farm, but the captain also had occasional militia duties. His father wanted Oliver to be a minister and sent him to Yale College in 1762. He left at the end of his second year, having displayed poor scholarship and conduct. He next enrolled at Princeton and graduated in 1766. Ellsworth returned home and studied theology with a local minister for less than a year. Next he turned to studying the law, and in 1770 was admitted to the bar.

At first Ellsworth's business was abysmal. To support himself he also chopped wood and took over his father's farm. He could not afford a horse and had to walk the ten miles to court in Hartford — and ten miles back to his farm. The estimated compensation for his first three *years* as a lawyer was 3 pounds. Part of Ellsworth's problem was location, and his prospects improved when he moved from Windsor to Hartford in 1775.

Ellsworth's first public office came in 1773 when the town of Windsor named him a deputy to the General Assembly. When the early stages of the Revolution began in 1775, he was named to a legislative committee that supervised expenditures for the Connecticut military. In 1777 Ellsworth became

OLIVER ELLSWORTH
(Reproduced from the Collections of the Library of Congress)

state's attorney for Hartford County, and remained in the post until 1785. The Assembly also selected him as a delegate to the Continental Congress, beginning in 1777 and continuing until 1783. The young man's prominence was evidenced by his selection to the Council on Safety that worked with the governor in managing the state's war effort. Ellsworth was an active member of both the state Assembly and the Congress. During this same period his legal business burgeoned. He was an energetic attorney, having over a thousand cases in his office at one time. Through his active practice and effective money management, he became quite wealthy as well as prominent.

Ellsworth had been named to the Governor's Council in 1780, and in 1784 this Council became the Supreme Court of Errors. That was the future chief justice's first judicial office. Shortly thereafter he moved up to the Superior Court. In 1787 Ellsworth became a delegate to the constitutional convention in Philadelphia. Appropriately, Ellsworth was an active member of the committee that prepared the judiciary article. He had to leave for judicial duties in Connecticut before the convention concluded its work, so he did not sign the constitution. Ellsworth was a powerful and influential voice urging ratification at the state convention called to consider the issue.

Ellsworth was elected as one of his state's first two United States Senators. His largest contribution to the new government was in being the principal author of the Judiciary Act of 1789. That Act established the structure of the federal court system that in large part is still the outline today. Ellsworth resigned from the Senate in 1796 to accept appointment as chief justice of the Supreme Court. His selection followed the Senate's rejection of John Rutledge for that position. He served three years without leaving a significant mark. In a poll of scholars rating the justices, Ellsworth was considered to have made an average contribution, not great, but not a failure.

President John Adams selected Ellsworth to journey to France and attempt to negotiate a reduction in tensions that were threatening to break out into war. The journey was physically taxing, and Ellsworth did not arrive in Paris until March of 1800. His health never recovered. Negotiations were unproductive. A modest set of agreements was reached that dealt with less controversial matters and deferred the larger issue of reparations for confiscated ships and cargoes. Once finished in Paris, Ellsworth sent his written resignation as chief justice back to America in October while he remained in England to seek improvements in his health. Finally in March 1801 Ellsworth sailed home. His public life was over.

ELLSWORTH BIBLIOGRAPHY

Brown, William G. *The Life of Oliver Ellsworth.* New York (1905).

Casto, William R. *The Supreme Court in the Early Republic: The Chief Justiceships of John Jay and Oliver Ellsworth.* Columbia, S.C. (1995).

Kraus, Michael, "Oliver Ellsworth," in Friedman, Leon & Israel, Fred L., eds. *The Justices of the United States Supreme Court 1789–1969.* New York & London (1969), vol. 1, pp. 223–235.

Lankevich, George J. *The Supreme Court in American Life.* New York City, et al. (1990), vol. 1, pp. 267–270.

Marcus, Maeva. *The Documentary History of the Supreme Court of the United States, 1789–1800.* New York City (1985), vol. 1, pp. 115–123.

Umbreit, Kenneth Bernard. *Our Eleven Chief Justices.* Port Washington, N.Y. (1969 reprint of 1938 publication), vol. 1, pp. 79–110.

Election of 1800

NOMINATIONS

Federalist Party Congressional Caucus (1st), in Philadelphia, Pennsylvania, May 3, 1800. *President*— John Adams, no ballots were taken. The party leaders had unenthusiastically decided to support Adams for a second term before the caucus was held. *Vice president*— Charles C. Pinckney, also chosen without any formal balloting since his name had been selected in private beforehand.

Democratic-Republican Party Congressional Caucus (1st), at Marache's Boarding House in Philadelphia Pennsylvania, May 11, 1800. *President*— Thomas Jefferson, who was not formally nominated because there was no opposition to his selection. *Vice president*— Aaron Burr, who received a unanimous vote of the 46 senators and representatives present. George Clinton had been considered before the caucus was held, but was unenthusiastic and wished not to be chosen.

GENERAL ELECTION

Thomas Jefferson — 73 electoral votes (7+ states)

Aaron Burr — 73 electoral votes (7+states)

John Adams — 65 electoral votes (6+states)

Charles C. Pinckney — 64 electoral votes (6+states)

John Jay — 1 electoral vote, cast to keep Adams and Pinckney from tying.

Jefferson and Burr having tied, the House of Representatives met to choose between them. From February 11 to 14 and February 16 to 17, 1801, the House voted. On the 36th ballot, Jefferson won with ten states, Burr four, and two abstained.

Winners

Thomas Jefferson, 3d president

Aaron Burr, 3d vice president

Losers

John Adams, Charles C. Pinckney

1800 presidential nominee —
Federalist Party

John Adams

No biographical sketch of Adams is included because he served as president from March 4, 1797, until March 4, 1801 (2nd president).

State Represented: Massachusetts.

Birth: October 30, 1735, at Braintree (now Quincy), Massachusetts.

Age on Inauguration Day (March 4, 1801): 65 years, 4 months.

Death: July 4, 1826, at Quincy, Massachusetts, age 90 years, 8 months.

1800 vice presidential nominee —
Federalist Party

Charles Cotesworth Pinckney

Full name: Charles Cotesworth Pinckney.

State represented: South Carolina.

Birth: February 25, 1746, at Charles Town, South Carolina.

Age on Inauguration Day (March 4, 1801): 55 years, ½ month.

Education: English schools, 1758–1764; graduated from Westminster School; entered Middle Temple, Oxford, for law studies, 1764–1769.

Religion: Church of England.

Ancestry: Father-in-law Henry Middleton was first president of Continental Congress; brother Thomas was vice presidential nominee (see election of 1796); Charles Pinckney, first cousin, was prominent South Carolina revolutionary leader; Charles Pinckney, son of first Charles Pinckney and second cousin of the candidate, was governor of South Carolina, U.S. Senator, and held other offices.

Occupation: Lawyer.

Public offices: South Carolina House of Commons, 1769–?; South Carolina Provincial Congress, 1774–1776; South Carolina General Assembly 1776–1786; delegate to constitutional convention; offered Supreme Court position by President Washington, but declined; declined Secretary of War, January 1794; offered Secretary of State, August 1795, but declined; Ambassador to France, 1796, but not received; special commissioner to resolve French-American differences, but not received by French government; Federalist vice presidential nominee 1800; elected South Carolina state Senate, 1801–1802; unsuccessful Federalist nominee for president 1804 and 1808.

Death: August 16, 1825, Charleston, at age 79 years, 5½ months.

Burial: St. Michael's Episcopal Church, Charleston, South Carolina.

Home: Belmont plantation, near Charleston.

Personal characteristics: Tall, heavy-set, imposing presence. Not a brilliant speaker, but concise and clear. Genial, fond of jokes, good humor.

Father: Charles Pinckney (Aug. 13, 1699/1700–July 12, 1758), prominent South Carolina colonial official, planter, and judge.

Mother: Elizabeth (Eliza) Lucas (Dec. 28, 1722–May 26, 1793), married on May 27, 1744; daugher of George Lucas, an Antigua and then South Carolina planter.

Siblings: George Lucas (June 14–29, 1747). Harriott (Aug. 7, 1748–Dec. 19, 1830), married Daniel Horry on Feb. 15, 1768, a wealthy South Carolina planter. Thomas (Oct. 23,

JOHN ADAMS
(From the author's collection)

1750–Nov. 2, 1828) — see sketch at election of 1796.

First wife: Sally Middleton (July 5, 1756–May 8, 1784), daughter of Henry Middleton, a large landowner in South Carolina and president of the Continental Congress in 1774; married Sept. 28, 1773.

Children: Charles Cotesworth (Sept. 10, 1779–?), died in childhood. Maria Henrietta (?–May 13, 1836), never married. Harriott (Dec. 17, 1776–March 15, 1866), never married. Eliza Lucas (?–April 16, 1851), married Ralph Izard.

Second wife: Mary Stead (1752–Jan. 14, 1812), daughter of Benjamin Stead and Mary (Johnson) Stead, granddaughter of South Carolina governor Robert Johnson; married July 23, 1786.

Children: None.

Son, brother, and cousin of prominent Revolutionary War leaders, Charles Cotes-

CHARLES COTESWORTH PINCKNEY
(From the South Caroliniana Library)

worth Pinckney was a member of an illustrious and talented family. His mother, Eliza Lucas Pinckney, had been the first to successfully grow indigo in South Carolina. As a young girl she had inherited a plantation after her father died, and almost by herself developed the techniques necessary for the crop. Pinckney's father, also named Charles, was a leader in the Charles Town legal community,

a colonial official in various capacities, and served as chief justice of the colony. Charles Cotesworth's cousin Charles was also a South Carolina political leader, but when affairs went badly for the colony during the war he had succumbed to political and financial pressure to renounce the rebellion. When the war took a turn for the better, he found himself despised by the now-successful rebels and died soon thereafter. That Charles' son, confusingly named Charles also, was a delegate to the United States Constitutional Convention, governor of and U.S. senator from South Carolina, and a diplomat. Thomas Pinckney, Charles Cotesworth's brother (the only prominent Pinckney not named Charles and therefore a unique man indeed), is the subject of a biographical sketch earlier in this book, having been the defeated Federalist nominee for vice president in 1796.

Charles Cotesworth received many advantages that perhaps explain his, and his family's, rise to influence. In 1753 his father had been appointed as South Carolina's agent in England for commercial and other affairs, and Charles Cotesworth and the rest of the family went with him. The boy of seven was enrolled in excellent schools, far preferable to those he would have attended in Charles Town. His father returned to South Carolina in 1758 and contracted malaria, from which he soon died. Charles Cotesworth remained on in English schools, performing exceptionally well at his studies. A legal career was his appointed course, and upon finishing at Westminster School in 1763 he entered Christ Church College in Oxford. In January 1764, Pinckney was admitted to the Middle Temple, one of the four Inns of Court in England at which all the country's lawyers received their training. While there he took coursework from William Blackstone, one of the great figures in the development of English law.

Charles Cotesworth's health was often bad and for a time he had to leave school, going to France and entering the royal military. The more rigorous life at the academy was thought conducive to good health. He completed his studies at Oxford in 1769 and was admitted to the English bar on January 27, 1769. After gaining practical experience during one circuit of court he returned to America, having spent 16 years in England. He settled in Charles Town, South Carolina, the family home.

The new lawyer quickly plunged into the practice of both his profession and politics. He was elected to the House of Commons. He also ran a plantation, as apparently did all the Pinckney politicians. Land and the money it represented was almost a prerequisite for political leadership in Charles Town and the South Carolina low country, as opposed to the more democratic up country. Charles Cotesworth also served on the vestry of St. Philip's Church, which in the absence of formal city government for Charles Town was the principal substitute. An early and unique honor was his selection as one of four curators for the Charles Town Museum, making him and the others the first such officials in America, a country that was so new that preserving the past seemed pointless. Devotion to science and education was a trait that marked Charles Cotesworth throughout his career.

Pinckney, in January 1775, became a member of the South Carolina provincial congress. One burning issue was whether to continue the Church of England, or Episcopal Church, as the established religion in the Colony. Pinckney voted, despite his strong allegiance to the church, to disestablish it and to permit complete religious freedom. The measure failed.

Pinckney began his military service early in the growing controversy between America and England. In 1772 he became an ensign in a Charles Town regiment. By April 1775 it was evident to most Carolinians that war was imminent, and rapid organization of military forces began. The Provisional Congress chose Pinckney and four others to be on a special secret committee to prepare the colony's defense. On April 21, 1775, Pinckney took his first "treasonous" step by leading a break-in at the State House armory where arms were seized from the British. The new rebel then was appointed to a Committee of Intelligence to work in the less revolutionary up-country areas in hopes of rallying them to the cause. Pinckney's boldness and leadership abilities achieved him a promotion to captain of the regulars in June 1775. He was sent to North Carolina to raise troops.

It was decided that the fort guarding Charles Town harbor, Fort Johnson, should be seized by the revolutionaries. This would block British attempts to enter the harbor. Pinckney was chosen as one of three captains that were to get troops ready to march on the fort. On September 15, 1775, he led one of two companies into the fort, causing a quick and wholly successful battle. Royal influence in South Carolina was, temporarily, at an end.

Throughout the Revolution Charles Cotesworth would be drawn first to military responsibilities and then would have to meet his political ones. Frequently he served on committees, which varied from examining defenses, to considering reprisals against Tories, or even debating the kind of government South Carolina should adopt after the Revolution.

Pinckney's military experiences continued to multiply. He was promoted to major and selected to prepare a battery across the harbor from Fort Johnson. In February 1776, he was promoted to lieutenant colonel, and in September was made a colonel. The South Carolina army became part of the Continental Army that same month. The war shifted to the north for a year and Pinckney for a time was able to devote himself completely to his legislative duties.

Few South Carolinians could speak French when General Lafayette visited on June 1777, and thus the multilingual Charles Cotesworth and his brother Thomas were singled out to assist in entertaining the French patriot. Lafayette and other foreign officers were going north to join General Washington's forces. Pinckney's father-in-law, Henry Middleton, as well as Pinckney's commanding officer wrote letters of introduction for him. Washington placed the South Carolinian on his staff and counseled with him on Charles Town defenses. Pinckney could not give an optimistic appraisal.

In September 1777 Pinckney was with Washington at the crucial Battle of Brandywine. This was a serious defeat for the Americans. Pinckney played an important role in rallying the defeated troops and directing their retreat, thereby preventing a complete rout. The following month he was still with Washington's staff at the Battle of Germantown. Taking his leave from Washington's army, Pinckney consulted with various leaders at the national capital, and then returned home to take command of the First South Carolina Regiment.

Again he divided his time between military and governmental responsibilities. Finally his efforts were rewarded in the adoption of a state constitution that permitted complete religious freedom and disestablished the Church of England. The formerly appointed upper house of the legislature was made elective.

Pinckney took his troops south to the Florida border (then Spanish territory) to end British occupation there. Supply problems as well as devastating malaria, heat, and other calamities thwarted the expedition and forced all the troops to return, with Pinckney responsible for assuring that the sick returned safely. The disaster caused a duel to be fought between the commanding officer of the Florida campaign and one of his subordinates who had criticized the expedition. Pinckney served as second to the commanding officer, Major General Robert Howe, but there were only slight injuries.

In November 1778, there was a new effort by the British to take command of the southern states. The British invasion began in southern Georgia. Pinckney was among the troops who were sent south to give battle. Arriving too late, Savannah having already fallen to the Redcoats, the army was unable to give serious resistance at this time. The rebels were forced in April 1779 to begin a retreat northward from Georgia and into Carolina. A numerically much superior British force began a campaign to roll the insurgents back. The Pinckney family home at Belmont was destroyed by the advancing British troops. Charles Cotesworth's mother had left the home before it was seized. Brother Thomas' Auckland plantation had likewise been destroyed by the British. Faced with the severe reduction in his family's fortunes, Charles Cotesworth offered to split all of what he had with his mother and brother.

Charles Town still had not fallen, and Pinckney backed a decision to strengthen Fort Moultrie, across the harbor from Fort Johnson, in an effort to prevent British ships from entering the harbor. Unfortunately the British were able to run the gauntlet successfully. Charles Cotesworth's troops at Fort Moultrie thereby were left out of the battle. A siege ensued. Pinckney participated in various councils to determine whether to surrender, and he argued against it. His objections were expressed strenuously and carried the day, but not the next when the decision to surrender was made. The British took command of Charles Town on May 11, 1780, and Charles Cotesworth began almost two years of effective removal from the war. He could not, under the chivalrous code of the day, join in battle against the British until he was exchanged with a British officer of equal rank who had been captured by the Americans.

Pinckney's town house in Charles Town was commandeered by the British. Pinckney stayed in his cousin Charles' house on a plantation, where, because of the nearness of mosquito-infested swamps, he contracted malaria. As were many prominent Charles Town leaders, Pinckney was pressured by promises of leniency and return of his lands to renounce his support for the Revolution. His cousin Charles' renunciation came at this time. Charles Cotesworth's response was of an entirely different order:

> The freedom and independence of my country are the Gods of my Idolatry. I mean to rejoin the American Army as soon after my exchange as I possibly can; I will exert my abilities to the utmost in the cause I am engaged in; and to obtain Success, will attempt every measure that is not cruel or dishonourable.

Though Charles Town remained under British occupation, patriot volunteers in the rest of the South were having considerable success in battles against British General Cornwallis. The crucial stronghold of Camden, South Carolina, had to be abandoned by the British in May 1781. As the military situation worsened, the British decided to send many of the most prominent prisoners in Charles Town to Philadelphia, Pinckney included, there to await their exchange. It was not until March 3, 1782, that Pinckney was finally exchanged, after one year and ten months of inaction as a prisoner. The war was effectively already over.

Pinckney again engaged in his duties with the General Assembly. He had been reelected in 1781 though he was still a prisoner who had not yet been exchanged. One of his disappointments in the Assembly was that he failed to prevent his cousin Charles' estate from being confiscated because of his renunciation

of the American cause. The humiliation was too much for the cousin and he died in September 1782. Formal end of Charles Cotesworth's military service in the war came on November 3, 1783, when he was discharged from the army commissioned as a brigadier general by brevet. He had served eight-and-a-half years in an effort to bring independence, and his cause had succeeded.

War had seriously injured Pinckney financially. His law practice had withered and his plantations were in disarray. Still, public duties consumed his time. In the legislature Pinckney strongly defended slavery, believing that it was necessary for progress of the southern economy. He also was an enthusiastic spokesman for education, knowing how difficult it would be for most to receive the foreign training he had gained. Three colleges were established by a bill he helped to pass in 1785.

Pinckney's next significant contribution came in his selection as one of South Carolina's delegates to what became the Constitutional Convention of 1787, but what was called merely to recommend changes to the existing Articles of Confederation. His brother Thomas had just been selected governor of South Carolina, and thus both simultaneously were embarking on major leadership responsibilities for their state. Once at the convention, Pinckney opposed the initial effort to discard the Articles and start anew on a constitution, his legalistic sensibilities being repelled by this technically doubtful decision. Yet he realized as much as any that a strong national government was necessary and acquiesced quickly to the sweeping proposal.

An aristocratic bent to Pinckney's positions at the convention was noticeable. As were many, he opposed an elected House of Representatives. He declared that it would be difficult to get a significant number of people to vote, and even when they did cast ballots the choices would as likely as not be poorly reasoned. The United States Senate should in his view be populated only by the wealthy, being the more educated and "stable" of society. To ensure this, he proposed making the Senate position non-salaried. As most Southerners, he also wanted slaves to be counted equally with whites in determining the population of a state and therefore the number of United States Representatives to which the state would be entitled. To perpetuate slavery, Pinckney also spoke for provisions to prevent future emancipation. Property and citizenship requirements should be imposed for all national officers, again ensuring that the uneducated would not rule.

Pinckney was pleased with the new constitution, believing that the bitter differences that surfaced at the convention between the slave interests of the South and the mercantile desires of the North had been satisfactorily compromised. He enthusiastically signed the document. Once back in South Carolina, Pinckney helped lead the fight for ratification of the new constitution.

Pinckney was a delegate to the ratification convention and was named chairman of the important Committee on Rules. Ratification came by a 149–73 vote. His service to the state seemed to be over, as he declined to stand for election to any office in the first ballots taken to fill the new government. The Departments of State and War were each offered to Pinckney by President Washington, but Pinckney declined. His legal affairs had been long neglected during his military service; another break would be difficult. In 1791, he also refused a remarkable offer made both to him and his law partner, Edward Rutledge, that one of them accept a position on the United States Supreme Court. Both lawyers were heavily in debt and could not afford to leave.

Perhaps feeling abler a few years later to leave his law practice, Pinckney accepted Washington's plea that he become ambassador to America's most important war ally, France. However, by the time of the appointment in 1796, France had gone through its own bloody revolution. The new radical leaders refused to receive Pinckney. America was remaining neutral in the French-English war then raging, and this infuriated the French. Pinckney went to Amsterdam to await further instructions, and he was furious over his treatment. President John Adams made a new effort after he took office in March 1797, and he appointed Pinckney one of three commissioners to France. He, John Marshall and Elbridge Gerry

met in Paris on October 4, 1797. The French foreign minister still was not ready to accept these envoys and instead secretly appointed three commissioners of his own to meet with the Americans. All agreed to keep the identity of the French representatives secret, and in negotiations and correspondence the Americans merely referred to the Frenchmen as X, Y, and Z. The French insisted on payment of a substantial bribe before substantive negotiations could begin, but Pinckney responded, "No. Not a sixpence." Further intransigence by the French caused the Americans to return home, though Gerry did remain behind in an unofficial capacity. In the subsequent furor in the United States over this French corruption, which was dramatically labeled the "XYZ Affair," Pinckney's comment was embellished to be "millions for defense, but not a cent for tribute."

Upon Pinckney's return to America he learned that President Adams had appointed him a major general, one of three under the command of Lieutenant General Washington. War with France seemed imminent. Alexander Hamilton, Pinckney, and Henry Knox were ranked in this order as major generals. Questions about this relative rank, raised petulantly by Henry Knox, caused Pinckney to offer to exchange places with Knox. "Let us first dispose of our enemies[;] we shall then have time to settle the question of rank." Pinckney traveled widely in his Southern department to prepare troops, build forts, and otherwise stand ready to repel any attack. With the fall of the French Directory and the takeover by Napoleon Bonaparte, the threat ended. Pinckney served from July 25, 1798, until June 18, 1800. Minor naval engagements occurred and several French ships were captured, but there was no land war.

Pinckney's brother Thomas had been nominated to run as vice president with John Adams in 1796. Charles Cotesworth was selected to run with Adams in 1800. The election promised to be close and the vote of South Carolina was thought to be, and it was, crucial. Presidential electors in South Carolina were to be selected by the state legislature, and the general election gave the Jeffersonian Republicans a legislative majority. When the legislature met, Charles Cotesworth's supporters suggested that a compromise be struck and the vote of electors chosen be given to Jefferson for president and Pinckney for vice president. Had the deal been made and South Carolina's eight electoral votes been taken from the Republican vice presidential nominee Burr and given to Pinckney, Jefferson would have become president and Pinckney vice president. Pinckney was offended and he rejected the suggestion. President Adams heard of his decision and thanked him warmly for his loyalty.

Pinckney's political career almost was over in 1800. In 1804 and 1808 he was the Federalist nominee for president but his selection was merely a token contest of the election that all knew would be won by the Jeffersonian Republicans. He devoted his life to his plantations, his law practice, and his sincere religious convictions. He did serve a term in the South Carolina Assembly in 1801, being elected at the same time that he and Adams were running for national office. His civic interests included work for the Society of the Cincinnati, the presidency of which he gained after Alexander Hamilton was killed by vice president Aaron Burr in an 1804 duel.

Analysis of Qualifications

A major difficulty in measuring Pinckney's possible impact as president is that he never served in any executive position other than in the military. He was a patriot, an excellent general, an open-minded if conservative legislator, and he was progressive on many religious and educational issues. He ultimately lost political power in South Carolina, but not the respect of those who had followed him, because his party represented the aristocratic wealthy and undemocratic elements of society that could not survive as a political influence in America's new politics. Pinckney was not a political leader who could be ranked with the pre-eminent men of his day.

He was a graceful, generous man, who gave freely of his time and money. His religious and civic activities marked him as a man with a supreme social conscience. His frequent disavowal of offers of public office, instead preferring the routine of his legal practice and his plantations, shows more than any other action that he did not crave political power. His legal abilities were not considered brilliant; he was not a forceful or dramatic orator. But he spoke clearly and concisely. He had much common sense. His height and bulk made him an imposing physical presence. His legal practice became extremely lucrative, indicating his appeal and success as an attorney.

As president in 1800 or after, Pinckney might have been troubled by an offer such as came to President Jefferson to secure under questionable authority the Louisiana Purchase. Just as he was reluctant at the Constitutional Convention to sweep away legal niceties and proceed to consider a completely new charter for the country, so he might have been reluctant to extend executive power as president. Yet also just as at the constitutional convention, his initial uncertainty may well have given way to concern for a strong national government. His affection for and understanding of England would have made him reluctant to begin war against it over the frequent seizure of American ships, and for the impressment or kidnapping of American sailors. Jefferson's answer to these insults was the embargo. In 1808, Pinckney attacked the Embargo, and there is no doubt that it would have been repealed had a Federalist Congress been elected with Pinckney. Instead, the Republican Congress repealed it after Jefferson had to admit the Act had been a failure. As war sentiment grew, Pinckney, with his military background, may have served admirably as president. He also would have seen the extreme danger lurking in the still-weak United States attempting to wage war against the most powerful country in the world.

Pinckney as president, on balance, would have been a solid, perhaps plodding leader. He never demonstrated originality of thinking. His role in the Constitutional Convention was as a defender of aristocratic Southern interests. He definitely was not a democrat, but believed in rule by the wealthy and privileged. Whether he could work well with Congress is uncertain, but he did serve several terms in the South Carolina legislature and was elected president of the senate, a sign that he was well respected by his peers. His natural conservatism would have kept him from dangerous foreign policy decisions during this heated period in American relations with many countries, including France, Britain, and the Barbary States, those north African countries whose pirates terrorized shipping and demanded tribute. He was an intelligent man, free from wild emotional excesses. He was incorruptible, placing honor before financial or political reward, as shown both by his refusal of favors from the British while a war prisoner and from the Republicans when a vice presidential candidate.

There were in Charles Cotesworth Pinckney the qualities of intellect, patriotism, integrity, and leadership to have made him a satisfactory, but not popular president. His administration would probably have been similar to that of John Adams — on balance effective, tinged with aristocratic views, conservative, easy prey for political attacks from the Jeffersonians. He does not appear to have had potential for greatness, but among the ranks of those who were thwarted in attempts for the presidency, he deserves to be classed as an eminently acceptable candidate.

PINCKNEY BIBLIOGRAPHY

(See bibliography for Thomas Pinckney, election of 1796.)

Williams, Frances Leigh. *A Founding Family: The Pinckneys of South Carolina.* New York City and London (1978).

Zahniser, Marvin R. *Charles Cotesworth Pinckney: Founding Father.* Chapel Hill, N.C. (1967).

Election of 1804

NOMINATIONS

Federalist Party public dinner: February 22, 1804, in Washington, a meeting of party leaders, congressmen, and others. *President*— Charles C. Pinckney, who was not specifically chosen for the top spot on the ticket at this time; a later meeting decided which of the two nominees named at this dinner would be a candidate for president, and which for the second office, and Pinckney received the top position then. *Vice president*— Rufus King, who along with Pinckney was selected at this dinner for one of the two places on the ticket; the decision was later made that King would be the candidate for vice president.

Democratic-Republican Congressional Caucus (2nd): February 25, 1804, held in the Capitol, Washington, D.C. *President*: Thomas Jefferson, selected without any formal vote being taken. *Vice president*— George Clinton, nominated on the first ballot with 67 out of 108 votes cast. Jefferson and his Cabinet had previously decided upon Clinton, but at the caucus a revolt against this dictation occurred, with John Breckinridge of Kentucky being the principal opposition choice.

GENERAL ELECTION

On September 25, 1804, the Twelfth Amendment to the Constitution was ratified, which provided for each member of the Electoral College to vote for one person for president, and to cast a separate ballot for vice president. No longer would electors cast two votes without distinguishing which was for president and which for the second office.

Jefferson and Clinton —162 electoral votes (15 states)

Pinckney and King —14 electoral votes (2 states)

Winners

Thomas Jefferson, 3rd president

George Clinton, 4th vice president

Losers

Charles C. Pinckney, Rufus King

*1804 presidential nominee—
Federalist Party*

Charles C. Pinckney

The biographical sketch for Pinckney appears at page 26, as he was a candidate for vice president and lost in the election of 1800.

State represented: South Carolina.

Birth: February 25, 1746, at Charleston, South Carolina.

Age on Inauguration Day (March 4, 1805): 59 years, ½ month.

Death: August 16, 1825, in Charleston, S.C., at age 79 years, 5½ months.

---

*1804 nominee for vice president—
Federalist Party*

Rufus King

Full Name: Rufus King.

State represented: New York.

Birth: March 24, 1755, at Dunstan Landing, part of Scarborough, Massachusetts, later Maine.

Age on Inauguration Day (March 4, 1805): 49 years, 11½ months.

Education: Local Scarborough school; then Dummer School, Byfield, Maine, 1766–1773; Harvard College, 1773–May 11, 1775, when college closed due to war; resumed at Harvard October 1775, in Concord, New Hampshire; returned to Cambridge in July 1776, graduated 1st in class, 1777; studied law in Newburyport; admitted to Bar in 1780.

Religion: Episcopalian.

Ancestry/prominent relatives: Grandfather arrived from England in late 17th century; Cyrus King (half-brother), a U.S. Representative from Massachusetts; William King (half-brother), 1st governor of Maine; John Alsop King and James Gore King (sons), U.S. Representatives from New York (John) and New Jersey (James); John also served as governor of New York.

Occupation: Attorney.

Public offices: Justice of the peace, 1781– 1783; elected to Massachusetts House of Representatives, 1783–1784; Congress of Confederation, 1784–1787; Federal Constitutional Convention in 1787; Massachusetts ratification convention in 1788; moved to New York, elected to General Assembly, 1788–1789; U.S. Senator, July 16, 1789–May 23, 1796, resigned; ambassador to Great Britain, May 20, 1796– May 18, 1803; defeated as involuntary candidate for U.S. Senate from New York, November 9, 1804; defeated as Federalist nominee for vice president, 1804 and 1808; declined to be special envoy to England, 1806; defeated for New York State Assembly, 1807; U.S. Senator, March 4, 1813–March 3, 1825; nominee for New York governor, 1816, defeated; defeated for president 1816; ambassador to England, May 5, 1825–June 16, 1826, resigned.

Death: April 29, 1827, at Jamaica, New York, at age 72 years, 1 month.

Burial: Grace Churchyard, Jamaica, New York.

Home: Large farm near Jamaica, New York.

Personal characteristics: 5'10" tall; short dark hair; ruddy complexion; broad brow; piercing eyes; musical voice.

Father: Richard King (1718–March 27, 1775); prominent merchant and ship-owner in Maine.

Mother: Isabella Bragdon (1731–October 1759); married November 20, 1753; daughter of Samuel Bragdon.

Stepmother: Mary Black (1736–May 25, 1816); married January 31, 1762; a first cousin of first wife and daughter of Samuel Black of York, Maine.

Siblings: Mary (November, 1756–March 30, 1824), married Dr. Robert Southgate in 1773. Paulina (March 1759–1833), married Dr. Aaron Porter in 1777.

Half brothers/sisters: Richard (December 22, 1762–1830), married Hannah Larrabee on January 14, 1790. Isabella (1764–1770). Dorcas (May 20, 1766–1833), married Joseph Leland on December 28, 1786. William (February 9, 1768–June 17, 1852), married Ann Frazier in 1800, was first governor of Maine. Elizabeth Lyden (1770–1853), married Benjamin Jones Porter in 1791. Cyrus (September 6, 1772–April 25, 1817), lawyer, U.S. Representative, married Hannah Storer in 1797.

Wife: Mary Alsop (October 17, 1769–June 5, 1819); married March 30, 1786; daughter of wealthy New York merchant John Alsop.

Children: Caroline (1790–1793). Henry (July 1792–September 1792). John Alsop (January 3, 1788–July 7, 1867), married Mary Ray on January 3, 1810; governor of New York, U.S. Representative, attorney. Charles (March 16, 1789–September 27, 1867), married Eliza Gracie in 1810, and after her death married Henrietta Liston Low on October 10, 1826; merchant, editor, president of Columbia College. James Gore (May 8, 1791–October 3, 1853), married Sarah Rogers Gracie on February 14, 1813; banker, railroad executive, U.S. Representative. Edward (1795–1836), married Sarah Worthington in 1816. Frederick Gore (1802–April 23, 1829), married Emily Post in 1825. Elizabeth (?–?).

Historic sites/memorials: King's home, "King Manor" in New York City is at 150th Street and Jamaica Avenue. It is now a municipal building.

King's early days were prosperous. His father owned several slaves, a sign of real wealth in colonial New England.

The senior King's prosperity caused many of his debtors to be resentful. Some of Rufus' early memories were of mob intimidation of his family. At least once the house was ransacked and the family held hostage by a mob of lawless debtors. To add to the King family troubles, Rufus' father was a Tory. He suffered as much humiliation for his political views as for his financial position. Nine months before the elder King's death, while he was in ill health, a mob held him at gunpoint and forced him to denounce his English views. Such were Rufus' experiences with the early days of the rebellion.

When Rufus was just 12, he was sent to a small private school called Dummer, one of the elite schools in America at that time. He then attended Harvard, where he was conspicuous at oratory. At Harvard he did not share his father's English sympathies. There is no record of King's opinion or reaction to his father's politics, but his own ardent rebel views may have been in part affected by his father's persecution.

After graduation from Harvard, Rufus moved to Newburyport, Massachusetts, to study law in the office of the future dean of the Harvard Law School, Theophilus Parsons. Parsons himself had only been a lawyer for three years, and thus the eminence of his later career was not yet evident. For a time after studying under Parsons, King returned to Scarborough, Maine, but his father's legacy of pro–British politics made the younger King suspect in the town. Rufus was even accused, along with his brother-in-law and three others, of being anti-revolutionary. They were to be tried in court for this charge, but Rufus stayed away from the jurisdiction of the court and eventually the charges were dropped. King decided to remain in Newburyport, but his legal practice was at first unsuccessful. He came into a sizable sum after he sold the land he had inherited from his father, thus easing the financial strain. King's revolutionary fervor was strong. He had enlisted in August 1778 for a short tour of duty to dislodge the British from Newport, Rhode Island. British reinforcements kept the maneuver from being successful, and King played no additional military role in the war. The following month King's military tour ended.

By July of 1780, King's study under Parsons was completed and he was admitted to the bar that month. By October 1781, he was a justice of the peace and was enjoying a thriving practice. Indeed his speaking skills and his quick intelligence placed him at the forefront of the bar in Newburyport, making him one of the city's prominent citizens.

King's first elective position came because of the unattractiveness of the office to more prominent citizens. Several men refused to serve in the Congress under the Articles of Confederation, and finally King accepted the job. Initially, Congress met at Trenton, New Jersey, and then later in New York City. In December 1784, when he took office as a Congressman, King was commencing almost 40 years of service in elective and appointed positions.

King's most important work in the Congress of the Confederation was his proposal that slavery be excluded in the new northwest territories. His early effort did not succeed but it became the foundation of the subsequent

Northwest Ordinance's exclusion of slavery. King's interest in the West was far surpassed by his concern for New England prosperity. Maritime issues were central, and King was provincial in his attitudes. His efforts on behalf of New England shipping oftentimes ignored Southern concerns about trade. He was little impressed with the need to open the Mississippi River to free American trade, which was a chief stumbling block in the treaty John Jay was negotiating with Spain in 1786. Though he foresaw that eventually America would expand across the Appalachian Mountains, he did not yet want the country's population to be so dispersed as to threaten the cohesiveness of the sections. Many Southerners, including James Monroe, saw King as the secret force behind the decision in the Jay Treaty negotiations to drop insistence upon having the Mississippi River open.

King's increasingly long stays in New York City because of his Congressional duties introduced him to New York society. From this select circle, he won the 17-year-old daughter of a wealthy dry goods merchant as his bride. King and Mary Alsop were married in 1786. She was considered a prize match for King, as the beauty and charm that had attracted many other suitors were matched by her considerable wealth. King's acquaintance and friendship with many of the leading men in New York City expanded after this marriage.

King's three terms as a delegate to the Congress of the Confederation showed him to be parochial in his protection of New England and his ignoring of the interest of other sections of the country. The three terms were the maximum permitted under the Articles of Confederation, but just as his duties as a con-

RUFUS KING
(Reproduced from the Collections of the Library of Congress)

gressman ended, he was selected as a delegate to the Constitutional Convention of 1787. King was fearful of a strong national government. At this stage in his career he was even perhaps considering the desirability of a separate confederation for the Northeast — if not completely independent from the rest of the United States, then at least largely autonomous. King's native Massachusetts was fertile ground for disunion at this point. Many agreed with King that the interests of the Northeast and those of the south were largely antagonistic.

Shay's Rebellion in Massachusetts, a revolt against paying taxes to the government and repaying debts to creditors, was a turning point for King. When the Massachusetts legislature declared the state in rebellion, King was delighted. So profound was the effect of Shay's Rebellion and similar episodes that anarchy, not a strong central government, became King's principal fear.

Also influencing King was his friendship and philosophical discussions with Alexander Hamilton. This great Federalist leader made almost a disciple out of King, as well as becoming a close friend. Hamilton's views on a strong national government based on the protection of property became King's views. On March 3, 1787, King was selected as a delegate to the Constitutional Convention. On May 25 a quorum at the convention was finally organized. King had little influence in the convention, but he did demonstrate his views on the major issues. He believed in a strong executive, and even proposed a term of as long as 20 years for the president. King may have even favored abolishing the states, but was eventually convinced that some minor authority should be left to them. Representation in the House he thought should be based not only on population but also on wealth, as he feared the uneducated masses would otherwise have too strong a voice.

In Massachusetts King was barely chosen a delegate to the constitution ratification convention, mainly because of his long absence from Newburyport and his increasing identification with New York City. At the beginning of the ratification convention in Massachusetts, a clear majority would have voted to reject the document. King was at the forefront of an effort to compromise with the opposition forces by proposing specific amendments that would answer the objections made. This initiative by King and others was probably the most important step in securing ratification in Massachusetts. Even with this compromise, ratification was only by a 187 to 168 vote in the convention.

For business and political reasons, King decided to move his official residence to New York. King was prominent both from being a delegate to Congress as well as from his efforts at the Constitutional Convention. It was a matter of considerable note in New York City that this eminent Massachusetts politician had, upon the creation of the new government, decided to move to that city.

New York Governor George Clinton and New Yorker Alexander Hamilton favored King as one of the state's new senators. When a special session of the legislature met, those who had favored the Constitution met in caucus and selected two other Senate candidates over King. The legislature as a whole, however, failed to give a majority to the caucus choice. After a protracted struggle, King was elected.

In the Senate, King became a strong Hamiltonian, voting for most of the measures proposed by the new Secretary of the Treasury. King supported creating the First Bank of the United States. On October 21, 1791, he was elected one of the first directors of that bank. He would be a director of banking institutions throughout his life. When British warships captured American shipping to the British West Indies, many in the country called for war. King and other Federalists did not think the country was capable of waging war against Great Britain at that time, and tried to calm the growing impetus towards conflict.

Though King was reelected to the Senate in 1794, his margin was narrow. A treaty had been negotiated with England, but it was generally thought unfavorable to the United States. Still, King favored ratification. It was King's suggestion that the worst of the articles in the treaty be sent back for negotiation, and this was probably the difference in the vote.

King was tiring of the Senate, but he was also selective in choosing an alternative. The secretary of state's office became vacant in 1795, but King rejected the offer of the post from President Washington by saying that he did not want to be the target for attacks by the enemies of the administration. In 1796 when Washington appointed him as the country's ambassador to England, he accepted. He arrived in London on July 23, 1796. The belligerent feelings between the two countries were still high. The principal issue between Britain and the United States was the impressment, or the seizure and enforced labor, of American sailors. King did not succeed in resolving the issue, but he did keep it at the forefront of American-English negotiations.

When the Irish rebellion of 1798 was over, King advised Britain not to exile any of the captured Irish leaders to the United States, because he feared that they would spread their revolutionary ideas in America. This request became public and made King the subject of bitter criticism by the American press. King's xenophobia was probably as strong as that of any Federalist back home.

When Thomas Jefferson became president, he retained King's services. King's freedom, however, was greatly curtailed. After little more than a year under the new administration, King resigned. His resignation fueled speculation that he would be a candidate for president or vice president in 1804. The former ambassador was indeed selected as the vice presidential nominee for the badly outnumbered Federalists. Alexander Hamilton had a less lofty but perhaps more achievable goal for King, which was for him to run for governor of New York. King refused, primarily because his chances were poor even for that position.

After a few years of Jeffersonian rule, many Federalists in New England began to talk again of secession. To them, Jefferson's policies favored the South and punished the maritime interests of the North. King gave no support to the disunion movement, but neither was he involved in trying to quiet such emotions. Indeed, one of the great failures of King's political career is that from his resignation as ambassador to Great Britain in 1802 until his election to the United States Senate over ten years later, he stayed almost completely out of politics. His enlightened, moderate views might have had a beneficial impact on the at-times strident Federalist leadership.

Alexander Hamilton's fatal duel with Vice President Aaron Burr on July 11, 1804, was one of the tragedies in King's life. Hamilton and King were great friends. More importantly to King's political career, Hamilton was also his mentor. King had advised Hamilton not to answer Burr's demand that he explain various remarks attributed to him that criticized Burr. Hamilton accepted the advice, and was challenged to a duel because of his silence. King tried to convince Hamilton not to go, but to no avail. Hamilton confided in King that he would participate in the duel, but he would not fire on Burr. For the rest of his life King took great interest in Hamilton's widow and children, and helped raise money for their welfare.

Though King was aloof from politics, he engaged in civic, church, and educational pursuits. He was a charter member of the Academy of Fine Arts in 1801 and a founder of the New-York Historical Society. He purchased a farm in Jamaica where he settled down to the life of a prosperous, gentleman farmer. Animal husbandry was his particular interest. He also was an active trustee of Columbia College for 18 years.

With war fever against Britain again rising in 1807, King spoke for restraint. The British seized and fired upon American shipping. King was fearful that war with Britain at that time would be disastrous, yet his call for restraint was seen as pro–British blindness.

By 1812, war with Britain was a reality. The Jamaican gentleman farmer saw it as a Democratic Party war and joined with most Federalists in opposing it. DeWitt Clinton, governor of New York, also was against the war. Though a Democrat, Clinton began to be spoken of as the Federalist candidate to defeat President Madison. King opposed any coalition with Clinton, believing then as he did throughout the Federalists' long decline that compromise with ambitious, renegade Democrats would only dilute Federalist principles. King reluctantly agreed to meet with Clinton, but never supported his presidential candidacy. King attended a convention in New York City that accepted Clinton as the Federalist nominee, and King may have been one of the three or four delegates at that convention who refused to accede to the choice. King was speculated upon as a running mate if a Southern presidential candidate were named, but that never materialized.

The military disasters that followed one another in the War of 1812 led to sweeping Federalist gains in the New York legislature. The Federalists found themselves in a position to influence the selection of a new U.S. senator from New York. Though the Democrats still were in a majority, they were badly disorganized. Bargaining occurred, allegedly with the Federalists agreeing to support a new Bank of the United States in return for electing a Federalist senator. King was selected and was completely surprised by his victory. He became the only U.S. senator in the new congress who had also served when Washington was president.

King's second tour of duty in the U.S. Senate was as a respected elder statesman. Anti-administration Democrats worked closely with King, and they along with the few other Federalists formed a significant block in the Senate. King played partisan politics, trying to embarrass the Democrats and President Madison wherever possible. Apparently he believed it possible for a Federalist resurgence in 1816. King was not blinded to the country's danger in the War of 1812, particularly after Washington, D.C., was burned and other cities were threatened. New defense measures became King's chief concern, and he even pledged substantial amounts of his own money in this endeavor. His political stock soared. He was seen as a good possibility for a high cabinet position. Such speculation was not fulfilled.

A Federalist resurgence in the election of 1816 also did not materialize. King's fairly narrow defeat in the spring of 1816 after a heated race for New York governor was a severe setback. He lost to Daniel Tompkins by 45,412 votes to 38,647. King had not wanted to be the candidate, but had succumbed to Federalist entreaties. King's tacit selection as the Federalist sacrificial presidential candidate was made because he was the only national leader who commanded respect. His unofficial candidacy received no sanction by any meeting of party members, and apparently only in New York, New Hampshire, Maryland, Massachusetts, Connecticut, and Delaware did his party seriously contest the presidential election. His paltry electoral vote total reflects this apathy. One final and self-destructive act of the Federalists was the holding of the Hartford Convention beginning on December 15, 1814. The anti-war and disunion statements that emerged from the convention stamped the Federalists as a short-sighted and provincial party that could not be trusted. It was to King's credit that he had nothing to do with that convention.

King's remaining years on the national stage were played out in the issues he faced in the U.S. Senate. In time, he became chairman of the Senate Committee on roads and canals, and his committee reported out bills that funded public improvements. In a foresighted fear, he felt the demand for internal improvements would lead to the day when the Treasury would be emptied by every pork barrel project imaginable.

The one great measure adopted by Congress which he authored was the Navigation Act of 1818. Stringent limitations on shipments to the United States from any port that did not accept American shipments were imposed. The reason for the act was the British practice of refusing to take shipments by non–British vessels, and thereby insuring their monopoly on maritime trade. King's desire to build an American merchant marine and to create a pool of sailors was foresighted, both economically and as a base for naval power in the future. He received wide and deserved praise for this measure.

Though King made no effort for reelection in 1819, some of the Democrats, again split with their own party, did see advantage to them in supporting King. Martin Van Buren was one of his Democratic backers in the New York legislature. King's elder statesman image, the fact that he was the last tie in the Senate to the American Revolution and George Washington, greatly aided his cause. The state senate voted unanimously for King's reelection, and there were only three nay votes in the House.

King's last term in the Senate was devoted to the anti-slavery cause. At first he spoke little about the morality of slavery, but saw the issue mainly in economic and political terms. Later his arguments evolved into the equality of all men, including men born as slaves. Many thought his heated and emotional comments on slavery and against the slave states were courting secession. Others saw his motivation as solely political, that he continued to hope for a Federalist rebirth. It is unlikely that King at this date was still trying to revive the Federalist Party, but it is also true that his sectionalism was becoming more pronounced.

As he approached the age of 70, King was quite portly, his hair was thinning, his face fleshy. As the last revolutionary in the Senate, he affected knee breeches, silk stockings and buckled shoes. To many he was a pompous and almost comical figure; to others he was merely aloof. In 1824 there was no chance for his reelection to the Senate and he retired from public office.

King's last years were suffered in bad health. His mind began to weaken as well as his body, and he was alternately petty to friends and servants and then contrite over his actions. Towards the end he began to suffer from hallucinations, and death finally called him on April 29, 1827.

Analysis of Qualifications

King was selected three times for either vice president or president—1804, 1808, and 1816. He was active in national life even before the Constitution was adopted; towards the end of his life he was the last Federalist United States senator. His career spanned the birth, brief command, and then slow death of his party. He was never a dominant leader. His principal biographer counts him as "in the second rank of political figures in the early years of the United States."

King never had a broad national view, and one of his chief failings was his short-sighted, New England viewpoint on many of the major issues he faced. These regional biases were mirrored by his antagonism towards foreigners. He distrusted the French in particular, but all foreign countries were on his suspect list.

The major international issues that followed the 1804 and 1808 elections, when he was defeated for vice president, dealt with America's relationship with Great Britain. During this period King rejected war against Britain, not only because he did not appreciate the hatreds evoked by various British actions, but because he did not believe America was strong enough to wage war against this great naval power. His diplomacy in England from 1796 until 1802 demonstrated real skill and understanding of the British. So long as his sympathies for England did not estrange him from Congress or public sentiment, he might have been a good president during the critical period that faced Jefferson in his second term and Madison in his first. By the time the War of 1812 erupted, King, unlike most Federalists, supported America's participation. Once the British attacked Washington, his support of war measures became fervent.

Had he been elected president in 1816, King would not have found himself facing international crisis so much as domestic problems. In the Senate he was a strong and bitter opponent of slavery, and his methods and words outraged many Southerners. King's emotional and unrestrained attacks against slavery during the 1820 debates over the admission of Missouri as a state would have been far more divisive had he been president than they were when he was a minority senator.

King was widely admired for his eloquence. Daniel Webster considered him in the Senate in 1814 "unequalled in dignity, force, and effectiveness as a speaker." He had a phenomenal memory. He loved books and amassed a large and expensive library in his Jamaica home. Perhaps his most pronounced personal characteristic was his aloof demeanor. He could be arrogant and cold, pompous and self-righteous, and particularly in his later years, was irritable in the extreme. He was a Federalist at heart, and believed in social or class distinctions. He wanted property qualifications for voting, and became incredibly suspicious and fearful of countries where democracy took a radical turn, as it did in France. King's concern about the protection of property, and his desire to exclude those without property or education from influence, marked him as a man who did not fit well into the mainstream of American politics after 1800. He did not want to stoop to the rough and tumble that the new political order required, and his elder statesman image in the United States Senate was probably just the image he had of himself—a man above the fray, serving in office for the good of his state and country but without personal ambition.

King had his personality and political flaws. It is also obvious that he had a strong and patriotic character. He eschewed the extremism of many of his Federalist brothers and genuinely understood, particularly in foreign affairs, the need for moderation. He would probably have served this country well, if not particularly imaginatively, as president.

KING BIBLIOGRAPHY

Brush, E.H. *Rufus King and His Times*. New York City (1926).

Ernst, Robert. *Rufus King, American Federalist*. Chapel Hill, N.C. (1968).

King, Charles R., ed. *The Life and Correspondence*

of *Rufus King.* New York City (6 vols., 1894–1900).

King, James Gore. "Rufus King, Young Statesman of Massachusetts, 1755–89." Unpublished 3 volume typescript, Harvard College Library.

Livermore, Shaw, Jr. *The Twilight of Federalism: The*

Disintegration of the Federalist Party 1815–1830. Princeton, N.J. (1962).

Some family information provided by Professor Robert Ernst, Adelphi University.

Election of 1808

NOMINATIONS

Democratic-Republican Congressional Caucus (3rd): held in the Senate Chamber in the Capitol, Washington, D.C., January 23, 1808. *President—* James Madison, nominated on the first ballot with 83 of 89 votes cast. George Clinton (N.Y.) and James Monroe (Va.) were mentioned as possibilities before the caucus was held, but Madison had been decided upon by most party members before the caucus. *Vice president—* George Clinton, nominated on the first ballot with 79 out of 88 votes cast. He was nominated by the caucus in anticipation that he would refuse, since he really wanted the presidential nomination. Surprisingly, he accepted.

GENERAL ELECTION

PRESIDENT:
James Madison —122 electoral votes (11+ states)
Charles C. Pinckney — 47 electoral votes (5 states)
George Clinton — 6 electoral votes

VICE PRESIDENT:
George Clinton —113 electoral votes (10 states)
Rufus King — 47 electoral votes (5 states)
Three others —15 electoral votes (2 states)

Winners:
    James Madison, 4th president
    George Clinton, 4th vice president
Losers
    Charles C. Pinckney, Rufus King

*1808 presidential nominee—
Federalist Party*

Charles C. Pinckney

The biographical sketch of Pinckney appears at page 26, as he was a candidate for vice president and lost in the election of 1800.

State represented: South Carolina.

Birth: February 25, 1746, at Charleston, South Carolina.

Age on Inauguration Day (March 4, 1809): 63 years, ½ month.

Death: August 16, 1825, in Charleston, South Carolina, at age 79 years, 5½ months.

*1808 vice presidential nominee—
Federalist Party*

Rufus King

The biographical sketch of King appears at page 35, as he was a candidate for vice president and lost in the election of 1804.

State represented: New York.

Birth: March 24, 1755, at Scarborough, Maine.

Age on Inauguration Day (March 4, 1809): 53 years, 11½ months.

Death: April 29, 1827, at Jamaica, New York, age 72 years, 1 month.

Election of 1812

NOMINATIONS

Federalist Party Convention (2nd): September 15–17, 1812, in New York City. *President*— DeWitt Clinton, not actually nominated at this convention. Three days of acrimonious debate occurred; on the third, it was generally agreed that Clinton was the best choice, but that later developments would decide the issue. The Pennsylvania correspondence committee was entrusted with the responsibility of announcing the nominee if events leading to the possible election of Clinton seemed promising. *Vice president*— Jared Ingersoll, nominated by a secret meeting of Clinton's supporters before this national convention was held. On August 26, 1812, in Lancaster, Pennsylvania, Ingersoll was chosen to run with Clinton, and in time this pairing was accepted as the most desirable. At the national convention, the Philadelphia correspondence committee was also entrusted with the choice for the second office. It is unclear if the committee ever officially placed its imprimatur on either candidate, or whether the choices were spread through other media.

Democratic-Republican Congressional Caucus (4th): May 18, 1812, in the Senate Chamber, Capitol Building in Washington, D.C. *President*— James Madison, nominated unanimously on the first ballot. *Vice president*— John Langdon, nominated on the first ballot with 64 votes out of the 82 cast. Elbridge Gerry was his only rival.

Democratic-Republican Congressional Caucus (4th, 2nd session): June 8, 1812, in the Capitol, Washington, D.C. *Vice president*— Elbridge Gerry, nominated on the first ballot with 74 out of the 77 votes cast. After the first session had adjourned, Langdon heard of his selection and declined to accept the nomination.

GENERAL ELECTION

Electoral Vote

President   James Madison —128 electoral votes (11 states)

DeWitt Clinton — 89 electoral votes (7 states)

Vice President   Elbridge Gerry —131 electoral votes (11 states)
Jared Ingersoll — 86 electoral votes (7 states)

Winners
James Madison, 4th president
Elbridge Gerry, 5th vice president

Losers
DeWitt Clinton, Jared Ingersoll, John Langdon

---

*1812 presidential nominee —
Federalist Party*

DeWitt Clinton

Full Name: DeWitt Clinton.

State represented: New York.

Birth: March 2, 1769, at Little Britain, New York.

Age on Inauguration Day (March 4, 1813): 44 years old.

Education: Local grammar school, then at Kingston Academy 1783–1784; Columbia College 1784–1786, No. 1 in class with B.A. degree; studied law with Samuel Jones, Jr., in New York City 1786–1789, and admitted to bar in 1789.

Religion: Presbyterian.

Ancestry/prominent relatives: DeWitt's grandfather, Charles Clinton, arrived from England in 1729; George Clinton (an uncle) was governor of New York and vice president of the United States; James Graham Clinton (half-brother) was a U.S. Representative.

Occupation: Attorney, but practiced only a short time.

Public office: Private Secretary to his uncle, Governor George Clinton 1790–1795; N.Y. State Assembly, January–April 1798; New York State Senator 1798–1802, 1806–1811; delegate

DeWITT CLINTON
(Reproduced from the Collections of the Library of Congress)

to state constitutional convention 1801; member of Council of Appointment of N.Y. 1801, 1802, 1806, 1807; U.S. senator (appointed to a vacancy) February 9, 1802– November 4, 1803, resigned; mayor of New York City 1803–1807, 1810, 1811, 1813, 1814 (appointive position); lt. governor of New York 1811–1813; unsuccessful Federalist nominee for president 1812; N.Y. state canal commissioner 1810–1824; governor of New York 1817–1821, 1825–1828; declined to be appointed minister to England 1825.

Home: Mansion on Richmond Hill, Greenwich Village, New York.

Death: February 11, 1828, at Albany, New York, age 58 years, 11½ months.

Burial: Clinton Cemetery, Little Britain, New York.

Personal characteristics: Over 6'3" tall, curly brown hair. Thin and strong. Called "Magnus Apollo" because of his handsome, imposing massive appearance.

Father: James Clinton (August 9, 1736–December 22, 1812); career military man.

Mother: Mary DeWitt (September 5, 1737–September 12, 1795); married February 18, 1765.

Siblings: Alexander. Charles. George, married Hannah Franklin. Catherine, married Samuel Norton. Mary, married R.B. Norton. Elizabeth, married William Stuart.

First wife: Maria Franklin (November 8, 1775–July 30, 1818); married February 10, 1796.

Children: Walter (1797–May 2, 1810). Charles Alexander (1798–?). James Henry (1802–July 1824). DeWitt (1805–?). George W. (1807–?). Mary (February 8, 1809–?). Juliana (August 1811–?). Franklin (1812–?). Julia Catherine (1817–?).

Second wife: Catherine Jones (?–?), married April 21, 1819.

DeWitt Clinton was a rare politician. He was at least equally if not more interested in history, the arts, and his hobby as a naturalist than in politics. Best remembered for his prominent, even indispensable role in the development of the Erie Canal, he should also be honored for his foresight in pressing for public education, religious freedom, and administrative reform in New York. Joining these facets of his political personality was his independence. He came close to being elected president as a renegade from the political party that had nurtured him. It was that kind of independence, at times even arrogance, that made his career one of constant controversy.

The Clinton family was an honored one in New York. DeWitt's grandfather, Charles Clinton, was a man of some property but no real wealth in England. He left his native country for America in 1729 to escape religious discrimination. Persecution aboard the ship that he and his comrades commissioned for the voyage was far worse than anything suffered in England. The captain apparently wanted to starve the several wealthy passengers to death and then claim their possessions. For five months, the vessel sailed aimlessly, as rations grew more scarce and the weak, both young and old, began to die. Finally a bargain was made with the captain — part of the passengers' wealth in return for their lives and passage to America. Two of the Clinton children had been buried at sea, and only one survived the journey. Settling in Ulster County, New York, the Clintons prospered. Four more children were born, including DeWitt's father. The royal governor took notice of the wealthy and influential Charles Clinton and offered him any office within his power to bestow. Charles Clinton declined, and preferment was then offered one of his sons, George. George Clinton would in time become governor of New York and vice president of the United States.

Another son of Charles Clinton, James, found his career in the military. He was called "a warrior from his youth" (Arthur Pound, *Native Stock*, New York [1931]). Early in his career, he commanded troops protecting the western frontier from Indians, and served during the French and Indian War. When the Revolution began, James became a colonel and then a brigadier general under the command of his brother, Governor George Clinton. DeWitt was General James Clinton's third son.

Young DeWitt was only seven when the war with England erupted. His schooling was satisfactory for the times, first under the tutoring of a Presbyterian minister, John Moffat. At age 13, DeWitt attended an academy in Kingston. Two years later, the Clintons decided DeWitt should attend Princeton. After these plans had been made, the New York legislature reestablished King's College in New York City, which had stopped functioning during the Revolution. The legislature renamed the school Columbia. Apparently part of the urgency in establishing the first class in 1784 was the embarrassment of seeing the governor's nephew, DeWitt, heading for neighboring New Jersey because no acceptable education was available in New York. DeWitt became the first student to matriculate at

Columbia, thoughts of Princeton having been banished from his mind. Two years later he graduated at the head of his class. Legal studies were conducted in the office of a prominent New York attorney, Samuel Jones, with admission to the bar in 1789, after three years of training.

The law would not be DeWitt's profession for long. After perhaps a year in private practice in New York City, Clinton became private secretary to his uncle, Governor George Clinton. In 1787, while barely begun in his legal studies, he had stepped onto the political stage by writing anonymous articles for a New York paper, opposing the ratification of the new federal constitution. These anti–Federalist sympathies led him, as did his uncle's own political leanings, into the Jeffersonian camp.

Uncle George treated Clinton well, gaining him appointments as secretary to the Board of Regents for New York University, and membership on the Board of Fortifications for the New York harbor. This latter post was significant because renewed war with England or even France was feared in 1794 and 1795, and harbor defenses were woefully inadequate. Such positions of influence were lost in 1795 when John Jay and the Federalists took over the governor's office. Clinton was forced to return to the practice of law for his livelihood. The following year he married Maria Franklin. Maria's father, Walter Franklin, was then deceased, but he had been a wealthy man whose estate provided well for his family. The family home had been so luxurious that it became the presidential mansion when the nation's capital was New York City.

Romance competed with a different love, Clinton's books and scientific interests. He was more scholar than lawyer, his wife's substantial inheritance making that possible. His own continuing education in the subjects that interested him became a passion. Natural history, zoology, mineralogy, literature, history, and a broad spectrum of other subjects occupied his time. Clinton read voraciously, and also studied under the direction of experienced scientists. Throughout his life, he would read and write in the areas of science, art, and history. Nonetheless, politics was clearly to be DeWitt's career of choice. A successful race for

the state assembly came in 1797. The following year he was elected to the state senate. There he was selected to be one of four senators who, along with the governor, chose the occupants for all the military and civilian appointive offices in the state. There were over fifteen thousand positions to be filled. Consequently, membership on the Council of Appointment was a choice political position. When Clinton began to push for wholesale replacement of Federalists appointed by Governor John Jay, he earned the historical reputation of being the father of the spoils system. Whether he was the father, or merely an enthusiastic descendant, Clinton brought the idea of party allegiance as the first criterion for office to full bloom.

Clinton's power in the Council of Appointment gave him a pre-eminent role in political affairs. His prominence was recognized in 1802 when one of the incumbent United States senators resigned and Clinton was appointed as his successor. A year in the Senate, then considered an inferior body to the House of Representatives, was sufficient for Clinton. In 1803, he resigned to take an appointment as mayor of New York City. The choice was crucial for Clinton's later political development. Becoming mayor turned his influence away from the national scene and concentrated it in New York State. The reasons he made the choice probably did not include recognition that he was at a turning point. Instead he was motivated more by the higher salary and proximity to his politically powerful uncle.

For almost all of the next 12 years, Clinton remained as mayor. His was a progressive regime. Clinton was concerned with establishing free public schools, humane asylums for the insane and for the orphans, and better defenses for New York harbor. His involvement with the arts and sciences increased, and included obtaining the presidency of the New York Academy of Arts. Disputes with Great Britain entered even the mayor's office. A $100,000 appropriation was gained by the mayor from a reluctant state assembly to fortify the harbor. The master plan for the development of Manhattan was also adopted during his tenure. All in all, it was a foresighted, forceful administration.

The forcefulness extended far beyond the city limits of New York. Clinton tried to exert influence over the political affairs of the entire state, and succeeded. George Clinton became vice president in 1805, and much of the elder leader's influence devolved on DeWitt. The party was badly factionalized. George Clinton had his own faction: the Livingstons had their bitter opposition party; and Aaron Burr supporters were ostracized in a third grouping. DeWitt Clinton did not want to be seen as a member of any faction, as he tried for political and personal reasons to remain friendly with all. Friends and enemies were being made and lost with every election and every issue. Strict divisions between these loose groupings were nonexistent. Clinton's political maneuverings took him from one alliance to another.

In 1808, DeWitt had wanted to see Uncle George elected president, and both Clintons were severely disappointed when James Madison was chosen instead. George Clinton dejectedly continued as vice president, but died in office in April 1812. DeWitt was no ally of Madison during these four years between presidential elections. Party squabbles in the three-sided Jeffersonian Party in the state were for a time subordinated as the Federalists gained ground in New York City and state. A Federalist-dominated Council of Appointment ousted Clinton as mayor in 1810, but not until bitter wrangling between Clinton and his soon-to-be allies, the Federalists, had soured many personal relationships.

A far more heart-rending loss occurred on May 2, 1810, when Clinton's oldest, most beloved son, Walter, died suddenly and quite unexpectedly at the age of 13. This tragedy shattered Clinton, and recovery came only gradually.

Before presidential politics consumed Clinton completely, the question of a canal in western New York, with which he would for all time be closely identified, came into public debate. Clinton quickly embraced the idea, as visionary and impractical as many thought it to be. The legislature accepted the vision of Clinton and many others, however, and a canal commission was formed in March 1810. Clinton was one of seven members. Clinton would never accept any compensation for his services on this commission, which would be on occasion a full-time job during the nearly 15 years he served on that and the successor commissions. Clinton and the other commissioners toured the western part of the state to determine the feasibility of the idea, as well as a route. A plan for a massive, publicly-owned canal project resulted from this investigation.

In 1811, Clinton returned to the mayor's office after a one-year absence. In March 1811, he was nominated for lieutenant governor to fill a vacancy caused by the death of the incumbent the previous August. Clinton's nomination precipitated bitter reactions from Tammany Hall regulars, who did not consider Clinton a sufficiently faithful party man. They nominated another candidate, and the Federalists a third. Clinton managed a narrow victory. Many Clintonians found themselves voting for Federalist candidates for state assembly and other offices because they so despised the Tammany men who were attacking Clinton. The assembly was by a narrow margin Federalist, and Clinton was able to keep his position as New York mayor as well as his new one as lieutenant governor. Through these twin offices, he could advance the canal scheme with considerable success.

The long-developing war with Great Britain was near the flashpoint. Clinton was not fervently for war, but many of the followers of President Madison were. Thus, a new issue was added into the list that divided Clinton and his brand of Jeffersonianism from the president's supporters. Clinton's reluctance for war was well known, and the Federalists and many Republicans looked to him as a sane candidate for president during the time of crisis. Some Republican gatherings in New York state nominated Clinton for president in 1812. Clinton was interested, and was also not loath to accept the support of Federalists. In time, only the Tammany men could be found willing to support President Madison in the state. When war was declared in June, the Clintonians opposed it.

Not all the Federalists were willing to concede that long-time Republican Clinton would lead them to victory in the presidential race. Even that conceded, not all members of this party of stubborn principle, so aptly exemplified by John Adams, were willing to regain power if it meant accepting a political apostate such as Clinton. Finally, however, in what amounted to a loosely organized convention in New York City, about 75 Federalist leaders agreed to accept Clinton as their candidate, although no formal nomination was made. For three days, the convention stalemated, but then agreed to accept him. The ensuing campaign presented Clinton to some voters as a man who would vigorously prosecute the war that had already begun, while to New Englanders with Federalist sympathies, he was pictured as the peace candidate. His clear support of the war after the election suggests Clinton's true feelings, but political considerations during the campaign did not require consistency. These efforts were unavailing, and Clinton lost in the closest election, indeed the only seriously contested one, between 1800 and 1824. David H. Fischer, an incisive historian of the Federalists has denigrated Clinton's worth to that party in 1812:

> Federalist strategy in the Presidential campaign of 1812 was doubly unfortunate. They gained nothing by [naming Clinton], and lost heavily in morale. Clinton proved unable to attract Democratic voters in significant numbers. Although he piled up an impressive total of electoral votes, only twenty short of success, he failed to run as strongly as avowed Federalist candidates in local elections. He was not able to carry as many states as the Federalists actually won in legislative and gubernatorial elections [*Revolution of American Conservatism*, p. 90].

Perhaps the hard-fought decision by the 1812 Federalist convention to accept expediency was, in political terms, not the right decision after all. It should be noted that Fischer's thesis, heavily documented as it is with statistics from local elections, is the minority one. Most historians have credited Clinton with being the necessary ingredient in the Federalists making a serious challenge for the presidency, the only time they did after 1800.

Clinton in defeat was hardly finished as a politician. Indeed, the best was still ahead. In office as mayor until 1815, Clinton wielded his political influence to see that New York participated vigorously in the difficult war against England. That effort took him from active participation in the canal project, but war's end brought the Erie Canal back to center stage in his efforts. He helped organize public meetings in every part of the state to support the project, which was increasingly being called either "Clinton's ditch" or "Clinton's folly."

With public support behind him, and petitions of thousands of New Yorkers in hand, Clinton went to Albany to lobby the state assembly in 1816. In April, the assembly agreed and a new canal commission was formed. Clinton was made a member, and the new organization set about planning the canal in detail. When Governor Daniel D. Tompkins resigned in 1817 to become vice president, Clinton was elected to succeed him, winning despite the now-traditional opposition of Tammany Hall. In this new role, Clinton could even more effectively push this massive public works.

Not all fellow Republicans saw Clinton's policies, particularly his even-handed distribution of patronage, as advantageous. The governor encountered strong opposition in 1820 when he ran for another term. His opponent was incumbent Vice President Tompkins, who saw the power of being New York governor as much more attractive than the inactivity of his present office. The plurality was small, but Clinton won reelection. Two years later, he retired from the governorship voluntarily.

Out of office in January 1823, Clinton was not out of mind. The wing of the party now dominated by Martin Van Buren wanted to punish him for his past infidelities, and in 1824, they voted Clinton off the canal commission. This was a stupid act of spite that was blatantly unfair and against the interests of the people since it removed the most knowledgeable advocate of the Erie Canal from its management. A wave of public sentiment returned Clinton to the governorship in November 1824, only seven months after he had been removed from the commission. It was fitting that when the canal opened in 1825, Clinton was chief executive and could take a prominent part in the ceremonies marking the event.

Clinton's name surfaced again in speculation about the presidency in 1824. At age 55, his health was not good. A shattered leg suffered in 1818 had left him an invalid. Perhaps due to ill health, Clinton declined appointment as minister to Great Britain in 1825, offered by newly-inaugurated President John Quincy Adams. The following year he was narrowly reelected governor. In 1827, a meeting in Ohio nominated him for president, but no serious movement toward him got underway. Death came during that election year of 1828, with Clinton having joined forces with those trying to put Andrew Jackson in the White House.

Death came only after his life's great work, the canal, had been completed, and some of its benefits of reduced transportation costs and opening of new markets had begun to be seen.

Analysis of Qualifications

Governor, mayor, would-be president, naturalist, devotee of the arts, historian. DeWitt Clinton was a man of immense talents, varied interests, solid achievements, and considerable ambition. Promoting himself to within grasping distance of the presidency when he was only 44, he more successfully promoted the Erie Canal. What he did, whether for good or ill, was attempted on a large scale.

Clinton's contribution to the acceptance of the spoils system in his state, and through New York's example the acceptance by the rest of the country, was probably not as significant as is sometimes noted. That the victors would in time realize they could take all the spoils was probably inevitable; Clinton just made the practice dominant a little before it otherwise might have been. Party warfare became the norm for his state, in part because of the Clinton personality. New York's political factions were built around personalities, and Clinton's was a dominating one. Oppressive, even arrogant, Clinton demanded loyalty but did not always return it. He was practical and innovative, with little acceptance of precedent if he found it useful to discard traditional ways. Clinton freely used patronage to reward and punish. Later, after his own defeat for the presidency, he seemed less interested in

strictly party grounds for selections of officeholders.

These techniques indicate an insightful, skilled politician. Few were the projects that he attempted that were not adopted, the Erie Canal being the most notable example. He was well known and respected, but somewhat aloof and not one who ingratiated himself with others. He gained influence through sagacious use of the power he could wield, whether it be through patronage, public opinion, or his Clintonian political party that for 20 years did battle with whatever other factions of the party existed. Clinton joined forces with the Federalists when it seemed advantageous; he sought alliance within his own badly splintered party as well. There was nothing cast in concrete in Clinton's political actions, and he understood well the need for flexibility.

Clinton's regimes as governor and mayor were contentious, but strong in accomplishments. As president during the critical period after 1812, Clinton would likely have shown the same political techniques, but on a larger stage. He was energetic, forceful, even dominating, but he knew how to compromise. He was never charged with dishonesty or self-dealing, and his failings mainly were in personal relations which were often strained. DeWitt Clinton had the look of an excellent president.

CLINTON BIBLIOGRAPHY

Bobbé, Dorothie. *DeWitt Clinton*. New York City (1933).

Clinton, Charles A. *Biographical Sketch of the Clinton Family*. New York City (1859).

Cornog, Evan William. "The Birth of Empire: DeWitt Clinton and the American Experience, 1769–1828." Unpublished doctoral dissertation, Columbia University (1996).

Evans, Thomas G. *The DeWitt Family of Ulster County, New York*. New York City (1886), reprinted from *New York Genealogical and Biographical Record* (Oct. 1886).

Fischer, David H. *The Revolution of American Conservatism*. New York City (1965).

Fitzpatrick, Edward A. *The Educational Views and Influence of DeWitt Clinton*. New York City (1969), reprint of 1911 edition.

Hanyan, Craig. *DeWitt Clinton: Years of Molding, 1769–1807*. New York City and London (1988).

Kass, Alvin. *Politics in New York State 1800–1830*. Syracuse (1965).

Lagana, Michael P. "The Political Career of DeWitt Clinton: A Need for Reinterpretation." *Niagara Frontier* 22 (1975), pp. 74–77.

McBain, Howard Lee. *DeWitt Clinton and the Origin of the Spoils System in New York*. New York City (1907).

Orth, Samuel P. "DeWitt Clinton, Father of the Spoils System." In *Five American Politicians*, Cleveland (1906).

Renwick, James. *Life of DeWitt Clinton*. New York City (1840).

Siry, Steven E. *DeWitt Clinton and the American Political Economy— Sectional Politics, and Republican Ideology, 1787–1828*. New York City (1989).

Walsh, William. "Tjerck Classen De Witt and Some of His Descendants." *Papers of the Historical Society of Newburgh Bay and the Highlands* IX (1902), pp. 37–50.

---

*1812 nominee for vice president—
Federalist Party*

Jared Ingersoll

Full name: Jared Ingersoll (Jr.)

State represented: Pennsylvania.

Birth: October 27, 1749, New Haven, Connecticut.

Age on Inauguration Day (March 4, 1813): 63 years, 4 months.

Education: Tutored at home, then Yale College, graduating 1766; studied law with his father, then with Joseph Reed, of the Supreme Executive Council of Pennsylvania; admitted to London's Middle Temple, 1774–1777, for his legal studies; admitted to Philadelphia Bar, 1773, before going to England.

Religion: Presbyterian.

Ancestry/prominent relatives: John Ingersoll emigrated from England to Massachusetts Bay Colony in 1629; Jared Ingersoll (the candidate's father), a prominent Loyalist during American Revolution; Jared's son, Charles Jared Ingersoll, was elected to Congress from Philadelphia; another son, Joseph Reed Ingersoll, was ambassador to Great Britain and a Congressman.

Occupation: Attorney.

Public offices: Continental Congress, 1780–1781; delegate to Federal Constitutional Convention, 1787; Philadelphia Common Council, 1789, Philadelphia city solicitor, 1798–1801; appointed attorney general of Pennsylvania, 1790–1799 and 1811–1817; U.S. district attorney for Pennsylvania, 1800–1801; refused to be appointed federal judge, 1801; unsuccessful Federalist nominee for vice president, 1812; presiding judge, district court for city and county of Philadelphia, 1821–1822.

Death: October 31, 1822, in Philadelphia, at age 73 years.

Burial: First Presbyterian Church Cemetery, Philadelphia.

Home: Philadelphia.

Personal characteristics: 5'9" tall, thin, erect and dignified; fair complexion, light-colored hair, slightly bald, near-sighted.

Father: Jared Ingersoll (June 3, 1722–August 25, 1781), lawyer, public official.

Mother: Hannah Whiting (Feb. 21, 1719–October 8, 1779), married August 1, 1743, daughter of Col. Joseph Whiting.

Stepmother: Hannah (Miles) Alling (?–?), widow of Enos Alling; married Ingersoll on January 6, 1780.

Siblings: James (April 21, 1748–?), died in infancy. Jonathan (June 17, 1741–?), died in childhood. Hannah (December 1752–?), died in childhood.

Wife: Elizabeth Pettit (?–?), married December 6, 1781; oldest daughter of Col. Charles Pettit.

Children: Charles Jared (October 3, 1782–May 14, 1862), married Mary Wilcocks on October 18, 1804; was a lawyer, author, and Congressman. Harry (?–?), died young. Joseph Reed (June 14, 1786–February 20, 1868), lawyer, writer, diplomat, Congressman; married Ann Wilcocks on September 22, 1813. Edward (July 7, 1790–July 7, 1841), married Catherine Ann Brinton.

Jared Ingersoll was a leader of the Philadelphia bar, a man whose legal counsel was sought and respected. He was, only quite incidentally, a politician. Ingersoll's one elective office was as a delegate to the Continental Congress, though he did serve in a handful of appointive positions. Jared Ingersoll simply was much more, almost entirely, interested in the practice of law than in any other pursuit.

Jared's father, for whom he had been named, was a prominent public official in colonial

Connecticut. Also an attorney, the elder Jared Ingersoll served as agent for Connecticut in London. While there in 1764 Ingersoll was instructed by the colony to oppose the Stamp Act, but of course the bill passed Parliament regardless of American opposition. Ingersoll was appointed by the British government as one of the agents for collection of the tax. Upon his return to America he found himself a despised representative of an increasingly despised British government. He was forced to resign his commission while surrounded by at least a thousand rebels in Hartford, whose "persuasive powers" overwhelmed him. Obviously his resignation was coerced, and Ingersoll withdrew it once in a position of safety. Yet a few months later the inevitability of acceding to the colonists' demands caused him to resign permanently. In 1766, long before Benedict Arnold's treason, Ingersoll defended the then-patriot from a charge of assault. In 1771 the Ingersoll family left Connecticut and settled in Philadelphia. There he tried to avoid involvement in the Revolution, as he was a Loyalist whose sympathies for the Crown were dangerous to espouse. Ingersoll was forced to leave Philadelphia and return to New Haven, Connecticut, by patriots in the "City of Brotherly Love," whose affection never seemed ample enough to include Loyalists. There he died in 1781.

It is against this family background that the development of the younger Jared Ingersoll stands in relief. After preliminary studies, Jared attended Yale College and graduated in 1766. Reading law under his father followed for a time, and he also studied in the office of a prominent Philadelphia attorney, Joseph Reed. He was admitted to the bar in 1773, but the

JARED INGERSOLL
(Reproduced from the Collections of the Library of Congress)

next year sailed for London and entered the Middle Temple, one of the four Inns of Court in London which were the exclusive colleges for studying law in that country. There, as well as for perhaps a year in Paris, Ingersoll would remain until 1778. The Revolution began in America while he was studying law, and Jared sided with the colonists. In 1775 he wrote his cousin, Jonathan Ingersoll, "I am now suffering the most humiliating news of a defeat of the provincials by the King's troops." While in London he also petitioned the government for payment of his father's salary that was two years in arrears. A few fervent debates with English legal comrades concerning the war no doubt enlivened his English stay. He was ready for home, however, and arrived on September 5, 1778, having traveled to Paris first on his way back to this new and rebellious country.

The elder Jared was a friend of Joseph Reed, who had become president of the Supreme Executive Council of Pennsylvania. President Reed had written Jared's father, calling the elder Ingersoll an "ancient and valued friend," and stated that Reed's election as president of the Executive Council had made it impossible for him to continue to practice in Philadelphia. Someone of learning was needed to fill the void in his office while Reed tended to political affairs. Reed asked that the younger Jared hurry home from England, and if he did Jared would receive "every assistance and advantage ... which his merit and my sincere esteem for him will justly claim." Jared was admitted to the Philadelphia bar in January 1779, far better trained than the vast majority of his fellow lawyers. Writing from Philadelphia in February 1779, Jared stated "I have clients, two clerks, and am engaged in the most important cases now pending."

Perhaps as a reaction to his father's well-known Tory sympathies, Jared asserted his own support for the Revolution by being selected for the Continental Congress in 1780, and served one year. He was also an assistant in the Pennsylvania attorney general's office.

Reed's health was poor, and his interest in politics far keener than his desire to tend to his law office. Thus Jared gained a substantial practice almost by default. Yet he also earned the position he was gaining. He was an excellent attorney, thorough, careful, well-versed in legal doctrine and an indefatigable battler for his client. Another prominent Philadelphia attorney, Horace Binney, would later call Ingersoll "without comparison the most efficient manager of an important jury trial among all the able men who were then at the Bar of Philadelphia."

As Ingersoll's reputation for prowess at the bar grew, he began to receive positions of considerable prestige. When delegates to the federal constitutional convention were selected in 1787, Ingersoll was sent as one of those representing his state. His role there was meager. His chief contribution, or at least his only recorded speech during the months of deliberations, uniquely appealed to the legal mind. The significance of the signature of any particular delegate, many of whom disagreed with important sections of the Constitution, was addressed by the delegate from Philadelphia. If several delegates refused to sign the document, great injury to the possibility of ratification by the requisite number of states could be inflicted. Ingersoll rose and said "that he did not consider the signing either as a mere attestation of the fact, or as pledging the signers to support the Constitution at all events, but as a recommendation of what, all things considered, was the most eligible." Ingersoll's statement was soon followed by a vote upon a motion presented by Benjamin Franklin, to the effect that the signatures indicated that the states represented at the convention had unanimously endorsed the document, even if every individual delegate making up the state's representation did not.

Governor McKean of Pennsylvania turned to Ingersoll as his appointee for attorney general of the state, being that commonwealth's first under the newly adopted state constitution. He would remain in the post from 1790 until 1800. His duties were not political, but legal. He moved from that post to an appointment for one year as United States District Attorney for Pennsylvania.

Though a few public duties did call him, Ingersoll was primarily engaged, actively so, in the practice of his profession. He was attorney for American merchant, banker, and philanthropist Stephen Girard. Girard would be a primary financial supporter of the War of 1812. After Girard's death, his will that created a college for poor orphan white boys was attacked by Girard's heirs, and other attorneys — Ingersoll was by then deceased — succeeded in preserving the scheme (see the sketch on Daniel Webster, election of 1836). He was counsel for one party or another in some of the major decisions of the early years of the United States Supreme Court. Federal-state relations, the constitutionality of an act of Congress, and even international questions were some of the issues involved.

Perhaps Ingersoll's most famous involvement was as defense counsel for United States Senator William Blount of Tennessee, who in 1797 was impeached by the House and tried in the Senate. Blount had in 1797 written a letter that clearly attempted to incite the Indians to revolt against the United States. His involvement in a scheme to assist the British in conquering West Florida was exposed by this letter. In quick succession the letter was published, the plot exposed, and Blount impeached. On December 17, 1798, the Senate became a Court of Impeachment. A week later Ingersoll and another lawyer appeared on Blount's behalf, denying the charges and also saying, regardless of the validity of the allegations, impeachment was an improper form of procedure. Blount's alleged conduct violated the laws applicable to all citizens, and he should be tried in an ordinary court, with ordinary protections that would there be afforded him. Ingersoll's lengthy appeal was that impeachment was historically misused in England, and a dangerous precedent must not be established in this new country. A trial by jury was the ultimate protection of society, and not just of individuals. A long survey was given of British legal history, from the Magna Carta, to giants in the law such as Blackstone, to historical events in which basic protections of the law were trampled. Blount was, despite Ingersoll's efforts, impeached and convicted.

Ingersoll's style before a court was described as colloquial — he virtually climbed into the jury box and made himself one of them, making the jury identify with his client at the same time as Ingersoll was showing his empathy with the jurors. When he found a weak point in his opponent's case, and he always discovered them, he would attack with a vengeance and leave the entire case in tatters. His sight was bad, at first being merely near-sighted, but then becoming more severely handicapped. He would pace his office and then the courtroom, preparing and then delivering his arguments. Ingersoll would prepare his argument for hours, took lengthy notes at trial, but then never looked at these papers and instead seemed to be talking extemporaneously.

The fame earned at the bar made him a logical choice in 1811 when the Pennsylvania governor had to fill the position of attorney general. Ingersoll had served in that post ten years before. One serious obstacle was that Ingersoll was a Federalist, and Governor Snyder was a Jeffersonian Republican. Apparently unable to find a qualified and willing candidate from within his own party, the governor decided to appoint Ingersoll, but wished to avoid the embarrassment of an appointment that would be refused. Snyder got a friend of Ingersoll's to contrive a meeting in which the governor's representatives could discreetly inquire concerning Ingersoll's reaction to an appointment. Ingersoll suggested at the meeting that though he would not seek the post, he would accept it. The appointment was consequently soon made, and he remained in office from 1811 until 1817. Ingersoll resigned only because the new governor in 1817 wanted the attorney general to live in Harrisburg, the capital. In December 1817, Ingersoll responded to the suggestion by saying "the Governor knew the inconveniences of his [Ingersoll's] residence when he appointed him; and that if they had increased, in his own apprehension, he would have saved the Governor the expression of his wish of his resignation…." Ingersoll then resigned.

In 1812 the unpopularity of the incumbent president, James Madison, mainly because of the recently commenced War of 1812, led many Federalists to believe their long drought in national power might soon be at an end. To succeed, however, they felt required to take the extreme step of nominating for President a member of the Democratic-Republican Party, DeWitt Clinton, who was among the strongest opponents of his own party's president. The convention that named Clinton had been called chiefly at the insistence of Philadelphia Federalists. The organizing committee for the convention was in that city. The battle between party purists, who could not accept the heresy of naming Clinton, and those who were more concerned with winning than in party consistency, finally was won by the pragmatists. No formal nomination for president occurred, nor was one for vice president. The delegates left the convention on September 17, 1812, however, with the impression that their tacit decision at the convention to accept Clinton would be given official sanction by the Philadelphia committee that had organized the convention. Two states were seen as crucial, Pennsylvania and North Carolina. Depending on the flow of events in the succeeding weeks, the committee would decide whether to name Clinton officially, as well as whom to nominate for the second spot on the ticket. A few weeks before the convention, a secret meeting of Clinton supporters in Lancaster, Pennsylvania, had not only named Clinton for president but also selected their state's highest Federalist official, Attorney General Jared Ingersoll, as his running mate. Pennsylvania was seen as so central to the success of the Federalists in 1812 that the decision to make Ingersoll the choice of the party was accepted nationwide. It is unclear whether formal nominations were ever made by the Philadelphia committee, but the two men were the accepted candidates of the party in the general election. The committee disseminated information throughout the remaining weeks of the campaign and informed the other sections of the country of Ingersoll's nomination in Lancaster.

Though unanimity was reached in the party, and a valiant run for the presidency made, it fell just short. The Clinton-Ingersoll ticket would have won except, ironically, the 25 electoral votes of Pennsylvania did not fall into the Federalist column even with Ingersoll on the ticket. Ingersoll had no base of political support in the state and probably attracted few votes. Yet it would have been hard to find a Federalist who did have a following in Pennsylvania as the state was strongly in the Jeffersonian camp. The Keystone State had given a majority of its electoral votes to the Jeffersonians in every election since the two unanimous selections of George Washington in 1789 and 1792.

It can hardly be said that Ingersoll retired from politics after the 1812 election, since in truth he had never been active in that arena. A high-powered legal practice in his adopted city of Philadelphia had commenced in 1801. He had once refused to be appointed chief judge of the U.S. Circuit Court in eastern Pennsylvania, wanting instead to remain in private practice. In 1821 he did accept a judicial position, that of presiding judge of the district court for the city and county of Philadelphia. He remained on the bench until his death the following year, four days past his seventy-third birthday. His final years had been spent in strained financial circumstances,

in part due to bad investments in unsettled western lands. It was said he narrowly missed making a fortune on coal lands, and instead lost his money in disastrous ventures. Perhaps this financial crisis is what convinced him in 1821 to take the steady if modest salary of a judge.

Analysis of Qualifications

Several glowing tributes were made to the memory of Jared Ingersoll when he died in 1822. Each of them without fail pointed to his high personal integrity, his intelligence, and his skill as an attorney. None of them could find much substance in his record of political leadership, simply because he had never been seriously a seeker of public office. As D.P. Brown said in his sketch of Ingersoll,

> His whole mind seemed to be devoted to his profession.... (H)e avoided participation in almost everything that did not, in some way, appertain to his profession. Eminently fitted to shine in every walk of life, his ruling attachment seemed to be entirely the law. To this, he looked through the medium of everything else, and he contemplated everything else through the lens of the law. His ambition was rendered perfectly subordinate to his love for his own peculiar science.

Horace Binney, a contemporary of Ingersoll's, stated "Mr. Ingersoll had, at no time of his life, a warm predilection for politics."

Why, one must then ask, did the Federalists in 1812 believe he was qualified for vice president? The obvious answer is that qualification for that office is almost always seen only in terms of political factors. Ingersoll's adopted state of Pennsylvania was thought to be and so it would prove, the key to the election. Ingersoll was a man of great talent, but he had never been called upon to lead in any political office. His only public service of any duration had been as a judge and as a lawyer — attorney general of Pennsylvania. He had never held executive office, never worked with a legislative body, never even been active in politics.

Ingersoll to many seemed cold and aloof. He had an almost military bearing, so ramrod straight did he stand and walk, so dignified and humorless did he appear in public. He was educated at the finest schools — Yale and the Inns of Court in England — that were available. Many thought him too proud to mingle with other men; his friends were few but highly valued; his dress was formal, even to knee-breeches and silk stockings, hair-powder, a cue, and buckled shoes, this well into the nineteenth century when almost everyone else had abandoned such attire. His fellow attorneys respected him and liked him, but never felt close to Ingersoll. As a public speaker he was thought competent but not dramatic. He was incredibly persuasive; his logic and the presentation of that logic were impeccable. But he was not prone to emotion, wild gestures, or other inciters of the public. His honesty in personal and professional affairs was never doubted.

In political terms Ingersoll was a conservative, a Federalist when few still existed, a mild one who did not incite the Jeffersonians. That Ingersoll could have proven himself able in the presidency must be admitted. Yet his nomination must be taken as a total failure by his party to choose a candidate who had proven himself in public office, or in some other capacity in which similar skills are needed. Ingersoll was one of the outstanding lawyers of his day. That certainly should not have been a disqualification, but neither should it have been the only qualification.

INGERSOLL BIBLIOGRAPHY

Avery, Lillian Drake. *A Genealogy of the Ingersoll Family in America 1629–1925*. New York City (1926).

Binney, Horace. *The Leaders of the Old Bar of Philadelphia*. Philadelphia (1859), pp. 77–110.

Brown, David P. *The Forum: or, Forty Years Full Practice at the Philadelphia Bar*. Vol. I, pp. 470–89 (1856).

Dexter, Franklin B. *Biographical Sketches of the Graduates of Yale College*. Vol. III, pp. 184–87, New York City (1903).

Gipson, Lawrence Henry. *American Loyalist: Jared Ingersoll* [the candidate's father]. New Haven and London (1971).

Meigs, William. *The Life of Charles Jared Ingersoll* [the candidate's son]. Philadelphia (1900), pp. 18–25.

Wainwright, Nicholas B., ed. *A Philadelphia Perspective: The Diary of Sidney George Fisher Covering the Years 1834–1871*. Philadelphia (1967).

*1812 nominee for vice president—
Democratic-Republican Party*

John Langdon

Full Name: John Langdon (Jr.), nicknamed "Jack."

State represented: New Hampshire.

Birth: June 26, 1741, on farm near Sagamore Creek outside of Portsmouth, New Hampshire. There is some dispute as to the precise date of birth.

Age on Inauguration Day (March 4, 1813): 71 years, 8½ months.

Education: Attended Portsmouth grammar school run by Major Samuel Hale; no other formal education.

Religion: Became interested in religion around 1805; joined the North Meeting House in Portsmouth.

Ancestry/prominent relatives: First Langdon arrived from England in mid–1600s; Woodbury Langdon (brother), member of Continental Congress.

Occupation: Seaman, merchant; extremely wealthy from shipping.

Public offices: Member of New Hampshire General Court, 1775; delegate to Continental Congress, 1775–1776, resigned to become New Hampshire's continental agent for marine affairs, 1776; judge of court of common pleas, 1776–1777; Speaker of New Hampshire House of Representatives, 1777–1780; member of several New Hampshire constitutional conventions, 1778–1783; elected delegate to Continental Congress, 1783, 1784, and 1786, but refused; New Hampshire state senator, 1785; president of New Hampshire, 1785; speaker of New Hampshire House of Representatives, 1786–1787; delegate to federal constitutional convention, 1787; governor of New Hampshire, 1788; U.S. Senator, March 4, 1789–March 3, 1801; elected first president pro tempore, April 6, 1789; declined to be appointed secretary of Navy 1801 and 1811; member of New Hampshire House of Representatives, 1803–1805; defeated for governor, 1802, 1804, 1809; New Hampshire governor, 1805–1809; 1810–1812; refused nomination for vice president, 1812.

JOHN LANGDON
(Reproduced from the Collections of the Library of Congress)

Death: September 18, 1819, Portsmouth, New Hampshire; 78 years, 3 months.

Burial: North Burying Ground, Portsmouth, New Hampshire.

Home: Large, castle-like mansion in Portsmouth, New Hampshire, 1777–1787; new mansion built and Langdons moved in 1787 (still standing).

Personal characteristics: Described as "a handsome man of noble carriage."

Father: John Langdon, Sr. (May 28, 1707–1759), a not-very-prosperous New England farmer.

Mother: Mary Hall (?–c. 1785), daughter of Josiah Hall of Exeter, New Hampshire.

Siblings: Woodbury (1739–January 13,

1805), married Sarah Sherburne in 1765. Elizabeth. Martha, married Thomas Simpson. Abigail, married a Mr. Goldthwait. Another sister.

Wife: Elizabeth Sherburne (1760–March 22, 1813), married February 3, 1777; daughter of John and Elizabeth (Moffatt) Sherburne, a Portsmouth merchant.

Children: Elizabeth (Betsey) (December 4, 1777–March 22, 1816), married Thomas Elwyn July 16, 1797. John, Jr. (March 1779–died in infancy).

Historic sites/memorials — John Langdon Mansion, 143 Pleasant Street, Portsmouth, N.H.

John Langdon served his country immeasurably during the pre–Revolution period by being a forceful proponent of independence. When others were still waiting to see which way the political and military winds were blowing, Langdon was publicly involved in the fight for liberty. It is for that recognition of duty and the vigorous fulfilling of it that Langdon should be remembered with respect today.

Langdon was born on a farm outside of Portsmouth, New Hampshire. The family was comfortable but not wealthy. John and his brother Woodbury attended a school in Portsmouth for a few years, but never attended college. They soon entered business, the older brother first and then young John. John became employed by Daniel Rindge in February 1760, in the counting room of Rindge's merchant ship company. By 1763, at age 22, John was a captain of his own vessel, the *Keppel*, carrying a cargo of New Hampshire goods to Antigua. By 1765 he was working for his brother's firm. Langdon stayed on the high seas as skipper of various ships for several years, making his first trans–Atlantic voyage in 1764 and 1765. By 1770 he owned his own vessels and no longer sailed himself. During this period he invested in several ships, sailed and then sold them. His life as a seaman — a dashing, handsome, bachelor captain — was lively and perhaps as ribald as the sailor image usually suggests. There is some evidence in letters written by Langdon that his family became quite concerned about his morals, but after he gave up sailing he apparently also gave up any immoral conduct. At this time he appeared to

be interested in a 16-year-old girl in Portsmouth, who flirted with him, at least by letter. Surprisingly to him, she married his brother Woodbury in March 1765. John was to remain a bachelor for several more years.

During the early protests over the Stamp Act and similar British measures, Langdon was on the high seas. New taxes on imports were a serious matter for one engaged in shipping, and many shippers attempted to slip goods by without declaring them, thereby avoiding the tax. One of Langdon's cargoes was involved in charges involving such attempted avoidance of the tax. In October of 1771, the *Resolution* was in Portsmouth harbor when it was discovered that 100 barrels of undeclared molasses were aboard. Under law, the collector at the port seized the vessel and all its cargo. On October 29, several masked and costumed men took over the vessel, tied up or ran off the officials on board, and removed the molasses. The culprits were never apprehended, but Langdon lost the cargo he had aboard after the vessel was condemned by the authorities. The reason for the confiscation of the vessel and cargo was a technical point concerning an alleged attempt to conceal the true owner. Langdon denied in his appeal of the order of confiscation that the vessel was his, but he lost. There was no doubt, however, that the cargo aboard was his, and that too was lost.

The Tea Act of 1773, complicated in form, basically permitted certain importers of tea, a staple in the New England households, to sell their tea at a lower price if they showed themselves to be loyal to the Crown. The Boston Tea Party of December 16, 1773, was but one result of this Act. Another was the formation of committees of correspondence in the various colonies to organize opposition. Langdon was appointed to such a committee in Portsmouth in 1773. He was becoming known as one of the radicals in Portsmouth. The decision was made by the committee not to permit the landing of any tea upon which the tax applied. In June 1774, a ship with a cargo of tea arrived in Portsmouth anyway, and Langdon was appointed to a committee to deal with the owners. After several days and some false starts, the tea was finally removed and was not sold. Langdon and eight others were commissioned to make certain, as much as possible anyway, that such importation did not recur.

A dramatic change had occurred in the climate in the American colonies in the aftermath of the Boston Tea Party of December 1773. The British closed the port of Boston where the disturbance had occurred, which in turn caused the colonists to call for a Continental Congress. Langdon was a delegate to the convention in Portsmouth to choose delegates for New Hampshire to Congress. Whether he hoped to be a delegate to the Continental Congress in Philadelphia is uncertain, but if so, he was disappointed. He was named, however, to a committee that was to continue meeting and examining the political situation monthly.

One of Langdon's more dramatic participations in rebellion involved the safeguarding of what limited guns and ammunition the Portsmouth rebels had in December 1774. Five British soldiers guarded a garrison, when Langdon and his group of 400 or so approached. A cannon was fired by the garrison, but no one was injured. Another party returned later and removed the cannon. Langdon was one of the acknowledged leaders of the expedition to seize the powder, and was in some danger of being arrested for his actions. He nonetheless remained in Portsmouth and no effort to seize him was ever made.

Langdon urged a ban on all trade with Britain. After such a policy was adopted by Portsmouth he was put on a committee to enforce the ban. In January 1775, Langdon's activities had gained him sufficient fame to cause his election to the Second Continental Congress. He had also been elected to the New Hampshire General Assembly. Langdon attended the Congress beginning in May, but was not of much influence.

On December 23, 1775, Langdon was back in Congress. He was put in charge of New Hampshire's obligation, imposed by Congress, to build one warship for defense of the country. Other colonies were also to build ships, the larger, more prosperous colonies to build more than one. Without detailed blueprints for the ship, Langdon returned to Portsmouth, procured a crew, signed a contract for the construction, and was well underway by the time

the plans finally arrived. Though the ship was completed over almost insurmountable odds and in short order, Langdon was unable to procure a cannon for the vessel until a year later.

In the summer of 1775, many British loyalists fled New Hampshire, including many government officials. Langdon wanted an independent government established and a constitutional convention was called that did just that. The break with England was clear. The same convention also chose Langdon as a delegate again to the Continental Congress, but he did not attend as he was busy with the ship construction. On June 14, 1776, New Hampshire declared itself independent. On June 25, one day before his thirty-fifth birthday, Langdon was put in charge of a proposed light infantry unit with the rank of colonel.

Despite Langdon's zeal for independence, at a critical juncture he appeared more interested in his financial advancement than in being in Congress. Congress had created the position of continental agent for each colony. The duties were somewhat nebulous, but it was clear that they would be lucrative positions. Langdon let it be known that he wished New Hampshire's appointment and was willing to resign his seat in Congress to get it. One of his closest friends thought Langdon should not take the position, that it spoke ill for his devotion to duty. Perhaps feeling guilty, Langdon responded that he believed there was very important work to be done for independence in this new position. Langdon did resign from Congress and was appointed as he desired. He was to take charge of all enemy vessels captured and returned to New Hampshire harbors, and would receive a percentage of the value of the ships. Langdon also equipped some of his own ships to engage in privateering and made substantial sums.

At 35, his apparently confirmed bachelorhood gave way to marriage. The bride, Elizabeth Sherburne, was 20 years younger than he. A castle-like mansion was selected to reflect his wealth and commemorate his marriage.

In 1777 Langdon was chosen speaker of the New Hampshire House of Representatives and a justice of the Court of Common Pleas. His political star was definitely ascending. Soon thereafter a threatened invasion of the state caused Langdon to donate three thousand dollars to the cause of raising and equipping an army to thwart the attack. He pledged "the plate in my house" for more arms. During the same crisis Langdon also raised volunteers and took to the field with the troops, but other than some long horse rides he saw no action and returned to Portsmouth. He rejoined the army in August of 1778, this time for three weeks. Still no engagement with the British occurred.

Langdon continued to be very active in politics by attending several conventions and conferences dealing with various aspects of the war and the economy. A new constitutional convention was held for New Hampshire in June 1778 and Langdon was a delegate, but the constitution that was drafted was voted down. Several more conventions were held before a charter was finally drafted that received the voters' approval in June 1783.

In 1783 and 1784, with the war over, Langdon's wealth enabled him to start construction of a mansion that took over three years to complete. It was perhaps the most impressive private home in New Hampshire; it took fabulous riches, which Langdon had accumulated, to build it. To operate the mansion the Langdons seemed to prefer black servants. Slavery had been abolished in New Hampshire by the 1784 constitution, so the servants were emancipated.

Langdon declined two elections to the Continental Congress in June 1783 and June 1784, but he did serve as a state senator from October 1784 to June 1785. The chief executive of New Hampshire was called the president, and when the incumbent New Hampshire president retired in the spring of 1785, Langdon ran for the post. No candidate received a majority, and therefore the state house of representatives was to choose two candidates from the list of contenders and the state senate then selected the winner. Langdon was one of the two choices and was selected by the senate in a 7–1 vote — not a very large senate. Hard economic times were afflicting the whole country. New Hampshire did not escape. Wealthy John Langdon was not a popular po-

litical figure to the impoverished voters when reelection time came the following year. Langdon was defeated. However, Langdon was chosen as a member of the house and was unanimously elected speaker. Coincidentally, the man who now served as president of the state had the year before been speaker, so the two men exchanged positions. One more time Langdon was elected a delegate to the Continental Congress, and another time Langdon decided not to attend but to remain with his same duties. The following year, 1787, another unsuccessful race for president of New Hampshire was made; this time Langdon received a plurality but was defeated by the incumbent in the senate "run-off."

Langdon was elected a delegate to the federal constitutional convention in Philadelphia in 1787. He arrived seven weeks after the convention had started. He did not make much of a contribution to the sessions, but his political principles are revealed by the votes he made: (1) he opposed property qualifications for election to Congress; (2) he favored letting the federal government have power to control the importation of slaves; (3) he wanted Congress to have authority to invalidate state laws that a two-thirds majority thought inimical to the interests of the federal government.

George Washington was the first delegate to sign the constitution, and Langdon was the second. After the signing Langdon attended the Continental Congress to vote for the new charter's adoption. He was extremely optimistic that it would be ratified by the necessary nine states.

To insure its acceptance, Langdon returned to New Hampshire. A convention was selected to vote on the constitution, and Langdon was a delegate. Despite his optimism, some of which had been communicated to such Federalist leaders as Washington, he was forced after the convention opened to seek a postponement because it appeared the vote would be negative. Many of the delegates had been instructed by the cities electing them not to vote for the constitution, and Langdon saw that something had to be done. Langdon somewhat sheepishly informed the Federalist forces that another try would be required. On June 18, 1788, with eight states having already ratified and only one more necessary, the New Hampshire convention reassembled. Langdon had been elected to the state house of representatives and was immediately and unanimously elected speaker. The next day he was informed that he had been elected president of New Hampshire. Thus by June 18 when the constitutional convention was reopened, Langdon was clearly the most dominant political force in the state. Ratification came with a 57–47 vote, and Langdon was ecstatic. Langdon's next move was to call a special session of the legislature to start the process of elections required under the new constitution. On November 12, 1788, the legislature elected him one of the state's first two United States senators; his vote was 60–3 in the house over another candidate. Langdon resigned the state presidency and in January left for New York, the national capital.

Most of the other senators were much less prompt in attendance, and Langdon and some few other timely attendees had to issue a call for the others to come. Finally a quorum was present and Langdon was elected the presiding officer in order to count the electoral votes for president and vice president. It was he who officially announced what was already a foregone conclusion, that George Washington was the first president of the United States. Langdon was named the first president pro tempore of the Senate, to preside whenever the vice president was not in attendance.

Langdon was extremely fond of George Washington, so much so as almost to amount to hero worship. This attraction helps explain his initial Federalist party affiliations. He supported Alexander Hamilton in the treasury secretary's early proposals on the economy. He particularly sided with the Federalists on the issue of a national bank. Yet as time progressed his allegiances began to change. Langdon had much in common with Thomas Jefferson, the leader of the opposition. Langdon had more faith in the wisdom of a democracy than apparently did the Federalists, Hamilton and President John Adams in particular. Moreover, he hated England and was drawn to France, which also allied him with the Republicans and Jefferson. Some loose talk by President Adams about a monarchy was particularly

offensive to Langdon. When Langdon's switch to the Jeffersonians became final and obvious, the Federalists were greatly distressed. President Adams was chagrined, and many saw anticipated political advancement as the cause for the change. Many thought Langdon hoped for the vice presidency. Yet actually the better analysis would be that he changed despite political considerations. Reelection by the New Hampshire legislature was imminent and the Federalists were in control there. The New Hampshire house voted for Langdon but the senate chose another. After a protracted battle Langdon was finally elected for a second term by a majority of one. For a time it appeared his brother Woodbury might instead be named.

After another term in the Senate, Langdon knew the Federalist legislature would not reelect him and therefore he retired. He was elected as a representative to the New Hampshire legislature, and was continually reelected though each year he was also attempting to be chosen governor of the state (the title of "president" had been discarded). Finally in 1805, he was elected governor, the first non–Federalist to be chosen. He served four one-year terms, but was then defeated because of President Jefferson's embargo against shipping to England, a measure that struck New Hampshire's shipping industry hard. Two more election victories for governor followed in 1810 and 1811, but Langdon was now feeling old and wanted to retire from politics. It is tradition that he even offered $2000 in 1811 to his party to induce them to find another gubernatorial candidate.

Langdon's selection as the vice presidential nominee by the Congressional caucus in 1812 was pure politics — an attempt to shore up New England support for the reelection of President Madison, whose first vice president, George Clinton, had died. Albert Gallatin, secretary of the treasury and a future vice presidential nominee who would decline his own nomination, urged Landon to accept. But Langdon was tired and no entreaties could succeed. He said he was too old, and in fact he was. On June 5, 1812, he left the governor's office and retired to his Portsmouth mansion.

Langdon's final years continued a growing

commitment to religion that had begun shortly after his beloved brother Woodbury's death in 1805. He had begun then to attend church regularly and became the founder of the New Hampshire Bible Society. Langdon's wife died in 1813, and this was a severe blow. His health and mental alertness failed badly thereafter, which was just the period that he would have been serving as vice president. He died in 1819.

Analysis of Qualifications

John Langdon was an extremely wealthy man, among the wealthiest in his native Portsmouth, if not in the whole state. His money was not inherited, but was gained through clever though ethical business practices. Langdon's career leaves little clues as to his fitness for high office. He did not receive much formal education, but he was reasonably well educated compared to his contemporaries. He was a radical patriot and early took up the call against England. It was in that capacity that he served his country most significantly.

Langdon was possessed with certain extraordinary skills. One was what would now be called a photographic memory. He was fond of quoting long passages of the classics, works many of which he had not read since childhood. He had the kind of dedication to a task, particularly one he believed in as fervently as the Revolution, that permitted him to overcome obstacles that might have defeated other men. His perseverance in constructing a sorely needed warship despite not even having plans for the construction was exemplary. His business sense must have been impressive, as he started on the lowest rung in a commercial shipping company and rose to be the owner of his own vessels. One question mark in his career was the fact that he emerged from the Revolution a very wealthy man, having equipped ships for privateering until that became unprofitable. He earnestly sought the position of "agent of prizes," the continental agent in New Hampshire for all affairs. He took this position even though it meant he had to resign his position in the Continental Congress. The choice disappointed several of his friends who thought that he was putting financial gain over

the needs of his country. Yet to say that Langdon here put his wealth ahead of his country ignores his pledging and spending substantial sums of his own money to equip units to fight in the war.

In sum, Langdon appears to have been a good business man, with common sense and cleverness. He was brave, as shown in his leadership of the radical, revolutionary forces in New Hampshire when it was far from clear whether "patriots" might not instead be found to be traitors and be hung. His antimonarchist views caused him finally to abandon the Federalists.

John Langdon respected the wisdom of the electorate. He was informal, exuberant and optimistic about all he was engaged in. He had considerable personal charm and was physically attractive. Still, little in his career marks him as a man who was brilliant or would have proven to be an outstanding national leader. Of course, Langdon declined the vice presidential nomination in 1812 on the basis that he was too old and his faculties too blurred. That appears to have been an accurate picture of Langdon at the age of 71. Had he become president it is doubtful that he would have been physically or mentally up to the challenge. In his prime he probably would have been a satisfactory, but hardly outstanding, president; by the time he was offered the nomination he was not physically fit for the position. For that reason Langdon must be classed with those who were not acceptable choices.

LANGDON BIBLIOGRAPHY

Batchellor, Albert, ed. "John Langdon." *New Hampshire Early State Papers* XXI (1892), pp. 804–812.

Lacy, Harriet S. "The Langdon Papers 1716–1841." *Historical New Hampshire* (Autumn 1967), pp. 55–65.

Langdon-Elwyn, John. "Some Account of John Langdon." *New Hampshire Early State Papers.* XX (1891), pp. 850–881.

Mayo, Lawrence Shaw. *John Langdon of New Hampshire.* Port Washington, N.Y., and London (1970), reprint of 1937 edition.

Election of 1816

NOMINATIONS

Federalist Party: *President*— Rufus King. The party made no serious effort to contest this election. The selection of King was accomplished mainly through letters between leaders and through a common, unspoken acceptance of Rufus King as the only choice for the meaningless honor. *Vice president*— John Howard. Party leaders in each state that presented slates of Federalist electors, about half of the total number of states, discussed whom they would support, without apparently any collaboration between states. The three states which elected slates of Federalist electors each had different candidates for the second office, though all voted for King for president. Howard received far more votes than any other Federalist candidate.

Democratic-Republican Party Congressional Caucus (5th): March 10, 1816, in the House Chamber of the Capitol, Washington, D.C. Only 57 senators and representatives appeared. It was decided at the caucus that any decision of so small a gathering would be of little effect, so a call for a new caucus was issued.

Democratic-Republican Party Congressional Caucus (5th, 2nd session): March 16, 1816, in the Capitol in Washington, D.C. *President*— James Monroe, nominated on the first ballot with 65 votes out of the 119 cast. All the rest of the votes went to William Crawford of Georgia. *Vice president*— Daniel D. Tompkins, nominated on the first ballot with 85 votes out of the 115 cast. All the rest of the votes went to Simon Snyder.

GENERAL ELECTION

Electoral Vote

PRESIDENT:

James Monroe—183 electoral votes (16 states)

Rufus King—34 electoral votes (3 states)

VICE PRESIDENT:

Daniel Tompkins—183 electoral votes (16 states)

John Howard—22 electoral votes (1 state)

James Ross—5 electoral votes (part of state)

John Marshall—4 electoral votes (part of state)

Robert Harper—3 electoral votes (1 state)

Winners

James Monroe, 5th president

Daniel Tompkins, 6th vice president

Losers

Rufus King, John Howard

1816 presidential nominee— Federalist Party

Rufus King

The biographical sketch for King is included in the section on the 1804 election, page 35.

State represented: New York.

Birth: March 24, 1755.

Age on Inauguration Day (March 4, 1817): 61 years, 11½ months.

Death: April 29, 1827.

1816 vice presidential candidate— John E. Howard

John E. Howard

Full name: John Eager Howard.

State represented: Maryland.

Birth: June 4, 1752, at "The Forrest" in Baltimore County, Maryland.

Age on Inauguration Day (March 4, 1817): 64 years, 9 months.

Education: Private tutors provided by his wealthy father.

Religion: Anglican (Episcopal).

Ancestry/prominent eelatives: Grandfather Joshua Howard arrived in Maryland from

England in 1667; George Howard (son), governor of Maryland; Benjamin Chew Howard (son), U.S. Representative; Benjamin Chew (father-in-law), chief justice of Pennsylvania Supreme Court.

Occupation: Developer, planter.

Public office: Committee of Observation, Baltimore County, 1774; committee to license suits of law, 1775; member of Continental Congress, 1784–1788; justice of Baltimore County, 1785–1787; justice, Baltimore County Orphans Court, 1786–1787; Maryland Senate elector, 1786; governor of Maryland, 1788–1791; Maryland Senate 1791–1795, declined his election in 1816; commissioner, Baltimore, 1792; associate justice, third district, May–July 1792; declined to be appointed secretary of war, 1795; U.S. Senator, November 30, 1796–March 3, 1803; unsuccessful Federalist contender for vice president, 1816.

Home: "Belvedere," near (now in) Baltimore, Maryland.

Death: October 12, 1827, at "Belvedere," near Baltimore, at age 75 years, 4 months.

Burial: Old St. Paul's Cemetery, Baltimore, Maryland.

Personal characteristics: Amazingly retentive memory; contemplative, cautious; scrupulously honest; stout; white hair, almost bald on the top of his head in later years; physically vigorous.

Father: Cornelius Howard (c. 1706–1777), wealthy landowner.

Mother: Ruth Eager (c. 1721–1796), daughter of John and Jemima (Murray) Eager.

Siblings: George (1740–1766). Rachel (1743–1747). Joshua (1745–1767). Ruth (1747–?), married Charles Elder. Rachel (1749–1750). Cornelius (1754–?), member of Maryland legislature. James (1757–1806). Violetta (1759–?), married Joseph West. Philip (1762–1764). Anne (1765–1770).

Wife: Margaret (Peggy) Oswald Chew (?–?), married on May 18, 1787; daughter of Benjamin Chew, a prominent Philadelphia attorney and chief justice of Pennsylvania Supreme Court.

Children: George (1789–1846), governor of Maryland; married Prudence Gough Ridgely, the daughter of another governor. John Eager, Jr. (?–1822), married Cornelia Reed. Benjamin Chew (Nov. 5, 1791–March 6, 1872), attorney, Congressman. Juliana Elizabeth (1796–1821), married John McHenry. Sophia (?–?), married William George Reed. Charles (1802–?). William (?–?). James (?–?), married Sophia J. Ridgely. Another child died in infancy.

Historic sites/memorials: Howard's home, "Waverley," is in Marriottsville, Maryland.

John E. Howard hardly needed the fleeting rewards of politics. He had fame earned justly as a Revolutionary soldier, a vast fortune inherited from his grandfather, and the tranquility gained from having a talented, successful cluster of children. He was only 50 when he left his final major public office in 1803, somewhat disillusioned by the turn of political fortune that had placed Jeffersonian Democrats in command two years before. For the rest of his life, Howard's participation in public life was as a civic-minded businessman, not as a candidate. His greatest contributions to his city and state occurred in that capacity, leaving a legacy of vast donations of land and money for public causes. Nomination for the vice presidency in 1816 came when his party had no chance for success, but it did have a handful of electoral votes with which to honor one of its most respected aging leaders.

Born into a wealthy Maryland family, Howard never had formal schooling, but instead was tutored by the best teachers the family fortune could provide. It was said that "he learned what he wanted to know and declined to study what did not appeal to him." Of his boyhood, little is known, other than he grew up in the protected surroundings of aristocracy. No career apparently had been selected for him. The Revolutionary War provided for the first time a serious commitment for his life, and for the next seven years he fulfilled it. In July 1776 he enlisted and, at least it was later reported, he declined a colonel's commission that his wealth and family connections made available. Instead, Howard settled for a captain's rank in the militia. Within three months, he was fighting in Colonel J. Carvil Hall's "Flying Camp" militia at the battle of White Plains. Little glory attended the first engagement, and by December, his enlistment period expired. Howard quickly attained the rank of major in a Maryland regiment of

JOHN E. HOWARD
(Reproduced from the Collections of the Library of Congress)

the regular army, and saw his first significant action at the battle of Germantown, Pennsylvania, in October 1777. George Washington commanded the army. The general determined to catch the British by surprise. Bad weather and poor visibility hampered the effectiveness of the troops, and soon the British were counter-attacking. Colonel Carvil Hall was injured, and Howard was called to take command of the regiment. Some British troops were using the home of Pennsylvania chief justice Benjamin Chew — later to be Howard's father-in-law — for cover, but they were sub-dued. The battle was a standoff, but Howard had commanded ably.

On March 11, 1778, Howard became a lieu-tenant colonel. For the next two years he saw little action, but in 1780 the Maryland troops were sent to the Carolinas to defend against the invasion of Cornwallis. The first major engagement was a disastrous defeat at the bat-tle of Camden, South Carolina. Fortunately, a disaster at Camden was soon followed by a signal victory at Cowpens, South Carolina, in which Howard played a vital role. The battle began January 17, 1781. The British had the Americans outnumbered and out-trained. The American commander, Daniel Morgan, no-ticed that the redcoats were threatening to outflank Colonel Howard. The Maryland reg-iment retreated when they mistook Howard's command to do just the opposite — attack. General Morgan spurred his horse towards Howard and asked if his men were beaten. Howard explained the confusion, and pointed out that this orderly if mistaken withdrawal hardly revealed defeat. Perhaps the confusion was propitious, because the British comman-der also believed Howard's men were demor-alized and therefore ordered his own men to attack. By then, Howard had turned his regi-ment and, much to the surprise of the British, charged forward and attacked. The astonished redcoats panicked and ran. Colonel Howard ordered his men to use bayonets, which fur-ther demoralized the British. They soon sur-rendered and threw down their guns. In what was perhaps considerable hyperbole, it was said that Howard soon had the swords of seven sur-rendered British officers presented to him. One defeated but brave British soldier caught Howard's attention, and Howard later wrote:

> An artilleryman … appeared to make it a point of honor not to surrender his match. The men, provoked by his obstinancy, would have bay-oneted him on the spot had I not interfered and desired them to spare the life of so brave a man. He then surrendered his match.

The unauthorized charge Howard had ordered was audacious and dangerous. Amer-ican commander Morgan rode up to Howard and told him, "You have done well, for you are successful; had you failed I should have shot

you." Howard's calm and accurate reply was, "Had I failed there would have been no need of shooting me." Several authorities have cred-ited Howard with converting American defeat into victory at Cowpens. Bold action had been needed, and Howard provided it at the right instant. Congress appreciated the Maryland colonel's role, as it voted him a medal on March 9, two months after the victory. Medals were also bestowed on General Morgan and another hero of the battle, the future presi-dent's kinsman, William Washington.

One last encounter with glory would com-plete Howard's military career. Preliminary to this final engagement, Howard's regiment served at the battle of Guilford Court House in North Carolina. Again, Howard's superior officer was wounded, and Howard was called upon to replace him during the remainder of the battle. The encounter saw the colonel's retreat from the field, but only after inflicting severe casualties on the British. At Hobkirk's Hill, South Carolina, Howard commanded the Maryland Second Regiment after Colonel Benjamin Ford was wounded. This experience well served Howard when on September 8, 1781, the battle of Eutaw Springs (South Car-olina) began. An experienced corps of Irish soldiers called the "Buffs" were the foe. Sav-age close combat ensued, with both sides ex-hibiting exceptional valor. Fortunately for How-ard's regiment, the remainder of the British troops finally gave way, forcing the Buffs to retreat as well. By then, Howard's regiment had been reduced to 30 men, and Howard was the sole remaining officer. The American gen-eral, Nathanael Greene, said:

> Nothing could exceed the gallantry of the Maryland Line. Cols. William and Howard, and all the officers, exhibited acts of uncom-mon bravery, and the free use of the bayonet, by this and some other corps, gave us the vic-tory.

Though victory had been gained, Howard had been severely wounded. A peace treaty would not come for two more years, but the war was already effectively over. Howard re-tired from the army with the rank of colonel. His final commander, General Greene, called him "as good an officer as the world affords. My own obligations to him are great — the public's still more so. He deserves a statue of gold no less than the Roman and Grecian heroes."

Romance and recuperation jointly occupied Howard's thoughts. With love letters written by his attending physician, Howard courted Peggy Chew, the daughter of former Pennsylvania chief justice Benjamin Chew. A rival, at least so-perceived by Howard, was a British officer. Years later Howard seemed still able to exhibit jealousy at the mention of the Englishman's name. Success at the courtship was not secured until 1787, when the 35-year-old Howard and Peggy Chew were finally married. Five days later, George Washington was a dinner guest at the Chew home. Howard revered Washington. The two men through war had become friends. Howard would remain loyal to the political party and philosophy of his old chief for the rest of his life.

Political involvement came naturally for the war hero and aristocrat. In the first few years after the war ended in 1783, Howard served as justice of the Baltimore County Court, elector of Baltimore County to the Maryland State Electoral Commission, which chose at-large senators for the assembly, and justice of the Baltimore County Orphans Court. Howard soon achieved higher office. He was elected by the general assembly as a delegate to the Continental Congress, serving from January until July 1788. The end of his service in Congress marked the beginning of the first of three consecutive one-year terms as Maryland governor.

Governor Howard was elected only after another, Thomas Johnson, declined to serve. Governors during this period were elected by the Maryland State Council and were not popularly chosen. Howard was Maryland's fifth governor, and the first to consider himself a member of a political party. Since his term began just as the federal constitution was being ratified, the idea of political party was also just getting its start. Howard, from the first, was a Federalist and eagerly supported the ratification of the new Constitution. George Washington was his inevitable choice for president.

On November 16, 1789, Howard was unanimously reelected governor by the State Council. He helped write a new militia law that was enacted. Relations with the new federal government were being formed, and Howard had such tasks as encouraging the new government to assume the debts of the states. That plea was presented for his state through the state's highest judges, whom Howard appointed with the realization that the more prominent the new justices were, the better they could present Maryland's case for debt assumption.

A third election to the governorship came in 1790. When that term expired a year later, Howard was barred under the state constitution from serving another successive term. For three years he served in the state senate, beginning in 1792. Howard was elected as an associate justice of Baltimore County, but refused the position. Declined also during the next few years was a major general's commission in the United States Army in 1794, and the position of secretary of war in 1795. Howard wrote President Washington that his shoulder wound incurred at Cowpens still bothered him, but moreover he did not feel worthy of the position. Howard would also be offered by Washington a commission as brigadier general in 1798, when war with France seemed imminent. That crisis soon ebbed and the position was not accepted.

By the time of the 1798 appointment as brigadier general, Howard was serving in the United States Senate. Richard Potts' unexpired term was filled by Howard beginning in 1796, and the following year the state legislature elected him to a full six-year term. The new senator supported strengthening the armed forces, as war with either France or England was considered likely. A larger army, vesting the president with wartime powers, arming merchant vessels, breaking treaties with France, and the creation of a Department of the Navy were all measures favored by Senator Howard.

Though a good Federalist on most issues, including Secretary of the Treasury Alexander Hamilton's financial measures, Howard did not toe the line on the Alien and Sedition proposals of 1798. Howard opposed this attempt by the Federalists to restrain criticism of the president or Congress.

When the senator's term expired in 1803, he retired to his substantial estate in Baltimore. Construction of "Belvedere" had been commenced in 1786, with the main dwelling completed in 1794. It was an elegant mansion surrounded by a wooded park. The house overlooked a "rapid water course" and falls, and much of the grounds were opened to the public. Graceful entertainment was the standard set at Belvedere. Included among the guests through the years were President Washington, justices of the United States Supreme Court, governors, and other public men. Though out of the scramble for elective office after 1803, Howard remained an active participant in public life in Maryland. His tastes in house guests, and in the use of his time, reveal that.

Howard's public service and philanthropy were sincere and considerable. Donations of land to public uses were often made from his vast estate. The site of the Washington monument in Baltimore, the surrounding parks, an entire city block for the construction of a Catholic church, the site of a rectory for an Episcopal church, and land for market houses, were some of his major contributions. Howard offered a substantial tract in the city of Baltimore if the state would move the capital there from Annapolis. The General Assembly rejected the offer by a one-vote margin.

Howard contributed his time as well as his money. Public activities included appointment as commissioner of the state penitentiary in 1804. In that capacity, he purchased land for and supervised the construction of a new state prison. During several elections for governor in the years after retirement from the Senate, Howard was given strong support, but was defeated. It is possible he would not have accepted the post had it been offered. When the War of 1812 erupted, Howard, unlike many Federalists, gave his active support. He was a member of the Baltimore Committee of Supply and helped raise money for the war effort. In 1814, Howard was elected a member of the Committee of Vigilance and Safety. That group gave assistance to other public officials in such things as caring for families of soldiers, raising money for defense, and helping at the local hospital. Perhaps more helpful than his time, Howard also contributed four sons to the war, all of whom served as officers. When other propertied men grew weary of the war and suggested surrender, Howard rebuked them:

> I have as much property at stake as most persons, and I have four sons in the field, but sooner would I see my sons weltering in their blood, and my property reduced to ashes, than so far disgrace my country.

Fortunately for father and sons, such sacrifices were not required.

Howard remained a figurehead leader in the national Federalist councils. A statewide Federalist organization was begun in Maryland in 1808 in response to the party's declining fortunes and the Jeffersonians' own successful organization. Young Federalists usually took the lead, while old war horses such as Howard, unused to the techniques of more modern political battles, remained aloof. Among the approaches used by the new leaders was to draw upon the sainted memory of George Washington in forming a patriotic organization called the Washington Benevolent Society. Howard, an admirer and comrade of the general, opposed the practice. When the Maryland chapter was formed in 1810, Howard refused to support it. The wife of the Federalist organizer, Robert Goodloe Harper, became so exasperated with Howard's obstruction that she said, "I think he does more harm to the cause by opposing everything that is proposed by the party, than any other man in the country." This reluctance to participate in, or see his party stoop to, the mundane necessities of a changed political world made Howard and many Federalists anachronisms.

In 1816 no formal nominations were made by his party for the presidential race. Rufus King was one of the few remaining national leaders and was the accepted, if almost tacit, choice for president. For a running mate, no unanimity was reached. In only a few states were electoral tickets presented. By far the largest state casting votes for King was Massachusetts. Those electors gave their votes to Howard for vice president. Ironically, another Marylander, the Washington Benevolent Society leader, Robert Goodloe Harper, received a few votes from Delaware. It does not appear that Howard considered himself a candidate that year, and in fact he never had a chance for victory.

In the same years as his unsuccessful consideration for vice president was Howard's election to the Maryland senate. He declined, but he did accept appointment by the legislature to a committee to survey new streets in Baltimore. His work on the committee continued until 1822. He was active in efforts to encourage colonization of former slaves, and served as president of the African Colonization Society of Maryland in 1817. He was also president of the Maryland Chapter of the Officer Veterans Group, Society of the Cincinnati, from 1804 until his death. This active, public spirited life was ended after the obstinately energetic Howard caught a severe cold while horseback riding, and died of pneumonia. President John Quincy Adams attended the funeral, as did many other of the nation's leaders.

Analysis of Qualification

This great soldier, civic leader, and philanthropist was one of Maryland's most public-spirited early leaders. His contributions on the battlefield were uniquely honored by his name being included in the third verse of the state song, "Maryland, my Maryland." "Remember Howard's warlike thrust..." the song declares. Howard was a vigorous and wealthy Baltimore booster, who by 1803 had completed his work in national affairs.

Howard's service in high public office ended 13 years before he was named for vice president. As an elder statesman in his party, Howard by 1816 had become aloof from political affairs. If called upon to lead a growing, restless country, whose eyes were on the west, on internal improvements to help growth, and just recently on slavery, Howard was out of touch. His talents had been utilized on a much smaller stage than that of national political power, and it is doubtful whether he was prepared to manage these larger responsibilities.

John Howard received the lion's share of his party's votes for vice president because of respect for his contributions in the Revolution and the early development of his state. Under that criterion, the party chose well. Under the test of whether the Federalists were naming a man who had demonstrated the capacity for presidential leadership, who without inordinate risk could be entrusted with the country's highest executive office, the party chose poorly.

HOWARD BIBLIOGRAPHY

Buchholz, Henrich Ewald. *Governors of Maryland from the Revolution to the Year 1908*. Baltimore (1908).

"Col. John Eager Howard of Maryland." N.p., n.d. (7-page pamphlet in the Maryland Room, University of Maryland).

Howard, Cary. "John Eager Howard: Patriot and Public Servant." *Maryland Historical Magazine* 62 (1967), pp. 300–17.

"A Memoir of the Late Col. John Eager Howard." Baltimore (1863), reprinted from the *Baltimore Gazette* of Oct. 15, 1827.

Municipal Art Society of Baltimore. *Fremiet's "Howard"; an equestrian statue... Addresses Delivered at the Unveiling*. Baltimore (1904).

Papenfuse, Edward C., et al. *A Biographical Dictionary of the Maryland Legislature, 1635–1789*. Vol. I, Baltimore and London (1979).

Powell, Henry Fletcher. *Tercentenary History of Maryland*. Vol IV. Chicago and Baltimore (1925), pp. 61–63.

White, Frank E., Jr. *The Governors of Maryland 1777–1970*. Annapolis (1970).

Election of 1820

NOMINATIONS

Democratic-Republican Congressional Caucus (6th): April 5, 1820, in the Capitol Building, Washington, D.C. *President*— James

Monroe. There was no opposition to the selection of Monroe for another term, consequently few people attended the caucus. *Vice president*— Daniel D. Tompkins. The main force behind the caucus were those men who wished to nominate Henry Clay of Kentucky for the vice presidency, the incumbent Tompkins being in a race for governor of New York. So few attended the caucus that it was decided to adjourn without reaching any decision. In June, Tompkins lost his race for governor, and so stood for another term as vice president.

The Federalists did not contest this or any later election.

GENERAL ELECTION
Electoral Vote
PRESIDENT:
    James Monroe — 231 electoral votes (24 states)
    John Quincy Adams —1 electoral vote
VICE PRESIDENT:
    Daniel Tompkins — 218 electoral votes (22 states)
    Four Others, 14 electoral votes
Winners
    James Monroe, 5th president
    Daniel Tompkins, 6th vice president
Losers
    None

Election of 1824

NOMINATIONS

In this election, the authority of the Congressional Caucus was not recognized by the multitude of contenders for the presidency. There were in effect no national nominations, but rather a mass of state nominations for men who were popular in the particular state making the nomination. A Congressional Caucus was held, but before that body met, there were already active nominees from local conventions and caucuses. The following is a partial listing of the states that nominated each of the candidates.

Nomination of William Lowndes. On December 18, 1821, by a resolution passed by the legislature of South Carolina. Lowndes died on October 22, 1822.

Nomination of John Quincy Adams. On July 20, 1822, by a resolution passed by the legislature of Tennessee. On March 4, 1824, by a state convention in Harrisburg, Pennsylvania, receiving 123 of the 125 votes cast. John C. Calhoun was nominated for vice president. Other meetings also nominated Jackson.

Nomination of Henry Clay. In November 1822, by resolutions passed in that month by both the Kentucky and the Missouri legislatures. In January 1823, by resolutions passed in both the Ohio and Illinois legislatures. In March 1823, by the legislature of Louisiana.

Nomination of William H. Crawford. November 24, 1823, by resolution passed in the North Carolina legislature. February 24, 1824, by a resolution passed in the Virginia legislature.

Nomination of John C. Calhoun. In November 1823, after Lowndes' death, by a resolution of the South Carolina legislature.

Democratic-Republican Congressional Caucus (7th): Dec. 27, 1823, in the Capitol, Washington, D.C. So few responded to a call for the caucus, that it was postponed.

Democratic-Republican Congressional Caucus (7th, 2nd session): February 14, 1824, in the House chamber, Capitol, Washington, D.C. *President*— William H. Crawford, nominated on the first ballot with 64 of the 68 votes cast. *Vice president*— Albert Gallatin, nominated on the first ballot with 57 of the 66 votes cast. After pressure from some of Crawford's supporters, who had second thoughts after the Caucus, Gallatin resigned his place on the ticket on October 2, 1824. No replacement was found.

Nomination of vice presidential candidates. In the legislative caucuses and in the various resolutions, usually no man for the second spot was named. Generally, these vice presidential candidates were selected by agreement of the various supporters of the different presidential nominees, with the desires of the candidate frequently being the determinant. After the Harrisburg convention's decision on March 4, 1824, which came as a serious shock to Calhoun, who had hoped to receive that meeting's endorsement for the presidency, the sights of the South Carolinian were gradually lowered to the second office. No definite time or date may be affixed to his withdrawal from the presidential contest, yet it was roughly in the summer of the election year. After Gallatin's resignation, the Crawford men turned to Nathaniel Macon, John C. Calhoun, and Martin Van Buren as their choices in various states. Henry Clay generally ran with Nathan Sanford. John Quincy Adams personally preferred Andrew Jackson for a running mate, thinking the vice presidency a fitting pasture for the man in his old age. It is generally supposed that the old man was not enthused over this graciousness, and most of Adams' votes came in tandem with Calhoun. Andrew Jackson, in most states, ran with Calhoun.

GENERAL ELECTION, November 2, 1824

It would not be until 1848 that all states voted on the same day. Yet, increasingly more states voted on the first Tuesday after the first Monday in November, and therefore that date will hereafter be given.

Popular Vote
```
Jackson . . . . . . . . . . . . . . . . . .151,271
Adams . . . . . . . . . . . . . . . . . . .113,122
Clay . . . . . . . . . . . . . . . . . . . . 47,531
Crawford . . . . . . . . . . . . . . . . . 40,856
Other . . . . . . . . . . . . . . . . . . . . 13,053
```

These figures are not a good indication of popular support for the candidates, because the totals are not complete due to the scarcity of voting records, and because in many states the people did not vote for president — the legislature in those states chose the presidential electors.

Electoral Vote
PRESIDENT:
```
Jackson — 99 (11 states)
Adams — 84 (7 states)
Crawford — 41 (3 states)
Clay — 37 (3 states)
```

VICE PRESIDENT:
```
Calhoun —182 (17 states)
Sanford — 30 (1+ state)
Macon — 24 (1 state)
Jackson —13 (1+ state)
Van Buren — 9 (1 state)
Clay — 2 (1 state)
```

No candidate for the presidency had a majority of the electoral vote, so the names of the three highest candidates were sent to the House of Representatives. On February 9, 1825, Adams was elected with a vote of 13 states, to Jackson's 7 and Crawford's 4.

Winners
John Q. Adams, 6th president
John C. Calhoun, 7th vice president

Losers
Andrew Jackson, William H. Crawford, Henry Clay, William Lowndes, John C. Calhoun (for president), Nathan Sanford, Nathaniel Macon

---

*1824 presidential nominee —
Democratic-Republican Party*

Andrew Jackson

No biographical sketch of Jackson is included because he later served as president, March 4, 1829–March 4, 1837 (7th president).

Birth: March 15, 1767, in Waxhaw, South Carolina.

State represented: Tennessee.

Age on Inauguration Day (March 4, 1825): 57 years, 11½ months.

Death: June 8, 1845, in Nashville, Tennessee, age 78 years, 3 months.

---

*1824 nominee for president—
Democratic-Republican
Party*

William H. Crawford

Full name: William Harris Crawford.

State represented: Georgia.

Birth: February 24, 1772, Amherst County, Virginia.

Age on Inauguration Day (March 4, 1825): 53 years, ½ month.

Education: Local schools in South Carolina and Georgia; hoped to attend University of Edinburgh, Scotland, but death of father ended scheme; Carmel Academy in Appling, Georgia, 1794–1796; studied law, admitted to bar in 1799.

Religion: No profession of religion, but considered himself a Christian. Member of American Bible Society.

Ancestry: Great grandfather born in Scotland in 1600; emigrated to Virginia in 1643.

Profession: Attorney.

Public Offices: Appointed as one of three commissioners to prepare digest of Georgia law, 1799–1801; Georgia legislature, 1803–1807; U.S. Senator, November 7, 1807–March 23, 1813; declined appointment as secretary of war, 1812; appointed minister to France, April 3, 1813–April 22, 1815; U.S. secretary of war, August 1, 1815–October 22, 1816; secretary of treasury, October 22, 1816–March 7, 1825, declined renomination by President Adams, 1824; defeated for president in 1824; appointed judge of Superior Court, Northern Circuit, June 1827, subsequently twice elected, died in office.

Home: "Woodlawn," Lexington, Georgia.

Death: September 15, 1834, at a home north of Lexington, Georgia, age 62 years, 6½ months.

ANDREW JACKSON
(From the author's collection)

Burial: "Woodlawn" home, near what is now Crawford, Oglethorpe County, Georgia.

Personal characteristics: 6'3" tall, well over 200 pounds, blue eyes, fair but ruddy complexion, powerful voice, somewhat awkward physically; affable, talkative, usually wore wig.

Father: Joel Crawford (October 16, 1736–October 1788), a farmer.

Mother: Fanny Harris (?–?), daughter of Robert Harris, married in 1760.

Siblings: Ann (1762–?), married Joel Barnett. Robert (1764–?), married Elizabeth Maxwell. Joel, Jr. (1766–?), married Ann Barnett. David (1768–?), married Mary Lee Wood. Lucy Ann (1770–November 11, 1809), married (1) a Richards, and (2) in 1801, James Tinsley. Elizabeth (1774–?), married (1) William Glenn, and (2) William Rhymes. Charles (1776–?), died unmarried. Fanny (1778–?), married David Crawford. Nathan (1780–?), died unmarried. Bennett (1786–1845), mar-

WILLIAM H. CRAWFORD
(From the Senate Historical Office)

ried (1) Nancy Crawford, and (2) Martha Crawford.

Wife: Susannah Gerardine (?–1863?), married in 1804.

Children: Caroline (March 1805–c. 1875), married George Mortimer Dudley. John (Feb-

ruary 1807–1876), married Sarah E. Bass in 1830; he was a local politician, postmaster, and lawyer. Ann (May 1809–?), never married. Nathaniel Macon (March 22, 1811–1872), married Anne Lesueur in 1840, a Baptist preacher. William Harris, Jr. (December 19, 1813–

November 1865), married Caroline E. Thomas; he was a minister. Robert (June 1816–1845), never married. Susan (?–1874/75), never married. William Bibb (1822–?), married Mary Knight; he was a minister.

Almost alone among presidential contenders, William Crawford magnanimously deferred to a friend and relinquished an opportunity to become president. Eight years later, when Crawford's "turn" arrived, he had been stricken by paralysis, abandoned by the incumbent president, and overtaken by a host of competitors who saw no reason to emulate Crawford's deference. Fate was not kind to this man, but he showed no bitterness. The story of William Crawford is a unique demonstration that a chance to grasp the brass ring of the presidency cannot be ignored, because it is likely not to be within reach again.

There were 11 children in William's family, and little money. Financial distress caused the Crawfords to move when William was seven from Virginia to South Carolina, where a new farm was started. During the Revolutionary War William's father was imprisoned for participating in the rebellion, but was released. Crawford's education was spotty, consisting of instruction in local schools and attendance at an academy in Georgia. Like John C. Calhoun, he also attended Moses Waddel's academy. In 1796 at the age of 24, Crawford became a teacher at Richmond Academy and there met his future wife, who was one of his students.

Crawford's first political involvement was the signing of a letter to President John Adams in support of Adams' anti–French policies. The letter, dated July 2, 1798, called for war if necessary. Later in his career Crawford's endorsement of these sentiments would cause the accusation that he supported the Alien and Sedition Acts that were passed shortly after the letter was sent. This momentary flirtation with Federalist principles soon passed.

In 1799 Crawford moved to Lexington and began a legal practice, after having studied law for one year at the Richmond Academy. His successes in that field came from his impressive appearance, good if not brilliant speaking ability, and direct, even blunt manner. He had a good memory, was witty, but perhaps most

importantly he committed himself completely to his client's cause. Crawford's political connections and legal skills earned him an appointment as a compiler of a digest of Georgia's laws, which he worked on with two other commissioners from 1799 to 1801. He received a professional and financial boost in 1802 when another attorney, Peter Early, turned his practice over to Crawford after Early was elected to Congress.

Crawford fought his first of several duels in 1802. It resulted from an attempt by a Federalist leader, John Clark, to end Crawford's growing political influence, either by killing Crawford or by embarrassing him should he refuse the challenge. Instead, Crawford killed his adversary, Peter Lawrence Van Allen. In frontier Georgia such an achievement added to his political clout. Crawford was not the innocent victim next time, as he seemed to accuse this same Federalist leader, John Clark, of attempting bribery to get a judgeship for an ally. The dispute grew through the years until in 1806 Clark challenged Crawford. When the contest was held, Crawford missed when he shot, and Clark badly injured Crawford's wrist. Clark would have continued the shooting except that Crawford's second called for a halt. After that experience Crawford denounced dueling.

In 1803 Crawford had been elected to the legislature. There he made a strong stand against the foreign slave trade. He also became a leader in one legislative faction that included the wealthier Georgia businessmen and attorneys. The year after he took his state assembly seat, Crawford purchased the first part of his plantation, "Woodlawn." It began at 260 acres and would gradually increase until it was more than a thousand. He loved the plantation and enjoyed experimenting with various crops. His special love was his apple and peach orchards.

Crawford's advance in politics was rapid. His affability as well as his ability earned him election by the legislature in 1807 to the United States Senate. There he showed little allegiance to his party, the Jeffersonian Republicans. On February 5, 1811, Crawford delivered a major speech on the extension of the charter of the national bank for 20 years, but the effort failed because of lack of administration support for the recharter legislation. Secretary of the Treasury Albert Gallatin, who in 1824 would be Crawford's running mate, resigned in disgust from the cabinet. Crawford was similarly piqued by President Madison's attitude.

As a second war with England became more likely, the Georgia senator became immersed in the debate over the country's preparedness. Crawford believed the United States was lacking in military strength. However, once war commenced, Crawford declined an offer from the president to become secretary of war. He said he was ill-suited for that position during wartime, but then became a critic of the administration's handling of the war.

After more than five years in the Senate, Crawford was well respected by his peers. Another who respected him was President Madison, who made a second offer of a high governmental post. This time Crawford accepted, and he left for Paris on June 18, 1813, to begin service as minister to France.

The Georgian's two years as minister were not successful, but perhaps no man could have solved the problems existing between the two countries. These included France's practice of seizing American ships on the high seas. Napoleon was losing his European war of conquest and was exiled to Elba; as Crawford was finishing his service in Paris, Napoleon escaped and returned to France. Never did Crawford find a stable government, nor one interested in responding to America's requests as presented by the ambassador. His most important service while in France was to act as the eyes and ears on European conditions for the American commissioners who at Ghent were trying to negotiate a treaty ending the American War of 1812. Crawford kept in continual contact with the commissioners, who included his future presidential adversaries Henry Clay and John Quincy Adams.

As Crawford set sail for the United States in 1815, he believed it likely he would be reelected to the Senate by the Georgia legislature. Instead, he learned that President Madison had appointed him secretary of war. His term there was short but hardly uneventful. One controversial event was the release of a report requested by Congress on the Indian

situation. On March 3, 1816, Crawford's report was presented to Congress. It created an immediate sensation. The policy of the government should be, according to the study, to bring these "savage neighbors within the pale of civilization." Ideas concerning the ownership of property must be inculcated. To civilize them, yet preserve their culture, they should be encouraged to intermarry with the white population. Further removal to lands west of the settled areas should not be made. In closing, Crawford's report stated that the country should be more interested in blending the Indians into national life than in accepting European immigrants, many of whom had left that continent because of crimes. These were unusual words for a government report, and they would be used against Crawford in later campaigns.

An even more significant result of Crawford's tenure in the War Department was his incurring the enmity of strong-tempered General Andrew Jackson. Jackson had secured a treaty with the Creek Indians ceding their territory to the United States, but Crawford decided that some of the lands actually belonged to the Cherokees. Renegotiation of the offending parts of the treaty was urged. This policy angered Jackson, and irritated many others who were anxious for possession of the lands. In Tennessee Crawford was burned in effigy, and suffered editorial abuse throughout the states affected by the treaty. Being fair to the Indians was not a popular policy in this period. Jackson would be blinded by hatred towards Crawford as a result of this incident.

In 1816 three main contenders for the presidential nomination existed: James Monroe, Governor Daniel D. Tompkins of New York, and Crawford. Resentment to the dynasty of Virginia politicians who had succeeded in making one of their own president every election except for 1796 caused Monroe much trouble. Monroe was Crawford's good friend, and the last of the Revolutionary War patriots with a claim on the presidency. New York Congressman Samuel R. Betts was quoted in a New York newspaper as saying that Crawford did not want the nomination. The statement was not authorized by Crawford, and many backers continued their work for the

Georgian. In this state of uncertainty, a direct inquiry as to Crawford's intentions was made. Crawford's response on February 1, 1816, was a strong disavowal of interest. Still, the activity on his behalf continued. On March 16, 1816, the Congressional caucus was held. Despite Crawford's statement that he wanted Monroe nominated, the vote was only 65 for Monroe and 54 for Crawford. Nine Crawford supporters voted for Monroe, providing the Virginian his margin of victory. Still other Crawford men did not attend. Crawford was embarrassed. Even though he wanted to be president, he also wanted to present a magnanimous image in 1816 by helping elect his good friend.

Crawford was offered the post of secretary of treasury by President Madison in the spring of 1816, after the caucus. The war secretary did not want the post and initially refused. Madison continued his entreaties. Finally Crawford agreed to the shift and in October 1816, he started his work at the treasury. He did not like the position at first, as the department was the largest in government, poorly organized, inefficient and unwieldy. The new secretary refused to remain in the post unless Congress permitted some changes. Hard work, the enactment of some of his recommendations, increased oversight of his subordinates all combined to increase greatly the effectiveness of the department. New President Monroe reappointed Crawford and the two friends worked well together. Monroe did not listen well to Crawford or to other cabinet members in making appointments to their departments, but he did nonetheless give them substantial responsibility and discretion. Crawford had the president's support in working to strengthen the second bank of the United States, which had been rechartered after Crawford left the Senate. It was in serious trouble, having expanded too rapidly after its recharter. At times Secretary Crawford ignored statutory restrictions in order to make certain that the bank did not fail. A hostile Congress made his efforts even more difficult, but in time the bank returned to a sound footing.

A second opportunity to antagonize the brittle Andrew Jackson occurred in 1818. Jackson had been instructed in general terms to deal with the Seminole Indian problem in Georgia. Jackson pursued the Seminoles into Florida, captured Pensacola, and hanged two British citizens. Crawford was afraid these unauthorized actions could precipitate a war with Spain, who controlled Florida. Jackson never forgave Crawford for criticizing him over these actions, and made increasingly vitriolic attacks on the administration, using Crawford as the foil. More important in the Florida situation than Jackson's ill temper were Crawford's efforts to gain that region from Spain. The secretary was tireless. Even after a treaty with Spain was signed but was not yet ratified by Spain, Crawford counseled for the occupation of the Floridas by American troops. This was eventually not necessary as the cession occurred in 1820.

Monroe was reelected without opposition in 1820, missing by only one electoral vote the unanimous election that only George Washington has received. Almost immediately three strong-willed members of his cabinet began jockeying for position for the 1824 succession: Secretary of State John Quincy Adams, Secretary of War John C. Calhoun, and Secretary of the Treasury Crawford. The internal feuding led to such charges as Calhoun's that the treasury secretary was reducing the appropriation request for the war department in order to weaken the influence and patronage available to him.

Political intrigue by partisans of the two men further soured cabinet relations. Beginning in 1822 Crawford considered leaving the cabinet, as so much infighting was occurring that governmental activities were being jeopardized. The president and Crawford had a candid series of letters in which suspicions of Crawford's conduct were aired. The president seemed satisfied by Crawford's avowal of innocence. Nonetheless, the relations between Crawford and Monroe were never as cordial as before.

Crawford was definitely the "frontrunner," to use more modern terminology, as the 1824 election campaign got under way. Monroe remained neutral. Charges were injected into the campaign that Crawford had been involved in the illegal slave trade; further controversy over Crawford's Indian report of 1816 flared, instigated by his old Georgia nemesis and dueling antagonist, John Clark. Despite these attacks, Crawford was in a good political position.

All favorable portents were shaken at the end of September 1823. Crawford became desperately ill from what may have been a stroke. The illness was also described as bilious fever (malaria), inflammatory rheumatism, or erysipelas. Aggravating the condition was the improper medical care he received, including perhaps laudanum, the same drug that wrecked Samuel Tilden's health (see election of 1876). For eight weeks Crawford's life was in the balance, then gradually he began to recover. He was blind, speechless, and paralyzed. He suffered from "thickened" speech the remainder of his life. By November 14, 1823, he unwisely decided to return to work, and became ill again. For the next three months he could barely see. In April 1824 he returned to the cabinet, but had a relapse in May.

While Crawford was almost completely incapacitated, the final Congressional caucus met. All but Crawford's supporters stayed away, and a smaller percentage of Congressmen attended than ever before. Only three states had a majority of their delegation present. Crawford won easily, and old friend Albert Gallatin won the second spot. The propriety of a caucus nomination became a major political issue; its secretive, undemocratic character was the center of abuse hurled by the supporters of each of the other candidates. A bitter opponent of Crawford's also had published a series of 15 letters anonymously accusing Crawford of mismanagement of public funds in the treasury department. By May and June the falsity of the charges was revealed, but the lie remained somewhat ahead of the truth in many areas of the country.

Former presidents Thomas Jefferson and James Madison each favored Crawford for president. His vice presidential running mate described Crawford in terms that these two old chief executives probably agreed with:

> [Crawford] united to a powerful mind a most correct judgment and inflexible integrity; which last quality not sufficiently tempered by indulgence and civility, has prevented his acquiring general popularity; but notwithstanding this defect (for it is one), I know so well his vast superiority over the other candidates for the office of President that I was anxious for his election and openly expressed my opinion.

Gallatin finally withdrew after pressure from some of Crawford's supporters who hoped that a politically stronger running mate could be obtained. No successor was ever named, and Crawford eventually was teamed with different men in different states. Crawford was not popular with the public. His frequently controversial actions — in favor of the national bank, against injustices to Indians, against Andrew Jackson — left a residue of bitterness. His defeat was evident to all, though he remained in the race and received the third highest vote. The deadlocked election caused the House of Representatives to select the new president. Crawford's health kept him from being a serious contender there. Crawford never expressed serious regrets about missing the presidency. To the contrary, in 1830 he remarked: "I then verily believed, and I do now believe, that had I been elected, my remains would now be reposing in the national burial ground...."

In 1825 and for some time thereafter, Crawford continued to be ill. A Crawford presidency would have coincided with continued illness, and might well, as he forecast, have caused his early death. For two years after the election he was unable to tend to plantation affairs, but by 1828 he had recovered. The only obvious remaining evidence was his thick speech. Crawford longed to return to the Senate, but the position was never offered. In 1828 his main ambition was to defeat Calhoun's ambitions for president. Calhoun alone among Crawford's 1824 adversaries was blamed for the disastrous defeat. Bitterness towards Calhoun's supporters, as well as toward Calhoun himself, would remain a driving emotion for Crawford until he died.

In February 1828, Crawford wrote Henry Clay saying that he approved of Clay's 1824 labors in electing Adams over Jackson in the House of Representatives, and that he (Crawford) would have done the same. Yet after four years of Adams, Crawford reluctantly supported Jackson. Crawford favored himself for vice president, and the lower house of the

Georgia legislature nominated him for the office. For a time he believed his election was possible, but then began to back Nathaniel Macon as an alternative to Calhoun. Crawford finally voted for Jackson for president, considering him the lesser of two evils.

Crawford's remaining years were spent as a judge on a Georgia superior court. His political involvement consisted of frequent letter writing outlining his views, and periodic hopes for election to office. In 1830 he wrote a strange letter to Clay about forming a coalition between the two men's supporters, electing Crawford president in 1832. Clay would then be appointed to a cabinet position, and could "hardly fail to succeed when I retire."

In the 1832 nullification crisis, Crawford argued against precipitate Southern actions, saying that nullification and secession should be avoided at all costs. His forays into the political arena kept his ambitions high, and in 1834 he wrote a friend that he hoped he would be appointed to a vacancy on the United States Supreme Court. Two days later he was dead.

Analysis of Qualifications

There are really two William Crawfords for purposes of evaluating his ability to serve as president. One is the Crawford who might have been elected president in 1816 — strong-willed, a good administrator, strong mind and memory, a giant physically whom Albert Gallatin could refer to as having a powerful mind and tremendous judgment. Then there was the Crawford of 1823 through 1828, who was wracked by debilitating illness, whose mind was not always sharp, whose judgment at least as to his political influence and position was sadly faulty, whose support had disappeared. One Crawford would have been a solid choice for president, capable even of greatness, or at the very least of steady and commendable leadership. The other Crawford, as he admitted himself, might not have been able to survive the rigors of office.

Crawford was an amiable, witty man who hated hypocrisy, was scrupulously honest and tirelessly hard working. He loved story-telling and a hearty laugh, but he was no man of the people in the manner of an Andrew Jackson. His legal talents had been sufficient to make him one of the most successful lawyers in his area of Georgia, and his imposing mental abilities and physical appearance caused his selection to the United States Senate after he had served in the legislature only four years. His prominence in Georgia soon was transformed into power in Washington. Consideration of Crawford as presidential timber occurred soon after he arrived in the capital. In the Senate, he revealed independence, intelligence, good speaking abilities, and integrity.

Perhaps Crawford's most significant contribution was in the cabinets of Madison and Monroe. He continued to work hard. Imaginative recommendations to solve some of the long-standing inefficiencies of the treasury department were of great benefit. Poor or nonexistent supervising of the various treasury agents who collected public money in customhouses, public land offices, and other places was corrected. Reorganization of the department was accomplished, not always for the better, yet the effort to modernize was unceasing. By the time Crawford left the treasury department both the number of employees and the payroll had been reduced to below the level of 20 years earlier.

Whether Crawford would have been elected without the blow of his illness is problematic. Certainly his stroke, if that is what it was, came at the worst possible time as the campaign was just getting under way. Whether he could physically have handled the presidency is even more subject to doubt. In December 1824, a friend and supporter, but a candid one, said that Crawford continued to suffer from his speech difficulty. His vision was troublesome, prohibiting him from reading more than a few lines. He could write, but it was nearly illegible; his feet and hands were painfully debilitated. Mentally, however, Crawford appeared as alert, forceful, and imaginative as ever. Whether the latter observation was honest or meant for political consumption is impossible to say. Regardless, his speech was so inarticulate as to make many doubt his alertness.

William Crawford is one of the great might-have-beens of the losing candidates. Esteemed by his peers, qualified by his government experiences and intellect, Crawford in 1816 stepped aside for a friend. Eight years later, even more experienced but now devastated by illness, he was denied the presidency forever.

CRAWFORD BIBLIOGRAPHY

Crawford, Fred. *William Harris Crawford Family Tree*. Chatham, Ill. (1989).

Green, Philip Jackson. *The Life of William Harris Crawford*. Charlotte, N.C. (1965).

Laurus Crawfordiana, Memorials of That Branch of the Crawford Family.... New York City (1883).

Mooney, Chase C. *William H. Crawford, 1772–1834.* Lexington, Ky. (1974).

Shipp, J.E.D. *Giant Days, or the Life and Times of William H. Crawford.* Americus, Ga. (1909).

Stephens, Lucinda Frances. *Crawford Genealogy.* Macon, Ga. (1936).

---

*1824 presidential nominee—
Democratic-Republican Party*

Henry Clay

Full Name: Henry Clay.

State represented: Kentucky

Birth: April 12, 1777, in the district known as the "Slashes" in Hanover County, Virginia.

Age on Inauguration Day (March 4, 1825): 47 years, 10½ months.

Education: No college; three years of county school; studied law and admitted to bar in 1797.

Religion: Raised as a Baptist, became an Episcopalian in 1847.

Ancestry/prominent relatives: English ancestors arrived in early 1600s; Thomas H. Clay (son), minister to Guatemala; James B. Clay (son), diplomat and congressman.

Profession: Lawyer.

Public Offices: Kentucky State Legislature, 1803; U.S. Senator, November 19, 1806 (not old enough under Constitution)–March 3, 1807; Kentucky House of Representatives, 1808–1809, speaker in 1809; U.S. Senate, January 4, 1810–March 3, 1811; U.S. Representative, March 4, 1811–January 19, 1814, resigned; speaker, November 4, 1811–January 19, 1814; commissioner to negotiate treaty with Great Britain, 1814; U.S. Representative, March 4, 1815–March 3, 1821; speaker, December 4, 1815–October 28, 1820, resigned; U.S. Representative, March 3, 1823–March 6, 1825, resigned; speaker, December 1, 1823–1825; defeated for president, 1824; U.S. Secretary of State, March 7, 1825–March 3, 1829; U.S. Senate, March 4, 1831–March 31, 1842; defeated for president, 1832 and 1844; unsuccessful candidate for presidential nomination, 1840, 1848; U.S. Senator, March 4, 1849–death, June 29, 1852.

Death: June 29, 1852, in Washington, D.C., at age 75 years, 2½ months.

Burial: Lexington Cemetery, Lexington, Kentucky.

Home: "Ashland"—estate of 600 acres near Lexington, Kentucky.

Personal characteristics: Great magnetism; dynamic, persuasive speaker; charming and graceful; tall, high forehead, gray eyes, large and expressive mouth.

Father: John Clay (1742–1781), a Baptist preacher.

Mother: Elizabeth Hudson (1750–December 4, 1829), married around 1765; after Clay's death, married Henry Watkins in 1791; daughter of George and Elizabeth (Jennings) Hudson.

Siblings: George (?–?), died as a young adult. Betsey Hudson (?–pre–1781). Henry (?–pre–1777). John (c. 1775–pre–1797). Sally (?–?), died young. Molley (?–?), died young. Porter (1778/79–February 16, 1850), married Sophia Grosch who died September 28, 1829, then married a Mrs. Hardin.

Wife: Lucretia Hart (March 18, 1781–April 6, 1864), married on April 11, 1799); daughter of Col. Thomas and Susanna (Gray) Hart.

Children: Anne Brown (April 7, 1807–1835), married James Erwin in 1823. Eliza (1815–1825). Henry, Jr. (1811–1847), in 1832 married Julia Prather. James Brown (1817–January 26, 1864). John Morrison (1821–1877), married Mrs. Josephine (Russell) Erwin in 1866. Laura (1816–1816), died at age 3 months. Lucretia (1809–1823). Susan (1805–1825), married Martin Duralde on April 22, 1822. Theodore Wythe (1802–1871), injured his head in his youth, and spent most of his remaining years in a mental asylum. Thomas Hart (September 22, 1803–March 18, 1871), married Marie Mentelle on October 5, 1837. Henrietta (1800–?), died in infancy.

Historic sites/memorials: "Ashland," his

home in Lexington, Kentucky, is open to the public. There is a Henry Clay Memorial Foundation based at Ashland. Clay's statue is in Statuary Hall in the U.S. Capitol. Huge painting of Clay in the Capitol arguing for the Compromise of 1850. There is a monument at the cemetery in Lexington. The Decatur House, located at 748 Jackson Place, N.W., Washington, D.C., was Clay's home for a time.

Henry Clay's father, a Baptist preacher, died when his best-remembered son was only four years old. The family knew more prosperity than many of its neighbors, but only marginally. A small country school provided Henry his entire early education, consuming no more than three years of his childhood. When Henry was 14, his mother remarried and the family moved to Richmond, Virginia.

In Richmond, Henry gained a position at a retail store. His stepfather's efforts earned Henry a position as a copyist in the office of the clerk of the High Court of Chancery, where he remained from 1792 through 1796. The Chancellor of the High Court, George Wythe, took an interest in the young clerk. Wythe directed Henry's reading and informal education, and also inculcated an interest in the law. In 1796, Clay began to study law in the office of Robert Brooke, Virginia's attorney general, and was admitted to the bar the following year.

Though his association with Attorney General Brooke and Chancellor Wythe had enabled him to make valuable contacts in Virginia, he decided that Kentucky offered more fertile ground for a new lawyer. Clay's mother now lived in this new frontier state, and in 1797 Clay moved to Lexington. He was only 20 years old, a newly licensed lawyer by the Virginia courts, tall, raw-boned, and ungainly, with much smoothing of rough edges still to be performed. The town had a similar appearance, and would grow from 2,000 people when Clay arrived to 4,000 ten years later. In a matter of only five or six years Clay became by common agreement one of the best lawyers in the city. Part of his prominence arose from his fortunate choice of a bride, Lucretia Hart, who was able to bring Clay into contact with

most of the important families in Lexington. Until his marriage, Clay was a carefree, gambling bon vivant whose reputation was justifiably poor. He seemed upon his marriage to leave most of these profligate habits behind. He never left behind, however, his open, winning personality that gained him strong admirers among male as well as female acquaintances. The political loyalty his supporters gave him became unbreakable.

Criminal law was Clay's forte. He was a showman of the highest sort, fluent and with a keen understanding of juries. He could be dramatic, crying at the proper cue, and also use sarcasm and humor to good effect. The makings of a great politician were clearly evident.

Clay's first involvement with the slave issue occurred in 1798 and 1799 when he fought to secure a new constitution for Kentucky, one which among other features would establish the gradual emancipation of all slaves. In later life, Clay strongly defended the rights of the slave owner, but he would also decry the existence of slavery. His remedy was for the states themselves to remove this evil by freeing the slaves when they reached a certain age, and then monetarily compensating their owners. Clay himself was a slave owner, but freed many of his own slaves. In his will in 1852, Clay followed his own earlier guidelines by requiring the emancipation of each slave when he or she reached the age of 25.

At the age of 29, still not old enough under the Constitution to serve, Clay was appointed to the United States Senate by the governor of Kentucky to fill an unexpired term. Returning to the legislature in Frankfort the following year, he was elected speaker of the Kentucky House of Representatives, and continued in that position until 1809. In the state house, the acrimony over the embargo imposed by President Jefferson against British goods became so intense that Clay challenged one of the few Federalist members, who had mercilessly abused him in debate, to a duel. On January 9, 1809, the duel was held and each party was slightly wounded. This sense of romantic honor that had to be preserved through dramatic means from time to time was a marked characteristic of the Clay personality. He was bold and decisive, yet also impulsive and emotional. He would be outraged by a personal slight, but would shortly thereafter be forgiving.

From his first service in the Congress, as a short-term, appointed U.S. Senator in 1806, Clay sponsored legislation for federal financing of internal improvements. Clay would soon more fully outline his "American System" for federal financing of public works, thereby increasing the productivity of American citizens. The obverse of his program was a high tariff to restrain foreign competition.

Clay returned to Washington in 1811 as a U.S. Congressman, and there at the capital he was to remain for nearly the rest of his life. He was given the rare honor as a freshman congressman to be selected as speaker of the House. He made a good presiding officer who commanded the respect of his colleagues. Along with other recently elected and youthful legislators, Clay became a War Hawk. The Hawks urged that the British be punished for their attacks on American shipping. England was also charged with encouraging Indians to disrupt American settlements west of the Alleghenies. Clay's placing of other War Hawks in prominent positions on House committees added to the momentum that resulted in a declaration of war against Britain in 1812. Throughout this difficult, inconclusive conflict the speaker maintained his zealous military support. In 1814, President Madison appointed Clay and four other men to be peace commissioners. Four and a half months of squabbling in Ghent, a city in the Netherlands, covered a whole range of disputes between the two countries. The treaty was completed in 1815, and Clay returned to the United States.

Clay was offered but refused positions of secretary of war and ambassador to Russia. Instead, he returned to the U.S. House and again was elected speaker. When James Monroe became president in 1817, Clay hoped to be appointed secretary of state, but John Quincy Adams was selected instead. Again, Clay was offered the positions of secretary of war or a foreign post, but he declined.

In Congress, he earned Andrew Jackson's permanent enmity by criticizing the general for his invasion of then–Spanish Florida and his mistreatment of the Seminole Indians there. He compared Jackson to the great military dictators of history, including Caesar and Napoleon. Jackson was not a forgiving man; the two would constantly clash throughout their careers. Clay's humanitarianism was demonstrated in this speech, as he condemned Jackson for his barbaric treatment of the Indians. This same issue would enliven the debate between the leaders ten years later.

The Kentuckian's first opportunity to play the role of the "great pacificator" occurred in the Missouri Compromise debate of 1820-1821. Clay was less concerned with the extension or limitation of slavery as he was with preservation of the Union. The dividing of the Louisiana Purchase lands by the 36°30' line prevented for 30 years the question of slavery in the territories from plunging the country into sectional conflict. This great accomplishment of a compromise won, Clay retired from Congress.

Clay's ten years in Washington caused him severe financial distress, resulting in large part from his gambling debts but also from some ill-advised signing of promissory notes for friends. Two years in Kentucky practicing law returned his private affairs to some order, and he returned to Congress in 1823, again being elected speaker.

The presidency was already the goal that would drive Clay for the remainder of his life. In 1822, the Kentucky Legislature nominated him for president. A few other states joined in the call. Clay's American System platform was an attempt to join the interests of his adopted West, which was mainly agrarian and in need of internal improvement, with the interests of the Northeast, which was mercantile in need of a high tariff. The South was interested in neither platform plank. Each section found a candidate more to its liking than Clay, and in the general election the great compromiser came in a close, but sufficiently far fourth, behind Crawford, Adams, and Jackson. No candidate gained a majority. Since only three candidates' names would be voted on by the House of Representatives in choosing a president, Clay became the king-maker. He might easily have been one of the top three candidates if a few Louisiana legislators who would have voted for him had not been waylaid by an accident and thereby prevented from attending the legislative session that chose Louisiana's electors. Even more damaging to his cause was the loss of electors in New York, largely by corruption. There seems a good possibility that Clay would have won in the House of Representatives which had selected him speaker almost unanimously since 1810, had he only been able to be on the ballot.

Some of Clay's friends visited Adams to discuss the possibility of Clay's receiving high office in an Adams administration. Adams made implicit but not firm promises of an appointment. It has never been conclusively determined whether Clay was directly involved in any contacts with Adams, and it seems definite that no explicit deal was ever made by Adams or Clay. What is clear is that Adams was the far preferable man to be president insofar as Clay was concerned. Jackson represented to Clay the worst excesses that democratic government could force upon itself. He never believed in a military man seeking high office, an opinion that caused him to be unnerved at his own Whig party's selection of generals to run in 1840 and 1848. There had already been several disputes between Clay and Jackson, and a deal was hardly necessary for Clay to vote for Adams. The Kentucky Legislature attempted to instruct all Kentucky Congressmen to vote for Jackson, but Clay ignored their recommendations and along with his supporters in the House made Adams president.

Soon thereafter Adams offered the position of secretary of state to Clay. This may have been the crucial decision in Clay's life; he decided incorrectly. When he accepted the position, the quite understandable, though probably unjustified, charge of "corrupt bargain" began. It would haunt Clay and Adams for the rest of their careers. Much of Clay's time until he left public office was consumed by refuting this charge.

Clay, as secretary of state, made no lasting contribution to American foreign policy. He did get along well with the president, and they agreed on most major objectives. Within a secretary of state's power was Indian policy. Thus Clay could further his life-long interest in a more humane approach towards Native Americans. Clay was probably unhappy as secretary of state. He did not find the work, particularly the routine of administration, to be enjoyable. Clay supported Adams for reelection in 1828 but the New Englander was overwhelmed by Jackson in the election rematch.

Clay remained in private life for two years. President Jackson was constantly disappointing to Clay. He believed Jackson's expansion of executive powers was creating a dictatorship and distorting the Constitution. In 1830, the Kentucky Legislature again nominated Clay for the presidency. Kentucky senator John J. Crittenden resigned from the Senate in order to make a vacancy for Clay. The most heated exchange with the president, and one which Clay thought would elect him chief executive, occurred over the rechartering of the second bank of the United States. Clay succeeded in getting a bill renewing the charter passed, but Jackson vetoed it. Clay most mistakenly believed that Jackson had hanged himself by the veto.

Another crucial issue of 1832 arose over South Carolina's attempt to nullify the "tariff of abominations," which had rates so high as to antagonize the South. Jackson's belligerently strong stand against nullification was to Clay an invitation for other Southern states to join in South Carolina's defense. Therefore, Clay was instrumental in preparing a compromise tariff in Congress that was adopted the same day that Jackson-backed measures permitting military force against South Carolina were also passed.

The issues Clay attempted to raise could not undermine Jackson's sweeping support in the country, and Clay was soundly defeated for the presidency in 1832. It was after this overwhelming defeat that the nullification crisis was resolved by Clay's compromise tariff. New issues soon arose, however. After the rechartering of the second United States bank was defeated, Jackson removed all governmental deposits from these banks, precipitating a nationwide financial crisis. Other factors contributed to the severe recession, but Jackson's vendetta against the bank and its officers probably played the crucial role in the panic. Clay became the principal spokesman in

Congress against Jackson's removal of the deposits, and though the president's actions could not be reversed, they could be condemned. A resolution of censure was introduced and passed, calling Jackson's actions a tyrannical abuse of executive power. The censure resolution also charged Jackson, with great validity, with undermining the United States Supreme Court and refusing to enforce its decision that prohibited Georgia from removing the Cherokee Indians from its boundary. Jackson's hatred, shared by many Americans, of the Indians led to the terrible "trail of tears" in which thousands of Cherokees died of starvation, exposure, and other abuses while being marched west of the Mississippi River. Abuse of the Indians was national policy for almost 100 years, and Jackson was only one of many who did not consider them worthy of fair treatment.

Clay was genuinely concerned that President Jackson ignored democratic procedures and was ruling as a dictator. Yet he also knew Jackson was extremely popular and could anoint a successor in 1836. This Jackson did by promoting the presidential candidacy of Martin Van Buren, his vice president. Clay thought it useless to contest the action, and did not seek the Whig nomination that year. The Democratic Party's success was sweeping, and the new Congress even expunged the resolution of censure that Clay had seen passed three years previously. The desecrating of the official journal of the Senate outraged Clay, and he remarked "the Senate is no longer a place for a decent man."

The Kentucky senator continued his opposition to Jackson's policies, as promoted by his successor Van Buren. The Panic of 1837 was a severe economic recession that made the Whig Party's victory in 1840 almost assured. Clay was confident that he would receive the nomination, but was concerned with the efforts of Daniel Webster and others to nominate the aged general and hero from almost 30 years before, William Henry Harrison. Probably the crucial individual in denying Clay the nomination this year was Thurlow Weed from New York, who first tried to convince Clay to withdraw his candidacy and, having been refused that, succeeded in outmaneuvering Clay at the

convention. A plurality of the delegates were for Clay, but he could never arrange a majority. After Harrison's election, Clay refused all offers of a cabinet position, as he believed he could run the country as leader of the United States Senate.

Clay pushed too hard against the new president and antagonized him. Harrison became so provoked at some of Clay's insistent demands that he said, "Mr. Clay, you forget that I am president." Harrison's death after only one month as president placed Clay's old friend John Tyler in the White House. Soon Tyler too found Clay arrogant and presumptuous. During the 1841-42 session of the U.S. Senate, Clay rammed through his version of bills, particularly in the area of a new Bank of the United States. Clay succeeded in getting his bill passed, but Tyler quite unexpectedly vetoed it. Holding his anger in check, Clay then secured the passage of an amended bill that he thought met Tyler's objections, but it too was vetoed. This caused Tyler's Whig cabinet to resign. Many of the Whigs in Congress wrote Tyler out of the Whig party. Clay was one of those who kept at Tyler's heels until the 1844 election.

As the next presidential election approached, most political observers saw the contest as being between Martin Van Buren as the Democratic nominee and Clay as the Whig. The crucial issue that loomed over the approaching campaign was the annexation of the Republic of Texas. This was an unattractive issue for either candidate to take a stand upon. The two of them met at Ashland, Clay's Kentucky plantation, in May 1842. There they probably made a deal to leave Texas out of the campaign. That arrangement went for naught when Van Buren was denied the nomination in lengthy convention balloting. An unknown Tennessee politician, James K. Polk, was nominated instead. Polk had no qualms about the Texas issue and announced completely for the annexation of the new state. Clay continued to try to straddle the issue and said that though he personally favored annexation, he would push for it only if it could be achieved without war, without national dishonor, and on fair terms. These positions were set out in two letters written to a correspondent in Alabama, and published by Clay. These "Alabama letters" outraged the abolitionists, who wanted no more slave states. They voted in large numbers for the abolitionist candidate, James G. Birney. The 15,000 votes for Birney in New York state threw the electoral votes there to Polk, and with them the election as well.

Texas was not the only reason for Clay's defeat. He continued to represent to most Americans the monied interests in the country. He had no expectation of defeat, and the loss was devastating. Clay made public statements of dropping out of politics and retiring to Ashland. In part because of his natural political inclinations, and in part because of the Mexican war, Clay soon returned to politics. The declaration of war against Mexico was senseless to Clay, and seemed totally provoked by the American government. His namesake and favorite son, Henry, Jr., was killed in the battle of Buena Vista. Not only was he concerned that America had initiated the conflict, but he feared the sole aim of the war was the annexation of Mexican territory, a fear that was well founded.

As 1848 approached, the urge to become president again overwhelmed him. He announced his candidacy in April 1848. Clay had too many losses burdening his candidacy, however, and even old friends deserted him. Another hero-general, Zachary Taylor, was nominated. The second nomination of a military figure by his party disturbed Clay, and he never endorsed Taylor's candidacy.

Taylor's election brought no peace to Clay. The growing sectional divisions again caused Clay to desire returning to the United States Senate and Kentucky obliged him. Clay argued that natural or geographical considerations made slavery in the new Mexican territories impossible. The South should therefore not insist on slavery being allowed there. Instead, they should be content with a strengthened fugitive slave act, requiring escaped slaves to be returned to their masters. He begged extremists both from the North and South to seek compromise. Clay was unable to have these and his other compromise measures adopted. In his absence, Senator Stephen Douglas of Illinois was able to pass each of the measures that became known as the Compromise of 1850. Clay died two years after his final legislative achievement.

Henry Clay suffered more than political defeats in his life. Almost all of his 11 children predeceased him, including all six of his daughters. One son became insane and spent much of his life in a Lexington asylum. The son of whom he was proudest, Henry, Jr., was killed in war. It was after the death of Henry, Jr., that Clay felt the need finally to receive holy baptism. On June 22, 1847, at the age of 70, Clay was baptized and joined the Episcopal Church. He had felt that a deep emotional experience was required before baptism, and perhaps his son's death provided that motivation.

Analysis of Qualifications

Clay as president would have been a bold, imaginative, but also impulsive leader. He could make bitter enemies, but he himself rarely held grudges against other politicians, with the notable exception of Andrew Jackson. He was a humanitarian of the first order, favoring liberty, even if gradual, for slaves at home, for Indians who were little more than savages to him, and for people struggling for independence in South America and in Europe. He could be extremely sentimental. His early years were marked by raucous living, apparently freely sampling the physical pleasures that life could offer. By the time of his first political involvement, however, Clay had matured and become much more concerned with his dignity and the earned respect of his constituents. He nonetheless remained a man of passion and energy.

A more dramatic contrast to Andrew Jackson would be hard to imagine. The incredible change to American politics caused by Jackson's election seemed a disaster to Clay. Jackson's policies and style were, to Clay, a debauching of government. Clay could not identify well with the common man. Jackson's use of patronage both to increase his own political power as well as that of his party was unacceptable to the Kentuckian, as was Jackson's stand on most of the major issues of the day.

It is Clay's almost constant advocacy of

gradual emancipation of the slaves that marks him as a truly foresighted politician. This issue, which eventually caused the incredible devastation of the Civil War, probably could not have been resolved, considering the passions on each side, by an approach such as Clay's. Yet he saw the danger that would eventually divide the country explosively in two. He devised, with others, probably the best approach to alleviate the tension short of war. Clay believed his proposals could have succeeded if not for the radical abolitionist attacks on slavery which he estimated had set gradual emancipation back by 50 years. He believed slavery an evil, and could not stomach such statements as those by Calhoun that slavery was a blessing. So concerned was Clay about colonization of ex-slaves that he presided over the first meeting of the American Colonization Society in December 1816, and was later president of that organization.

Clay was better presidential material than most of the men who defeated him. There is little doubt that he would have far surpassed the accomplishments of the two Whig generals, Harrison and Tyler, who defeated Clay for the nomination in 1840 and 1848. If ever a country needed a man of Clay's temperament, a humanitarian, a man who sought to reduce the most bitter of passions dividing the country, it was America in the period of 1820 to 1850. He was an outstanding statesman who helped preserve the country by his compromises in 1820 and 1850, though other men played major roles in both achievements. Clay was extremely popular with Congress, and in both the House and the Senate he became the leader of the Chamber in which he served. There is every reason to expect he would have worked extremely well with Congress as President.

Henry Clay was one of the truly outstanding presidential possibilities among those who tried, and in Clay's case, tried and tried again, but failed.

CLAY BIBLIOGRAPHY

Baxter, Maurice G. *Henry Clay and the American System*. Lexington, Ky. (1995).
Eaton, Clement. *Henry Clay and the Art of American Politics*. Boston and Toronto (1957).

Hopkins, James F. et al., eds. *The Papers of Henry Clay*. Vols. 1–10. Lexington (1959–91). Supplement (1992).
Mayo, Bernard. *Henry Clay, Spokesman of the New West*. Boston (1937).
Morgan, William G. "The 'Corrupt Bargain' Charge Against Clay and Adams: An Historical Analysis." *The Filson Club History Quarterly* 42 (1968), pp. 132–149.
Poage, George R. *Henry Clay and the Whig Party*. Chapel Hill, N.C. (1933).
Remini, Robert. *Henry Clay: Statesman for the Union*. New York (1991).
Schurz, Carl. *Henry Clay*, 2 vols. Boston (1887).
Van Deusen, Glyndon G. *The Life of Henry Clay*. Boston (1937).
Winkler, James E. "Henry Clay: A Current Assessment." *Register of the Kentucky Historical Society* 70 (1972), pp. 179–186.
Family information provided by Lorraine Seay, Curator of the Henry Clay Home, Lexington, Kentucky.

---

*1824 presidential nominee —
Democratic-Republican Party*

William Lowndes

Full name: William Jones Lowndes.
State represented: South Carolina.
Birth: February 11, 1782, Horseshoe Plantation, near Jacksonborough, South Carolina.
Age on Inauguration Day (March 4, 1825): Would have been 43 years, 1 month, but Lowndes died October 27, 1822).
Education: Local tutor, then English boarding school, 1789–1792; School of Henry Osborne, in Charleston, 1792–1795; School of Reverend Doctor Simon Felix Gallager, 1795–1798, Charleston; studied law in office of Charleston firm, 1800–1803; admitted to bar in 1808.
Religion: Episcopalian (?).
Ancestry/prominent relatives: Thomas Lowndes came from Overton, England, in 1725 and received four "baronies" of 12,000 acres each in South Carolina; Rawlins Lowndes (father) was first post-independence governor of South Carolina in 1778; Thomas Pinckney was William's father-in-law (see election of 1796); Thomas Lowndes (brother) was a U.S. Representative.

Occupation: Attorney, planter.

Home: Horseshoe Plantation, and a summer residence at "The Grove," a house outside of Charleston, South Carolina.

Public offices: South Carolina House of Representatives, 1804–1808, defeated in 1809. U.S. Representative, March 4, 1811–May 8, 1822, resigned; nominee for president in 1824 election, died before election.

Death: October 27, 1822, at sea between American and England on the ship, the *Moss*; age 40 years, 8½ months.

Burial: At sea.

Personal characteristics: 6'6" tall, slender, almost emaciated. Loose limbed, large features; face thin, long and pale. Black hair; usually appeared grave and thoughtful.

Father: Rawlins Lowndes (1721–August 24, 1800); planter, politician.

Father's first wife: Amarinthia Elliott (c. 1728–January 14, 1750); daughter of Thomas and Mary Elliott; married August 15, 1748.

Father's second wife: Mary Cartwright (?–?); married December 23, 1754.

Half brothers/sisters: Amarinthia (July 29, 1754–?), married Roger Sanders on September 26, 1776; after his death married a Mr. Champney. Mary (August 1755–?), died unmarried. Rawlins (November 5, 1757–?), died in childhood. Harriet (?–?), married a Mr. Brown. Thomas (January 22, 1766–July 8, 1843), lawyer, U.S. Congressman, married Sarah Bond on March 8, 1798. James (1769–1839).

Mother: Sarah Jones (1757–1800), married February 25, 1773.

Siblings: First child, born January 1774, and died in infancy. Second child died in 1778.

Wife: Elizabeth Pinckney (c. 1780–1847), married September 10, 1802; daughter of Thomas Pinckney (see election of 1796).

WILLIAM LOWNDES
(From the original in the South Caroliniana Library)

Children: Rawlins (1804–1834), married Emma-Raymond Hornby in 1827. Thomas Pinckney (October 1808–?), married Margaret Washington May 17, 1829. Rebecca Motte (1810–?), married Edward L. Rutledge on June 16, 1829.

He might have been ranked in America's history with the Clays, Calhouns, and Websters, a man of great influence, a colossus on the national scene who would be remembered for generations. Instead, and perhaps because of a childhood dare, he died almost before his political career had fairly begun. Yet even when he died at the age of 40, William Lowndes could be described by another giant, Henry Clay, as the wisest man he had ever known in Congress. The speaker of the House said "the highest and best hopes of the country looked to William Lowndes for their fulfillment." This South Carolinian mental and physical giant is the only also-ran who died before the election for which he was nominated; his personal papers have been depleted to almost nothing by two destructive fires; no portrait was ever painted of him, and his physical likeness was captured only in a caricature after Lowndes refused to sit for a painting; the first, and apparently most thorough biography of him was lost in manuscript form. It is as if there existed a conspiracy of obscurity against this statesman. William Lowndes has almost completely faded away, proving that early promise, even the presence of genius, is not enough to preserve a politician in history if he dies too young.

The Lowndes family of South Carolina were prosperous, influential individuals who traced their roots to Charles Lowndes. Charles migrated to South Carolina from the Leeward Islands in 1730, after financial troubles in that island province made him want to seek fortune elsewhere. Matters had deteriorated by 1735. He almost killed himself that year, confessing that he would have killed all his family as well. By the spring of 1736 he was imprisoned for abandoning his wife and children, and on May 22, 1736, he killed himself. The mother and elder son returned to the Leeward Islands, but two younger boys remained in America. One, Rawlins, was William Lowndes' father. Rawlins rose quickly and prosperously as a lawyer. His legal skills and financial resources made him a leading planter and politician in the colony. After independence was declared in 1776, Rawlins Lowndes became the first president (governor) of the state of South Carolina. His administration lasted one year, and by 1780 the British had retaken control of the rebellious colony. Rawlins, in ill health and none too enamored with war, retired to his plantation.

William's mother was Rawlins Lowndes' third wife. She was 16, he past 50 and ailing when the wedding occurred. Two children died in infancy, and finally William was born in 1782. Mrs. Lowndes was in weak health, and by the time William was six the family had decided that he would accompany his mother to England, where she would try to recover. There, from 1789 until 1792, Mrs. Lowndes gradually recovered her health, and William permanently lost his. The incident was tragic, not only because of its sweeping effect on William's career, but also because of its initial harmlessness. The following explanation appears in the William Lowndes papers:

Being at school, he had a wager with a school mate to reach the top of a high and steep hill first. It was winter and snow was on the ground. The adversaries set out together, and toiled on with varying success — at last Lowndes found himself at the top and alone — very much exhausted he lay down to rest, and fell asleep upon the snow — he slept for several hours — far in the night he was roused by messengers sent to look for him and then on awaking he felt pain in every limb.

Poor subsequent treatment that evening led to rheumatic fever. He would never fully recover. Though Lowndes would during several periods of his life seem temporarily free of illness, in fact these times were but respites that could not hold off an early death.

William was a brilliant student, far superior to his peers and a marvel to instructor and fellow students alike. Returning to South Carolina in 1792, he attended the best schools Charleston had to offer, and completed his preparation for a career by studying law in the offices of prominent local attorneys. In 1800 his father died; the close relationship established between the two, in part because of William's feeble health and consequent need for attention, made the loss an especially severe blow. Perhaps even more traumatic was the death of his mother, which William probably blamed on himself. While driving her in a carriage, William lost control, was too weak to restrain the frightened horse, and the carriage overturned after a wild ride through the trees alongside the road. Mrs. Lowndes was thrown from the carriage and killed, while William was knocked unconscious. He never again would drive a carriage if women or children were riding.

For the ten years from 1802 to 1812, William seemed relatively free of his physical afflictions. He watched his two half brothers enter politics and resolved to follow. Both elder Lowndes were Federalists, to the extent party allegiances were recognized in relatively non-partisan South Carolina. At first William probably also was a Federalist. This did not hurt when he began courting the daughter of a Federalist leader, losing 1796 vice presidential nominee, Thomas Pinckney. Major Pinckney at first objected to the romance because, or so it is remembered, of William's poor health. These objections were in time overcome and Eliza Pinckney and William Lowndes were married in September 1802. Soon they established residence at Horseshoe Plantation. A summer home was made outside of Charleston where they could escape the "vapors," i.e., the unknown cause of yellow fever that every year ravaged the swampy regions of the state.

After being admitted to the bar in 1804, William remained only one year as a lawyer and then returned to his life as a planter. Later a friend mentioned to Lowndes the shortness of his legal career, and the response was "Yes, very short; and in that time I had but one case in which my conscience and my duty concurred."

The year Lowndes abandoned the law was also the year he entered politics. Elected in 1804 to the state legislature, William led the ticket. His impact on deliberations was slight, but he did establish his opposition to the slave trade if not to the institution of slavery itself. Perhaps his most significant contribution, but one in which his role remained a secret for years, was in forging the compromise that permitted redistricting the state legislature. Previously the rich planter regions had held tight control over the legislature because of their disproportionate representation. Lowndes drafted a bill that based representation half on population and half on property. Both sides were satisfied. Lowndes made no effort to take credit and thereby to advance his career.

Several terms of service went uneventfully, but in 1809 Lowndes suffered his only electoral defeat when he tried for a fifth term (he was elected in 1804, 1805, 1806, and 1807, but did not run in 1808). He seemed reluctant to reenter politics, but was convinced in 1810 to run for Congress. In a strong, nationwide tide of youth replacing experience, Lowndes was elected. Another first-term Congressman from his state was John C. Calhoun. Henry Clay was sent for his first term from Kentucky. Lowndes traveled to Washington in the following autumn and roomed with these two fellow freshmen. They would become among the most vocal of the "War Hawks," who called for reprisals against England.

At first Lowndes complained of not having much work to do. His new friend and fellow Hawk, Henry Clay, was elected speaker, but even this did not earn Lowndes a top committee spot. The session seemed interminable, as battles over war preparations, and then the declaration of war itself occupied the Congress. Yet when vocal support for war measures was needed, Lowndes participated actively. When war was declared the weak but martial-spirited Lowndes wanted a commission in the army, and was promised as high a rank as he desired. Yet the secretary of war informed him he would not be assigned to the front unless strong political pressure forced him to. Lowndes did not want to gain his position in such a way and decided to remain in Congress.

In 1814 a new issue appeared in Congress with the question of the chartering of a second bank of the United States. Alexander Hamilton's effort to create a national bank had succeeded, but that institution had gone out of existence in 1811. State-chartered institutions had then taken over, issuing their own currency, following their own banking policies, and generally permitting inflation and financial uncertainty to run rampant. Lowndes strongly favored a second national bank, though he did quibble with some of the details of others' proposals. During the debate over the bank, this weighty issue was put aside with the news of General Andrew Jackson's startling victory in New Orleans in early 1815. That, on the heels of the favorable Treaty of Ghent ending the War of 1812, postponed the national bank question until the next Congress. Lowndes, as the rest of the country, was elated over the military news. In time, however, he was greatly troubled by the central character in the New Orleans story, Andy Jackson.

When Congress reconvened in December 1815, Lowndes was named chairman of the prestigious Ways and Means Committee by Speaker Clay. Lowndes clearly had the respect of his peers necessary to succeed in so exalted a position, but certain peculiarities bothered those who wanted strong leadership in the committee. Lowndes' weak health was well known. His weak voice was listened to keenly not only because of respect for the wisdom Lowndes exhibited but also because of the difficulty with which his words could be heard. Kind and unambitious in manner, deferential and unassuming, Lowndes was thought perhaps too friendly to lead. He proved otherwise. The South Carolinian became a central figure in legislative battles during the rest of his life. For three years he was chairman of Ways and Means.

The first battleground was a fight over a protective tariff. Lowndes was for mild protection, and gained a national reputation for the skillful manner in which he won that battle. He ably assisted the passage of the chartering of the second national bank. Lowndes worked on a bill to establish a sinking fund to pay off the national debt, and it succeeded in doing so by 1835. Lowndes succeeded by persuasion. His style was to consider all arguments dispassionately, even to review fairly in debate the good points of an opponent's position. John Randolph remarked after hearing one particularly even-handed summary by Lowndes, "He has done that once too often; he can never answer" his own description of the opposing position. But then Randolph had to admit that Lowndes proceeded to do just that, to devastate the argument he had apparently so masterfully presented.

Rumors that this rising star in the House would proceed to additional glory in the president's cabinet circulated in 1816. That year Lowndes refused to be appointed secretary of war by President Madison; the following year President Monroe was thought to be considering Lowndes for the same post, but apparently no offer was made. One of the attractive features of the young, if not vigorous, South Carolinian was that he was a strong nationalist. Sectionalism was becoming a growing concern. Lowndes seemed to bridge the widening chasm between North and South. Federal financing of internal improvements was favored by Lowndes, as was a moderately protective tariff. These were the two legs of Clay's "American System." Lowndes opposed the slave trade, but was a large slave owner. Both sides in the sectional conflict had reason to sense that Lowndes was a friend.

It was not only slavery that divided Congress. In early 1819 a new, politically charged issue struck Washington. General Andrew Jackson had taken upon himself to invade Spanish Florida, occupy Pensacola, and hang two British subjects for allegedly inciting the Indians against the Americans. The House Military Affairs Committee reported a resolution censuring Jackson for his conduct, and Lowndes supported the move. Many, however, liked what Jackson had done to assert American authority, and wished to see Florida annexed. Lowndes tried to direct the debate to the constitutional and legal issues, and away from the personalities and politics that so many dwelled upon. Jackson had the more appealing position and censure was not passed.

The Jackson dispute merely warmed up Congress for a far more significant fight, over the admission of Missouri as a state. When the first fight began, and the battle lines were being drawn between pro-slavery and anti-slavery forces, Lowndes' weak health forced him to seek improvement by a voyage to Europe. He arrived there in March 1819 and returned in mid–November. The Missouri controversy had hardly been resolved by the time of his return, and soon Lowndes was deeply, coolly and objectively involved. Lowndes presented his arguments favoring slavery in the territories on constitutional grounds. Yet he was also just as strongly in favor of compromise. In the weeks during which Congress wrestled with the topic, Lowndes played a significant moderating role. When four anti-slavery men were absent from the House, Lowndes urged a vote on the compromise. Opponents protested, but a vote was taken and the measure passed by three votes.

It became known that Speaker Clay planned to resign, and Lowndes was approached to run for the position. At first Lowndes refused, but in November 1820, when Congress reconvened he agreed to be a candidate. Seventy-three votes were needed for reelection and on the seventeenth ballot Lowndes received seventy-two. So extreme were the sectional feelings, however, that he could gain no additional vote. On the twenty-second ballot a moderate anti-slavery advocate, John Taylor, was elected instead. Lowndes along with the other two defeated candidates, John Sergeant (see election of 1832) and Samuel Smith of Maryland, were appointed by the new speaker to a committee of three to report on the request by Missouri to be admitted as a state. Missouri had drafted a state constitution in response to the action of Congress at the previous session. Lowndes argued that Missouri was already a state, that Congress had no authority to review her constitution. A provision Missouri had inserted in its constitution prohibiting free Negroes or mulattoes from entering that state was the bone of contention.

On February 9 or 10, 1821, while laboring on committee work to reach another compromise on Missouri, Lowndes was felled by a severe attack of rheumatic fever. For a time he lay near death, but slowly he strengthened sufficiently that the immediate danger seemed past. In fact, Lowndes would never again be sufficiently strong enough to participate actively in Congress.

Despite his feebleness, Lowndes was nominated at a South Carolina legislature caucus on December 18, 1821, for president of the United States. By a 58 to 54 vote, Lowndes' supporters managed to defeat an effort by partisans of fellow South Carolinian John C. Calhoun to prevent any presidential nomination at all at the gathering. Then all in attendance joined in voting for Lowndes, the Calhoun men having seen they were beaten. Lowndes was surprised by his nomination, but decided that he could not refuse: "The Presidency is not an office to be either solicited or declined." It appears that Calhoun and Lowndes met, and both men decided to remain in the presidential race.

Despite remaining an official candidate, Lowndes did not take his chances seriously. In April 1822, Lowndes requested a leave of absence from Congress because of health problems, and he resigned in May. A voyage to Europe was decided upon as a possible remedy. With his wife and daughter joining him, Lowndes embarked for England on the *Moss* from Philadelphia on October 21. He would not make it, as a friend, John Connell, later recounted in a letter describing the events:

> Mr. Lowndes was very feeble, but still able to sit up a part of the day until the succeeding Friday, when he became greatly exhausted. On Saturday night his symptoms became alarming, and early on Sunday morning it was evi-

dent that his dissolution was at hand; and about 9 o'clock on Sunday morning, the 27th Oct., 1822, his immortal spirit winged its way to the God who gave it.

Connell stated that since no preparations had been made to preserve Lowndes' body, it was decided he had to be buried at sea. The passengers and crew assembled the next afternoon, and after a short service Lowndes' remains were dropped overboard. Mrs. Lowndes and her daughter remained below in their room, but hearing the splash in the water, the new widow screamed. She lived until 1857, but never remarried.

Analysis of Qualifications

William Lowndes was constantly described as a precious individual. As a child he stood out from his peers in intelligence; as an adult, despite weak health, an emaciated, gawking appearance, and little strength as a speaker, he was a natural leader because of his wisdom and compassion. Little ambition seemed to be involved in driving William Lowndes forward, but instead a devotion to public service. Recognition for accomplishments was not sought and indeed at times even avoided. He was in fact a most unusual individual, whose untimely death was a great loss to the warring sections in America.

Part of his even-tempered approach to politics might be traced to the almost non-partisan nature of South Carolina politics, in which he entered the fray apparently (but not definitely) as a Federalist. With little fanfare he gradually shifted to the Jeffersonians. Nationalist in outlook, a believer in federally-funded internal improvements, moderate on the slave issue, Lowndes antagonized no one. He led the fight for a moderately protective tariff in 1816, supported a second bank of the United States, and then defended that bank from attacks that might have led to its dissolution because of bad management decisions it had made.

His service in Congress commenced simultaneously with that of Henry Clay and John C. Calhoun. Despite that these other two leaders are now remembered far more easily than is Lowndes, the three seemed to be of equal prominence during the 12 years they served together in Washington. Lowndes' speeches were carefully followed by his peers; his thoughtful observations were the basis of many changed opinions by fellow Congressmen. Though his voice was weak, his logic was strong and compelling. Perhaps the disinterest Lowndes had in his own political career added to his persuasiveness. Lowndes remarked that had he been in better health he would have preferred a military career to the life of a politician. In 1807, when animosity toward Britain threatened to start a war, Lowndes was made a captain in the state militia, and seemed greatly to enjoy the experience. Five years later he sought a commission when war between these two countries finally did erupt.

The increasingly bitter feelings between North and South could have benefitted from a Lowndes presidency. A nation struggling with opening up her vast interior would have profited from his views on internal improvements. The ending of the "Era of Good Feelings" and the reappearance of party animosities would have found the compassionate, modest, ingratiating Lowndes a helpful influence. For all his good qualities, it cannot be overlooked that had Lowndes lived to serve as president, it is likely he would have been wracked with ill health. How strongly he could have participated in the administration of government is open to serious question. Despite that unavoidable fact, the South Carolina leaders who nominated William Lowndes should be credited with having presented to the country an exceptionally able and timely leader.

LOWNDES BIBLIOGRAPHY

Chase, George B. *Lowndes of South Carolina.* Boston (1876).

Ravenel, Mrs. St. Julien (Harriott). *Life and Times of William Lowndes of South Carolina 1782–1822.* Boston and New York (1901).

Vipperman, Carl J. *William Lowndes and the Transition of Southern Politics, 1782–1822.* Chapel Hill, N.C. (1989).

A manuscript biography was prepared by William J. Grayson during the American Civil War, based on Lowndes' papers which had been collected by his widow. Grayson died before the work was published, and the manuscript was lost.

1824 presidential nominee — Democratic-Republican Party

John C. Calhoun

Full name: John Caldwell Calhoun.

State represented: South Carolina.

Birth: March 18, 1782, Abbeville District (now McCormick County), South Carolina.

Age on Inauguration Day (March 4, 1825): 42 years, 11½ months.

Education: Two years at Willington Academy; Yale College, 1802–1804, graduated Phi Beta Kappa; legal education at Litchfield, Connecticut, in Tapping Reeve's school; admitted to bar in 1807.

Religion: Raised in Calvinist family; attended Episcopal Church; at times seemed to support Unitarianism as "the only true faith."

Ancestry/prominent relatives: Scotch-Irish forebears, first arrived in America and settled in Pennsylvania around 1733; John Ewing Calhoun (father-in-law), a U.S. Senator from South Carolina; Joseph Calhoun (cousin), a U.S. Representative from South Carolina.

Occupation: Lawyer, planter.

Home: "Fort Hill," now part of Clemson University campus in South Carolina.

Public offices: South Carolina Legislature, 1807–1809; U.S. House of Representatives, March 4, 1811–November 3, 1817, resigned; U.S. secretary of war, December 10, 1817–March 3, 1825; unsuccessful candidate for president, 1824; vice president, March 4, 1825–December 28, 1832; resigned; U.S. Senator, December 29, 1832–March 3, 1843, resigned; unsuccessful candidate for president, 1844; U.S. secretary of state, April 1, 1844–March 6, 1845; U.S. senator, November 26, 1845–March 31, 1850.

Death: March 31, 1850, Washington, D.C., age 68 years, ½ month.

Burial: St. Philip's Churchyard, Charleston, South Carolina.

Personal characteristics: Massive, "leonine"

head; piercing eyes beneath huge brows; 6'2" tall; gaunt and angular; hair gray or almost white; walked with long rapid strides; wore plain, usually black suit; did not drink or gamble.

Father: Patrick Calhoun (1728–February 15, 1796), was a prosperous plantation owner and Indian fighter.

Mother: Martha Caldwell (his father's third wife) (?–May 15, 1801), married c. 1770.

Siblings: James (?–?), married Sarah Caldwell Martin on May 4, 1802. Catherine (?–1795), married Rev. Moses Waddel. William (?–?), married Catherine Jenna de Graffenreid. Patrick (?–?).

Wife: Floride Bonneau Calhoun (John's second cousin), (February 15, 1792–July 25, 1866), married on January 8, 1811; daughter of John Ewing Calhoun, a U.S. Senator, farmer.

Children: Andrew Pickens (October 1811–?), married (1) a Miss Campbell, and (2) Margaret Green on May 5, 1836. Floride (January 1814–April 7, 1815). Anna Maria (February 13, 1817–September 22, 1875), married Thomas Clemson in November 1838. Elizabeth (October 1819–March 22, 1820). Patrick (February 9, 1821–June 1, 1858), never married. John Caldwell (May 17, 1823–July 31, 1855), married (1) Anzie Adams, and (2) Kate Kirby Putnam in January 1853. Martha Cornelia (April 22, 1824–May 2, 1857). James Esard (April 23, 1826–?), died unmarried. William Lowndes (August 13, 1829–September 18, 1858), married (1) Margaret Cloud, and (2) Kate Putnam Calhoun, his brother's widow.

Historic sites/memorials: His home, Fort Hill, is preserved on the Clemson University Campus. Calhoun's statue is in Statuary Hall in the Capitol in Washington, D.C. John C. Calhoun State Community College is in Decatur, Alabama.

Calhoun ranks far above the anonymity of most defeated candidates. For over 100 years he has stood as a symbol of an entire section of the country, the South. Unfortunately for his memory, that symbol is one of unbending resistance and final defeat. The large, white marker over his grave in Saint Philip's churchyard in Charleston has carved on it merely one word, "Calhoun." An irreverent but insightful Northern soldier stood over the grave in April 1865, and pronounced a more informative epitaph: "The whole South is the grave of Calhoun." This graveside scorn accurately reflected Calhoun's own remorse at the likely events that would transpire after his death.

Calhoun's childhood was austere. He was born in a frontier community in South Carolina, where his father had to become an Indian fighter in order to survive. The father, Patrick Calhoun, had seen his own mother and brother killed by Cherokee Indians 20 years before Calhoun's birth. There was apparently little levity in the Calhoun household. The Calhoun children received no education until their teenage years. John had learned to read and write at home and to perform simple arithmetic tasks, but that was all. At age 13 he began more formal instruction under Moses Waddel, his brother-in-law. The school was in Columbia County, Georgia, and after only a short time Waddel's wife, John's sister, died. Waddel abandoned Calhoun, who had been staying with him, and began wandering in the wilderness. The abandoned pupil, completely alone for over six weeks at age 13, began self-education by attempting to read the many books that Waddel left behind. Calhoun returned home, but the next year his father died, leaving five farms and 31 slaves. The two older sons had left home by then, and it fell mainly on John's shoulders to manage the entire plantation.

Calhoun might well have remained a planter if not for the entreaties of neighbors who thought they saw something unique in Calhoun's extreme fondness for books. Unique John was, even tying books onto his plow so that he could read in the fields. The neighbors first tried to convince John's mother of the need for his education. His mother turned to her two older sons for advice. In the summer of 1800, these brothers returned to the Calhoun farm, convinced their mother that John should receive some further education, and then argued incessantly with John. Their thought was that he would return to Moses Waddel's school for a few months and then get a rudimentary legal education. John, however, when finally persuaded of the need, decided that he wanted a complete education that included attendance at one of the best colleges

JOHN C. CALHOUN
(From the original in the South Caroliniana Library)

in the country. He estimated the entire process would take seven years. Instead, after two years of intensive study with Waddel, he joined the junior class at Yale College in New Haven, Connecticut, and graduated in 1804. The amount of work that Calhoun had to devote to his education in the four-year period was simply incredible. A fair inkling of the greatness that was in Calhoun can be gained by realizing how much Calhoun was able to achieve towards his own education in such a short period of time — two years were spent with Waddel to learn essentially what normally would take 12 years; he then entered Yale

College in the junior class, having never attended college at all, and graduated two years
later. The following year he was at Litchfield,
Connecticut, at the law school of Judge Tapping Reeve. He completed his studies there at
the age of 24, and his formal education was
complete.

While a student at Yale and then Litchfield,
John corresponded with a widow of one of his
cousins. The widow's daughter, Floride Calhoun, was ten years younger than Calhoun,
but he began to court her first by mail and
then more directly. They were married in January 1811. Floride was the daughter of a cousin
of John Calhoun's father, and therefore was
John Calhoun's second cousin. Floride brought
a substantial fortune to the marriage, which
John insisted be put under his control. In time
he would build a substantial plantation named
"Fort Hill," the grounds of that plantation now
being part of Clemson University.

Upon finishing law school, Calhoun went
to Charleston, South Carolina, to continue
studying law. He did not like Charleston,
finding it a decadent city, certainly from his
cloistered perspective, and was particularly
appalled at the lack of interest in religion there.
In 1807 he returned to Abbeville to live. He
was chosen to give a speech in June 1807,
attacking a recent British insult against the
United States. The speech was well received.
As a result, John was elected without opposition to the legislative seat that his father had
long held. In 1810 he campaigned for a seat in
the United States House of Representatives,
and won in a landslide.

Calhoun immediately joined the group of
young Representatives known as the "War
Hawks." Every British affront led to cries for
war. In 1812, Calhoun introduced a resolution
to declare war against Great Britain and it was
adopted. Throughout that conflict the South
Carolina congressman was a central figure in
debate over war measures. When the war
ended, he became House majority leader for
the Jeffersonians, working closely with Henry
Clay on such issues as federal financing of
canals, highway construction, and the creation
of a national bank.

In 1817, Calhoun, as a recognition of his
leadership role in the House during the War

of 1812, was appointed secretary of war by the
new president, James Monroe. He was to serve
in that post for eight years. He is generally
credited with achievements ranking him
among the most outstanding secretaries of war
ever to serve. One event that was to haunt him
later occurred in 1817, when General Andrew
Jackson without authority led a raid into
Spanish Florida. Secretary of War Calhoun,
along with almost all of the rest of the cabinet
except Martin Van Buren (a crucial exception),
sought to have Jackson reprimanded. Those
who supported such a reprimand were to find
themselves Jackson's bitter enemies.

After President Monroe was reelected in
1820, the three top cabinet leaders began
maneuvering to succeed him. Secretary of the
Treasury William Crawford and Secretary of
State John Quincy Adams both began their
campaigns. Calhoun was only 39 years old in
December 1821, but in that month he announced his candidacy for president. He believed that he would ride the tidal wave of new
nationalism that he had strongly espoused
since arriving in Washington ten years earlier.
There were candidates from every region in
the country already, including another candidate that had been nominated by the legislature in his home state, William Lowndes.
Most of Calhoun's friends advised against running for president in 1824, but his ambition
was too strong.

Since three cabinet officers were running
for president, there began to be serious dissension in the Monroe administration. Secretary of the Treasury William Crawford lowered
the appropriations for Calhoun's war department, which severely decreased the political
patronage available to Calhoun. Calhoun then
sponsored bitter attacks against Crawford in
newspapers around the country. The candidates were making offers to each other to withdraw from the race in exchange for either the
vice presidency or cabinet positions. When
Andrew Jackson finally entered the campaign,
much of Calhoun's support went to him. Long
after the inevitability of defeat became apparent to others, Calhoun acknowledged it
himself and withdrew. He did not endorse
any of the candidates, but tried to remain
friendly with both John Quincy Adams, the

candidate of the North, and with Jackson, who drew support from all regions. Calhoun became the candidate for vice president with both the Jackson and Adams supporters, and he was elected easily. No presidential candidate received a majority, however. Henry Clay allegedly bargained with John Quincy Adams, enabling Adams to be chosen by the House of Representatives. Clay was then appointed secretary of state, a presumed barter of the nation's highest office that infuriated Calhoun.

When General Jackson was elected president in 1828, Calhoun again was elected vice president. Calhoun's hope was that Jackson would retire after four years and Calhoun would succeed him. Almost immediately, however, Calhoun and Jackson became estranged over the Margaret (Peggy) Eaton affair. Floride Calhoun, her Southern mores deeply ingrained, would not associate with the Secretary of War John Eaton's new wife, who allegedly had engaged in sexual relations with many men, including her husband, before their marriage. The remainder of the cabinet wives took their lead from Floride; Peggy Eaton was effectively ostracized. The first snubbing appeared at the inaugural ball in 1829. Jackson was outraged and came to Peggy's defense. Martin Van Buren, a bachelor and ambitious politician, became Peggy's friend. Jackson was greatly pleased with Van Buren's conduct and correspondingly outraged at Calhoun. The next blow to Calhoun's hopes of succeeding Jackson came over the growing sectional crisis. The dispute was not yet over slavery, but instead covered the tariff. The industrialized North wanted high tariffs on imports to protect their own markets, while the South, with mainly agrarian economies, wanted low tariffs. Some in the South saw "nullification" as the answer. They felt a state could declare any federal act that directly affected that state to be null and void. January 1830 saw a historic debate over this issue on the floor of the Senate, with South Carolina senator Robert Y. Hayne arguing for the South and nullification, and Massachusetts' Daniel Webster waxing eloquently for the North. Calhoun periodically sent notes of encouragement and advice to Haynes. President Jackson's stand still had

not been made public. At a Jefferson Day dinner in 1830, Washington political society expected a revelation of the president's position. The answer came in the form of a toast: "Our Federal Union! It must and shall be preserved!" Calhoun's response was a toast of his own: "The Federal Union — Next to our liberty the most dear." The battle lines were clear and Jackson and Calhoun were adversaries.

The final, irrevocable break came the next month. The long-dead issue, but one Jackson would not let be forgotten, of Jackson's invasion of Spanish Florida in 1817 again was the center of controversy. Calhoun's bitter enemies, Van Buren, William Crawford, and Sam Houston revealed to Jackson that Calhoun had opposed Jackson's actions in 1817 and had desired an investigation. Opposing or criticizing Jackson was tantamount to declaring war upon him. Jackson was livid. The controversy after six months cooled somewhat and Jackson desired a reconciliation. Calhoun, embarrassingly shortsighted, then undertook to have printed the entire affair — letters between Calhoun and Jackson, summaries of confidential Cabinet discussions, and other documents. Calhoun thought that Jackson had approved the publication of these materials when in fact Calhoun's old nemesis John Eaton had only led him to believe so. In fact Jackson knew nothing of the plans and exploded again when the publication occurred. It was the end of Calhoun as an anointed successor to Jackson.

With subservience to Jackson now pointless, Calhoun's stand with the South became more salient. Calhoun publicly admitted that the nullification doctrine that had been presented three years before in an anonymously authored document adopted by the South Carolina legislature had been his work. The tariff was still the issue, and an intolerably high tariff had been passed. South Carolina particularly was incensed and planned to declare the tariff ineffective within its borders. Calhoun resigned from the vice presidency in order to return to South Carolina. A convention was held there in November 1832. The convention voided the tariff acts within the state. The gauntlet had been thrown down to President Jackson.

Calhoun was elected to the Senate by the

legislature in order to carry on the fight. Senator Hayne resigned to become governor and thereby made the vacancy. A lower tariff, with Senator Henry Clay's help, was passed by Congress. This satisfied Calhoun. Also passed was the Force Bill that enabled Jackson to employ troops to make certain the tariff was enforced in South Carolina. It was up to Calhoun to return to his native state and convince the people to abide by the compromise and not to secede from the Union. The state convention that had declared the tariffs void reassembled and repealed its earlier action. In spite, it then declared the Force Bill inoperative in the state, an empty gesture since acquiescence in the tariff removed the necessity of the Force Bill.

Nullification had failed because there was a president strong enough to force one state, acting alone, to buckle under. Calhoun realized then that the South had to act in concert in order to protect its sectional interests.

During the next four years, with Jackson reelected to the presidency and Van Buren now vice president, Senator Calhoun joined forces with the Whig Party in opposing Jackson. He apparently toyed with becoming a Whig, but finally became the leader of his own Southern faction within the Democratic Party. The main, insurmountable problem with joining forces with the Whigs was their substantial abolitionist sentiment.

Calhoun became the Southern leader in Congress. He sponsored legislation, which invariably failed, preventing abolitionist material from being sent through the mails, denying the right of citizens to interfere in any way with slavery either in states or territories, and in many other ways seeking to protect slavery and the South from interference from the North. He had not given up on the presidency, however. Calhoun anticipated that with a solid South behind him and by picking up enough anti-abolitionists in the North, he could yet gain his prize. The defense of slavery became his overriding passion. In 1842, tired from arduous labor in the Senate on many fronts, Calhoun resigned and returned to South Carolina.

In 1844 one last strenuous effort would be made for the presidency. His old comrade-turned-adversary, Henry Clay, also made

another race. In 1842, as it had in 1822, the South Carolina legislature endorsed Calhoun for president. Calhoun's campaign was centered around tariff reform and free trade. The battlegrounds were the smoke-filled rooms and the state and lower level conventions that controlled not only who the delegates would be, but preparatory to that, the method by which they were to be named. Van Buren was the frontrunner and his control of the state machinery was strong. Calhoun's plan to break Van Buren's advantage was to insist on an open convention process where an equal number of delegates would be freely chosen from each Congressional district. Not only did the Van Buren machine control the convention process in many states, but Van Buren's advantage was increased by the disproportionately large number of delegates that his states were entitled to elect. The district system was an uphill battle from the start. By the fall of 1843 it was clear that it had failed, and with it Calhoun's hope to break the lock on the party machinery held by Van Buren. On December 21, 1843, Calhoun wrote a letter to his supporters, published in various periodicals, withdrawing from the race. He admitted that he had no chance of selection by a convention whose delegates would be chosen by Van Buren–controlled state party machinery. Calhoun then condemned the Van Burenites on the tariff and other sectional issues, letting it be known that even in defeat he would not be silenced. The letter was not as spiteful as Richard Nixon's "last press conference" after a 1962 defeat for California governor, but the sentiment of renouncing all future political activity was similar. Both vented their anger and frustrations in parting shots at their adversaries.

On February 28, 1844, a tragic event occurred that thrust Calhoun back into the center of national affairs. One of the massive guns on a newly commissioned battleship, the *Princeton*, exploded while the vessel was being inspected in a public relations exercise by the president. The president was spared, but killed were Secretary of State A.P. Upshur, Secretary of the Navy Thomas Gilmer, and several others.

With great reluctance, for Calhoun had proposed to remain out of public office unless he could gain the presidency, the South Carolinian accepted President Tyler's offer to become secretary of state. Calhoun saw a storm of immense force brewing over the admission of Texas and Oregon as states, and he hoped to play a role in averting disaster. Calhoun continued the diplomacy necessary to bring Texas into the Union but a firestorm erupted when a letter he had written to the British government was published. The British foreign minister had written before Calhoun's appointment that the British wanted to see slavery abolished throughout the world. They, therefore, opposed the annexation of Texas as a slave sate. Calhoun wrote a scathing reply, denouncing British interference with American events. An embarrassing section of the letter stated that the United States must admit Texas as a slave state to thwart the British designs on Texas and to prevent Texas from emancipating its own slaves. Freedom there potentially would start a chain reaction throughout the South. Emancipation was bad for the South and for the slave, Calhoun concluded, and therefore Texas must be admitted as a slave state. When the letter was leaked to the press by a Van Buren partisan in the Senate, it momentarily stalled the annexation process.

Leaving the cabinet in March 1845 when James K. Polk was inaugurated, Calhoun was a tired and dying man. Tuberculosis was now clearly evident. His eyes were sunken, his face ashen, his body emaciated. Physically he was failing; mentally he was burning brilliantly. He was returned to the Senate by the South Carolina legislature and fought the remaining five years of his life for equality and protection for the South. Slavery in the territories became the key, because if more free states were admitted than slave the numerical balance in the Senate between slave and free state senators would be lost. When President Zachary Taylor began to lean towards admitting California as a free state in 1849, Calhoun warned that the South would secede. The battle raged for over a year, and it took the death of President Taylor, the compromise efforts of Henry Clay and Stephen Douglas, along with the death of Calhoun himself, to get the country through the crisis. Clay proposed that Cali-

fornia be admitted as a free state, but that the territories of New Mexico and Arizona be organized with no prohibition of slavery. A new, draconian fugitive slave act would be passed to give security to the South. Henry Clay, John Calhoun, and Daniel Webster, the great Senate triumvirate that had dominated political debate since 1820, locked in battle one last time. Clay led off with his compromise. Calhoun followed. The compromise, he said, was insufficient. Absolute equality must be had in the territories between slave and free. Antislavery activities must be halted. The final cure, one left unsaid during the Senate speech, was a dual presidency, one from the North and one from the South. Calhoun was not yet ready for the South to secede, but to remain within the Union the South would demand concessions. Daniel Webster replied that this strife was without basis. Equality of the territories was impossible since climate and geographical conditions made slavery unsuited to the new West. The nation, he concluded, could not be dissolved. Calhoun's reply on the Senate floor was brief: "No, Sir, the Union can be broken."

Three weeks later Calhoun was dead. In his dying throes he cried, "The South. The poor South." Though his life closed with these words his influence did not. Posthumously published were the results of feverish theorizing that commenced in 1843 upon his retirement from the Senate. The books were *A Disquisition on Government* and *A Discourse on the Constitution and Government of the United States*. In them he explained his views on the nature of government and man. His solution of the differences between the sections was based on reforming constitutional checks and balances. His theory was dubbed the "concurrent majority." The gist of his view was that minorities within the majority were unprotected unless they had an effective veto over legislation and policies inimical to their interests. Farmer and industrialist, North and South, or any other "major" interest could not be expected to protect the other. Therefore each had to be able to protect itself against the eventuality of being in the minority. A veto was necessary, but the very right of veto would make each interest more aware and amenable to the conflicting interests of others. It was a theory designed to protect the South and other inevitable minorities, a plan that ironically would continue the subjugation of the most deprived minority of all, the Negro slave. The Civil War mooted the doctrine but the genius of Calhoun's effort both to describe government and to remake it continues to sparkle.

Analysis of Qualifications

Eighteen hundred and twenty-four catches John Calhoun in mid-career and in the height of his strong nationalism. An eight-year Calhoun presidency would have encompassed the years of the greatest transformation in his national image.

The historical interpretations of Calhoun during this period widely vary as to what degree he was exhibiting mere political opportunism. There is no doubt that Calhoun was a proud, aloof, intensely ambitious politician who craved the presidency. Many contemporaries thought that Calhoun's arrogance was looming large when at age 39 he had the audacity to announce for the presidency. He indeed had made a substantial impact both as a War Hawk in Congress and as secretary of war at age 35. He was a strong supporter of such nationalistic ideas as federal funding of internal improvements, a strong military, and a moderate tariff that would neither threaten the North's industrialization nor the South's agrarian economy. There is some evidence that the incumbent president, James Monroe, supported Calhoun. His campaign did seem to be credible, and indeed it might have succeeded if not for the entry, initially doubted, of Andrew Jackson into the race. Before Jackson's campaign began to snowball, however, Calhoun believed he was the strongest candidate in the South and the second choice in every other region. Even Daniel Webster reportedly favored his election. He considered himself a Jeffersonian, but he was hardly a man of the people, and never a democrat such as Jackson. He was an aristocrat, slaveowner, a believer in the "elite" ruling the masses. He was also a hardball political player who in his campaign against the early frontrunner, Secretary of the Treasury William Crawford, stooped to anonymous and almost libelous attacks against him

in the newspaper he controlled. To Calhoun's defense, however, it should be noted that this was very much the style of politics of the time.

The Missouri Compromise that helped bank the fires of dissent in 1820 was not rejected by Calhoun. At this stage in his career he supported the proposition that Congress could control slavery in the territories. That this meant Calhoun in 1824 would have been a flexible president than in his later years is certainly conceivable. In the mid–1820s his insistence on a Union on the South's terms was not nearly as pronounced as it would later become.

Calhoun was a poor politician on the national level. He dimly understood what moved other men and that cold logic did not have the effect on others as it did on him. Calhoun's will was rock hard — "cast iron" in a later biographer's view. The question, of course, is to what ends that will would have driven him.

Calhoun first espoused, anonymously, the doctrine of nullification in 1828 in response to the crisis over the extremely onerous tariff. His entire drift from strong nationalist to strong sectionalist drew its impetus from the growing loss of influence the South experienced. As long as the South and its institutions were not threatened, Calhoun could support the strengthening of the nation; when the South was endangered, then his focus shifted. Yet never did he want secession, not even in his most extreme final years defending the South and slavery. He did forecast the split but did not desire it. Nullification itself was an attempt to avoid the need for secession, by making each affected interest or region able to nullify an offending law and thereby end the grievance that otherwise would lead to rebellion. It is difficult to conclude other than that Calhoun as president would have been a strong champion of the South, but particularly in the mid- and late–1820s he would also have been a strong champion of any efforts to avoid conflict and needless animosity.

He had more daring and imagination than John Quincy Adams, under whom he served his first term as vice president, and less vindictiveness than did Andrew Jackson, under whom he served his second term. In many respects, Calhoun had the ability, if he would not have been sidetracked down narrow sectional paths, to have bettered both performances of the chief executives under whom he served.

CALHOUN BIBLIOGRAPHY

Barlett, Irving H. *John C. Calhoun: A Biography.* New York (1993).

Capers, Gerald M. *John C. Calhoun — Opportunist: A Reappraisal.* Gainesville, Fla. (1960).

Coit, Margaret L. *John C. Calhoun: American Portrait.* Boston (1950).

Current, Richard C. *John C. Calhoun.* New York City (1966).

Dillenback, Bruce L. "The Decade After Moses: The Political Legacy of John C. Calhoun." Unpublished doctoral dissertation, Florida State University (1990).

Hay, Thomas R. "John C. Calhoun and the Presidential Campaign of 1824." *North Carolina Historical Review* XII (1935), pp. 40 ff.

Marmor, Theodore R. *The Career of John C. Calhoun.* New York (1988).

Niven, John. *John C. Calhoun and the Price of Union.* Baton Rouge (1988).

Peterson, Merrill D. *The Great Triumvirate: Webster, Clay and Calhoun.* New York (1987).

Starke, William P. "Account of Calhoun's Early Life." *Annual Report of the American Historical Association* II (1899).

Styron, Arthur. *The Cast-Iron Man, John C. Calhoun and American Democracy.* New York City (1935).

Wilson, Clyde Norman. *John C. Calhoun: A Bibliography.* Westport, Conn. (1990).

_____, ed. *The Essential Calhoun: Selections from Writings, Speeches and Letters.* New Brunswick, N.J. (1992).

Wiltse, Charles M. *John C. Calhoun, Nationalist 1782–1828.* Indianapolis (1944).

_____. *John C. Calhoun, Nullifier 1829– 1839.* Indianapolis (1949).

_____. *John C. Calhoun, Sectionalist 1840–1850.* Indianapolis (1951).

---

*1824 vice presidential nominee —
Democratic-Republican Party*

Nathan Sanford

Full name: Nathan Sanford. He dropped the "d" in his surname early in adult life, "to save time," he said.

State represented: New York.

Birth: November 5, 1777, in Bridgehampton, New York.

Age on Inauguration Day (March 4, 1825): 47 years, 4 months.

Education: Clinton Academy in Easthampton, New York; entered Yale College 1793, left in 1795; studied law in the office of Samuel Jones in New York City, admitted to bar in 1799.

Religion: Episcopalian (?).

Ancestry/prominent relatives: First Sandford arrived in Connecticut from England by 1640; Nathan's third wife (Mary Buchanan) was granddaughter of Thomas McKean, a signer of the Declaration of Independence.

Occupation: Attorney.

Public office: U.S. commissioner of bankruptcy, 1802; U.S. attorney for the district of New York, 1803–1816; member of State Assembly, 1810–1811, speaker 1811, retired because of ill health; member of N.Y. State Senate, 1812–1815; U.S. Senate, March 4, 1815–March 3, 1821, defeated for reelection; delegate to state constitutional convention, 1821; chancellor of New York, August 1, 1823–January 24, 1826; unsuccessful candidate for vice president, 1824; U.S. Senator, January 14, 1826–March 3, 1831.

Home: "Sanford Hall," "an elaborate and costly structure" in Flushing, Long Island, built in 1835, demolished c. 1924.

Death: October 17, 1838, at Flushing, Long Island, at age 60 years, 11½ months.

Burial: Episcopal Churchyard, Flushing, Long Island, New York.

Personal characteristics: Erect, slightly below average height, dark eyes, dignified.

Father: Thomas Sandford (1715–February 23, 1787), influential, prosperous landowner, farmer.

Father's first wife: Mary Topping (1718–?), married c. 1738.

Mother: Phebe Baker (2nd wife of father) (February 29, 1740–January 22, 1796); had been married to Dr. Theophilus Howell (1738–1775); married Deacon David Hedges after Thomas Sandford died; daughter of Nathaniel and Sarah (Ludlow) Baker.

Half brothers/sisters: Thomas (1742–February 25, 1789). Sylvanus (1743–March 1778), married Damaris Howell. Mary (1752–July 8, 1785), married Jeremiah Miller, Jr.

Siblings: Phebe (October 26, 1779–March

29, 1842), married Dr. Rufus Rose.

First wife: Eliza Van Horn (?–1811), married May 1, 1801).

Children: Eliza (?–?), married John Le Breton. Edward (July 8, 1805–August 28, 1876), journalist and poet. Charles, died unmarried. Henry, died at age 21.

Second wife: Mary E. Isaacs (?–?), married April 14, 1813.

Child: Mary (1814–February 5, 1841), married Judge Peter Gansevoort in 1833.

Third wife: Mary Buchanan (?–April 23, 1879), daughter of Andrew and Ann (McKean) Buchanan; granddaughter of Thomas McKean who signed the Declaration of Independence; married May 27, 1828.

Child: Robert (December 10, 1831–January 13, 1908), married Helen Mary Hooker Stuyvesant on May 23, 1867).

Nathan Sanford's ancestors, who spelled their name "Sandford," settled in Connecticut in the 1640s. This first Sandford settler's son moved to Long Island, and there, through several generations, mostly prosperous ones, the family remained. Nathan's father, Thomas Sandford, "was a quite influential man — an Esquire, Justice of the Peace, *etc*." Just what the "etc." was is not altogether clear, but his life had been long and full even before Nathan's birth, which occurred when Thomas was 62 years old. The father was known as "Squire Sandford of Sandford's Neck," a wealthy man who at his death (when Nathan was only nine), left substantial land, some slaves, and a good name. Nathan's mother remarried, but for a time Nathan lived with his mother's relatives, for reasons that are unclear.

NATHAN SANFORD
(From the Senate Historical Office)

Education was gained at the Clinton Academy in Easthampton, six miles down the road in easternmost Long Island. When he was 16, Nathan matriculated at Yale, but left after two years and did not graduate. The law had become the young man's chosen career, and to reach that goal he entered the office of Samuel Jones, an eminent New York City attorney. With admission to the bar in 1799 came another change in Nathan's life — he dropped the first "d" in his surname in order to "save time," he said.

Twenty-three years old and with a freshly printed law license, Nathan became a commissioner in bankruptcy. Three years later, President Thomas Jefferson appointed him United States district attorney for the southern district of New York, there to remain for the next 12 years. Just when Nathan's political involvement began is unknown, but at some stage it appears evident that he must have become an active supporter of the Jeffersonian party and of the Society of St. Tammany in particular. New York politics was badly fractured, with the weakened Federalists contesting two different opposition factions, the Martling men (Tammany) and the followers of George and later DeWitt Clinton. The factions were somewhat free-floating, with politicians changing sides depending on the issues and personalities. Sanford early allied himself with the anti–Clinton faction, and the decision paid handsome financial as well as political dividends.

D.S. Alexander, in his work entitled *A Political History of the State of New York*, called Sanford "the pet of the Martling Men and the enemy of DeWitt Clinton…. His activity gave him strength and his loyalty to the Martling Men, [later] known as Tammany, supplied him with backers enough to keep him continuously in office for thirty years." Though loyal and long-serving, Sanford left little record of having an impact on public affairs during this period. The papers of most leading politicians in the state leave few references to Sanford, and until 1810 he seemed little noticed. The United States district attorney in New York received his compensation from fees charged through his office. Sanford has variously been estimated to have made the astronomical sums of $30,000 or as much as $100,000 per year. He owed his post, and his money, to Tammany and through it to the president. Loyalty was a lucrative attribute to exhibit.

In 1808, while continuing his duties as United States district attorney, Sanford was elected to the state assembly. There he followed the Jeffersonian line by defending the embargo. Sanford confessed that it was a painful measure, but insisted that the times required it. As D.S. Alexander reported Sanford's speech:

> He recalled how England had searched our ships, impressed our seamen, killed our citizens, and insulted our towns. The ocean, he argued, had become a place of robbery and national disgrace, since Great Britain, by its orders in Council, had provoked France into

promulgating the Berlin Decree of November, 1806, and the Milan Decree of December, 1807, which denationalised any ship that touched an English port, or suffered an English search, or paid an English tax — whether it entered a French port, or fell into the power of a French privateer. Thus, since England had blockaded one-half of Europe and France the other half, he thought it time for dignified retirement, until England felt the need of additional supplies, and France awoke to the loss of its luxuries.

In 1810, Sanford was again elected to the Assembly, and on January 29, 1811, was chosen speaker with a 31-vote majority over the Federalist candidate. His service may have set a record for brevity, as ill health forced the speaker to resign on February 14. His illness was serious. The problem was a pulmonary affliction that soon caused him to lose the use of one of his lungs. He annoyed his physicians by disproving their prognosis and living for 25 more years. Intra-party feuding became intense in 1811, when Sanford was presented as the Martling candidate for the state senate. He was named over strong objections from the supporters of DeWitt Clinton. Subsequent maneuvering by both factions resulted in the Clintonians also naming Sanford on their election ticket, hoping to gain some Sanford voters to their candidate for lieutenant governor. Sanford won with ease.

DeWitt Clinton was as different in political personality from Sanford as could be imagined. Where Sanford clung to party loyalty and a passive, noncommittal public image, Clinton was independent and forceful. When James Madison was nominated for a second term instead, Clinton began to court the Federalists as well as Republican dissidents. On May 29, 1812, 90 out of 95 Republican members of the state assembly who attended a nominating caucus in Albany named Clinton as their presidential candidate. Sanford and many other Martling legislators had refused to attend the caucus. The general election resulted in a narrow Clinton defeat. For the moment Clinton's foes, to whom Sanford owed his political advancement, had control in New York.

Martin Van Buren was fast rising to political prominence in New York. As a leader of the

"Albany Regency," as the tight-knit group of political kingpins in the state was called, Van Buren increasingly had the ability to direct political events. In 1815, a successor to United States Senator Obediah German had to be named; Van Buren decided Sanford should get the position. General John Armstrong also wanted to be named. Armstrong had resigned as secretary of war from President Madison's cabinet in September 1814, and certainly had a strong claim. Powerful Judge Ambrose Spencer was backing Armstrong, but Van Buren would not consent to push Armstrong's selection. Van Buren offered to assist the election of Spencer himself, but the judge for the moment declined. Van Buren outmaneuvered Spencer and finally Armstrong was dropped. Judge Spencer proposed at least one other name, but finally Van Buren's well-organized forces succeeded in gaining Sanford the party legislative caucus nomination.

Opposing the long-entrenched Ambrose Spencer was considered suicidal. Queasy Nathan Sanford asked Van Buren if he did not regret having bested Spencer. The consummate political operative quickly, and certainly honestly, said he had no qualms. The badly outmaneuvered Spencer withdrew his own late-blooming candidacy and said he would not compete "with so young a man as Mr. Sanford." The new senator was 37; Spencer was 51.

Sanford's term began on March 4, 1815, but the first session did not commence until December. The New Yorker made no lasting impression in his first six-year term. In 1816, he introduced a proposed constitutional amendment to make a federal judge removable from office should a majority of Congress vote to oust him. The Senate did not act on the proposal. He introduced few other measures, though once every session he proposed at least one bill.

Sanford in 1821 would need new employment. Van Buren was no longer his benefactor, but instead his rival for the Senate seat. Sanford was no match. Meticulous in his organization, Van Buren prepared to oust the incumbent. When the legislature met in the winter of 1820-21, the first item of business was the succession. Intra-party squabbling played a role, as Sanford had angered some in the Tammany, anti–Clintonian wing by not vigorously opposing the election of New Yorker John W. Taylor to the speaker's chair in the federal House of Representatives. As all New York politicians probably realized, Sanford rarely did anything vigorously. Sanford had been slowly weakening in his allegiance to the foes of DeWitt Clinton. The Clintonians found him palatable because he was never strident in his partisanship. The legislative nominating caucus met on February 1, 1821. Six of Van Buren's supporters were missing, as was one of Sanford's. A member who attended the caucus wrote in explanation of what happened:

> Mr. [Clarkson] Crolius then rose and asked [the] gentlemen to offer some reason for the nomination of Mr. Van Buren in opposition to Mr. Sanford against whom no charge or complaint had been made. If there was cause for dissatisfaction he should be the first to oppose his re-election; if however it should be satisfactorily proved that he had been an undeviating republican and a faithful senator in the councils of his Country, that he should then rely upon the support of every man in the meeting.... He was followed by Mr. [Samuel B.] Romaine, ... [who said] If Mr. Sanford should fail to receive a majority of the votes of this meeting the consequences would be the destruction of his political character in the public estimation, and a suspicion that he had either neglected the duties of his high station or had fallen from the faith which he had so long professed....

Argument was senseless, and Van Buren won the caucus endorsement by 58 to 24. On February 6 the full legislature voted. Many Federalist votes went to Van Buren. Two years earlier, for reasons that could hardly be called altruistic, Van Buren had helped re-elect to the Senate the Federalist Rufus King. Perhaps many Federalists were returning the favor by voting for Van Buren. The future president won with 86 votes to Sanford's 60; the 30 Federalist votes that went to Van Buren decided the outcome.

Speaker Taylor's reaction was one of horror: "How miserably mistaken is the policy of our State. She sacrifices her best men [Sanford?] to gratify a ferocious spirit of party, thus degrading herself...." The Clintonians had supported Sanford as the lesser of evils.

Clinton wanted to defeat his new and increasingly dangerous nemesis, Martin Van Buren, and Sanford was the weapon at hand. Many Federalists were dismayed that Federalist assembly members had furthered Van Buren's ambitions.

Sanford was no sooner an ex–Senator than he was chosen to New York's constitutional convention. Most prominent state politicians were delegates when the convention opened in August 1821. Sanford worked on a committee that reported a provision that abolished property qualifications for voting, but the provision restricted suffrage to white males. Sanford stated that the provision was what the voters wanted; conservatives were aghast at this liberalization of the vote. Sanford's argument won.

The practice of law was apparently not enticing to the former Senator, and Sanford sought help from political comrades to gain an appointment to a foreign mission. He had called upon Vice President Tompkins even while Sanford was still a Senator, to be named as ambassador to Great Britain. Party regularity proved inadequate to gain such a prestigious assignment. In 1822, President Monroe was faced with naming ambassadors to new republics that were being formed in South America. Senator Rufus King of New York thought Sanford might be named, but Secretary of State John Quincy Adams told King that Adams had previously discussed the question of a mission to Spain or Portugal with Sanford, and felt that the former Senator was not interested. If these established posts were not enticing, Adams felt Sanford would have no interest in South America. King thought there had been a misunderstanding, and therefore had a report of his conversation relayed to Sanford. Sanford was disappointed he had been overlooked and informed King he was indeed most interested in a diplomatic post. Sanford blamed opponents in New York for undermining him and spreading rumors that he would not take an ambassadorship. King then told Secretary Adams of Sanford's position. Adams elaborated to King on his earlier conversation with Sanford, saying that Sanford had felt it necessary that any country to which he was sent have adequate schools to educate his young children. Adams knew that South American countries could not provide that luxury, and therefore he had mentioned the New Yorker's name as a possibility to the president without any confidence that Sanford would accept.

While these concerns with a foreign mission were being discussed, Governor Yates of New York named Sanford to be chancellor of New York. The state senate unanimously confirmed him, and he took office on August 1, 1823. The chancellor was the highest judge in the state equity court. It was said that during this three-year service he performed ably, giving clear, well-reasoned opinions on the cases before him. Sanford was forced to content himself with the position, because no foreign mission was offered him.

In 1824, Henry Clay's candidacy for president had strong support in Kentucky and other western states, but many of his partisans felt a New York running mate would be crucial if he would have any chance of winning nationally. Peter Porter, who served with Sanford in Congress, wrote Clay in April 1824 saying Sanford would be a good choice for vice president. Clay responded the same month that his friends in Congress were inclined towards Sanford also. In June Clay wrote, in a letter marked "Confidential":

> In considering the pretensions of Chancellor Sanford, I take it for granted that his merits and qualifications have been principally, if not exclusively regarded. What may finally be the disposition of the Western States towards him cannot be certainly known at present. All that can be safely affirmed is that he seems to be well spoken of in several places.

On June 15, 1824, Clay and Sanford were named as candidates at a meeting held in the federal courthouse in Columbus, Ohio. A statewide committee was organized for the campaign. As late as September, Clay was still asking advisers whom to add to the second spot on the ticket. The presidential candidate thought he saw good support for Sanford among Clay's followers in Ohio and New York. One letter from Sanford to his erstwhile partner on a national ticket, written in October 1824, does not imply that Sanford considered himself Clay's running mate. Instead the letter merely reports on Clay's prospects in New York. Official partners or not, the two candidates went down to defeat together, both receiving the electoral votes of Ohio. Some New York electors also voted for both men, while Kentucky gave all its votes to Clay for president, but divided its ballots for the second spot equally between Sanford and John C. Calhoun.

Rufus King would not a second time by the grace of Van Buren be given extended service in the United States Senate. For over a year, the factions of the Republican Party divided over the succession. Nathan Sanford was finally unanimously elected as a compromise candidate by the legislature in 1826. In the Senate, he allied himself with the Administration Party of John Quincy Adams and his secretary of state, Henry Clay. Adams was not certain how strongly he could depend upon the New Yorker. When Sanford married for the third time in 1828, his bride was apparently a relative of the president. President Adams wrote in his diary that it was a marriage

> first projected when she [Sanford's bride] passed the winter with us in 1819. To that — Sanford has kept his peace nine years. My wife and I were invited to the wedding but could not conveniently attend. ... Mr. Sanford was formerly a cool political friend of mine; but in the lapse of time has estranged himself from me, and during the recent session of the Senate has avoided visiting me almost entirely.

The year before, Adams had referred to "Sanford's pertinacious refusal to take any part in sustaining the General Administration." Jabez Hammond, whose work on New York politics has become a standard text for the period, places Sanford among the administration backers, but then describes Sanford as "timid and over cautious." Hammond then added: "Strange delusion! If the Jackson Party succeed his political annihilation is as certain as it is that the sun will rise on the 4th March 1829." It is such indecision and timidity that made both Adams and opponents of the administration despair of being able to depend on the Senator from New York.

A few measures were introduced by Sanford during this second and final Senate term. The Senator argued for the creation of a department of the interior and the upgrading of the attorney general's office to a department of justice. He made a lengthy, detailed report in 1830 on coins, and legislation consistent with his proposals was subsequently passed. He was chairman in 1826 of the senate foreign relations committee and proposed a policy towards the often-hostile France that was later adopted by President Andrew Jackson. In 1828, Sanford was prominently mentioned as a candidate for governor of New York. DeWitt Clinton was again in power, and many thought Sanford was one of the few men with a chance to defeat him. The summer of 1827 Sanford spent traveling around New York, "to make friends." President Adams wanted him to win the governorship, even though he felt Sanford "had not chosen to make active exertions as a friend. But if elected governor of New York, he would have no spirit of hostility to the Administration, and the neutrality of his course hitherto would perhaps be more favorable to his success than if he had been more anxiously devoted to our cause." Sanford apparently withdrew from the canvass and was not an active candidate as the election of 1828 came closer.

Sanford's Senate term expired in 1831. His contemporary, Jabez D. Hammond, stated that "it was I believe at the time of his election [in 1826], understood that his political life was to terminate at the expiration of his senatorial term." William L. Marcy was picked to succeed Sanford by the Albany Regency, which was still controlled largely by Van Buren. Van Buren wanted a stout-hearted friend in the Senate in 1831, as his presidential ambitions were clashing constantly against those of Vice President Calhoun. Sanford would not provide the assistance in the Senate Van Buren needed to protect that flank, and thus on February 1, 1831, Marcy was chosen by an obedient state legislature.

Sanford played no political role after his retirement from the United States Senate. He hardly lived in exile, however. A magnificent home, derisively referred to as Sanford's Folly, was built in 1835 for him at Flushing, Long Island. "Sanford Hall," as he preferred it to be called, was enormously expensive and built on far too grand a scale to survive as a residence beyond his death. He lived to enjoy it only three years, as he died in 1838. The building alone cost the then-astronomical sum of $90,000. After his death it sold for $16,000. Around the turn of the century, it was being used as a private mental asylum.

Analysis of Qualifications

The most striking fact that appears after researching the life of this two-term United States Senator, chancellor of the state of New York, and long-serving United States district attorney, is how rarely he is mentioned in the papers and biographies of leading New York public figures who were Sanford's contemporaries. He apparently was not consulted in the major governmental or political decisions of his time. For 30 years he served in significant public offices, but his impact was almost non-existent.

The key to Sanford's obscurity lies probably in a facet of his personality that frustrated friends and caused opponents to ignore him. A political historian and ally of Henry Clay, Jabez D. Hammond, described Sanford as a friend of Clay's in 1827 and of the Adams administration, but bemoaned his political impotence by saying, "If Mr. Sanford would act with decision and energy he would effect much — but he is timid and over cautious...." Another Clay correspondent in 1827 discussed the growing danger that Andrew Jackson would be able to defeat President Adams in the 1828 election. New York was a wavering state, but it was speculated that Sanford would not be a factor — "such are the views of Mr. Sanford, such the current of things in N York, and such Mr. Sanford's characteristic indecision, that he will not break ground strongly in any direction." A few months later another New Yorker wrote Clay that the state legislature was wary of opposing Van Buren, who was laboring to elect Jackson. Sanford could not be depended upon either, as "he had neither the courage nor stability to oppose the man [Van Buren] he distrusted and hated."

The belief that Sanford was an almost apolitical figure was expressed in 1821 by then-Secretary of State John Quincy Adams, who described the New York Senator as "a most useful and very able member of the Senate;

but he has not been ardent enough as a partisan in the New York politics, and, the Bucktail, or Anti-Clintonian party having now the ascendancy in the State, the Legislature have displaced him to provide for one of their own leaders.' He was placed in the Senate by Van Buren, and when Sanford had proved himself less than dynamic in his partisanship, he was displaced by Van Buren. One gets the impression that he was a pawn used by the larger men of his day; he received high offices because of his party regularity, but he lost them because he withdrew from the forceful political action that was expected of him.

D.S. Alexander in his *A Political History of the State of New York*, thought that Sanford's long public service "did not leave a memory for eloquence, scholarship, or for great ability; though he was a ready talker and a willing friend, quick to catch the favouring breeze and ready to adopt any political method that promised success." Sanford had personal charm and warmth. He was scholarly, a master of French, Spanish, and Latin, and avidly read the works of Latin poets. He had no great enemies, and no ardent supporters. He apparently was simply a man of mediocre talents but affable nature. When Henry Clay needed to balance his appeal by finding a New York running mate in 1824, Nathan Sanford was geographically perfect. He was also such a political cipher that he would antagonize no one. Those are frequent partisan qualifications for the vice presidency. Those characteristics hardly bode well, however, for success had there been a Sanford presidency.

SANFORD BIBLIOGRAPHY

Adams, Charles Francis, ed. *Memoirs of John Quincy Adams*, 12 vols. Freeport, N.Y. (1969). Vols. IV–VIII, reprint of 1874–1877 edition.

Adams, James Truslow. *History of the Town of Southampton*. Port Washington, N.Y. (1962), p. 226, reprint of 1918 edition.

Adams, James Truslow. *Memorials of Old Bridgehampton*. Bridgehampton, N.Y. (1916).

Adams Family Papers, microfilm edition prepared by Massachusetts Historical Society, reels 30–48 (Diary of John Quincy Adams), especially reel 40.

Chester, Alden. *Legal and Judicial History of New York*. 3 vols. New York City (1911), vol. 1, p. 336.

Curts, Paul H. *Bridgehampton's Three Hundred Years*. Bridgehampton, N.Y. (1956).

Fitzpatrick, John C., ed. *The Autobiography of Martin Van Buren*. New York City (1973), reprint of 1920 edition.

Grande, Joseph A. "The Political Career of Peter Buell Porter, 1797–1829." Unpublished doctoral dissertation, Notre Dame University (1971).

Hammond, Jabez D. *The History of Political Parties in the State of New York*. 3 vols. Syracuse (1852), vols. I and II.

Hopkins, James F., ed. *The Papers of Henry Clay*, vols. 1–10. Lexington, Ky. (1959–91), vols, 3, 5 and 6.

Irwin, Ray W. *Daniel D. Tompkins, Governor of New York and Vice President of the United States*. New York City (1968).

Jenkins, John S. *History of Political Parties in the State of New York*. Auburn, New York (1849).

King, Charles R., ed. *The Life and Correspondence of Rufus King*, 6 vols. New York City (1900), vol. VI, pp. 498–99.

Lynch, Denis Tilden. *An Epoch and a Man: Martin Van Buren and His Times*. New York City (1929).

Myers, Gustavus. *History of Tammany Hall*. New York City (1970), reprint of 1917 edition.

Nevins, Allan, ed. *The Diary of Philip Hone 1828–1851*, 2 vols. New York City (1970), reprint of 1927 edition.

Niven, John. *Martin Van Buren: The Romantic Age of American Politics*. New York City and Oxford (1983).

Pelletreau, William S. "Chancellor Nathan Sandford." *Sag Harbor Express* (May 21, 1908), p. 1.

Sanford, Carlton E. *Thomas Sanford, the Emigrant to New England, Ancestry, Life and Descendants*. 2 Vols. Rutland, Vt. (1911), vol. II.

Sanford, Grover Merle. *The Sandford/Sanford Families of Long Island: Their Ancestors and Descendants*. Baltimore (1975).

Spencer, Ivor D., *The Victor and the Spoils: A Life of William L. Marcy*. Providence (1959).

Thompson, Benjamin F. *History of Long Island from Its Discovery and Settlement to the Present Time*. New York City (1918).

*1824 nominee for vice president—
Democratic-Republican Party*

Nathaniel Macon

Full name: Nathaniel Macon.
State represented: North Carolina.
Birth: December 17, 1757, at "Macon Manor," in Edgecombe, now Warren County, North Carolina.

Age on Inauguration Day (March 4, 1825): 67 years, 2½ months.

Education: Local school under Charles Pettigrew, 1766–1773; College of New Jersey (Princeton), 1774–1776; left when school closed during Revolutionary War; studied law 1777–1780 in Butte (later Warren) County Courthouse.

Religion: Baptist.

Ancestry/prominent relatives: First Macon arrived from France in second half of seventeenth century; Nathaniel was distantly related to Martha Custis Washington; Willis Alston (nephew)—U.S. Representative; Micajah Hawkins (nephew)—U.S. Representative; Charles Henry Martin (great grandson)—U.S. Representative.

Occupation: Attorney; most of adult career spent in politics.

Public offices: Elected to North Carolina Senate, 1781–1786; elected to Continental Congress, but declined, 1786; North Carolina House of Commons, 1790; U.S. Representative, March 4, 1791–December 13, 1815; speaker, 1801–1807; U.S. Senator, December 13, 1815–November 14, 1828; president pro tempore, 1827–1829; defeated for vice president, 1824; member of state constitutional convention, 1835.

Death: June 29, 1837, in Buck Spring, at age 79 years, 6½ months.

Burial: On his farm in Warren County, North Carolina.

Home: "Buck Spring," in Warren County, North Carolina.

Personal characteristics: Of middle height, "a round, shining, playful countenance, bald and gray, always dressed in the same plain but not inelegant manner" (Charles Jared Ingersoll, *Historical Sketch of the Second War*, vol. 1, p. 209, et seq.).

Father: Gideon Hunt Macon (c. 1720–c. 1761), prosperous tobacco farmer, and a justice of the peace.

Mother: Priscilla Jones (?–?), married c. 1744; she was the daughter of Edward and Abigail (Shugan) Jones; after Macon's death she married James Ransom and had six children.

Siblings: Ann Hunt (c. 1745–April 1798),

NATHANIEL MACON
(From the North Carolina Division of Archives and History)

Plummer and Betsy Kemp.

Children: Betsy Kemp (September 12, 1784–November 10, 1829), married William John Martin on November 5, 1801. Plummer (April 14, 1786–July 26, 1792). Seignora Donald (November 15, 1787–August 16, 1825), married William Eaton in 1807, wealthy Roanoke resident.

Nathaniel Macon was a major leader of the Jeffersonian Republicans during the ten years before his mentor became president in 1801. He continued as a valued servant of the sage of Monticello during most of Jefferson's presidency. After a brief parting of allegiances, Macon returned and thereafter remained a Jeffersonian. Macon's political life is dominated by the theme of small government and states' rights. He could be unyielding, obstructionist, and dogmatic, known as the most negative man in Congress. He was also kind, warm, well-respected, and popular. For almost 40 years he served his state and region in the highest counsels of government and left, if no permanent mark of leadership, then at least a high standard of integrity and consistency.

Nathaniel's immediate ancestors were prosperous, substantial men of the South. He was born in Macon Manor in North Carolina and remained at the sizable plantation until he left for school at the College of New Jersey (Princeton) in 1774, when he was 17. Princeton closed in 1776 because of the start of the Revolution, but Macon was only briefly stirred with patriotic impulses. A "tour" in the New Jersey militia lasted a year, but in 1777 he returned to the calm surroundings of his home in North Carolina and began to study law. When Cornwallis entered the state in 1780,

married (1) John Alston on March 17, 1760, who died in 1784; then married William Green on June 7, 1790. Sarah (c. 1747–April 11, 1808), married (1) John Hawkins, and (2) James Alston. Martha (February 20, 1749–September 17, 1820), married Joseph Seawell on August 28, 1771. Harrison (c. 1751–c. 1790), married Hannah Glenn c. 1772. Mary (c. 1753–after May 1814), married James Johnson. John (March 10, 1755–February 9, 1828), married (1) Joanna Tabb about 1776; (2) Betsy Williams; and (3) a Mrs. Joyce. Gideon Hunt, Jr. (c. 1761–March 27, 1809), married (1) Mary Green on July 1, 1779, and (2) Mary Hartwell about 1791.

Wife: Hannah Plummer (August 25, 1760–January 11, 1790), daughter of William

Macon left his studies and joined a volunteer company helping to repulse the invasion. It is unclear, but Macon probably participated in the key battle of Camden in August 1780. Macon had enlisted as a private and refused to serve as a lieutenant after having been elected to that rank. Nathaniel's brother John was a captain in the same regiment.

Macon remained with the company even after he was elected in 1781 to the state senate. He ignored the request to all legislators to take their posts at the capital until General Nathaniel Greene ordered him to do so, Greene insisting the soldier could provide the army considerable assistance in the assembly. Macon's response was that he was of more benefit as a soldier; not surprisingly the general's point of view won out. He was an active member from the start, speaking out on issues of state versus national government prerogatives. Macon served until 1786, and was elected in the latter year to the Continental Congress, but refused to serve.

Macon's marriage allegedly followed a game of cards with another suitor of young Hannah Plummer. The two men agreed that the loser of the game would forego future claims on her. Macon lost. He immediately rose from his chair and said "love is superior to honesty — I cannot give you up!" Hannah and Nathaniel were married in 1783. After bearing three children, Hannah died in 1790. Macon never remarried.

Macon and his bride made their home near Roanoke, in an isolated, heavily forested region. Macon seemed to love the primitiveness. He had built a rather eccentrically designed house. It was a two-story, two-room house, 16 feet long on each side. One room was upstairs, the bedroom, and one room downstairs. Slave quarters circled this curious main dwelling, and various other buildings completed the scene. The plantation consisted of about 500 acres inherited as Nathaniel's portion of his father's sizable estate, along with 26 slaves. When Nathaniel died in 1837, he owned 77 slaves. His fortune, as well as his ownership of slaves, increased markedly if not continuously, due to the profitable crops of tobacco he grew.

Macon declined in 1786 to serve as a delegate to the Continental Congress because the pay was too little. He also did not participate in the federal constitutional convention in Philadelphia during 1787. Macon was already such a strong states' rights advocate that he rejected the new Constitution that was proposed. He used his influence in the state to try to thwart ratification. The rest of his career would be consumed by trying to keep to a minimum the power of the national government. A majority of his fellow Carolinians probably disagreed with these opinions and the Constitution was ratified. Ironically, considering his opinions about the new government, Macon was elected to the United States House of Representatives to represent his home district.

Hannah Macon's death in 1790 left her widowed husband distraught, but this did not deflect him from his growing political career. From the earliest battles on the floor of the House, Macon was an opponent of the Federalists and their chief financial architect, Secretary of the Treasury Alexander Hamilton. Energetic exception was taken by the North Carolinian to Hamilton's proposals dealing with a national bank. At times Macon would become emotional and almost abusive towards these administration measures. Also from the beginning of his Congressional service Macon can be seen as an ardent defender of the South's "peculiar institution," slavery. As a strong believer in both economy and democracy, Macon rebelled against efforts by some Federalists to give the national government, and particularly the president, the trappings of a monarchy. Any pomp or ceremony Macon rejected; tributes given to President Washington when a session of Congress opened were opposed. Claims by individuals who lost property during the Revolution, or from foreigners who served the American cause and wanted to be compensated, were also anathema. Macon was parsimonious with the public purse, and he also believed patriotic service should not be for financial profit.

For the ten years leading up to the election of Thomas Jefferson in 1800, Macon worked for the Virginian's programs. He also became a close friend of eccentric, brilliant John Randolph of Roanoke, who at this stage was also a supporter of Jefferson. When the Jay Treaty was proposed in 1794 as a compromise of American-British disputes, Macon joined those who violently protested the treaty's terms as favoring England. Extreme anti–English sentiments frequently surfaced in Macon's speeches. He was a true friend of France even during the trying months of 1798–1799 when differences with the French revolutionary government were causing many Federalists to demand war. President Adams wisely kept calm and rejected the bellicose demands of his party, one of the few times the dour Federalist president and Macon, an ebullient Jeffersonian Congressman, agreed on so important a matter of policy. Macon and Adams were on opposite extremes of the Alien and Sedition Act proposals. Macon condemned these restraints on free speech and press. He warned of widespread abuse of the liberal grant of powers made under those measures.

When Thomas Jefferson was elected president in 1800, Macon finally had a president who shared his belief in limited national powers and strong state authority. Macon had been instrumental in bringing his home state into the president's column. Macon himself, starting at least by 1789, usually had no election opponent. Macon's tireless labor in Congress for ten years earned him easy election on the first ballot in 1801 as speaker of the House. Two years earlier, he had come within five votes of being chosen. The relationship of friendship and mutual respect that had grown up between John Randolph and Macon during their years together in the House was evident when Speaker Macon appointed Randolph chairman of the most important House committee, Ways and Means. Macon's independence from his party was clear even during this period when the speakership was bestowed by his fellow Jeffersonian Representatives. During the politically-motivated impeachment effort against Supreme Court Justice Samuel Chase, led by the Jeffersonians, Macon opposed his own party. In 1804 when the Congressional caucus met to renominate Jefferson for president and find a successor to the rebellious, upstart Aaron Burr as vice president, Macon protested that this was an abuse of Congressional authority. Many Federalists

counted Macon as their friend, as did most of his fellow Republicans. It was that popularity, and not party consistency, that earned him three consecutive elections as speaker.

Though Macon's power in his home state was rarely challenged, his grip on the speaker's chair was never certain. Macon's troubles were an outgrowth of his "Old Republican" principles. He remained consistent to the view that states' rights and a limited national government were the key to progress for the country. At every turn, even when the legislation was sponsored by his own party's presidents, Macon would vote against programs that enlarged the power of the federal government. Reelection as speaker in 1803 came easily, but in 1805, it was begrudgingly given, taking three ballots. Friendship with the increasingly acerbic, abusive Randolph hurt Macon's fortunes, as Randolph was becoming one of the most colorful and extreme critics of President Jefferson in the House. When Macon nonetheless reappointed Randolph as chairman of Ways and Means in 1803 and 1805, the speaker lost considerable support in his party. Randolph's appointment made Jefferson and his lieutenants frequently bypass the speaker when important matters were being directed through the House. Another blow came when Macon sympathized with the scheming to keep Secretary of State James Madison from being Jefferson's successor in 1808, but instead worked for James Monroe. Jefferson tried to reconcile these differences with Macon, writing the speaker "that some enemy whom we know not, is sowing tares among us." Such words did not mollify Macon, who was hurt and angry over his treatment by the administration. Randolph became so extreme in his criticism that Macon finally had to abandon his old friend and more often than not was on the opposite side of issues from Randolph as the third term of Macon's speakership ended. Perhaps equally irritating to his fellow Democrat-Republicans was that Macon was nonpartisan in his committee appointments and procedural rulings. Favoritism and loyalty were shown to a few of his friends, but by and large the speaker was objective, fair, and irritatingly independent.

There was never any question in 1807 but

that a new speaker would be named due to Macon's lack of loyalty to Jefferson's programs. Macon did not even attend Congress until well into the session, not only because of his deposing as speaker was preordained, but also because of a severe family tragedy. Macon's namesake grandson, Nathaniel Martin, died at the age of five. Fifteen years earlier Macon's only son, Plummer Macon, had died at the age of six. The new disaster was intensified by the memories of the previous one. Macon when he arrived in Washington was a depressed, politically beaten man. He began to reveal greater consistency in support of administration proposals and was a particularly warm advocate of the embargo against Britain that was imposed in 1807. Macon was fearful, however, that the country was rushing headlong into a war, this time with Britain, which should at all costs be avoided. War over "national honor," Macon said, would be ludicrous. But by 1808 Macon was supporting an increase in the size of the army to prepare for a war that increasingly seemed inevitable. It was a decision that was very painful for Macon to make, in part because he thereby opposed Randolph.

Though war with Great Britain was looming in 1810 and 1811, Macon urged at every opportunity a reduction in the army and navy, both in manpower and in weaponry expenditures. This was done even though he thought war would occur. Never a believer in strong central government, Macon was also fearful of a strong military organization, preferring instead to rely on the state militias if a crisis arose. Yet Macon, as a large planter with much tobacco to market, felt acutely the interference Britain was having on American commerce. By 1812 he could say, "We must either prepare to maintain the right to carry our produce to what market we please, or be content without a market...." Macon had come a long way from his feelings in 1798 favoring France, for in 1812 he stated, "The Devil himself could not tell, which gov't, England or France, is the most wicked." War with England became necessary, in Macon's view, "to prevent oppression and maintain our rights." Never an enthusiastic war hawk, Macon's support for war measures was mixed. He did vote to declare war in 1812, but in 1813 voted against a series of

measures to finance the conflict. He seemed very willing to let technical disagreements with bills cause him to oppose them. Macon's uneasiness about the war led to his being sounded out for vice president by the Clintonians in 1812, but his loyalty to the party of Jefferson made refusal an easy and quick decision.

While battles over war legislation were ongoing, Macon joined actively in other heated conflicts. Henry Clay and other young leaders were proposing that the federal government become involved in internal improvements in the various states — canals, roads, and other important projects. Further, a new national bank was sought to provide the capital for expansion. For the rest of his life Nathaniel Macon was a vigorous critic of these schemes, arguing that they were unconstitutional. Rarely could Macon be called a man who followed public opinion or changed with new situations. It was said that "no ten members gave so many negative votes" in Congress as did Macon (Ingersoll, *Historical Sketch of the Second War*, vol. 1, 212). It was playfully told Macon that if he should drown, his body should be looked for upstream since Macon never floated with the current (Ingersoll, p. 209). Macon seemed to feel he was holding the Jefferson line of restricted national government against the onslaughts brought by one-time followers of the former president. Jefferson appreciated Macon's stance, and wrote him in 1824:

> I am particularly happy to perceive that you retain health and spirits still manfully to maintain our good principles of cherishing and fortifying the rights and authorities of the people in opposition to those who fear them, who wish to take all power from them, and to transfer all to Washington.

It was the agrarian South that interested Macon, not a national bank, not internal improvements, not any of the measures of the new generation in Washington. Reelected to the House in 1815, Macon was that same year also given a United States Senate seat by a respectful North Carolina legislature. His "old fogey" image was emphasized by his affectation of wearing such clothes as a suit in the style used in the Revolution, of "superfine navy blue," much as Rufus King (see election of 1804) continued to wear such clothes, complete with buckled shoes. Many called him "Father Macon." Fine linen and a fur hat, and trousers tucked inside his boot, completed his appearance. Macon was respected for his long service and for integrity so pronounced that despite the lenient standards followed by most Congressmen, he was meticulous in keeping his expense reports for mileage and other matters.

In 1820 Macon joined the fight against the Missouri Compromise measures proposed by Henry Clay. The admission of Missouri as a state divided the country, and Macon opposed all parts of the Compromise. So great a defender of slavery was the North Carolina Senator that he could not accept the concessions eventually made by the South as a result of the Compromise.

In 1822 Senator Macon endorsed Secretary of the Treasury William H. Crawford for president in the election to be held in 1824. The Congressional caucus, poorly attended and much criticized, had nominated Macon's favorite, Crawford, and then added Albert Gallatin as his running mate. Gallatin was persuaded somewhat later to remove himself from the ticket. Henry Clay rejected overtures that he joined the Crawford ticket. Some of Crawford's backers suggested that no running mate be named. Because of Crawford's poor health, consideration was given to having him drop out of the race and his place be taken by his friend, adviser, and supporter, Nathaniel Macon. Instead, Crawford remained in the race. At a Virginia legislature caucus, Macon was nominated as Crawford's running mate for that state.

When the electoral votes were counted, Crawford received 41. The largest number were from Virginia — 24 — and Macon received that state's votes for vice president. The only other state Crawford carried, Georgia, gave its nine electoral votes for vice president to another Crawford insider, Martin Van Buren.

Though briefly in the speculation for president, and the principal running mate for vice president with Crawford, Macon never had any illusions about his own election chances

that year. Macon continued to enjoy the affection of his peers, and in 1826 was elected president pro tempore of the Senate. He was a compromise selection after the first 16 ballots had failed to produce a winner. In 1828, President John Quincy Adams tried to convince Macon to join his ticket for vice president, but the aging veteran of so many elections refused. Macon was not even a regular supporter of President Adams, but he did respect the president's honesty and sincerity. By December of 1827 Macon had endorsed Andrew Jackson's election as president, even though in 1824 Macon had found little to attract him to Old Hickory.

In December of 1828, Macon announced he would not stand for reelection when the North Carolina legislature met the next year to choose a Senator. He almost totally withdrew from public life. He managed his sizable plantation, engaged in fox hunts and his principal addiction, horse racing, entertained frequently if simply, and partook of his favorite drink (with moderation), corn whiskey. This simple, honest, patriotic man died suddenly in June 1837, having remained alert and active almost until the end.

Analysis of Qualifications

In 1824 the country was not yet facing the bitterest of the divisions between the North and South — over slavery, over the tariff, and other issues — that would lead to countless minor verbal battles leading up to the Civil War. America had just emerged from the first crisis, satisfactorily resolved by the Compromise of 1820. Nathaniel Macon was an obstructionist during that controversy in 1820, insisting on the undiminished rights of the South's slaveowners. Macon clearly did not have the compromise spirit. He was as extreme a supporter of slavery as could be found in the South, and as ardent a defender of state's rights. He quite simply was not the man the country needed in 1824.

Macon's reputation in Congress, despite his nearly 40 years of service in the House and Senate, was not for measures promoted but for his negative votes. While many in the country looked to the national government for help in internal improvements, Macon argued that federal funding of construction was unconstitutional. More importantly to him, but generally left unsaid in his public speeches, was that stretching the Constitution on this issue would eventually be rued by the slavery forces, as Congress would in time try to ban slavery itself. Funding for just about any program was opposed by Macon. He was personally thrifty, and insisted that the government be as well. It was said that his "economy of the public money was the severest, sharpest, most stringent, and constant refusal of almost any grant that could be proposed" (C.J. Ingersoll, quoted in *Dictionary of American Biography*, "Nathaniel Macon"). Good programs and bad were rejected by Macon, as in truth he did not believe the federal government had much of a role to play in American affairs.

Despite his states' rights vision, Macon was one of the best-liked members of Congress. As an "Old Republican," one whose federal service could be traced to the very first days of the Republic, Macon was a link to the past. Many thought he was still in the past, but they respected him nonetheless. Not a brilliant orator, he was frequently and dogmatically on his feet criticizing one measure or another. Senator Thomas Hart Benton called Macon "the real Cincinnatus of America," showing both the reverence in which he was held, and the moldy image that he projected.

Macon was an odd choice for the Crawford supporters in 1824. However, Crawford had a difficult time in finding a running mate since the Georgian's chances for victory were so minimal. Macon was a man from a different age, the great negater, an arch–Southerner who would add nothing to the ticket. A good and decent man, Henry Adams called him, and added:

> A typical, homespun planter, honest and simple.... An ideal Southern republican, independent, unambitious, free from intrigue, true to his convictions, a kindly and honorable man....

Henry Adams, *John Randolph*, 1882), p. 54. He was a leader of the Jeffersonians in Congress for 15 years, and helped mold a formidable opposition party in Congress before

Jefferson finally gained them a majority. The negatives outweigh the positive features in his background, and it is difficult to see how Macon could have performed creditably or beneficially as president.

MACON BIBLIOGRAPHY

Barry, Stephen John. "Nathaniel Macon: The Prophet of Pure Republicanism, 1758–1837." Unpublished doctoral dissertation, State University of New York at Buffalo (1996).

Battle, Kemp P. "Letters of Nathaniel Macon, John Steele, and William Barry Grove." *James Sprunt Historical Monographs*, no. 3, Chapel Hill, N.C. (1902).

Cotten, Edward R. *Life of Nathaniel Macon*. Baltimore (1840).

Cunningham, Noble E., Jr. *The Jeffersonian Republicans: The Formation of Party Organization, 1789–1801*. Chapel Hill, N.C. (1957).

———. "Nathaniel Macon and the Southern Protest Against National Consolidation." *North Carolina Historical Review* 32 (1955), pp. 376–384.

Dodd, William E. *The Life of Nathaniel Macon*. Raleigh, N.C. (1903).

———, ed. "Nathaniel Macon Correspondence." *The John P. Branch Historical Papers of Randolph-Macon College* III (1909), 27–93.

Dodd, William E. "The Place of Nathaniel Macon in Southern History." *American Historical Review* VII (1902), pp. 663–675.

Edwards, W.N. *Memoir of Nathaniel Macon*. Raleigh, N.C. (1862).

Gilpatrick, Delbert Harold. *Jeffersonian Democracy in North Carolina, 1789–1816*. New York City (1931).

Helms, James Marvin, Jr. "The Early Career of Nathaniel Macon: A Study in 'Pure Republicanism'." Unpublished doctoral dissertation, University of Virginia (1926).

Ingersoll, Charles J. *Historical Sketch of the Second War Between the United States of America and Great Britain*. Philadelphia (1845–1849).

Lemmon, Sarah McCulloh. *Frustrated Patriots: North Carolina and the War of 1812*. Chapel Hill, N.C. (1973).

Macon, Alethea Jane. *Gideon Macon of Virginia and Some of His Descendants*. Macon Ga. (1956).

Miller, Zane L. "Senator Nathaniel Macon and the Public Domain, 1815–1828." *North Carolina Historical Review* 38 (1961), pp. 482–499.

Risjord, Norman K. *The Old Republicans. Southern Conservatism in the Age of Jefferson*. New York City and London (1965).

Wilson, Edwin Mood. "The Congressional Career

of Nathaniel Macon." *James Sprunt Historical Monographs*, no. 2, Chapel Hill, N.C. (1900).

---

*1824 vice presidential nominee—
Democratic-Republican Party*

Albert Gallatin

Full name: Abraham Alfonse Albert Gallatin.

State represented: Pennsylvania.

Birth: January 29, 1761, in Geneva, Switzerland.

Age on Inauguration Day (March 4, 1825): 64 years, 1 month.

Education: Private tutors in Geneva; College of Geneva, 1773–1775; Geneva Academy, 1775–1779.

Religion: Not religious "in orthodox sense," but became convinced of the existence of God near end of his life.

Ancestry: Swiss ancestors, 11 generations in Geneva; moved to America in 1780.

Occupation: Public official, banker, teacher.

Public offices: Pennsylvania Constitutional Convention, 1789; Pennsylvania House of Representatives, 1790–1792; elected U.S. Senator, presented credentials on February 28, 1793, took seat on December 2, 1793, and then petition was presented that he was ineligible because not a U.S. citizen long enough; February 28, 1794, Senate declared seat vacant; elected member of Pennsylvania House of Representatives, 1794, but election contested and seat declared vacant; U.S. Representative, March 4, 1795–March 3, 1801; secretary of the treasury, January 26, 1802–February 9, 1814; commissioner to negotiate Treaty of Ghent, 1814; ambassador to France, 1815–1823; nominated but then resigned as candidate for vice president, 1824; ambassador to England, May 10, 1826–October 4, 1827.

Death: August 12, 1849, Astoria, Long Island, New York, at age 88 years, 6½ months.

Burial: Trinity Church Cemetery, New York City.

Home: "Friendship Hill," Fayette County, Pennsylvania; later settled in New York City.

Personal characteristics: Thin hair, bald at old age; long hooked nose, pointed chin; heavy French accent; slow speaking style; 5'9" or 5'10" tall, dignified, thin; dark eyes, almost black.

Father: Jean Gallatin (1733–1765), married 1755; was a partner in his father's watch business in Geneva.

Mother: Sophie Albertine Rolaz du Rosey (?–April 1770).

Siblings: Susanne (1756–1777), was hospitalized from infancy because of a nervous affliction.

First wife: Sophie Allegre (?–October 1789), married May 14/15, 1789, daughter of William Allegre.

Second wife: Hannah Nicholson (1766–May 14, 1849), married November 11, 1793, daughter of Commodore James Nicholson.

Children: James (December 18, 1796–?), succeeded his father as head of New York National Bank. Albert Rolaz (January 8, 1800–?), married Mary Lucille Stevens November 7, 1838, and lived idly on wife's fortune. Catherine (August 22, 1801–April 21, 1802), died from measles and whooping cough. Frances (February 3, 1803–?), married businessman Byan Kerby Stevens April 6, 1830. Sophia Albertine (?–?). Hannah Maria (?–?).

Historic sites/memorials: Statue in front of U.S. Treasury Building, Pennsylvania Avenue, Washington, D.C. His Friendship Hill house, three miles north of Pt. Marion on PA 166 (near Pittsburgh), still stands.

This son of Switzerland, who was denied a seat in the United States Senate and a chance at the vice presidency because he was foreign-born, is the only nominee who was not an American native. He was at least the eleventh generation of Gallatins to live in Geneva, and until he was 19 Albert too seemed destined to have his career there. When Albert was five his father died. His mother desired to pursue her own interests and convinced her good friend, Mlle. Pictet, to care for the boy. When he was nine, Gallatin's mother died as well. Education in eighteenth century Geneva was available to all, thanks to the reform efforts of the great theologian John Calvin. At the age of 12 Albert entered the College of Geneva, a boarding school taught entirely in Latin, with one hundred children to a class. After two years he then entered the Geneva Academy, again taught in Latin but with a different curriculum. It was an intense, monotonous, difficult course of study, but it probably taught Gallatin disciplined use of his great intelligence.

Upon graduation at age 19, Gallatin was without definite plans. Opportunities in Geneva seemed too limiting to the romantic youth. Careers in the law, medicine, the clergy, or the military were all possibilities but all unattractive. He was even offered a commission as an officer in a mercenary army that the British were raising to fight in America. Gallatin reportedly replied, "I would never serve a tyrant," meaning King George III of England. Instead, with two other youths he discussed and dreamed about the adventures available in the New World. Finally, on April 1, 1780, he secretly left Geneva with one of these two friends. His guardian would not discover his destination until he wrote her from a safe distance. He set sail for America from Nantes, France, on May 27, 1780, with a little money as well as a small cargo of tea he had decided to try selling once he reached the United States.

On July 15, 1780, Gallatin and his comrade finally set foot in their New World. Speaking little English, and trying to sell a product, tea, that seemed almost unpatriotic to many in America, Gallatin wandered about Boston for two months without fortune smiling upon him. Exchanging his tea for other goods, he went to Maine to spend the winter, hoping prospects were better there. Instead he only waited out a frigid winter. It was at that dreary time that his only claim to service in the military arose. A rumored British attack caused a

ALBERT GALLATIN
(Reproduced from the Collections of the Library of Congress)

handful of volunteers to gather and march on Passamaquoddy Bay. There was never an attack, but Gallatin was left temporarily in command. He would say later, "As I never met the enemy, I have not the slightest claim to military service." Gallatin's seeming lack of personal commitment in the Revolution would later be used against him politically.

Gallatin's obvious intelligence earned him a position as an instructor in French at Harvard College during 1781 and 1782. More appealing to Gallatin's sense of adventure was the lure of the west, which in 1782 was western Pennsylvania. He purchased a large block of land between the Monongahela and Kanawha rivers, hoping to sell some of it to pay for the rest. In this endeavor he gained a partner, M. Savary. Savary put up most of the money, knowing that Gallatin would come into a sizable inheritance when he became 25 years old. Crossing the mountains with a small party, Gallatin established a town in Fayette County, Pennsylvania. He named his house "Friendship Hill," apparently in honor of the three friends, Gallatin and his two fellow Genevese dreamers, who had longed to sail for America. In 1784, Gallatin met George Washington, who was also interested in investing in western lands. The Swiss immigrant impressed the general with his knowledge, but Gallatin rejected Washington's offer to become his land agent. Land promotion intrigued Gallatin, but in later years he would say that the venture had been a waste of time and money.

When not engaged in establishing a western outpost, Gallatin was in Richmond, Virginia. He met such luminaries as Patrick Henry and John Marshall, the latter offering to take him in as a law student at no charge. Gallatin clearly stood out from the uneducated in America, and such offers from those who saw great promise in him were frequent. In Richmond he stayed at the boarding home of Jane Allegre, a widow whose younger daughter Sophie soon attracted Gallatin's attention. Though the two decided to marry, Mrs. Allegre was adamant that this foreign dreamer, whose land ventures were souring and whose prospects for steady income appeared meager, would not become her son-in-law. The young couple therefore eloped. The marriage was in May 1789, and in October, after a few months at "Friendship Hill," the bride of only five months died. After this devastating blow Gallatin considered returning to Geneva, but Mlle. Pictet wrote discouragingly about prospects back in his native city.

Fortunately for America, Gallatin's heartsickness did not drive him back to Geneva. One reason was his growing political involvement. On August 18, 1788, eight months before his marriage, Gallatin had attended a public meeting in Fayette County. There he was elected a delegate to a statewide convention, whose purpose was to propose amendments to the newly ratified, but not altogether accepted, federal constitution. At the statewide convention the new politician felt no reticence, as he proposed a radical set of amendments to create a single-chamber Congress, greatly circumscribed powers for the Supreme Court and president, and other surprises. His efforts failed, but his political career was launched.

Gallatin was elected to the state legislature and served from 1790 until 1793. Prophetic of his later efforts on the national level, Gallatin's contribution in the legislature mainly concerned financial matters. Gallatin's own summation of his position in the legislature was far from humble: "I enjoyed an extraordinary influence in that body, the more remarkable as I was always in a *party* minority." Perhaps it was the deep indoctrination of Rousseau he had received in Geneva, but Gallatin was from the first a Jeffersonian Democrat. Gallatin's popularity with his fellow legislators came in part from his prodigious capacity for work. Each session he served on at least 40 committees, and would become the "laboring oar" (Gallatin's metaphor) on many of them. He spoke frequently on the floor of the house. Gallatin had also been indefatigable in breaking a party deadlock that had prevented the Federalist Senate from agreeing with the anti–Federalist, Democratic House on a United States Senator to replace one who had retired two years previously. When his name was proposed for the vacancy, Gallatin vigorously denied any interest in the position. He also said he doubted he had been a Pennsylvania citizen long enough. He received 45 votes, while his Federalist opponent received only 35. The legislature would miss his influence.

In June 1793, Gallatin enjoyed a boat ride up the Hudson River from New York City to the falls of the Mohawk. Among his fellow passengers was Hannah Nicholson, the daughter of a retired Navy officer. The next month Gallatin proposed to Hannah, and she accepted. They were married in November.

The next month, on December 2, 1793, Gallatin was sworn in as a United States Senator. Within minutes of taking the oath, Gallatin heard Vice President John Adams read a petition of 19 residents of York, Pennsylvania, protesting his election to the Senate on the grounds he had not for nine years been a resident of the United States, a constitutional requirement for the office. On February 28, 1794, a vote was taken on Gallatin's eligibility, and on strictly party lines Gallatin lost, 14–12. The legal requirements were too confused to be certain exactly when Gallatin had become a citizen of one of the states. It seemed evident that Gallatin had not technically complied with the laws of at least some of the states in which he had resided regarding the taking of an oath of allegiance. His defense was premised on the language of the Articles of Confederation, adopted in 1781, stating that "free inhabitants" were to have "all the privileges and immunities of free citizens in the several states." Gallatin had inhabited the United States since 1780, he argued, and had also served as a volunteer during the Revolution. The Federalists were too concerned about preserving their slender majority in the Senate to be swayed by such arguments. Before learning of the negative verdict against him, but fearing the worst, Gallatin and his new bride had decided to return to "Friendship Hill" if he was ousted from the Senate.

The "Whiskey Rebellion" was under way when the Gallatins reached their frontier home. The dispute was over payment of taxes on liquor, which many of Gallatin's neighbors distilled themselves and were refusing to subject to the tax. Gallatin attended a meeting on July 27, 1794, to consider the issue. Gallatin was made clerk of the meeting, and recorded the resolutions that were adopted opposing the tax and calling for a statewide convention on the issue. Hotheads continued to use violence and not rely just on resolutions. On August 21 in Pittsburgh, a meeting clerked by Gallatin issued an even more strident denunciation of the tax. All citizens were urged to shun the tax collectors and treat them with "the contempt they deserve." A more moderate statement was prepared by Gallatin, but it never reached the federal government. A few months later, when the Whiskey rebels were being condemned for their lawlessness, Gallatin began to regret his actions. He thought this episode "my only political sin." Gallatin became more energetic at similar meetings in restraining the emotions of the more radical westerners. Through his persuasion and courage, the committee that had been formed to determine what course to follow decided to submit to the law.

Gallatin's stand on the rebellion had endeared him to western Pennsylvanians. Without being on the ballot, he was elected by a comfortable margin of write-in votes to Congress in the August 1794, election. He was also elected to a fourth term in the state assembly. What was even more remarkable was that he did not reside in the Congressional district that had elected him, and the plan to put him in Congress was hatched only three days before the balloting by a handful of men disgusted with the candidates who were running.

For six years Gallatin served as a U.S. Representative. His greatest impact was in the area of finance. First, he proposed the establishment of a standing committee on finance, which would become the Ways and Means Committee. It received and reviewed all reports from the Treasury Department, thereby subjecting the Treasury to much more systematic review than in the past. Alexander Hamilton was offended by the detail being sought and correspondingly irked at the new Congressman. Just as forcefully, Gallatin expressed his opposition to the Jay Treaty with England, which many saw as a disastrous capitulation to the British.

After being easily reelected to a second term, though still making no pretense of living in the district, Gallatin became the acknowledged Republican leader in the House. New issues faced him, especially the growing animosity towards France expressed by the Adams administration. The Alien and Sedition Acts were passed over his vigorous protests. Some of the provisions seemed aimed at his participation in the early stages of the Whiskey Rebellion. Sentiment in his district was sharply divided over his opposition to the Federalist administration, but again he was reelected in 1799.

Gallatin's brilliance in leading his party in attacks on Hamilton's Treasury Department left little doubt that when Thomas Jefferson became president in 1801, Gallatin would be named secretary of the treasury. He would hold the office for 12 years, longer than any other man in history. Gallatin and the Treasury Department were a perfect match. One of his most importance problems was to reduce the national debt, which stood at $80,000,000 when he took office. His plan was to reduce that sum by seven million dollars annually. In 12 years at that rate it would have been eliminated. The extraordinary expense of the War of 1812 made that plan obsolete, though debt reduction had been until 1812 essentially on schedule despite the financial drain from conflicts with the Barbary pirates, as well as the loss of revenues due to the embargo against Britain in 1807.

During the prosperous years of Jefferson's first term, budget surpluses caused Gallatin to derive an elaborate plan with Jefferson on expensive internal improvements. These would include canals and highways to join the North to the South. The years were not so flush after the 1807 embargo, and rather than scheming to spend money Gallatin became, in his own melancholy admission, "a mere financier, ... a contriver of taxes, a dealer of loans...." He was reappointed as secretary by new president James Madison, but economic times were bad. Import duties fell precipitately, and internal taxes had to be imposed. The secretary failed in his attempts to procure the rechartering of the Bank of the United States in 1811. Opposition in New England to the War of 1812 made compliance and cooperation in that region with treasury laws increasingly difficult. Opposition in Congress to his regime also became intense. Gallatin's escape from these adversities was to become America's delegate to proposed Russian mediation to end the War of 1812.

After 12 years as secretary, Gallatin's financial views had been revealed in every detail. He abhorred public debt, as well as taxes, and sought to reduce both by duties on imports and careful budgetary restraint. Specific appropriations by Congress, with every dollar authorized, was Gallatin's proposal and it became American tradition. He attempted to influence Congress on such issues as the National Bank, even though his own president opposed him. He did not agree with the embargo because it undid his carefully knit financial plans, but supported the president nonetheless. It was a tempestuous 12 years of political infighting that Gallatin was leaving behind when he sailed for St. Petersburg in May 1813.

His mission to Russia was in vain, as Rus-

sia's offer of mediation was rejected by England. Gallatin was not even confirmed as a peace officer, the Senate showing its petulance toward Gallatin by rejecting his nomination. President Madison believed Gallatin would return as secretary of the treasury, but instead he became one of the peace commissioners when Britain agreed to negotiate directly with the United States. Gallatin's role was to give a national view to override the regional concerns of fellow commissioners (and in 1824, fellow candidates) Henry Clay and John Quincy Adams. He prepared and revised most of the important drafts of American proposals. His determination and patience kept the delegation from being worn down by British stubbornness. Adams would later say that Gallatin was the most important member of the commission that finally achieved the Treaty of Ghent on December 24, 1814, closing the War of 1812.

His work completed, the peace commissioner was able to visit his native city for the first time since he furtively left 35 years before. In France Napoléon had just retaken power, while King Louis XVIII was leaving the throne. Gallatin met both. In April 1818, he sailed across the Channel to London and again negotiated with England in the company of Adams and Clay over a commercial treaty. September found him back in the United States, with more job offers than he could handle. Profitable business ventures, election to Congress and the treasury department were all offered. Gallatin's family insisted on yet another alternative. President Madison had requested that he become minister to France. There was not much important work to be accomplished there, but Gallatin as well as his wife and children longed for the society and culture of Paris. For the next seven years he served in Paris, conscientiously if not successfully. France was not ready to solve Franco-American problems. Finally after few victories and many frustrations, with his children becoming more French than American, with Gallatin himself homesick, the minister took the excuse of the conclusion of a commercial agreement between France and the United States in June 1822, to announce his intention to return. Because of his own second thoughts, as well as some confusion on the part of the State Department, Gallatin did not leave until May 21, 1823.

The return was at first thought to be only temporary, but Gallatin discovered that some business ventures he had left in the care of others had soured bitterly. Other expenses had drained what little savings he had, and there just was no possibility of making Paris their home again. Domestic political concerns soon intrigued the former minister. William Crawford was one of five or six aspirants for the presidency, and Gallatin liked him. The two men's friendship had begun a decade earlier when Crawford had supported Gallatin's economic proposals in Congress. Gallatin thought that Crawford had continued the desired direction of the treasury department when the tall Georgian was appointed as secretary by President Madison. Gallatin was approached by Crawford forces, after Crawford's paralysis, regarding whether he would consent to run as vice president. Gallatin remained cool to the proposal, but did not reject it. The poorly attended Congressional caucus that met on February 14, 1824, included few backers of presidential candidates other than Crawford. It nominated the talented but sick Crawford, with Gallatin as his running mate.

Gallatin could see that there was little support for his candidacy, even in Pennsylvania. Followers of General Andrew Jackson attacked Gallatin for his supposed treason in the Whiskey Rebellion, and for being foreign-born. Hannah Gallatin urged her husband to withdraw. On September 29 a Crawford partisan visited Gallatin with news that because Jackson and Calhoun had joined forces, it was thought necessary to gain a stronger vice presidential partner for Crawford. Henry Clay would be that man. Gallatin easily agreed to write a letter withdrawing his candidacy, but Clay never agreed to substitute for him. Gallatin would refer to this episode as a "miscalculation," one made because of his affection for his fallen comrade, William Crawford. It is likely that had Gallatin been elected, the stridency by which his opponents were already arguing that he did not have the constitutional qualifications for the office would have been magnified many times. A vice president must

have been a citizen of the United States when the Constitution was adopted in 1789. Again, the same confusion as to whether Gallatin had fulfilled citizen requirements in any of the states in which he lived prior to 1789 would have made deciding the question a totally political point.

After a year at Friendship Hill, Gallatin was appointed to replace Rufus King as ambassador to the Court of St. James. In London for a year, the ambassador enjoyed some success in securing commercial treaties and in compromising a dispute over rights to Oregon. Upon his return to the United States in 1827, his career in public office was over. Gallatin's friend John Jacob Astor placed him at the head of the new National Bank, later renamed the Gallatin Bank. He rendered important public services in the areas of banking, the currency, and economic matters in general. In 1845 Gallatin demonstrated his continued zeal and courage by standing in front of a hostile mob and condemning their insistence upon the annexation of Texas. A particular interest of Gallatin in the years he spent as a banker was the cause of the American Indian. He wrote many articles on various aspects of Indian culture and history. In 1842 he helped found the American Ethnology Society.

This man of many brilliant talents, of varied interests, of manifold achievements, died at the age of 88, only a few months after the death of his wife Hannah.

Analysis of Qualifications

Albert Gallatin's public record is one of almost unblemished accomplishment. Gallatin left his mark on the treasury department that remains to this day. He never achieved the presidency, but influenced policy of two presidents, Jefferson and Madison, for 12 years.

Gallatin so stood out from his peers that continual offers of positions from veritable strangers were given him. Future Chief Justice John Marshall offered to take him in as a law student at no charge. General George Washington was ready to make him land agent for Washington's investments after only the briefest of encounters. The people of western Pennsylvania sent this foreign-born, heavy-accented land speculator to the state assembly despite his dramatic dissimilarities with them. In Congress he became the leader of the Democratic-Republicans in obvious recognition for his exceptional talents. But it was as secretary of the treasury that Gallatin demonstrated his brilliance most expansively. He was a nationalist, who saw in broad panorama how the mercantile and shipping interests of the North had to be reconciled with the farming interests of the South. He developed a sweeping proposal for internal improvements that would have benefited all sections and tied them together in common interests. President Jefferson's belief that such a scheme would require a constitutional amendment was disputed by his treasury secretary.

For four years Gallatin presided over flush economic times, and his policies took full advantage of the foreign trade that replenished the government's coffers and made elimination of the national debt a possibility. When leaner times arrived he adjusted, though unhappily, to the new exigencies. Gallatin showed his independence when he opposed Jefferson's embargo, and favored the rechartering of the Bank of the United States. No more hated institution existed in government insofar as the Jeffersonians were concerned, but Gallatin wanted the economic stability that a national bank offered. He failed on the issue but was bold in the attempt. Throughout his career Gallatin revealed vision, but was practical in what he attempted. What he called his one "political sin," support for the Whiskey Rebellion, was indicative that even in crisis he was unemotional and restrained. Unlike his radical neighbors, Gallatin counseled for obedience to the laws at the same time as the right to petition against unfair ones was exercised.

At the negotiations over the Treaty of Ghent that ended the War of 1812, Gallatin showed patience, persistence, and moderation in pressing American views yet controlling the conflicting viewpoints among his fellow American commissioners.

Gallatin was one of the outstanding men of his age. His nomination for the vice presidency came late in his career, and Gallatin was never enthusiastic for the position. Even though he was then 64 years old, his health and mental faculties were strong. Indeed, he would live 25-five more years. Few more capable men have ever received the honor he rejected, that of a nomination for vice president of the United States.

GALLATIN BIBLIOGRAPHY

Adams, Henry. *Life of Albert Gallatin*. Philadelphia and London (1879).

——. *The Writings of Albert Gallatin*. 3 vols. Philadelphia (1879).

Aitken, Thomas. *Albert Gallatin*. New York City (1985).

Bacon, William Plumb, ed. *The Ancestry of Albert Gallatin ... and of Hannah Nicholson*. New York City (1916).

Balinsky, Alexander. *Albert Gallatin: Fiscal Theories and Policies*. New Brunswick, N.J. (1958).

Burrows, Edwin G. *Albert Gallatin and the Political Economy of Republicanism, 1761–1800*. New York (1986).

Ferguson, E. James, ed. *Selected Writings of Albert Gallatin*. Indianapolis and New York City (1967).

Kuppenheimer, Louis B. "Albert Gallatin's Vision of Democratic Stability: An Interpretative Profile." Unpublished doctoral dissertation, University of Illinois at Chicago (1993).

Stevens, John Austin. *Albert Gallatin*. Boston (1884).

Walters, Raymond, Jr. *Albert Gallatin: Jeffersonian Financier and Diplomat*. New York City (1957).

Election of 1828

NOMINATIONS

National Republican Party. *President—*

John Quincy Adams. Adams was nominated at several state level conventions of local party members in 1827 and 1828. *Vice president*— Richard Rush. Rush was nominated for the vice presidency at several state conventions to run with Adams. Others such as J. Andrew Shulze (Pennsylvania) were nominated at various gatherings, but Adams finally accepted Rush as his running mate.

Democratic-Republican (or Democratic) Party. *President*— Andrew Jackson. Jackson was nominated by the Tennessee legislature in October 1825, and by various other meetings thereafter. *Vice president*— John C. Calhoun. Some of the state level meetings nominated Calhoun with Jackson. It was generally thought that Jackson wanted Calhoun as his running mate.

GENERAL ELECTION

Popular Vote
Andrew Jackson 642,553
John Q. Adams 500,897
Other 4,568
Electoral Vote
PRESIDENT
Andrew Jackson —178 (15 states)
John Q. Adams — 83 (9 states)

VICE PRESIDENT
John C. Calhoun —171 (14 states)
Richard Rush — 83 (9 states)
William Smith — 7 (1 state)
Winners
Andrew Jackson, 7th president
John C. Calhoun, 7th vice president
Losers
John Quincy Adams, Richard Rush

---

*1828 presidential nominee—
National Republican Party*

John Quincy Adams

No biographical sketch of Adams appears because he served as president from March 4, 1825, until March 4, 1829 (6th president).
State represented: Massachusetts.
Birth: July 11, 1767.

Age on Inauguration Day (March 4, 1829): 61 years, 8 months.
Death: February 23, 1848.

---

*1828 vice presidential nominee—
National Republican Party*

Richard Rush

Full name: Richard Rush.
State represented: Pennsylvania.
Birth: August 29, 1780, at Philadelphia, Pennsylvania.
Age on Inauguration Day (March 4, 1829): 48 years, 6 months.
Education: College of New Jersey at Princeton, 1794–1797, graduated as youngest member of his class; studied law in Philadelphia attorney's office.
Religion: Presbyterian (probably).
Ancestry: First Rush in America came from Oxfordshire in 1683. Benjamin Rush (father) was prominent doctor and patriot during the Revolutionary War, signed the Declaration of Independence; Richard Stockton (grandfather) was prominent patriot and signer of Declaration of Independence.
Occupation: Lawyer.
Public offices: Appointed attorney general of Pennsylvania, February–November 1811; appointed comptroller of U.S. Treasury, December 30, 1811–February 1814; appointed U.S. attorney general, February 10, 1814–November 13, 1817; minister to England, November 1817–1825; U.S. secretary of treasury, March 7, 1825–March 5, 1829; unsuccessful nominee for vice president, 1828; minister to France, 1847–1849.
Death: July 30, 1859, in Philadelphia, at age 78 years, 11 months.
Burial: Christ's Church graveyard.
Home: "Sydenham," a farm outside of Philadelphia, Pennsylvania.
Personal characteristics: Prematurely gray, then bald; "remarkable eyes"; a high forehead; fastidious, highly intelligent and sociable.
Father: Benjamin Rush (December 24, 1745 o.s.–April 19, 1813); married January 11, 1776; physician, revolutionary patriot.

JOHN QUINCY ADAMS
(From the author's collection)

Mother: Julia Stockton (March 2, 1759–July 7, 1848); married January 11, 1776; daughter of Richard and Annis (Boudinot) Stockton.

Siblings: John (July 17, 1777–August 9, 1837), never married. Anne Emily (January 1, 1779–April 27, 1850), married Ross Cuthbert March 12, 1799. Susannah (January 7, 1782–May 27, 1782). Elizabeth (February 14–July 2, 1783). Mary (May 16, 1784–November 2, 1849), married Major Thomas Manners. James (March 15, 1786–May 26, 1869), married Phoebe Ann Ridgway. William (November 8, 1787–January 15, 1788). Benjamin (January 3, 1789–July 21, 1789). Benjamin (January 18, 1791–December 17, 1824), never married. Julia (November 22, 1792–April 18, 1860), married Henry Jonotha Williams. Samuel (August 1, 1795–November 24, 1859), married Anne Wilmer in 1828. William (May 11, 1801–November 20, 1864), married Elizabeth Fox Roberts, July 18, 1827.

Wife: Catherine Elizabeth Murray (?–?), daughter of Dr. James and Sarah Murray; married August 18, 1809.

Children: Benjamin (January 23, 1811–June 30, 1877), married Elizabeth Simpson April 24, 1849. James Murray (July 10, 1813–February 7, 1862), married (1) Eugenia Francis Sheaff, and (2) Elizabeth Upsur Dennis, November 29, 1853. Richard Henry (March 11, 1815–October 29, 1826). Sarah Maynadler (September 17, 1817–?). Julie (November 11, 1818–?). Anne Marie (April 23, 1820–1887). Madison (July 28, 1821–?), married Marie Blight. Sarah Catherine (June 29, 1823–July 17, 1905), never married. Richard Henry (January 14, 1825–October 17, 1893), married Sarah Ann Blight in February 1851. Julia Stockton (July 21, 1826–January 20, 1858), married John Calvery.

Richard Rush's father and maternal grandfather were each signers of the American Declaration of Independence. His father and younger brother James were prominent physicians. Richard Rush himself never held elected office, but was an adviser, cabinet member and ambassador under four presidents. It was an illustrious family in which Richard more than upheld the tradition of public service.

Entering Princeton at the age of 14, Richard was attending the alma mater of both his father, Dr. Benjamin Rush, and his grandfather Richard Stockton. The classes were small, but there was little that singled Richard out as a student other than his interest in debate. At age 17, Richard was the youngest graduate in the class of 1797. No particular career interested him. Until more permanent plans could be made, Richard read law in the office of William Lewis, a distinguished Philadelphia attorney. Rather than practice law, Richard hoped to join an American ambassador as a private secretary, but the good offices of his father proved insufficient. Seeing the world would have to wait. Instead, Richard spent six years reading about it, immersing himself in literature, history, government, and law. Rush's lifelong interest in writing saw its first fruits in print with the publication in 1803 of essays on hard work and study, attributes Richard had in abundance.

Though his father had been a Federalist, Richard gravitated to the Republicans. Establishing himself as a speaker in 1807 by denouncing the British attack on the vessel *Chesapeake*, Rush also was establishing himself as a politician with his frequent pamphlets and other writings on political subjects. Governor Thomas McKean of Pennsylvania brought a libel action against Republican newspaper editor William Duane. Rush's defense of the editor in the politically-charged trial brought him further laurels as a bright new star for his party. His fervent remarks during the trial caused him to be challenged to a duel, but that matter was settled without bloodshed.

As a result of his growing fame, Rush's private law practice was profitable. He became solicitor to the Guardians of the Poor, for the Board of Health, and also was selected for membership to the Academy of Fine Arts. Rush's wide range of interests made him a patron of several historical and artistic associations. An offer to run for Congress was refused. Still greater recognition came in 1811 when the incumbent governor, striving to strengthen his political position in Philadelphia, appointed the well-known Rush to be attorney general of the state. Financial strain in his new position, especially in trying to meet expenses in the fashionable society of Philadelphia, made the office unattractive. Rescue came at the end of the year when President James Madison appointed Rush to be comptroller of the currency.

The office is now abolished, but during Rush's tenure the comptroller was an important check on the Treasury Department operations. All authorizations for expenditures necessary for the functions of the department were handled in his office, and legal opinions also had to be issued. It was a tedious, monotonous, time-consuming position. It was not,

however, a policy-making position. It symbolized the type of appointments Rush held throughout his career — a loyal assistant to other men, carrying out their policies.

The War of 1812 was erupting just as Rush took his place in Washington. On July 4, 1812, Rush gave an impassioned speech in the House chamber, commemorating American independence as well as condemning recent acts of British injustice. Rush became a principal administration spokesman for the defense of the war. The House speech was well received, being distributed widely in pamphlet form.

This speech and Rush's growing identification with the Republican Party widened the gulf between him and his father. Still, father and son were constantly in correspondence. The elder Rush provided an important sounding board for the younger. In 1813 Dr. Rush died, leaving Richard with an emotional but also political void to fill. Long-time family friend John Adams, the former president, eventually substituted for the deceased Dr. Rush in the frequency of his letters and the helpful criticisms he gave. The volume of letters was substantial, and would continue until the former president's death in 1826.

In February 1814, President Madison offered Rush his choice — the Treasury or the Justice Department. Rush chose to become attorney general. His most singular contribution in that post was to edit a five-volume *Laws of the United States*, which was published in 1815. No great achievements as an advocate before the Supreme Court, or in other capacities, marked his administration of the department. Political ridicule was leveled for his presence in Washington during the British capture and burning of the capital in 1814. He and President Madison were almost captured by the British but they escaped. The defense of the capital was not Rush's responsibility, but neither did Rush encourage meaningful measures to prevent the assault.

With the election of James Monroe in 1816, Rush added the function of acting Secretary of State to his other duties. John Quincy Adams was the actual head of the State Department, but he was in England and would not return until the summer of 1817. Rush's relations with Madison and Monroe were excellent. He had

RICHARD RUSH
(Reproduced from the Collections of the Library of Congress)

There were serious negotiations for Ambassador Rush. The issues were varied and seemingly insoluble, given the prejudices of the two countries. The Oregon boundary was critical; the question of American fishermen's use of Nova Scotia and other British territory for preparing their catch was heated, but the most controversial, divisive issue was the British practice of stopping American vessels and removing sailors on the pretext that they were British citizens attempting to evade their obligation to serve on English ships. The impressment of American sailors into British naval service was little short of slavery, and it rankled America. With British military might so dependent on their large navy, the English felt that "drafting" sailors in any way possible was crucial. Finally England agreed to the pre-conditions America wanted for a conference, and Albert Gallatin joined Rush for the actual meetings that then ensued.

The Convention of 1818 that resulted did not resolve all Anglo-American conflicts, but Rush and Gallatin were able to extract some important concessions. Fishing rights were granted to Americans off Nova Scotia and New Brunswick; the United States–Canada boundary was established from Lake of the Woods, the northernmost point in the continental United States (in what is now Minnesota), extending to the Rockies. The boundary farther west would not be resolved for almost 30 years, after the United States' acquisition of the massive western territories following the Mexican War. A procedure was established for arbitrating compensation for the American slaves captured by the British.

In 1823 the two countries again were in heated conflict on boundaries and trade. In the summer of 1823, Secretary of State John Quincy Adams sent detailed instructions to

the ear of each when they were in the White House. He also earned their loyalty by his hard work in the tasks they gave him. Carrying the twin and divergent responsibilities of two cabinet positions from March until September 1817, Rush was incredibly overworked. Twelve-to fifteen-hour days were commonplace. One measure that bore his name, but that was merely a factor of being acting secretary when others' work finally was concluded, was the Rush-Bagot Treaty with England. Armaments in the Great Lakes dividing America from British-controlled Canada were a constant source of concern to both countries. The agreement reached in 1817 limited those armaments in a way satisfactory to the United States. When Adams returned in September, Rush met at length with him to explain recent events in the department. The two exchanged offices, for Rush was appointed in October to become minister to England. Adams and Rush became good friends as well as mutual admirers as a result of these months of association at the State Department.

Ambassador Rush to open negotiations with the British on a wide range of issues. Rush met with foreign minister Canning on August 16, 1823, to begin discussions. Among the issues Rush raised was French designs on some of Spain's South American colonies. Canning named situations in which Britain might wish to aid Spain militarily in South America.

After receiving additional advice from Secretary of State Adams, Rush insisted that Britain recognize independent South American countries. Rush made this a precondition for America's taking joint action with England to block the French in South America. Britain rejected the condition.

The question of recognition stopped the move towards a joint guarantee against French designs. Such an agreement would probably have been unpopular in the United States, as nationalistic, anti–British sentiment was high. On December 2, 1823, the president announced an entirely different method of resolving conflicts in the hemisphere. The Monroe Doctrine declared the Americas off-limits to Europe. Rush had played an important role in precipitating the announcement, helping to shape its rejection of any American association with England in the region. The Doctrine was ridiculed in England. The fact that the Monroe Doctrine denounced the creation of new European colonies caused a complete breakdown in discussions of the Russian-American-British boundaries in the Northwest. Rush was tiring of the frustrations of negotiations. He was also financially strapped by the great discrepancy between the expenses of his large family and the paltriness of his salary.

With John Quincy Adams' election in the disputed 1824 presidential contest, Rush's good friend was in the White House. Adams had first asked William H. Crawford to continue as secretary of the treasury, and then offered the position to Albert Gallatin. Both having refused, the cabinet position was given to Rush. As secretary, Rush could further his beliefs in Henry Clay's American System. A high protective tariff and federal expenditures for internal improvements — the former protecting American industry from competition, the latter financing its growth — were the twin prongs of the scheme. Rush was opposed to

slavery. He was a long-time supporter of the American Colonization Society that desired to repatriate slaves in Africa or South America. As Treasury head, Rush argued for a government subsidy to help the Society's programs.

Congressional interference with the administration was debilitating. All cabinet officers were the targets of harsh criticism by the Jacksonians, who felt cheated out of the presidency and its spoils in 1824. In an article by eccentric John Randolph of Virginia attacking each cabinet officer, Rush was singled out for the worst abuse. Rush's participation in the flight from the British soldiers when Washington was burned was mentioned. The balding and white-haired Rush, son of the brilliant Dr. Benjamin Rush, was described as follows:

> And as for R___, his early locks of snow,
> Betrays the frozen region that's below,
> Though Jove upon the race bestow'd some fire,
> The gift was all exhausted by the sire.
> A sage consum'd what thousands might well
>   share,
> and ASHES! only, fell upon the heir.

A well-quoted line from Randolph's diatribe against Rush was that "Never were abilities so much below mediocrity so well rewarded; no, not when Caligula's *Horse* was made Consul." (Caligula was Roman emperor in the first century, A.D., whose disdain for his subjects caused him to name his horse one of the chief magistrates of the empire.)

Perhaps the abuse stung more than it should, for Rush wrote an anonymous article about Randolph that responded in kind. Randolph's speech, appearance, accomplishments and manner were all viewed sarcastically. Other, sometimes more thoughtful, usually anonymous pieces flowed from Rush's pen during the 1828 campaign, when Jackson and Adams again fought for the White House. A caucus in Harrisburg, Pennsylvania, named Governor Shulze as Adams' running mate, but the governor refused. Rush was substituted, the administration forces thinking that Rush's native Pennsylvania would be an important battleground in the campaign. Rush was pleased with his selection, but had few misconceptions about his chances for victory. After the ticket was defeated, Rush prophesied that Jackson would serve less than one term. Jackson would be overcome by the amount of work involved and the pressures and controversies of office, would resign and let vice president Calhoun take charge. It did not happen.

For the next 18 years Rush was out of major office, almost exactly matching the years he had just completed in office. Rush was selected as an agent for promoters who wanted to build a canal to link the Chesapeake and Ohio rivers. He left for Europe and in 1829 successfully negotiated a loan. Even so, the promoters refused to pay him in full for his labors. Rush slowly gravitated to Jackson's Democratic Party, despite Rush's just-completed 1828 campaign against the old Hero of New Orleans. The main reason for the change was the question of the recharter of the Bank of the United States. Rush and Jackson both opposed the bank. In 1832 Rush's opposition to the recharter and his support for the removal of federal deposits from the bank cost him a good chance at a Pennsylvania U.S. Senate seat.

More political involvement occurred on behalf of the anti–Masonic movement, including, as always, writing pamphlets and articles. During 1831 Rush became a leading contender for the anti–Masonic presidential nomination. Hoping that Henry Clay could be convinced to renounce Masonry, Rush publicly declined interest in the presidential nomination while urging Clay to accept it. John Quincy Adams likewise was mentioned, but Adams insisted he was not a candidate and instead asked Rush to run. The ex-president said that taking the nomination might become Rush's "indispensable *duty*." Adams confided to his diary that he greatly regretted Rush's refusal. Rush genuinely opposed the secret Masonic Order, which was subject to widespread criticism during the 1830s. In time, however, he drifted away from the anti–Masons. This broke the close relation he had enjoyed with Adams, and the breach would not be repaired until the 1840s.

Rush wrote two books at critical times in American-English relations, hoping to explain the controversies between the countries in a way that reduced the tensions. In 1835 President Jackson recognized Rush's adoption of

Democratic Party principles by rewarding him with a position as a commissioner to adjust a disputed boundary between the states of Michigan and Ohio. The following year he was appointed to represent the United States in securing the bequest from an Englishman, James Smithson, who had left a fortune to the United States for creating an "establishment for the increase and diffusion of knowledge." For two years in London Rush pressed to get the lawsuit over the estate settled. When a favorable decision was reached, Rush then converted the assets in the estate into gold for return to America. A half million dollars (when a half million dollars was still worth something!) was realized from Rush's efforts. For eight years Rush would encourage Congress to decide how to use the money. Rush's idea for creation of an institution were largely followed. He would become one of the first regents of the Smithsonian Institution. The success of this battle was one of the most satisfying achievements in his life.

From 1838 until 1847, Rush remained in his estate outside of Philadelphia. During the 1840 election Rush supported Van Buren's reelection, and was disgusted with the victory of General William Henry Harrison. Polk's election in 1844 was more satisfying, but soon he became concerned over the new president's bellicose attitude towards Britain, arising out of the dispute concerning the rightful boundary for Oregon. Rush could not accept the Polk cry, "Fifty-four Forty or fight!" Another book setting out the background for the current Anglo-American dispute seemed a chance to quiet passions. Rush wrote of his years as minister to Great Britain and of the Oregon controversy at that time.

Polk took an interest in Rush as a result of Rush's labors against a British war. In 1847, after the Senate rejected the first nominee, Polk appointed Rush as minister to France. Rush made no substantial progress on any issue, in large measure because King Louis Philippe was deposed by a revolution while Rush was ambassador. The creation of a provisional republican government after the king fled presented Rush with a crisis. He could not possibly get timely instructions from Washington regarding whether to recognize the new government; French exasperation over any delay in recognition might injure relations between the governments. So Rush, much to the surprise and some objection of other European ambassadors, presented his credentials to the new government. Even though the Whigs were victorious in the 1848 presidential election back home, Rush hoped to remain as minister in order to prevent making his recall look like a repudiation. His wishes were not honored. Rush in disgust left for America in 1849. He lived ten more years, serving in no further office, but counseling for moderation on the sectional crisis over slavery.

Analysis of Qualifications

It is difficult to evaluate a person's career as a lieutenant when attempting to judge his ability to serve as captain. Richard Rush presents that problem, as he was a dedicated and able administrator of the programs of others.

There was no question that Rush was a hardworking, diligent man. As secretary of the treasury, as acting secretary of state, a position he held simultaneously with being attorney general, and as comptroller, Rush worked long hours without complaint. As a minister abroad, first to the Court of St. James, then in Paris, Rush was unflagging and often effective in his efforts to compromise the disputes between the United States and other countries.

Perhaps the greatest independent action ever taken by Rush as an ambassador occurred when he was sixty-eight years old. The French Revolution of 1848 left the American minister to decide whether to grant recognition to the republic. Future relations between the two countries could be greatly strengthened, or soured, depending on what Rush did. His acceptance on behalf of the United States ensured some American influence.

Rush was a prolific writer. He authored several books while perhaps hundreds of political tracts were anonymously published. He was a nationalist, a believer in the American System of internal improvements and a high pro-

tective tariff. He also loved and strove for peace. Each time that a conflict loomed that might lead to war between the United States and England, Rush would write a book, present speeches, or otherwise attempt unemotionally to explain the basis of the dispute and the desirable compromise that would end it.

In personal relations Rush was companionable, a good listener as well as talker, a quiet wit who wrote and spoke easily, clearly, and appealingly. His grace and manners made him a favorite in England, and earned him few enemies even in the heated political wars in this country. His interests were broad, his knowledge of wide-ranging subjects considerable.

Richard Rush was a fine if not exceptional diplomat. He was learned and had common sense. He was neither lazy nor passive, but worked hard and asserted himself in situations in which he felt his opinions would contribute. Whether he would have made a good president is almost impossible to estimate, as he was never placed in a position in which he had to demonstrate leadership, initiative, or daring. That Rush did succeed in the tasks he undertook places him above many who share his fate as a defeated candidate. Though political parties should choose individuals who have shown some capacity for leadership, Richard Rush was at least a satisfactory choice for second-in-command.

RUSH BIBLIOGRAPHY

Adamson, Jason. *Captain Peter Rush of Pa., and His Descendants.* Turlock, Calif. (1965).

Bemis, Samuel F. *John Quincy Adams and the Union.* New York City (1956).

Brescia, Anthony Mark. "Richard Rush and the French Revolution of 1848." Unpublished doctoral dissertation, St. John's University (1968).

Keller, Eliza. "Richard Ruch, Early Pennsylvania Lawyer and Diplomat." Unpublished master's thesis, University of Pittsburgh (1939).

Powell, J.H. *Richard Rush: Republican Diplomat 1780–1859.* Philadelphia (1942).

Election of 1832

NOMINATIONS

Anti-Masonic Party Convention (first national nominating convention for any political party): September 26, 1831, in Baltimore, Maryland. *President—* William Wirt, nominated on the first ballot, with 108 of 109 votes cast. Henry Clay and John McLean had been approached, but refused the nomination. *Vice president—* Amos Ellmaker.

National Republican Party Convention (1st): Dec. 12–15, 1831, in the Athenaeum, in Baltimore, MD. *President—* Henry Clay, nominated on the first ballot by a unanimous vote of the 157 delegates present. *Vice president—* John Sergeant, nominated unanimously on the first ballot.

Democratic-Republican Party Convention (1st): May 21–23, 1832, at the Athenaeum, in Baltimore, MD. *President—* Andrew Jackson, not nominated at the convention, the only purpose of its gathering being to choose a vice president. *Vice president—* Martin Van Buren, nominated on the first ballot with 208 votes. The nomination by a convention was not accepted by Democrats everywhere, and William Wilkins received the party's vice presidential votes in Pennsylvania.

GENERAL ELECTION, November 6, 1832

Popular Vote

Andrew Jackson	701,780
Henry Clay	484,205
William Wirt	100,715
Other	7,273

Electoral Vote

PRESIDENT:
  Andrew Jackson — 219 (16 states)
  Henry Clay — 49 (6 states)
  John Floyd — 11 (1 state)
  William Wirt — 7 (1 state)

VICE PRESIDENT:
  Martin Van Buren — 189 (15 states)
  John Sergeant — 49 (6 states)
  William Wilkins — 30 (1 state)

Henry Lee — 11 (1 state)
Amos Ellmaker — 7 (1 state)

Winners
  Andrew Jackson, 7th President
  Martin Van Buren, 8th Vice President

Losers
  Henry Clay, John Sergeant, William Wilkins, William Wirt, Amos Ellmaker

---

*1832 presidential nominee—
National Republican Party*

Henry Clay

The biographical sketch for Clay is included in the section on the 1824 election, pages 78–84.

State represented: Kentucky.
Birth: April 12, 1777.
Age on Inauguration Day (March 4, 1833): 55 years, 10½ months.
Death: June 29, 1852.

---

*1832 nominee for vice president—
National Republican Party*

John Sergeant

Full name: John Sergeant.
State represented: Pennsylvania.
Birth: December 5, 1779, at Philadelphia, Pennsylvania.
Age on Inauguration Day (March 4, 1833): 53 years, 3 months.
Education: College of New Jersey (Princeton), 1792–1795; studied law under Jared Ingersoll, 1797–1799; admitted to bar in 1799.
Religion: Probably Episcopalian.
Ancestry/prominent relatives: First Sergeant in New Haven, Connecticut, by 1644; great grandfather, Jonathan Dickinson, was first pres-

JOHN SERGEANT
(From the Jenkins Memorial Law Library)

ident of Princeton; father, Jonathan Dickinson Sergeant, was member of the Continental Congress; brother Thomas Sergeant, local politician and judge, Pennsylvania attorney general, and important writer of legal works.

Occupation: Attorney.

Public office: Governor appointed him deputy attorney general for Chester County and Philadelphia, 1800; appointed by President Jefferson to be commissioner of bankruptcy for Philadelphia, 1801; state legislature, 1805–1806, declined reelection; reelected, 1808–1810; U.S. House of Representatives, October 10, 1815–March 3, 1823, March 4,

1827–March 3, 1829, defeated; March 4, 1837–September 15, 1841; president of Board of Canal Commission for Pennsylvania, 1825–1826; member of Panama Congress, 1826; defeated as National Republican Party nominee for vice president, 1832; defeated for U.S. Senate, 1834; president of Pennsylvania Constitutional Convention, 1837–1838; declined appointment as minister to England, 1841.

Death: November 23, 1852, in Philadelphia, at age 72 years, 11½ months.

Burial: Laurel Hill Cemetery, Philadelphia, Pennsylvania.

Home: Philadelphia.

Personal characteristics: Short, delicate in appearance, dark eyes, prominent nose, large mouth, well-dressed at all times.

Father: Jonathan Dickinson Sergeant (1746–October 8, 1793), lawyer and Congressman.

Mother: Margaret Spencer (January 5, 1759–June 17, 1787), married March 14, 1775; daughter of the Reverend Elihu and Joanna (Eatton) Spencer.

Siblings: William (January 1, 1776–March 7, 1807), married Elizabeth Morgan, September 3, 1801; a lawyer. Sarah (January 1, 1778–?), in October 1801, married the Reverend Samuel Miller, a professor at Princeton. Thomas (January 14, 1782–May 8, 1860), married Sarah Bache on September 14, 1812; she was a granddaughter of Benjamin Franklin; he was a lawyer and judge. Henry (January 14, 1782–March 24, 1824). Elizabeth (January 3, 1784–December 31, 1845). Jonathan (January 4–July 4, 1786). Elihu Spencer (May 29, 1787–August 4, 1824), married July 1, 1819, to Elizabeth Fox Norris.

Stepmother: Elizabeth Rittenhouse, married December 20, 1788; daughter of David Rittenhouse.

Half brother/sisters: Esther (October 16, 1789–June 4, 1870), in 1814 married William P.C. Barton, M.D. David Rittenhouse (July 1, 1791–August 8, 1872). Frances (November 17, 1793–November 3, 1847), married John C. Lowber, a lawyer, on November 10, 1819.

Wife: Margaretta Watmough (?–?), married June 23, 1813.

Children: Ten children.

John Sergeant was one of the most acclaimed attorneys in Philadelphia during the first half of the twentieth century. Forgotten today, Sergeant once ranked with the elite handful of members of what was probably the most esteemed bar in the country. His success brought public honors and private luxuries. Jonathan Dickinson Sergeant, the future vice presidential nominee's father, had known substantial public acclaim himself. Also an attorney, the elder Sergeant served in the Continental Congress, in the New Jersey Provincial Congress, and as attorney general for Pennsylvania. The family's move to Philadelphia occurred in 1777 after their home in Princeton had been burned on Christmas Day 1776, by Hessians employed as mercenaries by the British.

When John was eight years old his mother died. His father remarried a little over a year later. In the midst of a yellow fever epidemic in 1793, John's father courageously aided the sick in fatal disregard for his own safety. Thus at age 14 John was left in the care of his stepmother, who had to raise eight stepchildren and three of her own. During his last years the elder Sergeant had been an outspoken supporter of the French Revolution and of radical republican ideals. President John Adams remarked that "Nothing but the yellow fever, which removed Dr. Hutchinson [another French advocate] and Jonathan Dickinson Sergeant from this world, could have saved the United States from a fatal revolution of Government." Years later the "agitator's son" would spend a considerable effort to clear his father's name from this charge. Education had to come first, and that was completed at the College of New Jersey at Princeton, where John began his studies in 1792 and graduated in 1795. First employment came at the "compting house" (a bookkeeping establishment) of Ellison and Perot in Philadelphia. John's ambition appeared directed towards a career in business, but he changed course.

In March of 1797 Sergeant decided upon the law as his profession, and began his studies in the office of Jared Ingersoll of Philadelphia. The two men would share the same fate in the future, to be nominees in a losing cause for vice president. Ingersoll had already established himself as a leading member of the city's legal community, and thus Sergeant's own career was substantially advanced by the fact he was able to study in the senior man's office. On July 17, 1799, Sergeant was admitted to the bar. The following year Governor Thomas McKean appointed Sergeant deputy attorney general for Chester County and Philadelphia. In 1802 President Thomas Jefferson appointed him Philadelphia's commissioner of bankruptcy. It is ironic that such a considerable boost to the young attorney's career came from these two Democratic-Republicans, a governor and a president, as in a few years Sergeant would become closely identified with Federalist causes. In these positions Sergeant was able to continue his private practice as well. Financial success accompanied his professional recognition. Known as a cautious, deliberate, logical but not dramatic advocate, he was effective before juries because he seemed to be able to identify with them. There was no dishonesty or tricks in his method, and he earned the respect of many of his professional rivals.

In 1805 Sergeant was elected to the state legislature. Declining to run again in 1806, Sergeant also refused the governor's offer to appoint him that year to be recorder of Philadelphia. The following year he was returned to the legislature and became an advocate of internal improvements. As chairman of the committee on roads and inland navigation, Sergeant was in a position to advance his ideas on the subject. He worked hard to gain passage of a bill to aid the construction of a turnpike road. Public morality was also his concern, and he introduced a bill to ban masquerades of any kind because he thought they encouraged licentious behavior. Yet politics gave way to the need to attend his legal practice, and he left the legislature to devote his energies to his clients. So lucrative was the practice that when Sergeant had an expensive home built for himself and his family, it was thought he was able to pay for it out of the income he made just during the period the house was under construction. He also made friends with the influential in Philadelphia's legal, banking, and business communities. Included among these lasting relationships was one with Nicholas Biddle, who as president of the Second Bank of the United States played an important role in Sergeant's subsequent career.

A return to public office came in 1815 with the prominent attorney's election to the United States House of Representatives. He would serve a total of 14 years in the House intermittently until 1841. Early recognition came as an advocate of Henry Clay's "American System" of internal improvements and a high tariff. Not all his business constituents found this position desirable, but Sergeant withstood the criticism and was even reelected without opposition to his third term. Perhaps his most significant contribution during this period was as special agent to Europe for the Bank of the United States. The termination of the First Bank of the United States in 1811, followed by the heavy expenses of the War of 1812, had led to high inflation and great quantities of depreciated state bank currency. When the new Bank of the United States was established, a return to the gold standard seemed the only answer. Large quantities of specie, that is, gold and silver, had therefore to be purchased by the bank. Someone of discretion, absolute honesty, and intricate knowledge of the banking world was needed to go to Europe and purchase specie for as good a price as possible. Sergeant was selected. Only 37 years old, Sergeant had been elected one of the directors of the new bank in 1816, and when appointed as the bank's European agent it was with full recognition of the enormity of the task.

The problem was that the sellers of specie would know the difficult position the bank was in. Rumors concerning how much gold and silver was to be bought would drive the price of the metals up and make the task even more unmanageable. The specie was to be paid for by loans with European banks, the securing of these also being Sergeant's function. The whole difficult financial arrangement was to be supported by United States government bonds. Arriving on January 18, 1817, Sergeant continued his negotiations with financial houses until March 12. Hard bargaining by the British financiers caused him to reject their proposals and make arrangements to leave for the Continent. Before that occurred, one of the financial houses who had made an earlier unreasonable offer made a new, far more acceptable one. Within two more weeks the deal had been concluded on terms, if not generous, at least acceptable to the fledgling

American bank. One personal dividend of this trip was that Sergeant was then able to travel widely in Europe before returning to the United States. He visited Antwerp, Amsterdam, Rotterdam, and then returned to London to start the voyage home.

This victory for the bank may not have impressed a great number of his constituents, but Congressman Sergeant had gained admirers among the wealthy and politically powerful. His association with the bank continued to grow. He became a leading adviser both as legal counsel and as a director. As counsel he argued several times before the United States Supreme Court in suits involving the bank and other commercial interests. Among his significant victories before the Marshall court, which upheld the power of the national bank and the federal government against attempts by states to limit that power, was the 1824 decision in *Osborn v. United States Bank*. That case sustained Sergeant's position that a state could not tax the bank. Many states were trying to tax the local branches out of business. With him on the suit were his future running mate, Henry Clay, and another also-ran, Daniel Webster.

It was not banking, however, but slavery that consumed much of his attention and that of Congress for the next few years. The Missouri controversy found this Pennsylvania Congressman on the side of the anti-slavery forces. Favoring prohibition of slavery in all of the territories carved out of the Louisiana Purchase, he voted against the Compromise that set for 30 years the latitude of 36°30' as the boundary between slavery and freedom. Other concerns included establishment of a nationally uniform bankruptcy law, the adoption of which Sergeant helped achieve. Public morality again was not ignored and he opposed a lottery bill. Not just national interests drew Sergeant's attention, but as a reasonably ambitious Congressman he looked after local affairs as well. A new breakwater for Philadelphia, a new mint, and a bill to establish a Chesapeake and Delaware Canal were all fervently supported.

Sergeant's service in the Congress lasted until 1823 when he retired for two terms. During this retirement he helped form a citizen's group calling itself the Pennsylvania Society for the Promotion of Internal Improvements in the Commonwealth. The recently retired congressman became its president and leading member. Based in Philadelphia, the Society propagandized, organized meetings, offered resolutions, and generally attempted to arouse the citizenry and legislature to the benefits of canals. Sergeant's concern was that the massive expenditures necessary for a canal that would enable his state to compete with the Erie Canal could not be made by private industry, that jealousies and profit motives would prevent private industry from banding together on this undertaking. He was also prominent in other citizens' groups organized to back the proposal, including a state-wide convention that began on August 4, 1825. Sergeant gave a lengthy speech proposing a canal between the Susquehanna and Allegheny rivers. The resolutions he presented supporting this proposal were enthusiastically adopted by the convention.

Legislation was adopted by the state calling for the appointment of five canal commissioners and Sergeant was one of those named. When the board first met, the other four members elected Sergeant as their president. Their report favoring the construction of the canal was given to the governor, complete with surveys, maps, and cost estimates, just after the legislature commenced its session in December 1825. This report was transmitted to the legislators, who were already deeply in debate over the issue. A bill was passed, and signed into law on February 25, 1826, ordering the commencement of construction on the Pennsylvania Canal. A year's worth of effort, with Sergeant very much in the fore, had led to victory for the adherents of internal improvements.

One more public service awaited Sergeant before his return to Congress, and that was appointment by the second Adams president to be a member of the Panama Congress. The first Adams had condemned Sergeant's father for his agitation during the French Revolution. Perhaps all was forgotten and forgiven. Disturbances in South America prevented the Congress from getting under way. After a brief period waiting in Mexico, Sergeant returned to the United States in July 1827, and soon thereafter took his seat in the House of Representatives, to which he had been elected in 1826. He served one term and retired. Sergeant became increasingly allied with the Adams and Clay party as the presidency of Andrew Jackson began to restructure the party system. Opposition to Jackson took him beyond the political realm and into the courtroom. In the celebrated Cherokee cases, Sergeant argued for the Indians that treaties entered with the United States protected them in their right to remain in Georgia. The state was attempting to force them to move out of Georgia. The case established the concept of domestic dependent nations for the Indian territories, in which state law had very little authority. The Acts of the Georgia legislature interfering with the status of the Indians were invalidated by the court and Sergeant had won a signal victory, at least in principle. In practice, President Jackson refused to permit the decision to be carried out. His famous comment, "The Supreme Court has made its decision, now let them enforce it," revealed that the president did not feel the court was supreme over him.

When the National Republicans met in 1832 to choose a presidential ticket to run against Jackson, Henry Clay was chosen as its nominee. On the next day, Sergeant was unanimously selected as Clay's running mate. The ticket was no match for "Old Hickory." Two years later Sergeant lost again, this time in an attempt to be elected United States senator.

In 1836 Sergeant returned to the public arena with his selection to the Pennsylvania constitutional convention and election as president of that gathering. His main interest appeared to be the judiciary article in the new document. One final return to Congress occurred in 1839 and he declined reelection. With the Whig Party victory in 1840, Sergeant was tendered a place in President William Henry Harrison's cabinet, but he declined. After Harrison died, the new president John Tyler offered him the post of ambassador to England, but that too was declined.

Full-time involvement in political affairs was continually rejected because this heavily-involved Philadelphia attorney just could not spare the time from his law practice. Another significant decision from the United States Supreme Court was achieved by Sergeant in 1844, in the Girard Will case. Sergeant devoted much of his time and money to charities, and was president of the House of Refuge and the Apprentice's Library Commission. In the Girard Will case Sergeant was arguing to preserve a bequest in a will that gave to the city of Philadelphia property for charitable uses. The heirs contended that these will provisions were invalid. Sergeant won his case. Over one hundred years later the will was back in litigation, needless to say with a different set of attorneys. Established as a result of the bequest had been a school for "poor white male orphans," as required under the will. The Supreme Court held in 1957 that members of all races had to be admitted. That issue never arose during Sergeant's work on the case.

Though occasionally in the last decade of his life Sergeant would accept a short-term public appointment, generally his term in Congress that ended in 1841 concluded his career. President Polk named him to be the arbitrator of a title dispute to an island in the Delaware River, when the rival claimants were New Jersey and the United States. When he died in 1852, there were several public meetings and eulogies commending his years of service, both in office and as an attorney. Two long-time legal rivals, Horace Binney and W.M. Meredith, both of Philadelphia, praised him effusively. A leader of the early bar of Philadelphia had died, and his peers in the legal community turned out in force to honor him.

Analysis of Qualification

Sergeant was a quiet, scholarly man, mild-mannered and cordial in personal relations. Rarely a party-goer, he was sociable mainly with a small circle of close friends.

Sergeant's mark was made not so much in the political world as in the legal one. He was called "one of the most brilliant and honored men in the legal profession." It was no small measure of his reputation in the law that even though he had served only in the House of

Representatives, John Sergeant was nominated for vice president.

As a lawyer, he was described as having

> great quickness, grasp of thought, and power of comprehension[;] he derived through an excellent education the art of arranging his argument with perfect skill, according to the rules of the most finished and effective logic....

His jury arguments were persuasive because of a talent that made him seem "rather to argue his case *with* them than *to* them," and in the language of one of his competitors, he virtually "got into the jury-box, and took part as it were, in the decision of his own case." Yet throughout his career Sergeant was known as a dry and undramatic speaker, even a nervous one:

> For some minutes after he rose to open his argument, in any important cause, he appeared to be oppressed, his hand shook, his lips quivered, and his whole frame seemed to be disturbed; but gradually a reaction took place, and *when* that result arrived, he was every inch an advocate — self-possessed, eloquent, confident, and generally successful.

His clients were wealthy; they could rightly be called the "vested interests," but to Sergeant they were also the key to improving society. They would provide the jobs; their money would fund the philanthropies that would uplift their communities.

With riches and fame from his legal practice, Sergeant felt a social obligation and upheld it throughout his career. Active in civic affairs and charities, he often seemed to run for office to take over leadership of an important issue. His work in furtherance of canals in Pennsylvania, his service at the constitutional convention of the state, and his sponsoring of legislation to write a uniform set of bankruptcy laws, demonstrate a merging of his public spiritedness and willingness to advance worthy causes with his representation of businesses that could be benefited by those measures. His biggest single contribution during his public career may have been his negotiations with foreign lenders to gain the funds necessary to buy gold and silver for the Second Bank of the United States. In that capacity he showed resolve, patience, and imagination in successfully concluding a quite complex feat.

As president during the 1830s, Sergeant would have brought his considerable intelligence, ability at negotiating, and resolve to bear in favor of rechartering the Second Bank of the United States, which President Jackson had prevented. Henry Clay's system of internal improvements balanced by a high tariff would have been central to a Sergeant administration. Though seen as a strong anti-slavery man, Sergeant would not likely have inflamed feelings over the issue, so recently sparked during the South Carolina nullification crisis of 1832.

Sergeant's career presented him with few responsibilities that tested the skills necessary to perform as president. His sole elective positions were in the state and national legislatures. Yet as an attorney, as a congressman, as a special agent for the Bank of the United States, and as a public-minded citizen who got involved in constitutional revision, canal construction, and other measures, Sergeant had always excelled. He was just the kind of man whom a national party could conscientiously attempt to advance to such a high office as vice president.

SERGEANT BIBLIOGRAPHY

Binney, Horace. *Remarks to the Bar of Philadelphia on the Occasion of the Deaths of Charles Chauncey and John Sergeant*. Philadelphia (1853).

Boyd, Julian P. "John Sergeant's Mission to Europe for the Second Bank of the United States: 1816–1817." *Pennsylvania Magazine of History and Biography* 58 (1934), pp. 213–231.

Brown, David Paul. *The Forum: Or Forty Years Full Practice at the Philadelphia Bar*. Philadelphia (1856), vol. II, pp. 205–218.

Halfield, Edwin F. "Jonathan Dickinson Sergeant." *Pennsylvania Magazine of History and Biography* II (1878), pp. 438–442.

Meredith, William M. *Eulogium on the Character and Services of the Late John Sergeant*. Philadelphia (1853).

Shelling, Richard I. "Philadelphia and the Agitation in 1825 for the Pennsylvania Canal." *Pennsylvania Magazine of History and Biography* 62 (1938), pp. 175–204.

William Wirt

Born November 8, 1772, near Blandensburg, Maryland; died February 18, 1834, in Washington, D.C. Married Mildred Gilmer on May 28, 1795; she died September 17, 1799; they had no children. Married Elizabeth Washington on September 7, 1802; they had 12 children, at least five of whom died before adulthood.

William Wirt was the last of three sons and three daughters born to tavern-keepers Jacob and Henrietta Wirt. Jacob died when William was just two, and Henrietta when he was eight. In 1779 William was sent to a school in Georgetown and boarded there with a Quaker family. The young orphan boy wrote 50 years later that he had been devastated after being left and cried for hours. He attended other boarding schools in other places. At age 15 William began as a tutor in a Blandensburg household, and continued for 20 months. After a stay in Georgia with his married sister, Wirt returned to Maryland where he began studying law. He heard of an opening for a lawyer in Culpeper County, Virginia. He went there and five months later was admitted to practice law. When he married in 1795, he moved to his wife's family home near Charlottesville. His wife's father died a year or two later, and the young couple received land and built a mansion that they called "Rose Hill."

What broke this peaceful progress was his wife's death after they had been married for five years. Wirt decided he could not live at Rose Hill any more, and moved to Richmond. There he was elected clerk of the House of Delegates in 1800. He service as clerk briefly overlapped Patrick Henry's as a delegate. Seventeen years later Wirt's most significant literary effort, a biography of Patrick Henry, was published. In 1800 Wirt was one of the attorneys — apparently at the suggestion of Thomas Jefferson — defending the pamphleteer James Thomas Callender in a prosecution under the Alien and Sedition Act. Wirt was elected by the legislature in 1802 to be a chancellor in one of three Virginia districts. Wirt moved to Williamsburg to assume his duties. In 1803 he anonymously published in a Richmond newspaper the first of "The Letters of the British Spy." It was an extremely popular set of writings, part-travelogue, part social commentary, that was to appear written by an English visitor. Throughout Wirt's career he wrote and published, but few if any productions were as successful as the "Spy."

In 1806 Wirt moved back to Richmond. His Jefferson connection gained him selection as a prosecutor of former vice president Aaron Burr for treason. He became famous from the trial, and Jefferson urged him to run for Congress. Wirt did not, but he was elected in 1808 and served one term in the Virginia House of Delegates. In 1817 President James Madison named him United States attorney general. Wirt tried to bring a degree of organization and continuity to the office. He presented the government's position to the Supreme Court in many of the cases that established important early constitutional principles. As was customary, he also continued a private law practice. Wirt was highly respected as attorney general and was continued in that post by President John Quincy Adams in 1825. He retired in 1829 when Andrew Jackson became president, having served for 12 years.

Wirt opened his law practice in Baltimore. Within two years he was nominated for president by the Anti-Masonic Party. That party had a meteoric rise in reaction to the abduction and apparent murder of a man named William Morgan by members of the Masonic order. The new party opposed all secret societies. Wirt had been a Mason as a young man, and in 1832 actually supported Henry Clay for president. Clay held the new party in contempt and refused the nomination. So Wirt became the Anti-Mason nominee. Wirt may have decided that since Clay rejected the anti–Masons, the only hope was for all the anti–Jackson forces to unite around Wirt. Or he may have planned to withdraw in favor of Clay, but Clay would never attack Masons or give Wirt some other credible excuse for withdrawing in favor of Clay. For a Clay supporter and friend, Wirt's actions were mysterious. Clay and Wirt both lost.

WILLIAM WIRT
(Reproduced from the Collections of the Library of Congress)

Not long after the election his "youngest and favorite daughter" died. (Hagan, p. 22.) This helped precipitate a rapid physical decline and Wirt died in 1834.

The house Wirt lived in from 1816 to 1818, now known as the Hancock-Wirt-Caskie House, stands at 2 North 5th Street, Richmond, Virginia.

WIRT BIBLIOGRAPHY
Baker, John F. "William Wirt." *American Law Register* VII (N.S.) (1868), pp. 63–74.

Burke, Joseph Charles. "William Wirt: Attorney General and Constitutional Lawyer." Unpub-lished doctoral dissertation, Indiana University (1965).

Cauble, Frank. "William Wirt and His Friends: A Study in Southern Culture, 1772–1834." Unpublished doctoral dissertation, University of North Carolina (1934).

Eriksson, Erik McKinley. "William Wirt: Anti-Masonic Presidential Candidate." *Grand Lodge Bulletin* 27 (April, 1926), pp. 120–125.

Hagan, Horace H. "William Wirt." *Georgetown Law Journal* VIII (May, 1920), pp. 12–23.

Haley, Jill. "I Can No Longer Live Here: Elizabeth Wirt's Decision to Buy a New House." Unpublished Master's thesis, University of Delaware (1995).

Jabour, Anya. "Heart's Divided: The Marriage and

Family of Elizabeth and William Wirt, 1802–1834." Unpublished doctoral dissertation, Rice University (1995).

Kennedy, John P. *Memoirs of the Life of William Wirt, Attorney General of the United States.* Philadelphia (2 vols., 1849).

McIntosh, Linda. "William Wirt and the Election of 1832." Unpublished master's thesis, Johns Hopkins University (1973).

Robb, Arthur. "Biographical Sketches of the Attorneys General: Edmund Randolph to Homer Cummings." Unpublished typescript, U.S. Department of Justice library (1936).

U.S. Department of Justice. *Attorneys General of the United States.* Washington, D.C. (1985).

*1832 vice presidential nominee —
Anti-Masonic Party*

Amos Ellmaker

Born February 2, 1787, at Walnut Bottom Farm, near New Holland, Lancaster County, Pennsylvania; died November 28, 1851, in Lancaster. Married Mary Rachel Elder on June 13, 1816; they had four sons.

Amos Ellmaker was one of eight children of Nathaniel and Elizabeth Fellenbaum Ellmaker. Nathaniel was a prominent farmer, state senator, and local public figure who witnessed the signing of the Declaration of Independence. Some sources state that Amos attended Yale College, but by 1803 he was at Princeton and graduated in 1805. He then studied law under Judge Tapping Reeve at Litchfield, Connecticut, at the same time as John C. Calhoun. He completed his legal training with his future father-in-law, Thomas Elder of Harrisburg, Pennsylvania. There he began his legal practice, and from 1809 to 1815 served as deputy attorney general — the local prosecutor — for Dauphin County. He was elected to the Pennsylvania legislature and served from 1813 to 1814. During the War of 1812 he was an aide to General Forster during the 1814 march to the defense of Baltimore. Also in 1814 he was elected to the United States Congress. The first session did not begin until December 4, 1815. Ellmaker resigned from Congress on July 3, 1815, without ever qualifying, in order to accept appointment as pre-

siding judge of the Dauphin-Lebanon-Schuylkill judicial district around Harrisburg. He served only until December 21, 1816, when Governor Simon Snyder appointed him attorney general of Pennsylvania. One year later William Findlay became governor, but decided to keep Ellmaker and most of the rest of the cabinet. Allegedly among Ellmaker's deputies were future president James Buchanan and future vice president George M. Dallas.

Several sources state that Ellmaker declined to be appointed United States secretary of war in 1817, as newly elected President James Monroe floundered in filling that Cabinet post with a westerner. No record of an offer to Ellmaker was discovered, though Monroe's offers were spurned by Henry Clay, Richard M. Johnson, and Isaac Shelby of Kentucky, William Henry Harrison of Ohio, and Lewis Cass of Michigan. Monroe appointed John C. Calhoun instead. Ellmaker remained attorney general until he was replaced by a close ally of Governor Findlay in 1819.

At some stage Ellmaker moved to Lancaster, Pennsylvania, and opened a law office. He was said to be future President James Buchanan's first close friend in Lancaster when Buchanan moved there and started his own legal practice. Buchanan would be the only bachelor president, but in 1819 he apparently was engaged to an Ann Coleman of Lancaster. Miss Coleman died, a tragedy that tortured young Buchanan for months. Ellmaker was a close-enough friend to write him a poignant and encouraging letter in December 1819. In the letter Ellmaker states that his advice "opens in my own bosom a wound which a dozen years have not cicatrized, and brings to my recollection a dark period of my own days, the remembrance of which yet chills me with horror" (Curtis, *Buchanan,* pp. 19–20). To what tragedy Ellmaker was alluding is unknown. He was 20 years old "a dozen years" before 1819, and did not marry until he was 29.

Ellmaker was reappointed state attorney general in 1828 by Governor John Andrew Shulze, and served until resigning in August 1829. During the 1828 presidential campaign Ellmaker's support for President John Quincy Adams caused him to remove any subordinates who publicly tried to assist Andrew Jackson's

AMOS ELLMAKER
(From the *Journal of the Lancaster County Historical Society*)

back a recommendation for nominating a candidate at a convention a year later in Baltimore. That recommendation was adopted. Ellmaker was concerned about just whom that nominee would be, and preferred Richard Rush, President John Quincy Adams running mate in 1828. Ellmaker and others wrote Rush asking him to run, and Rush responded encouragingly. A significant campaign for Rush never developed and Rush ultimately did not compete. Ellmaker's worry was that "if a man be nominated who is not a firm, open, and decided antimason, the party will be deserted in disgust." He considered President Jackson the Mason candidate. At the September 1831 national convention, Wirt — not a committed Anti-Mason — was selected for president. Ellmaker was nominated for vice president by acclamation, perhaps because Pennsylvania was considered a key state. Ellmaker considered his ticket's victory to be "an

election. Surprisingly, in correspondence during the 1832 campaign, Ellmaker stated that he had supported Jackson in 1824 and 1828.

Ellmaker was an early activist in the anti-Masonic movement in Pennsylvania. Among other anti–Masons with whom Ellmaker corresponded were Thaddeus Stevens and William Henry Seward. The first Pennsylvania convention of the party was in June 1829. Ellmaker was not a delegate, but was chosen the next year as one of the delegates to the first national convention in Philadelphia to be held in September 1830. There a committee was named to advise on whether a presidential candidate should be nominated. Ellmaker was made chairman, and his committee reported

event manifestly impossible." He was correct, though he may have been surprised the ticket did so poorly in his home state.

Ellmaker had one more political race in him. In 1834 the Pennsylvania legislature chose a new U.S. Senator to replace William Wilkins. Ellmaker was the candidate for the Anti-Masons, the Whigs had Joseph Lawrence, and the two Democratic factions were behind Joel B. Sutherland and James Buchanan. One historian has written that if "the anti–Masons and Whigs had been able to work together they easily could have elected a senator, but they found it impossible to cooperate" (Klein, *Buchanan*, p. 102). Buchanan won on the fourth ballot, with Ellmaker as his closest competitor.

Ellmaker practiced law in Lancaster and stayed interested in politics, but apparently never again ran for office.

ELLMAKER BIBLIOGRAPHY

Ammon, Harry. *James Monroe: The Quest for National Identity.* New York (1971).

Beal, Rebecca J. *Jacob Eichholtz 1776–1842: Portrait Painter of Pennsylvania.* Philadelphia (1969).

Biographical Annals of Lancaster County, Pennsylvania. Vol. I. Spartanburg, S.C. (1985 reprint).

Chase, James S. *Emergence of the Presidential Nominating Convention, 1789–1832.* Urbana (1973).

Curtis, George Ticknor. *Life of James Buchanan, Fifteenth President of the United States.* New York (1883), pp. 19–20.

Diffenderffer, Frank Reid. "Politics 75 Years Ago." *Papers Read Before the Lancaster County Historical Society* VIII (1903), pp. 36–47.

Hamilton, Stanislaus Murray, ed. *The Writing of James Monroe.* 7 vols. New York (1898–1903), especially vol. 7, pp. 136–137.

Harris, Alexander. *A Biographical History of Lancaster County.* Lancaster (1872)(over half of Harris's sketch is a review of Ellmaker's character and personality).

Klein, Philip Shriver. *Pennsylvania Politics 1817–1832: A Game Without Rules.* Philadelphia (1942).

_____. *President James Buchanan: A Biography.* University Park, Penn. (1962).

Martin, C. H. "Sons of Lancaster County Who Won Congressional Honors at Home and Elsewhere." *Papers Read Before the Lancaster County Historical Society* XXXVI (1932), p. 114.

McCarthy, Charles. "The Antimasonic Party." *American Historical Association Annual Report for the Year 1902* I, Washington (1903), pp. 369–574.

McNeal, John Edward. "The Antimasonic Party in Lancaster County, Pa.: 1828–1843." *Lancaster County Historical Journal* 69 (1965).

"Notes on Amos and Elias E. Ellmaker." *Papers Read Before the Lancaster County Historical Society* XII (1908), pp. 175–183.

William Henry Seward Papers, microfilm edition.

Thaddeus Stevens Papers, microfilm edition.

Appreciation is expressed to Assistant Archivist Daniel J. Linke, Princeton University, for finding a record of Ellmaker's attendance.

1832 vice presidential nominee — Democratic-Republican Party

William Wilkins

Born December 20, 1779, in Carlisle, Pennsylvania; died June 23, 1865, in "Homewood," near Pittsburgh. Married Catherine Holmes in 1815, who died in 1816. Married Mathilda Dallas on October 1, 1818; they had three sons and four daughters. Mathilda was the daughter of Alexander J. Dallas, the U.S. secretary of the treasury from 1814 to 1816, and the brother of George M. Dallas, who among other high offices was U.S. senator and vice president from 1845 to 1849.

William Wilkins was the son of John and Catherine Rowan Wilkins. His father was a Revolutionary War veteran. The family moved to Pittsburgh in 1783, where John Wilkins established a store and held various local public offices. William was educated at local schools, then attended Dickinson College in Carlisle. Wilkins studied law in a Carlisle law office, was admitted to the bar on December 28, 1801, and began a practice in Pittsburgh. Wilkins spent 1806 in Kentucky with his brother after being censured for serving as a second in a duel.

In 1810 Wilkins was an organizer of the Pittsburgh Manufacturing Company. He became the first president when that company was chartered as the Bank of Pittsburgh in 1814, and continued in that position until 1819. Wilkins was also president of the Pittsburgh Common Council from 1816 to 1819.

After being defeated in two earlier elections, Wilkins was elected as a Federalist to the state house of representatives in 1819. In December, 1820 he resigned to become president judge of the fifth judicial district, receiving his commission at almost midnight on the last day of his friend Governor William Findlay's term. President James Monroe appointed him a federal district judge in May 1824, and he served until 1831. Still serving as a judge, Wilkins ran for Congress in 1826 and was defeated. He ran again as a Democrat in 1828, was elected, but his judicial colleagues asked that "if consistent with his views of the public

WILLIAM WILKINS
(From the U.S. Army Center for Military History)

ern business. Dallas refused, but Wilkins agreed to promote the idea with President Jackson. Within a few days his enthusiasm for taking a position so hostile to Jackson waned. Still, on June 11 Wilkins and Dallas voted in favor of the bank recharter. In July Wilkins headed the Senate conferees meeting with representatives from the House on a compromise tariff bill. Wilkins refused to accept in conference the tariff reductions already accepted 32–16 by the full Senate. Henry Clay considered this a betrayal, and believed as did some other senators that Wilkins was currying favor with Jackson in hopes of being selected as vice president in the election later that year. Wilkins was chairman of the Senate committee that reported the "Force Bill." Written by Daniel Webster to satisfy Administration demands for authorization, the bill was labeled the "Wilkins' alias Webster bill." It authorized military means to end South Carolina's attempt to nullify the tariff.

good," that he remain a judge. For whatever reasons, Wilkins declined to take his congressional seat. The Pennsylvania legislature in 1830 elected him a United States senator, a position he did accept. He and his brother-in-law George Dallas were the two Pennsylvania senators.

Wilkins was a staunch Jacksonian. In one of the most divisive issues of the day, the recharter of the Second Bank of the United States, Wilkins split with Jackson and favored recharter. That issue was boiling at the same time as the South Carolina nullification crisis, which arose over the Tariff of Abominations that Wilkins also favored. Charles Jared Ingersoll, an emissary from Nicholas Biddle at the bank, proposed to Wilkins and Senator Dallas that they pursue a lower tariff to appease the South and a bank recharter to please north-

In the 1832 elections, several prominent Pennsylvania leaders insisted that their state deserved finally to have one of its own serving as vice president. It was clear that the national Jackson leaders had decided to hold a convention so that New Yorker Martin Van Buren would be named as Jackson's running mate. Pennsylvania refused to send delegates, but instead nominated Wilkins for vice president at the March 10 state convention, by a vote of 67 to 62 for brother-in-law Dallas. The national convention nominated Van Buren. Pennsylvania stood alone when it cast all its electoral college votes for Jackson and Wilkins. Wilkins had managed to antagonize Jackson over the bank question and Van Buren over the vice presidency. Perhaps to make amends, ex-banker Wilkins was a forceful if not altogether sincere defender of Jackson in 1833 as the financial panic that year started to be blamed on Jackson's anti-bank policies.

On June 30, 1834, Wilkins resigned from the Senate to accept President Jackson's appointment as minister to Russia. It was a hardship post, and not necessarily a reward. Wilkins' principal negotiations were over trading rights in North America and for a treaty for neutral rights. Both initiatives failed. He resigned the foreign post in December 1835, and returned home. In 1840 he lost, but in 1842 won a seat in Congress. He served less than a year, as on February 20, 1844, he was sworn in as secretary of war by appointment of President Tyler. Tyler's previous pick was rejected by the Senate. He served until Tyler left office March 4, 1845.

Wilkins returned to Pittsburgh. His land investments proved profitable, ending the severe financial problems he had suffered for years. In 1855, and with the proceeds he built a mansion on a 650 acre estate outside Pittsburgh, that he called "Homewood." He was elected a Pennsylvania state senator and served from 1855 to 1857. During the Civil War and at age 80, he was named a major general of the Pennsylvania Home Guards. His role mainly was to give speeches and seek volunteers. He lived to see the end of the war, but no more.

WILKINS BIBLIOGRAPHY

Belohlavek, John M. *George Mifflin Dallas, Jacksonian Patrician.* University Park, Penn. (1977).

Chase, James S. *Emergence of the Presidential Nominating Convention, 1789–1832.* Urbana (1973).

Chidsey, Donald Barr. *And Tyler Too.* Nashville and New York (1978).

Gammon, Samuel R. *The Presidential Campaign of 1832.* Baltimore (1922).

Morgan, Robert J. *A Whig Embattled: The Presidency under John Tyler.* (1954).

Peterson, Merrill D. *The Great Triumvirate: Webster, Clay and Calhoun.* New York (1987).

Shenton, James P. *Robert J. Walker: A Politician from Jackson to Lincoln.* New York (1961).

Slick, Sewell E. "The Life of William Wilkins." Unpublished master's thesis, University of Pittsburgh (1931).

_____. "William Wilkins: Pittsburgher Extraordinary." *The Western Pennsylvania Historical Magazine* 22 (1939), pp. 217–236.

Election of 1836

NOMINATIONS

Whig Party. The infant Whig Party considered a national convention, but determined to maximize its vote by having several regional candidates. This could throw the election into the House of Representatives, where the most popular Whig might be able to defeat the Democratic nominee. *President—* Hugh L. White, candidate for the South, nominated on December 29, 1834, at at caucus of Whig congressmen from Tennessee opposed to Andrew Jackson. Also named by Alabama legislators on January 2, 1835; by Tennessee legislature on October 16–17, 1835; by Virginia Whig legislators on December 11, 1835, and by North Carolina Whig legislators on December 22, 1835. A Georgia states' rights convention named White on June 15, 1835, and Georgia states' rights legislators nominated White and Philip P. Barbour on December 18, 1835. *President—* Daniel Webster, candidate for the Northeast and especially Massachusetts, nominated by Massachusetts legislators on January 22, 1835, and by Rhode Island convention on June 24, 1835. Public meetings at Faneuil Hall on May 28, 1835, and later in Maine, Pennsylvania, and New York City also endorsed Webster. *President—* John McLean, candidate

WILLIAM HENRY HARRISON
(From the author's collection)

in Northwest, nominated by Whig members of Ohio legislature in December 1834. On August 31, 1835, he withdrew from the race. *President*— William Henry Harrison, candidate in remainder of country, nominated by Whig and Anti-Mason state conventions in Pennsylvania, December 14, 1835, with Francis Granger for vice president. Indiana state Whig convention on December 22-23, 1836 (Columbus), selected Harrison with John Tyler as running mate; New York state convention, February 3-4, 1836, in Albany, named Harrison with Francis Granger as running mate; the Maine Whig convention named Harrison, and the one in Connecticut nominated him along with Granger; on June 1, 1836, the New Jersey Whig convention nominated Harrison and Granger. *Vice president*— Francis Granger, nominated with William Henry Harrison in Ohio, Vermont, Connecticut, New Jersey, and probably other

states. *Vice president*— Philip P. Barbour, nominated with White in Georgia on December 18, 1835, but declined the nomination. John Tyler replaced him when the Georgians named him in May 1836. *Vice president*— John Tyler, named to run with White in North Carolina, Virginia, Maryland, Georgia, and other states.

Democratic Party Convention (2nd), held May 20-22, 1835, Fourth Presbyterian Church in Baltimore, Maryland. *President*— Martin Van Buren, nominated unanimously on first vote. *Vice president*— Richard Mentor Johnson, nominated with 178 of 265 votes on the first ballot, ahead of Sen. William Rives of Virginia. Virginia Democrats remained unhappy with Van Buren and gave their electoral votes to Senator William Smith.

GENERAL ELECTION

Popular Vote

Van Buren 764,176
Harrison. 550,816
White. 146,107
Webster 41,201
Others 1,234

Electoral Vote
PRESIDENT:
   Van Buren — 170 (15 states)
   Harrison — 73 (7 states)
   White — 26 (2 states)
   Webster — 14 (1 state)
   Willie P. Mangum — 11 (1 state)
VICE PRESIDENT:
   Johnson — 147
   Granger — 77
   Tyler — 47
   William Smith — 23

As no vice presidential candidate received

a majority, the senate elected Johnson by 33 votes to Granger's 16.

Winners

Martin Van Buren, 8th president

Richard M. Johnson, 9th vice president

Losers

William Henry Harrison, Hugh White, John McClean, Daniel Webster, John Tyler, Francis Granger, Philip P. Barbour, William Smith

---

*1836 presidential nominee—
Whig Party*

William Henry Harrison

No biographical sketch of Harrison is included because he served as president from March 4 to April 4, 1841 (9th president).

State represented: Ohio.

Birth: February 9, 1773.

Age on Inauguration Day (March 4, 1837): 64 years, 1 month.

Death: April 4, 1841.

---

*1836 vice presidential nominee—
Whig Party*

John Tyler

No biographical sketch of Tyler is included because he served as vice president from March 4 to April 4, 1845 (10th vice president), and as president from April 4, 1841, until March 4, 1845 (10th president).

State represented: Virginia.

Birth: March 29, 1790.

Age on Inauguration Day (March 4, 1837): 46 years, 11 months.

Death: January 18, 1862.

---

*1836 presidential nominee—
Whig Party*

Hugh White

Full name: Hugh Lawson White.

State represented: Tennessee.

Birth: October 30, 1773, Iredell County, North Carolina.

Age on Inauguration Day (March 4, 1837): 63 years, 4 months.

Education: Instructed at home, then received tutoring from Presbyterian minister at age 15, the Reverend Samuel Carrick, who would become his father-in-law, 1788–1791; studied law in office of Archibald Roane, later governor of Tennessee; then studied for two years in Pennsylvania, including a year in Lancaster in office of James Hopkins, attorney, 1794–1796.

Religion: Presbyterian.

Ancestry/prominent relatives: Scotch and Irish background; earliest White in America arrived from North Ireland in 1726; John Williams (brother-in-law), U.S. senator from Tennessee.

Occupation: Attorney.

Public Offices: Judge of Tennessee Superior Court for Law and Equity, 1801–1807, resigned; state senator, 1807–1809, declined reelection; appointed U.S. district attorney for East Tennessee, 1808–1809; Tennessee Supreme Court, 1809–April 1815, declined subsequent appointments in 1822 and 1824; state senate, 1817–1825; commissioner for Spanish land claims, 1821–1824; U.S. senator, October 28, 1825–January 13, 1840, resigned; elected president pro tempore of Senate, December 3, 1832; declined appointment as secretary of war, 1831; unsuccessful Whig candidate for president, 1836.

Death: April 10, 1840, on farm outside Knoxville at age 66 years, 5½ months.

Burial: First Presbyterian Church Cemetery, Knoxville, Tennessee.

Home: "Freeland," outside Knoxville.

Personal characteristics: 5'11" tall, very slender. Blue eyes, deeply set; full gray hair, curling down over his shoulders; habitual sad facial expression.

JOHN TYLER
(From the author's collection)

Father: James White (1747–August 14, 1821); state legislator in North Carolina and Tennessee; public office holder.

Mother: Mary Lawson (1742–March 10, 1819), married April 14, 1770; daughter of Hugh Lawson.

Siblings: Margaret (April 8, 1771–August 27, 1827), married Charles McClung. Moses (April 22, 1775–?), married Isabella McNutt. Andrew (May 9, 1779–October 6, 1806). Mary McConnel (November 11, 1782–?), married Dr. F. May, who died November 26, 1817, and then Judge John Overton. Cynthia Berry (April 7, 1786–August 11, 1855), married General Thomas Adams Smith on September 17, 1807. Melinda (February 15, 1789–March 2, 1838), married Col. John Williams, U.S. Senator and diplomat.

First wife: Elizabeth Moore Carrick (1783–March 25, 1831), married December 13, 1798; daughter of the Reverend Samuel Carrick.

Children: (The Whites had 12 children; all but two died before their father, most from tuberculosis.) A son and a daughter died in infancy. Carrick (1799–1826), a lawyer. Betsey (?–July 1828), married Newton Scott. James (?–November 1828), an attorney. Mary L. (?–1828), married a Mr. Swan. Lucinda (?–March 20, 1827). Margaret W. (?–September 1831), married Ebenezer Alexander in 1829. Cynthia (1812–January 1829). Melinda (?–April 20, 1830). Isabella Harvey (February 9, 1820–July 13, 1872). Samuel Davies Carrick (May 26, 1825–March 9, 1860/61?), never married.

Second wife: Mrs. Ann E. Peyton (?–April 1847), married on November 30, 1832.

For almost 30 years Andrew Jackson and Hugh L. White were close political allies and friends. Tennessee's two most eminent men were thorough Democrats, fellow judges, similar in appearance, with one succeeding the other in the same United States Senate seat. They shared another characteristic, and that was sensitivity to any perceived slight. White's feeling that President Jackson had not properly rewarded his loyalty and friendship, coupled with Jackson's growing resentment that White occasionally opposed him on some issues, made them caustic enemies at the end of their careers.

Hugh White's father, James White, had received land from the government as a result of his service during the American Revolution. Selling this land, White used the proceeds to purchase a large tract near the center of what later became Knoxville, Tennessee. The elder White moved his large family there when Hugh was 12 years old. It was dangerous territory, with Indians and whites trading atroci-

HUGH WHITE
(From the Senate Historical Office)

ties. Beginning in 1785, James White was involved in the State of Franklin, attending the constitutional convention for that short-lived effort to create a new state out of present-day eastern Tennessee. The senior White was also closely allied with speculator and politician William Blount, who from 1790 until 1796 was governor of the territory that became Tennessee. When Hugh was 20 he became Blount's private secretary. From Blount, Hugh acquired a considerable knowledge and interest in politics as well as in Indians, since

Blount also served as local commissioner of Indian affairs.

Hugh's educational preparation was meager. The family fortune was inconsiderable, and instruction at home under his mother's tutelage was all that was available on the frontier until, at the age of 15, Hugh began a three-year period of studies with a Presbyterian minister. That minister would later become his father-in-law. Other instruction came from a local attorney, followed by training in mathematics and perhaps other subjects in Philadelphia. This disorganized education was culminated by a year with a Lancaster, Pennsylvania, attorney, James Hopkins. White returned to Knoxville in 1796.

Interspersed with this helter-skelter education were many adventures on the frontier. As Blount's secretary, White became involved in the defense of Knoxville against Indian attack in 1793. After the Indian raid, White volunteered for the retribution. At the Battle of Etowah, White apparently was the one who killed the Indian chief, King Fisher, and ended the battle by that achievement. As significant as prowess and bravery in battle was to a political career in this raw western territory, it is remarkable that White refused to have the deed publicized. His granddaughter and biographer, Nancy Scott, stated that her ancestor was so horrified by the killing that he could not bear to have the fact mentioned. He allegedly also pleaded with a historian to leave the matter out of his book on Tennessee, to no avail. Regardless, White had a dramatic and effective event to use politically, but always refused to do so.

Politics was still in the distant future when White first made contact with his almost life-long friend, Andrew Jackson. Jackson had been recently elected a Tennessee congressman. White received help from him in pressing a claim for compensation to cover the expenses of the Etowah expedition. Jackson achieved payment not just for White but for all the soldiers.

White opened his law practice in Knoxville in 1796 upon his return from studying with the Philadelphia attorney James Hopkins. His practice developed apace, and soon White was recognized as a leading attorney in the community. The legislature selected the 28-year-old as a judge for one of the highest courts in the state, the Superior Court for Law and Equity. Also serving on that court for a short time was Andrew Jackson. Jackson served from 1798 until 1804, while White's tenure was from 1801 until 1807. The acquaintance developed into a mutual respect and a good friendship during these years.

The court system was in serious need of being revamped; no Supreme Court existed to rectify inconsistencies caused by the various superior courts. Perhaps in part because he wanted personally to be involved in correcting this and other judicial deficiencies, White resigned from the superior court in 1807 and ran for the state senate. White won, served one term, then did not stand for reelection; the court reforms were just about completed and he may have wanted to be completely "available" for appointment to one of the new posts. In 1809 White was appointed to one of the new Supreme Court seats and served until 1815.

Since Judge White's court duties were not burdensome and the remuneration was not generous, he remained in private practice in addition to being a judge. He also served as president of the Bank of Tennessee, headquartered in Knoxville. The year after his appointment was consumed with work starting up the bank. Economic times were severe, and it was difficult to keep the bank's doors open. Conservative management, which limited bad loans during rampant speculation in public lands, helped save the institution from the insolvency that afflicted many of its sister banks. White refused any salary during the whole period he was bank president. The institution finally closed in 1827, shortly after White resigned as president.

Banks were under attack from many quarters in the middle of the second decade of the nineteenth century, as they would be again during many critical economic periods. As a result, White decided to return to the legislature in 1815 to work for protective legislation. Elected by more than a three-to-one margin, White bided his time during the early part of the session. He tended to other proposals, including a bill prohibiting dueling. White had always found the "Code of Honor" to be completely dishonorable and barbaric. White drew up a bill taxing any out-of-state bank $50,000 per year. That effectively kept a federal bank out of the state. White wanted his and other state banks protected. Authorization to establish state banks in several Tennessee cities was also passed. Bank president White hoped that some of these cities would be able to establish branches of his bank. It is unlikely that he was defeated in 1819 for reelection, though there is some evidence he announced as a candidate. Nonetheless, he did not serve another term in the state senate.

The next public service to call White away from his banking and legal responsibilities was on a commission to resolve claims against Spain. A treaty had been entered with that country in 1819 that resulted in the cession of Spanish Florida to the United States. For three years White and two other commissioners labored with the almost two thousand claims that ultimately were filed, deciding which were meritorious and for what amount.

Though White refused election by the state legislature to the Tennessee Supreme Court in 1824, arguing bad health and press of business affairs, no such excuse was used the next year when he was named to the United States Senate. Andrew Jackson had resigned his seat in order better to prepare for another run for the presidency. White had supported Jackson during Old Hickory's unsuccessful 1824 campaign for president, but had some reservations about the race. A complication for White was that his brother-in-law, Tennessee Senator John Williams, was working against Jackson. A family split resulted that was never healed.

White soon established himself as a Jackson stalwart. President Adams' request to send delegates to a Panama Congress called by Simón Bolívar was condemned in the senator's maiden speech. One of the problems White foresaw was that the Panama Congress was to consider abolition of the slave trade, which he as the owner of 24 slaves could not endorse. White opposed Secretary of State Clay's long-held plans for internal improvements financed out of the federal treasury. He also fought the high protective tariff, the so-called "Tariff of Abominations" that would lead to the nullification crisis in 1832. On all issues, White was in the states' rights and strict constructionist camp.

Though gaining influence in the Senate, White was being continually rocked by tragedies at home of so serious a nature as to cause him to consider dropping out of politics. In 1826 his 27-year-old son died of tuberculosis, the same disease that made White's health precarious throughout his adult life. A year later both a daughter and daughter-in-law died of the same consumptive malady; in

a few weeks, another daughter died. In November of 1828 a son died, in January 1829 a daughter, and in April still another daughter. In all, in a six-year period closed by his wife's death from tuberculosis in 1831, ten children died, most from tuberculosis. In one nine-month period he buried four of his children. A contributing cause was that apparently White distrusted doctors and never called for help.

In the midst of these tragedies, White was attempting to help his old comrade Andrew Jackson be elected president on the second try. When the general won, White remained a confidant. Jackson told White that he could be secretary of war if he wanted the post, but if not to try to convince John Eaton, another Jackson partisan from Tennessee, to take the post. Eaton apparently wanted it sufficiently to try the ploy of writing White, telling him that the offer by the president was really to both of them, and that Jackson wanted White and Eaton to decide together which would take the appointment. Eaton professed a longing for the job, but he would defer to White if the senator wished it. Under the circumstances, White felt compelled to remove himself as a roadblock to Eaton. Other versions of the story insist that Jackson was part of the scheme and never intended to name White; still another is that White did not want the war department position, but instead desired to be secretary of state or of the treasury. Regardless, Eaton was in the cabinet and White's feelings were ruffled.

White did not approve of Jackson's cabinet, perhaps revealing his pique and estrangement. He wrote one friend that selfish and narrow-minded men were misleading Jackson. Nonetheless, in what became a litmus test for loyalty to the president, White passed easily. Doubts about the moral rectitude of John Eaton's wife, Peggy, caused a scandal in Washington. The wives of many prominent politicians, including some in the cabinet, refused to have their soirées and other social occasions spoiled by her presence. The ostracism of Peggy Eaton struck Jackson as a personal insult. It was a reminder of the comments about his own, now deceased wife, that had frequently been made behind his back. Part of the pressure was lessened on White since his ill wife was back in Tennessee. The senator made several public displays of gallantry toward the lady whose character, allegedly, was not that of a lady.

John C. Calhoun, the vice president, was one of those politicians whose wife was not back home. The vice president became Jackson's enemy and no longer his potential successor as a result. The maneuvering that Jackson began to put Martin Van Buren in line for the succession irritated Senator White. Eaton was forced by the whole episode to resign in 1831 from the war department. The president offered the post to White, but he declined, saying ill health, as well as multiple tragedies in his family made him unfit for the position. Constant attendance in Washington, required of a cabinet official but not of a senator, was incompatible with his domestic situation. The president tried again; the answer was no different. Though health and family disasters were certainly important, White apparently also refused the offer because he was displeased with the Van Buren machinations, undertaken by the president, and wanted no official role in that unsavory matter. This marked the start of serious differences between White and Jackson. Not surprisingly, the twin rejections by White made Jackson feel no special continuing desire to keep White as a confidant. White took the lack of contact with the president as a lack of appreciation. The senator became sensitive to any slight that seemed to emanate directly or indirectly from the White House. An additional irritant was what White took to be a refusal by the Jackson-controlled Washington paper to give him proper credit for the support he had given to the administration.

That some credit was due is clear. On Indian problems in the southeast, White approved of Jackson's policy of forced removal from Georgia that the Supreme Court had declared illegal. However, White felt compassion for the Indians and supported the policy more as an inevitability than out of other motives. From 1829 until 1836 White was chairman of the Senate Committee on Indian Affairs and generally tried to ensure that monetary obligations under treaties with the Indians were upheld, that fair treatment by the white man towards the red was maintained. White voted with the administration against recharter of the Second Bank of the United States.

The issue of the bank, in which Jackson could generally depend on White for support, was also an issue in which petty semantic differences further separated the two men. Jackson withdrew all federal deposits from the bank, causing a tremendous outcry. The senate followed this September 1833 presidential order with a resolution censuring him for the action. Thereafter, the Jacksonians fought to have that censure expunged from the Senate journal, an attempt White found to be dishonorable. It denied the occurrence of something that everyone knew happened. Thus White consistently voted against expunging. Jackson never understood.

Southern Democrats were in revolt over the imposed succession to the presidency of New Yorker Martin Van Buren. White became the favorite alternative to Van Buren among his party. In 1833 the Tennessee legislature almost nominated White for president to succeed Jackson in 1836, but White heard of the move and blocked it. The pressure for White continued, and Jackson told him that if he accepted a nomination that would place him in Van Buren's path to the White House, Jackson would make the Senator's name "odious" throughout Tennessee. Such words would have offended a far less sensitive man than White, and the break now was probably irreparable. In December 1834 the Tennessee Congressional delegation nominated White for the presidency. White answered the call by saying that even though he did not seek the position, it was any citizen's duty to accept an office thrust upon him by the people. The following February the administration struck back when it ignored White in the naming of a federal district attorney in Tennessee. The dispute was becoming increasingly public.

John Bell, himself defeated for president (election of 1860), became the most significant Tennessee Democrat to aid White's cause. Four powerful politicians from the same state were now drawing up battle lines, White and Bell on one side, and Jackson and speaker of the House (and future president) James K. Polk on the other.

White was up for reelection in 1835, and Jackson through Polk made every effort to defeat him. Instead, the legislature slapped the president with not only White's unanimous Senate victory, but it also nominated him for president. The Tennessee insurgents' success against Jackson ended in December 1835, when Bell lost a fairly close race for speaker against Polk. This signaled that the Democrats were lining up behind Jackson rather than against him. White's support began to fade. Many thought he might withdraw. Instead, he became the accepted candidate in the South for the opposition while other candidates were pushed by that party in the rest of the country. In all, ten states listed White on the electoral ballot, nine as a Whig and in one, Tennessee, as a Democrat. He swept his home state in the 1836 general election, and also won Georgia.

The public bickering between Jackson and White continued, and in 1839 the old general found the method for revenge. The recently elected, heavily Democratic legislature instructed White and the Whig senator that they had to vote for the Van Buren subtreasury bill. White believed in the right of the legislature, which selected him, to tell him how to vote. As a few other senators before him had done, White resigned rather than submit, just as Jackson had hoped. The public outcry was nationwide, and White was perceived as a martyr. Though never officially changing parties, White backed the Whigs in 1840. Henry Clay even approached White in advance of the Whig Presidential Convention to see if he would run, and if not whether the old senator would support Clay. White dismissed any personal interest in the position, and stated Clay was his choice for president. He was a Whig elector for Tennessee in 1840.

Resignation came when White's health was dreadful. Tuberculosis was completing its decade-long assault on his lungs. Bitter, sick, almost alone, White died three months after resigning from the Senate.

Analysis of Qualifications

A White presidency would not have been spectacular. Never bold or dramatic, Hugh L. White was a dignified, mild-mannered man. Ambition was hardly foreign, but respectability and decorum came first. Not unusual for his day was a coyness about running for office, and White had that characteristic to a pronounced degree. Yet White wanted recognition and influence as much as any politician and was willing to go to the political battlefront to achieve it. It is a delicate balance of personality traits that marks this solid, poorly remembered public servant.

No charge of dishonesty was ever seriously made against White, even in the vitriolic political age in which he did battle. A gentleman throughout, he was serious-minded with little sense of humor. His stern countenance was almost never broken by a smile. But he was an amiable man when the business before him could be set aside for the day, and had a humanitarian side demonstrated by his concern for the Indians. Though gentleness was a virtue frequently attributed to him, White was also stubborn and self-confident. Slow to make up his mind, with a good lawyer's requirement that he receive as much information as possible on an issue before reaching a well-considered conclusion, he was thereafter almost impossible to dislodge from his course. There was also nothing of the public orator in him. His speeches were dry, colorless, lacking in energy or excitement. His age was one of great orators, Clay, Webster, Calhoun, and many others, and among then White always failed to shine.

His political problems came from none of his just-mentioned virtues or failings, but rather from his independence. A rigidly consistent man on issues, there was nothing pliable or compromising in his nature. White was counted among the Jacksonians. Yet he outraged Old Hickory when he stood his ground, pleading that any other course would be morally dishonest, and voted against a resolution to expunge an earlier entered censure against Jackson. White himself described the situation: "For many years I have been on the most intimate and confidential terms with the chief magistrate. We have conversed with, and written to each other, perhaps with as much freedom as if we had been brothers." When

White did not get the cabinet post he wanted in 1829, his resentment began to affect the relationship. As sensitive as White was, Jackson returned the characteristic in equal measure. Jackson's pushing Van Buren toward the presidency offended and embittered White, in part out of jealousy, in part out of Jackson's unseemly dictation of the succession. White in time would call his old friend a despot, and harsh words would destroy any hope of a reconciliation. Jackson, for his part, could not brook any opposition — to oppose him was to make the president an enemy. Many old Jackson friends could, by the end of his two terms, be counted in that group.

White's virtues were many — honesty, intelligence, usually calm personality that was free from vindictiveness and spite. By experience and achievement, by intellect and honesty, Hugh White merited his chance at the presidency. His health was collapsing and he died before the end of the term to which he sought election. Ironically, his running mate had been John Tyler. Tyler was elected vice president four years later on his second try for the office. His second running mate also died, this time only one month into his presidency.

WHITE BIBLIOGRAPHY

Amburn, Floyd H. "The Political Career of Hugh Lawson White." Unpublished master's thesis, University of Tennessee (1933).

Bartus, Sister M.R. "The Presidential Election of 1836." Unpublished doctoral dissertation, Fordham University (1967).

Caldwell, Joshua William. *Sketches of the Bench and Bar of Tennessee*. Knoxville, Tenn. (1898), pp. 109–135.

Crook, Virginia, et al. *The Descendants of James Crook and Related Families 1746–1978*. Austin, Tex. (1978).

Foote, Henry S. *The Bench and Bar of the South and Southwest*. St. Louis (1876), pp. 116–125.

Gresham, L. Paul. "Hugh Lawson White as a Tennessee Politician and Banker, 1807–1827." *East Tennessee Historical Society Publication* 18 (1946), pp. 25–46.

_____. "Hugh Lawson White, Frontiersman, Lawyer, and Judge." *East Tennessee Historical Society Publication* 19 (1946), pp. 3–24.

_____. "The Public Career of Hugh Lawson White." Unpublished doctoral dissertation, Vanderbilt University (1943).

_____. "The Public Career of Hugh Lawson White." *Tennessee Historical Quarterly* III (1944), pp. 291–318.

Maury, Abram P. *Address of the Honorable Abram P. Maury on the Life and Character of Hugh Lawson White*. Franklin, Tenn. (1840).

Scott, Nancy N. *A Memoir of Hugh Lawson White, with Selections from His Speeches and Correspondence*. Philadelphia (1856).

Williams, Samuel C. *History of the Lost State of Franklin*. New York City (1932).

---

*1836 presidential nominee —
Whig Party*

Daniel Webster

Full name: Daniel Webster.

State represented: Massachusetts.

Birth: January 18, 1782, Salisbury, New Hampshire.

Age on Inauguration Day (March 4, 1837): 55 years, 1½ months.

Education: Learned to read in local rural schools, then largely taught himself; at 13 went to Phillips Academy at Exeter, New Hampshire, 1795–1797; Dartmouth College, graduated, 1801; "read law" in office of Thomas Thompson, in Salisbury, New Hampshire, and then in Boston office of Christopher Gore; admitted to bar in 1805.

Religion: Presbyterian.

Ancestry: First Webster arrived in America in 1635 from England.

Occupation: Attorney.

Public Offices: U.S. representative from New Hampshire, March 4, 1813–March 3, 1817, defeated; delegate to Massachusetts Constitutional Convention, 1820; Massachusetts House of Representatives, 1822; U.S. representative, March 4, 1823–May 30, 1827, resigned; U.S. senator, May 30, 1827–February 22, 1841, resigned; defeated for president, 1836; U.S. secretary of state, March 5, 1841–May 9, 1843, resigned; U.S. senator, March 4, 1845–July 22, 1850, resigned; secretary of state, July 22, 1850, until his death October 24, 1852.

Death: Died October 24, 1852, in Marshfield, Massachusetts.

Burial: Winslow Cemetery, Marshfield, Massachusetts.

Home: "Marshfield," a 1,400-acre farm near Boston.

Personal characteristics: Average height, massive chest, huge head considerably out of proportion to body; heavy, dark eyebrows and sunken eyes; skin was a dark pallor, making him appear to some to be Indian; called "Black Dan," initially at least because of dark skin.

Father: Ebenezer Webster (April 22, 1739–April 22, 1806.

Father's first wife: Mehitable Smith (?–March 28, 1774); married January 18, 1761.

Half brothers/sisters: Olle, or Ollivia (January 28, 1762–died in infancy). Ebenezer (July 16, 1764–died in same epidemic as older sister, as infant). Susanna (October 25, 1766–March 23, 1804), married John Colby. David (May 1, 1769–?), married Rebecca Huntoon, and was a farmer. Joseph (March 25, 1772–January 20, 1810), unmarried.

Mother: Abigail Eastman (July 19, 1737–April 25, 1816), married October 13, 1774; daughter of Major Roger and Gerusha (Fitz) Eastman.

Siblings: Mehitable (September 21, 1775–July 14, 1814), never married. Abigail (February 8, 1778–December 13, 1805), married William Haddock. Ezekial (March 11, 1780–April 10, 1829), married (1) Alice Bridges, and (2) Achsa (?) Pollard. Sarah (May 13, 1784–March 19, 1811), married a cousin, Ebenezer Webster on August 21, 1808.

First wife: Grace Fletcher (1781–January 21, 1828), married May 29, 1808; daughter of Rev. Elijah Fletcher.

Children: Grace (April 29, 1810–January 24, 1817). Daniel Fletcher (July 23, 1813–August 30, 1862), on November 27, 1836, married Caroline Story White, a niece of Supreme Court Justice Story; died at Second Battle of Bull Run. Julia (January 16, 1818–April 28, 1848), married Samuel Appleton on September 24, 1839. Edward (July 20, 1820–January 23, 1848), died of typhoid. Charles (December 31, 1822–December 18, 1824).

Second wife: Caroline LeRoy (September 28, 1797–February 26, 1882), married on December 12, 1829; daughter of wealthy New York businessman Herman LeRoy and Hannah Cornell LeRoy.

Historic sites/memorials: Statue at Scott Circle, Washington, D.C., where Massachusetts Avenue and Rhode Island Avenue meet. His statue is also in Statuary Hall, one of New Hampshire's two statues. The Webster family house, "The Elms," is located in West Franklin, New Hampshire.

Movie: *The Devil and Daniel Webster* (1941), with Edward Arnold as Webster.

Young Daniel Webster found no exuberance in work on the family's small New Hampshire farm. Instead, he was the one scholar among ten children in the family. He entertained and impressed with his precocious memory, his reading ability, and his talent at reciting scripture. An admiring lawyer helped pay his way to Phillips Academy at Exeter, New Hampshire. Among these strangers he was shy and withdrawn, but excelled in the classroom. After two years at Exeter, 15-year-old Daniel began teaching at a country school. A neighboring minister became interested in Daniel's abilities, and helped send him to Dartmouth College. His work there was mediocre, other than excellence in public speaking. Daniel unenthusiastically decided upon a legal career. He read law in Boston in the office of a prominent attorney, Christopher Gore, who became his friend as well as instructor. Daniel's parents' financial and physical needs caused him to open an office near them in Boscawen, New Hampshire, but after his father's death Daniel moved to Portsmouth. His fellow attorneys marked him as an outstanding talent, one attorney saying the secret to Daniel's success was that he was a born actor.

From the first, Webster's allegiances were with the merchants and businessmen whom he met in his legal practice. During the 1807 embargo imposed by President Jefferson, Webster was an outspoken critic because New England merchants were adversely affected. On July 4, 1812, Webster spoke before a group of New England Federalists and bitterly attacked what he called the "administration's war" against England. He warned that the South and President Madison might drive New England into secession should they continue

DANIEL WEBSTER
(From the Senate Historical Office)

the conflict. The response to Webster's Fourth of July denunciation of the war was electric. He was nominated and easily elected to the United States House of Representatives in 1812. The new congressman introduced countless resolutions to embarrass President Madison. He called for an explanation of the war and alleged that Madison had been tricked into it by Napoléon, the French leader who was seeking thereby to relieve English military pressure on France. Fortunately, Webster did not join the ill-starred Hartford Convention.

That meeting of disgruntled Federalists resulted in a demand for constitutional reforms that would give New England greater influence as the price for remaining in the Union. Webster thought that such a meeting was bad politics, even if he perhaps agreed with the sentiments expressed there. The successful conclusion of the war made the Federalists appear to be weak-kneed secessionists. Political charges would later swirl around Webster, which he strenuously denied, that he had given support to the Hartford Convention.

Webster fought against the military draft during the war. Conscription, Webster argued, was unconstitutional and constituted murder of any citizen forced to serve and who was subsequently killed in action. Webster therefore pronounced that states were permitted to interpose themselves between national government and the citizens and prevent the draft in that state. This was an ironic forerunner of John C. Calhoun's nullification argument of 20 years later. Webster was almost gleeful over the problems the American war effort encountered. He forecast the demise of Madison's party because of constant battlefield defeats. General Andrew Jackson's stunning victory at New Orleans in December 1814, which was soon followed by news of a satisfactory peace treaty entered at Ghent, dispelled the gloom and seemed to make mockery of the criticisms against the war he and other Federalists had made. Webster's reward for three years of opposition to the war was defeat by the voters in 1816 when he sought a third term.

After the defeat Webster moved to Boston. Portsmouth had suffered seriously from the embargo; Webster's legal practice correspondingly had dwindled. His home had been destroyed by fire and he was without insurance to rebuild it. Boston was clearly to be the center of New England commercial life, and a good lawyer's practice there could be most lucrative. Webster proved that in his case, and was soon earning the fortune of $20,000 per year. When in 1823 he was elected to Congress from Boston, he continued to take and even solicit legal business, particularly for hearings before the United States Supreme Court. During the 1820s, Webster was perhaps the most highly remunerated attorney in

the country. His clients were shipowners, insurance companies, large commercial enterprises, and the other representatives of "big business." His deserved reputation as an attorney focused on his outstanding speaking ability, composed of seemingly inescapable logic and the ability to express that logic in dramatic ways. Former president John Adams heard him once and said he was "the most consummate orator of modern times." Webster was a lead attorney in several watershed opinions by the United States Supreme Court. In each case Webster defended corporations and other large institutions. He had a willing ally in another old Federalist, John Marshall, who was chief justice of the United States Supreme Court for 35 years. His success ratio before the court dropped considerably after Marshall was replaced by a Jacksonian chief justice, Roger B. Taney in 1835.

Webster's first wife, Grace Fletcher, was plain in appearance, shy, but affectionate and considerate. She was the morally upright daughter of a preacher, and was a one-time schoolteacher. Webster's frequent and extended absences at Washington made her melancholy; her letters to Webster were filled with loneliness and feelings of inadequacy. Yet she apparently was a strong, needed restraint on Webster's more profligate habits. Throughout his career Webster was charged with being morally deficient, with rumors about excessive drinking and philandering. The truth of any of those charges is difficult to determine, but it does seem without question that Webster was a heavy drinker in an age where men were expected to drink. It also appears he held his liquor as well as most.

Grace Webster died in 1828. Webster married at the end of the next year the daughter of a wealthy New York businessman. Caroline LeRoy had none of the social fears that seemed to plague his first wife. Unfortunately the needed brake on Webster's habits was now missing. There is a tradition in the Van Rensselaer family of New York, which was then one of the wealthiest families in the state, that without ever meeting Catherine Van Rensselaer, Webster, a few months after his first wife died, asked her father for permission to marry her. For whatever reason, the match was not made. Though perhaps Webster approached the idea of a second marriage for political reasons, neither Daniel nor Caroline ever seemed to regret their wedding.

One profligate habit that no spouse was able to control was Webster's constant demand for money from all of his relatives and acquaintances. He seemed a compulsive spender who made and then frittered away fortunes. On several occasions large sums were raised from political supporters as the price to keep Webster in politics. Loans made by friends were legion, and in time most all creditors realized that a loan to Webster would never be repaid. In a political era in which conflicts of interest were much less recognized as a problem, Webster was so heavily indebted to so many wealthy businessmen that political opponents and even supporters questioned his objectivity.

That Daniel Webster was no ordinary man, either in talents or excesses, was apparent to all. He was drafted to run for a U.S. House seat from Boston in 1822, and won. In Congress slavery was one issue Webster sidestepped at first. Though repulsed by slavery, he did not wish to drive the wedge between the North and South any deeper by emphasizing the slavery question. Yet, Webster's oratorical abilities could not forever be restrained on the question. Southern rebelliousness over the high protective tariff led to the nullification crisis in the early 1830s. The famous debate with South Carolina Senator Robert Y. Hayne set out brilliantly each side's arguments in the bout between national power and states' rights. Webster's reply to Hayne in his January 1830 speech was that the Constitution was made by the entire people in the country, and could only be broken by them. No single section could argue, as Webster himself had argued during the controversy concerning the War of 1812, that it could ignore unpopular laws or secede from the nation. His concluding remarks have probably been repeated in every American history text covering this period: "Liberty and union, now and forever, one and inseparable." His speech was an overnight success. Thousands of copies were distributed nationwide. Webster gained tremendous national prestige, even being acclaimed in the South where fire-eating secessionists were still significantly in the minority.

Class war was developing in the country alongside the sectional North and South conflict. Nullification had put Webster and Jackson on the same side of a great national issue, while controversy over whether to recharter the Second Bank of the United States made them bitter opponents. Andrew Jackson partisans attacked big business and the creation of a national bank, while men of Webster's stripe were repelled by Jackson's attempt to pit the poor against the business classes. Webster's reputation as a unionist, which gained him high acclaim, was tainted by this equally widespread reputation as a defender of the monied interests. It was that reputation that made his election to the presidency an impossible dream, though he would never admit it.

Webster had begun preparing for the 1836 presidential election by solidifying his Massachusetts base. He achieved that when the Whig members in the legislature nominated him unanimously on January 21, 1835. Still, Whigs in the East and Northeast could not unite on a candidate. Webster also attempted to curry favor with the anti–Masons, seeing them as a growing and influential force. When he failed in December 1835 to get the nomination from the Pennsylvania convention of anti–Masons for president, it was clear that Webster's presidential hopes were dashed.

Since the Whigs and other anti–Jackson groups could not unite on any candidate, regional nominees appeared. Webster became the Northeastern candidate for the Whigs. They hoped so to split the vote as to deny the Jacksonian nominee, Martin Van Buren, from gaining a majority, thereby throwing the election into the House of Representatives. This scheme almost prevailed, as a shift of 2,000 votes in Pennsylvania would have deadlocked the election. Instead, Van Buren won the presidency, while Webster trailed badly in fourth place.

Webster began to plan for 1840 almost immediately. He proposed to leave the Senate in 1838, and to keep his name before the public by traveling the country giving frequent speeches. In 1837 he took an extended tour in the West to drum up support. Henry Clay was perceived as his chief rival for the Whig nomination, but in time Webster also recognized the problem posed by William Henry Harrison. In June 1838, Clay asked Webster to drop out of the race, but Webster refused. Many friends also encouraged him to quit. Webster realized the futility by the time he left for England in May 1839, to take a long-planned vacation. Webster could never escape the onus of being big business's candidate. In England he was treated as royalty. Perhaps this softened the chagrin he felt when upon his return in December he faced the inevitable and endorsed William Henry Harrison for the nomination.

Harrison's election placed Webster and Clay, and not the new president, at the head of the Whig party. Clay hoped to dominate the government by his power in the U.S. Senate, while Webster hoped to control by being named secretary of state. Webster saw the cabinet post as his first opportunity to wield real power. For almost 30 years, first as a Federalist, then as a National Republican and supporter of John Quincy Adams, and finally as a Whig who lost most of his battles to Andrew Jackson, Webster had known fame but not power. He was loath to relinquish that power after John Tyler succeeded to the presidency upon Harrison's death in April 1841. Tyler's Whig principles are summarized best by saying he was a nationalist and an opponent of Jackson. Beyond these points, the new president was a Southern Democrat. Tyler refused to go along with the northern branch of the Whig party in rechartering the Bank of the United States. His veto in September 1841, of the Bank recharter bill caused all of his cabinet to resign, except for Webster. The secretary of state explained that he felt he could continue to be useful. An equally significant if private reason was that he did not want to throw himself in with Henry Clay, whose efforts on behalf of the rechartering had been thwarted by Tyler. Webster became estranged from the rest of the Whig party because of his refusal to resign. In time he felt he and Tyler could create a new third party, but each man wanted to head it. Webster also felt he was performing valuable service as secretary of state. Webster's real hope was that he could get an appointment as minister to Great Britain, but the incumbent ambassador would not quit. He sought other posts as well. Finally, in May 1843, he resigned over the question of admitting Texas to the Union.

Webster made a slow march back to the Whig Party. He no longer believed that he could gain the presidency independently of the Whigs. Webster even hinted that he could support his old adversary Clay for president in 1844, and secretly pursued the vice presidential nomination with Clay. In the spring of 1844, Webster announced his complete opposition to the extension of slavery that would result from making Texas a state. Clay was nominated in May, but passed over Webster as his running mate. In January of 1845, Webster was narrowly elected to the U.S. Senate as a Whig. Within a short period it became public that he had run only after being promised a $100,000 fund by wealthy supporters, from which he could draw to pay debts and collect expenses. The fund actually only reached $37,000, and it established an annuity at a life insurance company for him, financed by 40 Boston supporters. Malfeasance as secretary of state was also charged, when it was pointed out that he had used public money to buy newspaper support for the treaty he negotiated settling the Maine-Canada boundary dispute.

His department's accounts finally were balanced when he paid $1,000 of his own money to offset a shortage there. The Congressional committee investigation found him not guilty of malfeasance, but discovered several indiscretions on his part. Daniel Webster's image as an orator and defender of the Union, coupled with his dominating physical presence, earned him the name, the "god-like Daniel." This public image of statesmanship was seriously darkened throughout his career by revelations such as these that there was another, meaner side to the picture. His boyhood nickname of "Black Dan," gained from his dark appearance, received added meaning because of his blindness in the area of personal finances. It is hard for many people to understand how the debtor of so many wealthy businessmen could be a servant of the people.

The constant pursuit of money helped finance two large farms. In 1832, he purchased a 160-acre farm near Boston called Marshfield, which would increase to 1,400 acres before he died. He also developed his family farm in New Hampshire to be a showplace. The contrast between statesman and farmer was stark. On the Senate floor he would be clothed in a costume of a Revolutionary soldier, wearing a dark blue coat with shiny brass buttons, and a brown vest. On the farm he would dress in hunting clothes or humbler attire, and would spend countless hours looking after his exotic and expensive livestock. The farm may have been a catharsis from the intense Washington atmosphere. He needed its calming influence throughout the latter part of the 1840s because of serious financial troubles, but even more poignantly because of the death of two children in 1848.

Texas was admitted in 1846 over Webster's objections. War with Mexico erupted accordingly. Webster favored a resolution that no new territory would be added as a result of the war, hoping thereby to prevent the inevitable furor that would result over the extension of slavery into such territories. The final, painful blow from the war for Webster was the death of his own son in battle.

In September 1847, the Massachusetts Whig state convention endorsed Webster for president. However, one of the heroes of the Mexican War, Zachary Taylor, seemed the likely Whig candidate. Webster became more interested in defeating Taylor than in winning himself. The 1848 convention in Philadelphia gave Webster scant support, and he finally had to acquiesce in Taylor's nomination.

President Taylor refused to support the Compromise of 1850. This compromise, first developed by Henry Clay, included admission of California — one of the plums of victory in the Mexican War — as a free state, and prohibiting the slave trade in the District of Columbia. The South would gain by having a strengthened fugitive slave law. Taylor's death in July 1850 removed a great roadblock. On March 7, 1850, in a speech that would subsequently be known by its date, Webster called for compromise in the following ringing words:

I wish to speak today not as a Massachusetts man, not as a northern man, but as an American.... I speak today for the preservation of the Union.

The speech of March 7 would antagonize Webster's Northern supporters and would gain precious little immediate support in the South. He stated that slavery in the territories was a false issue, because the climate in what is now the American Southwest was far too severe to permit slavery to flourish. The speech outlined what he saw as the historical reasons for slavery's existence and the North's forbearance of it. Webster's solution was to adopt the Compromise of 1850, and to strengthen and *enforce* the fugitive slave law.

When Millard Fillmore succeeded to the presidency on July 9, 1850, Webster had a good friend in the White House. On July 17, Webster gave his farewell address to the U.S. Senate, because the new president had asked him to be secretary of state. The new secretary was leaving a heated political war behind. Many Southern Unionists and Southern Whigs rallied to his cause after the speech of March 7. Yet Webster was also burned in effigy each time a runaway slave was caught in the North and returned South. The prosecution of anyone who assisted escaped slaves found little support in the North, and Webster's insistence upon such prosecutions made him despised among abolitionists. As secretary of state, Webster thought he might be able to turn America's attention from the internal conflict and focus it on international affairs, but his efforts to support Hungarian independence from Austria proved too meager an answer.

Even though a good friend and appointee of Fillmore, Webster again angled for the presidency in 1852. Webster's hope was that a new party would form composed of men who, like himself, were willing to compromise in order to preserve the Union. The Whig convention that was held saw Webster, Fillmore, and General Winfield Scott as the three contenders. Fillmore and Webster's votes together would have nominated either, but both were obstinate. Finally, enough Fillmore delegates went to Scott to give him the nomination. Webster and the president remained on fairly good terms despite the rivalry for the nomination.

Webster did not live to see the election held, as he died of cirrhosis of the liver on October 24, 1852. His last years had seen an intensifying of his religious fervor, which had always been great. His belief that organized religion was the foundation of a civilized society was unshakable. On October 10 he had dictated an epitaph for his tombstone, which stated in part: "Lord, I believe; help Thou mine unbelief. Philosophical argument ... has sometimes shaken my reason for the faith that is in me; but my heart has assured, and reassured me, that the Gospel of Jesus Christ must be a Divine Reality." On the morning of October 23 he told his doctor that he would die sometime that evening. He died at 2:37 A.M. the following day.

Analysis of Qualifications

Each member of the "Great Triumvirate" of Webster, Clay, and Calhoun spent a political lifetime attempting to gain the presidency. None made it, and Daniel Webster's campaigns were the most quixotic. Calhoun for a time after he became vice president, and Clay in 1824, 1840, and 1844 each had serious prospects for election to the presidency; Webster ran in 1836, 1840, 1844, 1848, and 1852, received a nomination only in 1836 and at no time was near victory.

Webster failed to reach the presidency for several reasons. Though many saw him as a statesman — the "god-like Daniel" — many others saw him as a money-grubbing defender of the privileged class. Webster's public statements included ample ammunition for the charge. To Webster, what helped business helped the country. He alternated between support for and opposition to a protective tariff. He changed positions depending on what his mercantile and manufacturing constituents felt was to their best interests. He loved being with the wealthy. His trip to England in 1839 opened his eyes to opulence that before he could only have imagined, while unseen was the equally pronounced squalor in English slums. The same blindness affected his perception of America. He did not appreciate the suffering of the masses who always found the appeal of an Andrew Jackson far more to their liking than that of Webster.

Webster also failed to gain the prize because he was an aloof, aristocratic figure in public. Certainly Webster was a great man, yet Webster himself was overly conscious of his status. Fellow senators became livid over his treatment of their friends, relatives or constituents when they tried to be introduced to Webster:

> Webster evidently felt such introductions to be an intolerable bore, and seldom took the trouble to conceal his annoyance.... Sometimes he did not even look at the person introduced, but mechanically extended his hand, and permitted the stranger to shake it if he had the courage to do so.

To thousands of voters, as well as hundreds of acquaintances, he would always be the stuffed shirt, the Federalist, the big business spokesman. He would never be president.

Yet what would a President Daniel Webster have been able to accomplish if only he had, by freak fortune, finally been able to reach the White House? The central issue that permeated political debate was slavery and its extension. Webster wanted to form a coalition, especially late in his career, of the property interests in both North and South who had a stake in the continuation of the Union. He disdained the tactics of the extremists of both stripes, abolitionists and secessionists. He abhorred slavery himself, and one of his most famous speeches — the Plymouth Address of 1820 — was filled with passages condemning slavery. Yet later in his life he decided that such oratory on the evils of slavery inflamed passions on all sides and accomplished nothing but greater division.

Webster's genius and greatness was shown in his pre-eminence as an orator. His oratory did not disguise an empty shell behind, as Webster had the intellectual equipment to match. For all his qualities, Webster also had tremendous flaws of ambition, financial profligacy, and gluttony in food and drink. He was a great man with great faults. The faults, however, were more often than not limited to his personal affairs. Though his fortunes, political and financial, were tied directly and constantly to Northern businessmen, he truly did believe that what benefited business and increased industry benefited the country as a whole. He would not have been a perfect president; he may not even have been a successful president, considering the passions and divisions of the time. That he had far greater credentials of intellect and experience than any man elected to the presidency after Andrew Jackson and until Abraham Lincoln seven elections later cannot be denied. In rejecting Webster, just as in refusing Clay's claims, the country chose mediocrity over greatness.

WEBSTER BIBLIOGRAPHY

Bartlett, Irving H. *Daniel Webster*. New York City (1978).

Baxter, Maurice G. *Daniel Webster and the Supreme Court*. Amherst (1966).

Brown, Norman D. *Daniel Webster and the Politics of Availability*. Athens, Ga. (1969).

Current, Richard N. *Daniel Webster and the Rise of a National Conservatism*. Boston (1955, reprinted in 1992).

Curtis, George T. *Life of Daniel Webster*. 2 vols. New York City (1872).

Dalzell, Robert F., Jr. *Daniel Webster and the Trial of American Nationalism 1843–1852*. New York City (1972).

Fuess, Claude M. *Daniel Webster*. 2 vols. Boston (1930).

Lodge, Henry Cabot. *Daniel Webster*. Boston (1883).

McIntyre, James W., ed. *Writings and Speeches of Daniel Webster*. 18 vols., National Edition, Boston (1903).

Nathans, Sydney. "Daniel Webster, Massachusetts Man." *New England Quarterly* 39 (1966), pp. 161–181.

Peterson, Merrill D. *The Great Triumvirate: Webster, Clay, and Calhoun*. New York (1987).

Remini, Robert. *Daniel Webster: A Conservative in a Democratic Age*. New York, 1997.

---

*1836 presidential nominee —
Whig Party*

John McLean

Full name: John McLean.

State represented: Ohio.

Birth: March 11, 1785, on a farm in Morris County, New Jersey.

Age on Inauguration Day (March 4, 1837): 51 years, 11½ months.

Education: Local Warren County, Ohio, school, did not begin until around 1795; then boarded in Cincinnati school of the Reverend Matthew Wallace; attended school of Robert Stubbs; studied law beginning in 1804 under guidance of Cincinnati attorney Arthur St. Clair, Jr.; admitted to bar in 1807.

Religion: Methodist.

Ancestry/prominent relatives: Fergus McLain (father) arrived in America around 1775 from Ireland; William McLean (brother), U.S. Representative.

Occupation: Attorney.

Public offices: Appointed examiner in United States land office in Cincinnati, 1811–1812; United States Representative, March 4, 1813–1816, resigned; declined to be a candidate for U.S. Senator, 1815; associate judge of Ohio Supreme Court, 1816–1822; unsuccessful candidate for U.S. Senate January 1822; commissioner of U.S. General Land Office, 1822–1823; U.S. Postmaster General, December 9, 1823–March 7, 1829; declined to be appointed secretary of war or navy, 1829; associate justice, U.S. Supreme Court, March 7, 1829–April 4, 1861; withdrew as Whig nominee for president in 1836; candidate for president in 1832, 1840, 1844, 1848, 1852, 1856; nominated, confirmed as secretary of war, September 1841, but declined.

Death: April 4, 1861, in Cincinnati, Ohio, at age 76 years, 1 month.

Burial: Spring Grove Cemetery, Cincinnati, Ohio.

Home: Clifton, near Cincinnati, Ohio.

Personal characteristics: About six feet tall, bald in front, disheveled appearance; Roman nose, firm jaw.

Father: Fergus McLain (1747–1837), born in Ireland; a weaver and farmer.

Mother: Sophia Blackford (1753–November 5, 1839), daughter of Nathaniel Blackford.

Siblings: Nathaniel (May 8, 1787–April 11, 1871), married Hester Nutt. Mary (August 7, 1791–September 15, 1863), married William Blair September 2, 1812. William (August 10, 1794–October 12, 1839), married Sarah Fox. Desire (?–?), married John Blair.

First wife: Rebecca Edwards (March 11, 1786–December 1841), married March 29, 1807; the daughter of a Doctor Edwards.

Children: Arabella Edwards (February 7, 1808–December 20, 1833), married E.J. Weed on March 27, 1827. Eveline Aurilla (November 17, 1809–January 17, 1887), married Capt. Joe P. Taylor, a brother of President Zachary Taylor, on November 20, 1827. Rebekah Eliza (August 16, 1811–September 23, 1837), married Augustus H. Richards, January 22, 1829. Sarah Ann (May 20, 1813–October 8, 1840), married Joshua H. Hayward, July 8, 1830. John (March 24, 1815–March 1871), married Mildred J. Taylor, December 1, 1835. Nathaniel Collins (February 2, 1818–January 4, 1905), married (1) Caroline Thew Burnet on September 5, 1838, and (2) Mary Louise Thompson, June 1, 1858. William Monroe (March 4, 1821–December 3, 1829).

Second wife: Sarah Bella (Ludlow) Garrard (?–?), daughter of Israel Ludlow and widow (with four children) of Jeptha D. Garrard; married March 2, 1843.

Children: Ludlow (1846), died after only a few weeks.

John McLean was known as the "politician on the Supreme Court." Few congressmen or senators, much less other supposedly nonpartisan, impartial justices of the nation's highest court, pushed their claims for the presidency as tirelessly and frequently as did John McLean. He served as an associate justice from 1829 until 1862, and for every presidential election during those intervening three decades, he was to one degree of seriousness or another, a candidate. Fortunately, McLean's ambition did not totally dominate the handling of his judicial responsibilities, and he made an adequate, though hardly exceptional, Supreme Court justice.

McLean's father was an immigrant from Ireland. He arrived in America in 1775, at the age of 28, soon married, started a family, and commenced the frequently-traveled trail west. John was the oldest child, and thus was old enough to recall the journeys, first to western Virginia, then to Kentucky. In 1797, when John was 12, he, his father, and another man traveled on a flatboat to Cincinnati. From there they went north and carved a small farm out of the wilderness in Warren County, Ohio. The frequent moves and the frontier areas in which the family had lived prior to Ohio kept John far from any schools. Warren County at last was a home in which an education could

be obtained. Odd jobs helped earn enough money to gain admission to an academy in Cincinnati. Beginning in 1804, John apprenticed himself for two years to the clerk of Hamilton County Court of Common Pleas. This provided the opportunity to study law under a local attorney, and in 1807, John was admitted to the bar.

The same year as McLean entered upon his legal career, he also married. Rebecca Edwards was the daughter of a Kentucky doctor. It was she who probably provided the impetus for McLean to settle into the significant chore of trying to make a living. He was able to buy some printing equipment, moved it to Lebanon, Ohio, and there started the weekly *Western Star*. The printing press was also used for other ventures, such as a book for the local Shaker community entitled *Christ's Second Appearance*. How much money was made on such enterprises is uncertain, but prospects were sufficiently bright as to entice John's brother Nathaniel to purchase the press in 1810. For the next two years, John devoted himself full time to the practice of law. He also went through a significant religious conversion in this period. A Methodist evangelist, John Collins, appeared in the Lebanon area and brought John, Nathaniel, and probably many others to experience Christianity in a way that previously they had lacked. John would remain devoutly committed to his faith for the rest of his life, and became a major national lay leader in the church.

After the 1810 census, Ohio's burgeoning population multiplied the state's representation in the national House of Representatives from one to six members. In 1812, these five new seats had to be filled, and McLean handily won the contest in the state's first district. Prominence had been earned by his skillful defending of a state supreme court justice against impeachment. Service as an examiner in the United States land office in Cincinnati also had gained him important political contacts. Only 27 years old, married, and with a growing family (the McLeans had three children and would soon have four more), McLean could ill afford the financial sacrifice of service in Washington. Within three years he would decide to return to Ohio. For now, however,

JOHN McLEAN
(Artist: John Wesley Jarvis; from the Collection
of the Supreme Court of the United States)

man court principally heard appeals from lower courts. Perhaps the biggest headache of his tenure was the rushed nature of deliberations. Each county was entitled to a court setting each year, and thus there were many miles and many cases that each judge had to endure. McLean revealed his sense of frustration when he said "every question, however important, must be viewed with haste, and often decided without much reflection."

McLean had his first opportunity to expound at length on slavery in 1817, when he decided a case brought by a slave seeking his freedom. McLean decided that the former slave was indeed free, and then, though "not strictly necessary that an opinion of any other point should be suggested," proceeded to declare his wish that all slaves could be freed. However, since he was bound by the Constitution, McLean could not declare such universal freedom. He believed that if a slave was brought into a free state by his owner and made to work there, the slave thereby earned his freedom. McLean was both a committed lay Methodist preacher and a politician. Both interests revealed themselves in his case opinions.

In 1822 McLean was a leading candidate for the U.S. Senate. He lost to another one-time member of the supreme court, Ethan Brown, who was then governor of Ohio. Later in the year, President Monroe finally rewarded McLean for his support in 1816 by naming him commissioner of the General Land Office. The salary was three times his pay on the state supreme court. The General Land Office was a major governmental agency in this period of rapid western expansion. Land sales were being made at a tremendous rate. The demands for

McLean joined the supporters of the War of 1812, mainly out of unavoidable acceptance of a fait accompli — the war had begun before he entered Congress. A charter for a Second Bank of the United States was then hotly contested in Congress. McLean did not attack the bank as unwise or unconstitutional, but he did believe the specific plan presented should be revised. Before leaving for home in 1816, he worked for the nomination of James Monroe for president. Monroe would later reward McLean's loyalty handsomely.

In 1816, McLean resigned from the House because of the low pay, and was appointed a justice of the Ohio Supreme Court. The pay was meager there as well, but at least he was close to his home and his family. The four-

political appointments to the various clerkships at McLean's disposal were almost equally frequent. Ten months after beginning his Washington career, McLean took a step upward when he was appointed by President Monroe to be postmaster general.

The Post Office Department was not yet of cabinet rank, but it had big-time responsibilities. About 27,000 employees were in the department, making it the largest civilian employer in the Executive Branch. Filling those spots in the era before civil service reform led to the making on average of five to ten appointments a day. Much money was dispersed in the form of postal contracts. New postal routes and post offices had to be established, something McLean did with relish. At a time of western growth, the need for new service was acute. During two years, McLean created as many new post offices as had existed for the whole country 20 years before. Though Monroe made the appointment, John C. Calhoun had been influential in convincing the president that McLean deserved the promotion. McLean returned the favor when he aided the South Carolina senator in his race for the presidency in 1824. When Calhoun settled for the vice president's office instead, McLean supported John Quincy Adams for president.

After Adams succeeded in his quest for the presidency, McLean was continued on as postmaster general. McLean's retention was doubtless owing to his support for Adams during the campaign, but it was also crucial that McLean had proved to be an exceptional administrator. He rationalized the department's operations, made local postmasters less subject to arbitrary dismissal and thereby increased their morale, and even increased the income of the department until it covered expenses and no Congressional subsidy was required. For over five years McLean served ably and gained considerable respect. When it was suggested that the salary of the office be raised, John Randolph of Roanoke argued that the increase be effective only so long as McLean held the position. President Adams praised his cabinet officer by calling him "an able and efficient worker."

The president's favorable comments were penned in his diary in 1827. Different sentiments were being expressed the next year when McLean became embroiled in the campaign to defeat Adams and replace him with Andrew Jackson. McLean had not been altogether comfortable in Adams' cabinet. The leading role played by Secretary of State Henry Clay, whom McLean personally did not like, irritated McLean. With substantial patronage at his disposal as postmaster general, McLean soon was accused of working against his boss, Adams, and furthering the challenger Jackson's campaign. Several advisers, including Clay, urged Adams to fire McLean. The president — to use more recent presidential terminology — never could find the "smoking gun" to prove McLean's duplicity. In May 1828, Adams confided in his diary that he was certain McLean was "double-dealing." McLean's substantial political clout, in the absence of clear evidence of betrayal, resulted in his retention.

When Jackson became president in 1829, McLean was offered secretary of war or secretary of the navy, but he declined. Remaining as postmaster general was made awkward by the Ohioan's opposition to Jackson's wholesale dismissal of postmasters, many of whom McLean had named. He told Jackson he could not remain in the cabinet and implement the removal policy. A vacancy on the Supreme Court presented itself, and two days after Jackson's inaugural he kicked McLean upstairs to the Supreme Court. Even then some Jackson advisers had reservations, fearing McLean would be too political on the Court. McLean's ambition was, at this juncture, already focused on the presidency. Assuming, as did many in this country, that "Old Hickory" would be content with one term, McLean hoped to succeed him in 1832. McLean had been torn between accepting the judicial appointment or else trying to secure a more political position. His fears proved well founded that the Supreme Court, though providing considerable prestige, would also remove him too sharply from politics. His political base in Ohio became severely weakened as his service in Washington permitted other local political leaders to take charge.

McLean quickly became disappointed in Jackson. Soon after the 1829 inauguration,

McLean told a friend that he had concluded that the new administration would be more disappointing to him than had the previous one. The Peggy Eaton affair, which President Jackson made a litmus test to determine friend from enemy, found McLean on the anti–Jackson, anti–Eaton side. In the early speculations for the 1832 presidential race, McLean was frequently mentioned, but his attempts to straddle the fence between Jacksonians and the party of Adams and Henry Clay proved destructive to his credibility. Frequent disputes over patronage in Ohio angered McLean. By 1831 there seemed little doubt that Clay and Jackson would be the candidates in 1832, and McLean would have to wait until another year. He for a time flirted with the anti–Mason movement. It was only when he decided that being a third candidate in a race between Clay and Jackson was fruitless that he informed the anti–Masonic party that he was not interested. Until his withdrawal as the party's national convention began, McLean had been the major possibility for the splinter party.

On public issues, McLean, though on the federal bench, made his positions clear. As his tenure on the Court continued, his support of Whig, anti–Jackson measures became increasingly evident through public letters and speeches. He supported Clay's "American System" of federal funding of internal improvements and a protective tariff. As the years passed, he became increasingly identified with the anti-slavery forces, though abolitionists distrusted him. Some positions became clear from his decisions on the court. His belief in a strong national government and his sympathy for American Indians, were revealed in two decisions that criticized Georgia's attempt to force the Cherokees from their homes in that state.

McLean kept a constant eye on politics. On 1836, he felt that if Ohio would first present him to the nation for president, he could build on that foundation and gain election. Several newspapers in his adopted state endorsed him as early as 1833. On October 25, 1833, a group of working men in Baltimore, Maryland, called for his election. His travels through Ohio, Kentucky, and Tennessee, hearing cases in his circuit responsibilities on the Supreme Court, enabled him to talk to local leaders in furtherance of his campaign. Future president Millard Fillmore of New York endorsed him. Public meetings in Ohio and other states continued to name him. In December 1833, meetings in Warren County and then in Cincinnati, Ohio, nominated McLean. Anti-Jackson members of the state legislature in December of the next year joined the bandwagon with a nomination. Despite such scattered indications of support, the movement never caught on other than in Ohio, and many Whig politicians even in that state were lukewarm towards him. When William Henry Harrison became the clear favorite of the old Northwest, McLean faced the inevitable and withdrew. This he did in a public letter published in September 1835. McLean's lack of aggressiveness, his almost passive public style, could never motivate large masses of voters or politicians. Others proved far more attractive candidates than he. McLean was also prone to finesse issues, to attempt to curry favor from all, but in fact to disappoint all.

Presidential politics remained McLean's quadrennial passion. He was displeased with President Martin Van Buren's performance, but thought little of William Henry Harrison, who defeated Van Buren. President John Tyler, in September 1841, offered McLean the cabinet post of secretary of war, and the Senate confirmed him. The Supreme Court justice decided that membership in the increasingly discredited president's cabinet would little advance his own political fortunes, and he declined. Henry Clay proved too formidable a candidate in 1844, and after Clay received the Whig nomination, McLean declined to be considered for vice president. That election was no sooner lost than McLean was looking to 1848. The Mexican War intervened. Despite his position on the Court, McLean felt no reluctance in stating his view on this political question. He opposed the war, finding it to have been instigated by the American government solely to acquire large parts of Mexican territory. Once the war was under way, he suggested that President James K. Polk offer peace to the Mexicans without any annexation of Mexican lands. The justice's condemnation of the war was clear and strong. Unfortunately for his prospects, Whig General Zachary Taylor insisted on winning major battles of the war. He thereby made himself an irresistible nominee of the very party that had largely opposed that war of conquest. Taylor was the brother of McLean's son-in-law, but such family relationships little tempered the distaste McLean felt at Taylor's nomination. McLean toyed with accepting the Free Soil Party's nomination. Hoping to gain the Whig nomination in 1852, McLean finally declined to be considered for the Free Soil ticket.

Though McLean had rejected the quite achievable Free Soil nomination in 1848, McLean, in the 1850s, revealed an increasing Free Soil tint. He stated that a slave was free once he was removed from a state that permitted slavery. Yet McLean did not shrink from enforcing the fugitive slave statutes, because he was charged under the Constitution with upholding the laws. Thus McLean was suspect among anti-slavery forces when the critical *Dred Scott* decision was being deliberated in 1856 and 1857. McLean hoped that this opinion would be handed down prior to the 1856 Republican National Convention and that his strong anti-slavery dissent would propel him to the presidential nomination. The Court postponed announcement of the decision and thereby thwarted McLean's hopes. *Dred Scott* raised the basic, nation-shattering question of whether a Negro could be a "citizen" under the Constitution. The majority said "no," but McLean in dissent argued forcefully for recognition of this basic status of the Negro. Once the majority found that slaves were nothing more than property, they proceeded to find that Congress was barred from preventing their admission to any territory in the West. The Missouri Compromise of 1820, which provided that slavery could not be introduced in any territory above the 36°30' latitudinal line, was unconstitutional. McLean opposed the judicial repeal of the 1820 Compromise, and instead held that slavery could only exist where it was permitted by law. There was a national uproar over *Dred Scott*. Many subsequently felt that McLean's strong, broad dissent had forced the majority into the extreme language that they had used; the case had actually been decided — all rights of the

parties concluded — on far narrower grounds than the ones that plunged the nation into bitter debate. McLean's dissent had gone so far afield from the necessary points of law that the majority wrote its opinion to respond to them. McLean became a hero to the abolitionists.

At the 1856 Republican Convention, McLean was given serious consideration for the presidency. At an informal ballot, McLean received 196 votes to John Charles Frémont's 359. The justice told friends that an earlier release of the *Dred Scott* decision might have so increased his support as to have gained him the nomination.

Four years later, McLean received his last convention ballots for president, a handful at the Republican gathering that chose Abraham Lincoln. The next year McLean died, his political ambitions finally silenced.

Analysis of Qualifications

Though serving one of the longest tenures on the Supreme Court, 32 years, McLean is not remembered for any great achievement in that capacity. Instead, his image is as the politician who also served as judge. His ambitions were as large as those of any who ever hungered after the presidency, yet fortunately as judge, McLean did not let that goal prevent him from serving competently. A poll of legal scholars ranked him as one of the average justices, spectacular neither for greatness nor for failure. Even had higher offices not distracted him for the entirety of those 32 years on the Court, there is little in McLean's career to suggest he would have been any abler as a judge. There was a solid, but limited, quality about John McLean.

McLean was a schemer. He wrote a good friend of Adams that year that he was trying mightily to avoid any interference with the president. In personal meetings with Adams, McLean professed good will. Yet secretly, McLean plotted for Jackson. A more direct man would have resigned his post and avoided the double dealing. While serving as an associate justice, McLean ignored judicial properties by announcing public positions, even some that ostensibly affected pending cases, in order to advance his political standing.

Yet McLean should be commended for his clear administrative skills exhibited as postmaster general. The department made considerable advances under his leadership. From President Adams on down, McLean was praised. He instituted reforms that made the postal service more profitable and effective, and at the same time made the local postmasters less subject to political reprisals.

On the Supreme Court, McLean had few opportunities to demonstrate political leadership. His lack of support in his home state of Ohio reveals both the limited political influence of a Supreme Court justice, but also the limited political appeal of McLean. He simply was not a "popular" politician. Reserved and not altogether imaginative when it came to campaigning, McLean had no large circle of supporters willing to further his ambitions. There is little in his background to suggest he would have worked effectively with other politicians, or in particular, with Congress. He could be cold and aloof, formal, perhaps revealing a basically shy personality. If he had the makings of a successful president in the period of increasing crisis in the 1830s and 1840s, the McLean record does not reveal the evidence. John McLean would have been a considerable risk to thrust into the presidency.

McLEAN BIBLIOGRAPHY

Gatell, Frank Otto. "John McLean," in Leon Friedman and Fred Israel, eds. *The Justices of the United States Supreme Court 1789–1969.* 4 vols. New York City (1969), I, pp. 535–546.

Haines, Charles Groves, and Foster H. Sherwood. *The Role of the Supreme Court in American Government and Politics 1853–1864.* Berkeley and Los Angeles 1957).

Hopkins, Vincent Charles. *Dred Scott's Case.* New York City (1967).

Warren, Charles. *The Supreme Court in U.S. History.* 3 vols. Boston (1922).

Weisenburger, Francis P. *The Life of John McLean, a Politician on the United States Supreme Court.* New York City (1971), reprint of 1937 edition.

Whipple, Charles H. *Genealogy of the Whipple-Wright, Wager, Ward-Pell, McLean-Burnet Families, Together with Records of Allied Families.* Los Angeles (1917).

1836 vice presidential nominee—
Whig Party

Francis Granger

Full name: Francis Granger.

State represented: New York.

Birth: December 1, 1792, in Suffield, Connecticut.

Age on Inauguration Day (March 4, 1837): 44 years, 3 months.

Education: Local schools and tutors, Yale College, entered 1808, graduated 1811. Studied law, admitted to bar in 1816.

Religion: Congregationalist.

Ancestry/prominent relatives: Launcelot Granger arrived in America in 1648, settling in Massachusetts. Gideon Granger (father), U.S. postmaster general.

Occupation: Attorney.

Public offices: New York State Assembly, 1826–1828, 1830–1832; defeated for lieutenant governor, 1828; defeated for governor of New York, 1830 and 1832; prominent in Anti-Masonic Party development, 1828–1834; unsuccessful Whig nominee for vice president, 1836; U.S. Representative, March 4, 1835–March 3, 1837, and March 4, 1839–March 4, 1841; defeated for reelection, 1836; U.S. postmaster general, March 6–September 18, 1841, resigned; U.S. Representative, November 27, 1841–March 3, 1843; member of Peace Convention, 1861.

Death: August 28, 1868, in Canandaigua, at age 75 years, 9 months.

Burial: Woodlawn Cemetery in Canandaigua, New York.

Home: Granger homestead, now a museum, in Canandaigua, New York.

Personal characteristics: Over six feet tall; commanding and extremely handsome appearance; silver-gray hair, full and flowing.

Father: Gideon Granger (July 19, 1767–December 31, 1822); married January 14, 1790. Lawyer, politician.

Mother: Mindwell Pease (August 31, 1770—April 17, 1860), daughter of Joseph and Mindwell (King) Pease.

Siblings: Ralph (November 22, 1790–1843), married Catherine Van Ness on April 16,

1821. John Albert (September 11, 1795–May 26, 1870), married first, Julia W. Williams, in 1820, and second, Harriet Jackson, in 1829.

Wife: Cornelia Van Rensselaer (1798–December 29, 1823), married May 20, 1817; died from complications in childbirth, daughter of Jeremiah and Sybella Van Rensselaer.

Children: Cornelia Adeline (1819–1894), married (1) John E. Thayer of Boston, and (2) Robert C. Winthrop. Gideon (August 30, 1821–September 3, 1868), married Isaphine Pierson in 1868. A third child, born December 1823, died January 21, 1824.

Historic Site: Granger House, Canandaigua, New York.

Francis Granger was an imposing man. Dignified, affable, strikingly handsome, he was a leading figure in New York politics as new parties were being formed in the late 1820s and during the decade of the 1830s. He won some important offices, including state assemblyman, U.S. congressman, and postmaster general under the first Whig president. Yet he failed in the two major positions he sought, New York governor and vice president of the United States. These defeats caused his retirement from politics while he was still a relatively young man. Urgings that he return were easily thrust aside.

Francis (always called Frank) was born in a house in Suffield, Connecticut, in which his father and grandfather both had lived. Gideon Granger, Frank's father, was prominent in early American party affairs. Few supporters of Thomas Jefferson could be found in New England when the Federalists and the Sage of Monticello battled for the White House in 1800, but Gideon Granger worked hard for Jefferson that year. Perhaps the most impor-

FRANCIS GRANGER
(From the Collection of the Ontario County Historical Society, Canandaigua, New York)

tant Jefferson leader in New England, Granger was rewarded by the new president in 1801 with appointment as postmaster general, an office he would retain through part of James Madison's presidency. His son Francis would 40 years later be appointed to the same seat in another president's cabinet.

Gideon, only 33 years old, moved his family to Washington, there to remain until 1812 when Granger secretly broke with the Democratic-Republican Party and supported turncoat DeWitt Clinton, who was running as a Federalist. After the election, Gideon Granger continued as postmaster general for a year, but then resigned in 1814. He soon moved to Canandaigua, New York, built a large house that still stands today as a museum, and there died in 1822.

Francis Granger in 1808 entered Yale College at the age of 16. A Yale College history states that in college Frank "was indolent and mischievous, but quick-minded and promising." He was quick-minded enough to graduate in 1811, and soon began to study law. When his father moved to Canandaigua, Frank followed in 1816, and was shortly thereafter admitted to the bar. The following year he married Cornelia, the daughter of wealthy Utica businessman Jeremiah Van Rensselaer. Frank was content with his law practice for a time, but ambition for political life soon drew him away from his legal books.

Like his father, Frank was loyal to the politics of DeWitt Clinton. There was only one party in the state, but many factions. In 1825, Granger was elected to the state assembly as a Clinton man, and was reelected the following year. His prestigious name as well as his own talents earned him considerable support for speaker in 1826, but he was defeated. Granger was no quiet backbencher, but spoke up forcefully on many issues. He soon joined the volatile Anti-Masonic movement, which swept New York in 1827 and 1828.

The Anti-Masons got their start in 1827, with the abduction of renegade Mason William Morgan. Morgan was an active Mason living in New York, but became angry with the Order. In 1826 he had published his *Illustrations of Masonry*, which described the secrets of the first three degrees of the Masonic society. Angry Masons had him arrested on a theft charge on September 11, 1826, arising out of a small debt he owed. After being acquitted in Granger's hometown of Canandaigua, Morgan was arrested again for the debt and jailed. When released, Morgan was kidnapped, it was supposed, by vengeful Masons. He was never seen again. This episode and the unproved assumption that the Masons had killed Morgan caused intense opposition to this secret order. In March 1827, memorials against the Order were presented to the New York Assembly. A select committee was formed to consider them, and Granger was made chairman. The result of the deliberations was to call upon the governor to offer a reward for the capture of Morgan's abductors. The second recommendation was to form a committee to investigate firsthand the facts of the case and to report back to the assembly. Granger refrained in the report and in his active participation in the debate from attacking Masonry as the cause of the crime. When others started to abuse the secret society, Granger protested. For a man who would shortly help lead the fight against Masonry, he was showing considerable objectivity during the early stages.

In what came to be known as the "infected district" of New York, around Buffalo and Rochester, Anti-Masonry soon developed as a political movement. Granger, along with the other two early leaders, William Seward and Thurlow Weed, initially did not want to make Anti-Masonry a separate political party. Citizens in some of the counties, angry over the Morgan affair, selected electoral tickets from which Masons were excluded. Soon the Masons became identified with the party of Andrew Jackson, while the Anti-Masons were principally supporters of President John Quincy Adams. The Masons themselves seemed to be engaging in secret manipulation of some elections, and this fired the opposition to make Anti-Masonry the issue in local political contests. Granger was avoiding close identification with the movement. He was an attractive, well-known figure who in 1827 was elected to a third term in the legislature and there loosely associated with the Anti-Masons. Therefore, when the new party searched for a statewide candidate in 1828, he was a leading contender from the start.

Political parties were fluid. Though all called themselves members of the party of Jefferson, supporters of President Adams and those of Jackson were clearly at odds. Those who favored Adams' reelection in 1828 as president saw the need to join forces with the Anti-Masons and select a state ticket attractive to them. Thurlow Weed was one of the major forces in the movement, and he decided Granger was the gubernatorial candidate most likely to gain support both from Anti-Masons and from Adams' men. Weed visited leaders throughout the state to argue the Granger cause. The putative candidate himself did not express any interest in the governor's nomination. The infected district in the west supported Granger, while the easterners, far from the Mason turmoil in the west, wanted U.S. Supreme Court Justice Smith Thompson. Thompson had played no role in the Anti-Masonic furor and was unlikely to attract the extremists in that movement. Weed was fearful that unless Granger was named, an independent, Anti-Masonic ticket would enter the field and assure that the Jacksonian candidate, Martin Van Buren, would win the governorship. Weed's efforts were unavailing, and the convention of Adams' followers who met in Utica on July 22, 1828, named Thompson over Granger in a close vote. Granger then received the nomination for lieutenant governor by acclamation. As Weed feared, ultra-opponents of the Masons were dissatisfied and denounced the Thompson candidacy. An Anti-Masonic convention at Utica, rather than ratifying the Adams party selection, named Granger for governor and John Crary for the second spot. Crary promised to withdraw as soon as Granger declined the gubernatorial nomination, so that there would be just one ticket in the field against Van Buren. Granger was in an awkward position. He sought no nomination, but now he had two conflicting ones. For the sake of unity, he decided to refuse the Anti-Mason nomination for governor and accept the Adams selection for lieutenant governor. Crary, however, then proved false to his word and remained in the contest. Rather than compromise, the Anti-Masons then named eccentric, aging newspaperman Solomon Southwick.

As feared, Thompson and Southwick split the opposition vote. Van Buren was elected with less than a majority of the votes cast. The vote was 136,785 Van Buren, 106,415 Thompson, 33,335 Southwick. Later observers such as D.S. Alexander, in his *A Political History of the State of New York*, felt "Granger would probably have received the aggregate vote of Thompson and Southwick, or three thousand more than Van Buren." That victory for the "Fox of Kinderhook" helped keep his march toward the White House unobstructed, and kept Granger from what was perhaps his needed boost for a career in major public office.

Though defeated for lieutenant governor, Granger remained an important political force. In 1829 he was reelected to the Assembly. One of his major concerns was the Chenango County canal bill. The previous year he had felt the legislation would pass the Assembly because of a deal he had worked out with the Anti-Masons who would support bank recharters if the bank supporters would favor the Chenango canal. The deal fell apart at the last minute. In succeeding sessions, Granger continued to work to put through legislation for the canal. His prominence earned him in 1830 the gubernatorial nomination he had rejected in 1828. The Anti-Masons met in Utica in August and unanimously named Granger for governor. Enos Throop was the Jacksonian party's opposition candidate, Van Buren having moved up to be Jackson's secretary of state after only 43 days as governor. Granger worked closely with Thurlow Weed during the election, a close relationship that would continue throughout almost his entire career. As the publisher of several newspapers through the years, Weed was a force in state politics. The campaign fell just short, and Granger lost with 120,361 votes to Throop's 128,842. Again, Granger had rolled up impressive majorities in the "infected district," but lost the eastern part of the state.

Granger continued to attract the support of the anti–Jackson leadership in New York. Future U.S. senator and Lincoln cabinet officer William Henry Seward gave his impression of Granger in 1831:

> I believe I have never told you all I thought about this star of the first magnitude in Antimasonry.... He is six feet and well-proportioned, as you well know, handsome, graceful, dignified, and affable.... He is a prince among those who are equals, affable to inferiors, and knows no superiors. In principle, he has redeeming qualities — more than enough to atone for all his faults — is honest, honourable, and just, first and beyond comparison with other politicians of the day. You will ask impatiently, "Has he a heart?" yes....

One anomalous line concludes Seward's praise of Granger: "There is yet one quality of Granger's character which you do not dream of— he loves money almost as well as power." That final comment was not repeated in others' estimates of Granger. Thurlow Weed gave Granger equal praise:

Francis Granger was also … a gentleman of accomplished manners, genial temperament, and fine presence, with fortune, leisure, and a taste for public life…. He sought to rise by an earnest and honest discharge of the duties of the various offices which he occupied, rather than by scheming or management.

Weed also said, "Than Francis Granger the people never had a more enlightened, upright, or patriotic representative."

Though a strong Anti-Mason and a good friend of Granger, Weed freely criticized his friend's actions when he was so moved. One example came during the 1830 campaign, after Granger had been elected as a delegate to the first national convention of the Anti-Mason Party held in Philadelphia, and was selected president. The gathering called for a national nominating convention the following year. Weed wrote Granger that his prominent position in national Anti-Masonry was "a mistake. The men from New York who urged it are stark mad." Granger's close identification with the national Anti-Masonic movement was an excuse Weed felt many voters would use to vote against Granger.

Granger won a seat in the assembly by 1831 and prepared for another statewide battle in 1832. That year was also a presidential election, and New York politics was shaped by the battle between the opponents and supporters of President Andrew Jackson. The Anti-Masons in 1831 nominated William Wirt for president at their national convention. In December 1831, the National Republicans nominated Henry Clay. The Anti-Mason New York convention was held in Utica on June 21, 1832, and it again unanimously nominated Granger for governor. A split presidential electoral slate was named, equally divided between Clay and Wirt. The Clay men later accepted the split slate. Jackson supporters called it the "Siamese twin party," but union of the anti–Jackson elements in New York was essential for victory. The Clay National Republicans did unite on Granger for governor, with William Marcy the Jacksonian Democrat's choice. The issues in the campaign degenerated into mere attacks on personalities. Marcy was ridiculed for having turned in an expense report while he served as a Supreme Court judge, which included a

charge of 50 cents for mending his pants. "Marcy pantaloons" soon became a symbol of the campaign, and other matters discussed were of equivalent weight. The western counties gave their usual strong support to Granger, and the eastern section, as usual, wiped out the margin and gave Marcy the victory with 166,410 votes to Granger's 156,672. The Anti-Mason Party started to disintegrate after his third successive defeat. Anti-Masonry as a single-issue movement had exhausted itself, and even the "infected district" began in 1833 to abandon the cause.

Granger, Weed, Seward and other Anti-Masonic leaders decided to join forces with the National Republicans in a new political party, which in time assumed the name of "Whig." By 1834 the Whig Party had been organized in New York and Granger was one of its leaders. Several candidates for governor were suggested. Granger was prominent among them, but he resolutely refused to be sacrificed again. Western support for another Granger nomination appeared at the September 1834 Whig state convention, but the three-time loser declined. William Henry Seward received the nomination, and Granger became a candidate for United States Representative. Seward was defeated, but Granger won his Congressional seat. He played no conspicuous role in Washington during his term.

With Old Hickory imposing on the Democrats his choice of Van Buren as his presidential successor, the new Whig Party struggled to choose its own candidate. There were several candidacies actively considered, with nominations occurring by state legislative caucuses, public meetings, and other ad hoc organizations. Little attention was given to the vice presidency during most of these gatherings. Francis Granger and John Tyler were the most frequently mentioned possibilities to run with the Whig presidential contenders. Suggestions from some quarters that a national Whig convention be held gave way to the counter-argument that regional nominations would most likely stop Van Buren's drive for election, with the final choice devolving upon the House of Representatives. Some of the early reluctance to name a running mate for the Whigs was due to the popularity of the Democrat's nominee, Colonel Richard M. Johnson of Kentucky.

Not all Anti-Masons had joined the Whigs. Several state Anti-Mason conventions, particularly in the northeast, were held for the purpose of nominating national candidates. A convention of Pennsylvania Anti-Masons was held in Harrisburg on December 14, 1835. It nominated William Henry Harrison for president and Granger was named his running mate by acclamation. Apparently, Granger had initially not wanted to be a candidate, but by the time of the Harrisburg nomination, he had decided to run. A national Anti-Mason convention was finally held in May 1836, in Philadelphia, but no nominations were made. Many Anti-Masons turned to Van Buren, however, rather than to the Whigs.

The same day as the Anti-Mason convention had been held in Harrisburg, a Pennsylvania Whig convention was held in the same city and ratified the choice of Harrison and Granger. A Massachusetts Whig convention on March 10, 1836, named Daniel Webster and Granger as their electoral ticket. Granger's name was included because it was felt he could bring the Anti-Mason element into the Whig Party. On February 3, 1836, a New York State Convention was held that unanimously nominated Harrison and Granger. Granger was formally notified of the nomination. He thanked his fellow New Yorkers for "this proud testimonial of public confidence." Granger was also nominated with Harrison at gatherings in Ohio (Whig), in Vermont (Anti-Mason), Connecticut (anti–Van Buren), New Jersey (Whig), and probably others.

The vice presidential candidates were rarely mentioned in this heated campaign. The presidential contest was the all-absorbing topic. Richard Johnson, the Democrat's nominee, did come into the public eye by charges he had a Negro mistress, and that he was a drunkard. Granger, fortunately, had nothing so dramatic to rouse newspaper writers. Johnson also was apparently the only vice presidential candidate to conduct an active canvass. Granger held on to his hope for victory even as late as November 30, 1836, because the nationwide returns for elections held weeks apart in the various states did not initially clearly indicate a Van

Buren victory. It soon thereafter was evident to all that Van Buren had won, but Richard Johnson had failed to secure a majority of the electoral votes for vice president. Therefore, for the only time in history, the Senate was called upon to choose between the two highest vote getters, Johnson and Granger. Some friends tried to make Granger think he had a good chance of victory. Granger wrote Weed that efforts to defeat him in the Senate included the charge that he was an abolitionist, an allegation Granger called a lie. In several states legislative caucuses were called to instruct their senators how to vote. Some of the caucuses, as have some historians since, believed that Granger as a New Yorker could not constitutionally serve with fellow New Yorker Van Buren as president. In fact, all the Constitution forbids is that electors from a state cannot vote for both a president and vice president from their own state. Thus, only New York electoral college members were barred from voting for two New Yorkers. The confusion hardly mattered. Johnson received 33 votes, Granger 16.

Granger served the next four years as a United States Representative. He gained the enmity of slaveowners by agreeing with John Quincy Adams that there should be no restrictions placed on the receipt of petitions to the House dealing with abolition of slavery. In March 1838, Granger became convinced that the antislavery forces were "gaining converts by the regiment.... They will have one-fourth of the votes of the states before the grand contest of 1840, and before that day men who now say, 'D___ 'em, put 'em down!' will beg not to be put down by them. They are engaged in it with the same honest purpose that governed the great mass of the anti-masons."

In 1838 victory in the New York gubernatorial campaign seemed assured for the Whig candidate, and Granger wanted a third nomination. Granger had the support of many who admired his work during the lean days of the party and wanted to reward him now that he could win. He had been a strong party spirit in Congress as well. Seward also wanted the nomination. Unfortunately for Granger, longtime friend and ally Thurlow Weed, also a Seward friend, had decided that Seward had the better chance of defeating the Democrats. Weed remained behind the scenes in the pre-convention maneuvering, but finally announced for Seward. Weed attended the convention in Utica on September 12, 1838. Granger and Luther Bradish, another contender, had agreed the one who fell seriously behind in the balloting would support the other. Four informal ballots were taken, and on the first Seward led with 52, Granger 39, and Granger's "partner," Luther Bradish, 29. On the second it was Seward 60, Granger 52, Bradish 10. Granger reached 60 on the next ballot, Seward 59, Bradish 8. Weed immediately buttonholed the delegates and argued that Seward was the electable candidate. On the fourth, Seward won with 67 to Granger's 48. Granger and his supporters were disappointed, some were bitter, but the candidate seemed stoic if hurt. He supported Seward in the general election, and the Whigs won. So did Granger, as a United States Congressman.

Though elected to Congress, Granger was disappointed. The next year, 1839, a vacancy in the United States Senate had to be filled, and Granger wrote a close friend that he would rather be a senator than hold any other office available. There was talk of a Democratic-Whig coalition to elect the popular Granger, but it did not materialize. In 1840, Granger probably supported Henry Clay for president, but quickly accepted William Henry Harrison's nomination and was pleased with the Whig's victory in November. Weed immediately tried to get Granger a place in the new cabinet, in part as recompense for the mistreatment Weed may have felt he had given Granger in recent years. Harrison was agreeable and offered Granger the post Granger's father had held 40 years before, postmaster general. Weed could not help but tweak his old friend a little. He wrote Granger shortly before the inauguration: "Now that you are to be more than ever a man of letters, pardon me for inflicting a brief one upon you...."

Granger's tenure in the cabinet was short. When John Tyler succeeded the deceased Harrison in April 1841, immediate tension between the long-time Whigs in the cabinet and the Democratic Tyler developed. By autumn a complete rupture in the government occurred over the issue of chartering a national bank, and all the cabinet resigned except for Secretary of State Daniel Webster. Granger was elected again to Congress to fill a vacancy, but when that term expired in March 1843, he refused to run for any other office.

During the remainder of his life, Granger only infrequently, and for brief moments, returned to politics. During the debate over slavery that dominated politics until the Civil War, Granger favored compromise. He did not desire to see Texas admitted to the Union in 1845. By then, Granger was estranged from Weed and Seward. Granger favored the compromise measures of 1850, while his two erstwhile political allies opposed them. On September 26, 1850, the Whig state convention met. Washington Hunt, a Weed-backed candidate, was named for governor. The convention then adopted resolutions praising Seward's course in the Senate, where he had opposed the Compromise of 1850 and favored the Wilmot Proviso. Granger had been elected president of the party convention and wanted party unity. Even so, when 40 delegates bolted after the anti–Compromise resolutions were adopted, Granger went with them. Granger had been reluctant to join the revolt, but nonetheless, his striking gray hair gave the seceders their party name for the next few years, the "Silver Grays." Granger presided over the rump session that was held, ratifying the state ticket adopted at the regular convention, but passing resolutions condemning Seward and praising the 1850 Compromise. Weed said in his memoirs that Granger had been made president of the regular convention to muzzle him, because his strong views were well known and might precipitate a revolt. So much for the best-laid plans.

Granger returned to private life. In 1856 he went to the last national convention of the Whig Party as a delegate from New York. There was really no Whig Party left that year. The nominee, old Granger ally Millard Fillmore, traveled also under the better-respected banner that year of the American Party. In 1860, Granger supported the Bell-Everett ticket, still hoping for compromise. The next year, he returned to politics, surprisingly for him, when the Washington peace convention was held in hopes of diverting the imminent Civil War. Weed was elected a delegate, but he declined in favor of Granger. Granger wrote Weed affectionately, showing that the wounds had healed in their ten-year earlier battle.

> I will tell you in candor how the idea [of accepting appointment as a delegate], which had never entered my head, struck me. Of course, it would be accepted as a most flattering honor, but you cannot imagine with what repugnance I even think of the possibility of ever again appearing before the public....

Granger seems to have definitely rid himself of political ambition. He finished out his years in the Granger homestead mansion in Canandaigua, dying there in 1868. His only son died the following week.

Analysis of Qualifications

Frank Granger was considered something of an aristocrat, but an open, honest, and friendly one. His political ally and adviser was the almost penniless Thurlow Weed. The two men formed an important political alliance in New York state. Probably no wealthier nor more prominent man associated with the Anti-Masonic movement or the Whigs in New York than Granger, and his image as being a cut above the rest of the party both helped and hurt. Weed and William Henry Seward were quite fond of Granger, but both would break with him as new political alliances were formed in the late 1830s.

Never elected to an office higher than United States Representative, Granger is remembered best in defeat, for governor of New York, and for vice president. He was appointed a member of President Harrison's cabinet in 1841, but only in the political role of postmaster general. Even there he suffered a major setback, for when President Tyler swung too far from accepted Whig dogma, Granger along with the rest of the cabinet, resigned. Seward though he had "no genius, in its restricted sense, not a very brilliant imagination, not extraordinary reasoning faculties; has no deep store of learning, nor a very extensive degree of information." Yet Seward thought highly of Granger, saying no man "is his equal in the skill of exhibiting every particle of his stores with great advantage." His refined man-

ners gave him the image of an aristocrat, but he seemed to have public service deeply rooted in him. Seward concluded by saying "very few men have fewer faults ... I mean, political great men."

Seward and Weed's judgments were those of political supporters. His public image was similar. Granger was a leader of the Canandaigua bar throughout his life. He was a favorite of women, and was described once as being dressed "in a bottle-green coat with gilt buttons, a model of grace and manhood.... He had youth, enthusiasm, magnificent gifts, and a heart of love. All his resources seemed to be at instant command..." (D.S. Alexander, *A Political History of the State of New York*, vol. II, p. 361). He was a good speaker, and attracted the loyalties of many who fought for him through several losing campaigns. He had few enemies because he was so kind-hearted, affable, and eternally optimistic.

Achievements in legislation or in executive leadership did not attend his career. His service was frequent in the state legislature of New York, less lengthy in Congress, and for only a few months in the national cabinet. His abilities were not quite fulfilled, and a far better estimate of his skills and character in office would have been possible had he only won one of his near misses for governor. Still, for a nascent political party, struggling to find as politically attractive a combination as possible in 1836, the Whigs selected a most credible vice presidential candidate in Frank Granger.

GRANGER BIBLIOGRAPHY

Aldrich, Lewis Cass. *History of Ontario County, New York*.... Syracuse (1893), pp. 469–473.

Alexander, DeAlva Stanwood. *A Political History of the State of New York*. 3 vols. Port Washington, N.Y. (1969), reprint of 1906–9 edition.

Benson, Lee. *The Concept of Jacksonian Democracy: New York as a Test Case*. Princeton, N.J. (1961).

Berger, Mark L. *The Revolution in the New York Party Systems, 1840–1860*. Port Washington, N.Y. (1973).

Dexter, Franklin B. *Biographical Sketches of the Graduates of Yale College*. Vol. VI. New York City (1912).

Granger, J.N. *Launcelot Granger of Newbury, Massachusetts, and Suffield, Connecticut: A Genealogical History*. Hartford, Conn. (1893).

Hammond, Jabez D. *History of the Political Parties in the State of New York.* 3 vols. Syracuse, N.Y. (1852).

Milliken, Charles. *A History of Ontario County, New York, and Its People.* New York City (1911).

Mushkat, Jerome. *Tammany: The Evolution of a Political Machine 1789–1865.* Syracuse (1971).

Seward, Frederick W. *William H. Seward: An Autobiography from 1801–1834.* New York City (1891).

Van Deusen, Glyndon G. *Thurlow Weed, Wizard of the Lobby.* Boston (1947).

_____. *William Henry Seward.* New York City (1967).

Weed, Harriet A., ed. *Autobiography of Thurlow Weed.* Boston (1883).

---

*1836 vice presidential nominee —
Whig Party*

Philip P. Barbour

Full name: Philip Pendleton Barbour.

State represented: Virginia.

Birth: May 25, 1783, Orange County, Virginia.

Age on Inauguration Day (March 4, 1837): 53 years, 9½ months.

Education: Local schools, studied law under several attorneys; admitted to bar in 1800; in 1801 went to William and Mary College, but did not graduate.

Religion: Episcopalian.

Ancestry/prominent relatives: His great-grandfather, James Barbour, emigrated from Scotland; James Barbour (brother), U.S. senator and Virginia governor.

Occupation: Lawyer.

Public offices: Member of Virginia House of Delegates, 1812–1814; U.S. House of Representatives, September 19, 1814–March 3, 1825; speaker, 1821–1823; appointed as judge on Virginia General Court, 1825–1827, resigned; U.S. House of Representatives, March 4, 1827–October 15, 1830; president of Virginia Constitutional Convention, 1829–1830; appointed U.S. District Judge, 1830–1836; between 1824 and 1835, declined the following offices: chancellor, Judge of Court of Appeals, U.S. attorney, governor, and U.S. senator; considered for vice president by some

Southerners, 1832, but refused; refused Whig nomination for vice president, 1836; associate justice of the U.S. Supreme Court, March 15, 1836–February 25, 1841.

Death: February 25, 1841, Washington, D.C., at age 57 years, 9 months.

Burial: Congressional Cemetery, Washington, D.C.

Home: Frascati, Orange County, Virginia.

Personal characteristics: Known for his industriousness and personal integrity; conscientious in his duties.

Father: Thomas Barbour, wealthy planter.

Mother: Mary Pendleton Thomas.

Siblings: Richard, died young. James (June 10, 1775–June 7, 1842) married Lucy Johnson; was a U.S. Representative and Virginia governor. Thomas, died young. Lucy. Nelly (?–1798), married Martin Nalle. Mary (also called Polly). Sally, married Gabriel Gray.

Wife: Frances Todd Johnson (?–?), married in 1804.

Children: Philippa, married Judge R.H. Field. Elizabeth, married J.J. Ambler. Thomas, married Catharine Strother. Edmund Pendleton (?–1851), married Harriet Stewart. Quintus, married Mary Somerville. Sextus (?–1849), died from cholera; never married; Septimus.

Historic sites/memorials: Home of James Barbour, Philip's brother, is in Barboursville, Virginia.

Philip Barbour descended from an old, well-established Virginia family. His ancestors were living in the colony at least one hundred years before the American Revolution. His great-grandfather apparently was a merchant who emigrated from Scotland in the mid-1600s. Philip's father had served in the old Virginia House of Burgesses, and had in 1769 signed the Non-Importation Act. After the Revolutionary War, he had been elected to the Virginia House of Delegates. His livelihood was his Orange County plantation. The fortune had largely been squandered by the time of Philip's birth in 1783. An early biographer of Philip Barbour merely describes the source of the poverty as "lavish hospitality, accompanied as it had been by a series of disasters...." Philip was a pupil of an Episcopal minister whose harsh discipline was his only legacy. He also attended rustic local schools.

Philip demonstrated academic ability, especially in foreign languages. His retentive memory also made him something of a scholar of Greek and Roman classics.

This early, poorly developed education came to an end in 1799, and the following year Barbour began studying law at home. He moved to Kentucky and late in the same year was admitted to the bar, "under great difficulty and embarrassment." Self-taught, Barbour at age 17 was poorly equipped for his chosen profession. He realized his own deficiencies. Responding to the urgings of his friends, Philip returned to Virginia and studied at William and Mary College. That interlude lasted only a few months, and an active legal practice was begun in Orange County, Virginia. Finding a bride came soon thereafter. He married the sister of his brother James's wife.

For the next eight years Barbour applied himself industriously to developing his legal skills and practice. The effort was apparently successful, as clients and fame came his way. His practice consisted of both criminal and civil matters.

Barbour took advantage of his fame in the courtroom by running for the state legislature in 1812, and winning. Of great significance to his victory was his brother James's prominence. The same year as Philip was elected to the state General Assembly, James was elected Virginia's governor. Philip's committee assignments appeared to have been significant, for he served on the judiciary and finance committees. The burning national issue was the War of 1812, which had begun just a few months before the new Assembly member took his legislative seat. Barbour sought to have the state lend to the federal government the money necessary to build a large war vessel, but he failed. In 1813, Barbour served on a military preparedness committee that removed the exemption from service in the army for college students.

Representative John Dawson died in office. In 1814 Barbour was selected to replace him. Another new resident of Washington was James Barbour, who had just been selected one of Virginia's United States senators. They would not share political philosophies through-

out their careers, but during the next few years they were on the same side of most issues.

Barbour supported what came to be known as "Virginian particularism"—a devotion to states' rights, a repudiation of growing national power, and an insistence on strict construction of the Constitution. These issues would eventually cause a political breach with his brother James. It would also leave Philip Barbour behind in the fast-moving politics of the period. Defense of his native state against increased federal power became Barbour's guiding principle. In this ultimately failed cause he was joined by many fellow Southerners.

In Congress Barbour constantly presented Constitutional arguments against new programs. For example, in 1817 Barbour opposed the enactment of the "Bonus Bill," a proposal to subsidize canals and roads. Barbour admitted the construction was needed, as it would increase the commercial wealth of the country by decreasing the costs and difficulties of transportation. Nonetheless, he opposed the bill because it infringed on the sovereignty of the states. He argued that the only proper role for the federal government in commercial matters was in the area of intercourse with foreign countries. Barbour argued that internal improvements were a matter solely for the states. One route proposed for a national road from Buffalo to New Orleans was through his congressional district. This fact did not weaken his opposition:

> This bill is entitled a bill for constructing a road from Buffalo in the state of New York, by way of Washington, to the city of New Orleans. But when I look into the provisions of the bill, when I see the stretch of authority there attempted, when I consider the profligate expenditure of money it proposes, while I view its partiality, its cruelty, its injustice, and its usurpation, and compare it with the constitutional power of the government, the title strikes me as inappropriate. It should be entitled, "A bill to construct a road from the liberties of the country by way of Washington to despotism."

President Madison agreed, and vetoed the Bonus Bill after each house had narrowly passed it.

The admission of Missouri as a state gave Barbour another opportunity to defend

PHILIP BARBOUR
(Reproduced from the Collections of the Library of Congress)

Southern rights. In February 1819, Barbour took the floor of the House to argue that any prohibition of slavery in a new state was unconstitutional. Any interference with slavery would make the new state a second-class entity in the Union. Barbour felt that the spread of slavery throughout the country, and not limiting it just to one section, would be beneficial. Wherever a slaveowner went, he should be able to take his "property" with him. Sound policy required that slavery not be isolated as a peculiar institution in the South, else it would lead to inexorable pressures of division.

The only route for Congress, therefore, was to accept or reject the application of a territory for statehood. The national government could not place limitations on admission. Despite such Southern objections, the Missouri Compromise was passed that barred slavery north of the 36°30' latitude, and permitted it south of that line.

At this stage in his career, Barbour not only defended the South but was also a protector of the image of Andrew Jackson. When General Jackson invaded Spanish Florida and hanged two British subjects because they were inciting the Indians to revolt against the United States, Congress considered a resolution of censure. Barbour thought Jackson entirely justified in his actions. Jackson had acted without clear direction from superiors, as unanticipated events had demanded a quick response. Barbour said the general had meted out "a stern justice, [and it] cannot be *morally wrong*." Such defenders were not forgotten by Old Hickory when he was later in a position to reward his supporters.

In 1821, Barbour argued an important case before the United States Supreme Court dealing with the power of the federal judiciary. Virginia employed Barbour to argue its position. He contended that the federal constitution only permitted the U.S. Supreme Court to review appeals from federal courts, and not from state courts. More specifically, Barbour contended that there was no reason to make the federal courts superior to state tribunals. Barbour did not convince the Supreme Court, but the Court also did not convince Barbour. A few years later he argued the same position in a Congressional debate over the reform of the federal judiciary.

Barbour's representation of the Southern diehards earned him important committee assignments. In 1820, Speaker Henry Clay decided not to run for another term in Congress, and Barbour was considered as his replacement. The early balloting for Speaker saw four other contenders at the forefront, but on the second day Barbour was brought forward as a compromise selection. His victory was gained on the twelfth ballot. The election of so consistent a Southern strict constructionist seemed a victory for his point of view, but in truth Barbour was a compromise that little represented the majority viewpoint. Clay

reclaimed his office in 1823, as his popularity was far too great for Barbour or any other Congressman to overcome. The speakership was but one of several contests between the two men. Since Clay was the chief spokesman for the "American System" of internal improvements and high tariff, he and Barbour were frequently at odds in floor debate on various measures. After one particularly strong and effective rejoinder by Clay, the Kentuckian was asked, "How does Mr. Barbour feel towards you after the prodigious beating you gave him?" Allowing for the possible prejudices of the questioner, it is nonetheless evident that Barbour was a poor match for the Kentucky orator.

After one term out of the speaker's chair, Barbour decided to retire from the House. In 1825, he was offered a law professorship at the University of Virginia, a post Thomas Jefferson urged him to accept. Instead, Barbour became a judge on the General Court for the Eastern District of Virginia. Two years later he returned to elective politics at the urging of supporters in Orange County. Again he was elected to the United States House of Representatives, and again he stood for election to the speaker's post. He received few votes, in part because even his friends abandoned him in order to concentrate their votes on another Southerner.

Barbour had returned to Washington in the middle of President John Quincy Adams' administration. James Barbour was secretary of war in the cabinet, but this did not prevent his brother Philip from becoming a severe critic of the president. Barbour attacked the government for profligate spending, for increased national assertions of authority, and in sum for the gradual acceptance of Clay's ideas of high tariffs and federal expenditures for internal improvements. Taking up another cudgel against the Adams regime, Barbour in December 1827 introduced a resolution calling upon the government to sell its one-fifth interest in the Bank of the United States. The proposal was overwhelmingly defeated in the House. Four years later the Bank would be the issue that separated loyal supporters of Jackson from the Clay partisans. Barbour was a few years premature.

With Jackson's election in 1828, many thought Barbour would receive a reward for his years of faithful service opposing Adams and Clay. He was passed over in the selection of the cabinet, and in 1830 received the much less prestigious appointment of a federal district judgeship in Eastern Virginia. The following year his name was bandied about as a possible replacement for attorney general, but he was not chosen. Nonetheless, Barbour's allegiance to Jackson did not seriously waver, and he commended the chief executive for his vigorous and novel use of the presidential veto to kill schemes both men opposed.

In October 1829, a state convention opened that was to consider adoption of a new constitution for Virginia. Former president Monroe was the presiding officer, but his ill health caused Barbour to be selected temporary president. Eventually Barbour was named permanent presiding officer.

When Barbour took office as a federal judge shortly after the constitutional convention, he gave a valedictory to his political career. Eschewing judicial nonpartisanship, Barbour urged continued allegiance to strict construction of the Constitution. He discussed the politics of his day and called for the perpetuation of the Jacksonian party. Even as a judge, Barbour did not stay out of public issues, as he served as chairman of a free-trade, no-tariff convention held in Philadelphia in 1831. Barbour denied the constitutionality of nullification, but not of secession. Nonetheless, Barbour assured the president that Virginia would not follow South Carolina's lead in nullification. The judge seemed pleased with Jackson's strong words against Calhoun and other nullifiers. What caused a break with the president was Jackson's clear aim to make New Yorker Martin Van Buren the next president. The means adopted to achieve that succession were to make Van Buren vice president in 1832. Many Southerners would not acquiesce, fearful that as a Northerner the "Sage of Kinderhook" would prove inimical to their interests. The Virginia legislature caucus almost nominated Barbour in March 1832, to run with Jackson, and in an informal vote Barbour was named. Meetings occurred elsewhere in Virginia, in Alabama, and also in North Car-

olina that named Barbour for the second position on the Jackson ticket. The Jacksonians' national convention was held solely to nominate Van Buren for vice president, but Southern forces gave Barbour 49 delegate votes.

For a few months, some dissatisfied Jacksonians in Virginia were promoting a Jackson-Barbour ticket, and ignoring the national nominations. Van Buren gradually mollified Southern concerns, and the Barbour boomlet died. In October Barbour gave up the fight and urged his supporters to back Van Buren.

The Jacksonians, now calling themselves the Democratic Party, met in May 1835, to choose their national ticket. Barbour was a contender for vice president, but Richard M. Johnson was selected instead. The poorly organized but growing opposition party — the Whigs — hoped to capitalize on the resentment Barbour and his supporters might feel at this snub. On December 11, 1835, the Virginia Whig members of the state assembly met and nominated Hugh L. White for the presidency, but left vice president open. One week later the states' rights advocates in the Georgia legislature, and also private citizens from throughout the state, met and nominated White for the presidency and Barbour for vice president. Upon being informed of the nomination, Barbour stated in a letter published on January 13, 1836:

> I never could consent to place myself in an attitude which would be in direct conflict with an immense majority of the political party, whose principles I have professed, and in whose ranks I have stood, since my first entrance on the theatre of public life, to act my part.

John Tyler, another Virginian who had entered Congress the same year as Barbour, was substituted.

When Barbour turned down the Whig nomination, he knew his appointment to the Supreme Court was imminent. Long angry over the direction the Court took under Chief Justice John Marshall, who interpreted the Constitution in a nationalistic light, Barbour wanted to change the Court's direction. Political opponent John Quincy Adams had been fearful as early as 1831 that Barbour might be put on the Court by Jackson, saying the nomination for a Court vacancy would go to "some shallow-pated wild-cat like Philip P. Barbour, fit for nothing but to tear the Union to rags and tatters...." Barbour was not named in 1831. He remained as a federal district judge, declining offers to run for governor and U.S. Senator, and appointments as attorney general or to a state appellate court.

President Jackson named Barbour to the Court, and he took office in March 1836. The most significant opinion written by Associate Justice Barbour came the year after his appointment, and perhaps suggests as closely as possible his attitudes at the time he would have been serving as vice president, or even president, had he been elected the previous year. It was clear that Barbour's feelings against federal encroachment on state jurisdiction had not waned. In *City of New York v. Miln*, 11 Pet. 102 (1837), the Court considered whether a state could require all ship captains from foreign countries, or from another state, to file reports on who their passengers were. Barbour found the New York law to be a valid exercise of state jurisdiction. "[T]he authority of a state [within its own boundaries] is complete, unqualified, and exclusive," he wrote.

Barbour's mark on the Court was small in the five years he served. Scholars, when polled in 1970, found Barbour an inconsequential judge whose Court career had been cut short and whose impact was minimal. After having been in ill health, Barbour returned to his judicial duties in February 1841. In the evening of February 24 he worked late with his fellow justices, not retiring from his labors until 10:00 P.M. When he failed to appear for breakfast the next morning, a worried justice sent a servant to discover the cause of the absence. Finally the chief justice and Justice Joseph Story went to Barbour's room and found him in his bed, apparently sleeping serenely, but it was a permanent sleep.

Analysis of Qualifications

In the years after the War of 1812, the country moved away from its eastern seaboard and its colonial roots. New ideas and men to champion them were brought forward. Still, a few leaders continued to hold to old Republican principles. Nathaniel Macon of North Carolina, a candidate for vice president in 1824, was the archetypical "Old Republican." Philip Barbour and the close-knit Essex Junto in Virginia that he represented so well, were also among those who tried to stem the tide of political, social, and economic change. Of course they failed in their effort to fight increased democratization and Constitutional liberalism, but they represented ably the conservative, almost aristocratic ideals of another age.

Barbour served in two widely different capacities in the national government. For 12 years he was a Congressman, for five more at the end of his life he was a Supreme Court justice. In the former he played a relatively significant role, mainly in debates concerning Barbour's view of the Constitution. His views were rejected as often as not, but he was a logical, vigorous debater who did not stoop to personal attacks. Barbour's careful, unembellished style was a sharp contrast to that of Henry Clay, whom Barbour replaced as speaker of the House. Barbour was not a strong speaker, and was replaced by Clay with little difficulty after a two-year stint in the speaker's chair. On the Supreme Court beginning in 1836, Barbour played no major role in reshaping the Court's direction, other than through his voting with Taney and other Jacksonians. He followed Taney in modifying the broad pronouncements of the Marshall court that had extended federal authority in many areas, but the change was undramatic.

In all his roles Barbour was an uncompromising defender of Virginia. Slavery was often the issue, and Barbour stood unalterably opposed to any limitations on the ability of slaveowners to take their "property" anywhere in the country. This same rigid understanding of Constitutional limitations made him oppose any expenditures for internal improvements, and to argue against a high tariff. He became a rallying point for fellow Southern conservatives as a compromise choice for speaker in 1821, and was the clear and unanimous choice back home in Virginia for president of the state's constitutional convention. Barbour earned the respect of both friend and foe. He was industrious, honest, and conscientious as a legislator and as a judge. In the eulogy delivered by Justice Story, Barbour was credited with having immersed himself in study of the law once he was appointed to the Supreme Court, devoting much of his leisure hours to filling in the abysmally weak preparation he had received for a legal career.

Intelligent but inflexible, nominated by the Whigs but still a Jacksonian Democrat, conscientious but ill-prepared by education or experience for the highest post in the country, Philip Barbour was a typically rational political choice as a vice presidential nominee. He was qualified in few other ways. There is more than a slight possibility that had he been elected vice president, and succeeded to the presidency as his own fellow Virginian Democrat-turned–Whig, John Tyler did four years later, Barbour would have been equally adept at becoming a man without a party. He would not have agreed with any of the Whig platform, but would have been ostracized from the Democrats because of his treason of running as a Whig. There is no reason to lament his failure to become a heartbeat away from the presidency.

BARBOUR BIBLIOGRAPHY

Bartus, Sister M.R. "The Presidential Election of 1836." Unpublished Ph.D. dissertation, Fordham University, 1967, pp. 53–54, 160–165.

Blaustein, Albert P., and Roy M. Mersky. *The First One Hundred Justices*. Hamden, Conn. (1978).

Cynn, P.P. "Philip Pendleton Barbour." *John P. Branch Historical Papers* IV (June 1913), pp. 67–77.

Gatell, Frank O. "Philip Pendleton Barbour." *The Justices of the United States Supreme Court, 1789–1969*. Edited by Leon Friedman and Fred Israel. 4 vols., New York City (1969), I, 717–734.

Green, R.T. *Genealogical and Historical Notes on Culpeper County, Virginia, Embracing a Revised and Enlarged Edition of Dr. Philip Slaughter's History of St. Mark's Parish*. Culpeper, Va. (1900).

Lowry, Charles D. *James Barbour: A Jeffersonian Republican*. University of Alabama (1984).

Slaughter, Philip. *History of St. Mark's Parish, Culpeper County, Virginia...*, pp. 118–121 (genealogical information), Baltimore (1877).

Story, Joseph (?). "Obituary. Philip Pendleton Barbour." *Peters' Report of Cases ... in the Supreme Court of the United States* XVI (1842) ii.

*1836 recipient of electoral votes
for vice president*

William Smith

Born c.1762, near the boundary between North and South Carolina; died June 26, 1840, in Huntsville, Alabama. Married Margaret Duff in 1781, when she was 14. They had a daughter.

William Smith's background is sketchy. Family lore held that Smith's father was wealthy, but lost much with the devaluation of continental money. William allegedly was a classmate of Andrew Jackson and William H. Crawford at a country school in South Carolina. Smith at least knew these future national leaders when all three were young boys. Smith attended the Mount Zion Collegiate Institute in Winnsboro and graduated in 1780. One friend told a later biographer that Smith was "wild, reckless, intemperate, rude and boisterous" in his early years, though a descendant said his only vice was tobacco. The same friend who thought him wild also said that his marriage at 19 to 14-year-old Margaret Duff reformed him. Smith remained vindictive towards foes, strong-willed and no conciliator. He became a lawyer in 1784, settled first in Pinckneyville and then in York, South Carolina, to practice. He also accumulated sufficient land to become a planter.

Smith served in the state senate from 1802 to 1808, the last two years as senate president. From 1808 to 1816 he was a judge of the state Circuit Court of Appeals. From the beginning of John C. Calhoun's lengthy political career, Smith appeared to resent the 20-year younger man's influence. Calhoun said that Smith was "a weak political intriguer." In 1816 Smith was elected to the U.S. Senate. He was a states' rights advocate, opposed to a national bank, to federal expenditures on internal improvements, and to a high tariff. Calhoun was a leading candidate for the 1824 presidential election. Smith supported Secretary of the Treasury William Crawford, and followed Crawford's orders to vote against Secretary Calhoun's War Department program. Calling Smith "narrow-minded" and "wedded to

Georgia politicians [i.e., Crawford]," Calhoun was instrumental in the legislature's electing Robert Hayne in 1822 to replace Smith in the Senate.

Back home in Carolina, Smith helped organize the so-called states rights' "Radicals" in opposition to Calhoun, who at this stage in his career was a strong nationalist. Smith was elected to the legislature in 1824. There he led the "Revolution of 1825" that saw adoption of resolutions declaring unconstitutional a protective tariff and any federally-funded internal improvements. In 1826 the legislature elected Smith by a 83–81 vote to the U.S. Senate to fill a vacancy. Smith's obsessive dislike for Calhoun was shaken by Calhoun's cordiality when Smith returned to Washington. Smith said that Calhoun "treated me with so much kindness and consideration that I could not hate him as I wished to do." Someone guessed that "Smith hated Calhoun the more for not being able to hate him!"

Smith backed Andrew Jackson's election in 1828. William Crawford's Georgia supporters gave Smith the state's electoral votes for vice president. Calhoun won most of the rest. President Jackson apparently offered Smith a seat on the U.S. Supreme Court in 1829, but he declined. Smith publicly disagreed with Calhoun's nullification doctrine in the crisis over the "Tariff of Abominations." Smith's unionist stand helped Calhoun's forces defeat him when he ran for a full Senate term in 1830. Smith served in the state senate from 1831 to 1832. He moved to Louisiana in 1832. Some thought Smith left because of Calhoun's clear control over Carolina politics. Smith had become a wealthy man, in part by investing in

WILLIAM SMITH
(From the collection of Dr. Caroline Smith Helms and Tybring Hemphill)

land in Louisiana and Alabama. After a brief Louisiana stay, he settled on a farm near Huntsville, Alabama. Smith received all of Virginia's electoral votes for vice president in 1836, largely due to that state's resentment that Virginia Senator William Rives had been passed over for vice president at the national convention. In March, 1837 Jackson appointed Smith to the U.S. Supreme Court. Smith was to have circuit riding responsibilities for what was then the Ninth Circuit, being Alabama, Mississippi, Arkansas, and Louisiana. All three Louisiana congressmen and one from Mississippi sent a protest to the Senate against Smith, saying he was too old at 75 and too long removed from the practice of law to be a judge. The Senate confirmed Smith, but he declined. He wrote a public letter saying that he declined not due to age or "any doubt of my legal learning," but because of a desire to stay active in Jacksonian politics. Smith was elected to Alabama's legislature, serving from 1836 to 1840.

Smith's called his Alabama estate "Calhoun Place." He died there in 1840.

SMITH BIBLIOGRAPHY

Boucher, Chauncy S. *The Nullification Crisis in South Carolina*. Chicago (1916).

Carson, Hampton L. *The History of the Supreme Court of the United States*. Holmes Beach, Fla. (1991, reprint of 1904 edition).

Hardin, Richard Larry. "William Smith and the Rise of Sectionalism in South Carolina." Unpublished master's thesis, University of South Carolina (1971).

O'Neal, John Belton. *Biographical Sketches of the Bench and Bar of South Carolina*. Spartanburg (1975, reprint of 1859 edition), pp. 106–120.

Smith, Caroline Patricia. "Jacksonian Conservative: The Later Years of William Smith, 1826–1840." Unpublished doctoral dissertation, Auburn University (1977).

_____. "South Carolina 'Radical': The Political Career of William Smith to 1826." Unpublished master's thesis, Auburn University (1971).

Swisher, Carl B. *History of the Supreme Court of the United States, the Taney Period*. Volume 5. New York (1974).

Warren, Charles. *The Supreme Court in United States History*. Boston (3 vols., 1922), vol. 1.

Wiltse, Charles M. *John C. Calhoun: Nationalist, 1782–1828*. Indianapolis (1944).

_____. *John C. Calhoun: Nullifier, 1829–1839*. Indianapolis (1949).

Election of 1840

NOMINATIONS

Whig Party Convention (1st): December 4–6, 1839, in Harrisburg, Pennsylvania. *President*— William Henry Harrison, nominated after two informal ballots. His first ballot total was 91 votes; he had 148 out of 254 on the final ballot. Henry Clay (Ky.) and Winfield Scott (N.J.) were his principal opponents. *Vice president*— John Tyler, nominated unanimously on the first ballot.

Democratic Party Convention (3rd): May 5–6, 1840, at the Hall of the Musical Association, in Baltimore, Maryland. *President*— Martin Van Buren, nominated unanimously on the first ballot. *Vice president*— no nomination was made. Richard M. Johnson was the favorite, and the incumbent, but had sufficient opposition that the convention decided to leave the choice of vice president to each state individually. No other serious contender arose.

GENERAL ELECTION, November 3, 1840

Popular Vote

Harrison 1,275,390
Van Buren 1,128,854
Other 7,564

Electoral Vote

PRESIDENT

Harrison — 234 (19 states)
Van Buren — 60 (7 states)

VICE PRESIDENT

Tyler — 234; Johnson — 48; L.W. Tazewell — 11; J.K. Polk — 1

Winners

William Henry Harrison, 9th president
John Tyler, 10th vice president

Losers

Martin Van Buren, Richard M. Johnson

*1840 presidential nominee —
Democratic Party*

Martin Van Buren

No biographical sketch of Van Buren is included because he served as president from March 4, 1837, until March 4, 1841 (8th president).

State represented: New York.

Birth: December 5, 1782.

Age on Inauguration Day (March 4, 1841): 58 years, 3 months.

Death: July 24, 1862.

MARTIN VAN BUREN
(From the author's collection)

*1840 vice presidential
nominee — Democratic Party*

Richard M. Johnson

No biographical sketch of Johnson is included here because he served as vice president from March 4, 1837, until March 4, 1841 (9th vice president).

State represented: Kentucky.

Birth: October 17, 1780.

Age on Inauguration Day (March 4, 1841): 60 years, 4½ months.

Death: November 19, 1850.

RICHARD M. JOHNSON
(Reproduced from the Collections of the Library of Congress)

Election of 1844

NOMINATIONS

Liberty Party Convention (2nd): August 30, 1843, in Buffalo, New York. *President—* James G. Birney, nominated by the 148 delegates from 12 states. *Vice president—* Thomas Morris.

Whig Party Convention (2nd): May 1, 1844, at the Universalist Church, in Baltimore, Maryland. *President—* Henry Clay, nominated unanimously by resolution. *Vice president—* Theodore Frelinghuysen, nominated on the third ballot with 155 votes of the 271 cast. He had 101 on the first ballot. John Davis (Mass.), Millard Fillmore (N.Y.), and John Sergeant (Penn.) also were in contention.

Democratic Party Convention (4th): May 27–29, 1844, in the Odd Fellows' Hall, Baltimore, Maryland. *President—* James K. Polk, nominated unanimously on the ninth ballot, after a stampede of vote changes had occurred; received his first votes, 44, on the eighth ballot, out of 262 cast. Martin Van Buren and Lewis Cass were the other main possibilities. *Vice President—* Silas Wright, nominated with 256 votes of the 266 cast. Wright refused the nomination by a telegram sent on May 29. On the 30th of May, George M. Dallas was named on the second ballot with 220 out of 256 votes cast. He received 13 votes in the first ballot. John Fairfield (Me.) was the other chief contender.

GENERAL ELECTION, November 5, 1844

Popular Vote

Polk	1,339,494
Clay	1,300,004
Birney	62,103
Other	2,058

Electoral Vote

PRESIDENT
Polk —170 (15 states)
Clay —105 (11 states)
VICE PRESIDENT
Dallas —170; Frelinghuysen —105

Winners
James K. Polk, 11th president
George M. Dallas, 11th vice president

Losers
Henry Clay, Theodore Frelinghuysen, Silas Wright, James Birney, Thomas Morris

---

1844 presidential nominee—
Whig Party

Henry Clay

The biographical sketch for Clay appears in the section on the 1824 election, pages 78–84.

State Represented: Kentucky.
Birth: April 12, 1777.
Age on Inauguration Day (March 4, 1845): 67 years, 10½ months.
Death: June 19, 1852.

1844 vice presidential nominee—
Whig Party

Theodore Frelinghuysen

Full name: Theodore Frelinghuysen.
State represented: New Jersey.
Birth: Franklin Township, Somerset County, New Jersey, March 28, 1787.
Age on Inauguration Day (March 4, 1845): 57 years, 11 months.
Education: Tutored at home; attended Queen's College grammar school (later Rutgers), 1798–1800; attended classical school of Dr. Robert Finley at Basking Ridge, N.J.; began Princeton College, 1802, graduated 1804; studied law under Richard Stockton, admitted to bar, 1808.

HENRY CLAY and THEODORE FRELINGHUYSEN
(From the collection of David J. and Janice L. Frent)

Religion: Presbyterian, then Reformed Protestant Dutch Church.

Ancestry/prominent relatives: The Rev. Theodorus Jacobus Frelinghuysen came from East Friesland, later part of Germany, in January, 1720; he was a pastor; Frederick Frelinghuysen (father), member of Continental Congress, U.S. senator; Frederick Theodore

Frelinghuysen (nephew and adopted son), U.S. senator and ambassador, secretary of state.

Occupation: Attorney, educator.

Public office: New Jersey attorney general, 1817–1829; defeated for Senate, 1826; declined to be appointed to N.J. Supreme Court, 1826; U.S. Senate, March 24, 1829–March 3, 1835; mayor of Newark, 1836–1839, resigned; unsuccessful Whig nominee for vice president, 1844.

Home: Grew up at Millstone, family homestead in Somerset County, N.J.

Death: April 12, 1862, at New Brunswick, N.J., at age 75 years, ½ month.

Burial: First Reformed Protestant Dutch Church Cemetery, New Brunswick, N.J.

Personal characteristics: A little under six feet tall, well-proportioned, muscular; broad forehead, soft dreamy eyes that could flash when aroused; amiable, tender. Bent slightly in later years.

Father: Frederick Frelinghuysen (April 13, 1753–April 13, 1804), U.S. senator, lawyer, Revolutionary War patriot.

Mother: Gertrude Schenck (?–March 11, 1794), married in 1775; daughter of Hendrick Schenck.

Siblings: Maria (March 1778–March 13, 1832), married the Rev. John Cornell. Catherine (?–?), married the Rev. Gideon N. Judd. John (March 21, 1776–April 10, 1833), married (1) Louisa Mercer in 1797, and (2) Elizabeth Van Vechten on November 1, 1811. Frederick, Jr. (November 8, 1788–November 10, 1820), married Jane DuMont, August 4, 1812.

Stepmother: Ann Yard (?–?), married in 1794.

Half brother/sister: Sarah, died at age 18. Elizabeth, married Dr. James Bruyn Elmendorf.

First wife: Charlotte Mercer (1784–1854), daughter of Archibald Mercer; married in 1808.

Children: None, but adopted the children of his deceased brother Frederick. These were: DuMont (February 16, 1816–1905), married Martina Vanderveer, and was a lawyer and prominent church lay leader; Frederick Theodore (August 4, 1817–May 20, 1885), lawyer, U.S. senator, and secretary of state; Gertrude Ann (1814–1886), married William Mercer;

Susan (1813–1863), married M.D. Waterman; and Maria Louisa (?–?), married John C. Elmendorf. They also adopted a nephew of Mrs. Frelinghuysen: William T. Mercer (1812–1886), married Gertrude Ann Frelinghuysen in 1835, another of their adopted children.

Second wife: Harriet Pompelly (?–?), married in 1857.

Historic sites/memorials: The school he attended, Basking Ridge Classical School, is in Basking Ridge, New Jersey.

The first Frelinghuysen in America was a Dutch Reformed Church minister who was sent to the New World in 1720, and settled a few miles west of New Brunswick, New Jersey. For 25 years, Theodorus Jacobus Frelinghuysen, whose father also had been a Reformed pastor, preached to a not always receptive flock. His message was stern, his words and demands unbending. All five of his sons were ordained into the ministry, while his two daughters married ministers. Grandson Frederick, Theodore's father, may have been rebelling against tradition, for despite his mother's urging he did not enter the ministry. Frederick entered the legal profession instead. After the Revolution, he gained a general's commission in 1794. Serving also in the United States Senate and various lower political offices, Frederick Frelinghuysen developed a different tradition of service from that of his forebears. Future vice presidential candidate, college administrator, and Christian activist Theodore Frelinghuysen took heed of both strains of family history.

The family home, called Millstone, was a comfortable dwelling along the Millstone River in central New Jersey. Educated at home until he was 11, Theodore then attended the grammar school connected with Queen's College (later Rutgers College) in New Brunswick. After two years, he received his father's permission to leave the school and return home, to devote himself to farming as a career. His mother having died when he was only seven, young Theodore received, at times begrudgingly, maternal direction from his stepmother. When Theodore's father was gone from home for an extended period on political matters, the stepmother packed Theodore up and sent him to a school in Basking Ridge, run by Dr. Finley. Once there, he gradually became resigned to and then enchanted by his education. Theodore graduated tied in his class with Joseph R. Ingersoll for top honors. Ingersoll would also later gain considerable distinction, serving as ambassador to Great Britain.

After graduation, Theodore returned to the family home, Millstone, which had come under the control of his brother John after their father died in 1804. John was an attorney and for a time Theodore read law in his office. Theodore then studied law with Richard Stockton of Princeton and was admitted to the bar in 1808. While studying for his own career, Theodore also tutored other boys. Theodore moved to Newark to open his law office. He developed a debating society with other young men and through these and other activities became well known, liked, and respected. The year after being admitted to the bar, he married Charlotte Mercer, daughter of Archibald Mercer. Their marriage was never blessed with any children, but the couple adopted several nephews and nieces.

Frelinghuysen had labored in obscurity as a lawyer until 1812, when he gained considerable publicity by defending a black man against a murder charge. There was no doubt the defendant had committed the act, but the question was whether it was done in self-defense. A masterful argument drawing on the sympathies of the judge and jury saved his client. His efforts made a tremendous impression on his fellow attorneys, as well as the public at large. This momentous boost led to an extensive private practice, lucrative and well publicized. Frelinghuysen understood human nature and made his arguments effectively. An imaginative mind, clear and precise diction, perfectly chosen phrasing, and a clear, mellow voice to project his thoughts made him an impressive advocate. Many contemporaries would forever believe, despite the fame and success that followed his subsequent careers, that he had made a serious mistake in abandoning the legal profession.

During the War of 1812, this gentle but intensely patriotic man volunteered for service. He had not been drafted but felt it his duty to participate anyway. Frelinghuysen never saw action but did raise and command a company of volunteers. It was only a momentary break in his legal rise, and success continued to crown his efforts in court. In 1817, the New Jersey legislature, though not in political sympathy with him, thought so much of his ability that they selected him state attorney general. The selection surprised the 30-year-old lawyer, but he accepted. Frelinghuysen would be reelected twice and did not retire from office until chosen for a still higher position. Frelinghuysen was in 1826 named to the state supreme court, but he declined the legislature's offer.

Several of his cases as attorney general were significant. He helped establish the proposition that when a religious society splits over philosophical differences, the faction that remains closest to the original principles of the organization should own the society's property. The principle was established in a case in which he represented a Quaker faction. A highly publicized 30-day court proceeding took place. Frelinghuysen's argument before the court was widely praised, and successful. No more financially significant case was tried than a dispute as to which entity, the state or the Board of Proprietors, owned all the land under the waters along the coast and tideland waterways. Frelinghuysen's position in favor of the board was upheld in the lower court, but after he had turned the representation over to other attorneys, the decision was reversed on appeal. Throughout his work, Frelinghuysen established a reputation for intuitive brilliance, hard work, but perhaps equal to all other attributes, a Christian influence on his own clients and on his opponents. His humility and openmindedness kept him from being sanctimonious, and his good humor and obvious affection for others assured his popularity with his acquaintances.

While serving as state attorney general, Frelinghuysen was elected by the legislature in 1828 to the United States Senate. He was not noted during his one term there for innovative proposals, but he was respected and loved for what William Lloyd Garrison termed in a poem written about Frelinghuysen, his "Christian statesmanship." A six-hour speech opposing the forced removal of the Cherokee and Creek Indians from Georgia and other southeastern states earned him initial fame. The New Jersey senator tried to amend a bill to permit those Indians who so desired, to stay in their ancestral areas and to be protected from the encroachment of the white man. No one, he insisted, should be forced to abandon his home. He said, as the conscience of the Senate, "If we abandon these aboriginal proprietors of the soil ... how shall we justify it to our country? ... Her good name is worth all else...." A lengthy debate ensued, one which Frelinghuysen — and the Indians — lost. Frelinghuysen called his efforts a "solemn duty to a most 'interesting' portion of my fellowman." The plea fell on too many deaf ears to change the result, and the Indians had to embark on the nightmarish "Trail of Tears" that led to countless deaths.

Frelinghuysen opposed other measures that seemed to place the desires of government or business above the demands of conscience. The New Jersey senator resoundingly opposed the idea of mail delivery on the Sabbath. He requested the president to declare a day of public humiliation because of an epidemic of cholera. Many well-known leaders, including Henry Clay and Daniel Webster, gave Frelinghuysen tribute for strengthening the moral sense of government.

It was not just matters of conscience that stirred the one-term senator. In 1832, he could be found espousing both the candidacy and the policies of presidential nominee Henry Clay, whom Frelinghuysen would join on another losing ticket 12 years later. Fervor for Clay was clear in a public letter Frelinghuysen had published in a newspaper:

> I say [he has] *just* claims [to the presidency] — for if eminent qualifications — if exalted talents, and persevering and unshaken devotion to the vital interests of the country deserve such distinction, his title is full. I have been investigating Mr. Clay's public character, for the whole session and for many years before; and the more I have studied, the more I have esteemed and admired.

Besides giving election support to Clay, Frelinghuysen voted consistently with the Kentuckian in the Senate. Both men favored the creation of a new Second Bank of the United States, wanted the proceeds from the sale of public lands to be distributed among all the states, and sought to broaden the class of veterans who could receive federal pensions.

Most significant, perhaps, of the issues facing these future running mates was the question of nullification. South Carolina attacked the very system of federalism by rejecting the authority of the national government in the area of the tariff. This threatened to cause civil war in 1833. The high tariff had caused considerable hardship in the South. Frelinghuysen's answer to attempted nullification of that tariff by South Carolina was to urge a reduction in tariff duties. "If this were a mere abstract question," Frelinghuysen said he would favor the high tariff duties. However, "it is vain to disguise this matter, that for the last nine or ten years, a constant, pervading, and almost universal discontent with our tariff system, has prevailed throughout the Southern section of the United States." The opposition had been so severe, so uncompromising, the senator believed, that national harmony demanded that the North compromise. Accordingly, Frelinghuysen voted in favor of Henry Clay's plan to reduce the tariff duties gradually. It was not a complete capitulation to the South, for the New Jersey senator favored a new look at the question in ten years.

That was the carrot. Frelinghuysen also supported the use of the very strong stick of the "Force Bill," whereby President Andrew Jackson was authorized to use troops in the South to enforce the tariff. Thus the senator clearly favored obedience to the law, sympathized with the commercial interests of his native state, but simultaneously sought to lessen the tensions between the regions of the country by compromise.

Nullification placed Clay and Frelinghuysen alongside President Jackson; few other issues did so. Jackson not only vetoed the bill creating a new national bank, but ordered the withdrawal of federal deposits from the existing one, whose charter still had a few years to run. Frelinghuysen could be counted as a constant opponent of Jackson on the question, despite that the Democratic New Jersey legislature instructed him to vote favorably on the president's measures. The senator voted to censure Jackson for his actions, and then voted not to expunge the resolution of censure after the Democrats had regained control of the Senate.

Such independence made Frelinghuysen's reelection by the Democrat-controlled legislature impossible, and thus, on March 4, 1835, he retired from his Congressional duties and was replaced by a Democrat. He reestablished his law practice in Newark. His fame was no longer limited just to his courtroom prowess, but was now augmented by a national political reputation. The people of Newark soon after the city was incorporated in 1836 elected Frelinghuysen their mayor. He served two one-year terms and then retired. Public work was now impossible to avoid, but then Frelinghuysen seemed to have no inclination to avoid it. His involvement in charitable and religious organizations was mammoth. At one time or another this apparently tireless man was president of the American Bible Society, the American Tract Society, the American Sunday School Union, the American Temperance Society, and the American Board of Commissioners for Foreign Missions. Local church work in Newark took considerable time. In 1835, his biographer states, he thought seriously of being ordained. With Henry Clay, he was a member of the American Colonization Society, which sought to solve the growing slavery crisis by resettling freed slaves in Africa or South America.

From 1839 until his death in 1862, Frelinghuysen was almost totally consumed, in addition to the just-stated civic responsibilities, with education. The Council of the University of the City of New York (now New York University) unanimously selected him as their chancellor. Talbot Chambers, who is the author of the first book-length biography of Frelinghuysen, said that the New Jersey attorneys who had been overwhelmed with Frelinghuysen's legal skills, thought "that to put him at the head of any university was like burying him in a marble mausoleum before his time." It was not a comfortable retirement the new chancellor sought, however, but instead a mechanism to further his considerable interest in, indeed almost reverence for, education.

The same year that he became chancellor of New York University, Frelinghuysen also served as vice president of the American Common School Society. Interest both in colonization and in education are seen in the chancellor's proposals that the colonies for freedmen not be founded until slaves first were educated. Immediate emancipation Frelinghuysen thought would be harmful, and instead, when the slave was colonized, he should already be nourished "by the lights of science, religion and liberty." In 1836 he declared, "We must, by schools and colleges there, render the colonies hopeful spots, toward which the colored man will turn his eye and his heart from the ends of the earth, when he thinks of himself and his children."

While serving as chancellor, Frelinghuysen could give his old friend and political comrade, Henry Clay, little more than moral support for the presidency. In 1844, Clay received the final of his three presidential nominations. With President William Henry Harrison's death and John Tyler's succession as chief executive fresh on the delegates' minds, a careful choice of a running mate had to be made. Clay was 67, not nearly as vigorous or healthy as in his younger years; the presidential nominee was thought to have unsavory aspects to his personal life, and was a Southern slaveowner, albeit also a staunch nationalist. Frelinghuysen provided balance to all these facets of the Clay candidacy. Apparently Clay was friendly with his running mate, but not enthusiastic over the convention's choice. Four ballots were taken before the New Jersey educator was named. The practice of creating campaign songs may have made Clay's lyricist wince at the prospect of rhyming Frelinghuysen with anything. Necessity did produce a few almost-memorable lines:

> Hurrah! Hurrah! The nation's risin'
> For Harry Clay and Frelinghuysen.

More of an albatross to the campaign than the songs were the efforts of the Democrats in immigrant neighborhoods to make Roman Catholics, principally the Irish, fearful of religious persecution if so prominent and devout a Protestant as Frelinghuysen should ever succeed to the presidency. New York and Philadelphia were particular targets of that nasty tactic. Horace Greeley discussed long after the election the desire of the Democrats to frighten uneducated Roman Catholics by identifying Frelinghuysen

> with an important religious sect, at whose bible anniversaries and missionary meetings he was frequently an active and influential attendant. He was known to belong to the presbyterian denomination of Christians; and this circumstance while it brought over a few additions to the Whig ranks, was destined to be used with great effect in prejudicing the minds of Roman Catholics and adopted citizens....

It is doubtful that fears over the second man on the ticket turned sufficient votes for defeat, and instead the narrow loss of Clay and Frelinghuysen in the general election should be attributed to other factors. Most notable was the abolitionist party's nominee, James G. Birney, taking enough votes in New York to give that state and the presidency to James K. Polk. The losing vice presidential candidate took defeat gracefully, resuming his duties at New York University.

Eleven years marked the length of Frelinghuysen's tenure as chancellor. In 1850, he resigned to return to his native state and accept the presidency of Rutgers University in New Brunswick. He was inaugurated on July 24, 1850. Besides serving as president, he also was a professor of international and constitutional law and of moral philosophy. His regime was not marked by any vast growth in the university; new buildings were not erected; more students were not attracted in large numbers. However, the new president tried to consolidate the position of the school by markedly increasing its endowment. He failed to make significant gains towards the goal, but marginal improvement was obtained. It seemed a quiet, undynamic presidency. Frelinghuysen was 63 when he assumed his Rutgers post and suffered severely from illness. He was past applying himself vigorously. A somewhat faster pace became necessary when Abraham Lincoln was elected president in 1860, and civil war loomed. Frelinghuysen had the honor of seeing the president-elect stop his train in New Brunswick on his way to his inauguration, and speak to the students and other citizens who crowded around. When war came, the Rutgers president urged his students to enlist, and proudly saw large numbers do so.

After 12 years at Rutgers, and one year of civil war, Theodore Frelinghuysen died at the age of 75. His last years had not been comfortable physically; his first wife had died in 1854, but he had remarried three years later. No children of his own comforted his old age, but he adopted the children of his brother Frederick, who died in 1820.

Analysis of Qualifications

A few other nominees have been in part selected because of their religious piety, but in none was that factor so dominant as in the case of Frelinghuysen. "The Christian Statesman," he was called, who acted as the conscience of both Congress and his Whig party. His involvement in social reform was likewise well known. Perhaps in no other case was it feared that a counter-balance to the presidential nominee's public image of immoral character was desperately needed.

There was achievement in each of Theodore Frelinghuysen's several careers. As an attorney, he was preeminent, rising to fortune and fame in New Jersey. He was considered a true loss to the bar when he forsook private legal practice for politics and then academia. As a politician, he served ably as attorney general of his state, was popular and effective in that role, and then rose to the United States Senate. A public-spirited man of the first order, he devoted himself to reform and religion. Becoming attorney general and foregoing a lucrative private practice indicates that fact; his service in charitable causes is still clearer proof. Once promoted to the United States Senate, he gained nationwide renown for his morality. He simply saw no issue as separate from his sense of right and wrong.

Frelinghuysen's most useful public office was probably that of senator. He was benevolent, wise, free from deviousness. He was also practiced and conciliatory. There was little to suggest the unbending ideologue in his public life. True, he saw public issues in moral terms; he was a warm, charming individual with sincere compassion for all his fellow men. These attributes did not prevent him from advocating the use of force, if needed, during both the nullification crisis and the Civil War. He was an intellectual, yet had lived far from the ivory tower of college life before he assumed an academic post at the age of 52. There was no sanctimoniousness to Frelinghuysen. He was a Christian who truly perceived his own lack of perfection.

Few men who failed to achieve the presidency have served in sufficiently varied capacities to permit a true measure of their fitness for that highest of public offices. That is particularly true in this case. In fact, Frelinghuysen only served eight years (as a senator and mayor) in a public capacity other than that of a practicing lawyer. Frelinghuysen was a gifted orator, intelligent, an incisive legal thinker, honest, effective as a United States senator, a competent if undynamic college administrator. Public-spirited and intensely religious, he was also practical. A lengthier tenure in legislative or other public office might well have given greater substance to the impression his career leaves, that he was an excellent candidate for high office. Even so, there are too many positive aspects, and a dearth of negative, to permit his placement anywhere except among the capable losing candidates.

FRELINGHUYSEN BIBLIOGRAPHY

Chambers, Talbot W. *Memoir of the Life and Character of the Late Hon. Theodore Frelinghuysen, LL.D.* New York City (1863).

Chute, William J. "The Educational Thought of Theodore Frelinghuysen." *Rutgers University Library Journal* 18 (1953), pp. 20–27.

Demarest, William H.S. *A History of Rutgers College 1766–1924.* New Brunswick, N.J.(1924).

Eells, Robert. *Forgotten Saint. The Life of Theodore Frelinghuysen: A Case Study of Christian Leadership.* Lanham, Md., and Palos Heights, Ill. (1987).

Hess, Stephen. *America's Political Dynasties: From Adams to Kennedy.* Garden City (1966), pp. 339–363.

Hunt, William Southworth. "Theodore Frelinghuysen: A Discussion of His Vice Presidential Candidacy in the Clay-Polk Campaign of 1844, and Its Reasons." *Proceedings of the New Jersey Historical Society* LVI (1938), pp. 30–40.

Lee, Francis Bazley, ed. *Genealogical and Memorial History of the State of New Jersey* I, New York City (1910).

McFarland, Emily Frelinghuysen, and Ross Armstrong McFarland. *The Frelinghuysen Family in New Jersey, 1720–1970.* Cambridge, Mass. (1970).

Parker, Cortlandt. *The Essex Bar, Inaugural Address of Cortlandt Parker, Esq.* Newark (1874).

_____. *A Sketch of the Life and Public Services of Theodore Frelinghuysen.* New York City (1844).

1844 vice presidential nominee —
Democratic Party

Silas Wright

Full name: Silas Wright, Jr.

State represented: New York.

Birth: May 24, 1795, Amherst, Massachusetts.

Age on Inauguration Day (March 4, 1845): 49 years, 9½ months.

Education: Middlebury (Vermont) Academy, 1808–1811; Middlebury College, 1811–1815; studied law with attorneys in Washington County, New York; admitted to bar in 1819.

Religion: Presbyterian.

Ancestry/prominent relatives: First Wrights arrived in Massachusetts in 1630; Silas Wright, Sr. (father) elected to Vermont state legislature.

Occupation: Attorney.

Public offices: During 1819 through 1823 served in several capacities, at various times being appointed surrogate of St. Lawrence County (1821–1824), postmaster of Canton, justice of the peace, commissioner of deeds, town clerk, and inspector of highways and common schools; New York state senator, 1823–March 1827; U.S. House of Representatives, March 4, 1827–February 16, 1829; resigned to become comptroller of New York, 1829–1833; U.S. senator, January 4, 1833–November 26, 1844; declined to be appointed U.S. secretary of treasury, 1845; declined vice presidential nomination, 1844; New York governor, January 1, 1845–January 1, 1847, defeated 1846.

Death: August 27, 1847, Canton, New York, at age 52 years, 3 months.

Burial: Old Canton Cemetery, Canton, New York.

Home: Canton, New York, farm.

Personal characteristics: Medium height, brown hair, blue eyes, balding; broad and powerful physique; husky, rough voice.

Father: Silas Wright, Sr. (March 17, 1760–May 13, 1843), tanner and shoemaker, then farmer.

Mother: Eleanore Goodale (?–c. 1846), daughter of Isaac Goodale; married September 17, 1780.

Siblings: Silas was the fifth child in his family.

Wife: Clarissa Moody (July 9, 1804–August 15, 1870), married September 11, 1833, daughter of Medad Moody of Canton, New York.

Children: None.

Few men have declined as many public offices as did Silas Wright — nomination for the presidency and vice presidency, governor, United States Supreme Court justice, United States senator, to name the major ones. He was a man of many talents and achievements, but he was also a pessimist and humble man who often doubted his capacity for high office.

Born in Massachusetts, Wright moved with his family to Vermont when he was only a year old. There his father as a farmer gained his first taste of financial security, if not luxury. The elder Wright was elected to the Vermont legislature, but rose no higher in public life. His son's education was typically sporadic until he was 14, when Silas was enrolled in Addison County Grammar School, and at 16 in the Middlebury, Vermont, Academy. The latter school was a highly religious one, but neither then nor later did Silas indicate much interest in spiritual matters. To help support himself he taught at another school in between his courses at Middlebury. Silas graduated in 1815 and began to "read" law under the guidance of an attorney in Sandy Hill, New York. Apparently Wright decided that opportunities in Vermont were too limiting and that New York would better accommodate his ambitions. In January 1819, he was admitted to the New York bar. Soon thereafter Wright met his future benefactor and ally Martin Van Buren. They became formally introduced when the two strangers got into a friendly scuffle aboard a steamboat. Wright either pushed him or else Van Buren just fell overboard. Van Buren took

it in good humor, and this unusual start of a solid political and personal relation was made.

A place for Wright to practice his newly acquired professional skills was no easy decision. The new lawyer began to ride through New York on horseback to find a suitable location. He stopped at the Canton, New York, home of an old family friend, Medad Moody. Moody agreed to build Wright a house. With that offer as an incentive, and with the additional attractiveness of one of Moody's daughters, Wright decided to stay. Not one to rush things, Wright married Moody's daughter fourteen years later.

The new attorney's political start came soon. Wright's legal mentor, Roger Skinner, was a political power in the state; Van Buren was well on his way in national politics. These and a few other men formed the powerful political force called the Albany Regency, which dominated New York politics for decades. After serving in several minor positions, Wright was elected to the state senate in 1823. He was an intelligent, practical politician who at this stage had few strong stands on issues. His first major task in the senate, and one which was solely partisan, was to secure the state for the Regency's choice for president in 1824, William H. Crawford. Previously in New York the state's electoral college votes had been determined by the legislature, and the Regency wanted to continue that practice for 1824. Particularly was this point crucial because Crawford was not popular in the state and had little chance to win a general election contest. When other approaches failed, Wright joined in postponing the consideration of any change in the procedure used to select presidential electors until after the November election. Wright also joined in the partisan effort to remove former governor DeWitt Clinton as canal commissioner.

Wright's faction lost its legislative control in the 1824 election. It appeared that the United States senator who was to be chosen in 1825 would come from the opposition. However, Wright and others in the party were able to deadlock the Senate's consideration of a successor for Senator Rufus King, and therefore no man was named. A year later, after another election had returned the Regency to power, they were able to choose the new senator. Once the Federalist Party disappeared, two factions of the Democratic-Republican Party had only each other to fight for control of state government, and fight they did. Wright, Van Buren and other "Bucktails" were more economy-minded than their opponents, were skeptical of banks and land speculation, and were hesitant to approve canal projects or other internal improvements. They opposed slavery's extension into the territories. The "Hunkers" held opposing views on each of these issues. Wright would always be opposed to banks. Later in his career, he would become so antagonistic to the financial community that he called it a moral, economic, and political blight on the country.

After four years in the legislature, Wright moved up to the United States Congress, serving from 1827 until 1829. The main issue Wright faced as a congressman was the tariff. He gradually became convinced that the only reason for a tariff was to produce revenue, and if instead the tariff was employed to protect local industries then it was wrong. The presidential election in 1828 found him and his ally Van Buren as staunch supporters of Andrew Jackson. Wright's election that same year was only by 45 votes, as Jackson was not popular in Wright's district.

In this same election, Van Buren was elected New York governor. The new governor soon sought to advance Wright's career. A United States Senate vacancy existed; the position of state comptroller was also open. Wright said the United States Senate was for wealthier men, that he could not properly fill the post. This was his first of many demurrers to office.

SILAS WRIGHT
(From the Senate Historical Office)

Instead Wright took the lucrative but difficult post of state comptroller. He found his new office complicated. He was the chief financial adviser for the state, required to sit on many boards and commissions. The government was operating in the red and part of the reason was corruption. Wright personally conducted an investigation of graft in a public works project that was supposed to drain swamps and improve navigation on a river channel. The detailed report charged the commissioners responsible with fraud. This and other publicity caused Wright constantly to be mentioned for higher office. In 1832 he refused to run for governor, but instead was mainly concerned with getting Van Buren elected as vice president. This accomplished, Wright agreed to be selected for the United States Senate even though he did not really want to leave Albany.

The nullification crisis in South Carolina was exploding as Wright took his seat at the Capitol. He visited President Jackson, who advised him to notify the Regency of the seriousness of the problem. Wright seemed confused, and he badly wanted advice. However, he eventually concurred in a bill to reduce the tariff sharply, which would alleviate the immediate cause for the South's anger. The bill passed, as did the crisis.

The nullification controversy resolved for the moment, the new senator returned to Canton, New York, finally to marry Clarissa Moody. Almost from the moment of the wedding, Wright's attitude toward politics was under domestic attack. Clarissa was an extremely, embarrassingly shy woman, who wanted nothing to do with public life. The stories of her difficulties in politically-required social gatherings were legion, and Silas was fully aware of the problem. Wright himself told the story of President Van Buren's escorting Clarissa to the dinner table and placing her next to Van Buren's own chair. There was pathos in his humor when Wright remarked, in mock surprise, that Clarissa "did not get under the table, and went through the whole ceremony in fine style."

The two made a strange match, the politician and the bashful bride. The marriage nonetheless was a strong one. One possible point of trouble was Wright's inordinate drinking. In an age of drinkers Wright was not often bested. His complexion was frequently florid from the effects, but his mental and physical abilities were not noticeably affected, or so it was said.

Wright backed Jackson's plan to remove all federal deposits from the congressionally-created national bank. He differed from the president only in the timing of the withdrawal, believing that Jackson should wait until Congress was in session. The attacks on Jackson because of the withdrawals were savage. Wright remained silent, causing vice president Van Buren to ask the reason. Again the feelings of inadequacy were apparent, as Wright announced that there were far abler advocates of the Jackson position than he. Van Buren firmly and helpfully rebuked Wright for his timidity, and Wright soon was involved in the

administration's defense. Yet Wright never was a good speaker. He was unemotional, coldly statistical on occasion, and without persuasive talents. Daniel Webster, a political opponent but obviously one capable of measuring oratorial ability, called Wright "the most inferior man in debate that sat in the Senate." Perhaps an exaggeration, but the remark had Wright properly placed in the lower ranks of orators.

Wright's hard-money, no-speculation views were obvious, as was his partisanship, when he endorsed President Jackson's Specie Circular in 1836 that barred payment for public lands except by coin. Wright called the speculation in land a form of "public gambling," and heartily supported Jackson on the issue. That same year he assisted Van Buren's election to the presidency. Thus it was Van Buren who was in office when several different factors combined to create the Panic of 1837. These included the effects of the Specie Circular, the probable attempt by the national bank to promote a recession and thereby discredit Jackson, and a worldwide recession. The economic distress of that year put the Democrats, and Van Buren in particular, on the defensive. Wright wrote a series of letters for publication in newspapers, explaining the tight-money policies of the president. Few people were convinced. Van Buren's solution was an independent treasury system, thereby removing the banks from government altogether. The New York senator introduced the measure and shepherded it for several sessions. It was finally passed in 1840.

Pessimistic, low on self-esteem, Wright did not take these controversies in stride. He became depressed and in January 1838, said he had "an unusual visitation of hypocondria." Defeats in the Senate on administration proposals were frequent. Wright often commiserated with the president, and was as close an adviser to Van Buren as existed. Slavery agitation did little for Wright's spirits either. He found the institution morally repugnant, but he also opposed involving Congress in this emotional, divisive issue. There was more to be despondent about in 1840, as Wright's political leader and tutor, President Van Buren, was ousted from the White House by the Whigs' "hard cider and log cabin" campaign.

During Van Buren's four years Wright had been chairman of the Finance Committee in the Senate; under the Whigs he lost his chairmanship and much of his influence. One defeat he did not mind was that of Democratic vice president Richard M. Johnson. Wright had for a time tolerated Van Buren's running mate, but by 1840 he found Johnson to be an eccentric embarrassment.

Again in 1840 this great decliner refused to run for an office. This time it was the New York governorship. Wright was afraid that should he be elected governor, the likely Whig majority in the legislature would select an unsatisfactory replacement for senator. The 1840 national election not only resulted in Van Buren's defeat, but also placed the Whigs in power in Congress. Wright's three-year effort to pass the independent treasury bill (1837–1840) was in vain as the Whigs quickly repealed the system. Wright found President John Tyler, who succeeded the deceased William Henry Harrison, an ally in the new fight over a national bank. Tyler twice vetoed bank bills passed by the Whigs. These political wars were more than Wright could stomach, however. With Clarissa lonely in Canton, the senator again discussed retirement.

Wright had been reelected to the United States Senate in 1837 without trouble. He again faced election in 1843. If a confused scramble for the seat would not have threatened to split the Democrats, Wright probably would have retired. Instead he again was selected by the New York legislature. As the battles between Tyler and the Whigs grew more intense, the president tried to make peace with the Democrats. One maneuver was to offer former president Martin Van Buren an appointment to the Supreme Court. Being rebuffed, Tyler offered the same nomination to Wright. This attempt to purchase Democratic support was blatant, but Wright was tempted. Even so, Wright eventually also refused.

At first Wright could not decide what position to take on the annexation of Texas. He knew he wanted no more slave states admitted to the Union, but he also feared dividing the country and destroying Van Buren's chances for a second election to the presidency.

Finally Wright concluded that politics be damned, the country could not afford to admit Texas. The Democratic nomination would require Southern convention delegate votes, which would be unobtainable to anyone who opposed Texas annexation. Still Wright counseled Van Buren to stand firmly against Texas, because it "involve[d] consequences much more momentous than the result of a single election."

Despite Wright's encouragement, Van Buren made no firm stand on the Texas question but tried to postpone a decision until after the election. The national convention opened with Van Buren's holding a clear majority of delegates. Two out of the first three Democratic conventions, in 1832 and 1836, had required a two-thirds majority for nomination. That total Van Buren could probably not get. The two-thirds rule was reimposed by the 1844 convention, dooming Van Buren. After several ballots in which the ex-president received a majority but then began to slip, a plan was developed to substitute Wright for president. Van Buren had given a letter to a delegate to use in case of a deadlock, asking to be withdrawn and for his supporters to vote for Wright. But Wright would not budge, as he wanted neither the presidency nor the suspicion of having been involved in a scheme to advance his own candidacy at the expense of Van Buren's.

After the dark-horse James K. Polk was nominated, Wright won the vice presidential nomination easily. A new invention, the telegraph, was used to communicate with Wright. The New York senator wired back his refusal of the nomination. Several messages were exchanged with Wright, but he only solidified his position. Of all of Wright's refusals of office, this rejection earned him the greatest accolades. To have rejected both the presidency and the vice presidency out of, it was supposed, respect for Van Buren and a sense of integrity, made Wright appear to be a very unusual politician indeed.

This new popularity only intensified the New York Democrat's insistence that he finally agree to run for governor. Van Buren himself argued that declining this offer would make him appear uninterested in the Democrats and particularly in Polk. The presidential nominee could use Wright's presence on the ticket to carry the state. Despite these entreaties, Wright urged supporters not to nominate him. When he received the nomination anyway, he said "never has any incident in my public life been so much against my interests, my feelings, and judgment." Clarissa stated that she wanted her husband's opponent, Millard Fillmore, to win. To the Wrights' and the Whigs' chagrin, Silas did win by ten thousand votes, 241,000 to 231,000.

The troubles facing the new governor were immense. Large, almost feudal land holdings by a few rich individuals had led to rebellion by tenants on these estates. Some bloodshed, much violence, and few easy answers characterized this anti-rent dispute. Wright opposed the violence and found it hard to sympathize with the tenants. His tough measures to end the violence by arresting the tenants were unpopular. An equally controversial stand was to veto a popular measure for canal extension.

The most obvious failure of the Wright governorship was his refusal to fulfill the role of party leader. The intraparty disputes were as vitriolic as ever, but the governor tried to stay aloof. Friends and opponents alike were surprised by his squeamishness, though in truth it seems in character. A President Wright would have been equally timid.

Unsolved and, in some areas, accelerating controversies led to Wright's overwhelming defeat in 1846 when he ran for reelection. A party split was of major importance in his defeat. His administration had succeeded in getting the first steps taken in reform of the anti-rent problems, including removing a landlord's right to seize and sell property to satisfy a tenant's rent obligations. A tax on landlords' income had also been imposed. The most important reform, limiting the length of future leases, failed.

At last, if involuntarily, Wright could retire. He became a teetotaler after decades of over-indulgent drinking. He worked strenuously on his farm and seemed to enjoy it. Involvement in politics was slight, but included was support for the Wilmot Proviso that would have barred slavery in any of the territories acquired as a result of the Mexican War. The physical exertion, the summer's heat, and perhaps even the total abstinence after so many years of drinking, were too much for Wright. He had quit the governorship in January 1847. That summer he suffered two mild heart attacks that gave him warning of his mortality. Finally, on August 27, 1847, he suffered a third and fatal seizure.

Analysis of Qualifications

At first Silas Wright thought politics was a necessary weapon to be used in whatever way necessary to achieve the results he desired. As a member of a powerful, patronage-hungry machine in New York, he saw firsthand how means were justified to achieve ends. But as his career progressed, he changed. Interest in politics waned; interest in specific issues became paramount. At the same time, Wright's innate lack of self-confidence made him shy away from continuing political involvement.

No sound educational foundation was laid for this future leader. Yet he was intelligent, and even if lacking in brilliance and breadth of knowledge, he had common sense. His speaking style was unimpressive, though he spoke clearly and to the point. Logic was his weapon, not emotion or rhetoric. Realizing how his style paled against the abilities of a Webster or a Clay, he was timid in speaking. Vice President Martin Van Buren was amazed at his silence in the Senate while their mutual friend and leader Andrew Jackson was assailed by the Whigs. Wright's only explanation was that he was incapable of giving as effective a defense as was required. Self-doubt dominated Wright. It explained as much as anything his constant refusal of high office. He rejected an excellent opportunity to be nominated president after the 1844 convention became deadlocked. One reason was that he did not want to appear a traitor to Van Buren. Yet Wright's fears concerning such an image of betrayal were grossly exaggerated. Van Buren himself had given a letter to a delegate stating that he wanted Wright to be the nominee if he, Van Buren, failed. The country was sorely in need of leadership, not excuses to avoid leading. A stronger man, equally honorable as Wright, would have taken the nomination.

On issues, Wright was part populist (ahead

of his time), part Free-Soiler, and part hard-nosed politician. He opposed wealth and privilege wherever found. Banks, manufacturers insisting on a high protective tariff, and those who wanted canal improvements and other public projects that would make their businesses more profitable were all targets of his condemnation. A long letter to President Polk about appointments bemoaned the morality of politicians. He said that men who wanted power soon forgot the functions of their office and remembered only the perquisites; they worried little about their obligations and much about their reappointment or reelection. Wright told Polk there was a "pervading thirst among our population" for the spoils of office. On slavery, Wright favored the Wilmot Proviso, but also favored efforts to quiet the sectional bickering. As he approached middle age, though unfortunately it was almost the end of his abbreviated life, Wright became more concerned with principle. As concerned as he was about Van Buren's reelection to the presidency, he would sacrifice that possibility just to add weight to preventing the admission of Texas to the Union. For the willingness to sacrifice political power, to speak honestly regardless of the consequences, he was called the Cato of America, after the Roman whose incorruptible honesty caused him to oppose Caesar.

Silas Wright was a great man in his personality, his honesty, and his devotion to his country. He was not a great leader, as fully demonstrated by his one term as governor of New York. He was an honest, sincere Cato, not a dominating, inspirational Caesar. He served well in the United States Senate. He served much less effectively as governor. The different talents required in each office show the strengths and weaknesses of Silas Wright. He would probably not have made a good president in the time of crisis the country faced in 1844.

WRIGHT BIBLIOGRAPHY

Garraty, John Arthur. *Silas Wright.* New York City (1949).
Gillet, Ransom H. *Life and Times of Silas Wright.* 2 vols. Albany (1874).
Gilpin, Henry D. *An Eulogy on Silas Wright....* Philadelphia (1847).
Hammond, Jabez D. *Life and Times of Silas Wright.* Syracuse (1848).
Jenkins, John S. *Life of Silas Wright.* Auburn, N.Y. (1847).
Mallam, William D. *Silas Wright— The Farmer Statesman.* Canton, N.Y. (1994) (pamphlet published by St. Lawrence County Historical Association).

1844 presidential nominee—
Liberty Party

James G. Birney

Born February 4, 1792, in Danville, Kentucky; died November 25, 1857, in Eagleswood, New Jersey. Married Agatha McDowell on February 1, 1816, who died in 1839. Married a Miss Fitzhugh in 1841.

James Gillespie Birney's mother died when he was three. His father, also named James, was an Irish emigrant. Settling in Kentucky, the elder Birney would eventually become one of the wealthiest men in the state and a large slave-owner. His son James attended Transylvania University and then Princeton, graduating in 1810. He went on to read law in an attorney's office in Philadelphia, where he was admitted to the bar in 1814. Returning to Danville, Birney developed a large law practice. His wife was the daughter of a U.S. district judge and niece of the state's governor. Besides being married in 1816, Birney was elected to the legislature. In 1818 Birney moved to Alabama. His antislavery views were becoming pronounced. He played a role, though not as a delegate, in seeing that the 1819 Alabama constitution barred the importation of slaves for sale in the state. That same year he was elected to the first Alabama General Assembly.

Birney incurred large gambling debts and was not managing his plantation effectively. He did well financially from practicing law in Huntsville, where he began living in 1823. He sold the plantation and slaves. Birney wrote legislation beginning in the mid–1820s restricting slavery in various ways. While visiting New York and New England in 1829 his anti-

JAMES G. BIRNEY
(From the collection of David J. and Janice L. Frent)

slavery views hardened as he became convinced that slavery was retarding the South's progress compared to the North. The American Colonization Society favored freeing slaves and sending them elsewhere, such as Africa. Birney became an agent for the Society in 1832 and lectured around the South espousing those views. He returned to live in Danville, Kentucky, because he believed that state offered the best opportunity to carrying on an effective anti-slavery campaign. By 1834 he changed his mind about colonization because he felt it ineffective and un–Christian. He freed his six slaves that year, as he moved slowly from wanting to limit slavery to being an outright abolitionist.

The next step was to form the Kentucky Anti-Slavery Society in 1835. He condemned slavery in meetings in New York and New England, and urged concerted, national efforts against slavery. The opposition to his planned start-up in Kentucky of an anti-slavery weekly newspaper became so strong that he moved across the Ohio River to near Cincinnati. From January 1836, to September 1837, he published the *Philanthropist*, which criticized both political parties for weakness on slavery. He summoned anti-slavery activists to forceful political involvement. His sharp tone led to many dangerous confrontations, but apparently he was never physically harmed. While in Cincinnati he hid a runaway slave named Mathilda. That action led to his indictment, but he represented himself at trial and was acquitted.

Since he was elected executive secretary of the American Anti-Slavery Society he moved to New York City in 1837. Birney had become so prominent an anti-slavery advocate that he was nominated for president at a New York state anti-slavery convention in 1839. He declined, in part because he thought it premature until the Whig Party nominee was known. In April 1840, dissatisfied with the Whig candidate, Birney accepted the Liberty Party presidential nomination at a convention of delegates from six states. Birney drew only 7,000 votes.

Birney was a vice president of the World Anti-Slavery Convention meeting in England in 1840. He had written several works, but his best known was published in 1840, calling churches "the bulwarks of American slavery." Leaving New York, Birney settled in Bay City, Michigan. His 1844 presidential race was somewhat more effective, but still he only polled 2.4 percent of the vote. Birney earlier in his career had admired Henry Clay, a good friend of Birney's father and a fellow Kentuckian. Birney finally decided, though, that Clay had "no conscience" on slavery. Clay's lack of conviction made him, "of all our public men, the most dangerous." Thus Birney may have received considerable personal satisfaction that the 15,000 votes he polled in New York caused Clay to lose that state, and the presidential election.

In the summer of 1845 Birney fell from a horse and was permanently paralyzed. There would be no more campaigns for office. He moved to Eagleswood, New Jersey in 1853, and died there four years later.

BIRNEY BIBLIOGRAPHY

Birney, James G., and F.H. Elmore. *Correspondence Between the Hon. F.H. Elmore and James G. Birney.* New York (1969, reprint of 1838 edition).

Birney, William. *James G. Birney and His Times.* New York (1969, reprint of 1890 edition).

Dumond, Dwight, ed. *Letters of James Gillespie Birney, 1831–1857.* Gloucester, Mass. (1966, reprint of 1938 edition).

Fladeland, Betty L. *James G. Birney: Slaveholder to Abolitionist.* Ithaca, N.Y. (1955).

Green, Beriah. *Sketches of the Life and Writings of James Gillespie Birney.* Utica, Jackson and Chaplin (1844).

Kraut, Alan M., ed. *Crusaders and Compromisers: Essays on the Relationship of the Antislavery Struggle to the Antebellum Party System.* Westport, Conn. (1983).

1844 vice presidential nominee — Liberty Party

Thomas Morris

Born January 3, 1776, in Berks County, Pennsylvania; died December 7, 1844, in Bethel, Ohio. Married Rachel Davis on November 19, 1797, and had three daughters and eight sons. Two of his sons would become U.S. congressmen.

THOMAS MORRIS
(From the Senate Historical Office)

Thomas Morris was the fifth of twelve children of Isaac and Ruth Henton Morris. Isaac was a Baptist minister, "preaching without failing in a single appointment for over sixty years, never taking a dose of medicine." He died at age 91 in 1830. Thomas's mother was the daughter of a Virginia planter, but refused at her father's death (well after Thomas had left home) an inheritance of four slaves. Both parents hated slavery, and Thomas probably absorbed those beliefs. The family moved to near Clarksburg, Virginia, when Thomas was young. They were poor, living in the mountains, and there were few schools. He had only three months in a common school, and otherwise was self-taught using his father's small library of Bibles. When he was 16 Thomas served several months as a member of a local militia fighting Indians. He left home and moved with some other immigrants to Ohio when he was 19. He became a clerk in a Columbia store owned by John Smith (later to be one of Ohio's first U.S. Senators). Morris married, and in 1800 moved to Williamsburgh, Ohio. There he was a brick maker. Morris was so impoverished that once he was imprisoned for debt.

The Morrises moved to Bethel in the winter, pulling all their earthly possessions on a sled across the snow. In 1802 he began studying law and was admitted to the bar in 1804. Over time, this barely educated and poorly trained lawyer would prove a great success, especially in his power over juries. Morris was elected to the legislature in 1806. He would serve five terms in the state house, and ten in the state senate at various times between 1806 and 1833. He labored for the common man, promoting public schools, fighting chartered monopolies, and proposing protection of part of a debtor's property from seizure. In 1809 he was named a judge of the supreme court, but a change in the law made him ineligible. In 1828 he was a passionate supporter of Andrew Jackson for president, and helped start the *Ohio Sun* newspaper to promote the campaign. In 1832 Morris again was a Jacksonian campaign leader, but the same year was defeated for a seat in Congress. Despite his defeat the Jacksonian's won control of the legislature, Morris was chosen by a 54 to 49 vote to be the next U.S. senator. In the Senate he was an ardent anti-bank spokesman and as a result gained some national press attention. Still, Morris's first four years in the Senate were relatively quiet, and in particular he was quiet about slavery. In January 1836, however, he took a surprisingly strong stand demanding that the Senate receive antislavery petitions sent to the Senate by abolitionist groups, while most senators for years had followed a "gentlemen's" agreement not to accept these memorials. After Senator John C. Calhoun condemned Morris's position, Morris moved to abolish slavery in the District of Columbia. In the months ahead Morris's stand became increasingly uncompromising and increasingly isolated, both in the Senate and back home in Ohio. His position weakened him politically in a party that was trying to mollify its large Southern base. In an 1837 Senate debate about slavery, Morris gave a nationally noticed response to a speech delivered by John C. Calhoun. Morris said that he did not believe "that this republic was a confederacy of separate and independent states"; it was an indissoluble union. He apparently hoped for reelection in 1838, but the Democrats abandoned him for a more moderate man, Benjamin Tappan.

Near the end of his term, a fellow resident of Bethel needed an appointment to West Point, but Morris had none to make. Morris suggested that Congressman Thomas Hamer still had an appointment, but was told that Hamer was angry at the father of the would-be cadet. Morris agreed to ask Hamer to make the appointment as a personal favor to Morris. It was made, and Ulysses Grant was on his way to West Point.

On February 9, 1839, less than a month before leaving the Senate, Morris replied to Henry Clay's speech that had urged compromise about slavery. Morris said, "Though our national sins are many and grievous, yet repentance, like that of ancient Nineveh, may yet divert from us that impending danger which seems to hang over our heads as by a single hair. That all may be *safe*, I conclude *that the negro must be free.*" Morris wanted no compromise.

The result of so strong a stand was to be booed and to have eggs thrown at him when he tried to speak back home in Ohio. He was chased by a mob in Dayton and had similar threats elsewhere. He became a political martyr to abolitionists and a role model for future Ohio leaders of the movement, like Joshua Giddings, Salmon Chase, and Benjamin Wade. Morris helped start a state Liberty Party in 1841, promoted the idea of choosing independent candidates for state office and no longer working with the Whigs. For the next several years Morris was a frequent abolitionist speaker. When the Liberty Party met in Buffalo in 1843, Morris was nominated for vice president. He campaigned actively, but the ticket got only 2.3 percent of the vote. He died a month after the election, and four months before he would have taken office had he won. As one biographer put it, Morris is "one of the forgotten men of the early antislavery movement" (Neuenschwander, p. 123). A likeness is engraved over the entrance to the Clermont County courthouse in Batavia, Ohio.

MORRIS BIBLIOGRAPHY

Blue, Frederick J. *Salmon P. Chase: A Life in Politics.* Kent, Ohio (1987).

Clermont County, Ohio, 1980: A Collection of Genealogical and Historical Writings. Batavia, Ohio (1980), vol. 1, pp. 65–66.

Galbreath, C. B. "Centennial Anniversary of the Birth of Ulysses S. Grant. *Ohio Archaeological and Historical Quarterly* XXXI (1922), pp. 221, 246–250.

Grant, Ulysses. *Personal Memoirs of U.S. Grant.* New York (1962, reprint of 1885 edition), p. 12.

Howe, Henry. *Historical Collections of Ohio.* Norwalk, Ohio (2 vols., 1896), vol. I, pp. 414–416.

Morris, Benjamin F. *The Life of Thomas Morris.* Cincinnati (1856).

Neuenschwander, John A. "Senator Thomas Morris: Antagonist of the South, 1836–1839." *Cincinnati Historical Society Bulletin* 32 (1974), pp. 122–139.

Swing, James B. "Thomas Morris." *Ohio Archaeological and Historical Quarterly* X (1902), pp. 352–360.

Appreciation is expressed to Amos Loveday and Leslie Floyd, of the Ohio Historical Society, for providing information.

Election of 1848

NOMINATIONS

Democratic Party Convention (5th): May 22–25, 1848, at the Universalist Church, Baltimore, Maryland. *President*— Lewis Cass, nominated on the fourth ballot with 179 votes out of 290 cast. He had 125 on the first ballot. James Buchanan and Levi Woodbury (N.H.) were his chief competitors. *Vice president*— William O. Butler, nominated on the second ballot with 169 of 290 votes; he had received 114 votes on the first ballot. John Quitman (Miss.) was his major rival.

Whig Party Convention (3rd): June 7–9, 1848, in the Museum Building, Philadelphia, Pennsylvania. *President*— Zachary Taylor, nominated on the fourth ballot with 171 votes out of 280 cast. On the first ballot Taylor received 111 votes. Henry Clay, Winfield Scott, and Daniel Webster were his main rivals. *Vice president*— Millard Fillmore, nominated on the second ballot with 173 of 266 votes, having received 115 votes on the first ballot. Abbott Lawrence (Mass.) was the other major contender.

Free-Soil Party Convention (1st): opened August 9, 1848, in Buffalo, New York. *President*— Martin Van Buren, nominated on the first ballot with 244 votes; John P. Hale (N.H.) received 181 votes. *Vice president*— Charles Francis Adams, nominated unanimously on the first ballot.

GENERAL ELECTION, November 7, 1848

Popular Vote

Taylor	1,361,393
Cass	1,223,460
Van Buren	291,501
Other	2,830

Electoral Vote

Taylor–Fillmore — 163 (15 states)
Cass–Butler — 127 (15 states)
Van Buren–Adams — 0

Winners

Zachary Taylor, 12th president
Millard Fillmore, 12th vice president

Losers

Lewis Cass, William O. Butler, Martin Van Buren, Charles F. Adams

---

*1848 presidential nominee —
Democratic Party*

Lewis Cass

Full name: Lewis Cass.

State represented: Michigan.

Birth: October 9, 1782, at Exeter, New Hampshire.

Age on Inauguration Day (March 4, 1849): 66 years, 5 months.

Education: Common schools in Exeter, then Phillips Academy, 1792–1799; studied law under Governor Meigs in Marietta, Ohio, admitted to bar in 1802.

Religion: Never joined a church, though attended his wife's Presbyterian church regularly.

Ancestry: First ancestor in America came as indentured servant in 1630s; most were farmers; mother's family came from England in 1638 and were much more prosperous than the Casses.

Occupation: Attorney.

Public offices: Prosecutor of Muskingum County, Ohio, 1804–1806; Ohio House of Representatives, 1806–1807; U.S. Marshal for Ohio, 1807–1812; appointed military administrator of Michigan and Upper Canada, October 14, 1813; appointed governor of Territory of Michigan, October 29, 1813–August 1, 1831; U.S. secretary of war, August 1, 1831–October 4, 1836, resigned; appointed minister to France, October 24, 1836–November 12, 1842; unsuccessful candidate for Democratic presidential nomination, 1844 and 1852; U.S. senator, March 4, 1845–May 29, 1848, resigned; unsuccessful Democratic nominee for president, 1848; U.S. senator, March 4, 1849–March 3, 1857, not reelected; U.S. secretary of state, March 6, 1857–December 14, 1860, resigned.

Death: June 17, 1866, Detroit, Michigan, at age 83 years, 8 months.

Burial: Elmwood Cemetery, Detroit, Michigan.

Home: Detroit, Michigan.

Personal characteristics: By the time of presidential nomination, he was fat, slow, balding. Wore wig; sagging jowls; dark, sunken eyes. Clear, low-pitched voice; 5'8" tall, wide shouldered; at earlier age, was muscular, powerful, heavy black hair, worn long and disheveled; large mole on left cheek.

Father: Jonathan Cass II (October 29, 1753–August 4, 1830), born in Massachusetts; drifted between laborer jobs, then appointed major in militia, commander of fort in Northwest Territory; became farmer, craftsman, and sold lots from his bounty land received for his Revolutionary War service.

Mother: Mary Gilman (?–1834), married December 20, 1781.

Siblings: Deborah Webster (April 16, 1784–?), married Judge Wyllys Silliman. George Washington (January 25, 1786–August 6, 1873), married Sophia Lord; a farmer. Charles Lee (August 15, 1787–June 4, 1842), married (1) Josephene Mount, and (2) Mrs. Sina Townsend; captain in army, federal agent for Indians; farmer. Mary Gilman (August 12, 1788–?), married Joseph F. Munro, a merchant. John Jay (February 28, 1791–April 29, 1792).

Wife: Elizabeth Spencer (1786–March 5, 1853), married in 1806; daughter of Revolutionary general, and doctor.

Children: Elizabeth (?–1832), died of cholera. Maria Sophia, married Capt. Augustus Canfield. Lewis, Jr., politician and mayor of Detroit. Matilda. Isabella, married Theodore Marinus Roest van Limburg, who was Dutch minister to the United States. A daughter and son died in infancy.

Historic sites/memorials: Cass's statue is in the national capitol as one of two placed by Michigan.

Few public careers can rival that of Lewis Cass. He held public office for over 50 years, from prosecuting attorney of a county to almost being president of the United States. His family had initially been poor, though as Cass approached young manhood better fortune came their way. If his name is little remembered today it is not for the lack of contribution or longevity. What he lacked in personal dynamism he compensated for with hard work, intelligence, and bulldog determination.

Cass's father, Jonathan, had held various laboring jobs until the American Revolution. At the outbreak of that war Jonathan Cass, then 23, and a blacksmith, enlisted and in time became an officer. He served until the conflict was over. Returning home, Jonathan married into a much wealthier and more successful family. Lewis was the first child. At the age of ten, after a rudimentary education in the common school, Lewis enrolled at Phillips Academy in his hometown of Exeter, New Hampshire, where he spent seven years. Edward Everett and Daniel Webster, two later fellow frustrated national candidates, were among his classmates. For a short period Lewis taught at Exeter, but then in 1799 or 1800 moved to Ohio where his father's service in the Revolution had gained as bounty land a sizable tract near Zanesville. The first winter there Lewis studied law in the Marietta office of a future Ohio governor, R.J. Meigs. With spring's arrival these scholarly pursuits had to give way to the backbreaking labor of clearing the land to start a farm. For several summers Lewis aided his father and his brothers in preparing the farms, but the law was to be his career. In the autumn of 1802, he became the first lawyer to be admitted to the bar under the new Ohio constitution.

The search for justice in the frontier of Ohio was little different than in other western states. Like Abe Lincoln would two decades later in Illinois, Cass rode the circuit with other lawyers and a judge, as advocates and arbiters went from town to town for court sessions. Cass held his own financially for the short period he practiced law. Soon, however, he was elected prosecuting attorney and shortly thereafter a state representative. While in the legislature Cass wrote resolutions asserting that Ohio played no part in the Aaron Burr conspiracy that planned, apparently, the establishment of a separate western confederacy with Burr at its head. President Thomas Jefferson, enraged by Burr and, subsequently, by Burr's acquittal on conspiracy charges, was quite solicitous to any man who publicly denounced Burr. Cass's reward was appointment as United States Marshal for Ohio, a position he retained from 1807 until 1812.

War against Britain had been threatening

for years. It finally erupted in 1812. No American politician would in his career show more hatred toward Britain than did Cass. He resigned his position, closed his law office, and helped raise troops. He soon was elected a colonel. Against orders from General William Hull, Cass led his troops into battle and was successful, but a weak-willed Hull continued to protest and ordered Cass to withdraw from his position. Another assignment was given Cass that took him away from the main American forces. In his absence General Hull, who had retreated to Detroit, surrendered to the British. Cass was surrendered as well, even though not actually captured. Rather than hand his sword over to the British, he broke it in two. His hatred and disdain for Hull would be permanent.

Hoping to convince the Madison administration of Hull's incompetence, Cass traveled to Washington to report personally concerning the reasons for the debacle. Later Cass would testify at Hull's courtmartial for treason and cowardice. Hull was convicted of the latter and sentenced to death. The sentence was remitted, however. Cass's remaining military exploits were much more satisfactory, as he was placed under the command of General William Henry Harrison. The two enjoyed considerable mutual respect and shared in the acclaim that came from defeating Indian chief Tecumseh's braves. Cass may have been the one who identified (accurately?) Tecumseh's body on the battlefield.

By the time Cass left the army he had become a general, a title he enjoyed using for the rest of his life, all 53 more years of it. His military career may well have continued except that President Madison in October 1813 appointed Cass territorial governor of Michigan. As governor his problems were mainly defense. The Indians were one adversary. Attacks that were almost as damaging were those made in the eastern media that described Michigan as a wasteland. Cass served 18 years as governor, a tenure longer than any other governor of an American territory.

Cass signed at least 19 different treaties with various Indian tribes, adding over a quarter of the territory of present-day Michigan, Wisconsin, Illinois, and Indiana to white control.

His fairness and courage made him a favorite among the Indians. He did not respect their civilization, but he believed the white man owed the Indian a fair price for his lands, and an honest following of a treaty after it was signed. Not only was Cass honored as a friend of the Indian, he was also respected by them for his daring. Cass the presidential candidate was a tired, fat, phlegmatic man of 66, and therefore it is difficult to perceive that Cass became famous for his reckless, dashing manner. Space permits recounting only one episode. One tribe with whom he was negotiating, which was armed, hostile, and fresh from battle, raised the British flag as a sign of defiance. Cass marched into their camp alone and unarmed. He pulled down the flag, tucked it under his arm, and berated the assembled warriors for their act. He turned and walked out, leaving dazed but slightly more respectful antagonists behind.

His Indian duties took him on thousand-mile journeys, by horseback, canoe, and other slow and exhausting means, throughout the territory. The secretary of war appreciated success, and in 1828 he asked Cass to assist in drawing up regulations for the government to follow in dealing with tribes throughout the country. Cass's proposals were fair for the times, and were based on the belief that the Indian and white man could not live together in harmony. Consequently, all tribes must be removed from near American settlements. Cass also believed that the source for much of the trouble between the race was liquor. He wished the sale to Indians be banned.

The false stories circulating in the east concerning the alleged inhabitability of Michigan were of almost equal concern to Cass as were the Indians. His effort to remove this impression included writing articles for eastern journals extolling Michigan's virtues. He encouraged migration. Over thirty thousand new residents came to Michigan during his governorship. Road construction was another focus of his efforts, and he encouraged Congress to improve transportation and communication.

As did most territorial governors, Cass enjoyed almost dictatorial powers. But throughout his tenure he attempted to democratize the territory. He sought the establishment of a legislative body. Counties multiplied and local or township governments were created. In 1817 he induced two eastern newspapermen to establish a paper in the territory. He promoted education by helping to organize a meaningful system of public schools and by trying to get teachers to migrate to Michigan. His civic involvement included active support of religion, though he never formally joined a church. The establishment of the Michigan Historical Society was pushed, and Cass became the first president. His personal fortune also burgeoned, as he had parlayed his share of his father's bounty land from Revolutionary War service into significant and lucrative investments, including ownership of much of downtown Detroit. His fortune became as large as any in the state, but there was little to suggest graft or financial self-dealing in his success.

There is evidence that President Monroe had considered Cass for secretary of war in 1817, and other appointments were probably considered. Nonetheless, Cass labored as territorial governor ably and popularly until 1831 when President Jackson offered to name him secretary of war. Cass accepted. His participation in the ugly "Trail of Tears" removal of the Cherokee Indians from Georgia shows both sides of his views on Indians. He agreed that the Indians should be removed from Georgia despite the Supreme Court's decisions invalidating those removals, but he opposed forced removal. Cass desired the Indians be given an attractive reason for agreeing to leave. During the Nullification crisis of 1831-1832, he played a behind-the-scenes role in strengthening Union military positions in South Carolina should war have been necessary. President Jackson gave him public praise for his assistance once the conflict had been resolved.

Cass's temperance concerning alcohol applied not only to Indians but also to the army. He banned liquor sales to soldiers on military bases, removed alcoholic substances from the list of items provided soldiers by the army, and advocated total abstinence. Cass practiced these beliefs in his personal life and became president of a temperance organization.

Five years as secretary of war were followed by an appointment as minister to France in 1836. The new ambassador had to reopen the embassy in Paris that had been closed two years before due to a dispute between the two countries. He became a friend of French King Louis Philippe and helped reestablish Franco-American relations on a friendly basis. He ended his first year of service in France by taking a long cruise through the Mediterranean on the *Constitution*, a vacation promised him as part of the incentive to accept the ambassadorship. He visited Greece, Italy, Turkey, Egypt, the Holy Land, and other ports of call for the frigate. He sent home long descriptions of his travel for publication.

Cass's tenure as minister continued beyond the change of administrations in Washington, but disputes with Daniel Webster's Whig State Department finally caused him to resign. By December 1842, he was back in the United States. Cass's return was the cause for public celebrations. His differences with Webster had centered on a treaty negotiated with the British over the Maine-Canada boundary and the asserted right of England to stop and search ships on the high seas, usually to see whether slaves were being transported. Cass had publicly denounced Webster's agreement to a treaty that did not deny the British the right to stop American vessels. This posturing against the still-hated British won Cass many adherents and much publicity. Cass stated that negotiations should not even have begun over other differences until Britain renounced the searching of ships. Webster and Cass exchanged several public letters that increased Cass's following. When Cass landed in Boston on December 6, 1842, he was surprised to find a large, enthusiastic reception for him. For four days he shook hands in a public meeting in New York's city hall. He was invited to address the House of Representatives. As he traveled through Pennsylvania he was greeted with parades, speeches, and a genuine outpouring of public support for his stands.

By 1842, the only major Democratic contenders for the 1844 presidential nomination were Cass and former president Martin Van Buren. The *New York Herald* in its November 3, 1842, edition endorsed the 60-year-old former governor, cabinet secretary, and ambassador. The only Whig candidate was Henry Clay. Both Clay and Van Buren announced their opposition to the immediate annexation of Texas. As the conventions approached, it became clear that Texas was the only real issue in the campaign. On May 10, 1844, Cass stated he wanted Texas in the Union, a stand that gained Cass important Southern support but also weakened his Northern position. The Baltimore convention opened on May 27. Van Buren's chances were poor, as his opposition to the Texas annexation would probably cause a Southern bolt from the party should he be nominated. The ex-president led on the first ballot, 143 votes to Cass's 83. The vote totals for the two candidates slowly crept towards each other until Cass passed Van Buren, and on the seventh ballot Cass led 123 to 99. A two-thirds majority was needed to win, and it looked as if Cass's momentum might achieve that. Nonetheless, movement towards him had been slow. Unfortunately for his cause, his supporters could not prevent an adjournment for the evening, which proved fatal. All-night negotiations led to a decision by many for James K. Polk, an obscure former House speaker from Tennessee. Once the session opened the next day the action of political power brokers became clear. Polk was put into nomination; major states such as Pennsylvania and Massachusetts showed they were part of the scheme. The bandwagon pulled out and delegations became anxious that they might be left behind. The eighth ballot closed with Cass holding 114 votes, Polk 44. Cass had earlier instructed a delegate from Michigan to announce his withdrawal as a candidate should it become clear that he was losing support. Cass's decision was read and the nomination of Polk was certain. He won on the next ballot.

Cass was a good loser and campaigned actively for Polk, who won. The Democratic legislature in Michigan elected Cass United States senator on February 4, 1845, and thus Cass and Polk both took their places in Washington on March 4, 1845. The new senator joined the new president in urging that all of Oregon be taken from the British, by negotiation or, in Cass's view, by war. The cry was "Fifty-four forty-nine or fight!" Cass opposed the concession to England reached by Polk that the forty-ninth parallel, instead of 54°40' be accepted. Cass eagerly supported war measures offered by the president to fight the war with Mexico that soon erupted.

The new territories acquired from Mexico after the war's conclusion became an even greater controversy than had the war. Cass opposed the Wilmot Proviso that would ban slavery in all territories acquired from Mexico. "Popular sovereignty" was Cass's approach — let the people of each territory decide whether it should be slave or free.

On December 24, 1847, Cass declared strongly for popular sovereignty and urged Congress to stay out of territorial slavery issues. The 1848 presidential race was under way. Conventions in Michigan, Ohio, Indiana, and other states endorsed Cass for president. At the national Democratic convention, Cass led on the first ballot but was well short of victory. On the fourth the break towards him started and he was nominated. As would prove fatal to his election chances, the New York "barnburners," those Democrats supporting the Wilmot Proviso, walked out of the convention. Their nomination of Martin Van Buren as the Free-Soil nominee doomed Cass.

Cass resigned from the Senate to wage his campaign. He promised to serve only one term, but would not get the opportunity. Cass was to many, despite his past contributions, an elderly, outdated and unexciting choice who was more a relic than a leader for the future. The election was close. The Van Buren total was more than twice the margin of victory attained by the Whig nominee Zachary Taylor over Cass. Even more importantly, Van Buren's total in New York state was more than Taylor's victory margin there. Had Cass won New York, he would have won the presidency.

As in 1844, Cass was able to receive the consolation of a Senate seat despite losing the presidency. The Michigan legislature sent him back to his old position after two lengthy, bitter weeks of voting. In the new Congress Cass continued to urge a non-divisive settlement of the growing sectional crisis. Though he did not favor the fugitive slave law features, Cass did support the remainder of the Compromise of 1850. Of different parties, Cass and Henry

Clay were close allies in the debate. The Michigan senator's image as a moderate with some appeal in the South as well as in the North gave him support in the 1852 national convention. Despite his 70 years, Cass even led on the first ballot, but his support soon fell away and Franklin Pierce was nominated.

The new Congress again was faced with a slavery crisis, this time over Kansas and Nebraska. Cass first opposed Douglas's measures on the territories, but then grudgingly gave his support because popular sovereignty was incorporated in the proposals. As did many of the less impassioned leaders, he saw the dispute over slavery in the Mexican territories as one of semantics and blind principle. Cass felt the extremists ignored the practical fact that slavery was ill suited for the American Southwest. Still, Cass's statements on slavery as a moral wrong were becoming stronger, perhaps as his hopes for a presidential nomination were growing dimmer.

In 1856, it was clear that the now–Republican legislature would not reelect Cass, and thus he sent a gracious if politically meaningless note requesting that he not be considered for reelection. The new president, James Buchanan, offered the 74-year-old political veteran the post of secretary of state, and Cass accepted. Both men were expansionists. Cass had long argued for the acquisition of Cuba; he also now urged the purchase of Alaska from the Russian czar. Much to his personal satisfaction, at long last Cass secured a British disavowal of any right to stop and search foreign vessels on the high seas. All his efforts were ignored by a populace caught up in the looming threat of domestic conflict. After Lincoln's election in 1860, Cass urged the passive Buchanan to strengthen federal troop positions in Southern forts, saying, "I demand it." The demand was rebuffed, and Cass offered his resignation.

Cass was a strong Unionist throughout the Civil War. He did give occasional advice to the new Secretary of State William Seward. In 1864, he stated he supported General McClellan over Lincoln, but he took no further role in the election. His health began to fail that year, but he lived long enough to see the Northern victory in 1865. After his death on June 16, 1866, President Andrew Johnson declared a day of national mourning. Sixty years after first being elected to office, general and would-be president Lewis Cass's public service was finally over.

Analysis of Qualifications

Not a great man, nor in truth one of the truly influential men of his age, Lewis Cass was nonetheless a seasoned, intelligent, thoughtful politician whose main shortcomings were his extreme ambition for the presidency and his age at the time of his nomination. His ambition is hardly unique among presidential winners or losers; his age, well, he cannot fully be faulted for that either.

Cass was extremely polite in personal relationships. Though having few warm friends because of his reserve, he also had few if any real political or personal enemies. He was fair and honest in all his dealings, whether in government or business. There was little invective in his speeches, and when he spoke it was for moderation and understanding, not war. The good life that his fortune could buy was richly enjoyed by Cass, and his love of food, but not drink, was clear.

Education had prepared Cass exceptionally well for his day. He had also acquired a love of books and scholarly matters rare among political leaders. His publications included articles concerning the Indians, the Battle of New Orleans in 1814, and on Michigan life and geography. While ambassador to France he wrote on the French king and his court, and wrote extensively concerning his observations during a Mediterranean tour. He was a scholar, a careful observer of men and events, and a lover of education.

Cass was also a thorough democrat, in the party sense but also as a principle of government. Though given broad powers as governor of the Michigan territory, he argued for the dispersal of these powers to local and legislative government. He favored popular sovereignty over Congressional dictation on the slavery question. In part he thought this a politically necessary compromise, but he also believed the people should make these crucial decisions.

Honest, educated, moderate, Cass's personal

qualities were depicted by some as amiable weakness, a lack of conviction. Andrew Jackson reportedly remarked, "It is hard for him to say *no* and he thinks all men honest." Cass was seen as such an ambitious seeker for the presidency as to be a trimmer on issues. One man's motivations are certainly not safely judged a century after the fact, but it is fair to say that if Cass did adjust his positions for political advantage, he was certainly not unique in that regard. Neither were his positions inconsistent over time. A 50-year public servant, Cass was no political hack who merely marked time waiting for advancement. He was energetic and effective as Michigan governor; he was less a force but still competent as War Department secretary under Jackson; as minister to France his powers were limited but he was well received and liked by a regime with which America was reestablishing official relations after an angry break. His Senate service was as a moderate and compromiser who wished to avoid war by avoiding Congressional decisions on slavery. As a presidential candidate, however, his most vigorous years were behind him. Horace Greeley was hardly fair, but his thrust was not entirely misdirected, when he called Cass a "pot-bellied, mutton-headed old cucumber." One cannot easily see Cass as a dynamic leader of the nation out of sectional conflict, but neither can he be seen as a Buchanan "dough-face" who lacked strength of character. Cass revealed his own likely actions when he described Buchanan's paralysis of nerve immediately after Lincoln's victory:

> The President is pale with fear, for his official household is full of traitors, and conspirators control the government.

Cass wanted a compromise, but he was not willing during the nullification crisis of 1831–1832, nor the secession crisis of 1860–1861, to let the South bolt from the Union. His experience and education would have been valuable in the White House; his moderation fringed with firmness on the Union was needed as well. He did not have the personal qualities to have been a great popular leader such as Jackson; even had he been president

he might today have faded into anonymity. Yet Cass was no minor league player suddenly thrust into the national arena through political maneuvering. Instead he was an able public servant whose chance at the presidency came late, but who deserved it nonetheless.

CASS BIBLIOGRAPHY

Burns, Virginia. *Lewis Cass, Frontier Soldier*. Bath, Mich. (1980).

Dunbar, Willis Frederick. *Lewis Cass*. Grand Rapids, Mich. (1970).

Gillman, Alex W. *The Gillman or Gilman Family*. London (1895).

Gilman, Arthur. *The Gilman Family*. Albany, N.Y. (1869).

Klunder, Willard Carl. *Lewis Cass and the Politics of Moderation*. Kent, Ohio (1996).

Lawrence, Ruth. *Genealogical History of Ledyard, Cass, Livingston, Prince, and Allied Families*. New York City (1925).

McLaughlin, Andrew C. *Lewis Cass*. Boston and New York City (1891).

Schoolcraft, Henry R. *Outlines of the Life and Character of Gen. Lewis Cass*. Albany, N.Y. (1848).

Shelby, C.K. "The Paternal Ancestry of Lewis Cass." Unpublished manuscript in Burton History Collection. Detroit Public Library (1947).

Smith, W.L.G. *The Life and Times of Lewis Cass*. New York City (1856).

Stearns, Ezra. *Genealogical and Family History of the State of New Hampshire*. New York City (1908).

Stevens, Walter W. "Michigan's Lewis Cass." *The Filson Club History Quarterly* 39 (1965), pp. 320–325.

Woodford, Frank B. *Lewis Cass, the Last Jeffersonian*. New York City (1973), reprint of 1950 edition.

Young, William T. *Sketch of the Life and Public Services of General Lewis Cass*. Detroit (1852).

1848 vice presidential nominee—
Democratic Party

William O. Butler

Full name: William Orlando Butler.
State represented: Kentucky.
Birth: April 19, 1791, Jessamine County, Kentucky.

LEWIS CASS and WILLIAM O. BUTLER
(From the collection of David J. and Janice L. Frent)

Age on Inauguration Day (March 4, 1849): 57 years, 10½ months.

Education: Local schools and tutors; Transylvania University, graduated 1812; for six months studied law in Lexington, Kentucky, attorney's office; admitted to bar 1817 after five years' absence in military.

Religion: Presbyterian.

Ancestry/prominent relatives: Grandfather came to America from Ireland; four uncles and father all fought in the Revolutionary War.

Occupation: Attorney, soldier, farmer.

Public offices: Kentucky General Assembly, 1817–1819; U.S. House of Representatives, March 4, 1839–March 18, 1843; defeated for governor of Kentucky, 1844; unsuccessful Democratic nominee for vice president, 1848; defeated for U.S. Senate, 1851; unsuccessful candidate for Democratic presidential nomination, 1852; declined to be appointed governor of Nebraska Territory, 1855.

Home: Farm on banks of Ohio River, near Carrollton, Kentucky.

Death: August 6, 1880, Carrollton, Kentucky, age 89 years, 3½ months.

Burial: Small family cemetery, foot of Butler's Hill, near Carrollton, Kentucky.

Personal characteristics: Tall, slender, dignified, muscular; some said he resembled Andrew Jackson; polished manner.

Father: Percival Butler, also called Pierce (April 4, 1760–September 9, 1821), first adjutant general of Kentucky.

Mother: Mildred Hawkins (January 3, 1763–May 29, 1833), married May 30, 1786.

Siblings: Eleanor (May 7, 1787–May 20, 1844), never married. Thomas Langford (April 10, 1789–October 21, 1880), married Sarah Hawkins. Richard Parker (September 27, 1792–January 8, 1885), married (1) Pauline Bullock, and (2) a daughter of Dr. Blythe. Percival (Pierce) (October 4, 1794–January 15, 1851), married Eliza Sarah Allen in 1822. Frances Maria (April 19, 1796–November 26, 1843), never married. Caroline Thomas (February 4, 1798–January 15, 1885), married Judge James Pryor. Edward (August 26, 1800–December 30, 1801). Edward (March 20, 1802–September 8, 1821). Jane Hawkins (February 4, 1804–August 8, 1877), married Dr. U.E. Ewing in November 1836. Mary Lang-

ford (January 1, 1807–August 27, 1861), never married.

Wife: Eliza Todd (?–April 16, 1863), married April 17, 1817.

Children: None.

Historic sites/memorials: General Butler State Resort Park, Carrollton, Kentucky, that incorporates his farm.

With an ancestry such as his, perhaps there was no course for William Butler other than to gain military glory. Four uncles and his father, all the sons in an Irish immigrant's family, fought ably in the Revolutionary War. George Washington responded, "When I wanted a thing well done, I ordered a Butler to do it." No less than his forebears, William Butler performed admirably in the military, and followed his father onto another battlefield as well, that of politics.

William's father had risen to a captaincy during the Revolution, fought with Washington, endured with him at Valley Forge, gloried with him at Yorktown. With the war over, Percival Butler moved to Kentucky, eventually settling in Port William, now called Carrollton. By 1800, he owned over a thousand acres of farmland and a dozen slaves. His trailblazing through the frontier in Kentucky made him an Indian fighter when necessary; he was by choice a politician and for over 20 years served as adjutant general of Kentucky, beginning his service in 1792 when that state entered the Union. William, his second son, received such education as was available in Port William, and then entered Transylvania University in Lexington, Kentucky. A legal career seemed his goal upon graduation, and for six months Butler studied in the office of a Lexington attorney, Robert Wickliffe. His studies ended after such a short tenure because the War of 1812 demanded soldiers, and Butler had to discover whether he was one.

Though the adjutant general was his father, no special route to distinction was set for William. He entered as a private, was elected to a corporal's rank, and was then commissioned an ensign. Butler accepted the latter rank on condition that he could remain with the same troops. General James Winchester was his commander. The winter of 1812-1813 was no pleasant time to be soldiering. Bitterly cold marches had to be endured and lack of supplies made conditions worse. Butler's first military fame came in the Battle of River Raisin on January 18 and 22, 1813, in southern Michigan. Butler's men crossed the frozen river and charged British-occupied Frenchtown across deep drifts of snow. Butler was at the head of the company as it raced for a crucial fence line that lay in the middle of a cleared field. He and his men won the grim dash and forced the British and their Indian allies to retreat. A small skirmish in the total conflict, yet Butler and his men's bravery cannot be denied. Four days later, bravery alone was inadequate. British reinforcements and bungling by the American general forced a surrender. The British commander promised safety for the troops, but Indians massacred large numbers of prisoners. A blow struck Butler, but his heavy clothing prevented serious injury and he was able to ward off another attack. Still he was a prisoner, and more exposure to the bitter cold followed with a march through the snow to Fort Niagara. As a grizzly reminder of what might have been, the men had to walk by the scalps and severed heads of some of the less fortunate soldiers. The prisoners were paroled, which meant they were to stay out of combat until an exchange was made with British soldiers captured by the Americans.

After a still longer, arduous trip, Butler finally returned to Port William and his astonished family, who had been convinced he was dead. After a brief rest, he was transferred to a new regiment and made a captain. The duties consisted of raising volunteers. Butler formed his own company and was placed under Andrew Jackson's command. This change in assignments would shape Butler's political future. A forced march to Jackson's position near Spanish Florida brought praise from the general. Other companies had failed to reach him, and Jackson wrote Secretary of State James Monroe that Butler was a fine example of what a soldier should be.

Jackson's invasion of Florida and the capture of Pensacola was not consistent with Spanish neutrality, and the general would be condemned for the maneuvers. There was no question, however, that as a subordinate But-ler performed courageously in the assault on the city. Butler had been with Jackson little more than a week and had already distinguished himself before his commander twice. Basking in glory was not possible, as a rapid march to New Orleans was necessary. On December 1, 1814, he arrived as part of Jackson's first troops in the city. When the superior officers in his company became injured, Butler took command of at first his company and before the Battle of New Orleans was completed, of three others companies. With some tactical skill, but more significantly due to his bravery and even rashness, Butler kept his forces at the forefront of his area of battle. By vigorous pursuit of the British, he deprived them of time to establish their defenses. At one stage, Butler was cornered by British troops in a dilapidated frame building. Saying he would surrender to the soldier who secured his sword, Butler threw it on the floor. In the momentary distraction, Butler burst through the rotted walls of the building and escaped. Jackson cautioned his young officer to be more cautious at one juncture in the battle.

After the battle, the somber duty of burying the British dead was detailed to a company under Butler's direction. Butler would write poetry throughout his career, and the pathos of the scene of carnage, even if suffered by the enemy, moved him to write a poem on the bravery and death that are shared by all participants in war. Captain Butler was given a brevet major rank at Jackson's request because of his action at New Orleans. Jackson would later describe Butler in this battle as follows:

> On all occasions he displayed that heroic chivalry, and calmness of judgment in the midst of danger, which distinguish the valuable officer in the hour of battle.

For a year after the war, Butler served as an aide to General Jackson; William replaced his brother Thomas in that capacity. Jackson and Butler would thereafter retain a warm friendship and respect for each other. In 1817, Butler returned to Carrollton and began the practice of law. That same year he was elected to the first of three terms in the Kentucky General Assembly. The quiet, private life of small-town legal practice agreed with the former soldier, and it was not with apparent enthusiasm that he abandoned this existence.

Butler's poetry played an important role in his life. Perhaps the idyllic scene of his farm along the Ohio River made him more productive poetically. Yet it was not just peace and solitude about which he wrote, but also his experiences in the War of 1812. Later he would publish a book of his poems, *The Boatman's Horn, and Other Poems*. Lew Wallace, the writer of *Ben-Hur*, considered Butler one of his favorite poets, though none of his work has endured.

For 20 years Butler practiced law in Gallatin County, with only a brief stint in the Assembly. Finally prevailed upon to run for Congress in 1839, he served two terms but was adamant about retiring after that stint. Part of his reluctance probably arose from the fact that Kentucky was Whig territory, while Butler was a Jacksonian Democrat. In Congress, Butler supported President Van Buren's subtreasury plan, favored the Tariff of 1842, opposed imprisonment for debt, and generally was an administration Democrat. The work was disagreeable to the Kentucky congressman, and he retired in 1843. Retirement from politics would be short-lived, as the Democratic state convention in January 1844, nominated him for the governorship. Whether he was playing coy or whether he was sincere cannot be certain, but his acceptance of the nomination was not enthusiastic:

> True, I cannot but regret that your selection did not fall upon one in every way better calculated to maintain that position than I pretend to be. I know myself full well. I am but a plain and unpretending man; one accustomed thus far in life, to achieve moderate ends by direct and open means.

However reluctant his acceptance might have been, the Democratic nominee immediately jumped into a hectic campaign schedule. His Whig opponent was respected Judge William Owsley. The two candidates agreed to campaign together across the state. The war record of Butler was closely examined and unfavorably interpreted by the Whigs; political motives were seen in many of his military accomplishments. For his part, Butler tried to wrap himself in the cloth of Andrew Jackson,

a not altogether popular effort in Kentucky, Henry Clay's bailiwick. With Clay running as the presidential nominee and with a strong Whig tradition in the state, Butler was defeated. His consolation was that he held the Whig majority well below expectations. Near the end of the campaign Butler broke off his tour with Owsley. He said he had to return home because of family illness, and for Owsley to give his regrets at the remaining stops. Instead, Butler began campaigning in another area of the state. Perhaps he felt his speaking talents were a poor match to those of his opponent, but regardless of the reason, the move was a deceitful one.

On June 29, 1846, President Polk appointed the Carrollton lawyer and farmer a major general in the army. The Mexican War had broken out, and Polk wanted some Democratic balance to the heavily Whig contingent of career generals that initially commanded the troops. In August, Butler arrived in Mexico and began a march towards Saltillo. General Zachary Taylor thought that little fighting would occur when the soldiers reached Monterrey, but that forecast was inaccurate. Bloody street fighting erupted. Butler personally reconnoitered for his troops and exposed himself to much enemy fire. There was little coordination among the various units, and even less understanding of the size of the Mexican forces and the layout of the city. Butler was injured by a musket ball that struck him just below the knee. Weakness from loss of blood caused him to be removed from the forward action, but as he was being helped to the rear, he advised a retreat. The Mexican positions were too strong for attack to be successful. Congress and the people of Kentucky each awarded him a sword for his bravery.

The knee injury was painful and caused the general to need crutches. While the recovery took place, Butler went back to Kentucky, only to be summoned to Washington. There was some speculation that he was to be made secretary of war, but in fact the president only wanted to consult with him on the condition of the war. Several meetings occurred, including a few with the cabinet. The summer of 1847 Butler spent recuperating in Carrollton. By November, he was in New Orleans with fresh troops for the reinforcement of General Winfield Scott. Scott had seized Mexico City on September 14 but needed help to hold it. To reach the capital a long march from Vera Cruz was required, and few soldiers blessed Butler for the pace he set for this hot journey, which was made infinitely more arduous because of sickness.

Butler engaged in no additional fighting against the Mexicans, but did help in curbing the bickering between the generals. The war successfully concluded, Scott left for the United States and Butler was made commander in chief of the occupation armies in Mexico. Winfield Scott was pleased with the performance of his successor. Praise for one officer by another was rare in this war. As part of his duties, the new commander was empowered to squelch all revolt in Mexico. Forceful action against a few early efforts helped end that threat. On May 29, 1848, Butler announced the end of the war, as ratifications of the Treaty of Guadalupe Hidalgo were to be exchanged the following day. Two days later, Butler left for the United States.

Upon his arrival in New Orleans, the general was greeted by a tumultuous crowd estimated at fifteen to twenty thousand. He was paraded in a coach pulled by four white horses. At a public dinner in the city, Zachary Taylor, the Whig presidential nominee that year, was reported to have said Butler was "a friend, a brother soldier, and a gentleman whom I respect, and to whom the country owes a debt of gratitude." The rarity of the tribute arises from the fact that Taylor headed one presidential ticket while Butler a few weeks earlier had been nominated to the tail of the other.

The Democratic convention that had met in Baltimore beginning May 22, 1848, had without a whole lot of bickering nominated Lewis Cass on the fourth ballot. John A. Quitman of Mississippi and Butler were the principal challengers for the vice presidential nomination. Quitman was the epitome of the firebrand radical Southerner who, with his Northern abolitionist counterpart, would together precipitate the Civil War. Butler, on the other hand, represented moderation. A slaveowner, Butler nonetheless did not press for extension of slavery into the new territo-

ries. Butler received the nod on the second ballot. He played no role in the campaign, did not even give speeches, as silence was the accepted style. The defeat Cass and Butler suffered in November turned on the votes the Democrats lost in New York state to the Free-Soil candidate, former Democratic president Martin Van Buren.

Defeat did not much bother Butler, and he returned to Carrollton. He no longer practiced law but instead worked on his sizable plantation. In 1851, several individuals began to see in Butler real potential for the Democratic presidential nomination the following year. Included were Francis P. Blair and Thomas Hart Benton, two Missouri politicians who considered Butler a moderate Southerner, with few well-publicized stands on issues, who could be hidden from view and elected. Blair secured a promise from Butler that he would not make public any stands on the issues of the day. A strong boom for the Kentuckian got under way, but some Southerners began to accuse him of the heresy of Free-Soil beliefs. The house of cards, built on silence and image, tumbled down when Butler strongly endorsed the right of a slaveowner to take his slaves anywhere in the country. His stand may have been made with full knowledge of the consequences, because Butler was irate over the treatment he was getting from many quarters. Butler apparently wished to end the dispute about his principles even if it meant ending his chance for the presidency.

George N. Sanders, an unprincipled but clever publicist for Stephen Douglas, also savaged the Kentucky candidate. In scurrilous charges that he would repeat against other candidates later, Sanders alleged that Butler had no principles, that he was only an opportunist. Allegedly, Butler's only achievements had been in war, and those not as a leader but as a rash subordinate who though brave was not level-headed.

Butler did not want the presidency by the time the national convention opened. Instead, he wrote the convention that he believed his superior on the 1848 ticket, Lewis Cass, should be given another chance. It was not to be. Butler received a momentary flurry of interest before the protracted and bitter voting finally compromised on dark-horse Franklin Pierce.

In a remarkable public display of candor, Butler explained his retirement from both politics and the legal practice. He stated that after he lost the 1844 election for governor his health was so bad that he had to quit the bar. He declared himself "utterly unfit to make a speech," specifically basing this admission on his ill health but also apparently believing himself inferior in oratorical skills. One speech had been given since this forced retirement, "which was attended with so much pain and difficulty, that I am unwilling to venture on a second attempt." This letter was written in the summer of 1852, and would signal the end of a political career that at times had shown much promise, but which never realized much actual success.

His only reentry into government occurred when Butler was named one of the commissioners to the Washington Peace Conference in February 1861. The conference achieved nothing other than some too-little, too-late recommendations for compromise. There would be war, and Butler was opposed to secession. At age 70 he was too old to fight, but he was for the Union. During the war, his wife of over 45 years died, leaving him alone at his Carrollton home. The old-soldier-turned-politician continued almost until the end to travel out to his farm daily, and until his health failed even walked at least six miles every day. At the age of 89, Butler breathed his last.

Analysis of Qualifications

In physical appearance, William O. Butler was another Old Hickory — Andrew Jackson. He sat tall and erect, exuding masculine strength and courage. Even in background, the two men shared several characteristics. Jackson and Butler gained military glory together in the War of 1812, especially at the Battle of New Orleans. Probably both were well suited for military careers, but both gravitated towards politics when that reward for their military service was thrust upon them. Yet one succeeded fabulously in politics, rising to the presidency and becoming the symbol for an entire era in America. The other failed in the four highest offices he sought — governor, senator, vice

president and president — and is a forgotten man today.

As a soldier, Butler was courageous, even reckless. Some of the abandon he had earlier demonstrated in the War of 1812 was restrained when, as a general in the Mexican War 30 years later, he was responsible for the lives of so many more men. Perhaps he was merely older and wiser. Butler's fame as a soldier was not for plotting grand strategy. Instead, it was for courageously leading by example, inspiring his troops to perform under difficult circumstances. General Butler was a man of action. Perhaps of extreme rarity in the Mexican War, he was a man without burning political ambition, who did not use his position and opportunity for fame to advance his presidential aspirations.

As a man, Butler was respected. He was called "in every sense of the word one of nature's 'noblemen.'" One of the striking aspects of his personality was humility. This modesty extended to his abilities as a speaker, and there Butler became almost unable to act. His statement blaming an illness for his withdrawal from public speechmaking has already been quoted. As a poet, Butler demonstrated imagination and a deep appreciation for nature. It was in his poetry that Butler revealed as much as anywhere that he was a man of an earlier age. He loved his peaceful Carrollton farm on the Ohio River. He loved to listen to the boatman's horn (the title of his best-known poem) and tend to his crops. It was not politics or modern economic realities that interested him. He was a Jacksonian who disagreed with the type of progress represented by his fellow Kentuckian Henry Clay's "American System" of vast internal, federally subsidized improvements. He did not want a national bank or other symbol of growing, increasingly concentrated economic strength.

William Butler was also a man of peace. Fighting in two wars, he wanted nothing to do with a civil war. Dislike for controversy, as well as love for the Union, caused him to urge restraint in the sectional crisis. Slavery should not be extended into the territories, but it should be protected where it presently existed. Though almost being elected vice president, and having a chance for the presidential nomination, in actuality Butler served in only two positions—six years as a legislator, and four years in Congress. When he was a candidate for the presidency in 1851-1852, the feature of his background that was most attractive to supporters was the absence of publicly known positions on issues. One modern writer even described him as a "dull, trusting and honest Kentuckian" who fitted the needs of his political sponsors perfectly. Still another writer called him "tractable, ignorant of politics, and honest in his good-natured simplicity." No one doubted his honesty or integrity, but many condemned him for political naïveté and simplicity that made him shapeless clay that could be molded by his managers. Butler never exhibited political leadership. What he had to offer political kingmakers was a popularity due to his military exploits and his striking appearance. He had never shown subtleties of political understanding. He was a reluctant candidate for every office he was offered, and seemed to doubt his abilities in them. It would seem that Butler was too great a risk for the nation's highest offices. He was a good man, but with no record of political performance.

BUTLER BIBLIOGRAPHY

Bell, Malcolm, Jr. *Major Butler's Legacy: Five Generations of a Slaveholding Family.* Athens, Ga. (1987).

Blair, Francis P. *The Life and Public Services of General William O. Butler.* Baltimore (1848).

Butler, William D., John C. Butler, and Joseph M. Butler, comps. *The Butler Family in America.* St. Louis (1909).

Clift, G. Glenn. *Remember the Raisin!* Frankfort (1961).

Ellis, James T. "General Wm. O. Butler, Soldier and Statesman." *Register of the Kentucky Historical Society* X (1912), pp. 65–67.

Life of General Lewis Cass: ... To which is appended, a sketch of the public and private history of Major-General W.O. Butler, of the volunteer service of the United States. Philadelphia (1848).

Roberts, Gerald F. "William O. Butler: Kentucky Cavalier." Unpublished master's thesis, University of Kentucky (1962).

1848 presidential nominee—
Free-Soil Party

Martin Van Buren

No biographical sketch of Van Buren is included since he served as president from March 4, 1837, until March 4, 1841 (8th president).

State represented: New York.

Birth: December 5, 1782.

Age on Inauguration Day (March 4, 1849): 66 years, 3 months.

Death: July 24, 1862.

1848 vice presidential nominee—
Free-Soil Party

Charles Francis Adams

Full name: Charles Francis Adams.

State represented: Massachusetts.

Birth: August 18, 1807, in Boston, Massachusetts.

Age on Inauguration Day (March 4, 1849): 41 years, 6½ months.

Education: Russian and English schools while father an ambassador; Boston Latin School; Harvard, 1821–1825; studied law in Washington, D.C., then in Daniel Webster's Boston office; admitted to bar on January 6, 1829.

Religion: Unitarian; in middle age began to find this religion too austere and cold.

Ancestry/prominent relatives: John Adams, president, 1797–1801 (grandfather); John Quincy Adams, president, 1825–1829 (father); Edward Everett (wife's brother-in-law), see Election of 1860; Henry Adams (son), writer and historian; Charles Francis Adams, Jr. (son), civic leader and historian.

Occupation: Attorney, public office holder.

Public office: Failed as Anti-Mason nominee for state representative, 1833; declined Whig nomination for state representative, 1838; state representative, 1841–1843; state senator, 1844–1845; unsuccessful nominee of Free-Soil Party for vice president, 1848; unsuccessful Free-Soil candidate for Congress, 1852;

MARTIN VAN BUREN and CHARLES FRANCIS ADAMS
(From the collection of David J. and Janice L. Frent)

U.S. Representative, March 4, 1859–May 1, 1861, resigned; U.S. ambassador to Great Britain, March 20, 1861–May 13, 1868; unsuccessful Liberal Republican candidate for president, 1872; declined Republican nomination for vice president, 1872; unsuccessful Democratic nominee for governor of Massachusetts, 1876; American arbitrator at Geneva, 1871–1872.

Home: Until 1837, Charles Francis had lived in "Old House" at Quincy, Massachusetts, with his parents; then built his own summer house one-eighth of a mile away.

Death: November 21, 1886, Boston, Massachusetts, 79 years, 3 months.

Burial: Mount Wollaston Cemetery, Quincy, Massachusetts.

Personal characteristics: Poor speaker; close physical resemblance to his presidential father and grandfather; cold, aloof, intensely serious.

Father: John Quincy Adams (July 11, 1767–February 23, 1848); president of the United States, 1825–1829.

Mother: Louisa Catherine Johnson (February 12, 1775–May 15, 1852), daughter of Joshua and Catherine (Nuth) Johnson; married July 26, 1797.

Siblings: George Washington (April 12, 1801–April 30, 1829), may have committed suicide. John II (July 4, 1803–October 24, 1834). Louisa Catherine (August 12, 1811–1812).

Wife: Abigail Brooks (1808–1889), married September 3, 1829.

Children: Louisa (1831–1870), married Charles Kuhn. John Quincy II (1833–1894), politician and farmer. Charles Francis, Jr. (May 27, 1835–1915), railroad executive and historian. Henry Brooks (1838–1918), writer and historian. Arthur (1841–1846). Mary (1846–1928), married Dr. Henry P. Quincy. Brooks (June 24, 1848–1927), writer and historian.

Historic site/memorials: Adams National Historical Site, 135 Adam Street, Quincy, Massachusetts. Beacon Hill Historic District, Boston, has an Adams home.

None of the other also-rans can claim as sterling a political lineage as could Charles Francis Adams. Son and grandson of presidents, Adams was himself destined for consideration in several elections for one or the other of the nation's highest offices. Yet few of the defeated candidates can claim so few actual electoral victories — a few terms as a state legislator, slightly more than two years as a congressman. He was a cold, self-centered man with little popular appeal. He had ability, but his entire political success, such as it was, arose from his parentage.

The earliest years in young Charles' life were spent in Europe. At age two he joined his father, future president John Quincy Adams, on a voyage to Russia where the elder Adams would serve as ambassador. French became his first language, English a lesser used one. Fame and attention became the norm. When he turned eight, he was in England, with his father now serving as minister to that country. Charles' poor progress in his studies worried John Quincy. Charles would never show much interest in schoolwork, though on rare occasions when a subject fascinated him, he excelled. In 1817, Charles was back in the United States, a country he did not remember and which was more foreign than Europe to this lad of ten. With his father preoccupied with public duties in Washington, Charles attended a boarding school in Boston. Two years later, Charles was freed from this unhappy exile and was allowed to join his father, who was then secretary of state. A few more years of indifferent study prepared him sufficiently for the minimal requirements for Harvard, which he entered when only 14.

Charles graduated from Harvard just as John Quincy Adams began his term as president. Living in the White House, the reserved, almost friendless boy enjoyed the attention. Adams' presidency was an unpopular one. Political opponents made life uncomfortable for not only the president, but also his family. Along with his older brother John, Charles served part-time as private presidential secretary.

Charles was going through the motions of studying law in the office of a Washington attorney. In 1827, he went to Boston and studied in Daniel Webster's office. Desultory in his studies, Charles nonetheless succeeded in passing the bar in 1829 and opened an office in Boston. Few clients came, but then Charles was rarely there to receive them. Charles and his father had not been close, but when the oldest Adams brother, George Washington Adams, died, the father seemed to show more interest and affection for both of his two remaining sons. The law office continued to be ignored as Charles took over business duties previously handled in Boston by his brother George. When Charles married Abigail Brooks, daughter of a wealthy Massachusetts businessman, in 1829, additional money came from his father-in-law. Despair over his brother's death, the lack of cordiality with his father, and a host of other real or perceived problems made Charles at this stage a melancholy and rather aimless young man. The marriage seemed to change that lack of direction. In later years, he said that if not for Abigail, he would never have accomplished anything in life. The statement has much evidence to support it.

Perhaps it was disgust over the treatment his father gave him, or memories of abusive treatment received by two presidents Adams, but for whatever reason Charles refused to be drawn into politics. Tending to family property, reading and writing on history and other subjects that interested him, Charles was relatively idle. Not until the Anti-Mason movement began to gather steam did Charles become sufficiently interested in public affairs to jump into the fray himself. His father was involved with the Anti-Mason movement, but refused suggestions that he become the party's 1832 presidential nominee. Charles had been fearful John Quincy Adams would embarrass himself by becoming involved in a hopeless try for vindication. Though wary of his father's ambitions, Charles was working for the Anti-Masonic movement by writing relatively unnoticed articles against the secret Masonic order. In 1833, Charles attended the state party convention, where he was nominated for state representative while John Quincy Adams received the gubernatorial nod. Both Adamses went down to defeat. The younger aspirant failed after he withdrew his name from consideration once a run-off became required, no candidate having received a majority.

Charles helped Congressman John Quincy Adams in his financial affairs. The son soon became an irritant to his father by his suggestions on investments and property, matters which seemed trivial to the old man who acutely perceived his own mortality and the relative insignificance of possessions. A bitter quarrel drove Charles from Washington, but the wound would soon heal and relations were restored.

Charles blamed Daniel Webster when his father lost the 1834 U.S. Senate election. In 1836, Charles became a bitter opponent of Webster's presidential candidacy. Instead, he supported Democrat Martin Van Buren, a bit of political apostasy that can be explained only as pique against Webster. Webster won Massachusetts, but no other state. Charles withdrew from a connection with any political party during the next few years. He was not politically disinterested, however, and spoke and wrote on many issues. Slavery gradually became the only issue that interested him. Charles Francis Adams, like his father, regretted the bitter abolitionist attacks on slavery at the same time as he considered the institution evil. Mob violence involving both abolitionists and slave sympathizers appalled Adams, and he sought a middle position.

Offers of nominations came his way on several occasions. He was drifting back to the Whigs after his defection in 1836, and that party first suggested he run for the legislature in 1838. He refused, but a second offer in 1840 was accepted and he was elected. Adams had turned against Van Buren because of his proslavery policies. Thus he was pleased when Van Buren was defeated for reelection in 1840, although he felt the victor, William Henry Harrison, was unqualified. For five years Charles would serve in the state house or senate, spending the summer and fall in Boston for the legislative sessions, returning to Quincy the rest of the year to write, tend to the building of a home near the family's Old House, and reading. In 1842. Adams first made his legislative mark by presenting anti-slavery petitions, including one signed by over sixty thousand individuals protesting the capture of an escaped slave and his return to his owner. Adams sought to have the capture of escaped slaves outlawed in the state. He tried to have Massachusetts congressmen instructed to oppose the admission of slave state Texas to the Union. If efforts to prevent annexation failed, Adams called for the creation of a Free Soil northern party. Such a party would later nominate him for vice president.

Adams worked for Henry Clay's election to the presidency in 1844, especially since it appeared that Clay opposed annexation. The pro–Texas James K. Polk was elected instead. When Texas was admitted even before Polk took office, Adams introduced a resolution in the Massachusetts legislature, calling on Congress not to admit any more slave states. The resolution passed overwhelmingly.

The year 1846 found Charles out of the legislature, having rejected another term because he wanted to return full-time to reading and his editing of his family's papers. Adams would before his death edit and publish the papers of both his presidential forebears, as well as write biographies of each. These labors were tragically interrupted in February 1846 by the death of his five-year-old son, Arthur. Grief kept Adams a recluse for months. To work himself out of his sorrow, Adams invested in a faltering Boston paper and became its editor. He made it a strident anti-slavery propaganda sheet. The new editor attacked his erstwhile party, the Whigs, for half-hearted anti-slavery positions. Old-line Boston businessmen who wanted to preserve their Southern markets were aghast.

The end of the Mexican War in 1846 added seemingly endless new territory to the Union. In Congress, the Wilmot Proviso was introduced that would have banned slavery from any of these lands. Adams urged adoption of the Proviso. On February 23, 1848, John Quincy Adams died, leaving a void for Charles, but also ending the pressure of measuring up to his father's challenging standards. Charles Francis Adams was most definitely on his own now, and he felt some relief. Almost immediately, Adams was mentioned as a replacement for his father in Congress. The anti-slavery editor wanted the position, but his Whig credentials were too suspect and Horace Mann received the nomination instead. Since the 1848 Whig presidential nominee was Zachary Taylor, a slaveowner who would not embrace the Wilmot Proviso, Adams joined the Free

Soil movement and severed all ties with the Whig Party. He called upon Massachusetts to send its "true-hearted" sons to an anti-slavery convention. In June 1848, New York Democrats opposed to the nomination of Lewis Cass for president chose Martin Van Buren to lead the anti-slavery fight. Adams considered Van Buren a suspect candidate whose anti-slavery fire was not heavily stoked. Adams addressed his state's Free Soil convention, and evoked images of his illustrious forebears by using his grandfather's words, "Sink or Swim, Live or Die, Survive or Perish, to go with the liberties of my country, is my fixed determination." He was chosen as a delegate to the national anti-slavery convention to be held in Buffalo. Adams saw Van Buren as a possible nominee for his new party, but wanted the ex-president to declare his slavery position more clearly and forcefully. Van Buren's reply to Adams on the issue only made Adams more uncertain about Van Buren. Adams himself received some votes at the convention, but Van Buren was nominated. The second spot seemed to require a western Whig to balance the eastern Democrat Van Buren. When western delegates were asked as to their candidate for vice president, it was Adams, another easterner, and not much of a Whig. John Quincy Adams in death undeniably aided his son's selection, as Charles was named because his father had so forcefully and tirelessly proclaimed the anti-slavery cause. Adams at first refused the nomination, but then accepted. The relationship between the two halves of the ticket was not cordial, and no prospect of victory existed to help ease the disagreements between the two men. The only pleasure Adams received out of the election results was that the Whigs were given a blow in Massachusetts that might prove fatal.

The Free Soilers began to lose what support the 1848 election had gained them when the Compromise of 1850 was adopted. Adams had opposed the compromise as a blot on Northern purity on the slavery question. Better to let the South secede with its peculiar institution, than to join forces in protecting it. Thus he found disgusting Webster's "Seventh of March" speech embracing the compromise; particularly galling was the Fugitive Slave Law that renewed the bitter feelings about the capture of runaway slaves.

Adams ran as a Free Soil candidate for Congress in 1852, but finished second out of four candidates. His influence in Massachusetts politics was waning. Adams represented anti-slavery agitation, and people wanted to put that behind them. Adams realized his political impotence and began to see himself and the Free Soil movement as political martyrdom. He refused to give up even a hopeless fight. Adams did decline being a Free Soil candidate for president when some of the delegates to the 1852 convention suggested him. The results of the 1852 elections — a tremendous Whig defeat — at least gave Adams hope that the Whig Party could be dissolved and a new, less compromising Northern party created.

Instead of political power, Adams had to content himself with his writings, especially his sorting of family papers for publication. From 1851 until 1856, ten volumes of his edited *Papers of John Adams* were published, as well as his biography of his grandfather. The death of the Whig Party and the emergence of the Republicans converted scholar Adams back into politician Adams. He attended the Republican national convention in 1856. Adams desperately wanted the new party to offer him the congressional nomination for his father's old seat, but in 1854 and 1856 he was rebuffed. From 1856 until 1858, he bided his time, rising to attack the *Dred Scott* decision, pro-slavery activities in Kansas, and other slavery excesses, but generally remaining aloof. The nomination he had so long coveted for Congress came in 1858. Adams was incredulous. The Republicans swept Massachusetts, and Adams ran ahead of the rest of the ticket in his district.

Two years later Congressman Adams supported William Seward for the presidential nomination. He was greatly surprised and disappointed with Abraham Lincoln's nomination. Adams thought Lincoln too inexperienced, though capable enough. Adams won easy reelection to his seat, and was soon in the middle of speculation about possible cabinet officers for Lincoln. That possibility did not arise, but Seward, who was named secretary of

state, convinced Lincoln to name the Massachusetts congressman minister to England. That post had been held by both his father and grandfather. When Adams thanked Lincoln for the appointment, he was enraged with Lincoln's response: "You are not my choice. You are Seward's man." Understandably, Adams' opinion of Lincoln took another step backwards.

Real problems faced the new American minister in London. British recognition of the Confederate States of America seemed almost a foregone conclusion, as most Britons were convinced that the rebels were going to win their war. Belligerent rights had already been extended to the Confederates, much to Adams' dismay. The South's slavery stance did not appeal to the Englishmen, who had banned slavery themselves, and Adams preyed on that sentiment in trying to reduce the likelihood of full recognition. Greatly exacerbating the situation was the seizure by an American navy captain of a British ship, the *Trent*, and the removal of two Confederate agents, James Mason and John Slidell. It was a *cause célèbre* in England, whose government was outraged by the interference with its own vessel and the seizure of diplomatic agents. Britain seemed ready to declare war against the North. The prime minister demanded a return of the agents and an apology, notifying the American government that refusal could lead to war. Tempers finally cooled and the British accepted the release of Mason and Slidell, without apology.

The minister also had to deal with the threat of British-built vessels being delivered to the Confederates. The raider *Alabama* was being built in a Liverpool port and Adams insisted that the British seize it. Continued Union losses on the battlefield encouraged the British to try joining with the French to intervene in the Civil War, and Adams was told by Secretary Seward to sever diplomatic ties if the South was recognized. The French rebuffed the English move, and Northern victories at Vicksburg and Gettysburg quieted British calls for recognition. Though encouraging news began to have effects on British favoritism to the South, a dangerous issue still remained unresolved in the form of two ironclad vessels under construction in Liverpool. The secretary of state instructed Adams that unless the British stopped Confederate use of British shipbuilding facilities, the United States might go so far as to employ privateers to destroy the vessels. The two ironclads were nearing completion. On September 5, 1863, Adams wrote the British foreign minister that unless the ironclads were seized, "it would be superfluous in me to point out to your lordship that this is war." Britain could not claim to be neutral if she let two such dangerous ships be constructed in her ports and sail to aid the Confederate cause. It appears that even before Adams' strongly threatening communication, the British government had decided to seize the Confederate ships and they did.

Though probably not decisive in convincing the British to seize the ships, Adams' bold language made him a hero at home, and highly respected among many Englishmen. James Russell Lowell said, "None of our generals, nor Grant himself, did us better or more trying service than he in his forlorn outpost of London." His duties lessened as a result of the settlement of the main issues of neutrality and as Britain recognized the impending doom of the Confederate cause.

Ambassador Adams publicly supported moderation towards the South during the last year of the war and at the start of the Johnson administration after Lincoln's assassination. Support for Johnson's conciliatory policies towards the South was unpopular and injured Adams' future political prospects, especially with Republicans. Adams tended to minor matters as minister after the war, but he longed to return to America. Finally, in April 1868, his resignation became effective.

His welcome back to the United States was lukewarm at best. Snubbed by Republicans from President Grant down to local politicians in Boston, he at least had the considerable satisfaction of being offered the presidency of Harvard, which he nonetheless refused. Adams consented to be one of the arbitrators of damage claims by Americans against the British arising from the Civil War. President Grant did not want to appoint him, but Secretary of State Hamilton Fish finally convinced Grant. December 1871 was the first session for the

arbitrations in Geneva, and then to Adams' dismay a six-month break was agreed to. He returned to Washington during the interlude and found himself high in speculation for the 1872 presidential nomination. Anti-Grant groups were beginning to form loose associations that in time coalesced as the Liberal Republican Party.

Adams was the frontrunner for the new party's nomination. The Liberal Republican movement got its impetus from Missouri politicians B. Gratz Brown and Carl Schurz, with Brown himself eyeing the presidential nomination. Being in Europe so long had kept Adams away from the bitter Reconstruction-era political wars. Also aiding his candidacy was wide press support as well as broad nationwide popularity. He had no headquarters and no staff. Charles Francis Adams was as disinterested an observer of his own "campaign" as could be found. Most of his supporters, including the delegates to the national convention, had never met him. These idealistic men, frustrated and disgusted with the graft in Washington, sincerely looked to Adams as the ablest man to clean up the national mess. Remaining aloof from the movement even as the convention opened, Adams could not determine whether the Liberal Republicans represented a legitimate national uprising or merely an amalgamation of disparate political egos that wanted a new vehicle for advancement. The erstwhile "candidate" even appeared to be trying to dampen his supporters' zeal, as he wrote to a supporter named David Wells a devastatingly haughty letter. In it Adams stated he did not want the nomination unless there was an "unequivocal call." If instead there were to be bargains struck before a nominee was selected, he wanted his supporters to "draw him out of that crowd."

When Wells' letter was published without authorization, delegates were offended by this supercilious language. Adams had left for Europe even before the convention opened. Several days after the convention had concluded, Adams learned he had been the frontrunner during the first five ballots. A long-brewing dispute between Missourians Gratz Brown and Carl Schurz had exploded. Brown, back in St. Louis, was told (erroneously) that at the convention Schurz had abandoned Brown's standard and was working for Adams. Brown rushed to the Cincinnati convention. The exact cause of Adams' demise is unclear, but Brown worked feverishly, promising rewards and punishments. He publicly abandoned his own candidacy and urged Greeley's selection. After the fifth ballot, Illinois determined to throw its support to Adams, and thought an avalanche towards the old statesman would result. Minutes before Illinois got the convention floor, however, a landslide had begun towards Greeley for reasons that are unknown. Brown received the vice presidential nomination. By such a slender margin, the final Adams opportunity for its third generation in the White House was lost.

The negotiations in Geneva concluded in September 1872, and a month later Adams sailed for home, his public career over. His mind failed faster than his body. Though rumors surfaced from time to time of high government appointments, he was little capable of such service. He died in 1886, barely aware of his surroundings.

Analysis of Qualifications

Charles Francis Adams as president would have much resembled the other Adams presidents. Cold, aloof, little interested in popular approval, each Adams had always done what he thought was right, not what was politic. All three had limitations, but they were not ones of intellect or dedication. It is likely that a third Adams president would have rated somewhat equal to the first two — highly competent, but disadvantaged by inadequate public support and an unwillingness to compromise.

As a diplomat, Charles Francis Adams excelled. He was restrained, not given to flights of emotion. Setbacks did not infuriate or frustrate him so much as they drove him to succeed. He was persistent, showing consistent resolve despite setbacks. At times as minister to England, he had to act independently of instruction from the State Department, and he acted wisely. Both as English ambassador during the war and as claims arbitrator afterwards, Adams was given unreasonable demands to make upon the British, and on each

occasion he handled his burdensome duties with skill.

This was a cold, sober man, who believed emotion was vulgar and rarely exhibited that "crass" trait. Study for self-improvement was his life's plan, and years of repose — reading, writing, reflecting — filled the void between public responsibilities. At all times, Charles Francis drove himself to succeed, as if previous generations were measuring his performance. There were few close personal friends. Social amenities were little understood, or at least appreciated, by this man who loved books more than parties. His family life showed the warmer side, as he was an affectionate father and husband. Even his often stormy relations with his father calmed and warmed as each aged. His natural reserve made him a poor politician, but it also made him appear a statesman rather than a party hack. Many saw him as an eccentric who was above the strife.

Adams was direct and sincere. A poor speaker, this scion of a form of American nobility found himself a political force because he evoked the images of a founding father and of an eloquent opponent of slavery. After the Civil War, he was swept into presidential consideration by those who opposed Grant. To his supporters, Adams represented incorruptibility and stability. His reputation was national; his following cut across party lines. He had no greatly original ideas that contributed to the advance of the nation, but no doubt he always sought to further the public interest. Political considerations were damned while he fought against slavery. When the Whigs compromised on the issue in 1848 by nominating Taylor, a slaveowner himself, Adams broke from the party and ran on a third party ticket.

Uncompromising, highly ethical, dedicated to his country, Charles Francis Adams felt a peculiar, probably indescribable responsibility to his family name and to his ancestors. Every office he did hold, though none of the highest public positions were ever his, was managed with distinction. The presidency would almost certainly have been no different. It is also quite possible that like the other two Adams' service, a four-year Charles Francis Adams presidency would have been so lacking in political finesse that he would have been defeated for a second term.

ADAMS BIBLIOGRAPHY

Adams, Charles Francis, Jr. *Charles Francis Adams.* Houghton Mifflin, Boston (1900), reprinted, Chelsea House edition, New York City (1980).

Diary of Charles Francis Adams. Vols. 1–2 edited by Aida DiPace Donald and David Donald; vols. 3–4 edited by Marc Friedlaender and L.H. Butterfield (1964–68).

Duberman, Martin B. *Charles Francis Adams, 1806–1886.* Boston (1961).

Rayback, Joseph G. *Free Soil: The Election of 1848.* Lexington, Ky. (1962).

Russell, Francis. *Adams: An American Dynasty.* New York City (1976).

Shepard, Jack. *The Adams Chronicles, Four Generations of Greatness.* Boston (1975).

Election of 1852

NOMINATIONS

Democratic Party Convention (6th): June 1–5, 1852, at the Maryland Institute Hall, Baltimore, Maryland. *President*— Franklin Pierce, nominated on the 49th ballot with 282 out of the 286 votes cast. Pierce had received his first votes (15) on the 35th ballot. The major rivals were Lewis Cass, Stephen Douglas, James Buchanan, and William Marcy (N.Y.). *Vice president*—William R. King, nominated on the second ballot with 277 out of 288 votes. He had received 125 votes on the first ballot.

Whig Party Convention (4th): June 16–18, 1852, at the Maryland Institute Hall, Baltimore, Maryland. *President*—Winfield Scott, nominated on the 53rd ballot with 159 of the 292 votes cast. He had received 132 votes on the first ballot. Millard Fillmore was his main rival, with Daniel Webster being a weak third alternative. *Vice president*— William A. Graham, nominated on the second ballot. There was much confusion, but the convention chairman said the nomination was unanimous. No formal vote was taken.

Free Soil (Democratic) Convention (2nd): August 11, 1852, in Pittsburgh, Pennsylvania. *President*—John Hale, nominated unanimously on the first ballot. *Vice president*— George Washington Julian, nominated nearly unanimously on the first ballot. Samuel Lewis (Ohio) and Cassius M. Clay (Ky.), were pre-convention favorites.

GENERAL ELECTION, November 2, 1852

Popular Vote
Pierce 1,601,274
Scott 1,386,580
Hale 155,825

Electoral Vote
Pierce-King — 254 (27 states)
Scott-Graham — 42 (4 states)

Winners
Franklin Pierce, 14th president
William R. King, 13th vice president

Losers
Winfield Scott, William A. Graham, John Hale, George W. Julian

---

1852 presidential nominee —
Whig Party

Winfield Scott

Full name: Winfield Scott.

State represented: New Jersey.

Birth: June 13, 1786, on the family estate, "Laurel Branch," 14 miles from Petersburg, Virginia.

Age on Inauguration Day (March 4, 1853): 66 years, 8½ months.

Education: Local tutors; high school in Richmond, Virginia, for one year, then William and Mary College, 1805; left to study law in office of Petersburg attorney David Robinson, and admitted to Virginia bar in 1806.

Religion: Episcopalian.

Ancestry/prominent relatives: Winfield's grandfather, James Scott, was a lowland Scot rebel, who escaped from Scotland around 1746 after having supported the Scot Pretender, Prince Charles Edward (Charles 1).

Occupation: Admitted to bar in 1806, but following year turned to the military; he spent the rest of his career as a soldier.

Public offices: Unsuccessful contender for Whig presidential nomination in 1840, 1844, and 1848; unsuccessful Whig nominee for president in 1852.

Death: May 29, 1866, in West Point, New York, at age 79 years, 11½ months.

Burial: National Cemetery, West Point, New York.

Home: No permanent home; moved frequently in military; last 20 years of career spent at Elizabethtown, New Jersey, or in New York City.

Personal characteristics: 6'5" tall, 230 pounds, strong, corpulent in later years; loved elaborate dress uniforms, called "Old Fuss and Feathers."

Father: William Scott (?–1792), gentleman farmer.

Mother: Ann Mason (?–1803), daughter of Daniel Mason, from distinguished Dinwiddie County, Virginia, family.

Siblings: James, married Martha Pegram. Rebecca, married Edward Henry Pegram. Elizabeth, married Joseph Wells Harper. Martha, married J. Thomas Field. Mary, married Theodore Scott.

Wife: Maria D. Mayo (1789–1862), married March 11, 1817, daughter of John Mayo of Richmond, Virginia.

Children: Maria Mayo (1818–?). John Mayo (April 18, 1819–September 23, 1820). Virginia (1821–?). Edward Winfield (March 23, 1823–May 17, 1827). Cornelia (1825–?). Adeline Camilla (1831–?). Marcella (January 21, 1834–?).

Historic site/memorials: Scott Circle in Washington, D.C., where Massachusetts and Rhode Island avenues meet, has in its center a giant equestrian statue of Scott (cast from captured cannon). A Winfield Scott house is at 24 W. 12th Street. Fort Scott historic area, Kansas, contains the fort named for him in 1842.

Few men rank higher in American military annals than does General Winfield Scott. His contributions in three wars — the War of 1812, the Mexican War, and the Civil War — were monumental. In 1807 he enlisted in the army, became a brigadier general by 1814, and remained in the military for the next 50 years. Achievements as a soldier only made Scott hunger for still greater honors. Only the presidency seemed capable of satisfying his ambition.

Born in 1786, Winfield came from a distinguished family. His grandfather had chosen the wrong side in one of the frequent efforts to place the father of Bonnie Prince Charlie on the English throne. Backing the wrong candidate in Scotland in 1746 had more significant repercussions than did losing an election in America one hundred years later, and thus James Scott fled to America. Winfield's father William fought in the Revolution. He then settled into the comfortable life of a Virginia gentleman farmer. Ann Mason, Winfield's mother, came from one of the most prominent and wealthiest families in Dinwiddie County, Virginia. All in all, Winfield was in a financially secure environment. Upsetting that tranquility was the death of his father when the boy was only six. His mother died 11 years later. The family fortune went to older brother James, and Winfield's share was much more modest. After short stints in various schools, Winfield studied in 1805 in a law office in Petersburg, Virginia. His legal career would be short, but he was admitted to the bar in 1806. Observing the treason trial of Aaron Burr was the high point of his abbreviated life in the law; the not guilty verdict disappointed him. He moved to South Carolina hoping to open his practice there, but war with England threatened. He decided to enlist, and his life was thereby permanently redirected.

Scott enlisted in the Petersburg cavalry.

Insignificant action resulted, and before the year was out Scott was back practicing law. Yet soon thereafter again the prospect of war seemed real, and Scott approached President Jefferson concerning a captain's position. On May 3, 1808, the commission was made and the new captain set about recruiting a company. Delays caused him not to arrive at his assigned post in New Orleans until April 1809. Scott was dissatisfied with army life, and was unimpressed with his fellow officers. Still unaware that his future was in the military, Scott determined again to return to the practice of law. On the way back to Virginia he learned that his courtmartial was being considered because of remarks he had made about his commanding officer, General James Wilkinson. The general had been implicated in the Burr conspiracy; too candid, or too indiscreet, Captain Scott made the remark that Wilkinson was as big a traitor as Burr. Wilkinson learned of the remark and pressed charges against Scott for conduct unbecoming an officer. The result was a fairly mild sentence of a one-year suspension from the service, which began in 1810. Winfield spent the year in Virginia, studying and reading on many subjects, including foreign authorities on warfare.

Back in the army, Scott traveled to Louisiana overland, blazing the first trail to Baton Rouge across Indian territory. He continued to study law. Throughout his life Scott was an omnivorous and eclectic reader. Training his mind was a ceaseless endeavor. With the War of 1812 starting, a new call for troops was made. Experienced men got promotions, and Scott found himself a lieutenant colonel, assigned to western New York. His first action came October 8, 1812, in a naval engagement near Buffalo. Scott was captured by the British later in the month at the battle of Queenstown Heights. The battle initially was an American victory, but turned to defeat when many volunteers refused to continue the fight. Parole came in November and Scott was next assigned to Philadelphia as an adjutant with the rank of colonel. This duty led to his being wounded in the attack on Fort George, but he recovered quickly. The colonel's next assignment was as commander at Fort George. Defenses had to be made quickly, which Scott

achieved by tireless efforts. Several other engagements occurred in ensuing months. With the war going poorly, Scott was sent to Albany to prepare for an offensive against the British. On March 9, 1814, Scott was commissioned a brigadier general. Two weeks later the new general was in Buffalo training troops for coming battles on the frontier. His methods and inspiring presence proved decisive in a lengthy engagement at Chippewa in early July. His outnumbered but inspired troops drove the British backwards for 16 miles. On July 25, one of the great engagements of Scott's career came at Lundy's Lane. Twice his mounts were killed beneath him. Scott himself became so badly injured that he was carried from the field. Though both sides suffered heavy losses, it was the British who retired from the field. The Americans were left, bleeding and reeling, with one of their few victories of this war. Scott was given the temporary rank of major general for his achievement; he also earned a nationwide reputation for valor.

So few were the military heroes in this conflict, in which most of the battles were lost though the war was won, that Scott's victories earned him a medal from Congress and accolades from the people as he journeyed to his next assignment. His wounds kept the general from further action in the war, and headquarters for him were established in Baltimore. There he presided over the postwar dismantling of the army. Five out of every six officers were discharged. The selections were principally made by Scott. A trip to Europe in 1815 and 1816 introduced him further to foreign military leaders and techniques. Scott used those experiences, as well as his vast reading, to write regulations and instructions for the military. One work, published in 1835, became the standard on infantry tactics until after the Civil War.

Peacetime army work was monotonous and hardly memorable. At least he found sufficient time to get married in 1817 to Maria Mayo. Their married life was frequently saddened by deaths among their children, only three of their seven offspring surviving their father.

Scott's temperament became increasingly irritable with age. Perhaps in peacetime, with promotions few and glory nonexistent, many military men are inordinately concerned with position. Scott was no exception. In 1828, when a junior officer was promoted over him as commanding general of the army, Scott tendered his resignation. He later withdrew it. His resentment was not borne silently thereafter, and relations between Scott and his commander were strained.

The Black Hawk War in 1832 was the first major military engagement by the American Army since the War of 1812. Scott sat it out when his troops became sick from cholera. While recovery was slowly occurring, Scott issued an order that any soldier found intoxicated should dig a grave and ponder that he would need one if he persisted in drinking. Scott wrote an article on intemperance and urged his soldiers to heed its teachings. Not all did.

Scott was summoned by President Andrew Jackson in 1832 to journey to South Carolina. The nullification crisis could erupt into civil war, and the president wanted Scott on the scene. No military force proved necessary, but Scott's presence and discreet display of strength played a role in keeping that crisis under control. Three years later relations between president and general were badly strained over the prosecution of the Seminole War in Florida. Jackson sent him to put down the Indians, but then became dissatisfied with his lack of immediate progress. A court of inquiry praised Scott for his work. The whole episode likely was affected by Jackson's spite over being criticized by Scott in 1817 for conduct during an earlier Seminole conflict.

In 1838 and 1839, the general used persuasion and a show of force to put down revolt along the New York–New England border with Canada. One episode had important political repercussions. New York revolutionists had seized an island on the Canadian side of the border. They used a steamboat called the *Caroline* to maintain contact with the shore. Scott quashed the *Caroline* rebellion and gained thereby great political support in western New York. Millard Fillmore, an important Whig politician in Buffalo, thought Scott would make a good presidential candidate. Fillmore communicated with New York political boss Thurlow Weed concerning Scott's

chances. Scott himself was quite taken with the idea, and considered himself a serious candidate. Few others did. At the Whig national convention in 1840 Henry Clay, William Henry Harrison, and Scott were contenders. Many were using Scott just to thwart Clay. In the end the convention turned to another hero for the War of 1812, Harrison. Scott blamed General Solomon Van Rensselaer for the defeat. Van Rensselaer was the father of the leader of the *Caroline* insurrection. Though he never forgave Scott for arresting his son, Rensselaer was probably not a sufficiently important New York delegate to have been the cause of Scott's defeat.

The presidential bee had stung Scott severely. His considerable disappointment over the 1840 loss could only be salved by victory at a later convention. In the meantime, there were military duties to tend. In 1841 Scott became commanding general of the army, 13 years after he first thought he deserved the post. Scott believed in looking the part of a general, and he imposed strict dress and grooming requirements for his officers as well. But Scott was an evenhanded commander, trying to reduce unnecessarily harsh discipline in the army. The next five years were quiet ones. His new duties in the army did not distract him from the 1844 presidential contest. Henry Clay of Kentucky was anointed unanimously at the national convention on May 1, 1844. Though never seriously in the running, Scott apparently again suffered severe disappointment at being passed over for the nomination.

Far more immediate concerns than politics came the following year. Threats of war against Mexico were real. Scott named Zachary Taylor to command the army in Mexico. President Polk became concerned that victories by this Whig general might make Taylor president. Polk called Scott and suggested he take personal command of the offensive. Scott was in a dilemma, for as much as he would like the assignment, he was loath to remove a successful general and place himself in command, at least not without some pretext. One convenient excuse would be if Scott could deliver reinforcements to the front. For the moment, however, there were no additional troops. Scott recognized Polk's political motives. The commanding general indiscreetly wrote a letter saying that Polk would appoint no Easterner, Whig, or West Pointer to command. The press unfortunately got a copy, and the general got some new enemies. Polk flailed about for a Democrat to replace Taylor, but finally on November 23, 1846, he named Scott to lead an expedition to Mexico. The seeds for bitter conflict between the generals over troops and glory were now planted.

Scott's first Mexican victory came at Vera Cruz, which he seized with nominal loss of life on March 26, 1847. Success followed at Contreras, Churubusco, and finally Mexico City on September 14. While these maneuvers were occurring, Scott ordered troops from Taylor's command to help in the conquest. Taylor reacted bitterly, but obediently. Taylor sent letters to Polk and the secretary of war protesting his treatment at Scott's hands.

Victory led to different problems. A civil government for the conquered territory had to be devised. Scott's occupation government proved effective, and a group of Mexicans even asked the general to become their dictator. While Scott was consumed with his duties, rival officers were undercutting him at home. In this most political of American wars, another sad chapter of backbiting and glory-hunting was begun when General Gideon Pillow wrote a report giving a different version than Scott's on the closing battles of the war. The Democrats seized upon it to discredit Scott, whom they feared as presidential material in 1848. In his report Pillow took the glory and criticized Scott's actions. Some of Pillow's officers agreed with the version. Scott demanded an explanation from these officers but was rebuffed. Scott brought charges, but President Polk saw his opportunity. The president dismissed Scott's claims, placed William O. Butler in Scott's command, and subjected Scott to a court of inquiry before politically selected officers. While the inquiry was occurring Scott refused to permit his name to be considered for president. Thus Taylor got the 1848 nomination without a real contest from Scott. Eventually the charges against Scott were withdrawn; the Democrats were defeated by Taylor just as Polk had feared; and Scott returned to his duties as commanding general of the army.

Scott's presidential ambitions were not quite exhausted. His last chance would be in 1852. He would be 66 years old then, hardly prime age for success, but still younger than Harrison had been. Fortunately for Scott, Fillmore was in the White House, Taylor having died in 1850. Fillmore had pressed Scott's cause in 1840, and when Scott's rival and one-time subordinate Taylor died, Fillmore said, "Now, General, your persecutions are at an end." Thurlow Weed and William Seward, powers in the Whig Party who had helped defeat Scott before, now worked for him. Counseling the indiscreet general to remain silent on important issues, these campaign managers worked behind the scenes. This was not a campaign to build public support, but one to consummate secret deals and thereby gain the nomination.

Though a friend, President Fillmore was hardly deferring to the aged general. The president, Scott, and Secretary of State Daniel Webster were the leading candidates. A "masterly silence" cloaked Scott's feelings on the Compromise of 1850, a compromise Taylor had opposed but Fillmore, upon his ascension, helped pass. Scott had done some unpublicized lobbying for the compromise, and his managers wanted that role to remain secret. At the national convention in 1852, Webster was never a serious contender. His votes and those of a few minor candidates merely prolonged the contest between Scott and President Fillmore. A bargain was finally arranged by Scott's managers, whereby Southern delegates were assured on eight points. The most important was that Scott accepted the 1850 Compromise, especially the vigorous enforcement of the fugitive slave law. An adjournment had occurred after 46 ballots. Fillmore and Webster men had a weekend to negotiate among themselves in an effort to block Scott. Webster declined, and on the fifty-third ballot Scott went over the top.

Victory in hand, Scott rebelled against his months of enforced silence. He rejected the plans of his convention managers. Anti-slavery Northeasterners whom Weed and Seward had hoped to keep in the fold by finessing the fugitive slave law promise, were immediately antagonized when Scott stated he accepted the entire Whig platform, including the slave provisions. The platform was no semantic quibble to many, and promises of vigorous enforcement of the fugitive slave law divided what was left of the disintegrating Whig Party. Webster was bitter over his own defeat, and advised some of his supporters to abandon Scott and vote Democratic. More serious to the campaign was the rejection of Scott by the Free-Soil convention when they nominated John P. Hale of New Hampshire.

It was a vicious campaign. Charges from both sides were scurrilous and deeply personal. Scott was easily ridiculed for his elaborate uniforms, his plumes and feather that he felt helped cultivate the image of distinction necessary for command. Events from the Mexican War were resurrected, including Scott's charge that Polk was making "fire upon my rear" at the same time that the general was facing the enemy in Mexico. An outraged President Polk had for a time threatened to relieve Scott of command. Scott had received notice of his threatened demotion while eating in a Washington restaurant. This resulted in another unfortunately phrased letter from Scott to the president: "Your letter, received as I sat down to a hasty plate of soup, demands a prompt reply." Scott's personality, prickly and vain, was excoriated with unnecessary exaggerations in the press. He was called anti–Catholic (a charge the Whigs themselves used against Democratic nominee Pierce), an incompetent commander, and assorted epithets too numerous to mention.

Few thought Scott would win, but the Whig candidate himself was one of those optimistic few. During a brief campaign swing Scott had proclaimed such hopeless inanities as that he was in love with the "sweet German accent" and the "rich Irish brogue." His whole campaign was awkward and ineffective. Franklin Pierce was almost equally inept, and would prove to be poorly qualified once elected. But Pierce had the advantage of a much more effective political operation in many states. Moreover, the South was becoming solidly Democratic as Whigs became increasingly identified with opposition to slavery. Still, Pierce's victory was only a narrow majority, 50,000 out of over three million cast, over the combined Whig (Scott) and Free-Soil (Hale) totals. The Whigs had been badly split, yet still a credible race had been run.

Scott's contributions to his country were far from over. He was 66 years old, but still commanded the armies of the United States. He would continue to do so until he was 75. In the next few years, Scott played an important part in settling a controversy over possession of the San Juan Island in Puget Sound. Conflicting British and American claims over the island again strained relations to the breaking point. Scott was in poor health and hardly ready for a trip to the Pacific Northwest. The dispute was settled in large part due to his mediation.

As the Civil War became a likelihood, Scott counseled the president to reinforce Southern forts. In October and then December 1860, he pleaded with President James Buchanan to strengthen federal positions in the South, but without success. During the inauguration in 1861 the safety of the new president, Abraham Lincoln, was Scott's personal responsibility and he handled that important duty effectively. Once the war erupted, military leaders who placed their loyalties with the Confederacy urged this native Virginian to join them, but Scott was a Unionist. Since his advice on the prosecution of the war was not generally heeded by the civilian leaders, Scott decided in October 1861 to retire. On November 1, 1861, the president and his cabinet went to the general's home, where Lincoln read a tribute. A few minor parts were given him as the tragedy of the war was played out, but in truth the army and the country had been given over to younger men. He died a year after the war ended.

Analysis of Qualifications

"Old Fuss and Feathers" he was called, though not to his face. The phrase poked fun at one of the outstanding characteristics that a Scott presidency might have stumbled on — the general's pervasive vanity. A brave and talented man whose career in the army was as illustrious as it was lengthy, Winfield Scott was no political leader. A better general than Zachary Taylor, Scott probably would have made a better president. His martial skills also far outdistanced those of Franklin Pierce, who had been a political general named by a Democratic president anxious to get some of the war glory for his party's men, no matter how militarily inexperienced. The Pierce presidency was inept, and it is likely that Scott would have surpassed that hapless man in the incredibly difficult tasks of chief executive in the 1850s. Yet is is also probable that a President Scott would have been as well remembered for failings as successes, for evidences of unsuitability for the White House as for fitness.

Scott entrusted his political fortunes in 1852 to William Seward and Thurlow Weed. Though he kept up with public affairs and had views on most of the issues of the day, Scott was inexperienced with the political world. A few men have made the transition effectively from career military men to president — most notably Dwight Eisenhower and Andrew Jackson. Scott had an incredibly thin skin. He was not politically realistic, as was revealed in his unreasonable beliefs in 1840 and 1844 that he had a meaningful chance for the presidential nominations. His impolitic statements concerning the fugitive slave law in 1852 demonstrated either refreshing candor or a lack of political sophistication, more likely the latter. After all, for months he had consented to complete silence on crucial issues, and it was frustration and probably vanity that finally caused him to speak out.

As age overtook Scott, so did increasing physical problems. In part because of these, the general was often irritable with his aides. He could be petulant. Disputes with his army comrades were many. Apparently there was far too little glory to go around during the Mexican War, for seemingly all involved from president on down were trying to steal the honor belonging to others. Scott was not above joining in these rivalries.

General Scott loved elaborate military uniforms, with bangles and plumes, sashes and swords. He was a majestic man, a giant in height and bulk, strong and erect. Few had a greater ambition than he, and great deeds filled his military career. Food was almost as much of a passion as military glory, and he fancied himself a connoisseur of wines. Reading was another kind of gluttony for Scott. Books on science, history, politics, as well as military matters were consumed. His knowledge was broad, if not necessarily deep in understanding. Despite all the egotistic strutting, Scott was scrupulously honest in business and personal relations. He was a poor businessman and was frequently financially strapped.

Likely Scott would not have been remembered as an exemplary president. It is easy to see him bumbling in office, becoming angry and irritable, becoming confused by the totally new world of politics. One hopeful counterweight to this negative forecast of a Scott presidency was his history of successful negotiations under the gun — with the Canadians over border disputes in New York, with Indians during potential bloody conflict in the Southeast, and with the British when San Juan Island threatened to become a crisis. Scott had tact, could use the carrot or stick when necessary, and apparently could use finesse, when he applied himself, in personal relations. Scott had greatness with all-too-obvious personal foibles. His outstanding qualities are matched by negative ones. He is a difficult Also Ran to measure, and on balance is given only a passing grade. At least it is easy to say that as between Scott and Pierce, the choice should have been "Old Fuss and Feathers."

SCOTT BIBLIOGRAPHY

Elliott, Charles Winslow. *Winfield Scott, the Soldier and the Man*. New York City (1937).

Johnson, Timothy Dwight. "Young Fuss and Feathers: Winfield Scott's Early Career, 1808–1841." Unpublished doctoral dissertation, University of Alabama (1989).

Mansfield, Edward D. *The Life and Services of General Winfield Scott*. New York City (1852).

Scott, Winfield. *Memoirs of Lieut.-General Scott, LL.D., Written by Himself*. 2 vols. New York City (1864).

Smith, Arthur Douglas H. *Old Fuss and Feathers: The Life and Exploits of Lt.-General Winfield Scott....* New York City (1937).

Wright, Marcus J. *General Scott*. New York City (1894).

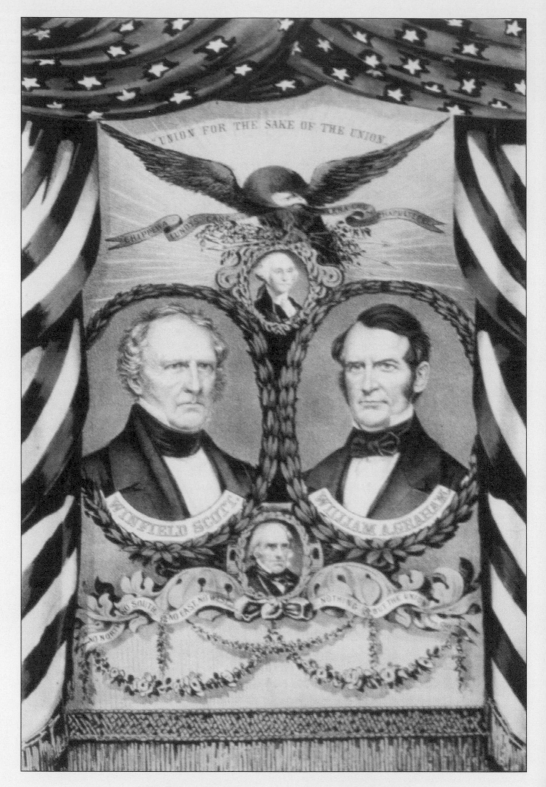

WINFIELD SCOTT and WILLIAM GRAHAM
(From the collection of David J. and Janice L. Frent)

1852 vice presidential nominee —
Whig Party

William Graham

Full name: William Alexander Graham.

State represented: North Carolina.

Birth: Vesuvius Plantation, Lincoln County, North Carolina, on September 5, 1804.

Age on Inauguration Day (March 4, 1853): 48 years, 6 months.

Education: Boarded at private academies in North Carolina, 1816–1819; final preparation for college at Hillsborough Academy, 1819–1821; University of North Carolina, 1821–1824; read law in office of Thomas Ruffin; admitted to bar in 1829.

Religion: Presbyterian.

Ancestry/prominent relatives: Scotch-Irish; first Graham arrived in mid–1700s from Ireland; James Graham (brother) U.S. Representative.

Occupation: Attorney.

Public offices: Representative to North Carolina General Assembly, 1833–1840; defeated for U.S. Representative, 1837; Speaker of the House of Commons, 1838–1840; declined to run for Congress, 1839; selected U.S. senator, November 25, 1840–March 4, 1843, defeated for reelection; governor, January 1, 1845–January 1, 1849; declined to be appointed ambassador to Russia or Spain, 1849; secretary of navy, July 22, 1850–July 25, 1852; declined nomination to Department of Interior, 1850–1851; unsuccessful Whig nominee for vice president, 1852; state legislature, 1854–1855; N.C. state senate, 1863–February 1864; Confederate senate, May 1864–1865; elected U.S. senator, 1866, not permitted to take seat; delegate to state constitutional convention, 1875, died before took seat.

Death: August 11, 1875; Saratoga Springs, New York; 70 years, 11 months.

Burial: Hillsborough, North Carolina, Presbyterian Church Cemetery.

Home: Hillsborough, North Carolina.

Personal Characteristics: Over six feet tall, erect, dignified, slender, considered extremely handsome; scrupulously neat in dress and grooming; hazel eyes.

Father: Joseph Graham (October 13, 1759–1836), planter, owner of iron foundry, local politician, major general of N.C. militia in War of 1812.

Mother: Isabella Davidson (?–January 15, 1808); married 1787; daughter of Major John Davidson of Rural Hill Plantation, Mecklenburg County.

Siblings: Sophia (1791–1865), married Dr. John Ramsay Witherspoon in 1815. Alfred (1803–1835), never married. Violet Winslow Wilson (1799–1868), married Dr. Moses Winslow Alexander in 1821. Joseph Jr. (1797–1837), married Sarah Kimbrough in 1827. James (1793–1851), U.S. Congressman, never married. George Franklin (1794–1827), married Martha Ann Harris in 1825. John Davidson (1789–1847), married (1) Elizabeth Epps Connor in 1815 and (2) Jane Eliza Johnston in 1840. Polly (1788–1801). Robert Montrose (1798–1821). Mary (1801–1864), married Robert Hall Morrison in 1824. Isabella (1807–1807).

Wife: Susan Sarah Washington (1816–1890), married June 8, 1836.

Children: Joseph (1837–1907), doctor. John Washington (1838–1936), state senator, college professor. William A., Jr. (1839–1923), farmer, state senator. James Augustus (1841–1909), lawyer and state senator. Robert Davidson (1842–1905), lawyer. George Washington (1847–1923), doctor. Augustus Washington (1849–1936), attorney, state legislator. Susan Washington (1851–1909), married Walter Clark. Alfred Octavius (1853–1854). Eugene (Genie) Berrien (1855–1863).

Historic sites/memorials: Graham's birthplace still stands at Vesuvius Furnace, Catawba Springs, North Carolina.

The youngest of 11 children, William Graham grew up in relative prosperity in rural North Carolina. His father had gained prominence during the American Revolution, rising from private to major, and demonstrating bravery by ignoring numerous wounds while continuing to fight. A minor political career, including county sheriff and delegate to the state convention that ratified the national constitution, added variety to the elder Graham's main occupation as a farmer and owner of an iron foundry on his Vesuvius Plantation. It was a fascinating childhood for William, full of stories about the Revolution and about politics. William's mother died when he was only four, and he seemed to gain an especial closeness to his father.

Rural North Carolina offered few educational opportunities that were not gained at home. William's father was his earliest tutor, and perhaps minor instruction was infrequently gained at nearby schools, though that is not recorded. At the age of 12 William journeyed to Lincolnton Pleasant Retreat Academy, where his father was a trustee. Family tradition holds that he had to be dragged from his hiding place beneath is bed when time to leave for boarding school came. Lincolnton Academy was only ten miles from Vesuvius Plantation. William next attended Statesville Academy. In both schools William excelled, showing far greater interest in his studies than was common. There was a reserve in William even as a teenager, which later unfairly would be called a haughty coldness by political opponents. Once while home from school, William was the manager of the ironworks for his father. Though only a lad of 14, he produced one of the greatest profits for the works until that time.

William entered the University of North Carolina in 1821. Active in several campus organizations, particularly the Dialectic Society, William became a campus leader. At graduation, he was one of only four honor students in the 34-person class, and was selected to give the class oration.

William had decided on a career in the law, at least preparatory to a try at politics. He read law for two years in the Hillsborough office of Judge Thomas Ruffin. Admitted to the bar in 1827, attorney Graham opened his office in that same city. There was much more competition among lawyers, but before long he was gaining more than his share of business. He was diligent, well organized, and wrote and spoke clearly and compellingly. In 1835, he was offered a judgeship, but declined. The more cloistered life of the judiciary did not appeal to the young lawyer who was becoming active in organizing the Whig Party in the state.

Graham's activities in the nascent Whig Party were inspired at least in part by his opposition to President Andrew Jackson's attempts to kill the national bank. The bank crisis established Graham's party in North Carolina, coalescing the Jackson opponents on one issue. For 14 years, beginning in 1836, the Whigs would control the state's governorship and most other offices. In 1833, Graham had been elected to the General Assembly by only one vote, but his margins thereafter were much more secure, not even being opposed in his next two elections. The first controversy to bring Graham prominence was the battle by the Whig-controlled legislature to instruct the state's two Democratic U.S. senators on how to vote. The question of whether legislators had the right to instruct United States senators divided the two parties. Ironically, the Whigs generally felt instruction was improper, but the prospect of forcing the two opposition senators to resign when they could not abide by the instructions was too appealing to let principles interfere. Graham's carefully prepared, persuasively delivered speech in favor of the instructions did not sway a majority, but it did place Graham as a Whig leader to watch.

In 1837, Graham tried to make the jump to Congress. He was not an enthusiastic candidate, as prospects for victory for any Whig in his district were small. He had also just married and was leery of the exile to Washington that would be required if he won. He need not have worried, as he lost by a small margin — 191 votes out of 4,991 cast. The following year his respectful colleagues in the legislature selected him speaker, a position he would retain until his next promotion. Declining more forcefully in 1839 some additional urgings to run for Congress, Graham was biding his time and preparing his case for the ultimate office within the power of the legislature to bestow. The strong Whig majorities in the legislature that were elected in 1840 made the ambition within reach. Instructions had finally been issued to the two Democratic senators, and in 1840 both resigned rather than follow the legislative demand. Two vacancies had to be filled. Long-time Whig leader Willie Persons Mangum got one. After much scrambling by various candidates, and after the leading contender had declined election, Graham got the seat. At the age of 36, he was off to join his hero Henry Clay and other luminaries in Washington.

Closely allied with Clay, Graham backed the "American System" of internal improvements, and with less vigor the principle of a protective tariff. Public education was also a high priority of the North Carolinian. However, it was support for the recharter of a national bank that brought him closest to the mainstream of the Whig Party. It also made him a bitter opponent of accidental president John Tyler, who had succeeded to the presidency on April 4, 1841, upon the death of William Henry Harrison. Graham had not been impressed by old Tippecanoe, thinking he looked too worn for his responsibilities. That foresight did not make him more of a supporter of Tyler, who after a few months was described by Graham as an "imbecile" who should be discarded by the party. Even so, Graham was more willing than some to compromise with the president.

Graham's ability to continue the fight in Washington was dependent totally on the results of the 1842 North Carolina elections. The unexpired Senate term he was filling only lasted two years, and therefore the legislature chosen in 1842 would either retain or replace him. Whig apathy permitted a sweeping Democratic resurgence that almost picked off the governor's chair, and did regain the legislature. Two competing Democrats deadlocked the deliberations over a successor to Graham, and each side threatened to vote for Graham unless the other gave in. That was not to be, however, and eventually the Democrats chose a compromise third candidate. Graham retired to his law practice and soon had a thriving business.

Graham was at this stage an extremely popular politician whose short career had few blemishes. He had declined to run for governor in 1842, but agreed to run in 1844 if there was a unanimous vote by the party state convention. That the Whigs saw him as their best hope is clearly shown by his unanimous endorsement. The gubernatorial campaign was conducted on national issues. This was a presidential election year. The crisis over the annexation of Texas cut across party lines, particularly in the South. Henry Clay tried to straddle the controversy, appealing to the North by saying he did not favor admission at this time, and seeking Southern votes by emphasizing the "at this time" caveat. Graham faced a dilemma of repudiating his presidential candidate or else offending large segments of North Carolina voters.

To make matters more difficult, in February 1844, Graham became seriously ill. Rumors that he was dying and would have to be replaced as the nominee slowed his campaign. A protracted recovery finally permitted him to return to the hustings by May. With his Democratic opponent he criss-crossed the state, though at the end the Whig nominee ignored the Democrats' stronghold in eastern North Carolina. Graham had finally decided to straddle the issue of Texas himself, by saying he did not want war with Mexico, which was sure to come if the United States admitted Texas. The war would be dishonorable and a blot on American reputations, a forecast that proved true. "In due time we shall have Texas without war, and without a violation of honor." His moderate stance on the question proved adequate, and he won with a comfortable majority in the August state elections. In November would be the national elections, and Graham devoted himself to helping Clay carry the state. That battle was also won, but the national war was lost with the election of Democrat James K. Polk. Graham was disheartened, seeing Polk's campaign as a territorial expansionist as a sure precipitator of war once he took office.

The North Carolina governor's office was not a powerful one, as the chief executive did not even have the veto power. The governor's early efforts were directed to such historically significant but politically inconsequential matters as securing all state records dealing with the Revolutionary War, a matter of considerable interest to this scion of a great hero of that war. A liberal bent was demonstrated by his support for measures creating schools for the deaf and dumb and for the blind. More controversial was Graham's effort to buy for the state a failing railroad that he had helped charter while a legislator. The Assembly authorized

Graham to purchase the road, and the governor used the entire appropriation as the state's bid. It was the only bid, and later in Graham's career he would be criticized for paying an exorbitant price for a railroad that continued to need a state financial subsidy.

The governorship agreed with Graham, and he decided to try for one more term. Trying to appear reluctant for office, Graham waited for a "call" from the people before announcing he would accept another term. There was little to show as accomplishments during his first two years. Many Whigs despaired of his electability. The Democrats, however, were having trouble determining their candidate. During the campaign the Mexican War began. Whigs nationwide decried the need or honor in "Polk's War" and Graham was no different. He doubted whether America was justified in fighting a war to ensure Texas's boundaries. Still, once war was declared, Governor Graham performed his responsibilities in raising troops. The election occurred in the midst of the war crisis, and Graham was reelected with twice the margin of his first victory.

Graham's second inaugural address ignored the national issues that were beginning to cause the governor political trouble. But the problems would not go away. New volunteers had to be raised for the war. The army was now requiring that all enlistees serve for the duration of the conflict. Earlier volunteers objected since they had only agreed to serve for one year. There was much difficulty in raising the two companies required from North Carolina, and Graham and his party were partly to blame. Their criticism of the war, justified as it might have been, had made the state a hotbed of anti-war sentiment. More controversy rained down on the governor when he refused to permit the regiments that were raised to elect their own colonels. Graham named them himself and chose only Whigs. The first two nominees failed to serve, one refusing the appointment and the other dying before taking command. The next two likewise refused, and the final candidates were again Whigs with little military experience. It was not a high point in Graham's career. That a Democratic governor might have done the same thing, and that the Democratic president

was also practicing politics with his appointment of generals, does however say a lot about the standards of the time.

In Mexico the North Carolina regiment mutinied against the petty, high-handed discipline of one of the colonels appointed by Graham. Politics so pervaded the war effort that even when President Polk visited the state to accept an honorary degree, the governor would not welcome him officially. Graham never did become reconciled to the merits of the Mexican War.

In 1848, the governor decided not to run for a third term. The Whig nominee barely won that year, presaging the fall of the party from power two years later. Governor Graham's closing message to the legislature made the slight reference to the political wars of the preceding two years, and instead focused on an ambitious plan to remake the state. Internal improvements were the focus, from detailed plans for railroad routes, to specific roads that ought to be built and canals to be dug. An asylum for the insane was urged, court reform supported, and a survey of agricultural and mineral resources of the state suggested. This plan did not meet instant success, but it did set a reformist tone for that session of the legislature.

In retirement, Graham returned to his law practice in Hillsborough. In 1849, with President Zachary Taylor in the White House, Graham was offered his choice of appointment either as ambassador to Spain or to Russia. Both were quickly rejected by the former governor. The burning controversy over slavery was again threatening to erupt, but the compromises suggested in the Senate by Graham's old friend Henry Clay gave prospects for cooling the flame. Taylor's opposition to the compromise made him only briefly mourned when he died; pro-compromise New Yorker Millard Fillmore assumed the presidency. The North Carolina Congressional delegation recommended their fellow Carolinian Graham to Fillmore for a cabinet position. Fillmore asked all Taylor cabinet officers to remain until the close of the Congressional session. Finally on July 25, 1850, Graham accepted the position of secretary of the navy.

Uninformed about naval matters, Graham

took the office as a typical political appointee. Demonstrating the dedication he had applied in his other public offices, Graham was in time able to take firm hold of his responsibilities. That he succeeded is shown by the rating of the novice naval head by scholar Samuel Eliot Morison, as one of the best nineteenth-century navy secretaries.

At least five matters received Secretary Graham's close attention. Reorganization of the coastal survey was badly needed. Promotions among career officers were solely based on seniority, and much deadwood existed as a result; younger, aggressive officers resigned rather than wait for death to thin the ranks above them. Another focus of Graham's tenure was to support even though not initiate, the significant opening to the Far East represented by the sending of a naval expedition to Japan. Commodore Perry headed the famous mission. Similar in intent, both expeditions being based on a desire to open new commercial opportunities for America, was the exploration of the Amazon valley in Brazil. Another purpose of the Amazon mission was to discover whether colonization of former slaves could be made there. With the improvements in steam-powered vessels, Graham was also faced with the difficult decision of whether to back the new innovation as a replacement for sailing ships, a controversy that separated far more experienced navy men than he was. No definite decision was ever made by the secretary, though he did suggest that new sailing vessels be equipped to change over to steam if that should later prove desirable.

In 1852, it was not surprising that cabinet member Graham supported President Fillmore for nomination to a full term. The selection of General Winfield Scott instead made Graham an attractive candidate to bridge the gap to Fillmore's supporters. Graham was also a Southerner who could bring valuable support from that region. Graham's selection had no significant impact on the campaign. Scott did not prove an attractive candidate and the ticket was badly defeated.

As a Whig in now solidly Democratic North Carolina, and as a Unionist in a state edging towards secession, Graham had few opportunities for elective office. The former

governor was elected to the state senate in 1854, and two years later backed the Know-Nothing (American) Party presidential candidacy of his old boss, Millard Fillmore. Graham denounced both the abolitionists and the secessionists, hoping all sides would moderate their demands and work for peaceful resolution of the conflict. During the 1860 Constitutional Union Party convention, a few states supported him for the presidential nomination, and when John Bell was nominated instead, Graham supported him. Abraham Lincoln's election was to Graham an insufficient cause for revolution. Lincoln's call for troops, however, and North Carolina's secession, finally convinced Graham to support the rebellion. He had initially opposed the call for a state convention to consider secession, but eventually he even attended the convention, was barely defeated for president of the gathering, and voted for the resolution of secession.

During the war Graham saw five of his sons fight for the Confederacy; the other two were too young to do so. Their father was a critic of the Confederate government's policies, especially on the suspension of habeas corpus, the restrictions on use of civil courts, and other limitations on freedoms. During the war, Graham served in the North Carolina legislature, and then was elected to the Confederate States Senate. Senator Graham wanted peace and urged the Hampton Roads Conference as a means to end the war. When it became clear that the Confederate government would continue to insist on independence as the price of peace, Graham encouraged the North Carolina government to seek a separate peace. The proposal came to naught, and the war ended not by negotiation, but by defeat.

This former Whig, constant Unionist until the war erupted, and critic of the Confederacy, was selected by the North Carolina legislature after the war to represent the state in the United States Senate. North Carolina's request for readmission to the Union was rejected, however, and thus Graham could not serve. Back in his native state he helped form the conservative Democratic Party, opposing Negro suffrage, but also rejecting the tactics of the Ku Klux Klan. In 1874, he was selected to arbitrate a boundary dispute between Virginia and Maryland, and died in New York state while serving in that capacity.

Analysis of Qualifications

William Graham represented a forgotten segment of the antebellum South — a Unionist Whig, a conservative, a man who saw in his own section's cries for more slave territory, as well as in Northern abolitionists' sentiments, the reprehensible ingredients that would cause rebellion and dissolution. Whether in 1852 his brand of conservatism could have helped slow the rush towards civil war is doubtful. Probably no one could have averted that crisis at that date. Yet there is reason to believe that this North Carolinian would have been better remembered by posterity, even if he ultimately failed in the crisis of the day, than the presidential ticket that defeated him.

For 30 years Graham represented North Carolina and the nation in varied capacities. His experience was broad and significant. He had served in both state and national legislatures; he had executive experience as governor of his native state; his administrative abilities were demonstrated as secretary of the navy for two years. As a politician Graham was well respected by his peers as well as his constituents. Even while fellow Whig candidates in North Carolina were becoming weaker, Graham maintained his popularity among the voters.

Family background and his own education placed William Graham in an advantaged position. The luster already attached to the Graham name by his father's exploits helped William get started in politics. With several years in private academies, and with a full four-year curriculum at the University of North Carolina, Graham had an exceptional education for the times. From these sources he gained a love of history and knowledge in general. He also gained a love of the Union that served him well during the difficult years of the 1840s and 1850s. A conservative in politics, Graham drew his Whig principles from the old National Republican wing of the party. A supporter of John Quincy Adams in 1828, a bitter opponent of Andrew Jackson, Martin Van Buren, and James Polk, Graham found

his party leader in Henry Clay. He shared Clay's vision of an "American System" that would build up domestic industry by using a tariff to protect it from foreign competition, and smoothing its growth by internal improvements such as roads, canals, and railroads.

In personal qualities Graham was reserved, modest, almost aloof. His demeanor made some feel he was cold and arrogant, but he felt a strong social responsibility, a noblesse oblige because of the advantages educationally and financially he had enjoyed. Graham not so much identified with the people as he felt responsible for them. He opposed universal suffrage, feeling that the better-educated classes were the only ones capable of governance. Governing by the privileged, however, must be on behalf of all people. Grace and dignity were the frequent descriptions of his appearance; many called him the most handsome man in state politics. Fair to his opponents, calm in debate, Graham exploded rarely and usually only when his personal integrity was attacked. In speaking style the North Carolinian was logical, unemotional but persuasive. He eschewed invective in the same manner as he avoided frivolity. Graham was fair; he was neither mean nor witty.

Graham was not afraid of government. As governor he wanted the state to assume responsibility for the disadvantaged — the blind, deaf, or dumb. He wanted a system of public works directed towards improving American industry. He was conservative, but also forward-looking. Most of all Graham desired sectional peace, and was willing to compromise to receive it. When the Confederacy was forming, Graham pleaded for calm, and Union. As president he would have demanded the same. His background suggests he would have performed well.

GRAHAM BIBLIOGRAPHY

Clark, William Alexander Graham, comp. *Descendants of James Graham (1714–1763) of Ireland and Pennsylvania*. Washington (1940), in William Alexander Graham Papers, the Southern Historical Collection, University of North Carolina.

Graham, William A. *General Joseph Graham and His Papers on North Carolina Revolutionary History*. Raleigh (1904).

Hamilton, Joseph Gregoire de Roulhac, ed. *The*

Papers of William Alexander Graham. Projected 8 volumes, Raleigh (1957–   ).

McGehee, Montford. *Life and Character of the Hon. William A. Graham*, printed in Joseph Gregoire de Roulhac Hamilton, ed. *The Papers of William Alexander Graham*, Raleigh (1957) I, 1–64, reprint of 1877 publication.

Nash, Frank. "Addresses at the Unveiling of the Bust of William A. Graham, by the North Carolina Historical Commission, in the Rotunda of the State Capitol, Delivered in the Hall of the House of Representatives, January 12, 1910." *North Carolina Historical Commission Bulletin* No. 7 (1910), reprinted in Joseph Gregoire de Roulhac Hamilton (ed.), *The Papers of William Alexander Graham*, I, 65–127.

Williams, Max R. "The Education of William A. Graham." *North Carolina Historical Review* XL (1963), 1–14.

_____. "Secretary William A. Graham, Naval Administrator, 1850–1852." *North Carolina Historical Review* XLVIII (1971), 53–72.

_____. "William A. Graham," in *Dictionary of North Carolina Biography*. Chapel Hill, N.C. (1986), vol. 2.

_____. "William A. Graham, North Carolina Whig Party Leader, 1804–1849." Unpublished doctoral dissertation, University of North Carolina (1965).

Family information supplemented by Professor Max R. Williams, Sylva, North Carolina.

1852 presidential nominee—
Free Soil Party

John P. Hale

Born March 31, 1806, in Rochester, N.H.; died November 19, 1873, in Dover, N.H.

Married Lucy Lambert; they had one daughter.

John Parker Hale, Jr.'s parents were John and Lydia C. O'Brien Parker. The senior John was a successful attorney who died when the future presidential candidate was 13. Young John was able, despite financial difficulties caused by his father's death, to attend Phillips Exeter Academy and graduate from Bowdoin College in 1827. After studying law in Rochester and Dover, Hale was admitted to the bar in 1830. He practiced in Dover, where his ability to appeal to juries was the cornerstone of his success. After just two years of practice Hale was elected to the state legislature. In 1834 President Jackson named him United States district attorney, a position he held until 1841. In 1842 Hale was elected as a Democrat to Congress, but broke with his party over its support for annexation of the slave state Texas. In a January 1845 letter to the voters in his district, Hale said bringing Texas into the Union would "provoke the scorn of earth and the judgment of heaven." He had already been renominated for Congress, but in February 1845, his nomination was revoked and he was evicted from his own party. Hale organized an independent party that took control of the New Hampshire legislature in 1846. He was elected speaker. In June 1846 Hale was elected by the legislature as what was said to be the first avowedly anti-slavery United States senator.

The votes that made him a senator came from a coalition of Whigs and independent Democrats, which left him with no true party home in Congress. In October 1847 a collection of anti-slavery activists met in Buffalo and, calling themselves the Liberty Party, nominated Hale for president. Hale rejected the nomination. The 1848 elections sent 13 Free-Soil representatives to Congress and Ohioan Salmon Chase to join Hale in the Senate. This small group of anti-slavery advocates would through fits and starts over the next decade grow in size to control Congress as Republicans. Hale's attacks on slavery were the hallmark of his service, but he was not vitriolic. Instead he showed good-nature for those who mistakenly would support so wrong an institution. His humor and good will was not always the most salient aspect of his speech. Mississippi Senator Henry S. Foote said he would hang Hale were he ever to venture to that Deep South state. Hale also took an interest in the navy and was, among other efforts, able to have flogging banned.

Hale's anti-slavery prominence made him a lecturer and frequent speaker throughout the North. Delegates from the former Free Soil Party, now calling themselves the Free Democrats, gathered in Pittsburgh in August 1852. They unanimously nominated the well-known Hale for president. Hale got about 5 percent of the vote in November.

Hale's senate term expired March 3, 1853,

JOHN P. HALE
(From the collection of David J. and Janice L. Frent)

and he was not re-elected. He again practiced law, and for a brief time lived in New York. In 1855 the state legislature — after a protracted battle — again sent him to fill an unexpired term in the Senate. He was now a Republican, and not just a third party, anti-slavery advocate. He became ill in what for a time was a famous outbreak of illness at the National Hotel in Washington in 1857, and his health would suffer thereafter. In 1859 he was elected to a full term, and served until March 3, 1865. During the Civil War he was chairman of the Senate Committee on Naval Affairs. He became embroiled in some controversy about loose oversight of navy contracts, rewarding New Hampshire contractors and even receiving a fee from one person who was defrauding the government. Though the statutes of the time did not apparently make anything Hale did illegal, he was defeated handily when the Republican state legislators met in 1864 to name a Senator for the next four years.

When Hale stepped down in March 1865, President Lincoln named him minister to Spain. He did not know Spanish, nor did he know diplomacy. By 1869 he was tangled in a bitter public dispute with the secretary of the legation, H.J. Perry, including being charged with violating import rules. The Spanish government was in turmoil at the time, as Queen Isabella II was deposed in September 1868, in part for her scandalous lifestyle. Hale was recalled in April. He was ill, and had a stroke in 1870 that left him paralyzed. Hale was an invalid until he died in 1873.

HALE BIBLIOGRAPHY

Baxter, Gerald D. "John Parker Hale, Constitutional Constructionist and Radical Republican: A Study in Intra-Communicative Conversion and Inter-communicative Persuasion." Unpublished Ph.D. dissertation, University of Southern California (1972).

Blue, Frederick J. *The Free Soilers: Third Party Politics, 1848–54.* Urbana (1973).

Foner, Eric. *Free Soil, Free Labor, Free Men: The Ideology of the Republican Party Before the Civil War.* New York (1970).

Julian, G.W. "A Presidential Candidate of 1852." *Century* (October 1856).

Sewell, Richard H. *John P. Hale and the Politics of Abolition.* Cambridge, Mass. (1965).

*1852 vice presidential nominee —
Free Democrat (Free Soil) Party*

George Washington Julian

Born May 5, 1817, near Centerville, Indiana; died July 7, 1899, in Indianapolis. Married Anne Elizabeth Finch in May 1845, who died in November 1860; they had three children, two of whom died young. Married Laura Giddings, daughter of Joshua Giddings, on December 31, 1863; they had two children. She died in 1884.

Isaac and Rebecca Hoover Julian lived in a log cabin when George was born. Isaac was a Quaker, a veteran of the War of 1812 and a one-time Indiana legislator. His death when George was six left his widow to care for six children. After attending local schools and teaching when he was 18, George studied law and was admitted to the bar in 1840. In 1845 George entered politics by being elected as a Whig to the Indiana General Assembly. For the first time in his career, but not the last, Julian's views on slavery were too radical for the voters and he was defeated after a two-year term. Julian attended the 1848 Free-Soil convention in Buffalo that nominated Martin Van Buren for president. The party did not propose abolishing slavery, but just not permitting it in any of the new territories acquired from Mexico after the Mexican War. Julian was an energetic campaigner in the losing cause. Julian announced for Congress in December 1848, and he won in the 1849 election.

The Compromise of 1850 had given many citizens a false sense that the divisive issue of slavery had been resolved. Many northerners seemed eager to have the slavery issue just go away. Julian's strong views were less popular in 1851 when he ran for re-election, and he lost. The lack of zeal by the major parties caused a committed band of Free-Soilers again to gather to nominate a presidential ticket in 1852, this time in Pittsburgh and this time calling themselves the Free Democrats. Neither of the preferred presidential candidates,

GEORGE WASHINGTON JULIAN
(From Indiana Historical Society Library, Negative No. C3702)

John Hale and Salmon Chase, wanted the empty prize of the nomination and urged each other to accept. Hale was nominated. Without much advanced planning, the convention then named the 35-year-old Julian for vice president. He had not been in Pittsburgh, but he did some traveling on the stump thereafter. Julian was heckled, at times felt threatened, but there was no violence. The Free Democrats' showing was even worse than Van Buren's in 1848.

The slavery issue again dominated political discourse because of the Kansas-Nebraska bill in 1854. Julian was now essentially an abolitionist, which made him radical by mid–1850s standards. He lost another race for Congress in 1854. By February 1856 Julian joined and became a leader in the new coalition party, the Republicans. In 1860 Julian was elected to Congress as a Republican. Julian was frequently at odds with the new President, Abraham Lincoln. Lincoln steered a moderate course on slavery, at least until 1863, trying first just to preserve the Union as various Southern states seceded. Julian was a prominent, aggressive member of the Joint Con-

gressional Committee on the Conduct of the War. Lincoln and his generals were frequently criticized by the watchdog committee. Julian's radicalism was now popular enough in Indiana for him to be reelected four times, the last being in 1868. Though dissatisfied with Lincoln's slow pace on abolition, he unlike some radicals favored the president's renomination in 1864. Julian also felt Lincoln was too conciliatory towards the South in 1865 as the war drew to a close. The congressman wanted no leniency shown the conquered rebels. In 1867 he had what to him was the honor of serving on the seven-person House committee that drew up articles of impeachment against President Andrew Johnson, who had tried to thwart the radical Republicans' post-war goals.

Julian's feud with influential Indiana politicians, including Oliver Morton, led to his district being reshaped in 1867. He barely won in 1868, and lost in 1870. As an opponent of Republican President Grant, Julian bolted from the regular Party and became a leader of the Liberal Republicans in 1872. They along with the Democrats nominated Horace Greeley for president, but he lost. Julian moved back to Indiana. He built an impressive mansion outside Indianapolis. He stayed active in politics, eventually rejoined the Democrats, and even became the surveyor general of New Mexico when the Democrats retook the presidency in 1885. In 1889, he returned to Indianapolis, participated from the sidelines in William Jennings Bryan campaign in 1896, and died in 1899.

JULIAN BIBLIOGRAPHY
Blue, Frederick J. *The Free Soilers: Third Party Politics, 1848–54.* Urbana (1973).
Clarke, Grace Julian (daughter). *George W. Julian.* Indianapolis (1923).

Hammerback, John Clark. "George Washington Julian: Hoosier Spokesman for the Slave." Unpublished Ph.D. dissertation, Indiana University (1970).

Julian, George W. *Political Recollections, 1840 to 1872.* Chicago (1884).

Knoblauch, Juliet. "George Washington Julian: Land Reformer." Unpublished master's thesis, Auburn University (1959).

Riddleberger, Patrick W. *George Washington Julian: Radical Republican.* Indianapolis (1966).

Seldon, Mary Elisabeth. "George W. Julian: A Political Independent," in Gray, Ralph D. (ed.). *Gentlemen from Indiana: National Party Candidates 1836–1940.* Indianapolis (1977), pp. 29–54.

Election of 1856

NOMINATIONS

Native American (Know-Nothing) National Convention, at National Hall, February 22–25, 1856, in Philadelphia, Pennsylvania. *president*—Millard Fillmore, nominated on the second ballot with 179 votes out of 182; Fillmore had received 71 votes out of 143 on the first ballot. Other contenders were Sam Houston (Texas) and George Law (New York). *Vice president*— Andrew Jackson Donelson, nominated on the first ballot, with 181 votes to 30 for other candidates; he had received less than a majority before votes were switched to him.

Democratic National Convention, held June 2–6, 1856, in Smith and Nixon's Hall, Cincinnati, Ohio. *President*— James Buchanan, nominated on the seventeenth ballot with a unanimous 296 votes; Buchanan had received 135 votes on the first ballot. Franklin Pierce (New Hampshire) and Stephen Douglas (Illinois) were the principal other contenders. *Vice president*— John C. Breckinridge, nominated unanimously on the second ballot, having received 50 votes out of 296 cast on the first. John A. Quitman (Mississippi), Linn Boyd (Kentucky), Herschell V. Johnson (Georgia), James Bayard (Delaware), and Aaron Brown (Tennessee) were the other main possibilities.

Republican National Convention, June 17–19, 1856, in the Music Fund Hall, Philadelphia, Pennsylvania. *President*—John Charles

Frémont, nominated on an informal first ballot with 359 out of 567 votes; in the formal balloting, Frémont received 520 votes. John McLean (Virginia), Salmon Chase (New York), and William Seward (Ohio) were also candidates. *Vice president*—William L. Dayton, nominated on an informal ballot with 253 votes. In the formal voting, Dayton received 523 of 567 votes. Abraham Lincoln (Illinois) was the leading other candidate.

GENERAL ELECTION, November 4, 1856
Popular Vote

Buchanan	1,836,072
Frémont	1,342,345
Fillmore	873,053
Others	3,177

Electoral Vote

Buchanan-Breckinridge — 174 (19 states)
Frémont-Dayton — 114 (11 states)
Fillmore-Donelson — 8 (1 state)

Winners

James Buchanan, 15th president
John C. Breckinridge, 14th vice president

Losers

John Charles Frémont, William L. Dayton, Millard Fillmore, Andrew Jackson Donelson

John Charles Frémont

Full name: At birth, John Charles Frémon; changed to Frémont at about age 25.

State represented: California.

Birth: January 21, 1813, at Savannah, Georgia.

Age on Inauguration Day (March 4, 1857): 44 years, 1½ months.

Education: Charleston, South Carolina schools; preparatory school of Dr. Charles Robertson, in Charleston, 1827–1829; Charleston College, 1829–1831, expelled for poor attendance.

Religion: Episcopalian; his wife, Catholic.

Ancestry/prominent relatives: His father arrived from France around 1800; Thomas Hart Benton (father-in-law), U.S. senator.

Occupation: Explorer, Army soldier, rose to major general during Civil War.

Public Offices: Appointed military governor of California, January 16, 1847, by Commodore Robert F. Stockton, who may not have had authority to do so; served only a few months; U.S. senator from California, September 9, 1850–March 3, 1851, defeated for reelection; unsuccessful Republican nominee for president, 1856; nominated for president in 1864 by splinter party, but declined; appointed territorial governor of Arizona, 1878–1883.

Death: July 13, 1890, in New York City, at age 77 years, 6 months.

Burial: Rockland Cemetery, Piermont (Nyack), New York.

Home: "Los Mariposas," in California.

Personal Characteristics: Small, lean, strong man; full bearded; curly, black hair, almost grizzled, parted in middle; restless, constantly in motion; dressed plainly and simply.

Father: Jean Charles Frémon (?–1818), born near Lyons, France, and moved to America around 1800; taught French, dance, and other subjects in various schools.

Mother: Anne Beverly Whiting (?–September 17, 1847), married Major John Pryor when she was 16, he 61, and stayed with him about 12 years; had an affair with Frémon and went away with him after they were discovered in July, 1811; may have married Frémon after Major Pryor died.

Siblings: Frank (?–1839). Elizabeth (?–1831).

Wife: Jessie Benton (May 31, 1824–December 27, 1902), married October 19, 1841; daughter of Senator Thomas Hart Benton of Missouri, and his wife Elizabeth McDowell.

Children: Elizabeth Benton (November 3, 1842–?). Benton (July 24–October 6, 1848). John Charles II (April 19, 1851–?), naval officer. Anne Beverly (February 1–July 1, 1853). Frank Preston (May 25, 1854–?).

Movies: *Dream West* (1986), a made-for-television miniseries with Richard Chamberlain portraying Frémont.

Historic sites/memorials: The Pathfinder Dam, near Casper, Wyoming, honors Frémont, the "Pathfinder of the West."

Scandal and ostracism marked the early years of John Charles Frémont. Frémont's mother, Ann Beverly Whiting, was the daughter of a well-established Virginia family that had long previously fallen on hard times. After her father died, she was forced into a marriage with Major John Pryor, a man two generations older than she. Young Ann had her own needs, and she found them satisfied by a young émigré from France, Charles Frémon, who was a teacher at a private school in Richmond, Virginia. The affair was conducted secretly for some time, but in July of 1811, Major Pryor confronted his wife with the accusations. Ann admitted them and said she would leave immediately with Frémon. John Charles was the first of three children born to this illicit relationship. Probably sometime after Major Pryor's death, Frémon and Ann did marry.

Their years together were happy enough, but Frémon longed to return to France. Moreover, American society had never accepted this unmarried couple and their bastard children. In 1818, only a short time before their planned emigration to France, Frémon became ill and died. John Charles was only five. The family was then living in Norfolk, Virginia, but Mrs. Frémon decided to move to Charleston, South Carolina. It was an important move. John

Charles entered a circle of friends with the children of the wealthy in affluent Charleston. He received an education probably unavailable in Norfolk, and he also was befriended by lawyer John W. Mitchell, who probably saw in Frémont a future lawyer of real promise. At Mitchell's own expense, he sent John Charles to a preparatory school, where John Charles received a short but good education. He then entered Charleston College, and subsequently became a country teacher.

Frémont became interested in the sciences, especially astronomy. He met Joel Roberts Poinsett, who had been United States minister to Mexico. After Poinsett's return to Charleston from Mexico, he invited Frémont and others to weekly breakfasts in which Poinsett's experiences of travel, of people, and of ideas, were the topics of discussion. Poinsett helped Frémont become a teacher of mathematics upon a Navy warship, the *Natchez,* and for two years Frémont traveled the coast of South America.

In June 1835, Frémont received his discharge from the *Natchez.* Next he helped survey a projected railroad route from Charleston to Cincinnati, Ohio. In the autumn of 1836, Frémont signed on with another survey crew to establish the common boundaries of North Carolina, Tennessee and Georgia.

With Poinsett's help, Frémont became the chief assistant to Joseph Nicolas Nicolett, a famous French scientist who came to America because its unexplored West was a land of opportunities for his talents. He was to make a survey of the Northern territory between the Mississippi and Missouri rivers. Frémont received from Nicolett his training as a scientist and a scholar. Frémont was transformed from an untrained assistant governmental surveyor to being an explorer who had the scientific talents and techniques to understand the wilds he was charting.

Frémont was involved in two surveys with Nicolett and sharpened his skills for his later leadership of similar expeditions. Frémont accepted an offer to work with the United States Coastal Survey. He and Nicolett lived at the home of an eccentric scientist who was the superintendent of the Coastal Survey. He met much of official Washington at the elaborate parties held at this home, including Thomas Hart Benton, a senator from Missouri. Through discussions with Benton and others, he began to view exploring as aiding the fulfillment America's destiny.

Perhaps even more important was that Frémont met Benton's daughter, Jessie. She was then 15 years old and was so beautiful and intelligent as to be the object of many older men's attentions. Mrs. Benton had hopes that widower President Martin Van Buren would marry Jessie. Yet the dashing young explorer Frémont and the even younger Jessie were immediately attracted to each other. The age difference, the lack of substantial income, and an army career which would cause frequent absences, made Frémont an unattractive candidate to the Bentons for their daughter's hand. They insisted on a one-year moratorium on any talk about marriage.

In June of 1841, Frémont left to lead a survey in the Iowa Territory. This was an important task in the new territory that was opening up for settlement, and upon his return Frémont was the talk and the toast of Washington. Jessie and Frémont became even more attracted to one another. Protestant ministers in Washington would not marry them for fear of incurring the wrath of Senator Benton. They were finally able to arrange for a marriage from a Catholic priest. For a time, they continued to live separately and kept the marriage secret. Finally, Frémont told the senator. Benton went into a rage. He ordered Frémont out of his house, never to return, and for his daughter to remain. Jessie immediately turned around this incredibly difficult situation by saying that wherever Frémont went, she would follow. She then proceeded to do so. The senator faced the inevitability of the marriage, and relented. He continued to assert what dominion he could, and demanded that the two live at the Benton home. That is what occurred, with Senator Benton's becoming the chief and indispensable benefactor of the Frémont career.

On May 2, 1842, Frémont left on his first major expedition to the West. One of the men he recruited in St. Louis was Kit Carson, doing so quite by accident. As he paced the deck of a steamboat, Frémont bemoaned the fact that he had not yet acquired a guide whom he could trust. Kit Carson, who had not introduced himself, said he could lead the men anywhere. When Frémont arrived at Fort Laramie he learned that the Sioux Indians were on the warpath. Frémont wished to continue, and gave his men an explanation of the alternatives and the dangers. He then said he would fully understand if any man wished to turn back. Frémont himself would go on and wanted whoever would go with him to do so. On other occasions similar opportunities were given by Frémont to his men to back out of the next dangerous step that had to be taken, but the men always went with him. They finally reached and mapped South Pass in the Rockies. The expedition then returned to St. Louis by the same route.

Frémont just barely reached home prior to the birth of his first daughter. Frémont and Jessie, despite her weakened condition after a difficult pregnancy, collaborated in the writing of a report on this first expedition. The report was published by Congress and became an inspiration as well as a guide for many who wished to travel to the West.

Planning immediately commenced for the next expedition. This time Frémont procured a cannon as well as other weaponry, ostensibly because of the Indian problems that arose during the first trip. When the secretary of war saw that a cannon had been obtained, his previous doubts about the expedition intensified. He ordered Frémont to return to Washington, but in St. Louis, Jessie intercepted and read the letter. She wrote Frémont and without telling him the reason, begged him to leave immediately. The relationship was already such that Frémont obeyed the instructions without question. Jessie then wrote Washington and told them what she had done.

This expedition lasted 14 months. Frémont and his men endured incredible difficulties. Hunger, near drownings in the rapids, tremendous thirst in the desert, and other deprivations abounded. Finally the men made it across the snow-covered Rockies, eating their mules and horses in order to stay alive. They arrived at Sutter's Fort, east of present-day San Francisco in what was then Mexican territory. Frémont and his men recovered from the

ordeal there and left a few days prior to the arrival of a Mexican force that might have imprisoned Frémont's party.

In May 1845, Frémont left on his third expedition. His instructions were extremely obscure, intentionally so. Ostensibly he was to explore the headwaters of the Arkansas River, and if possible survey the Red River around Texas. Yet the true purpose of this trip was intertwined with events in Washington, Mexico City, and London. The Mexican War was about to break out. The U.S. government had ambitions on the vast territories that are today the American Southwest. The British, who then claimed the Pacific Northwest, were aware of America's covetous gaze. Frémont may actually have been sent secret orders, perhaps only oral ones, to be in California with an American military presence should war break out.

In late September, Frémont and his men had reached the Great Salt Lake. Because of approaching winter, Frémont decided to travel across the Great Salt Lake Desert. The mountain men and Indians thought he was crazy for doing so, but it was the only way to make it across the Rockies before the winter snowstorms. Part of the trek was through Donner Pass, which the following year would cause such hardship to be faced by a different party that it would reduce men to cannibalism. Yet Frémont was lucky, and he made it through this rugged area, not easily, but successfully. Again they arrived at Sutter's Fort, but appeared to have no plans. Frémont told all who asked that he was surveying a route from the United States to the Pacific Ocean.

Over the next few months Frémont ignored repeated Mexican orders to leave. Finally, in late June 1846, Mexican General José Castro began to move against Frémont in order to drive him out of California. Some Americans had already declared California a republic. Frémont wanted to help, but delayed pending receipt of orders. Before any real battle occurred, Castro and the Mexican leaders escaped to Mexico and the remaining Mexican army disbanded. Commodore Robert Stockton, who led the U.S. Naval forces off the coast of California, asserted command based on nebulous orders he had received many months before. Stockton told Frémont that he would make him governor of California. It would not prove to be quite that simple.

Lines of authority were quite broken in the territory. No one had orders authorizing the creation of a government in California, because communications were too slow to react to the changing situation. Both Stockton and U.S. Army General Stephen Kearny claimed authority in California. Kearny had recently arrived from the fighting near Santa Fe. Frémont alone negotiated a treaty with the Mexican forces, though General Kearny clearly outranked Lieutenant Colonel Frémont. After the treaty was concluded, Kearny was outraged, but knew he did not yet have the means to retaliate.

On January 16, 1847, Commodore Stockton finally appointed Frémont governor of California. Kearny wrote Frémont and said that Kearny himself was in charge. Frémont's response was that he could not obey Kearny until the leadership question was resolved between Commodore Stockton and Kearny. Frémont's written response was handed to Kearny when Frémont was present. Kearny gave Frémont an immediate opportunity to retract and destroy the statement, saying he would forget he ever saw it. Frémont stood firm. By February 12, Kearny learned that he himself had been officially appointed governor of California. General/Governor Kearny did not tell Frémont. Frémont's dispute with one of Kearny's officers, Colonel Mason, became so serious that Frémont challenged Mason to a duel. Eventually the duel was canceled.

In June of 1847, Kearny ordered Frémont and his original party back to Washington. When they reached Fort Leavenworth in August, Kearny had Frémont arrested. This totally surprised Frémont, as he had no idea matters had reached such a low ebb.

The court-martial that was held became a *cause célèbre*. The papers daily carried accounts. Jessie Frémont, who was then pregnant with their second child, sat in on each day of the three-month trial. Frémont was not allowed a private attorney, and thus he conducted all questioning for the defense himself Three charges were leveled against him, all

based on Frémont's failure to recognize Kearny's authority. One, mutiny, carried a possible death sentence. After three days deliberations, the military judges found him guilty. Yet the judges then immediately stated in complete contradiction of the guilty verdict that his errors were not intentional, that the lines of authority were too blurred for him to have known who was truly in charge. A recommendation was made in the verdict itself that the president pardon Frémont and permit him to remain in the service. The pardon was given, but Frémont refused and resigned in protest. When the Frémonts' second child died shortly after birth, both parents blamed the military for causing such a terrible strain on Jessie.

Since he was now out of the army, Frémont could not get a governmental survey job. Senator Benton secured him the job of surveying the route for a railroad from St. Louis to the West. Frémont had already been planning to move to California and live on a ranch that he had purchased the previous year.

By November 15, 1848, Frémont arrived at Bent's Fort, in southeastern Colorado. The weather was already extremely cold, and the time for passing through the Colorado mountains was past. Frémont wanted to make this trip as quickly as possible by taking a shortcut through dangerous and uncharted mountain territory. He believed he could make it across the mountains into the Sacramento Valley in 35 days, but his reasoning proved fatally in error. The cold and snow were unbearable, and at times the men could make no more than a half mile's journey in a day. Other times they sank down into the incredibly deep snow, and could not travel at all. Before the journey was over, ten men died, and some had to be left behind in order for others to travel forward and attempt to get help in Taos, New Mexico. Frémont was among the Taos group. He was too weakened by the journey to return, and indeed only one man was strong enough to lead the rescuers back. When some of the survivors were discovered, evidence of cannibalism was found, though all denied that this had occurred. Perhaps Frémont was no more rash in this particular effort than he had been during some earlier episodes; he just was not as lucky.

Frémont and the remaining party traveled on to California. There Frémont's fortune continued to be bad. He discovered that the ranch that had been purchased on his instructions was poorly suited for raising anything. Miraculously, within months it became clear that the ranch was at the southern end of a large gold discovery. Frémont became tremendously wealthy. His ranch was named "Los Mariposas," and there he built his home.

In 1850, John Charles Frémont was elected one of the first two U.S. senators from California. The two senators drew lots to see who would get the long term and who would have to seek re-election the following year. Frémont got the short term. California was admitted as a state on September 9, 1850, and Frémont took his seat. He declared himself a Democrat "by association, feeling, principle, and education." Generally he followed the lead of his father-in-law, Democratic Senator Benton. He finished out that session of Congress and headed back to California. In choosing the next senator the legislature deadlocked for 142 ballots in February 1851, and decided to forgo further balloting until January 1852. Frémont was no longer a candidate when that occurred. Four years later Frémont would say that pro-slavery legislators had blocked him because of his opposition to slavery. In fact, Frémont's views on the issue were too nebulous to have played a role.

The next few years were not as filled with adventure as before. He traveled with Jessie to England and to Paris, where a daughter was born in February of 1853. They returned to Washington in June. After being ignored for command of a federal surveying expedition to discover a practical Rocky Mountain railroad route, Frémont undertook a private winter expedition to determine the same thing. He succeeded. Such dangers no longer excited him, though, and it was his last expedition. The daughter who had been born in Paris died in July. Both parents were devastated, Jessie so much so that she almost seemed not to recognize that the death had occurred.

Frémont withdrew from politics after the deadlocked Senate voting in 1852. However, in 1856 no one under consideration for the presidential nomination of the brand-new

Republican Party was making much progress. Frémont's well-publicized and heroic adventures were far more appealing qualifications than were the long and often controversial public records of other potential nominees. Francis P. Blair, Gideon Welles, and Nathaniel P. Banks were prime movers in the Frémont cause. There was little national publicity for Frémont until April 1856. At that time Frémont wrote a letter to the leader of the free-state movement in Kansas, encouraging him in the struggle there and falsely asserting that his anti-slavery views had defeated him for the Senate in 1851. The Frémont campaign would thereafter be an avowedly anti-slavery movement. It was enough to win the Republican nomination over Supreme Court Justice John McLean, Salmon Chase, and William Seward.

In Democratic campaign literature and in speeches, Frémont was criticized for his illegitimate birth, for his court-martial, for the entire Mexican War episode, and for being a Catholic (he wasn't). Frémont himself frightened moderates North and South by taking a strong anti-slavery position. Former President John Tyler said that he thought disunion would follow a Frémont victory. The Know-Nothing Party nominee Millard Fillmore sought the middle-of-the-road voter. Frémont lost, but the new party that refused to soft-pedal the slavery issue had shown that it could make a credible run for the presidency.

Frémont returned to his ranch in California, title to the property having been confirmed in him by the United States Supreme Court in 1855. When the Civil War started, Frémont was in Europe raising money to help erase the substantial debt he had incurred in his California businesses. President Lincoln apparently desired to appoint Frémont minister to France, but Secretary of State Seward protested. So Frémont was appointed a major general in the army. Frémont was placed in charge of the Department of the West with headquarters in St. Louis. He had many obstacles to overcome. The greatest one was self-imposed when the new general emancipated all slaves owned by supporters of the Confederacy, without having first received approval for the order from Washington. Frémont refused to retract the order and Lincoln was forced to do so himself. Frémont was removed from his post and placed in charge of the Mountain Department in Western Virginia. He probably had insufficient forces for the command. After being overwhelmed by Stonewall Jackson in May and June 1862, he was placed under the command of General John Pope. This was a demotion and resulted in Frémont's requesting that he be relieved. Lincoln was relieved.

In 1864, some dissident members of both parties nominated the explorer/general for president, but in September Frémont withdrew from the race at Lincoln's urging. He was to play no further part on the national scene. His business endeavors began to dominate. Serious financial losses followed, particularly because of his involvement with various failed Western railroads. Frémont's later years were spent almost in poverty. From time to time the government would attempt to assist him, as when he was appointed territorial governor of Arizona from 1878 until 1883. Finally, a few months prior to his death, he was returned to his rank of major general, which he had held during the Civil War. This gave him a major general's pension. This substantial pension came too late to be of help, and he died while visiting New York City in 1890.

Analysis of Qualifications

Frémont has several claims to uniqueness among the defeated candidates. He is the only illegitimate child, the only explorer among the candidates, and the first Westerner to be nominated for president. His career was one of physical action. He demonstrated tremendous physical courage as well as leadership in his expeditions to explore the West. He was a brave if not successful military leader during the Civil War. His failure on the battlefield was not the result of lack of courage, but instead resulted from an inability to work successfully with other commanders. The men among whom he demonstrated the greatest leadership were the rough, wild, physical men of the frontier. Frémont was aloof, even imperious. He was easily affronted when he did not feel he got deserved respect from others. On expeditions, this attitude, when coupled with his obvious courage, may have added to his leadership image. Frémont had always demonstrated single-mindedness to the point of inflexibility. Such a trait made it possible for him to lead five expeditions across hazardous terrain, but it also cost him almost a quarter of one expedition when he rashly insisted on continuing across the Rockies during some of the worst weather that area had faced in memory.

By 1856 Frémont was unalterably opposed to slavery. He had not until then been identified with the antislavery movement. Still his election would have antagonized the South almost as severely as did Lincoln's in 1860. The man who defeated Frémont, James Buchanan, has justly been regarded as one of the worst presidents in history. The reason for his abysmal historical respect is that at the time of great crisis, he was a passive president. Frémont was the opposite: strong-willed, staunchly unionist, abolitionist President Frémont likely would have reinforced federal positions in the South and tried to hinder the developing secessionist movement wherever possible. Yet if Frémont's election or subsequent policies had precipitated a civil war, the skills of a Lincoln would have been sorely missed. Frémont was impetuous, not reflective, never showed an ability to work well with others. Time and again the "Pathfinder" was impractical. His headstrong actions resulted either in glory or in disaster.

Frémont failed as a military commander when he tried to make political decisions. When the Civil War had barely begun, when the direction the border states were to fall teetered in the balance, Frémont risked antagonizing all border slaveowners by issuing his own, unapproved emancipation proclamation. President Lincoln had to rescind the order himself when Frémont refused to do so. President Frémont would have been similarly lacking in political finesse.

John Charles Frémont was an honest, intelligent, fearless man, but the Republican Party sought glitter rather than the substance of political leadership when it selected him as its first presidential nominee. It chose a military hero solely to win votes. He was not a hero who, like Dwight Eisenhower almost exactly a hundred years later, rightly could claim a

JN? C. FREMONT.   W? L. DAYTON.
THE CHAMPIONS OF FREEDOM.

JOHN CHARLES FRÉMONT and WILLIAM DAYTON
(Reproduced from the Collections of the Library of Congress)

military record that showed some presidential attributes, such as administrative skills or the ability to negotiate and compromise. Frémont was more like a Custer, whose achievements were dramatic, but irrelevant to this new field of battle.

FRÉMONT BIBLIOGRAPHY

Bartlett, Ruhl. *John C. Frémont and the Republican Party*. New York (1970, reprint of 1939 edition).

Dellanbaugh, Frederick S. *Frémont and '49*. New York City (1914).

Egan, Ferol. *Frémont: Explorer for a Restless Nation*. Garden City, N.Y. (1977).

Eyre, Alice. *The Famous Frémonts and Their America*. Boston (1948).

Frémont, John Charles. *Memoirs of My Life*. 2 vols. Chicago and New York City (1887).

Hart, Pamela. *Jessie Benton Frémont—A Biography*. New York City (1987).

Jackson, Donald, and Mary Lee Spence. *The Expeditions of John Charles Frémont*. 2 vols. Urbana, Ill. (1970 and 1973).

Nevins, Allan. *Frémont: Pathmarker of the West*. New York City (1955).

Phillips, Catherine Coffin. *Jessie Benton Frémont: A Woman Who Made History*. San Francisco (1935).

Rolle, Andrew. *John Charles Frémont: Character as Destiny*. Norman (1991).

---

*1856 vice presidential nominee—
Republican Party*

William Dayton

Full name: William Lewis Dayton.

State represented: New Jersey.

Birth: February 17, 1807, at Baskingridge, Somerset County, New Jersey.

Age on Inauguration Day (March 4, 1857): 50 years, ½ month.

Education: At age 12, entered academy in

Baskingridge of Dr. Brownlee; Princeton College, graduated 185; studied law in office of Peter Vroom (became governor in 1829); admitted to bar, May 1830.

Religion: Probably Presbyterian.

Ancestry/prominent relatives: Great-uncle Elias Dayton a brigadier general in American Revolution; Jonathan Dayton (first cousin, once removed) member of Federal Constitutional Convention, 1787, speaker of House of Representatives, U.S. senator.

Profession: Attorney.

Public offices: Legislative Council, 1837–1838; justice of New Jersey Supreme Court, 1838–1841, resigned to resume law practice; U.S. senator, appointed July 2, 1842–March 4, 1851, not reelected, replaced by his future daughter-in-law's grandfather; unsuccessful Republican nominee for vice president, 1856; attorney general of New Jersey, 1857–1861; declined to be considered for U.S. senator, 1858; minister to France, March 18, 1861–death, December 1, 1864.

Death: December 1, 1864, Paris, France, 57 years, 9½ months.

Burial: Riverview Cemetery, Trenton, New Jersey.

Home: Trenton, New Jersey.

Personal characteristics: As a youth was unusually slender, in feeble health. In later life, his appearance was dignified, and even became rather fat. Health never robust.

Father: Joel Dayton (September 5, 1776–May 3, 1833); farmer.

Mother: Nancy Lewis (April 23, 1787–August 9, 1866); daughter of Edward and Nancy (Crowell) Lewis.

Siblings: Alfred Bailey Dayton (December 25, 1812–?); married Elizabeth Vande Vere of Somerville, New Jersey. Marcia Dayton (?–?); married Samuel D. Beach. James Brinkerhoff Dayton (December 29, 1822–November 1886); married (1) Maria Louisa Clark and (2) Sarah Thompson; a lawyer. Anna F. Dayton (February 11, 1825–?); married Peter Voorhis, a lawyer.

Wife: Margaret Elmendorf Vande Vere (?–?); married May 22, 1833.

Children: William L., Jr. (April 13, 1839–July 28, 1897); married Harriet Maria Stockton on December 27, 1894; attorney, diplomat. Ferdinan. Anna. Edward.

His family was not wealthy, but it was illustrious. Dayton's father has been described as both a farmer and as a mechanic, but in either event he did not know luxury. His first American ancestor arrived in 1650, and more recent forebears included a general during the American Revolution, a member of the Constitutional Convention in Philadelphia, and the commissary of the American Army during the Revolution. Dayton received his formal education starting at age 12, at a well-established and respected academy in Baskingridge, New Jersey, first run by Dr. Finley, and in Dayton's time by the Reverend Dr. Brownlee. One of William's brothers became a doctor, and another a lawyer. William's career was pointed towards the law as well when he graduated in 1825, at the age of 18, from the College of New Jersey at Princeton. His legal studies began later that year in the office of prominent Democratic attorney Peter D. Vroom, in Somerville. In 1829, Vroom was elected New Jersey governor. Despite their political differences, Vroom and Dayton maintained a solid friendship throughout their careers.

By 1830, Dayton was admitted to the bar. He moved to Middletown Point and subsequently to Freehold, both in Monmouth County. His career received a well-publicized boost when his careful legal reasoning succeeded in getting not only the indictment against his client quashed, but also resulted in the voiding of the indictments against all other defendants who had been charged by one particular term of the grand jury. Such sweeping success against the prosecution by one so young and inexperienced made people notice.

Dayton's continued success as an attorney also led to political opportunities. His county had been a Democratic stronghold, but economic distress had made an opening for the Whigs, with whom Dayton identified. The Panic of 1837 led to the Whig triumph of the same year in New Jersey. The young attorney was swept into the Legislative Council along with the remainder of the Whig ticket. Dayton became chairman of the important judiciary committee. In this position he spearheaded the legislation that created a new county court system in the state, greatly reducing the burden on the judges of the Supreme

Court to conduct trials. The Supreme Court was given broader appeal powers, and for that reason it was decided to increase the number of judges on the court from three to five. As one of the principal architects of the new system, and though only 31 years old, Dayton was appointed to one of the two new seats on February 28, 1838.

His stay on the high court was short, lasting only three years. Judge Dayton made no lasting contribution to the jurisprudence of the state, and apparently served without controversy. Judicial life, and more particularly judicial salary, did not satisfy the Daytons' needs, and after frequent expressions of a desire to resign he finally did so on February 18, 1841. The leading New Jersey newspaper said, "He will carry with him to the less arduous pursuits of private life, the consciousness and the credit of having discharged his public functions with honor to himself and the court." Life in private practice was renewed in Trenton, and though brief was apparently profitable.

The death of incumbent United States Senator Samuel L. Southard, a cousin of Dayton's mother, occurred on June 26, 1842. Governor William Pennington, finding fellow Whig and popular former judge Dayton a politically appropriate choice, appointed him to the vacancy. The appointment was only valid until the next session of the state legislature, but that body confirmed the governor's selection by unanimous vote of the Whig majority in October 1842. That Whig unanimity would be repeated in 1845 when Dayton was elected to a full six-year term.

Dayton made few speeches, but he attempted to pick his spots well. His first noteworthy speech came on February 15, 1843. America and its institutions had been receiving abuse overseas as well as at home because of delinquencies by state governments in paying interest on their debts. The national debt was growing alarmingly, having reached the dizzy heights of almost forty million dollars. Resolutions as well as substantive measures to deal with the problem were introduced. Dayton's response was to denounce those who overlooked the long history of the federal government's honoring its debts, starting with

Alexander Hamilton's insistence in 1789 that the new nation assume and pay in full all debts incurred with foreign lenders as well as domestic ones. That state governments rightly were distrusted should not lead to criticism of the financial integrity of the national government. Dayton reviewed the repayment habits of the very foreign governments that were attacking America, and found much hypocrisy in their statements. His metaphors were dramatic:

> With these budgets of iniquity upon their backs, (the fruits of rapine and war), they stagger along like the old sinner of Bunyan's Allegory, reading homilies to us.... *We*, in lusty youth, carrying the weight of a thistle down, and with an inheritance stretching from sea to sea.

A more concrete issue than national pride was the Tariff of 1842. The preceding tariff had gradually reduced duties on imports until a minimum was reached in July 1842. The tariff proved inadequate as a revenue measure, but also inadequate to Northern interests in protecting domestic industries. The Whigs succeeded in raising the duties on many goods that competed too closely with native manufacturers. The junior New Jersey senator agreed with the protection principle and in April 1844, responded to attempts to lower the duties by praising the 1842 tariff. He decried those who would say a protective tariff hurts the farmers while lining the pockets of the industrialists. Instead, the interests of both groups were closely tied: the gain by one raised the economic well-being for all. Dayton was no Daniel Webster–style apologist for the growing commercial and industrial classes, but he identified with and championed their cause nonetheless.

New Jersey swung back to the Democratic party in 1843, which boded ill for Dayton as the legislature would choose two years later whether to reelect Dayton or replace him. An early round in the battle occurred in December 1843, when the Democratic legislature, following frequent practice of the 1800s, instructed Dayton how to vote. The substantive issue was minor but politically volatile. Dayton's response was firm:

I hold my place on this floor, subject to no limitation save that affixed by the constitution; and responsible to no power save that of the people. Between them and me, I acknowledge no such go-between.

The answer, in short, was "no." Fortunately for Dayton, the Democrats who instructed him on how to vote were no longer in command of the New Jersey legislature when his reelection was considered.

War was never Dayton's answer to solve difficult problems of national self-interest. In the dispute with Great Britain over Oregon, which threatened to break into hostilities in 1844, Dayton counseled for negotiations: "The question of Oregon is the very question of all others, properly the subject of negotiation, and even of arbitration, in preference to war." Though presidential candidate James K. Polk argued "Fifty-four forty or fight," Dayton properly saw that settlement for a compromise line near the forty-ninth parallel would be mutually agreeable. Dayton also suggested that Oregon would be of little use to the growing country, that it would for the foreseeable future be too distant from the Eastern states to be a viable part of the nation.

Along with Abraham Lincoln and many other prominent Whigs, Dayton believed the war with Mexico in 1846 was dishonorably provoked by an ambitious president who wanted to acquire more territory. Dayton opposed the annexation of the Republic of Texas into the Union, which precipitated that war. In June 1844, Senator Dayton stated that it was "asking too much" of the North to require the admission of any more slave states. In February 1845, he argued in the Senate that the admission of Texas was unconstitutional. Since Texas was then an independent republic it could not be made a state — only territories could gain statehood. He lost that argument. Dayton also insisted that the Missouri Compromise that permitted slavery in all territories south of the 36°30' line was never meant to apply to anything other than the Louisiana Purchase territories; the fact that all of Texas lay south of that latitude would cause an unconscionable dilution of the influence of the free states. He closed by saying, "We ask our southern friends not to press us too far."

The outbreak of the Mexican War following the admission of Texas sorely tried Dayton's principles. He eventually decided to vote for measures to prosecute the war under the rationale that the men in the field could not be abandoned. The war was a fait accompli, as much as he abhorred it. In order to prevent still more slave influence from growing out of that war, Dayton joined those sponsoring the Wilmot Proviso, named for Representative David Wilmot of Pennsylvania who proposed that no territory gained as a result of the war could allow slavery. "If nothing but free territory is to be acquired, depend on it," he argued, "a Southern President [Polk] will scarcely hold it worth the millions of money and the blood it will cost to obtain it." There was no sense of manifest destiny in Dayton's speeches.

February 1848 saw the concluding of a treaty that brought peace. Dayton's arguments soothed few of the raw nerves the new territories exposed. The Compromise of 1850, proposed by Henry Clay, championed by Webster, and ramrodded through Congress by Stephen Douglas, was rejected by Dayton. To satisfy the North the compromise would admit California and abolish the slave trade in the District of Columbia; the South would be presented the offsetting advantage of having no restrictions on slavery in the territories, the Fugitive Slave Law would be strengthened, and the Texas boundary disputes would be settled.

In this battle Dayton was unwavering in his support of President Zachary Taylor's rejection of the compromise. On March 23, 1850, the New Jersey senator argued against the Fugitive Slave Law and the organization of any more territorial governments. Basically, however, Dayton wished to minimize the bitterness in the controversy by showing how academic the whole question of slavery in the Mexican territories really was. Slavery simply could not exist in the barren Southwest, he argued, because the plantation economy that needed slavery could not thrive there. "We have the North and South contending with each other to desperation," he concluded, "upon the small chance (an admitted decimal only) of slavery going where it is said it cannot…. The subject matter is not worth the effort…."

Since Dayton believed the Compromise unnecessarily conceded too much to the South, he voted against it when final passage of the measures was achieved. His spirited speech on June 11 and 12, 1850, against the measures led Senator Henry Foote of Mississippi to speculate in his own speech that Dayton had his eye on being rewarded by President Taylor with an administrative appointment. Dayton firmly denied the charge, which had no apparent foundation.

The Democrats having retaken control of the New Jersey legislature, they elected Commodore Robert F. Stockton to replace Senator Dayton. (Stockton's granddaughter would one day marry Dayton's son.) Dayton left the Senate on March 3, 1851, having served nine explosive years. He returned to the practice of law in Trenton. His practice thrived, but politics never avoided him completely.

As the Whig Party disintegrated, Dayton gravitated easily to the Republicans. At the first Republican National Convention in 1856, vibrant, exciting, somewhat unsettling John Charles Frémont was selected for president. An old-line Whig was considered essential for balance. Late on the eve of the presidential balloting, the name of Abraham Lincoln for the number two spot began to circulate, first just among his home state delegation, but then among those of Pennsylvania and Ohio. Dayton received support from those seeking geographical and political balance. An informal ballot was taken prior to actual nominations for vice president, and Dayton led with 159 votes, Lincoln second with 110, Governor Nathaniel Banks of Massachusetts with 46, and 12 others with a handful each. Lincoln was gracious, telling a friend: "When you meet Judge Dayton, present my respects and tell him that I think him a far better man than I for the position he is in, and that I shall support him and Col. Frémont most cordially."

Apparently Dayton had no idea that he might be considered. In a brief speech in Trenton after being formally notified of the nomination, Dayton condemned the repeal of the Missouri Compromise and supported the admission of Kansas. Many commentators,

then and later, thought Dayton a politically uninspired choice, and that a strong favorite of Pennsylvania, such as Simon Cameron, might have taken that state from Buchanan and the election as well.

After the Republicans' defeat, the would-be vice president returned to Trenton, once more to serve in public office. Governor Newell appointed him state attorney general, a post Dayton would hold for four years. He resigned upon being appointed minister to France by his former, gracious vice presidential opponent, Abraham Lincoln. Dayton had received the votes for president of his state's delegation at the 1860 national convention for three ballots, but had then been a helpful campaigner for Lincoln in the general election. Many expected a cabinet post for him. It was reported by New Jersey Judge Nixon that Lincoln had informed the New Jersey Congressional delegation that his hope had been to appoint Dayton Secretary of State, but William Seward had a politically stronger claim. The Treasury also was a possibility, but again politics counseled for another choice. Lincoln thought that a prominent ambassadorial post was the next best position. France was second in prestige to England, with Charles Francis Adams the favorite for the London post.

Dayton's three years in Paris significantly contributed to the Union's war effort. He was on good terms with the French emperor, and worked diligently to prevent French recognition or assistance of the Confederate government. His achievements included preventing the fulfillment of French contracts to construct Confederate warships, some of which would have been ironclads. His vigilance helped restrain the French government, during bleak periods of Union military misfortune, from accepting Confederate entreaties for recognition.

It has been recorded that Dayton loved food and partook far too sumptuously of it. On December 1, 1864, Dayton died suddenly from apoplexy after a large dinner in Paris. He left a large estate, valued at over $100,000. The details of his death left one of the few blemishes on his career, and that only because of speculation. Dayton died in the apartment of a woman (needless to say, not his wife) in Paris, and his body was immediately sent to the American legation. The woman insisted on making an explanation, but her story was suppressed by the Lincoln administration for fear of unfavorable publicity. The doctor's account of her story and Dayton's death was that "after some pleasantries (?) upon entering the apartment, [Dayton] called upon his hostess to give three cheers for Abraham Lincoln, the news of whose reelection had just reached Paris. He soon complained of feeling unwell," and died before a physician could reach him. The matter did not get exposed in the press either in Paris or Washington.

Analysis of Qualifications

William Dayton was not a man of brilliance, great learning, or dynamic personality. He was, however, a solid and well-respected politician with the experience and intelligence to have served reasonably capably as president. His failings took the form of indolence and love of pleasure, and there is doubt concerning the intensity and energy he would have brought to the White House.

The New Jersey senator made his mark as a strong if not rabid opponent of the extension of slavery. He opposed the Compromise of 1850 because it gave the South too many concessions, unnecessary ones in his view. Yet he did not want the Union split over the semantics of whether slavery would be legally permitted in the Mexican territories. Geography and climate would prevent the slave economy from flourishing there, and though he would not desire to be counted with those who voted slavery's extension, he thought preservation of harmony counseled in favor of giving the South this essentially meaningless concession. Compromise was not the dominant thrust of his Senate career, but rarely could he be numbered with the extremists. He was patient, deferential, endowed with ample common sense. The South would not have been able to trust his instincts, as they were anti-slavery. Though Dayton can in no measure be credited with qualities of leadership equal to Lincoln's, both men did represent a conciliatory brand of Republicanism that nonetheless invoked hatred and distrust in the South.

One early biographer, generally sympathetic with Dayton, stated:

> He was not, properly speaking, an indolent man; his acquirements in after life forbid any such position; but it always required a great exertion to bring the powers of his mind into full exercise [Elmer, *Constitution*, p. 374].

In conclusion, that biographer thought that "the whip and spur of necessity" were required to bring Dayton's full abilities to play. Dayton's love of food, a fondness he indulged fully, may reflect the same essentially lethargic personality.

Frequent appointments to high office demonstrate an appreciation at least for Dayton's political influence, and probably also for his abilities. Only 31 when appointed a New Jersey Supreme Court judge, 35 when appointed to the United States Senate, Dayton was well-liked and made his mark early. He was also appointed as state attorney general, Lincoln's ambassador to France, and in a quasi-appointive manner, selected for vice president by the Republicans. He did not receive these honors by the caliber of his public speaking, which was adequate if uninspiring. He rose fast in politics, maintained his position in high office, and left few enemies or controversies.

Such is not the stuff of greatness. In the world of also-ran vice presidential candidates, however, it marks William Dayton as an acceptable nominee.

DAYTON BIBLIOGRAPHY

Biographical Encyclopedia of New Jersey of the Nineteenth Century. Philadelphia (1877), pp. 5–7.

Bradley, Joseph P. "A Memorial of the Life and Character of Hon. William L. Dayton, Late U.S. Minister to France." *New Jersey Historical Society Proceedings* 4 (series 2) (1875), pp. 69–118.

Elmer, Lucius Q.C. *The Constitution and Government of the Province and State of New Jersey....* Newark (1872), pp. 372–396.

"Hon. William L. Dayton." *United States Magazine.* (August 1856), pp. 249–251.

"The Hon. William L. Dayton, U.S. Senator from New Jersey." Photocopy of article in Princeton University Library's alumni folder on Dayton, from unknown source, dated January 1849.

Jacobus, Donald Lines, and Arthur Bliss Dayton.

MILLARD FILLMORE and ANDREW J. DONELSON
(From the collection of David J. and Janice L. Frent)

The Early Daytons and Descendants of Henry, Jr. New Haven (1959).

Lewis Letter, vol. 3 (Nov.–Dec. 1889), pp. 135–138.

MacCarthy, John Peters. "William L. Dayton, United States Minister to France." Unpublished senior thesis, Princeton University (1954).

MacCrellish, William H., Jr. "The Diplomatic Career of William Lewis Dayton: France and the Union 1861–1864." Unpublished senior thesis, Princeton University (1944).

Sandburg, Carl. *Abraham Lincoln: The War Years.* New York, Sangamon Edition (6 vols., 1940), vol. 5, p. 658.

Snell, James P., comp. *History of Hunterdon and Somerset Counties, New Jersey, with Illustrations and Biographical Sketches of Its Prominent Men and Pioneers.* Philadelphia (1881), pp. 582–583.

Whittlesey, Walter Lincoln. "William Lewis Dayton, 1825…." *Princeton Alumni Weekly* XXX (May 9, 1930), pp. 797–802.

---

*1856 presidential nominee —
Native American Party*

Millard Fillmore

No biographical sketch of Fillmore is included since he served as president from July 10, 1850, until March 4, 1853 (13th president).

State represented: New York.

Birth: January 7, 1800.

Age on Inauguration Day (March 4, 1857): 57 years, 2 months.

Death: March 8, 1874.

---

*1856 vice presidential nominee —
Native American Party*

Andrew J. Donelson

Full name: Andrew Jackson Donelson

State represented: Tennessee.

Birth: August 25, 1799, in Sumner County, Tennessee.

Age on Inauguration Day (March 4, 1857): 57 years, 6½ months.

Education: Had a private tutor in Andrew Jackson's home, then Cumberland College, graduated 1816; U.S. Military Academy, 1817–1821, graduated second in his class; Transylvania University, 1822–1823; admitted to bar, 1823.

Religion: Unknown.

Ancestry/prominent relatives: First ancestor in America was John Donelson (great-grandfather), who arrived in 1716; Andrew Jackson was his uncle; Daniel Smith (grandfather) was a U.S. senator from Tennessee.

Occupation: Attorney.

Public Offices; Clerk in General Land Office, and in that position served as President Jackson's secretary, 1829–1837; American chargé d'affaires to Republic of Texas, September 16, 1844–1846; minister to Prussia, 1846–1848; U.S. minister to Germany, 1848–1849; unsuccessful Native American nominee for vice president, 1856; delegate to Constitutional Union convention, 1860; state conservative party convention delegate, 1867.

Home: "Tulip Grove," a plantation adjacent to Andrew Jackson's "Hermitage," in Nashville; sold, and moved in 1858 to Memphis, with a plantation in Bolivar County, Mississippi.

Death: June 26, 1871, at Memphis, age 71 years, 10 months.

Burial: Elmwood Cemetery, Memphis.

Personal characteristics: Handsome, good-natured; tendency to be haughty.

Father: Samuel Donelson (c. 1764–c. 1803); after father died Andrew was raised by Andrew Jackson and his wife.

Mother: Mary Ann Michie Smith (April 26, 1781–1857); married June 20, 1796; only daughter of Daniel Smith.

Stepfather: James Saunders.

Siblings: John Samuel (?–1817); unmarried. Daniel Smith (June 1801–April 1863); married Margaret Branch in 1832; Confederate brigadier general.

First wife: Emily T. Donelson (Andrew's first cousin) (June 1, 1807–December 19, 1836); married September 16, 1824.

Children: Andrew Jackson (June 6, 1826–1859); West Point graduate, engineer, became ill and died while on duty. Mary Emily (August 31, 1829–1905); born in the White House; married General John A. Wilcox, U.S.

representative from Mississippi on May 27, 1852. John Samuel (1832–1863); born in White House; captain in army, killed at battle of Chickamauga. Rachel Jackson (1834–1888); born in White House; married General William B. Knox.

Second wife: Elizabeth Martin Randolph (a niece of his first wife) (1796–?); married on November 10, 1841; daughter of James G. Martin; her first husband was Lewis Randolph, Thomas Jefferson's grandson.

Children: Daniel Smith (December 2, 1842–January 1864). Martin (June 26, 1847–); Mississippi planter. William Alexander (January 18, 1849–?); Tennessee planter. Catherine (February 25, 1850–1868). Vinet (August 30, 1854–?); businessman. Lewis Randolph (February 14, 1856–?). Rosa Elizabeth (June 14, 1858–?). Andrew J. Donelson (January 21, 1860–?).

Historic sites/memorials: "Tulip Grove," his Nashville home, is adjacent to Andrew Jackson's "The Hermitage." Another Donelson house is two and a half miles southwest of Duncan, Mississippi (private).

Trained as a lawyer and soldier, Andrew Jackson Donelson ignored both professions for a career in politics. The nephew and namesake of a president, a vice presidential nominee himself, the Tennesseean never held elective political office. His abilities were never tested in high office, and his fame rested far more on the reflected glow from his famous uncle rather than from actual achievements.

Future president Andrew Jackson first met the Donelson family when he moved to Nashville in 1788 and boarded in the home of Donelson's widowed grandmother. Among the children were Samuel and Rachel; one would become Donelson's father, the other Jackson's wife. Jackson helped Samuel elope with Mary Smith. The future president was the godfather of the Donelson children, and not surprisingly one of the sons was named after him. Thus a close relationship existed between the families at the time that young Donelson's father died in 1803. Mrs. Donelson remarried and Jackson took the three Donelson sons to live with him. Andrew Jackson Donelson became his famous uncle's favorite ward, as Jackson had no children of his own.

Growing up at the Hermitage, Jackson's plantation in Nashville, must have introduced Andrew to many of the nation's famous and powerful. General Jackson secured an appointment for his namesake to West Point in 1817. Applying himself arduously to his studies, Andrew finished the normal four-year curriculum in three and ranked second in his graduating class. Throughout Andrew's West Point years the general paid close attention to his progress and wrote often with parental suggestions on personal habits. In every way conceivable, except by formal adoption, Andrew had become Jackson's son.

Donelson became a second lieutenant in the corps of engineers, and was assigned at Jackson's request to be the general's aide-de-camp. Getting orders was protracted, and for a time Donelson waited at the Hermitage. His first assignment from the general was to proceed to Louisiana in order to advise his uncle on fortifications there in case the threatened war with Spain spread that far west. However, there was almost no fighting and a treaty ceding Florida to the United States was entered with Spain. With peace seemingly assured and no other foreign adversaries likely, General Jackson advised Donelson to resign. Promotions would be few and infrequent; military glory was nonexistent in a peacetime army. To Jackson, and to his nephew, a peacetime commission was a waste of time.

His resignation took effect on February 1, 1822. Donelson was soon studying law at Transylvania University in Lexington, Kentucky. That also was Jackson's suggestion. One of the reasons for the choice was Jackson's belief that his nephew would meet many of his contemporaries who would in the coming years play important roles in politics in the South. Jackson added, "I will not disguise, I look forward, if you live, to the time when you will be selected to preside over the destinies of America." For about a year after graduating in 1823, Donelson practiced law in Nashville with another attorney. Much of his work even then was to look after General Jackson's affairs.

In Jackson's first campaign for the presidency in 1824, someone was needed to help with his massive correspondence. Donelson was asked if he would journey to Washington to help. Just married in September 1824, Donelson and his new bride moved to the capital to work on the campaign. It was a relatively short stay, and after John Quincy Adams won the presidency, the Donelsons returned to Nashville. Jackson also returned, to plan for another assault on the White House. All the family were convinced that he had been kept from his goal only by a corrupt bargain between Adams and Henry Clay. Vengeance was in their mind, not just victory.

For four years, Donelson was Jackson's confidential secretary, handling the correspondence and tending to political chores of a minor nature. In 1828, victory was theirs, and Donelson accompanied his uncle to Washington to continue his duties as secretary. Shortly after the election, Rachel Jackson, the general's wife and Andrew's aunt, died. President Jackson blamed the emotional strain of the campaign, in which Rachel's character had been questioned. The social responsibilities of a White House hostess were assumed by Donelson's wife Emily. With Emily acting as surrogate first lady, and Andrew as one of the inner circle of advisers called the "kitchen cabinet," the Donelsons were among the most important people in the capital.

Within the inner circle there were considerable rivalries. Donelson found himself opposed to the political ambitions of Major John Eaton, W.B. Lewis, and Martin Van Buren. What became the *cause célèbre* of the administration rose out of Secretary of State Eaton's choice of Peggy O'Neill as his wife. The new Mrs. Eaton's morals were questioned by most of Washington society, including the cabinet wives. Emily Donelson refused to have Peggy Eaton participate in any of her social functions, to the fury of President Jackson. The president took it as a personal affront that she was refused invitation to many of his cabinet members' homes.

The "Peggy Eaton affair" split Jackson from his nephew. There was much politics involved in addition to the social code. Martin Van Buren and his supporters used the affair to estrange Jackson from Vice President John Calhoun, whose wife would not socialize with Mrs. Eaton. Jackson's view was that to oppose Peggy Eaton's social acceptance was to oppose the president politically. Jackson was sensitive to criticism, his appreciation of different sides of an issue limited. There was more than just the stigma of an immoral past that many found objectionable in Peggy Eaton, for Emily Donelson among others also thought she was meddlesome and rude. By April of 1829, just a month after Jackson's inauguration, the controversy was in full flame. The opposition newspapers were making much of the affair, which caused Jackson even more readily to consider those who would not accept Peggy Eaton to be his political enemies. Donelson was the link with Jackson for those who wanted Eaton out of the cabinet and his wife out of the city. Donelson conveyed information to the president that he thought conclusively demonstrated her previous unchaste character, but this only infuriated Jackson more. Donelson was warned by other Jackson friends not to be seen as too anxious to question Mrs. Eaton's character. Calhoun was Donelson's friend, and it was increasingly easy for Calhoun's enemies to use the Eaton affair not only to antagonize Jackson towards the vice president, but also against his own nephew.

As 1830 began, Donelson was seriously looking at leaving Jackson and returning to Tennessee. Since Emily Donelson was White House hostess, her refusal to accept Peggy Eaton meant the president's own house was off limits to the star of this controversy. Jackson wrote Eaton that the Donelsons would have to respect his wishes in the matter or else quit his employ. A long note of explanation of his position was sent by Donelson to the president. Pleading his continued support and affection for Jackson, Donelson said he could not continue in his confidential capacity with the president if Jackson continued to insist on loyalty on this point. Donelson was certain that his political opponents were making it impossible to continue, particularly scheming by Martin Van Buren and W.B. Lewis, both of whom were trying to advance Van Buren's fortunes at the expense of Calhoun's. A two-year impasse, with Emily Donelson even leaving the White House and returning to Tennessee, severely strained family relations. John Eaton resigned his post as secretary of state in

1831, and he and his wife moved from Washington. Eaton's absence from the scene made the question of the Donelsons associating with the Eatons academic. The furor was finally over, and in time the breach between uncle and nephew would be healed. The fires of conflict may even have forged a closer bond.

Donelson's duties were to handle the president's correspondence, sometimes from the roughest of notes given him by Jackson. Annual messages to Congress as well as other reports were written by Donelson. Sometimes he made noticeable changes in Jackson's language. In one particular report to Congress Donelson had weakened the harsh language used by Jackson, and these changes became a public issue. Political duties also consumed much of the secretary's time. Technically, Donelson was a clerk with the General Land Office. His performance of political tasks led to criticism by Jackson's opponents that politics permeated the supposedly nonpartisan departments of the government.

Towards the end of Jackson's presidency, Emily Donelson's health began to fail. In September 1834, it became obvious she was ill; by June of 1836 the end seemed imminent. Donelson returned to Nashville to be with her, but after a momentary rally he returned to Washington to assist Jackson in preparation of his final message to Congress. Before Donelson could rejoin his wife, she was dead from tuberculosis. Five years later, Donelson married Mrs. Elizabeth Martin Randolph. She was, as his first wife had been, his cousin.

When Jackson retired in 1837, both he and Donelson returned to Nashville. The new president, Martin Van Buren, offered Donelson a cabinet post but then withdrew it, saying he began to fear political repercussions in naming the inexperienced nephew of a former president. Donelson readily accepted the explanation and did not appear to have a real desire to serve in the cabinet. Jackson had other plans for his nephew, which included running for Congress against John Bell. Donelson turned down the opportunity to lose against the popular Bell. Donelson did become involved a few years later in fellow Tennesseean James K. Polk's efforts to be nominated vice president. That effort failed in 1840, but continued towards the 1844 election. Donelson was a delegate to the 1843 state Democratic convention that named Polk for vice president. Donelson wrote leaders in other states urging their vote for Polk at the national convention. Donelson and Jackson initially supported Van Buren for the presidential nomination, but the general soon soured on Van Buren because of his lukewarm support for annexation of Texas. It was Donelson's unhappy duty to inform Van Buren that Old Hickory was dumping him in favor of Polk for president.

At the 1844 national Democratic convention, Donelson in the early balloting voted for Lewis Cass, but on the eighth ballot switched to Polk. On the next ballot Polk won. During the general election campaign Donelson actively worked for him, but in September he was called away from his campaigning to handle an important diplomatic responsibility. President John Tyler needed someone to replace the American envoy to the Republic of Texas, who had recently died. On October 21, 1844, Donelson set off for Texas.

Through Andrew Jackson, Donelson was a close friend of the Texas president, Sam Houston. Arriving in Texas on November 10, Donelson requested a meeting with Houston. Houston appeared to be cozying up to France and England as a result of previous rejections by the United States of Texas's request for annexation. In fact, Houston was just trying to gain leverage in one final effort at annexation, but his tactics worried even his old comrade Andrew Jackson. Donelson was convinced after a private meeting with Houston that there was no danger that the Texas president would work against annexation.

Donelson left in January 1845 for Nashville. Congress passed a resolution annexing Texas just before President Polk was inaugurated in March, but the new president sent the envoy back to Texas to gain Lone Star acceptance of the Congressional action.

Texas had also selected a new president, Anson Jones. President Jones indicated disenchantment with the American terms for joining the Union, and many scholars have considered him in favor of having Texas remain independent. There is evidence that Donelson sometimes worked through Texas Vice

President Kenneth L. Anderson, who had earlier in Tennessee been a political ally of President Polk. Donelson in time would almost hate Jones, so obstructionist did the Texas chief executive become to Donelson's efforts for annexation. Yet even former president Houston was unhelpful because the terms offered by the American Congress were unfavorable. Finally the Texas Congress did issue a call for a convention to consider the American Congressional action, as required under the annexation proposal. Once that call was issued, Donelson was confident the battle was won. He was right.

Those in America who had favored annexation gave Donelson unstinting praise for his diligence and skill in pressing Texas leaders for acceptance of the terms offered. Donelson took his leave from Texas and rushed to the Hermitage. Jackson's health was bad and he appeared near death. The nephew arrived too late. Sam Houston made a similar rush to the old general's bedside, but also failed to arrive prior to Jackson's death on June 8, 1845. In Jackson's will Donelson, who was badly in debt during his entire life, received no money or property other than the general's sword. The will stated "that he fail not to use [the sword] when necessary in support and protection of our glorious Union, and for the protection of the Constitutional rights of our beloved country should they be assailed by foreign enemies or domestic traitors."

Donelson had strong support from many in the party for a substantial role in the new Polk administration, even a cabinet post. Andrew Jackson before his death had met with Polk and informed his nephew that Donelson's interests would receive consideration. Jackson was almost an impediment, however, for Polk feared that Old Hickory's nephew in the cabinet would appear to be nothing more than blatant politics. Donelson had no experience in any office except for personal secretary to a president, and a short stint as an envoy. Instead, Polk and other prominent Democrats wanted Donelson to take control of the party's Washington newspaper, as vigorous new editorial discretion was needed. The would-be journalist eventually declined and asked for and received a foreign mission. In July 1846 he arrived in Prussia.

For three years Donelson wrestled with commercial treaties, uncertainties concerning whether to recognize as legitimate the short-lived movement to unite the German principalities, and monitoring the spate of revolutions that occurred in 1848 in Europe. Though socially an enjoyable interlude, his diplomatic post proved frustrating and financially unrewarding.

When Zachary Taylor and the Whigs won the presidency from the Democrats in 1848, Donelson's diplomatic days were numbered. He was held over for a few months in his post, but finally arrived back in the United States in January 1850. The Mexican War that had transpired in his absence had never received his support, as it appeared little more than a war of conquest to him. The former diplomat was also concerned about the increasing sectional divisions resulting from the rush of both slavery and abolitionist forces to control the new territories gained from Mexico. So fierce was the controversy that a convention of Southerners was called to meet in Nashville in 1850 to consider secession, with old friend John C. Calhoun as the principal promoter. Donelson wished to be a delegate, but only so that he could argue for Union.

On June 3, 1850, the Nashville Convention opened. The potential for a clarion call for secession had been lessened by the Compromise of 1850 measures in Congress. Donelson was pleased but not complacent as the convention closed without calling for disunion. A radical remnant of the convention reassembled in November, and these extremists did vote resolutions of secession. Donelson tried to speak at the gathering but was refused an opportunity. With his fervent objective being sectional peace, Donelson agreed to take over the editorship of the Washington *Union* newspaper in April 1851. He made it a clear advocate of the 1850 Compromise measures and all other moderate sectional proposals. Secession was a strong force in many states for over a year after the 1850 Compromise, and Donelson's constant pleading of the cause of moderation may have played some role in quieting these passions by late 1851, when Unionists took control in most of the Southern states.

In May 1853, Donelson resigned from the

paper, as he was not being paid for his work — a matter of considerable concern to the always-destitute Donelson. Even his Nashville plantation, Tulip Grove, which was adjacent to Jackson's Hermitage, was sold to pay debts. Fortunately, a cousin purchased it and Donelson's family could remain. His plantations elsewhere performed poorly. Elizabeth Donelson's substantial fortune was frittered away keeping up with her husband's exorbitant spending habits. For two years this somewhat embittered former diplomat and journalist, angry at his own party's failure to provide more substantial rewards for his considerable services, remained out of politics.

By 1854, the nativist, anti-foreigner Know-Nothing Party was a force in Tennessee and most other states. Donelson disliked Catholics, was prejudiced against immigrants, and also wished to abandon the Democrats who he felt had abandoned him. Thus he became a leader in the Know-Nothing movement. Donelson attended the national convention in 1855 which laid the groundwork for a vigorous national campaign the following year. His speeches were stridently anti–Democratic, and particularly violent against President Franklin Pierce, whom he blamed for his problems as editor.

On February 22, 1856, the national convention of this new party opened in Philadelphia. The northern and southern wings were badly divided, with the abolitionists looking for an excuse to bolt and join the new Republican Party. Moderates and Southerners backed a resolution that no platform be adopted, thereby hoping to avoid a self-destructive party debate. Ironically, the Free-Soilers used this excuse to leave the convention. Some Southern states were unrepresented for other reasons. After former president Millard Fillmore won the presidential nomination, several names were placed in nomination for vice president. One of these nominees, Richard Call of Florida, then rose and withdrew his own name and proposed Andrew Jackson Donelson. Donelson did not initially receive a majority, but after all the states had voted several started switching to the Tennesseean, and he won with 181 votes to only 30 for others.

Since Fillmore was then in Europe, Donel-son had the initial campaign to himself. He delivered a few speeches, a practice not considered quite seemly for a national nominee, but well before November had retired to his plantation. Donelson's most embarrassing problem was the bitterly anti–Fillmore editorials he had written in 1851–1852 as editor of the *Union*, but those were, rather unconvincingly, explained away as meaningless accusations that the then–Democrat editor had to make against the then–Whig president.

The Know-Nothings became demoralized. From the heady days of 1855 when they seemed to be sweeping local election after election, the party had fallen off dramatically in support. The question for many came down to which, the Democrats or Know-Nothings, had the better chance to defeat the arch enemy, abolitionist Republicans. After a narrow Democratic victory in October elections in Pennsylvania, much of the fire seemed to go out of the Know-Nothing cause. The party carried only Maryland.

For the remaining years of his life Donelson mainly tended to his precarious financial affairs. In 1858 he moved to Memphis, and operated a plantation there as well as in Bolivar County, across the state line in Mississippi. In 1860 he was a delegate to the Constitutional Union convention that nominated John Bell for president. He would have preferred old Texas friend Sam Houston. Secession was rejected as an acceptable resolution of the South's grievances, and for this opposition Donelson was arrested by the Confederates in August 1861, but soon released. As the war progressed this Southern unionist wished for the old order to be restored, with slavery, but as one country. It was of course a vain hope.

After the war, Donelson briefly reemerged in politics by attending a state nominating convention in 1867, but the conservative candidates it selected went down to defeat in Reconstruction Tennessee. Negro suffrage repulsed him. The whole trend of Southern politics caused him to abandon public life one last time. He died in 1871.

Analysis of Qualifications

Andrew Donelson was one of those occasional national party nominees who has very few achievements in his background, but did have some overriding political asset. In Donelson's case that asset was his identification with Andrew Jackson, not only in name but also in personal association. As a former Democrat and Jackson protégé, Donelson was thought capable of giving the Know-Nothing Party credibility. Millard Fillmore's experience as a Whig president was the bridge to the other major political party. With a Fillmore-Donelson ticket the Know-Nothings hoped to provide something for everyone, but the election returns revealed they barely presented anything for anyone.

Whether Donelson would have made a good president is problematic. Twice in his life he had been called to perform in an important public office, as special envoy to Texas and as minister to Prussia. His service was credible but hardly sufficient testing of the skills required for a president. For ten years he was Andrew Jackson's private secretary, which put him in a very menial way at the center of important decisions.

Since his roles were always subordinate, it was difficult for him to achieve much of a personal reputation for accomplishment. Martin Van Buren called him "a man ... of much more ability than he had credit for...." Perhaps, but still it was not good government, though it might have been good politics, for a national party to present him to the American public as presidential material. The White House is no place to be tested for leadership and administrative ability, particularly not at such a crucial time in the country's history as the 1850s. He shares with Sargent Shriver one hundred years later the background of minor appointive office and a family relationship to a president. It would seem that in both cases, their parties failed in their responsibility to select men whose capacity for the presidency could be fairly weighed.

DONELSON BIBLIOGRAPHY

Burke, Pauline Wilcox. *Emily Donelson of Tennessee.* 2 vols. Richmond, Va. (1941).

Clayton, W.W. *History of Davidson County, Tennessee.* Philadelphia (1880), pp. 479–480.

Hall, Allen A., ed. *The American Banner,* no. 5, Nashville (April 19, 1856), pp. 65–86, a campaign biography of Donelson, perhaps written by himself.

Middleton, Annie. "Donelson's Mission to Texas in Behalf of Annexation." Master's thesis, University of Texas (1920), published in *Southwestern Historical Quarterly* XXIV (1921), pp. 247–291.

Moore, John T., and Austin P. Foster. *Tennessee, the Volunteer State, 1769–1923.* Chicago and Nashville (1923), pp. 112–113.

Owsley, Harriet Chappell. "Andrew Jackson and His Ward, Andrew Jackson Donelson." *Tennessee Historical Quarterly* XLI (1982), pp. 124–139.

Satterfield, R. Beeler. "Andrew Jackson Donelson, a Moderate Nationalist Jacksonian." Unpublished doctoral dissertation, Johns Hopkins University (1961).

_____. "The Early Public Career of Andrew Jackson Donelson, 1799–1846." Unpublished master's thesis, Vanderbilt University (1948).

Sioussat, St. George L., ed. "Letters of James K. Polk to Andrew Donelson, 1843–1848," III, 51–73; "Selected Letters, 1844–1845, from the Donelson Papers," III, pp. 134–162; "Selected Letters, 1846–1856, from the Donelson Papers," III, pp. 257–291." *Tennessee Historical Magazine* (1919).

"Sketch of the Life of Andrew Jackson Donelson," in *Life of Millard Fillmore.* New York City (1856).

Election of 1860

NOMINATIONS

Democratic Party Convention (8th): April 23–28, and May 1–3, 1860, at Hall of the South Carolina Institute, Charleston. *President* and *vice president*— 57 ballots were taken, with no candidate ever receiving a two-thirds majority as required for nomination. Stephen A. Douglas for all ballots had between 145 and 152 votes, out of 303 cast. Robert M.T. Hunter (Virginia) and James Guthrie (Kentucky) were his two main rivals. On May 3, the convention adjourned to reassemble in Baltimore.

Constitutional Union Party Convention (1st): May 9, 1860, in Baltimore, Maryland. *President*— John Bell, nominated on the second ballot with 138 of 251 votes cast. Bell had 68 votes on the first ballot. Sam Houston (Texas) was his main rival. *Vice president*— Edward Everett, nominated unanimously on the first ballot.

Republican Party Convention (2nd): May 16–18, 1860, at the Wigwam, Chicago, Illinois. *President*— Abraham Lincoln, nominated on the third ballot. After the roll call, Lincoln had 231 of 465 votes; shifts before the official tally was announced gave him 340 votes. His principal competitors were William Seward (New York), Simon Cameron (Pennsylvania), Salmon Chase (Ohio), and Edward Bates (Missouri). He had received 102 votes on the first ballot. *Vice president*— Hannibal Hamlin, nominated on the second ballot with 367 of the 466 votes. He had garnered 194 votes on the first ballot. Cassius Clay of Kentucky was the major rival for the nomination.

Democratic Party Convention (Reassembled): June 18–23, 1860, at Front Street Theatre, Baltimore, Maryland. *President*— Stephen Douglas, nominated on the second ballot with 190½ of 203½ votes cast. He had 173½ of the 200½ cast on the first ballot. The Southern delegates walked out before the first ballot was taken, but initially it was determined that the nominee would have to get two-thirds of all delegates to the convention, even those who had bolted. After the second ballot this interpretation was discarded and Douglas was declared the winner. *Vice president*— Benjamin Fitzpatrick, nominated on the first ballot, nearly unanimously. Fitzpatrick refused to accept. Herschell V. Johnson, nominated by the National Committee since Fitzpatrick's refusal of the nomination occurred after the convention had adjourned.

National Democratic Party (convention delegates who had bolted from the regular party convention): June 23, 1860, at Maryland Institute Hall, Baltimore, Maryland. *President*— John C. Breckinridge, nominated on the first ballot with 81 of 105 votes. Daniel Dickinson received all the remainder of the votes. *Vice president*— Joseph Lane, nominated unanimously on the first ballot.

GENERAL ELECTION

Popular Vote

Lincoln 1,865,908
Douglas. 1,380,202
Breckinridge`.   848,019
Bell. 590, 901
Others.   531

Electoral Vote

Lincoln-Hamlin—180 (18 states)
Breckinridge-Lane—72 (11 states)
Bell-Everett—39 (3 states)
Douglas, Johnson—12 (1 state)

Winners

Abraham Lincoln, 16th president
Hannibal Hamlin, 15th vice president

Losers

Stephen Douglas, Benjamin Fitzpatrick, Herschell Johnson, John C. Breckinridge, Joseph Lane, John Bell, Edward Everett

1860 presidential nominee —
Democratic Party

Stephen Douglas

Full name: Stephen Arnold Douglass; in 1846, he dropped the final "s."

State represented: Illinois.

Birth: April 23, 1813, in Brandon, Vermont.

Age on Inauguration Day (March 4, 1861): 47 years, 10½ months.

Education: Tutored by his bachelor uncle; attended Brandon (Vermont) Academy, and then in 1832 entered Canandaigua Academy to study law; in January 1833, began to study under an attorney; admitted to bar in 1834.

Religion: No strong religious identification, but leaned to Baptist Church; his second wife was a Roman Catholic.

Ancestry/prominent relatives: First of family in America was William Douglass, who arrived in Boston from Scotland in mid–1600s.

Occupation: Attorney.

Public offices: Illinois state's attorney, First Judicial District, 1835; state representative, 1836–1837; register of Springfield Land Office, 1837–March 2, 1839; nominated in 1837 for U.S. Representative, but lost election by 36 votes; appointed Illinois secretary of state, served, 1840–1841; appointed to Illinois Supreme Court, served, 1841–1842; defeated for U.S. Senate, 1842 (before was old enough to serve); U.S. Representative, March 4, 1843–March 3, 1847, resigned; U.S. senator, March 4, 1847–death, June 3, 1861; unsuccessful contender for Democratic presidential nomination in 1852 and 1856; defeated Democratic nominee for president, 1860.

Home: Jacksonville, then Chicago, Illinois.

Death: June 3, 1861, in Chicago, at age 48 years, 1½ months.

Burial: In Chicago at site overlooking Lake Michigan, which he had picked out as place to build his home; it is now called Douglas Monument Park.

Personal characteristics: 5'4" tall; large, deep-blue eyes; dark eyebrows; large, round head with massive neck; small, chubby hands and feet; boisterous, much nervous energy; smoked cigars, drank whiskey, and chewed tobacco, all to excess.

Father: Dr. Stephen A. Douglass (1781–July 1, 1813).

Mother: Sarah Fisk (?–May 30, 1869), daughter of Nathaniel and Sarah (Arnold) Fisk of Brandon, Vermont.

Stepfather: Gehazi Granger (c. 1775–October 15, 1869), married Sarah Douglass on December 2, 1830.

Siblings: Sarah Arnold (October 29, 1811–?), married Julius N. Granger in February 1830.

First wife: Martha Denny Martin (1824–January 19/23, 1853), married April 7, 1847; daughter of Col. Robert Martin, a planter in Rockingham County, North Carolina.

Children: Robert Martin (January 28, 1849–?), married Jessie Dick on June 23, 1874. Stephen Arnold, Jr. (November 3, 1850–?). Ellen (January–February 1853).

Second wife: Adele Cutts (1835–?), married November 20, 1856; daughter of James Madison Cutts, a Washington government clerk.

Children: First child lived only a few hours, February 1858. Ellen (September 20, 1859–June 1860), had been sickly since birth.

Historic sites/memorials: Douglas's statue is on the lawn of the Illinois capital in Springfield. Douglas's birthplace is in Brandon Village, Vermont, historic district.

This great spokesman for the West, champion of "squatter sovereignty" was actually a sixth generation New Englander, born in Vermont in 1813. Douglas's father, a physician, died while Douglas was still an infant. Family tradition is that Douglas was in his father's arms in front of a fireplace when his father suffered a fatal heart attack. A neighbor's fortuitous arrival kept the infant Stephen from being burned and perhaps killed when his father dropped him into the flames. After the father's death, the Douglass family moved in with a bachelor uncle and farmer, Edward Fisk. There, grandfather Benajah Douglass played an important role in young Stephen's development. Benajah served five terms in the Vermont General Assembly, was a town selectman, and proved a valuable role model for Stephen's own political development.

Douglas received very little schooling, perhaps three months a year. Farm work was exhausting and Stephen helped run both his Uncle Edward's farm and the farm Stephen's mother inherited when her father died. Apparently Stephen resented the harshness of his uncle's discipline. Becoming restless and deciding to leave home, Douglas in 1828 traveled 14 miles north of Brandon to Middlebury, where he worked with a cabinetmaker. There he was both servant and apprentice, and after eight months of such drudgery he returned home. While still in Middlebury he had begun to read intently, particularly in politics. Andrew Jackson quickly became his political idol.

Back in Brandon, Stephen worked at another cabinet shop, but in the winter of 1829-1830, he became seriously ill. The boy was told that less strenuous work might be all he would ever be able to handle. In his autobiography, Douglas said that a probable life as a craftsman was transformed by bad health into the life of political achievement he eventually led. College seemed the answer and the local preparatory school, Brandon Academy, was his first stop. In 1830, he moved with his mother and new stepfather, Gehazi Granger, to Ontario County, New York. There he attended Canandaigua Academy. This school was a political tempest, with Freemasonry and Anti-Masonry seething. In this politically charged environment, Douglas apparently decided to study law. On January 1, 1833, he left school to "read law" with two practicing attorneys. After six months, Stephen decided it would take too long in New York to become eligible to practice law and he started west.

Cleveland, New York, was his first extended stop, in large part because Douglas again became prostrated by illness. Disease of one sort or another plagued Douglas his entire life. Rheumatism and a serious throat problem that required annual attention were frequent maladies. After recovering to some degree, Douglas left for St. Louis, Missouri, and finally to Jacksonville, Illinois. There he was told that he could open his own law office with no further training than he already had. After a short period, he decided that the prospects for success in these circumstances were small. Douglas went to Winchester, Illinois, and in order to support himself, opened a school and taught some local children.

No real strides towards financial success were made, but nonetheless Douglas did manage to continue studying law. Finally he took an examination before a Supreme Court justice and was granted the required certificate to be an attorney. Douglas had no delusions about the quality of his legal education. He applied himself industriously to learning the law. He decided the county seat was a more promising community in which to practice, and returned to Jacksonville.

At age 21, Douglas became the criminal prosecutor for the fastest growing section of the state, a feat accomplished through lobbying with his Democratic associates in the legislature to make the prosecuting attorney position elective. He was not yet a skilled attorney, and was probably not competent for the position. What he lacked in education, he tried to remedy with common sense, with varying degrees of success. The position, which involved traveling a circuit for court, gave him valuable political contacts.

Douglas labored long and successfully for the establishment of local party organizations, complete with nominating conventions. At such a convention he was nominated and subsequently elected a member of the legislature in 1836. Another first-term legislator was Abraham Lincoln. The issue of the day was internal improvements, and Douglas, along with a majority of the legislature, voted for a package that came close to bankrupting the state. Douglas later defended himself by saying he was only deferring to the wishes of his constituents, even if he actually knew the projects were impractical.

Douglas left the legislature after adjournment and became register of the Springfield Land Office. This was an incredibly lucrative position, particularly for one who was impoverished when he first arrived in Illinois less than three years before. His duties were few, but again he was able to travel a large area and make the political contacts that were later to serve him immeasurably.

Douglas's tireless effort for the party and his courageous championing of Andrew Jackson gained him the Democratic nomination for Congress. Douglas was not yet 25. The Whigs chose Lincoln's law partner, John Todd

Stuart, as their candidate. In the political style of their day, the candidates campaigned together, and even at times slept in the same bed together in the poor excuses for lodging that could be found. Douglas lost by only 36 votes out of the 36,495 cast. The final results were not known for several weeks, and for a while it appeared that Douglas had won.

The next political position Douglas held was especially designed for him. Douglas for political reasons desired to see the Whig-dominated Illinois Supreme Court changed from four to nine members. This accomplished, Douglas was appointed one of the new judges. The Illinois electorate was not fooled, and Douglas and the Democrats were roundly criticized. Yet Douglas spent two years as a justice and was generally believed to have, at least under the standards of frontier law then present, acquitted himself fairly well. During this period, 1841 to 1843, Douglas also attempted to be elected to the United States Senate, though he was one year short of the required age of 30. He was defeated by five votes in the legislature. The following year, 1843, in a specially gerrymandered Congressional district, the voters elected him their U.S. Representative. During the campaign, he again fell seriously ill, but recovered and was able in December of 1843 to take his seat in Washington.

The 1844 presidential race was in full swing by the time the new Congressman arrived in Washington. After James K. Polk was nominated for president by the Democrats, Douglas threw himself into Polk's campaign. Douglas won his own reelection with a landslide and saw his party's nominee squeak through to the presidency.

Polk soon disappointed Douglas. Douglas had taken the campaign rhetoric seriously, particularly "Fifty-four forty or fight." When Polk showed willingness to compromise America's claim to the Oregon Territory at something less than 54°40', Douglas fought him. Douglas did support the president vigorously on most Mexican War issues.

After a third election to the House in 1846, Douglas was elected to the United States Senate in 1847. Again, Douglas's maneuverings had accomplished victory, as long before the legislature finally voted Douglas had the Sen-

ate seat sewed up. On taking his seat in December of 1847, Douglas was made chairman of the Committee on Territories. The issues faced in that crucial committee were to dominate the rest of his life. Slavery was the focus, and whether it would be allowed to spread to the territories was the question, Douglas's question in particular. Slavery was no mere abstraction to Douglas. The need for voter support in southern Illinois, which felt greater kinship with the slaveholding South than with the abolitionist North, was a political reality he had to appreciate. A more personal problem existed. His wife, North Carolina born and raised, had inherited a substantial Mississippi plantation with over a hundred slaves when her father died.

Compromise became Douglas's hallmark. A sweeping test of his nerves and skills came in the Compromise of 1850. It was Douglas, after the initial compromise efforts of Clay and Webster had failed, who resurrected the separate pieces of the legislative package and labored them through both the Senate and the House. With President Taylor, an early compromise opponent, dying in office, Webster out of the Senate and serving in the cabinet, Clay absent because of bad health, and Calhoun dead, Douglas succeeding in passing what many thought saved the Union for the next ten years.

In 1852, Douglas sought the presidency. Ambition was ever pushing Douglas forward, and at age 39, he was given a fair chance of gaining the presidential nomination. He started early and campaigned brashly. He even named a running mate before he received the nomination, a tactic Ronald Reagan would use 124 years later with no better result. He selected Senator Robert M.T. Hunter of Virginia, thereby pairing himself with a Southerner who had opposed the 1850 Compromise. Yet if ever a candidate had his friends to blame for defeat, it was Douglas in 1852. An editor in Illinois, George N. Sanders, used the newspaper Douglas had helped him start to launch scurrilous attacks on Douglas's rivals for the nomination. This backfired, causing Douglas to lose credibility and support. At the national convention, Franklin Pierce became the compromise choice on the forty-ninth ballot.

Douglas had led on the thirtieth ballot, but never got close to winning the nomination.

Douglas was a good loser, and plunged into campaigning for the Pierce ticket. The election had just ended when his young wife, only 28 years old, died because of complications in the delivery of a baby. The baby also failed to survive. Douglas went into a severe depression. He began drinking heavily, and eventually made most of his friends and acquaintances doubt his ability to cope with this tragedy. After the adjournment of Congress, Douglas took a European tour. The months-long travels seemed to revive him. His sister, Sarah Granger, came to live with him and raise his sons. Drinking continued to be excessive; his clothes were shabby and in general his personal habits remained careless for some time.

Though Douglas's 1850 Compromise had bought some time, by 1854 passions were high again, this time over Kansas. A bitter fight, both in Washington and in Kansas, developed over whether Kansas would be slave or free. Every kind of political chicanery and intimidation were used in Kansas to influence the outcome. Again Douglas sought compromise. He believed that the status of a state as free or slave should be determined by its own people at the time a territory was admitted to the Union as a state. This famous "popular sovereignty" principle meant that such artificial mechanisms as the 1820 Missouri Compromise, which set the 36°30' parallel as the boundary between slave and free states, should be discarded. Douglas believed that geography and climate would determine the true viability of slavery in the territories, not votes in Congress. In 1854, therefore, Douglas was willing to yield much that was important to the North in order to buy the restraint of the South. The bill finally approved gave the citizens of Kansas the right to make the decision on slavery. This had the effect of repealing the Missouri Compromise. Also included in the bill was a strong Fugitive Slave Act. These two features of the 1854 legislation on Kansas doomed the Democratic Party in the North during the next election. Only seven of the 42 Northern Democratic Congressmen who had supported the 1854 measures were reelected.

The Kansas compromise, which permitted each territory to regulate its domestic institutions, led to divisive attempts by each warring group of extremists to control what the people of Kansas and Nebraska decided. Less than two years after the 1854 legislation, two rival governments had been formed in Kansas, one slave and one free. People from neighboring states, most notably Missouri, were pouring into Kansas in order to vote on the issue of slavery.

While these developments were occurring, Douglas again sought the nomination for president. Bitter feelings over Kansas persisted, and despite Southern support, his weakness in his own Northwest spelled defeat. On the sixteenth ballot at the Democratic convention, with Buchanan leading with 168 votes to Douglas's 122, Douglas instructed his supporters to vote for Buchanan and to end the stalemate. Douglas would never be rewarded for his willingness to concede the fight, but instead was largely cut out of the inner circle in the Buchanan administration. His party suffered rejection in Illinois where the Republicans gained the governorship and made a close race out of the presidential contest in November.

Douglas had remained a widower for three years. In November 1856, he married the beautiful Adele Cutts, the daughter of a governmental clerk and great-niece of Dolley Madison. Her lavish entertaining became the social centerpiece of Washington society. The shabby, rumpled and at times inebriated Douglas now became much more conscious of his appearance. He seemed to settle into the role of the wealthy, well-positioned politician that he was, with frequent entertaining of the rich and powerful. Adele was a marvelous match for him, and the marriage appeared to have been a true success.

There was dramatic further weakening of the Democratic Party in 1857 by its acceptance of what the North perceived as a bogus Kansas constitution drafted by a convention in Lecompton, Kansas, composed almost entirely of slaveholders. When President Buchanan for political reasons urged the acceptance of Kansas as a state based on the Lecompton constitution, the Northern moderates, including

Douglas, were outraged. In large part due to Douglas's insistence, the issue was submitted to the Kansas voters and the Lecompton constitution was overwhelmingly rejected.

Lecompton was a complete break by Douglas with the pro-slavery wing of the Democratic Party. The slavery forces had dominated the party for decades, and it was difficult to see how he could ever be nominated for president without their support. Buchanan turned on Douglas and used all of the tools at his command to punish him. Yet, Douglas's party in Illinois rallied around him. The Democratic state convention in April 1858, announced their complete support for his reelection to the Senate. Many Republicans sensed Douglas might switch parties, and such Eastern leaders as Horace Greeley urged that the Illinois Republicans adopt Douglas as their senatorial standard bearer. Abraham Lincoln had too great a lock on the Republican nomination to be turned aside, and the historic Lincoln-Douglas battle began.

Douglas was much better known than Lincoln, both nationally and in Illinois. Lincoln's challenge to Douglas to debate was, perhaps like most such challenges, an effort by the weaker candidate to gain an advantage over the frontrunner. These debates caused the clarification and perhaps hardening of both candidates' views. Douglas in expressing his Freeport doctrine, elaborated on his previous arguments that the Supreme Court and the laws of Congress notwithstanding, slavery could exist in no state without the support of that state's citizens. Lincoln, in turn, made his "House Divided" speech, stating that the nation could not long remain half slave and half free, a position that Douglas thought foolish and erroneous and which the South thought was cause for revolution.

Until the adoption of the seventeenth amendment in 1917, Senators were elected by the vote of each state's legislature. Thus, Lincoln and Douglas really were campaigning to convince voters to cast ballots for legislative candidates of their respective parties. The Republicans won a statewide popular vote majority, but the Democrats won enough close legislative seat contests to gain a majority of members in both houses. When the legislature met on January 6, 1859, Douglas was elected with 54 votes to Lincoln's 46.

Though Douglas had won, his future in the larger, national arena, was clouded. The Buchanan administration saw to his removal as chairman of the Territorial Committee in the Senate. Southerners viewed him as an apostate on slavery and untrustworthy generally. Perhaps angered by the viciousness of some of the attacks upon him, the Illinois senator began speaking out even more forcefully on his differences with the Southern radicals.

Douglas announced his candidacy for the presidential nomination in June of 1859. By the time the presidential convention opened in Charleston, South Carolina, in April 1860, a bitterly divided Democratic Party existed. Douglas was the clear favorite of the North, but was anathema to the South. Some Southern states withdrew from the convention due to the platform that was adopted. After the convention voted that two-thirds of all the delegates eligible to vote, including those who had withdrawn, were necessary for victory, success for any candidate was hopeless. After 57 ballots, the convention adjourned to meet in June in Baltimore. Some attempt was made in various states to replace the delegates who had withdrawn, the Douglas and more moderate forces attempting to get pro–Union delegates. Another bitter squabble occurred in the Baltimore convention on the seating of these new delegates. Again, the South withdrew in a huff, and this time Douglas was nominated on the second ballot. Upon hearing that Lincoln would be his opponent, he brushed aside the optimism of some of his supporters and said that Lincoln was the strongest nomination that the Republicans could have made.

Initially, it appears that Douglas was relatively confident of victory. By midsummer his confidence had waned, and he, at least privately, acknowledged the likelihood of Lincoln's victory. Northern abolitionists were completely behind Lincoln; Southern extremists backed vice president John Breckinridge whom the Southern states nominated after bolting the Baltimore convention. Border state moderates lined up with John Bell, a moderate Democrat and former Whig. Hoping to slow the rush to secession if Lincoln won, Douglas decided to undertake a uniquely active campaign tour through the South. This was at a period when presidential candidates did not campaign. Physical exertion in one's own cause was considered unseemly. During visits to border states, Douglas first began confronting the secession issue and called it treason. In September, early returns in Vermont and Maine showed the likelihood of a Republican sweep. Douglas was heavily pressured to withdraw and seek fusion with John Bell. It is thought, but hard evidence is difficult to find, that Bell and Breckinridge agreed to withdraw if they, with Douglas, could agree on a compromise choice. Horatio Seymour of New York was frequently mentioned. Douglas reportedly refused, thinking there was no compromise candidate who could hold onto his votes. Towards the end of the campaign, Douglas did seek fusion with the Bell slate in certain states, but never with Breckinridge.

Lincoln swept the North in the November elections. Even had all the votes for Lincoln's three opponents been combined, Lincoln would still have won enough Northern states, who by now had a majority in the electoral college, to win the election. Douglas immediately counseled the South to give Lincoln a chance. To retreat from a difficult position was hardly Douglas's style, and after his defeat he again traveled to the South, allegedly in order to inspect his wife's plantation in Mississippi, and gave speeches in several cities urging moderation.

One person impressed by Douglas's eloquence, or so one of Douglas's biographers reports, was Ulysses S. Grant. The man who eventually saved the Union as general of its armies was contemplating fighting for the South, but fellow Illinoisian Douglas persuaded him to stay with the North.

With the start of the next Congressional session after the election, Douglas embraced one compromise measure after another in the Senate. He worked for the Crittenden Compromise. This plan would have repealed Douglas's popular sovereignty concept by forever prohibiting slavery north of the 36°30' line and permanently protecting it to the south. Another tactic was to prevent Congress

from legislating on slavery in the territories. The Fugitive Slave Act should be vigorously enforced. But no compromise was meaningful, Douglas believed, unless it banished the slavery question from Congress forever. Proposal after proposal was defeated either by the hard-line Republicans or by the Southern ultras. Neither side seemed to want compromise. The only compromise that was ever adopted was a constitutional amendment to be submitted to the states, that would have prohibited the Federal government from interfering with slavery in any state. Had it been adopted, it would have been the thirteenth amendment, but the Civil War intervened. Ironically, the thirteenth amendment that was finally added to the Constitution freed the slaves, instead of insuring their bondage.

The very day that Lincoln arrived in Washington in preparation for his inauguration, Douglas met with him. In time, Douglas became almost Lincoln's confidant. Douglas stated publicly that though he vastly disagreed with Lincoln politically, they were in complete harmony where the issue of disunion was concerned. Lincoln was inaugurated on March 4. By mid–March, Douglas seemed to be Lincoln's spokesman in the Senate, giving speeches that, because of his frequent meetings with Lincoln, many thought reflected Lincoln's own positions. Once the secession conventions throughout the South had occurred by mid-April, Douglas realized that further compromise was impossible.

The Illinois senator supported the calling of volunteers. He even urged that more volunteers be requested than had Lincoln. At the president's insistence, he went on a tour of the Northwest to urge support of Lincoln's policies. After a few weeks, Douglas became ill. On May 1, it appeared merely to be a cold, but by May 10, it was clear he was suffering from one of his serious bouts with inflammatory rheumatism. At first it was believed Douglas could survive, but then other ailments, from an ulcerated throat to liver problems, flared. At last, on June 3, Douglas succumbed. Even had he won the presidency, he would have served less than three months.

His last words, instructions for his two sons, were, "Tell them to obey the laws and support the constitution of the United States." This bequest to his sons expressed the benchmarks of his life. The country would miss him.

Analysis of Qualifications

Stephen Douglas had the misfortune to be defeated by the man whom most scholars have selected as the greatest president in history. Who then can mourn the failure of Abraham Lincoln's opponent? Yet it is possible that the country missed the opportunity of having another firm and insightful leader who would have been hailed since for his achievements.

Douglas was a born politician who loved being among the people. He was a persuasive orator, the equal of Clay or Webster. His personal magnetism endeared him not only to friends but to political adversaries as well. Close personal friendships helped him greatly in his political quests, and he built an Illinois political organization on those friendships. Perhaps above all, he was a showman. His vitality and exuberance, and perhaps also his diminutive stature won him converts.

Douglas's spectacular political successes and defeats were achieved while he was still young. His death came when he was 48. His youth attracted a following of other youthful, energetic, ambitious men who identified strongly with the Little Giant.

This persuasive force was perhaps his most outstanding attribute. Douglas would have been an honest, powerfully persuasive president, who nonetheless would have used every political tool possible to achieve his ends. Politics was his vocation and his quick rise to prominence showed he had mastered his profession.

What would Douglas have done that might in time have caused a war to become unnecessary to resolve the sectional differences? Douglas put much stock in economics and specifically in trade relations between the North and South to make each section dependent on the other. He would not have attacked slavery, and that issue would have had its resolution deferred. Indeed, Douglas can justly be criticized as well as distinguished pointedly from Lincoln in that he took no public stand on the morality of slavery. Politically, not morally, was how he viewed slavery, and he believed each state should decide the question for itself. Upon that stand he based his "popular sovereignty" principle. There are those who since the Civil War have argued that slavery as a viable economic factor was on the wane, and in time the South would have had to give up on its institution. Perhaps slavery could have been abolished short of war, but it would not have occurred within Douglas's presidency.

It may have a national tragedy that Douglas did not receive the Democratic nomination and been elected president in 1856, rather than Buchanan. Douglas was intelligent, strong-willed, and not prone to let the country drift as did Buchanan. He had enormous energy and was at times even reckless. His strong stand on the Kansas-Nebraska question would have been far more effective from the White House than from the Senate. Alexander Hamilton Stephens, who became vice president of the Confederacy, believed Douglas's election in 1856 would have saved the Union without war. Douglas would not have become subservient to the South as did Buchanan, but neither would he have frightened the South so severely as did Lincoln.

It would be fascinating to be able in some historical sleight-of-hand to give the Little Giant a chance to be president rather than Lincoln, to see what this strong-willed Democratic nationalist could have done. Douglas said during the campaign that if secession came, he would if necessary coerce the South to return to the Union. When Civil War did erupt, Douglas was foursquare behind Lincoln in raising volunteers. Though a President Douglas may in time have failed to thwart secession, he may also have limited the number of states that seceded much more successfully than did Lincoln. With Douglas in the White House, the moderate elements in many Southern states would have a fairer chance of success, and the Southern extremists may more effectively have been isolated. Mollification of the South would have threatened a Northern backlash, and the Northern majority in the country might have swept Douglas and his policies out. It would have been a fine line to travel even to avoid war, and an even more difficult one if any closing of the sectional divisions could have been achieved.

STEPHEN DOUGLAS and HERSCHELL JOHNSON
(From the collection of David J. and Janice L. Frent)

One final, somber note is that it should not be forgotten that even had Douglas won the presidency in 1860, his illness and death by June 3, 1861, or just three months after he would have been inaugurated, might still have occurred. Herschell V. Johnson, Douglas's running mate and a Georgia moderate, would then have been president.

DOUGLAS BIBLIOGRAPHY

Capers, Gerald M. *Stephen A. Douglas: Defender of the Union*. Boston and Toronto (1959).

Douglas, Charles Henry James, ed. *A Collection of Family Records, with Biographical Sketches and Other Memoranda of Various Families and Individuals Bearing the Name Douglas or Allied to Families of That Name*. Providence (1879).

Johannsen, Robert W. *The Frontier, the Union, and Stephen A. Douglas*. Urbana and Chicago (1989).

_____. *Stephen A. Douglas*. New York City (1973, reprinted 1997).

Johnson, Allen. *Stephen A. Douglas: A Study in American Politics*. New York City (1908).

Milton, George Fort. *The Eve of Conflict: Stephen A. Douglas and the Needless War*. Boston and New York City (1934).

Nevins, Allen. "Stephen A. Douglas: His Weaknesses and His Greatness." *Journal of the Illinois State Historical Society* XVI (1949), pp. 385–410.

Stevens, Frank E. *Life of Stephen A. Douglas*. Springfield, Ill. (1923).

Willis, Henry P. *Stephen A. Douglas*. Philadelphia (1910).

1860 vice presidential nominee —
Democratic Party

Benjamin Fitzpatrick

Full name; Benjamin Fitzpatrick.

State represented: Alabama.

Birth: June 30, 1802, Greene County, Georgia.

Age on Inauguration Day (March 4, 1861): 58 years, 8 months.

Education: Limited schooling, perhaps six months in all; studied law under another attorney; admitted to bar in 1821.

Religion: Unknown.

Ancestry/prominent relatives: In 1720, Benjamin's great-grandfather emigrated from Ireland; Dixon H. Lewis (brother-in-law), Alabama U.S. senator; Franklin Elmore (brother-in-law), U.S. senator from South Carolina.

Occupation: Attorney, planter.

Public Offices: Deputy sheriff of Autauga County, Alabama, around 1817; solicitor of Montgomery Circuit, 1819–1823; defeated for Democratic nomination for governor, which he had not sought in 1837; governor of Alabama, 1841–1845; appointed U.S. senator, November 25, 1848–November 30, 1849; defeated for election to full term; appointed again to U.S. Senate and served January 14, 1853–March 3, 1855, and November 26, 1855–January 21, 1861; declined Democratic nomination for vice president, 1860; president pro tempore of Senate, 1857–1860; president of Alabama Constitutional Convention, 1865.

Home: "Oak Grove," a large plantation about six miles west of Wetumpka, Alabama.

Death: November 21 (or 25), 1869, at Wetumpka, Alabama, age 67 years, 4½ months.

Burial: Oakwood Cemetery, Montgomery, Alabama.

Personal characteristics: Considered one of the most handsome politicians in state; courteous, honest, frank, somewhat bland in personality.

Father: William Fitzpatrick (1744–1809), soldier, for 19 years a Georgia legislator.

Mother: Anne Phillips (?–1809), daughter of Joseph and Sarah (Lindes) Phillips.

Siblings: Joseph, married Sarah Tranum. Phillips (December 18, 1787–October 28, 1835), married Frances Tranum on June 25, 1810. William, married Evalina Wasmer. Alva (June 3, 1801–1863), married (1) Sophia Herron on November 20, 1833, (2) Mrs. Catherine (McGowan) Vickers, and (3) Mrs. Frances Long in 1849/50. Bird, married Dorothy Graves. Celia, married William Owens Baldwin. Nancy, married Benjamin Baldwin. Elizabeth, married a Mr. Evans.

First wife: Sarah Terry Elmore (1807–1837), married July 19, 1827; daughter of General John Archer and Anne (Martin) Elmore.

Children: Elmore Joseph (June 3, 1828–July 27, 1884), married (1) Rosalie Armistead on December 6, 1854, and (2) Elizabeth Thornton Marks on August 6, 1868. Phillips (March 15, 1830–April 29, 1901), married Mary Ann Bethea on March 3, 1858, and (2)

Jennie Kelly on January 5, 1882. Morris Martin (November 30, 1831–September 1853). James Madison (December 6, 1833–April 29, 1852). Thomas Sumpter (November 13, 1835–?). John Archer (December 14, 1836–?).

Second wife: Aurelia Rachel Blassingame (January 3, 1825–1872), married on November 29, 1846.

Children: Aurelia (April 20, 1848, died same day). Benjamin (December 29, 1854–November 1892), married Evelyn Hewitt Sheppard.

Benjamin Fitzpatrick was one of the many conservative men of the South who saw in the Civil War nothing but suffering for his region. A states' rights and slavery advocate, he was a fabulously wealthy planter whose fortune could not survive emancipation. Yet he still favored the Union. When war broke out, he retired from the United States Senate and from politics, and watched the bloody conflict from the sidelines.

There was little in young Benjamin's upbringing that presaged fame and fortune. His parents died within a few days of each other when he was only seven years old. Frontier Georgia, where he was born, had no rural school system and, at most, Benjamin received six months of quite rudimentary instruction. When his parents died, an attentive older sister and elder brothers raised him, but before long Benjamin was called on for rather adult responsibilities. In 1816, when he was 14, Benjamin was sent to Alabama to help manage lands owned by the brothers there. In later years, Fitzpatrick liked to point out the field near Montgomery where he tended hogs for his brothers.

Hogs and farming continued to demand his attention, but Benjamin's interests broadened when he became a deputy to the Autauga County sheriff. That lasted long enough for Benjamin to get a job as a clerk in a trading house in Wetumpka, Alabama. These chores were apparently not fulfilling, and young Fitzpatrick decided to become a lawyer. For a few months he read law in the office of Judge Nimrod E. Benson, who would later become Fitzpatrick's law partner. He applied himself sufficiently, or standards were such that he was able to become solicitor for the county within a year after beginning his work with Judge

Benson. When Alabama became a state in 1819, he was elected the first solicitor of the county. Formal admission to the bar came two years later. At first Fitzpatrick remained in Wetumpka, but then moved to Montgomery. His first case was defending an Indian against a charge of stealing a horse. The novice attorney's legal skills proved adequate, and so did his common sense. After the not-guilty verdict, Fitzpatrick urged his client to flee from the unsympathetic county.

For six years Fitzpatrick practiced law. During that period he married Sarah, the daughter of General John Elmore. One of Sarah's sisters was married to Dixon Lewis, whom in 1848 Fitzpatrick would replace in the United States Senate. Fitzpatrick gained a sizeable practice in Montgomery and was well-respected by his peers. However, ill health forced him to retire to his plantation outside of Wetumpka, where, except for occasional forays into politics, he would remain for the rest of his life. Land was added to the plantation through the years until, by 1860, it consisted of almost 16,000 acres, valued at the then-astronomical sum of $60,000. His personal estate in 1860 was valued at $125,000. His life on the plantation, Oak Grove, involved hard work, but also extravagant comfort. An article was written for a nationally distributed periodical in 1860 describing a visit to the Fitzpatrick mansion. Oak Grove then extended along the Coosa River for two-and-a-half miles. Cotton, corn, and vegetables were the principal crops. Described in the language of the day as a "compassionate slaveowner," Fitzpatrick owned over one hundred slaves. He allowed them to earn money at their labors, grow some of their own crops for sale, and otherwise seemed to treat them as humanely as the slave system permitted.

The comforts of the mansion kept Fitzpatrick satisfied for 12 years. A painful break in the peaceful existence occurred in 1837 when his first wife died, leaving him six children ranging from nine years to less than one year of age. That same year Fitzpatrick was given, without his knowledge, serious consideration by the Democratic legislative caucus as a candidate to replace Governor Clay, who had resigned to take a Senate seat. Fitzpatrick lost by only a few votes, but his popularity was evident. More direct political involvement arose in 1840 with his selection as a presidential elector for Martin Van Buren. A condition of the nomination was that the elector campaign actively in his congressional district. This Fitzpatrick did, energetically and successfully. Fitzpatrick's efforts added measurably to his political stock.

The first fruit of this newfound fame was nomination for governor in 1841. William L. Yancey, editor of the influential *Argus* paper, backed Fitzpatrick's candidacy. The issue of the day was the deplorable condition of the state banks. Despite the Oak Grove planter's 14 years of farming, he had not become entangled with the local bank. Fitzpatrick announced that he had never and would never receive a loan from a bank. The impression left by Fitzpatrick's 1840 canvass as a presidential elector, tied with his association with the bank reformer element in the party, were sufficient to gain Fitzpatrick the nomination. These credentials were also adequate to cause the bank element to bolt from the party and support the Whig candidate, James W. Mc-Clung, a prominent lawyer and former speaker of the state house of representatives. Fitzpatrick won with 27,974 votes to McClung's 21,219. On November 22, 1841, the planter-politician was inaugurated as the still-young state's ninth governor.

Bank reform was not easily achieved. Worthless bank paper littered the state. Loans had been made to state legislators and not repaid, in violation of the statute. One of the largest debtors was the state senate president. Forty-five Whigs who were either members of the legislature or directors or presidents of the various banks had outstanding loans of over $500,000. To combat this serious problem, Fitzpatrick had urged John A. Campbell of Mobile to run for the legislature. He wanted Campbell to lead the fight for reform. Campbell won election and became chairman of the banking committee. He would later be a United States Supreme Court justice.

The first order of business was to investigate the condition of the banks. Campbell's committee issued a report revealing the deplorable loans that had been issued by the par-

ent bank in Tuscaloosa and the four branches in other parts of the state. The committee recommended liquidation of two of the branches. The governor gave his endorsement to the plan, and the legislature in 1842 did liquidate. Of equal significance, a bill was passed requiring all nominees for state legislator to sign affidavits setting out their liabilities to the bank. In the next election, Governor Fitzpatrick campaigned to educate the state on the importance of electing men who were not tied irrevocably to the banking problem, but were instead free to make the dramatic reforms that were needed. His campaign helped elect a reform-minded legislature. All four bank branches were liquidated during the four years Fitzpatrick was governor, and in 1845, the charter of the parent bank was not renewed. Suits were instituted to collect the unpaid loans. The governor was authorized to investigate bank expenditures and to bring suit to recover illegal payments.

Other problems confronted Governor Fitzpatrick during his two terms. Because of profits expected from the state banks, the 1836 legislature had repealed all forms of taxation in the state. Fitzpatrick had the politically unpopular duty in 1842 of informing the legislature the experiment had failed and that taxation would have to be reimposed. The first series of taxes proved inadequate, and additional levies had to be made by the following session. Reforms in education were urged by the governor. Less frequent legislative sessions were encouraged. Fitzpatrick believed that no sooner had a bill been passed than the next session repealed it without giving the measure a chance to work. In sum, Fitzpatrick as governor evidenced extreme fiscal conservatism, personal honesty, and a willingness to take strong stands for reforms he thought were required. He had been practical, but firm, and his four-year tenure led to significant strides for the state.

In national affairs, Fitzpatrick opposed the national bank and disapproved of a protective tariff and any internal improvement bills. As a rigid states' rights Democrat, he wanted the federal government to exercise only such limited powers as were clearly enumerated in the Constitution. Fitzpatrick revealed no inclination to run for federal office and retired to his

BENJAMIN FITZPATRICK
(From the Alabama Department of Archives and History)

tutions but wary of encouraging sectional ill will. In December 1848, the just-named senator opposed efforts to prohibit slavery in New Mexico. He voted against printing a resolution from New York that demanded the outlawing of slavery in all new territories. When he returned to the Senate in 1853, Fitzpatrick renewed his support for slavery in the debate over the Kansas-Nebraska bill. Yet largely, Fitzpatrick stayed out of debates and avoided adding to the strife. He voted to repeal the 1820 Missouri Compromise and thereby remove any restriction on territorial slavery. In 1858 he said the admission of Oregon could not be opposed just because it would be a free state. The people of the Oregon Territory had voted to exclude slavery, and Fitzpatrick said that was their prerogative. He did object to Oregon's admission before any credible information had been received concerning just how many people were in that territory. "I would as promptly vote to admit a free state as a slave state when she presents herself with a clear record, showing clearly that she is entitled to admission."

Fitzpatrick wanted the two increasingly divided sections of the country to live in harmony. Controversy over the Mexican territories reached crisis proportions in 1850. He attended the Nashville convention in June 1850, being selected as a delegate at large by the Alabama legislature. The convention had been called, at John C. Calhoun's behest, to get all slave states together to devise and adopt some mode of resistance to the Northern "aggressors." In Nashville, Fitzpatrick fought alongside most of his state's delegates to preserve the Union. He endorsed the Clay

plantation in 1845 after completing his two terms as governor. There he remained until 1848 when his brother-in-law, Senator Dixon Lewis, died. Governor Chapman appointed Fitzpatrick to the vacancy, where he served from November 1848 to November 1849. Selection of a permanent successor was in the hands of the legislature, and sufficient enemies from the bank reform days must have remained to cause Fitzpatrick's narrow defeat, losing on the sixth ballot. When Senator William R. King resigned in 1853 to assume the vice presidency, Governor Collier appointed the Oak Grove planter to the vacancy. This time the legislature elected him to the remainder of the term, and in 1854, to a full six-year term.

In the Senate, Fitzpatrick was a conservative, quick to defend the South and its insti-

Compromise proposals of that year as a means of ending the crisis. In the Senate a few years later, the Alabaman denied any desire for secession, and stated the South merely wanted slavery protected. Abolition agitation threatened the Union, he argued, but Alabama would remain loyal.

As the war clouds of rebellion became increasingly turbulent and widespread, Fitzpatrick still argued for union. In 1860, when war was imminent, Fitzpatrick asked for an increased defense expenditure for North and South, in order to complete the construction of forts that had been started years earlier. He was a member of the Committee on Military Affairs in the Senate. He never attempted to slight the North in defense appropriations, even when war between the two sections seemed unavoidable. His evenhandedness and moderation earned him the friendship of all his peers. This respect gained him election in 1857 as president pro tempore of the Senate and he continued in that prestigious role until 1860.

There were a few in the South who refused even to consider secession. The majority of the Unionists, however, were, like Fitzpatrick, moderates who would not favor secession except under the most extreme provocation by the North. Fitzpatrick's image as a Unionist was clear in the public mind. The pro-secession wing of the state party and the moderates prepared in 1859 and 1860 for the national convention in the latter year. During those preparations, Fitzpatrick announced that he did not favor the nomination of Stephen Douglas for the presidency. Fitzpatrick wanted delegates to be sent to the national convention who would "secure to our section all our rights, as well as justice to every portion of the Union...." The Charleston convention ended in deadlock between the Douglas forces and the Southerners, and adjournment was ordered. Some Southerners wanted to back Fitzpatrick for the nomination as a substitute for Douglas. That never became a serious movement, in part because Douglas failed to yield. When Douglas was nominated following the bolt of most of the Southern delegates from the reassembled convention in Baltimore, Fitzpatrick was named for the vice presidency,

receiving all but one vote. It was traditional geographical ticket-balancing.

Prior to the convention, Fitzpatrick had informed friends that he would not accept the vice presidential nomination unless a platform acceptable to him was adopted, and unless he received a two-thirds majority of all the delegates originally sent to the convention. The latter was a numerical impossibility after the Southerners walked out and were not present to vote. Douglas's "squatter sovereignty" was rejected by Fitzpatrick and there was no more central issue to the campaign than slavery in the territories. Fitzpatrick said that to have accepted the nomination with Douglas, his would-be running mate "would have subjected me to the imputation of having abandoned opinions, well settled and declared to the world, for power and place."

Also influencing the nominee was a plan, ironically initiated by Jefferson Davis, to have all three tickets opposed to Lincoln withdraw so that a unity candidate — perhaps Robert Hunter or James Guthrie — could be named. Fitzpatrick made the decision which he called "not only unpleasant but painful," to refuse the nomination. He praised Douglas's character, called the presidential nominee a personal friend, and said that outside of their differences on the territorial question they were in harmony. Since the Illinois senator had made squatter sovereignty the issue of the campaign, he could not run with him. Fitzpatrick ultimately endorsed John Breckinridge as there never was a single Democrat unity candidate.

When Lincoln won the election, Fitzpatrick said that no action should be taken by the South unless an "overt act" by the new administration was taken to injure the South's rights. When fellow Southern senators resigned from the Senate in January, Fitzpatrick joined them. He told the Senate:

> I acknowledge no loyalty to any other power than that of my sovereign state; and shall return to her with the purpose to sustain her action, and to share her fortunes for weal or woe.

During the war, Fitzpatrick stayed on his plantation and made no effort to gain a military commission. He was helpful to passing soldiers, never failing to open his doors to his seceded country's weary warriors. Destitute families, widowed and orphaned by battle, would also receive his generous assistance. When the war ended, Fitzpatrick was imprisoned as a traitor by the Northern military. Released within a few months, he was then elected a delegate to and then unanimously chosen president of the state convention that declared slavery abolished, found secession to have been null and void, and then provided for the election of new government officials. Fitzpatrick never again held public office. In 1867, he was disfranchised because he had been a member of Congress prior to the war but had sided with the South. Two years later he died.

Analysis of Qualifications

Though tributes from contemporaries are prone to gloss over blemishes and emphasize the positive in just-deceased politicians, there is much truth in the following statement about Benjamin Fitzpatrick that appeared in the New Orleans *Picayune* just after Fitzpatrick's death:

> In his social and domestic relations he was faithful and true. In all the conditions and circumstances of life he was honorable, considerate and just. Having personal honor, consideration, fidelity, truth and warmth of affection, combined with a clear, sound, and practical understanding, ... he escaped all imputations on his personal character. No one supposed that he could be corrupt, or would sacrifice a public interest for his private emolument. He was never accused of deserting a principle, abandoning a friend, or failing to perform a public or personal obligation ... he was habitually firm, prudent, circumspect, and moderate. He was courteous, affable, and of a genial and obliging disposition.

Overblown, no doubt, but this summary by Justice John A. Campbell reveals the truth about this solid, unspectacular, and unambitious public servant.

His education was minimal. His early career consisted of odd jobs. Though poorly trained, he received brief success as a lawyer but then retired due to ill health. From that time, when he was only 25 years old, until his death at age 67, he spent only 12 in public office. The remainder of his life he enjoyed the comfortable, at times arduous, apparently quite satisfying existence of a Southern planter.

When Fitzpatrick served for four years as governor of his state, he revealed conviction and courage in opposing the existing banking system. A wealthy man did not need banks; Fitzpatrick boasted of owing the banks nothing, financially or politically. The bank reform movement was not founded by Fitzpatrick, but he did ably lead it as governor. The governor was no vicious demagogue, but encouraged conservative reforms that saved his state from financial embarrassment.

On national issues, the salient feature of his career was consistent support for the South's interests, especially slavery. Though not an extremist, Fitzpatrick did believe in what became known as the "Alabama Platform," which denied that Congress had any right to interfere with slavery in the territories. Yet, Fitzpatrick doubted the desirability of secession, even if the North continued to interfere with territorial slavery. Both he and Stephen Douglas represented the moderates in their respective sections of the country. Still, Fitzpatrick could not ignore his differences with Douglas on the major issue of the day, squatter sovereignty. Never ambitious, when offered one of the nation's highest offices, he rejected it at least in part because acceptance would have meant being untrue to his past positions.

It is difficult to measure Fitzpatrick's qualifications for the presidency since he always withdrew from forcing himself into a leadership role. For four years, he demonstrated ability as governor, yet then he retired to his plantation. Service for about eight years in the United States Senate is marked by moderation and integrity, but not by assuming the mantle of leadership for his section. If placed into a position of authority, there is little doubt Fitzpatrick would have applied himself to the fullest of his abilities. He was very much among the second rank of politicians of his day in influence. Fitzpatrick would have had to reveal still untapped abilities if he was to be a superior president. Nonetheless, he appears to have been a most adequate choice, a Southern man of peace and moderation.

FITZPATRICK BIBLIOGRAPHY

Brewer, Willis. *Alabama: Her History, Resources, War Record and Public Men, from 1540 to 1872.* Spartanburg, S.C. (1975), reprint of 1872 edition.

Davis, William C. *Breckinridge: Statesman, Soldier, Symbol.* Baton Rouge (1974).

Duncan, William Watson. "Life of Benjamin Fitzpatrick." Unpublished master's thesis, University of Alabama (1930).

Keller, Mark. "Alabama Plantation Life in 1860— Governor Benjamin Fitzpatrick's 'Oak Grove.'" *Alabama Historical Quarterly* XXXVIII (1976), pp. 218–227; reprint of article in *Spirit of the Times* XXX (July 14, 1860), pp. 272–273; summarized in Ulrich B. Phillips, *Life and Labor in the Old South*, Boston and Toronto (1963), reprint of 1929 edition, pp. 282–284.

Moore, Albert Burton. *History of Alabama.* Chicago and New York (1927).

Owen, Thomas M. *History of Alabama and Dictionary of Alabama Biography.* 4 vols. Chicago (1921), III, pp. 582–584.

Riley, B.F. *Makers and Romance of Alabama History.* Birmingham (1915), pp. 33–37.

Roberts, Shepherd H. "Benjamin Fitzpatrick and the Vice-Presidency." *Transactions of the Alabama Historical Society* IV (1904); also published as reprint no. 17, Alabama Historical Society.

Stewart, John Craig. *The Governors of Alabama.* Gretna, La. (1975), pp. 80–84.

Wynn, Adaline Evans. *Southern Lineages, Records of Thirteen Families.* Atlanta (1940).

---

*1860 vice presidential nominee —
Democratic Party*

Herschell V. Johnson

Full name: Herschell Vespasian Johnson.

State represented: Georgia.

Birth: September 18, 1812, in Burke County, Georgia.

Age on Inauguration Day (March 4, 1861): 48 years, 5½ months.

Education: Private schools in Georgia; then Monaghan Academy, 1826–1838; University of Georgia (then called Franklin College), 1831–1833, graduated 1834; studied law under Judge W.T. Gould, admitted to bar September, 1834.

Religion: First Presbyterian, but then joined Swedenborgian Church in 1848.

Ancestry/prominent relatives: Probably of English ancestry, family long in America (before the Revolution). His wife was the niece of President James K. Polk and a cousin of General Leonidas Polk of the Confederate Army.

Occupation: Attorney.

Public offices: Declined to be nominated for U.S. Congress, 1841; unsuccessful Democratic nominee for Congress, 1843; refused to be considered for governor, 1845; defeated for Democratic nomination for governor, 1847; appointed to U.S. Senate, February 4, 1848– March 3, 1849; state circuit judge, November 13, 1849–August 1853; governor of Georgia, November 9, 1853–November 6, 1857, retired; unsuccessful Democratic nominee for vice president, 1860; elected as delegate to Georgia secession convention, January 1861; Confederate States senator, December 1862–May 1865; president of state constitutional convention, 1865; elected U.S. senator, 1866, but prevented from taking his seat; appointed judge of Middle Circuit, Georgia, January 1, 1873–death.

Home: Sandy Grove plantation in Jefferson County, Georgia.

Death: August 16, 1880, in his home in Jefferson County, Georgia, at age 67 years, 11 months.

Burial: Louisville, Georgia, Old Louisville Cemetery.

Personal characteristics: Large, impressive man; weighed 245 pounds in middle age; reduced to about 200 pounds towards end of his life; deeply religious; high integrity; considered noncombative and almost lazy, but when aroused was dramatically forceful and compelling.

Father: Moses Johnson (1776–1836).

Mother: Nancy Palmer (June 27, 1785– August 28, 1855), daughter of George and Mary (Crueton) Palmer.

Siblings: There were nine sons in the family, but only two, Herschell and another boy, lived to maturity.

Wife: Ann F. Polk (October 10, 1809–January 14, 1884); married, first, Robert T. Walker; then married Johnson on December 19, 1833); she was a daughter of William

Polk, Maryland Supreme Court judge, and was a niece of President James K. Polk.

Children: William Walker (April 26, 1829–January 18, 1854), was a son of Mrs. Johnson's first marriage. Two daughters died at birth. Emmett R. (?–?), married Geraldine Griffin. Winder P. (?–?), married Leonara Johnson. Herschell V., Jr. (?–?), married Caroline Roberts; a doctor. Tomlinson Fort (?–?), married Emmer Arkwright on January 12, 1882; public official. Tallulah (August 15, 1840–June 17, 1925), married Elijah Pearce Horne on February 19, 1862. Ann Fromentine Polk (?–?), married Charles Hardwick; died in childbirth. Gertrude (?–?), married Col. John M. Stubbs.

In old age, Herschell V. Johnson advised a much younger man not to get into politics: "Whatever triumphs one won in the political arena, he would find them apples of ashes, and however high one rose in popular favor, he would live to see the day when he would sink lower in popular esteem than when he started." It is doubtful that all of the also-rans and their running mates felt quite as fatalistic about political life, but most must have felt at least a twinge of these emotions after suffering their own defeats.

Nine children were born into the Moses Johnson family in the piney woods of Burke County, Georgia. Only Herschell and a brother lived to majority. Local schools provided Herschell's early education. When he turned 14, he was off to Monaghan Academy for two years. In 1831, Herschell matriculated at the University of Georgia, where future Georgia leaders Howell Cobb and Alexander H. Stephens were then in attendance. Two years' study prepared him for graduation, but he postponed taking the final examinations and instead began the study of law for eight months in a school run by a judge in Augusta. Admission to the bar and graduation from the university both came in 1834. Herschell was also married that year to a widow, Ann Walker, who was the niece of Tennessee politician and future president, James K. Polk. Ann and Herschell would be partners throughout Johnson's 40 years in politics. A family friend would assay the impact Mrs. Johnson had on Herschell in this way:

She was the opposite of him in many respects. He was given to pessimism. She was full of optimism. He was inclined to look on the dark side of the picture. She was always looking at its bright side…. She always looked for the good qualities of people, and if she noticed their faults, it was to correct them with the love of a mother and in the spirit of an angel…. I have no doubt that the success and honors won by Governor Johnson were due more to her than to himself [J.K. Hines, 1924].

Even allowing for some Southern chivalry in the description, it is likely that Mrs. Johnson significantly strengthened her husband in his many gloomy periods.

Trying to establish a law practice occupied Johnson until 1840. More than one partnership was made, and a move from Augusta to Jefferson County occurred in 1839. In his new home, he settled in the spacious luxury of "Sandy Grove," a plantation that would grow to 3,652 acres and 117 slaves during the days immediately before the war that ended the plantation system. In 1840, Johnson got what was apparently his first taste of politics when he helped campaign for the Democratic presidential ticket headed by Martin Van Buren. The next year he was prominently mentioned for the Democratic nomination for Congress, but he refused and insisted that former classmate Howell Cobb be selected by the convention. The next election, however, Johnson did receive the nomination for United States Representative, only to be defeated in the general election.

As an attorney and as a Democratic politician, Johnson was progressing rapidly. In 1845, when he was 33, Johnson was a leading contender for governor. After determining that he could not gain the two-thirds majority necessary at the party convention, however, he deferred to another. Nonetheless, Johnson played a leading role in the campaign by agreeing to take over the editorship of a Democratic newspaper during the remainder of the election.

In 1846, Johnson condemned, in rather personal words, the actions of United States Representative Alexander H. Stephens in grandstanding about the Mexican War.

Stephens quite naturally took offense, and his response was to challenge Johnson to a duel. Johnson refused to accept the challenge. Ironically, those would-be combatants on the field of honor would a few years later be the closest of personal and political friends.

At the next election in 1847, Johnson was again a candidate for the nomination as governor, and again was defeated. The victor, George Towns, appointed Johnson after the general election to a vacancy in the United States Senate. It was not a bad consolation prize.

In the Senate the only issue seemed to be slavery. From his first entry on the Senate floor until the Civil War made the point moot, Johnson believed that Congress should not interfere with slavery in the territories. Congress should neither guarantee nor prevent slavery's entrance into any area in the newly conquered Southwest and West. The Southern point of view on the virtues of slavery was a subject of some of his speeches, as were attacks on the North for being hypocritical when it said the forcing of slavery on any territory was unconstitutional, while at the same time it pushed for Congressional exclusion of slavery. To Johnson, if Congress had the power to exclude slavery, it certainly had the power to permit it. Johnson only served the last year of a Senate term and then returned to Georgia. He made strong friendships with John Calhoun and William O. Butler while in Washington, and he signed the "Southern Address" authored by Calhoun.

For the next four years, Johnson was a judge traveling the circuit with fellow attorneys. He also stayed an active participant in politics. The Compromise of 1850 repulsed him, and he urged Southern congressmen not to yield on the issue. "Concession will invite further insult," he stated. He argued that the day was near when the South would have to defend itself. During this period, Johnson was as ardent a states' rights advocate as could be found and seemed to be countenancing war. Ten years later, he would just as vehemently be urging the South to stay in the Union. In November 1850, Johnson had progressed so far in his advocacy of slavery that he wanted a Southern "States' Rights Party" that would join Whigs and Democrats concerned about Southern principles. When Franklin Pierce was nominated by the Democrats in 1852, however, Johnson was greatly relieved, since he believed the New Hampshire "dough-face," a Northern man with Southern sympathies, would right the balance between the sections.

After four years as judge, in which he earned the plaudits of many for his courage in rooting out crime despite threats and being burned in effigy, Johnson was unanimously nominated by the Democrats for governor. In a friendly, well-mannered campaign, Johnson and Whig candidate Charles Jenkins traveled together and even, at times, slept in the same room because of primitive accommodations along the campaign trail. The issues included the national one of slavery in the territories, mixed with some local concerns as temperance — which Johnson favored — and education. The Democrat candidate won with only a 510 vote margin.

Johnson would serve two successful and respected terms. His reelection in 1855 was contested by the Know-Nothing or American Party. Johnson campaigned actively. The governor could not limit himself just to local problems and frequently spoke out on the Kansas-Nebraska Act pending in Congress, beseeching his colleagues to remain calm and not insist on secession. He wanted Kansas admitted as a slave state to restore equality between the slave and free states in the United States Senate. Abolitionists frequently came under attack by the Georgia governor, as did "Black Republicans," all of whom were called enemies of the South, out to destroy the region and its institutions. These pronouncements, as well as the fact that Johnson was a popular governor in a strategic Southern state, made him a serious contender for vice president in the 1856 Democratic national convention. Johnson received a sizable vote, but John C. Breckinridge of Kentucky was selected.

After his four years as governor were concluded, Johnson retired to his plantation. He was not a delegate in 1860 to the national convention in Charleston, but favored Stephen Douglas for the presidency. When that bitter convention split, with Southern delegates walking out, Johnson felt the precipitating cause for the division was less the conflict between Southern and Northern principles than it was conflicting ambitions of the two regions' leading politicians who were seeking the presidency. Once the convention deadlocked, Johnson felt that Douglas should be abandoned. The reaction of the Southern delegates convinced Johnson that Douglas could not hope to carry the South in the general election and, therefore, a compromise candidate was needed. When citizens of Macon, Georgia, asked for his opinion of the current political situation, he responded in a public letter printed on May 10. Johnson urged the South to return to the national Democratic Party and not go its separate sectional way. The adjourned national convention would reopen in Baltimore and the former Georgia governor thought all bolting delegations should return to the fold. Johnson attended the state convention in June that would decide Georgia's course, and he again urged unity with the North. He was in a distinct minority, and thus he bolted the convention and with a few others was elected a delegate to the Baltimore convention.

At the national election, the Johnson delegation was not seated, and the hard-line delegates sent by the state convention were. Soon that accepted delegation bolted the convention again. Douglas was nominated by the Democrats that were left; Johnson was disappointed. Benjamin Fitzpatrick was nominated as Douglas's running mate, but within days had declined the honor and the party had to turn to the National Executive Committee to name a successor. Johnson was the unanimous, and the wise, selection. He was an important former governor of an important Southern state, an ardent unionist, and a Douglas supporter. Despite the last credential just stated, Johnson confided in Alexander Stephens about his partner on the national ticket: "Douglas and his friends have displayed great folly, but that augments the necessity of greater effort to maintain the principles which I honestly believe are essential to the well-being of the South & the Union." He was pessimistic about the ticket's chances for victory. About the country's future, he was equally despondent.

"The sky is dark. The fires of sectionalism in the South are waxing hot and Black Republicanism in the North already exhibits the insolence of conscious strength." He would have preferred someone other than Douglas have been nominated since the "Little Giant's" chance for victory was so meager. Instead, Johnson had supported his would-be dueling adversary from 14 years before, Alexander H. Stephens, as a compromise that was not accepted.

Johnson conducted an active canvass. He found sullen audiences even in his native Georgia. The abandonment by long-time friends and political allies was painful, and the memory of the 1860 election is probably what prompted the sentiments quoted at the beginning of this sketch. In mid-campaign, he met with a hopeful Douglas, but told him of the slim chances in the South for victory. Douglas seemed surprised, and responded, "if you be correct in your views, then God help our poor country." The unpopularity of Johnson's personal decision to join the ticket was obvious in the returns in Georgia. The sectional Breckinridge ticket won the state with 51,800 votes, while the unionist Bell ticket garnered 42,800. Douglas and Johnson were hardly to be seen, with only 11,500 votes. Lincoln was not on the ballot in Georgia nor in any other Deep South state.

Johnson, A.H. Stephens, and others in Georgia soon were fighting the growing sentiment for secession. Johnson did not believe the mere election of a "Black Republican" was sufficient grounds for disunion. Stand firm for the South, he counseled, but stand within the Union. When a convention was held in January 1861 to determine whether Georgia would secede, Johnson was a delegate. His views were well known and found many adherents. He had hoped that popular "Little Aleck," Alexander Stephens, would take the lead in the convention for the unionists, but the prickly and pessimistic Stephens refused, believing the cause was lost and not worth the effort. Thus, the leadership was thrust upon Johnson, and he proposed a resolution that would guarantee Georgia's remaining within the Union as long as possible and called for a Southern convention to be held to adopt an acceptable plan to be presented to Congress. He felt there were certain basic Southern rights that must be upheld: no interference with slavery in the territories, return of fugitive slaves, penal sanctions for assisting fugitive slaves, and a few other measures to perpetuate this "peculiar institution." Rather than vote on Johnson's proposal, a resolution for secession was adopted by a 166 to 130 vote. Johnson was then appointed a member of the committee to draft an ordinance of secession. When the time came to vote on the ordinance, a motion was made to vote on Johnson's earlier resolutions in favor of remaining in the Union; they were rejected narrowly, 164 to 134. Johnson voted in favor of the final secession ordinance, saying that now Georgia had chosen its course, and he would be loyal to her. Johnson never doubted the right to secede from the Union existed, but merely argued against the desirability of taking that step prematurely.

For the next year and a half, Johnson remained out of politics and tended to his plantation, Sandy Grove. Again he supported Alexander H. Stephens' presidential ambitions, this time the presidency being that of the Confederate States. When Stephens was instead named vice president, Johnson declared loyalty to and general satisfaction with President Jefferson Davis of Mississippi, but wrote Stephens his disappointment that "Little Aleck" had been passed over. In short order, however, Johnson was criticizing the president's cabinet and many of the administration's measures, particularly in the area of finance. At the end of 1862, he got the opportunity to join the highest counsels of the government when he was elected to the Confederate States Senate from Georgia. There, his opposition to Davis would gain a national platform.

The inveterate pessimism of Johnson was continually expressed in letters to Stephens, with whom he maintained a lively correspondence for years. He hoped and prayed for success, he told the vice president, but did not expect it. Because the Southern cause was doomed, so was slavery. The measures Davis took out of military necessity, many of which were similar to Lincoln's, brought condemnation from the Georgia senator. Johnson

believed that the military draft made Southern independence unworthy. Conscription of soldiers was a violation of states' rights, Johnson believed, and crushed the volunteer spirit. He opposed the suspension of habeas corpus because it was so liable to abuse. He did not want a national Supreme Court because each state should be able to declare a Confederate Congressional enactment unconstitutional within its own borders. Thus, Johnson espoused in the Confederate Senate, the same argument John C. Calhoun had pled for during the 1832 nullification crisis. Johnson offered an amendment to the Confederate Constitution that would permit nullification, and if a state still found itself aggrieved, would have permitted peaceful secession from the Confederacy. The amendment was not adopted by Congress.

Though numbered with President Davis's most consistent critics, Johnson saw the effect this opposition had on the national effort and stated that "warfare on his administration will be disastrous." Throughout the war, he pleaded with his friend Stephens to attend the sessions of Congress and perform his duties as vice president. Instead, the Confederacy's second highest official sulked in Georgia throughout the war and added ammunition to Davis's critics. Georgia was the leading state in opposition to Davis, and when General Sherman entered the state in 1864 and conquered Atlanta, he made an effort to treat with these opposition leaders, particularly Governor Joseph Brown, and reach a separate peace for the state. Georgians were not quite that disloyal, however, and the attempted peace failed. Johnson tried to finesse Stephens by first emphasizing the merits of their common opposition to Jefferson Davis, but then urging on Stephens a sense of national loyalty to fight "the war according to the President's plan and policy and try to cause, so far as I can, the best results to flow from which I may not approve. This may be an error, be it so, it is an honest error and accords best with my views of patriotic duty and sound Statesmanship."

When the war ended in 1865, Johnson was a financially ruined man. His slaves were free, his plantation burned by the marauding troops of General Sherman, and his law practice of little value because few citizens had any money to pay lawyers or anyone else. As a prewar unionist, however, Johnson was seen as a man who could gain the state quick reentry into the Union. He was made president of the state constitutional convention that abolished slavery and ratified the thirteenth amendment to the national constitution. Johnson argued that the South should be left alone in working out a new relationship with the freedman, but, of course, that was not to be permitted until ten years of reconstruction had been attempted. Johnson spoke kindly of the former slaves and said that the two races must begin to live harmoniously. Johnson was elected to the United States Senate, but like other representatives from the recently conquered states, he was refused his seat. Stephens was the other rejected Georgia senator.

For the next few years, Johnson, seemingly disgusted with politics under the radical reconstruction rule of blacks, "carpetbaggers" and "scalawags," worked at his farming and his law practice. He spoke out against what he felt was imposed Negro domination of his state, which to him was rule by the illiterate and incompetent. Yet he also counseled for obedience to the government, much as throughout his life, he urged individuals to work within the system to change it.

In 1873, Johnson was appointed a judge by the incumbent governor, and remained in the post until he died. His most noteworthy service while judge was when he charged a grand jury that was investigating a Negro riot, "deal with them as free and as if they were white and award to them the full legal right to your impartiality." Johnson was concerned with the deepening racial antagonisms, and though no friend of equal rights, believed the former slaves should be treated with humanity and fairness. As was perhaps common, and not always accurate, Johnson before the war was described as a kind master to his slaves. But considering his actions after the war in attempting to afford the Negroes fair treatment, it seems probable he was an enlightened slaveowner.

In religion, Johnson converted to the Swedenborgian Church, or the Church of the New Jerusalem, in 1848. His wife had first become interested in the teachings of Emanuel Swedenborg, and out of fairness to her keen interest in the religion, Johnson agreed to study it himself. He was soon committed. Religion played a vital role in the Georgian's life, and particularly after the war he would comment frequently about the fleetingness of life and the need to tend to the "passage to the spiritual world." His religious intensity is also revealed by the statement in a letter, again to Stephens, that "the subject of prayer ... never fails to challenge my serious and delighted contemplation.... Prayer opens the windows of the soul, and lets in the ever shining light." It was probably with considerable peace of mind that he faced his own mortality. After a sudden illness, he died in 1880.

Analysis of Qualifications

The course of American history might well have been profoundly changed in 1860 had a states' rights, unionist Southerner been elected president. Though it is difficult to say that any permanent rapprochement between the sections would have been achieved merely by the election of a president with Southern sympathies — Pierce and Buchanan had exhibited those — at least the war would have been averted for another four years. The immediate dispute over slavery concerned its extension into the territories. There were other sectional arguments that extended far beyond slavery and included general economic issues such as the tariff. Perhaps the North and South were inexorably proceeding along a path to conflict, and that peaceful or bloody separation, but separation undoubtedly, was inevitable. The election of Herschell Johnson to the presidency would have given the country four more years to disprove that perception if it could.

Johnson was ardent on many things, and on Southern rights perhaps more than anything else. When the Compromise of 1850 was being formed, Johnson called for Southern resistance to any effort to weaken equal Southern privileges in the territories. He joined in the movement in Georgia to found a separate Southern or States' Rights Party. Yet two years later, he was back in the national Democratic Party fold, and thereafter there was little doubt that Johnson stood strongly, not only for states' rights, but also for union. He joined the Confederacy out of loyalty to his state, just as throughout his public career he could argue forcefully for a position but then accept the majority will if his position was not accepted. It was that capability that strongly distinguished him from fellow Georgian unionist Alexander H. Stephens. Yet they were good friends and political allies even while they disagreed.

One overwhelming personal characteristic that Johnson's letters and speeches indicate is an innate pessimism. Throughout the 1850s, he despaired for the continuance of the Union. During the four-year existence of the Confederate States of America, he frequently commented that there was little chance of ultimate victory. His 1860 race for the vice presidency seemed to him doomed from the start. That all these things were in fact eventually lost causes does not make his attitude any less negative and, probably, counterproductive. Still, Johnson was courageous in many of his stands. The prime instance was when he knowingly subjected himself in 1860 to the rejection by his own state that accepting the vice presidential nomination entailed, because he believed so strongly in preserving the Union.

Herschell V. Johnson had the respect of the South, earned by his honesty and devotion to the Southern cause. Though this esteem was severely damaged by his acceptance of a place on the Douglas ticket, it was nonetheless capable of being tapped. He had the fortitude to work with Congress to reach solutions on the territories that might have been a new Compromise of the 1860s. He was probably as good a choice as the national Democratic convention could have made for vice president.

JOHNSON BIBLIOGRAPHY

Avery, I.W. *The History of the State of Georgia from 1850 to 1881....* New York City (1881).

Collins, William B. "Herschell V. Johnson in the Georgia Secession Convention." *Georgia Historical Quarterly* XI (1927), pp. 330–333.

Flippin, Percy Scott. "From the Autobiography of Herschell V. Johnson, 1856–1867." *American Historical Review* XXX (1925), pp. 311–336.

_____. *Herschell V. Johnson of Georgia, State Rights Unionist.* Richmond, Va. (1931).

Hines, James K. "Herschell V. Johnson." *Report of the 41st Annual Session of the Georgia Bar Association* (1924), pp. 179–230.

Johnson, Herschell V. "Autobiography." Unpublished manuscript in possession of Duke University.

Ramage, C.J. "Herschell Vespasian Johnson." *Virginia Law Register*, vol. 7, new series (1922), pp. 736–743.

White, George. *Historical Collections of Georgia....* New York City (1854), pp. 254–258.

Family information provided by Mrs. Jane Johnson Terrell, Charlotte, North Carolina, and by Mrs. Carolina Berckmans Davis, Atlanta, Georgia.

1860 presidential nominee —
National Democratic Party

John C. Breckinridge

Full name: John Cabell Breckinridge.

State represented: Kentucky.

Birth: January 16, 1821, at Cabell's Dale, near Lexington, Kentucky.

Age on Inauguration Day (March 4, 1861): 40 years, 1½ months.

Education: Church boarding school; Kentucky Academy, 1831; Centre College in Danville, November 1834–September 1838 (B.A.); six months at College of New Jersey (Princeton); studied in office of attorney, then Transylvania University, 1840–1841, graduated LL.B., admitted to bar in 1840.

Religion: Presbyterian.

Ancestry/prominent relatives: Scotch-Irish descent; first Breckinridge arrived in America around 1728; grandfather (John Breckinridge), lawyer, was Kentucky Attorney General, legislator, U.S. senator (1800–1805), and U.S. attorney general, 1805; father (Joseph Cabell Breckinridge) was lawyer, state legislator, Kentucky secretary of state; son (Clifton Breckinridge) was U.S. Representative, minister to Russia; uncle (Robert Jefferson Breckinridge), minister, college president, Kentucky Union leader.

Occupation: Attorney.

Public offices: Kentucky House of Representatives, 1849–1850, declined reelection; U.S. House of Representatives, March 4, 1851–March 31, 1855, declined reelection; declined appointment as governor of Washington Territory, 1853; appointed and confirmed minister to Spain, but declined February 8, 1855; vice president, March 4, 1857–March 4, 1861; offered ambassadorship to Spain, 1858, declined; U.S. Senator, March 4–December 4, 1861, expelled; Confederate Secretary of War, February 7, 1865, until fled country at end of May 1865.

Death: May 17, 1875, Lexington, at age 54 years, 4 months.

Burial: Lexington Cemetery, Lexington, Kentucky.

Home: Lexington, Kentucky; after Civil War, lived in exile in Canada and England for several years.

Personal characteristics: 6'2" tall, slim and well-proportioned; almost black hair; large, deep-set eyes; large nose; clear and sonorous voice.

Father: Joseph Cabell Breckinridge (July 24, 1788–September 1, 1823), speaker of Kentucky House of Representatives.

Mother: Mary Clay Smith (August 30, 1787–October 8, 1864), married May 11, 1811; daughter of Samuel Stanhope Smith, who was president of Princeton; her maternal grandfather was John Witherspoon, revolutionary leader.

Siblings: Francis Ann (February 24, 1812–November 2, 1837), married the Rev. John Young November 3, 1829. Caroline Laurens (October 12, 1813–November 4, 1867), married the Rev. Joseph J. Bullock on October 31, 1832. Mary Cabell (January 7, 1815–August 13, 1835), married Dr. Thomas P. Satterwhite on June 6, 1832. Letitia (October 26, 1822– May 15, 1852), married Charles Parkhill September 6, 1847. Mary Ann Cabell (February 15, 1824–August 10, 1827).

Wife: Mary Cyrene Burch (August 16, 1826–October 8, 1907), married December 12, 1843.

Children: Joseph Cabell (December 29, 1844–c. 1901), married Sallie Johnson December 1, 1869, a cotton planter in Arkansas. Clifton Rhodes (November 22, 1846–December 3, 1932), married Katherine Carson on November 21, 1876, U.S. Representative and diplomat. Frances (June 21, 1848–?), married John Andrew Steele in 1879. John Cabell (August 7, 1849–March 18, 1850). John Witherspoon (December 1850–May 9, 1892), married Louisa Tevis; California lawyer. Mary Desha (February 1853–?), married Anson Maltby.

His life was tragically short and ironically complex considering the simplistic image he gained as a champion of secession. Depicted as the candidate of those who would destroy the Union unless slavery was protected, Breckinridge was appalled by slavery and wished for gradual emancipation. A leader of a rebellion, he was actually almost obsessively deliberative, believing that compromise was the solution of almost all great national crises. Elected vice president when he was only 35, nominated for the presidency when he was 39, Breckinridge held no further U.S. public office after the age of 40. Precocious achievement, followed by complete and rapid defeat, characterized his short but eventful life.

J. Cabell Breckinridge, John's father, was only 34 when he died three years after John's birth. John was raised by his mother, with help that varied from beneficent to teasingly cruel from his older sisters. His uncles, particularly Robert Jefferson Breckinridge, also influenced young John, as did his grandfather Breckinridge. The household was strongly religious, in the Calvinist-Presbyterian mold. Two uncles were ministers. Bible study and other religious training inculcated strong moral values and a sense of restraint and respect for authority. The family also adopted the view, which was in turn embraced by John, that slavery was an evil and that voluntary emancipation was the answer to this social stigma.

Breckinridge's education was excellent for his day. He attended a boarding school beginning at the age of ten, after his mother had taught him to read and write. Following graduation from Centre College in 1838, when he was only 17, Breckinridge began studying law in the office of Judge William Owsley, a Whig politician of considerable prominence who was later to become governor of Kentucky. For a time Breckinridge tried to establish a practice in Frankfort. The competition for legal business there was too keen for a novice attorney, and the somewhat chagrined lawyer moved with his cousin Thomas Bullock to the Iowa Territory, settling in Burlington. He befriended the local Indian tribe and even went on a buffalo hunt with them. Though success did not come instantaneously, within three years Breckinridge and Bullock, attorneys at law, was a well-established and respected firm. Breckinridge returned to Kentucky for a visit. John's sister Letitia played Cupid, with his assent, and while in Lexington he became engaged to one of his law partner's cousins, Mary Cyrene Burch. Living permanently in Iowa was not in her plans, and perhaps not in Breckinridge's either. The young lawyer's brief exile to Iowa seemed more an opportunity to prove himself than anything else. Having succeeded in Iowa, John could return to Kentucky with his self-respect restored. He went back to Burlington only long enough to close out his legal affairs, and then returned to Kentucky and opened a law office with yet another Bullock cousin, Samuel R. Bullock. Samuel handled the Lexington office, and Breckinridge and his new bride lived and worked in Georgetown, Kentucky.

The following year, 1844, Breckinridge was deeply into his first serious political involvement, the campaign of James K. Polk for the presidency. Polk's running mate, George M. Dallas of Pennsylvania, as well as third-party presidential candidate James G. Birney, had both been roommates of Breckinridge's father in college. Breckinridge gave some thought to running for office himself, but the entreaties of his law partner who needed his assistance in the firm dissuaded him. Breckinridge's forensic skills became evident, and the frequent speeches he was asked to give on behalf of the Polk-Dallas ticket established his reputation throughout the state.

Breckinridge, his wife, and their child moved to Lexington in early 1846. They purchased the comfortable home of an ex-congressman, and also purchased a slave girl for household duties. Breckinridge's dislike of slavery did not prevent him from employing it, at least on a small scale. The Mexican War was starting and he volunteered. His legal mentor and now governor, William Owsley,

appointed him a major in the Kentucky volunteers in September 1847, and Breckinridge was off for Mexico. He was placed under the command of General William O. Butler, who was to be the Democrats' unsuccessful vice presidential nominee in 1848. By the time Breckinridge arrived in Mexico City in mid-December 1847, the city had already been conquered. He spent three months with the occupation forces, making influential friends among the military, especially Butler. He also gave legal representation to soldiers in various disputes. Breckinridge's most notable case was the defense of General Gideon Pillow against charges leveled against him.

Upon his return to Kentucky, Breckinridge announced his candidacy as a Democrat for the state house of representatives from Fayette County. This was a Whig stronghold, and the Whigs would not permit the election even of a war veteran with a well-known family name without a fight. The Whigs were justifiably confident. Breckinridge promoted emancipation, an issue the Whigs had pushed vainly for years in the legislature. He did not believe in racial equality, however, and wanted all freedmen to leave the state. He would later be a proponent of the African colonization of freed slaves. Breckinridge was tireless in the canvass, articulate, and far more dynamic than the Whigs were used to. The Breckinridge name was still powerful in Kentucky, a vestige of grandfather John Breckinridge's long and significant political career. The vote tally was close, but Breckinridge turned the usual Whig county into a personal political stronghold, winning with 43 percent of the vote in a three-cornered race. He was the first Democrat ever elected from the district, and his political future seemed limitless. It almost was.

Breckinridge was nearly elected speaker of the House, so strongly did his surprising election and his personality capture the imagination of his party. In the legislature he was a strong voice in favor of the Union. Shortly after his election he met his future antagonist Abraham Lincoln, when Lincoln and his wife Mary Todd were visiting her relatives in Lexington. At this stage in their careers the two future presidential candidates would have been generally in agreement, even on slavery. Breckinridge did not run for re-election. Politics was hardly out of his blood, however, and in 1850 he announced his candidacy for the Whig seat in the United States Congress long held by Henry Clay. In 40 years only two Democrats had been elected in the district. Breckinridge seemed to receive the blessing of the old Whig leader Clay, for after an effusive speech by Breckinridge praising Clay at a testimonial dinner, Clay prophesied that Breckinridge would use his talents for the benefit of the country. Clay then embraced the youthful politician. Clay did seem strongly interested in Breckinridge's career. Breckinridge reciprocated by being almost fawning in his respect for Clay. The Whig lock on the seat was broken, and Breckinridge won by the margin of 500 votes out of over 11,000 cast. On June 29, 1852, less than a year after Breckinridge's election, Clay died. His successor in Congress was at his bedside, having been with him almost daily as death neared.

A second term was not necessarily Breckinridge's preference as the next election approached. At first he hoped that President Pierce would appoint him governor of the Washington Territory. But when the appointment came, Breckinridge refused it. He won a narrow reelection to Congress. He then faced his first critical test on the divisive issue of slavery in the territories. During the debate on the Kansas-Nebraska bill, Breckinridge generally favored the program submitted by Senator Stephen Douglas, a man whom Breckinridge became increasingly allied with during the Kentuckian's congressional and then vice presidential years. Breckinridge was a key figure in convincing President Pierce to back outright repeal of the old Missouri Compromise line that prohibited slavery in the territories above the line of 36°30'. Breckinridge wanted territorial expansion and favored the admission of Nebraska as a state. The debate over the bill became so heated that Breckinridge, after retorting savagely to the verbal assault upon him made by New York Congressman Francis Cutting, was challenged by Cutting to a duel. Breckinridge refused to retract his allegation that Cutting had lied on the floor of the House, and the duel was

arranged. Before it could be held, however, the adversaries were cooled down by the intervention of friends, including perhaps President Pierce. Nothing, other than Breckinridge's gaining a reputation as a Southern hothead, ever came of the challenge.

The 1855 elections approached with Breckinridge declining to assume the nearly impossible task of winning after the Whig legislature in Kentucky had gerrymandered his strongest supporters out of his district. He toyed with the idea of accepting an offer from President Pierce to be ambassador to Spain. The pay was low, and Breckinridge was already facing economic strain as a Congressman. His wife was also opposed to the diplomatic post, and therefore it was refused.

Breckinridge's seat and most other Kentucky offices were swept by the Know-Nothing Party in the 1855 elections, despite Breckinridge's earnest campaigning for the Democrats. The Whigs were now a defunct party, the Republicans just forming, and the Know-Nothings gained primacy for a few years as the opposition to the Democrats. The 1855 election was an overwhelming setback for Breckinridge's attempt to build a vibrant Democratic Party in the state, and he immediately began to restructure the organization.

Breckinridge wanted Pierce to win a second term in 1856. Some leaders suggested that Breckinridge himself should be a candidate, though he had only in January of the election year become old enough to serve in the office. The presidential speculation was shortlived, but he was an early favorite for the vice presidency. The main requirement for him to be selected was that Stephen Douglas not receive the presidential nomination, for then a Southern follower of Douglas, as Breckinridge was, would not be needed on the ticket. Breckinridge voted for Douglas at the national convention, and when Pennsylvanian James Buchanan was nominated instead, Breckinridge was the easy victor for the second spot. Breckinridge took to the campaign trail when several states asked for his help. The speech-making was intense but not long lived; after a few weeks' tour through certain critical states he returned to Kentucky. Buchanan and Breckinridge won comfortably. Included in the victory was the first Kentucky plurality for a Democratic ticket since 1828.

Breckinridge was almost immediately shunted to the sidelines, if not out of the game altogether, by the new administration. Appointments were not discussed with him, much less policy. The cold, secretive Buchanan, who like Pierce is disparaged for his presidential efforts by historians, did not know Breckinridge before the election and made no effort to enlist his support after. Breckinridge could feel the chill, and his own sensibilities probably intensified the cold. Before the month of the inauguration had passed, Breckinridge was wondering how his glorious victory could so soon have become empty. Breckinridge was not cheered by the equally distressing news on his finances, and he was forced to sell his Lexington home and his slaves.

Though ignored by the administration, Breckinridge did have a role to play in the debates in the Senate. And the debates concerned the never-ending controversy over slavery in the territories. Breckinridge believed that Congress could not interfere with slavery in the territories, and only upon a territory's admission as a state could slavery be prohibited. The immediate focus of the controversy was the Kansas-Nebraska problem that had first arisen three years before when Breckinridge was in the House of Representatives. For months Breckinridge remained silent on the controversy. The issue was whether to admit Kansas as a state under the Lecompton constitution, adopted by an almost entirely pro-slavery territorial convention. Abolitionists had boycotted the delegate selection process. Breckinridge finally followed the South on this issue, saying that a boycott of an election, though unfortunate, was not sufficient grounds to reject the election results.

In 1859, Breckinridge seemed to be weighing the odds for a presidential race. No strong encouragement came from any section of the country; there were many other Southern candidates in the race, and the Kentuckian's prospects were not good. His possible candidacy was postponed if not cancelled. Breckinridge decided that he wanted to be elected senator. The Kentucky legislature obliged. He was elected in 1859 even though the seat would

not become vacant until 1861 when his term as vice president concluded.

After the Senate selection Breckinridge went to Frankfort to accept the post and to thank his supporters. While there he denounced the Republicans in a speech that seemed to signal a sharp break from his years as a nationalist on sectional issues. He accused the Republicans of favoring Negro equality, and said the natural consequence of Republican victories would be armed conflict. He defended the South and slavery in his strongest language up until that time, and demanded the enactment of a federal slave code. The speech ended Breckinridge's presidential ambitions. He could no longer present himself as a Southern nationalist in the John Bell mold. Stephen Douglas saw this result clearly, and said that Breckinridge had forfeited any hope for the Democratic nomination because of the Frankfort speech.

The vice president did not allow his name to be put into nomination at the 1860 national convention in Charleston, South Carolina. His state had endorsed James Guthrie for president after Breckinridge had effectively taken himself out of the race. When no nomination was made and the convention subsequently reassembled in Baltimore, Douglas could not be stopped. The bolting Southerners who would not accept this nomination met in rump session in Baltimore and nominated Breckinridge without his knowledge. He was stunned and wished to reject the nomination. The most fearful thing to him was a Republican victory. He did not wish to engage in a hopeless race for the presidency whose only result would be a splitting of the anti–Republican vote. Jefferson Davis convinced him, however, that if Breckinridge accepted the nomination the resulting inevitability of Lincoln's election wold force Douglas to compromise. All candidates could then withdraw in favor of another. Douglas would not give in, however. Breckinridge felt committed, and went through the motions of continuing the campaign even though he saw it as hopeless. There was some hope that if no candidate received a large majority it might be possible for him to win in the House of Representatives, but Lincoln's sweep of the North made that speculation moot.

After the election Breckinridge did not attempt to cool the passions that swirled around him. He continued to appear to stand for those who would secede unless sufficient concessions were made. He made a list of demands on December 8, 1860, saying that unless slavery was protected in the territories, a stronger fugitive slave law enacted and enforced, and other measures adopted, secession would be the last, but nonetheless the only resort. He helped name a compromise committee in the Senate to attempt to resolve the conflict. He was even-handed in naming representatives from all factions to participate. The Republicans on the committee would not compromise, and all of Breckinridge's requirements for staying in the Union were rejected. Breckinridge saw secession as inevitable, primarily because of the Union's refusal to countenance compromise. His first reaction was to seek a border state convention that would decide what could be done to avert disaster. He invited the governors of the border states to issue a call for a convention, but he could not get much support for his idea. Many felt Breckinridge's motives were to use the convention as a means to declare war.

Breckinridge's position during these critical months was ambiguous. He desired peace but only on the South's terms. There were minimum guarantees he demanded for states' rights, and secession was the alternative if the guarantees did not come. He suggested to Lincoln that all federal troops be removed from the South so as to avoid the possibility of inadvertent conflict that could spark a much larger conflagration. He wanted the Union to survive, but not through the destruction of principles he believed more important than the Union.

After the Senate adjourned on March 28, 1861, Breckinridge returned to Kentucky. When Fort Sumter was fired upon he believed secession was the only recourse, but Kentucky did not agree. In June he returned to the Senate and frequently criticized Lincoln's preparations for war. He did nothing directly to hinder Northern war mobilization, but to many he was a symbol of treason who brazenly remained on the floor of the Senate. Opponents feared he was passing secret information

on to the new Confederacy. He said he was committed to neutrality, but all of his kind words were reserved for the South.

In August the Senator returned to Kentucky and found the state, though divided, to be dominated by unionists. The legislature was criticizing his stands, including his attack on Lincoln's call for troops. Breckinridge rightly feared he was going to be arrested for treason. On September 19, 1861, he made the most fateful decision of his life, which was to flee from Kentucky and join the Confederacy. He did not want to fight the Union, indeed had no military experience in combat, but neither did he want to be a bystander. The North had forced him to choose, and he chose the Confederacy. Breckinridge would later regard this decision as a great mistake. On December 2, 1861, the Senate expelled him as a traitor. Kentucky never did secede, and thus Breckinridge was an outcast in his own state.

Breckinridge journeyed to Richmond where he received a brigadier general's commission. President Jefferson Davis considered appointing him secretary of war, a position in which Breckinridge would probably have far outclassed the other occupants of that office during the Confederacy's short history. Davis eventually decided to select another instead. As a general, Breckinridge was superb. His lack of military experience led to early mistakes, but he learned quickly. He fought at Shiloh in 1862 and at Vicksburg later that same year. General Braxton Bragg became a bitter opponent during Breckinridge's assignment to his army. Breckinridge received his orders too late to help Bragg on his invasion of Kentucky, but did join with him at the battle of Murfreesboro, in which Breckinridge's forces admirably fought to cover the retreat of the main army under Bragg. Other leading battles in which Breckinridge participated were at Chickamauga and Missionary Ridge in 1863. The following year he was assigned as head of the department of southwest Virginia, and was then ordered to the Shenandoah Valley by General Robert E. Lee. The battle of Cold Harbor is probably the engagement in which he demonstrated the most skill. Breckinridge also fought alongside General Jubal Early in his raids on Washington, D.C.

Breckinridge was head of the department of southwest Virginia when President Davis finally did ask him to become secretary of war in 1865. The war was virtually lost by then, and Breckinridge immediately tried to take stock of the desperateness of the situation. For the first time there was as head of the War Department a strong-willed politician who would stand up to President Davis and inform the president when he was wrong. General Lee voiced especial pleasure in Breckinridge's appointment, saying that of all the generals in the Confederacy Breckinridge was the one to whom he would entrust his army. High praise indeed. The cause was hopeless, however, and by April Breckinridge knew it. He spent much time arranging for the evacuation of the government from Richmond when the inevitable occurred and Lee was no longer able to hold the federals out. This finally occurred on April 2, 1865. Breckinridge remained behind while the president and the rest of the cabinet left by train. Breckinridge later met with Union general William Tecumseh Sherman to help negotiate the surrender of Joseph E. Johnston's army. The secretary's influence helped gain lenient terms, which unfortunately were later rejected by the U.S. War Department. President Davis was not ready to give up the fight, but Breckinridge convinced him that there was no honor in having the Confederacy continue as no more than isolated guerrilla actions throughout the South. The secretary of war, the president, other civilian officials and a small army continued its flight across Virginia, the Carolinas and Georgia. Breckinridge became divided from the president's party, however, and before he could rejoin him the president was captured. Breckinridge then saw his only hope to be escape from the country. Breckinridge, as a former vice president and as a senator who continued in Washington after secession had become a reality, was perhaps vilified as a traitor to a degree matched only by the attacks on Davis himself. Many were calling for his execution. His last official act as secretary of war was on May 26 to promote to lieutenant colonel a man who helped him escape and find a boat. Breckinridge and a few companions made it to Cuba after several close encounters with federal troops, and

from there Breckinridge traveled by way of England to Canada.

In Canada Breckinridge began a life of exile. Though amnesty was granted to most ex–Confederates after the war, the high government officials were not included. Former President Davis was in prison. Breckinridge made the cause of raising money for his legal defense a high priority. Breckinridge's family joined him in Canada, but his wife Mary's health was bad and they went to France. They traveled to the Middle East, Greece, Turkey, and many other countries. After 20 months the exiles returned to Canada, there joining a society of ex–Confederates who could not or would not return to the United States. Finally on December 25, 1868, President Andrew Johnson issued a complete amnesty for all ex–Confederates. Breckinridge was finally free to return.

Back in Kentucky by March 1869, Breckinridge refused all suggestions that he return to public life. He did become active in several railroad ventures as well as becoming president of an insurance company. His recreation more often than not was found at the racetrack. In company with a vast number of his fellow Kentuckians, Breckinridge would often profess that his first love was thoroughbred horses.

Breckinridge's health had been poor ever since the war. The last few years of his life were a series of illnesses followed by short-term recoveries. He finally succumbed on May 17, 1875, at age 54.

Analysis of Qualifications

This most able man was presented as a presidential candidate at the occasion of the country's greatest sectional crisis. He had immense talents. His speeches were exceptional, being noted for their dramatic style and clarity. His appearance was inspiring, as he was a tall, handsome, and graceful figure. His manners were old South — gracious, open and friendly. He had considerable personal courage, as demonstrated both in politics and in war. He had magnetism, even charisma. For all the bitter hatreds that the divisive issues preceding the Civil War engendered, Breckinridge was singular in his friendships with even the most diametrically opposed politicians. He fought them verbally but then dined graciously. Respect for Breckinridge was not limited to his political friends. Yet for all these qualities, Breckinridge would not have served the country well as president during this impossibly complex time. Though civil war would have been postponed by his election, it would not have been avoided. He might even have made a Southern secession more effective because four years of a Breckinridge presidency would probably have facilitated growing Southern preparations for conflict.

Breckinridge was a conservative man. He believed in certain simple and time-proven virtues. Respect for authority and religion were among these. He also was exceptionally deliberative in his decisions. He was a methodical but indefatigable worker once his mind was completely engaged on a project. Emotions did not govern Breckinridge's will. These virtues also created in Breckinridge a certain rigidity once his mind had become fixed on a point. The point that would have destroyed a Breckinridge presidency was the perception he held of states' rights. As a greater and greater segment of the country was viewing slavery as an evil, Breckinridge was increasingly seeing it as an unalterable constitutional right. The Supreme Court in the *Dred Scott* case accepted his thesis that Congress could not interfere with slavery in the territories. As president, Breckinridge would have demanded guarantees in order for the Union to be preserved, and he would not have seen the South's plight as resolvable unless he received those guarantees. Such rigidity would not have resolved this almost intractable slavery controversy, but would have intensified it.

Breckinridge was no firebreather. Yet it is likely that much of the country would have perceived Breckinridge in the White House in the same manner that it did with him in the U.S. Senate. That perception was one of a Southern operative who was trying to undermine the North while preserving the institutions of the South. He would have led a divided country, in some ways one as sharply divided about the president as Lincoln found. Lincoln resolved the conflict his presidency caused by fighting and winning the bloodiest war America would know. Breckinridge's res-

olution of the conflict is more difficult to fathom. Breckinridge would have been faced with conflicts largely beyond his power to resolve, bitterness beyond his ability to quiet. He would have been distrusted by many and hated by still more. It would not have been a formula for success. There is nothing in the prospect of a Breckinridge presidency that argues convincingly that he would have lessened the pressures that propelled the country towards war.

BRECKINRIDGE BIBLIOGRAPHY

Breckenridge, James Malcolm. *William Clark Breckenridge: His Life, Lineage, and Writings.* St. Louis (1932).

Brown, Alexander. *The Cabells and Their Kin.* Boston (1895).

Davis, William C. *Breckinridge: Statesman, Soldier, Symbol.* Baton Rouge (1974).

Harrison, Lowell H. *John Breckinridge, Jeffersonian Republican.* Louisville (1969).

Heck, Frank H. *Proud Kentuckian: John C. Breckinridge, 1821–1875.* Lexington (1976).

O'Connor, John R. "John Cabell Breckinridge's Personal Secession, a Rhetorical Insight." *The Filson Club History Quarterly* 43 (1969), pp. 345–352.

Stillwell, Lucille. *Born to Be a Statesman: John Cabell Breckinridge.* Caldwell, Idaho (1936).

1860 vice presidential nominee— National Democratic Party

Joe Lane

Full name: Joseph Lane.
State represented: Oregon.
Birth: December 14, 1801, Buncombe County, North Carolina.
Age on Inauguration Day (March 4, 1861): 59 years, 2½ months.
Education: Common school in Henderson County, Kentucky.
Religion: Baptized as Roman Catholic in 1867.
Ancestry/prominent relatives: Lafayette Lane (son), a U.S. representative; grandson Harry Lane, senator from Oregon, 1913–1917, and a doctor.
Occupation: Soldier, businessman.

JOHN C. BRECKINRIDGE and JOE LANE
(From the collection of David J. and Janice L. Frent)

Public offices: Indiana House of Representatives, 1822–1823, 1831–1833, 1838–1839; state senate, 1844–1846; governor of Oregon Territory, March 3, 1849–June 18, 1850, resigned; territorial delegate to Congress, March 4, 1851–February 14, 1859; governor, May 16–19, 1853, but he resigned the governorship when he heard of appointment; U.S. senator, February 14, 1859–March 3, 1861; defeated vice presidential nominee for Southern Democrats, 1860; defeated for Oregon senate, 1880.

Death: April 19, 1881, Roseburg, Oregon, at age 79 years, 4 months.

Burial: Masonic Cemetery, Roseburg, Oregon.

Home: Vanderburg County, Indiana farm, until moved to Oregon in 1849; then established a farm in Roseburg, Oregon.

Personal characteristics: Approximately 5'8" tall; thin; dark brown hair; bow-legged, high forehead.

Father: John Lane (1758–?).

Mother: Elizabeth Street, married in 1798.

Siblings: Jessie (1799–?), married (1) Mary McLaughlin and (2) Eulila Garrett; was a Methodist minister. Mary, born in Kentucky; married a Mr. Spencer. Winnifred, born in Kentucky; married Edward Henry White in 1866. Lorena. Floyd. John. Simon (May 16, 1812–November 14, 1881.

Wife: Mary Hart (called "Polly") Pierce (March 16, 1802–August 16, 1870), married June 1820.

Children: Nat(haniel) (?–July 1878), married 2 wives while still in Indiana; married Eliza Jane in Oregon. Joseph Samuel (October 14, 1827–August 6, 1910), married Annie Higgins. Ratliff (c. 1826–December 20, 1848), married Alice? Melissa (c. 1821–1895), married Andrew Barlow. Emily (1834–November 1907), married Creed Floed. Mary (1830–?), married Aaron Shelby. Simon (February 29, 1832–May 20, 1919), married (2nd) Katherine Drain. John (1837–December 24, 1914), married Elizabeth Sherrard on December 15, 1875. Winnifred (called "Winnie") (c. 1840–?), married Lafayette Masher in July 1856. LaFayette (November 12, 1842–November 23, 1896), married Amanda Mann in 1867; U.S. Representative.

Historic sites/memorials: Creed Floed (son-in-law) house, 544 S.E. Douglas Street, Roseburg, Oregon, was where he ate his meals; Lane lived across the street.

Though born in North Carolina, Joe Lane and his family soon moved to Henderson County, Kentucky. There he received little formal education, attending the country schools infrequently and briefly. At the age of 15 he started out on his own, crossing the Ohio River and settling in Warrick County, Indiana, where he worked as a store clerk. Married at 19, he became a state legislator at 21. His whole early years were apparently lived at high speed, with little patient waiting.

Lane served intermittently in the Indiana legislature ten years out of the next twenty-four. He settled on a farm on the banks of the Ohio River in Vanderburg County, Indiana. His business pursuits included buying produce and being involved with the flatboat trade in New Orleans. He and his wife had ten children, found relative financial prosperity, and were well-respected by political and personal friends. In politics he sided with Jackson, Polk, and the Democrats. A break with this comfortable existence came with the Mexican War. Lane volunteered as a private after resigning from the state senate. He was soon elected colonel of the regiment which he joined. President Polk rewarded his political allies, and commissioned Lane a brigadier general. Some waiting in Texas ensued, but within three months the new general was in Mexico, fighting at Saltillo and then at Buena Vista. In the latter engagement Lane was severely wounded in the arm. His bravery and military skill were obvious. After his first command was disbanded when its enlistment period expired, Lane joined General Winfield Scott at Vera Cruz. His troops captured Major Iturbide, the son of the former Mexican emperor, at the Battle of Huamantla. Lane's achievements earned him the brevet rank of major general. Successive engagements, all successful, occurred at Puebla, Matamoras, and Orizaba. The final battle of the war for Lane was at Sequalteplan on September 25, 1848.

Lane returned to Indiana a hero. He had earned the sobriquet of "Marion of Mexico" for his bravery and skill. The name was borrowed from Francis Marion, the "Swamp Fox" of the American Revolution whose rapid cavalry thrusts and withdrawals kept the British off balance. Lane's political benefactor Polk then named him territorial governor of Oregon, an offer that proved highly attractive to the ambitious, restless Lane. On August 29, 1848, he left Indiana with his son Nat. Reaching the military outpost at Jefferson Barracks in St. Louis, he insisted on continuing even though winter was fast approaching. With 25 men loaned by General Stephen Kearny, Lane set out for Santa Fe and southern California. The desert and desertions depleted this small force. The trip was arduous, but Lane finally reached San Francisco and then took a ship for Oregon. Only eight of the party that started with Lane at St. Louis made it as far as Oregon City.

The new governor immediately issued a proclamation establishing the government. The date was March 3, 1849, the last full day of office back in Washington for Lane's political godfather, President Polk. Lane's efforts included ordering a census, setting elections, establishing a court system, encouraging the immigration of teachers, and fighting — at times personally — the Indians. Governor Lane also took a tour of his new domain, traveling by canoe up the Columbia River and then exploring the Pacific coast. It was not long before he decided to settle permanently in Oregon. He loved the beauty, the openness, and perhaps most of all, the political potential there.

Lane's involvement in various Indian skirmishes showed him unusually conscious of the fact that the Indian was not always the villain. This did not mean he fully avoided traditional frontier attitudes about the "savages." In June 1850, Lane resigned the governorship to join a party tracking down Indians who had attacked Oregon citizens who were traveling to the gold mines in California. This posse reached the Indian camp and sat down to parlay. The whites were badly outnumbered, and when some of the Indians broke for their weapons during the negotiations, Lane had the chief seized and a knife held under his throat. Such quick thinking led to the Indians leaving peacefully and the chief being held until a

final treaty could be reached. The chief took a liking to the brave, fair Lane, and asked to use Lane's name as his own. Permission for only part was given, and the Indian was thereafter called "Chief Jo."

The gold mines beckoned Lane as they did many less illustrious Oregon citizens. He found some gold, much hard work, and considerable danger. An Indian slave that he had been given by Chief Jo saved his life during one particularly close encounter. No fortune appeared, and Lane returned to Oregon.

Back in Oregon Lane agreed, with little persuasion, to run as a territorial delegate to Washington. In one of the turns of fortune that can make a political career, the popular incumbent whom Lane had not expected to defeat, died suddenly. What started as an opportunity to make himself better known ended in an overwhelming victory. Though Washington would soon be more home to Lane than Oregon, he decided to go to Indiana where most of his family, including his wife, still lived, and bring them to Oregon. He traveled by way of Panama, and then learning of an attempt to capture Cuba, he traveled to Havana. The attempted invasion had already ended with the capture of the invaders. The day after Lane arrived, the leader of the invasion was executed.

Lane journeyed on to Indiana, where he was met with rousing receptions throughout the state. He argued forcefully and jingoistically, for the capture of Cuba from the Spanish. Lane also praised the Compromise of 1850, passed the previous year by Congress. The Fugitive Slave Act he called "the best measure of all." Agitation over slavery was anathema to Lane; though he supported Southern rights he did not wish to see the issue divide the country. Much far-fetched speculation was occurring at least in Indiana concerning Lane as a presidential nominee for the Democrats in 1852, but he denied any presidential aspirations. While in Indiana he sold his remaining holdings there and then left for Washington.

Lane's maiden speech in Washington was a continuation of the emotional binge started in Indiana concerning Cuba. His vision had widened, however, and he now spoke of the spread of American democracy throughout the continent, the Pacific, and especially to Cuba, which was "almost ours already." His subsequent speeches were generally more about provincial issues, as befitted a new delegate still solidifying his position back home. Appointments to territorial offices were especially crucial, as was repayment of various debts incurred in organizing the territory and in fighting the Indians. Lane's ability to get appointments accepted by the president and Congress and his willingness to use this authority to strengthen his political power at home, led to the establishment of what approximated a political machine in the territory. "The Clique," as it became known, at first greatly assisted Lane's career, but his ruthless tactics eventually gained him as much enmity as power.

Lane's 1852 presidential prospects never spread beyond support by the Oregon and Indiana delegations to the Democratic convention. Lane pronounced himself pleased by the selection of Pierce. His hope that the convention would deadlock proved out, but Pierce had been the beneficiary of the impasse. It took 30 ballots for Indiana to give up on Lane, which is not bad allegiance.

In the new Congress Lane successfully backed a resolution to separate the northern half of Oregon and form a separate Washington Territory. He continued to push for the conquest of Cuba, though he apparently believed Cuba shortly would ask to become part of the United States. The session over, Lane returned to Oregon with 29 members of his family. His welcome was enthusiastic, which was helpful since a reelection campaign was then under way. Lane initially had attempted to be coy about reelection, but when far more people took him at his word that he would not run again than urged him to reconsider, he soon dropped any pretense and announced his "availability." He would never repeat that mistake. A party split was developing over patronage, with Lane the target for those who were dissatisfied with the status quo. The explosion that would develop eventually over the issue was still a few years distant.

The searing issues of slavery and its extension to the territories were not principal ones for Lane. Slavery was outlawed in Oregon, as were free Negroes and mulattoes. Lane attempted to avoid taking strong positions on an issue that was academic, even if controversial, in Oregon. Lane's efforts back in Washington were more directed towards such matters as army troops to help control the Indians, government salaries in the territory, and as always, getting his suggested appointments approved. In the summer of 1854 he was struck with a serious fever, and President Pierce visited him daily. To receive better care, as well as somewhat cooler temperatures, he was moved into the White House. The president himself waited on Lane. At last he began his recovery and was returned to less exalted lodgings.

Renomination as Oregon's Congressional delegate became troublesome in 1855. The Clique was becoming restless at some of Lane's surprising appointment suggestions, while anti–Clique politicians longed to break their opponents' stranglehold on office. The Whig party was beginning to organize, as were the Know-Nothings. Mention of Lane for the presidency was gaining frequency, particularly back in Indiana, which continued to make quadrennial claims on its former adopted son. Strong-arm efforts by Lane put down the growing rebellion in the Oregon ranks and gained him renomination and easy election as delegate. The campaign had been bitter, even leading to a fistfight between Lane and his opponent, John P. Gaines.

Lane was clearly siding with the South and the slave system in the growing sectional crisis. The provoked, but despicable attack by South Carolina Congressman Preston Brooks on Senator Charles Sumner found Lane taking Brooks' side, arguing both that the attack was justified based on Sumner's verbal attacks on Brooks' uncle, and that Sumner's injuries were grossly and politically exaggerated (which they were not). Lane even served as a second for Brooks in some aborted duels scheduled against defenders of Sumner.

The hopes by some Indianans that Lane could be the 1856 nominee never materialized into delegate votes, as very little effort was expended in Lane's behalf at the convention. Lane's chief fear was the election of the Republican Frémont, since he believed the Republican would cause civil war. The Democrat Buchanan won instead, and rumors of a cabinet post for Lane spread but never proved accurate. Again the Oregon delegate was primarily concerned with Oregon issues, especially statehood. Unfortunately, statehood for that territory became embroiled in the debate over slavery. Though twice passing the House, the bill admitting Oregon as a state died in the Senate. Lane's standing back in Oregon was suffering because of this failure to gain admission. Returning to Oregon in April 1857, Lane fought hard for renomination. The issues were slavery and the "Clique," with Lane's performance closely tied to both issues. Despite early speculation that Lane would have a fight for victory, he won comfortably with more than 60 percent of the vote.

After the Oregon delegate returned to Washington with another term won, the territory adopted a constitution for itself, which would become effective once admission to the Union was won. Lane's eyes were clearly on one of the Senate seats that would come with statehood, and he worked behind the scenes to solidify his support. These machinations took the form of secretly encouraging, financially and otherwise, the establishment of a newspaper friendly to his interests. This was despite the existence of competing papers that were friendly to him. Apparently Lane doubted their fealty and effectiveness and began to seek other media partisans. The result was a fight between rival publishers for political domination in the territory. Lane found himself in the center of the dispute, each paper claiming him as its own.

Far more important to the nation than Oregon was the crisis over Kansas. Again Lane sided with the South and slavery, arguing that Congress should admit Kansas as a slave state, even though the constitution adopted in that territory permitting slavery was subject to justifiable charges that it did not represent the sentiment of most Kansas residents. The Kansas crisis injured Oregon's chances for admission. Once that issue was settled there was little time left in the session to take up Oregon. It appeared to many back in Oregon that Lane was waiting to have his territory admitted as a state until he knew whether he

wold be one of the first United States senators. That charge of holding statehood hostage to his political ambition began to circulate widely in the territory. The Kansas-Nebraska controversy also split the Democratic Party into administration supporters who with President Buchanan wanted to accept Kansas with the slavery constitution, and those who followed Illinois senator Stephen Douglas, who described the Kansas charter as a fraud. Lane was with Buchanan. The party split spread to Oregon.

Though buffeted by criticism and party rivalries, Lane did succeed in being elected one of the first senators when the legislature met in July 1858. Oregon was not yet a state but was preparing eagerly for admission. Lane hurt his cause when earlier he had prophesied that statehood was imminent, and then the House failed to vote favorably. However, finally the bill was reported out of committee in January 1859. Republicans were opposed because they sought leverage against the Kansas bill. Nonetheless, Oregon statehood did pass the House by a narrow margin. Lane's goal of a Senate seat became a reality, and he was sworn in on February 14, 1859. New Senators had to draw lots to see who would get the term expiring in 1861, and which the term ending on March 3, 1859, eighteen days later. Lane "won" that contest and got the longer term. The party realignment in Oregon had proceeded so quickly from the previous year that the eighteen-day senator failed to be reelected, as the legislature deadlocked and no successor was named immediately.

As in 1852 and 1856, Lane's name began to surface as a compromise presidential nominee in 1860. President Buchanan was rumored to favor him. Newspapers North and South spoke of him among the second rank of possibilities, those just behind Douglas if he could not gain the two-thirds majority required. The Oregon senator was a delegate to the Charleston convention, journeying there with his state's convention endorsement for the presidency. He soon joined the South again on slavery questions. Lane professed to be strongly unionist, but only at the price of preserving the rights of Southern states. This meant permitting slavery in every territory until a final decision was made by the voters at the time of state-hood. Lane was not optimistic. He apparently not only failed to see much prospect of gaining the presidential nomination, he also despaired of being reelected in Oregon. Douglas could not get the necessary majority, but he did succeed in getting a plank adopted for "popular sovereignty" in the territories. The Southern delegations began to walk out. Lane was asked what the Oregon delegates should do, and he encouraged them to walk out as well. A story printed much later, and which is subject to question, states that Lane had been accepted as the compromise choice for president by both the Douglas and the slavery forces. Though no definite commitment had been made, the story insists that Lane's nomination the following day appeared certain. Yet that evening Lane, not knowing of the compromise, sent a telegram to the Oregon delegation encouraging them to walk out with the South. Though the telegram was kept secret by its recipients, someone in the telegraph office leaked the story and killed Lane's presidential prospects. We shall never know, but there are strong indications that the basic thrust of the story is accurate.

After a lengthy impasse the convention was adjourned for six weeks. Again the Southern delegates bolted the convention. At the rump meeting, Lane received the unanimous nomination for vice president. Union was still Lane's stated hope, but he seemed to resign himself that secession was inevitable because Lincoln's election seemed inevitable. Once the election prediction proved sound, he suggested that anything short of secession would be dishonorable for the South. Lane even offered to give his services to a Southern confederacy if requested. He was not reelected to the Senate, and left Washington for Oregon with this farewell thought:

> I now serve notice that, when war is made upon that gallant South for withdrawing from a Union which refuses them their rights, the northern Democracy [Democratic Party] will not join in the crusade.

He was right about some Democrats, certainly himself, but the forecast was essentially erroneous. His description of Lincoln's party was equally blind, and prejudiced: an "infernal Black republican sectional hypocritical fanatical negro-loving party." Lincoln himself was a "miserable creature" that did not understand government.

Lane retired bitterly, and quietly, to Oregon. His pro-slavery, pro-secession stands had not been popular there and he was burned in effigy. Rumors that he had returned to the state with crates full of arms for rebellion or for the creation of a Pacific Republic were false but widespread. He did not seek elective office again until he was almost 80, though he did campaign occasionally for other Democrats. One fellow Democrat was his son LaFayette, who would become a Congressman.

Lane remained on his farm outside Roseburg. He was baptized a Roman Catholic in 1867 along with his wife and some of their children. When Mrs. Lane died in 1870 he became a recluse, living only with a Negro boy. Finally in 1878 his family convinced him to move to Roseburg. In 1880 he tried unsuccessfully to be elected to the state senate. Lane died the following year.

Analysis of Qualifications

There were many attractive facets of the Joe Lane character. The courage exhibited in the Mexican War and in battles against Oregon Indians was repeated in many political encounters. It was courage tempered with reason, as he did not act rashly or blindly. He was fair in most of his personal and political dealings. Unlike many of his political contemporaries, he was scrupulously honest. There were no Daniel Webster–like skeletons of financial indebtedness and conflicts of interest in his closet. His son even remarked, with some exaggeration it is supposed, that father "was very much in the habit of paying debts [he] did not owe." Some of his political opponents admitted to themselves even as they were trying to discredit Lane that he simply could not be attacked on charges of dishonesty.

These qualities were tied with a restless energy and ambition. That drive took him to Oregon and made him a political force of the first rank there. The drive also made him part of a political machine that he manipulated with patronage. His actions were at times quite disconcerting to his would-be allies, but his clear goal was perpetuating himself in office and advancement to the United States Senate. Such energy also made him ineffective or at least bored in the one administrative position he held, the governorship of the Oregon Territory. The detail of day-to-day governance was not for him, not when there were Indians to fight or gold to find. He used the Clique when it was to his advantage, and then turned on it when that seemed advantageous. He was the kind of politician who seemed to believe the political universe, or so much of it as he could claim, should revolve around him. His egotism made his political friends short-term ones, and made him longer-term enemies. There was no strong Lane partisan group back in Oregon after his 1860 fiasco of preaching Southern and secession doctrine. The moral problems of slavery did not trouble or apparently even interest Lane. Secession to him seemed perfectly acceptable and even honorable as a reaction to Northern attempts to restrict the institution. His positions took an extreme states' rights cast. He was probably the most popular non–Southern politician in the South. Had the Democrats united on Lane, rather than split their vote among Douglas and Breckinridge, a much closer presidential campaign would have resulted, though Lincoln could well still have won. He was a man of principle, and the principle was not slavery so much as it was states' rights. He owned no slaves and could not personally have benefited from the basically academic arguments over territorial slavery.

A Lane presidency may have succeeded at an earlier time in our history, when war was not imminent and passions were not inflamed. Though the South would have been pleased, the North would have been repelled by his view of Southern rights. There would at most have been a postponement of the sectional conflict, not a resolution. A Northern moderate, willing to compromise on slavery with the South but not concede, able to gain the support of moderates on both sides of the Mason-Dixon line, but strong in his Union principles, such a man might have held the Union together and brought the country back from war. Probably no such politician existed; Joe Lane was not such a man. He was essentially another James Buchanan, who probably would have caused a continued drift towards war without himself provoking it. It would have been a failed presidency.

LANE BIBLIOGRAPHY

Brackett, Albert G. *General Lane's Brigade in Central Mexico*. Cincinnati (1854).

Hendrickson, James E. *Joe Lane of Oregon: Machine Politics and the Sectional Crisis, 1849–1861*. New Haven and London (1967).

Kelly, Sr. M. Margaret Jean. *The Career of Joseph Lane, Frontier Politician*. Washington, D.C. (1942).

1860 presidential nominee— Constitutional Union Party

John Bell

Full name: John Bell.

State represented: Tennessee.

Birth: February 18, 1796, at Mill Creek, Tennessee (some sources have given birth as February 15, 1797).

Age on Inauguration Day (March 4, 1861): 65 years, 2 weeks.

Education: Local county schools; Cumberland College (later University of Nashville), 1810–1814; admitted to bar in 1816.

Religion: Presbyterian.

Ancestry/prominent relatives: Robert Bell (grandfather), a captain in Revolutionary War, and native of North Carolina.

Occupation: Attorney.

Public offices: Tennessee state senate, 1817–1819, declined reelection. U.S. representative, March 4, 1827–March 3, 1841; speaker, 1834–1835, defeated by James K. Polk for second term as speaker; some votes for U.S. senator, 1833; U.S. secretary of war, March 5, 1841–September 12, 1841, resigned; defeated for U.S. Senate, 1841, declined to run for Senate in 1843, defeated in 1845; Tennessee house of representatives, 1847, selected speaker but declined; U.S. Senate, November 22, 1847–March 3, 1859, defeated; offered secretary of navy post by President Fillmore in July 1852, declined; unsuccessful presidential nominee of Constitutional Union Party, 1860.

Death: September 10, 1869, at Cumberland Furnace, near Nashville, Tennessee, age age 73 years, 7 months.

Burial: Mt. Olivet Cemetery, near Nashville, Tennessee.

Home: On banks of Cumberland River, near Cumberland Furnace, Tennessee.

Personal characteristics: Short, nearly obese; serious in appearance, even glum; not distinguished for his intelligence, a plodder and hard worker; dignified to point of aloofness; not a good politician, poor speaker; apparently somewhat irritable, self-centered, miserly.

Father: Samuel Bell (February 11, 1766–1836); married on June 16, 1791; was farmer and mechanic in Mill Creek area, southeast of Nashville.

Mother: Margaret Edmiston (January 23, 1773–1830).

Siblings: Sarah (July 3, 1792–?), married William Gaines. Robert (1794–died in infancy). Catherine (February 21, 1798–1852), married Andrew Crockett. Thomas (September 26, 1802–?). Martha (January 15, 1805–?), married James Crockett. Elizabeth Ann (?–?), married Crymer McEwen. Mary (?–?), married Littleton J. Dooley. James (?–?), married Mary Dickinson.

First wife: Sally Dickinson (?–September 28, 1832); sister of brother James's wife, and daughter in wealthy family.

Children: Mary, married David Maney. John, Jr., married Fanny Maney. David Dickinson, married Kate Gibbs. Fanny, married Thomas Maney. Sally, married Edwin Keeble.

Second wife: Mrs. Jane Erwin Yeatman (October 22, 1798–October 15, 1877), daughter of Col. Andrew and Jane (Patton) Erwin, was first married to Thomas Yeatman in 1817; he died on June 12, 1833; married Bell in 1835.

Children: Jane Erwin. Ann Lorraine. Mrs. Bell also had four children from her first marriage: James Erwin (August 27, 1818–?); Emma (July 1822–?); Thomas (July 20, 1827–?); Henry Clay (?–?).

John Bell was raised on a farm in central Tennessee, a few miles southeast of Nashville. Though his family was hardly wealthy, he was able to secure a rudimentary education that was capped by graduation from Cumberland College in Nashville, later to become Nashville University. The school was then struggling. It did not have a curriculum to challenge young John's talents, but at least he took his studies seriously and far exceeded the educational attainments of the vast majority of his contemporaries. John followed the then-accepted route to a legal career of studying in a law office. In October 1816, Bell began practicing in Williamson County, Tennessee, and formed a partnership with another attorney. His practice struggled considerably. At the age of 21 he was elected to the Tennessee state senate. He was only to serve one term and then returned to his law practice, this time more successfully establishing his office in Franklin, Tennessee. His notoriety as a state senator had helped build his reputation as a lawyer.

In 1818, Bell married and moved to Murfreesboro, wanting to take advantage of that city's designation as the state capital. The designation did not remain long and neither did Bell. In January 1822, he followed the state capital to Nashville.

At first, Bell was a staunch supporter of Andrew Jackson, a necessary viewpoint for any ambitious man in Tennessee at that time. In September of 1826, Bell announced for Congress to succeed Sam Houston who was running for governor. His opponent was former Congressman Felix Grundy, an equally partisan Jackson man who charged, presciently, that Bell was not as diehard a Jackson supporter as Bell professed to be. Jackson may have been doubtful of Bell's fidelity also, and Jackson announced his vote for Grundy. Bell won easily despite Jackson's opposition. Bell was joined in Washington as Congressmen from Tennessee by Davy Crockett and James K. Polk, two men destined for far more fame than Bell.

Bell's first term was dominated with questions concerning the cession of territory to Tennessee and other states for support of the public schools. Bell unsuccessfully supported legislation that would have provided land to Tennessee. He opposed bills for internal improvements, such as the construction of the Cumberland Road which ran from Cumberland, Maryland, to the Ohio River. Bell's objection, and an accurate prediction, was that voting for expenditures in favor of one state would be predicated on the benefited state's representative agreeing to vote for legislation favoring other states. The pork barrel philosophy of federally funded internal improvements was obvious to Bell even in 1827.

Andrew Jackson was swept into the presidency in 1828 with Bell's fervent backing. Bell was selected chairman of the House Committee on Indian Affairs, a post he was to hold during his entire remaining tenure in the House except for 1833 until 1835, when he was chairman of the House Judiciary Committee. Jackson wanted the Cherokee Indians moved out of Georgia, and Bell agreed to the wisdom of the plan. The forced march of the Indians down the "Trail of Tears" to the West, leaving countless dead from exhaustion, malnutrition, and other causes, was the result of this policy. Bell may not have been quite as rabid an Indian hater as Jackson, but he did think the Cherokees had no claim to the land they occupied and should be removed away from the white settlements. He wanted to exchange land with the Cherokees but not to use troops to force them to move. The next year Bell's future running mate, Edward Everett, argued for repeal of the bill removing the Cherokees, but Bell opposed him. Bell's agreement with Jackson on most issues put him in good stead with the administration. He was considered for the post of secretary of war, but someone else was nominated.

The genesis of Bell's permanent break with Jackson probably was their positions on the rechartering of the national bank. Jackson was unalterably opposed to the bank. Bell remained silent for a substantial period. Adding persuasiveness to his philosophical reasons for believing the national bank should be continued was Bell's substantial personal indebtedness to the bank. Bell finally endorsed a new charter. Yet on most issues Bell was agreeable with the president's position. Opposition on the crucial bank issue was sufficient to make him Jackson's enemy. When the nullification crisis loomed, Bell favored Jackson's strong stand against the doctrine. This placed him squarely in the unionist camp and somewhat

out of step with many of his Southern colleagues. The sectional divisions were still poorly formed, however, and he escaped serious political trouble in Tennessee.

In 1834, Bell was elected speaker of the House of Representatives when the incumbent resigned. Though nominally a Democrat and a Jackson adherent, he was elected with only a few Democratic votes but with substantial Whig party backing. The rumors began to multiply that he was a closet Whig who was undermining Jackson. The president was still not ready for a final break with his fellow Tennesseean, and professed to believe that Bell was still with him. Bell's bitter antagonist in the speaker contest was future president and fellow Tennessee congressman James K. Polk, who as a result of the speaker battle became Bell's irreconcilable enemy. Polk tried to drive a wedge between President Jackson and Bell. He was the source of much of the innuendo that, as it would turn out, properly charged Bell with unfaithfulness to Old Hickory.

Bell's financial difficulties were relieved somewhat by his remarriage in 1835 after his first wife's death. His second wife, Mrs. Jane Erwin Yeatman, was the widow of a wealthy cotton and tobacco merchant. She brought a sizeable fortune to the marriage. Bell was never successful in business, and probably did not have sound business judgment. Yet his obligations to the national bank were retired and he, for some period at least, was free from financial worry. He was to return to deep indebtedness later after other business ventures failed.

Bell definitely was gravitating towards the Whigs. The abuses of the Jackson-imposed spoils system antagonized the dignified, aloof Bell. The bank controversy, though his position was not yet publicly clear, also drove Bell away from Jackson and to the politics of Henry Clay and the Whigs. By 1835, the break with the president became permanent. Jackson's singlemindedness in insisting that Vice President Martin Van Buren had to succeed him, grated on Bell. The dismissal of federal employees who refused to assist the Van Buren campaign was corrupt politics as far as the speaker was concerned. Bell supported fellow Tennesseean Hugh Lawson White for the presidency. Despite Jackson's opposition Bell ran unopposed for reelection. Jackson could not believe the failure of his party to find a candidate to defeat Bell.

With the adjournment of Congress in July 1836, Bell's efforts on behalf of Hugh Lawson White and against Jackson and Van Buren intensified. Most Tennessee newspapers supported Bell and White; many denounced Jackson in much the same terms as did Bell. The White victory in Tennessee was consolation enough for Bell, who never did appear to have real hope that White would win the presidency. He just wanted to defeat Jackson, Polk, and Van Buren in his home state. That he did, though Martin Van Buren won a national majority and the presidency.

Though Bell received the satisfaction of victory in Tennessee over Polk and Jackson, his joy was short-lived. The Democratic majority in the House replaced Bell as speaker with his enemy Polk by a 132–84 vote.

With the opening of the new Congress there was no more pretense that Bell backed Jackson or Van Buren. The division became so sharp that Bell called for an investigation into whether Jackson should be impeached for abuse of his appointment powers. Jackson was, or so Bell accused, interfering with elections by requiring absolute loyalty to Jackson and to Van Buren. The ousting of the opponent's friends from federal jobs or intervention in their political campaigns, were the alleged tactics.

Surprisingly, at least from the perspective of 160 years later, Bell's opposition to Jackson was good politics even in Tennessee. Bell succeeded in keeping Tennessee in the Whig column during presidential elections through 1852. So popular was the Bell attack on the old general that again he drew no opponent when he ran for reelection to his House seat in 1837. Bell's pro–White, anti–Van Buren faction captured the Tennessee legislature. Felix Grundy, Bell's first opponent for Congress back in 1826, was the incumbent U.S. senator. He clearly could not be reelected. Bell's driving ambition was to be returned to his post as speaker of the House. Ephraim Foster won the Senate seat, and Bell started his campaign for speaker.

Bell was to be severely criticized in Tennessee for doing so, but he opened his assault on Speaker Polk by traveling to New England in an attempt to gain Northern Whig support. He spoke in Boston at a dinner in which he received a florid introduction from Massachusetts Senator Daniel Webster, who was already anathema to many Southerners. He then spoke at other Northern cities in an attempt to gather in the old-line Federalist and now Whig support. The first serious charges began to be made that he would sell the South out in order to gain high office.

Bell had run unopposed for Congress in 1835 and 1837, but in 1839 the Democrats finally convinced a candidate to enter the race against Bell. The Democrats had an excellent year in Tennessee, electing James K. Polk governor, gaining control of the legislature, and electing six of thirteen Congressmen. Bell, however, survived the Democratic resurgence and again put his sights on the now-vacant speaker's chair. The Whigs could not agree on a candidate, and though Bell was a leading prospect, another was elected on the eleventh ballot. In 1840 Bell first supported Henry Clay for president. Bell was rewarded for his prominence among the Whig ranks, and Whig president William Henry Harrison appointed him secretary of war. When President Harrison died only one month after his inauguration, the states' rights Democrat-turned-Whig, John Tyler, became president. Tyler immediately began opposing the Whigs' programs in Congress. He vetoed several bills that were litmus tests for one's faithfulness to the party. The veto of the bill rechartering the national bank was the most serious denial of the Whig faith, but there were other apostasies. Finally four of the five cabinet members resigned, all except for Daniel Webster. Bell did not really want to resign for he enjoyed being head of the War Department. He grudgingly did tender his resignation only out of the need to abide by the wishes of the Whig leader, Henry Clay. It was Clay's programs that were being vetoed by President Tyler, and Clay demanded that a show of outrage by the cabinet be made. This sacrifice made for Clay was to embitter Bell and cause him to lose whatever earlier admiration he held for the Kentuckian.

Bell was out of a job, and he did not like it. In 1841, state elections were held in Tennessee. Governor Polk was voted out of office, and the new legislature was also Whig. Two senators were to be selected and though Bell probably wished to receive one of the positions, he was not in a good position to do so. He diplomatically deferred to other candidates. He probably felt that a defeat at that time could seriously jeopardize his future political career. The Democrats had a one vote edge in the House while the Whigs had a more sizeable majority in the Senate. The result was that no senator was elected for two years while the two houses wrangled. Though neither party covered itself in statesmanship, the apparent chief cause of the impasse was the Democrats, who refused to follow the general procedure of the two houses meeting jointly in order to select the senators. Agreement to that approach would have meant both senators would be Whigs. The obstructionism backfired and the Whigs gained both legislative chambers in the 1843 elections. They immediately elected two Whig senators after the state had been without representation in the Senate for two years. Again Bell deferred to the interests of other Whigs and did not make the probably futile effort to be elected.

Bell had returned to his law practice after leaving the cabinet in 1841. He could not stay removed from politics for long and he seemed to be waiting for the right opportunity. In 1844, he again backed Henry Clay for the presidency. Zeal was particularly easy to exhibit when Polk became the Democrat's nominee. Bell's frenzied activity helped carry Tennessee over home-stater Polk by 113 votes, though Polk did win the presidency. The next definite steps back into politics occurred in 1847 when he ran for the state house of representatives. For a former cabinet officer to be satisfied long with such a lowly post did not seem possible, and his sights were obviously much higher. The realization of that ambition came later in 1847 when he won election as United States senator. He was a compromise candidate and did not win until the forty-eighth ballot.

In Washington, Bell attempted to end the differences he had with President Polk. The effort was only slightly successful. He opposed the war with Mexico and found the covetous aims on Mexican territory to be demeaning. On the day the treaty was being signed in Mexico that ended the war, a fact that was not known in Washington until days later, Bell argued that no war should be fought just to gain territory. California and New Mexico should not be acquired unless Mexico was willing to cede them. The only justification for the war would be to establish that Texas was part of the United States and its border was the Rio Grande; any other ambition was akin to the greed of the old Roman emperors, and he wanted none of it. Bell gained some admirers for his unpopular stand against manifest destiny, but probably more enemies.

The Compromise of 1850 was to occupy Bell's and the nation's attention during 1850 and 1851. The dispute over what to do with the territory added as a result of the Mexican War threatened to precipitate a civil war ten years prior to its eventual explosion. The admission of California and New Mexico, a strong fugitive slave bill, and retaining slavery in the District of Columbia, were all bitterly debated. On all these questions Bell wavered. He delivered a speech over the course of three days in which he seemed to change positions daily, almost as if he was thinking and reflecting as he talked. President Zachary Taylor opposed the compromise. Taylor's death and the ascension of Millard Fillmore who strongly backed the compromise changed the complexion of the battle. Each part of the compromise package eventually passed. Bell voted in favor of admitting California as a state, did not vote on the New Mexico territory question, was against abolishing slavery in the District of Columbia, and did not state his position on toughening the fugitive slave laws.

The passing of the compromise killed the Whig party as a national influence. Northern abolitionists who backed the admission of California and the prohibition of slavery in the new territories were Whigs. Southern Whigs, who were as likely to be slaveowners as were any Southern Democrats, could not politically coexist with them. Bell began to consider establishing a national conservative party that would attract moderates from the North and South. In this period of bitter passions, however, there was little support for compromise parties.

Bell's health was poor in 1852. He even considered resigning from the Senate. He did not resign and instead helped lead the Whigs to a narrow victory in Tennessee, though the national total favored the Democrats. The Whig party could not continue long, and that fact was becoming more and more apparent.

In 1853, Bell was up for reelection. The Tennessee Senate was Democratic and the House was Whig. Bell's long record made him controversial. Bell ignored the suggestion that the Whigs unite on a new candidate. He stood for reelection, and two other Whigs entered the fray. The battle was long and rancorous; Bell emerged the victor but the party was badly split.

As the Whig Party disappeared, and Bell could not become an abolitionist Republican, he joined the only other party then attempting to establish itself with some degree of success, the Americans or Know-Nothings. This episode in Bell's career is not particularly appealing, since the Know-Nothings were a secret organization of anti–Catholic, xenophobic and narrow-minded men who were only used by Bell as a convenient vehicle for his continued political existence. Most of his fellow Tennessee Whigs also joined, some as reluctantly as did Bell. Bell hoped the party would expand from its narrow principles, and endorsed the American presidential candidate, former president Millard Fillmore. The Democrats finally retook Tennessee in a presidential race, and the Democrats also controlled the legislature. They decided to elect a successor to Bell even though his term had over two more years to run. Alfred Nicholson easily defeated Bell, 58 votes to 35. The legislature also sent instructions to Bell to vote for the admission of Kansas as a slave state under a controversial constitution. Bell's conduct since 1854 during the entire Kansas-Nebraska controversy was also condemned. Bell rejected the legislature's attempt to control him and said he would continue to vote as he thought was best. The Democratic senator, future president Andrew Johnson, engaged in caustic, personal attacks on Bell on the floor of the Senate, attacks that Bell returned in kind. The

time for compromise and reason seemed at an end.

Bell's hatred of extremism, both Northern and Southern, placed him at the forefront of those still trying to resolve the sectional crisis on terms other than total victory for one faction or the other. On February 12, 1859, the old Tennessee Whigs nominated him for president. The party was merely known as the Opposition, and it won six of ten Congressional seats in the state. Other nominations and endorsements of Bell for president followed. Finally, a new party, calling itself the Constitutional Union Party, held a convention in Baltimore on May 9, 1860. Bell, John J. Crittenden, and Sam Houston were the chief candidates; Crittenden declined, and the battle devolved into a two-man contest. Bell led after one ballot and secured the victory after an overnight postponement. Bell was not an exciting choice, and the addition of Edward Everett as a vice presidential nominee did not strengthen the ticket.

The party intentionally declined to present a platform, saying that the only issue was the Union. The effort was to avoid all comment on slavery since it was a cause of such bitter divisions. Bell himself refused to be pinned down on his plans if elected, other than that he would use all his authority as president to preserve the Union and the Constitution. He was not overly hopeful of victory, seeing his chief avenue for success to be remaining friendly towards all the other parties. If the selection fell to the House of Representatives, then perhaps he could be the compromise choice. In some states he agreed to fusion with other candidates in order to stop the election of Abraham Lincoln. He saw Lincoln as the sure way to civil war, and therefore every effort to prevent Lincoln's election should be made.

Bell counseled for restraint. The South should not let its grievances lead to war. As late as July he thought his approach had a real chance to gain him the South's electoral votes. The result, however, was his winning only three states. The calamity, as he saw it, of Lincoln's election came to pass.

Bell urged that the South give Lincoln a chance. He stated that secession was rebellion. These statements make his conversion a few months later from unionist to Confederate all the more surprising. When Tennessee finally voted to secede, Bell went with his home state. When Lincoln on April 18, 1861, called for troops to be raised to put down the rebellion, Bell insisted Tennessee ignore the order. If the North started war, he said, the South must resist. At the same time he was urging Lincoln, in at least one personal conference with the president, not to use force but to continue reconciliation efforts. He even looked to establish a border state confederacy that would ignore pleas from both North and South for help; it would instead act as a neutral, pacifist buffer that might help quell the rebellion passions. Yet when the passions were not eased, Bell joined the secessionists. Many of his supporters saw this as treason, for just six months earlier they had backed him as the one true Union candidate.

Bell spent the Civil War trying to avoid Union troops, moving in advance of the approaching armies whenever that became necessary. The end of the war found him in Georgia. After the war he attempted to reopen some of his collapsed mining ventures. He lived only a few more years, dying on September 11, 1869.

Analysis of Qualifications

John Bell was nominated for president because he represented those Americans who desired for the sectional crisis to pass without war. Ironically, once war began he joined the South and secession. Throughout his career he was a Southerner with Northern leanings, a slaveowner who nonetheless realized the limits to which slavery could be taken. He never joined the extremists from his section until civil war had actually erupted. Unfortunately, on balance he was an indecisive man who at times of crisis could not be depended upon to offer strong leadership. One is left with the conclusion that a Bell presidency in the early 1860s would have been a continuation of the haphazard stumbling towards greater and greater crisis that had characterized every president since his fellow Tennesseean (and bitter opponent) James K. Polk had left the presidency in 1849.

Bell's personal style was cold and aloof,

even haughty. The 1840 log cabin and hard cider presidential campaign by the Whigs was repulsive to the dignified Bell. He was a poor politician despite his many electoral victories. He did not know how to relate to people. The very necessary ability to be able to tell people "no" gracefully never appeared in Bell. He made enemies rather than friends when office seekers sought his support. His mind was on issues and programs and not on people. Often his political opponents accused him of being cold-blooded and without compassion, devious and not open. The charges had validity.

Bell deserves praise in addition to the criticism. He was genuinely concerned about alleviating the passions that threatened and then did split the country. He hated the spoils system and the effect on the integrity and freedom of office holders. This concern led him to propose an early, but defeated bill to make federal employees ineligible to participate in politics. He hoped thereby to remove the pressures to support the incumbent administration. His early years in the House of Representatives revealed his concern for funding schools by using proceeds from the public lands, a foresighted if not unique proposal. Bell was intelligent and interested in the welfare of his country. Yet his personal austerity and aloofness prevented him from being able to lead. When crisis came in 1850 over the admission of California and the organization of the territories gained from Mexico, he was at a loss on what to do. In 1854, he was more forthright and stood against slaveowners who tried to force a tainted constitution and government on Kansas, despite the instructions from his own legislature to support the bill. In neither crisis was he a leader, however, being slow to decide on what side of the issue he should be on. In the last great crisis of his career, the 1860 election, Bell stood for reason and restraint. Yet when Lincoln was elected, he gradually shifted positions and joined the South's rebellion sentiment.

Bell's career leaves no strong images. He frequently was changing political course, from Jacksonian Democrat (perhaps a reluctant one) to Clay Whig to anti–Clay Whig to Know-Nothing to unionist to secessionist. No major legislation was left behind when he finally

JOHN BELL and EDWARD EVERETT
(From the collection of David J. and Janice L. Frent)

retired from Congress in 1859, after almost 26 years in the House and Senate. He was not one of the greats in Congress, but neither was he one of the counterproductive forces. He was one of those many individuals whom one party or another has tried to promote from an arena in which they served adequately into the presidency in which they had little prospect for success.

BELL BIBLIOGRAPHY

Bell, Getha G. *The Bells in U.S.A. and Allied Families, 1650–1977.* Ann Arbor (1977).

Caldwell, Joshua W. "John Bell of Tennessee." *American Historical Review* IV (1898–99), pp. 652–664.

Grim, Mark Sillers. "The Public Career of John Bell." Unpublished master's thesis, University of Tennessee (1930).

The Life, Speeches, and Public Services of John Bell. New York City (1860).

Parks, Joseph Howard. *John Bell of Tennessee.* Baton Rouge (1950).

Parks, Norman L. "The Career of John Bell of Tennessee in the U.S. House of Representatives." Unpublished doctoral dissertation, Vanderbilt University (1942).

---

*1860 vice presidential nominee —
Constitutional Union Party*

Edward Everett

Full name: Edward Everett.

State represented: Massachusetts.

Birth: April 11, 1794, in Dorchester, Massachusetts.

Age on Inauguration Day (March 4, 1861): 66 years, 11 months.

Education: Village school in Dorchester, Massachusetts; then in Boston schools; Phillips Academy at Exeter, New Hampshire; Harvard College, 1807–1811, graduated with highest honors; Harvard divinity degree, 1814; Göttingen, 1815–1817 (Ph.D.) (first American to receive German Ph.D.).

Religion: Unitarian.

Ancestry/prominent relatives: English ancestors, arrived in America around perhaps 1634 or 1635; sister-in-law's husband was Charles Francis Adams (see election of 1848); Alexander Everett (brother), editor and diplomat; William Everett (son), U.S. representative.

Occupation: Ordained minister; university professor.

Public offices: U.S. representative, March 4, 1825–March 3, 1835, declined reelection; governor of Massachusetts, January 7, 1836–January 18, 1840, defeated for reelection; ambassador to Great Britain, September 13, 1841–August 8, 1845; declined appointment as special envoy to China, 1843; U.S. secretary of state, November 6, 1852–March 3, 1853; U.S. senator, March 4, 1853–June 1, 1854, resigned; defeated for vice president, 1860.

Death: January 15, 1865, Boston, age 70 years, 9 months.

Burial: Mount Auburn Cemetery, Boston, Massachusetts.

Home: Boston.

Personal characteristics: Tremendously gifted; extraordinary memory; inspiring speaker, perfect timing, graceful, almost too polished; one of the preeminent orators of his day; dignified, courteous, upright, fond of ceremony; methodical and attentive to detail.

Father: Oliver Everett (June 11, 1752–December 19, 1802); minister; judge of Court of Common Pleas.

Mother: Lucy Hill (January 12, 1768–May 4, 1824), married November 6, 1787; daughter of Alexander Sears and Mary (Ritchie) Hill, Boston.

Siblings: Oliver (May 15, 1788–August 11, 1864), married Ann (Vincent) Gardner, February 17, 1811. Alexander Hill (March 19, 1790–June 19, 1847), married Lucretia Orne Peabody, September 21, 1816; editor and diplomat. Sarah Preston (September 5, 1796–?), married Nathan Hale, 1816. Thomas Huse (February 67, 1799–?). Lucy (October 17, 1791–?), married Francis S. Durivage, August 22, 1812. John (February 22, 1801–February 12, 1826), never married; a lawyer and politician. Enoch Huse (July 27, 1803–1826), did not marry.

Wife: Charlotte Gray Brooks (November 4, 1800–July 2, 1859), daughter of Peter C. Brooks, a leading Boston businessman; married May 8, 1822.

Children: Grace Fletcher (?–January 6, 1836). Anne Gorham (March 3, 1823–October

18, 1844). Charlotte Brooks (August 13, 1825–December 15, 1879), married Capt. Henry Augustus Wise, U.S.N., on August 20, 1850. Grace Webster (December 24, 1827–January 8, 1836). Edward Brooks (May 6, 1830–November 5, 1861), married Helen Cordis Adams, October 24, 1855. An unnamed daughter (January 30–February 9, 1833). Henry Sidney (December 31, 1834–October 4, 1898), married Katherine Pickman Fay on June 26, 1866, diplomat, civic leader. William (October 10, 1839–February 16, 1910), educator, U.S. Representative.

One of the great orators in American history, Edward Everett is perhaps best remembered for finishing second best to another master, Abraham Lincoln, in their addresses at Gettysburg. His life demonstrated brilliance at scholarship, devotion to public service, and remarkable but short-lived efforts as a minister of the Gospel.

Everett's father, as his son later would be, was a Harvard graduate and a minister. Oliver Everett's bad health caused him to retire from the ministry and, again like the son, he was nominated for Congress. There the similarity ends, as Oliver Everett was defeated in his campaign as the Federalist nominee. When Edward was eight his father died, and the family moved to Boston. For a short period Edward received instruction from young Daniel Webster. Webster's older brother — the regular instructor — had taken ill. This association began a lifelong friendship. More formal schooling was received at Phillips Academy in Exeter, New Hampshire. Everett distinguished himself at Phillips, as he did in every school he attended. Classical subjects fascinated the boy. At age 13 Edward started his studies at Harvard. General literature and foreign languages were staples of his curriculum, but theology perhaps intrigued him most of all. He would become proficient in German and French, and knowledgeable in Greek and Latin as well. Poetry was a pastime for the student, both reading and writing it. Edward graduated from Harvard at age 17 with highest honors, though he was the youngest member of his class. Divinity studies at the same institution then occupied him for three years, at which time he received his Masters. The year of his

graduation Edward desired to visit the South. He acquired a letter of introduction to Thomas Jefferson from John Adams. Unfortunately Edward did not meet the sage of Monticello.

The prestigious honor of appointment as pastor at Brattle Street Unitarian Church, Boston, came when Everett was only 20. Though he would serve only one year, his skills at the pulpit were remarkable. He had been reluctant to accept the post, as he wanted to go to Europe to study. The privilege of ministering to the largest church in Boston was too appealing, however. Even at age 20, Everett proved a more effective preacher than his beloved predecessor, a renowned minister with decades of experience. Everett's speaking style was not to change radically throughout his religious, academic, and public careers. He was eloquent, dramatic, almost (in Henry Clay's words) "too theatrical." The listener would become spellbound; the diction, phrasing, and delivery were almost perfect. At times he was too perfect, appearing artificial and too formal. Altogether, however, he had an overpowering effect.

Yet for all his success, Everett found the pulpit unfulfilling. He longed to take up his deferred plans to study in Europe. The opportunity came when his alma mater offered him the first professorship of Greek literature. A two-year leave for travel and study in Europe would precede his teaching duties. This Everett eagerly accepted. The two years were spent at Göttingen, Germany, and then two years happily stretched to four. It was 1819 before the professor-to-be returned to Harvard and assumed his responsibilities. He had met kings, poets, historians, the leaders of science, politics, and the arts. He was well prepared, overprepared, for his professorship.

There was little in teaching young college students that could long hold Everett's fascination. Ralph Waldo Emerson was a student, and Emerson worshiped his youthful instructor. Their friendship would continue throughout Everett's life. The professor also took on the duties of editing the *North American Review*, an important literary periodical that had been poorly written and edited for years. Circulation increased fivefold under Everett.

It was a critical success as well, many of the articles being written by its editor.

Restlessness was Everett's constant goad. Marriage to the daughter of a wealthy merchant made his financial state secure and enabled his thoughts to wander to loftier matters. The Greek Revolution so stirred the emotions in Everett that he campaigned for appointment as a special ambassador to that country to report on the revolution. Even his friend Daniel Webster could not gain Everett the appointment. Some grand outlet for his interests was needed. Finally Everett decided on a race for Congress in 1824. The young professor thought he had received permission to continue at the university should he win. Win he did, easily. A factor in his success was sudden fame gained by giving a stirring oration on the occasion of Lafayette's visit to Boston. Everett had not yet announced for Congress, but the speech made his selection and eventual election an easy task. The vote was 1,529 to 603. Somewhat cooler was the reaction from the Harvard administration. They perhaps had little appreciated Everett's abandoning the pulpit, since many of them were ministers themselves. Even less appealing to them was his clear lack of dedication to teaching. Everett unhappily resigned his position at the school, but the decision seemed the right one for both sides.

For five terms Everett would serve in Congress. His relations with President John Quincy Adams, also from Massachusetts, were good. The new Congressman gained influence on Capitol Hill and in the executive branch. In a speech dealing with a constitutional amendment changing the method of electing presidents, Everett gratuitously spoke on the slavery question. In words that would immediately bring him condemnation in the North, he cited the Bible's language, "Slaves, obey your masters." Everett argued slavery was a positive good that in time would fade away but for now should be supported. Everett would spend much of the succeeding months defending and explaining his sentiments. More humane was his call for civilized treatment of American Indians. Everett's indignation was obvious at the forced removal of Creek and Cherokees from Georgia to west of the Mississippi River.

On other matters, he was President Adams' champion in the House. After Andrew Jackson's election in 1828, Everett's influence was greatly reduced. His chairmanship of the House Committee on Foreign Relations was lost in the political revolution wrought by Jackson.

Everett represented eloquently and consistently the conservative, established citizens of Massachusetts. He supported the rechartering of the Second Bank of the United States and a high tariff favorable to the manufacturing North. Only on the slavery question did he show deference to the South, but he was also an active member of the Colonization Society. Tiring of his back-bench role as a minority Whig member of the House, Everett retired in 1834 and returned to Boston. He then stood for election as governor of the Commonwealth, receiving the nomination of both the Whig and the Anti-Masonic parties in 1835. A sizeable majority of the voters agreed to advance the ex–Congressman's political career.

The day before his inauguration in 1836, the new governor's daughter died. Public life gave him little time to recover from his depression. He filled his administration with capable subordinates. Being a good judge of character and talent was one of Everett's many virtues. Public education, not surprising for the scholar and former educator, was a high priority. Great improvements in education occurred during his four successive one-year terms. A frequent traveler throughout the state, Everett was a vigorous and diligent chief executive. As he would prove in other posts, the governor also enjoyed ceremony; he was dignified and a little pompous in his high position, but he was also effective.

For four elections he beat the same man, Marcus Morton, for the governorship. Morton finally succeeded on the fifth. In Massachusetts at that time a majority of the popular vote was needed for election, and in 1839 Morton got a majority over Everett, by exactly one vote. Morton had 51,034 of the 102,066, or the exact minimum for victory. Everett received approximately three hundred fewer votes, with the rest scattered to other candidates. There were many grounds upon which to contest the election, but Everett retired gracefully and without protest. Nonetheless, he felt rejected by the defeat. Any personal or popular rejection of his ambitions would always be painful.

After a brief rest, Everett toured several countries in Europe. While there he learned he had been appointed ambassador to England. It was a post he had before leaving for Europe let Secretary of State Webster know he wanted. Southerners opposed him because of a statement made during the previous campaign. Everett had unequivocally opposed the slave trade and the extension of slavery into any new territories. The vote for confirmation was close, but Everett won. There were many conflicts between the two countries, including the boundary between Maine and Canada, the British interdiction of American ships on the high seas to discover whether they were engaged in the importation of slaves, and the compensation for vessels and cargo retained by the British under these circumstances. Of more interest to the ambassador than any substantive matters, was his opportunity to meet so many of England's great writers and thinkers. Everett always reveled in the conversation of learned people, and there was much reveling during his four years in London. His own reputation as a scholar, writer of poetry, translator of foreign works, and other literary achievements made him accepted by the intelligentsia as an equal at the very least. So enjoyable was the experience that in April 1843, Everett refused a suggestion from President John Tyler that he undertake a mission to China.

As his tour of duty to England drew to a close, Everett began to be mentioned as a candidate for vice president on the 1844 Whig ticket. That did not transpire. With Democrat James K. Polk becoming president in 1845, it was only a matter of time before the recall of the Whig ambassador. Everett would be charged with being too friendly with England during his service there. Yet as much as he admired that country, he never forgot that America's interests had to come first.

A new position was waiting for Everett when he returned to Boston in September 1845, after a five-year stay abroad. The presidency of Harvard University was available. The post had surprisingly little attraction for

Everett. He rightly foresaw that it would be arduous labor and drudgery, with little time for scholarly pursuits. There was no dean at the school, and the disciplinary responsibilities of the presidency at times seemed to overwhelm his larger administrative tasks. Yet at the behest of almost all his friends, Everett accepted reluctantly. The lack of freedom and the incredible workload became immediately apparent. He became sensitive and critical of every student defect, as well as many in the faculty. His three years' service was not particularly successful, though he achieved a measure of calm at the school.

So total was his relief in 1848 at being free of the Harvard presidency, that his frequent problem with ulcers was alleviated. Doctor's orders had finally caused him to take the step of resigning, even though he felt he had not accomplished many goals at the college. With the Whigs back in the White House, Everett had hopes of being returned to his favorite post in London, but it was not to be. Other suggestions were that he run for Congress. The University of Missouri wanted him as their president, but he had enough of that kind of chore. Literary pursuits enticed him, including writing a history of the United States, but those endeavors died aborning. Finally he began a collection of his dear friend Daniel Webster's speeches.

Webster's famous Seventh of March (1850) speech was not one of the reasons Everett so fervently supported Webster. The Massachusetts senator's call for compromise by offering the South vigorous enforcement of the Fugitive Slave Law fell on Everett's unsympathetic ears. Slavery was anathema to Everett by now, and participating in the return of escaped slaves made him feel a party to slavery's outrages. The death of President Zachary Taylor enabled the new president, Millard Fillmore, to fill his own cabinet, and Senator Webster was made secretary of state. Again political disappointment haunted Everett, as his longheld dream of being a United States senator was denied when someone else was chosen to replace Webster. Everett did greatly assist Webster in one of the most popular state papers issued while Webster was secretary. The cause of Hungarian freedom was a popular concern in the early 1850s. The new secretary of state found a haughty letter on his desk from Austrian authorities, who then controlled Hungary, protesting American interference in the revolution. Webster requested that Everett draft a reply to Austrian chargé d'affaires Hulsemann, which Everett did in bombastic, patriotic, forceful terms. American reaction was uniformly favorable, but Everett's authorship was not announced. Webster might well have identified Everett after the administration had left office, but by then he was dead. A later and poorly conceived effort by Everett to show his authorship was condemned by many who thought this would-be friend of the deceased Webster was trying to steal glory from his grave.

With Webster's death, the vacancy in the State Department was offered to Everett, and accepted. Before Everett took office in November 1852, Democrat Franklin Pierce had won the presidency. It was clear Everett's State Department leadership would be short-lived. His most significant achievement in that short period was the authoring of a dramatic but diplomatic response to a French and English suggestion that American interests in making Cuba a part of the United States be discarded, and that instead the three nations declare Cuba to be the property of Spain. The special interest America had in this island was carefully explained by the secretary; the history of territorial expansion was detailed. The secretary then insisted it was beyond the power of the executive to bind America from purchasing Cuba at some future date.

On February 2, 1853, the Massachusetts legislature elected Secretary of State Everett to the United States Senate. The office to which he had so long aspired would not prove satisfying, as Everett was constantly embroiled in controversy. The Kansas-Nebraska bill was introduced by Senator Stephen Douglas, and Everett was shocked. The repeal of the Missouri Compromise, leading to the opening of all territories to the possibility of slavery, was repugnant to the Massachusetts senator. He delivered a forceful speech denouncing Douglas's bill, but Everett was quite ill at the time. An all-night Senate session preceded the final vote on the legislation, and because of his ill-

ness Everett went home in the early morning after being assured no vote would be taken. Surprisingly, a roll call was made, the bill passed easily, and Everett was absent. The charge was immediately made that he was dodging the issue; many said Everett's sights were on the presidency and he was therefore trying to avoid taking a stand. The charge was ludicrous. The senator's opposition was clear. A few days after the voting Everett tried to have his vote recorded, but he was refused. Another bitter outcry against Everett soon arose when he prepared a pamphlet demonstrating that he had been the secret author of the Hulsemann letter concerning America's support for Hungary. Everett was aghast at allegations that he was stealing Webster's glory.

On May 12, 1854, Everett sent a letter to the governor stating he wanted to resign. Ill health was the reason given, and that was accurate enough. Also true, however, was his brother-in-law Charles Francis Adams' statement that the senator was "stuff not good enough to wear in rainy weather, though bright enough in sunshine." He just could not stand the abuse and controversy. Everett was not a fighter. Public issues in the 1850s made the weak-willed out of place.

Boston was the place of retreat. Everett established himself as a literary and civic leader, contributing to the founding of the public library among other endeavors. Eighteen hundred fifty-six was the one hundredth anniversary of George Washington's first Boston visit, and Everett wanted to commemorate the occasion. He wrote the Boston Library Association inquiring as to their interest in his delivering such a speech on February 22, and they were enthusiastic. In time, Everett would deliver the speech on over a hundred different occasions. "The Character of Washington" became his best-known and most successful, if not his best, oration. A Ladies Mt. Vernon Association had been formed to purchase and preserve Washington's home. Everett decided to give the proceeds of his Mt. Vernon speeches to the association and traveled nationwide in the effort. Before he was finished, almost $70,000 was raised for the project.

Though the Whig party had almost disappeared by 1856, Everett continued to count himself among its members. In the campaign of 1860, a new party was formed. The Constitutional Union Party was composed of very respectable, conservative, and for the most part, old men who rejected the extremism of secessionists and of abolition. In May their convention met in Baltimore. Everett had informed his supporters that he did not want to presidential nomination and his wishes were heeded. He had never conceived that he might then be given the vice presidential spot, but he was, unanimously. It took two weeks of encouragement by friends for him to accept. He knew the cause was hopeless. He and presidential nominee John Bell had served in Congress together, each had similar views on the divisive issues in the campaign, and they were good friends. Everett's lengthy statement accepting the nomination gave the reasons why he did not want it. It was one of the most half-hearted agreements to a place on a national ticket ever written.

The outcome of the election was no surprise. With Lincoln's inauguration in March 1861, and the secession of the South, the old Massachusetts statesman began his last act of great public service. Support for the war was weak in many areas of the North. Everett undertook another strenuous tour, delivering 23 separately composed speeches, many of them delivered several times. His most renowned address was his two-hour speech at Gettysburg. The dedication of that great battlefield and its cemetery was an occasion calling for a tremendous oratorical effort, and Everett undertook one. He studied the battlefield firsthand in order to get a better understanding of the ebb and flow of the battle. On November 19, 1863, he delivered a stirring and brilliant two-hour speech that kept his audience rapt for the entire period. Unfortunately for its place in history, a two-minute address by the Civil War president followed, meant only to be a short statement consecrating the grounds. There were two Gettysburg addresses that day, but history has effectively recorded only one. In truth, history remembers accurately. Everett admitted, in a letter to Lincoln, that the president had captured in two minutes more of the essence of the occasion that Everett had in two hours.

During the war, Everett became increasingly fond of Lincoln. He believed the president the perfect man for the times. Everett's unequivocal support for the war effort also caused a break with many of his longtime friends. One beneficial change in opinion came from Charles Francis Adams, who admitted that in this ultimate crisis Everett had at last demonstrated he could shake off his fears and timidity. On occasion Adams believed Everett was "almost like ... a woman" in his desire to avoid conflict, but during the war he "spoke forth at last with all his power what he really felt. To me [Adams] his four last years appear worth more than all the rest of his life...." It was the last cause Everett would espouse, as he died on January 15, 1865, after the result of the bloody conflict was at last evident.

Analysis of Qualifications

Edward Everett wore many hats in life. He was a clergyman, college professor and president, a diplomat and a statesman. His literary brilliance became obvious at an early age, but because of his restlessness, the scholarship he could have left for posterity far exceeded his actual effort. Though serving only one year as a pastor in a Boston church, his powers as demonstrated from the pulpit were extraordinary. Most of all, Everett was a tremendously, uniquely effective orator, one of the greatest in this country's history. Francis Jeffrey of the *Edinburgh Review* told Everett in December 1813, "I do not hesitate to say that I consider you the most remarkable young man I have seen in America." Everett's uniqueness was in his intellectual brilliance, not in his skills as a politician.

Everett's speaking style was ornate, graceful, perfect in organization and delivery. He committed his speeches to memory, but made extemporaneous additions and deletions as he was delivering them. His magnetic presence added much to the effect of his style, as did a tremendous breadth of allusions drawn from his extensive, almost encyclopedic knowledge. His career is dotted with incredibly successful orations that left his listeners at first stunned and silent, but finally deafening in their cheers.

In the diplomatic field Everett's contributions were in his writings and speeches. His explanation of America's position in relation to Cuba, and his ghostwriting of Webster's famous Hulsemann letter explaining American support for Hungarian independence, were perhaps the high points of his diplomacy. He engaged in no extensive negotiations, contributed no bold policy, but excelled in delineating eloquently America's position.

It was in the political world that Everett failed to dominate. For ten years he was a United States congressman, and for one year a U.S. senator. No crucial legislation was shepherded through Congress by him, but he did lend his oratorical abilities in support of a high tariff, the rechartering of the national bank, and other conservative issues. At first Everett spoke in favor of protecting slavery, even quoting Biblical support for his position. Always Everett showed religious zeal, as befits a former Unitarian minister. Though he would come to oppose the extension of slavery into any new American territories, Everett still attempted to prevent slavery from dominating Congressional debate and dividing the country.

Charles Francis Adams thought highly of Everett, but also thought him incapable of performance during times of controversy and conflict. So exhausted, and ulcerous, was Everett as a result of his three-year presidency at Harvard, that he had to resign. He admitted some of his reluctance for conflict during his Gettysburg Address: "A sad foreboding of what would ensue, if war should break out between North and South, has haunted me through life, and led me, perhaps too long, to tread in the path of hopeless compromise, and the fond endeavor to conciliate those who were predetermined not to be conciliated." It is hard to imagine Everett performing vigorously in the trials of the presidency at so critical a time as the 1860s. His greatest achievements were in scholarship and learning, not in government.

Edward Everett should be remembered fondly and respectfully as an intellectual, literary giant of the nineteenth century. His failure to receive the presidency, however, should not be regretted.

EVERETT BIBLIOGRAPHY

Dozer, Donald M. "Lincoln's Rival at Gettysburg." *Filson Club History Quarterly* 45 (1971), pp. 77–81.

Everett, Edward Franklin. *Descendants of Richard Everett of Dedham, Mass.* Boston (1902).

Frothingham, Paul Revere. *Edward Everett, Orator and Statesman.* Boston and New York City (1925, reprinted 1971).

Long, Orie William. *Literary Pioneers, Early American Explorers of European Culture.* Cambridge, Mass. (1935), pp. 63–76.

Reid, Ronald F. *Edward Everett: Unionist Orator.* Westport, Conn. (1990).

Varg, Paul A. *Edward Everett: The Intellectual in the Turmoil of Politics.* Selingsgrove, Penn. (1992).

Yanikoski, Richard A. "Edward Everett and the Advancement of Higher Education." Unpublished doctoral dissertation, University of Chicago (1987).

Elections of 1861

CONFEDERATE STATES OF AMERICA

Provisional government. Forty-three delegates from Mississippi, Florida, Georgia, Alabama, Louisiana and South Carolina held a convention in Montgomery, beginning on February 4, 1861. Texas had also seceded, but did not get delegates to the convention. On February 9, the delegates voted for provisional leaders who would serve until a permanent constitution became effective.

President— Jefferson Davis, named unanimously by the six states, each state having one vote. Robert Toombs (Ga.), Alexander H.

Stephens (Ga.), Howell Cobb (Ga.), Robert Barnwell Rhett (S.C.), and William Lowndes Yancey (Ala.) were also prominently mentioned. The convention was intent on making its choice unanimous, thereby duplicating the consensus achieved in 1789 when George Washington was named. Each state caucused prior to the formal balloting, and after it appeared Davis had strong support all states agreed to vote for him. *Vice president*— Alexander Hamilton Stephens, named unanimously after Georgia, whose three candidates for the presidency were all defeated, was given the consolation prize of choosing the vice president.

CONVENTION, February 9, 1861
Winners
   Jefferson Davis, Alexander Stephens
Losers
   None
   Government under permanent constitution. The Confederate government provided for a general election to be held on the first Wednesday in November 1861, to elect a president and vice president for six-year terms beginning February 18, 1862. No nominations

were made, but the incumbents were continued in office without meaningful opposition. General Pierre G.T. Beauregard (La.) made a feeble effort to gain support, but did not receive serious consideration. The states involved in the election were Alabama, Arkansas, Florida, Georgia, Louisiana, Mississippi, North and South Carolina, Tennessee, Texas, and Virginia. Missouri and Kentucky were admitted to the Confederacy after the election.

GENERAL ELECTION, November 8, 1861
Popular Vote
   Jefferson Davis 403,760*
Electoral Vote
   Davis-Stephens — 109 (11 states)
Winners
   Jefferson Davis, Alexander Hamilton Stephens
Losers
   None

BIBLIOGRAPHY
Rable, George. *The Confederate Republic: A Revolution Against Politics.* Chapel Hill (1994).

Election of 1864

NOMINATIONS
   Republican Party (National Union Party) Convention (3rd): June 7–8, 1864, at Front Street Theatre, Baltimore, Maryland. *President*— Abraham Lincoln, nominated on the first ballot with 494 of 519 votes. *Vice presi-*

dent— Andrew Johnson, nominated on the first ballot, after numerous vote changes (had 200 before vote switching started) with 492 out of 519 votes cast. Hannibal Hamlin (Me.) and Daniel Dickinson (N.Y.) were the other contenders.

This total is an extrapolation from available returns from congressional races that were held on the same day. Davis was apparently on the ballot in all, or nearly all, of the congressional districts. No record of any votes for any other presidential candidate has been discovered. Some vote totals for Davis have been found. Complete returns from Georgia show that he and Stephens got 50,813 votes, and none were reported for anyone else; the total cast for congressional candidates in Georgia was 47,928. Thus using available totals in other states' congressional races appears a close approximation for a total, nationwide presidential vote. Sources: "Election Returns for Electors for President and Vice President of the Confederate States of America," Executive Minutes, Georgia Department of Archives and History; Martis, Kenneth C., *The Historical Atlas of the Congresses of the Confederate States of America, 1861–1865,* New York (1994), esp. p. 76 n. 51; Rable, George C., *The Confederate Public: A Revolution Against Politics,* Chapel Hill (1994); "Returns of Electors for President and Vice President of the Confederate States of America," War Department Collection of Confederate Records (Record Group 109), National Archives, Washington.

Democratic Party (9th): August 29–31, 1864, at the Amphitheatre, Chicago, Illinois. *President*— George McClellan, nominated on the first ballot with 202½ of 231 votes cast. *Vice president*— George Pendleton, nominated on the second ballot with a unanimous vote, having received 55 of 226 votes on the first ballot. James Guthrie (Ky.), Lazarus Powell (Ky.), and George Cass (Pa.), were other candidates.

GENERAL ELECTION, November 8, 1864

Popular Vote

Lincoln 2,218,388
McClellan 1,812,807
Others.   692

Electoral Vote

Lincoln-Johnson — 212 (22 states)
McClellan-Pendleton — 21 (3 states)

Winners

Abraham Lincoln, 16th president
Andrew Johnson, 16th vice president

Losers

George McClellan, George Pendleton

---

*1864 presidential nominee —
Democratic Party*

George B. McClellan

Full name: George Brinton McClellan.
State represented: New Jersey.
Birth: December 3, 1826, in Philadelphia, Pennsylvania.
Age on Inauguration Day (March 4, 1865): 38 years, 3 months.
Education: Preparatory schools in Philadelphia; University of Pennsylvania, 1840–1842, but did not graduate; West Point Military Academy, 1842–1846, graduated second in his class.
Religion: Presbyterian.
Ancestry/prominent relatives: Family had come from Scotland in early eighteenth century. Great-grandfather Samuel McClellan was a brigadier general in the American Revolution. George B. McClellan, Jr. (son), was a U.S. representative. George B. McClellan, Sr. (father), and John H. McClellan (brother) were eminent Philadelphia surgeons. Henry Brainerd McClellan (cousin) was a Confederate officer and Virginia educator.
Occupation: Soldier and engineer.
Public offices: Unsuccessful Democratic nominee for president, 1864; chief engineer, New York City Department of Docks, 1870; governor of New Jersey, January 15, 1878–January 18, 1881.
Home: Orange, New Jersey.
Death: October 29, 1885, in Orange, New Jersey, age 58 years, 11 months.
Burial: Trenton, New Jersey.
Personal characteristics: 5'8" tall; huge chest; broad, muscular shoulders; bore himself proudly with true soldier image; auburn-red hair and mustache.
Father: George McClellan (December 23, 1796–May 9, 1847), prominent Philadelphia physician.
Mother: Elizabeth Brinton (?–?), married in 1820.
Siblings: John Hill (August 13, 1823–July 20, 1874), a physician. Arthur (c. 1838–February 22, 1904). Frederica (?–?), married T.C. English. Mary (?–?).
Wife: Ellen Mary Marcy (?–February 12, 1915), married May 22, 1860, daughter of Randolph B. Marcy, McClellan's commander in Red River exploration and first cousin of Gov. William L. Marcy of New York.
Children: George Brinton, Jr. (called "Max") (November 23, 1865–November 30, 1940), born in Dresden, Germany; a lawyer, U.S. representative, mayor of New York City, and college professor; married Georgiana Heckscher in 1889. Mary (called "May") (October 12, 1861–September 11, 1945); married Paul Desprez; lived in France.
Historic sites/memorials: Statue at intersection of Connecticut Avenue and Columbia Road, N.W., in Washington, D.C.

Few of the also-rans are as controversial as George B. McClellan, and in McClellan's case the debate never centers around his political career. McClellan's service as general-in-chief of the Union armies for part of the American Civil War has been the subject of countless books, articles, student theses, not to mention heated private arguments. It is not on that facet, which is probably the most important, of his career that this sketch will focus, but instead on his development into a major political figure.

Born in 1826 into the home of a prominent medical doctor in Philadelphia, George was an energetic, intelligent child who excelled in school. After finishing his preparatory education in Philadelphia, George left for the University of Pennsylvania in 1840 at the age of 13. There he remained for two years. Though technically not old enough to be admitted, McClellan entered West Point in June 1842, after the 16-year age minimum was waived due to his precocity, mental as well as physical. He performed brilliantly; his appreciation of that fact was revealed by a growing, if restrained conceit about his own abilities. Because he excelled, at graduation he would have a choice as to the branch of the service he would enter. He finally decided upon the engineers.

On June 30, 1846, Brevet Second Lieutenant McClellan graduated second in his class and looked forward eagerly to service in the just-developing war in Mexico. He was assigned to a company of miners and sappers in Mexico. McClellan early revealed his skills at training troops and was selected to help prepare a new company for the war then raging south of the Texas border. By January 1847, the troops were marching towards Tampico, working on road and bridge construction. In the battle of Cerro Gordo he led an impressive assault, and within a week of his achievement was promoted to second lieutenant. Gallantry and skill in subsequent battles at Contreras and Churubusco gained him a first lieutenant's rank, and then a captaincy was given him after the assault on Chapultepec.

After gallant service in Mexico, McClellan was placed back at West Point, serving as an instructor in practical engineering from 1847 until 1851. His intelligence and fluency in several languages was put to good use when he translated the French regulations on bayonet exercises and modified them for use in the American Army. These regulations were soon adopted by the army as standards. In the summer of 1851, McClellan moved out of the classroom and into practical application of his engineering knowledge in construction of Fort

Delaware. McClellan then joined an expedition exploring the Red River between Texas and Indian Territory. Engineering work took him next to Texas for rivers and harbors improvements. Surveying a railroad route brought him to the attention of Secretary of War Jefferson Davis, future president of the Confederacy. Davis was so pleased with the young engineer's work that he asked him to continue his railway studies.

Such projects as these were McClellan's life for his first years in the army. When an increase in the size of the regular army was authorized in 1855, McClellan was made a captain in one of the new cavalry regiments. But rather than join the regiment, McClellan was sent to Europe with several other officers to study military operations in the Crimean conflict. Studying the Russian army was McClellan's particular responsibility. McClellan's report on his observations included several recommendations for changes in American practices, including a new type of saddle for use by the cavalry. The McClellan saddle was soon the standard in the army. The design remained in use virtually unchanged until the cavalry stopped being a factor in the American military in the 1930s.

Though recognition and some promotions had been given McClellan, there seemed little future in the peacetime army. There was certainly little income. Therefore, in January 1857, he resigned from the army and became chief engineer for the Illinois Central Railroad, based in Chicago. Within a year McClellan was vice president of the road, in charge of Illinois operations.

McClellan's opportunity to become a part of the Illinois Central came in November 1856, when the railroad's president offered the promising, young, ambitious army engineer a salary of three thousand dollars per year, more than twice his army pay. The vice presidency of the road was to be his as soon as he became familiar with operations. The Panic of 1857 soon hit, and McClellan was put in charge of paring all unnecessary expenses. He took a tour of the entire line in order to determine where expenses could be cut. The duties of railroad vice president brought him into frequent contact with one of the railway's attorneys, Abraham Lincoln. The same month that Lincoln was nominated for president in 1860, McClellan won another type of prize, marriage to Nellie Marcy. She was the daughter of an old army friend. A few weeks later McClellan and his new bride moved to Cincinnati where he took the position of president of the Ohio and Mississippi Railroad. This was an important east-west railroad that intersected and interchanged freight with the Illinois Central. Soon thereafter he was named president of the St. Louis, Missouri, and Cincinnati Railroad.

The future conflict between McClellan and Lincoln was presaged in 1858 when Lincoln and Senator Douglas were conducting their famous series of debates as part of their campaigns for the Illinois senate seat then held by Douglas. McClellan, as a vice president of the railroad, on several occasions placed at Douglas's disposal the private railroad car maintained by the road for its president. No similar privilege was accorded Lincoln.

McClellan's railroading career lasted until April 23, 1861, when he was appointed a major general in charge of all of the Ohio volunteers. The governor of Ohio had offered him the assignment, but since McClellan was not an Ohio resident a quick enactment was needed from the legislature to permit him to serve. This was accomplished in a day. McClellan had been well thought of for his ten-year army career. Soon he was getting additional offers. Training the Ohio volunteers was his first task, but the national authorities wanted him too. McClellan was named on May 3 to be a major general in the regular army, with command of the Department of the Ohio. His responsibilities included Ohio, Indiana, and Illinois, and this area was later enlarged to include additional states. McClellan was ordered to take control of western Virginia, thought to be strongly unionist in sentiment, and keep it from joining the Confederacy. McClellan succeeded in taking control of the area's railroads, and then personally conducted the military campaign that gained the region for the North. Lee's attempt to reverse the loss failed. Congress voted its unanimous thanks for the achievement.

Within days of McClellan's well-published victory in Virginia, General McDowell was suffering ignominious defeat at the battle of Bull Run. Lincoln began to cast about for McDowell's replacement, and ordered McClellan to Washington. The president appointed him to command the Army of the Potomac. McClellan had now found his most useful rule. Frantically immersing himself in the details of training the vast collection of civilian soldiers that had been raised since Fort Sumter, McClellan soon heard delightful praise, much of it extravagant, for his skills. The savior of the North he was called, his small but impressive victories gained earlier in Virginia were magnified into stupendous martial achievements. McClellan had no experience with operations as large as were now expected of him; no American general had ever commanded as large an army as was now under this 35-year-old's control. The significance went to McClellan's head quickly. He reported to his wife from Washington, "I find myself in a new and strange position here ... all deferring to me. By some strange operation of magic I seem to have become the power of the land.... When I was in the Senate chamber today and saw these old men flocking around me;.... I began to feel how great the task committed to me; ... who would have thought, when we were married, that I should so soon be called upon to save my country? ... I shall carry this thing *en grand* and crush the rebels in one campaign." He added, "The people call on me to save the country. I must save it, and cannot respect anything that is in the way.... I would cheerfully take the dictatorship and agree to lay down my life when the country is saved."

T. Harry Williams, the eminent Civil War historian, looked at the numerous letters McClellan wrote to his wife at this stage and said

> Here ... are most of the ingredients of George B. McClellan — a fascination with people in the mass but at a proper distance; a conviction that these people who stare at him so intently are thinking that only he can save them; a determination to save those who so adore him, whether they be civilians or soldiers; a rising doubt that he may not be able to accomplish his purpose because the enemy, who at first appeared so contemptible, was

suddenly increasing in numbers; and a gnaw-ing fear that men on his own side, men in high places, are for mysterious but sinister reasons conspiring to overthrow him [*McClellan, Sher-man, and Grant*, p. 21].

McClellan's first impression of the com-mander-in-chief, Abraham Lincoln, was unfa-vorable. He thought Lincoln out of his league as president, a kind-hearted but hopelessly ill-schooled man. In time McClellan would refer to the president as the "original Gorilla."

Few people have ever denied McClellan recognition as an able, even magnificent trainer of troops. Even Ulysses Grant, who in the early stages of the war had sat for three days vainly trying to see McClellan in order to get an appointment to his staff, felt McClel-lan was a unique inspiration to the army. Yet McClellan never wanted to use, to soil, to injure this fine-tuned machine that he was constructing, the Army of the Potomac. Pres-ident Lincoln and his advisers by the end of the year were impatient. Winfield Scott retired in November as general-in-chief of the armies, and McClellan received the appointment. The new commanding general feared, indeed grossly exaggerated, the Rebels' strength and refused to move on Southern positions until he was reinforced. Finally Lincoln took the ini-tiative and issued General War Order No. 1, requiring all Northern armies to advance on February 22, 1862. McClellan had a different plan for attacking the Confederates than did Lincoln, and a compromise was finally reached. McClellan personally joined the Army of the Potomac in this campaign, and was consequently relieved of his position as general of the armies. The ensuing series of battles was called the Peninsular Campaign. The attempt to capture Richmond, the Con-federate capital, ended in disaster. McClellan blamed the civilian authorities for preventing reinforcements from General McDowell, whose troops had been ordered back to Wash-ington to thwart an expected attack by "Stone-wall" Jackson. The bloody battle of Cold Har-bor, in which waves of Union troops were sacrificed against strong Southern positions, was a disaster. McClellan wrote the secretary of war a report on the battle, and revealed his persecution complex when he said, "If I save

the army now, I tell you plainly I owe no thanks to you or any other person in Wash-ington. You have done your best to sacrifice this army."

Before McClellan would advance from the position he had taken after the defeats around Richmond, he insisted on more reinforce-ments. Finally in August the army was ordered withdrawn, and McClellan was relieved of command.

McClellan was placed in charge of reorga-nizing the troops. But soon his replacement as commanding general, Henry Halleck, suffered even graver defeats. In September 1862, Mc-Clellan was placed back in command, rejoined the army, and ordered an advance on General Robert E. Lee. The Battle of Antietam was the result, a Union victory that was not followed up with pursuit of the retreating Confederate troops. Lee's army escaped because of McClel-lan's uncertainty about further sacrifice of his troops. McClellan had a basic, understandable squeamishness about war, understandable that is except in a general whose duty was to pros-ecute the conflict. He became almost ill at the grisly sight of wounded and dead soldiers, and was reluctant to give orders which would inevitably lead to more killing. These delays led to McClellan's being replaced by General Ambrose Burnside on November 7, 1862. McClellan was sent to Trenton, New Jersey, to await further assignment. The assignment never came. By this time, Lincoln and his advisers had become seriously concerned about McClellan's growing political involvement, and were not going to reappoint him to a high command.

McClellan's procrastination at several crit-ical junctures during his command led the press and others to charge him with disloyalty. McClellan struck back at his critics through speeches, but also through action. It is not hard to conclude that the principal reason for his political career was to gain vindication for what he though was mistreatment at the hands of Lincoln and the war department.

The general was forbidden from moving to New York City, for Lincoln feared he would develop into a strong political force there. Top Democratic officials were in frequent corre-spondence with the deposed commander, and fears of an alliance between them were understandable. His first blatant foray into politics came when he endorsed the Democratic candidate for governor of Pennsylvania. A lifelong Democrat, states' rights advocate and anti-abolitionist, McClellan had become even more certain of his Democratic allegiance since the war began. The Lincoln administration and Republicans in general were outraged at this high-ranking officer in the army endorsing a political candidate, but it seems evident that the administration had given him little else to occupy his time. By January of 1864, he was touring New England, testing the waters of a presidential race. His name was high on almost every Democrat's list of possible candidates in 1864, mainly because of his treatment at the hands of the federal government. Many thought he was persecuted, and McClellan agreed with that sentiment. Election to the presidency would not only redeem his honor, it would in most supporters' minds end the war. McClellan was disgusted with the direction the war had taken, particularly since the Emancipation Proclamation in September 1862. The war to restore the Union, which McClellan heartily endorsed, had been turned into a war to abolish slavery. The latter direction of the conflict was repugnant to McClellan's states' rights sensibilities.

Three candidates were prominent in the Democratic speculation: Horatio Seymour, Governor Thomas Seymour of Connecticut, and General McClellan. Horatio Seymour did not want the prize. A groundswell of popular support seemed to be propelling McClellan towards the nomination, but he never definitely announced his interest. At no time did he encircle himself with advisers and supporters to work to gain the nomination. At the convention no one with authority to speak for McClellan was trying to line up delegates. McClellan's sense of honor, and perhaps his unfamiliarity with politics, made him recoil from direct involvement during the nomination process. The peace Democrats who were willing to sue for peace on almost any terms, and the war Democrats who criticized many of Lincoln's policies but not the basic concept of military victory, were bitter enemies. The party still had not recovered from the self-

destructive emotions that had rent the party in two in 1860. Copperheads (Northerners with Southern sympathies) such as the discredited Clement Vallandigham insisted that McClellan not be nominated, since McClellan supported the war. They succeeded in getting the following plank in the platform:

> Resolved. That this convention does explicitly declare, as the sense of the American people, that after four years of failure to restore the Union by the experiment of war, during which, under the pretense of a military necessity of war-power higher than the Constitution, the Constitution itself has been disregarded in every part, and public liberty and private right alike trodden down, ... justice, humanity, liberty and the public welfare demand that immediate efforts be made for a cessation of hostilities, with a view of an ultimate convention of the States, or other peaceable means, to the end that, at the earliest practicable moment, peace may be restored to the basis of the Federal Union of the States.

Despite the success of the peace Democrats in securing the platform, the war Democrats named their candidate easily on the first ballot. McClellan won 150 of the 225 votes. Vallandigham, of all people, rose to make the nomination unanimous, but it was not. The party remained badly divided when it left the convention, and the split would greatly hinder the chances of success.

McClellan procrastinated in politics as well as in war, and did not at first decide whether to accept the peace plank in the platform. Nine days later, however, in his formal letter acknowledging his accepting the nomination, he rejected the platform. Secession would not be accepted, he said, and it was his desire to return to the status quo before the war. That meant one Union, and it also meant slavery. Yet he would not immediately stop the hostilities, and until the South agreed to these terms the fighting must continue. McClellan called the peace platform a political vehicle for what was only one faction of the party, and he felt no compulsion to accept it. The peace Democrats were outraged, but in truth they had nowhere else to turn.

McClellan could not decide whether to resign from the army. It might have been his hope that he would be recalled to command

and he did not want to forego that opportunity. He was strongly criticized by the Republicans for remaining in the army, drawing his sizeable salary, but running for president. Yet McClellan did not run; he sat. Remaining in his Trenton, New Jersey, home, McClellan neither campaigned himself nor directed personally any coterie of supporters who campaigned for him. Few Democratic leaders conducted campaigns for the ticket in states other than their own, and little uniformity therefore developed. McClellan tried to make Lincoln's policies on civil liberties an issue. He condemned the frequent arrests of civilians and holding them without trial, the suppression of the press, and other actions taken in the name of military necessity. The high inflation rate and tremendous national debt were also criticized. Republicans counterattacked by charging McClellan with being little more than a traitor, with masquerading as a soldier when in fact he was as much of a Copperhead as any of the peace Democrats. Inefficiency, corruption, and tyranny were McClellan's issues, but they were not enough. He lost decisively to Lincoln, carrying only three states.

It has been charged that the counting of the soldier vote in 1864 was so irregular as to cause serious questions about who actually won the contest. The official total for the soldier vote, which was parceled out to the home states of the soldiers, was 116,887 for Lincoln, 33,748 for McClellan. For a man who was apparently revered by the vast majority of his soldiers when he was their commander, this total represents a dramatic, and perhaps questionable, reversal. Regardless of whether such practices affected the actual outcome, widespread fraud, intimidation, and other election abuses seemed to have been practiced against McClellan. Perhaps these too were in the name of military necessity, for many Republicans in high places thought the entire war would be lost if McClellan won the election.

McClellan, still a young man, hardly faded away. He resigned from the army on election day, and quietly accepted the results. For the next three years he was in Europe. Business ventures took up much of his time. His engineering background was put to good use when he was made chief engineer of the New York City Department of Docks in 1870, and he resigned after serving two years. The only political office he ever held, and only the second he sought, was the governorship of New Jersey from 1878 until 1881. It was a successful governorship, one apparently gained with very little effort expended on McClellan's part. He could not under the state constitution run for reelection. He died at his home in Orange, New Jersey, four years later.

Analysis of Qualifications

Few men could have inspired the devotion of his subordinates as did George McClellan during the Civil War. His obvious concern, even empathy, for his men made them love him. Another Union general, John Pope, said, "The effect of this man's presence upon the army of the Potomac — in sunshine or rain, in darkness or light, in victory or defeat — was electrical and too wonderful to make it worth while attempting to give a reason for it." McClellan's charisma, whatever its source or explanation, does not dispel the fact that he was an extremely troubled commander. He considered himself a savior, and many of his fellow soldiers and some civilians encouraged that belief and accepted it themselves. That he did not save the Union was, in his mind, solely explained by the interference of the Lincoln administration. The battle over the quality of McClellan's generalship will go on as long as there is interest in the Civil War. Even without resolving the conflict, however, conclusions can be reached about the McClellan personality that throw great light on his capacity for presidential leadership.

McClellan did not seem to have a good grip on reality. His dislike of combat made him constantly overestimate the Rebels' troop strength and demean his own. His self-image made it possible for him to create a messianic role for himself, and to see as conspiratorial miscreants all those who criticized any of his strategies or actions. He seemed to see things as he wanted to see them, not as they were. McClellan, basking in the glow of popular tribute, neither accepted praise objectively nor took the necessary action to make that faith justified. McClellan had many of the qualities of a great general, and perhaps he was merely called into the highest military command much too early. However, being called into a still higher command as president would have been an equally too abrupt promotion for the 38-year-old McClellan.

McClellan had absolutely no experience in politics. His preconvention passivity, which continued into the general election, indicated McClellan wanted more to be rewarded than to fight for the prize of the presidency. He was a man of many accomplishments — intelligent, fluent in almost all the western European languages, and an expert in many fields including engineering. He did not, however, seem to understand politics as the art of the possible. The general encountered disappointments that seemed to render him incapable of making a decision. Disagreements with others were viewed as persecutions; political opponents would have been enemies. A Republican Congress might easily have impeached a recalcitrant, abusive McClellan just as they did Andrew Johnson, who shared some of McClellan's personality deficiencies and many of his views on treating the South. There would have been no Thirteenth Amendment abolishing slavery, or later civil rights amendments and legislation if McClellan could have had his way. He wanted a Union reconstructed on the same order as before the war. It might be concluded then, that four years of war would have achieved nothing in the decades-long controversy between the North and South over slavery. A McClellan-sponsored peace might have had many seeds for decades more of bitter controversy over slavery.

McCLELLAN BIBLIOGRAPHY

Campbell, James Havelock. *McClellan*. New York City (1916).

Eckenrode, H.J. and Bryan Conrad. *George B. McClellan: The Man Who Saved the Union*. Chapel Hill, N.C. (1941).

Hassler, Warren W., Jr. *General George B. McClellan, Shield of the Union*. Baton Rouge (1957).

Kamaras, Nicholas P. "George B. McClellan and the Election of 1864." Unpublished doctoral dissertation, University of Delaware (1976).

Macartney, Clarence E. *Little Mac: The Life of General George B. McClellan*. Philadelphia (1940).

Michie, Peter S. *General McClellan*. New York City (1901).

Myers, William S. *General George Brinton McClel-*

lan: A Study in Personality. New York City (1934).

Nelson, Larry E. *Bullets, Ballots and Rhetoric: Confederate Policy for the United States Presidential Contest of 1864*. University, Alabama (1980).

Sears, Stephen W. *George B. McClellan: The Young Napoleon*. New York City (1988).

_____, ed. *The Civil War Papers of George B. McClellan*. New York City (1989).

Waugh, John C. *The Class of 1846: Stonewall Jackson, George McClellan and Their Brothers*. New York (1994).

Wheeler, Richard. *Sword Over Richmond*. New York City (1986).

Williams, T. Harry. *McClellan, Sherman and Grant*. Westport, Conn. (1976), reprint of 1962 edition.

1864 vice presidential nominee —
Democratic Party

George H. Pendleton

Full name: George Hunt Pendleton
State represented: Ohio.
Birth: July 19, 1825, Cincinnati, Ohio.
Age on Inauguration Day (March 4, 1865): 39 years, 7½ months.
Education: Woodward High School (Cincinnati), 1833–1835; Cincinnati College until 1841; private tutors, 1841–1844; Heidelberg (Germany) University for short period; studied law, admitted to bar in 1847.

Religion: Episcopalian.

Ancestry/prominent relatives: Descended from Henry Pendleton of Norwich, England, whose two sons emigrated to America in 1674; great-grandfather (Nathanael Pendleton) was aide-de-camp to General Nathanael Greene during Revolution, was later a federal judge, and was Alexander Hamilton's second in fatal duel with Aaron Burr; father (Nathanael Pendleton) was U.S. representative as Whig, 1841–1843; George's wife was the daughter of Francis Scott Key, and niece of Chief Justice Roger B. Taney.

Occupation: Attorney.

Public Offices: Ohio state senator, 1854–1856; defeated as Democratic nominee for U.S. representative, 1854, elected 1856, served March 4, 1857–March 4, 1865; defeated

GEORGE B. McCLELLAN and GEORGE H. PENDLETON
(From the collection of David J. and Janice L. Frent)

Democratic nominee for vice president, 1864; defeated for U.S. representative, 1864 and 1866; defeated for Democratic nomination for president, 1868; unsuccessful Democratic nominee for Ohio governor, 1869; U.S. senator, March 4, 1879–March 3, 1885, defeated; ambassador to Germany, 1885–1889.

Death: November 24, 1889, Brussels, at age 64 years, 4 months.

Burial: Spring Grove Cemetery, Cincinnati, Ohio.

Home: Cincinnati, Ohio.

Personal characteristics: Tall, handsome, had a glistening black beard; friendly and well-mannered; known as "Gentleman George."

Father: Nathanael Greene Pendleton (August 25, 1793–June 16, 1861), born in Savannah, Georgia; married 1820.

Mother: Jane Frances Hunt (1802–1839), daughter of Jesse Hunt.

Siblings: George was the oldest of ten children. The others whose names are known were as follows: Elliot H., married Anna James. Nathanael. Susan L. Martha E. Eva. Half brother was Edmund H. Pendleton, who married the only daughter of New York governor William L. Marcy. Charlotte was a half sister.

Wife: Mary Alicia Loyd Nevins Key (1823–May 25, 1886), married in 1846; she was the daughter of Francis Scott Key; died in carriage accident.

Children: Francis Key, lawyer and judge. Mary. James Frances. Alice.

Historic site/memorial: Pendleton's house in Cincinnati is at 559 E. Liberty Street (private).

Fame is indeed fleeting. George Hunt Pendleton's name was in the years following the Civil War the title by which two nationally controversial proposals were known. One dealt with the funding of governmental debt, the other with the elimination of governmental graft. Perhaps this obscurity is only fitting, however, since Pendleton was the author of neither proposal but merely became their best-known advocate.

Nathanael Greene Pendleton, George's father, was born in Georgia, moved to New York in 1796, and then finally settled in frontier Cincinnati, Ohio, in 1818. Marrying the daughter of a Cincinnati pioneer, Jesse Hunt,

Nathanael became a minor political actor in the new state. In 1840, he was elected as a Whig to the United States House of Representatives, but retired after one term, never to return to elective politics. His son would not be so quickly satisfied with the political arena.

George was the first of ten children. His education was exceptional for the era, and was capped with a tour of Europe from 1844 through 1846. Nineteen years old, freshly graduated from Cincinnati College, George sailed for France. A few weeks in Paris were followed by a tour through Belgium, Switzerland, and finally Italy, where he spent the winter. In the spring of 1845 he continued on to Vienna, Prague, and Berlin. Holland was next, and then London. Travel was difficult, as there were as yet no railroads. For a few months George returned to Germany and attended the University of Heidelberg. Having joined a group of German students, he then traveled by foot through Germany, Switzerland, and Italy. Greece was next, and then the Holy Land. Pendleton returned to Paris by way of the ancient ruins of Egypt, a sea voyage to Trieste, and other side trips. Final sojourns to England, Scotland, and Ireland capped his travels. George finally sailed for home in the summer of 1846. This was a rare experience for an American, especially one from a sparsely settled frontier area such as Ohio. Knowledge of French and German languages greatly aided his travels, knowledge that marked him even more as an exceptionally well-educated American.

The year of his return from Europe, George married the daughter of Francis Scott Key, the famed author of "The Star Spangled Banner." Alice Key was a beautiful, talented, and intelligent woman who was also the niece of Chief Justice Roger B. Taney. Pendleton's own climb to fame started the following year when he was admitted to the bar in Ohio, forming a partnership with George E. Pugh. Pugh would five years later be elected attorney general of Ohio, and subsequently a United States senator.

After six years in private practice, Pendleton in 1853 was unanimously nominated by the Democratic party for the state senate. His election was easily attained, making him the youngest member of the senate. His sights were raised in 1854 with his nomination for the U.S. House, in an attempt to fill the same seat his father had held 12 years earlier. The Kansas-Nebraska crisis split the Democratic party and made the appeal of the Know-Nothing party even stronger. The Know-Nothings swept the Ohio elections and kept Pendleton out of Congress. It proved a short-lived tide, and the Democrats ousted the Know-Nothings two years later. That year Pendleton finally was elected to a congressional seat.

The new congressman proved a supporter of Stephen Douglas. He joined the "Little Giant" in opposing the Kansas Lecompton constitution on the grounds that it had been fraudulently derived. Yet Pendleton was a fence-straddler on many issues, attempting to avoid controversy and extreme positions. He stayed out of the slavery debates, and was conciliatory in his speeches. A narrow victory in the 1858 elections was followed by a much more comfortable margin in 1860.

With war clouds looming ominously, Pendleton sought compromise. The Crittenden Compromise or any other negotiated settlement of the crisis between the North and South was far preferable to Pendleton than war. Yet if secession should come, Pendleton thought no attempt should be made to keep the Southern states in the Union. The Ohio congressman urged that the North listen to the South's grievances and redress them:

> They say they have fears for their safety. Allay those fears. They say they have apprehensions of wrong. Assuage them. Gentlemen, remove every cause of agitation and irritation, however unfounded you deem it.... Let me beg of you to grant all their reasonable demands.... I beg you, in God's name, do it! Do a patriotic duty! Give us peace instead of discord!

Peaceful secession did not come, and Congressman Pendleton was a constant critic of Lincoln administration policies in waging war against the South. Throughout the war he believed peace should be accepted at any price since there was no justification for the conflict. He voted only for those war measures necessary to sustain the Union armies in the field. He characterized his stand as one in favor of "all measures necessary to enable the govern-

ment to maintain its honor and dignity, and prevent disaster to its flag.... The faith of the government was pledged to the troops in the field, and must not be forfeited by inadequate supplies." He would vote for such appropriations as were required to support the army and navy, but never favored vigorous prosecution of the war.

Pendleton's party was badly divided. The war Democrats joined the Republicans in backing every measure to prosecute the war. The peace Democrats, or as they would become known, the Copperheads, opposed in varying degrees those measures deemed necessary by the Lincoln administration to carry on the conflict. Pendleton opposed the suspension of habeas corpus, all measures to prosecute civilians in military courts, and the legal tender act which helped finance the war. The most notorious Copperhead, Clement L. Vallandigham, was a fellow Ohio congressman, and Pendleton never engaged in the excesses of his Ohio colleague. The two were quite similar in political views, but fortunately Pendleton never slid into the near-treason that ruined Vallandigham. In 1862, Pendleton signed a controversial document criticizing the government's arrest of civilians in the border states, such arrests being made in an attempt to round up secessionists and keep these states in the Union. Pendleton followed with attacks on the military draft, and voted against conscription. In the spring of 1863, to Pendleton's credit, he did urge peaceful enrollment for the draft, while some Copperheads were encouraging fellow believers to oppose enrollment.

These views greatly endangered Pendleton's reelection in 1862. Fortunately Pendleton demonstrated far more tact and restraint than many Copperheads. Despite a gerrymandering of his district by the Ohio Republican legislature, Pendleton was able to eke out victory.

The rest of the war found Pendleton on the side of the peace Democrats. He became seriously embroiled in the Vallandigham controversy of 1863. In December 1862, Pendleton traveled with Vallandigham, who had recently been ousted as an Ohio congressman, and the two Copperheads delivered speeches against the war in New York and other cities. Pendleton called the Lincoln administration a "reign of terror." Attacking the Lincoln war measures as unconstitutional, he accused the government of being little more than a tyranny. To the extent dissension existed in the North, Pendleton blamed Lincoln. The Emancipation Proclamation was savagely opposed, as was the enlistment of Negro soldiers. With emancipation being proclaimed, Pendleton saw a conspiracy in the entire Republican war effort. Pendleton blamed Lincoln for having inveigled the North into a war that allegedly was intended only to preserve the Union, when in fact Lincoln's true intent, so Pendleton charged, had been abolition. In a flight of rhetorical excess, Pendleton charged that "cooperation with you [on abolition] is a treason to the country. Before you ask for unity, return to your avowed purpose and policy in carrying on the war." Pendleton feared Negro political equality and eagerly preyed on the racial prejudices of his constituents to oppose the war.

Vallandigham had been jailed because of allegedly treasonous remarks about the administration and because he encouraged opposition to the war. Rather than imprisoning him, however, Lincoln ordered that Vallandigham be released to the Confederates. Pendleton had sat on the podium during the speech that caused Vallandigham's arrest. He then served as Vallandigham's counsel during the military trial that returned a verdict of treason. The case became a cause célèbre among Democrats. Whether there was justification for the government's patent infringement of civil rights in the case became a nationally debated issue.

Vallandigham did not stay long in the South, but made his way to Canada. Pendleton joined him there and helped plan the exiled political leader's race for governor of Ohio in 1863. It was a surreal campaign, with the candidate secreted in Canada while comrades such as Pendleton carried on the fight for him. Towards the end of the campaign, the candidate himself entered Ohio, but he was not arrested. Anti-Negro banners and slogans were everywhere at Democratic rallies, and Pendleton joined in the furor of race-baiting. Few campaigned as hard for Vallandigham as did Pendleton. Many Democrats sat out the campaign, fearing that the party would be permanently besmirched with an image of treason because of this candidacy. Republicans elected their candidate and despite claims of fraud by the Democrats, Vallandigham was finished politically.

The president in 1864 proposed that a provisional governor be appointed for each seceded state, and a regular civil government organized once one-tenth of the population took an oath of allegiance to the Union. Pendleton's response was bitter.

> Admit you are in revolution; admit you are revolutionists; admit that you do not desire to restore the old order. Avow that you are not bound by the constitution, but by your own sense of right.

The war had been going badly, and many Democrats thought they were assured of ousting Lincoln in the 1864 election. The Democratic convention, despite a strong peace Democrat contingent, nominated for president one of the prominent generals of the war, George McClellan. McClellan opposed the administration policies, but not on the basis of the peace Democrats. Instead, he believed Republican interference with his generalship had prevented victory in the field. After his nomination, the convention went to the opposite end of the political spectrum and chose Pendleton for vice president. The Ohioan did not lead on the first ballot, but overtook James O. Guthrie of Kentucky and won on the second. Pendleton was a sop to the Vallandigham supporters. To many observers, the Democratic cart had two drivers and they were going in opposite directions. Pendleton in September quietly traveled to visit Vallandigham in Ohio. He begged the controversial leader to endorse McClellan. A crowd gathered outside Vallandigham's house while Pendleton was meeting with him, and called upon the two politicians to speak. Pendleton made only brief remarks, and then called upon his host in hopes that he would publicly embrace McClellan. Pendleton was not disappointed. Vallandigham's endorsement was hardly sufficient. Military victories for the Union armies spelled the defeat of the Democratic politicians. The Democrats' bright hopes of summer turned to defeat in the November general election.

With the war clearly headed toward Union victory, post-war measures gained serious consideration in Congress. In January of 1865, Pendleton voted against adoption of the Thirteenth Amendment to the Constitution that would prohibit slavery. In an extended speech, he argued the Thirteenth Amendment was, in essence, unconstitutional. The Constitution could only be amended in certain limited ways, Pendleton argued, and to abolish slavery was to change the very nature of the compact initially entered between the states. The "spirit, scope and intent of the constitution," was being violated. Fortunately, Pendleton was outvoted.

After the war, Pendleton endorsed the greenback movement. This was the first great political issue to adopt his name. The "Pendleton Plan," also called the "Ohio Idea," got some of its impetus from the conviction by many Democratic leaders that a new issue was necessary to take power away from the Republicans. The issue chosen was governmental finance. The bonds that had been issued during the Civil War to finance that tremendously expensive conflict became the focal point of a dramatic controversy in the late 1860s. Many thought that the bonds that had been issued during the war should be paid back in specie, that is, in gold or silver coin. Pendleton had stood for "hard money" until very recently, and had opposed paper money with the statement that "gold and silver currency is the law of the land at home, the law of the land abroad: there can, in the present condition of the world, be no other currency." Yet in 1867, Pendleton abandoned his hard money views and supported repayment of bonds in greenbacks. It was an inflationary scheme that appealed to the debt-burdened northwestern farmers, who were Pendleton's main constituents. In the 1867 Ohio campaign, Pendleton spread his newly discovered financial doctrines throughout the state. There was a dramatic comeback for Ohio Democrats in that election, though future Republican president Rutherford B. Hayes did narrowly win the governorship. A formidable political force had been created by the greenback issue. Pendleton himself became a principal beneficiary of the movement.

The Pendleton plan of paying off war bonds with greenbacks became a major issue in the 1868 presidential campaign. Pendleton was the leading candidate for the Democratic nomination that year; the national party platform endorsed his views. The money issue made him the leading candidate, but it also prevented his ever gaining the necessary two-thirds majority at the convention. His views antagonized the hard money eastern Democratic businessmen, and with a two-thirds majority needed, his chances for nomination were nil. He led the voting for 16 ballots, and got within three votes of a majority. After the twenty-first ballot, Vallandigham read a letter from Pendleton that withdrew him from consideration. A reluctant candidate, Horatio Seymour, was subsequently nominated. Had there not been a two-thirds majority rule, it seems evident that Pendleton would have been nominated for president.

Pendleton's defeat in 1864 for the vice presidency had begun a 14-year retirement from public office. His abortive attempt in 1868 to be nominated for president had been followed the next year by his nomination for governor of Ohio, but he was defeated by the incumbent, Rutherford Hayes. The issue of Negro suffrage proved the major issue in the campaign. Hayes' courageous endorsement of the Fifteenth Amendment that insured black voting rights did not spell defeat for the Republicans, as many in that party feared. Thus, rather than politics, Pendleton turned to business. In 1869, he was chosen president of the Kentucky Central Railroad, and would remain in that position for ten years.

Pendleton finally returned to public office in 1878 when he was elected to the United States Senate by the Ohio legislature. As chairman of the Senate Committee on Civil Service, Pendleton became a champion of reform. Few expected the old Democrat to urge such reform, and many thought politics was his sole motivation for embracing the issue. It appears, however, that Pendleton was sincere. The actual bill that became known as the Pendleton Act was drafted by Dorman B. Eaton. It created a Federal Civil Service Commission which would administer a competitive examination for applicants for a small portion of governmental positions. The assassination of

President Garfield in 1881 by a disappointed office-seeker gave great impetus to the reform movement. In December 1882, the House easily passed Pendleton's plan, but the Senate hotly debated the issue. Many saw the measure as a Republican one, and charges were made that it would solely serve to perpetuate Republicans in office, since they now controlled governmental patronage. Nonetheless, the first tentative step towards reform did pass. It created a "classified" service to be governed by the new commission, mainly consisting of Washington clerks, custom-house personnel, and some post office employees.

Pendleton was not reelected in 1884 by the legislature. His support for civil service reform was unpopular with Ohio Democratic bosses and Pendleton's loss of his Senate seat was the price he had to pay. The following year he was appointed by newly elected President Grover Cleveland as minister to Germany. In 1886, Pendleton's wife was killed in a carriage accident while she was visiting in New York City and was riding through Central Park. After this tragedy, it was thought Pendleton lost his zest for life. He was "but a ghost of his former self, and many of his friends declared that they scarcely knew him." In 1888, Pendleton suffered a paralytic stroke, lingered for a year, and then died.

Analysis of Qualifications

A shrewd, moderate, popular politician, George Hunt Pendleton nonetheless allowed himself to be swept up in the anti-war movement centered among the Midwest Democrats. His historical reputation (slim as it is) has permanently been damaged by that fact. That facet of his career does suggest he was not the man to be leading the country at the critical time in the Civil War, when Northern intensity for continuing the war was waning almost as rapidly as the South's military fortunes. The rest of his career, however, suggests that this Ohio Democrat was an able and principled public servant who rendered valuable services to his country. He and a few other Midwest politicians are the link between the peace movement of the Civil War, and the equally anti-government, states' rights–oriented Greenback and still later Populist causes.

Pendleton's 1864 vice presidential nomination was a concession to the strong Democratic Party peace movement. He was to balance the martial policies of General George B. McClellan, who headed the ticket. Few Copperheads were as reviled, then or since, as fellow Ohio congressman Clement Vallandigham. Few Democrats were as close personally or politically to that alleged traitor as was Pendleton. Despite sharing views with the outcast leader, Pendleton escaped the extreme political abuse hurled at Vallandigham because he was much less strident in his rhetoric, less frequent in his denunciations, less prone to slip into negotiations with the Confederates. Pendleton called Lincoln's government a tyranny, and accused the president of secretly plotting a war against slavery while publicly only calling Northerners to arms in order to preserve the Union. Throughout the war Pendleton used the race issue to advance the Democratic cause. He opposed the constitutional amendment that abolished slavery, opposed the Emancipation Proclamation, and called frequently upon the president to return solely to reunification as the goal of the war. In 1864, had Pendleton been elected vice president and then come into the presidency, the South would have been emboldened to continue the conflict. The Union armies would have been reined in and the South likely offered terms for ending the war that would have preserved their "peculiar institution."

Yet it cannot be denied that Pendleton was an able leader. Despite the end of the war and the establishment of reconstruction governments, the South would be one hundred years in the process of ending the vestiges of slavery. Nonetheless, unless he had been elected with a strong Democratic Congress, Pendleton would have faced the same frustrations as did accidental president Andrew Johnson. At odds over Reconstruction, and abused by the Northern press, Pendleton would have more skillfully than Johnson attempted to blunt the radical Republican programs. Perhaps he would have been more politically skilled and better able to thwart the landslide Republican victory in the 1866 Congressional elections that ensured continued conflict between Congress and President Johnson. A more moderate

Reconstruction might have been the result. Black civil rights would not then have enjoyed its brief, ten-year flourishing in the South, but the bitterness of that reconstruction and the savage reaction to it when the Democrats reclaimed in the 1870s may also have been avoided.

The Greenback movement that Pendleton endorsed in 1867 may not have had Pendleton as a champion should he have been serving as president. Much of the reason for Pendleton's embrace of Greenback arguments despite his long standing, extremely public hard-money views, was his attempt to restore Democratic political fortunes. A President Pendleton may have experienced entirely different pressures.

In sum, George Pendleton was a capable, well-respected, but opportunistic, political leader. His strong Southern sympathies, tied with vigorously expressed states' rights and pro-slavery views, might have thwarted most of the political gains achieved by the Civil War, even if many of those achievements were temporary. His pro–Southern beliefs may have saved the country from much divisiveness, or instead might only have accentuated the kind of conflict that actually occurred between President Andrew Johnson and Congress. George H. Pendleton would have been a gamble.

PENDLETON BIBLIOGRAPHY

Angle, Paul. "Dirty Politics." *Chicago History* 8 (1967), pp. 58–60.

Biographical Cyclopedia and Portrait Gallery ... of Ohio I (1883), pp. 143–144.

Bloss, G.M.D. *Historic and Literary Miscellany.* Cincinnati (1875).

_____. *Life and Speeches of George H. Pendleton.* Cincinnati (1868).

Cox, Samuel S. *Three Decades of Federal Legislation, 1855–1885.* Providence, R.I. (1894).

Destler, Chester McA. "The Origin and Character of the Pendleton Plan." *The Mississippi Valley Historical Review* XXIV (1937), pp. 171–184.

du Bellet, Louise Pecquet. "Pendleton Family," in *Some Prominent Virginia Families.* Lynchburg, Va. (1907), vol. IV, pp. 224–281.

Ford, Henry Jones. *The Cleveland Era: A Chronicle of the New Order in Politics.* New Haven (1921).

Gray, Wood. *The Hidden Civil War: The Story of the Copperheads.* New York City (1964), reprint of 1942 edition.

Klement, Frank L. *The Copperheads of the Middle West.* Chicago (1960).

_____. *The Limits of Dissent.* Louisville (1970).

Mach, Thomas Stuart. "'Gentleman George' Hunt Pendleton: A Study in Political Continuity." Unpublished doctoral dissertation, University of Akron (1996).

Milton, George Fort. *Abraham Lincoln and the Fifth Column.* New York City (1942).

Morgan, H. Wayne. *From Hayes to McKinley, National Party Politics 1877–1896.* Syracuse (1969).

Rittenhouse, George H. "George Hunt Pendleton, with Special Reference to his Congressional Career." Unpublished master's thesis, Ohio State University (1932).

Shipley, Max L. "The Background and Legal Aspects of the Pendleton Plan." *The Mississippi Valley Historical Review* XXIV (1937), pp. 329–340.

Unger, Irwin. *The Greenback Era: A Social and Political History of American Finance, 1865–1879.* Princeton (1964).

"U.S. Civil Service Hits 100." *Retirement Life* 59 (Jan. 1983), pp. 4, 20–21.

Election of 1868

NOMINATIONS

Republican Party Convention (4th): May 20–21, 1868, at Crosby's Opera House, Chicago, Illinois. *President—* Ulysses S. Grant, nominated by a unanimous vote of the 650 delegates. *Vice president—* Schuyler Colfax, nominated on the fifth ballot with 541 votes of the 648 cast. He had received 115 on the first ballot. Benjamin Wade (Ohio), Reuben Fenton (N.Y.), and Henry Wilson (Mass.), were the chief alternatives.

Democratic Party Convention (10th): July 4–9, 1868, at Tammany Hall, New York City, New York. *President*—Horatio Seymour, nominated on the 22nd ballot with a unanimous vote from the 317 delegates. He had received his first votes (9) on the fourth ballot; his name was not formally put into nomination until the 22nd ballot. George H. Pendleton, Andrew Johnson, Winfield Scott Hancock, and Thomas A. Hendricks all made serious attempts at the nomination on earlier ballots. *Vice president*—Francis P. Blair, Jr., nominated unanimously on the first ballot.

GENERAL ELECTION, November 3, 1868

Popular Vote
Grant 3,013,650
Seymour 2,708,744
Others.   46
Electoral Vote
Grant-Colfax — 214 (26 states)
Seymour-Blair — 80 (8 states)
Winners
Ulysses S. Grant, 18th president
Schuyler Colfax, 17th vice president
Losers
Horatio Seymour, Francis P. Blair, Jr.

---

*1868 presidential nominee —
Democratic Party*

Horatio Seymour

Full name: Horatio Seymour.
State represented: New York.
Birth: May 31, 1810, Pompey Hill, Onondaga County, New York.
Age on Inauguration Day (March 4, 1869): 58 years, 9 months.
Education: Local academy in Pompey Hill, then Utica Academy, Oxford Academy, 1820–1822, and Geneva Academy, 1822–1824; then military academy at Middletown, Connecticut, 1824–1826; read law under two attorneys in Utica; admitted to bar, 1832.

Religion: Episcopalian early in life, but confirmed in Trinity Church in 1831.

Ancestry/prominent relatives: Richard Seamer/Seymour emigrated from England to New England in 1638; Roscoe Conkling (brother-in-law) U.S. senator from New York; Horatio Seymour (uncle), U.S. senator from Vermont; Thomas Seymour (first cousin), governor of Connecticut.

Occupation: Attorney, but never practiced; owned large farm near Utica, New York.

Public offices: Military secretary to New York governor William Marcy, 1833–1839; New York Assembly, 1841–1842; mayor of Utica, 1842–1843, defeated in 1843 by 16 votes; New York Assembly, 1844–1845; elected speaker in 1845; defeated Democratic nominee for governor, 1850, 1854, 1864; governor of New York, 1852–1854, 1862–1864; nominated for governor but declined, 1876; refused to be considered for Democratic presidential nomination, 1860; defeated for U.S. Senate, 1862; unsuccessful Democratic nominee for president, 1868; refused to accept sure election to U.S. Senate, 1875.

Death: February 12, 1886, in New York City, age 75 years, 8½ months.

Burial: Forest Hill Cemetery, Utica, New York.

Home: Farm of 500 acres he called "Marysland"; at Deerfield, north of Utica; lived in small frame cottage.

Personal characteristics: Excellent orator, well-read, handsome and charming; almost six feet tall, slender, erect; hazel eyes, fringe of beard from ear to ear; balding.

Father: Henry Seymour (May 30, 1780–August 26, 1837), businessman, politician, banker; committed suicide during financial panic of 1837.

Mother: Mary Ledyard Forman (February 18, 1785–September 16, 1859), married January 1, 1807; daughter of General Jonathan and Mary (Ledyard) Forman.

Siblings: Mary Forman (September 15, 1807–?), married Rutger Bleeker Miller, July 18, 1828. Sophia Apolina (August 2, 1812–?), married Edward F. Shonnard. John Forman (September 21, 1814–February 22, 1890), married (1) Frances Antill Tappan, May 4, 1839, and (2) Helen Lincklaen Ledyard. Helen

Clarissa (March 1, 1818–June 4, 1894), married Ledyard Lincklaen on December 7, 1843. Julia Catherine (May 4, 1827–October 1893), married Roscoe Conkling, June 25, 1855, a U.S. senator.

Wife: Mary Bleecker (April 12, 1812–March 8, 1886), married May 31, 1835; daughter of John Rutger and Hester (Barley) Bleecker.

The vast majority of Horatio Seymour's fellow defeated candidates would not have been able to understand this New Yorker. Throughout his career he refused nominations for various high offices; sometimes he relented, as in the case of his selection as the Democrats' presidential candidate in 1868, but always only because of a sense of duty. Seymour died at the age of 75, and during only eight years in that lengthy life did he serve in public life. Politics, it would seem, was not this man's lifeblood.

Pompey Hill was a small central New York community when Horatio was born there in 1810, the second of six children in a politically active, financially comfortable family. His father Henry was a political lieutenant in the Albany Regency, the powerful machine constructed and directed primarily by Martin Van Buren. Through this connection Henry became a member of the state assembly, served one year on the five-member state Council of Appointment, was a member of the important canal commission, was mentioned for governor in 1822, but retired from public office to enter banking. He was honest, capable, but moody and frequently depressed. His mental malady caused him to commit suicide in 1837 when the nationwide financial panic of that year made the senior Seymour feel he was ruined. In fact, he had left a substantial estate behind which, with Horatio's careful management, enabled the family to continue quite comfortably.

Horatio attended several local academies. His delicate health caused his family to decide the stimulation of physical exertion was needed. Accordingly, Horatio was sent off to a military academy in Middletown, Connecticut, when he was 14. Just what was learned is uncertain, but Horatio's two years there certainly did not prevent, and may have helped cause, a lifelong suspicion of the military.

After completing his studies at the age of 16 in Middletown, Horatio returned to Utica (where his family had moved in 1820) and began reading law under two local attorneys. One, Greene C. Bronson, would 30 years later run for governor the same year as did Horatio. The law would not be Horatio's career, however, and after being admitted to the bar in 1832 he practiced for no more than two years. Marriage in 1835 to the daughter of a wealthy landowner added to obligations he had already assumed in dealing with his own family's lands. Farming and both families' investments occupied him sufficiently that a law practice was out of the question. His lack of interest in a legal career made its abandonment a simple decision.

William L. Marcy, a Martin Van Buren protégé, was elected New York governor in 1832. The Seymour family's close relations with Van Buren led to the appointment of 22-year-old Horatio to the position of military secretary for the new Democratic governor. For six years Marcy retained his office, and Horatio his. The young secretary met most of the prominent Democrats of his day, learned valuable lessons from watching the inner workings of a most effective political machine, and was ready for his own role in public life when the voters retired Marcy from the governorship in 1838.

The Democratic Party in New York was badly split, both on issues and over conflicting ambitions of various leaders. Seymour would throughout his career try to bridge these divisions. He was largely successful in this, and remained personally popular throughout the party due to his even-tempered, unruffled disposition, and constant desire to seek a middle ground on most issues. In 1841, Seymour was elected to the New York Assembly as a Van Buren supporter. His conservative, business-oriented principles soon had him loosely identified with the faction of the party colorfully called the "Hunkers." Their intraparty adversaries were called the Barnburners. The next year Seymour was elected mayor of Utica in a narrow victory over the Whig candidate. Financial reforms that he forced upon city government proved unpopular — the voters had grown used to having the government spend more than it taxed. As a consequence, Seymour was defeated in 1843 when he ran for a second one-year term. The margin of defeat was only 16 votes. The mayoral elections were in the spring, and by the fall of 1843 Seymour was running again, hoping to return to the state assembly.

Seymour won his second term in the assembly and was mentioned for speaker. The honor went to another, as Seymour declined to run. Instead, this son of the former canal commissioner became chairman of the canal committee in the assembly. No firmer supporter of canals could be found. Seymour's report on the Erie Canal in 1844 called for funding improvements in the canal with the money acquired from tolls. Many legislators felt a foreign loan would be necessary, but Seymour convinced a majority that the prospects for growth in the canal would more than pay for deepening and widening the canal, as well as lengthening the locks. Seymour's figures actually proved too conservative, and the tolls brought in more money than he had forecast. The canal report established Seymour's reputation in the assembly and greatly increased his influence. In 1844, he was the only one of all the Democrats who served in the previous year's assembly who was reelected. Most retired, and therefore Seymour was the senior legislator for his party. This position made him an early favorite for the speaker's chair in 1845, and he won easily, despite the internecine feuding in the party. The constant intraparty controversy was distasteful to the mild-mannered Seymour, and he decided to retire from the assembly after one term as speaker.

For the next few years Seymour refrained from active politicking. When the Whigs routed his party in New York in 1848, Seymour reentered politics to help the Democrats recover. In 1848, he was a central figure in the Democrats' state convention that compromised the differences between the Hunkers and Barnburners. Soon, however, there were new factions that appeared, one called the "Hards" that could not accept the party compromises and sharply identified with Southern slave interests. Seymour and a majority of New York Democrats were called "Softs." In September 1850, Seymour's long service in the party earned him the gubernatorial nomination. That year the Whigs had their own party problems, over the issue of slavery in the territories. (See discussion in sketch of Francis Granger, election of 1836.) Seymour went down to defeat by the narrow margin of 214,614 for the Whig, Washington Hunt, and 214,352 for Seymour — 262 votes! Two years later the roles of victor and vanquished were reversed, and Seymour beat Hunt 264,121 to 241,525, with 20,000 for the Free Soil nominee.

Seymour's authority as governor was limited, as the state constitution created a weak governor's office. Ironically, one of his first acts was to sign a law authorizing the creation of the New York Central Railroad, a huge collection of smaller lines that soon put Seymour's favorite public works project — the Erie Canal — almost out of business. Seymour was faced with a Whig legislature, which sent him a bill adopting prohibition of alcohol in the state. Seymour vetoed it, calling it unconstitutional and unwise. The state's press condemned the veto, and the governor was called a drunk himself. In fact, Seymour never drank. Soon after the ensuing election, in which Seymour was defeated largely on this issue, the state's highest court upheld Seymour's view that the act was unconstitutional. Seymour had wanted to step down after one term, but in 1854 the party insisted that he run again. Seymour had somewhat wanly suggested to former Governor Marcy, who was then the U.S. secretary of state, that he would like to be appointed governor of Nebraska, or perhaps serve in a diplomatic post. Seymour finally relented to the pressure that he stand for a second term, but he was defeated in a four-cornered race. The Democratic vote was badly split among three of the candidates. Seymour lost by only 309 votes out of more than 450,000 cast. To use a sports cliché of a much later day, Seymour just could not win the close ones. His former legal mentor, Greene Bronson, drew off 33,850 votes that would almost certainly have gone overwhelmingly to Seymour.

The just-defeated governor had favorably impressed many in the Democratic party. His name started to be mentioned for the presidential nomination in 1856. In April of that year, Seymour had a letter published in which he declined to be considered for the office. The only campaign issue was slavery, and though Seymour objected to that institution, he also denounced abolitionists as causing more havoc than benefit. Instead, he believed that slavery could effectively, and safely insofar as the Union was concerned, only be abolished by the voluntary action of the Southern states themselves. When in 1858 the former governor was again mentioned for another term, he firmly refused to be considered. His life was focused on his business interests, and he did not want to return to public life.

In 1860 the Democrats were badly split over a presidential candidate. Seymour was given consideration by many moderates. The South saw him as a friend because he denounced abolitionists and defended the right of the South to continue slavery until they decided to abandon it. Once again Seymour published a denial of interest in a presidential candidacy, and he did not figure in the divisive convention balloting that transpired. After Lincoln's election Seymour called for calm. He wanted the Crittenden Compromise adopted, and when that failed, he helped organize a convention of moderates at Tweddle Hall in Albany, New York, held in late January 1861. He urged the North to extend conciliatory gestures to the South, and to abandon force as an instrument of reunification. When Fort Sumter was fired upon, Seymour was in the Northwest looking after business interests. That absence from New York at the crucial moment when war broke out would lead political adversaries to charge he had hidden in the woods at the time of crisis. This was only one of several events in Seymour's life that were maliciously misinterpreted by future election opponents. Actually, while Seymour was in the Northwest, he tried to encourage enlistments in the Northern army. Seymour himself never attempted to join the army, another factor that brought him condemnation.

In 1862, Seymour was nominated a fourth time for governor. During the first year of the war he had been allied with the critics of the Lincoln administration, and he campaigned for governor by attacking the conduct of the war. His opponent was General James Wadsworth, who remained at the front lines during the election campaign. Throughout the North the 1862 elections were a severe setback for the Republicans. The war was proceeding poorly, severe measures had been taken to stifle dissent in the North, and Seymour was one of many Democrats who benefited. Even so, his margin of victory was small — 306,649 to 295,897. The Republicans continued to control the legislature.

The governor believed the war must be prosecuted to a successful conclusion, but that Lincoln was violating the Constitution in doing so. Peace and reunification should be held out to the South at all times if they would just lay down their arms. Seymour and his fellow peace Democrats' slogan after the announcement of the Emancipation Proclamation was "The Constitution as it is, the Union as it was." Slavery should not be abolished, because that would make it impossible for the South to agree to end the war. Suspension of habeas corpus was condemned by the governor as being unconstitutional. Relations with the Lincoln administration were poor, but Seymour worked conscientiously to fill the state's enlistment quotas and otherwise to bear his state's share of the war burden. At times he felt the state was being overburdened. The arrest of Vallandigham in 1863 (see George Pendleton sketch, Election of 1864), outraged Seymour. He accused the administration of treating the Constitution as a "fair weather thing," something to be respected in times of peace and ignored during a crisis.

When New York's new draft quotas were to be announced in July 1863, Seymour feared the worst. The governor gave a speech on July 5, the day after both Gettysburg and Vicksburg had been taken by Union armies, in which he implied that the war situation was worsening and that prospects of victory offered by the national administration were false. His timing was atrocious. The twin Fourth of July victories at Gettysburg and Vicksburg were a great lift to Northern morale. Six days after this speech, serious draft riots broke out in New York City. Subsequent reports, even in reputable history texts, stated that a thousand lives were lost in the conflict. In fact, 18 people were killed, a serious enough matter but not the statewide insurrection that the larger figure suggests. The rioting began on Saturday, July 11. Seymour was out of town but arrived back Monday evening, July 13. Upon his return he made some remarks at city hall to a crowd that had gathered. The speech was impromptu, and no rioters were apparent. Horace Greeley bitterly opposed Seymour as being a traitor for failing to support the Lincoln administration's vigorous policies. Greeley's *Tribune* newspaper's account of the speech is therefore unreliable. However, Greeley reported, and it was accepted throughout the country, that Seymour had from the city hall steps addressed a mob of rioters and opened his remarks by calling them "my friends." No other newspaper quoted the governor as using those words, but the myth of Seymour addressing a mob of draft rioters as "my friends" became part of political lore. Seymour never denied the use of the phrase, but he simply could not remember whether he had used that innocuous phrase to open his statement to what appeared to him to be a crowd of peaceful citizens who had gathered to hear him speak.

In 1864, Seymour was severely crippled politically by the adverse publicity he had received during his two years as governor. Frequently he was grouped with the extreme peace Democrats, the Copperheads, who were thought little more than traitors. A public battle with the Lincoln War Department occurred during the election year over the state's draft quota, and finally a commission investigated and found Seymour to have been correct. Twenty-five thousand fewer conscriptees were taken from the state as a result. George McClellan became the Democrats' presidential nominee, and Seymour found that distasteful. Seymour was permanent chairman of the Democratic National Convention in 1864 and supported the nominee only grudgingly. His own nomination for another term as governor came at the September state party convention. He declined to accept, but the convention did not relent and he finally agreed to campaign. It was for naught, as Republican Reuben Fenton defeated him in a hotly contested race. The soldier vote turned the contest against the Democrats, and many felt the vote was so fraudulently taken in the army camps that the result was suspect.

Actually Seymour was pleased with the defeat, as he had not wanted another term. The next few years Seymour remained in private life, though he frequently criticized the Reconstruction policies enacted by the Radical Republican Congress. Negro suffrage in Seymour's opinion should be left to the individual states, and he opposed the Fourteenth and Fifteenth amendments. As the leading Democrat in the most important state in the Union, Seymour was again viewed by many as a presidential candidate. Again he rejected the idea. George Pendleton was becoming the leading alternative candidate, and Pendleton's "Ohio Idea" of paying back government bonds with greenbacks was anathema to the hard-money Seymour. Soon Seymour was backing Thomas Hendricks of Indiana as an alternative, and when Hendricks faltered, the former New York governor considered Chief Justice Salmon Chase as his favorite. Seymour was named permanent chairman of the 1868 convention, just as he had been in 1864. For 18 ballots Hendricks, Pendleton, Chase and others fought to a standstill. Pendleton withdrew, and the convention seemed to be moving inexorably to Hendricks. Yet for reasons that apparently developed in the proverbial smoke-filled room meeting of power brokers, a delegate from Ohio rose and changed all of his state's votes to Seymour. The reluctant candidate was placed in nomination, the Ohio delegate stated, "against his intentions but no longer against his honor." Seymour, as convention chairman, was then on the podium. He protested that he could not accept. He then left to consult with the New York delegation. While he was absent from the stage, massive vote shifting occurred and Seymour was named unanimously. Twice Seymour rejected the nomination, yet the convention, weary from balloting and probably genuinely fond and respectful of the New York governor, would not abide by his wishes.

Seymour was not interested in the nomination. He seemed by nature to shy from controversy, and nothing could be more bitter than a run for president against the candidate of the Radical Republicans. He apparently had no optimism he would win, nor did he think if he did win he would have any power — Congress would thwart his every move, just as it had Andrew Johnson. His friends sometimes did more harm than good, as an enthusiastic endorsement by the arch–Copperhead Vallandigham damaged Seymour's credibility. During most of the campaign he remained inactive, which was the accepted standard for presidential candidates. When the October elections held in Indiana, Iowa, Pennsylvania, and Ohio went completely for the Republicans, many Democrats urged Seymour to drop out of the race and let another be substituted. It was too late for that, and Seymour knew it. Instead, he went on an extensive campaign tour of six Northern states. He stayed at the top of the ticket, and though the expected defeat did come, it was not by the margin many expected. He lost by 300,000 votes out of almost six million cast, or less than five percent. It is clear many Northerners had their doubts about Grant as presidential material.

In defeat Seymour was content. During the next few years he did not seek office, but did try to reform the state Democratic party by "cleaning up the Augean Stables" of Tammany Hall. In that he failed. The national stench of corruption emanating from Congress was also the subject of his frequent comment. He saw Reconstruction as a policy of revenge, not one of reconciliation. Seymour did not believe Negro suffrage was an answer to the South's problems, but that it only aggravated that region's difficulties. Seymour was outraged when his own party accepted Horace Greeley, his near-lifelong adversary, as its presidential nominee in 1872. He could not have been too unhappy to see Greeley lose by a larger margin than had Seymour.

Over another one of his objections, Seymour was nominated for governor in 1876. This time he made the refusal stick, even though the state convention had already disbanded and gone home. Two years earlier he had been equally emphatic when he rejected certain election by the Democrat-controlled state assembly to be the next United States senator. Seymour was retired and he meant to stay that way. Thereafter he quickly spurned any suggestions he run for office.

Business pursuits occupied his remaining years. His large, comfortable but hardly luxurious farm outside of Utica was his home. The Seymours never had children, but a namesake nephew and other relatives filled some of that void. A serious sunstroke in 1876 had been one of the reasons Seymour had so adamantly refused the gubernatorial nomination that year. His health never recovered. Both he and his life's companion of 50 years, Mary Bleecker Seymour, became seriously ill in 1886. On Lincoln's birthday in 1886, Seymour died. Within a month his wife passed away as well.

Analysis of Qualification

It has been argued that the suicide of Horatio Seymour's father in 1837, when the son was 27 years old, was the momentous event in molding Seymour's character. From that day forward he was wary of controversy, of becoming too seriously committed to a bitterly divisive cause, for in such causes he saw the danger of mental pressures that had led to his father's self-inflicted demise. Horatio Seymour was tagged the "Great Decliner," but these were declinations that more often than not were followed by acceptances.

Like his contemporary, fellow New Yorker Samuel Tilden, Seymour lacked nerve and confidence. Seymour could be strong-willed, but usually he attempted to take the middle road and compromise. It is absurd that a politician's image could be ruined by the possible use of the phrase "my friends," but somehow it is fitting that Seymour, who always tried to remain friendly to all factions in his party, should encounter this difficulty. He did not want to take risks, but instead tried to remain above the fray. Still, he had sufficient ambition that he would relent to take the office when pressure was brought to bear. He said in 1869, a few months after his defeat for president, that one defeat for that office cured him of any ambition to attempt it again. Perhaps that was right. He had a dual nature, one which urged him to serve his state and country, and another that was repulsed by the conflicts that had to be foreborn to earn high office.

Seymour was a conservative, business-oriented Democrat, with substantial investments that tied him to banks, railroads, and other commercial interests. He was wealthy if not lavishly so. On slavery he had always been an opponent, but he almost equally opposed Northern abolitionists who would wreck the Union to end the institution of slavery. His service as governor put him in contact with prison issues, and he became a concerned penal reformer. He once gave a speech to prisoners, and sardonically referred to it later as "my talk with 'my friends' in prison walls." He was a wise, concerned, humane man, filled with kindness and respect for his fellow man. He seemed loved in his home state by many voters, but his election victories were few and his defeats at least equal in number. Had he been president during the Reconstruction period, he might have been constantly at odds with a Republican Congress, but then a Seymour presidential victory might also have given Congress a much more Democratic cast. He would have returned the Southern states to Southern rule as quickly as he could, rather than postpone until 1876 that retreat from the experiment of equal civil rights in the South. A President Seymour would probably not have been an innovator, or a dynamic leader. Instead, he would have tried to reconcile differences. He once said, "The longer I live and the more I learn of men, the more I am disposed to think well of their hearts and poorly of their heads." Praise for Seymour as a political leader must be tempered; he just was not made to lead during a period of crisis.

SEYMOUR BIBLIOGRAPHY

Carroll, Howard. *Twelve Americans, Their Lives and Times.* New York City (1883), pp. 1–47.

Hartley, Isaac S. *Hon. Horatio Seymour, LL.D., Ex-Governor of the State of New York....* Utica, N.Y. (1886).

Jacobus, Donald Lines, comp., under general direction of Seymour, George Dudley. *A History of the Seymour Family, Descendants of Richard Seymour of Hartford, Connecticut....* New Haven (1939).

Mitchell, Stewart. *Horatio Seymour of New York.* Cambridge, Mass. (1938).

Wall, Alexander J. *A Sketch of the Life of Horatio Seymour 1810–1886, ...* New York City (1929, reprinted 1991).

1868 vice presidential nominee —
Democratic Party

Frank Blair

Full name: Francis Preston Blair (Jr.).

State represented: Missouri.

Birth: February 19, 1821, Lexington, Kentucky.

Age on Inauguration Day (March 4, 1869): 48 years, ½ month.

Education: Private schools in Washington, D.C.; entered Yale October 1837, expelled January 1838; University of North Carolina, 1838–1839, expelled; Princeton 1839–1841; studied law at Transylvania University; admitted to bar in 1842.

Religion: Had not been overtly religious. Gave comfort to his family when, after his 1872 stroke, he formally expressed his Christianity.

Ancestry/prominent relatives: First Blair, Scotch-Irish, arrived in America in the mid-eighteenth century; William C. Preston (first cousin, twice removed), senator from South Carolina; James Blair (grandfather), attorney general of Kentucky; B. Gratz Brown (see Election of 1872), a cousin; family intermarried with Breckenridges, McDonnells and Floyds; was preeminent family in Virginia.

Profession: Attorney.

Public offices: Appointed attorney general of the New Mexico Territory; member of the Missouri house of representatives, 1852–1856; elected as a Free-Soiler to Congress (March 4, 1857–March 3, 1859); successfully contested the election of John R. Barret to the 36th Congress and served from June 8 to June 25, 1860, when he resigned; unsuccessful candidate for reelection to the 36th Congress to fill the vacancy caused by his own resignation; delegate to the Republican National Convention at Chicago in 1860; elected to Congress and served from March 4, 1861, until his resignation in July 1862, to become a colonel in the Union Army; presented credentials as a member-elect to the 38th Congress and served from March 4, 1863, to June 10, 1864, when he was succeeded by Samuel Knox, who contested the election; unsuccessful Democratic candidate

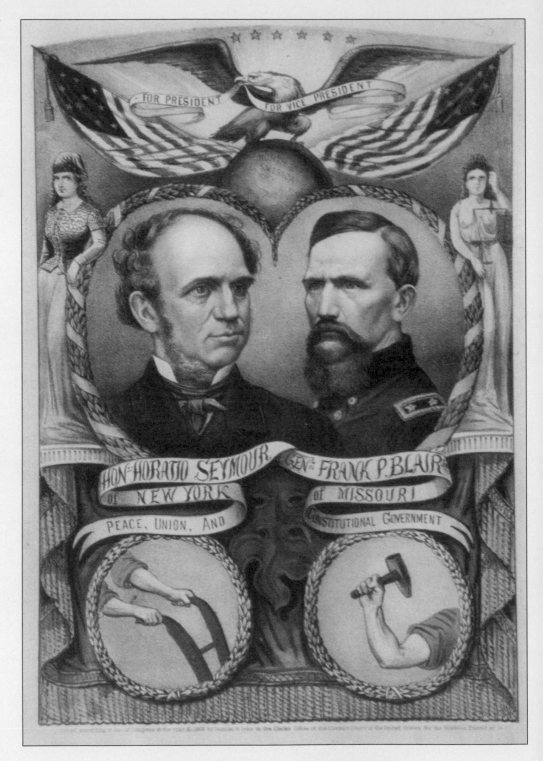

HORATIO SEYMOUR and FRANK BLAIR
(From the collection of David J. and Janice L. Frent)

for vice president of the United States in 1868; member Missouri house of representatives in 1870; elected as a Democrat to the U.S. Senate and served from January 20, 1871, to March 3, 1873; was not a candidate for reelection owning to ill health; state insurance commissioner in 1874.

Death: July 8, 1875, St. Louis, Missouri, at age 54 years, 4½ months.

Burial: Bellefontaine Cemetery, St. Louis, Missouri; large bronze statue placed in Forest Park, St. Louis, on May 21, 1886.

Home: St. Louis, Missouri.

Personal characteristics: 5'11" tall, 175 pounds; wiry, lean; small hands and feet; long drooping mustache.

Father: Francis Preston Blair (called "Preston") (April 12, 1791–October 19, 1876), politician, journalist.

Mother: Eliza Violet Gist (1795–July 5, 1877); married July 21, 1812; daughter of Col. Nathaniel and Judith (Bell) Gist; her father had an illegitimate child by an Indian woman, and this child — Sequoyah or George Gist — became a prominent Indian chieftain and developed the first Cherokee alphabet.

Siblings: Montgomery (May 10, 1813–July 27, 1883) married (1) Caroline Buckner, and (2) Mary Elizabeth Woodbury; a politician, U.S. postmaster general. Juliet (1814–1816). Laura (February 22, 1816–October 30, 1819). Elizabeth (June 20, 1818–?), married S.P. Lee. James (October 7, 1819–December 15, 1852) married Mary Serena Eliza Jessup.

Wife: Appoline Alexander (1825–?), married September 8, 1847; granddaughter of Gov. George Madison of Kentucky, and daughter of Andrew and Myra (Madison) Alexander; after Blair's death, she married Franklin Dick.

Children: Andrew Alexander (September 20, 1848–January 1932), married Anna Biddle in 1871; a metallurgist. Christine Biddle (April 5, 1852–?), married Benjamin B. Graham. James Lawrence (April 2, 1854–January 16, 1904), married Appoline Alexander (?) in 1883. Francis Preston (October 18, 1856–?), married Florence Price in 1882. George Madison (April 18, 1860–1881). Cary Montgomery (March 3, 1868–?), married Emily Johnson in 1890. Caroline Martin (August 22, 1870–1876). William Alexander (June 8, 1872–1893).

Memorials: Each state is authorized to place two statues in the Capitol. Missouri's are Blair and Thomas Hart Benton. Family lived at Blair House, 1651 Pennsylvania Avenue, N.W., Washington, D.C.; house is now used for foreign dignitaries who are staying in Washington.

Though born in Kentucky, Frank Blair, Jr., moved to Washington, D.C., in 1830 at the age of nine when his father helped establish the *Globe* newspaper. Preston Blair, Sr., was an Andrew Jackson confidant and made himself a national political force through his newspaper. In Washington, young Frank was educated in private schools and began to show early his spoiled, irresponsible, but brilliant personality. The family was extremely close, with parents and children relying upon and adoring each other to exceptional degrees. No school could long interest or restrain Frank, and he was expelled first from Yale College for pranks, then from the University of North Carolina for poor grades and dismal attitude. He completed his work at Princeton, having been admitted only because of the political influence of his father. Still, Frank was at first denied a degree because of a wild week of partying immediately before graduation. The year after his studies at Princeton he spent at Transylvania Law School in Lexington, Kentucky, and began the practice of law with his brother, Montgomery Blair, in St. Louis. He also occasionally worked on the *Washington Globe* staff, and was left in charge in 1843 while his father took a short leave of absence.

A few years of legal practice in St. Louis ravaged his health, and he decided to take the Santa Fe Trail west in an attempt to recuperate. He was at Brent's Fort in New Mexico when the Mexican War broke out. After General Stephen Kearny conquered the territory, Blair was appointed attorney general by Kearny. It was a short term position, but he did help establish the legal code for the new territory.

By 1847, Frank had returned to St. Louis. Appoline Alexander was the granddaughter of the Revolutionary War hero and Kentucky governor, George Madison. Madison was also Blair's father's uncle. Thus, "Appo" and Frank were cousins, and on September 8, 1847, they also became husband and wife. Appo never became comfortable in the extremely close relationships of Blair siblings and parents. It is possible that the reason Frank remained in St. Louis after his brother Montgomery moved to Washington was that Appo desired to keep as much distance from the rest of the family as could be maintained. Her marriage never was an easy one, as Frank's constant financial difficulties as well as many of his political positions were an embarrassment to her. A few years after Frank's death, Appo wrote her mother-in-law that she doubted the worth of the many political battles Frank had fought. All in all, Frank and Appo were not the perfect match.

Though nominally a Democrat, Frank demonstrated his Free-Soil beliefs. He owned slaves himself, but still was a firm supporter of the Missouri Compromise and an opponent of the Kansas-Nebraska Act. In Missouri, Frank found his champion in Thomas Hart Benton and worked strenuously for the reelection of the racially moderate senator in 1850. Apparently because of Frank's views on slavery, in March of 1849 someone shot at him on a dark street in St. Louis. An opposition newspaper editor named Pickering was indicted for the attempted murder, but insufficient evidence was produced and Pickering was acquitted. Benton's efforts also failed, and Blair saw his candidate defeated.

In 1852, Blair was elected to the state house of representatives. Four years in the legislature identified Frank more clearly as a Free-Soiler and enemy of slavery. Campaigning as a Free-Soil Democrat, and advocating a free Kansas, Blair was elected to the United States House of Representatives in 1856. Blair supported the Republican nominee for president that year, and Thomas Benton for governor. Blair was the only Free-Soil candidate elected to Congress from a slave state in 1856. His anti-slavery sentiments caused an even more difficult election campaign in 1858. Both Blair and his opponent claimed victory. The House finally voted 93 to 91 to seat Blair.

Throughout his congressional career and until the end of the Civil War, Blair supported colonization in Latin America as the answer to slavery problems. In 1859, he addressed the Mercantile Library Association of Boston on "the destiny of the races on this continent." Though denouncing slavery, Blair also criticized racial mixing and the dangers of creating a "hybrid race." He used arguments both of morality and of self-interest in calling upon the South to throw off the burden of slavery. His lengthy speed was published in pamphlet form and made Blair well-known as an anti-slavery advocate. Abraham Lincoln as well as many other prominent leaders praised his speech highly. Most of Frank's speeches were prepared by his father, who apparently was much the more gifted speechwriter. This speech along with the fact that he was the only Free-Soil congressman from the South made him a national figure. Many invitations to speak came, and Frank informed his father that he would accept invitations only if the senior Blair would write the speeches for him. His father eagerly agreed.

In 1860, Blair was a delegate to the Republican National Convention in Chicago and supported fellow Missourian and U.S. Senator Edward Bates. Blair would accept no candidate that would inflame the South as much as William Seward. The Blair family heartily endorsed Lincoln's nomination. Yet as the election approached, Frank became convinced that far from dousing the fires of secession, Lincoln's election would cause war. Once Lincoln's election was assured, Blair proceeded to organize the unionist forces in Missouri to keep that state from seceding.

His first step was to organize unionist delegates to be elected to the Secession Convention that was called by the slaveowning, rebellion-sympathizing governor. The Lincoln Clubs that Blair had organized during the election campaign were converted into "Wide-Awake" Clubs. He began secretly drilling and arming these for potential battle with the governor and his supporters. Blair was in frequent contact with General Winfield Scott, commander of the federal armies, and with Lincoln. On April 17, 1861, Blair had the pleasure of delivering personally from Lincoln the orders to the aggressively pro–Union Nathaniel Lyon that placed Lyon in charge of all Loyalist forces. Blair was elected a colonel of the first regiment under Lyon and soon participated in the capture of a Confederate encampment of 750 men. A bullet was fired through his window and just missed his head while he was sitting in his St. Louis home.

Blair had been reelected to Congress in 1860 and journeyed to Washington in June of 1861 for the special session. He finished second in the election for speaker of the House. As consolation Blair was appointed chairman of the Committee on Military Affairs. When the session concluded, Frank returned to St. Louis with Lincoln's orders to keep him informed on all conditions there. For the time being, Blair refused the offer to be appointed a general in the army and instead desired to remain in Congress. John Charles Frémont was now the head of the military department that included Missouri. Blair soon bemoaned Frémont's selection, as he found Frémont to be a poor organizer, to exhibit confusion and bad judgment in all of his decisions, and to seem paralyzed by events. At first, Frank attempted to maintain cordial relations with Frémont and many of his suggestions for appointments were accepted by the general. On August 30, 1861, Frémont disbanded the provisional government that had been appointed after the Confederate governor withdrew to the South, and declared martial law. The slaves of all supporters of the rebellion were liberated. Two days later, Frank wrote his brother Montgomery Blair, who was now postmaster general and a confidant of Lincoln's, setting out his criticisms of Frémont and asking that he be replaced as soon as possible. Frémont's wife traveled from St. Louis to visit Lincoln and demanded an audience with the president. She laid the blame for Frémont's troubles upon Frank Blair. Frémont arrested Frank, who was still in the militia, and charged him with insubordination. The arrest became a cause célèbre nationwide. Montgomery Blair sent a telegram to Frémont telling him to release Frank. Frémont did release his prisoner and told Blair to "avoid so evident a breach of military propriety" in the future. Blair was livid, not only for his arrest, but for the release order that charged him with military impropriety. A copy of the release order and a personal letter were mailed by Blair to Adjutant General

Lorenzo Thomas. Blair asserted he had only been doing his duty.

Frémont's reactions to the criticism that was coming from many quarters were to arrest the critics. The arrest of a newspaper editor and the closing down of an offending newspaper were the final straw to Blair. A few days later he made formal charges to the military against Frémont. Again Blair was placed under arrest. Montgomery Blair and Francis Preston Blair, Sr., became concerned that Frank would destroy himself in his battle against Frémont. The final decision was with Lincoln. After consultation with various other generals, all of whom agreed with Blair's charges, Frémont was removed from command. There was much personal animosity in Blair's running battle with Frémont, but it is also clear that Blair was genuinely concerned that Missouri was being lost to the Confederacy because of the incompetence of General Frémont. He courageously, or perhaps recklessly, risked his future because of this conviction.

In June of 1862, Blair was made a brigadier general and attempted to recruit forces in St. Louis. The recent Frémont controversy hampered his efforts, but in time seven regiments were raised and he went with them to Arkansas to join General William T. Sherman. Though he was tired of politics and continued in his military service far more often than his political duties, Blair was reelected to Congress in 1862, but only by 153 votes over his opponent, Samuel Knox. In 1864, this election would be overturned by the House and Knox would be declared the winner.

Blair's military career was exceptional. A biographer of the Blair family described Blair's qualifications:

> Whatever his deficiencies in professional and business affairs, Frank was a man of fierce determination, boundless energy, vivid imagination, instinctive courage, and a taste for grand homicide on a massive scale if exercised in a noble cause. In short, he was eminently qualified to be a great soldier, and the Civil War gave him the opportunity [Smith, *Francis Preston Blair*, p. 290].

His personal heroism was frequently exhibited. He joined Grant at Vicksburg in December of 1862, and had two horses shot from beneath him. He shortly became a major general and was put in command of the second division of the 15th Army Corps, where he made important contributions in various engagements. When Vicksburg surrendered on July 4, 1863, he was with generals Grant and Sherman to accept the surrender. He saw further action with General Sherman at Corinth, Mississippi, and at Chattanooga. His commanding officer, William T. Sherman, praised him frequently for his contributions. On December 11, 1863, Blair relinquished his command to another future vice presidential nominee, John A. Logan, and returned to his congressional seat. The congressional session was short, and Blair alternated between military and political duties by taking a new appointment as a major general and taking command of the 17th Corps in May 1864. Blair was with Sherman and joined in the infamous, but brutally effective, march to the sea. The final surrender of the war, by Confederate general Joseph E. Johnston, was received by Sherman, Blair, and a few other generals on April 17, 1865.

Blair had the temperament for battle; he was one of the few politicians-turned-general who excelled in uniform. Yet Blair was also an important factor in Congress. He was a lightning rod for Lincoln's opponents, and he sent crushing bolts back at Lincoln's attackers. Both personally and through his brother and father, Blair advised Lincoln on many matters, including urging the appointment of Ulysses Grant as commander of all the armies.

Blair made many enemies because of his abrasive style. He took the offensive against Salmon P. Chase, a member of the cabinet but also one of Lincoln's unannounced rivals for the 1864 presidential nomination. Chase eventually resigned because of the abuse he suffered at Blair's hands. Blair's enemies made several efforts to retaliate. Article I, Section 6 of the Constitution states that no person holding an office under the United States can be a member of either House of Congress, and a member of the army does hold office "under the United States." Previously the argument had been made that Blair was a member of the state militia and therefore not subject to this restriction. Lincoln had joined in this interpretation. While the constitutional question was being

debated, a committee investigating charges of irregularities in Blair's 1862 election voted five to four to oust him from his congressional seat. By a small majority, the House of Representatives agreed there were sufficient defects to void the election.

Just as Francis Preston Blair, Sr., had been one of the most intimate friends of Andrew Jackson, so had he and his family become extremely close to Abraham Lincoln. Frank Blair was in the Carolinas at the time of Lincoln's assassination, but his sister, Lizzie, and the wife of Gideon Welles, the secretary of the navy, were the only two people Mary Todd Lincoln wanted to see after her husband had been killed. For days Lizzie was constantly with Mrs. Lincoln.

Frank Blair's activities leading up to the Civil War and throughout the conflict were clearly as an opponent of slavery. Yet once slavery was destroyed by the war, he began to align himself with the former slaveowners and against the radical Republicans who desired a stringent reconstruction of the South. Frank Blair and his father frequently transmitted requests for pardons of various Confederate officers to the new president, Andrew Johnson. For a time he was a Johnson supporter, but soon decided Johnson was incompetent and unable to control the radicals. Frank began to praise the former Confederates in various speeches. Though not finding anything to applaud in the cause for which they had fought, Blair did find much to commend in their character. Nothing favorable was said about the former slaves, and he particularly was distressed at the idea of giving the vote to the freedmen.

As the Fourteenth Amendment was being debated in Congress, Blair took a strong stand in opposition. The clear indignities and outrages visited upon the former slaves, revealed in testimony in Congress, did not sway Blair. In his mind, states' rights could not be surrendered to the federal government; in time, he felt the Southern whites could be trusted with the proper treatment of their former slaves.

At least in the privacy of their home, as well as with other family members, Blair's wife Appo defended the radical Republican policy and criticized to the extent women were permitted to do so, her husband's position. As was true throughout Frank's life, he was seriously in debt. In 1860, he had been almost bankrupt, but had found support from friends to avoid public embarrassment. Frank would also borrow heavily from his family, much to the disgust of his wife. At no time during his life did Blair exhibit any self-restraint in his financial affairs, nor any intelligence. His father continued to support him primarily because, despite Frank's faults, his father believed he was destined for great things.

Since Frank and his family had discarded Andrew Johnson as a possibility in 1868, they searched around for another Democratic presidential possibility. Though a Free-Soiler before the war, and a Republican during it, Blair had quickly returned to his family's antecedents as Democrats once the radical Republicans took charge in Congress. Frank himself was a dark horse candidate for the Democratic nomination. The first act of any new president should be, Frank thought, the voiding of all of the radical reconstruction programs because they were unconstitutional. His first choice was Winfield Scott Hancock, who would not get the nomination until 1880. In July 1868, the Democratic National Convention opened in New York City. The convention was full of ex–Confederates whose names the Republicans flung back at the party as the election approached. It was far too early in the North to say forgive and forget. The Democrats were not being even reasonably discreet in their attempts to regain national power. Frank Blair perhaps was the least discreet and most unreasonable of all. To present his position, he wrote a public letter to Missouri lawyer James Broadhead. His warning to the nation was that unless a Democrat was elected in 1868, before the next election occurred in 1872, reconstruction would be an accomplished fact. All states would be admitted with black suffrage and carpetbaggers in charge. The 1868 election must therefore result in the canceling of all reconstruction acts. The new president must "compel the army to undo its usurpations at the South, disperse the carpetbag state governments, allow the *white people* to reorganize their own governments and elect

senators and representatives." After long balloting, Horatio Seymour finally received the presidential nomination. Since Seymour had been a peace Democrat during the war, a strong military record was needed in the vice presidential candidate. Frank Blair easily and quickly filled that bill.

The campaign was almost too easy for the Republicans. The Democratic presidential nominee could easily be criticized as having been against winning the war, while the vice presidential nominee was charged with trying to lose the peace. Frank would not be quieted, and throughout the campaign he pressed his views that control of the South must immediately be returned to the whites. All attempts to give the blacks civil and political rights must end. Blair's position is not all that inconsistent with his Free-Soil view before the war, since at no time did he desire that the former slaves remain in this country and receive equality. His answer before the war was colonization of slaves in Latin America; his answer after the war was the disfranchisement of Negroes.

As November approached, there were efforts by various Democrats to select new candidates. On October 17, Blair offered to withdraw if his father and Samuel J. Tilden of New York could agree that he should do so. On October 19, the Democratic national committee decided to stay with the same candidates, but some efforts to muzzle Blair were made. With all these problems, and with Grant's image as the savior of the North, it is surprising that the election was as close as it was.

Blair seemed to love conflict over compromise. In early 1869, he essentially invited himself to a banquet for former Union officers. He gave a speech after several other former Union generals had spoken, in which he praised the great Southern generals from the war. He was angrily hooted out of the room and not allowed to finish his talk. Blair had proceeded too far in his identification with the South, and though he could in the future count on strong Southern support in a presidential bid, he was antagonizing far too many Northern voters ever to make a credible choice for president. Yet the family continued to think Frank had a good future, particularly with the end of reconstruction looming closer.

With Blair's encouragement, Senate Democrats supported the nomination of Missouri senator Charles Drake for the Court of Claims. Blair then successfully ran for the Senate vacancy. Appo was particularly pleased by the sizeable, and stable, $7,500 salary in the senate. In his new post Blair continued his attack on reconstruction. He condemned various bills to control the Ku Klux Klan by increased federal judicial authority in the South. In 1872, he recognized that his prospects were dim for election to the presidency. He postponed his ambitions and helped secure the nomination of Horace Greeley.

In the summer and fall of 1872, Blair began to lose the use of his right hand. During his adult life he had been bothered by frequent and severe headaches, in part due to his smoking of over 30 cigars a day and his heavy drinking. Yet it seemed that he also suffered from high blood pressure or heart problems, for in October of 1872, he became paralyzed on his right side from a stroke. He taught himself to write left-handed, and considering his poor penmanship before, there probably was not much loss of clarity. His paralysis caused him to be defeated for reelection to the Senate in 1872. In the summer of 1873, he went to Clifton Springs, New York, because of its hot mineral waters, and seemed to be improving. A reporter who saw him in 1873 found him "a noble wreck stranded on a rocky shore...." Later in 1873, he returned to St. Louis and his improvement continued. However, he suffered another stroke and had to return to Clifton Springs. His finances were no better than at any other time in his adult life, and gifts and loans from his family became necessary. He gradually lost all control over his speech and continued to be paralyzed. While alone in the house in July 1875, he was knocked unconscious in a fall and died within a few hours.

Analysis of Qualifications

The Civil War demonstrated Blair's talents to the fullest. He was an able, courageous military leader whom his commanding officer, William T. Sherman, valued highly. He was too uncontrollable to have made a satisfactory peacetime career soldier, but he was fully suited for the demands and excitement of war. He was extravagant financially as well as physically. His political positions throughout his career showed great courage and determination. As the only Free-Soil congressman from a slaveowning state prior to the Civil War, Blair obviously was not only a man of conviction but also one of considerable political skill. He would today be called charismatic in his ability to inspire and excite others. Though able to handle himself well extemporaneously, Blair also called upon the considerable talents of his father to write many of his best speeches. He was never easy on his political enemies. Twice he was the subject of assassination attempts, probably because of his vitriolic attacks.

Once the Civil War had ended, Blair's emphasis shifted dramatically. As radical Republicans took control of the national government, Blair more and more found himself the advocate of the rights of white Southerners. Such advocacy placed him on the side, even if unconsciously, of racial hatred and the reenslavement of the black race. The association was unconscious, as Blair did believe in time that former masters would become benevolent leaders. Since in Blair's view the ex-slave was incapable of governing himself, and certainly incapable of governing the whites, the paramount point was to prevent them from having any voice in Southern government. To that end, Blair opposed the Fourteenth Amendment to the United States Constitution, as well as any other legislation that would give federal authorities the power to interfere with states' rights.

Francis P. Blair as president during this critical period would have advanced the end of reconstruction, probably without significantly altering the final result of that process. All Southern governments were "redeemed" between 1870 and 1876; all threw off the black and Republican dominated governments, and all imposed Black Codes and other restraints on the former slaves. Probably any man would have been a better president than Ulysses S. Grant, and Blair is no exception. Blair wished only that the Southerners would be left entirely to their own devices, as in time they would be. What the country probably could best have used during this sad period was a moderate president who would have restrained the excesses on both sides such that the backlash that eventually did occur both in the North and South could have been avoided or ameliorated. It was that loss of will on the part of the North that enabled the South to be "redeemed" in reconstruction, and it was the severity of the reconstruction that caused Southerners to seek redemption so forcefully.

Perhaps it is too much to expect that any president could have saved the country from much of the one hundred years of Southern despair and the need for a second reconstruction in the 1960s. Whether such a man did exist, Frank Blair almost certainly was not he.

BLAIR BIBLIOGRAPHY
Preston, William B. *The Preston Genealogy*. Salt Lake City (1900).
Smith, Elbert B. *Francis Preston Blair* (the candidate's father). New York (1980).
Smith, William Ernest. *The Francis Preston Blair Family in Politics*. 2 vols. New York (1933).
Sontag, David L. "Frank Blair in the American Civil War." Unpublished master's thesis, Central Missouri State University (1990).
Wurthman, L.B. "Frank Blair, Lincoln's Congressional Spokesman." *Missouri Historical Review* 64 (1970), pp. 263–288.

Election of 1872

NOMINATIONS

Liberal Republican Party Convention (1st): May 1, 1872, in Cincinnati, Ohio. *President—* Horace Greeley, nominated on the sixth ballot with 482 votes out of 726 cast, having received 147 on the first ballot. Charles Francis Adams (Mass.), Lyman Trumbull (Ill.), B. Gratz Brown (Mo.), David Davis (Ill.), and Andrew Curtin (Pa.) were other possibilities. *Vice president—* B. Gratz Brown, nominated on the second ballot with 435 votes out of 696 cast, having been given 237 on the first vote. Lyman Trumbull (Ill.), George Washington Julian (Ind.), and Gilbert Walker (Va.) also were contenders.

Republican Party Convention (5th): June 5–6, 1872, at the Academy of Music, Philadelphia, Pa. *President—* Ulysses S. Grant, nominated unanimously on the first ballot. *Vice president—* Henry Wilson, nominated on the first ballot with 364½ votes of the 686 cast. Schuyler Colfax (Ind.) received the rest of the votes.

Democratic Party Convention (11th): July 9–10, 1872, at Ford's Opera House, Baltimore, Md. *President—* Horace Greeley, nominated on the first ballot with 686 votes out of 732 cast. *Vice president—* B. Gratz Brown, nominated on the first ballot with 713 votes out of 732 cast.

GENERAL ELECTION, November 5, 1872
Popular Vote

Grant	3,598,235
Greeley	2,834,761
Others	34,683

Greeley died on November 29, 1872, before the electoral college met. The votes due to him (66) were scattered among other men.

Electoral Vote
PRESIDENT
Grant — 286 (29 states)
Greeley's 66 votes (6 states) went to:

Thomas Hendricks	42
B. Gratz Brown	18

Charles J. Jenkins   2
David Davis   1
Horace Greeley   3
(Greeley's 3 votes were not included in official total.)

VICE PRESIDENT
Wilson 286
B. Gratz Brown   47
7 others   19

Winners
Ulysses S. Grant, 18th president
Henry Wilson, 18th vice president
Losers
Horace Greeley, B. Gratz Brown, Thomas A. Hendricks

1872 presidential nominee—
Liberal Republican and Democratic Parties

Horace Greeley

Full name: Horace Greeley.
State represented: New York.
Birth: February 3, 1811, Amherst, New Hampshire.
Age on Inauguration Day (died before this date; March 4, 1873): 62 years, 1 month.
Education: Infrequent education in local schools, left at age 13; apprenticed in art of printing.
Religion: Universalist.
Ancestry/prominent relatives: Horace's great-great-grandfather, the first Greeley in America, arrived from England in 1640; Horace's mother was Scotch-Irish.
Occupation: Printer, newspaper editor and publisher.
Public offices: U.S. House of Representatives, December 4, 1848–March 3, 1849; defeated for U.S. senator, 1861 and 1863, for U.S. House, 1868 and 1870, and for New York state comptroller, 1869; declined appointment as minister to Austria, 1867; elected to New York state constitutional convention, 1867; unsuccessful Liberal Republican and Democratic nominee for president, 1872.
Home: Farm in Chappaqua, New York.

Death: November 29, 1872, Pleasantville, New York, at private sanitarium; age 61 years, 10 months.
Burial: Greenwood Cemetery, Brooklyn, New York.
Personal characteristics: 5'10" tall; disheveled; wore poorly fitting, if immaculately clean clothes; trademark was long white coat or duster, pant legs sitting on top of his boots, and white broad-brimmed hat; eyes pale, skin almost ghostly white, hair blond; high and shrill voice; affected throat whiskers though his face was clean-shaven.
Father: Zaccheus Greeley (March 23, 1782–December 18, 1867), farmer and day laborer.
Mother: Mary Woodburn (1788–1855), daughter of David and Margaret (Clark) Woodburn; married in 1807.
Siblings: Horace, died young. Nathan Barnes (June 12, 1812–December 11, 1894), married Sally A. Hines in January 1838, and after her death married Polly R. Conn on December 24, 1856. Arminda (December 26, 1813–died young). Arminda (1814?–?), married Lovell Greeley. Esther Senter (?–January 10, 1890), married John F. Cleveland. Margarette Woodburn (?–?), married William O. Bush.
Wife: Mary Young Cheney (October 20, 1811–October 30, 1872), daughter of Silas E. and Mary (Young) Cheney; married on July 5, 1836.
Children: First two children died at birth, a son in 1838 and a daughter in 1842. Arthur Young (called "Pickie") (March 22, 1844–July 12, 1849), died of cholera after only a four-hour illness. Raphael Uhlman (1851–February 28, 1857). Mary Inez, died at age six months of croup. Ida Lillian (November 17, 1848–April 11, 1882), married Nicholas Smith, May 1, 1875. Gabrielle Rosamond (March 26, 1857–?).
Memorials/statues: Greeley's statue is in City Hall Park, New York. The New Castle (N.Y.) Historical Society has a Greeley Room.

Horace Greeley published and edited the most influential newspaper in the North. His brilliant, persuasive, aggressively moralistic editorials helped mold public opinion for 30 years. Horace Greeley was one of the most intellectually impressive men ever to be nominated for president, yet he was also without a doubt the most eccentric and unpredictable.

As a child, Greeley knew few comforts. His father struggled to provide for his family through farming, for which he seemed to have no aptitude, and by hiring himself out as a laborer. His New Hampshire farm was sold at foreclosure, along with many of the family possessions. Greeley's father fled the state in order to avoid imprisonment for debt. The whole family moved to Vermont to escape this legal threat. It was not until after Horace had left home for the newspaper business that the remainder of the family enjoyed any success at farming.

Horace was a precocious child who, according to some perhaps exaggerated stories, was at the age of four winning spelling bees against children twice his age; had read the entire Bible at age five; and by the time he was 13 was sent home from school because he knew more than the teacher did. His obvious brilliance caused the trustees of a school in a neighboring town to vote that the only pupil from a town other than their own who could attend was Horace Greeley. Leading citizens from the village offered to pay for his education at Phillips Academy in Exeter, but the parents rejected the offer out of pride and perhaps out of reluctance to send Horace so far from home. Greeley would become the quintessential self-made man, whose natural brilliance was never honed by the discipline of formal education.

The family decided to move to Wayne, Pennsylvania, to start afresh, but Horace, only 15, remained behind and was apprenticed to a newspaper owner in East Poultney, New York. Just when he became convinced that the newspaper and printing business would become his career is uncertain, but at least by the time of his apprenticeship, his life's work seemed set. The paper collapsed in June 1830, causing Greeley to walk most of the way to Erie County, Pennsylvania, where his parents lived. Seven months working for the *Erie Gazette* and at other jobs indicated little success would be found in Erie, and Greeley set out for New York City.

Arriving in August 1831, he had only ten dollars to his name, knew no one in the city, and had no job. He was tall, slender, and pale, the ultimate country unsophisticate in the big city. A succession of positions in the printing and newspaper business permitted him to save enough money that by January 1833, he could form a printing firm with Frances V. Story as his partner. Story drowned in July, and a new partnership was formed with Jonas Winchester. The partners' principal income came from printing lottery numbers, a mundane but lucrative task. Greeley could not be satisfied with such efforts and longed to be publishing his political views. In March 1834, Greeley founded the *New Yorker*, a literary and news journal that every week printed some news as well as short stories, poems, and music. Its circulation was impressive, but its profits were not. However unprofitable the *New Yorker* was, it did establish Greeley as a rising talent in the newspaper field.

Greeley's political enthusiasm as well as his financial needs caused him to write frequently for various political journals, and in 1838 he began to edit a campaign paper, the *Jeffersonian*. His two political partners were Thurlow Weed and William H. Seward, who were to remain closely allied with Greeley until shortly before the Civil War. The *Jeffersonian* established Greeley as a political publisher, and in 1840 the Whigs called upon him again for another weekly paper. The *Log Cabin* began publication on May 2, 1840, and was an astounding influence on the campaign. Greeley edited the *Log Cabin*, continued his publishing of the *New Yorker*, and also made speeches and involved himself tirelessly in other ways for the campaign. The Whigs' success in that election, Greeley believed, was in large measure due to his efforts. His self-importance was exaggerated, but the *Log Cabin* made a significant contribution.

Greeley began publishing the *New York Tribune* on April 10, 1841. There were 12 daily newspapers in New York City in 1841, but there was no penny newspaper that identified itself with the Whigs. He borrowed some money, threw his own savings into the venture, and after a few weeks of doubt saw the paper grow to 6,000 circulation by its fourth week and 11,000 by its seventh. Thomas McElrath was brought in as the business manager and partner of the paper, an important addition that complemented Greeley's talents, which clearly were not in the business area. Later in the year he merged the *Log Cabin* and the *New Yorker* into his new paper.

As political as Greeley was, his paper set a new standard for taste and high moral standards. It was certainly a biased newspaper, but it was well written and informative. The journalism of its competitors, in which police reports and various scandals dominated the headlines, was not repeated in the *Tribune*. It was a radical newspaper, in that it reflected the radical political views of its publisher.

One of the more intriguing social movements that Greeley embraced was Fourierism, named for Frenchman Charles Fourier. Fourier desired that society be reorganized on a decentralized basis. All of society would be carved into units, called phalanxes, consisting of 620 men working 5,000 acres of land. It was a self-sufficient community, but trade would arise between the various phalanxes. All people within one community would share proportionately according to their efforts and initiative. Greeley became so enamored with Fourier that three times a week he permitted a Fourierist article to appear on the first page of the *Tribune*. Greeley was the center of two efforts to fund phalanxes, one in northern Pennsylvania, and the other in New Jersey. Greeley also was influential in converting Brook Farm in West Roxbury, Massachusetts, into a Fourierist community. It disbanded in 1847, and the other two phalanxes withered.

Also vigorously espoused in the *Tribune* was a generous homestead law, which would give free government land to settlers. He compared the exploitation of workers in the cities to Negro slavery. He supported women's rights generally, but not women's suffrage. Unionism posed no threat in Greeley's mind, though liquor did. He also opposed capital punishment. The total number of political issues that found their way onto Greeley's editorial pages is almost countless.

Through Greeley's moral fervor and the general quality of the *Tribune*, the newspaper achieved tremendous national influence. Its peak came during the years immediately prior to the Civil War, when it received a revered place almost next to the Bible in many Northern, and particularly rural homes. The cause most loudly trumpeted by Greeley in these years was abolition. Though not at first being radical in his views, Greeley increasingly found himself among the rabid abolitionists. He opposed the Compromise of 1850 and for that matter the very acquisition of the Mexican territories, because he saw this as increasing the ability of the South to extend slavery. The Kansas-Nebraska Act, which permitted the majority of the Kansas and Nebraska residents to decide whether these territories would be slave or free, and which also repealed the Missouri Compromise line, was anathema to Greeley and he urged resistance to its operation. He advised Northerners to ignore the Fugitive Slave Act and to assist in the escape of any fugitive blacks. No issue was more crucial to Greeley during the last half of the 1850s and during the Civil War than the complete abolition of slavery.

Greeley's emotions and interests were in the political issues that burned within him. He paid little heed to the economics of the newspaper, and he gradually lost control. He was a bad businessman because he did not care about the business end of his work. The *Tribune* made enormous amounts of money, but what he easily could have enjoyed of that amount he permitted other owners of the paper to take disproportionately. His own income was in large part given away to charities as well as to scoundrels who touched his generosity.

Greeley's private life was equally disorganized. Of seven children born to his wife, only two daughters lived to adulthood. Their first child to survive birth, who was the brilliant light in his parents' lives, died at the age of five almost without warning, having first exhibited the symptoms of cholera only four hours before he died. Mrs. Greeley retreated to her home and became increasingly irritable and hypochondriacal. There is no hint that Greeley was ever critical of his wife's terrible temper and lack of support for him, but his home life must have been close to unbearable. Mrs. Greeley was strong-minded and a perfectionist. She complained about everything and everybody. There was little domestic common sense in Greeley's wife, and she could neither attend to the housework herself nor coexist with the domestic servants who were hired. It has been said that she seemed to delight in affronting those who met her. One of Greeley's best friends, Alice Cary, stated that she never once visited the Greeleys without being insulted. For all of Mrs. Greeley's intolerable habits, Horace probably never serious considered divorce as he believed uncompromisingly in the sanctity of marriage. Starting in 1853, the Greeleys lived on a farm in Chappaqua, New York, where his experiments in farming were recounted in the *Tribune*. Greeley's relaxation was on his farm as well as among a wide circle of friends, many of whom were women of strong political influence, such as Elizabeth Cady Stanton and Alison and Phoebe Cary.

As the Civil War loomed, Greeley's impassioned arguments against slavery did not subside. Various commentators have given Greeley considerable "credit" for so inflaming passions of both North and South as to make war inevitable. As wide as the *Tribune* circulation was in the North, it was nonexistent in the South. So hated was Greeley and his views in the South that any representative of the *Tribune* had to travel incognito.

Greeley initially did not support Abraham Lincoln for the Republican nomination in 1860, and as a delegate to the Republican National Convention he was primarily interested in defeating his old political partner, now enemy, William Seward. On the eve of the balloting, Greeley started counseling delegates to support Lincoln. After Lincoln's election, Greeley continued to fight any prospect of compromise on slavery. He preferred secession to any action that might aid slavery. If the South wanted to secede, so be it, and no effort should be made in the name of compromise that would perpetuate this dreaded institution. As war began, his newspaper trumpeted the cry "Forward to Richmond." This helped compel the Union generals and politicians into precipitous action that resulted in disaster at the first battle of Bull Run.

Throughout the war, Greeley was a thorn in Lincoln's side. Lincoln's hesitation on the slavery question drew the sharpest barbs. Greeley wished for a general emancipation to be declared immediately, ignoring Lincoln's own studied decision that the border states, which had not seceded, be appeased on this issue as encouragement to remain in the Union.

In 1864, Greeley belatedly and reluctantly supported Lincoln for renomination and election, having declared in early 1864 that many of the candidates would make as good a president as Lincoln. In mid–August, he believed Lincoln was a certain loser in the November election and that he should be dumped from the ticket. Finally by September, he did endorse Lincoln's election, perhaps on the basis, which cannot be proved, of an alleged offer by Lincoln to appoint Greeley postmaster general. Such an appointment never came.

Greeley's interest in a negotiated settlement to the Civil War showed itself on the pages of the *Tribune* as well as in private activities. In July 1864, he informed Lincoln that two Confederate agents were in Canada and had informed Greeley that they were ready to negotiate a peace. In his letter to Lincoln, Greeley said that "our bleeding, bankrupt, almost dying country also longs for peace; shutters at the prospect of fresh conscriptions, of further wholesale devastations, and of new rivers of human blood...." If Greeley had given up hope and was grasping at any straw, Lincoln had not. The president approached this opening gingerly, looking for hidden dangers. He informed Greeley that if these representatives from the South had full authority to negotiate a settlement, that he, the president, would meet with them. He told Greeley to go to Canada to open negotiations. This suggestion greatly surprised and perplexed the editor. Greeley discovered there that the Southern agents indeed did not have full authority that would have been required to decide upon peace terms, and the hope was abandoned. Greeley's despair over the Union's chance for victory was displayed daily at the *Tribune*. His criticism weakened Lincoln's support at home, but also weakened many readers' opinions of Greeley.

Once the Appomattox surrender was concluded, Greeley joined the radical Republicans in support of the Fourteenth and Fifteenth Amendments to the Constitution. He did not want a conciliatory policy towards the defeated states and desired to complete the revolution in racial conditions quickly and decisively. Andrew Johnson became an impediment to the Republicans' reconstruction plans. Greeley strongly backed Congress's impeachment effort. Though Greeley supported all efforts to end the vestiges of slavery, he also favored a general amnesty for the Confederates. The most controversial act of his entire career was his joining the signing on May 13, 1867, of the bond that permitted the release of Jefferson Davis from prison. His paper lost more than half of its circulation, and thousands of orders for the just-completed second volume of his popular book, *The American Conflict*, were canceled. When Greeley was nominated for president a few years later, this particular act hung as an albatross around his neck, though it was hardly the only reason for his defeat.

The first two years of the Grant administration were favored with strong *Tribune* support. However, Greeley then began criticizing the flagrant corruption and lack of direction in the executive branch. There were also personal political problems concerning federal patronage in New York, which was being distributed by local politicians whom Greeley distrusted. On September 15, 1871, the *Tribune* publicly rejected the idea of a second term for Grant. The best approach seemed to Greeley to be the creation of a new, anti–Grant party, and gradually such a coalition of diverse political factions joined as the Liberal Republican Party. The editor himself did not at first believe he would carry the banner against Grant, but his lifelong interest in political office made him readily accede to the suggestion that he be a candidate. Greeley engaged in no active campaign prior to the new party's convention. The contest at the Cincinnati convention that began on May 1, 1872, was between Greeley and Charles Francis Adams, the son and grandson of former presidents. When Greeley finally secured the nomination on the sixth ballot, it was a bitterly divided convention. The normal acquiescence in making the nomination unanimous was rejected, and many delegates left the convention refusing to work for Greeley. The Democratic convention also was not excited about seconding the nomination of this man who through his newspaper

had attacked the Democratic Party for 30 years. The Democrats did nominate Greeley, but again many refused to accept the decision.

The campaign against Greeley was vicious. Greeley's constant criticism of Lincoln during the Civil War, as well as his joining in the release of Jefferson Davis, were used to depict Greeley as a traitor. One of the nominee's most fervent political positions was reconciliation with the South, and he used the phrase that both sections were "eager to clasp hands across the bloody chasm." Many Northerners were not yet ready to forget the war, and Greeley's conciliatory approach gained him few votes. Resigning from the editorship of the *Tribune*, he began a strenuous campaign through the North, giving speeches and meeting with political leaders. He could not stem the tide and was swamped in a solid Grant victory.

Five days before the election the almost tragic marriage that had sapped Greeley's energy and emotions for 35 years ended with his wife's death. That blow was followed by his surprisingly strong rejection from the American voters. A third strike came when Greeley discovered that the control of the *Tribune* was slipping from him. Other owners and editors were weary of Greeley's political activities that were sapping the strength of the paper. There was more than a little greed in their putsch as well. Greeley thought his protégé, Whitlaw Reed, was at the center of the overthrow effort, but this was untrue. The rigors of the campaign as well as the tribulations of these successive defeats, caused his mind to break. His decline was rapid, and he died on November 29. He did not die forgotten, and his funeral was attended by the president, the vice president, and much of the cabinet and Congress.

Greeley was an eccentric, high-strung yet brilliant man, and it is probably accurate to say that the personal and political devastation he suffered during the fall of 1872 was too much. Defeat literally killed him.

Analysis of Qualifications

Greeley was a frustrating mix of features. He was a brilliant and remarkably influential editor who for 30 years carried the banner of great reform causes in America. His simple, incisive style of writing was both understandable and convincing. He was a power in politics, particularly in the use of the *Tribune* to promote first the Whig Party and later the Republicans. Yet perhaps as a result of his lack of formal education, he was poorly disciplined. As one biographer stated, Greeley "was prone to quick decisions and deemed his judgment infallible, for as a self-made man he had little else upon which to rely. He lacked the ability to see all facets of a problem...." He was idealistic and dynamic, a combination that through his editorials in the 1850s helped make the Civil War inevitable. Greeley was hardly the cause of that conflict, yet his fulminations made the sectional chasm more difficult to bridge.

Greeley was not driven by the same forces that propelled other men. He had no interest in money, and so little sense about business that it is doubtful that the *Tribune* would ever have amounted to the force it was if not for the early hiring of a business manager. Though he could be thoughtlessly cold to people he met, much of this should be attributed to his absentmindedness and his total devotion to his work. Visitors to his office would not even be honored by Greeley with a quick glance, and a curt conversation would be conducted while Greeley continued with his head buried in his writing. In contrast to this business demeanor, Greeley was easy prey for the downtrodden. He moralized on the great national issues in the newspaper, and he also contributed to just about any charity that requested money. Many scoundrels took advantage of his soft heart that could not discriminate between the needy and the greedy.

Greeley was a reformer, humanitarian and philanthropist. He was also an undisciplined and abrasive visionary who had little appreciation for the art of the possible. Greeley's stumbling in 1864 in dealing with the possibility of a negotiated settlement to the war contrasts poorly with Lincoln's careful analysis. Both men longed for peace, and probably Lincoln desired it just as passionately as Greeley, since the burden of the war was daily and personally upon the president. Greeley charged forth without asking questions, his criticisms being reserved for Lincoln's lack of similar

blithe enthusiasm. As president, Greeley would constantly have been hampered by his failure to appreciate the nuances inherent in any difficult political situation.

The great substantive political issues in 1872 were corruption and Reconstruction. The corruption in the Grant administration was already evident, and calls for civil service reform were mounting. Greeley opposed such reform, thinking that the problem with political patronage could be cured not by eliminating it but by limiting presidents to one term. The issue of Reconstruction in the South and the still-recent memories of the war probably explained the severity of Greeley's defeat. His hope that the two sections could reach across the "bloody chasm" struck many Northerners as a treasonous desire to forget the suffering caused by the war.

A not-to-be-forgotten factor was Greeley's own bad health. Though Greeley's death probably was accelerated by the bitterness of the crushing blows he suffered during this period, only one of which was his election defeat, even had he received good news from the polls it is hard to imagine that his delicate constitution would have carried him through a full term. Equally hard blows would have pounded him as president, and a similar disintegration into insanity and death could easily have occurred.

It is not likely, then, that Greeley could have performed with distinction or even safe mediocrity as president. As editor of the *New York Tribune* he found the position that best suited his talents and most served his country. From that high and influential position he helped shape public opinion for three decades. The actual last year of his life was an unfortunate ending to this unusual man's successful career. A Greeley presidency would probably have been an even sadder conclusion.

GREELEY BIBLIOGRAPHY

Archer, Jules. *Fighting Journalist. Horace Greeley.* New York City (1966).

Greeley, George Hiram. *Genealogy of the Greely-Greeley Family.* Boston (1905).

Greeley, Horace. *Recollections of a Busy Life.* New York City (1868).

Hale, William Harland. *Horace Greeley: Voice of the People.* New York City (1950).

HORACE GREELEY and B. GRATZ BROWN
(From the collection of David J. and Janice L. Frent)

Horner, Harlan Hoyt. *Lincoln and Greeley*. Westport, Conn. (1974), reprint of 1953 edition.

Linn, William A. *Horace Greeley*. Woodstock, N.Y. (1975).

Lunde, Erik S. *Horace Greeley*. Boston (1981).

Parton, James. *The Life of Horace Greeley*. Salem, N.H. (1972), reprint of 1855 edition.

Schulze, Suzanne. *Horace Greeley: A Bio-Bibliography*. New York (1992).

Seitz, Don C. *Horace Greeley*. Indianapolis (1926).

Stoddard, Henry Luther, *Horace Greeley, Printer, Editor, Crusader*. New York City (1946).

Zabriskie, Francis Nicoll. *Horace Greeley, the Editor*. Philadelphia (1980), reprint of 1890 edition.

1872 vice presidential nominee—
Liberal Republican and Democratic Parties

B. Gratz Brown

Full name: Benjamin Gratz Brown.

State represented: Missouri.

Birth: May 28, 1826, in Lexington, Kentucky.

Age on Inauguration Day (March 4, 1873): 46 years, 9 months.

Education: Tutored at home; Transylvania University, 1841–1845; Yale College, 1845–1847; studied law with father, then entered Louisville Law School; admitted to bar in 1849.

Religion: Presbyterian.

Ancestry/prominent relatives: Scotch-Irish family, great-grandfather (John Brown) arrived from Ireland in 1740; grandfather (John Brown) was first U.S. senator from Kentucky; great uncle (James Brown) was Kentucky secretary of state and U.S. senator from Louisiana; father was Kentucky secretary of state, commissioner of Indian Affairs; maternal grandfather (Jesse Bledsoe) was U.S. senator from Kentucky; one of his mother's aunts married Francis Preston Blair, Sr.; cousin was Francis P. Blair, Jr. (see election of 1868).

Occupation: Attorney.

Public offices: Missouri house of representatives, 1852–1858, defeated 1858; defeated for governor 1857; U.S. senator, November 13, 1863–March 3, 1867; governor of Missouri, January 1871–January 1873; defeated for Liberal Republican presidential nomination, 1872,

unsuccessful Liberal Republican and Democratic nominee for vice president, 1872; master in chancery, 1885.

Home: Country home near Ironton, Missouri; in 1880 moved to Kirkwood, a St. Louis suburb.

Death: December 13, 1885, Kirkwood, Missouri, at age 59 years, 6½ months.

Burial: Oak Hill Cemetery, Kirkwood, Missouri.

Personal characteristics: In twenties was slender, average height, red hair and large head; long red beard in mid-thirties; blue eyes; during 1872 campaign described as 5'8" tall, 120 pounds, fair complexion, blue eyes, light and fine auburn hair.

Father: Mason Brown (November 10, 1799–?), lawyer, judge, and political leader.

Mother: Judith Ann Bledsoe (?–September 28, 1827), married March 10, 1825; daughter of Judge Jesse Bledsoe of Lexington, Kentucky.

Siblings: None.

Stepmother: Mary Yoder (?–?), married December 8, 1835; daughter of Capt. Jacob Yoder; they had three sons and three daughters.

Wife: Mary Hansome Gunn (1841–1887), daughter of Calvin Gunn; married August 12, 1858.

Children: Lillian Mason (1860–?). Van Wyck. Gratz Knox. Mary G., married Presley Carr Lane. Violet Gratz, married William M. Tompkins. Margaretta Mason. Eliza Eloise. Judith B., married Leslie Dana. Robert Bruce.

Historic sites/memorials: Brown's home is in the Celebrities' Historic District in Frankfort, Kentucky. Another Brown home is now the Cole County Historical Society Building, 109 Madison Street, Jefferson City, Missouri.

The future vice presidential nominee's family was as prominent as any that ever sired a candidate. Three United States senators graced his family tree; three ancestors had been secretary of state for Kentucky; many other honors had been bestowed on his several luminous forebears. B. Gratz Brown, named for his great-uncle Benjamin Gratz, in whose home he was born, had quite a tradition to follow.

When Gratz was still a young boy his mother died. The boy was tutored at home and not only in traditional subjects. Political education was also received in strong measure in his house, with Whig doctrines the text. His mother had refused to permit slaves to be owned by the family; later the restriction was removed, but emancipation came to many of the family slaves when they were 25.

While attending Transylvania University in his home town of Lexington, Kentucky, Brown decided to study law. The decision seemed to have been reached to advance his real goal: being a politician. Brown's background had made him a strong supporter of Henry Clay, but he would not become at any stage in his career a blind partisan. Indeed, the constant feature of Brown's political life was the frequency in which he switched parties and positions. In 1849 and 1850, a strong emancipation movement was gathering steam in Kentucky. Brown played no active role in the campaign, but his convictions were clearly favorable to emancipation. The movement failed, however, and a heinous provision was added to the state constitution that any emancipated slave must leave the state or be imprisoned. Perhaps the political climate seemed too negative, or perhaps Brown merely saw greater political opportunity, but in 1849 he moved west to St. Louis to join his cousins Frank and Montgomery Blair. His relatives would give him the entree he needed to start afresh.

The Blairs were well established. "Old Bullion," as Thomas Hart Benton was called, was an incumbent United States senator who was very close politically to the Blairs. Yet Benton was losing favor because of his moderate stands on slavery. There was neither opportunity nor perhaps inclination on Brown's part at first to become too greatly involved in the political wars, and instead he joined the Blair law firm. Slowly he came around to Benton's viewpoint on many issues. The Whig Party was disintegrating, and the moderate Bentonites were Brown's most acceptable intermediate home. Brown's political involvement began with writing editorials for the St. Louis *Democrat*, published by the Blairs and others friendly towards Benton's policies. Within two years Brown was editor-in-chief.

Benton's unpopular slavery opinions caused him to lose reelection to the United States Senate. In 1854, he ran for Congress, while Brown

made his first election foray as a candidate for the state house of representatives. Brown won but Benton did not. Benton next sought election to the other Senate seat, which would be filled by the legislature that was just elected. Brown searched for any political coalition that could be put together for Benton, including moderate Whigs together with Benton Democrats. While the battle for the Senate seat raged, Brown found his own chair in jeopardy. His election had been by only 12 votes and his opponent was not yet willing to concede. The house, by one vote, decided Brown could keep his seat. Brown's election difficulties were part of a several-pronged effort to remove prominent and vocal Benton supporters from positions of influence.

The legislature voted for United States senator for 41 ballots, but neither side would budge. The session ended with no senator being elected. During the battle tempers flared, and Brown challenged a particularly offensive opponent to a duel. At the last moment the adversary withdrew his offending words and the duel was canceled. Besides using the dueling field, Brown also pushed Benton's cause through vigorous editorials in the *Democrat*. Brown was particularly successful in rallying German-American voters to the Benton cause, a group of supporters Brown would find quite helpful in his own later campaigns.

A reorganization of parties in Missouri was under way. Brown hoped to be able to form a moderate party of disaffected Democrats and old-line Whigs. Benton was now old and discredited; the Republican Party was too abolitionist to gain support, and thus Brown was without a party. In 1856, his political and familial cousin, Frank Blair, became a Republican and began organizing the state in the party's behalf. Brown was not yet ready to follow suit. Throughout their twin careers, however, it would appear Blair was the first to show the way and then Brown, sometimes only after a period of savage denunciation of Blair's actions, would conform. Brown was no abolitionist in this pre-war period, but he was a mild emancipationist and a Free-Soiler. He worked strenuously to get Benton to support Benton's son-in-law, John Charles Frémont, for the presidency, but failed. Secret meetings between Know-Nothings and Brown were held in the 1856 campaign. Early elections in St. Louis showed the Know-Nothings to be unpopular, and thus Brown dropped any plans for a coalition and turned to Benton Democrats to help Frémont.

Though a Frémont partisan, Brown was chosen as a delegate to the 1856 Democratic National Convention. He and other Bentonites were not permitted to take their seats because a rival, anti–Benton delegation from Missouri succeeded in pressing their credentials. Brown damaged his group's chances when he physically broke into the convention hall after having been denied admission, and sought to take his place as a delegate. His brashness and strong temper then was not out of character. Brown had continued to hope that Senator Benton could be persuaded to support Frémont, but when Benton made his unequivocal endorsement of Democrat James Buchanan, Brown felt compelled to follow his lead. Brown said later that he felt that in one of the great watershed elections in American history, he had in the end allowed himself to be counted on the wrong side. Frémont and Benton both lost.

Brown's abrasive and fiery character caused another duel during this election campaign. Brown's editorial attacks on Thomas C. Reynolds had inflamed partisans of each man. Reynolds was a prominent, hot-tempered anti–Benton Democrat who was a political power in St. Louis. For months Brown fired salvoes at Reynolds. At last Reynolds challenged him to settle this matter "honorably." On August 26, 1856, the two met on an island in the Mississippi (thereby avoiding state laws prohibiting dueling). Brown was injured in the knee, while Brown's bullet just barely missed Reynolds' head.

The Republican Party increasingly appeared to Brown as the future force in Missouri. In the legislature Brown made an impassioned speech for emancipation, again rousing the hatred of the slavery forces. Brown's arguments did not focus on the moral necessity of freeing the Negro, but rather the economic requirement that white workers not be priced out of jobs by slavery. Benton broke with his protégé after this speech, because the former

senator had never favored emancipation. Benton's view had been to defuse slavery as an issue. His former pupil had once agreed with those sentiments, but was now performing just the opposite task by declaring for emancipation. Brown's hope was to join moderate former Whigs and the Democratic moderates into a new coalition by appealing to the economic interests of business as well as white laborers. Brown's speech was not taken as moderation, however, but instead as an avowal of abolitionism.

Emancipation under whatever title defeated Brown in his attempt to be reelected to the Missouri house in 1858. There was little question that year as to his political stripe, even though he continued to call himself an "Opposition" candidate instead of a Republican. Brown gave frequent editorial support to Abraham Lincoln in his Illinois campaign against Senator Stephen Douglas. The *Democrat* gradually became, ironically, a Republican paper. Brown's increasingly strident political stands caused a breach with Blair and the *Democrat* in the spring of 1859. These two ambitious politicians could not work in harness on the paper, and on April 11, 1859, Brown was fired.

The first Republican convention in Missouri was held March 10, 1860, and Brown presided. Again Blair and Brown were divided, Blair being a supporter of Missourian Edward Bates for president while Brown remained uncommitted. Brown was selected as a delegate to the Republican National Convention in Chicago, and there helped swing Missouri's delegation to Lincoln.

Secession was becoming a reality throughout the South after Lincoln's election. Brown helped organize a Union regiment and became a colonel. For three-and-one-half months he served patrol duty in St. Louis and throughout southwest Missouri. Brown's military career then ended, as he had no interest in soldiering. This was not to say he was indifferent to military matters. John Charles Frémont was appointed to command the Department of the West and established headquarters in St. Louis. Brown was one of his sponsors. The Blairs began to criticize Frémont, and Brown saw an alliance with Frémont as a way to decrease the Blairs' power. The most significant and controversial action taken by Frémont was his proclamation on August 30, 1861, placing all of Missouri under martial law. The slaves of any resident who was aiding the rebellion were declared free. Lincoln feared making emancipation a war aim so early would drive the border states into the Confederacy, and therefore asked Frémont to modify the proclamation. The request was refused. Lincoln personally modified the order and shortly thereafter Frémont was removed from his post.

Brown agreed with Frémont's approach and slowly became a radical Republican. Increasingly, Brown criticized the president as being too moderate on war aims. Brown was definitely allying himself with the abolitionists. He wanted all secessionists to be treated as enemies, with their property confiscated and their rights as citizens forfeited. All slaves should be emancipated and Negro regiments formed to fight the rebels. When Lincoln finally announced the Emancipation Proclamation, Brown was delighted. His pleasure turned to dismay when he discovered Missouri was not included within the states affected by the proclamation.

Abolition was in part a means to an end. The goal was Brown's election to the United States Senate. He refused to run against his cousin Blair for Congress. Instead, Brown laid the political groundwork that led to smashing radical victories in the fall legislative elections which gained control of the legislature. The ensuing balloting for U.S. senator became deadlocked between Brown and other candidates. Thirty ballots were taken, at times highlighted by Brown's furious speeches against Lincoln, Blair, the incumbent governor, and any other politician who wavered on the radical program. A year would pass before the twin vacancies in the U.S. Senate would be filled. In the interim, Brown participated actively in a state emancipation convention held in September 1863. Brown demanded immediate abolition, and charged that it was Lincoln who constantly had stood in the way of freedom for Missouri slaves. Never should rebels be allowed to return to participation in the electorate. The convention drew up demands and sent a delegation to call upon Lincoln to press their grievances. Shortly thereafter Brown had a more personal victory to celebrate, as he was elected to the Senate after an apparent bargain was made with the supporters of another candidate. Many were surprised that such a radical Republican could be elected from Missouri. It would become clear shortly that such radicalism would not long remain a force.

The new senator was quick to join the extreme Republicans in Congress in condemning Lincoln's moderate reconstruction policies. Brown went so far, so presumptuously, as to read Lincoln out of the Republican Party. He joined those who were trying to prevent renomination of the president. All Southern plantations should be confiscated and the lands redistributed; Southern governments should be dissolved and military dictatorships established. With such views, it is not surprising Brown found himself in the forefront of the fight to nominate John Charles Frémont as the radicals' candidate for president. He failed to convince Missouri radicals to join in the formation of a third party. In late May, Brown attended the radical convention in Cleveland that nominated Frémont. Brown was given serious consideration for vice president but the nomination went elsewhere.

Brown was severely disappointed to find after both the radical and then the Republican conventions had made their selections that most radicals supported Lincoln. Brown began to worry that he was on the wrong side of another major election. Evidence that he began to back off from his extremism in response to political realities came in his objection to the stringent Wade-Davis bill that would have disfranchised all Confederate officials and soldiers. Under the bill no new civilian government could be formed until a majority of the citizens had pledged loyalty, whereas Lincoln's approach called for only 10 percent to pledge loyalty. Brown tried to get consideration of the bill postponed as he felt the matter too significant to rush through in the closing days of a session. Mainly, Brown was stalling for time, not in order to decide the practical merits of various proposals but instead their political ramifications.

The Republicans swept to victory in Missouri in November. Brown called for universal emancipation and suffrage. "Freedom and franchise are inseparable," he declared, making him one of the few leaders, even among the radicals, who sought genuine political equality for the former slave. A new Missouri constitution was being formed, and he desired these protections to be written into it. He no longer fervently argued for "eternal punishment" for the rebels, and only reluctantly endorsed the "ironclad oath" that was required of all voters that they had in no way participated in the rebellion. Yet for the next few months he continually flip-flopped on the key reconstruction issues; after the constitution had been adopted, Brown switched his public stand and stated his opposition not only to the constitution in general but to the oath in particular. Then in Washington he opposed President Johnson's moderate reconstruction proposals, which seemed inconsistent with his stand on the state constitution. Brown, like many other Southern radicals, was in transition and could not decide just where he stood on many issues.

Brown was slowly rejoining the Democratic Party. He announced that bad health would prevent his standing for reelection to the Senate. He called for several leading Missouri radicals to meet with him in November 1866, to determine the direction they should take. Universal suffrage and universal amnesty became his principles, one a reflection of his radical past and the other the recognition of his Democratic future.

Brown was, in fact, ill. He was glad to be out of the Senate wars that were intensifying and would lead to the impeachment and near conviction of Andrew Johnson. New residence was taken up outside of St. Louis at Ironton, where Brown operated a granite quarry. For the next few years, Brown was an observer more than a participant in the political wars, but his name continued to be mentioned. The radicals were losing influence but still winning elections because of the disfranchisement of thousands with the test oath. Universal amnesty became the key for moderates and conservatives throughout the state. Brown's name with increasing frequency was mentioned for governor. A revolt against the radicals seemed imminent in Missouri and the entire country

waited to see if this strongly unionist state during the war would turn its back on the Republicans. If so, then the future of Republicanism in the South was definitely clouded.

Powerful forces in business, journalism, and elsewhere saw Brown as the perfect vehicle to retake the state. A former radical, a native Southerner, a unionist during the war, Brown represented the kind of solid respectability that would be needed for victory. The realignment of parties that was inevitable after the war was accelerating. The radicals were using influence, financial and otherwise, to increase the Negro turnout. Brown hoped to gain the 1870 Radical Party nomination for governor, but representation to the convention was so discriminatory as to leave Brown with little prospect of success. Early balloting on key procedural issues showed the anti–Brown forces to be in command, and thus the minority in favor of Brown left the convention. Two hundred fifty out of 800-plus delegates bolted, formed the Liberal Republican Party, and made Brown their nominee for governor. The incumbent governor, J.W. McClurg, was the radicals' nominee.

The Liberal Republicans conducted a frenetic campaign. Brown campaigned on the basis of universal suffrage and universal amnesty, and by doing so became the center of national attention. President Grant did all within his patronage power to defeat Brown. The Republicans were fearful of the fall of other Southern Republican strongholds once Missouri left the radicals. It was a smashing Brown victory, in which he won the governorship by over forty thousand votes and the Democrats and Liberal Republicans controlled the legislature. The Democrats took much credit for the victory, and Brown agreed. Many of his Republican supporters were aghast at how far, how fast Brown was traveling in his conversion from radicalism. Many hoped for the formation of a coalition containing disaffected radical Republicans, moderates from both parties, and conservative Democrats still concerned with the "bloody shirt" of Southern Democratic rebellion.

Brown was already considering the 1872 presidential nomination. He did not know what party to seek it from, whether a new, national Liberal Republican Party, or the Democrats. In part to solidify his Democratic support, Brown now endorsed his one-time ally, then enemy, and now ally again, cousin Frank Blair, for the United States Senate. As the drive for the nomination intensified, long-running rumors about Brown's drinking resurfaced. Throughout his career, political opponents had labeled Brown a drunk. It is possible that a factor in his moving from Kentucky to Missouri in 1850 was the reputation he was trying to escape as having a drinking problem. Reports that Brown had been drunk at one public event or another were rife, from commencement exercises at the University of Missouri, to the emancipation convention in 1863, or being sick from drink during the 1870 convention that nominated him for governor. Brown devoted much time to denying these charges, but they were true in substance if not always in detail. How severe a drinking problem Brown had is difficult to determine, but it does seem certain that in an era when strong drink was the accepted passion of countless men in and out of public life, Brown's intemperance was noticeably extreme.

On January 24, 1872, a convention of Missouri Liberal Republicans was held in Jefferson City. It endorsed the holding of a national convention in Cincinnati in May. Brown was frequently mentioned in the front rank of contenders for the presidency, along with Greeley, Charles Francis Adams, and a few others. One of Brown's supposed partisans was Missouri senator Carl Schurz, but word got to Brown that Schurz was working for Adams. A telegram informing Brown of the duplicity caused Brown to race by train to the convention. Upon arriving he announced that he was now backing Horace Greeley for the nomination. The endorsement was startling, for there had been no previous friendly relationship between Brown and Greeley. Greeley had some support in the South through his efforts to have Jefferson Davis released on bail from federal prison. Yet the probable spur to the change in heart by Brown was that his anger towards Schurz, once Brown realized the hopelessness of his own cause, made him desire to foist on this would-be friend the one candidate Schurz most detested: Greeley. It was understood that in return for the support Greeley would give Brown the vice presidency. Greeley and Brown were nominated, and the convention left in anger and confusion. The only common issue for the delegates had been their dissatisfaction with Grant, and probably no nomination would have appeased more than a sizeable minority. Many called on Greeley to step down as the nominee; Brown began to regret having played a crucial role in the nomination. He was tired and ill. In his distress Brown even went to a phrenologist "to have his head examined." Defeat was clearly anticipated by all except for Greeley.

One of the low points in the campaign was Brown's attending ceremonies at Yale University commemorating the twenty-fifth anniversary of Brown's graduating class. He got painfully, embarrassingly drunk and gave an incomprehensible, rambling speech. He even praised his running mate Greeley with the phrase "he's got the largest head in America." The next day Brown collapsed. The official explanation was that he had cholera morbus from eating soft-shell crab. The political opposition, and probably many of his friends, had a different diagnosis.

The presidential campaign closed out the last few months of Brown's governorship. Some progressive programs were espoused by the governor, including the establishment of a state board to handle the taxation of railroads, condemnation of inhumane treatment of prisoners, creation of a juvenile reform system, and opposition to capital punishment. Adding to the ridicule he received for his support of Negro voting rights was Brown's call for female suffrage.

Brown would live for 12 more years, but politics seldom occupied his time. He became active with the St. Louis street railway. His granite quarry was the source for the stone to build a bridge across the Mississippi at St. Louis. The Panic of 1873 severely affected his business interests and he had to return to his abandoned legal practice. By 1874 Brown was an avowed Democrat, but did not run for office under any party's banner. His life was centered on his family, his business, and writing small volumes on his lifelong interests of mathematics and geometry.

In 1880, Brown and his still-growing family moved to Kirkwood, a St. Louis suburb. He developed pneumonia in December of 1885 and would not sufficiently rest to recover from it. He suffered a relapse and died on December 13.

Analysis of Qualifications

B. Gratz Brown could be charged with many things during his career. One allegation that would have been totally unfounded is that he was consistent. He started public life as a Whig, having been raised in a family where worship of Henry Clay was inherited. Upon arrival in Missouri and forming an alliance with the Blairs, he became a Benton Democrat. He shortly dropped the moderation that was the key to Thomas Hart Benton, and joined the abolitionists and secession-hating radicals. For a time he avoided the Republican label and merely considered himself part of the opposition; in time he would gladly adopt the radical Republican banner. His next step was as a Liberal Republican, and in that incarnation he was nominated for the vice presidency. Finally he became a Southern Democrat.

One unique characteristic of Brown is that he did not equivocate in his various political stances. When he was a radical Republican, he was an extreme radical. He called for the rejection of Lincoln, the permanent disfranchisement of rebels, the complete political equality of Negroes. When he became a Liberal Republican, he adopted the slogan "universal suffrage and universal amnesty." As a Benton Democrat he decried the extremism of secessionists and of abolitionists; as a radical he decried Lincoln's moderation in the cause of emancipation.

Perhaps as partial explanation of his wide swings in principle, Brown was a quick-tempered, passionate man. He was involved in at least three duels or challenges during his life, and in none of them was he the innocent victim of abuse but gave equally in invective with what he received. Brown simply could not do things by halves. He reacted to political pressure by counterattacking. Announcing his support for Greeley in part as spite against his supposed ally Carl Schurz was certainly in character.

There was a streak of progressivism in Brown. Few leaders adopted the cause of former slaves quite as warmly as he. Certainly part of his motivation was the continuation of radical political fortunes by ensuring maximum Negro voting. But rare was the radical who called for equality of the former slave. As governor, Brown supported attempts to reform the state prison system; he wanted juvenile reform programs; he was against capital punishment. Brown even adopted the cause of women's suffrage at a time when national champions of that cause were few. As a senator, he had called for civil service reform and desired the shortening of the work day for government employees.

In personal habits, Brown was hardly a role model. His drinking was an embarrassment on several occasions. It interfered with the performance of many of his political duties; whether it was a serious enough problem that it would have crippled him as president is beyond knowing now. Brown was well educated for his day, having attended both Transylvania and Yale universities. He was intelligent and in debate could be persuasive. His oratory was never considered unusually skilled, but apparently he could more than hold his own against most political antagonists.

Brown fairly well typifies the vice presidential nominee. He never rose to great prominence in his career; never was he a significant national leader. He had performed with some distinction at the state level and had been a major if hardly dominant force in Missouri. His experience in government was not extensive, having served six years as a state legislator, a truncated term as a United States senator, and was finishing his two-year term as governor when nominated for the vice presidency. Weighing Gratz Brown's qualifications for serving as president is difficult because his career had not been significant. He had shown courage and he had shown social liberalism. On the negative side he had never revealed an ability to work well with the political opposition; he was far too quick-tempered and adversarial. In sum, Brown was an adequate if uninspired choice for the vice presidency. He falls in the great mass of candidates whom the country need not mourn having missed, but neither is there cause for rejoicing.

BROWN BIBLIOGRAPHY

Hardin, Bayless. "The Brown Family of Liberty Hall," in *Genealogies of Kentucky Families*. Baltimore (1981), pp. 90–103, reprinted from *The Filson Club History Quarterly* XVI (1942).

Judson, Frederick N. "The Administration of B. Gratz Brown." *Missouri Historical Society Collections* II.

Peterson, Norma L. *Freedom and Franchise: The Political Career of B. Gratz Brown*. Columbia, Mo. (1965).

---

*1872 presidential nominee —
Democratic/Liberal Republican parties*

Thomas A. Hendricks

Born September 7, 1819, near Zanesville, Ohio; died November 25, 1885, in Indianapolis.

Married Eliza C. Morgan on September 26, 1845; they had one child, who died at age 3.

Thomas's parents were John and Jane Thomson Hendricks. Thomas's uncle William Hendricks was elected Indiana's first congressman in 1816, and in 1822 was elected governor. In 1820, when Thomas was one year old, he and his family moved from Ohio to a farm in Uncle William's Indiana. The family prospered, both from farming and from other businesses. Thomas attended local academies, and then from 1837 to 1841 was a student at Hanover College. After graduation, Hendricks went for eight months to a law school in Chambersburg, Pennsylvania, operated by his mother's brother, Judge Alexander Thomson. He returned to Shelbyville, Indiana, where starting in 1843 his practice grew "steadily, but not rapidly" (Gray, p. 124).

Hendricks was elected as a Democrat to the Indiana House in 1848. As a nine-year-old boy he had become enamored of Andy Jackson, and was a lifelong Democrat as a result. In 1849 he was elected a state senator, and in 1850 was a delegate to the state constitutional convention. His rapid promotions saw him elected to Congress in 1850, and he served until 1855. His support for Stephen Douglas's "popular sovereignty" — let each territory's voters decide whether there would be slavery or not — and

general lack of zeal on anti-slavery issues, caused his defeat for reelection in 1854. He remained in Washington, however, because President Franklin Pierce selected him as commissioner of the General Land Office, where he served from 1855 to 1859. Hendricks then resigned and returned to Indiana, briefly to Shelbyville and then to Indianapolis.

In the heated political climate of 1860, Hendricks became the Democratic nominee for governor. He lost narrowly. The 1862 elections were more to Hendricks' liking, as the Democrats took control of the legislature, which then elected Hendricks to the United States Senate. He served from 1863 to 1869. He did not oppose the war with the South, but did protest Lincoln's strong military rule. His was a logical, conservative argument, but he was at times misunderstood and placed with the virulently anti-war Copperheads, i.e., northerners sympathetic to the South and opposing the war. His publicly voiced view that blacks were inferior and needed to be separate also played into this characterization of his goals. After Lincoln's assassination, the public's identification of Hendricks with weak support for the war caused him to be shouted down when he rose to speak at an Indiana memorial service. In Congress he opposed the three constitutional amendments that banned slavery, extended equal protection of the law to blacks, and granted ex-slaves the vote. While still in the Senate, in 1868 Hendricks ran for governor. He lost by about 961 votes in a possibly stolen election. The Democratic presidential nominee that year lost Indiana by 20,000 votes. Hendricks had been a strong contender at his party's 1868 national convention, and led on the next to last ballot before a bandwagon for Horatio Seymour started rolling.

Hendricks returned in 1869 to his Indianapolis law practice. He was elected governor in 1872. The same year Horace Greeley, the fusion presidential candidate of the Democrats and dissident Republicans, died after losing the election, but before each state's electoral college members met to cast their votes. The 63 votes that Greeley won nationwide were distributed to others, with Hendricks receiving 42. Hendricks served as governor from 1873 to 1877. At the end of his term he was an active candidate for the 1876 Democratic presidential nomination. His presidential bid failed, and the conservative, hard-money candidate New York Governor Samuel Tilden won. Hendricks was a good geographic and economic balance, a Greenback Indianan. He was chosen as vice president. The ticket gained more votes than their Republican opponents. In a controversial election that failed to prove conclusively which side had more fraudulently procured votes, the Republicans were declared the winners.

Though physically weak and out of public office since 1877, Hendricks in 1884 again received substantial support at the presidential nominating convention, though he publicly protested he was not a candidate. He was a good geographic and philosophical balance to the New York governor nominated for president, Grover Cleveland. Cleveland-Hendricks became the first successful Democratic ticket since 1856. Hendricks did not live long to enjoy it. He became vice president on March 4, 1885, and died about eight months later.

The Hendricks Cabin Historic Site is in Shelbyville, Indiana.

HENDRICKS BIBLIOGRAPHY

Goen, Annie Lee. "Senator Thomas A. Hendricks in the Civil War and Southern Reconstruction, 1863–1869." Unpublished master's thesis, University of Texas (1935).

Graham, Hope. "Thomas A. Hendricks in Reconstruction." Unpublished master's thesis, Indiana University (1912).

Gray, Ralph D. "Thomas A. Hendricks: Spokesman for the Democracy," in Gray, Ralph D., ed., *Gentlemen from Indiana: National Party Candidates 1836–1940*, Indianapolis (1977), pp. 117–139.

Guse, Dennis A. "Thomas A. Hendricks: Civil War Speaker." Unpublished master's thesis, Indiana University (1961).

Hatch, Lewis Clinton. *A History of the Vice-Presidency of the United States.* Westport, Conn. (1970, reprint of 1934 edition), pp. 289–322, *passim.*

Holcombe, John W., and Hubert W. Skinner. *Life and Public Services of Thomas A. Hendricks with Selected Speeches and Writings.* Indianapolis (1886).

Savich, Yovanka. "The Senatorial Career of Thomas A. Hendricks, 1863–1869." Unpublished master's thesis, Butler University (1961).

Young, Klyde, and Lamar Middleton. *Heirs Apparent: The Vice Presidents of the United States.* Freeport, N.Y. (1969, reprint of 1948 edition), pp. 203–209.

Election of 1876

NOMINATIONS

Republican Party Convention (6th): June 14–16, 1876, at Exposition Hall, Cincinnati, Ohio. *President*— Rutherford B. Hayes, nominated on the seventh ballot with 384 votes of the 756 cast. He received 61 on the first ballot. Almost all the rest of the votes on the last ballot were cast for James Blaine of Maine, who had led by almost three to one over Hayes until the last ballot. Oliver Morton (Ind.), Benjamin Bristow (Ky.), Roscoe Conkling (N.Y.), and John Hartranft (Pa.), were other major contenders. *Vice president*— William

Wheeler, nominated by acclamation on the first ballot after the few votes for others were changed.

Democratic Party Convention (12th): June 27–29, 1876, at the Merchant's Exchange, St. Louis, Missouri. *President*— Samuel Tilden, nominated on the second ballot with 535 votes of the 738 cast. He had received 401½ on the first, but had not received the necessary two-thirds majority. Thomas Hendricks (Ind.) was a distant second on the first ballot. *Vice president*—Thomas Hendricks, nominated unanimously on the first ballot.

GENERAL ELECTION, November 7, 1876

Popular Vote

Tilden 4,288,546
Hayes 4,034,311
Others   90,244

Electoral Vote

Hayes-Wheeler —185 (21 states)
Tilden-Hendricks —184 (17 states)

A special Electoral Commission had to be appointed to decide several contested returns from Southern states. They reached their decisions, all in favor of Hayes, from February 1 through March 2, 1877.

Winners

Rutherford B. Hayes, 19th president
William Wheeler, 19th vice president

Losers

Samuel Tilden
Thomas Hendricks

---

*1876 presidential nominee —
Democratic Party*

Samuel J. Tilden

Full name: Samuel Jones Tilden.
State represented: New York.
Birth: February 9, 1814, at New Lebanon, New York.
Age on Inauguration Day (March 4, 1877): 63 years, 1 month.
Education: Little formal education; privately tutored at home, attended for three months an academy associated with Williams College, Williamstown, Massachusetts; attended Yale for one year in 1834; then New York University, first entering class; irregular attendance, but apparently did graduate from law school.
Religion: Presbyterian.
Ancestry/prominent relatives: Nathaniel Tilden emigrated to New England in 1634.
Profession: Attorney, admitted to New York bar in 1841.
Public offices: Elected corporation counsel for New York City by New York Common Council, 1843–1844; elected to New York general assembly, 1846; delegate to New York constitutional convention, June 1–October 9,

1846; defeated for corporation counsel, 1856; Democratic state party chairman, 1866–1874; state legislature, 1874–1876; delegate to 1867 constitutional convention; governor of New York, 1875–1877; defeated Democratic nominee for president, 1876.
Home: "Greystone," a massive estate at Yonkers, New York; he purchased it in 1879; prior to then lived in New York City.
Death: August 4, 1886, at Greystone, age 72 years, 6 months.
Burial: Tilden lot in New Lebanon, New York.
Personal characteristics: Medium height, slender, round face, all teeth had to be removed and replaced with artificial ones; chestnut colored hair; after 1877 defeat, overcome with "numb palsy"; started shuffling in his walk, yellowish complexion, feeble constitution; frequently ill, even hypochondriacal.
Father: Elam Tilden (December 31, 1781–April 10, 1842); married February 8, 1802; storekeeper, farmer, political leader.
Mother: Polly Younglove (March 20, 1782–December 11, 1860); adopted daughter of Dr. Moses Younglove.
Siblings: John (1802–1823). Mary B. (1809–June 1878?), married A.F. Pelton (?). Moses Y. (1811–September 8, 1876). George F. (1817–1835). Henry A. (May 21, 1821–March 12, 1884), married a Miss Gould; businessman. Henrietta (1821–1839).
Wife: Never married.
Historic sites/memorials: Tilden house at 14-15 Gramercy Park is now the headquarters of the National Arts Club.

Samuel Tilden was the only bachelor among the defeated candidates. Perhaps fittingly, he was also among the coldest and most arrogant. Tilden was raised in a family that was quite close-knit. His relationship with his father was particularly important. Sam was something of a hypochondriac, but he was also subject to very real ailments all of his life. Sam's father, a farmer and subsequently a general store owner, perhaps encouraged this obsessive concern with health because of the elder Tilden's keen interest in patent medicines and other questionable cures. Tilden's health was permanently damaged by an overdose of laudanum, an opium medicine, administered accidentally to him during a severe illness. This likely caused his constant troubles as an adult with digestive and stomach ailments. Perhaps the health worries also made his introspective manner more pronounced, not only as a child when he had few friends and did not engage in outside games, but also as an adult.

Tilden's boyhood was politically and intellectually precocious. His father was a close advisor of such New York political giants as Martin Van Buren and Silas Wright, and their company at the Tilden household was frequent. It appears that young Samuel was welcomed in the circle of conversation. His opinions, at a quite early age, were respectfully listened to. Though political development was advanced, Tilden's formal education was limited severely. Sam's bad health was part of the reason he did not attend school with other children. When he finally attended Williams College in Williamstown, Massachusetts, he left there after a short period due to ill health. After several other stays at various schools, including Yale for a term and New York University, he finally attended the first law school opened in the state. This was at New York University. Sam remained for three straight years and graduated, a unique achievement for him.

Tilden's first political involvement beyond the conversations with the visitors at the family home was during the 1832 presidential race between Andrew Jackson and Henry Clay. Sam gave a speech in behalf of Jackson, and also helped Van Buren, Jackson's vice presidential running mate and a Tilden family friend. Van Buren was so impressed that Tilden became a trusted and intimate friend.

In 1837, Tilden entered John W. Edmunds' office as a law clerk. It was while working in the office that Sam decided to attend the law school of New York University. Tilden also continued writing and delivering speeches, becoming more and more active, particularly for Van Buren. During Van Buren's unsuccessful reelection campaign for president in 1840, Tilden devoted six months to the campaign and abandoned all other activities.

Admitted to the bar in May 1841, Tilden opened his own office. On April 10, 1842, his beloved father died. The loss of his advisor

and confessor was a severe blow. Tilden nonetheless continued his legal practice, which was growing but far from lucrative. To expand his contacts, Tilden drew upon his political connections and was appointed corporation counsel for the city of New York. This appointment gave Tilden a substantial part of the city's legal business. A new administration in the city in 1844 caused him to be replaced, but his practice had already started to bloom.

As a delegate to the 1844 Democratic National Convention, Tilden worked arduously for Van Buren's renomination. When "dark horse" James K. Polk was nominated instead, Tilden plunged into that campaign, helping to establish a Democratic newspaper to promote Polk's election. The paper folded in 1846, its mission accomplished.

Though not enthused at the amount of time away from his private practice that would be required, Tilden agreed at Governor Silas Wright's insistence to run for the state general assembly. Tilden won and became one of Wright's legislative leaders. The new assemblyman was extremely close, politically and personally, to the governor. Tilden gained statewide recognition as a reformer by leading the successful fight to break up the huge manorial estates that existed in New York since the first land grants from England. The compromise that was reached was to phase out these large estates gradually. The interests of both the landowners and lease owners were balanced, and that compromise was mainly Tilden's creation.

Tilden only served one term. He then was a delegate to the state constitutional convention, from June 1 until October 9, 1846. He served with distinction in the drafting of the constitution that still serves New York.

These activities first brought Tilden in contact with the railroad, mining, canal and other business interests that would make him, through his law practice, one of the wealthiest men in the state. As was evident throughout his life, Tilden was dedicated to pursuing a career in the law. After his successes in 1846, he turned down an opportunity to be his party's candidate for Congress. Still, a full-time political career might have been in the offing had Governor Wright, who was renominated, been reelected. Wright's career itself might have sky-rocketed, even to the presidency. It seems probable that any Wright political fortunes would have been shared with Tilden, one of his closest advisors. Wright lost reelection in 1846, however, and Tilden settled into a lucrative legal business.

Though each presidential and gubernatorial election seemed to find Tilden hard at work for the Democratic nominees, Tilden's time was basically devoted to his burgeoning law practice. He handled several important, apparently hopeless cases that, when he was victorious, gained him considerable fame and fortune. The arrival of impressed railroad and other industry clients also established him financially. His new prominence, both political and professional, caused some of his shyness to dissolve. Yet Tilden never would become a success of much note before a jury, for his genius was not in the emotional jury presentation, but rather in the cold, clear, incisive distillation of complex business problems into workable solutions. He was a problem solver of unique skill. He built a fortune on his ability to reorganize distressed railroads, particularly in the boom period after the Civil War. He did not make people love or identify with him, but he made them respect or even stand in awe of his legal and business acumen.

Tilden's quick rise in the New York Tammany Hall organization might cause some initial doubts concerning his political integrity. Yet prior to the domination of Tammany by Boss William Tweed, it stood as an honored and powerful Democratic Party organization in New York City. In 1856, Tilden was elected a sachem in Tammany, a position of considerable power. After the Civil War, however, he would earn his greatest fame as a reformer for his battles against Tammany.

Tilden was sorely troubled by the prospect of Lincoln's election as president in 1860. During the campaign, he wrote what was perhaps the most influential pamphlet for the Democratic Party, explaining his position on why any candidate, but particularly Douglas, was better than Lincoln. Lincoln's election, Tilden argued, meant that the Union was lost. Tilden saw the probability of Lincoln's victory and began to urge the fusion of all the tickets for candidates other than Lincoln in order to avert this "disaster." Yet once war began, Tilden was foursquare behind the president. He did not participate in any part of the war effort, instead remained aloof in his law practice. Tilden criticized the extreme measures adopted by Lincoln, such as suspension of habeas corpus and the expulsion of some of the more radical Northern sympathizers of the Confederacy. Ironically, however, it was the Civil War that was greatly responsible for Tilden's wealth, since his investments in railroads and mines increased in value manyfold.

Once the war was over and Lincoln's assassination brought Andrew Johnson into the presidency, Tilden began an intimate relationship with the new president. Johnson's mild reconstruction policies against the South appealed to Tilden. The idea of a Union Party was embraced by Tilden, where Democrats and Republicans supportive of Johnson would run together. Little came of this idea.

Though Tilden had long been an opponent of slavery, a speech he gave at the 1868 state Democratic convention shows that he, like the vast majority of those who had opposed slavery, believed that the Negro did not have the intelligence to be given equal political rights with the whites in the South. The South should be readmitted to full rights in the Union. The reconstruction governments, composed of Republicans and recently emancipated Negroes, should not continue.

There has been some speculation that Tilden's favorite candidate for the presidential nomination in 1868 was himself. Yet Tilden publicly was a backer of Horatio Seymour. Tilden agreed after the convention to be Seymour's national campaign manager. General Ulysses Grant won, but the margin was not large.

Tilden became the central reform politician in New York because of his challenge to Boss Tweed and Tammany Hall, beginning in 1869. Tilden had remained a member of Tammany throughout this period, and probably knew of Tweed's corruption as early as 1865. Yet Tilden's vastly profitable and time-consuming legal career kept him from denouncing Tweed publicly. Tilden may also have hoped that some other way besides public condemnation could be found to deal with this central Democratic Party organization. Tilden was state chairman for the Democrats from 1866 until 1876, and during this period Tweed attempted to have Tilden removed. Tilden had outraged Tweed by having some fraudulent orders rescinded that had been entered by Tweed-dominated judges. The real battle resolved itself into years-long court trials of principal Tweed ringleaders. The fraudulent overcharges and hidden payments in New York City were exposed through these trials. Tilden gave key legal assistance, though he was not the prosecutor.

Tilden also undertook to amend the charter for New York City and thereby destroy Tweed-dominated government. Tilden was initially seen as naive in his attempts, and an almost unanimous legislature refused to challenge Tweed's money and power. The reformer himself was divided between his desire to cleanse the city and his fear of damaging the Democratic Party. Yet the revelations in the investigation finally brought the pressure of public opinion strongly behind Tilden. In the next city elections the reform candidates swept the city. Tilden also succeeded as a member of the state legislature in having three Tweed judges impeached.

The reform movement had claimed Tilden as its leader. Beginning in 1872, he curtailed his law practice in order to devote his energies to politics. After a four-month vacation to Europe beginning in the spring of 1873, a trip he had at least once before planned but abandoned, he returned to the political fray. The nomination for governor at this time was by convention. Shortly before the convention, on August 21, 1874 (or so Tilden recorded), he first considered seeking the nomination. Many of his supporters, including former governor Seymour, were pessimistic about his chances. He had made countless enemies in the reform battles, but he had made powerful friends as well. A large number of newspapers vocally were behind him. On September 16 the convention opened, and Seymour nominated Tilden. Tilden won on the first ballot and went on to defeat the incumbent Republican governor.

Tilden's victory was nationally riveting. As soon as the returns were counted, he began to be considered for the presidency. He was inaugurated on January 1, 1875. In his address he concerned himself with conditions in the South and with other national issues, indicating the new governor was thinking about the 1876 presidential campaign. He found a new corruption target in the Canal Ring, a group of officials who through fraudulent contracts and doctored construction estimates milked the state for vast sums in the operation and maintenance of the canal network in New York. Tilden asked for and received a commission to examine these frauds. He continued his push for municipal reform, but continued to be thwarted.

Tilden's one term in the governor's mansion was permeated with the universal feeling that he would be the nominee for president. Many in the state, his long list of enemies from the reform fights chief among them, were against him. The State Democratic Committee nominated him unanimously. He began a careful newspaper campaign to promote his candidacy. His chief opponents were Thomas A. Hendricks of Indiana and Winfield Scott Hancock of Pennsylvania. At the convention, Tilden came near victory on the first ballot and won on the second. Hendricks initially refused the running mate position, but finally assented. Tilden was immediately faced with those in his party who thought his vast wealth should be the primary campaign funding source, while Tilden expected contributions from the party. No resolution of the differences occurred and the funding never was satisfactorily handled.

The campaign was vicious, with mud being slung from both camps. Tilden was condemned for his aloofness during the Civil War, his extreme wealth and apparent income tax avoidance, and his connection with railroads. The tax issue had to do with a mild, but novel, income tax passed during the war that he avoided by demonstrating business losses and taking advantage of other legal arguments.

On election night, it appeared Tilden had won. New York was considered the pivotal state, and Tilden's victory there was apparent. Hayes granted an interview in which he said he thought he had been defeated. The states in the South that in the ensuing months would become the key battleground were also thought won during the night of the election by the Democrats, but the Republican leaders there were kept from conceding defeat by the Hayes and Grant White House campaign leaders.

The key states were Florida, Louisiana, and South Carolina. One elector in Oregon was also contested, since even though Hayes had clearly won the state, one of his electors was arguably not legally qualified to serve and the Democrats argued that the next highest vote getter, a Democrat, should win. The Oregon Republican elector was allowed to cast his vote.

The problem with deciding who legitimately won any of the questionable Southern states is that vote fraud and intimidation were practiced by both parties, and probably more successfully by the Democrats. Each of the three contested Southern states initially reported a Tilden majority, but vote canvassing resulted in several thousand Tilden votes being discarded for alleged irregularities. The backbone of the Republican strength, the Negroes, were fairly effectively intimidated and failed to vote in the numbers they might have in a fair election, and therefore neither side could claim clean hands.

The dispute appeared unresolvable, since there were two sets of returns sent to Congress for each of the disputed states. Tilden was severely criticized by his own party for his passivity. Tilden's apparent position was that reason would prevail; he was certain he had won and he could not believe the election would be stolen. Hayes apparently believed he and the Republicans had fairly won, but did not presume his victory with the certainty that Tilden did his.

Congress was constitutionally required to open and report the election returns, but it was divided along party lines as to what should be done. The idea of a commission to resolve the dispute gained favor. Tilden never desired such an approach. He insisted upon the House of Representatives counting the electoral college votes and if no candidate had a majority, then under the Constitution the House would choose among the highest candidates. Since the House was Democratic, this plan obvi-

ously appealed to Tilden. Yet both the Tilden and the Hayes forces eventually acquiesced in the idea of an electoral commission. The decision was to have a commission of 14 members evenly divided along party lines, with a fifteenth member to be nonpartisan. The fifteenth member ended up being partisan enough to vote for Hayes on every disputed ballot. There is some evidence that this member, Justice Joseph Bradley of the U.S. Supreme Court, had initially on the evening before the vote decided upon Tilden, but was visited later the same evening by some Republican leaders and for reasons that can only be assumed changed his mind.

Hayes was therefore president by an electoral college vote of 185 to Tilden's 184. Many Democrats vowed to fight in order to get Tilden seated as president. Some supporters advised that Tilden go to Washington anyway and be inaugurated. No such move was made. The rumored bargain between the Southern Democrats and the Republicans for the removal of federal troops and the ending of Reconstruction was consummated, and this evidence of a deal was widely reported in the press. The public image of the day was clearly that Tilden had won, but the election was stolen from him in return for federal surrender in the South.

Tilden left for Europe in July 1877, for a rest. There and for the remainder of Hayes's term, he considered himself and expected to be treated as the president who was merely prevented from being seated by the fraud of the Republicans. The renomination and "reelection" of Tilden in 1880 seemed assured. Then in October 1878, evidence appeared of a plot by the Democrats, obviously unsuccessful, to buy electors in Florida after the dispute over the returns arose in November 1876. This scandal dubbed the "Cipher Telegrams," probably kept Tilden from making another presidential challenge in 1880. The income tax evasion charges also dogged Tilden, and he was prosecuted by the federal government for unlawful failure to pay. He entered a settlement in 1882. After he refused to be nominated for governor in 1879, thinking it belittling for a "president-elect" to run for governor, the state party became badly split and was defeated.

Tilden's reluctance to run again for president became more pronounced.

Yet Tilden remained silent on his plans. Many states in 1880 elected strong Tilden delegations. His health again was a problem, and this may have been a prime reason for his reservations. Finally, as the New York delegation met to go to the national convention, Tilden told them that he did not want the nomination unless it was unanimous. He then sent a letter to be read to the delegation that he wished to be "honorably discharged" from renomination. Perhaps Tilden was being too clever in seeking a draft by the convention. The party never even placed his name in nomination, and Winfield Scott Hancock won on the second ballot.

Tilden did not withdraw from politics, and he was mentioned prominently for the nomination in 1884. His health had deteriorated even more by then, and he did decline early enough to get the New York party strongly behind that state's new governor, Grover Cleveland. Tilden was seen as a likely "gray eminence" in the new administration, but never took advantage of what potential there may have been.

Tilden's last years were devoted to improving the mansion, Greystone, he had purchased. He worked arduously on a genealogical record of his family that he completed and published. There were also frequent rumors of an impending marriage with one woman or another, though no marriage ever occurred.

His last year was spent almost as an invalid. He had suffered an apoplectic stroke that paralyzed one leg, arm and eye. His hands became so weak that someone had to feed him. When he died in 1886, he left his huge estate to establish a public library in New York City. Heirs protested and after lengthy court battles, only one-third of his estate went to that purpose.

Analysis of Qualifications

Samuel Tilden is the losing presidential candidate who came the closest to being elected. As such, the question of just how capable a president he would have been has special poignancy.

People did not like Tilden at first meeting. What close friends that he did have were as often infuriated by his brusque manner as were individuals he only just met. His public speaking style was somnolent, without emotion or magnetism. Yet the unappealing style of his public speaking was matched by its precision and careful, almost irrefutable reasoning, the very trait that made him so hugely successful as an attorney. His mind has been called scientific, coldly analytical. The salient fact is that the image of Tilden that grew out of his passivity during the post-election controversy in 1876 is accurate. He was a slow, almost plodding thinker that would have all of his options considered and all of his facts before him prior to making any decision.

The dominating problem facing the president elected in November 1876 was the still-divided country, a South still under federal troop control to varying degrees, and a North whose politicians would wave the "bloody shirt" of Southern treason and civil war in order to gain votes. Rutherford Hayes probably did make a deal with the South to end federal reconstruction of the South. Tilden, though not in the form of a deal, would have accomplished the same because he believed the South should be returned to white rule.

Once Reconstruction was dealt with, the remaining dominant problem was the corruption that had ravaged the federal government during the Grant presidency. Tilden's bona fides on being a zealous investigator of corruption were well-established by his attacks on Tammany Hall.

Tilden was credited for being a superb administrator, an invaluable skill in the presidency. His executive experience from 1874 until 1876 as governor of New York was meaningful preparation for still higher office. His reform program had initially encountered defeat in the state legislature, but with sufficient evidence to indict the malefactors, he was able to incite public opinion so successfully that he forced the legislature to follow his requests. The finances of state government had been unsound, but through his efforts they were placed on a much more secure footing. These achievements augured well for a Tilden presidency.

Another necessary presidential attribute is political skill sufficient to deal both with

SAMUEL J. TILDEN and THOMAS A. HENDRICKS
(From the collection of David J. and Janice L. Frent)

Congress and public opinion. As a political strategist Tilden was masterful; his own election campaigns for governor and for president were conceived by him and implemented personally to the smallest detail. He was perhaps the most valued adviser to President Van Buren, even when Tilden was barely in his twenties; the Democratic Party in New York turned to him as a strategist for several successful gubernatorial and other campaigns. Tilden rarely ran for office himself, and thus his political career until he was elected to the governorship was mainly as a political manager. Those skills of organization and execution would have been transformed into the not-too-different political talents needed by a president.

Tilden is a difficult man to measure in the "what might have been" category. Brilliant yet cold, politically skilled but not greatly experienced as an executive, careful and reflective to the point of indecisiveness, once certain of a course he could be stubborn and unwavering. On balance, it would appear that Tilden would have succeeded as did Hayes in ending the worst of the corruption in government, would have removed the troops from the South, and would have inspired confidence and respect both in his intelligence and his personal integrity. But it does not seem likely that Tilden, any more than Hayes, would have been ranked among the great presidents, since so much of what was great about the man was counterbalanced by less laudatory characteristics. He would have been a good president for the period, which, in truth, is all the country need ever desire.

TILDEN BIBLIOGRAPHY

Adkins, Brian Christopher. "Samuel Jones Tilden and the 1880 Democratic Presidential Nomination." Unpublished master's thesis, University of Wisconsin–Milwaukee (1992).

Bigelow, John. *Letters and Literary Memorials of Samuel J. Tilden*. New York City (1908, rep. 1971).

_____. *The Life of Samuel J. Tilden*. New York City (1895).

_____. *Public Writings and Speeches of Samuel J. Tilden*. New York City (1885).

Flick, Alexander C. *Samuel Jones Tilden: A Study in Political Sagacity*. Westport, Conn. (1973), reprint of 1939 edition.

Severn, Bill. *Samuel J. Tilden and the Stolen Election*. New York City (1968).

---

*1876 vice presidential nominee—
Democratic Party*

Thomas A. Hendricks

No biographical sketch of Hendricks is included here since he served as vice president from March 4 until November 25, 1885 (21st vice president). However, see the sketch at the election of 1872, since Hendricks was that year a recipient of more than 5 percent of the electoral votes for president.

State represented: Indiana.

Birth: September 7, 1819.

Age on Inauguration Day (March 4, 1877): 57 years, 6 months.

Death: November 25, 1885, while serving as vice president.

Election of 1880

NOMINATIONS

Republican Party Convention (7th): June 2–5, 7–8, 1880, at Exposition Hall, Chicago, Illinois *President*— James Garfield, nominated on the 36th ballot with 399 votes out of the 755 cast. He had received his first votes (10) on the second ballot. James Blaine and Ulysses Grant were the frontrunners for most of the balloting. *Vice president*—Chester A. Arthur, nominated on the first ballot with 468 out of the 751 votes cast. Elihu Washburne (Ill.) was a distant second.

Greenback Party Convention (2nd): June 9–11, 1880, at Exposition Hall, Chicago, Illinois. *President*—James B. Weaver, nominated on the first ballot. In an informal ballot, Weaver received 224½ votes out of 716 cast. When formal balloting began, Weaver passed 500 votes and other states switched to him, making the nomination unanimous. Edward P. Allis (Wis.), and Benjamin Butler (Mass.) were his strongest competitors. *Vice president*—B.J. Chambers, nominated on the first ballot with 403 votes to 311 for General Absalom M. West (Miss.).

Democratic Party Convention (13th): June 22–24, 1880, at the Music Hall, Cincinnati, Ohio. *President*—Winfield S. Hancock, nominated on the second ballot. Before ballots were switched, he had received 320 votes; after the vote changes he held 705 of the 738 votes. He had received 171 votes on the first ballot. Thomas Bayard (Del.) and Samuel Randall (Pa.) were the other major contenders. *Vice president*—William English, nominated by acclamation on the first ballot.

GENERAL ELECTION, November 2,1880
Popular Vote

Garfield	4,454,416
Hancock	4,444,952
Weaver	308,578
Others	11,000

Electoral Vote
Garfield-Arthur — 214 (19 states)
Hancock-English —155 (19 states)
Winners
James Garfield, 20th president
Chester A. Arthur, 20th vice president and 21st president
Losers
Winfield S. Hancock, William English, James B. Weaver, B.J. Chambers

---

1880 Presidential Nominee—
Democratic Party

Winfield Scott Hancock

Full name: Winfield Scott Hancock.
State represented: Pennsylvania.
Birth: February 14, 1824, Montgomery Square (North of Norristown), Pennsylvania.
Age on Inauguration Day (March 4, 1881): 57 years, 3 weeks.
Education: Norristown, Pennsylvania schools; West Point Military Academy, 1840–1844, 18th in class of 25.
Religion: Baptist.
Ancestry/prominent relatives: English forebears on father's side; paternal grandmother was born in Edinburgh, Scotland; mother's family arrived from England around 1730.
Profession: Soldier.
Public offices: Reconstruction military governor of 5th Military District, August 26, 1867–March, 1868; given consideration by the Democrats for president in 1868, 1872, and 1876; unsuccessful Democratic nominee for president, 1880.
Home: No permanent home, as he lived wherever he was stationed by the army; at time of presidential nomination lived at Governor's Island, New York Harbor.
Death: February 9, 1886, at Governor's Island, New York, at age 62 years.
Burial: Norristown, Pennsylvania; in 1896 reinterred in Arlington National Cemetery.
Personal characteristics: 6'2" tall, strikingly handsome, blond or light brown hair, powerful and graceful; by his mid-fifties had become fat, perhaps 250 pounds; dignified with flashes of fiery temper that quickly waned.
Father: Benjamin Franklin Hancock (October 19, 1800–February 1, 1867); lawyer and school teacher; son of Richard and Anna Maria (Nash) Hancock.
Mother: Elizabeth Hoxworth (December 8, 1801–January 25, 1879), daughter of Edward and Mary (Hoxworth) Hoxworth, a farmer in Pennsylvania.
Siblings: Hilary Baker (identical twin brother) (February 14, 1824–1908), lawyer. John Hancock (March 23, 1830–?).

Wife: Almira Russell (c. 1833–April 20, 1893); married January 24, 1850; daughter of St. Louis merchant Samuel Russell and wife Almira DuBois.

Children: Russell (October 29, 1850–December 30, 1884), married Elizabeth Gwynn, April 30, 1872. Ada Elizabeth (February 24, 1857–March 18, 1875), died of typhoid fever.

Historic sites/memorials: Large equestrian statue at Pennsylvania Avenue and Seventh Street, Washington, D.C.

Movies: Hancock's role in the Gettysburg battle was portrayed in the 1994 television and theater movie, *Gettysburg*.

Winfield Scott Hancock and the man for whom he was named, Winfield Scott, are the only presidential also-rans who lived their entire adult lives, even the period of races for the presidency, in the military. Yet most of the more politically experienced candidates were probably less qualified to be president than Hancock. Hancock's life knew few failures, because few were the obstacles that his talents could not overcome. Hancock had a generally calm disposition, a quick intelligence and great diligence, and a devotion to peace and democratic institutions. He was, as Union commanding general George B. McClellan called him, "superb."

Hancock's father was a moderately prosperous lawyer in Norristown, Pennsylvania, where Winfield was born in 1824. Benjamin Franklin Hancock, himself a namesake of a great American, named his firstborn son after the general he had served under during the War of 1812. Winfield's identical twin brother Hilary received neither a famous name nor apparently the personality of Winfield. Hilary would show some talent in his early years as an amateur geologist, artist, cartoonist, and even as an experimenter with electricity. But he descended to alcoholism and spent many years as a bum on skid row.

Hancock's appointment to West Point was the turning point in his life, putting him on the road to military glory that in turn led to his presidential nomination. A former congressman, John Benton Sterigere, had been embittered by the deceitful actions of the father of another boy who was interested in going to West Point. Sterigere procured the appointment for Hancock in order to thwart the other candidate. Hancock was then only 16 and not fully prepared for becoming a West Point student. When he entered, he was a small, weak, 5'5" fellow, whose good nature and good looks enabled him to escape some of the hazing he might otherwise have faced. By the time of his graduation four years later, he had matured into a 6'2" specimen of young manhood, ready to take on the world. His class was not noted for excellence, and Hancock was no standout. But Hancock was popular and respected among his peers, who in his four years at the Point included Stonewall Jackson, George McClellan, James Longstreet, and Ulysses Grant.

When war with Mexico erupted in 1846, Hancock immediately requested an assignment to the fighting. He had spent his first years in the army along the Red River in Texas and in Indian fighting on the frontier. Most of the fighting, though, had been against wild game while stationed in some of the army's more remote outposts. Two years had passed since graduation, and he had few achievements to gain him favor in his request to be sent to Mexico. One advantage he did have was his name and the fact he had met General Winfield Scott while he was at West Point. The general appreciated the young soldier's eagerness to fight and saw to his assignment. By the time Hancock reached Mexico, the war was half over. His brief involvement with this short war did enable him to win commendation for bravery in battles at Contreras, Churubusco, Molina del Ray and Chapultepec. Hancock remained in Mexico City with an occupation force until after the Treaty of Guadalupe-Hidalgo was signed. He then returned to less exciting assignments in the United States.

Wisconsin and Minnesota were his next stations. Hancock was not advancing quickly in the army; few soldiers do in peacetime. An old classmate and future Civil War general Don Carlos Buell introduced Winfield to his future wife, Almira Russell, whose father was a St. Louis merchant. The courtship was short. The Hancocks were married in an elaborate ceremony that featured the bride's gown of spun glass, a novelty that almost caused a riot of uninvited spectators who wanted to see it.

Hancock had graduated from West Point in June of 1844, but it was 1853 before he became a first lieutenant. It took a request to be assigned to the Quartermaster Corps, the army's supply organization, before he received a promotion to captain. In February 1856, he was ordered to Florida to fight against the Seminole Indians. Mrs. Hancock was the only officer's wife to accompany them on the expedition. Next stop was Fort Leavenworth, Kansas, where he remained until March 1858. He was selected to proceed with a force across the Rockies to Utah and California. The trails blazed by John Charles Frémont were now sufficiently marked that even an army could pass over them. The problems of logistics and supply for such an undertaking were immense, and Hancock was responsible for these. He was gaining a reputation as one of the best quartermasters in the army, partly because he paid meticulous attention to detail, even the paperwork that was usually neglected.

Hancock's political opinions were not pronounced, but he was a Democrat. It is unlikely Hancock ever voted until 1880. Even apolitical men began to have opinions as talk of secession spread. Hancock did not want to appease the South but wished for the Union to be preserved. When war broke out, there was no doubt that Pennsylvania-born Hancock would fight for the Union. Just as definite was his sympathy for those from the South who felt compelled to resign from the service and join the Confederates. He and Mrs. Hancock held a dinner party for the departing Southerners on June 15, 1861. Though no dinner list was kept, Mrs. Hancock later said that three of the six Confederates attending the party were killed by Hancock's men in the battle of Gettysburg two years later.

Again Hancock requested orders for combat. This time his benefactor was General George B. McClellan, who three years later would fail in his own race for the presidency. McClellan succeeded in getting Hancock appointed a brigadier general of volunteers, not a bad promotion for a captain. The task of all brigades in the burgeoning army was organization and training, and Hancock went to work. Hancock had never led a large command in combat but he proved well prepared for the task. His brilliant field generalship played a prominent role in the battle of Williamsburg in May of 1862. His rout of the Confederates caused General McClellan to telegraph Washington with the tribute "General Hancock was superb today." The nickname of "Hancock the Superb" stuck and became more appropriate as the war progressed. He earned it that first battle by refusing to withdraw when ordered to do so. Hancock realized the supreme importance of his position and did not want to concede it to the Confederates. After he had procrastinated on the withdrawal for hours, hoping that reinforcements would come and that the retreat order would be reversed, he saw the enemy advance. Hancock positioned his troops to maximum advantage on the terrain, and then when the battle began he braved the hail of bullets to ride back and forth along the line urging his men to stand fast. When the Rebels' advance stalled, Hancock ordered a counterattack. This bold move caught the Confederates unprepared and they were beaten back. Many Rebels were captured. The victory was one of the few for the Union to savor at that early date. Hancock's bold actions earned him the respect and affection of his men.

Hancock's participation in the Peninsular campaign of 1862 earned him McClellan's praise as well as a recommendation for promotion to major general. In September of 1862, that battle of Antietam was waged, and again Hancock performed admirably. When a division commander was killed, Hancock was promoted on the field to replace him and commanded the center of McClellan's army during this crucial battle. This promotion to commander of a division of the Second Corps placed Hancock with the corps that was to become his for almost the remainder of the war.

Hancock was quite fond of General McClellan, but there were few victories under his leadership. On November 7, President Lincoln replaced McClellan with Ambrose Burnside, a most unfortunate choice. Hancock advised his soldiers, bitter over McClellan's departure, "We are serving our country, not any man."

Burnside ordered an ill-conceived, or not conceived, attack on entrenched Confederate fortifications at Fredericksburg on December 13, 1862. Hancock counseled against the attacks, as did many others, but Burnside was insistent. The Union losses were staggering, the Confederate casualties negligible. Burnside was finally convinced to halt the action but only after Hancock's troops suffered horrendous casualties. Hancock was against the order to attack, but once it was given he was a committed soldier who spurred his men on to extreme sacrifice.

Burnside's disaster was followed by command being given to the inappropriately named "Fighting" Joe Hooker. Hooker's generalship was the equivalent of Burnside's and further defeat followed. This new disgrace caused repercussions throughout the army. Hooker was sacked, but not before the corps commander for Second Corps resigned in disgust over Hooker's actions. On June 9, 1863, Hancock was named by President Lincoln to lead the Second Corps. It was less than one month to Gettysburg.

The Union army's defeat under Hooker at Chancellorsville encouraged General Lee to invade the North. The badly managed Union army desperately needed a leader, and George Meade was selected by President Lincoln. On June 28, Meade began to position the army to thwart Lee's advance. Hancock was instructed on July 1 to proceed to Gettysburg to take personal command of the forces there. The First Corps commander, General Reynolds, was killed in the early skirmishing at Gettysburg and Meade ordered Hancock to replace him on the field. At this stage in the pre-battle positioning, Meade believed that the main engagement would occur not at Gettysburg but some distance away at Pipe Creek. Hancock arrived at the Gettysburg countryside and found confusion and desperation. Meade had instructed Hancock that if he believed the Gettysburg area was a better location for the battle, that he should so inform Meade and the army would be moved to the new location.

Many credit Hancock for selecting Gettysburg. The Union gained important tactical advantages on this terrain. Other military historians give credit to competitors for the prize

of foresight in choosing Gettysburg. Regardless, Hancock at least approved of the battle site and informed General Meade that the Army should be moved into position there. When Meade arrived, Hancock took command of the army in the most crucial area of the battle. His very presence inspired the troops that had been wavering prior to his arrival. He rallied the men, and to keep them from turning when the Rebel fire became particularly intense, he mounted his horse and with a few staff members rode slowly along the front of the line. It was miraculous that he was not killed. Infantrymen who had been trying to keep as low as possible to evade the rain of fire took courage from his foolhardy example.

Hancock's luck did not quite hold, and he received a painful injury to his thigh. He remained on the battlefield until the fighting was over, refusing to leave while the firing continued. It was his men that fought off the brave charge by General George Pickett, which actually was "the high water mark of the Confederacy."

Hancock had to be relieved of his command while he recovered from his serious wound, a wound that never quite healed. In early 1864, while Hancock was still incapacitated, Congress voted its thanks for the success at Gettysburg to three generals: Meade, who was the commanding general; Hooker, who did have a considerable role to play; and General Howard, who far from being a hero at the battle, had almost squandered the potential victory prior to Hancock's arrival. Hancock was noticeably excluded from the thanks, primarily because he was a Democrat. In 1866, he was finally given official congressional thanks for his role. While Hancock was still incapacitated, General Meade complained about the absence of vigorous subordinate officers, and named Hancock expressly. Meade believed that Hancock would be a good commanding general of all the armies, but a man named Grant received that assignment.

Finally in March 1864, Hancock was able to return to duty. He participated in the Wilderness battle of early May, but the result was inconclusive. Probably the worst episode for the Union army during the Civil War occurred at Cold Harbor on June 3, 1864, when Hancock was ordered over his objections to attack entrenched Confederate positions. Horrible losses were suffered. The casualties were so severe as to threaten Grant's leadership of the army as well as Lincoln's reelection for president. Despite Grant's reputation as a man who would sacrifice his troops willingly and rashly, Hancock had very cordial relations with his commanding general. Hancock as early as 1864 was being mentioned as a Democratic nominee for president, and Grant and Hancock's relationships were such that Grant would good-naturedly rib his subordinate about the rumors.

After the Wilderness campaign, Hancock was assigned to recruiting duties in an attempt to keep veterans, after their tour of duty was over, from quitting the army. Hancock's wound also continued to trouble him, and the recruiting duty seemed a good time for recuperation. In February 1865, Hancock was reassigned to command in the Shenandoah Valley and mainly dealt with the raids of Colonel Mosby.

In his memoirs General Grant spoke highly of Hancock: "Hancock stands the most conspicuous figure of all the general officers who did not exercise a separate command. He commanded a corps longer than any other one, and his name was never mentioned as having committed in battle a blunder for which he was responsible.... His personal courage and his presence with his command in the thickest of the fight, won for him the confidence of troops serving under him." He had strong tactical sense about organizing his troops for battle, and selecting the proper positions, and his courageous example and commanding appearance inspired his troops on countless occasions. Whether he would have been able to take a more strategic role, such as in the command of the entire armies, cannot be answered by the successes he found in a lesser role, but at least he deserved and received tremendous respect for his leadership.

After the war was over, Hancock was placed in charge of the military department that included the District of Columbia. In that capacity, he had military authority over the conduct of the trials as well as execution of the conspirators for the assassination of President Lincoln. He took special interest in the case of Mrs. Mary E. Surratt, who was the only woman executed as a conspirator. After Mrs. Surratt was condemned to death, Hancock was distressed. He hoped that her sentence could be commuted and made every effort to assist Mrs. Surratt's daughter and others to receive a presidential pardon. He remained at the prison where the execution was to take place until after it was over, so that he could halt the execution immediately if a reprieve arrived. It never did, and Hancock obeyed orders and allowed the execution to proceed.

Hancock, unlike the other principal generals of the Civil War who later became presidential candidates, remained in the army. In 1866 he was promoted to be major general of the regular army. In 1867 he was engaged in Indian fighting, but President Andrew Johnson removed him from that command in order that he could become a military governor of the Fifth Military District, which included Louisiana and Texas. Hancock made his headquarters in New Orleans and immediately endeared himself to the South by his removal of the harsh restrictions imposed by the earlier reconstruction authorities. Hancock was already considering himself a moderate Democrat who would be depicted as an enemy by the radical Republicans. Before he left for New Orleans he told his wife

> I am expected to exercise extreme military authority over those people. I shall disappoint them. I have not been educated to overthrow the civilian authorities in time of peace. I intend to recognize the fact that a civil war is at an end, and shall issue my orders or proclamations accordingly.

Probably the most controversial action in Hancock's career occurred very soon after his arrival in New Orleans. On November 29, 1867, he issued his famous General Order No. 40. This restored civilian control in Texas and Louisiana. It caused a sensation. The civil authorities were given control in almost all areas; he reinstated the right of trial by jury, habeas corpus, and a free press and free speech. Almost every newspaper in the country gave front page coverage, and while the South cheered him, many in the North criticized him as a rebel sympathizer. That charge could hardly be supported, as no general performed more admirably in the Civil War than had Hancock. But Hancock's whole attitude was that the war was over. The important matters ahead were the reconciliation of the two sections, not their continued division.

President Johnson strongly supported Hancock's decision. Many radical Republicans who favored continued military control over the South were outraged. Hancock's future presidential opponent, James Garfield, said in the House of Representatives that Hancock had totally exceeded his authority and it was for Congress, not Hancock, to determine whether civil or military authority applied in the South. Despite the hot words from Washington, General Order No. 40 was allowed to stand.

Hancock deferred to the civilian authorities on matters he thought outside the proper military interest. Pressure from Washington was increasing, however, and as President Andrew Johnson faced his own impeachment in Congress, Hancock realized he could receive no help from the chief executive. He said, "I may expect one humiliation after another until I am forced to resign. I am prepared for any event. Nothing can intimidate me from doing what I believe to be honest and right." An effort was brought in Congress to reduce him to the rank of brigadier general, and Representative Garfield introduced it in January of 1868. Garfield was later to apologize to Hancock for his actions. Realizing Hancock's popularity, the attempt to demote him was withdrawn. The final straw to the radical Republicans was Hancock's removal of nine aldermen from the New Orleans City Council when they appointed a city official over Hancock's warning not to do so. The position was elective, and when the aldermen made the appointment, Hancock removed them. General Grant, who was still commanding general of the army, overruled Hancock's decision, saying "your order of removal is based on certain charges which I did not think were sustained by the facts as they were presented to me." Hancock requested that he be relieved, and with no reluctance, Grant acceded. Grant and Hancock's relations were strained thereafter, and Hancock showed his distaste for Grant by ignoring the commanding general on

almost every occasion that they met in Washington. This attitude was greatly to injure Hancock's career, as Grant as president passed over him on promotions and assignments. For example, Hancock was ignored when a successor as commander of the western division of the army was made. Hancock, never deferential when it came to such promotions, wrote to General Sherman. Sherman talked with Grant and then responded:

> The President authorizes me to say to you that it belongs to his office to select the Commanding Generals of Divisions and Departments, and that the relations you chose to assume toward him, officially and privately, absolve him from regarding your personal preferences.

Hancock protested that he had right cause to feel cold towards Grant, but meant no disrespect. When Grant did notice him for appointment, Hancock may well have wished to be overlooked. He was banished to the Department of the Dakotas, at that time perhaps one of the worst assignments in the army. The breach between Hancock and Grant was never successfully healed.

Hancock had received mention for the presidency at the 1868 Democratic convention and got 144 votes on the twenty-eighth ballot. Yet Hancock stayed completely out of politics himself, and the efforts on his behalf were made without his encouragement.

General Meade died on November 6, 1872, and as the senior major general in the army, Hancock could not be ignored for appointment as Meade's successor. Hancock took command of the division of the Atlantic and moved to Governor's Island, New York City. General Hancock began to grow quite fat, and he perhaps weighed as much as 250 pounds as a result of his comfortable existence at Governor's Island. He became involved with the National Rifle Association, and was selected president. He also involved himself in various patriotic endeavors, but continued to stay out of politics. In 1872, he asked that he not be considered by the Democrats for president, and in 1876, he received 75 votes on the first ballot for the presidency.

It was 1880, however, that finally saw his nomination. The main reason for his success that year was the weakness of other candidates. Samuel J. Tilden, the former governor of New York and the 1875 presidential nominee, had been tainted by scandal and was suffering from paralysis. Senator Thomas Bayard had alienated Tilden, and could not be nominated. Governor Thomas Seymour may have been a strong candidate, but he did not want the nomination. Basically Hancock was a man with a good reputation from the Civil War, whose absence from public life meant he had no liabilities in the public mind. On the second ballot at the Cincinnati convention in June, Wisconsin made a switch to Hancock that, for whatever reason, triggered a rush towards the general. It was after almost an hour of wild cheering, marching and general bedlam before order could be restored and the states who wanted to switch to Hancock could be recognized.

During the campaign, Hancock was criticized in the North by the strong support he was receiving in the South. Republicans parodied this support by singing

> In the Union War I fought so well
> That my name is greeted with the
> "Rebel yell."

"Waving the bloody shirt" was a frequent tactic by the Republicans after the Civil War, and the issue still had appeal among the hundreds of thousands of Union army veterans and their families. General Grant campaigned against Hancock, which may have turned the tide against the Democratic nominee in a few states. One of the critical problems in Hancock's campaign was the depiction of him as being naive about the great public issues. Hancock gave an interview to a New Jersey newspaper that was printed on October 8, 1880, in which he stated, "the tariff question is a local question." Since the protective tariff was probably the crucial issue in the campaign, the Republicans characterized General Hancock's statement as being absurd and indicating a complete ignorance of the issue. Hancock probably was simplistic about important public issues, as indeed he had no experience with them. Thomas Nast, the great and caustic cartoonist, created a devastatingly effective anti–Hancock cartoon that received wide cir-

culation, showing a confused Hancock asking New Jersey's Theodore F. Randolph, "Who is tariff? And why is he for revenue only?" As close as the election was, Hancock's statement about the tariff, which rather than being naive could also be interpreted as being quite sophisticated, may have cost him the presidency.

Hancock's nonchalance and grace under pressure showed on election night when he went to bed early without knowing the election results. His wife woke him at 5:00 the next morning and told him he had been defeated. Hancock responded, "That is all right. I can stand it." He then went back to sleep.

Hancock remained as commanding general of the Department of the Atlantic until his death, his last significant accomplishment being the organization of an impressive funeral rite for General Grant when he died in July of 1885. Grant's attitude towards Hancock had somewhat mellowed in his last years, and the ex-president had given Hancock applause in his memoirs.

Analysis of Qualifications

"Hancock the Superb" may well have been superb as president. Ending the bitter divisions between North and South was the great necessity of the period, and Hancock beautifully bridged the gap between the two formerly warring sections. Hancock had excelled as a general on behalf of the Union, and had subsequently shown his benevolence towards the South after the war in the issuing of General Order No. 40. Hancock probably failed to achieve the presidency because of warring Democratic factions in New York, and that state went very narrowly for Garfield. A few thousand additional votes would have given New York and the presidency to Hancock.

Hancock's greatest liability as president would have been his inexperience. The presidency is a political position, and political skills are required. Hancock's intelligence and great courage could never be questioned, nor could his benevolence and personal strength of character. What can be questioned is his understanding of the give and take, the command and then the compromise required in order for Congress to accede to his wishes. He did not have a politically astute staff that would have joined him in the White House, and as the first Democratic president since James Buchanan he would not have had a cadre of experienced Democratic administrators to call into his administration.

Hancock would not have been passive as president, as his actions as military governor of the Department of Louisiana and Texas after the Civil War revealed. Though a general in the army, he had supreme confidence in the abilities and appropriateness of civil authority. His respect for civil authority not only appeared when he was military governor, but after the disputed election of 1876, he refused to lead a Democratic army to seat Samuel Tilden, who many felt had a just claim on the presidency after that election. General Hancock allegedly was ordered to the Pacific coast by President Grant in order to prevent him from leading an effort to seat Tilden, and the further rumor was that Hancock had refused the order. Hancock said, "I have not refused to obey such an order, for the simple reason that I have received no such order. Nor would it be conceivable for me to think of renewing warfare and bloodshed." Hancock, a general of war, was constantly a man of peace.

Hancock was a commander. He was used to issuing orders and having a staff to carry them out. The inability to achieve such results as president would have been frustrating. One of the great unknowns of presidential election history is whether this great and good general who had succeeded so admirably both at war and in the governing authority he had been given after that war, could have managed the intricacy of the highest civilian office. The evidence is that the Democratic Party indeed had given the country a man who deserved the opportunity to serve.

HANCOCK BIBLIOGRAPHY

Cole, J.R. *The Life and Public Services of Winfield Scott Hancock*. Cincinnati (1880).

Forney, John W. *Life and Military Career of Winfield Scott Hancock*. Philadelphia (1880).

Goodrich, Frederick E. *Life of Winfield Scott Hancock*. Philadelphia (1886).

Hancock, Almira Russell (Mrs. Winfield S. Hancock). *Reminiscences of Winfield Scott Hancock*. New York City (1887).

Jenkins, Howard M. "Genealogical Sketch of General W.S. Hancock." *Pennsylvania Magazine of History and Biography* X (1886), pp. 100–106.

Jordan, David M., *Winfield Scott Hancock: A Soldier's Life*. Bloomington and Indianapolis (1988).

Thede, Peter J. *Winfield Scott Hancock: A Study in Leadership*. Carlisle Barracks, Penn. (1990).

Tucker, Gene. *Hancock the Superb*. Indianapolis and New York City (1960).

---

*1880 vice presidential nominee —
Democratic Party*

William H. English

Full name: William Hayden English.

State represented: Indiana.

Birth: August 27, 1822, Lexington, Indiana.

Age on Inauguration Day (March 4, 1881): 58 years, 6½ months.

Education: Local schools, then attended Hanover College; studied law, and admitted to bar in 1846.

Religion: Baptist (?).

Ancestry/prominent relatives: Paternal ancestors came from England, arriving around 1700; a son, William E. English, U.S. Representative from Indiana.

Occupation: Attorney; banker.

Public offices: Postmaster of Lexington, Indiana, 1841–1843; clerk of Indiana house of representatives, 1843–1845; worked as clerk in U.S. Department of Treasury, 1845–1849; clerk of claims committee, U.S. Senate, 1849–1850; secretary of Indiana constitutional convention, 1850–1851; state representative, 1851–1852, elected youngest speaker in history; U.S. Representative, March 4, 1853–March 3, 1861, retired; unsuccessful Democratic nominee for vice president, 1880.

Home: "Governor's House," mansion in Indianapolis on site originally intended for the state's governors; then moved to "Hotel English" in that city.

Death: February 7, 1896, in Indianapolis, at age 73 years, 5½ months.

WINFIELD SCOTT HANCOCK and WILLIAM H. ENGLISH
(Reproduced from the Collections of the Library of Congress)

Burial: Crown Hill Cemetery, Indianapolis.

Personal characteristics: 5'9" tall, full beard, clear, gray eyes; erect bearing; high, broad forehead; dignified; retiring and reserved; could appear cold to strangers, but much more relaxed and affable with friends; strict personal morality and aggressive businessman.

Father: Elisha English (?–November 14, 1874); sheriff and member of state legislature.

Mother: Mahala Eastin (1798–?), daughter of Philip and Sarah (Smith) Eastin; married in 1818.

Siblings: None.

Wife: Emma Mardulia Jackson (?–November 14, 1877), married November 14, 1847.

Children: William Eastin English (November 3, 1850–April 29, 1926), married Annie Fox; was a U.S. congressman, attorney. Rosalind (?–?), married Dr. Willoughby Walling.

Historic Sites: English Foundation Building, near northside in Indianapolis. English's mansion, and the English Hotel and Opera House, were on the Soldiers and Sailors Monument Circle that he was instrumental in having built. The mansion was razed in 1896 and the hotel in 1948.

While other also-rans and running mates have hungered for political office, William English was an infrequent office-seeker who spent the bulk of his adult life in business pursuits. He was chastised as a shylock banker who took advantage of the Panic of 1873 to foreclose on hundreds of debtors, and probably deserved some of the taunts even though he was never guilty of illegal tactics. He was an unemotional, conservative, shrewd businessman who during the 1880 campaign was depicted by the Republicans as a monster skinflint.

English was an only child in a frontier Indiana family. English's maternal grandfather fought in the American Revolution; English's father was one of 14 children who moved to Indiana in 1818 from his native Kentucky. Politics was in young William's blood, for his father served as sheriff, United States marshal, and for 20 years a member of the senate or house of representatives of Indiana. Investments in real estate had made the English family financially comfortable if not rich. William received from this heritage a strong devotion to the Democratic Party. He also enjoyed the benefits of prominent benefactors, such as his father's good friend, Indiana U.S. Senator Jesse D. Bright.

English's early education consisted of what instruction could be obtained in the schools of rural Scott County, Indiana, and then three years of Hanover College. The respected Madison attorney, Joseph G. Marshall, was his legal instructor. When English was only 18, he was admitted to the bar, and that same year his political involvement began when he delivered a speech about that year's emotional presidential campaign between Harrison and Van Buren. Though the Whigs won, when President Harrison died the Democratic vice president, John Tyler, succeeded to the nation's highest office. Tyler rewarded the promising young Democrat in Lexington, Indiana, with appointment as postmaster of his home town. English took the oath of office on his twentieth birthday. The next year he rose further from small-town obscurity by his selection as clerk of the Indiana house of representatives, a post his long-time legislator-father was instrumental in securing. Jesse D. Bright was then lieutenant governor of the state, but the following year would be elected to the United States Senate.

English threw himself into the election for president in 1844, and was a partisan campaigner for the Democratic nominee, Tennesseean James K. Polk. When Polk won, English assumed he was due an appointment from the new president. English got recommendations from prominent Indiana Democrats, all of the party's state senators, most of the Democratic state representatives, and from several statewide officials, the most significant of which was the newly-elected Senator Bright. English took these written endorsements to Washington, added the support of the congressional delegation, and in April of 1845 was appointed as clerk in an auditor's office in the Treasury Department. English had used very heavy weaponry in order to secure a quite minor position.

In 1848, English supported Lewis Cass for the presidency and voted for him at the national convention. English's father, Elisha and an uncle, Revel W. English, were vice presidents of the convention. Two other uncles were delegates. These four English brothers were members of their respective state legislatures in four different states, all as Democrats. William was destined to follow their substantial lead. When Cass lost to General Zachary Taylor in November, English submitted his letter of resignation from the Treasury position, a strongly-worded, partisan document that was reprinted with laudatory comments in the party press.

Senator Bright had taken particular interest in fellow Indianan English, and helped gain the younger man the position of clerk for the claims committee of the Senate in 1849 after English's resignation from the auditor's office. The next year English was back in his native state as secretary of the Indiana constitutional convention, which lasted four months. As principal secretary of the convention, English kept the notes of convention proceedings, attested to the final version of the constitution proposed to the voters, and was charged with publishing the convention's journal and other records of the proceedings. Fresh from these successes, English was nominated unanimously for the state house of representatives in 1851 and was elected easily over a substantial Whig competitor. Though only 29 years old, English was elected on March 8, 1852, as the youngest speaker in the history of the state house. One hundred years later Birch Bayh, later to be a United States senator, would come close to that record by being elected when he was a month shy of 31 years old. It was quite an honor not only for a young man, but also for a first-term state representative. It was a measure of how prominent were English's political contacts.

The speaker's chair in Indianapolis could not hold English for more than a few months; later in 1852 he was a candidate for United States Representative. Nominated and then elected in October, English campaigned not only for himself but also for Democratic presidential nominee Franklin Pierce. Thus upon entering the Capitol in Washington, English was seen as a political ally of the new president. He soon demonstrated on the floor of the

House that the assumption was an accurate one. The decade before the Civil War consumed Congress with one issue, the extension of slavery into the territories. English was made a member of the House Committee on Territories, and almost immediately became embroiled in the debate over the admission of Kansas. He advocated that there be no congressional restrictions on slavery, but instead supported Illinois Senator Douglas's conception of "popular sovereignty," i.e., letting the people of the territories themselves decide upon their domestic institutions. English's views on slavery were ambivalent. No owner of slaves himself, and generally antagonistic to slavery, the Indiana congressman nonetheless wished that Southerners not feel endangered by Northern agitation on the issue:

> I am a native of a free state, and have no love for the institution of slavery. Aside from the moral question involved, I regard it as an injury to the state where it exists, and, if it were proposed to introduce it where I reside, would resist it to the last extremity.

With these sentiments expressed, he then left it to the people of each state or territory to make a final decision:

> We do not like this institution of slavery, … but consider that it is a matter which, like all other domestic affairs, each organized community ought to be allowed to decide for itself.

Though support of the admission of Kansas as a slave state was the death knell of political fortunes for most Northern Democrats who supported it, English was one of only three in that category who survived the Northern voters' wrath in the 1854 elections. Know-Nothing Party members formed coalitions with the remains of the Whig Party in the North. English deprecated the anti-foreign, nativist attacks of the Know-Nothing opposition. English's almost unique survival among Northern pro-slavery Democrats in 1854 can in large part be credited to the fact that his district lay on the very southern tip of Indiana, separated only by the Ohio River from Kentucky and its slavery. At the end of his second term English desired to retire from Congress, but the convention that attempted to nominate a successor failed after 42 ballots to agree on an alternative, and it turned unanimously to English and requested he relent on his decision to retire. Elected a third time, English found himself chairman of the Committee on Post-offices and Post-roads, an important and taxing post in the rapidly developing America of the 1850s.

The Kansas-Nebraska fight of 1854 was renewed with heightened emotionalism in this new Congress, for Kansas was now applying for admission as a state under the Lecompton Constitution, a controversial document written at a convention held in the small Kansas town of that name, attended by pro-slavery delegates and boycotted by anti-slavery men. The Congressional debates of 1858 presaged the Civil War, only three years away. As a member of the Committee on Territories, English had played a significant role in the House fight over the issue. When the House and Senate could not agree on legislation, English was made a member of the joint conference committee to resolve the differences. This six-member committee initially could not break the deadlock, but then the senators asked if the House had a compromise to offer. English requested a delay to finalize some ideas he had. The resulting proposal, which came to be known as the "English bill," was the only significant piece of legislation in his eight years of service in the House to bear his name. Many saw English's work as a bribe to the Kansas voters. It proposed that the Lecompton Constitution be submitted to the voters of that territory. Should they accept it, and its pro-slavery features, then additional free government land would be offered to the Kansas people. The bill narrowly passed both houses, but not without bitter charges being hurled at the scheme. President Buchanan was grateful for the compromise and offered English some high government post in reward for his labors, but English refused. The compromise did not resolve the issue because despite the bribe the Kansas voters overwhelmingly rejected the Lecompton Constitution at the polls.

Reelected in 1858, English began what would prove his last term in public office with the largest majority he had ever received. He was selected as a member of the Democrats' national campaign committee in 1860, and though not a delegate he did attend the national convention in Charleston as an extremely interested, active observer. English hoped for moderation and compromise. He appealed to his Southern comrades not to join the secession movement:

> the great Democratic party, that has so long and so justly boasted of its nationality, must not degenerate into a mere Southern sectional party, or a party that tolerates the sentiment of disunion; if it does, its days are numbered and its mission ended.

The appeal was of course in vain. He lent his name to Breckinridge's candidacy, but did not apparently campaign for him. Wanting no part in the conflict, English this time irrevocably refused to be renominated for Congress and retired in March 1861. He refused the command of a regiment offered to him by Governor Oliver Morton. Instead he devoted himself for the next year to trying to redirect his life away from politics. A year back home was a restless time, and any desire to recommence his legal career soon faded. Instead, he got into banking. With a sizeable fortune developed from wise real estate investments during 20 years in office, English had already been a frequent lender to friends and political allies, including Senator Bright. Bright in turn introduced English to George Riggs, a Washington banker. Other banking acquaintances were made through additional political friendships. A partnership was made with Indiana politician and banker Hugh McCulloch, and in May 1863, they opened the First National Bank of Indianapolis. In the credit-hungry, boom times of civil war, the bank grew rapidly. Soon English was one of the leading financial lights in the Indiana capital. On January 1, 1865, he moved into prestigious Governor's Circle, initially named because it was to be the site of the state governor's mansion. He would remain there until he moved into the English Hotel of Indianapolis, but that was several years and several million dollars later.

English lived a happy, extremely prosperous life. Yet as is perhaps not uncommon among bankers, his reputation spread for cold business judgments. The panic of 1873 left many people without the means to pay mortgages held by English's banking empire. Though his bank and other interests withstood the effects of the recession, many businesses were forced to close and English more often than not picked up the pieces at foreclosure. In 1880, a bitterly critical Republican campaign document, *The Life of William H. English*, by Charles S. Keyser, received broad publicity for its attacks on the "English reign of ruin." Listed was each debtor upon whom foreclosure was made; a few individual debtor's stories were told; their sad plight was depicted, especially the fact they still owed substantial sums on their debts even after foreclosure because English, as the only bidder, had bid much less than the debt secured by the property. English was a Scrooge, forced to hide behind the iron fence of his Indianapolis mansion, afraid to venture forth. Keyser stated, "There are but few men who have no redeeming virtue." But English was depicted as one of those few.

The truth would appear to be much less harsh, but still somewhat negative. True he evicted hundreds of individuals who had not weathered the fearful economic storm of the 1870s. His obligation to investors in his bank and other interests made it difficult to ignore the delinquent payments. He did not seem to exhibit compassion to the hundreds of misfortunates, but felt that emotion had little place in the business world. He cried out during the 1880 campaign, in anger and frustration, "What do they do with mortgages elsewhere — burn them?"

All was not comfort and pleasure for the wealthy banker. His father died in 1874. His wife became an invalid in 1876, and the following year she died. His only son, later to be a United States congressman, at this stage in his life seemed to be directionless. His wife's illness had caused English to retire from the constant work he was devoting to the banking business, and with his wife's death he began to look for something to fill the empty hours. A return to politics was the choice.

The first step was helping see his son elected to the state legislature in 1878. This completed three generations of English men in this post, grandfather Elisha, father William H., and now William E. English. In 1876, William H. English had been a loyal supporter of the

Tilden ticket, which included Indianan Thomas A. Hendricks in the running mate position. When Hendricks took himself out of consideration for that same spot in 1880, instead trying for the presidency, English began his own campaign for the vice presidential nomination. He wrote Tilden in 1878 and offered support for the presidency in two years. Besides the vice presidency, English had alternative ambitions for a cabinet post, particularly the Treasury. As an important Indiana banker, English could count on being listened to by those who wanted his party's nomination.

A publicity campaign was initiated in 1879. Newspaper editors were written as early as February of that year. The general technique was to write and include newspaper clippings that depicted English as a good candidate for high office in the next election. Important political leaders were contacted across the country and asked for support. Some wanted part of the English fortune before they would help, usually discreetly requesting it in the form of a campaign contribution to get the English candidacy across in their respective states. English was not afraid to use his fortune to advance his candidacy, but he also feared its adverse political impact. The English image as a skinflint was countered by trying to involve himself in civic affairs, such as a sizeable contribution to enlarge the Indianapolis library. While these political efforts were under way, additional publicity was gained by the construction in Indianapolis of the English Opera House. It opened in September 1880. News of the details of its ornate construction had kept his name at least before Indiana citizens. It was meant not only to increase the family fortune, but also to provide a business to occupy his son, who would become manager of the house.

At the state party convention in June 1880, English's publicity campaign, and his money, had gained him sufficient recognition that he was chosen chairman of the state central committee. Some Democrats were resentful that a relative novice had leapt over far more consistent workers in the party to gain this position. Soon after the state party organized, the national party convention began its delibera-

tions to select a presidential ticket. Indianan Thomas A. Hendricks had foresworn the vice presidency, stayed as a contender for the top spot until the convention, but his first ballot total was a severe disappointment to him. He finished well back in the pack. Included with Hendricks among the not-so-serious contenders was Connecticut governor James English.

After Winfield Scott Hancock was named for president on the second ballot, consideration for vice president began. Alabaman, former Confederate general, feeble but unbowed Edmund W. Pettus nominated English. Every state except two seconded the nomination. English was selected because he balanced the ticket geographically. It was also hoped he would open his bank vault to the needs of the party in the general election.

English soon became a campaign issue. Not only was he accused of enlarging his wealth by mortgage foreclosures during hard times, but publicized also were his pro-slavery votes preceding the Civil War. During the 1850s, English had frequently spoken disparagingly of the Negro. As a state legislator he had voted to exclude Negroes and mulattoes from Indiana. He had once argued

> I have come to the unequivocal conclusion that the African is a distinct species of the human race, differing radically and as definitely, to the careful observer, in mental construction and intellectual bias, as in physical conformity and external appearance.

Republicans publicized an image of English as barricaded in his iron house. He was said to have offered fifty thousand dollars to be nominated but then contributed only five thousand. Actually, he may have contributed as much as fifteen thousand. One of the most damaging stories, because it was mainly true, was that after the disastrous Chicago fire, he had been asked to make a contribution for relief and had given exactly one dollar. He was then informed that this miserly offer would injure him politically, and he gave one hundred dollars instead, saying he had misunderstood what he had been asked to contribute to. There were many reasons for the extremely narrow Democratic loss in the general election, but the negative publicity aroused by

English may have played a meaningful part. There had been some efforts to get English to withdraw from the ticket, but these failed.

English did not again run for public office. His son's political career occupied some of his time, but the career never proved viable and was abandoned. More significant were his historical efforts. English wrote frequently and well on his state's history and on the West in general. A two-volume work on the exploration of George Rogers Clark consumed several years of work. English became president of the Indiana Historical Society, which he had helped organize in 1886. His first historical work had been a biography of the constitution and lawmakers of Indiana; the last ten years of his life were spent on a history of Indiana. His home on Governor's Circle, and then his rooms at the Hotel English, because a veritable historical museum, containing relics and papers discovered during his researches. His legacy included his writings, the English Hotel and the English Opera House. In 1893, his wealth was estimated at the vast sum of four million dollars. His living expenses, however, were thought to be less than one thousand dollars annually.

Analysis of Qualifications

A few men have been nominated for vice president for the principal reason that it was hoped they would help bankroll the national campaign. The most obvious example was Henry Gassaway Davis, who at age 81 had few remaining contributions to bring to the campaign other than monetary ones. William H. English was another prime representative of this class of nominees. Unlike Davis, English did at least partially fulfill his end of the tacit bargain.

Never a prominent politician, English served only eight years in elective office, those as Congressman, plus a few months as a state legislator. In Washington, English was a Democratic backbencher, whose only significant notoriety came from the English bill which attempted to bribe the people of Kansas into accepting the tainted, pro-slavery Lecompton Constitution. For 20 years, English devoted himself to public life, serving in various appointive positions before being elected to

the state legislature, and almost immediately thereafter, the federal house of representatives. At the age of 40, English abandoned this career almost completely, and turned his energies to an area he apparently took to naturally, the making of substantial sums of money. As a banker, English rose rapidly and could soon be counted among the wealthiest of the state's citizens.

English was an upright, moral man who revealed aggressiveness and good business aptitude. He was a miserly man, with little sympathy for the downtrodden. His interests were broad, and he made significant contributions to the field of history and culture in his native state. As a politician he was a conservative Democrat who understood and profited from the spoils system when his party was in power before the Civil War, and could have been expected to continue the system if he had helped his party regain national office in 1880. Civil service reform was one of the key issues of the day, and in English, advocates of that reform would have found little support.

English had little personal warmth, and many thought him cold and arrogant. Strong-willed, a doer and achiever, English dominated many lesser men. Never a bitter partisan, English had friendships with many Republicans in the state, perhaps in part because he did business with so many of them.

There was little to suggest greatness in William English. He had been a success at what he had attempted, and had revealed executive ability if not always a compassionate heart. He was inexperienced in national affairs since he had withdrawn from them 20 years before his nomination for vice president. English was not an inspired choice. His selection had the normal ulterior party motives of geographical balance and, in this case, of pecuniary support to the party. All is not negative, for at least he had demonstrated some capacity for achievement. He would have managed governmental affairs efficiently, conservatively, and quietly should he have been called to the presidency. What his goals would have been are certainly questionable, as for the previous 20 years his only ambition had been the accumulation of money, an accumulation apparently for its own sake, as he did not spend it. In sum, there appears to have been too little statesmanship, too miserly an interest in the public welfare, for English to have been as president anything other than a banker tending to the country's financial balance sheet. It is well he was only an also-ran's running mate, and never had the opportunity to manage the country's affairs in the same manner as he accumulated his fortune.

ENGLISH BIBLIOGRAPHY

A Biographical History of Eminent and Self-Made Men of the State of Indiana.... 2 vols. Cincinnati (1880), vol. II, pp. 209–227.

Clancy, Herbert J. *The Presidential Election of 1880.* Chicago (1958).

Cole, James R. *Life and Public Services of Winfield Scott Hancock, ... also, The Life and Services of the Hon. William H. English.* Cincinnati (1880).

Dunn, J.P. *Commemorative Biographical Record of Prominent and Representative Men of Indianapolis and Vicinity....* Chicago (1908), pp. 8–18.

_____. *Greater Indianapolis; the History....* 2 vols. Chicago (1910).

_____. *Indiana and Indianans.* 5 vols. Chicago (1919), V, pp. 2154–2158.

Forney, John W. *Life and Military Career of Winfield Scott Hancock..., also contains a succinct Biographical Sketch of Hon. Wm. H. English.* Philadelphia (1880), pp. 483–502.

Goodrich, Frederick E. *The Life and Public Services of Winfield Scott Hancock, Major-General, U.S.A.* Boston (1880), pp. 329–365.

Handfield, F. Gerald, Jr. "William H. English and the Election of 1880," in Ralph D. Gray, ed., *Gentlemen from Indiana: National Party Candidates 1836–1940.* Indianapolis (1977), pp. 83–116.

Huffman, Danna Lansley. "The Life and Public Career of William Hayden English, 1822–1896." Unpublished master's thesis, Butler University (1946).

Keyser, Charles S. *The Life of William H. English, the Democratic Candidate for Vice President of the United States.* Philadelphia (1880).

Pierpont, Frederick L. "The English Bill." Unpublished master's thesis, Indiana University (1935).

Reed, George Irving, ed. *Encyclopedia of Biography of Indiana.* 2 vols. Chicago (1895), pp. 41–46.

Schimmel, Eliot L. "William H. English and the Politics of Self-Deception, 1845–1861." Florida State University (1986).

1880 Presidential Nominee— Greenback Labor Party

James B. Weaver

Born June 12, 1833, in Dayton, Ohio; died February 6, 1912, in Colfax, Iowa.

Married Clara Vinson on July 13, 1858; they had five daughters and two sons.

James Baird Weaver was the fifth of 13 children born to Abram and Susan Imlay Weaver. The Weaver family moved first to Michigan, and then to Davis County, Iowa, in 1843. They farmed the Iowa prairie, with James attending country schools. They moved to the small county seat of Bloomfield after Abram Weaver was elected to a local office. Starting when he was 14 and continuing for four years, James had a rural mail route, some of it where there were no roads. He spent a few months in 1853 searching for gold in California. For a time James clerked at a store in Bonaparte. His public speaking skills finally convinced him to become a lawyer. Borrowing one hundred dollars he began studies in 1855 at Cincinnati Law School. The legal, but outrageous interest rate on the loan was 33⅓ percent per year. He finished law school in a year and began his practice in Bloomfield.

Weaver's interest in politics first led him to be a Democrat, but the issue of slavery drove him to the Republican Party. When the Republican National Convention was held in Chicago in mid–May 1860, Weaver traveled there to observe the nomination of Abraham Lincoln as president. With Lincoln's call for volunteers, Weaver joined and became a first lieutenant in an Iowa infantry unit. He fought at various important engagements in Tennessee and Mississippi, including at the 1862 battle at Shiloh. He rose quickly in rank due to his bravery and skill, and was advanced over senior officers to major and then to colonel. His enlistment expired in May 1864, allowing Weaver to return home for the rest of the war. He resumed his law practice in Des Moines. On March 13, 1865, he received the brevet (temporary) rank of brigadier general for "bravery in the field."

Weaver failed in 1865 to receive the Republican nomination for Iowa lieutenant governor, but the next year was elected local district attorney. From 1867 to 1873 he served as the appointed federal assessor of internal revenue in one of the Iowa regions. Refusing to bend with prevailing winds, Weaver was a frequent opponent of the powerful railroad interests that were so vital to a state like Iowa. He was also a prohibitionist and a believer in the inflationary monetary policies of what became known as the Greenback movement. These differences with the Republicans caused him, he thought by trickery, to be defeated for the Republican nominations for Congress in 1874 and for governor in 1875. In 1877 he renounced the Republicans and joined the Greenback Party. He was elected to Congress the next year. In 1880 he was nominated for president at his party's June convention in Chicago, winning on the first ballot. He gave speeches touring the country "from Arkansas to Maine, and from Lake Michigan to Mobile." He thought he had spoken to over a million people, but not nearly that many voted for him.

GEN. JAMES B. WEAVER.

JAMES B. WEAVER
(From the University of Michigan Library, Ann Arbor, Michigan)

He had relinquished his congressional seat to run for president, and was defeated in 1882 when he tried to reclaim it. He retook the seat in 1884 and 1886. The Greenback Party's narrow focus limited its success. It was absorbed into the Farmer's Alliance movement and then into the Populist or People's Party. Weaver ran for the Populist Party presidential nomination in 1892. He was a dynamic speaker, striking in appearance, a reminder of the glories of Union Civil War victories, all of which combined to give him a strong following. The connection with the War and the old parties also was a negative, as he seemed to embody the charge that the Populists "did not represent new ideas, but old ones relabelled" (Hicks, page 235). Weaver still gained the nomination with a strong first-ballot majority. He got more popular votes in November than in 1880, but was a distant third.

Weaver remained active in the political monetary fray, and was a strong booster of William Jennings Bryan in 1896 when Bryan gained the Democratic and Populist presidential nomination. That was the beginning of the end of the Populists as a separate party. Weaver in time became a Democrat. His remaining political office was as mayor of Colfax, Iowa, where he spent his last years.

Weaver's home in Bloomfield, Iowa still stands on U.S. Highway 63 (private).

BARZILLAI J. CHAMBERS
(From the University of Michigan Library, Ann Arbor, Michigan)

WEAVER BIBLIOGRAPHY

Allen, E.A. *The Life and Public Services of James Baird Weaver*. Cincinnati (1892).

Evans, Harry C. *The Pioneers and Politics of Davis County, Iowa*. Bloomfield, Iowa (1929).

Haynes, Fred E. *James Baird Weaver*. Iowa City (1919, reprinted 1975, Arno Press).

Hicks, John D. *The Populist Revolt*. Lincoln, Nebr. (1961, reprint of 1931 edition)

Lilley, Lin S. "Entering the Presidential Race, A Comparison of Entrance Speeches of Minor Candidates and Major-Party Nominees." Unpublished Ph.D. dissertation, University of Iowa (1992).

Nger, Irwin. *The Greenback Era: A Social and Political History of American Finance, 1865–1879*. Princeton (1964).

Wilkens, Kenneth G. "A Rhetorical Study of the Speechmaking of General James B. Weaver." Unpublished Ph.D. dissertation, Northwestern University (1954).

1880 Vice Presidential Nominee — Greenback Labor Party

Barzillai J. Chambers

Born December 5, 1817, in Montgomery County, Kentucky; died September 16, 1895, in Cleburne, Texas. Married Susan Wood in 1852; she died in 1853. Married Emma Montgomery in 1854; she died after having one child, and then the child died in infancy. Married Harriet A. Killough in 1861; they had three children. He has been referred to as "Benjamin" in many histories.

Barzillai J. Chambers was one of eight children in the farm family of Walker and Talitha Cumi Mothershead Chambers. He apparently attended some local schools, but nothing definite is known of him until at age 20 he was a volunteer Kentucky soldier who went to Texas to help in the revolution against Mexico. His uncle Thomas Jefferson Chambers raised the volunteers and appointed his nephew a captain and his aide-de-camp. Independence had already been won before they arrived. Barzillai was discharged and became a surveyor in the Houston area. He moved to north central Texas, a less settled region that exposed him to several Indian attacks. Chambers was elected surveyor. When his term ended, he settled on a farm in Navarro County. He became a lawyer in 1860, but rarely practiced.

Chambers was an ardent secessionist when the Civil War began, but at age 44 he did not serve in the army until he enlisted for six months in 1864. When the war ended he moved to north central Texas, bought substantial land, and donated the site for the town he founded: Cleburne. From 1871 to 1875 he was half-owner of a bank. He also invested in and promoted a narrow gauge railroad that was to run to Dallas. In 1868 Chambers gave a speech attacking the big business interests that had funded Ulysses Grant's campaign for president. He opposed all interest-bearing loans to the federal government, considering such loans unconstitutional. The new Texas constitution of 1876 contained tax and other provisions that Chambers disliked. He campaigned for the state senate as an opponent of the constitution. The document won easily; Chambers lost the same way. He was at some point elected a Cleburne alderman.

Chambers was disgusted with the failure of the 1876 Democratic national convention to adopt a strong greenback plank. Chambers wanted the party to stand firmly for continuing the use of the paper money that was issued during the war, and not to resume specie (coin) payments. This was an inflationary practice, as it was much easier for debtors such a farmers to repay in paper money as opposed to needing gold or silver coin. The Greenback Party began organizing in Texas in 1877. Chambers attended the party's first statewide convention in 1878 and was nominated for commissioner of the state land office. He later withdrew from the race and switched to a campaign for the state legislature. Chambers wrote a pamphlet, quoted by some newspapers, that sharply criticized government bondholders and the politicians who were supported by them. One of his particular targets was popular Senator Richard Coke. He lost his legislative race, but gained notoriety across much of the state for his attack on Senator Coke.

In 1879 Chambers attended the national convention of a splinter, mainly Southern Greenback group, called the Union Greenback Labor Party. He was elected to the group's national executive committee. In March 1880 he attended the splinter group's second convention. After New Yorker Stephen Dellaye was nominated for president, Chambers was nominated for vice president. Chambers bought the *Cleburne Avalanche* in April to publicize his views. In June, Chambers attended the national convention of the principal Greenback party and sought union between the different factions. Chambers was nominated for vice president. His opponent, General A.M. West, moved to make the nomination unanimous. Chamber's campaigning was halted in July when he slipped and fell from a train in Texas, fracturing two ribs. Several weeks of bed rest caused him to consider withdrawing, but he did not, nor did he ever resume campaigning.

After the ticket's defeat in November, Chambers remained active in the party. He accused the party's chairman of being dictatorial in 1882, and thought the party was "disintegrating" due to bad leadership. In 1884 he disagreed publicly both with the party's gubernatorial and its presidential nominees on certain issues. He drifted towards populism by 1890, as he continued to seek a new political party that would focus on the hardships faced by farmers.

CHAMBERS BIBLIOGRAPHY

Barr, Alwyn. "B.J. Chambers and the Greenback Party Split." *Mid-America* 49 (1967), pp. 276–284.

_____. "Barzillai J. Chambers." *The New Handbook of Texas.* Austin (1996), vol. 2, p. 29.

_____. *Reconstruction to Reform: Texas Politics 1876–1906.* Austin (1971).

"Brief Biographical Sketch of Colonel B.J. Chambers," in *Biographies of Leading Texans*, typescript in Texas State Archives (n.p., n.d.), pp. 142–143.

Byrd, A.J. *History and Description of Johnson County.* Marshall, Tex. (1879).

A Memorial and Biographical History of Johnson and Hill Counties, Texas. Chicago (1892).

Jill Currie of the Layland Museum and Tina Williams of the Cleburne (Texas) Public Library provided research material on Barzillai Chambers.

Election of 1884

NOMINATIONS

Republican Party Convention (8th): June 3–6, 1884, at Exposition Hall, Chicago, Illinois. *President*— James G. Blaine, nominated on the 4th ballot with 541 out of the 813 votes cast. He had garnered 334½ on the first vote. Chester Arthur was his chief rival. *Vice president*— John A. Logan, nominated on the first ballot with 779 votes out of the 786 cast.

Democratic Party Convention (14th): July 8–11, 1884, at Exposition Hall, Chicago, Illinois. *President*— Grover Cleveland, nominated on the second ballot with 683 votes out of 820 cast. He received 392 on the first ballot. Thomas Bayard (Del.) was his major opponent. *Vice president*— Thomas A. Hendricks, nominated unanimously on the first ballot.

GENERAL ELECTION, November 4, 1884

Popular Vote
    Cleveland 4,874,621
    Blaine 4,848,936
    Others.   326,197
Electoral Vote
    Cleveland-Hendricks — 219 (20 states)
    Blaine-Logan —182 (18 states)
Winners
    Grover Cleveland, 22nd president
    Thomas A. Hendricks, 21st vice president
Losers
    James G. Blaine, John A. Logan

1884 presidential nominee —
Republican Party

James G. Blaine

Full Name: James Gillespie Blaine.
State represented: Maine.
Birth: January 31, 1830, at West Brownsville, Pennsylvania.

Age on Inauguration Day (March 4, 1885): 55 years, 1 month.

Education: Washington College, Washington, Pennsylvania, 1843–1847; then studied law, but never admitted to bar.

Religion: Congregationalist.

Ancestry/prominent relatives: Scotch-Irish Protestants on paternal side; Roman Catholic Irish on maternal side; great-great-grandfather (James Blaine) arrived from Ireland in 1745; great-grandfather (Ephraim Blaine) prominent in Revolution, friend of George Washington.

Occupation: Newspaperman at early adulthood, before entering politics.

Public offices: Delegate to 1856 Republican National Convention; Republican State Committee, 1859–1881; Maine legislature, 1859–1863, speaker of Maine House, 1861–1863; declined nomination for Congress, 1860; U.S. House of Representatives, March 4, 1863–July 10, 1876; speaker of U.S. House, 1869–1875; U.S. senator, July 10, 1876–March 5, 1881; unsuccessful candidate for Republican presidential nomination, 1876 and 1880; U.S. secretary of state, March 5–December 12, 1881, resigned; unsuccessful presidential nominee, 1884; secretary of state, March 7, 1889–June 4, 1892, resigned.

Home: "Blaine House," in Augusta, later became Maine's Governor's Mansion; vacation home at Bar Harbor, Maine.

Death: January 27, 1893, in Washington, D.C., at age 63 years.

Burial: Oak Hill Cemetery, Georgetown, Maryland; reinterred near Forest Grove Cemetery in Blaine Memorial Park, Augusta, Maine, June 13, 1920.

Personal characteristics: Large head, strong in appearance, pleasing voice; inspirational speaker; dignified; tall, commanding figure.

Father: Ephraim Lyon Blaine (1796–June 28, 1850), farmer, minor public official, businessman.

Mother: Maria Louise Gillespie (1801–1871), daughter of Neal Gillespie, Jr.; married in 1820.

Siblings: James (1821–1822). Neal Gillespie (1823–?), married in 1847 to Rebecca A. Officer. Ephraim Lyon (1825–1850). Eliza Gillespie (1827–1885), married Maj. Robert C. Walker in 1845.

Wife: Harriet Baily Stanwood (1828–1903), married June 30, 1850, secretly, and when legality of ceremony was questioned, remarried March 29, 1851.

Children: Stanwood (1851–1854). Robert Walker (1855–January 15, 1890), never married; was a lawyer and solicitor of U.S. State Department. William Emmons (1857–June 1892), married Anita McCormick September 26, 1888; served as assistant to later vice presidential candidate Henry Davis (1904) on West Virginia Railroad. Alice Stanwood (1860–February 2, 1890), married Col. J.J. Coppinger. Margaret Isabella (1865–July 27, 1949), married Watler Damrosch May 27, 1890. James Gillespie, Jr. (1869–?), married Marie Nevins in 1886, divorced February 20, 1892; married Mrs. Beryl Whitney Wheeler. Harriet Stanwood (1871–?), married Truxton Beale in 1894, divorced 1896.

Historic sites/memorials: Blaine's Washington home still stands at 2000 Massachusetts Avenue, N.W. Blaine's house in Augusta, Maine, is now the Governor's Mansion.

Many prominent ancestors preceded James G. Blaine onto the American stage. The presidential candidate was the fifth generation from James Blaine, who arrived from Londonderry, Ireland, in 1745. That James Blaine's son fought in the French and Indian Wars and then was commissary general for a large part of General Washington's army during the Revolution.

The next generation Blaine made his mark in business, moving westward and acquiring substantial property. James G. Blaine's father was a lawyer but chose business for his career. The Blaines had been Presbyterian, but this did not dissuade James' father from marrying a Catholic woman of almost equally prominent lineage. During the religious bigotry of a later age, James G. Blaine would be "accused" of being a Catholic, but he never took the religion of his mother but instead became a Congregationalist.

No brilliance exhibited itself in James' early years. He was a shy child with a speech impediment. The family was comfortable enough financially, neither rich nor poor. James grew up on his mother's family farm in Pennsylvania, the nearest town being West Brownsville, insignificant except for its location on the National Road. At the age of 13 James began studies at Washington College in Washington, Pennsylvania. He graduated in 1847 as the youngest and third highest member of his class. Yale Law School was his ambition, but it was too great a financial strain on his parents. Work to earn the funds required sent him to Lexington, Kentucky, where he stopped long enough to hear his and his family's political idol Henry Clay speak and to discover a job opportunity at a military academy in nearby Georgetown. Blaine would remain in the South from 1847 until 1851, acquiring a deep disgust for slavery, or so he would later say when campaigning in Maine. Nonetheless, while in Kentucky he voiced the opinion that abolitionists' activities were counterproductive.

At the military school he met Harriet Stanwood, a teacher at a nearby girls' academy. After a secret marriage in June 1850, they were remarried the following year because of doubts concerning the validity of the first ceremony. Blaine's hopes for legal studies had to be postponed again by the death of his father and by his own marriage. Money now took priority over education. A short stint at the Pennsylvania Institute for the Education of the Blind in Philadelphia was only a stopgap. A more promising opportunity appeared when Harriet's family back in Maine told the couple of the possibility of editing the Kennebec *Journal*, a strong Whig paper in Augusta, Maine. Blaine quickly accepted and was shown in the edition of November 6, 1854, to have taken charge.

Blaine's rise in Maine political life was greatly aided by his position with the newspaper. He took up the Northern cause on most major issues, from abolition to the tariff. He abandoned his goal of a law degree, which was probably just a perceived requirement for a political career; the paper now sufficed for that. In 1854, the new Republican Party took control of Maine state government. As the editor of the leading Whig, now Republican, paper in the capital, Blaine got the lucrative state printing contract. His business was good and investments in lands and other ventures were also profitable. Blaine's rise in Maine was meteoric. After 20 months in the state he was elected a delegate to the Republican National Convention of 1856. His political insight, remarked upon in his earlier years, proved increasingly perceptive. He accurately forecast that the pre-convention favorites, Seward and Chase, could not be nominated. After Frémont was chosen, Blaine was energetic in his cause, but the first Republican ticket failed.

The budding politician's next move was to Portland, Maine, when he was offered the editorship of a daily newspaper at a good salary. The Republican governor then asked him to participate in an investigation of the state's prisons. Several reforms were suggested, saving the state much money. In 1858, Blaine was elected to the state house of representatives. His leadership qualities were quickly appreciated: Blaine was made speaker after one term. In 1859 this recent Maine immigrant became chairman of the state Republican Party, a position he was to hold until he became United States secretary of state in 1881. One constant in Blaine's career was his ability to become liked immediately, whether by legislative colleagues or by the voters. He genuinely liked people and they returned his friendship. His ingratiating manner was keynoted by his fantastically retentive memory, particularly for names and faces. He inspired devotion in his followers, bringing him to the verge of the ultimate political prize in America. Blaine was magnetic in his speaking style. Even his extemporaneous speeches were magically filled with perfectly phrased jewels of either tribute or disparagement, Blaine being the master of each.

The outbreak of the Civil War found no firmer unionist than Blaine. Still, as did many other influential men in that war, he paid for a substitute to fight for him. Blaine's future presidential opponent Grover Cleveland avoided military service in the same fashion. Instead of military glory, Blaine was seeking and gaining greater political laurels. He was elected to the United States House of Representatives in 1862 and would continue in that

post until 1876, when he resigned to become United States senator. Blaine's energies were tireless in pursuit of a strong Republican majority in his home state in 1862. Maine's elections were held two months before those in the rest of the nation, and traditionally the momentum from one party's victory in Maine would propel it to national gains as well (thus the saying, "As Maine goes, so goes the nation"; for a corollary to this maxim, see Alfred Landon sketch in the 1936 election). In 1862, the North suffered continual defeat in the war, and Blaine saw danger to the Union cause if his party lost in Maine. Though hardly the sole cause, Blaine could be proud of his contribution to preserving the Republican Maine majority.

In Congress Blaine frequently clashed with arch-rival Thaddeus Stevens of Pennsylvania. Yet as always with his political adversaries, Blaine tried to remain on friendly personal terms. When the war ended Blaine generally agreed with the Radicals' Reconstruction aims, though he was not extreme. He wished for a conciliatory approach. Yet the South's refusal to act as if they realized the war had been lost hardened Blaine's views. Southern states rejected the Fourteenth Amendment to the Constitution, returned Confederate officers and political leaders to Congress at the first postwar election, and otherwise tried to regain politically some of what they had lost militarily. Such intransigence led to a three-to-one Radical majority in the 1867 Congress and caused the confrontation with Andrew Johnson. As did every other Republican in the House, Blaine voted to impeach Johnson, but he would say 15 years later that he came to consider that vote his worst political decision. He would realize Johnson had committed no impeachable offense, but had only been bull-headed. As the 1868 election approached, Blaine joined most Republicans in a frenzy for Ulysses Grant. His fervor increased when the Democratic vice presidential candidate, Francis P. Blair, stated that the only issue in the campaign was the end of Reconstruction. Blaine knew the South had yet to accept the verdict of war and he would not rest until that victory was confirmed at the polls.

Though at times in the Reconstruction debates he would join the Radicals, Blaine maintained a moderate or even liberal voting record. Universal suffrage — ensuring the former slaves the right to vote — and universal amnesty — removing political disabilities from the ex–Confederates — were the cornerstones of his policy towards the South. North and South had reason to find Blaine an appealing candidate for high national office.

House Speaker Schuyler Colfax was elected vice president with Grant in 1868, and Blaine was a candidate for the speaker vacancy. No opponent contested him from the Republican side of the aisle and thus he was easily elected. He was a well-respected speaker, seldom engaging in debate but making what were conceded to be impartial rulings from the chair. By the time he left the speaker's chair, because the Democrats had gained a majority in the House in 1875, he was in a powerful position to win the Republican presidential nomination in 1876. A few storm clouds nonetheless loomed menacingly.

In 1866, Blaine had stooped to sarcastic and bitterly personal debate on the House floor with arrogant and powerful New York congressman Roscoe Conkling. The substance of the dispute was minor; its political repercussions perhaps cost Blaine the presidency. After Conkling had ridiculed Blaine, the Maine congressman retorted:

> The contempt of the large-minded gentleman is so wilting, his haughty disdain, his grandiloquent swell, his majestic, supereminent, turkey-gobbler strut has been so crushing to myself and all the members of the House, that I know it was an act of the greatest temerity for me to venture upon a controversy with him.

Blaine would regret to his grave his characterizing, appropriately enough however, Conkling's bearing as a "turkey-gobbler strut," and otherwise ridiculing the haughty and unforgiving New Yorker. Conkling was a powerful enemy, perhaps one enemy too many for a man with Blaine's ambitions.

Another storm warning came in the form of an accusation of corruption. Blaine's historical image has been largely molded by one fact, the allegations arising out of the so-called "Mulligan Letters." These letters exploded upon the Republican candidate in the spring of 1876, just months before the convention. The con-

troversy began with unsubstantiated charges that Blaine had gotten a loan from a railroad with no obligation that he repay. He counterattacked in the House, denying any participation in any transactions with the railroad. Initial public reaction after Blaine's speech was that the charges were politically motivated. Then one James Mulligan testified before a Congressional investigatory subcommittee on May 31, 1876. He said that he had letters from Blaine in his possession. Blaine, who was present at the hearing immediately looked distressed. Mulligan had been a clerk in Blaine's brother-in-law's office and had come into possession of some of Blaine's business letters. Blaine succeeded in getting a recess called for the day. Blaine then went to Mulligan's hotel and demanded the return of the letters. He took them from Mulligan only on the promise that he would return them. Blaine returned them. Mulligan and Blaine then went to Mulligan's room. The ensuing events there are uncertain other than that Blaine emerged with the letters. Mulligan's testimony the next day was that Blaine had asked to examine the letters a second time and, upon being promised that Blaine would return them, Mulligan consented. This allegedly came after Blaine had pleaded with Mulligan and even attempted to bribe him with a diplomatic appointment. Blaine's side of the story was that he had indeed asked for the letters but had not promised to give them back. Blaine said that he had given these letters to two lawyers whose sworn affidavit stated they found nothing there that was properly subject to the inquiry of the committee.

Blaine partisans believed, perhaps wistfully, that he had successfully answered the charges. The national convention was near and Blaine knew that further efforts to dispel the odor of corruption were needed. Before a packed House and gallery, Blaine selectively read portions of the letters to show their innocence. His defense was that these letters were of an intimate business nature and it was only by the foulest political chicanery that he was forced to read them to the public. Despite no doubt being edited by Blaine, the excerpts did show that Blaine had acted as an agent for the railroad to sell some of their bonds. In fact, he had lost money on the sales since he later agreed to buy the bonds back when they had lost much of their value. Yet the letters also showed that contrary to the defense he had earlier made, Blaine had been intimately involved in selling these bonds. Much suspicion was left concerning just how far from the truth the remainder of his assertions were.

The allegations were blunted, but Blaine was clearly suspect in the minds of the reformers who were appalled at the corruption of the Grant administration. On June 11, Blaine collapsed and was unconscious for two days. The convention opened on June 14, and rumors that Blaine was near death were rampant. With scandal and illness enveloping his candidacy, Blaine at least had the good fortune to have a dramatically effective nominating speech given by Robert G. Ingersoll. Besides stirring the crowd, it also gave him the appellation of the "plumed knight" from Maine. After the speech a recess was called until the following day. The emotional peak could not be sustained overnight. Blaine was the clear favorite of the largest bloc of delegates, but with certain favorite son candidates remaining firm, Blaine would not get a majority. The final ballot was 384 for Rutherford B. Hayes, governor of Ohio, and 351 for Blaine. Conkling can probably be credited with denying Blaine the nomination.

When the secretary of the treasury resigned three days after the convention, one of the incumbent Maine senators was appointed to replace him. Blaine was then appointed by the governor to the vacant Senate seat. In his new position, Blaine fought President Hayes' decision to remove federal troops from the South. Blaine did not believe that the black man had achieved his freedom — a fact well-accepted — but Blaine also believed that the federal government should not stop trying to gain that freedom. That sentiment put Blaine definitely in the minority. Blacks in the South represented Republican votes. Blaine did not want to concede that whole region to an indefinite but certainly lengthy period of Democratic dominance. His forecast was accurate, and the Republicans as well as the former slaves were the losers. Hayes' decision broke the friendship between the two Republicans and it would never be healed. Many of Hayes' proposals were

criticized by the Maine senator. Blaine had no interest in civil service reform but instead saw the partisan distribution of political jobs as good government. Blaine did join the president in opposing free coinage of silver, a complicated issue that essentially determined whether there would be a plentiful money supply or, instead, stabler, tighter money. On balance, however, Blaine gave little comfort to the man in the White House.

After 1876, Blaine's enthusiasm for the presidency seemed to wane. He would try again in the next four elections, but never would he have the same intense desire for the office. Part of his decreased enthusiasm may have been caused by the fratricidal war between the Grant (Stalwart) branch of the party that included such men as Conkling, and the "Half-Breeds" who opposed the former president's reelection. Blaine was definitely anti–Grant but did not want to contest the 1880 nomination. Nonetheless, it was support for Blaine that prevented Grant's renomination and eventually caused a stampede towards James A. Garfield at the convention. Blaine saw Garfield's election as a tremendous personal boon, as the two men were exceedingly close. Blaine was offered any position in the cabinet he desired, and the State Department was the obvious choice.

Once selected for the chief cabinet position, Blaine attempted to dictate other personnel decisions. Though not a Grant supporter, Garfield wished for a reconciliation with the Stalwarts. Garfield even proposed to Blaine that Conkling be secretary of state and Blaine take the Treasury. Blaine was steadfast in counseling against reaching out to the Stalwarts, and the political feud grew more intense. Within a few months, patronage jobs that had been promised to Stalwarts were withdrawn. Conkling's New York Republican allies were livid. The political infighting led crazed Stalwart C.J. Guiteau, a thwarted office-seeker, to shoot President Garfield, crying as he did that now Chester A. Arthur would be president and the Stalwarts would be in power. Garfield's death was Blaine's political death as well, since Blaine turned from being the real power in the Garfield administration to being an outsider in Arthur's. His resignation came in December 1881. Blaine had foreseen eight or at least four years of a Garfield-Blaine administration, but instead he served less than ten months.

Blaine's achievements during this short stint as secretary of state were necessarily few. As he would prove later in his second tour of duty in the office, Blaine's major interest was in forging greater ties within the hemisphere, particularly with Latin America. The United States would be protector, but the Latin American countries would not be treated as subservient colonies. It was the Monroe Doctrine with a greater emphasis on balancing our interests with those of our neighbors.

Upon leaving the State Department, Blaine began writing his memoirs, to be called *Twenty Years of Congress*. Money was a significant reason for the venture, as Blaine was for a time financially embarrassed. A large Washington mansion that was begun when Blaine became secretary of state had to be rented to others. His children were being schooled in Europe, an expense which, tied with his ownership of two homes in Maine and the mansion in Washington, was more than Blaine could handle. Besides personal problems, Blaine was also being broadsided from Democrats for his handling of the State Department. He was accused of being belligerent, attempting to meddle in the affairs of many foreign countries. Such "meddling" would become an issue in the 1884 campaign. The investigations into his administration came to naught, however, and his memoirs were extremely well received. Both his political and personal affairs started to improve.

Blaine was now out of politics. From being Garfield's prime minister, he was now without political portfolio. Blaine's sense of loss probably colored his comments, but he was frequently critical of new President Arthur's handling of foreign affairs. As 1884 approached, those within the party who felt Blaine had been unfairly denied the nomination in 1876 and 1880 would not be stopped from pushing their champion again. Blaine himself, a masterful reader of the political winds, thought 1884 would not be a good Republican year and apparently did not want the nomination. The several anti–Blaine factions could not coalesce around one man, however. Blaine received the nomination on the first ballot.

Mulligan resurfaced to plague Blaine. There were more letters than those Blaine earlier had seized. None were particularly damaging, but they did renew the affair even if no new light was shed. One more recent letter about Blaine's handling of the initial 1876 exposures also became public. Attempting to have a vindication written by one of the principals in the railroad bond controversy, Blaine had written a letter to one Warren Fisher, Jr., on April 16, 1876, requesting assistance. Enclosed by Blaine was a letter Fisher was to send back to him, stating categorically that the corruption charges were false. His letter asking for the vindication closed by saying "Kind regards to Mrs. Fisher. (Burn this letter)." The juxtaposition of the two phrases seemed to highlight Blaine as hollow and deceitful. The simultaneous revelations about Grover Cleveland that he had an affair with a woman, who then bore his child, seemed to pale in significance when compared with Blaine's self-inflicted wounds.

Blaine would unintentionally strike two more blows for Cleveland. Late in the contest he took to the campaign trail, at that time still not an accepted practice for "dignified" presidential nominees. Towards the end of his tour he went to New York City, there to meet a group of Protestant clergy. Their spokesman had at the last minute been unable to attend, and a bigoted, dull-witted preacher named Samuel Burchard was substituted. Burchard's remarks to Blaine referred to the Democrats as the party of "Rum, Romanism, and Rebellion." Blaine either did not hear or else failed to appreciate the significance of the remarks. An attack on Roman Catholics could be suicidal in heavily Irish sections of New York. Blaine's later repudiation of the comment was too late; many of the early reports had even falsely, perhaps deliberately, attributed the alliterative slur to Blaine. Many people probably heard one or more versions of the minister's comment and never (at least until after the election), heard Blaine's response. Blaine's next disaster was to attend a dinner in his honor at Delmonico's with a group of the wealthiest men in New York. That impolitic event was labeled the next day as "Belshazzar's Feast," and Blaine was identified to the poor and hungry as the uncaring candidate of the rich.

The election was incredibly close. The

winner of New York state would win the presidency. After days of counting votes, Cleveland
was given an 1149 vote plurality in New York
out of more than one million votes. In his correspondence Blaine little regretted his defeat,
saying that he had not wanted to run that year
as he had feared victory could not be his. In
fact, however, victory was tantalizingly close
to being his. Had only 600 of the Catholics,
or impoverished workers, or others his ill-
designed campaigning had antagonized in New
York the last week of the election, voted for
him instead of Cleveland, James G. Blaine
would have been our twenty-second president.

Defeat returned Blaine to the task of completing his memoirs. His financial success from
the first volume also permitted him to start
construction of a beautiful island home at Bar
Harbor on the Maine coast. In 1887, he took
a European tour that many believed was just a
prelude to running for president again.

Blaine wrote from Europe that he did not
desire the Republican nomination unless it
came his way unanimously. Victory would be
too hard to gain unless he could start with a
united party, an unlikely event. On January 25,
1888, he wrote these sentiments to the chairman of the Republican National Committee.
Blaine was also ill and did not desire the strain
of another campaign. But Blaine did not lose
his interest in politics, and took advantage of
President Cleveland's call for a reduction in the
protective tariff rates to give his views on the
issue. Blaine denounced Cleveland and said
that the only parties to gain by lowering the
tariff would be the British, who would then be
able to flood America with their manufactured
goods. Blaine's stand was a far more popular
one than Cleveland's though perhaps it was not
economically as sound. Despite Blaine's protest, many of his friends continued to work for
his nomination. While in England, Blaine
stayed with Andrew Carnegie. Carnegie telegrammed the delegates that if the convention
could not agree on a candidate, Blaine would
accept. Blaine's sons were also working strenuously to push their father's cause. Despite
these efforts, Blaine continued to insist he
would not run. Seeing that the decision was
final, Carnegie telegrammed supporters that
Benjamin Harrison would be acceptable to

Blaine. Harrison did receive the nomination
and privately acknowledged his debt to Blaine.

Blaine's prominence in the party, as well as
his energetic campaigning for the victorious
Harrison, made it clear that Blaine would be
secretary of state. Yet this would not be the
close political relationship that Blaine had
enjoyed under President Garfield. Harrison
seemed to take a perverse pleasure in making
known that he would be independent from
Blaine, and delayed notifying Blaine that he
would be appointed to the State Department.
Relations with Harrison were never cordial. It
became almost impossible for Blaine to get one
of his appointments as a State Department
position approved. In May of 1891, Blaine's bad
health caused him to go to Bar Harbor, Maine,
for recuperation, and he would not return to
his post until October. Harrison became bitter that Blaine gave no credit to the president
for the increased work the chief executive had
to take on during Blaine's absence.

Harrison was a cold, inconsiderate man, and
it was not just Blaine who was ignored and even
punished by the president. Harrison was in
deep political trouble; Blaine was the candidate of many of his Republican opponents. In
February 1892, Blaine announced he would not
run for the nomination, yet again many Blaine
supporters would not accept that statement.
His health left him in no condition to seek the
presidency, however. On June 4, Blaine surprisingly submitted his resignation to the president. The exchange of cold, formal notes
between the two concerning the nomination
shows how strained their relationship had
become.

The resignation came only three days before
the Republican national convention. Whether
Blaine had a serious interest in gaining the
nomination at that late date is uncertain. He
had too much political savvy to think he had
a chance to thwart Harrison's renomination.
Blaine did receive a few votes at the convention but Harrison easily won. He would be
defeated in the general election.

Blaine's three years as secretary of state were
productive. Relations with Canada and Britain
were strained because of the Canadians'
destruction of seal herds in the Bering Sea off
the coast of Alaska. Drawn-out negotiations

with the British minister to the United States eventually did result in a treaty that recognized the need to protect the seals. Of equal interest to Blaine were relations with Hawaii. Blaine favored annexation of those islands to the United States, but that would not be achieved until after his death.

Though many foreign policy problems faced the secretary of state, he focused most of his attention on South America. He mediated in several disputes in Latin countries. He threatened Chile with intervention by the independent nations of this hemisphere. In October 1889, Blaine was the guiding force behind a Washington conference that would discuss greater ties between the countries of North and South America. Finally, he attempted to use tariff reductions as a negotiating tool to receive reciprocal reductions from other countries. He saw vast markets for all countries' goods if trade barriers would be relaxed.

Blaine's interest in foreign policy almost made twice being secretary of state a sufficient substitute for his failure to become president. Unfortunately for Blaine, both stints in the State Department ended unhappily, in the first because of a president's death and the second because of the animosity of the president.

Though Blaine did resign in anger and disgust, he nonetheless campaigned for Harrison's election in the fall. Blaine's health was failing rapidly, and he did not live to see the victor in that election, Grover Cleveland, inaugurated in March. Blaine died of Bright's Disease, tuberculosis, and a weakened heart.

Analysis of Qualifications

The "Plumed Knight's" accomplishments in 30 years on the national stage were meager. His political life is usually depicted as a series of quadrennial bursts of activity to gain the Republican presidential nomination. On many of the significant issues of his day he represented preservation of the status quo and was against what would today be considered progress. Even though the marks of achievement in the form of legislation or great causes espoused may be few, James G. Blaine was to millions an idol, to probably a majority of his party for at least four elections the choice for president, and to all who met him a gregari-

ous, concerned, warm individual. There was definitely much that merits praise in this contradictory character.

On the negative side, Blaine was an extreme partisan. He saw little virtuous in the Democratic Party, and little to condemn in the Republican record, though he would frequently condemn Republican presidents. Some of this partisanship made Blaine blind to the merits of civil service reform. For all of Rutherford B. Hayes' term, Senator Blaine was an obstructionist to the president on the issue, in part because he perceived the form a nostrum sponsored by fuzzy-headed idealists, and also because he had become personally estranged from President Hayes. He let personal feelings frequently interfere with his public duties. His dislike for Hayes, Arthur, and Harrison made him a carping critic. He was well-liked and respected for his speaking skills. He could be savage or serene in debate, and few could equal him in either technique. With such skills, Blaine is still best remembered for such relatively insignificant oratorical contributions as a eulogy for Garfield and the characterization of Conkling as a turkey-gobbler.

On the credit side of the ledger must be placed the extremely valuable contributions Blaine made to the foreign policy of the country as secretary of state. He turned the Monroe Doctrine from a jingoistic excuse for interventionism in South America, into a call for international cooperation in this hemisphere. This was farsighted even if ultimately little practiced by later administrations. His civil rights record during Reconstruction was admirable, even if politically motivated. He had become a real friend to black Americans when few politicians were continuing to speak on their behalf.

The evidence is inescapable that Blaine did engage in manufacturing evidence to hide his relatively innocent involvement in the "Mulligan Letter" affair. Indeed, his major sin was not in the underlying event but instead in the effort to conceal that involvement. That other, far better remembered politicians have engaged in similar efforts should prevent Blaine from being discounted solely on this basis. Blaine's basic character flaw that caused these indiscretions is that he saw no conflict of interest, no disservice to his constituents by both voting for big business schemes and then participating in the profits from them. These promoters did not have to buy his vote because he believed in their proposals. Blaine realized the political risks involved in such activities and tried to prevent discovery. Thus the Mulligan letters.

Blaine was no avaricious scoundrel using his position at the public trough solely for personal gain. He was generous and revealed little aptitude or interest in money, other than to ensure that his debts did not drag him into embarrassing straits. His wife primarily handled the day-to-day business affairs in the home.

Blaine had no executive experience until he became secretary of state. He performed well in that position, though his indiscriminate belief in the primacy of American interests over all others at times made him subject to a justifiable charge of meddling in and bullying other countries. Yet as no other office did, the State Department demonstrated that Blaine's partisanship could be directed towards useful goals, and that he was capable of innovative and farsighted proposals to deal with problems. No better indication of this exists than his Latin American policy.

In summary, Blaine would have brought consummate political and personal skills to the presidency, yet would have been hampered by excessive partisanship and moral shortsightedness. It is not unreasonable to assume that the image of Blaine, just as had been the image of Chester Alan Arthur before his presidency, as a political and moral scoundrel would have proved unfair. Neither man was a saint, yet neither man was worthy of the abuse heaped upon him by political enemies and a press too eager to condemn. It is likely that Blaine would have made a good president, more politically savvy and experienced in Washington than was Arthur, yet less attuned to the movement in the country against even the appearance of corruption and the evils of the spoils system than were Hayes and Cleveland. Each had his faults and his offsetting virtues. Blaine might have been considered, as were Hayes, Arthur, and Cleveland, a solid, unspectacular, average president. His performance would have been uneven, but adequate.

BLAINE BIBLIOGRAPHY

Balestier, C.W. *James G. Blaine: A Sketch of His Life*. New York City (1884).

Blaine, James G. *Political Discussions: Legislative, Diplomatic and Popular*. Norwich, Conn. (1887).

_____. *Twenty Years of Congress: From Lincoln to Garfield*. Norwich, Conn., vol. I, 1884; vol. II, 1886.

Blaine, John Ewing. *The Blaine Family*. Cincinnati (1920).

Crawford, T.C. *James G. Blaine: A Study of His Life and Career*. Philadelphia (1893).

Dodge, Mary Abigail (Gail Hamilton). *The Biography of James G. Blaine*. Norwich, Conn. (1895).

Hoogenboom, Ari. "John Sherman and James G. Blaine: Two Who Failed," in *Statesmen Who Were Never President*. Lanham, Md. (1996).

Muzzey, David S. *James G. Blaine: A Political Idol of Other Days*. New York City (1934).

Ridpath, J.C. *Life and Work of James G. Blaine*. Memorial Edition, Philadelphia (1893).

Russell, Charles Edward. *Blaine of Maine: His Life and Times*. New York City (1931).

Sherman, Thomas H. *Twenty Years with James G. Blaine*. New York City (1928).

Stanwood, Edward. *James Gillespie Blaine*. Boston (1905).

Tutorow, Norman E. *James Gillespie Blaine and the Presidency: A Documentary Study and Source Book*. New York (1989).

---

*1884 vice presidential nominee —
Republican Party*

John A. Logan

Full name: John Alexander Logan.

State represented: Illinois.

Birth: February 9, 1826, in Brownsville (now near Murphysboro), Illinois.

Age on Inauguration Day (March 4, 1885): 59 years, 1 month.

Education: Tutored at home, then school in Brownsville, Illinois; Shiloh Academy, Shiloh Hill, Illinois, 1842–1845; private tutor at home; Louisville University Law School, 1850–1851; admitted to bar, 1851.

Religion: Member of Trinity Church of Chicago.

Ancestry/prominent relatives: John Logan (father) came as boy to America from Ireland

JAMES G. BLAINE and JOHN A. LOGAN
(From the collection of David J. and Janice L. Frent)

in early 1800s. Alexander Jenkins (uncle) was Illinois lieutenant governor.

Occupation: Attorney.

Public offices: Elected clerk of Jackson County, Illinois, 1849–1850, resigned; prosecuting attorney, Third Illinois Judicial District, 1851, resigned after a few months to run for legislature; Illinois house of representatives,

1852–1853; elected prosecuting attorney again in 1853–1856, resigned; state house of representatives, 1856–1858; U.S. representative March 4, 1859–April 12, 1862, resigned to take brigadier general commission; declined appointment as ambassador to Mexico, 1865, and Brazil or Japan, 1866; U.S. representative March 4, 1867–March 3, 1871; declined to run for governor, 1868; U.S. senator March 4, 1871–March 3, 1877, March 4, 1879–December 26, 1886; unsuccessful candidate for president, 1884; defeated Republican nominee for vice president, 1884.

Death: December 26, 1886, in Washington, D.C., at age 60 years, 10½ months.

Burial: Rock Creek Cemetery, Logan mausoleum, Washington, D.C. Reinterred December 26, 1888, at National Cemetery, Soldiers' Home, Washington.

Home: Moved to Chicago 1871, and by 1877 built home overlooking Lake Michigan; lived in boarding house in Washington, 1885, then bought home of John Sherman, the "Stone Mansion."

Personal characteristics: Vigorous, medium height, thin (approximately 140 pounds), bright eyes, swarthy complexion that earned him the name "Black Jack," straight black hair, large drooping mustache.

Father: John Logan (1788–November 4, 1852), medical doctor, farmer, local politician.

Father's first wife: Mary Barcune (died c. 1817).

Half sister: Louisa (November 17, 1816–?).

Mother: Elizabeth Jenkins (September 19, 1805–October 22, 1874); married in 1825.

Siblings: Thomas M. (August 1, 1828–June 26, 1907). Dorothy Adeline (July 23, 1830–August 26, 1864). Margaret Caroline (August 17, 1832–February 1833). Darthulia [Dorthulia] Ann (May 26, 1834–September 15, 1894). William Henry (December 1, 1836–June 29, 1868). James V. (1839–?). Philip Benton (February 2, 1841–December 27, 1846). George Marion (April 27, 1842–December 24, 1846). Solomon J. (March 23–24, 1845).

Wife: Mary Simmerson Cunningham (August 15, 1838–February 22, 1923), married November 27, 1855, daughter of Capt. J.M. Cunningham and Elizabeth Hicks La Fontaine.

Children: John Cunningham (August 22–September 6, 1856). Mary (Dolly) (1859–March 16, 1940), married William F. Tucker in November 1887. Manning Alexander (changed his name to John A. Logan, Jr., after his father's death) (July 24, 1865–November 11, 1899), married Edith Andrews on March 22, 1887; died in his first day of battle in the Philippines. Kate (?–March 1872), an adopted daughter and distant relative.

Historic sites/memorials: An equestrian statue of Logan is in Logan Circle, Rhode Island and Vermont avenues, Washington, D.C. Another Logan statue is in the Vicksburg Military Park, Mississippi. John A. Logan College is in Carterville, Illinois.

In 1824, Dr. John Logan crossed the Mississippi River and settled in "Egypt," that triangular portion of southern Illinois with Altoona and Vandalia on the north and Cairo on the south. Its political and cultural attitudes were in many ways unique in Illinois. Egypt was more Southern than Northern, most particularly in its attitudes towards slavery and the Democratic Party. John Logan, Jr., would be nurtured in that environment, would grow to manhood identified with both those causes, but in the crucible of the Civil War would reject both. For that apostasy, and the image of opportunism it projected, Logan would for the remainder of his life be more often condemned than praised.

John grew up on his family's comfortable farm, the income from which was augmented by the fees from his father's medical practice. When obligations on the farm permitted John to leave school behind, he took the opportunity. This was particularly necessitated by the father's devotion of considerable time to the duties imposed upon him after his election to the state legislature in 1836. The senior Logan became a good friend of another rising Illinois politician, Abraham Lincoln. It was at Lincoln's suggestion that a new Illinois county was named for Dr. Logan in 1839. John was at age 16 enrolled in Shiloh Academy, where he was a good student and excelled in oratory. He remained for three years.

The fiery, aggressive spirit that would always be a Logan hallmark exhibited itself in his eagerness to participate in the Mexican War in

1846. Because of family responsibilities he remained in Illinois until 1847, but that year he was made a second lieutenant in the army. In July he began a long trek to Santa Fe. It was a hot, tiring march for a young man who was not robust. He was efficient and energetic, however, and sufficiently noticed by his superiors for these traits that he was made adjutant general of the fort at Santa Fe. Instead of taking advantage of an opportunity to return to Illinois for recruiting duties, Logan decided to remain in New Mexico in hopes of getting in the fighting. It was never to be, and after the Treaty of Guadalupe Hidalgo was signed he returned to his native state, disappointed in his unheroic fate.

A different kind of combat was now taking possession of Logan. Politics attracted the recently discharged soldier, and to further the ambition he decided to become a lawyer. His license barely gained, in February 1851 he announced for the prosecuting attorney position in his county. He won, but then resigned in a few months to run for the state legislature. Ambitious, popular, fun-loving, an able speaker, Logan made an appealing figure. His swarthy complexion and raven hair earned him the nickname "Black Jack" Logan. His innate abilities and dramatic appearance, when coupled with his father's considerable political experience and contacts, made these first forays into elective politics successful.

At this stage in his career the Democrat Logan, true to his father's political party and principles, was bitterly anti–Negro. He wished to exclude all free Negroes from the state and pushed for appropriate legislation. That effort attracted considerable statewide attention to the youthful legislator, and made good political points back in "Egypt." There were few Negroes in the state, and the danger of an invasion of freedmen was not nearly as significant a reason for Logan's crusade as was a desire to make political capital. He succeeded in getting a law adopted that imposed a fine for bringing in free blacks. To many the legislation was harsh, and Logan's image as a ruthless, caustic politician was becoming formed.

A term in the legislature had gained Logan considerable notoriety. He decided that it would advance his political career to try again for the position of prosecuting attorney, which a year before he had resigned in order to run for the legislature. He won, and in the spring of 1854 began to travel the circuit with other attorneys. In the process Logan became a close friend of fellow lawyer, Democrat, and ambitious politician Stephen Douglas. In 1856 Logan determined to return to the legislature. The electorate did not seem to mind his constant change of heart on which office he desired to hold, and sent him to Springfield with a resounding majority. The political life, as well as the circuit-riding responsibilities of Logan's legal career, put a considerable strain on his marriage to Mary Cunningham, whom he had wed in November of 1855. Frequent, plaintive letters from wife to husband described her loneliness, accentuated by the fact that she was pregnant. In 1857, she wrote him "politics, if you will allow, can destroy our happiness together." Despite these early feelings of abandonment, and perhaps also feeling secondary to her husband's political and legal ambitions, Mary Logan remained a faithful wife. She would write a strikingly laudatory book on her husband after his death.

As a new state representative, but one with considerable statewide notoriety, Logan was selected by the Democrats to lead a highly publicized attack on the new Republican governor, arguing that under the state constitution he was ineligible to serve because of an alleged duel he had participated in during the Mexican War. Logan led this offensive even though the new governor was seriously ill.

With political as well as legal success behind him, Logan announced for Congress in 1858. A bitter fight between Senator Douglas and President Buchanan in Washington had split the party in Illinois and in other states. Logan aligned with the Douglas wing. He appeared alongside Douglas at three of the famous Lincoln-Douglas debates in Illinois that fateful election year. For Logan there never was any real contest. He won with 15,000 votes to a total of 3,000 for two opponents. The young congressman-elect made his first trip to the East when he took his seat in Washington.

The Logan image as a mudslinger and fiery battler soon had additional facets. In the

House he got into an argument with another Illinois representative. The words became so heated that the two men rushed each other to start a fight. They were separated, but only after — according to some reports at least — Logan had drawn a pistol. There were equally hot, if not quite so personally directed, words from Logan on the desirability of the Fugitive Slave Act. He defended the capture and return of slaves, and criticized those who called it "dirty work." Many newspapers and political opponents started using the sobriquet "dirty work Logan." He condemned John Brown and issued wild charges and warnings of future violence in America. Such displays made him feel he was the best debater in Congress. He took advantage of every speaking opportunity, often with slavery as his topic, and always with a strong pro–Southern point of view.

With reelection gained in 1860, but with disunion threatened because of the victory in the presidential race by another Illinoisan, Logan soon had the issue of secession to face. Secession itself he opposed, but also denounced the use of force by the North to prevent it. He encouraged the South to wait and see what Lincoln would do, and not to rush into irreversible action. During the next few months, Logan said he would support any compromise that would satisfy the South and keep that region in the Union. He wanted Congress to renounce interference with slavery in the territories, and to protect the slave trade. Even the attack on Fort Sumter did not drive him into the Northern camp. There would be charges throughout the remainder of his career that Logan contemplated enlisting in the Southern army and seeking a commission. Letters were produced during later political races supposedly proving he encouraged certain individuals to join the Southern cause. The truth of most of these charges is now beyond proof or denial. There is a blank in the detailed collection of Logan papers concerning this period, suggesting at least the possibility that his extremely protective wife, whose book on her husband laundered his life story severely, may have destroyed such incriminating documents as did exist. It is clear that he defended the South and condemned those he felt were abandoning her, including his for-

mer mentor, Stephen Douglas. In savage terms he abused all who called for strong action by the North to suppress the incipient rebellion.

The Illinois papers picked up the story of alleged Logan treason. There were rumors that a Northern military commander had decided to arrest him. He was called the "chief traitor" in Illinois. Unionists insisted that Logan resign from Congress. It was not until June that he definitely sided with the Union. Logan gave a fervent speech that called for enlistments in the Northern army, much to the surprise of many observers. The conversion was so complete that he went to President Lincoln and asked for a commission. The president urged him instead to remain in Congress for the short term, and later perhaps a commission would be forthcoming. Nevertheless, Logan did see limited action in the first engagement of that bloody war. Permission had been given him by General Winfield Scott to accompany the troops to Manassas Junction to witness the battle. There he picked up a musket from a fallen soldier and fired off a few shots at the rebels. Logan became obsessed with gaining a military commission, saying "the stain upon our family must be wiped out," meaning the charges against him for disloyalty.

Lincoln in August finally gave Logan his coveted appointment, as a colonel in charge of a regiment. Logan soon raised the necessary troops and within two months was in battle. On August 19 he had given an impassioned speech for union and for enlistments in Cairo. General Ulysses Grant would later credit Logan for completely changing the sentiments in "Egypt" away from the rebels and in favor of the Union. It was with hope not only of "wiping out the stain" but also of painting an entirely new picture of a heroic soldier-politician that Logan marched off to war.

The story of Logan's courageous and effective military service is beyond the scope of this sketch. A brief summary is the best that can be achieved. In late 1861, he joined General Grant's forces in time for the Battle of Belmont, Missouri. His first taste of battle as a commissioned officer was exhilarating and successful. His gallantry would often descend into rashness, and during this first engagement he had a horse shot from beneath him. In

February 1862, he took part in the fighting at Fort Donelson. Logan's regiment helped save that battle from becoming a rout of the Union army, for his troops plugged a dangerous breach in the Union line that threatened to split it in two. The fighting was intense, and Logan was in the middle of it encouraging his men to overcome the fearsome odds. At least two bullets struck him, in the shoulder and the ribs. He had to be helped from the field, seriously injured.

Colonel Logan was taken to Cairo for medical treatment. The recovery was slow and painful. When a new division commander was needed, Logan was appointed but was too weak to take command. Many analysts have felt that Logan's missing this early and demanding promotion saved his career, because he still needed far more seasoning in less awesome commands. In late May 1862, he rejoined the army and took part in the capture of Corinth, Mississippi. Throughout the remainder of the year the still-weak colonel took command of guarding and rebuilding an important railroad line in western Tennessee and Kentucky.

After Fort Donelson he had been promoted to brigadier general, and after another engagement — Vicksburg — in which he participated gloriously, he earned the additional star of a major general. In what some experts believe was a critical battle of the Civil War, the Battle of Champion's Hill, Mississippi, in May 1863, Logan was a central figure in sustaining the Northern victory. Champion's Hill, a difficult, dynamic battle in which the fortunes of war seemed to swing back and forth between the contending sides, finally was won by the North, preserving Grant's invasion of Mississippi and eventually permitting the siege of Vicksburg.

With Vicksburg's surrender on July 4, 1863, Logan sought permission to return to Illinois. He campaigned actively for the Republicans, and his war hero mantle earned him wide audiences. Lincoln himself encouraged Logan's trip to Illinois, telling the secretary of war, "please give Gen. Logan the extended leave asked for, unless you know a good reason to the contrary." After the election he returned to the army. In 1864, he took part in General

Sherman's invasion of Georgia, but again left the army to campaign, with Lincoln's blessing, for the Republicans in the fall elections. Thus the obloquy of having participated in Sherman's bloody march "from Atlanta to the sea" was never rightfully placed on Logan. During the fighting around Atlanta, Logan was promoted to command a corps of the Army of Tennessee. When General McPherson was killed in July 1864, he took temporary command of that army. Though he would return to the army after the 1864 elections, his fighting days were essentially through after the Atlanta engagement. General Sherman did not think Logan equal to the command of the entire army of Tennessee and promoted another to the permanent position. Logan was upset but publicly gracious. Many other men had quit the army in rage over far lesser slights.

Logan is generally regarded as the best of the "political generals" in the Civil War, those men chosen from the political ranks and promoted to military command in hopes their prestige would bring support to the war effort. When he returned to private life after Appomattox with military laurels aplenty, he had established himself as an undeniable contender for high political office. That he would not make those future fights in his old uniform as a Democrat was not initially clear. For 14 months after the war he remained aloof from politics. Many felt, including Logan himself, that he had missed a golden opportunity to be elected United States senator in early 1865 when he returned to the army rather than remain in Illinois and campaign for the post.

Logan resigned his commission in August 1865, and began to lay the groundwork for election to the Senate. A long-discarded law practice occupied him for a short time, as did real estate and other business ventures. A fraternal organization of soldiers became his concern, partly to advance his political fortunes. President Johnson appointed Logan ambassador to Brazil, but Logan wanted neither to be removed from the maneuvering for the Senate seat, not to be associated with the increasingly discredited presidency of Andrew Johnson. Thus he declined the offer. The Grand

Army of the Republic organization proved another helpful boost to his political ambitions, and he would within a few years become its president. Radical reconstruction was in full swing in Washington. It was not long until Logan threw his fortunes in with the radicals. He called the president a demagogue, and gave vicious speeches about others who disagreed with the radicals' policies. The abuse was returned in kind, and Logan was described as an 1861 Copperhead who had tried to hide his treasonous past.

In July 1866, Logan definitely announced his conversion to Republicanism. He lost a race for chairmanship of the Illinois Grand Army of the Republic, an important political plum that would have eased his election to the Senate. That Senate seat seemed to be slipping away. Logan just stepped up his strident speeches in favor of radical reconstruction and against President Johnson. The local press in "Egypt" delighted in ridiculing the abusive convert to Republicanism, who four years before had spoken equally strongly for Southern rights. Some even charged that he gave support to a scheme in 1866 to take over the federal government in a military coup d'état, with Logan as the possible dictator should it succeed, but the evidence is slim.

The Senate seat seemed to be going aglimmering. Therefore, both as a means of increasing his chances for the higher office and to give himself an alternative should he lose, Logan ran for the position of Illinois congressman-at-large. He was elected by a large majority, and immediately began to turn to the legislative campaign for the Senate seat. The incumbent, Lyman Trumbull, had secured far too many pledges of support while Logan was campaigning for Congress, and the effort was futile.

The attacks on President Johnson became more vociferous. Logan was named one of the seven House members to draw up Articles of Impeachment of the president. Logan was so constantly on the attack in Congress that even some of Johnson's other opponents feared Logan was gaining sympathy for the president. Despite the stridence of the speeches, Logan appeared ready to compromise with the president if just some way could be found. Logan

began to doubt conviction in the Senate could be achieved, even after the House had impeached Johnson, and thus he wanted a face-saving compromise. Instead, with Logan exposed politically, the Senate did acquit Johnson by the margin of one vote.

Though Johnson was acquitted, the radicals had lost little momentum in getting their favorite in the White House, Ulysses Grant. Logan heartily supported his old commander. Despite strong urgings, Logan refused to be a candidate during the fall election for governor. Probably he was afraid of being taken out of the running for the Senate seat, which would be contested during the middle of the new governor's four-year term. In 1870, Logan made his bid for the Senate. Logan's position as thrice-elected national president of the Grand Army of the Republic immeasurably advanced his cause. Interestingly, it was as president of the GAR that Logan in May 1868, established May 30 as a day to commemorate the war dead. That day would later be adopted as a national holiday, Memorial Day.

Logan had two simultaneous campaigns, one for reelection to the House and the other as a candidate for U.S. senator. He and his senatorial opponent campaigned in the county party conventions, insisting that legislative candidates who were selected at those conventions declare which man they would support for senator. In November he won his congressional seat, and the following January the legislature chose him United States senator.

In the Senate scandal soon touched Logan. The issue was whether he had tried to use the leverage of the pending impeachment proceedings in 1868 to get President Johnson to consider favorably the claims of some American businessmen to an island in the Caribbean, Alto Vera. Nothing came of the attempt, which involved far more men than just Logan, but additional evidence of an unsavory political morality seemed to be added to the public perception of Logan. The new senator was under constant attack for other matters as well. One cause of the persistence of the criticism perhaps was the fact that Logan always seemed to strike back in kind, with little regard for political consequences. He was a street fighter who, though mellowing to a degree with age, could be incited to riot.

When Grant sought a second term in 1872, Logan opposed him, perhaps because of the president's rejection of a pet Logan legislative proposal. The scandal that soon thereafter enveloped the Grant administration and much of Congress touched Logan as well. The Credit Mobilier scandal involved bribes of key government leaders by proponents of a gigantic railroad scheme. Logan had received ten shares of stock in the company without paying anything for them. He was then offered a dividend in the company, saying that the remainder of the dividend had paid for the stock. Somehow Logan became concerned about the potential explosiveness of the matter and returned the stock and dividend. By that fortunate decision Logan escaped the career-ending disgrace that many politicians suffered because of the Credit Mobilier.

The presidency was becoming Black Jack's consuming ambition. As early as 1876 Logan was already beginning to consider the possibility seriously. He was in a tough battle for reelection to the Senate that year however, and was defeated by the legislature after a protracted session. He may have been a victim of a Republican ploy to remove from the national Electoral Commission a Supreme Court justice who was meant to be the independent, objective vote in determining whether Rutherford Hayes or Samuel Tilden had been elected president that year. The Justice, David Davis, was elected senator, and was then unavailable for the Electoral Commission. Another Supreme Court justice was named in his place who did vote for Hayes and caused the Republican's election.

Logan was easily elected to the Senate in 1879. His obvious ambition and his still caustic manner made him many enemies. Logan energetically worked for Grant's nomination for president in 1880. Even when James Garfield won the nomination, Logan declared immediately for Grant's nomination in four years. Logan's last chance for the presidency was 1884. Outside of Illinois he had few supporters for the nomination. Thus, during the third ballot Logan wired the convention and asked his supporters to give up the manifestly futile

effort and vote for James G. Blaine. When Blaine was nominated on the next ballot, Logan was an obvious choice for the vice presidency. The two men had been close for a few years, and basically agreed on the principal issues. Both had somewhat corrupt reputations, which suggested a type of harmony on the ticket not particularly desired by the Republicans. Civil service reform was not important to Logan, and indeed he seemed to favor the unlimited application of the spoils system. He had to face during the campaign the charges of disloyalty, and again Logan reacted violently. He spit in the face of one man, probably a Democratic plant, who told him at a campaign stop that he wanted to shake the candidate's hand because Logan "raised the first rebel flag in Illinois." Besides expectorating, Logan also called the man a "liar." The Democratic press made much ado about the uncouth antics. At campaign's end the running mate was worn out from too many speeches, too many miles, and too much pessimism. He thought the ticket would lose. He had advised Blaine not to attend the sumptuous banquet given him by New York's wealthy on election eve which received the beautifully biting caricature by Thomas Nast in his famous cartoon, "Belshazzar's feat." That gluttony during the depressed economic times, along with a few other last-minute indiscretions by Blaine, made Logan's pessimism appropriate.

After the defeat, Logan still had to defend his Senate seat when the legislature met in Illinois in January. The two political parties were exactly evenly divided, and from February until May the legislature wrangled over the Senate election. Finally, after three members had died and had been replaced in special elections, Logan could claim his seat for another six-year term.

He would not have six more years, however. Logan was only 60 years old, but he was worn out from 40 years in politics and in war. In 1886, he had just completed a poorly-received book, *The Great Conspiracy*, which in partisan style blamed the Civil War on a conspiracy of long standing among certain Southern leaders. After a short illness, Logan died the day after Christmas 1886.

Analysis of Qualifications

"Black Jack" Logan's political manner well suited his nickname. In appearance he was dark and swarthy, with what was called the biggest mustache in America. He looked to many to be an Indian, and his fiery personality seemed to add credence to the speculation. In public he was relentlessly on the attack. In private he could be warm and fun-loving.

As a general, Logan was widely commended. General Grant praised him in his *Memoirs*, but mixed the praise with some reservations when he described his subordinate as impetuous as well as brave. Few corps commanders had served as well as Logan, but Sherman in particular doubted he could have taken on still higher command. Logan was obedient and industrious as a soldier, two qualities lacking in an inordinate number of Civil War generals. Perhaps the best service he rendered in a 40-year public career was the four years he served outside of political office as a military leader.

Politics was Logan's life. From early adulthood he realized politics would be his career. The courage he exhibited on the battlefield was equally alive in political skirmishes. Never one to back down or apologize, Logan was in a lifelong series of heated disputes with one opponent or another. He made as many political enemies as he did friends. George Hoar described Logan as a man of ability, but that his merit was marred by a manner that was "exceedingly imperious and domineering, impatient of contradiction in any matter...." He was, Hoar summarized, "a rather uncomfortable man to get along with." Equally prevalent was the concern about his public morality. Scandal seemed to hover around him in public office. The loose sense of public honor then rampant among politicians was in no way tightened by Logan. He did live in an age in which a great proportion of the public servants seemed also to be serving themselves, and Logan only added to that public perception.

If any quality stood out about Logan it was his harshness. He was bombastic, flamboyant, crude, even vicious in public debate. To oppose Logan was to stand subject to the most biting personal criticism. He could be ruthless and unforgiving for the smallest slight. He was intolerant of many things and exaggerated these prejudices for public impact. When he turned from being a Democrat to a Republican, the change was neither gradual nor only by degrees. What was his party home before the war became little more than a den of thieves and traitors to him after the war. He was an opportunist who tried to stay abreast of political changes. He was as partisan for the Republicans as he had been partisan in favor of the Democrats. Logan never did things by halves, nor by compromise. Whether the Senate or the presidency was the goal, Logan was persistent and domineering. In sum, Logan was not a man with whom to be trifling.

As president, there is little reason to believe Logan could have taken command of his many personal excesses and led the country harmoniously. His political career had been a continuous controversy, and a Logan presidency would not have changed these characteristics, but only intensified them. To many he was the very symbol of graft that was the bane of late nineteenth-century politics. He was a divisive, unrepentant, self-seeking political animal. He had no views which he desired to further in the presidency, no programs waiting for an opportunity to be enacted. He was simply a poor choice, politically as well as substantively, for vice president.

LOGAN BIBLIOGRAPHY

Andrews, Byron. *A Biography of General John A. Logan* (1884).

Cottingham, Carl D. *General John A. Logan: His Life and Times*. Carbondale, Ill. (c. 1982–89).

Dawson, George F. *Life and Services of General John A. Logan as Soldier and Statesman*. Chicago and New York City (1887).

Dickinson, John N. "The Civil War Years of John Alexander Logan." *Journal of the Illinois State Historical Society* 56 (1963), pp. 212–232.

Hawkins, May Strong. "The Early Political Career of John A. Logan." Unpublished master's thesis, University of Chicago (1934).

Jones, James P. *"Black Jack": John A. Logan and Southern Illinois in the Civil War Era*. Tallahassee (1967).

_____. *John A. Logan: Stalwart Republican from Illinois*. Tallahassee (1982).

Kent, Gary W. "Evolution of Change: The Ideological Migration of John A. Logan During the Civil War Era." Unpublished doctoral dissertation, Southern Illinois University (1989).

Logan, Mary S.C. *Reminiscences of a Soldier's Wife.* New York City (1913).

Messamore, Ford. "John A. Logan: Democrat and Republican." Uunpublished Ph.D. dissertation, University of Kentucky (1939).

Wallace, Joseph. "A Biography of John A. Logan." Unpublished manuscript in Illinois State Historical Library, Springfield.

Some family information provided by Roger D. Bridges, Director of Research, Illinois State Historical Library, Springfield.

Election of 1888

NOMINATIONS

Democratic Party Convention (15th): June 5–7, 1888, at the Exposition Building, St. Louis, Mo. *President*—Grover Cleveland, nominated by a resolution passed without opposition. *Vice president*—Allen G. Thurman, nominated on the first ballot with 684 votes out of 822 cast. Isaac P. Gray (Indiana) was a distant second.

Republican Party Convention (9th): June 19–25, 1888, at the Civic Auditorium, Chicago, Ill. *President*— Benjamin Harrison, nominated on the eighth ballot with 544 votes out of 830 cast. He had received 85 votes on the first ballot. John Sherman (Ohio), Walter Gresham (Ind.), Chauncey Depew (N.Y.), Russell Alger (Mich.), and William Allison (Iowa), were his major rivals. *Vice president*— Levi P. Morton, nominated on the first ballot with 592 votes out of 826 cast. William Walter Phelps (N.J) and William O. Bradley (Ky.) were far behind.

Prohibition Party Convention (5th): May 30–31, Tomlinson Hall, Indianapolis, Indiana. *President*— Clinton B. Fisk, nominated by acclamation on the first ballot. *Vice president*— John A. Brooks, nominated by acclamation.

GENERAL ELECTION, November 6,1888

Popular Vote

Cleveland 5,540,309
Harrison 5,444,337
Fisk 249,506
Others 150,000

Electoral Vote

Harrison-Morton — 233 (20 states)
Cleveland-Thurman —168 (18 states)

Winners

Benjamin Harrison, 23rd president
Levi P. Morton, 22nd vice president

Losers

Grover Cleveland, Allen G. Thurman, Clinton Fisk, John A. Brooks

---

*1888 presidential nominee—
Democratic Party*

Grover Cleveland

No biographical sketch of Cleveland is included since he served as president from March 4, 1885, to March 4, 1889, and March 4, 1893, to March 4, 1897 (22nd, 24th president).

State represented: New York.

Birth: March 18, 1837.

Age on Inauguration Day (March 4, 1889): 51 years, 11½ months.

Death: June 24, 1908.

GROVER CLEVELAND and ALLEN G. THURMAN
(From the collection of David J. and Janice L. Frent)

*1888 vice presidential nominee —
Democratic Party*

Allen G. Thurman

Full name: Allen Granberry Thurman.
State represented: Ohio.
Birth: November 13, 1813, at Lynchburg, Virginia.
Age on Inauguration Day (March 4, 1889): 75 years, 3½ months.
Education: Chillicothe, Ohio, public schools; then Chillicothe Academy, 1825–1830; studied law in his uncle William Allen's office, 1830–1833; admitted to bar, 1835.
Religion: Episcopalian.
Ancestry/prominent relatives: English ancestors, settled early in Virginia. Both grandfathers fought with General Washington during the American Revolution. Joseph Hewes,

a great-great-uncle, was a signer of the Declaration of Independence. Uncle William Allen was an Ohio governor.
Occupation: Attorney.
Public offices: U.S. representative, March 4, 1845–March 3, 1847, declined reelection; elected Ohio Supreme Court justice, 1852–1856, chief justice, December 4, 1854–February 9, 1856; declined reelection; defeated for governor, 1867; U.S. senator, March 4, 1869–March 3, 1881, defeated 1880; Electoral Commission 1877; president pro tempore of the senate, 1879–1881; unsuccessful candidate for Democratic presidential nomination, 1876, 1880, 1884; delegate to International Monetary Convention, 1881; defeated for U.S. Senate, 1886; declined to run for governor, 1887; refused appointment to Interstate Commerce Commission, 1887; defeated Democratic nominee for vice president, 1888.

Death: December 12, 1895, Columbus, Ohio, at age 82 years, 1 month.

Burial: Green Lawn Cemetery, Columbus, Ohio.

Home: Columbus, Ohio.

Personal characteristics: Medium height, careless dresser, portly, broad-shouldered; large, square head and ruddy complexion, whitish-gray hair and full beard; always had a red bandanna as a pocket handkerchief.

Father: Pleasant Thurman (October 23, 1783–February 13, 1856), a minister, married May 21, 1811.

Mother: Mary Granberry Allen (October 20, 1789–1851), daughter of Col. Nathaniel Allen of North Carolina.

Siblings: Thurman had a brother and five sisters, but only a sister survived infancy. She was Henrietta Jennings, married the Rev. C. Riemensnyder.

Wife: Mrs. Mary Dun Thompkins (May 2, 1812–1893), married Gwyn Thompkins in 1835 and he died in 1838; married Thurman on November 14, 1844.

Children: Elizabeth (?–?), married Richard C. McCormick on November 11, 1873; he was a territorial delegate from Arizona and U.S. representative from New York. Allen W. (?–?). Mary (?–?).

As a boy, Allen Thurman was called "right-angled-triangled" Thurman because of his love of mathematics. During the Civil War he was called a "Copperhead" because of his opposition to the Lincoln administration. In 1879, Thurman was toasted at a public dinner as the leader of the Ohio Democratic Party and was described as the "noblest Roman of them all." From that, until the end of his life Thurman was called the "old Roman." Each of these appellations reveals a facet of Thurman's life: a distinguished and conservative man, with side interests in the sciences, mathematics, and other disciplines, who stood his party ground even during wartime. Though he tried for three successive elections to receive the presidential nomination, all he received for his efforts was finally a vice presidential try on a losing ticket, a nomination he, at age 75, did not even want.

Born in Virginia, Thurman stayed there until at age five he was taken with his family across the Alleghenies to Ohio. Pleasant Thurman, Allen's father, was a Baptist preacher and slaveowner who, at least according to his son's campaign biographers, left that state and emancipated his slaves because he had become convinced of the moral repugnance of slavery. With a huge six-horse wagon, containing children, spouse and household belongings, Pleasant Thurman in 1819 set off for a farm in Chillicothe, Ohio. There the elder Thurman became a school teacher and businessman as well as local politician. Though Pleasant Thurman was a Whig, his son became a staunch Democrat. Allen's mother was a strong-willed, talented woman who opened a boarding school in 1825. A teacher there was a Frenchman who started Allen on a lifelong fondness for French literature and a not-quite-so-cultured appreciation for snuff. In later years the red bandanna he used as his snuff handkerchief was a trademark. Throughout his education Allen revealed industry and intelligence; he excelled particularly, in addition to French and snuff, in mathematics and Latin. His hard study made him physically weak. A job as a surveyor got him outdoors and in more vigorous health.

From 1830 until 1833, Thurman studied law in his uncle William Allen's office. Uncle William would in 1834 be elected to Congress, and he subsequently became Ohio governor. The two politicians would in their later years be political opponents. With William Allen in Congress, Allen Thurman needed both a new employer and a legal instructor. The employer was Governor Robert Lucas. Future Supreme Court justice Noah Swayne became the legal tutor. Duties for the governor went from 8:00 A.M. until 8:00 P.M. daily, while studies for Judge Swayne consumed substantial additional hours. Four or five hours of sleep a night were all the harried young man allowed himself. In 1835, the efforts paid off in Thurman's admission to the bar. Back home in Chillicothe, the new lawyer opened up a practice with his uncle.

Uncle William failed to be reelected to Congress and thus the two men practiced law actively together for a short period. Political interests soon consumed increasing amounts of the ex-congressman's time; Thurman took over most of the legal practice. He traveled the circuit with the judges and other lawyers, gaining a favorable reputation among his peers for legal competence. In 1837, William Allen was elected to the United States Senate, and Thurman now had to assume sole control of the practice.

It was hardly all work and no politics, as Thurman became involved with and eventually was elected president of the state Democratic Young Men's Club. He was a good and willing speaker. His contacts spread, helping both his professional and his potential political career. In 1844, after practicing law for nine years and dabbling in politics, Thurman became seriously involved in the fight to nominate Martin Van Buren for president. That attempt earned Thurman his party's nomination for Congress, even though he was out of state at the time and did not participate in the nominating convention. Only 31 years old, Thurman made an active canvass, defeating the incumbent Whig congressman by 363 votes. A few weeks after the election the congressman-elect married widow Mary Dun Thompkins, whose first husband died in 1838. She was the daughter of a wealthy Chillicothe merchant and landowner.

The issues of the day primarily concerned "manifest destiny." Once war with Mexico started because of the annexation of Texas, Thurman insisted all politicians should support it. When Americans were fighting in the battlefield, there was not time nor place for criticism; there was only the necessity to give all required aid. These words would be eaten 15 years later when Thurman actively opposed the North's prosecution of the war against the Southern secessionists. At this stage of his career, with a Democratic war being waged by a Democratic president, Thurman equated opposition by the Whigs to Federalist criticism of the War of 1812. In words that would later apply to Thurman himself, the Ohio Democrat warned:

> he who loudly proclaims that we are prosecuting a war that is unholy, unrighteous, and damnable — he who dwells upon its costs and dilates upon its horrors — in short, he whose almost every word is calculated to condemn the country, to dishonor and disgrace her in the eyes of mankind, ... [l]et my colleague take warning by what history teaches, and beware!

One term in Congress was all he financially felt able to serve, and he declined reelection in 1846. His Chillicothe law practice occupied him until 1851, when a new constitution was adopted by Ohio. In that document a five-member state Supreme Court was provided for, and Thurman was elected to one of the five seats. He got a four-year term, and for two of them served as chief justice. From this experience Thurman earned the title of "Judge," which throughout his career in other offices was still used. He was well-respected as a judge, but again the remuneration of public office could not compare to that of his private law practice, and Thurman retired after his term expired.

Now living in Columbus, where he had moved to serve on the court, Thurman took an active interest in politics even though he did not run for office. He opposed the repeal of the Missouri Compromise that resulted from passage of the Compromise of 1850. Though Thurman supported Stephen Douglas for president, he could not support the Illinois senator's view of "squatter sovereignty," i.e., that each territory could decide for itself whether it would be slave or free. An important political enemy was made in 1857 when, because of a misunderstanding, Thurman was publicly rude to Henry Payne, then a candidate for governor and subsequently a United States senator from Ohio. That enmity would harm Thurman in subsequent races, most noticeably his try for the presidency in 1880. An early sign of internal party opposition was when Thurman was denied election as a delegate to the 1860 Democratic National Convention.

The start of the Civil War brought Thurman actively back into politics. The Ohioan opposed secession and believed it was probably unconstitutional. However, he questioned the efficacy of attempting to force the South to remain in the Union once it had decided to leave. During a Jackson Day dinner in 1861, Thurman pleaded for every conciliatory step necessary to be made to the South. Never a friend of slavery, neither was Thurman an advocate of abolition. Though Thurman said he had no ill will for Negroes, neither did he want large numbers of them migrating to Ohio or other Northern states.

When the Lincoln administration began to prosecute war dissenters in the North and arguably violated their civil liberties, Thurman, fellow Ohioan George Pendleton, and other Democrats protested loudly. A trial of a civilian by a military court raised Thurman's ire; the suspension of habeas corpus by presidential decree was attacked. The Emancipation Proclamation seemed a mistake to Thurman, since he felt it converted a war to preserve the Union into an unnecessary war to end slavery. He hurled such epithets as "despot" and "tyrant" against the national administration.

With these viewpoints, it was easy for Thurman to play a major role in the movement to nominate the ultra–Copperhead Clement Vallandigham for Ohio governor. The campaign occurred with the candidate out of the country, since he had been exiled by the Lincoln administration following his conviction for, essentially, treason. The Republican victory in the fall elections was a shock for Democrats, and it marked the end of the momentum of the Democratic peace movement.

Thurman was a restraining influence on the more radical Copperheads. When the war was over, the Democratic Party would for a decade or more be fighting its image as a band of traitors and fifth columnists. "Waving the bloody shirt" of the late war was all the Republicans had to do for victory. Thurman felt the voters' animosity early after the war's end when his strenuous efforts for the state Democratic ticket failed. The Republicans elected their candidate governor with a 43,000 vote majority. Two years later, in 1867, Thurman himself was the sacrificial lamb for his party. But Thurman did not feel the cause was hopeless. Thurman opened his campaign by calling for a reduction in expenses for the army, demanding the rich pay their fair share of taxes, and ending land giveaways to railroads. Though victory eluded Thurman, he reduced the overwhelming Republican margin of 1865 to just 3,000 votes. He had given 100 speeches in 65 nonstop days of campaigning. The victorious Republican, future president Rutherford B. Hayes, commended Thurman's gentlemanly conduct. Though the Republican margin had been seriously reduced, Thurman should not

be given undue credit. His opponent had been dragged to the edge of defeat by the issue of Negro suffrage. Ohio voters overwhelmingly rejected a Republican-sponsored state constitutional amendment guaranteeing blacks the vote. The rest of the GOP ticket went down to defeat. Only Hayes stood as a Republican survivor.

Fortunately for Thurman, the Democrats' takeover of the state legislature meant that they could select the next United States senator. Though Vallandigham had been the party's preelection choice for the post, a new situation put Thurman in the lead for the seat. A party legislative caucus selected Thurman by 51 to 24 over Vallandigham. When he took his place in the capitol in March of 1869, he found only six other Democrats there. During only two years of Thurman's 12-year Senate career would his party be in the majority.

Radical Republican Reconstruction was the issue. Thurman opposed making ratification of the Fifteenth Amendment that would give blacks the right to vote, a condition for Southern states' readmission to the Union. Thurman pointed out that his state had emphatically rejected Negro suffrage, and to force Georgia or Mississippi to ratify it was to force Ohio to live under that amendment. Since in his view the Southern states were never out of the Union, conditions on their "return" could not be imposed. Civil rights measures were almost uniformly opposed by the Ohio senator. When Charles Sumner presented his bill in 1866 to guarantee equal rights for the former slaves in public transportation, theaters, inns, schools, churches, and other public facilities, Thurman was loud in his rejection. He argued that this bill was social legislation that did not just mandate legal changes, but social ones. Thurman's belief that some of the Act was unconstitutional was accepted in a subsequent Supreme Court opinion.

Reconstruction was one issue the Democrats had to use against their opponents, but a far more effective one was needed. The "Ohio Idea" became a key approach. Increasing the money in circulation by printing greenbacks — paper currency — which would not be redeemed in silver or gold, and permitting them to be used to redeem bonds that had been issued to fund the Civil War, was one panacea. Many Westerners found the shortage of money an impossible burden; debtor classes everywhere supported the inflation that would be a natural consequence of paper currency. Thurman never fully supported the "Ohio Idea" though his fellow Ohioans, George H. Pendleton and Clement Vallandigham were conspicuous proponents. The divergent views of the Ohio Democratic Party did not erupt just yet, and the party was able to get through the 1873 election and elect Thurman's aged uncle, William Allen, as governor. Threats of disunity and of voter satisfaction had led to suggestions that a new political party be organized, composed of disgruntled members from both existing parties. Thurman stood firm against entreaties that he join the movement.

Though Thurman supported a slight increase in currency, he was a hard money man who believed all currency should be redeemable in gold or silver. In the Senate he said that if an increase in currency was made now, then backers would return in the next session and ask for more, and the process would never end. This stand infuriated many Ohio Democrats, and it kept him from getting his bid launched for the presidency in 1876. At the state convention on June 17, 1875, the greenback supporters won the platform battle. At Mansfield, Ohio, on July 31, 1875, Thurman condemned his own party's position. He would not leave the party, however, because he argued fluctuations would always occur in a party's direction. Furthermore, the state convention which had created the platform only nominated state candidates, not federal ones. Thurman refused to alter his views just because a "temporary" majority of a state convention had reached a different conclusion on this issue. Generally his speech seemed to have irritated friends and foes alike as a senseless fence-straddling. He rejected outright neither the platform nor the people nominated on it, nor did he endorse the platform. His uncle became a permanent enemy as a result. Thurman apparently saw his position as loyalty to his party, but also to his principles. At the state convention in May 1876, William Allen received the state's endorsement for president over Thurman, even though at Allen's advanced age he had no chance for the nomination. Thurman received some votes at the national convention.

The 1876 presidential contest ended in dispute; neither party had a clear victory. Controverted returns from three Southern states had to be resolved by Congress. Thurman was named as one of two Democratic senators on a committee of seven to decide the approach to take. An electoral commission of 15 members was the plan derived, and Thurman was then named one of seven Democrats on that commission. In deciding how to award the electoral votes of a state, each member of the commission voted in each instance for his party's candidate. Thus each of the three states was given to Republican Rutherford Hayes by an 8–7 vote. Before the commission had completed its work, Thurman's frequent bouts with neuralgia caused him to resign. He was reported to have cried when the decision for Hayes was announced.

Thurman's hard money views appealed to Eastern businessmen, but on other issues Thurman was repugnant to them. Chinese labor was important to Western railroad interests, but Thurman opposed additional Chinese immigration. In 1878 Thurman supported repeal of the act that would require resumption of payments on government currency in gold or silver, and instead wanted to substitute a single national paper currency. The final straw for businessmen, if one was necessary, was the Thurman Act of 1877. In this bill, Thurman proposed that repayment be required for loans that had been made by the government through the years to individual railroads. These loans for construction had been allowed to go uncollected, and the Thurman Act created a procedure for collection.

When the Republicans took control of the state legislature in the 1879 election, Thurman's days as a senator were effectively over. He was replaced by a Republican when his term ended in 1881. That Republican was James A. Garfield, who in addition to being elected senator by the legislature in 1879 (but he could not take his seat until March 1881), had been elected in 1880 to the U.S. House of Representatives and at the same election, chosen president of the United States. Garfield decided to take the presidency.

In 1880 Thurman made another try for the presidency. Again opposition from within his own state's delegation destroyed his chances. Thurman received the endorsement of his state party's convention in 1880, but many in the delegation worked against him. He seemed to consider this race his retirement from politics. In 1883, he refused to run for governor. The following year some supporters pressed his candidacy for president, but he was unenthusiastic. At the national convention, without exerting any effort in his own behalf, the Old Roman received 88 votes on the first ballot. Grover Cleveland won on the second. Thurman's age and poor health prevented him from receiving serious consideration for a cabinet post; what offers were made during the Cleveland administration were refused. He allowed his name to be used for the Senate in 1886, but since the Republicans had a legislative majority the cause was doomed. The following year Thurman against refused to run for governor and announced he would never seek public office again.

Nonetheless, at age 75, Thurman became Cleveland's running mate in 1888. His supporters had gone to the convention well-supplied with red bandannas, his trademark. When his name was placed in nomination, the crowd waved a sea of the cloths. Cleveland did not object to his nomination, and it was hoped by many Democrats that Thurman could help in the South and West. In truth, though, his health was not up to the rigors of the campaign. His age was frequently mentioned in the press and by the opposition. At a major rally in Madison Square Garden, his cholera-morbus prevented him from giving a speech to the accumulated thousands of partisans. His brief comments at the gathering referred to the charges that he was too old, and he apologized that perhaps his appearance that night would give credence to the allegation. An unhappy fact was that Cleveland's first running mate, Thomas Hendricks, had died shortly after taking office in 1885, when he was about Thurman's age. The Cleveland-Thurman ticket got a popular vote plurality, but lost the electoral college count to the Republicans. This

time it was final—the Old Roman was out of politics.

Thurman's last seven years were spent in semi-retired law practice in Columbus, in reading and studying, and one would suppose, in contemplating his long career. As a lawyer he was well-compensated and honored with some major suits. Perhaps the most far-reaching was his work for the government in trying to set aside the patents granted to Alexander Graham Bell for his telephone, on the basis that Bell had procured them by fraud. That suit failed after lengthy litigation. He served on a three-man committee to arbitrate a dispute between four great trunk line railroads as to their freight rates. In 1890, Thurman was honored with an elaborate banquet in Columbus, to which even former president Cleveland came to salute his former running mate.

Analysis of Qualifications

Why was Allen G. Thurman nominated for vice president? There seems no reason other than his popularity within the party, and the hope that he could gain votes in doubtful areas of the country where President Cleveland was weak. Those are not unusual "qualifications" for vice president, but they are hardly the standards by which potential presidential performance can be judged. In truth, Thurman was an old man in ill health. His fame had been made as an obstructionist Democrat during the Lincoln administration. As a lawyer he was well known and respected, and he had a lawyer's tendency to be more concerned with the legal effects of proposals than with their broader ramifications. Thurman had never held an executive office, and his lack of experience in that capacity would have been magnified by the absence of a strength of will, a ruthlessness, in carrying out measures. Allen Thurman was a good man who simply had never indicated he deserved a chance at the presidency.

Certainly the Ohio politician was well liked by men from both sides of the political aisle. Staunch Radical Republican Senator Charles Sumner counted staunch Democrat Thurman as his good friend. Flinty Republican Senator George F. Edmunds of Vermont and Thurman were ideological opposites. Nonetheless, frequently when one was absent from a vote the other would refuse to vote, since had they both been present their votes would have canceled each other out. Edmunds described his friend as having a "command of pure and strong English. He was powerful in debate, never mincing words, but calling things by what he considered their right names. He was brave in his convictions and was always working for what he thought the good of his country...." Even the egotistical, dapper Roscoe Conkling of New York found a friend in the slovenly Ohioan. Fellow Ohio senator, but a Republican, John Sherman, placed Thurman "in the first rank of able and notable men." No man seemed to doubt Thurman's honesty; few ever felt the sting of a harsh word. He was fair and skillful in debate, a sound reasoner. As a lawyer he was logical and aggressive, winning his share and more of his cases because of hard work that went with his native skills.

Even though not doubting his good humor and friendliness, many took exception to his doctrinaire states' rights attitude. Thurman spent the whole Civil War debating the legality of measures taken by President Lincoln. He was a stalwart for Vallandigham in 1863, though by the following year Thurman hoped the party could keep Vallandigham at a distance because his extremism was threatening the party's fortunes. He was known as one of the great Senate constitutional lawyer, and one a contemporary historian said had been surpassed in the Senate only by Webster, Calhoun, and Fessenden. Debates on constitutional matters seemed to stir his soul more than arguments over the purpose and need for programs.

Many were disconcerted when Thurman was nominated in 1888. A member of the Democratic National Committee had before the nomination referred to the Old Roman as a "corpse." One of his frequent opponents in Ohio politics said that Thurman would lose votes for the ticket. The narrowness of the ticket's defeat suggests that concerns about Thurman's health, which on a few occasions got vivid publicity such as at the Madison Square Garden debacle, may have played a significant negative role. Opposition to Thurman had always been strong within his own Ohio party, indicating a failure to be able to control, or perhaps want to control, even his own political house. A fractious Congress might have shown similar lack of obedience.

Thurman should be remembered as a good and significant man from the period during and immediately after the Civil War. He should not be recalled, however, as a politician whose failed attempts at the presidency should be mourned.

THURMAN BIBLIOGRAPHY

The Biographical Cyclopedia and Portrait Gallery with an Historical Sketch of the State of Ohio. Vol. I. Cincinnati (1883), pp. 195–197.

Boyd, James P. *Biographies of Pres. Grover Cleveland and Hon. Allen G. Thurman.* Philadelphia (1888).

Brown, H. Gertrude. "Allen G. Thurman and Reconstruction." Unpublished master's thesis, University of Chicago (1932).

Carroll, Howard. *Twelve Americans, Their Lives and Times.* New York City (1883), pp. 331–354.

Dieck, Herman. *The Life and Public Services of ... Grover Cleveland ... to Which Is Added the Life and Public Services of Allen G. Thurman....* Philadelphia (1888).

Hare, John S. "Allen G. Thurman: A Political Study." Unpublished doctoral dissertation, Ohio State University (1933).

Hensel, W.U. *Life and Public Services of Grover Cleveland ... with a Sketch of Allen G. Thurman....* Philadelphia (1888).

Seymour, Henry James. "Allen G. Thurman." *Magazine of Western History* III (1885), pp. 42–49.

*1888 presidential nominee —
Prohibition Party*

Clinton B. Fisk

Born December 8, 1828, in Clapp's Corners, now Greigsville, New York; died July 9, 1890, in New York City. Married Jeannette Crippen February 20, 1850; they had three children.

Clinton Bowen Fisk was the fifth son of Benjamin B. and Lydia Aldrich Fisk. He was named for DeWitt Clinton. Benjamin was a blacksmith, wagonbuilder, and militia captain. According to Fisk's campaign biography, this future nominee of the Prohibition Party was born in a converted distillery. When Clinton was a year and a half old the Fisks moved to an 80-acre farm in the wilderness of Michigan. Tragically, the father Benjamin died of typhus when Clinton was four. When he was nine Clinton went to Deacon Elijah Wright's house, apprenticed until he turned 21. Clinton studied at night before the fireplace fire. After two years, Clinton's mother convinced Deacon Wright to let her boy come home. There was a stepfather there now, William Smith, who made their home a stop on the Underground Railroad for runaway slaves trying to escape north.

When Clinton was 15 he spent a year at Albion College, a Methodist school. After a one-year break, Clinton returned to Albion, met his future wife there, but ended his education because of acute eye disease. The family thought it resulted from Clinton's too frequent reading in front of the fireplace light. Clinton then clerked at local stores. In 1848 he moved to Coldwater, Michigan, and starting working for a business owned by his future father-in-law. The business thrived. Fisk also started a bank and in 1853 bought a farm. In 1855 he ran for justice of the peace on a prohibition ticket. Fisk had long been a teetotaler. Perhaps too few of his neighbors were, and he lost. In 1857 he lost his business too, in the financial Panic of 1857.

Fisk became a St. Louis agent for the Aetna Insurance Company. The seeming imminence of civil war caused Fisk to drill secretly with others who favored preserving the Union. When war began, this formerly secret group became the Missouri Home Guards with Fisk as one of the privates. On September 5, 1862, Fisk became a colonel of the 33rd Missouri Infantry. After organizing a brigade he was commissioned a brigadier general on November 24, 1862. He saw action almost exclusively in Missouri and Arkansas. General Fisk commanded the District of Southeast Missouri, and later the Department of Northern Missouri.

When the war ended, Fisk was made assistant commissioner of the Freedman's Bureau in Kentucky and Tennessee. President Andrew Johnson allegedly explained the appointment by saying, "Fisk ain't a fool. He won't hang everybody." Fisk made available a former Union army barracks in Nashville for the establishment of a school for freed slaves. The first students at Fisk School in 1866 ranged from age seven to seventy. On August 22, 1867, the institution became Fisk University. Over the years General Fisk made substantial financial as well as other contributions to the school.

Moving to New York, Fisk became a successful banker. President Grant named him in 1874 to the Board of Indian Commissioners. He was its president from 1881 until he died. Fisk had a near–nervous breakdown in 1877, and took an European tour to recover. He also participated in numerous Methodist Church mission activities.

In 1884 the presidential ticket for the Prohibition Party received 15 times more vote — 150,000 — than it ever had before. This excited temperance leaders such as Fisk, who hoped it presaged bigger successes. New Jersey prohibitionists convinced Fisk to run for governor in 1886. He conducted an active campaign, traveled 5,000 miles, and gave 125 speeches. Though he lost, his 19,808 votes was three times what the party had previously received. At the national convention in 1888, Fisk was nominated for president without opposition. The party platform went well beyond prohibition issues, and called for several reforms including abolishing the Internal Revenue Service, "equal wages for equal work" for the sexes, and for women's suffrage. Fisk gave a speech to an overflow crowd in the New York Metropolitan Opera House, one of the largest auditoriums in the world. He planned an active campaign, but his health became bad. Fisk's 250,000 votes increased the party's 1888 vote by two-thirds, but was only 2.2 percent of the total.

After the election Fisk joined a company that was making plans to build in Tennessee a liquor-free town and industrial site. Fisk became ill before much progress had been made, and died in his New York home.

Fisk University in Nashville is named for the General. Fisk also paid for the construction of a chapel for use by a black church in Fairhaven, New Jersey, and it is named for him. It is located on Cedar Avenue.

FISK BIBLIOGRAPHY

Cabell, Foraker A. "Clinton B. Fisk." *The Greater Fisk Herald* (Fisk University publication, March, 1927), pp. 23, 36.

"Clinton B. Fisk, 1850, Presidential Candidate." *IO Triumphe* (Albion College publication, July 1947), pp. 53–55.

Colvin, D. Leigh. *Prohibition in the United States.* New York (1926).

Hopkins, Alphonso A. *Life of Clinton Bowen Fisk....* New York (1969, reprint of 1888 edition).

Scott, George R. "Sixty-One Years Out of Congress." *The Voice* (Prohibition Party newspaper, unknown date, copy of article in Fisk University file on General Fisk).

Storms, Roger C. *Partisan Prophets: A History of the Prohibition Party, 1854–1972.* Denver (1972).

Warner, Ezra J. "Clinton Bowen Fisk," in *Generals in Blue: Lives of the Union Commanders.* Baton Rouge (1964) pp. 154–55.

Beth M. Howse, special collections librarian, Fisk University, was extremely helpful in gathering information on General Fisk.

1888 vice presidential candidate —
Prohibition Party

John A. Brooks

Born June 3, 1836, in Mason County, Kentucky; died February 3, 1897, in Memphis. Married Sue E. Osborn on October 13, 1857. Three weeks later she died. Married Sue Robertson in 1859. They had five children, one of whom died a few weeks after birth.

John Anderson Brooks was one of four children and the only son of John T. and Elizabeth Anderson Brooks. John T. was a preacher and lawyer as well as a farmer. Squire Brooks he was called, but his education came only from a local log-cabin school. Squire Brooks' son, John A., worked in the fields alongside the slaves. The Brooks' family crop in Kentucky was tobacco, a back-breaking, time-consuming product that left little opportunity for school. At age 12 he became part of a debate society. The organizer was a temperance leader, and John heard much about the evils of alcohol. When John was 17, he entered Bethany College in northwestern Virginia, the part that later became West Virginia. In this border state region, Brooks identified strongly with the South and slavery. Bethany was founded by Alexander Campbell in 1840. Campbell was a minister's son who had a passion for Christian unity and an aversion to denominations. He and his followers called themselves "Disciples of Christ," and their church simply "Christian." Campbell proclaimed that "The church of Christ upon earth is essentially, intentionally, and constitutionally one." For Brooks, Campbell's teaching and preaching "changed the whole direction of his life." He became committed to being a preacher.

In 1854, Brooks and two other students earned "first honors" ranking as undergraduates in the school of chemistry in 1854. Brooks graduated in 1856 and gave a commencement address in French. There were addresses in four other languages, even English. After graduation, Brooks returned to Macon County to preach. He was for a time pastor at the Flemingsburg church. His campaign biography alludes to Brooks' being "drawn into religious controversy" with Methodists. The Methodists and the Disciples apparently had heated public clashes, verbal ones, and Brooks was a defender of his church. This was absorbing entertainment. Large crowds gathered for such debates, and a transcript of at least one of Brooks' encounters was printed and circulated as a pamphlet.

Brooks' Flemingsburg church established a college to serve northeastern Kentucky. It was nearly bankrupt after a year. Brooks agreed in 1861 to take charge as president. In two years the school was financially sound. Brooks' Southern sympathies several times nearly caused his arrest by Union commanders in Kentucky, a slave state that did not secede. Brooks at least once went into hiding with Confederate troops to avoid arrest, then returned to his church when it seemed the danger had passed. As the war ended in 1865, Brooks became pastor at a church in Winchester. There he remained until

Opposite: **CLINTON B. FISK (left) and JOHN A. BROOKS**
(Reproduced from the Collections of the Library of Congress)

1870, when he moved to the First Christian Church in St. Louis.

Over the next 20 years Brooks pastored at Missouri churches, including ones in Mexico, Warrensburg, Belton, and finally Kansas City. In the last-named city he was pastor of the Independence Avenue Christian Church from 1887 to 1892. For three years he was president of the church's state General Conference. Brooks was also a committed Mason. He rose through the different levels until in 1886 he was unanimously elected the Supreme Master Workman, meaning he was head of the entire order.

Brooks participated in the so-called "Murphy movement" that arrived in Missouri in 1878 and 1879. The Murphyites wanted legal prohibition, and did not just try to persuade individual drinkers to abstain. Brooks helped form and became president of the Prohibition State Alliance in 1880. He first tried to work for state prohibition laws through the Democratic Party. In 1882 the state election campaign centered on prohibition, with Brooks the leading spokesman for one side and U.S. Senator George Vest the champion of the opposition. From Brooks' viewpoint, an unsatisfactory legislature was chosen. Most Democrat leaders opposed prohibition. Brooks stayed with the party for one more election, but in 1883 found no better climate. Republicans were equally uncooperative. Brooks decided an independent party was needed.

In August 1884, the state Prohibition Party nominated Brooks for governor. Brooks ran a competitive race, and felt that substantial fraud had occurred in many counties. The prominence Brooks gained led to his being sent by national prohibition leaders to speak for the cause in several Southern states, and later in New York, Pennsylvania, and Ohio. At the party's 1888 national convention, several other candidates were nominated for vice president, but Brooks won on the first ballot. The ticket lost, but got 66 percent more vote than four years earlier.

Brooks continued his ministry, in the Christian Church and as a vigorous prohibition speaker. He "accepted a call" in 1896 to be pastor at the West End Tabernacle in London, but after only eight months ill health caused him to return to the United States He died three months later.

BROOKS BIBLIOGRAPHY

Brooks, John A. "The Non-partisan Prohibition Movement." *Evangelical* (1885), p. 212.

Cherrington, Ernest Hurst. *Standard Encyclopedia of the Alcohol Problem.* Westerville, Ohio (1925), pp. 431–432.

"Church at Sixth and Prospect Streets, Kansas City." *Christian Standard* (July 23, 1892), pp. 1, 7.

Durban, W. "English Topics." *Evangelist* (1896), pp. 280–81.

Hopkins, Alphonso A. *Life of Clinton Bowen Fisk with a Brief Sketch of John A. Brooks.* New York (1969, reprint of 1888 edition).

"John A. Brooks" (obituary). *Christian Evangelist* (1897), p. 85.

Millenial Harbinger (Bethany College journal), scattered issues from 1854, 1856, and 1863.

R. Jeanne Cobb, archivist and coordinator of Special Collections at Bethany College, generously photocopied articles from religious and college periodicals in her library.

Beth Weinhardt responded to an e-mail request and graciously searched for materials at the Westerville Public Library, Ohio.

Election of 1892

NOMINATIONS

Republican Party Convention (10th): June 7–10, 1892, at the Industrial Exposition Building, Minneapolis, Minnesota. *President—*

Benjamin Harrison, nominated on the first ballot with 535⅙ votes out of 904⅓ cast. James Blaine (Me.) and William McKinley were in a distant tie for second. *Vice president*— Whitelaw Reid, nominated by acclamation.

Democratic Party Convention (16th): June 21–23, 1892, in a specially constructed building in Chicago, Ill. *President*—Grover Cleveland, nominated on the first ballot with 617⅓ votes out of 909½ cast. David Hill (N.Y.) and Horace Boies (Iowa) were other contenders who were quite far behind Cleveland. *Vice president*— Adlai E. Stevenson, nominated on the first ballot with 652 votes out of 909 cast; he had only 402 before vote changes began. Isaac Gray (Ind.) was a close rival.

Prohibition Party Convention (6th): June 29–30. 1892, at Music Hall, Cincinnati, Ohio. *President*— John Bidwell, nominated on the first ballot with 590 votes; Gideon Stewart (Ohio) had 179, and W. Jennings Demarest (N.Y.) had 139. *Vice president*— James B. Cranfill, nominated on the second ballot; Joshua Levering (Md.) was his principal opponent.

People's Party (Populists) Convention (1st): July 2–5, 1892, at Convention Hall Coliseum, Omaha, Nebraska. *President*— James B. Weaver, nominated on the first ballot with 995 votes of the 1,263 votes; James H. Kyle (S.D.) had 265 votes. Leonidas L. Polk of North Carolina had been a likely nominee for one of the positions, but he died June 11. *Vice president*— James G. Field, nominated on the first ballot with 733 votes to 554 votes for Ben Terrell (Tex.).

GENERAL ELECTION, November 8, 1892
Popular Vote
Cleveland 5,551,883
Harrison 5,179,244
Weaver 1,024,280
Bidwell 264,138
Others. 30,000
Electoral Vote
Cleveland-Stevenson — 277 (23 states)
Harrison-Reid —145 (16 states)
Weaver-Field — 22 (4 states)
Winners
Grover Cleveland, 24th president
Adlai E. Stevenson, 23rd vice president

Losers
Benjamin Harrison, Whitelaw Reid, James B. Weaver, James Field, John Bidwell, James Cranfill

---

*1892 presidential nominee —
Republican Party*

Benjamin Harrison

No biographical sketch of Harrison is included since he served as president from March 4, 1889, until March 4, 1893 (23rd president).
State represented: Indiana.
Birth: August 20, 1833.
Age on Inauguration Day (March 4, 1893): 59 years, 6½ months.
Death: March 13, 1901.

---

*1892 vice presidential nominee —
Republican Party*

Whitelaw Reid

Full name: James Whitelaw Reid; was christened without the name "James," but as infant was given this extra name in honor of a family friend; Whitelaw dropped the "James" soon after becoming an adult.
State represented: New York.
Birth: October 27, 1837, outside Xenia, Ohio.
Age on Inauguration Day (March 4, 1893): 55 years, 4 months.
Education: Xenia Academy; tutored by his uncle; Miami University, 1853–1856.
Religion: Presbyterian.
Ancestry/prominent relatives: James Reid (paternal grandfather) emigrated from Ireland in late 1700s, but was of Scottish descent; Ogden Mills (father-in-law) was prominent businessman and philanthropist; Ogden Mills Reid (son) became president of New York *Tribune*.
Occupation: Journalist.
Public office: Declined appointment as ambassador to Germany, 1878 and 1881;

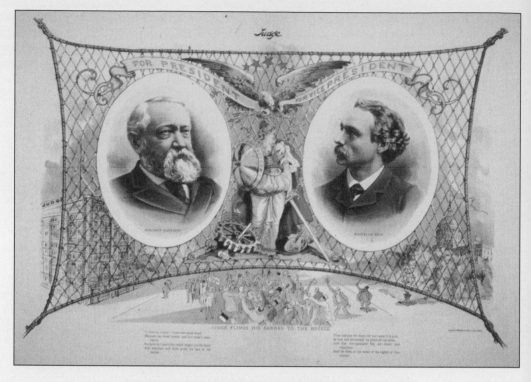

BENJAMIN HARRISON and WHITELAW REID
(From the collection of David J. and Janice L. Frent)

minister to France, 1889–1892; unsuccessful Republican nominee for vice president, 1892; ambassador to Great Britain, 1905–1912.

Home: Seven-hundred-acre estate in Westchester County, New York, called Ophir Farm; also a mansion across the street from Columbia College; also a lodge called Wild Air.

Death: December 15, 1912, in London, at age 75 years, 1½ months.

Burial: Sleepy Hollow Cemetery, Tarrytown, New York.

Personal Characteristics: 5'10" tall, thin, frail, slight droop in his shoulders; high forehead, thin nose, prominent cheekbones; black hair worn long and combed straight back; full mustache and imperial.

Father: Robert Charlton Reid (1795–1865), a farmer.

Mother: Marion Whitelaw Ronalds (1803–1895), married in 1826, daughter of George Slater Ronalds.

Siblings: Gavin (April 8, 1828–1862), married Nettie _____. Chestina (June 12, 1844–1876), married in 1867.

Wife: Elizabeth (called "Lizzie") Mills (January 6, 1858–April 29, 1931), married April 26, 1881; was the daughter of Darius Ogden Mills and Jane Templeton (Cunningham) Mills, a distinguished capitalist and philanthropist.

Children: Ogden Mills (May 16, 1882–January 3, 1947), married Helen Rogers in March 1911; became president of the New York *Tribune*. Jean Templeton (1884–May 1, 1962), married John Ward on January 23, 1908; he was son of Earl of Dudley and was the equerry (cared for the horses) of the King of England; the King and Queen attended their wedding.

Historic sites/memorials: Reid Hall, his home in Purchase, New York, is now part of Manhattanville College (Ophir Hall).

He shares with Horace Greeley, James Cox, Warren Harding, and Frank Knox the distinction of being the only career newspapermen to be nominated by a national convention. Greeley and Reid, for four years together as publisher and managing editor respectively for the New York *Tribune*, share the additional background of never having served in a major political office prior to their nominations. It is doubtful Greeley or Reid would have excelled if they had gained the presidency.

Young Whitelaw's health had been frail. Growing up in Xenia, Ohio, on his father's farm, he distinguished himself as a bookish, intelligent child who avoided athletics. The Reid household was not prosperous, but neither was it in embarrassingly strained circumstances. Religion was important to the family, and among Whitelaw's few early reading sources was the Bible. Culture, especially the enjoyment of music and literature, separated the Reids from the typical frontier Ohio family. Education was gained at local schools, including the Xenia Academy. At Miami University in Oxford, Ohio, Whitelaw received honors in foreign languages and in any course that called upon felicity in expression. Even during school he was having pieces accepted for publication in newspapers. Politics was at times the topic, including an article for a Kansas newspaper on the bitterly controversial bill on that territory introduced by Senator Stephen Douglas. Graduating at the head of his class from Miami, Reid was still uncertain what to do with himself. A small grade school in South Charleston, Ohio, took him as a principal, though he was only 19. For two years he taught French, Latin, mathematics, and several other subjects in addition to his duties as principal. This was unsatisfactory work and he returned to his home to give himself time to plan his next step.

A chance conversation at a local store led him into purchasing one of the two Xenia newspapers, the *News*. Whitelaw became the editor, his brother Gavin the business manager, and their father the chief bankroll. Political issues, most particularly slavery, often were discussed on the editorial page. Whitelaw was from the first a loyal Republican, and he often accused far better-known members of his party of straying from party principles. Frémont was supported by young Reid in 1856, and a few years later the journalist recognized Lincoln as the likely best candidate for the Republicans in 1860. Reid had exceptional political instincts.

Bad health, constant work with no break,

and poor if any profits caused the Reids to give up the *News*. A strenuous trip for his health was taken, traveling three thousand miles into the wilderness of Minnesota and other areas. Reid wrote articles about the adventure for publication in the Cincinnati *Gazette*. After an interlude of other odd jobs in Xenia and nearby towns, Reid got a job reporting the state legislative session for the Cincinnati paper, and soon was the capital reporter for two other papers. It was drudgery, with little of interest to write about, but for the first time Reid began to make noticeable money from his labors. He was made city editor for the *Gazette* in recognition for the paper's satisfaction with his work during the legislature. But Fort Sumter and the start of the Civil War made him more useful to the paper as a war correspondent. Traveling with General Rosecrans in West Virginia as an aide-de-camp and reporter, Reid revealed considerable skill in writing of battle. He was also a frequent and accurate critic of inefficiency, lack of nerve on the part of commanders (especially General George B. McClellan), and inadequate training of the troops. Quite by luck, because of the absence of other war news during the period, Reid's extremely well-written report of the Battle of Shiloh received nationwide publicity, and the Whitelaw Reid name gained prominence in journalistic circles. Using the pen name "Agate" for his reports, Reid criticized the army's lack of preparation for the attack by Confederate General Albert Sidney Johnston's troops, and described poignantly the ebb and flow of the battle. Generals, including the Shiloh commander Ulysses Grant, were irritated over the criticism. In time Reid would be barred from the front line because of his negative comments.

Journalism was not Reid's sole concern. In 1860 he had advocated Lincoln's nomination for the presidency and had helped persuade the Ohio delegation to abandon their previous favorite, Salmon P. Chase, in favor of Lincoln. During the 1860 general election campaign he served as county Republican chairman. Visits to Washington as part of his reporting duties placed him in contact with such leaders as Garfield, John Hay, Sumner, Chase, and others in Congress and the administration. For a time he served as clerk of a congressional committee. He also was able to invest in the Cincinnati *Gazette*, which was a necessary inducement to get him to stay with the paper after offers from other papers were made.

The last battle that Reid personally viewed was Gettysburg, and he barely made it to the conflict before it was over. As at Shiloh, Reid's report of the progress of the fighting became the most popular and widely published.

In 1864, the rising young reporter had no enthusiasm for another term by Lincoln, as Reid felt the president was incapable of handling the office. Active in the dump Lincoln effort, he continued to urge the president to withdraw even after the convention had selected Lincoln for another term. After the assassination, Reid became an opponent of Andrew Johnson's lenient policies towards the defeated South. With Salmon Chase, Reid toured the South in May 1865, and formed indelible impressions of a recalcitrant, noncontrite if defeated region in which the vast majority of the whites continued to be rebels. One reason for his tour was to examine investment opportunities, particularly in cotton plantations. He purchased some Louisiana acreage, which yielded just sufficient profit to induce a second try in Alabama, which then wiped out his earlier gains. In 1867, Reid gave up on the ventures. Reid actually lived on very little of what he made and was always attempting to find long-term investment opportunities.

As a result of his tour of the South, Reid wrote a book, *After the War*, which explained his view of the effects of the war on that region. A detailed history entitled *Ohio in the War* was published in 1868, a scholarly, well-documented work that has stood the tests of time and critical analysis as well.

These experiences of war, the heady involvement in reporting to a national audience, helped convince Reid to remain in the East and not return to Ohio. In September 1868, Reid walked into the offices of Horace Greeley's New York *Tribune*, one of the nation's largest and most influential papers. He was soon caught up not just in the myriad of chores, many of them totally new, as editor, but also in Greeley's politics. In 1872, Reid

helped press Greeley's presidential nomination by the newly-formed Liberal Republicans. He proposed convention rules in the *Tribune* (anybody come who wanted to, and organize by states once you arrive), and then attended the convention as one of the self-appointed delegates. With Greeley's nomination, Reid took over full control of the paper. The devastating defeat suffered in November returned Greeley in name to the editor's chair, but he never filled it in fact as his health rapidly deteriorated. His death before the new year began left his subordinates battling over control. At first despairing of victory, Reid was finally able to piece together a syndicate, including robber baron Jay Gould in the partnership, and won the fight. A shadow was nonetheless cast over the paper by Gould's presence, and in fact the industrialist, financier and political operator no longer received the criticism from the *Tribune* that had appeared frequently prior to the ownership change.

Greeley had run a loose operation. Reid soon changed that. Labor problems were frequent as the panic of 1873 caused Reid to force three wage reductions. Technological advances were applied rapidly to the production of the paper. With the invention of linotype (some credit Reid with naming the invention when he exclaimed, "Why, it's a line of type"), labor unrest increased as Reid insisted that the formerly skilled position of typesetter was now a no-skill, much lower-wage position. The paper's circulation suffered at first from the change of editors, but in time grew beyond what it had been under Greeley. As a business move to boost circulation, Reid publicly aligned his paper with the Republican Party, and encouraged the party organizations nationwide to help with subscriptions to the weekly edition of the *Tribune*. As part of the new regime, Reid had the old Tribune Building torn down and a new tower built in its place. The workers on the building struck over low wages, and Reid had them replaced.

In politics Reid was constantly opposed to the Republican president Ulysses Grant. Refusing ever to support a Democrat for president, the *Tribune* nonetheless did give help to Democratic gubernatorial hopeful Samuel

Tilden in the 1874 New York race. By 1876, when Hayes had received the Republican presidential nomination, the *Tribune* returned to the party fold. Still, had a Grant regular rather than a man like Hayes, who could be seen as representing reform, been nominated, Reid was ready to bolt the party. The day after the election the *Tribune* "erroneously" reported that Tilden had been elected, but by the next day had fallen into line with the rest of the country's Republican press and called the election a deadlock that had yet to be broken. When charges of corruption and bribes surfaced with Hayes' election, Reid was eager to find evidence of Democrat bribes. The publication in 1878 of the "cipher dispatches," involving Tilden's nephew's attempt to bribe election officials in the South, made the Democrats' charge of "theft" a hollow one. The publication also made Reid a hero to many in his party. Soon thereafter he was offered the ministry to Germany, but turned down the offer as conducive neither to a future political role nor to retaining his control of the *Tribune*.

When Grant sought a third term in 1880, Reid attacked him. Reid was pleasantly surprised with old friend and fellow Ohioan James Garfield's nomination. For six months of Garfield's presidency, the New York editor was one of the most influential men in America. The new president respected Reid's judgment on cabinet and other appointments, and on policy. Few New York contacts were as well known to Garfield as was Reid, and that placed the journalist in a strong position to influence patronage in his state.

Yet while the new administration was taking shape, Reid was preoccupied with ending his bachelorhood at the age of 42. Lizzie Mills was the 22-year-old daughter of fabulously wealthy Darius Ogden Mills, whose palatial home in San Francisco would give his daughter tastes in comfort beyond her future husband's ability to provide. Some time from matrimony was taken to secure the election of a friendly senator from New York, and Thomas Platt was that man. Reid also helped name the principal Grant opponent in the state, Judge W.H. Robertson, as the collector of the New York Customs House. This was perhaps the most important patronage posi-

tion in the country, because it was the most profitable to the occupant. The selection, and the battle in the Senate over confirmation, indirectly led to Garfield's assassination by a disgruntled office-seeker who identified himself with Robertson's New York adversaries. By that time, however, Reid was enjoying a several months' honeymoon in Europe. When he left in May for Europe, he could foresee at least four years of intimate relations with the American president; upon his return, Reid was definitely on the outside, with barely even a view into new president Chester Arthur's administration.

James G. Blaine, the plumed knight from the state of Maine, was now the savior of Reid's political fortunes. Long-denied the presidential nomination, Blaine was now actively pushed by Reid for the 1884 election. "Accidental" president Chester Arthur was strongly criticized in the pages of the *Tribune*, and Reid wielded little influence as a result. While fighting Arthur on the national level, journalist Reid was active in promoting the Associated Press wire service. In 1885, he was secretly involved with others in taking control of the United States Press organization as well. His paper was not the best seller in New York, and trailed several others. He was not interested in stooping to the yellow journalism then in vogue, but instead wanted to appeal to the intellectuals, or at least the educated.

As 1884 approached, Reid found ways to assist Blaine's candidacy. The national press realized the connection and frequently showed Reid as one of the major national leaders in the Blaine campaign. In the famous cartoon of "the Belshazzar Blaine and the Money Kings," Reid was shown at the shoulder of Blaine while the assembled millionaires looked on. Blaine lost narrowly, and Reid was devastated. A Blaine election would have placed him almost as close to the White House as Garfield's election had four years earlier. Twice Reid had been denied, by the whims of fate, the opportunity to share meaningfully in power. A better chance would never come.

With Grover Cleveland's election, the *Tribune* became a severe administration critic. Blaine was still Reid's candidate, and the *Tribune* published the "Paris letter" from Blaine that condemned Cleveland's message on the tariff. The letter said in essence that the only people benefited by Cleveland's stand were the British, who could make vast profits with a lower tariff on their goods. With much less eagerness, Reid published a little later the letter from Blaine that announced he would not be a candidate in 1888 for the presidency.

Though Blaine was not to be president, a Republican did win in 1888. Benjamin Harrison owed little to Reid for his election, but the influential New York editor could not be ignored as a party power. Speculation was rife that he would get a cabinet post or high ambassadorial position. The recent publication of Blaine's Paris letter, strongly anti–British in tone, had disqualified Reid for the London ministry. He was called Blaine's "chief henchman," not the best credential for British ambassador. Harrison sent Vice President Levi Morton to Reid to soften the blow of rejection, as Reid had been quite forward in his request for the London post. Instead, after refusing to accept anything less than London, Reid was persuaded to accept the mission to France as his consolation prize. He had little knowledge or interest in European affairs. Fortunately, little significant occurred during his three years there. A favorable commercial treaty was negotiated, permitting the importation of American pork, and an extradition treaty was also produced that enlarged the offenses for which extradition would be permitted.

Reid's return to the United States in 1892 found him in the midst of speculation for the vice presidency. Incumbent president Harrison was in trouble for renomination, and Reid doubted Harrison's chances. The New York state convention endorsed Reid for vice president after someone reported, accurately or not, that Vice President Morton did not want to be renominated. Many people were placed into nomination for vice president, but all withdrew or were dropped before the balloting began and Reid was named by acclamation. The campaign was lifeless; no candidate, Republican or Democrat, generated much excitement. Grover Cleveland returned to the presidency after having been in private life for four years, and Reid returned to his newspaper.

Reid was no longer interested in newspaper work. For three years the former national candidate seemed despondent over the 1892 defeat. He had desperately wanted this high office and he had seen it slip, surprisingly to him, away. He blamed the McKinley high tariff for defeat. His public career, never really begun except on the sidelines, was viewed as finished. A tour of North Africa, frequent and extended vacations to California and Arizona, and far more horseback riding and resting than politics dominated his life. One helpful result of his absence from the paper was that a 20-year-old labor dispute was finally settled when other managers were temporarily in control of the paper.

A momentary revival in Reid's optimism and interest occurred with William McKinley's election to the presidency in 1896. An Ohioan like Garfield, McKinley was well known to Reid, was assisted greatly by the *Tribune* in the campaign, and had consulted with the editor over such significant matters as the selection of a vice presidential candidate at the convention. Reid wanted to be the secretary of state, and was indiscreet, even insistent, in informing McKinley of his desires. The explanation given by the incoming administration for selecting another was that Reid's ill health, which for three years had caused him to seek the warmer and drier climates of Arizona and Africa, meant he was physically incapable of applying himself to the stringent routine of the State Department. Reid continued to hope he might still receive the ambassador position to England, but instead the editor's old lieutenant, John Hay, was selected. Reid was bitter. The consolation prize came in June 1897, when Reid was named as the leader of America's delegation to Queen Victoria's Jubilee in celebration of the sixtieth anniversary of her coronation.

The Spanish-American War in 1898 found Reid arguing for restraint, but backing the president when events finally caused McKinley to ask for a declaration of war. When the war was quickly won, Reid's leading role in the public debate over the war caused his appointment to the Peace Commission to seek terms from Spain. The five-man commission met in Paris with Spain's representatives, finally leading to a favorable treaty with which Reid was greatly pleased. He totally accepted the desirability of taking all of the Philippines and Cuba, but he wanted the possessions made independent as soon as they were ready for that transformation. Another chance for strutting on the English social stage came in 1902 when Reid was made an American delegate to the coronation of Edward VII.

After returning from France in 1892, Reid had almost abandoned active involvement with the *Tribune*. Reid spent great amounts of time at his various estates in New York, California, or on vacation. From this semi-retirement he established the editorial policy of support for Theodore Roosevelt when he succeeded to the presidency upon McKinley's death. Neither Roosevelt nor Reid initially was a fan of the other, but mutual respect began to grow. This friendship finally achieved for Reid his goal of being named ambassador to Great Britain.

Reid set sail for London on May 27, 1905. He established a standard of living there that was the equal of his sumptuous existence in America. Newspaper comment upon the extravagance only gained from him the retort that he had no more of a luxurious style in England than in the United States. The ambassadorship was uneventful in the area of policy. In 1908, he supported Taft's election, and when he asked the new president to allow him to stay on a few months as minister until after his daughter's London wedding, those months stretched into almost the entire Taft presidential term. Bronchial troubles that had weakened him for a lifetime finally conquered him. He died in London in 1912.

Analysis of Qualifications

Whitelaw Reid's motives were often controversial. Friends saw him as a cool, reflective, intelligent man who was too dignified to be a glad-hander. Opponents saw the same actions and called Reid aloof and calculating, with no human emotion or compassion. The basic thrust remains the same, that Reid made friends only with difficulty, that he acted cautiously, and that he was tremendously concerned with appearances and receiving the honors he felt himself due.

Through shrewd investments and conservative management of the *Tribune*, greatly augmented by his financially fortuitous marriage to Elizabeth Mills, Reid became quite wealthy. His lived in sumptuous style. Worker wages were a constant concern during his reign at the *Tribune*, and labor disputes were so heated and protracted that he had a national reputation for tight-fisted intransigence on labor matters. A Reid presidency would have had strong union opposition.

Horace Greeley had made the *Tribune* a popular, cause-fighting newspaper with considerable nationwide circulation. It had a reputation for integrity and independence, as well as for eccentricity. Reid straightened out the loose management of the paper, but also incurred suspicion because of the partners with whom he operated, most notably Jay Gould. There was a clear public identification of the paper with the Republican Party.

One of Reid's bitterest opponents during his tenure on the *Tribune* was fellow New Yorker, Senator Thomas Platt. Therefore Platt's opinions are colored, but still seem near the mark when he described Reid as "selfish and unscrupulous, ... a fawning and unctuous friend while he is a friend. ... I have never known the time when he could be induced to look beyond ... his personal advantage." The inaccuracy in the comment is to make Reid's sole motivation one of personal gain. Reid was fawning, insistent, embarrassingly forthright to President McKinley in wanting an appointment as secretary of state, and he said he would accept nothing less. Of course there was nothing greater. Yet Reid was also a fighter for what he thought was good government and good journalism, refusing to permit his paper to engage in the sensationalism that was then gaining large circulations for other New York papers. He also considered himself, perhaps presumptuously, as a defender of worthy virtues not only in journalism but also in politics. He wanted his paper written for and to be read by educated gentlemen, and not incidentally, by Republicans.

There was little in Reid's past to prepare him for the myriad responsibilities of the presidency. His intelligence could not be doubted; his skill in writing was superb. These talents would have only been a weak start to a successful presidency. He had few skills in working with other men; he antagonized and irritated more frequently than he convinced or ingratiated. He hungered for office. The recognition that went with his three mainly ceremonial missions to Great Britain seemed the perfect satisfaction for his ambition. The despondency that followed his 1892 defeat for vice president revealed how deeply he had wanted that office. There would have been a country full of dissatisfied observers had he attained this goal.

REID BIBLIOGRAPHY

Campbell-Copeland, Thomas, comp. *Harrison and Reid: Their Lives and Record.* 3 vols. New York City (1892).
Cortissoz, Royal. *The Life of Whitelaw Reid.* 2 vols. New York City (1921).
Duncan, Bingham. *Whitelaw Reid: Journalist, Politician, Diplomat.* Athens, Ga. (1976).
Gallagher, Gary W., ed. *Two Witnesses at Gettysburg: The Personal Accounts of Whitelaw Reid and A.J.L. Fremantle.* St. James, N.Y. (1994).
Jones, Robert H. "Whitelaw Reid," in *For the Union: Ohio Leaders in the Civil War,* edited by Kenneth W. Wheeler. Columbus, Ohio (1968).
Smart, James G. "Whitelaw Reid: A Biographical Study." Unpublished doctoral dissertation, University of Maryland (1964).
_____. "Whitelaw Reid and the Nomination of Horace Greeley." *Mid-America* 49 (1967), pp. 227–243.

1892 presidential nominee—
Populist Party

James B. Weaver

(The biography on Weaver appears at the election of 1880, pages 376–378, as he was the Greenback-Labor Party nominee for president that year.)
State represented: Iowa
Birth: June 12, 1833, in Dayton, Ohio;
Age on Inauguration Day (March 4, 1893): 59 years, 8½ months
Died: February 6, 1912, in Colfax, Iowa.

1892 vice presidential nominee—
Populist Party

James G. Field

Born February 24, 1826, in Walnut, Culpeper County, Virginia; died October 12, 1901, in Gordonsville, Virginia. Married Frances Elizabeth Cowherd; they had six children. She died in the spring of 1877. Married Elizabeth Logwood (she was 27 years younger, and the aunt of future President Woodrow Wilson's wife, Edith Bolling Galt Wilson) in 1882; they had three sons.

James Gaven Field was the son of Lewis Yancey and Maria Duncan Field. A playmate was Ambrose Powell Hill, the future Confederate general. James attended local schools, clerked for A.P. Hill's father in a Culpeper store, and also did some teaching. Adventure beckoned, and in 1848 Field left for California with Major Henry Hill, who was the Army paymaster for soldiers fighting in the Mexican War and who needed a clerk. Field returned to Virginia in 1850.

Field read law in his uncle Henry Field's law office and was admitted to the bar in 1852. He married into a wealthy Albemarle County family. Field now had a home in Culpeper, and as a gift from his father-in-law, a country home on 270 acres that they called "Breitstein." In 1859 Field became commonwealth's attorney for Culpeper County. That ended in April 1861, the same month that Fort Sumter was fired upon. Field left home to serve in the 13th Virginia Infantry.

General A.P. Hill made his old friend a major and named him chief quartermaster, i.e., supply officer. Field was at the battles of Williamsburg, Cold Harbor (where he was wounded), Seven Pines, Gaines' Mill, Fraser's Farm, and Malvern Hill. At Cedar Mountain, Virginia, in August 1862, Major Field was seriously injured and one leg was amputated. He convalesced for 11 months back home at Breitstein. Field rejoined Hill in Pennsylvania in July 1863, for the third day of a momentous battle. He probably witnessed Pickett's charge. Field had not seen the whole battle, but he had seen enough of Gettysburg. Field was with Hill's Corps for the rest of the war.

JAMES B. WEAVER and JAMES G. FIELD
(Reproduced from the Collections of the Library of Congress)

After Appomattox, Field resumed his law practice in Culpeper. He also accumulated substantial land holdings, and began to farm. Field, only a major in the Confederacy, became a brigadier general in the Virginia militia. He was active in the Grange and other agricultural groups. At political rallies and patriotic gatherings, the one-legged general was often a speaker. In 1877 the incumbent Virginia attorney general died just days after the party convention renominated him. Field was appointed to fill the remaining months of the term, and was elected to a full term. After four years, he declined reelection and returned to Albemarle County and his law practice.

Field took an aggressively pro-farmer tone in his speeches by 1887. He asked, "What is the Democratic party *except* the farmers of Virginia?" The failure of the Democrats on farm issues led Field to advocate the creation of an independent party. The Farmers' Alliance, or Southern Alliance, was a successor to the Grange and not yet a political party. Field spoke at various Alliance rallies and was closely identified with the movement. Field wanted the various farmers' groups to unite. Democrats tried to placate the Alliance with various promises on farm issues, but Field became increasingly disenchanted with his old party. In the spring of 1892, the absorption of the non-political Farmers' Alliance into the new People's or Populist Party was well under way. A Populist Party state convention was held June 23, 1892, in Richmond. The seventy-five delegates elected Field as permanent chairman of the meeting and sent him as a delegate-at-large to the national convention in Omaha.

Former Union General James Weaver was nominated for president. A Southerner was needed to balance the ticket. Field was the choice. He was a good speaker and conducted an active campaigner. The flavor of his fervent oratorical style is captured by these lines: "All hail the power of the People's name/ Let autocrats prostrate fall./ Bring forth the royal diadem/ And crown the People sovereign, all." Field campaigned across the South and had a few joint appearances with General Weaver.

Field remained active with the Populists and chaired their state convention in 1893. He was chairman of the state's Bimetallic League, pushing for the free and unlimited coinage of silver, as were some Democrats like William Jennings Bryan. Field counseled the Populists to fuse with the Democrats in 1896 when Bryan was nominated. Field was one of the few who attended the 1900 Populist Party national convention in Sioux Falls, South Dakota, as the party was all but dead. The old general was in about the same condition. He

died in 1902 while riding his horse "Nimrod" across the rolling farmland near his home.

FIELD BIBLIOGRAPHY

Argersinger, Peter H. *Populism and Politics: William Alfred Peffer and the People's Party.* Lexington, Ky. (1974).

Goodwin, Lawrence. *Democratic Promise: The Populist Movement in America.* New York (1976).

Knoles, George Harmon. *The Presidential Campaign and Election of 1892.* Stanford (1942).

Moore, John. "The Life of James G. Field, Virginia Populist." Unpublished master's thesis, University of Virginia (1953).

Peffer, William (edited by Peter H. Argersinger). *Populism: Its Rise and Fall.* Lawrence, Kans. (1992, reprint of 1899 edition).

Sheldon, William DuBose. *Populism in the Old Dominion: Virginia Farm Politics, 1885–1900.* Princeton (1935).

1892 presidential candidate—
Prohibition Party

John Bidwell

Born August 5, 1819, in Ripley Hills, New York; died April 4, 1900, in Chico, California. Married Annie Kennedy in 1868. They had no children.

John Bidwell was the son of Abram and Clarissa (Griggs) Bidwell. When John was ten the family moved to Erie County, Pennsylvania; two years later they moved to Ohio. John had gotten little education. When he was 17, he walked three hundred miles to Ashtabula to enter Kingsville Academy. The academic standards were apparently minimal, because after one year he was made the principal. In 1838 he taught in Darke County, then decided to move farther west. Bidwell settled near Fort Leavenworth, Missouri, and again taught school.

Bidwell at age 22 was with the first overland party bound for California that gathered at Independence, Missouri in May 1841. Sixty-nine people started west, eventually to split up so some could go to Oregon. Bidwell was with the group of 32 who arrived November 4, 1841, at Mt. Diablo, California. It had been such an arduous journey that the group lost all their wagons. He lived at Captain Sutter's settlement, which became Sutter's Fort and, eventually, the city of Sacramento. Bidwell became Sutter's bookkeeper and general assistant for matters requiring some education. He was still working with Sutter when the first stages of a revolt began in December 1844 by Mexican soldiers against the local Mexican governor. Bidwell and Sutter joined the forces defending the governor. They were captured and imprisoned when the insurgents took control, but both were released soon thereafter.

Bidwell was at Sutter's Fort when American Captain John Charles Frémont's force arrived, in December, 1845, led by Kit Carson and pulling cannon. Frémont's orders were obscure, but he was probably sent from Washington, D.C., to be available if war against Mexico began. Frémont was looking for Sutter, and recorded an unfavorable impression of Bidwell. Frémont considered him stuffy, a little arrogant, and entirely too reluctant to make a decision about the supplies that Frémont desperately needed. Bidwell gave him many of the supplies he asked for, but not all.

Within a few months there was war between Mexico and the United States. Bidwell was a member of the committee that drew up the declaration of independence for the Bear Republic of California. Bidwell joined Frémont's force, the two men now getting along marginally better. He was made a lieutenant, then magistrate for Los Angeles after the Mexicans there surrendered, but then had to escape when the city again came under Mexican control. When the war ended he returned to Sutter's Fort.

Bidwell became wealthy as a result of the California gold discovery. He was the first successfully to prospect on the Feather River. In 1849 he was able to buy 22,000-acre Rancho Chico north of Sacramento. It extended east of the Sacramento River for 14 miles. Agriculture dominated his life. He had 1,200 acres of fruit orchard. Various industries were constructed, such as flouring mills, a fruit cannery, vinegar works and a dairy. The "keynote of Bidwell's management policy was diversity, and this plus innovation ... soon brought him

unparalleled success" (*Bidwell Mansion,* p. 6). Over two hundred Indians lived on the ranch. The Bidwells personally conducted religious services each Sunday for them.

Bidwell was chosen, but did not serve as a delegate to the convention that wrote the state's constitution in 1849 — he was in the mountains and did not learn of his selection until too late. He was then elected to its first state senate. In 1860 he was a delegate for Stephen Douglas to the national Democratic convention. He supported the union after the Civil War began. The governor appointed him a brigadier general in 1863. His politics had changed enough that he was a delegate to the Union Party (Republican) national convention in 1864. That same year he was elected to Congress, was named chairman of the Agriculture Committee, and served one term. Bidwell was one of the first proponents of a transcontinental railroad. He declined to run for reelection, and returned to California to run a losing race for governor in 1867. His nomination by the Republicans was blocked by railroad interests, fearful of Bidwell's independence. The railroad lobbyist that they nominated was defeated. Disgusted, Bidwell left his brief home in the Republican Party and became an independent. In 1875 he lost a race for governor as the candidate of the Anti-Monopolist Party, receiving about a quarter of the vote.

Bidwell's prohibition views were evident at least by the 1860s when he became concerned that his wine was turning too many people into drunkards, and so he destroyed his vineyards. In 1890 Bidwell was the Prohibition Party candidate for California governor. In 1892 he won one of the more spirited contests for his party's presidential nomination. The Westerner beat out three Easterners. He had hoped to make an active campaign, but a financial crisis caused him to focus on his businesses in California. He got the most votes of any Prohibition Party candidate ever — 271,000.

Bidwell Park in Chico, California, is the second largest municipal park in the country (New York's Central Park is the largest), and was a gift from Bidwell's widow to commemorate his life. The Bidwell Mansion State Historic

Park in Chico is adjacent to Chico State University.

BIDWELL BIBLIOGRAPHY

Adrian, Frederick Wayne. "The Political Significance of the Prohibition Party." Unpublished doctoral dissertation, Ohio State University (1942).

Benjamin, Marcus. *John Bidwell: Pioneer.* Washington, D.C. (1907).

Bidwell, Annie Kennedy. "The Character of John Bidwell." *Publications of Historical Society of Southern California* II (1919), pp. 53-55.

_____. *Dear General: The Private Letters of Annie E. Kennedy and John Bidwell, 1866–1868.* Sacramento (1993), edited by Linda Rowlings.

Bidwell, John. "The First Emigrant Train to California." *American History Illustrated* XX (April 1985), pp. 36–47.

Bidwell Mansion State Historic Park. Pamphlet by California Department of Parks and Recreation (revised December 1991) (contains excellent biographical articles on both General and Mrs.Bidwell).

Cherrington, Ernest Hurst, ed. *Standard Encyclopedia of the Alcohol Problem.* Westerville, Ohio (1925), pp. 343–44.

Cody, Cora Edith. "John Bidwell: His Early Career in California." Unpublished master's thesis,University of California (1927).

James, George Wharton. *Heroes of California: The Story of the Pioneers of the Golden State....* Boston (1910), pp. 45–55.

Mathes, Valerie Sherer. "Annie E.K. Bidwell, Chico's Benefactress." *California History* LXVIII (spring/summer 1989), pp. 14–25.

Nunis, Doyce B., Jr., ed. *The Bidwell-Bartleson Party: 1841 California Emigrant Adventure. The Documents and Memoirs of the Overland Pioneers.* Santa Cruz, Calif. (1991).

Ottley, Allan R., ed. *John A. Sutter's Last Days: The Bidwell Letters.* Sacramento (1986).

Royce, Charles C. *John Bidwell: Pioneer, Statesman, Philanthropist, a Biographical Sketch.* Chico, Calif. (1906).

Storms, Roger C. *Partisan Prophets: A History of the Prohibition Party, 1854–1972.* Denver (1972).

Turner, James R. "The American Prohibition Movement, 1865-1897." Unpublished doctoral dissertation, University of Wisconsin (1972).

Beth Weinhardt, Westerville Public Library, Ohio, graciously provided some of the cited sources.

1892 vice presidential candidate—
Prohibition Party

James B. Cranfill

Born September 12, 1858, in Parker County, Texas; died December 28, 1942, in Dallas. Married Olivia (Ollie) Allen at a Methodist camp meeting on September 1, 1878. Their only child died at age two.

James Britton Buchanan Boone Cranfill was the son of Eaton and Martha Jane Galloway Cranfill. He attended local schools of Gonzales County, Texas, but never went to college, medical school or seminary. In 1877 and 1878 he taught school in Crawford, and married one of his students. He studied medicine with his father, passed the state medical examination, and practiced medicine from 1879 until 1882 in Turnersville. He also during this period operated a shoe shop, a general store, and a corn and flouring mill and gin. In order to publicize his various businesses, he published a monthly newspaper in 1881 and 1882, the Turnersville *Effort.* Cranfill left that paper, and medicine, and moved to the county seat in Gatesville to publish the weekly *Advance.*

As a Baptist writer later said, Cranfill as a young man "played the fiddle, smoked, danced, and indulged in a weakness for cards" (Story, *Baptist Leadership*, p. 16). Cranfill's religious conversion came in July 1876, at a brush-arbor (outdoor camp) meeting, held along Hog Creek four miles outside Turnersville. He was a hard-shell Baptist who was licensed to preach by his parents in 1876. Cranfill disagreed with his church on certain issues and in 1877 stopped preaching. Nine years later, in 1886, he returned to the ministry, shortly after his 2½-year-old son died. He was zealous about politics too. Through his newspaper Cranfill issued a call for the first Prohibition Party convention in Texas, which was held in September 1886. Cranfill became chairman of the state executive committee.

At the end of 1886, Cranfill moved to Waco. He established a daily Waco newspaper, the *Advance.* From January to October 1889, he was financial secretary for Baylor University, a Baptist school. For the rest of his life

JOHN BIDWELL and JAMES B. CRANFILL
(From the Bidwell Mansion Association; candidate drawings are from
The Voice newspaper, the remainder being the author's conception)

Cranfill's activities revolved around the Baptist Church, prohibition, and writing. There was much overlap. Ordained a Baptist minister in 1890, he was called "young, active, unusually bright, resourceful and popular" (Riley, *History of Baptists*, p. 322). From 1890 to 1892 he was superintendent of Baptist mission work and in that capacity began publishing the *State Mission Journal*. In March 1892, Cranfill and another minister purchased the *Western Baptist* in 1892, moved it from Dallas to Waco, and renamed it the *Texas Baptist Standard*.

As leader of the Texas Prohibition Party, Cranfill was a delegate to the 1892 national convention. After a Californian was named for president, most delegates agreed that a Southerner should be his running mate. Five people were nominated, but one withdrew. Cranfill would not be old enough to serve as vice president until six months after the next year's inauguration, but even so was nominated on the second ballot. Cranfill began an active personal campaign in the South. In Wesson, Mis-

sissippi, a local lawyer spoke for the Democrats after Cranfill's speech. C.A. Hobbs, a friend who published the *Brookhaven Leader*, invited Cranfill to respond. Cranfill said too many people unthinkingly followed party labels. Cranfill read aloud from part of what he called the Democratic platform, and asked everyone who endorsed it to stand. Hundreds did, including his debate opponent. Cranfill then confessed that he had actually read from the hated Republican Party platform. The crowd laughed, and national news stories were made about his Wesson trick. It was hardly enough for victory: the party gained 2.3 percent of the national vote.

There were 50 years left in Cranfill's active life. A newspaper war was fought through the 1890s between Cranfill's *Texas Baptist Standard* and another Texas Baptist paper published by Samuel Hayden. The church became divided between the two men. In 1898 Cranfill moved his newspaper and himself to Dallas. He finally sold the paper in 1904 to George W. Carroll, who was the Prohibition Party's vice presidential nominee that year.

In politics, Cranfill opposed woman's suffrage, favored the unlimited coinage of silver as advocated by William Jennings Bryan in 1896, and took strong stands against labor unions. He applauded — as many prohibitionists did not — Carrie Nation's saloon-busting in Kansas. In 1908 he received some votes for president at the Prohibition Party's convention.

Cranfill wrote and edited extensively, particularly books about the Baptists and religion generally. During the resurgence of the Ku Klux Klan in the 1920s Cranfill courageously spoke out against them. Thirty-six years after his brief national campaign, Cranfill still found prohibition the central issue in 1928, and opposed Democratic presidential nominee Al Smith, a "wet" on the issue.

CRANFILL BIBLIOGRAPHY

Bailey, Emory E. *Who's Who in Texas.* Dallas (1931), p. 43.

Baker, Robert A. *The Blossoming Desert—A Concise History of Texas Baptists.* Waco (1970).

Blocker, Jack S., Jr. *Retreat from Reform: The Prohibition Movement in the United States, 1890–1913.* Westport, Conn. (1976).

Carroll, J.M. *A History of Texas Baptists.* Dallas (1923).

Colvin, D. Leigh. *Prohibition in the United States: A History of the Prohibition Party and of the Prohibition Movement.* New York (1926).

Cox, Norman Wade, et al., eds. *Encyclopedia of Southern Baptists.* Nashville (1958), vol. I, pp. 328–329.

Cranfill, J.B. *Dr. J.B. Cranfill's Chronicle: A Story of Life in Texas.* New York (1916).

_____. *From Memory: Reminiscences, Recitals, and Gleanings from a Bustling and Busy Life.* Nashville (1937).

_____. "Reminiscent," in Lowry, James H. comp., *History of the Texas Press and the Texas Press Association.* Wichita Falls (1929), pp. 174–181.

Elliott, L.R., ed. *Centennial Story of Texas Baptists.* Dallas (1936).

Gould, Lewis L. *Progressives and Prohibitionists: Texas Democrats in the Wilson Era.* Austin (1973).

Howe, Edgar F. *Biographical Sketches of General John Bidwell ... and Dr. James B. Cranfill, Prohibition Nominee for Vice President.* Redlands, Calif. (1892).

Knoles, George Harmon. *The Presidential Campaign and Election of 1892.* Stanford (1942).

Riley, B.F. *History of the Baptists of Texas.* Dallas (1907).

Storey, John W. *Texas Baptist Leadership and Social Christianity, 1900–1980.* College Station, Tex. (1986).

Summerlin, Travis L. "James Britton Buchanan Boone Cranfill," in *The New Handbook of Texas.* Austin (1996) p. 392.

Walker, J.L., and C.P. Lumpkin. *History of the Waco Baptist Association of Texas.* Waco (1897).

Election of 1896

NOMINATIONS

Republican Party Convention (11th): June 16–18, 1896, at a specially built auditorium, St. Louis, Mo. *President*—William McKinley, nominated on the first ballot with 661½ votes out of 902 cast. Thomas B. Reed (Me.), Levi Morton (Ind.), William B. Allison (Iowa), and Matthew Quay were also contenders. *Vice president*—Garret A. Hobart, nominated on the first ballot with 523½ votes out of 893 cast.

Henry Clay Evans (Tenn.) was the major other contender.

Democratic Party Convention (17th): July 7–11, 1896, at the Coliseum in Chicago, Ill. *President*—William Jennings Bryan, nominated on the fifth ballot with 652 votes out of 930 cast. He had received 137 on the first ballot. John R. McLean (Ohio), Joseph Sibley and Robert E. Pattison (Pa.), and Richard Bland (Mo.) were the other contenders. *Vice president*— Arthur Sewall, nominated on the fifth ballot with 602 votes out of 679 cast, after having received 100 on the first ballot.

Populist Party Convention (2d): July 22–25, 1896, the Auditorium, St. Louis, Missouri. *Vice president*— Thomas E. Watson, nominated on the first ballot with 539¾ votes to 257 for Arthur Sewall, and a scattering for others. The convention voted 738 to 638 to take up the nomination of a vice president first, because this was the central question — would the Populists join the Democrats and name Sewall, or make a separate ticket. *President*— William Jennings Bryan, nominated on the first ballot with 1042 votes; Seymour Norton (Ill.) had 321, with 12 scattered for others. Bryan had wired the convention after Watson had been nominated, saying he would not accept the Populist nomination without Sewall.

GENERAL ELECTION, November 3, 1896
Popular Vote

McKinley 7,104,779
Bryan (D) 6,502,925
Bryan (P) 222,253
Others 315,000

Electoral Vote
PRESIDENT

McKinley — 271 (23 states)
Bryan —176 (22 states)

VICE PRESIDENT

Hobart 271
Sewall 149
Watson 27

Winners

William McKinley, 26th president
Garret Hobart, 24th vice president

Losers

William Jennings Bryan, Arthur Sewall, Thomas E. Watson

1896 presidential nominee —
Democratic Party

William Jennings Bryan

Full name: William Jennings Bryan.
State represented: Nebraska.

Birth: March 19, 1860, at Salem, Illinois.

Age on Inauguration Day (March 4, 1897): 36 years, 11½ months.

Education: Whipple Academy in Jacksonville, Illinois (preparatory school), 1875–1877; Illinois College, 1877–1881; Union College of Law, Chicago, 1881–1883, admitted to bar, 1883.

Religion: Presbyterian.

Ancestry/prominent relatives: Scotch-Irish ancestors; William Smith Bryan arrived in America in 1650, settling in Virginia; Ruth Bryan Owen (daughter), U.S. representative from Florida. Charles W. Bryan (brother)— see Election of 1924.

Occupation: Attorney; lecturer; publisher and editor.

Public offices: U.S. representative, March 4, 1891–March 3, 1895; unsuccessful candidate for U.S. Senate, 1894; unsuccessful Democratic nominee for president, 1896, 1900, 1908; secretary of state, March 4, 1913–June 9, 1915, resigned.

Home: Lincoln, Nebraska; in 1902, built "Fairview," a country estate outside of Lincoln; in 1921 moved to Miami, Florida.

Death: July 26, 1925, in Dayton, Tennessee, at age 65 years, 4 months.

Burial: Arlington National Cemetery, Virginia.

Personal characteristics: Tall, broad-shouldered, at times almost fat; enormous head in proportion to his body; deep musical, "lute-like" voice with amazing carrying power.

Father: Silas Lillard Bryan (November 4, 1822–1880), farmer and local politician.

Mother: Maria Elizabeth Jennings (May 24, 1832–June 27, 1896); married on November 4, 1852, daughter of Charles Waters and Mariah W. (Davidson) Jennings).

Siblings: Virginia Ann Bryan (September 8, 1853–December 26, 1857). John Henshen Bryan (June 4, 1856–December 31, 1857). Frances Maria Bryan (March 18, 1858–December 6, 1934), married (1) Alfred C. Millson on March 6, 1877, and (2) married James W. Baird on June 8, 1893. Hiram Lillard Bryan (October 4, 1862–July 19, 1863). Russell Jones Bryan (June 12, 1864–August 11, 1881). Charles Wayland Bryan (February 10, 1867–March 4, 1945), married Elizabeth Louise Brokaw on

November 29, 1892. Nancy Lillard Bryan (November 4, 1869–January 30, 1904). Mary Elizabeth Bryan (May 14, 1872–April 25, 1962), married Thomas Stinson Allen on June 28, 1898.

Wife: Mary Elizabeth Baird (June 17, 1861–January 21, 1930), married on October 1, 1884, daughter of John and Lovina (Dexter) Baird.

Children: Ruth Baird Bryan (October 2, 1885–July 27, 1954), married (1) William Homer Leavitt on October 3, 1903, and (2) married Reginald Altham Owen on May 3, 1910, and (3) married Captain Borge Rohde on July 11, 1936; she was a U.S. representative. William Jennings Bryan, Jr. (June 24, 1889–?), married (1) Helen Virginia Berger on June 24, 1909, and (2) Ellen Bent Ballinger on January 30, 1929. Grace Dexter Bryan (February 17, 1891–September 1945), married Richard Lewis Hargreaves on June 7, 1911.

Historic sites/memorials: Lincoln, Nebraska, home, called "Fairview," is at 4900 Summer Street. Boyhood home in Salem, Illinois, is at 408 S. Broadway. Bryan's statue is one of two from Nebraska in Statuary Hall, in the Capitol. Bryan College, founded in 1930 and named for the candidate, is in the city in which the "monkey trial" took place — Dayton, Tennessee.

Movies: Two movies based on the Scopes "monkey trial" have been made: *Inherit the Wind* (1960), with Fredric March portraying Bryan and Spencer Tracy as Clarence Darrow; *Inherit the Wind* (1988), a made-for-television movie with Kirk Douglas as Bryan and Jason Robards as Darrow.

William Jennings Bryan's father was a lawyer, an unsuccessful candidate for Congress and, according to the son in his *Memoirs*, a devout Christian, as was his mother. The seeds of his own religious fervor were planted by this intensely religious household. His life became a crusade, with politics and religion being inextricably joined. His substantive accomplishments were meager, but he dragged his party, kicking and screaming, away from its conservative past into its first contact with the reform-minded attitudes that would be its future under such leaders as Woodrow Wilson and Franklin Roosevelt.

Though the family lived in Salem, Illinois, William was sent to Jacksonville, Illinois, in 1875 in order to get what was thought to be a more substantial education. While there he met Lyman Trumbull, Lincoln's friend and United States senator. Bryan "read" law in Trumbull's office and also attended law school. For a short time after completing his education he practiced law in Jacksonville, remaining at this from 1883 until 1887. While still not fully established in his profession, but feeling prosperous enough, he married the daughter of a merchant in 1884. She too became a lawyer and was a dominant influence in Bryan's life.

Bryan was restless in Jacksonville. He had become active in the local Democratic Party, but had not become prominent nor would prominence have really mattered, as Jacksonville was staunchly Republican. One firm dominated the legal profession in the city. He therefore sought appointment either to a post in Springfield or one in Washington. These efforts failed. Bryan took a seemingly insignificant journey to Kansas on legal business in the summer of 1887, and then continued on to Iowa to examine some land owned by his father-in-law. On his way he stayed with a law school friend in Lincoln, Nebraska, and immensely enjoyed his week-long visit. He decided to open a partnership with his friend and began his new career in Lincoln on October 1, 1887. His interest in the law continued to be secondary to his fascination with politics. In 1890, not yet in Nebraska three years, Bryan was elected to Congress by a substantial margin in what had been a safely Republican district. Farmers in Nebraska and throughout the Midwest were in the grips of a severe depression. Agrarian organizations were sprouting up. In Bryan's district an independent farmer's nominee for Congress was selected, who would have siphoned off valuable protest votes from Bryan. Yet before the election the independent candidate withdrew, leaving Bryan to face a much weaker farmers' candidate and the Republican incumbent William J. Connell. Vigorous campaigning by the energetic, youthful and dynamic Bryan, coupled with the economic hard times, gained the victory for Bryan.

Bryan was reelected in 1892 but by a much-reduced margin, primarily due to gerrymandering of his district by the Republican legislature. In 1894, perhaps fearing defeat for a third term, Bryan campaigned for the United States Senate. Prior to the adoption of the 17th Amendment in 1913, senators were elected by the states' legislatures. Bryan's Senate campaign was therefore in behalf of legislative candidates he thought would be favorable to him. Bryan's chief political issue was his unswerving support for the free coinage of silver. He argued in Congress and on the stump in behalf of his theories. No assemblage was too small to attract his zealous advocacy. The arcane details of the silver argument are too convoluted for quick explanation. In simple terms, though, advocates of the unlimited coinage of silver were attacking an act of Congress passed in 1873 that removed any statutory provision for the coinage of silver. This act was passed at a time when the value of silver was sufficiently high that few owners of silver presented their metal for coinage, since there were other, more profitable uses. When the price of silver fell after the 1873 act, the government mints would not accept the silver for coinage since there was no law authorizing it. To individuals already suspicious that the monied interests controlled the federal government, the omission of the coinage of silver appeared to be a plot to keep the money supply and prices low. So long as inflation was checked, creditors who loaned money could be assured of repayment with dollars that were worth at least as much if not more than the dollars they had earlier loaned. Several economic panics occurred after the new law, one during 1873 itself; many hurt by the recessions blamed the economic disaster on the restricted money supply. The battle cries were "free and unlimited coinage of silver" and "sixteen to one." The latter phrase referred to the ratio of coinage between gold and silver that had existed from 1837 until the 1873 congressional enactment. This became Bryan's issue, one that took him to his party's presidential nomination, but no further. Both facts significantly map the breadth, but also the limits, of the silver issue.

Bryan's oratory had been impressive during his first race for Congress. It became far better appreciated while he was a congressman.

His labors brought him wide familiarity in the silver movement. When the 1896 Democratic convention opened in Chicago, it was controlled by the silver forces. Bryan was chosen as one of the speakers for silver, and his immortal phrasing swept the convention:

> You shall not press down upon the brow of labor this crown of thorns; you shall not crucify mankind upon a cross of gold.

The effect on the crowd was incredible. The well-remembered lines were but two in a host of phrases that enraptured his already silver-crazed listeners. These closing lines of Bryan's speech left his listeners emotionally drained and almost overcome with the power of his delivery; he was almost to his seat before the stunned and awestruck silence of the convention hall was shattered by an explosion of cheers and applause that lasted half an hour.

Bryan was not an innocent participant in a great drama. Bryan wanted the nomination desperately, and he laid his groundwork well. His prime strategy was to avoid too early an appearance before the convention so that his oratorical powers would be saved until the most propitious moment. Complicated maneuvering was necessary even to get his delegation seated, as a rival anti-silver Nebraska delegation was also competing for a seat on the convention floor. Bryan even had to prevent his election as permanent chairman of the convention, a position that would have thrust him forward too soon and diluted his impact. For all his efforts he was rewarded with the nomination on the fifth ballot.

Bryan was the youngest man ever nominated for president. His thirty-sixth birthday had been in March, so Bryan would on inauguration day in 1897 be only two years beyond the constitutional minimum of 35. His youth as well as his inexperience, with merely two terms in Congress, were focal points of the opposition's attack on him. The strategy of the Republican nominee, William McKinley, was to remain home in Canton, Ohio, while others conducted his campaign. Bryan, perhaps thereby intentionally emphasizing his youth and energy, took the exact opposite approach of vigorous, nationwide personal campaigning. Eighteen thousand miles by train and other conveyances passed by before election day arrived, which was probably the most demanding schedule attempted by any presidential candidate to that date. Bryan made the election a referendum on silver and on the big businesses he felt were draining the workingmen of all their livelihood.

The election was close. Shortly before the balloting, the depressed farm prices that had been boosting Bryan's candidacy suddenly soared because of crop failures in other countries. The price of gold began to drop because of new gold discoveries and new processing techniques. Bryan's issues were turning against him. He was also faced with a splinter Democratic ticket peeling off votes, enough to cost him a few key states. As it was, Bryan was short 600,000 votes out of 13,600,000 cast. He was left, however, the dominant voice in the Democratic Party and primed for a rematch.

After this defeat, Bryan's efforts were primarily directed towards advancing the silver cause through speeches, the organization of speakers' bureaus to blanket the country, and the election of candidates who were committed to silver. Bryan also attempted to purge the Democratic Party leadership of any gold standard supporters, including those in state party leadership positions. Bryan's sights were clearly and candidly aimed at 1900.

The Spanish-American War intervened, and Bryan became a vigorous supporter of American involvement. The governor of Nebraska authorized Bryan to raise a regiment for service in Cuba, but the former presidential nominee languished in Florida preparing for service throughout the short war and never saw combat. Camp life was rigorous, and the extreme Florida heat and the tropical insects severely wracked the regiment that had volunteered to serve with Bryan, many because they were avid Bryan and silver supporters. Typhoid ravaged the regiment as well. Bryan became ill, but continued his efforts to make certain that his troops were well tended. The silver regiment became something of a political pawn, with the McKinley administration and the army itself apparently considering political questions in determining whether to allow it to go to Cuba, remain in Florida, or to disband. Once Spain's surrender was announced on August 12, 1898, President McKinley declared that a substantial number of the volunteers would be released from service. If Bryan and his regiment were released, then Bryan would be freed to return to the political wars. Instead, they were left on active duty, forcing Bryan to choose between political inactivity in Florida or the dangerous appearance of resigning from service and returning to politics while his regiment remained in Florida. The decision was put off until December 10, when Spain signed the peace treaty. Bryan took the occasion to resign his commission after serving for five months.

The Spanish War brought the new issue of imperialism. Bryan merely added a new section to his stock speeches on silver and now also attacked the evils of expansion. However, he desired that the treaty already negotiated with Spain that gave the United States control of Cuba and the Philippines, be accepted for the interim and later efforts be made to withdraw from the newly occupied territories. The attempt to argue both for expansion and his push for a Congressional resolution supporting eventual Filipino independence seemed too nice a political distinction for many voters. Bryan lost support among some of his old silver allies, who primarily were also antiimperialists.

Bryan spent 1899 preparing for the next presidential election. The candidate seemed intent on besting his travel record set in the 1896 campaign. Many new groups were potentially receptive to Bryan because of imperialism and the trust questions, but were frightened away by Bryan's continued silver advocacy. Silver was beginning to dwindle in popular acceptance and even interest. The country appeared to be moving on to new battles, but Bryan was not. This led to a perception of Bryan that continued throughout his career — obstinate and even naive refusal to accept a changing world.

As the 1900 Kansas City Democratic national convention approached, several efforts were made to push forward an alternative to Bryan, but with little impact. Still, Bryan had a difficult time at the convention itself in getting the silver plank he wanted. He even had to issue an ultimatum that unless silver was again endorsed, he would refuse the nomination. By a single vote in the platform committee, the plank was adopted. Knowing of the need for broadening his appeal, however, Bryan permitted imperialism to be characterized as the dominant issue of the campaign. Bryan's moral crusade against McKinley's foreign policy was unpopular. The American people generally supported the territorial ambitions expressed by the Republicans. As vocal and energetic as the cause of anti-imperialism was, it was no more than a determined minority. Bryan also tried to make the election a class war. What in 1896 was only a footnote, accusing the Republicans of being the party of the rich and unfeeling few while the Democrats were the party of the people, became a much more pronounced chapter in 1900.

The result was the same as 1896. Defeat was somewhat greater, increased by general prosperity, the satisfaction with the war results, and Bryan's growing image as a radical with unsound ideas.

Bryan in defeat was not yet ready to give up the struggle. He began the *Commoner*, a newspaper that was distributed by mail nationwide. On January 23, 1901, the first weekly issue appeared. Bryan was the principal editorialist and the editor. Though many lucrative business offers came his way, he continued to have his sights on the presidency. Public lecturing became Bryan's chief occupation in an attempt to keep his name prominent. His issue more frequently was imperialism, particularly after the aggressive Theodore Roosevelt succeeded McKinley following the president's assassination in 1901.

Bryan became sufficiently wealthy from his lecturing and other ventures to move from the modest home in Lincoln into a country estate named Fairview. The completed home was ready in 1902, but Bryan had begun his serious planning of the estate in 1893 when he purchased the property. Shortly after the house was completed he also indulged himself and his wife with a long-discussed tour of Europe, one that permitted him a several-day visit with Russian author Leo Tolstoy. Both participants apparently were impressed.

The 1904 national convention in St. Louis was a rout of Bryan forces. Even the venerated silver issue was discarded and those in favor of gold wrote the platform. Bryan was a delegate and carried the fight for his principles to the floor of the convention. Bryan endorsed no candidate, but was unalterably opposed to the eventual nominee, New York judge Alton B. Parker. Parker had remained silent on the money question, but after his nomination he sent a telegram to the convention that he would not run unless the convention accepted his support of the gold standard. The convention attempted to sidestep the issue, merely saying that there was no expectation that the monetary standard would be involved in the 1904 election and a supporter of the gold standard was therefore acceptable. Bryan spoke forcefully to the contrary, but did not prevail.

Parker was more overwhelmingly defeated than had been Bryan in either of his previous campaigns. Parker sought Bryan's support but never received more than acquiescence in the nomination. Bryan was in some respects vindicated by the results, though in truth the explanation for the election outcome lies much more in the fascinating appeal of Theodore Roosevelt than in any other factor.

The routing of the anti–Bryan forces in November 1904 opened the door to yet another Bryan nomination in 1908. President Roosevelt's own progressivism, in which he adopted many of Bryan's anti-wealth attacks, made Bryan himself seem less radical. The young Bryan had scared many people, but an older one seemed more acceptable, if only because of familiarity. Bryan performed his pre-convention tasks well, and no serious opponent for the 1908 nomination surfaced. Bryan's third election attempt was his most disastrous; he received a lower percentage of the vote in the 1908 election than in his other two campaigns. His time seemed to have passed, though he was only 48 years old.

In defeat Bryan returned to the lecture circuit. He continued to push progressive ideals to an eager audience, though apparently always less than a majority of the country. Bryan wanted to retain his position as the leader of the national Democratic Party and to prevent a conservative candidate from gaining the 1912 nomination. Bryan remained publicly neutral between several rival candidates, foremost among whom were Woodrow Wilson, governor of New Jersey, and speaker of the U.S. House of Representatives, Champ Clark. More and more, however, Bryan appeared to be favoring Wilson. At the convention the battle between Clark and Wilson continued through ballot after ballot. Bryan delivered a speech in the convention that accused Clark of being supported by the corrupt and monied New York interests. Unless they withdrew their support he would vote for Wilson, even though for all previous ballots he had voted for Clark. Bedlam ensued. Bryan's tactics made many believe he was trying so to disrupt the front-runners that he finally would become the nominee. His wife Mary's own insistence that he become a candidate, and the prospect of an easy Democratic victory over the fragmented Republicans, lends credence to the theory. After 46 ballots, Wilson was nominated, however, and Bryan for whatever motivations was partially responsible for preventing Clark from gaining the prize.

As reward for his position in the party, Bryan was offered his choice of cabinet posts by the victorious Wilson. Bryan chose the State Department, a post for which he had no training. Wilson acceded. Bryan served from 1913 until June 1915, when Wilson's increasingly militaristic and anti–German statements caused Bryan's resignation. Bryan was a complete pacifist at this time. He probably felt that his singular achievement as secretary of state was the negotiation and signing of peace treaties with 29 nations. When Wilson no longer maintained strict neutrality with the warring European factions, Bryan felt he could no longer serve. Yet Wilson and Bryan parted on friendly terms and Bryan continued to support the president in almost every respect. When Wilson ran for reelection in 1916, Bryan worked on his campaign.

Bryan faded from prominence in Democratic Party affairs. He continued to advise Wilson during the Democrat's second term. During Wilson's greatest failure as president — his obstinacy on the League of Nations Treaty — Bryan advised compromise, which of course was rejected. During the 1920 presidential race, Bryan again went to the convention as a delegate. Prohibition and support for the League of Nations were his passions. The decline in Bryan's influence is obvious from the fact that the eventual nominee, James M. Cox of Ohio, was against prohibition.

In 1921, Bryan moved to Florida, where his wife's bad health would with luck improve. His religious fundamentalism, perhaps gained from his parents' own religious fervor, led to the final major chapter in his life. In 1924, Bryan wrote a statute passed by the Florida legislature prohibiting the teaching of evolution or any other theory that linked man with lesser animals. He carried the message to college audiences and to churches, trying to stem the tide of modernism that he saw as anti-religious. Tennessee in 1925 passed a bill similar to Bryan's. John Scopes ignored the statute in a test case managed by the American Civil Liberties Union. An attorney for the prosecution invited Bryan to participate in the trial, rightly believing that Bryan would gain a national audience for the affair. On July 19, 1925, the trial began. World attention had indeed been gained. The trial proceeded for ten days. Though fireworks at times erupted, the real drama began with the unexpected but strategically planned calling of Bryan to the witness stand by the defense, led by Clarence Darrow. Bryan felt he could not refuse and maintain his self-respect. He therefore acquiesced, though legally he need not have. Clarence Darrow, almost as nationally famous as was Bryan, attempted to force Bryan into logical dilemmas by asking the witness to explain his beliefs regarding whether each statement in the Bible was literal truth, from Eve being created from Adam's rib, to the serpent tempting Eve, to the swallowing of Jonah by a whale. Bryan emerged from the ordeal exhausted and sweating profusely. Not only were Darrow's questions heated, but the courtroom itself was sweltering in the unairconditioned summer heat. The popular perception of Bryan's statements on the Bible was that he was an unthinking, narrow-minded fundamentalist whose low-wattage intelligence caused him to be trapped into absurd defenses. Other fundamentalists accused Bryan of acknowledging too frequently that some of the Bible was allegorical or metaphorical, and that some of the Biblical statements were merely instructive and not to be taken as actual events. Bryan failed both his audiences.

Apparently Bryan did not feel that he had failed, and many of his supporters agreed. Bryan desired the next day to examine Darrow himself in a reversal of the previous day's roles, but the long trial made his fellow prosecution attorneys veto the plan. Neither side made closing arguments. This was a second defeat for Bryan since apparently he had labored for months over the speech he would deliver to the jury. Thus another chance for clarification and vindication was thwarted. The jury deliberated briefly and found the defendant Scopes guilty. He was given a fine and not imprisoned.

Bryan desired to stay on in the Dayton area for several days to dictate the speech he was denied an opportunity to give. He was to address a few scattered audiences and vacation in the gorgeous scenery at the nearby Smoky Mountains. Five days after the verdict, Bryan died in his sleep. The place that history records as the site of his greatest humiliation was, perhaps not quite fittingly, the place of his death.

Analysis of Qualifications

The image of William Jennings Bryan today is negative. It is one of defeat. What is most remembered is the "Monkey Trial," the Dayton evolution vs. creation trial that has always been considered his humiliation. Compounding that image is the fact that his political career is noted for three other rejections, his races for the presidency. Though the image is too one-sided, nonetheless history has properly considered Bryan not to have been suited to the presidency.

Bryan was an ideologue, in politics and in religion. He was a moralist and evangelist, not a statesman. He became fixed on an idea and could not be shaken. Though he was too much criticized for lacking intelligence, particularly after the Dayton trial, it does appear that he had neither imagination nor intellectual brilliance.

Bryan's ideas were heavily glossed with his religious fervor. This was particularly obvious in his later years, but throughout his career he was a moral and religious leader who was sincere in his professions of faith. His pacifist reign as secretary of state in President Wilson's cabinet was the one opportunity in an official position to further his principles.

Bryan's first race for the presidency revealed starkly his belief that America's economic strength lay not in big business or business leaders but in the common man who would escape economic depression by the simple fact of being given free and unlimited coinage of silver. He believed that the causes of America's troubles were a conspiracy, by those Theodore Roosevelt would call the "malefactors of great wealth," to exclude all but themselves from America's bounty. Bryan truly was the father of the Democratic Party's alliance with small business, blue-collar workers, the Negro voters, and the remainder of what first elected Woodrow Wilson and later became the Franklin D. Roosevelt coalition. Not only did Bryan champion the cause of the underprivileged and the common man, he identified with them. His newspaper was called the *Commoner*, and he himself was tagged the "Great Commoner."

He was an outstanding, uniquely gifted orator, who moved even his opponents not so much by the substance of his speeches, but instead by their form and delivery. He was energetic and set new and at times ridiculed standards for campaigning for a presidential candidate. He also had courage, the courage of a man sure of his positions and certain of his opponents' error and even venality. Yet for all this, Bryan shares with Henry Clay the distinction of being the only man to be three times nominated and three times defeated for president.

Bryan was defeated because people were afraid of Bryanism. This represented to a majority of Americans who each time voted for his opponent that he was an economic heretic who little understood the complexities of the business world and who, if placed in charge of the country, would bring the economy to ruins. The fear appears justified. Free silver and the money supply are but parts of a much more complicated monetary and fiscal fabric. The chances that "free silver" would have righted the economy in 1896 or continued its boom in 1900 are slim. Silver was but one example of Bryan's great failing, his view of the whole world and its complex problems as black and white, good vs. evil, big business vs. the people.

To his credit, Bryan was a man somewhat ahead of the electorate in sponsoring progressive ideas. Much of what he promoted in 1896 and 1900 was, by 1904, being championed by Teddy Roosevelt. Yet for all of his mass appeal, his oratory, his attractiveness physically, Bryan must be summarized as a brilliant package that appeared to have not much substance. His heart was as golden as his tongue, his morals as untainted as his record of defeat. He was a lifelong teetotaler, a devoted family man, a religious tower. Yet there is nothing in his record of public life that makes one believe he had the administrative skills, the imagination, or the mental agility to govern. The likely result of election would have been continued rigidity and continued support for policies that could neither have caused domestic prosperity nor dealt realistically with foreign affairs.

BRYAN BIBLIOGRAPHY

Ashby, Leroy. *William Jennings Bryan: Champion of Democracy*. Boston (1987).
"Bryan Family Genealogy." Typescript in collection of Nebraska State Historical Society, Lincoln.
Bryan, William Jennings. *The First Battle*. Chicago (1896).
_____, with Mary Baird Bryan. *The Memoirs of William Jennings Bryan*. Philadelphia (1925).
Cherny, Robert W. *A Righteous Cause: The Life of William Jennings Bryan*. Glenview, Ill. (1985).
Coletta, Paolo E. *William Jennings Bryan*, vol. I: *Political Evangelist, 1860–1908*; vol. II, *Progressive Politician and Moral Statesman, 1909–1915*; vol. III, *Political Puritan, 1915–1925*. Lincoln, Nebr. (1964–1970).
Ginger, Ray. *William Jennings Bryan: Selections*. Indianapolis (1967).
Glad, Paul W. *The Trumpet Soundeth: William Jennings Bryan and His Democracy, 1896–1912*. Lincoln, Nebr. (1960).
Heinlein, Robert A. *JOB: A Comedy of Justice*. New York (1984) (novel: in each of several alternate universes Bryan and Sewall's success or failure in 1896 is the pivotal event in American history).
Hibben, Paxton, completed by C. Hartley Grattan. *The Peerless Leader: William Jennings Bryan*. New York City (1929).
Koenig, Louis W. *Bryan: A Political Biography of William Jennings Bryan*. New York City (1971).
Larson, Julie. "A Narrative Analysis of the Scopes Trial." Unpublished doctoral dissertation, University of Southern California (1995).
Levine, Lawrence W. *Defender of the Faith, William Jennings Bryan: The Last Decade, 1915–1925*. New York City (1965).
Long, J.C. *Bryan, the Great Commoner*. New York City (1928).
Rosser, Charles McDaniel. *The Crusading Commoner: A Close-up of William Jennings Bryan and His Times*. Dallas (1937).
Vickers, Sarah Pauline. "The Life of Ruth Bryan Owen...." Unpublished doctoral dissertation, Florida State University (1994).

---

*1896 vice presidential nominee —
Democratic Party*

Arthur Sewall

Full name: Arthur Sewall.

State represented: Maine.

Birth: November 25, 1835, in Bath, Maine.

Age on Inauguration Day (March 4, 1897): 61 years, 3½ months.

Education: Bath, Maine, common schools.

Religion: Attended the Bath Swedenborgian Church (Church of the New Jerusalem).

Ancestry/prominent relatives: First Sewall arrived in America in 1634, settling in Massachusetts; among Arthur's ancestors were three chief justices of Massachusetts, another was named first president of Harvard College but declined; distantly related to Longfellow and Grover Cleveland; Arthur Sewall's son Harold March Sewall was a politician and diplomat.

Occupation: Shipbuilder.

Public office: Bath city council member; Bath alderman, 1876–1877; defeated for U.S. Senate, 1893; defeated Democratic nominee for vice president, 1896.

Home: Summer home at Small Point, Maine; large, comfortable home in Bath.

Death: September 5, 1900, at Small Point, Maine, at 64 years, 9½ months.

Burial: Maple Grove Cemetery, Bath, Maine.

Personal characteristics: Heavy build, almost 6 feet tall; always handsomely and expensively tailored; dignified air, almost aristocratic; mustache.

Father: William Dunning Sewall (Novem-

WILLIAM JENNINGS BRYAN and ARTHUR SEWALL
(Reproduced from the Collections of the Library of Congress)

ber 27, 1795–January 30, 1877); shipbuilder, politician.

Mother: Rachel Trufant (October 26, 1797–November 14, 1878), daughter of William Trufant.

Siblings: Edward Sewall (September 23, 1833–March 21, 1879), shipbuilder. Harriet Hyde Sewall (?–?), married Joseph Ropes. William Dunning Sewall (1827–1851). Frank Sewall (September 24, 1837–December 7, 1915), a minister. Alice Worcester Sewall (?–?).

Wife: Emma Duncan Crooker (September 17, 1836–September 29, 1919); married 1859; daughter of Charles and Rachel (Sewall) Crooker of Bath; Emma was a distant cousin of Arthur's.

Children: Harold March (January 3, 1860–October 28, 1924), politician; married Camilla Loyall Ashe in September 1893. Dummer (August 15, 1864–October 7, 1866). William Dunning (April 14, 1861–April 25, 1930), ship-

builder; married Mary Locke Sumner on June 9, 1886.

Historic sites/memorials: Sewall House, 963 Washington Street, Bath, Maine; the 1844 Sewall mansion is part of the Maine Maritime Museum. The year he died, a ship named the *Arthur Sewall* was launched by his company. It disappeared after setting sail from Delaware Breakwater for Seattle on April 2, 1906, with a cargo of 4,900 tons of coal.

Like a few of his fellow losing running mates, Arthur Sewall was a businessman first, a politician a distant second. A few years before his nomination for vice president, it was said that he had four major interests — his family, the American Merchant Marine, politics, and railroads. Sincerely and openly religious, Sewall found many outlets for his energy other than politics. As a Democrat in overwhelmingly Republican Maine there were few election offices to which he could aspire.

Arthur would before reaching his twentieth birthday form a partnership with his older brother for the purpose of constructing ships. Their father had begun the family's shipbuilding business in Bath, Maine, in 1823. The elder Sewall was among the earliest and most prominent shipbuilders in Bath, and also was active in political and railroad circles. An 1877 newspaper article said of Arthur's father:

> At the time of his marriage and before and sometime after he was managing his grandfather's farm. Within two or three years afterward he began trade with the late Freeman Clark.... After being engaged in trade two or three years he purchased the York lot.... The lot was at that time covered with excellent ship timber. Immediately after the purchase of this lot, Mr. Sewall began the great business of his life, shipbuilding. He built at first a small vessel of some two or three hundred tons. He continued to be steadily and actively occupied in this business for fifty years....

Arthur's education was in the local Bath schools, but a more significant education for the future shipbuilder was the practical experience he gained at home and at sea. While still a teenager, he was sent to purchase ship timber at Prince Edward Island, and in 1854 he formed a partnership with his older brother, Edward, using the name of E & A Sewall. The brothers' first ship was the *Holyhead*, of over 1,000 tons. This partnership lasted for 25 years, and on average one ship per year was built during that period. Before the Sewall brothers started their own shipbuilding business, their father's company had in 1841 completed what was then the largest merchant ship sailing under the American flag, the *Rappahannock*. Almost 50 years later, Arthur Sewall would himself build a ship called the *Rappahannock*, which would then be the largest wooden sailing vessel under the American flag.

Five years after Arthur Sewall began his shipbuilding career, he married Emma Crooker, the daughter of another longtime shipbuilder. She was a highly educated woman for her day, who had traveled extensively, had learned French fluently, and was described as "an artist with pen and camera, and a historical student." Three sons were born to the marriage, two of whom grew to adulthood.

As a young man of 23, Arthur visited the South, there to learn firsthand about the ports and to gain practical knowledge of the cotton industry, such a vital part of shipping to the Sewall partnership. For 30 days he lived aboard one of his ships, seeing the problems of the ship's captain, understanding the difficulties with crew and cargo on a long voyage. In ways like these, Arthur Sewall soon became more than a youthful heir to a shipping business; he became an experienced and capable manager of that business.

During the 25 years the two Sewall brothers operated their business, the old construction yard tripled in size. The ships grew larger, and the number of employees increased steadily. They continued to build wooden sailing vessels even after the Civil War, when many companies, particularly in England, were building steam-powered and even steel vessels. The company never built any clipper ships, but specialized in large merchant vessels.

In 1879, brother Edward Sewall was fatally injured at the shipyard, and the company was reorganized as A. Sewall & Co. The Sewall company craftsmen, as well as the captains of Sewall ships, were invariably natives of the Bath and Kennebec Valley region. The family atmosphere at Sewall & Co. was intensified by the fact that the senior partner was able to and at times did perform every task in the shipyard.

During the Civil War, the Sewalls refused to hide the American origin of their ships by having them sail under foreign flags. As a result, one of their vessels was captured on her maiden voyage by a Confederate raider.

While finding his work as head of one of the largest shipbuilding firms in Maine exciting and fulfilling, Sewall was drawn to other pursuits as well. He was a director of the Maine Central Railroad beginning in 1875 and its president since 1884. Until he resigned in 1893, Sewall had been president of at least one of the Maine two-foot gauge railroads, the Phillips & Rangeley. He had also been a director of president of at least four other railroads. His management of the Maine Central for nine years made that rather small, regional railroad sufficiently successful to make it an attractive target for takeover. The larger Boston and Maine did just that in November 1893 and ousted Sewall as president. He lost interest in being actively involved with railroads, perhaps out of disgust. Besides railroading, Sewall had found banking a major sidelight interest. For almost 30 years he was president of the Bath National Bank.

The shipbuilder's political involvement was much constrained by the strong Republican voting habits of the Maine electorate. The highest and only elective offices he ever held were as a city councilman and city alderman of Bath. He attended every Democratic national convention from 1872 through 1900 except for the one of 1876. That year, though not in attendance at the convention, he was a strong admirer of Samuel J. Tilden. Sewall would always believe that Tilden had victory stolen from him in that controversial election. In 1888 and 1892, he was elected at the national convention to the Democratic National Committee. He was not a strong supporter of Grover Cleveland and totally disagreed with Cleveland's support of the gold standard. In 1893, the same year he was defeated in the Maine legislature for the United States Senate, Sewall wrote a friend to discuss his opinion of President Cleveland. In the letter he castigated the president for supporting the gold standard, and instead called for the free and unlimited coinage of silver. Three years later he would have his opinions adopted by the Democratic Party when it selected William Jennings Bryan as its presidential candidate, and Sewall himself for vice president.

Between the conventions of 1892 and 1896, Sewall started the last great episode in his shipbuilding career. He realized that the day of the wooden sailing ship would soon be over and decided to begin construction of the first American-built steel vessels. A good friend, Thomas Hyde, had begun a sizeable iron works in Bath. Sewall's shipbuilding craftsmen knew little about working with iron and steel, and therefore Sewall imported the builder of a British ship for the project. The new superintendent of construction brought plans from England for the new vessel. The first American steel vessel, the *Dirigo*, was soon under

construction at the Sewall yard. Sewall and his imported superintendent were both hard-headed individuals, and before the ship was completed the superintendent had left. The *Dirigo* slid into the Kennebec River in 1894. The firm built four additional steel sailing vessels, still avoiding the use of steam as the motive power. One of these ships, the *William Frye*, would in 1915 be the first American merchant ship to be destroyed by the German navy when it was sunk in route to Liverpool.

When Sewall began his steel vessel construction, the country was in a severe depression. Few people were building ships at that stage, and after construction was finished, there was not sufficient cargo for the ship to carry. Nonetheless, Sewall continued to build the steel vessels. Three years after Sewall's death, the shipyard closed. Most of the ships in the 50 years that Arthur Sewall had been involved in the business were built for his own company. Sewall's successors continued to operate the ships until 1916, when the firm of A. Sewall & Co. finally was dissolved.

The great shipbuilder and railroad executive held a tight grip on the state's minuscule Democratic Party. When the delegation to the 1896 national convention was selected, most desired ridding the party of Sewall's influence. As an advocate of free silver, Sewall was in the minority among Maine Democrats on this central issue in the campaign. The delegation from Maine removed Sewall as its member on the national committee, and "The Senior," as he was called within his company, wired his wife that he was now forever done with politics. She could not have been more pleased. He could not have been more wrong.

William Jennings Bryan's capture of the national convention in 1896 is a story told elsewhere (see pages 425–426). Sewall's nomination also needs to be explained. It was a free silver convention; to that degree the Maine shipbuilder's selection can be understood. Yet Sewall was also a millionaire businessman, opposed to free trade and in favor of the high tariff, unabashedly American and almost imperialistic in his foreign policy views. Thus on most issues other than the monetary one, Bryan and Sewall did not see alike. Many of the other possibilities for vice president refused to be considered, being afraid of the association with the boy orator from Nebraska. Bryan in his *Memoirs* years later said he had no preference for a running mate, thought a Southerner would be a good choice, but left the matter to the convention with some veto right. The leading contender, John R. McLean of Ohio, might have won easily except Bryan threatened to resign from the ticket if the wealthy McLean were named. Many men were nominated, and Sewall remained at the convention for four ballots. He did not appear to be a serious contender during this early voting, and he therefore left the convention and went to the train station to leave. There, waiting for his train, he was notified that he had received the vice presidential nomination. Sewall's selection seemed to be an attempt to give the ticket respectability, to join the "radical" with a dignified businessman who could calm the more conservative elements in the party.

Since Sewall had been so little involved in national politics, the initial reaction to his nomination was "Who is Sewall?" Those curious about Sewall would not find out much more about him during the campaign, as he and Bryan agreed that Sewall would give few speeches and let that particular task remain with the presidential candidate.

Bryan was also nominated by the Populist Party. The Populists saw no reason to accept the conservative compromise of Sewall as a running mate. Instead, they nominated Georgia Populist leader Tom Watson. Watson and Sewall bickered some during the ensuing campaign as to who should quit the ticket with Bryan. Watson caustically described Sewall as "a wart on the ticket. He is a knot on the log. He is a dead weight to the ticket." Bryan had telegraphed the Populist convention and told them to "withdraw my name if Sewall is not nominated." They did not follow his instructions. Different versions of the telegram circulated among the Populists, including a rumor that Sewall would be replaced by whomever the Populists named. Sewall sent some messages of his own, stating "any statements or inferences that I propose to withdraw from the ticket are without foundation. I never had and have not now the remotest intention of doing so."

The campaign turned so much into a class war between the "people" represented by Bryan and the property interest represented by McKinley that Sewall seemed out of place on the Democratic side of that conflict. Yet he was a loyal Bryan supporter and was optimistic about the ticket's chances of success. The vote was relatively close, but still a clear defeat for the Democrats. Sewall had eagerly joined in making the free coinage of silver the major issue of the campaign. On that score and many others the people of Bath by and large disagreed with their native son. Nonetheless, Sewall received a warm reception in his hometown during the campaign, was treated to a large parade, and spoke when Bryan came to join his running mate to one of the largest crowds ever gathered in Bath. Despite these showings of respect, the people of Bath overwhelmingly rejected the Bryan-Sewall ticket, as did Maine as a whole. Sewall was an aloof figure in Bath; few people knew him well. Those who were mere acquaintances more often than not thought him cold and almost arrogant. An issue in 1896 had been the allegations that he was an exploiter of his labor force, but many of his workers came to his defense. It is probably true to say that labor relations were not enlightened in many industrial settings during the 1890s, and Sewall's was little better but certainly no worse than most.

Despite his stilted public demeanor, Sewall was a warm and charitable individual with friends. He remarked in 1893 that he seemed to have few friends in the world, "and my experience is teaching me every day to value them more and more, and I hope their number, though very few, will not grow less." One of his closest friends and advisors was the Swedenborgian minister in Bath, Dr. Samuel Dike. They were often seen together walking or riding in a carriage, talking about religious issues. So devoted did the two men become, that in 1890 upon Dr. Dike's retirement, Sewall sent him on an around-the-world tour with no limit on his expenses. Sewall's charities included being a director of the Old Ladies' Home in Bath, as well as being an active member and leader of the Swedenborgian church.

"The Senior's" nomination for vice president made him no more of a political force in Maine than he had been before. In the remaining four years of his life after the 1896 convention, he continued his work as a shipbuilder, calmly if somewhat sadly resigned to his defeat. His health was bad the last few years of his life, and he traveled both to the South and to the dry far West in search of his health. Three years before his death, a large life insurance company refused to issue him a policy because a medical examiner thought he had Bright's Disease. Apparently he did not have that particular ailment, and the cause of his death was diagnosed as apoplexy.

Analysis of Qualifications

One of the questions asked after the Democratic national convention of 1896 was "Who is Arthur Sewall?" After that question was answered — millionaire banker, merchant, and shipbuilder — the next inquiry was "What is he doing on the ticket with William J. Bryan?" So many could not give a rational answer to the second question that the Populist Party rejected Sewall at its subsequent convention, even over the threat that Bryan would not accept their presidential nomination unless Sewall was named as his running mate.

There was more to Arthur Sewall than the few details that filtered out during the campaign. Rumors that he had serious labor problems at his shipyard were apparently exaggerations, though his defense is almost as suspect that there was an esprit de corps and family atmosphere at the Sewall shipyard. As a businessman, Sewall was eminently successful, in the rather parochial setting of Bath, Maine. He was president of the small Bath National Bank, president of the small Maine Central Railroad, and one of the largest shipbuilders in the state. He was not innovative in his business, but instead was conservative and safe. Perhaps his best-remembered accomplishment was the construction of the first steel vessels in America, but that was long after Britain had begun the construction not only of steel ships, but ones that were powered by steam. The latter was an advance that Sewall ignored; they continued to build even into the twentieth century only sailing ships. Sewall never served in a higher public office than the city council of Bath, and that only for one year.

As a politician Sewall was one of the major forces in the completely insignificant Maine Democratic Party, whose existence could be compared to that of the Republican Party in one of the Deep South states during the first decades of the twentieth century. His grip on the party had antagonized many, as had his apostasy in the business community of favoring the coinage of silver. Ironically, just prior to his vice presidential nomination he was ousted from party leadership in the state. Sewall was no leader of men, but instead a dignified, somewhat aloof, intelligent man who did not appeal to a broad spectrum. He himself remarked how few friends he seemed to have. Still, he was a decent man who just did not have the natural abilities or inclination to be an outgoing, graceful and sociable politician.

Arthur Sewall may well have risen to the occasion of being thrust into the presidency. However, nothing in his past gives much basis for being confident that this small town banker and businessman, successful though he was, had the stuff of which good presidents are made. He had not demonstrated political leadership capability, nor experienced the give and take of legislative battles. Sewall had no familiarity with national issues, nor with national leaders. He did have opinions — he wanted the free coinage of silver, favored the annexation of Hawaii, and wanted an independent Cuba. But he had dealt with no national problems on a first-hand basis. The Democrats were indeed risking greatly when they offered this intelligent, but inexperienced and aloof Maine businessman, as a man to stand within a heartbeat of the presidency. He should not have been nominated.

SEWALL BIBLIOGRAPHY

Baker, William Avery. *A Maritime History of Bath, Maine and the Kennebec River Region.* Bath, Maine (1973).

Brown, John Howard. *Bryan, Sewall and Honest Money Will Bring Prosperity!* New York City (1896).

Coe, Harrie B. *Maine: Resources, Attractions and Its People: A History.* New York City (1931), V, pp. 206–207.

Goodwyn, Lawrence. *Democratic Promise, the Populist Movement in America.* New York City (1976), pp. 477–512.

Hatch, Lewis. *Maine: A History.* 5 Vols. New York City (1919), V, pp. 13–18.

Hennessy, Mark W. *The Sewall Ships of Steel.* Augusta, Maine (1937).

Illustrated Historical Souvenirs of the City of Bath. (1899), p. 80.

Jones, Robert C. *Two Feet Between the Rails.* Vol. I. Silverton, Colo. (1979).

Jones, Stanley L. *The Presidential Election of 1896.* Madison, Wis. (1964).

Little, George Thomas. *Genealogical and Family History of the State of Maine.* 4 vols. New York City (1909), II, pp. 518–525.

Obituary. *The Bath Independent.* September 8, 15, 1900.

Plummer, Edward Clarence. *History of Bath, Maine.* Bath (1976), reprint of 1936 edition, pp. 296–297.

Schlup, Leonard. "Bryan's Partner: Arthur Sewall and the Campaign of 1896." *Maine Historical Society Quarterly,* 1977, pp. 189–211.

Woodward, C. Vann. *Tom Watson, Agrarian Rebel.* New York City (1963), reprint of 1938 edition, pp. 296–300, 308–326.

Yakowicz, Susie. *Steel Glory: The Life of Shipbuilder Arthur Sewall.* Eagan, Minn. (1996).

Some family information provided by Harold E. Brown, Curator, Bath Marine Museum.

1896 vice presidential nominee —
Populist Party

Thomas E. Watson

Born September 5, 1856, in Columbia (now McDuffie) County, Georgia; died September 26, 1922, in Washington D.C. Married Georgia Durham on October 9, 1878; they had three children.

Thomas Edward Watson was the first son of John Smith Watson and Ann Eliza Maddox Watson. They lived in a log house on a 600-acre farm worked by five slave families. Named Edward Thomas, he later inverted his names. Tom's father and many other family members fought in the War Between the States. Private John Smith returned home in 1865 wounded and broke. In defiance of the new realities, the penniless ex-soldier built a grand, white-columned mansion. It was foreclosed three years later, and the family moved to a small farm house.

Tom attended Mercer University from 1872 until 1874, but lack of funds caused him to leave and teach in a country school. While teaching he studied law and was admitted to the bar in 1875. During this time and for the rest of his life he wrote — poetry especially but not exclusively. He married, lived in the home of his physician father-in-law, and then settled into

THOMAS E. WATSON
(Reproduced from the Collections of the Library of Congress)

his own home in Thomson, Georgia. Watson established a highly successful criminal defense law practice. The income allowed him to buy a better house in 1878 for his father and three sisters.

The decline of Watson's family into poverty after having been planters and slave-owners, was an embarrassment and a goad. He was called an "agrarian avenger," and fought the businessmen and northern industrialists who displaced the old South. He was a rebel and fighter by nature. Watson, Watson's brother Julius, and a legal and political rival, W.D. Tutt, were jointly indicted for carrying concealed weapons, probably to use against each other because of earlier altercations. In January 1882, the Watsons pled guilty. Within weeks a chance meeting led to an argument. Tutt hit Watson, and Watson shot Tutt in the hand. Watson was indicted for assault with intent to murder, but the matter was "settled" halfway through trial. Watson managed a narrow election victory for the state assembly later in the year. He served one term.

Watson was elected to Congress as a Populist in 1890. In 1891 he founded a Populist newspaper. The Democratic Party machine back in Georgia made sure that his district boundaries were changed. He was defeated in 1892 in a violent and potentially fraudulent election. Georgia's Governor William J. Northen was accused in 1892 of having said "Watson ought to be killed...." Watson lost again in 1894. In 1896 the Democratic Party nominated William Jennings Bryan for president. The Populist Party's convention came two weeks later. There was a strong movement among the Populists to accept Bryan as their nominee as well, but the Democratic vice presidential nominee, Maine banker and shipbuilder Arthur Sewall, was too much a "plutocrat" for the Populists. Watson was nominated for vice president instead. Watson accepted under what may have been a perception that Sewall had agreed to withdraw. That did not happen. The next few months were filled with confusion and hard work to get two overlapping tickets on state ballots. Watson campaigned, but was treated as a pariah by Democrats and ignored by Bryan. C. Vann Woodward, Watson's best biographer, said, "It

is doubtful if any candidate ever to appear on a presidential ticket found himself in quite the humiliating position that Tom Watson occupied in 1896." The humiliation ended with a resounding defeat.

For the next eight years Watson was out of politics. He wrote several volumes of history and a novel. In 1904 he was the Populist candidate for president, but came in fifth. He did even worse in 1908. He started *Tom Watson Magazine* in 1905 to publicize his political views. Watson was becoming bitter and vengeful, and creating chaos among supporters and party and elected officials in Georgia. He let loose with diatribes in speeches and magazine articles against Catholics, blacks, socialists, and various individuals. At the approach of the First World War, Watson fiercely argued against intervention. Defeats for Congress in 1918 and in his state's presidential primary in 1920 were followed by an overwhelming victory for the U.S. Senate later in 1920. His platform was isolationist, pro-labor, and even pro–Soviet. He died in Washington after serving less than two years.

The Thomas E. Watson Home is located at 310 Lumpkin Street, Thomson, Georgia (private). Watson's statue is on the capitol grounds in Atlanta.

WATSON BIBLIOGRAPHY

Brewton, William W. *The Life of Thomas E. Watson.* Atlanta (1926).

Brown, Walter J. *J.J. Brown and Thomas E. Watson: Georgia Politics, 1912–1928.* Macon, Ga. (1989).

Carto, Willis A. *Profiles in Populism.* Old Greenwich, Conn. (1982), pp. 40–63.

Durden, Robert F. *The Climax of Populism: The Election of 1896.* Lexington, Ky. (1965).

Glad, Paul W. *McKinley, Bryan, and the People.* Philadelphia (1964).

Hicks, John D. *The Populist Revolt: A History of the Farmers' Alliance and the People's Party.* Lincoln, Nebr. (1959, reprint of 1931 edition).

Goodwyn, Lawrence. *Democratic Promise: The Populist Movement in America.* New York (1976).

Schipper, Martin P., comp. *The Thomas E. Watson Papers* (1991), microfilm, with guide.

Watson, Thomas E. *The Life and Speeches of Thomas E. Watson.* Nashville (1908).

Woodward, C. Vann. *Tom Watson: Agrarian Rebel.* New York (1963, reprint of 1938 edition).

Election of 1900

NOMINATIONS

Republican Party Convention (12th): June 19–21, 1900, at the Exposition Auditorium, Philadelphia, Pa. *President*—William McKinley, nominated unanimously on the first ballot. *Vice president*—Theodore Roosevelt, nominated unanimously on the first ballot by the 925 delegates.

Democratic Party Convention (18th): July 4–6, 1900, at Convention Hall, Kansas City, Mo. *President*— William Jennings Bryan, nominated unanimously on the first ballot. *Vice President*—Adlai Stevenson, nominated on the first ballot with 559½ out of 936 votes. David Hill (N.Y.) was a distant second.

GENERAL ELECTION, November 6, 1900

Popular Vote
McKinley 7,218,039
Bryan 6,358,345
Others 394,086

Electoral Vote
McKinley-Roosevelt — 292 (28 states)
Bryan-Stevenson —155 (17 states)

Winners
William McKinley, 25th president
Theodore Roosevelt, 25th vice president

Losers
William Jennings Bryan, Adlai Stevenson

WILLIAM JENNINGS BRYAN and ADLAI E. STEVENSON
(From the collection of David J. and Janice L. Frent)

1900 presidential nominee—
Democratic Party

William Jennings Bryan

The biographical sketch for Bryan appears in the section on the 1896 election, pages 423–430.

State represented: Nebraska.
Birth: March 19, 1860.
Age on Inauguration Day (March 4, 1901): 40 years, 11½ months.
Death: July 26, 1925.

1900 vice presidential nominee—
Democratic Party

Adlai E. Stevenson

No biographical sketch of Stevenson is included since he served as vice president from March 4, 1893, until March 4, 1897 (23rd vice president).

State represented: Illinois.
Birth: October 23, 1835.
Age on Inauguration Day (March 4, 1901): 65 years, 4½ months.
Death: June 14, 1914.

Election of 1904

NOMINATIONS

Socialist Party Convention (2nd): May 1–6, 1904, delegates from 36 states met at Brand's Hall, Chicago. *President—* Eugene V. Debs, nominated by acclamation on the first ballot. *Vice president—* Benjamin Hanford.

Republican Party Convention (13th): June 21–23, 1904, at the Coliseum, Chicago, Ill. *President—* Theodore Roosevelt, nominated unanimously on the first ballot. *Vice president—* Charles W. Fairbanks, nominated by acclamation on the first ballot.

Democratic Party Convention (19th): July 6–9, 1904, at the Coliseum, St. Louis, Missouri. *President—* Alton B. Parker, nominated on the first ballot with 679 votes out of 1000 cast. William Randolph Hearst (N.Y.) was a distant second. *Vice president—* Henry G. Davis, nominated on the first ballot, received 654 out of 977; the nomination was then made unanimous. Robert Williams (Ill.) and George Turner (Wash.) were rivals.

GENERAL ELECTION, November 8, 1904

Popular Vote

Roosevelt 7,626,593
Parker 5,082,898
Debs 402,283
Others 407,190

Electoral Vote

Roosevelt-Fairbanks — 336 (32 states)
Parker-Davis —140 (13 states)

Winners

Theodore Roosevelt, 26th president
Charles W. Fairbanks, 26th vice president

Losers

Alton B. Parker, Henry G. Davis, Eugene Debs, Benjamin Hanford

1904 Presidential Nominee—
Democratic Party

Alton B. Parker

Full Name: Alton Brooks Parker.
State represented: New York.

Birth: May 14, 1852, near Cortland, New York.

Age on Inauguration Day (March 4, 1905): 52 years, 9½ months.

Education: Local public schools; the Cortland Academy and Cortland normal school; Albany Law School, graduated 1873 with LL.B.

Religion: Episcopalian.

Ancestry: First Parker arrived in America from England in 1638, settling in Andover, Massachusetts.

Occupation: Attorney.

Public office: Clerk of Board of Supervisors, Ulster County, 1873–1876; county surrogate, 1877–1885; declined appointment by President Cleveland to be assistant postmaster general, 1885; chairman of state Democratic executive committee, 1885; appointed judge, Supreme Court, third division, 1885–1889; appointed to New York Court of Appeals, second division, 1889–1892; appointed to general term of first department, 1892–1896; appointed judge of appellate division of supreme court, 1896–97; elected chief judge, New York Court of Appeals, January, 1898–August 5, 1904, resigned; unsuccessful Democratic nominee for president, 1904.

Home: "Rosemount," a country estate at Esopus, New York.

Death: May 10, 1926, at New York City, age 74 years.

Burial: Kingston, New York.

Personal characteristics: 6' tall, almost 200 pounds; large head, reddish brown hair, severely receding by time of his nomination; brown, expressive eyes, large walrus mustache.

Father: John Brooks Parker (August 5, 1823–April 15, 1882); farmer.

Mother: Harriett F. Stratton (January 14, 1825–September 19, 1914), married in 1851; daughter of Joseph and Sarah (Beers) Stratton.

Siblings: Gilbert (died young). Harriet Olive (died young). Fred H. (May 11, 1862–July 5, 1949), married Catherine Zillah Ogle on June 5, 1918; bank examiner. May L. (?–?), married James A. Miles.

First wife: Mary Louise Schoonmaker (?–April 2, 1917), married October 16, 1873; daughter of Moses Schoonmaker, a farmer.

Children: John M. (?–?), died at age seven.

Bertha (August 26, 1874–April 20, 1936), married Reverend Charles Mercer Hall on January 25, 1898.

Second wife: Amelia Day Campbell (c. 1872–August 20, 1960); married January 16, 1923, daughter of Andrew Arthur Campbell and Amelia Parsons (Day) Campbell.

Children: None.

Historic sites: Parker's home still stands in Esopus, New York, looking down an embankment upon the Hudson River. It is not open to the public.

Judge Alton Parker has the distinction of being the only nominee for president whose life has been deemed so colorless, so lacking in dramatic detail, that no book has been published about him. That Alton Parker's life was insignificant or not useful would be the wrong conclusion, however. Judge Parker was a conservative, intelligent, honorable man who rendered valuable service as a member of the highest court in New York State, and as an attorney in successful private practice for the 22 years following his defeat for the presidency. Even if it is understandable that he never captured the imagination of his contemporaries or historians, nonetheless Alton Parker deserves to be remembered.

Alton's family was a typically poor, pre-Civil War farming family. John Brooks Parker, Alton's father, is remembered for his love of books, his intelligence and curiosity, and his seeming unsuitability for farming. Local schools provided the fundamentals of an education for young Alton, but family financial difficulties blocked the boy's dream of attending Cornell University. Instead, after completing all the studies that the local village could offer, Alton taught school at the age of 16. Tradition holds that the young schoolmaster gained the respect and attention of his pupils when he thrashed the class bully. Later, Alton had agreed to accept a particular teaching position. Later that same day his father secured a better-paying offer for Alton. John B. Parker convinced Alton that he had to refuse the better-paying post, saying "You made a contract; it is your duty to uphold it."

That contract and other ones were upheld for a time, but the young man had different ambitions. Early in life Alton determined to become a lawyer. Attending court with his father one day as a boy, Alton had been swept along by the power of the arguments presented by one attorney. Parker was convinced from that moment on that he would one day emulate that lawyer. The first step was to read law in the Kingston-on-the-Hudson office of Schoonmaker and Hardenburgh.

With the clerkship as preparation, Alton entered the Albany Law School in 1872, and graduated the following year. Admission to the bar came in 1873. The novice attorney set up practice in Kingston with another lawyer. For 12 years he remained an active attorney, until appointment to judicial positions removed him from private practice.

Private practice could not alone hold the ambitious, industrious Parker. His former boss, Augustus Schoonmaker, Jr., had been defeated for reelection as a judge; Parker vowed to restore him to office. Only 24 years old, Parker campaigned county-wide, visiting countless voters and presenting Schoonmaker's case so convincingly that the judge was returned to the bench at the next election. Parker's own election to office came in 1877 when he easily gained the Democratic nomination for county surrogate and then won the general election with ease. At the next election the Republicans conceded the office to the effective and popular young politician, and put up no opponent against him.

Such leaders as Samuel Jones Tilden, recently defeated Democratic nominee for president, recognized Parker's potential. Tilden summoned the 29-year-old attorney and asked for help in political organization in Parker's home county. Parker never asked for any named position in the party during this period. He helped secure comfortable majorities in Ulster County for the Democrats, in what had before his involvement been a safely Republican county.

In 1880 and 1884, Parker attended the Democratic national conventions as a delegate from New York. Between those two national campaigns, Parker actively assisted Grover Cleveland's election to the New York governorship in 1882. Cleveland's election to the presidency in 1884 broke a 24-year lock on the White House by the Republicans. The new president called Parker to his office for a suitable reward. Cleveland wanted Parker in the politically important Post Office Department. When the young New Yorker rejected the offer of the first assistant postmaster general's post, a five thousand dollar salaried position, Cleveland turned to the postmaster general and indicated his surprise. The cabinet officer asked Parker the reason. The response was that he could not afford to leave his smaller salary as county surrogate, but with the potentially sizable supplement of an increasingly established private practice. The postmaster general said that he had given up twenty thousand dollars a year to take an eight-thousand dollar Cabinet position. Parker's quick rejoinder left all smiling: "If I had been making twenty thousand dollars a year for ten years, I should not mind taking a five thousand dollar place in Washington."

Parker had firmly placed his career in the legal field, not in politics. His abilities in both fields were recognized at high levels. When David Hill decided to run for governor of New York in 1885, he turned to the 33-year-old surrogate and attorney to be his campaign manager. Much like the work for Schoonmaker a few years earlier, Parker made the campaign a personally exhausting one. He visited every region of the state in a tireless series of organizational meetings and campaign speeches. When the election was won, the opportunities for Parker's advancement were manifest to all. Thus it was no surprise that when a member of the New York Supreme Court died, Parker was appointed by Governor Hill to the vacancy. The Republicans in 1886 again paid him the honor of running no opponent against him when Judge Parker had to face his first election test in his new position. Though still a child prodigy in terms of the age of most judges, Parker received the considerable honor in 1892 to sit on the general term of the Supreme Court. Despite its name, the Supreme Court was not the highest court in the state, but had trial level jurisdiction. The general term was a short-lived experiment to have Supreme Court judges sit in panels of three or four to review the decisions of the lower courts. His fellow judges requested that Parker be appointed to replace an ailing judge on the newly created appellate division of the Supreme Court. He was elected to be chief judge of the New York Court of Appeals in 1897, which is the state's highest court. The two hundred fifty thousand vote Republican majority in the statewide elections of 1896 was erased the following year, and Parker was elected to this judgeship with a sixty thousand vote margin.

During the next seven years, Parker served with distinction as the highest judicial officer in New York. On several occasions he refused offers to run for what more traditional politicians would have considered higher office — lieutenant governor, governor, and even United States senator. Parker's temperament and ambition were well-suited for a judgeship. To serve elsewhere would have been a demotion in Parker's eyes. His record as chief judge was progressive in many areas, most notably in labor cases. Many times in dissent, but on other occasions being able to command a majority of the court for his position, the chief judge argued for upholding laws that gave unions the right to strike (no minor issue during the late 1800s), imposed limits on hours of work in some industries, and prohibited the employment of any child under 14 years of age. In a case dealing with trusts, Judge Parker held that it was immaterial whether a certain combination restraining trade was reasonable or not. Even without a statute prohibiting such combinations, general legal principles prohibited them. In contract matters Parker was more conservative. Private parties should abide by their contracts even when arguably they were pressured into the agreements by what later proved to be unconstitutional laws.

Throughout his judicial career, Parker's position was that a judge should be above politics. When Tammany Hall proposed him for governor, a thought seconded by Governor Hill's faction, Parker remained noncommittal. So well respected had Parker become that his party kept returning to him for other offices. After the Democrats made him their consensus choice for United States senator, Judge Parker demurred:

> Gentlemen, I have no wish to be a candidate. I beg you to choose another. My ambition is to serve my state and my profession on the bench of the court. And it is not seemly that a judge of that court should be a candidate for a political office.

If Parker lusted for any higher office, it was for appointment to the United States Supreme Court. With few Democratic presidents during his adult life to pluck him from his state court post, that ambition was never fulfilled.

The Democrats had suffered through two increasingly severe defeats with William Jennings Bryan as their candidate for president. Conservatives began to consider the dignified, nonpolitical chief judge of New York. A New York organization was formed, partially as a reaction to the budding candidacy of William Randolph Hearst, the activist owner of a nationwide newspaper chain. Former governor and United States senator David Hill was a major force in the Parker movement. Hill worked to convince other states' conservatives that Parker was available and a potential winner. A major boost to the Parker campaign came at the 1904 New York State Democratic Convention. Parker's opponents were routed and Hill's maneuvering gained formal instructions from the convention that the state's delegates vote for Parker. Conservative Democrats across the country had the upper hand as organization for the national convention progressed.

Through it all Parker remained silent. Even vigorously pro–Parker commentators demanded that the judge declare himself not only as a candidate, but also on the important issues. The burning issue, to many the only issue, continued to be whether the country should have a gold standard, or permit the free and unlimited coinage of silver, the latter being the gospel according to the Bryan disciples. Since Parker's unalterable rule was that judges should make no statements on political questions, the country did not know where he stood. Parker's only response to the pressure was a letter written to a reporter friend, not published until after the nomination:

> You may be right in thinking that an expression of my views is necessary to secure the nomination. If so, let the nomination go. I took the position that I have maintained — first, because I deemed it my duty to the court;

second, because I do not think the nomination for such an office should be sought.

Parker's silence did not mean disinterest. Governor Hill's biographer alleged Parker had decided that he would run for president as early as the fall of 1903, but Parker denied this. On November 17, 1903, the chief judge gave a speech in tribute to Revolutionary patriot and first American Chief Justice John Jay, saying:

> [Jay] gave to the public service the day of his vigorous manhood, the best years of his life, ... [thus setting] aside every personal interest, laboring with fidelity and unselfish effort....

He sounded like someone declaring himself available if called. State conventions were held throughout the country as the national convention drew near. No clear-cut favorite emerged from these, but the New York Parker organizers won important victories in these state-by-state skirmishes. Anti-Bryan forces coalesced around Parker. So successfully routed were the Bryanites at the convention, that Parker was within ten votes of having a two-thirds majority after the first ballot roll call. Quick changes in states' votes gave him a unanimous total when the official balloting was completed.

The nomination was secured at five o'clock in the morning. In the afternoon, 81-year-old Henry G. Davis was named as Parker's running mate. With these proceedings completed, the convention was then put into an uproar by a declaration of independence and integrity rarely witnessed at one of these quadrennial gatherings. Parker sent the following telegram, firmly and irrevocably revealing his position on the principal issue of the campaign:

> I regard the gold standard as firmly and irrevocably established, and shall act accordingly if the action of the Convention shall be ratified by the people. As the platform is silent on the subject, my views should be made known to the Convention, and if it is proved to be unsatisfactory to the majority, I request you to decline the nomination for me at once, so that another may be nominated before adjournment.

For a time it appeared the party, which twice had nominated the silver-activist Bryan, could not so completely reverse form and accept an avowed gold-standard bearer. To reject the man just nominated unanimously was too politically unpalatable, though, and cooler heads prevailed upon the convention to endorse Parker even after the telegram.

It was decided that Parker should remain safely, dignifiedly ensconced in his New York home during the campaign. Resigning the judgeship he had held for seven years, Parker declared that if elected he would serve only one term. The interests of the country were too vast, and questions presented of "such overwhelming magnitude," that it must be clear the president was independent and not constantly concerned with what would be advantageous for his reelection. Parker was presented as the safe, sane choice to counter the excesses of the "Rough Rider," Theodore Roosevelt. Parker's liberal labor record was submerged as the campaign progressed. Delegations visited his New York home, and his short, carefully prepared addresses to them were published in papers across the nation. With the campaign obviously in trouble, Parker criticized Roosevelt more sharply as the election neared. He alleged that the government's treatment of citizens in the occupied Philippines was cruel and unjust. Subsequent revelations proved the validity of this charge, though Roosevelt was not involved in the scandal. He also charged that the Republican campaign manager had been selected because, as a former secretary of commerce, he could use his knowledge of corporate misdeeds to extract large contributions from businessmen.

Nonetheless, in the main the campaign was a gentle, lackluster one. The exciting and dynamic Roosevelt was simply too well liked, too enjoyable as president, for the people to turn him out in favor of the colorless Parker, who did not even have the semblance of a united party behind him. Parker won the solid South, and nothing else.

For the next 20 years Parker was active in his profession, but did not withdraw totally from politics. In 1912, he played a prominent part in the next soul-searching by the Democrats at a national convention, regarding whether to reject the policies of Bryan or to take a more conservative approach. Parker's selection as temporary chairman of the convention became the test of the respective strengths of each faction, and Parker won. In the legal profession his contributions multiplied and diversified after the presidential defeat. He was elected president of the American Bar Association, the New York State Bar, the New York County Bar, and other organizations. Several significant cases were handled during these next two decades, and his practice was extremely lucrative. At times he again could give free reign to his strong pro-labor views, and he represented the American Federation of Labor and Samuel Gompers in two significant cases. Because of his prestige, he was asked to be the state's chief counsel in impeachment proceedings brought against New York governor William Sulzer.

Living a comfortable life, tending to his legal and political interests, Parker had the wherewithal to create a magnificent country estate outside of Esopus, New York. There he could indulge his passion of riding horses at least an hour every day. He would rise early each morning, take a swim in the nearby Hudson River, ride his horse, and then tend to the sizable farm. He was a muscular, athletic man, fond of the outdoors and physical labor. His vitality, not nearly as dramatic as Teddy Roosevelt's, was no less real.

Parker was never again seriously in consideration for high state office. The presidential race also seemed to foreclose his first and only goal, to be a member of the United States Supreme Court. Running for president had been an unwanted duty, and it had drastically changed the direction of his career.

Analysis of Qualifications

In 1904, the American people were faced with one of those rarities in presidential election history: two exceptional men were being presented by their respective parties for the highest office in the country. That they chose Theodore Roosevelt over Alton Parker was understandable for many reasons. With Roosevelt's ranking by historians as one of the country's top four presidents, it must be conceded that there is little basis to criticize their

decision. Yet, Alton Parker's failure to grasp the brass ring should be mourned not because of who defeated him, but because of who Parker was.

As a legal scholar and jurist, Parker made a lasting impression on his contemporaries and on his state's history. As a driving force in national bar associations, Parker's influence spread far beyond New York. Duty characterized Parker's adult life. He perhaps lived out the lesson taught by his father that day when he encouraged his son to honor a commitment to a teaching position, despite that the salary would be less than another, later offer. Fair and cordial to all who appeared before his court, Parker was particularly kind and helpful to young lawyers who were still finding their way and could easily be intimidated by the court. When offered the presidential nomination of his party, he was willing to discard it immediately if the party would not accept his views on the most significant public concern, the gold standard. His opponent that year, President Roosevelt, called the telegram that announced Parker's support of the gold standard "a bold and skillful move ... he now stands forth to the average man ... as one having convictions compared to which he treats self interest as of no account." A later Democratic also-ran, John W. Davis, said Parker was "one of the outstanding figures in public life in the United States, a man of great courage, loyalty, and devotion to his convictions."

Parker was an even-tempered man, not prone to descend into attacks on personalities no matter what the provocation. He had good political instincts, demonstrated considerable talent as a political organizer and campaigner, but was lackluster in personal appearances before large audiences. Parker was incorruptible, and saw service as far more important than personal gain. He was not experienced in major national affairs, and would have been a novice in dealing with Congress. Foreign policy was totally alien. Twenty years as a judge had little prepared Parker for the highest office in the country, and there might have been a difficult period of adjustment to the new responsibilities had he been elected. Still, he had excelled in every other demand made upon him in his long and varied career, and there is good reason to believe the presidency would have been graced by his presence.

Roosevelt and Parker were both honest, intelligent, deeply principled men. Both enjoyed active, physical lives, loved the outdoors, played as hard as they worked. Parker was more conservative than Roosevelt, and would have had fewer crusades than did the president who called his office a "bully pulpit." There would have been differences in their performance, but they both would have been good.

PARKER BIBLIOGRAPHY

"Alton B. Parker." *Oklahoma Law Journal* 3 (1904), pp. 26–28.

Creelman, James. "Alton B. Parker: A Character Sketch." *The American Monthly Review of Reviews* XXX (August 1904).

*Field, Robert M., Jr. "Alton B. Parker: His Life and Times." An authorized biography accepted for publication by John Day & Co., but withdrawn by Parker's widow (1932).

*_____. "From Tilden to Wilson." Unpublished manuscript (c. 1930).

Grady, John R. *The Lives and Public Services of Parker and Davis.* Philadelphia (1904).

O'Brien, Morgan J. "Alton Brooks Parker." *American Bar Association Journal* XII (1926), pp. 453–455, 465.

_____. "Memorial of Alton Brooks Parker." *New York County Lawyers' Association Yearbook, 1926,* pp. 313–319.

Obituary. *New York Times,* May 11, 1926, p. 1.

Papers of Alton B. Parker, in possession of Library of Congress, Manuscript Division; see especially container 16, "Autobiographical and Biographical File, ca. 1920–1937."

Parker, Alton B. "Alton Brooks Parker." Unpublished manuscript of his memoirs, ending in 1904, in possession of Library of Congress, Manuscript Division.

Parker, Amelia Campbell. "Alton Brooks Parker." *Proceedings of the Ulster County Historical Society,* 1934–35, pp. 28–56.

Schlup, Leonard. "Alton B. Parker and the Presidential Campaign of 1904." *North Dakota Quarterly* 49 (1981), pp. 48–60.

Sykes, M'Cready. "Alton B. Parker, Chief-Judge of the New York Court of Appeals." *The Green Bag* XVI (1904), pp. 145–152.

Wheaton, James O. "The Genius and the Jurist: A Study of the Presidential Campaign of 1904." Unpublished doctoral dissertation, Stanford University (1964).

Some dates and names for the Parker family were obtained from obituaries for the relevant dates in the *New York Times.*

---

*1904 vice presidential nominee—
Democratic Party*

Henry G. Davis

Full name: Henry Gassaway Davis.

State represented: West Virginia.

Birth: November 16, 1823, in Baltimore, Maryland.

Age on Inauguration Day (March 4, 1905): 81 years, 3½ months.

Education: Brief education in local schools, then found first job at age fourteen.

Religion: Presbyterian.

Ancestry/prominent relatives: First Davis ancestor arrived in Maryland from England in 1688; Arthur Paul Gorman (cousin), U.S. senator; Stephen B. Elkins (son-in-law), U.S. senator from New York, secretary of war; Thomas B. Davis (brother), U.S. representative from West Virginia; Davis Elkins (grandson), U.S. senator from West Virginia.

Occupation: Railroad, timber, other businesses.

Public office: State House of Delegates, 1865–1866; state senator, 1868–1871; U.S. Senate, March 4, 1871–March 3, 1883; American representative to Pan American conferences, 1889, 1901; unsuccessful Democratic nominee for vice president, 1904.

Home: "Deer Park," summer home and farm on crest of Alleghanies, in Garrett County, Maryland; "Graceland," his house in Elkins, West Virginia.

Death: March 11, 1916, in Washington, D.C., at age 92 years, 4 months.

Burial: Maplewood Cemetery, Elkins, West Virginia.

Personal characteristics: Physically vigorous, tireless, loved outdoors and horseback riding throughout life; tremendous aversion to waste; cool business judgment; honest, amiable, philanthropic.

Location not discovered; the author would appreciate hearing from anyone with knowledge of either Field manuscript; please write care of McFarland & Company, Inc., Publishers.

ALTON B. PARKER and HENRY G. DAVIS
(From the collection of David J. and Janice L. Frent)

Father: Caleb Dorsey Davis (March 7, 1792–September 4, 1850), businessman.

Father's first wife: Sarah Rowles, married April 1815, died 1819; one child, Nathan, who died young.

Mother: Louisa Warfield Brown (March 10, 1799–July 23, 1868, married March 9, 1819).

Siblings: Elizabeth (died young). John B. (c. 1820–1889). Thomas Beall (April 25, 1828–November 26, 1911), never married, businessman, U.S. representative. Eliza A., married Opton Buxton. William Robinson (August 23, 1833–April 22, 1879), married Mary H. _____.

Wife: Catherine Ann Salome Bantz (December 22, 1827–December 6, 1902), married February 22, 1853.

Children: Hallie D. (December 19, 1853–March 1, 1933), married Stephen Benton Elkins on April 14, 1875, who would become a U.S. senator and took over many of Davis's businesses. Maria Louisa (1854–?). Kate Bantz

(December 1, 1856–January 21, 1903), married Lt. Commander R.M.G. Brown. Anderson (1859–1862). Grace Thomas (October 19, 1869–1931), married Arthur Lee on September 19, 1898. Henry Gassaway, Jr. (1872–April 24, 1896). John T. (March 31, 1874–1935).

Historic sites/memorials: Elkins and Davis College in Elkins, West Virginia, named for him. His home, Graceland, is on the campus.

Henry G. Davis was past 80 years of age when he received his party's nomination for vice president. He was the only octogenarian ever nominated by a major party, but was more vigorous mentally and physically than many far younger candidates.

The start of this long and useful life came in 1823, when Davis as the fourth of seven children was born into a moderately successful businessman's family. They unfortunately tried to live somewhat beyond their means. When construction contracts to build part of the Baltimore and Ohio Railroad grade proved unprofitable, a situation then aggravated by the nationwide Panic of 1837, the family lost most of what it had. Henry's father suffered an emotional collapse as a result of his impoverishment and was incapable of further work. He died in 1850. Henry's mother became the sole support for the family, and opened a school for girls. Henry had never been overly interested in school, and the family exigencies were an easy rationale for dropping out of school and beginning to work himself. A variety of odd jobs presented themselves, with Henry finally working in a quarry. Then Maryland governor George Howard, the son of another defeated vice presidential nominee, offered Davis a job working on his sizeable plantation. Henry moved to Waverly and worked there until he was 20 years old.

If ever a man worked his way up through an enterprise, Henry Davis did in railroading. His first employment at age 20 was as a brakeman on the Baltimore & Ohio; years later he would own his own railroad. The brakeman's responsibilities were arduous, for he had to turn the brake wheel on each car, hopping from roof to roof, to stop or slow the train down. Davis's quickness and strength made him a natural. His superiors noticed his intelligence and willingness to work and promoted him to a conductor's position. Beginning in 1847, Davis was a supervisor of a division on the Baltimore & Ohio. For ten years he continued his work for the B&O, but had his sights set considerably higher than remaining for a lifetime in the lower reaches of the business. In 1852 he asked to be made a station agent at Piedmont, Virginia (later West Virginia), an important central point on the B&O. Though there was considerable train traffic at Piedmont, there was little else in that primitive settlement. Recently married, with in-laws who were hardly enamored of their daughter marrying a railroad worker, Davis set up housekeeping in a boxcar. Considering the flimsiness of most Piedmont dwellings, the boxcar may have been a relatively substantial abode. During his first year there his wife stayed in more civilized circumstances with her parents in Maryland, and then moved to Piedmont after Henry had completed construction of their house.

Being a railroad employee took second place to Davis's development of his own business in Piedmont. With two of his brothers, Davis opened a general store, selling feed, grain, hardware, and virtually every other necessity to the farmers in the area. In 1858, he resigned from the B&O and devoted himself full time to H.G. Davis & Bros.

Davis's interests and income grew. He bought farm products and shipped them on the railroad. He became president of the bank he founded in Piedmont the same year he resigned from the B&O. His lifelong involvement with the lumbering and coal mining business began when he established a company to exploit the neighboring abundance of both products. The Civil War made Davis's business prosper far beyond their humble beginnings. Davis was a strong Union man who at least once had to escape Confederate raiders. Davis secured lucrative contracts with the government to provide lumber. Frequent destruction of parts of the vital local railroad system by marauding rebels made even more business for Davis, for he supplied the lumber to rebuild. When Davis suggested that he might enlist in the army as his patriotic duty, President Lincoln himself in a personal meeting suggested that far greater service would be rendered by remaining in his position as supplier for the army. This farsighted entrepreneur purchased during the war, over the objection of one of his brother-partners, large tracts in the interior of the state for development of timber and coal. It would be a tremendously wise investment.

Though a strong Union man during the war, Davis was equally adamant for conciliation between the reunited sections after Appomattox. In 1863, the pro–Union western counties of Virginia had split from the rebel majority of the state. The new state of West Virginia formed its own government, and in 1865 Davis was elected to its House of Delegates. The war was over, and making peace was the main concern of the legislature. Davis opposed the test oaths to prove loyalty to the Union. During his one short term, Davis saw the passage of the charter for the Potomac and

Piedmont Coal and Railroad Company, which later would become the basis for his railroad empire in West Virginia. When the term was over, Davis returned to his business pursuits instead of seeking reelection.

In 1868, however, Davis decided again to seek public office, this time the state senate. He had become a prominent businessman in the state, added still larger sections of forest and coal lands to his control, and laid out the lumbering town of Deer Park. He was therefore a major figure in the senate. In 1871, his prominence led to an easy victory when the legislature selected the United States senator to replace an outgoing Republican incumbent who was a vestige of postwar Republican dominance in West Virginia. Six years later his reelection would be more difficult, but he won in 1877 on the fourth ballot taken by the legislature.

In the Senate, Davis opposed most civil rights legislation and favored general amnesty bills for ex–Confederates. The remonetization of silver was becoming a crucial issue; Davis allied himself with the soft-money, silver forces. During his first term, Davis's party was in the minority, but beginning his second six years in the Capitol Davis was chairman of the Appropriations Committee when the Democrats took control of the Senate. From that significant position, Davis's views favoring a high tariff and supporting the establishment of Cabinet-level departments for commerce and agriculture had added impact. Davis also backed legislation that demanded greater efficiency in government and provided far clearer and more accurate recordkeeping of expenditures and income. Davis could not understand why the government could not achieve what was taken for granted in private business — intelligible bookkeeping.

Business success was developing so rapidly that Davis decided that he could not stand for reelection to a third term. He announced his decision in November 1882; when the legislature met the following spring to choose his replacement, they gave him their unanimous vote of thanks. Republicans and Democrats alike respected his earnest devotion to West Virginia. Among his most devoted friends were Republicans James G. Blaine and Benjamin

Harrison. Blaine, in his book *Twenty Years in Congress*, says about his friend:

> Mr. Davis has honorably wrought his own way to high station, and had been all his life in active affairs as a farmer, a railroadman, a lumberman, an operator in coal, and a banker. He had been uniformly successful. He came to the Senate with the kind of practical knowledge which schooled him to care and usefulness as a legislator. He steadily grew in esteem and confidence of both sides of the Senate, and when his party obtained the majority he was entrusted with the responsible duty of the chairmanship of the Committee on Appropriations. No more trustworthy man ever held that place. While firmly adhering to his party, he was at all times courteous, and to the business of the Senate or in local intercourse never obtruded partisan views.

Blaine and other political friends would frequently be given, and accept, opportunities to invest in a Davis venture after he left the Senate. It was a mutually beneficial association.

The vast northern part of West Virginia was largely undeveloped after the Civil War. The reason was the absence of transportation into the region. Davis set about constructing a railroad to take advantage of the tremendous timber and coal reserves there. Horseback riding over much of the territory during a period of over ten years had convinced Davis firsthand of the value of the area. Many political friends were given shares in the business, including Blaine and Delaware senator Thomas Bayard. Stephen Elkins, a delegate from New Mexico, later would become Davis's son-in-law and a United States senator from New York. Elkins also invested in many of Davis's businesses. Davis's cousin, Senator Arthur Gorman, was another relative in high places who received financial success by permitting Davis to invest his money. During the last few years Davis was a senator, his scheme for the railroad began to take shape, and the line was completed in November 1881. The coal deposits that were mined, and the timber that was cut, added greatly to the Davis fortune.

Davis became keenly interested in building a railroad that would link the entire western hemisphere from South America to the United States. For almost 30 years Davis was a promoter of a Pan-American railway. His first involvement came when Republican President Harrison selected Democrat Davis as one of ten delegates to the first international conference for American affairs. He was appointed to several committees, one of which concerned the proposal of an international railroad. From October 1889 until April 1890, Davis and the other delegates worked on problems of mutual interest to the Americas. A second conference was held in October 1901. Davis was one of five delegates from the United States to that conference, and was chairman of the delegation. His tireless efforts on behalf of Pan-American unity, particularly in the form of a railroad, led to his nomination as president of the conference, but he begged not to be considered. During other conferences, and as a member of a continuing committee studying the matter, Davis worked to promote the feasibility, desirability, and profitability of a Pan-American railway. At several junctures the idea seemed achievable, but finances and political problems always quashed the project.

Even if business success kept Davis from full-time involvement in public affairs, he never fully withdrew. During the Democratic national conventions from 1868 until 1892, he was a delegate from West Virginia, and headed his state's delegation in 1880, 1884, and 1888. In 1884 he was the principal competition to successful vice presidential contender Thomas A. Hendricks at the Democratic convention.

While helping on the sidelines, Davis was also frequently begged to come onto the field as a candidate. In 1888, he declined to run for governor, saying he was too busy with his railroad ventures, which he was. In 1896 and 1900, he did not get involved in the campaigns even to the degree of being a delegate to the national convention. Never enamored with William Jennings Bryan, he nevertheless always supported the party nominee. When Bryan was defeated in 1900, Davis said that he hoped the party at last could be rid of Bryanism. Hoping to retake West Virginia from the Republicans who had swept the elections there in 1896, many friends encouraged the 75-year-old businessman to run for governor. He declined the chance to run for that office, and further refused to be a candidate for the United States Senate that year.

These refusals of candidacy can easily be understood by seeing how far his railroad, mining, and timber empire was growing in the state. So profitable was the West Virginia Central Railway that a Jay Gould group of investors bought the company in 1902. Several million dollars were available either to draw interest or to be put into active use. The 79-year-old Davis was still aggressive and far from ready to retire. With this money he bought a small railroad line, and then began construction to connect it to another undeveloped region of West Virginia, this lying in the heart of the state. New towns were laid out, with such family names as Gassaway and Elkins. The Coal and Coke Railway Company was the result of these labors. He retained almost complete control in this new venture until 1907, and did not remove himself completely until 1912 when his son-in-law, Stephen Elkins, took over.

The "grand old man" of West Virginia, as he was known, not always appreciatively by him, found himself in the center of the political fight in 1904. He was a key figure at the state convention, as he wanted to rid the party of the Bryan influence and did not trust others to accomplish that. At the national convention he was a delegate who continued the fight for a conservative nominee. After a conservative platform was adopted and Parker was nominated for president, Davis felt his work had been accomplished. He therefore left for home by train. While Davis was on his journey, the Parker forces met to decide on a running mate. As the cousin of Senator Arthur Gorman, who had delivered valuable support to Parker for the nomination, Davis may have been part of a bargain for the Gorman delegates. He was nominated unanimously. A telegram had to be sent to catch Davis with the news.

At 81 years of age, out of public office for 20 years, Davis was a surprise choice. His views were acceptable to the Parker supporters. No desire had been expressed to make peace with the liberal Bryan faction, but since Davis had worked for the Bryan campaign in his state in the Great Commoner's two earlier races for president, he at least could be seen as a friend if not fellow believer. Along with these political considerations was the hope that Davis would contribute a sizeable chunk of his fortune to the national campaign. Davis was surprised, but the vigorous, assertive businessman accepted the nomination without hesitation.

During the campaign the Republicans made an issue of Davis's age. With the memories of President McKinley's assassination less than four years earlier fresh on people's minds, the grisly possibility could not be ignored. Davis conducted an active canvass in part to dispel these concerns, giving 90 speeches by his own count. He did not delude himself with false hope of victory, however, and accepted the ticket's defeat in November with equanimity.

The remainder of his life was devoted to his business and charitable interests. The West Virginian had throughout his adult life, upon achieving his fortune, been liberal with his money to worthy causes. Included as recipients of his largess were hospitals, schools, orphanages, churches, and just about every other institution of social concern. He also gave generously to individuals whose plight touched him. Religion played a substantial part in his life. The Sabbath was rigidly observed, so much so that in his younger years (say, before he became 80), the family horses were put out to pasture until the Sabbath was over; swings were tied to the trees so children would not be enticed to play; and even food was to the extent possible prepared on Saturday for the Sunday meals. Alton Parker shared that zeal for the Sabbath.

Enjoying himself with vigorous exercise even in his nineties, Davis finally began to succumb to the inexorable effects of age. His passion of horseback riding across his sizeable estate, sometimes 12 hours a day, had to give way to simpler pleasures. Finally in 1916, having caught a bad cold that developed into a debilitating case of grippe, he began to fade. After what appeared to be a marked turn for the better, his health suddenly faltered again and he died peacefully in his sleep.

Analysis of Qualifications

For 50 years Henry Davis methodically kept a careful journal of events, impressions, and personalities. It was a very big journal. It contained a record of achievement in business, politics, and philanthropy, that could be approached by few men and not only because of the gift of so many years that he received. He had excellent business sense, and parlayed his energy, foresight, and willingness to work into a considerable fortune for himself and for those who invested with him. He also developed large portions of his state, established towns, factories, and schools, and generally made a broad mark across over 50 years of West Virginia history.

Henry Davis abhorred waste. He disliked it in government as well as in his private businesses. Never quite developing into eccentric behavior, this passion for economy and orderliness would have served him well in public office, even if it had caused untold frustrations in dealing with so many who did not share his propensities. His life was active, filled with physical exercise, love of the outdoors, devotion to his family, as well as tireless effort in his public and business affairs. He was born while James Monroe was president, first achieved prominence when Lincoln was in the White House, was nominated for vice president when Theodore Roosevelt was cutting a dramatic swath through American and world affairs, and died on the eve of World War I. Henry Clay as well as Woodrow Wilson had been acquaintances; Whig, Union and Democratic parties had been his political homes through different periods. A high tariff and internal improvements were sponsored by Davis before the Civil War. New issues that were encountered included bimetallism or the silver controversy, and Davis sided with Bryan on that. Imperialism during the turn of the century became a new concern, and Davis frequently stated that America was venturing too far down the road to colonialism in the Philippines and elsewhere. Few men have ever lived so long in public life, encountered so many critical and diverse public issues, yet remained so flexible to these changes.

The West Virginian was no narrow partisan, but found ideas and friends on both sides of the political fence. Allen G. Thurman and George H. Pendleton, veritable Civil War "Copperheads," could be counted as friends by the same man who was intimate with

Republicans James G. Blaine and Benjamin Harrison.

The negatives in Davis's career need also to be admitted. No great achievement marked his 12 years in the United States Senate. He was not an innovator of legislative programs. His administration skills and his executive ability were tested and found admirable on the small scale of West Virginia railroading, but no test had ever been given him that could match the daily worries of a president. Long out of public office, at 81 and far from the pinnacle of his mental and physical abilities (though still vigorous for his age), Davis was not as in touch with the issues as was desirable. He was one of the great beneficiaries of the industrial revolution in America after the Civil War. It might be asked whether he should be included in that suspect class of individuals — the Goulds, Carnegies, or Vanderbilts — who now are called the "robber barons." There is no hint of that in Davis's career. His labor relations were good for the times; his many philanthropies seem more than token conscience pacifiers but instead were manifestations of an overall approach to life, namely concern about those far less fortunate than he was.

Henry G. Davis justly deserved his nomination, though his party may have waited a little too long to give it to him. Perhaps he would have been a caretaker president, one who ably if quietly and conservatively managed the affairs of the country without dramatic new innovations. Yet that is not a bad standard for achievement.

DAVIS BIBLIOGRAPHY

Elkins-Randolph County (West Virginia) Public Library, and genealogist William H. Rice, provided the family data.

Pepper, Charles M. *The Life and Times of Henry Gassaway Davis 1823–1916.* New York City (1920).

Ross, Thomas Richard. *Henry Gassaway Davis: An Old-Fashioned Biography.* Elkins, W.V. (1994).

Williams, John A. "Davis and Elkins of West Virginia: Businessmen in Politics." Unpublished doctoral dissertation, Yale University (1967).

1904 presidential nominee —
Socialist Party

Eugene Debs

Born November 5, 1855, in Terre Haute, Indiana; died October 20, 1926, in Elmhurst, Ill. Married Katherine Metzel on June 9, 1885; they had no children.

Eugene Victor Debs was one of ten children and the first son born to Jean Daniel Debs and Marguerite Marie Bettrich Debs. Both parents were natives of Colmar, Alsace, in northeast France. They arrived in America in 1849, were married the same year, settled in Terre Haute and operated a grocery. Eugene left school at age 14 to take a menial job for a railroad in Terre Haute, but worked his way up to being a fireman. After four years he quit his dangerous job, partly at his mother's urging, and came home. Debs became a billing clerk at a large wholesale grocery. He had dropped out of school early, but read avidly, as had his father, and briefly attended a business school. He formed a weekly debating club in Terre Haute that was able to attract prominent national speakers. Debs also became secretary to the local chapter of the Brotherhood of Locomotive Firemen in 1875. Over the next few years he rose to high national office in the union. By 1880 he was editor-in-chief of the union magazine.

In 1879 Debs was elected as a Democrat as city clerk, and then in 1885 elected to the Indiana house of representatives. The experience was frustrating. He tried but failed to have passed a bill requiring railroads to compensate injured workers. He said he would never run for election again. Five presidential campaigns were still ahead.

In 1893 Debs helped organize the American Railway Union and was elected president. When Pullman Company workers struck in Chicago, Debs' union voted not to move Pullman cars. Debs was charged with contempt for violating a federal court's injunction against the strikers. He served a six month sentence in a county jail in Illinois. He used that "free" time to read and study socialism. On January 1, 1897, Debs announced that he was a socialist.

That year he converted the remnants of the Railway Union into the Social Democratic Party. In 1900 Debs was nominated for president and received almost 100,000 votes (0.6 percent). In 1901 the two major American socialist parties merged. Debs was much more successful in 1904 with a relatively, but not completely united socialist movement and garnered over 400,000 votes (2.9 percent). Socialist unity was a constant Debs concern. He became associate editor of a socialist weekly. He also helped found in 1905 the International Workers of the World, nicknamed the "Wobblies." It was one of the most radical American union groups yet organized. Debs was frustrated with the group and resigned in 1908.

Debs in 1906 took the public relations lead in defending three union activists who were indicted for the bombing murder of a former governor of Idaho. He thought they were framed, and even got into a public debate with President Roosevelt. A jury in August 1907 acquitted the first to be tried; the other two were never convicted either.

As a presidential candidate in 1908, he toured the country on a train that even he called the "Red Special." He got about the same vote as four years earlier. In 1912 Debs made another active campaign. The Socialist Party officially renounced crime, sabotage, and other violence in the cause of social change. Debs got his highest vote to date, 900,000 (6 percent). Debs did not seek the nomination in 1916, but ran for Congress instead. He finished third, but the votes he received in this race were triple those he received from Terre Haute in 1912. The Socialist Party in 1917 issued a declaration, endorsed by Debs, that all possible means should be used to stop American entry into World War I. When Congress declared war, that act was called "a crime against the people of the United States." At a party state convention in Ohio, Debs angrily denounced the government for its sedition prosecutions. Debs was indicted four days later as a result, convicted under the Espionage Act, and sentenced on September 14, 1918, to ten years in prison. The U.S. Supreme Court upheld the verdict in 1919, and Debs began serving his sentence on April 13, 1919. The 1920 Socialist Party convention named the federal prisoner its presidential candidate. Without much personal campaigning, he got 900,000 votes. On Christmas Day, 1921, the winner of the 1920 election, Warren Harding, released Debs but did not restore his citizenship.

Debs edited a new national socialist weekly. He prepared articles about prison conditions that after he died were collected into a book called *Walls and Bars*. He had radical views, but he was described by friends and foes as warm, kind to a fault, with the purest of motives.

The Eugene V. Debs Home is located at 451 North 8th St., in Terre Haute. A Debs Foundation operates the house museum.

DEBS BIBLIOGRAPHY

Constantine, J. Robert, ed. *Gentle Rebel: Letters of Eugene V. Debs*. Urbana, Ill. (1995).

Currie, Harold W. *Eugene V. Debs*, Boston (1976).

Debs, Eugene V. *Eugene V. Debs Speaks*. New York (1994).

Fitrakis, Robert J. *The Idea of Democratic Socialism in America and the Decline of the Socialist Party*. New York (1993).

Ginger, Ray. *The Bending Cross: A Biography of Eugene Victor Debs*. New Brunswick, N.J. (1949).

Morgan, H. Wayne. *Eugene V. Debs: Socialist for President*. Syracuse (1962).

Radosh, Ronald, ed. *Debs* (Great Lives Observed series), Englewood Cliffs, N.J. (1971).

1904 vice presidential nominee — Socialist Party

Benjamin Hanford

Born in 1861 in Cleveland, Ohio; died January 24, 1910, in Brooklyn. Married Alice M. Burnham.

Benjamin Hanford was the son of George Byington Hanford and Susan Elizabeth Martin Hanford. Ben's mother died when he was still an infant, and his father married Frances Jane Thompson. Hanford's stepmother was said to be "a woman of rich and cultivated mind and rare and beautiful character, and Hanford declares his debt to her is incalculable" (Wanhope, p. 3). The extent of his formal education is unknown, but he was encour-

EUGENE DEBS and BENJAMIN HANFORD
(From the Debs Foundation)

aged by his stepmother to be an avid reader. Hanford learned the printer's trade in Iowa at the Marshalltown *Republican*. In 1879 he moved to Chicago. On February 26 he joined the Chicago's Typographical Union No. 16. For the rest of his life he was a union member. Over the next decade he was, with some exaggeration, said to have "worked in printing offices in every city east of the Missouri River."

Hanford became a socialist while in Philadelphia in 1892. In 1898 he was the Socialist Party nominee for governor of New York. Teddy Roosevelt, fresh from his charge up San Juan Hill, won by 18,000 votes over the Democrat, Augustus Van Wyck, in an election in which over 1,300,000 votes were cast. Hanford received 23,860, while the Prohibition candidate received 18,383. As the *New York Times* noted, either minor party's "vote if added to the Democratic vote would have defeated" Roosevelt (*New York Times*, December 30, 1898, p. 2). Teddy Roosevelt's rocket-like career nearly fizzled at launch in 1898, and Hanford arguably had unconsciously kept that from occurring. In 1900 Hanford got 12,000

votes and in 1902, 23,300 votes for New York governor. In 1901 Hanford was the party's candidate for New York mayor.

For many years Hanford took three months off from work each year to campaign and lecture, and then after the election or other endeavor he returned to his printing trade. He wrote and spoke and labored tirelessly for a "worker's paradise," in which capitalism had been overthrown, and the "mines, mills, factories, foundries, workshops, land, railways, tools and machinery" were the collective property of the workers. Hanford's socialist politics and his firebrand union activism went together. In 1899 the New York *Sun* newspaper locked out its union printers. Hanford wrote most of the literature that his Typographical Union No. 6, the "Big Six," used to rally its members and educate the public. In 1904 he was in Colorado speaking and organizing on behalf of striking coal miners, and wrote a book *The Labor War in Colorado* (1904).

Hanford created the fictional character of "Jimmie Higgins" in his writings. Higgins was the symbolic rank-and-file, virtually unknown socialist who did the work while others took credit. An army of Jimmie Higginses is what Hanford wanted to enlist with his writings. Hanford was considered a dynamic speaker, as he had "a burning earnestness, as evident in his daily private life as in his appearance on the platform, and an ability to clothe his thoughts and feelings in the simplest and most direct language...." (Mailly, p. 10). At the 1904 national convention Debs was nominated for president. Hanford was then unanimously selected for vice president.

Hanford's health had never been robust, but in 1905 he became ill and never recovered. He had to avoid all public speaking, but was able to keep writing. Hanford later described his "broken health and acute physical suffering, and said it was the love and support of 'Comrades the world over'" that gave him the strength to continue. In 1907 he was elected to the national party executive committee, receiving the highest number of votes of the 128 candidates for the seven positions.

In 1908 an effort to replace Eugene Debs as the presidential nominee was aided by rumors that he was too ill to run. Hanford wrote him in May, urging Debs to run. At the national convention Hanford rose from his seat in the New York delegation, waving a piece of paper. It was Debs' letter responding to Hanford's request that he run. Hanford had saved it for use at the opportune time. He read Debs' comments that "My general health is about all that could be desired. So far as strength is concerned, I have never had more to my credit, if

as much." Debs was nominated, and then so was Hanford for vice president. Hanford proved to be the one too ill to campaign.

Hanford was one of the first trustees of the Rand School of Social Sciences, where socialist thought could be taught by socialists. In a book he wrote the year before his death, he said, "Until I joined the movement I had never lived." He died in January 1910.

HANFORD BIBLIOGRAPHY

Constantine, J. Robert, ed. *Gentle Rebel: Letters of Eugene V. Debs.* 3 volumes. Urbana, Ill. (1995).

Fine, Nathan. *Labor and Farmer Parties in the United States, 1828–1928.* New York (1961, reprint of 1928 edition).

Ginger, Ray. *The Bending Cross: A Biography of Eugene Victor Debs.* New Brunswick, N.J. (1949).

Hanford, Benjamin. *Fight for Your Life!, Recording Some Activities of a Labor Agitator.* New York (1909).

Hunter, Robert. "The Socialist Party in the Present Campaign." *American Monthly Review of Reviews* 38 (Sept. 1908), pp. 293–299.

Kipnis, Ira. *The American Socialist Movement, 1897– 1912.* New York (1952).

Mailly, William, ed. *National Convention for the Socialist Party Held at Chicago, Illinois, May 1 to 6, 1904.* Chicago (1904), pp. 9–10.

Morgan, H. Wayne. *Eugene V. Debs: Socialist for President.* Syracuse (1962).

Shannon, David. *The Socialist Party of America: A History.* Chicago (1967, reprint of 1955 edition).

Wanhope, Joshua. "Biographical Sketch of Ben Hanford," in Hanford, Benjamin, *Fight for Your Life*, New York (1909), pp. 3–6.

Election of 1908

NOMINATIONS

Socialist Party Convention (3rd): May 10-17, 1908. At Brand's Hall, Chicago, Illinois. *President*— Eugene V. Debs, nominated on the first ballot with 159 votes, and 39 cast for three others. *Vice president*— Benjamin Hanford, nomi-

nated on the first ballot with 106 votes, 46 for Seymour Stedman (Ill.) and 33 for 4 others.

Republican Party Convention (14th): June 16-19, 1908, at the Coliseum, Chicago, Ill. *President*— William Howard Taft, nominated on the first ballot with 702 votes out of 979

WILLIAM JENNINGS BRYAN and JOHN W. KERN
(From the collection of David J. and Janice L. Frent)

cast. *Vice president*—James S. Sherman, nominated on the first ballot with 816 votes out of 979 cast.

Democratic Party Convention (20th): July 7-10, 1908, at the Civic Auditorium, Denver, Colorado. *President*— William Jennings Bryan, nominated on the first ballot with 888½ votes out of 1002 cast. *Vice president*—John W. Kern, nominated by acclamation.

GENERAL ELECTION, November 3, 1908
Popular Vote
Taft 7,676,258
Bryan 6,406,801
Debs 420,793
Others. 378,882
Electoral Vote
Taft-Sherman — 321 (29 states)
Bryan-Kern —162 (17 states)
Winners
William Howard Taft, 27th president
James S. Sherman, 27th vice president
Losers
William Jennings Bryan, John W. Kern, Eugene Debs, Benjamin Hanford

1908 presidential nominee—
Democratic Party

William Jennings Bryan

The biographical sketch for Bryan appears in the section on the 1896 election, pages 423–430.
State represented: Nebraska.
Birth: March 19, 1860.
Age on Inauguration Day (March 4, 1909): 48 years, 11½ months.
Death: July 26, 1925.

1908 vice presidential nominee—
Democratic Party

John W. Kern

Full name: John Worth Kern.
State represented: Indiana.
Birth: December 20, 1849, at Alto, Indiana.
Age on Inauguration Day (March 4, 1909): 59 years, 2½ months.

Education: Kokomo public schools; Old Kokomo Normal School; taught a few years; then attended law school at University of Michigan, 1867-69; admitted to bar in 1869.

Religion: Presbyterian.

Ancestry/prominent relatives: First Kern emigrated from Germany in middle eighteenth century.

Occupation: Attorney.

Public office: Defeated for Indiana legislature, 1870; elected by Kokomo City Council as city attorney, 1871–1884; defeated for county prosecuting attorney, 1880; reporter of state supreme court, 1885–1889; Indiana Senate, 1893–1897; Indianapolis city solicitor, 1897–1901; defeated Democratic nominee for governor, 1900 and 1904; defeated for U.S. Senate, 1905; unsuccessful Democratic nominee for vice president, 1908; defeated in party caucus for U.S. Senate, 1909; U.S. senator, March 4, 1911–March 3, 1917; defeated for reelection; Senate majority leader, 1913–1917.

Home: Kerncliffe, in the Blue Ridge Mountains, a thousand-acre estate four miles from Hollins, Virginia; a home also in Indianapolis.

Death: August 17, 1917, at Asheville, North Carolina, at age 67 years, 8 months.

Burial: Kerncliffe, near Hollins, Virginia; reinterred in Crown Hill Cemetery, Indianapolis, in 1929.

Personal characteristics: Tall, thin, usually poor health; full beard, always smoking a cigar; for years affected a Prince Albert coat, but then started wearing dark business suits.

Father: Jacob Harrison Kern (December 1813–?), a physician.

Mother: Nancy Leggett (March 5, 1823–February 9, 1859).

Siblings: Sarah, an older sister, married a Mr. Engels.

First wife: Julia Anna Hazzard (October 31, 1849–September 1, 1884), daughter of David Hazzard of Kokomo, Indiana; married on November 10, 1870.

Children: Frederick Richmond (September 26, 1871–c. 1900), did not marry. Julia Anna (October 3, 1883–c. 1974), married George Bilton Lawson, December 25, 1914.

Second Wife: Araminta A. Cooper (1866–January 1954), daughter of William Cooper, a Kokomo doctor; married December 23, 1885.

Children: John Worth, Jr. (1900/1901–January 29, 1971), married Bernice Winn; mayor of Indianapolis, judge of U.S. Tax Court. William Cooper (August 9, 1903–November 10, 1967), married Mary Florence Malott, September 24, 1929.

Few men have been nominated for vice president with less experience in high office than John Kern. He had served for 13 years as city attorney for Kokomo, Indiana, and for four years as reporter of the Indiana Supreme Court. He spent two years as an Indiana state senator. What is most salient about Kern's prenomination political life is defeat — for the state legislature, twice for Indiana governor, and once for the U.S. Senate. Yet even though the Democratic Party in 1908 chose inexperience, the party also found an intelligent, gifted man. Kern's political problem was that he was an uncompromising Democrat in the traditionally Republican state of Indiana.

In 1838, John's father, Dr. Jacob Kern, moved to Shelby County, Indiana. Shortly thereafter he moved to Ohio where his first child was born; then he returned to Indiana before John's birth. The senior Kern was a serious, stern man, a good physician, apparently a restless man who picked up stakes again when John was five years old and moved to Iowa. John's mother died in 1859, and the family returned to Alto, Indiana, at about the time that the Civil War was ending. John attended what was for rural Indiana a good school, but he had to travel about six miles each way, every day, to reach it. He excelled in school, easily outshining his peers, and decided to become a lawyer. Though Dr. Kern had sufficient money to pay for his education, John wanted to provide for himself. Even before he turned 16, John had taken the Indiana Teachers Exam and was given a certificate for two years. Many in his first class of students were older and larger than their instructor.

Saving his money diligently, John was able to commence his law studies at the University of Michigan in 1867, shortly before he turned 18 years of age. Two years later he had graduated, received his admission to the bar, and had opened a law office in Kokomo. Apparently some consideration was given to moving to Iowa, but since that state definitely embraced Republicanism as its majority position, the politically ambitious Kern decided to remain in Indiana.

Kern was a precocious young lawyer, popular with the younger men in his community, and active in local politics. So political was Kern that when his wedding announcement appeared in the local newspaper, it referred to his Democratic allegiance. The Republican paper allowed that he was an admirable fellow anyway. Kern had not yet turned 21.

Probably the young attorney's earliest fame came as special prosecutor of a man who was charged with killing a member of a prominent Kokomo family. The defense attorney was future vice president Thomas A. Hendricks. Kern won the case and the admiration of Hendricks, who prophesied that the time would come when Kern would be a political leader in the state. Other laurels came for this successful trial lawyer. At times he was careless in preparing his case, but so effectively did he ingratiate himself with the jury, command their attention by his style and the logic of his argument, that he won far more than his share of cases. He was known as an honest, persuasive lawyer, who nonetheless was not above trying to confuse the opposition. Kern's skills as an orator were not just used in the courtroom, but he became a popular community speaker, thereby spreading his fame and influence.

Though not yet old enough to vote, Kern upon his move to Kokomo immediately became a major mover in Democratic politics. The county convention held in 1870 was dominated by Kern's persuasive influence, and the convention turned to this youthful political novice as its state legislative candidate. Kern at first refused the nomination, but eventually acquiesced. The overwhelmingly Republican county narrowly elected Kern's opponent in the general election. The same year, Kokomo's newest and perhaps youngest lawyer contributed significantly to establishing a Democratic paper in the city. He encouraged the publisher to get started, canvassed the town for subscriptions, and otherwise advanced the cause of the newspaper. The following year

Kern was selected Kokomo city attorney. For 13 years, regardless of the changing political complexion of the city council, Kern retained this position.

For the next decade Kern did not himself run for office, but worked arduously for Democratic candidates. In 1876 he vainly pushed Thomas Hendricks' claim on the presidential nomination, but supported Samuel Tilden when the convention was over. Though Kern's influence was growing, he seemed to be getting nowhere on the county level and looked to a run for state office to get his political career on firmer ground. The position of reporter for the state supreme court was a lucrative office and would cause him to be known at a much larger level. In 1884, Kern was unanimously nominated for reporter at the state convention. He conducted an active campaign, was elected and moved to Indianapolis.

Four years as reporter significantly advanced Kern's political career. His duties were simple — editing and publishing the opinions of the state supreme court. He also had time for a private law practice. Retiring after one term, Kern remained in the capital to practice law. In 1892, he ran for the state senate and was elected. There his reputation as a pro-union, progressive defender of the poor was firmly established. One of his more significant legislative efforts was to fight, successfully, for a bill that protected employees when they attempted to form a union. An employer liability law was passed in 1893 largely by Kern's efforts, as was a child labor law.

Kern's health was never robust. An early indication of problems to come arose in 1895, and on doctor's orders he went to Europe for an extended rest. In London he met Judge Alton B. Parker, who in 1904 would become the Democrats' presidential nominee. They formed a lasting friendship during their days together as American tourists.

Ironically for a future running mate for William Jennings Bryan, John Kern was at first not enamored with the free and unlimited coinage of silver. But when the state convention took the issue up in 1896, he said he would abide by the platform that was adopted. During Bryan's first race for president, Kern agreed with the Great Commoner that the election represented a class struggle. He met Bryan that year, and the two men would remain political and personal friends.

From 1897 to 1901, Kern served as city attorney for Indianapolis. From that not very lofty springboard, Kern attempted to jump to the governorship in 1900. Democratic fortunes looked bleak that year, but many people encouraged Kern to run for the state's highest office. It was only when another Democratic candidate, whose principles Kern disliked, announced for the governorship, that he agreed to jump into the race. Party loyalty always had a strong pull on Kern. Kern easily won the nomination on the first ballot at the state convention, but lost badly in the general election, the whole party ticket going down to defeat. Four years later the pattern was repeated.

Kern's good friend, Alton Parker, was on his way to the presidential nomination. Parker urged Kern to run for governor in order to help the party in Indiana. Kern was not nearly as enthusiastic for Parker's candidacy as he had been for Bryan's. When Parker repudiated the silver issue after his nomination, many of Bryan's men abandoned the ticket. Friendship and party loyalty worked to force Kern into the governorship race. He lost again in a Republican landslide. He was the party's candidate the following year for senator, but lost that as well.

Another tour of Europe for health reasons occurred in 1906; when he returned he seemed even weaker than when he had left. A bad cold degenerated into other ailments, and a doctor finally diagnosed his condition as incipient tuberculosis. A sanatorium at Asheville, North Carolina, was his home for the next three months. Upon his return to Indianapolis, he had decided because of the delicacy of his health to avoid serious future political involvement.

Regardless of Kern's determination to eschew politics, well in advance of the Democratic national convention held in Denver in 1908, the possibility of Kern's nomination for vice president was frequently discussed. Bryan was the clear favorite for the presidential nomination. Kern's close friendship with Bryan, Indiana's key position in a national campaign,

and the Indianan's skill as a public speaker all made him a logical choice. Health seemed less of a problem, as there was no recurrence of the tubercular symptoms. Nonetheless, Kern went to Denver intent on avoiding the nomination. After Bryan was named for president, Thomas Riley Marshall placed Kern in nomination for the second spot. Though other candidates were nominated, they all withdrew or were abandoned and Kern was nominated without a ballot even being taken.

Bryan telegraphed congratulations to his running mate:

> Accept my warmest congratulations. Your nomination gratifies me very much. We have a splendid platform and I am glad to have a running mate in such complete harmony with the platform....

Somewhat morbidly, Bryan later paid effusive tribute to potential vice president Kern:

> I do not know how I can better express my feeling on the subject than to say that if I am elected president and Mr. Kern is elected vice-president, I shall not be afraid to die, because I shall feel that the policies outlined in the platform, which I shall endeavor to put into operation, will be just as faithfully carried out by him as they would be by me.

It was a strenuous campaign, but one Kern jumped into eagerly. His responsibility was to secure the South and East, while Bryan's prairie populism from Nebraska was thought particularly attractive in the West. During the campaign one of Kern's sons, John, Jr., was stricken with polio. The candidate hurried home whenever he could, then left on the campaign trail only when little John rallied. Death seemed imminent as the campaign entered its own final days. On the morning after the election, the boy rose from his sickbed and asked if his father had been elected. The honest reply told of the defeat. The boy then exclaimed, "What fools the people of the United States are to turn down such a man as father." Miraculously, young John did recover. Two years later the successful vice presidential candidate, James S. Sherman, visited the Kern home and was told of what the boy said. Sherman was brought almost to tears, and stated, "My boy, the more I have seen of your father and the better I know him the more I am inclined to think you were right." In defeat, Kern became close to the new vice president.

All was not lost in the Bryan-Kern debacle, as Indiana's Democrats had captured control both of the governor's office and the state legislature. Kern felt assured he would be the victor when the legislators met to choose a new United States senator. Other hopefuls did not defer to the just-defeated national candidate. They far out-organized Kern. Kern's complacency was shaken by reports from the capital that a secret ballot would be held. Kern's popular appeal in his native state meant few legislators could openly snub the people's will, but the call for a secret caucus augured ill for Kern. A still-overconfident Kern was defeated on the twentieth ballot by Benjamin F. Shively, 42 votes to Kern's 36. The loser would, in a too-candid interview, blame the "brewery crowd" for arm-twisting legislators to defeat this progressive consumer-minded politician. When the legislators were asked to say publicly how they voted, Kern ended up with a majority, proving some were lying to protect their careers.

Kern was depressed, but resigned himself to retirement from politics. Ironically, immediately after his release from the sanatorium two years earlier, he had seemed to prefer a quiet withdrawal from public life. In 1910, the governor suggested that legislators be instructed in the choice of a U.S. senator by the state party convention's first deciding upon a nominee. That idea was accepted. The 1910 state convention selected Kern in a landslide. In doing so they ignored Kern's wishes that he be passed over. The incumbent Republican senator, Albert Beveridge, was abandoned by many progressives in his own party. A national referendum seemed in the making as Teddy Roosevelt campaigned for the Republican senator and Bryan and Alton Parker did their part for Kern. Democrats carried the legislature, and they quickly chose Kern.

An embarrassing episode soon occurred in Washington over the selection of new members for the prestigious Senate Finance Committee. Fellow Indiana Democrat Shively wanted the seat, and Kern endorsed Shively. Yet in Kern's absence from a meeting of the selection committee, Kern was named to the vacancy. Shively could not help but feel betrayal, and many of the senior Indiana senator's supporters agreed.

Kern's initial fame in the Senate arose from a special committee that he headed, one to investigate charges that Illinois Republican senator William Lorimer had bribed his state's legislators to name him. After a whitewash investigation cleared Lorimer, Kern and a few others remained unconvinced. They continued to press for a thorough investigation; in time they succeeded. Kern and two likeminded but younger men were included on the special committee. They pulled the laboring oar in the investigation, and stood as the only three of the eight members who at the conclusion of the hearings wanted to recommend expulsion of Lorimer. Kern forcefully presented the minority report to the full Senate, arguing at length for four days on the details of the evidence. He was in ill health, and feverishly worked to complete each day's speech just before he had to deliver it. When the majority report was given, Kern was uncharacteristically contentious, raising frequent challenges to the remarks. An overwhelming vote, 55–28, agreed with Kern's position and found Lorimer guilty of the bribery charges. He was ousted, and Kern's vigilance was rewarded.

In 1912, the split among the Republicans caused by Theodore Roosevelt's Bull Moose party made the Democratic presidential nomination a grand prize indeed. Kern wanted Indiana Governor Marshall, or at least some other progressive to be the nominee. During opening battles at the convention, Kern supported William J. Bryan for temporary chairman. This had turned into a test vote on who would control the convention, the conservatives or the progressives. Alton Parker was presented as the conservative alternative for temporary chairman. Bryan nominated Kern himself. Kern rose to speak, withdrew his own name and then called passionately and sincerely for Parker to withdraw as well in the spirit of harmony. This Kern said would allow the convention to choose a compromise man. Parker sat mute, and thus Kern called upon New York's Tammany Hall leader, but he too would not budge. With those tacit refusals, Kern threw down the gauntlet and said the battle was between the people and the "powers," and insofar as Kern was concerned, he was for the people and Bryan. Bryan and Parker were both surprised by Kern's approach, and Bryan later praised Kern for his sincere desire for compromise. Compromise did not appeal to everyone, and Parker won narrowly.

A deadlock over the presidential nomination seemed to be developing between the conservatives and progressives. Kern's name surfaced as a nominee who would appeal to both factions. He refused to allow his name to be used even when promised that if Indiana would take the lead in voting for him, Illinois and a few other states would immediately follow. Instead, when the deadlock finally broke, Woodrow Wilson was named.

With the Democrats winning the presidency and control of Congress, Kern could expect a considerable boost in his influence. What he did not expect was selection as Senate majority leader, the only time that a senator with as few as two years' service in that body had been named. His reputation as a conciliatory bridge between the party's factions was his main credential. His friendliness and good humor were an added bonus. Kern in a revolutionary move refused to name committees on the basis of seniority. Such novelty helped prepare the Senate for the dynamic new programs that his president would shortly start sending up to Capitol Hill in a never-ending stream.

In one of the most public episodes of his Senate term, Kern became active in an investigation of labor unrest in West Virginia coal mines. A strike there had led to the imposition of martial law. Violence, arbitrary arrests, imprisonment and murder were the result. On April 12, 1913, the majority leader introduced the "Paint Creek Resolution," responding to a request from the United Mine Workers. While many pointed to violence and greed on both sides of the dispute, Kern retorted that he could not see greed in workers' wanting to be free from effective slavery. The resolution asked that a committee be established to determine whether a system of peonage existed at these mines. The controversy was on the front

pages of the nation's newspapers. Old friends called, many to ask Kern to stop his crusade. Anti-union feelings were high, regardless of the evidence of egregious abuses by the mine owners. Kern responded to the requests to stop: "I'll see you in hell first!" The committee vindicated Kern's charges by reporting arrests without warrants, imprisonment without fair trials, and civil liberties of all sorts ignored.

Kern frequently championed labor's cause. The Kern-McGillicudy Workman's Compensation Act provided for federal employee compensation when there was an injury on the job. Passage of a child labor law was also spearheaded by Kern. The majority leader's careful marshaling of forces, counting of votes, and arm twisting of a most persuasive sort resulted in laws passing the Senate that established the Federal Reserve and the Federal Trade Commission. Antitrust laws were strengthened and modifications in the tariff passed. It was a hard fight to keep the progressive troops marching together. The broad-sweeping proposals sent up by the president seemed to be antagonizing businessmen everywhere. Kern's style of leadership did not involve many speeches on the Senate floor, but instead took him well behind the scenes to persuade the wavering.

A tough reelection campaign faced the first term senator in 1916. He had no personal organization in the state, nor any money. The passage of the 17th Amendment in 1913 had given the voters the right to select the U.S. Senator, not the legislators. Kern had enthusiastic supporters who thought he was the hero of the oppressed, but it was not enough. His health was poor as well. Entering the campaign with a bad cough, Kern got worse and in time he lost his voice. Weak, sick, tired, carrying the weight of four tough years passing legislation many saw as radical, Kern lost the election to Republican businessman Harry S. New. After giving his valedictory in the Senate in March 1917, Kern had the honor of praise being bestowed upon him from both sides of the aisle. A particularly moving tribute came from a man who held one of the most dramatically opposing political philosophies. This man was Henry Cabot Lodge, who would become President Wilson's mortal enemy in the League of

Nations battle a few years later. Kern reciprocated the warm emotions, having once called Lodge the senator "whose career I envy more" than that of any other man.

The senator was not just defeated, he was wracked with illness. Another short stay at the Asheville sanatorium was followed by a strenuous Southern speaking tour on behalf of the president's policies. In August 1917 he began to decline in health again and returned to Asheville. He was dead within a matter of days.

Analysis of Qualifications

Ironically for a man who first held principles opposed to the soft-money views of William Jennings Bryan, John Kern became a symbol of progressivism in Indiana. He was, moreover, a leader of the progressive forces in the United States Senate when Woodrow Wilson came to power in 1912. He was a loyal Democrat, a decent and honest man, a man who nonetheless chose Republican Indiana as the state in which to conduct his political career. Not surprisingly, defeat far more often than victory crowned his efforts.

What was most remembered about John Kern was his magnetic, loving personality. He was captivating in a crowd, large or small. His political career was immeasurably advanced by his prodigious memory for names and faces. Ambition did not drive him; most of his adult life was spent not in public office but instead in his law office. A good storyteller, a humorous public speaker, Kern could never be identified with the bitterly partisan politicians. Some thought him lazy in politics, but only because he was disinterested in organizational details. He was careful in making decisions, so much so as to be a procrastinator. His biographer and former aide, Claude Bowers, stated that he liked to retire to complete solitude, and there spend hours alone while he wrested with difficult issues.

Wrestling with these ideas led him firmly into the progressive camp. Farmers, workers, and other less advantaged in society were his particular concern. He wanted lower tariffs on agricultural and industrial products, large businesses to be regulated by the government and the banking system to be under the oversight of a federal agency. Women's suffrage, direct election of senators, and party primaries were other progressive ideas that he endorsed. Such principles did not lead him into socialism, but his human rights views required him to argue forcefully for the right of free speech for socialists. Eugene V. Debs, frequent presidential candidate of the Socialist Party, simultaneously acknowledged Kern's lack of sympathy for socialist views but his support for Debs's right to express them.

Kern was not the first choice by Bryan for vice president in 1908, but after the nomination was spurned by several other leading contenders, Kern was a readily accepted substitute. He mirrored Bryan's views closely. His outspoken defense of labor unions was seen as potentially helpful among that segment of the voters. As a campaigner, Kern played an important role in making the pro forma stops in the solid South and then concentrating on the East, permitting Bryan to campaign in the West. Kern was unable even to hold his home state of Indiana. Nonetheless, he emerged from the election with heightened respect. It enabled him to realize, somewhat belatedly, his ambition to be a United States senator. As senator, and particularly as majority leader from 1913 to 1917, Kern played his most important role in public life. Substantial legislation was passed because of Kern's prodding, cajoling, and constant devotion to the task.

Kern would have brought the same equanimity, energy, and progressive principles to the presidency that he demonstrated as majority leader. He worked well with others, was anything but a prima donna, and was cautious and objective about what was possible and what was visionary. Though little experienced in national affairs at the time of his vice presidential nomination, two years later Kern as senator began to show just how quick a study he was. His selection for the vice presidency was an entirely satisfactory decision by the 1908 convention.

KERN BIBLIOGRAPHY

Bowers, Claude G. *The Life of John Worth Kern.* Indianapolis (1918).

Haughton, Virginia F. "John Worth Kern and Wilson's New Freedom." Unpublished doctoral dissertation, University of Kentucky (1973).

Moore, Betty Jane. "The Majority Leader of the United States Senate: The Leader's Effectiveness as a Major Determinant in the Leadership Model." Unpublished doctoral dissertation, University of Maryland (1986).

Sehlinger, Peter J. "John Worth Kern—A Hoosier Progressive," in Ralph D. Gray, ed. *Gentlemen from Indiana, National Party Candidates, 1836–1940.* Indianapolis (1977), pp. 189–217.

Family information from Kern family Bible, in possession of George Lawson, Salem, Virginia; examined by Mrs. Fitzhugh L. Brown, Sewickly, Pennsylvania. Additional assistance was provided by Judge John W. Kern, III, Washington, D.C.

---

*1908 presidential nominee—
Socialist Party*

Eugene Debs

No sketch appears here of Debs, but see the election of 1904, pages 451–452.

State Represented: Indiana.

Birth: November 5, 1855, in Terre Haute, Indiana.

Age on Inauguration Day (March 4, 1909): 53 years, 4 months.

Death: October 20, 1926, in Elmhurst, Illinois.

---

*1908 vice presidential nominee—
Socialist Party*

Benjamin Hanford

No sketch appears here of Hanford, but see election of 1904, page 452–454.

State Represented: New York.

Birth: 1861, in Cleveland, Ohio.

Age on Inauguration Day (March 4, 1909): 48 years old.

Death: January 24, 1910, in Brooklyn.

Election of 1912

NOMINATIONS

Socialist Party Convention (4th): May 12–16, 1912, in Tomlinson Hall, Indiana. *President*— Eugene V. Debs, nominated on the first ballot with 163 votes; Emil Seidel had 56, and Charles Edward Russell (N.Y.) had 54. Seidel moved that the vote be made unanimous. *Vice president*— Emil Seidel, nominated on the first ballot with 159 votes, Dan Hogan (Ark.) had 73, and John W. Slayton (Penn.) had 24. Many others were nominated, including Kate Richards O'Hare (Mo.) and Anna Agnes Mahley (Wash.), but no one else got votes. The nomination was made unanimous.

Republican Party Convention (15th): June 18–22, 1912, at the Coliseum in Chicago, Ill. *President*— William Howard Taft, nominated on the first ballot with 556 votes out of 723 cast, with 348 present but not voting. Theodore Roosevelt was the chief other candidate. *Vice president*— James S. Sherman, nominated on the first ballot with 596 votes out of 654 cast, 424 either present and not voting or absent. Sherman died on October 20, 1912, so the Republican National Committee met and chose Nicholas Butler.

Democratic Party Convention (21st): June 25–29, July 1–2, 1912, at the Fifth Maryland Regiment Armory, Baltimore, Md. *President*— Woodrow Wilson, nominated on the 46th ballot with 990 votes out of 1086 cast. He received 324 on the first ballot. Champ Clark (Mo.), Judson Harmon (Ohio) and Oscar Underwood. (Ala.) were the major rivals. Clark led Wilson until the 30th ballot. *Vice president*— Thomas R. Marshall, nominated on the second ballot with 644½ votes out of 1043⅓. He had received 389 on the first ballot, John Burke (N.D.) was the other contender.

Progressive Party Convention (1st): August 5–7, 1912, at the Coliseum in Chicago, Ill. *President*— Theodore Roosevelt, nominated by acclamation without a ballot. *Vice president*— Hiram W. Johnson, nominated by acclamation.

GENERAL ELECTION, November 5, 1912

Popular Vote
Wilson 6,293,152
Roosevelt 4,119,207
Taft 3,486,333
Debs 900,369
Others 241,902

Electoral Vote
Wilson-Marshall — 435 (40 states)
Roosevelt-Johnson — 88 (6 states)
Taft-Butler — 8 (2 states)

Winners
Woodrow Wilson, 28th president
Thomas R. Marshall, 28th vice president

Losers
Theodore Roosevelt, Hiram W. Johnson, William Howard Taft, James S. Sherman, Nicholas M. Butler, Eugene Debs, Emil Seidel

---

1912 presidential nominee —
Progressive Party

Theodore Roosevelt

No biographical sketch of Roosevelt is included since he served as president from September 14, 1901, until March 4, 1909 (26th President).

State represented: New York.
Birth: October 27, 1858.
Age on Inauguration Day (March 4, 1913): 54 years, 4½ months.
Death: January 6, 1919.

1912 vice presidential nominee —
Progressive Party

Hiram Johnson

Full name: Hiram Warren Johnson.
State represented: California.
Birth: September 2, 1866, in Sacramento, California.
Age on Inauguration Day (March 4, 1913): 46 years, 6 months.
Education: Sacramento public schools; University of California (Berkeley), 1884–1886, dropped out; studied law and admitted to bar in 1888.
Religion: Apparently not a member of any church; buried after a nonsectarian service in San Francisco.
Ancestry/prominent relatives: English ancestors; father, Grove Johnson, was a U.S. congressman for one term.
Occupation: Attorney.
Public office: Corporation counsel for Sacramento, 1895–1897; assistant district attorney in San Francisco graft cases, 1906–1909; governor of California, January 2, 1911–March 15, 1917; unsuccessful Progressive Party nominee for vice president, 1912; U.S. senator, March 16, 1917–August 6, 1945; unsuccessful contender for Republican presidential nomination 1920 and 1924; refused to be appointed secretary of interior, 1933.
Home: For many years rented Calvert Manor, a Georgian mansion in Prince George's County, Maryland, built in 1753 by Lord Baltimore; then moved to home on Capitol Hill.
Death: August 6, 1945, Bethesda, Maryland, at age 78 years, 11 months.
Burial: Cyprus Lawn Cemetery, San Francisco, California.
Personal characteristics: Short, stout, square-jawed, round face, almost always wore formal attire — cutaway coat and vest with a derby; then when fashions changed, wore double-breasted suits.
Father: Grove Lawrence Johnson (March 27, 1841–February 1, 1926); attorney and local politician; U.S. congressman.
Mother: Ann Williamson de Montfredy (May 23, 1842–1903); married on January 23, 1887.

THEODORE ROOSEVELT and HIRAM JOHNSON
(From the collection of David J. and Janice L. Frent)

Stepmother: Helen Alice Hassett (?–?), married September 1, 1908; she was the daughter of a former mayor of Sacramento, W.J. Hassett.

Siblings: Albert de Montfredy (September 16, 1861–September 1907); was an attorney. Josephine (May 1863–January 1952), married Adolph Fink. Mary (September 1872–?), married Henry O'Neil. Mabel (October 1879–January 1951), married Bruce Dray, a bank clerk.

Wife: Minnie Lucretia McNeal (1868–January 25, 1955), married on January 23, 1887; daughter of Archibald McNeal, of Sacramento.

Children: Hiram, Jr. (Jack) (August 10, 1887–?); married Amy Bowles in 1912; she died September 17, 1918; a lawyer. Archibald (1890–August 1, 1933), committed suicide.

Historic sites: Hiram Johnson house, 122 Maryland Avenue, N.E., Washington D.C., Johnson's home while he was a U.S. senator (private) (also called Mountjoy Bayly House).

Hiram Johnson's father gave him a heritage of political ambition, but not one graced with a style that Hiram cared to emulate. As a Sacramento, California, politician, Grove Johnson in 1867 began his career with a scandal. He pleaded no contest to the charge that as an election inspector he had added the names of at least 60 nonexistent individuals to the voter list. Four years later his attempted return to politics brought the allegation that he had his and his opponent's names printed on ballots with a special ink which, after enough time had passed for them to be marked by the voters and cast in the ballot box, would fade out and reveal the candidates in the opposite order on the ballot. Grove Johnson switched parties from Union (Republican) right after the war, to Democratic and then back to Republican. He was a political opportunist to the extreme, with fraud an acceptable aspect of his political technique. Grove was an attorney, and he built a profitable practice in Sacramento. As an attorney he frequently defended the Southern Pacific Railroad, a position that would in time bring him into sharp conflict with his two sons.

Hiram went through the Sacramento public schools and then two years at the University of California at Berkeley. An unexpected pregnancy by his girlfriend caused him to drop out of school, marry her, and return to Sacramento to work as a stenographer in his father's law office. The marriage begun in haste continued strong and supportive for 60 years. In the family law office Hiram studied, and in 1888, after a year and a half of legal education he was admitted to the bar. He joined his father and older brother in a three–Johnson firm. When Grove Johnson won a seat in Congress in 1894, Hiram was his campaign manager. Politics intrigued the young attorney. So did the law, and he gained considerable respect for his courtroom skills.

Hiram and his brother Albert soon parted political as well as personal company from their father. Grove remained in Congress only one term, and then was defeated by a more progressive, less railroad-oriented candidate. Grove's unscrupulous political conduct, as well as his rejection of reform programs both on the state and national level, led his sons to drop out of the law firm and start their separate practice. Hiram's political ambitions received their first boost when he was elected in 1892 as president of the county Republican Party. In 1895, he became corporation counsel (city attorney) for Sacramento, a reward for his valuable assistance to the successful mayoral candidate. When Hiram began to support reform candidates who were trying to free the city from the shackles of machine politics, a break with Grove was unavoidable. In 1901, the two took opposite sides in the mayor's race, and Hiram's choice won. Grove publicly attacked his sons, saying, "Children make mistakes, but the old man never does." Later he referred to his boys as his "two chief enemies down the street; one, Hiram, full of egotism, and the other, Albert, full of booze." Cruelly, but perceptively, Grove had accurately described his offspring. In 1907, Albert would die from his alcoholism. Hiram would live on.

After the split occurred in the family firm, followed by a serious political setback in the reform fight in Sacramento, the Johnson brothers left for San Francisco in disgust and opened a new law office there. That was in 1902, and two years later Hiram began practicing law on his own, perhaps finding too many personal difficulties in continuing to work alongside his alcoholic brother. Hiram achieved major recognition for being involved with the prosecution of scores of San Francisco public officials for graft. Johnson's flair as a trial lawyer gained him a dramatic conviction of the mayor of the city, Eugene Schmitz, in 1907. Johnson then managed the campaign of the district attorney who would carry on the fight against city corruption. The chief prosecutor was shot in 1908, and Johnson returned to the scene of his earlier triumph against Schmitz and secured the conviction of San Francisco's political boss, Abraham Ruef. The image he gained from these highly publicized trials was a forceful, absolutely incorruptible reformer.

The national headlines from the Ruef trial made Johnson immensely attractive to a reform group organized in 1907 in the state, the Lincoln-Roosevelt Republican League. A bitter confrontation with his father in 1909 during a hearing in a legislative committee on which his father served, marked him even more as a man who was independent and fearless. The only issue in the 1910 campaign was ending the control of state politics exerted by the railroad: "Kick the Southern Pacific out of politics" was the theme, and it swept Hiram into office.

Governor Johnson immediately set about fulfilling his campaign promises of kicking special interests out of government. A strongly progressive legislature backed the new governor. Soon a flood of bills dear to the progressives' hearts poured forth. Included were recall, initiative and referendum, an advisory direct primary law for U.S. senators, a state civil service system and strong labor legislation. Eight-hour work days for women and strong guidelines for child labor were passed. Yet it was the battle against the railroads that put Johnson in the governor's mansion, and it was his success in crippling their power that made him nationally known. Passage of a state Public Utilities Act gave new powers to the already-existing railroad commission, and regulation of the Southern Pacific became a reality.

Johnson's election as governor enabled him to become acquainted with former president Theodore Roosevelt. The two men soon had a mutual interview, and they found themselves eminently compatible. Roosevelt became Johnson's political mentor, almost his surrogate father. Until Roosevelt's death in 1919, Johnson turned to him for advice and encouragement. At this initial stage Johnson was encouraging Roosevelt, insisting that he get in the race to defeat President William Howard Taft for the 1912 Republican nomination. The governor led a strong Roosevelt delegation from California to the national convention. Twice he walked out with the delegation over disputes with the old guard in charge of the convention. The second bolt from the convention was to form a progressive party to nominate Roosevelt for president. Johnson was chosen as national chairman for the Bull Moose Party. California progressives had been organizing to place Johnson second on the ticket with Roosevelt. They had begun their efforts with the expectation that the ticket would be the Republican one, but easily shifted their focus to the Progressive nomination. Almost five months of work, largely unaided by Roosevelt himself, culminated in success at the Progressives' convention. By this time ultimate defeat in November was certain, and Johnson reluctantly agreed to accept nomination only after Roosevelt said, "You must come along with me, Hiram." On August 7, 1912, Johnson was nominated as Roosevelt's running mate.

Johnson's campaign style was frantic, loud, and at times vicious. Johnson denounced the Republicans as strenuously as the Democrats. For ten weeks, across 22 states by train, Johnson delivered almost 500 speeches. The split Republican vote between Taft and Roosevelt doomed the Progressives, and Woodrow Wilson easily won the general election. Roosevelt was impressed with his comrade, and by 1914 was touting Johnson as his favorite for the 1916 Republican nomination.

Most of his desired reforms having been accomplished in the first session of the legislature under Governor Johnson, the just-defeated national candidate had little to interest him on the state level in 1913 and 1914. Johnson's personal popularity remained high, however, and he won easy reelection the latter year despite that most Progressive Party candidates were defeated. He did not run as a Republican that year, and tried to keep the

Progressives' third party a separate movement. Roosevelt continued his praise, writing to Johnson, "I cannot imagine anything so good for this country as to have you President. ... I do not know of any one man in this country who I should be so glad to see President of the United States as yourself." It was not to be in 1916, and instead Johnson found himself running for the United States Senate. He said in the campaign he would try to revive the faltering Progressive movement. It was during that campaign that he played one of the critical roles of his life, quite possibly causing the defeat of the extremely able Republican nominee, Charles E. Hughes. Johnson saw Hughes as a representative of the old-guard, conservative Republicans, even though Hughes as New York governor had established an unmatched record for reform. The California party was badly split, and Johnson as usual was going his own way without party support. When Hughes campaigned in California, it was Johnson's intraparty enemies who conducted the presidential nominee on his tour. A few days after arriving, Hughes stayed at the same hotel as did Johnson, but Hughes was unaware of Johnson's presence. Johnson took no steps to meet with his party's presidential candidate, perhaps believing that the first move should come from Hughes. When Hughes discovered Johnson was there, he was only moments from departing for the next campaign stop. The story got picked up in the press as a mutual snub between the principals. Johnson's lack of enthusiasm for Hughes was obvious among California Progressives. While Johnson won election to the Senate by a 300,000-vote margin, Hughes lost the state by 4,000 votes, and with it lost the presidency.

In the United States Senate, Johnson for almost the next 30 years was intimately identified with isolationist, "Fortress America" political principles. The clear trend in 1917 towards involvement with the war in Europe troubled Johnson, and he finally but reluctantly acceded to the need for participation. Soon after America declared war, Johnson regretted the decision. He then became a consistent critic of the Wilson administration.

After the war was won, Johnson believed Wilson was involved in secret negotiations over the Treaty of Versailles. He called for release of the complete text of the treaty. The presence of 14,000 American troops in Russia after the war was over, fighting to try to overturn the Bolshevik regime, was violently criticized. Johnson was strident in condemning the League of Nations proposal. Johnson throughout his career feared foreign entanglements, and to him the League was just a giant guarantee that we would be constantly at war to fulfill the stated commitments of mutual security. Johnson and a few other hardliners came to be called the "irreconcilables." He was anti–British. He viewed the League as an attempt to perpetuate the British Empire through guarantees of the colonial possessions of Great Britain. Wilson would not compromise, and thus the Treaty was defeated. Since such senators as Henry Cabot Lodge would have been willing to compromise, Johnson felt his own unalterable objections to the treaty were crucial in preventing a settlement between the White House and the Senate.

Wilson considered Johnson a member of the "little band of willful men" who obstructed the treaty's passage. Just as important to the defeat, though, were the despair and urge for "normalcy" that dominated the country. The League was shrouded in suspicion and secrecy, and Johnson fed upon that by arguing Americans must not be committed to foreign wars by the whim of European dictators.

As a leading advocate of isolation, Johnson was a prime candidate for president in a war-weary America of 1920. He was initially reluctant to announce his candidacy, but many saw him as the heir to the tradition of his beloved Theodore Roosevelt, who had died the year before. Johnson had conducted a coast-to-coast crusade against the League, and had drawn huge crowds. With the encouragement of some Roosevelt advisers Johnson finally became convinced a presidential candidacy was viable. He won primary victories in every state that held one, but there were not nearly enough delegates to be won that way. He was not acceptable to many of the conservative, immensely powerful leaders in the party, and despite Johnson's national appeal he was never in a position to gain the nomination. Johnson's opposition to the League lost him support from among the Progressives. With large segments of both the old guard and the reform wing against him, he was doomed. When the convention deadlocked, Johnson was offered the vice presidency in exchange for support by each of the major candidates, including Warren G. Harding. He rejected all the offers. Ironically, all the candidates who came to him were dead before the presidential term they were all seeking was completed on March 4, 1925. It was reported by one writer that after Harding had been selected in the smoke-filled room machinations, but before he was nominated, he went to Johnson's room and informed him of his imminent nomination. He then told the California senator, "Hiram, I want you for my vice-presidential candidate." Johnson's reply was, "I don't care to consider it." Four years as a spare wheel in a Harding administration, working subserviently to a man he did not respect or think fit for the presidency, was probably a key motivation in the rejection. Three years later Harding would be dead. Johnson was also disgusted, almost despondent, over his own defeat for the nomination. He had little taste for politics for several years.

For the next 12 years, with Republicans in the White House, Johnson was usually a critic and opponent of the administration. He toyed with running for president in 1924, particularly while Harding was still alive. Coolidge's ascension indicated the futility of a race for president, but still Johnson got into the hopeless contest. He lost most primaries to Coolidge, and never was a serious threat. He did not endorse Coolidge's election nor the progressive Robert La Follette who was in the race as a third party candidate.

Johnson's Senate record was a mixture of isolationism, progressivism, and parochial California concerns. He criticized the treaties proposed during the 1920s to limit the production of arms. The Four-Power Treaty negotiated by Secretary of State Charles E. Hughes seemed suspect because it violated his cardinal principle of diplomacy, that all discussions be held publicly. It also seemed an indirect way to force the United States into the League of Nations, because the treaty provided that each of the countries play a role in policing the world and preserving the peace. Johnson turned from being a friend of disarmament to being bitterly opposed to such treaties, wanting instead for America to have a strong navy in order to protect its own interests without having to rely on any ally. Admission into the World Court was objected to for many of the same reasons — it was an indirect way to ease the United States into the League, and an undesirable means to force the country into peace-keeping commitments.

The only national legislation to bear Johnson's name was the Johnson Act of 1934. It was a reaction to efforts to reduce the reparations owed this country by European nations as a result of World War I. Johnson's bill made it illegal for financial institutions to lend money or sell or purchase securities of any foreign country that had defaulted on its obligations to the United States. It was the opening triumph in a decade-long neutrality and isolation battle that would not be finally resolved until Pearl Harbor.

A six-year fight, beginning in 1922, to construct the nation's first large flood control and power generation project — Boulder Dam — was probably Johnson's most lasting contribution as a senator. Bitter fights between the states that would participate in the project, and between senators uninterested in assisting the Southwest and California with such a massive and unique government project, finally were overcome and construction began on what was later renamed Hoover Dam on the Colorado River. Johnson also helped preserve Muscle Shoals as a governmental and not private power project. He generally took an anti-private utility stance. Though seen as a liberal on most issues, Johnson favored a high protective tariff to protect California agricultural products.

The conservative administrations of Harding, Coolidge, and Hoover found Johnson a consistent critic of their policies. When the Depression deepened and President Hoover seemed incapable of responding to the crisis effectively, many progressives urged Johnson to challenge Hoover. He had no desire to take on another fruitless challenge of an incumbent president, but remained a strong critic. When Franklin Roosevelt was nominated by the Democrats, he courted Johnson and won. Johnson liked the New Yorker, a distant relative of his hero Theodore Roosevelt, but he still feared some of the candidate's positions. Those fears and doubts would turn into bitter opposition by the end of Roosevelt's first term, but during 1932 Johnson endorsed the Democratic Roosevelt and campaigned for him. Roosevelt was appreciative and after the election offered Johnson the secretary of interior post. Johnson had no interest in being someone else's assistant, and refused the offer. "I have lived so long in absolute independence that it is a very difficult thing for me to see myself as a member of any group where I would discipline myself to the view of any one, or any few men."

For four years Johnson voted for almost all New Deal legislation. However, when Roosevelt's programs called for increasing federal, and usually presidential authority, Johnson feared the president was trying to establish an effective dictatorship. The court-packing scheme of 1937 was the final break with Roosevelt. The president's demand for power seemed now to threaten a dismantling of all checks and balances imposed by the Constitution. Johnson's health was bad—he had a stroke in 1936. His mental health was not good either, in part because of the suicide of one of his sons, Archibald, in 1933. He was increasingly irritable and bitter in his attacks. Foreign policy differences were frequent with Roosevelt. Johnson was not blind to the evils of Hitler and Mussolini, but he warned that in "fighting a European dictator, we would create one of our own." Lend Lease was called the "Wickedest piece of legislation that has ever been presented to the American Congress." Every new indignity imposed on Europe by Hitler received little more than a shrug from Johnson. He laughed at any fears that Germany or Japan could conquer America, and he wanted the United States to strengthen her own defenses and ignore the rest of the world. As soon as Pearl Harbor was attacked, however, even Johnson knew isolation no longer was possible.

Johnson's loyal support of the war did not cause him to favor some of Roosevelt's war aims, most notably the formation of the United Nations. In November 1943, the Californian was one of only six senators to vote against a resolution calling for a postwar organization of nations. On July 13, 1945, he was the only vote on the Senate Foreign Relations Committee cast against the United Nations, and one of only three in the full Senate. His health had just about collapsed. He had suffered another stroke in 1943 from which he physically and emotionally never recovered. On the day the atomic bomb was dropped on Hiroshima, Johnson died.

Analysis of Qualifications

Hiram Johnson is remembered today chiefly for two fairly early episodes in his political career. In 1912, he was Theodore Roosevelt's running mate on the Bull Moose ticket. Four years later, he is credited with having caused his fellow Republican Charles Evans Hughes' defeat for the presidency, because in pique he refused to help Hughes' candidacy. Some recall he was one of the leading isolationist senators from the aftermath of World War I all the way until World War II was declared. These high points are in fact good summaries of his career. The 1912 campaign marked his early and sincere progressivism. Isolationism drove him throughout his Senate career. The image as an egocentric, easily antagonized, even vindictive politician is an appropriate one. His life on the national political stage began meteorically, with his election to the governorship of California after having no previous experience in elective office. Two years later he was on a national party ticket. For the next 12 years he was seriously mentioned for the presidential nomination. Many credited him with having the makings of an outstanding chief executive. Yet even during these early periods there were hints of the obstructionist, suspicious attitudes that would dominate the last 20 years of his life.

Johnson was rarely a constructive force. His hallmarks were opposition and criticism. His speaking style was abrasive, with his clenched fist constantly being pounded into his open palm. He could generate enormous public enthusiasm, angrily deriding the forces that he felt oppressed the people. He began his two terms as governor with little idea of what progressive legislation should be adopted in California, bringing with him little more than a campaign slogan of kicking the Southern Pacific Railroad out of politics. Once the focus shifted from "throw the rascals out" to "what do we do now?" Johnson struggled. That considerable reform did emerge owes as much to the strength and character of the California progressive movement as it does to Johnson himself.

The flinty, irascible politician's ego was constantly exposed, from the pique over Charles E. Hughes that led to the famous "snubbing" incident, to his animosities toward every president, Republican or Democrat, who served after his hero Theodore Roosevelt. He was distrustful and vindictive. He created a powerful political machine, built on and subservient to his personality. It permitted much reform to occur in a formerly corporation-run California; it also personalized and embittered politics in the state. He was a sincere if singleminded believer in his goals. It was easy to incur his wrath by the slightest opposition. Governor Hiram Johnson was a most useful and significant leader in California, whose force of will and dynamism permitted the strides taken by that state in the second decade of the twentieth century. Yet his style of governance, particularly as displayed when serving in the U.S. Senate, was short-sighted, parochial, and caustic. It is easy to see a Johnson presidency as a series of pitched battles, a contentious administration with a progressive domestic program and an isolationist foreign policy. He may have been forced by events finally to recognize America's interests in Europe; he may instead have divided the country bitterly in battling to keep us out of the first world war. This mix of might-have-beens, the risks weighed with the potential, causes Johnson to be placed in the category of satisfactory nominees, neither a likely failure nor a sure success. He can in fact be viewed as both, a man whose administration would probably have been crowned both with triumph and dismal failure.

JOHNSON BIBLIOGRAPHY

Boyle, Peter. "The Study of an Isolationist: Hiram Johnson." Unpublished doctoral dissertation, University of California at Los Angeles (1970).

Davenport, Frederick M. "Did Hughes Snub Johnson?—An Inside Story...." *American Political Science Review* XLIII (1949), pp. 321–332.

Finney, Ruth. "Hiram Johnson of California." *American History Illustrated* I (1966), pp. 20–28.

Fitzpatrick, John James, III. "Senator Hiram W. Johnson: A Life History, 1866–1945." Unpublished doctoral dissertation, University of California, Berkeley (1975).

Johnson, Hiram. *The Diary Letters of Hiram Johnson, 1917–1945.* New York (7 vols., 1983).

Liljekvist, Clifford. "Senator Hiram W. Johnson." Unpublished doctoral dissertation, University of Southern California (1953).

Lincoln, A. "Theodore Roosevelt, Hiram Johnson, and the Vice-presidential Nomination of 1912." *Pacific Historical Review* XXVIII (1959), pp. 267–283.

Lower, Richard Coke. *A Bloc of One: The Political Career of Hiram W. Johnson.* Stanford (1993).

_____. "Hiram Johnson: The Making of an Irreconcilable." *Pacific Historical Review* XLI (1972), pp. 505–526.

Lowry, Edward G. *Washington Close-ups: Intimate Views of Some Public Figures.* Boston (1921).

McKee, Irving. "The Background and Early Career of Hiram Warren Johnson, 1866–1910." *Pacific Historical Review* XIX (1950), pp. 17–30.

Olin, Spencer C., Jr. *California's Prodigal Sons, Hiram Johnson and the Progressives, 1911–1917.* Berkeley and Los Angeles (1968).

Tucker, Ray, and Frederick R. Barkley. *Sons of the Wild Jackass.* Freeport, N.Y. (1969), reprint of 1932 edition.

Weatherson, Michael A., and Hal Bochin. *Hiram Johnson: A Bio-Bibliography,* Westport, Conn. (1988).

_____, and _____. *Hiram Johnson: Political Revivalist.* Lanham, Md. (1995).

Willis, William L. *History of Sacramento County.* Los Angeles (1913), pp. 500–503.

1912 presidential nominee— Republican Party

William Howard Taft

No biographical sketch of Taft is included here since he served as president from March 4, 1909–March 4, 1913 (27th president).

WILLIAM HOWARD TAFT (left) and JAMES S. SHERMAN
(From the collection of David J. and Janice L. Frent)

State represented: Ohio.
Birth: September 15, 1857.
Age on Inauguration Day (March 4, 1913):
55 years, 5½ months.
Death: March 8, 1930.

1912 vice presidential nominee —
Republican Party

James S. Sherman

No biographical sketch of Sherman is included since he served as vice president from March 4, 1909, until October 30, 1912 (27th vice president).

State represented: New York.
Birth: October 24, 1855.
Age on Inauguration Day (March 4, 1913): 57 years, 4½ months; died before then.
Death: October 30, 1912, while serving as vice president.

1912 vice presidential nominee —
Republican Party

Nicholas M. Butler

Full Name: Nicholas Murray Butler.
State Represented: New York.
Birth: April 2, 1862, in Elizabeth, New Jersey.
Age on Inauguration Day (March 4, 1913): 50 years, 11 months.
Education: Columbia University, graduated 1882, masters 1883; his thesis was on "Permanent Influence of Immanuel Kant"; Ph.D. 1884, his dissertation was "The History of Logical Doctrine," University of Berlin 1884–85.
Religion: Episcopalian.
Ancestry/prominent relatives: Paternal great-grandfather a rector in Church of England; maternal grandfather also a minister. Paternal grandfather a seaman; father-in-law was a leading Presbyterian clergyman in New Jersey.
Occupation: Educator.
Public offices: Member of New Jersey state board of education, 1888–1895; president of

**WILLIAM HOWARD TAFT (left)
and NICHOLAS M. BUTLER**
(From the National Archives)

New Jersey Council of Education in 1891; appointed to Paterson, New Jersey, Board of Education, 1892; president of Conciliation Internationale, 1905–1924, an international peace organization; refused several offers of appointment to various presidents' cabinets; named by the Republican National Committee in 1912 to substitute on the ticket for deceased vice presidential nominee James S. Sherman; unsuccessful candidate for Republican presidential nomination in 1920.

Home: New York City.

Death: December 7, 1947, in New York City, at age 85 years, 8 months.

Burial: Cedar Lawn Cemetery, Paterson, New Jersey.

Personal characteristics: Brown hair in ear-lier days; receded by age 40 and graying; blue eyes, mustache. Solidly built; medium height.

Father: Henry Leny Butler (March 11, 1833–September 23, 1904), small businessman; born in London, arrived in America in 1835; his father's name was John Thomas Butler Buchanan, but by time the family arrived in America the "Buchanan" had been discarded.

Mother: Mary Jones Murray (June 7, 1838–February 3, 1912), daughter of the Rev. Dr. Nicholas and Eliza Jones (Rhees) Murray; married October 4, 1860.

Siblings: Henry Meldrum (February 6, 1864–August 22, 1940), married Mary L. Brobst; a New York businessman. William Curtis (c. 1865–January 6, 1944), married Eleanor Hughes; engineer, then banker in Everett, Washington. Mary (?–November 2, 1945), married Walter B. Mahoney, a New York businessman. Eliza Rhees (October 22, 1872–September 18, 1935), an educator; never married. Two other children died young.

First wife: Susanna Edwards Schuyler (1863–January 10, 1903); married February 7, 1887; daughter of J. Rutsen Schuyler, wealthy owner of a munitions firm in New Jersey.

Child: Sarah Schuyler (1893–February 21, 1947), married Neville Lawrence of London in 1933; he was a businessman and banker.

Second wife: Kate La Montagne (May 5, 1865–May 4, 1948), married May 5, 1907; daughter of Auguste La Montagne and Annie Davis.

Children: None.

It was a close-knit, comfortable, politically active family in which Murray Butler was raised. His brilliance could not be doubted, and he showed his genius almost immediately. There were those who referred to him as having "a man's wit in a child's body." He also had an egotist's sharp tongue, and would correct his teachers even in elementary school. At home, he would participate in esoteric philosophical discussions, particularly with his grandfather. There is little in young Murray's life that did not show brilliance.

At the age of 13, Butler graduated from high school. Paterson, New Jersey, to which his family had moved in 1864, had not provided the education sufficient to prepare him for college. For the next two years he would be tutored in Latin, Greek, advanced mathematics, and other subjects. In the most frivolous of ways, Butler became infatuated with Columbia College. The frivolity was his watching a boat race between various colleges, and it was Columbia's blue colors that most appealed to him. From that basis he would first choose the school for his own education, and later for his career. Professors found him the most brilliant student they had ever instructed. While attending school he was also paying his own way by writing articles for the New York *Tribune* and by teaching other students. He was also intensely involved in almost all campus social functions. He was editor-in-chief of the student newspaper and of the junior class annual. There was little modesty in Butler, and other students almost instinctively deferred to him for leadership positions.

The president of Columbia recognized Butler's genius. Frederick A.P. Barnard called Butler into his office frequently, and they engaged in long discussions about the school and on other subjects. Though Butler had not earlier thought of education as his career, these discussions led him in that direction. President

NICHOLAS M. BUTLER
(From the collectio of David J. and Janice L. Frent)

Barnard wanted Butler to join the college faculty and in time become its president. Barnard's ambitions for Butler began when Butler was still a teenager.

After graduation Butler remained at Columbia for both his masters and his doctorate. The traditional route for scholars was then to attend a European school for post-graduate work. Butler went to Germany and attended the University of Berlin in 1884 and 1885. The experience was one of the high points of his life, as he found the work intellectually challenging, a difficult feat for Butler. Upon his return to Columbia there were few openings. Butler was only an assistant to a professor of philosophy from 1885 until 1886. From 1886 until 1889 he was a tutor, but finally was placed at the head of a department in 1889 when he was made professor of philosophy, ethics, and psychology.

Butler's forte was not in teaching but in administration. He had little interest in entering discussions with his students. He would read his lectures in class, with only a modicum of time left for questions at the end. It was said that his lectures flowed so smoothly that they almost lulled his listeners to sleep, and made no impression upon them. Teaching would not be Butler's career. In 1890 he devised a plan for the establishment of a department of philosophy at Columbia. In order to implement it he would leave teaching that year, never to return in a full-time capacity.

Even while teaching at Columbia, Butler would until 1895 keep his home in New Jersey. He drafted several pieces of legislation for New Jersey, organizing and improving public libraries, establishing vocational education, and reorganizing schools. In 1891, he was president of the New Jersey Council of Education. He also authored the legislation creating nonpartisan school boards in cities of intermediate size. He then became Paterson's first president of a nonpartisan school board.

There seemed no end to the avenues that Butler's interest in education took. He was the driving force in establishing in 1887 the New York College for the Training of Teachers; the school became affiliated with Columbia in 1898. In 1890, he founded and began editing the *Educational Review*, which became a very successful periodical for teachers and other students of education. In 1892, his *Great Educators Series* was begun, being book-length biographies of major world educators. Still other periodicals were either edited or strongly influenced by his efforts. In 1898, he published his first book, *The Meaning of Education*.

Butler's involvement in education was at all levels of instruction, from primary schools through post-graduate work. He advocated the raising of standards for college admissions and was a major force behind the creation of the College Entrance Examination Board in 1899. This board established uniformity in college entrance examinations. He was the first chairman of the board and continued in that position until 1913. A list of other educational associations in which he played a leadership role is almost endless, including the National Council of Education, the College Council of New York State, the National Education Association, and the Association of Colleges and Preparatory Schools. As his fame and achievements multiplied, he increasingly was contacted by other universities and offered

their presidencies. One list of the schools included the following: the state universities of Ohio, Indiana, Illinois, Wisconsin, Iowa, Colorado, Washington, and California; he was offered the opportunity to become the first president of Stanford University. He also declined several offers of political positions, including United States Commissioner of Education in 1889. Butler's commitment to Columbia, which was now far beyond his infatuation with the school colors, became paramount in his professional life. He would remain with the university for almost 60 years.

Politics was almost as much of an obsession with Butler as was education. He grew up in an unbendingly Republican family. James G. Blaine, the Republican presidential nominee in 1884, was a personal friend of Butler's father and visited occasionally, as did other political leaders. Butler would later confess that Blaine was his first, and perhaps strongest, political idol. Blaine's defeat in 1884 was a crushing blow to the then 22-year-old student in Berlin. New York's political leader Garret A. Hobart, later to be vice president under William McKinley, offered him the opportunity to be elected to a safely Republican state assembly seat, but Butler demurred. He also turned down offers to run for mayor of New York City, and for New York governor in 1904, 1912 and 1926. He refused to become secretary of state in 1921 or to be appointed ambassador to England, Germany, or Japan. In 1904, even President Theodore Roosevelt gave some support to Butler for the New York governor's nomination. Roosevelt was actually more enamored with the possibility of Charles E. Hughes' becoming New York governor that year. Though Butler craved political influence and seemed to collect letters from influential politicians in the same way others collect stamps, he only once sought political office. His short-lived campaign for the presidency in 1920 will be discussed subsequently.

Seth Low was serving as Columbia's president when he resigned in 1901 to become the Republican candidate for mayor of New York City. Butler first served as acting president, but in 1902 received the permanent appointment, which he would continue to hold until

1945. Columbia had already begun its move to its new campus under the leadership of President Low, but it was largely through Butler's efforts that the school experienced its tremendous growth both in size and prestige. In Butler's first year the student enrollment was 4,300. It peaked at 32,000 shortly before World War II began. The faculty and staff increased eight-fold, while the budget increased more than ten times. Forty years of Butler administration made Columbia University one of the principal universities in the country. Before Butler was appointed president the administration took a poll of educators in the country to determine their feelings about Butler being offered the position. There are no preserved dissents in this poll, and perhaps there were none given. The choice by the trustees on January 6, 1902, was unanimous, and Butler became Columbia's twelfth president. The next 40 years were to prove the choice a wise one.

The new president's energy was almost incomprehensible. A collection of his writings shows 3,200 published essays, speeches, reviews, interviews, and other works. So infatuated was he with his own writing that he had published his high school valedictory address. He made annual summer trips to Europe for educational purposes, in part to recruit new teachers for Columbia. He read endlessly, boasting, with the college librarian confirming, that he used the college library more than anyone else, student or faculty. He devoured newspapers, the *Congressional Record*, and untold numbers of books and articles. His chief interests were politics, economics, philosophy and, of course, education. He had no ghost writer for his many published works, and he even did his own research. One particular effort, the preparation for a lecture on "building the American dream" resulted in Butler personally examining over 2,000 volumes in the library.

This work was anything but drudgery to Butler. He loved to give speeches and to see his work published. He would not prepare speeches beforehand other than mentally to work the matter over for about an hour prior to delivery. Thus the speech was almost entirely extemporaneous. He had a stenographer take notes so that the speech would be pre-served. His natural, easy flowing speaking style could be dramatic, and it commanded his audience's attention.

This frenetic activity does cause Butler's motives to be questioned. His personality was cold and pompous. He had the ego of the man who knows he is intellectually superior to almost all those with whom he deals, and showed it. He could be condescending and snobbish, with an incredible belief in his own ability. Such belief became almost a sense that he was infallible. Yet coupled with this self-confidence was a strong need for recognition. He sought out great men of his age, whether political leaders or people in private life. For many years he was a confidant of presidents, but even after his political influence had waned, he continued to write the incumbent presidents for almost no reason other than to get a written response. This he would immediately place in his presidents' file. He also collected degrees, achieving honorary awards from 37 universities. Educational awards were almost equally matched by foreign governmental decorations, including one from both Mussolini's Italy and Trujillo's Dominican Republic. He received almost as much satisfaction from his foreign correspondence, always meticulously filed away, as from his presidential letters.

Also on the darker side of his career was his pitiful home life. His first wife was in perpetual bad health and died in 1903, leaving him a nine-year-old daughter, Sarah. His second wife was insufferable. Kate Butler in public would appear the loving wife, concerned and understanding. At home she was a constant complainer, hysterical and jealous. Butler hardly knew how to react around her. So jealous was Kate that she forbade Butler's daughter Sarah from visiting. The rest of his family was also banned. The man who carried on such lengthy correspondence with presidents and kings could not face his own wife. When his daughter or other relatives would arrive unexpectedly, he would seem frightened that Kate might discover their presence. There was nothing to hold the Butler marriage together other than the Columbia president's fear that the scandal of a divorce would bring harm to his beloved university.

Close friendships with U.S. presidents earned Butler a reputation as a political power. Beginning with President Benjamin Harrison, Butler was an adviser to every Republican president through Calvin Coolidge. President McKinley praised him as follows: "In my opinion, the ablest politician in the United States, with a single exception, is Nicholas Murray Butler. He also has high qualities for diplomatic service." The closest relationship he had with a president began with his meeting Theodore Roosevelt at the 1884 Republican convention. In 1900, Butler advised Roosevelt not to accept the vice presidency but to remain as governor of New York. When Roosevelt accepted the vice presidency, he still continued to seek advice from Butler. McKinley's assassination made Roosevelt president, which increased the flood of letters exchanged between the Columbia campus and the White House. The first serious breach between the two occurred in 1908 when Roosevelt selected William Howard Taft as his successor instead of Charles Evans Hughes, whom Butler supported. Roosevelt also did not accept gracefully the biting criticism by Butler concerning some of the president's public statements. An exchange of antagonistic letters resulted. Thus when Taft became president, a rupture in the Roosevelt-Butler friendship had already occurred. During the next four years, Butler would become increasingly separated from the ex-president, beginning to see him as an arrogant dictator who lusted for political power. When the Taft reelection campaign began, Butler was one of Taft's key advisers and supporters. Butler's ambition was not only to reelect Taft but also to finish Roosevelt politically. He gave speeches, wrote letters, and otherwise performed every task asked of him on behalf of Taft. Though the campaign for the Republican nomination against Roosevelt succeeded, the general election was an overwhelming defeat for Taft. In honor of Butler's contributions to the campaign, he was selected as the replacement for Vice President James S. Sherman when Sherman died late in the campaign. It was an empty honor by the time it was bestowed upon Butler, as the election was over.

The educator's most conspicuous political involvement was his association with the international peace movement. When Russian czar Nicholas II called for a peace conference in 1898, the Columbia professor pleaded with President McKinley to send a delegation. He and a French pacifist helped found the Conciliation Internationale. Beginning in 1905 and lasting until World War II, Butler was a major participant in almost all peace society meetings in the United States and England. His reputation as an international political force largely grew out of these conferences.

Simultaneous with his growing involvement with the peace movement was his increasing friendship with Andrew Carnegie, which began in 1892. Carnegie's wealth made the industrialist a dominant force in the peace movement. In 1898, he asked Butler how best to use a five to ten million dollar sum to improve human conditions. Butler's ready, and self-serving, suggestion was to create an endowment for Columbia. Carnegie rejected this suggestion. A few years later, however, Butler and others did convince Carnegie to create the Endowment for International Peace. Butler became a trustee when it was founded in 1911, and would remain in that position until his death. In 1925, he succeeded Elihu Root as president of the endowment, not resigning until December 1945. The endowment became a vehicle to consolidate the various organizations within the peace movement. It also became bitterly distrusted, as its wealth made playing favorites among the various organizations life-threatening to those groups which it disapproved. Butler personally decided how to funnel the huge funds from the endowment, making him a figure of great power.

Butler's education in Germany and his respect for German culture made him initially side with that country as World War I approached. He did not expect war to begin, and certainly not to be started by Germany. He had been a frequent correspondent with Kaiser Wilhelm II and thought him a great man, and a man of peace. As Anglo-German disputes began to intensify in 1909, it was England that he found militaristic. He insisted that America maintain strict neutrality in the war and not increase defense appropriations. America was to Butler the greatest moral influence in the world and any efforts to militarize seemed to blemish that image. As war became more of a reality overseas, Butler began to reverse his position and became ardent for England's position. The same Germany he earlier found peace-loving he decided now was a ruthless enemy of all peace-loving countries. Germany must be completely vanquished and its ideals repudiated.

After the war was over, Butler was a lukewarm supporter of the League of Nations. He accepted the idea of international involvement in improving the condition of backward nations; he embraced an international court to settle disputes. Yet his moralistic bent made him reject diplomacy as a tool of international relations, since he did not believe compromising disputes was a satisfactory approach. He did not wish for good and evil, right and wrong, to be compromised into a result, but instead wished for a court to seek out the just result even if it meant one party receive nothing.

The Kellogg-Briand pact of 1928 was achieved in no small measure because of Butler's influence. This treaty called upon every signatory to renounce war as a means of achieving national goals. Butler would later take credit for suggesting such a treaty to Briand, but it is unlikely that his efforts really initiated the conference. His pride also made him furious when Frank Kellogg received the Nobel Peace Prize in 1929, not only because it slighted Butler's efforts, but also because he considered Kellogg of little consequence in the whole matter. In 1930, he persuaded Pope Pius XI to endorse the treaties and worked frantically in the United States for its acceptance here. Butler's 30-year involvement with the peace movement as of 1931 earned him the Nobel Peace Prize for that year.

Among Butler's most controversial activities were his close relationships with many world dictators. He had several conversations with Benito Mussolini, who Butler found to be a cultivated, intelligent man who was remaking Italy into a powerful world force. Butler would express his beliefs that dictatorships brought forth stronger, more intelligent leaders than did democracy. Even with World War II raging in Europe, he would never criticize Mussolini.

As a second world war threatened in Europe, Butler became less identified with the international peace movement and more with demanding increased defense measures at home. Though he had rejected after World War I the idea of collective security by nations, he now invited an alliance to control Nazi Germany.

After William Howard Taft's presidency, Butler became much less of an influence in national affairs. After eight years of Woodrow Wilson, he believed that continued Democratic control of national government would plunge the country into communism. He became New York's favorite son candidate at the 1920 Republican convention, and was considered for a time as a serious contender. The New York *Times* endorsed him as clearly the most qualified candidate in the race. His not very stimulating slogan was "Pick Nick for a Republican Pic-Nic in November." Once it became clear at the convention that he had no chance to win, he worked hard to defeat Leonard Wood. He eventually supported Warren Harding and would later praise the man considered as the country's worst president. Defeat at the convention made Butler bitter and he reacted angrily in public. It was to Butler that Harding confided, "I am not fit for this office and should never have been here." President Harding offered Butler any office he wanted in his cabinet, but all Butler wanted was to advise the new president on whom to appoint.

Presidents Coolidge and Hoover were more often the subject of Butler's criticism than support. He was particularly strong against prohibition and gave countless speeches nationwide seeking the repeal of the prohibition amendment. The New York *Times* in November 1927 said that Butler had criticized almost all Republican presidential candidates of being cowards on this issue. At the 1928 convention he was one of the few who fought for prohibition repeal.

Butler was now more of a gadfly than a political force. When Hoover was nominated in 1928, Butler publicly separated himself from the Republican candidate, and praised Alfred E. Smith, the Democratic nominee. As the Great Depression deepened, Butler's opinion of Hoover became more intensely negative. Butler became an early supporter of Franklin

D. Roosevelt and was exceedingly happy over Hoover's defeat. Yet he soon turned against even Roosevelt, as he opposed all efforts of the new president that appeared to be creating a welfare state.

Though Butler would remain mentally alert until the time of his death, his physical abilities were failing him. He refused to retire, either as a political spokesman or as president of Columbia. At age 75, Butler said he would die in office, and increasingly hard of hearing and almost blind, but still worked five to six hours per day. The trustees of the University told him in 1946 that he would have to resign, and on October 1, 1946, he did so. Perhaps his last major achievement was to encourage his successor as president of Columbia, Dwight D. Eisenhower, to take the job. He told the general, "I shall be only too happy to be your close advisor, companion, and friend." Within little more than a year from his resignation, Butler was dead.

Analysis of Qualifications

Few men who have been nominated for either of America's two highest offices had the brilliance of Nicholas Murray Butler. Yet, McKinley's evaluation of him as one of the great political minds seems grossly misplaced. Butler's abilities as an administrator could not be doubted. His turning Columbia into a major national educational institution was an achievement of the first rank. He accomplished that through his tireless involvement in educational affairs, writing, speaking, and lecturing. He made himself and his university a force in educational progress. He attracted strong faculty and students. He was also an inspirational public speaker, who held the attention of his audience and could sway them with his words. His advice on national affairs was sought eagerly by a lifetime of presidents. Yet a great politician is more than these things; he is also an individual who can identify with the needs and ambitions of the people. He is a man who must have the strength of his own convictions, but also the humility to listen to and accept advice. If he lives in an ivory tower, or an ivy one, he will become lost.

There is no doubting Butler's convictions. His lifelong involvement with the interna-

tional peace effort was a proud accomplishment. Yet each time when world war challenged his convictions, he reversed himself and became as militaristic as any in government. He distrusted the common man and was no great believer in democracy. His praise for Mussolini and other "enlightened" dictators brought him into disrepute among national leaders. Many saw him as a defender of the status quo. His associations as president of Columbia brought him into contact with great business leaders, and he identified with them. He wanted the "best people" to rule with a kindhearted benevolence towards those unfortunate in society. Yet the benevolence would not take the form of governmental assistance to the impoverished. As the Depression began, his solution was that each employed individual should set aside one day's pay for those who were unemployed. If there were those who still did not receive sufficient funds, then businesses and other groups should assist them. Yet none of this should be administered by the government. The New Deal was not the answer, but instead what was needed was "a change of heart and a change of point of view" among business leaders. Governmental handouts would weaken the moral fiber of American workers, and he saw creeping socialism in all that the second Roosevelt attempted. He has been characterized as a nineteenth-century English liberal, and Butler's combination of autocratic tendencies and concern for, but rejection of governmental help to, the poor and oppressed, makes the description an apt one.

Nicholas Murray Butler found his great station in life as a preeminent education administrator and publicist. He could well have served admirably in many of the appointed positions he was offered through the years. Yet it is also likely that he was correct in refusing the elected positions that at times were dangled before him. He simply did not have the personality for leadership in a democracy. Great men were impressed with him, for indeed he was an exceptionally learned, insightful man. Yet he was also cold, pompous and embarrassingly egotistical. Though he would have brought many admirable qualities to high national office, they would have been counter-balanced by equally negative ones. His greatness would have been severely tainted by his limitations.

BUTLER BIBLIOGRAPHY

Butler, Nicholas Murray. *Across the Busy Years: Recollections and Reflections*. 2 vols. New York City (1939-1940).

Bromley, Dorothy Dunbar. "Nicholas Murray Butler: Portrait of a Reactionary." *American Mercury*, March 1935, pp. 286-298.

Coleman, McAlister. "Nicholas Murray Butler: The Open Mind of Morningside." *Modern Monthly*, May 1933, pp. 200-209.

Johnston, Alva. "Cosmos: Dr. Nicholas Murray Butler." *Profiles from the New Yorker*. New York City (1938), pp. 219-238.

Marrin, Albert. *Nicholas Murray Butler*. Boston (1976).

Whittemore, R.F.W. *Nicholas Murray Butler and Public Education, 1862–1911*. New York (1970).

Dates and names for the Butler family were mainly acquired from obituaries for the relevant dates in the *New York Times*.

1912 Presidential Nominee— Socialist Party

Eugene V. Debs

The sketch on Debs appears in the section on the 1904 election, pages 451–452.

State represented: Indiana.

Birth: November 5, 1855 in Terre Haute, Indiana.

Age on Inauguration Day (March 4, 1913): 57 years, 4 months.

Death: October 20, 1926, in Elmhurst, Illinois.

1912 Vice Presidential Nominee— Socialist Party

Emil Seidel

Born December 13, 1864, in Ashland, Pennsylvania; died June 24, 1947, in Milwaukee. Married Lucy Geissel; they had two children, one of whom died in infancy. They were divorced on April 28, 1924, on grounds of desertion.

George Lukas Emil Seidel was the oldest of nine sons and two daughters of Otto Carl Ferdinand Seidel and Henrietta Christine Friederika (Knoll) Seidel. Seidel's father was a carpenter who was born in Prussia and traveled to the United States in 1859 when he was still young. He established himself as a carpenter in Prairie du Chien, Wisconsin, when Emil was one year old. In 1867 the family moved to Madison, and two years later to Milwaukee. Emil finished elementary school, but at age 13 was apprenticed as a woodcarver in the furniture plant where his father worked. Seidel participated in a strike and in helped to organize the Wood Carvers Association of Milwaukee.

When he was 22, Seidel went to Germany. Besides improving his wood carving skills at the Berlin Art Craft School, Seidel also developed into a radical socialist by the end of his six-year German stay. Back in Milwaukee by August 1892, Seidel spent the next ten years at his craft. He helped establish an interior decorating company that went broke in a financial panic, worked as a carver and designer for a stove company, and for seven years operated his own business.

Seidel continued his political activism by joining a loose-knit group of Milwaukee socialists in 1893. Victor L. Berger was the guiding force. By 1897 Seidel joined the Social Democratic Party of Eugene Debs and Berger. A large percentage of the members were foreign-born. Seidel's American birth and excellent English and German language skills helped propel him to a leadership role. Seidel lost his race for Wisconsin governor in 1902. In 1904 he was elected to the Milwaukee Common Council, and re-elected in 1906. He ran for Milwaukee mayor in 1908, and got 33 percent of the votes in losing narrowly in a three-way race. In 1909 he was elected an alderman-at-large. By 1910 the city had the largest foreign population base of any American city. Sixty percent of the foreign-born were from Germany and had familiarity with socialism. Seidel and other socialists literally spoke their language. Corruption had engulfed local Democratic and Republican officials. Seidel tried again for mayor in 1910. In a three-way race, Seidel won with 46.4 percent of the vote

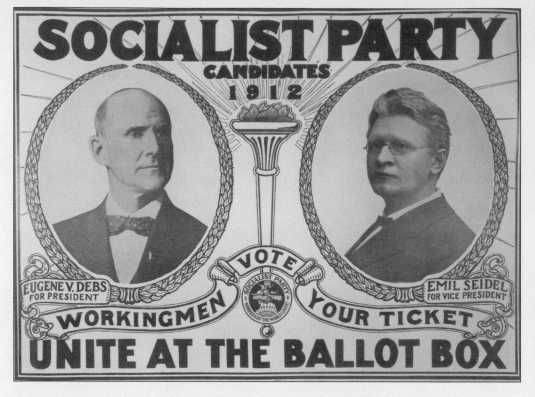

EUGENE V. DEBS and EMIL SEIDEL
(From the Debs Foundation)

and became the first Socialist to be elected mayor of a major American city. The party won all citywide races, 21 of 35 council seats, and won control of the county board. The year saw a surge of Socialists elected in other states. Fifty Socialists were elected as county and municipal officials in the Milwaukee area. They were called simple "mechanics and trade unionists," but they impressed people with their work ethic and their honesty. Carl Sandburg was Seidel's secretary. Over the two years Seidel oversaw increased regulation of businesses, inspections of factories, adoption of an eight-hour work day for city employees, and increased rights and recognition of unions. It was a fairly moderate administration, without radical reforms that doctrinaire socialists wanted. The party was "really civic and social reform. It was mild and gentle and uplifting and thoroughly housebroken" (*Saturday Evening Post*, Dec. 31, 1910, p. 23).

Seidel said that he wanted not only public ownership of utilities, but also publicly owned businesses competing in such areas as bakeries, slaughterhouses, and coal docks. He also promoted public construction of low-cost housing. The new mayor thought he was realistic and said that he did "not expect to usher in the co-operative commonwealth in one or five years." He did not in fact have that much time. The Wisconsin legislature, in part responding to the threat of socialism, passed a statute for non-partisan municipal elections. In 1912 Seidel did not have the luxury of a split opposition vote, but ran against the unity candidate supported by both major political parties, Dr. Gerhard Bading. Seidel got 40 percent of the vote, and was out of office in April.

Seidel was a strong candidate for his party's presidential nomination in May 1912, but won the vice presidential spot instead. He travelled more than 25,000 miles campaigning in a losing effort. He continued to travel for the cause. By October 1914, a party paper said that he and an anti-socialist publisher, Adam Bede, had debated in 100 cities to 100,000 people on the desirability of socialism. Debs thought Seidel's weak debating skills were making him a "laughing stock" and socialism "appear ridiculous and contemptible." Debs asked a friend to dissuade Seidel from continuing on the debate tour. Seidel had another losing race for mayor and for the U.S. Senate, both in 1914. The next year socialist Daniel Hoan was elected mayor, and remained in that office for the next 24 years. Seidel did organization work for the national party. He was elected alderman at large in 1916 and served until 1920 when he lost for city treasurer. That same year Seidel became secretary of the state organization until he suffered a nervous breakdown in 1923. He retired to his brother's farm and gradually recovered. In 1926 Seidel was appointed a member of the board of civil service commissioners by Mayor Hoan and continued until 1932. His last election was to the city council in 1932, and he retired in 1936. For the last 25 years of his life he lived in a cooperative housing development started by socialist mayor Hoan.

SEIDEL BIBLIOGRAPHY

Austin, H. Russell. *The Milwaukee Story: The Making of an American City.* Milwaukee (1946).

Constantine, J. Robert, ed. *Letters of Eugene V. Debs.* Urbana & Chicago (1990), vol. I.

England, George Allan. "Milwaukee's Socialist Government." *American Monthly Review of Reviews* (October 1910), pp. 445–455.

Gregory, John G. *History of Milwaukee, Wisconsin.* Chicago & Milwaukee (1931), pp. 41–43.

Howe, Frederic C. "Milwaukee, a Socialist City." *Outlook* (June 25, 1910), pp. 411–421.

Miller, Sally. "Casting a Wide Net: The Milwaukee Movement to 1920," in Critchlow, Donald T., ed. *Socialism in the Heartland: The Midwestern Experience, 1900–1925.* Notre Dame (1986), pp. 18–39.

_____. "Milwaukee: Of Ethnicity and Labor," in Stave, Bruce M., ed. *Socialism and the Cities.* Port Washington, N.Y. (1975).

Morgan, H. Wayne. *Eugene V. Debs: Socialist for President.* Syracuse (1962).

Olson, Frederick I. "The Milwaukee Socialists, 1897–1941." Unpublished doctoral dissertation, Harvard University (1952).

_____. "Milwaukee's First Socialist Administration, 1910–1912: A Political Evaluation." *Mid-America* 43 (1961), pp. 197–207.

Salter, J.T. *The Pattern of Politics.* New York (1940), pp. 135–159.

"Socialist Platform and Candidates." *Outlook* (June 1, 1912), p. 235.

Still, Bayard. *Milwaukee: The History of a City.* Madison (1948).

Thompson, Carl D., ed. *Socialist Campaign Handbook.* Chicago (1912), pp. 17–19.

Wachman, Marvin. *History of the Social Democratic Party of Milwaukee, 1897–1910.* Urbana (1945).

Election of 1916

NOMINATIONS

Socialist Party Mail Referendum (1st). To appear on the referendum ballot, candidates had to be proposed by at least ten party local organizations from around the country. The locals voted from November 1 to December 31, 1915. On January 1, 1916, the Chicago party headquarters prepared ballots, and sent them to each local. Only dues-paying members of the Party could vote. Ballots had to be returned by the end of February. The vote was announced March 11. *President*—Allan Benson received 16,639 votes, James H. Maurer (Penn.) got 12,264, and Arthur LeSueur (N.D.) 3,495. *Vice president*—George Kirkpatrick, who received 20,607 votes to defeat Kate Richards O'Hare with 11,388.

Republican Party Convention (16th): June 7–10, 1916, at the Coliseum, Chicago, Illinois. *President*—Charles Evans Hughes, nominated on the third ballot with 949½ votes out of 987 cast. He had received 253½ on the first ballot. John Weeks (Mass.), Elihu Root (N.Y.), Albert Cummins (Iowa), Theodore Burton

(Ohio), Charles Fairbanks, Lawrence Sherman (Ill.), Theodore Roosevelt, Philander Knox (Penn.), Henry Ford (Mich.), Martin Brumbaugh (Penn.), Robert La Follette (Wisc.) split the remainder more or less evenly on the first ballot. *Vice president*— Charles W. Fairbanks, nominated on the first ballot with 863 votes out of 987 cast.

Democratic Party Convention (22nd): June 14–16, 1916, at the Coliseum in St. Louis, Mo. *President*— Woodrow Wilson, nominated on the first ballot with 1092 votes out of 1093 cast. *Vice president*— Thomas R. Marshall, nominated by acclamation.

GENERAL ELECTION, November 7, 1916
Popular Vote
    Wilson 9,126,300
    Hughes 8,546,789
    Benson   585,113
    Others.   250,000
Electoral Vote
    Wilson-Marshall — 277 (30 states)
    Hughes-Fairbanks — 254 (18 states)
Winners
    Woodrow Wilson, 28th president
    Thomas R. Marshall, 28th vice president
Losers
    Charles Evans Hughes, Charles W. Fairbanks, Allan Benson, George Kirkpatrick

---

1916 presidential nominee—
Republican Party

Charles E. Hughes

Full name: Charles Evans Hughes.
State represented: New York.
Birth: Glens Falls, New York, April 11, 1862.
Age on Inauguration Day (March 4, 1917): 54 years, 11 months.
Education: Madison College (now Colgate University), 1876–1878; Brown University, 1878–1881, Phi Beta Kappa; Columbia Law School, 1882–1884, graduated with highest honors.
Religion: Baptist.
Ancestry/prominent relatives: Father was Welsh, mother Dutch and Irish; Charles E. Hughes, Jr. (son), was U.S. solicitor general.

Occupation: Attorney; taught at Cornell University Law School for two years.
Public Offices: Special counsel for legislative utility and insurance investigations, 1905–1906; Governor of New York, 1907–1910, resigned; associate justice, U.S. Supreme Court, 1910, until resigned, June 10, 1916; unsuccessful Republican nominee for president, 1916; U.S. secretary of state, March 4, 1921–March 4, 1925; judge, Court of International Justice, 1928–1930; chief justice, U.S. Supreme Court, February 24, 1930–July 1, 1941.
Home: New York City, moved to Washington, D.C., when served on Supreme Court; summer home at Cape Cod.
Death: August 27, 1948, Osterville (Cape Cod summer home), Massachusetts, 86 years, 4½ months.
Burial: Woodlawn Cemetery, New York City.
Personal characteristics: Striking full, reddish-brown beard and bushy eyebrows, piercing eyes; could appear cold in public, little public warmth, but humorous and even playful in private; very thin, even emaciated until his late thirties (weighed only 127 pounds early in career); began to exercise and eat more regularly and filled out to 170 pounds, 5'11" tall.
Father: David Charles Hughes (June 24, 1832–December 15, 1909), born in Tredegar, England; a Baptist preacher, son of Nathan and Jane (Evans) Hughes.
Mother: Mary Catherine Connelly (November 22, 1830–December 30, 1914), schoolteacher; daughter of William and Margaret Ann (Terpenning) Connelly.
Siblings: None.
Wife: Antoinette Carter (September 14, 1864–December 6, 1945), married December 5, 1888; daughter of Walter S. and Antoinette (Smith) Carter.
Children: Charles E. Hughes, Jr. (November 30, 1889–January 21, 1950); married Marjorie Bruce Stuart on June 17, 1914; attorney, U.S. solicitor general. Helen (January 11, 1892–April 18, 1920), died of influenza and pneumonia. Catherine (August 11, 1898– December 31, 1961); married Chauncey L. Waddell (who founded an investment firm) on June 10, 1922. Elizabeth (August 19, 1907–April 25,

1981), married William Thomas Gossett on December 19, 1930, who was an attorney in Hughes's firm, then general counsel for General Motors.

Historic sites/memorials: Hughes's Washington homes are still standing: 2100 16th Street, N.W., is now the Bulgarian Embassy; 2223 R Street, N.W., is privately owned.

Charles E. Hughes stands as one of the most brilliant men ever nominated for the presidency. He never hungered for political office but was given four years as New York governor because the people, and President Theodore Roosevelt, insisted that he take the job. He almost became president because the progressive wing of the Republican Party demanded he take the nomination. The law was his vocation, and in the law he met his greatest triumphs. Fame and fortune sought him. He had little care for either, yet achieved both. Charles Evans Hughes has the misfortune of missing the White House by the narrowest of margins, yet American history still places him in the highest ranks of its public servants. He was, simply put, a great man.

Hughes's father was an abolitionist Baptist preacher in New York. His father's life, like his much more famous son's, was one of achievement. His wealth was in the acclaim he received from his congregation, and the constant appeals from other churches for him to become their pastor. Religious fervor bloomed where the elder Hughes preached. The Hughes household was at times equally intense. Hughes's mother was a schoolteacher, but when Charles was born Mrs. Hughes stopped teaching and devoted herself to her only child.

Hughes's basic instruction came from his parents. He was sent to school at the age of six, after having been instructed at home for several years. At his new school he found himself bored and apathetic. After only three weeks he devised, at the age of six, the "Charles E. Hughes's Plan of Study" in which this tyke established a schedule of subjects he would study. The future chief justice won his first case, as his parents relented to his request. This tremendously precocious child had been reading at a very early age, and by the age of eight was studying Greek by himself. Finally, when

Hughes turned 12 he attended what was probably the best public school in New York City, Public School 35. After only a few weeks, his parents moved from the neighborhood of this school, leaving young Charlie a long ferry journey and walk each day if he wanted to continue to attend. The school had interested Hughes as no other ever had, and he made the long trek every day. He continued to excel in his studies, particularly in the precocious essays he would write. At the age of 13 he graduated, and was still a year short of the minimum age for attending college.

Hughes's father hoped that Charlie would join the ministry. Yet the intensity of the home religious life, the constant attendance at revivals, church meetings, and services, made the young, studious, but fun-loving Charlie want to leave home for college as soon as possible. A visit with a family friend whose nephew attended Madison University (now Colgate) caused him to prepare his second big case. He convinced his father that by carefully preparing for the entrance examinations, with his father's help, he could be ready. His case won, he devoted himself to the examination and passed easily.

As would be a constant throughout his educational career, Hughes stood at the top of his class at Madison. After receiving a small scholarship and special consideration because he was a minister's son, he matriculated at Brown University in September 1878. The honors continued to flow, including election to Phi Beta Kappa.

Though school was one triumph followed by another, Hughes still did not know what career to follow. He thought of medicine, apparently had dismissed the ministry, but only infrequently thought of the law. After a stint at teaching at a preparatory school in Delhi, New York, at which he so excelled that the school principal begged him to remain, Hughes began to study law in the office of a practicing attorney. After a short period, he decided a more formal legal education was necessary. In the fall of 1882, he began studies at Columbia Law School. Soon after classes started he applied for a clerkship at a local firm, Chamberlain, Carter & Hornblower. After being rebuffed by Hornblower, he literally ran into Carter. While each was picking himself up from the collision, Carter inquired as to the reason for Hughes's presence and heard of his desire for a clerkship. Carter opposed law students' trying to work during the school term, but suggested that Hughes come back in the summer. Both Carter and Hughes's professors liked what they saw. Hughes was chosen the outstanding graduate of Columbia in June of 1884 and was offered a three-year tutoring position at the school. He was also offered a permanent position in Carter's law firm. He would not know of his grade for 50 years, but he made an almost perfect score on his bar examination — 99½.

Carter thought Hughes the most intelligent clerk who had ever worked for him. Hughes began to be rewarded financially in ever-increasing fashion. Hughes did not know how to pace himself, or rather, he had only one pace, all-out. His health suffered immensely and he took a long vacation to Ireland after his first year. The following year he took another long cruise. In three years this intensity moved Hughes from the bottom of this small firm to the top. As other firm members left, only Carter, who merely acquired the clients and then turned them over to the others, was above Hughes. It was a general commercial law practice, dealing with importers, dry good merchants, and other significant if not giant firms.

Though dedicated to his work, Hughes did not ignore his social life altogether. Then again, perhaps he merged the two. He first met the senior partner's daughter, Antoinette Carter, a year after he joined the firm. The courtship was neither immediate nor hurried, but in the succeeding years he began to see Antoinette more frequently. The bond that developed was incredibly strong, and the frequent absences from one another that would occur in later years would pain each severely. They were married on December 5, 1888, and neither apparently would ever regret the decision.

Married life was immensely satisfying to Hughes and Antoinette, but his legal work continued unabated. He became so drained by his activity, so worried and at times depressed, that he was almost emaciated. His several

attempts to receive life insurance were rejected, because no company thought him a suitable risk considering his health. The ambition that drove Hughes to such precarious health was not one for power or fame, but mainly for the satisfaction received from being as good a lawyer as was possible. The young lawyer finally decided to leave his father-in-law's firm and to accept a full professorship at Cornell Law School. His father-in-law was incredulous, telling Hughes point blank that the idea was absurd, financially if for no other reason. Yet in September 1891, Hughes and his family moved to Ithaca, New York. Three satisfying years followed, but the financial sacrifice was too great for him to continue. With the entreaties of his father-in-law, and the pinch of his pocketbook, Hughes decided to return to New York City and retake his place in the firm. He left Cornell in June 1893, leaving the experience that he would later call perhaps the most enjoyable of his life.

Hughes's political involvement was minor and casual. He was more active in the organized bar association and in his church. At age 43, however, he begrudgingly entered public life.

Henry W. Taft, the younger brother of future president and Supreme Court justice William Howard Taft, was in 1905 made counsel to a New York legislative committee established to investigate inflated gas and electric utility rates. Taft suggested that Hughes be appointed as investigating attorney for the committee. The early reports of Hughes's appointment focused on the fact that he taught a Bible class attended by John D. Rockefeller. By implication he was tainted with the evils he was named to investigate. Within a few weeks of observing Hughes's skills in handling witnesses, his incredible performance in unraveling the intricacies of the utilities' financial arrangements, and his tireless energy in performing all this work, the most skeptical reporter was convinced that this was a man of unusual ability and dedication. His exposures showed that the city of New York was paying greatly inflated rates for service. Substantial reductions in costs for both the city and individuals resulted. A recommendation in his report called for the establishment of a public service commission, a new and somewhat radical idea that would soon be adopted.

Following close on the heels of the gas and electric scandals, and based solely on his performance in that capacity, Hughes was asked to act as counsel for an investigation of insurance companies. Again he showed how the manipulation of the few had greatly affected the rates and service provided. He also showed the close connection between insurance companies, other big organizations, and political parties, especially his own Republican Party. The insurance investigation started in September 1905, and lasted for the rest of the fall. Partly as an attempt to end Hughes's exposure of the Republican Party's involvement in the scandal, local Republican leaders tried to convince Hughes to run for mayor of New York. The ploy was transparent and was refused. It was no ploy the next year when President Theodore Roosevelt insisted that only Hughes was a suitable candidate for the party in the gubernatorial campaign. Hughes had become a significant national figure due to his investigatory work, and a man of his stature was required to defeat the popular demagogue and wealthy newspaper publisher, William Randolph Hearst. The campaign was bitter, and the margin of victory was slim. Hughes was the only Republican candidate to win a statewide race in New York that year.

Hughes was an unusual governor. He rejected political patronage as an accepted part of governing, and angered many Republican leaders for his failure to accept their suggestions for appointments. Surprisingly, Hughes eschewed private meetings and instead transacted business in a large public room in which everybody sat waiting their turn. Secret conferences were few.

Hughes was a good administrator, and sought out other men with similar abilities. His programs were progressive. He outlined the legislative reforms necessary to correct the abuses he had uncovered as counsel for both the utility and the insurance investigations. Two public service commissions were established during his administration, one for the state and one for New York City. Prior to that time, only the state of Wisconsin had such a commission. He sought election reform as

well, hoping to establish a modest primary system rather than continuing to use state conventions to nominate candidates.

Hughes's record as governor boosted his national prestige. He showed himself to be open-minded and progressive, and gave voice to the better sentiments of the people. It was while he was finishing his second term as governor that President William Howard Taft offered him an appointment to the United States Supreme Court. He allegedly also held out the prospect of naming him chief justice when the incumbent retired. The lawyer in Hughes would not permit him to reject such an offer. The appointment met with universal acclaim. Hughes's five-year record in public service had few if any blemishes, and his image as a reformer and progressive was unrivaled.

Perhaps one of the most significant decisions he wrote during his first tour of duty on the court was in a railroad rate case. The decision he drafted was a complex document for which Hughes earned the respect of his fellow justices. He was particularly close and shared mutual respect with Oliver Wendell Holmes.

Hughes's standing on the court was reflected to some extent in political party affairs. There was considerable interest in 1912 in nominating Hughes for president in an attempt to heal the bitter party wounds caused by the Taft-Roosevelt clash. Hughes firmly refused, saying it was improper to take a judge who was supposed to be making impartial decisions and dangle the prospect of political office in front of him. The Supreme Court must be kept out of politics. This insistence weakened greatly in 1916 when again he was called upon, this time with more vigor, to be the presidential nominee. Hughes finally did succumb to the pressure, but then ran a singularly uninspired campaign. He chose poor organization people to run his campaign, and his prospects accordingly suffered. Hughes began to attack President Wilson as not being sufficiently pro–English or sufficiently prepared for war. The issue appeared to be, as the Democrats stridently termed it, Hughes and war or Wilson and peace. The telling blow, the one that may well have cost him the election because it cost him California, was his unintentional but negligent snubbing of

Senator Hiram Johnson, who had been Teddy Roosevelt's 1912 running mate on the Bull Moose ticket. No effort was made to placate the California senator after Hughes had failed to meet with him when each man had for a short period, unknown to Hughes, been in the same hotel. The switch of California's few thousand vote majority for Wilson would have made Hughes president. Indeed, Hughes went to bed the night of the election believing he had won, as he had unexpectedly swept the Eastern states. Then equally unexpectedly he began to lose by close totals many of the Western states he was thought to have. His campaign had been negative, critical, and uninspired. It was the low point in his public career.

After his defeat, Hughes returned to private practice in New York. His wealth began to grow, but he did not avoid unpopular cases, many of which he took for no fee. He headed a Bar committee urging the seating of five socialist members of the New York state legislature who had been barred from taking their seats solely because they were socialists. Seymour Stedman, the 1920 Socialist Party candidate, was personal attorney to the assemblymen. Hughes defended Senator Truman H. Newbury in 1918 who was being tried for violation of campaign and expenditure laws, violations that likely did occur, but without the senator's knowledge. Hughes opposed President Wilson's efforts to have the covenant of the League of Nations adopted. This covenant would have required members of the League to insure the mutual security of all nations, even, implicitly, to the providing of military support if any nation were threatened.

Hughes did not choose to run for president in 1920. The Republican who was elected, Warren Harding, named him secretary of state. Hughes abandoned the Versailles Treaty and the League of Nations once he took office. Instead he sought a separate peace treaty with Germany. This seemed the practical alternative, since Hughes continued to believe that the U.S. Senate would reject any attempt to join the League and adopt the Versailles agreements. Throughout his stint as secretary of state he was unsympathetic to ideas involving collective security of nations. He was even cau-

tious in having America participate in the World Court, an attempt at international judicial resolution of disputes. He gradually convinced himself and then President Harding to join the Court under certain conditions. As secretary of state, Hughes had unusually free rein. A poll of scholars would later rate Hughes as the third greatest secretary of state ever to serve, ranking just behind John Quincy Adams and William H. Seward. Among the toughest issues he faced were in relations with Japan, a country that seemed to have a "manifest destiny" of its own in China, Russia, and the Pacific. His biggest achievements were in the area of naval and military armaments. The secretary successfully managed a conference in Washington that set specific ratios of naval equipment between the great powers. This required the demolition or halting of construction of many vessels by the major countries. The Washington disarmament conference opened in November 1921. Secretary Hughes immediately insisted upon disarmament. The concrete nature of his proposals astounded the delegates, as he called for a ten-year moratorium on the construction of major war vessels and for the sinking or scrapping of specific ships in each of the navies of the United States, Great Britain, Japan, France and Italy. Ratios of war vessel tonnage between these powers were finally adopted, an achievement due mainly to Hughes.

In 1925, Hughes retired as secretary of state. His renewed private law practice finally enabled him to begin accumulating a substantial fortune. Business poured in from large corporations and other sources that could afford the legal fees commanded by an ex–Supreme Court justice, presidential candidate, and cabinet officer. After five quick and successful years in private practice, Hughes was again called upon for the Supreme Court. President Herbert Hoover needed a successor to Chief Justice William Howard Taft. Hughes was the logical choice. Far from receiving the unanimity that greeted his appointment to the court in 1910, Hughes's nomination now was attacked by those who disagreed with his active participation in politics since he left the Supreme Court in 1916. Others were more concerned with the type of clients he had represented since his last judicial service, including the Oil Institute of America and electric companies. The monopolies and vested interests that to many were evil big business had tainted their attorney. Senator George Norris of Tennessee said, "No man in public life so exemplifies the influence of powerful combinations in the political and financial world as does Mr. Hughes." The final vote for confirmation in the United States Senate was 52 to 26. Hughes took office as chief justice of the United States on February 24, 1930.

Unlike his previous term on the court, the next 11 years involved the court in decisions on some of the most bitterly contested economic and political controversies in history. The deepening depression and the election of Franklin Roosevelt called for dramatic measures, ones that did not fit the mold of past governmental relief measures. The role of the chief justice can be one of great leadership, depending on the personality and intellectual qualities he possesses. Another judge, Felix Frankfurter, said in 1953 about Hughes, "to see him preside was like witnessing Toscanini lead an orchestra." The court during these years was bitterly divided on many issues. Hughes's talents were needed to keep the justices operating smoothly. Justice Frankfurter also said that Hughes "took his seat at the center of the Court with a mastery, I suspect, unparalleled in the history of the Court, a mastery that derived from his experience as diversified, as intense, as extensive, as any man brought to a seat on the court, combining with a very powerful and acute mind that could mobilize these vast resources in the conduct of the business of the court."

As chief justice, Hughes was a protector of the Bill of Rights and civil liberties. As he defended the socialists as a private citizen in 1920, so he defended other political expressions that were unpopular. In a 1931 decision he declared unconstitutional a state criminal statute outlawing the display of a red or Communist flag. He struck down censorship statutes that he felt not only injured the libelous newspapers but also the good-intentioned publications. Civil rights also received his protection, as he agreed with the majority of the court that facilities for the legal education of blacks must be provided by states regardless of how small the demand by blacks was. Though a few of Hughes's decisions did support the New Deal economic program, beginning in 1935 he joined the majority of the court in striking down the more extreme measures that tested the limits of constitutional authority. A unanimous court agreed that farm mortgage relief that had been passed by Congress was unconstitutional. An attempt to control farm prices was also declared unconstitutional. A string of decisions followed that undercut the New Deal program.

The series of anti–New Deal pronouncements by the Supreme Court led to President Franklin Roosevelt's decision to "pack" the court, that is, to add one judge to the court for each sitting judge who was over 70 years of age and would not retire. Though the president explained the proposal on the basis of the workload of the court, it was clear that he wanted to dilute the votes of the conservative members that were thwarting his program. During the battle that followed in Congress, the Supreme Court began to soften its opposition to New Deal legislation. In a series of decisions, with "The Chief" voting in the majority, the Supreme Court upheld a revised form of a mortgage relief act, upheld minimum wage legislation for women, and declared constitutional the National Labor Relations Act of 1935. It was this last pronouncement that particularly highlighted the change in attitude on the Supreme Court. Chief Justice Hughes said that the right of employees to bargain with their employer, free from fear of reprisals, was a fundamental right that could be protected by congressional legislation. Chief Justice Hughes's basic attitude seemed to be that the Constitution should always be interpreted to meet current exigencies. When innovative, imaginative approaches were required, he interpreted the Constitution to permit these changes.

On June 2, 1941, the chief justice wrote President Roosevelt saying that his health and age made it necessary for him to retire, effective July 1, 1941. He was 79 years old.

His achievements on the Court were immense. Not only did he help direct the

Court through the difficult trials of the Depression, but he left his mark in substantive ways of interpreting the Bill of Rights and the interstate commerce clause. He was an innovative leader of the Court, holding reign over a bitterly divided group of nine judges when they were being attacked from all political viewpoints. Legal historians in 1970 rated the one hundred men who had been justices on the Supreme Court. They ranked Charles Evans Hughes as one of the 12 greatest justices of all time.

Analysis of Qualifications

Hughes's brilliance at every stage of his life, in several different careers as a politician, judge, and statesman, was remarkable. He showed exceptional administrative ability as governor, and a real understanding of the use of politics and public pressure to get his programs adopted. He was a progressive reformer, a Republican in the style of Theodore Roosevelt, though he was much more cerebral and less gregarious than the Rough Rider. Hughes had a most unusual mind, capable of storage of vast quantities of information with the ability to synthesize in brilliant ways. He was driven, driven much harder by his will to succeed than by any quest for power or fame. His legal career exhibits this more than any other part of his life, as he drove himself to ill health and even temporary retirement after only three years of private practice, to the more sedentary life of a law school professor. The drive continued, however, and in order to provide better for his family he returned after two years of teaching to the hectic pace of private practice. He became so exhausted at times that he had to take long ocean cruises or other vacations, without the wife and children he loved, in order to recover. As he matured, this inability to work without becoming exhausted became less troublesome.

A Hughes presidency would have been a war administration. What Hughes knew about the military was minor, but what he lacked he would quickly have gained. He had become an expert after only a few weeks in a complicated gas and electric utility investigation, and then later in insurance fraud scandals. His introduction to foreign affairs was meager prior to becoming secretary of state in 1921, yet he was quick student there and became one of our outstanding State Department leaders.

If the country missed greatness in not choosing him for president, there was still no shortage of other areas in which his intelligence, drive, respect for individuals' needs and rights, and his outstanding administrative ability found their expression. In no station in life did Hughes ever fail to excel — as a student, a lawyer, governor, secretary of state, or Supreme Court justice. The presidency would almost certainly have been no different.

HUGHES BIBLIOGRAPHY

Blaustein, Albert P., and Roy M. Mersky. *The First One Hundred Justices*. Hamden, Conn. (1978).

Glad, Betty. *Charles Evans Hughes and the Illusions of Innocence*. Urbana (1966).

Hendel, Samuel. "Charles Evans Hughes," in Leon Friedman and Fred Israel, *The Justices of the United States Supreme Court, 1789–1969*. 4 vols. New York City (1969), III, pp. 1893–1915.

_____. *Charles Evans Hughes and the Supreme Court*. New York City (1951).

Johnson, William Lee. *A Genealogical Study of the Family of Charles Evans Hughes, 1862–1948*. Washington, D.C. (1994).

Miller, Karen Ann Justin. "The Republican Insurgency and Foreign Policy Making, 1918–1925...." Unpublished doctoral dissertation, Columbia University (1992).

Perkins, Dexter. *Charles Evans Hughes and American Democratic Statesmanship*. Boston (1956).

Pusey, Merlo. *Charles Evans Hughes*. 2 vols. New York City (1951).

Ransom, William L. *Charles E. Hughes*. New York City (1916).

Wessner, Robert F. *Charles Evans Hughes: Politics and Reform in New York, 1905–1910*. Ithaca (1967).

Some family information was acquired from obituaries in the New York *Times*.

FOR PRESIDENT   FOR VICE PRESIDENT

CHARLES F HUGHES   CHARLES W FAIRBANKS

CHARLES E. HUGHES and CHARLES W. FAIRBANKS
(From the collection of David J. and Janice L. Frent)

*1916 vice presidential nominee —
Republican Party*

Charles W. Fairbanks

No biographical sketch of Fairbanks is included since he served as vice president from March 4, 1905, until March 4, 1909 (26th vice president).

State represented: Indiana.
Birth: May 11, 1852.
Age on Inauguration Day (March 4, 1917): 64 years, 10 months.
Death: June 4, 1918.

---

*1916 Presidential Candidate —
Socialist Party*

Allan L. Benson

Born November 6, 1871, in Plainwell, Michigan; died August 19, 1940, in Yonkers, New York. Married Mary Hugh on November 19, 1899; they had four children.

Allan Louis Benson was the son of Adelbert and Rose Morris Benson. Allan attended public schools in Otsego, Michigan. He became a newspaperman at the age of 19, and for seven years worked as a reporter or sub-editor for papers in Chicago, Salt Lake City, and San Francisco. He was the assistant managing editor for the Detroit *Journal* (1897–1901), and managing editor for the *Detroit Times* (1901–1904) and the Washington *Times* (1906–1907).

Benson voted for the Democrat Bryan in 1896, but then turned to the Republican McKinley in 1900 because he then thought that "we ought to be a world power and hold the Philippines." Benson said that he got started in socialism at the *Detroit Times* in 1902 when he saw an article in another newspaper. Someone he respected was quoted as saying that "Nothing can stop socialism, and nothing ought to stop it." That day he began to read about socialism, starting with just an article in an encyclopedia in the newspaper office. He felt "an internal sensation that I had never felt up to that time or since." He had found the answers to his life's questions in socialism. He wrote his first book in 1904, *Socialism Made Plain*. His editorials at the *Detroit Times* took on an obvious pro-socialism slant. Benson's attacks on capitalism and praise of the "glory of Socialism" did not at first seem to affect newspaper profits adversely, but in the spring of 1904 the publisher, James Schermerhorn, ordered that all Benson editorials were to be approved before publishing. Benson quit and for a while sold life insurance. In 1906 he began work for a Washington, D.C., paper, and then for another year and a half he worked as an editor in New York for the same publisher's group of magazines. Benson said he was fired in 1908 because the publisher hired someone at a lower salary to do his job. He became a full-time free-lance writer on political and economic subjects from a socialist perspective. Many of his articles appeared in *Pearson's* magazine, a struggling (it was published from 1899 until 1925), but respected publication that he correctly decided would take a chance on his controversial views. He not only wrote editorials from 1914 until 1916 for the national socialist newspaper, *Appeal to Reason*, he took the professional and personal risk of signing his name to them.

Benson was largely unknown nationally until he wrote some widely circulated socialist tracts. Most were collections of articles first published in *Pearson's*. The pamphlet *The Usurped Power of the Courts* (1911) was said to have sold a million copies, but 300,000 may have been more accurate. A book, *The Truth About Socialism* (1913), went through nine printings. Another booklet, *The Growing Grocery Bill*, sold 1,700,000 in six months in 1912. Many of these sales were in bulk to socialist organizations for distribution as propaganda. What placed Benson in the front rank of socialists was a 1915 book that proposed that no future war should be declared until a popular referendum was held. Former Secretary of State William Jennings Bryan in February 1917 would advocate the same thing. Benson conducted a nationwide campaign on the issue as the Great War in Europe began to threaten to involve the United States. His antiwar editorials for the *Appeal to Reason* reached millions of socialists and radicals of other stripes.

Eugene Debs was in poor health in 1916. He declined to be the party's presidential candidate after losing in the previous four elections. Reformers in 1913 had adopted a proposal that the 1916 candidates would be chosen by a referendum of all the dues-paying members. Pennsylvania state legislator James Maurer and People's College (a Kansas socialist school) vice president Arthur Le Sueur contended with Benson. Benson was the best-known of the poorly known candidates, and won narrowly. Benson's campaign was primarily a newspaper attack on Wilson's war preparedness policies. Benson demanded a referendum on the war, and even argued that those who voted in favor should be the first to go into the Army. How that would work with a secret referendum ballot was never explained. Benson finished a weak third, with 30 percent less vote than Debs received in 1912. Many socialists had abandoned the party and supported Woodrow Wilson's re-election. German militarism was seen as more a threat to socialists than was Wilson.

World War I caused even more socialists to leave the party. In 1918 Benson publicly abandoned the party after it issued a manifesto saying that Germany and the allies were equally to blame for the war. Benson believed that foreign-born leaders were now dominating the party and were advocating near anarchy. To Benson, the defeat of Kaiser Wilhelm was essential to social progress. By 1920 only a handful of major leaders, like Debs (then in prison), Morris Hillquit, and Victor Berger remained in the party. Benson's belief in socialism, if not in the Party, remained strong.

A reporter described presidential candidate Benson as a "stockily built, ruddy-faced man forty-six years of age, with grayish hair, gold-bowed spectacles, and the look of a thinker" (*Outlook*, April 12, 1916, p. 865). He was not a dynamic or particularly accomplished public speaker. Benson wrote Debs in August 1916, saying the speaking campaign was about to begin, an event he had "dreaded" for six months. He read voraciously, perhaps six books at a time, while his phenomenal memory meant he did not even need book marks to keep his places in the various works. The combination of incessant reading and steel-trap memory gave him an impressive if somewhat haphazard knowledge of a wide range of subjects. Benson was described as an agnostic, though perhaps that was not true as he grew older. He was a self-educated man who did not value formal education. Benson was a first-class polemicist, more than he was a politician or historian. He had a profitable free-lance writing career, including writing biographies of Henry Ford and of Daniel Webster and numerous magazine articles. Contacts made for his writings made this socialist a friend of such men as Henry Ford and Thomas Edison. Less surprising perhaps were friendships with Clarence Darrow and a wide circle of literary men, including Mark Twain.

BENSON BIBLIOGRAPHY

Benson, Allan L. "I Wouldn't Have Missed It." Unpublished autobiography (c. 1939), copy in possession of Mrs. Mary Currie.

_____. Our Dishonest Constitution. New York (1914).

_____. A Way to Prevent War. Girard, Kans. (1915).

_____. "Why Mr. Benson Is No Longer a Socialist." Current Opinion (August 1918), p.85.

Constantine, J. Robert, ed. Letters of Eugene V. Debs. Urbana (1990), 3 volumes.

Currie, Harold W. "Allan L. Benson, Salesman of Socialism, 1902–1916." Labor History 11 (1970), pp. 285-303.

_____. Eugene V. Debs. Boston (1976).

_____. "A Socialist Edits the Detroit Times," Michigan History, vol. LII (1968), pp. 1-11.

Davenport, Frederick M. "The Pre-Nomination Campaign: The Presidential Choice of the Socialists." Outlook (April 12, 1916), pp. 865-869.

Fine, Nathan. Labor and Farmer Parties in the United States, 1828–1928. New York (1928).

Fitrakis, Robert J. The Idea of Democratic Socialism in America and the Decline of the Socialist Party. New York (1993).

Jackson, L.B. (Benson grandson). Telephone conversations with author in April, 1997.

Morgan, H. Wayne. Eugene V. Debs: Socialist for President. Syracuse (1962), pp. 149–153.

Obituary. "Allan L. Benson, 68, an Author, Is Dead." New York Times (August 20, 1940), p. 19.

*1916 vice presidential nominee—
Socialist Party*

George Kirkpatrick

Born February 24, 1867, in West Lafayette, Ohio; died March 17, 1937, in San Gabriel, California. Married Mrs. Marian (Patullo) Monheimer on July 13, 1913. They had one son, and were divorced in 1926. Married Mrs. Florence (Hall) Slocum on July 10, 1926.

George Ross Kirkpatrick was the son of Robert and Sarah Heslip (Williams) Kirkpatrick. He graduated from Albion College in 1893. Albion's alumnus Clinton Fisk ran for president on the Prohibition Party ticket the year before George began college; the 1892 Prohibition nominee James Weaver got an even larger vote. Prohibition was such a central issue during this period that there were intercollegiate oratorical contests on the question. George won first honors at the state competition. At the national contest in Illinois on June 30, 1893, George was ranked first for thought and composition of his speech. For the next two years he performed post-graduate studies at Vanderbilt University and the University of Chicago.

From 1895 to 1898 Kirkpatrick was a professor of history and social sciences and principal of the normal department (teacher college) at Southwestern College in Winfield, Kansas. He resigned and for two years lectured for the Kansas State Temperance Union. In 1901-1902 Kirkpatrick taught history and political economy at Ripon College in Wisconsin. Kirkpatrick during this period had become attracted to and then a student of socialism, almost at the exact same time as his 1916 running mate Allan Benson was doing the same in Detroit. Kirkpatrick joined the Socialist Party in 1903. The national party office funded his lecture tour across Michigan that same year. His then moved back into teaching, first at the Rand School of Social Science in New York City, and then at the School of International Socialism in Kansas City, Kansas. He became a lecturer for the New York City schools for five years, frequently wrote pamphlets about socialist issues, and lived in Newark.

ALLAN L. BENSON and GEORGE KIRKPATRICK
(From Craig Hardy, Barrington, New Hampshire)

Kirkpatrick shared Allan Benson's opposition to Woodrow Wilson's war preparedness program. Kirkpatrick was a dynamic antiwar speaker and pamphleteer. His best-known writing was *War— What For?* published in 1910. The book attempted to convince workers that war was part of an eternal class struggle. Five-time Socialist presidential nominee Eugene Debs respected Kirkpatrick's writings, and said, "no other book ever written on war" was more compelling than Kirkpatrick's. In late 1915 the Socialist Party conducted a referendum of party members to decide the 1916 presidential ticket. Kirkpatrick beat popular speaker and "wild-eyed Socialist evangelist" Kate Richards O'Hare of St. Louis (Shannon, *Socialist Party,* p. 25). Kirkpatrick hoped that the presidential nominee would be James Maurer, but it was Benson. Kirkpatrick wrote an election-year book, *Think—or Surrender,* but none of his writings had the impact of his antiwar proclamation.

Benson and Kirkpatrick did not draw the crowds, nor ultimately the votes that the charismatic Debs had. Both candidates tried to characterize Woodrow Wilson's slogan "He kept us out of war" as a sham. The effort was futile, and the ticket got a third less vote than had Debs in 1912.

Kirkpatrick remained active in the party. He served as editor of the nationally circulated and influential socialist newspaper, *Appeal to Reason,* published in Girard, Kansas. He was a member of the board of the socialist People's College, in Fort Scott, Kansas. The national party office was in Chicago, and Kirkpatrick lived there during part of the 1920s. He served briefly as national executive secretary of the party and also served as party publicity/publication director. Kirkpatrick wrote Debs in May 1926, urging him not to go on speaking trips because they were too tiring. Kirkpatrick used the letter also to reflect on being blacklisted from meaningful college teaching positions. "This does not make me sore at all," he wrote. For Kirkpatrick, the financial sacrifice of being an active socialist was less than the intellectual sacrifice of not being one.

Kirkpatrick moved to San Gabriel, California, in about 1929. In 1934 he ran for the U.S. Senate and Upton Sinclair ran for governor. Sinclair got only 3,000 votes, but Kirkpatrick's 108,000 votes were a record for a California Socialist candidate. In the party's 1934 national convention, a new Declaration of Principles was debated. It was strongly pacifist, but then also said socialists should oppose war by "massed war resistance..., in a general strike of labor unions," and by other means. Kirkpatrick argued that this language of rebellion was "putting swords and ropes in the hands of our enemies," but he was outvoted. Kirkpatrick resigned from the party and helped in 1936 to create an alternative called the Social Democratic Federation. He was a member of the new group's national executive committee until he died at his home in 1937. Kirkpatrick's last book was *Is Plenty Too Much for the Common People?* (San Gabriel, Cal., 1940), which worried about a comfortable society's neglecting of its social duties.

KIRKPATRICK BIBLIOGRAPHY

Constantine, J. Robert, ed. *Letters of Eugene V. Debs.* Urbana (1990). 3 volumes.

Egbert, Donald Drew, and Stow Persons. *Socialism and American Life.* Princeton (1952).

Kirkpatrick, George. *War—What For?* West Lafayette, Ohio (1910; reprinted, New York, 1971).

Morgan, H. Wayne. *Eugene V. Debs: Socialist for President.* Syracuse (1962), pp. 149–153.

Shannon, David A. *The Socialist Party of America: A History.* Chicago (1967, reprint of 1955 ed.).

Election of 1920

NOMINATIONS

Socialist Party Convention (5th): May 8–14, 1920, at Finnish Socialist Hall, New York. *President*—Eugene V. Debs, nominated unanimously. *Vice president*—Seymour Stedman, who was nominated with 106 votes over Kate Richards O'Hare (Mo.), who got 26.

Republican Party Convention (17th): June

8–12, 1920, at the Coliseum in Chicago. *President*— Warren G. Harding, nominated on the tenth ballot with 692 of 984 votes; before vote shifts, he had received 644. Harding garnered 65½ votes on the first ballot. Leonard Wood (N.H.), Frank Lowden (Ill.), and Hiram Johnson (Calif.) were the leading candidates on the first ballot. *Vice president*— Calvin Coolidge, nominated on the first ballot with 674½ votes to Irvine Lenroot's (Wisc.) 146½, with 163 votes scattered among 5 more contenders.

Democratic Party Convention (23rd): June 28–30, July 1–3, 5–6, 1920, at Civic Auditorium in San Francisco, Calif. *President*— James Cox, nominated on the 44th ballot with a unanimous vote, having received 699½ votes out of 1094 cast just before the motion for a unanimous vote was made. He had received 134 on the first ballot. William McAdoo, A. Mitchell Palmer, and Al Smith were the other contenders. *Vice president*— Franklin D. Roosevelt, nominated by acclamation on the first ballot.

GENERAL ELECTION, November 2, 1920
Popular Vote

        Harding. 16,152,200
        Cox 9,147,353
        Debs 919,799
        Others 559,789

Electoral Vote

        Harding-Coolidge — 404 (37 states)
        Cox-Roosevelt — 127 (11 states)

Winners

        Warren G. Harding, 29th president
        Calvin Coolidge, 29th vice president

Losers

        James Cox, Franklin D. Roosevelt, Eugene Debs, Seymour Stedman

---

*1920 presidential nominee —
Democratic Party*

James M. Cox

Full name: James Middleton Cox.
State represented: Ohio.
Birth: March 31, 1870, at Jacksonburg, Ohio.

Age on Inauguration Day (March 4, 1921): 50 years, 11 months.

Education: Attended one-room schoolhouse in Jacksonburg irregularly until he was 16; tutored by his brother-in-law in preparation for getting a teacher's certificate.

Religion: Episcopalian.

Ancestry/prominent relatives: First Cox ancestor, Thomas Cox, came to America from England in 1665.

Occupation: Newspaper editor.

Public Offices: U.S. representative, March 4, 1909–January 12, 1913; governor of Ohio, 1913–1915, defeated in 1914, again governor, 1917–1921; unsuccessful Democratic nominee for president, 1920; declined appointment to Senate, 1946.

Home: "Trailsend," large stone and brick mansion east of Dayton, overlooking the Miami Valley.

Death: July 15, 1957, at Trailsend, Ohio, at age 87 years, 3½ months.

Burial: Woodland Cemetery, Dayton, Ohio.

Personal characteristics: Short, stocky, wore wire-rimmed glasses, intense.

Father: Gilbert Cox (April 25, 1834–?); married September 21, 1852, divorced.

Mother: Eliza Andrews (?–?).

Siblings: William. Ann. Scott (c. 1857–August 28, 1949), newspaperman. Catherine. John. Charles.

Wife: Mayme Simpson Harding (?–?), married May 25, 1893, divorced in 1912.

Children: James M. Cox, Jr. (c. 1903–Oct. 27, 1974), married Betty Lippett; newspaper publisher. John W. Cox. Helen, married Daniel J. Mahoney.

Second wife: Margaretta Parker Blair (c. 1890–November 6, 1960), married September 15, 1917; died in fire that burned her Oakwood, Illinois, home.

Children: Barbara, married Garner Anthony. Anne, married Robert Chambers.

Only three newspapermen have been nominated for president, and two of them succeeded the same year: 1920. Unfortunately, the wrong one was elected, with Marion, Ohio, *Star* publisher Harding besting Dayton, Ohio, *Daily News* owner Cox. With the country resentful and angry after eight years of Democratic rule, with a war fought, but the peace to end all wars not yet won, it is almost inconceivable that in 1920 any Democratic candidate could have defeated any Republican candidate for president. Elections are often won for reasons far separated from the qualifications of the nominees, and the 1920 presidential race eminently demonstrates that fact.

James Middleton Cox grew up in a broken home. As an adult he would see his own first marriage fail. Born in small, getting smaller Jacksonburg, Ohio, Jimmy Cox and his six siblings were worked arduously by a father who seemed more interested in his children's labor than in their education. Jimmy grew bitter seeing neighbor children trekking to school while he plowed or planted. What schooling he got came infrequently from a one-room schoolhouse. The drudgery made Jimmy an ambitious boy fascinated with education. At 16 he left the farm, where he had been staying with his father following the parents' divorce. He moved to Middletown, eight miles away, and stayed with his mother. It was a fortuitous change, for there he was able to be tutored by his brother-in-law John Q. Baker, a teacher at a local school. At 19 Jim passed the Ohio teacher examination and received his certificate. That achievement probably says more about Ohio teacher standards of the time than it does about Cox's diligence at his studies.

In the space of three years Cox taught at three schools, but was soon drawn into his life's work, journalism. Brother-in-law Baker was the publisher of the *Middletown Weekly Signal*. Jim was thrust into learning just about every facet of that small paper's operations, from reporting to typesetting to distributing. The paper became a daily in 1891 and Cox started working full-time, dropping his teaching career completely and permanently. Baker had to look elsewhere for assistance after a year, because Cox had moved up in the newspaper world to being a local reporter for the *Cincinnati Enquirer*. Though Cox did not mention the incident in his autobiography, *Journey Through My Years* (1946), apparently he got the full-time job with that paper after imaginatively monopolizing the telegraph one day. He had the day's entire paper sent over the wire, while he raced to the scene of a railroad

accident. The facts in hand, Cox returned to the cooperative telegraph office and filed his scoop.

The *Enquirer* entrusted him with covering the stories on railroads, not just accidents but also planned events. Investigatory zeal led to stories on alleged corruption by an important local railroad magnate. The outraged, powerful businessman demanded that Cox be fired, but the reporter was transferred to another position instead. The warning was clear, however, and inquiries concerning other employment were made. The election of a new Democratic Congressman, Paul J. Sorg, proved fortunate. Sorg hired the 24-year-old newspaperman as his secretary.

Washington opened Cox's eyes to politics and its possibilities. Democrats were traditionally weak among Civil War veterans, and a large contingent of vets lived in Sorg's district. Cox suggested Sorg introduce special pension legislation for ex-soldiers. Sorg won by only 202 votes in 1894, and increased votes from veterans more than equaled that victory margin. In 1896, a strong Republican year, Sorg decided not to seek reelection. He did assist his aide Cox in purchasing the Dayton *Evening News*, a struggling daily that sorely needed imagination and energy. The paper had for a brief period before the Civil War been owned by Clement Vallandigham, the Copperhead Dayton congressman. Now it was a small circulation, uninspired sheet that failed to keep pace with the Cincinnati papers that dominated the market. Cox would change that.

The new owner improved the paper markedly, improvising a better press, aggressively seeking advertisement, purchasing wire services and reporting in depth on local news. In short order he drove the Cincinnati competition from their dominance. His stories were muckraking in content. Cox prided himself on the number of libel suits filed against the paper — and dismissed. Crusades were brought involving railroads; political bossism; labor relations; police, fire, sewage, and other governmental services; and a raft of other concerns. As circulation spread, so did the crusading publisher's fame and influence, not to mention wealth.

All was not liberal enlightenment at the newspaper office, for Cox championed causes that would limit foreign immigration. He once declared in the paper that the "Anglo Saxon race is the grandest race that evolution has produced." Negroes also came in for discrimination, since Cox felt that segregation was necessary to prevent chaos. These views would remain with him throughout his career. He seemed more in the mold of liberal Democrats in pressing for labor reform, including ending the use of strikebreakers. Child labor and female work hours also received his attention.

For all his crusading zeal, Cox was foremost a businessman making his enterprise a profitable one. In 1905, he purchased the Springfield, Ohio, *Press-Republic*. The News League of Ohio was created by Cox to serve as the publishing company for his growing chain of papers. With these two papers firmly established as leaders in their markets, Cox's sights turned to a different, but to him closely related, field. Politics would for the next 12 years dominate his life.

The opportunity for Cox to win office in 1908 seemed great. The Republicans were badly divided, their incumbent congressman being challenged by a rival Republican. In a three-way race, the Democrat was virtually assured of victory. Cox prepared well to be the nominee, and by the time of the nominating convention he was the only serious contender. He was named by acclamation, and began an active campaign. His experience with Congressman Sorg was not forgotten, and especial attention was directed to veterans because the large — 7,000 men — National Soldiers Home was in his district. Cox was elected easily, getting 49.5 percent of the vote and the other two candidates splitting the remainder equally. Having campaigned as a progressive Democrat, Cox now turned to serving in a boss-controlled House of Representatives.

"Uncle Joe" Cannon, the dictatorial, arch-conservative Republican speaker of the House, struggle to maintain power after the 1908 elections. Led by progressive George W. Norris of Nebraska, but with Cox playing an important role as well, the insurgents succeeded in stripping the speaker of some of his power to name committee members. When the Democrats took control of the House after the 1910 elections, still further democratization of procedures was achieved, with Cox supporting the changes. On other issues, Cox clearly staked out his progressive positions. The freshman congressman opposed the Payne-Aldrich Tariff that increased duties on many goods. National attention was directed to the young Ohioan by his effort to have established a children's bureau within the federal government. Better veteran pensions were urged, revealing his constant attention to this important constituency back home.

Governor Judson Harmon wanted to move from the Ohio executive mansion to the one in Washington, D.C. Cox became Harmon's ardent backer. His motives were not completely disinterested, as Cox wanted to run for the vacated governor's chair. On May 16, 1912, Cox announced his candidacy for governor. Progressives were cheered when he called for passage of the initiative and referendum amendments to the state constitution. Cox endorsed a state-wide primary to choose party candidates, prison reform, legislation to protect state workers, and other reforms. Other Democratic candidates began to drop out in the face of the Cox juggernaut. By the time of the convention he was the only contender. The GOP graciously divided their votes again between two candidates, and Cox won in a three-way race, getting 41.5 percent to outdistance the Republican and Progressive party nominees.

The new governor intended to be a strong one. Before his term of service was completed, many complained that "Boss Cox" had run roughshod over his opposition. Patronage was used skillfully to work his will over the legislature. Every 12 Democratic legislators had a Cox man as whip to keep their votes in line. Many positions were made appointive by the governor rather than elective; bureaucratic duplication was eliminated, further consolidating power in the hands of the governor. These and many other tools enabled the first two years of Cox's governance of Ohio to burst forth with liberal legislation. New laws were passed protecting workers, establishing work safety standards and maximum hour rules. An

Ohio Agriculture Commission was established to police that segment of the economy, the Ohio Industrial Commission to regulate another. Prison improvements took the form of "education, reform, and probation." To Cox, criminals were the product of heredity and poverty; it was up to the prison system to reform them, not punish. He became personally involved and visited prisons on several occasions.

Educational improvements were perhaps his most prized reform. Complete reorganization of the state's schools was achieved. As with many of his programs, Cox first sought a survey of the problem by a blue-ribbon panel and then received recommendations for changes. The need to bring rural school standards to a level approximating urban schools was obvious. Cox's legislation attempted to do that. School districts were consolidated; salaries increased. Better roads were a constant concern as well, since Cox believed that improvement in the state's economy would depend on transportation. The effort was politically controversial, since counties that already had good roads were in no mood to subsidize counties that had neglected theirs. Workman compensation laws, bank regulation, and municipal home-rule were a few more of the seemingly never-ending list of additional targets attacked by the still crusading newspaperman-turned-governor.

The governor was, politically, too successful with his legislative package. Ohioans became dismayed over the change being wrought. In 1914, they wanted a halt to the reform. Cox achieved a politically inspired tax cut, but it was not enough to preserve the Democrats. The voters assured themselves a respite by ousting Cox and electing Republican Frank Willis. In the same year, Warren G. Harding won a narrow primary victory for the United States Senate nomination, and went on to victory along with Willis in the general election. By a margin of thirty thousand out of over a million votes, Governor Cox was retired.

Cox returned to his newspapers. It was not long though before Cox was laying the groundwork to return to politics and the governor's chair. Wary of emphasizing progressive issues, Cox made honesty his campaign theme in 1916. He stated that most of the reform laws needed were already on the books, and no new wave of legislation would be passed. With Woodrow Wilson winning the state by 89,000 votes, Cox eked through with a 6,616 vote majority.

The second Cox term mainly was concerned with war measures. Wilson may have won reelection because of the slogan "He kept us out of the war," but soon that phrase became obsolete. With World War I now an American conflict, constant problems occurred at home with manpower, product shortages, and transportation. At one critical juncture the governor seized a shipment of coal bound for the Great Lakes, since it appeared that Ohio's allocation of that fuel for the winter of 1917–18 was grossly inadequate. Another Cox worry was the loyalty of foreign-born residents in the state. Many statements were issued from the governor's office that suggested those opposed to the war or some of its measures were engaged in treason and sabotage.

In 1918 Cox faced the same Republican opponent for the third time, Frank Willis. It was a sweeping Republican year nationwide and in Ohio, but Cox was able to hold on to office by an 11,000-vote plurality. Once the war ended, Cox became a nationally recognized advocate of demobilization planning to reduce the unemployment and other problems of adjusting from a war to a peacetime economy. Nativism again was stressed, with Cox stating, "Every germ of Prussian poison must be squeezed out of the organic law of Ohio." Legislation was passed banning the teaching of the German language in Ohio schools; Cox pressed for strengthening this law by extending its application to private schools. Else, Cox feared, there wold be pockets of treason that still would fester. Loyalty laws of many types were sponsored or supported by the governor. Labor dislocations caused constant problems in postwar Ohio. Cox mediated disputes and attempted to keep passions and violence under control. One issue Cox tried to avoid was prohibition, but finally he sided with the liquor interests. State regulation of alcohol was preferred over national prohibition.

Reelection in 1918 had made Cox a Democrat to be considered for the next presidential nomination. It was difficult to imagine a Democratic victory in 1920, with frustrations over the war and economic hard times being rampant. Cox admitted that the prospects for eventual election of a Democrat were bleak, but nonetheless selection as a nominee for president by one of the major parties was a great honor that was not to be rejected. One issue that gave Cox national attention was criticism of the Wilson administration's refusal to involve itself in postwar domestic planning. Cox's proposals included some public works jobs to lower the high unemployment rate, encouragement of businesses to increase their employment through various federal and state incentives, and a nationwide program of road and railroad construction. As a businessman himself, Cox placed primary emphasis on the private sector curing the employment ills, and would use public jobs primarily in the area of construction and repair of public works.

When the Democratic convention opened June 28, 1920, in San Francisco, the presidential field had three main candidates, two from the Wilson administration. In addition to Cox, the leading candidates were Attorney General Mitchell Palmer and wartime railroad director William Gibbs McAdoo, who was Wilson's son-in-law. In all, 23 candidates received votes on the first ballot. The first serious move in Cox's direction came on the seventh ballot, when New York and New Jersey abandoned their favorite sons to vote for Cox. By the twelfth ballot Cox was in the lead, but then his momentum stalled. On the thirtieth ballot, McAdoo supporters had reason to cheer, but the march towards his candidacy also stopped well short of the two-thirds majority required. The crucial moment came on the thirty-eighth ballot when Palmer finally quit the race and a majority of his support went to Cox. A McAdoo effort to adjourn was defeated as momentum towards Cox started to mount. He won on the forty-fourth.

Soon after the final ballot, a mutual friend of Cox and Franklin D. Roosevelt suggested to Cox that Roosevelt be named as vice president. It was perfect balance for the ticket, geographically sound, and with the added advantage of Roosevelt's famous name and known independence, both of which could be expected to add at least a few votes. There was little unity after the convention, however, and many Democrats went home to sit the election out. Those in favor of prohibition deserted the cause. Though the convention had endorsed the League of Nations, the fight for the League was put in the background, as Cox feared the unpopular issue was too strong a drag on his candidacy. This irritated the Wilson supporters, not to mention the president himself. Yet Cox was inconsistent in his treatment of the issue, and during the last week of the general election again gave the League prominence. Little money came in to finance the campaign. The pessimism among the candidate's supporters was stifling. It was an accurate premonition. Cox suffered one of the great electoral defeats in presidential history, carrying 11 states in the "Solid South," but nothing else. Cox blamed his defeat on pent-up resentment resulting from the war. In essence, Cox agreed that Harding's call for a "return to normalcy" had irresistible appeal. The loser was so disconsolate he never did issue a formal concession statement.

Politics still stirred the defeated presidential candidate, and in 1922 he made a much-publicized tour of Europe to examine the international situation. Cox tried to convince Americans to participate in the League of Nations. As the next presidential election approached, Cox was at the vanguard of the fight that was continuing for admission to the League. The former nominee was not himself running again, but he wanted the candidate who was selected to be "right" on the issue. His name was placed on the Ohio primary ballot because Cox wanted to prevent McAdoo from getting the state's votes. McAdoo had abandoned support for the League, despite being Wilson's son-in-law.

In New York City a badly split Democratic Party gathered to choose a nominee. The Wets and Drys, the pro–League and anti-League advocates, all were mortally opposed to those who disagreed with them. It led to the longest convention in history—103 ballots. Cox played a crucial role first in convincing one of the leading candidates, Governor Al Smith of New York, that he did not have a chance and should drop out, and then in getting a pledge from the candidate whom many had decided to vote for as a compromise, John Davis, that he would support the League of Nations. It hardly mattered, and another overwhelming Democratic defeat was suffered.

There were no more political races for Cox after his 1920 defeat. He turned down suggestions he run for Senate, or accept an ambassadorial post. A newspaper empire became his consuming passion. Papers were bought in other cities in Ohio, but the empire was formed when papers in Miami, Florida (1923) and Atlanta (1930) were purchased. The competing Atlanta paper was brought into Cox control in 1950. Florida first and then Atlanta became objects of his boosterism. Cox accurately forecast that Atlanta would become the major city linking the Northeast to the Southeast. He was a wealthy man, with a mansion built for him overlooking the Miami Valley east of Dayton.

The last public service rendered by Cox came in 1933, when his former running mate Franklin Roosevelt, now president, appointed him vice chairman of the American delegation to the London World Monetary and Economic Conference. The world depression demanded international solutions, but the conference failed to discover any. Cox in time opposed Roosevelt, as did other former Democratic presidential nominees Al Smith and John Davis. Cox feared Roosevelt was a demagogue, but he never joined the Liberty League or other anti–Roosevelt organizations as did many other Democrats, including Al Smith.

His career was a full one, holding high public office, but perhaps performing more lasting service as a lifelong advocate of civic improvements in the cities in which he owned his newspapers. In 1946, he wrote his autobiography, leaving out facts, such as his opposition to Roosevelt, that he felt detracted from the message he was trying to relate. *Journey Through My Years* explained Cox's past as a consistent weave with the New Deal. There was some truth in his analysis, but the omissions were equally important to understanding the full story.

In 1957, Cox died at his Ohio home, aptly named "Trailsend."

Analysis of Qualifications

The choice between intellect, personality, and past achievements now seems embarrassingly clear — Jim Cox was a far superior candidate for president than was Warren Harding. What cannot be said with much assurance was whether the choice as presented to the American people in 1920 was quite so one-sided. The people were tired of conflict and controversy, tired of progressives in domestic policy and wagers of war to end wars internationally. Harding represented a rebuff to eight years of very active government, and the people voted overwhelmingly for tranquillity.

Cox was a liberal, with a few imperfections, in a mold that would later produce the New Deal. As a newspaperman he was a muckraker and crusader for good government, locally and nationally. Running for Congress in 1908, the Dayton journalist embraced the progressive issues of the day. Presidential candidate William Jennings Bryan shared his platform on opening day of the campaign. As governor of Ohio Cox almost frantically rammed through changes in the manner government related to business, labor, agriculture, and education. The initiative and referendum were endorsed to make government more responsive to the people. Simultaneously, consolidation of government bureaus and changing many elective positions to appointive ones made the government more responsive to the governor, James Cox. By one count, 56 bills were passed by the legislature as Cox tried to reform Ohio. He was sympathetic to labor, but with the restraint of his experience as a businessman. He was "Boss Cox" to many, grabbing for power to assure that his measures passed and then were effectively administered. What Cox demonstrated by six years as governor is that he understood the relationship between the legislative and executive branches, that he could compromise when necessary but that he willingly used power and patronage to achieve his ends when that was necessary. That Cox understood government and could operate it effectively is perhaps the most striking contrast with the man who defeated him for president.

There was little humor in Jim Cox. As a journalist or a political leader, action and results were his passions. He was a booster, a

JAMES M. COX and FRANKLIN D. ROOSEVELT
(From the collection of David J. and Janice L. Frent)

hustler; he was in constant motion and attempted nothing halfway. Coming up through business, Cox had acquired an appreciation for the interdependence of government, business, labor and the press.

A Cox administration would have been an efficient, dynamic one. Graft would have been ferreted out; his advisers would not have been cronies known for their card-playing or joke-telling skills, but instead for their efficiency in getting things done. As governor, Cox demonstrated that he did not just create programs when there were problems, but first he wanted studies to see just what the problems were. That would have been repeated on the national level. Cox, simply put, had earned by experience a chance at the White House. That he was discarded in favor of Warren G. Harding was one of the poorest selections ever made by the American electorate.

COX BIBLIOGRAPHY

Babson, Roger. *Cox, the Man.* New York City (1920).

Bagby, Wesley M. *The Road to Normalcy: The Presidential Campaign and Election of 1920.* Baltimore (1962).

Cebula, James E. *James M. Cox.* New York City and London (1985).

Cox, Henry Miller. *The Cox Family in America.* Somerville, N.J. (1912).

Cox, James M. *Journey Through My Years.* New York City (1946).

Craig, Douglas Bryden Stuart. "Rehearsal for Revolt: The Ideological Turmoil of the Democratic Party, 1920–1932." Unpublished doctoral dissertation, University of Virginia (1989).

Graham, Robert O. "James M. Cox and the Reform Movement in Ohio." Unpublished master's thesis, Ohio State University (1931).

Grant, Philip A., Jr. "Congressional Campaigns of James M. Cox, 1908 and 1910." *Ohio History* 81 (1972), pp. 4–14.

*1920 vice presidential nominee—
Democratic Party*

Franklin D. Roosevelt

No biographical sketch of Roosevelt is included here since he served as president from March 4, 1933, until April 12, 1945 (32nd president).
   State represented: New York.
   Birth: January 30, 1882.
   Age on Inauguration Day (March 4, 1921): 39 years, 1 month.
   Death: April 12, 1945.

---

*1920 presidential nominee—
Socialist Party*

Eugene V. Debs

The biographical sketch on Debs appears at the Election of 1904, pages 451–452.
   State represented: Indiana.
   Birth: November 5, 1855, in Terre Haute, Indiana.
   Age on Inauguration Day (March 4, 1921): 65 years, 4 months.
   Death: October 20, 1926, in Elmhurst, Illinois.

---

*1920 vice presidential nominee—
Socialist Party*

Seymour Stedman

Born July 14, 1871, in or near Hartford, Connecticut; died July 9, 1948, in Chicago. Married Irene Moulton (1872–1956), the daughter of Granville and Harriet Taylor Moulton of Portland, Maine. No children survived him.
   Seymour Stedman was one of at least two sons of Frank and Henrietta Chamberlain Stedman. His campaign biographical sketch said that his "ancestors were of revolutionary stock," and that he was related to poets Ed-

mund Clarence Stedman (1833–1908) and William Cullen Bryant (1794–1878) (Rand, *Political Guide*, p. 15). The family initially had a comfortable living, probably from a fruit shop called Stedman and McLean, but financial reverses caused the Stedmans to move to Solomon City, Kansas. A series of droughts further reduced them financially. Seymour before he was ten years old was helping by tending sheep for five dollars per month. In about 1881 the family moved to Chicago. Seymour's formal preparatory education ended in the third grade. By the age of 11, he was working at the Crane Brothers iron foundry for three dollars per week. Later he worked as a messenger for the American District Telegraph Company and then Western Union. His first exposure to union activism may have been his participation as a 13-year-old in the 1884 telegrapher's strike. Stedman said they struck "because the work was too hard." As a messenger he worked until seven o'clock four nights a week, and until nine or eleven o'clock the other three nights. He subsequently worked for another telegraph company, for an abstract company, and finally in a law office. There he had little to do and spent much time reading about economics, among other subjects.
   At the age of 17 Stedman met with the dean of the Northwestern University law school and asked to be admitted. The dean questioned Stedman for an hour and then admitted him to the school. Stedman continued to work at his undemanding job during the day, reading more than working, and then attended law school at night. He graduated in 1891 and was admitted to the Illinois bar the next year.
   Stedman was initially a Democrat. Eugene Debs helped organize the 1894 American Railway Union (A.R.U.) strike against the Pullman Company. Stedman wanted to be a strike spokesman and had to overcome suspicions about his Democratic ties. Stedman abandoned the Democrats when President Grover Cleveland sent federal troops to end strike violence. As a Populist, Stedman ran for city attorney and for state attorney. He was among the third of the delegates at the 1896 Populist national convention who supported Debs for president. A Debs telegram stating that he

FROM ATLANTA

All socialists are, always were, and always will be, opposed to war and its cause --- capitalism.

CAMPAIGN SPECIALTY COMPANY
1101 CHESTNUT ST., ST. LOUIS

To hell with war, to hell with all who crave it. When masters rule the world no more, we'll need no wars to save it.

EUGENE V. DEBS
(From the Debs Foundation)

would not accept and urging support for William J. Bryan ended the effort. By 1897 Debs and Stedman were socialists. Stedman attended the 1897 national convention of the A.R.U., which organized itself into the Social Democracy of America. Stedman helped found 20 Chicago branches within a month.

A battle for the soul of the party was especially intense from 1898 to 1901. Stedman was a leader of the more moderate forces against

EUGENE V. DEBS and SEYMOUR STEDMAN
(From the Debs Foundation)

the anarchist and communist elements. In 1898 Stedman attended the second national convention of the party, where a 53-delegate majority adopted a proposal to make Colorado a communist colony for the unemployed. Col-

onization in various forms had been and would remain a point of division among socialists. Stedman was the final speaker opposing colonization. Debs, Stedman and the remainder of the 37 who opposed the motion bolted from the convention at 2:30 A.M. By the time the sun came up they were organizing a competing party. Stedman was chosen secretary and served with Debs on the five-member executive committee of the new faction, which called itself the Social Democratic Party. Among Stedman's interests was to form an alliance with farmers. Others found the idea of socializing the farmers to be ludicrous.

Within little more than a year of the new party's formation, there were efforts to unify the factions. On some core issues such as public ownership of the means of production and distribution, and substitution of a "Socialist cooperative commonwealth," the factions agreed. The 1900 national convention named a unity committee with Stedman as a member. The convention ultimately nominated Debs for president and Job Harriman, the presidential nominee of the main rival group, for vice president. Debs opposed unity and found Stedman too willing to harmonize with other factions. In fact, Stedman had serious reservations about union. His work on the unity committee over the next several months led him to believe the rival party would not sufficiently compromise over key issues. Though Stedman's point of view was maintained by the leadership of his party, a referendum was held among the party rank and file, who overwhelmingly approved union and the name of Social Democratic Party. By 1901 unification was declared, but new factional splits would follow. Stedman remained a member of the executive committee.

Stedman established a law practice in Chicago. Much of his time was spent on socialist legal problems. He would for many years be the party's general counsel and attended most national conventions. Stedman spoke out for his more conservative views in party splits with the radical elements. Many working-class members distrusted lawyer Stedman and other mainly professional men who as a small group of insiders dominated the management of the party. In 1908 Stedman rose at the national convention and to outcries of "no" and booing said that Debs's recent throat operation meant that someone new should be nominated for president. He proposed Algie M. Simons,

a relatively moderate editor of a socialist periodical. Ben Hanford followed by reading a letter from Debs saying that he was fully recovered. Hanford announced that Stedman had seen the letter before proclaiming Debs too ill. The opinion was rampant that Stedman was part of a conspiracy to thwart the will of the majority. Debs was easily nominated. For vice president, Stedman received 46 votes compared to Hanford's 106, and 33 for four others. Stedman's split with Debs would be mended in the years ahead and they were good friends.

A national scandal resulted from an explosion at the Cherry Mine in Michigan in 1909. On behalf of the United Mine Workers, Stedman conducted an investigation and presented a report that was published in 1910. It condemned serious safety violations by the mine owners. Stedman conducted a similar investigation of a mine explosion in West Virginia in 1913, and of a copper mine strike in Calumet in 1914.

Stedman was one of four socialists elected to the Illinois legislature in 1912 and became the leader of the small group. A Chicago newspaper classified him "among the best rough and ready debaters upon the floor of the house. In fact some believe he is the ablest...." (*Chicago Daily News*, April 17, 1913). After serving one two-year term, he ran for mayor of Chicago in 1915. He was among four candidates defeated by William Hale Thompson when that long-serving mayor was chosen for his first term.

After a 1917 socialist convention adopted a strident anti-war policy, even to violent opposition to war preparations, many of the less radical members left the party. Stedman stayed active. Another pivotal event was the October 1917 Bolshevik Revolution in Russia that ended the brief experiment with democracy that had followed the abdication of Czar Nicholas II. The arrival of a Soviet-style collective caused an immediate reaction of "unsurpassed joy" among most American socialists (Miller, *Berger*, p. 177). However, bloody revolution was not quite what many socialists said that they were promoting. Stedman and others on the national executive committee were condemned by enthusiastic American supporters of Bolshevism as being too hesitant to embrace Lenin and Trotsky. It was only a matter of degree, as in November 1918 Stedman favored a resolution that extended "the hand of comradeship to the revolting working class of Europe."

The aftermath of the Great War saw an obsession with espionage, Bolshevism, and revolution. Many American socialists were indicted under the federal Espionage Act as a result of their attempts, at least by speeches, to hinder the government's war policies. Stedman defended more than 50 of them, in part because another socialist attorney, Morris Hillquit, came down with tuberculosis in the summer of 1918 and turned all his cases over to Stedman. For personal reasons prominent socialist Kate Richards O'Hare did not want Stedman to represent her, but relented after other leaders insisted. Two days before her trial was to begin, or so the O'Hares said, Stedman "confessed" that he had been so busy with other cases that he forgot about hers. She quickly got another attorney, and was quickly convicted. Former socialist congressman Victor Berger was indicted for espionage one week before the November 1918 election returned him to Congress from Wisconsin. Stedman's defense could not prevent conviction and a 20 year prison sentence. In 1921 Stedman argued the appeal to the United States Supreme Court. On a 6–3 vote the conviction was overturned.

The struggle between socialist factions came to a head at the 1919 party convention in Chicago. The Old Guard still dominated and elected Stedman chairman of the convention by 88 votes to 37 for Joseph Coldwell. The minority filed out and immediately formed the Communist Labor Party, with Bolshevik enthusiasts like John Reed dominating that new party. The relationship between American socialists and militant international communism was an inevitable concern to many Americans. In January 1920 five socialist members of the New York state assembly were suspended from the body. They were called agents of the alien and invisible Bolshevik conspiracy. Stedman was part of a team of socialist attorneys who defended them in a hearing held before the assembly's Judiciary Committee. Reflecting the nationwide focus on subversives, on the first day of the hearing

in Albany, 38 socialists and communists were indicted for espionage in Chicago. Stedman gave a five-hour closing argument in March 1920, but he could not prevent the legislators' expulsion.

Another leader in prison for espionage was Debs himself, who was indicted in June 1918 after giving an antiwar speech in Canton, Ohio. Stedman was the lead defense counsel in a September 1918 trial held in Cleveland. After the prosecution finished, the defense called no witnesses, a decision Stedman announced by saying, "Let's see, you rest. We rest." Debs made his own unsuccessful jury argument. Stedman's arguments on appeal to the U.S. Supreme Court were rejected in March 1919.

When the 1920 national convention met, Atlanta federal prisoner 2253 received the presidential nomination. Stedman gave a speech favoring an international peace conference, opposing the League of Nations as a capitalist tool to exploit workers, and promoting strikes to improve workers' conditions. Stedman and Kate Richards O'Hare were nominated for vice president. Stedman was described as a "barefoot newspaper boy, as a loyal and faithful servant of the working class" by nominating speaker Lena Morrow Lewis of California. O'Hare had already begun serving her prison sentence for espionage, and there was a concern that both candidates being in prison might handicap the campaign. Stedman won the nomination easily.

Stedman made a plea to President Wilson's secretary Joseph Tumulty to pardon both Debs and O'Hare. Two weeks after the socialist convention Wilson commuted O'Hare's sentence. It would be another year before Debs was released. Stedman conducted an active campaign. He reported to federal prisoner Debs that the party was in bad shape, but the socialist movement was in great condition. Stedman was not surprised by the ticket's November defeat.

Stedman had run for many offices, jokingly saying he had run for everything except U.S. Senate and avoided that race because he might win. After the 1920 campaign, espionage trials and being a candidate were in Stedman's past. He was a trustee of the Cooperative Society of America, a one million dollar chain store venture that went into receivership in 1921. Stedman also was a vice president, trust officer and director of the City State Bank of Chicago. He also represented this institution in court. On November 2, 1929, the bank was placed into receivership by the state of Illinois. Stedman and others were indicted 18 months later for allegedly accepting a large deposit knowing that the bank was insolvent, in order to embezzle the money. Stedman was convicted and sentenced to serve one to three years in the state penitentiary. Thus both members of the 1920 Socialist ticket were convicted of felonies. An appellate court in 1935 reversed the conviction. It found that Stedman did not know that the bank was insolvent when the deposit was accepted. The evidence showed that Stedman had himself made a substantial deposit the day before the bank closed, and had lost most of it. He had invested in real estate bonds and mortgages through the bank, which also largely became worthless. Stedman was a victim of the financial collapse, not a perpetrator. Many socialists saw the indictment as politically motivated.

Stedman continued to practice law in Chicago until a few years before his death in 1948.

STEDMAN BIBLIOGRAPHY

Buckingham, Peter H. *Rebel Against Injustice: The Life of Frank P. O'Hare.* Columbia, Mo. (1996).

Coletta, Paolo E. *William Jennings Bryan: Political Evangelist, 1860–1908.* Lincoln (1964).

Constantine, J. Robert, ed. *Letters of Eugene V. Debs.* 3 volumes. Urbana and Chicago (1990).

Death certificates of Seymour and Irene Stedman, Illinois Department of Public Health, Division of Vital Records.

"Debs Is Nominated by the Socialists." *New York Times* (May 14, 1920), p. 3.

Fleischman, Harry. *Norman Thomas, a Biography: 1884–1968.* New York (1964).

Ginger, Ray. *The Bending Cross: A Biography of Eugene Victor Debs.* New Brunswick (1949).

Harris, Frank. "My Political Creed." *Pearson's* (November 1920).

Hartford, City of, Vital Records Department, could find no birth certificate for Stedman, thus he may not have been born in Hartford.

Hartford city directories, 1871–79.

Heath, Frederic Faries, ed. *Social Democracy Red Book: A Brief History of Socialism in America.* Terre Haute (1900), pp. 116–117.

Kipnis, Ira. *The American Socialist Movement, 1897–1912.* New York (1952).

Laidler, Harry W. "The Socialist Convention." *The Socialist Review* IX (June, 1920), pp. 26–29.

Miller, Sally. *Victor Berger and the Promise of Constructive Socialism, 1910–1920.* Westport, Conn. (1973).

Minor, Robert. *Stedman's Red Raid.* Cleveland (1921), pamphlet.

Morgan, H. Wayne. *Eugene Debs: Socialist for President.* Syracuse (1971).

People v. Stedman. 279 Illinois Appellate Court Reports 630 (1935) (unpublished opinion obtained from clerk of court). Thanks are due to Ken Raigins for acquiring this opinion.

Pratt, Norma Fain. *Morris Hillquit: A Political History of an American Jewish Socialist.* Westport, Conn. (1979).

Quint, Howard H. *The Forging of American Socialism: Origins of the Modern Movement.* Columbia, S.C. (1953).

Rand School of Social Science, Department of Labor Research. *A Political Guide for the Workers, Socialist Party Campaign Book 1920.* Chicago (1920), pp. 15–23; copy filmed with *Socialist Party of America Papers,* microfilm edition.

"Report of the Eighth National Convention of the Socialist Party Held at Finnish Hall." Unpublished transcript, in *Socialist Party of America Papers,* microfilm edition, reel 76 (especially speeches nominating and seconding Stedman for vice president).

"Seymour Stedman, Chicago Lawyer" (obituary). *New York Times* (July 10, 1948), p. 15.

"Seymour Stedman, Ran on Debs Ticket" (obituary). *New York Herald-Tribune* (July 11, 1948), p. 36.

Shannon, David A. *The Socialist Party of America.* Chicago (1967, reprint of 1955 edition).

Stedman, Seymour. "Debs as the Standard Bearer." *The Socialist World* (September 1920), pp. 6–8.

_____. "How the Workers Vote Themselves into Jail." *The Socialist World* (July 15, 1920), pp. 8–9.

_____. "Nine Steps to a New Age." *The Independent* (October 9, 1920), pp. 39–40.

_____. "To Straphangers Who Vote." *Issues of 1914.* Socialist Party pamphlet, Chicago(1914).

_____. Papers, Wisconsin State Archives, Madison.

"Stedman Defines Socialist Aims," *New York Times* (August 2, 1920), p. 3.

Waldman, Louis, with introduction by Seymour Stedman. *Albany, the Crisis in Government: The History of the Suspension, Trial, and Expulsion from the New York State Legislature....* New York (1920).

Election of 1924

NOMINATIONS

Republican Party Convention (18th): June 10–12, 1924, at the Municipal Auditorium in Cleveland, Ohio. *President*— Calvin Coolidge, nominated on the first ballot with 1,065 votes out of 1,109 cast. *Vice president*— Frank Lowden, nominated on the second ballot with 766 votes out of 1,109 cast, after vote switches. He had received 413 on the second ballot before the changes, and 22 on the first ballot. William Kenyon (Iowa), Charles Dawes, and Theodore Burton (Ohio) were other possibilities. Lowden, who was at the convention, refused to accept the nomination. Charles Dawes was nominated on the next ballot, the third, with 682½ out of 1,109 cast. Herbert Hoover received the bulk of the remainder.

Democratic Party Convention (24th): June 24–July 9, 1924, at Madison Square Garden, New York City, New York. *President*— John W. Davis, nominated on the 103rd ballot, after vote switching, with 844 out of 1,098 cast. Before the switching, he had received 575½ votes; on the first ballot Davis got 31 votes. William McAdoo, Al Smith, and Oscar Underwood were the other candidates. *Vice president*— Charles W. Bryan, nominated on the first ballot after switching, with 740 votes out of 1,098 cast. He had received 238 before the vote changes. George Berry (Tenn.) led before the votes were changed.

Progressive Party Convention: July 4, 1924, Cleveland, Ohio. *President*— Robert M. La Follette, nominated unanimously. *Vice president*— Burton K. Wheeler, nominated unanimously.

GENERAL ELECTION, November 4, 1924

Popular Vote

Coolidge	15,717,553
Davis	8,386,169
La Follette	4,814,050
Others	158,187

Electoral Vote

Coolidge-Dawes — 382 (35 states)
Davis-Bryan —136 (12 states)
La Follette–Wheeler —13 (1 state)

Winners

Calvin Coolidge, 30th president
Charles G. Dawes, 30th vice-president

Losers

John W. Davis, Charles W. Bryan, Robert La Follette, Burton K. Wheeler, Frank Lowden

---

*1924 presidential nominee —
Democratic Party*

John W. Davis

Full name: John William Davis.

State represented: West Virginia.

Birth: April 13, 1873, in Clarksburg, Harrison County, West Virginia.

Age on Inauguration Day (March 4, 1925): 51 years, 10½ months.

Education: Taught at home; at age 12 enrolled at Clarksburg Female Seminary; September 1887, went to Pantops Academy near Charlottesville, Virginia; Washington and Lee College, 1889–1892; Washington and Lee law school, 1894–1895; admitted to bar in 1895.

Religion: Presbyterian, but with no real belief in religion.

Ancestry/prominent relatives: Welsh, Scotch-Irish ancestors; father a state assemblyman, U.S. congressman.

Occupation: Attorney.

Public offices: West Virginia House of Delegates, 1898–1900; U.S. House of Representatives, March 4, 1911–August 29, 1913, resigned; U.S. solicitor general, 1913–1918; U.S. ambassador to England, November 21, 1918–March 31, 1921; declined to be appointed to U.S. Supreme Court in 1922; unsuccessful Democratic presidential nominee, 1924.

Death: March 24, 1955, in Charleston, South Carolina, at age 81 years, 11½ months.

Burial: Locust Valley Cemetery, Glen Cove, New York.

Home: Apartment on Fifth Avenue in New York; home in South Carolina; rented home on Long Island also.

Personal Characteristics: 6' tall, 190 pounds, white hair, ruddy complexion; witty, gentlemanly, graceful; liked by almost all who knew him; tremendously persuasive and logical as attorney.

Father: John James Davis (May 5, 1835–March 19, 1916), married August 21, 1862; an attorney and politician; served two terms as congressman.

Mother: Anna Kennedy (November 14, 1841–1917); daughter of William Wilson Kennedy, a lumber merchant.

Siblings: Lillie, married John A. Preston (?–July 29, 1939). Emma A. (?–February 1, 1943), never married. Moselle, died in infancy. Anna (Nan) (c. 1874–June 14, 1945), married Hilary Goode Richardson on December 31, 1901, a minister. Estelle, died at age six of scarlet fever.

First wife: Julia McDonald (c. 1874–August 17, 1900), married on June 20, 1899, died after childbirth; daughter of Major Edward and Julia (Leavell) McDonald, who lived on a farm near Charles Town, West Virginia.

Child: Anna Kennedy (1900–   ), renamed Julia after her mother died; married Charles P. Healy, who died in 1957.

Second wife: Ellen Graham Bassell (Nell) (c. 1869–July 13, 1943), married January 2, 1912; daughter of John and Martha L. Bassell.

Children: None.

Movies: *Separate but Equal*, a 1991 made-for-television miniseries on ABC, based on the *Brown vs. Board of Education* Supreme Court case. Burt Lancaster played Davis, while Sidney Poitier played Thurgood Marshall.

Nothing so pleased John W. Davis as being a lawyer, arguing his client's position and battling the legal opposition. Nothing was so thrust upon the man as the insistent demand that he run for public office. He lost only one election, but it was for the country's highest office. Three other times he won. Win or lose, he always seemed to long for return to the excitement of the courtroom.

Davis was the only son among six children of a small town West Virginia lawyer, who also served two terms in Congress. Discipline was taught Davis by his mother. Tutored at home and then at a female academy in his native Clarksburg, John completed his education at Washington and Lee University in Lexington, Virginia. He would maintain a close relationship with his alma mater throughout his life.

Since he could not immediately afford law school, Davis secured a position as a tutor to several children in Charles Town, West Virginia. Davis stayed with the family, there getting to know particularly well one of his female students, who would six years later become his wife. Not much money was being set aside for law school, so Davis agreed to read law in his father's office. That proved intellectually unsatisfying to Davis. With his father's financial assistance, he did finally take the one-year law school program at Washington and Lee.

Davis's education poorly prepared him for small town practice. Like many lawyers he found himself frustrated by his ignorance of technical pitfalls that could trip him. Financial rewards were limited as well, and he agreed to take a professorship at Washington and Lee law school with a good salary. There was too little to satisfy his combative nature in the cloistered life of a professorship and thus after a year Davis returned to his father's firm. His second try at private practice was more successful.

Until his success was secure, however, Davis put off the responsibilities of marriage. Young Julia McDonald, his former student, was tiring of waiting as were both sets of parents. Finally in 1899 Davis procrastinated no longer and the two were married. A year later their first child was born. A drunk doctor failed to sterilize his instruments, and soon Julia was suffering from puerperal fever. Fourteen months after their marriage, Julia was dead. Davis could not be consoled, even by his newborn daughter. Davis had little religious conviction to support him during this trial, and friends were inadequate. For years he could suddenly be wracked with anxiety over the memory of this senseless tragedy.

Some of Davis's early cases revealed a willingness to take liberal positions on legal issues, depending on the needs of his clients. His defense of miners who had been arrested while marching in protest of mine conditions and in defiance of a court injunction, was spirited and successful. A jam-packed courtroom saw this still raw attorney give a compelling closing argument at trial that caused the anti-labor judge to give only light sentences to the miners. Davis quickly earned respect for his integrity. His identification with his clients, whoever they might be, was almost total. As any good lawyer, he believed in what he was doing. Years later, as a prospective nominee for president, he would be called upon to explain the at-times unpopular causes and clients he espoused. He was more than equal to the task.

Davis's income and fame grew as his clients multiplied. The once humble, small-business clients brought in by his father gave way to more lucrative assignments from larger companies. The railroads saw in young Davis a legal talent they wanted on their side, as did several mining companies. This strained the relations between the two Davis lawyers, as not only was the elder attorney somewaht jealous of his son's apparent superiority as an attorney, but he also could not sympathize with the legal arguments made by the younger Davis in defense of some of these companies.

In 1898, Davis was forced into his first political race. His success and fame as an attorney, his strong speaking ability and his winning personality made the nominating convention choose him to oust the Republicans from their 20-year lock on the legislative seat from the county. Davis's reaction was to refuse the nomination, but finally he relented. The campaign repulsed him, as he was no flesh-presser who enjoyed crowds and false shows of emotion. Since his opponent had made enemies by supporting railroad interests, it was politic but ironic that Davis won his first office by denouncing the railroads.

At the only session of the state legislature in which Davis served, he was touted for speaker, but finally settled for the position of Democratic floor leader. Few if any in the body could match his legal abilities. The freshman legislator became the acknowledged authority on the language in almost all bills. His abili-

ties were sorely needed, as while dozing during one particularly boring debate he was suddenly stirred by hearing the final reading of a bill changing public executions of murderers to a private affair within the prison. The unfortunate phrasing of the bill that caught Davis's ear was, "all convicts confined in the State penitentiary shall suffer death in private within the walls of the prison." Davis thought a helpful additional phrase would be to limit the executions to those "under sentence of death." But Davis was more than a wordsmith. His forthright stands on several controversial issues, in which he refused to take the politically safe route, marked him for integrity and courage. As his service in the legislature ended, there were those who clearly thought higher office would be his, certainly the governorship.

Though for 12 years following his one term as a legislator Davis would be county party chairman, his real interest remained the law. In 1904, he was a delegate to the Democratic national convention, and voted for fellow attorney Alton Parker. William Jennings Bryan's populist stands never interested the increasingly business-oriented Davis, and thus he was pleased to see the Democrats turn toward more conservative leadership.

His legal success grew out of many factors. His memory was keen; his speaking abilities clear and concise. His gifts were less of intellectual brilliance than of the discipline of hard work, clarity of expression, and synthesizer of facts. His temper was not well under control early in his practice. Once he struck an opposing attorney in court; another time he threw an inkwell at another lawyer during a trial. A Republican newspaper editor who had verbally abused his father was chased by Davis through the streets of Clarksburg as the outraged attorney tried to strike the newspaperman with a whip. Fortunately he learned to control such excesses of zeal.

Davis was less reluctant about bar association office than about governmental service, and he accepted the post of president of the West Virginia Bar Association in 1906. Four years later his dislike of political office again rose to the fore when he begged not to be nominated for Congress. The Democrats had decided that he was their best hope for claiming the seat, despite Davis's assertion to the press immediately before the convention delegates balloted that he would not accept the nomination. The report of his refusal was never filed by the newspaperman, who had become too drunk to make it to his office. Two telegrams from Davis's father demanding him to stand firm in his refusal to accept were pocketed by a supporter and never shown to the reluctant candidate. His father threatened to throw him out of the house, but eventually resigned himself to Davis's decision to run. Even Republicans found Davis an attractive candidate. The Democratic candidate was supported by both miners and mine owners, a rare feat in West Virginia. Such bipartisan backing gave Davis a large majority in the general election. He was the first Democrat to win the seat since 1894.

His reputation as an outstanding lawyer earned him appointment to the Judiciary Committee. Speaker Champ Clark would later say that never had he known a freshman congressman to earn so great a reputation in so short a time. Davis throughout his legal practice had been outraged that a judge could issue an injunction against miners and other laborers almost at will. He therefore framed an anti-injunction bill and shepherded it through the House committee and onto the floor. The West Virginian was reelected in 1912. He supported many of the progressive features of new president Woodrow Wilson's "New Freedom" program, including the child labor law and eight-hour work day. Winning reelection narrowly partly due to the three-way presidential race, Davis wondered about his future in the House. His influence was small and his frustrations many. His progressive record had been slowly developing, but he continued to be opposed to female suffrage and to favor literacy tests for voting, hoping therefore to reduce immigration. He won some notice and respect for his skilled involvement in the impeachment of a federal judge and in the prosecuting of a Washington banker who had struck a congressman because of his remarks in a speech.

While his congressional career was unsatisfying, his private life improved. In 1912, he married the daughter of one of his principal Charlottesville legal rivals. She was divorced, her first husband having been a drug addict and adulterer, whose unsavory reputation stained his new wife's image as well. Davis's parents were not pleased with the match, and Davis broke off the engagement. Eventually finding the courage to ignore his parents' objections, he married Nell Bassell on January 2, 1912. Her gracious beauty finally won over Davis's parents; the marriage seemed in every respect to have been a happy one.

President Wilson gave Davis the position of solicitor general. The responsibility of that official is to present the government case in appeals to the United States Supreme Court. For five years David developed further his already exceptional advocacy skills, always on behalf of the progressive programs of President Wilson. Sometimes he personally disagreed with his legal position. One such occasion was in presenting the case against the Oklahoma "grandfather clause" for voting. This exempted from a literacy test any citizen whose ancestors had been able to vote prior to 1866. Since there was slavery prior to that year, the intent of the law was clear. Davis had the professional if not the personal satisfaction in seeing the Oklahoma statute become the first ever act held unconstitutional on the basis of the 15th Amendment to the Constitution. In this and many other cases, Davis was making a brilliant impression on the Court and other attorneys. He was tremendously respected, but also revered as an individual. Justice Hughes said it was an "intellectual treat" to hear Davis; another judge doubted that Davis's opponents could receive "due process" because of the persuasiveness Davis brought to his advocacy.

> When he appeared in a Supreme Court chamber every interested observer used to be reminded ... of doting grandfathers enjoying the performance of a precocious and favorite grandson. The Court fairly hovered over Mr. Davis in solicitude....

By 1917, Davis was tiring of his post. Three times she had seriously been considered for an appointment to the Court, in large part because of the encouragement from the justices themselves. Chief Justice White particularly communicated his hope that President Wilson appoint Davis. Once in 1914 and twice in 1916 he was passed over. In 1913, Davis had been anxious for the appointment to an intermediate federal court vacancy, and the entire West Virginia congressional delegation, the two West Virginia federal judges, and county bar associations all urged President Wilson to appoint Davis, but to no avail. Davis was severely disappointed, and this experience seemed to sour him on a judgeship.

In 1918, Wilson appointed Davis as ambassador to England. First Davis served as one of four commissioners to a German-American conference on prisoners-of-war, but the Germans, despite their losses on the battlefield, were recalcitrant and little progress was made. There was little communication between Wilson and Davis, and the ambassador was left out of most policy decisions. Davis became a much-revered figure in England, however, primarily because his tact prevented the worst of the American government's insensitivities to the British from becoming major issues in England. King George called Davis the most perfect gentleman he had ever met.

As his tenure drew to a close, Davis began to be mentioned as a possible 1920 Democratic presidential nominee. He almost resigned as ambassador in February 1920, because of President Wilson's dismissal of Davis's old friend and secretary of state, Robert Lansing. Davis was advised that a resignation then would appear to be the opening shot in a presidential race, and thus Davis stayed at his post. West Virginia Democrats were working for his nomination; former Secretary of State Lansing pushed his cause. In May 1920, the *New York Times* created a sensation by endorsing him as a "great man, a great American, and a great Democrat." Wilson's attitude was coldly negative, saying, "if you want to stand still, he is just the man...." For a time at the convention, it appeared Davis might be able to win, but finally the nod went to James Cox of Ohio.

As Davis returned to his legal practice in New York City, he said that ten years was what every man should give in public service. He had just completed his decade of involvement and wanted to retire permanently to private law practice. The offers from prestigious firms had been overwhelming. Davis finally chose

Stetson, Jennings & Russell, the same firm in which Grover Cleveland had worked between his two terms as president. Davis had found his life's work; Wall Street practice suited him perfectly. He developed a huge, profitable business. He was indefatigable. His industry amazed the partners who had invited him into the firm, for they thought he would be an administrator and client developer, but hardly a practicing attorney. The courtroom was Davis's battleground, and he won far more than he lost. His clients were big business, including J.P. Morgan, the fabulously wealthy head of a colossal financial empire based on the U.S. Steel Company and railroads. Davis's clients perhaps imperceptibly refined his political views. Davis opposed regulation of the coal, gas, and iron industries; he desired the reduction of taxes on the rich (feeling personally oppressed by such taxes). He publicly opposed the equal rights for women amendment that was periodically proposed in Congress. His anti-progressive character was not generally noted in the press when Davis continued to be mentioned as a Democratic presidential possibility for 1924. In 1922, President Harding agreed to appoint Davis to the Supreme Court after Chief Justice Taft and other judges had beseeched him to do so. Much to Taft's chagrin, Davis declined the appointment on the basis that he could not afford the financial sacrifice. At the same time as a Supreme Court justice's salary was $15,000, Davis's income was several hundred thousand annually.

Though Davis did not seek the 1924 presidential nomination, neither did he wish to refuse it. His continued work for politically unattractive clients such as J.P. Morgan showed that the Democrats would have to take him on his terms. Davis was silent on the major political issues. Progressives could look to his role as solicitor general and think he was a progressive; conservatives could see his present legal practice and think him conservative. The Democratic field was crowded. The issues were farm relief, the Klan, and a long list of social reforms. William Jennings Bryan took strong exception to Davis and did not trust him. For one hundred ballots the progressives at the national convention stayed with Al Smith and

William Gibbs McAdoo; the conservatives were for Oscar Underwood and others. The party was too badly split, views on the issues too divergent for compromise. Finally in relief but also in resignation, a move to Davis started on the one hundred second ballot, and Davis won on the following vote.

Davis tried to start his campaign with an appeal to the progressives in his own party by selecting as his running mate Governor Charles Bryan of Kansas, William Jennings Bryan's brother. Bryan accepted only after Senator Thomas J. Walsh of Montana, former Secretary of Agriculture Edward T. Meredith, and former Secretary of War Newton Baker all refused. Much like George McGovern was to discover 48 years later, it is hard to get a candidate to be second in command on a doomed ship.

Davis himself recognized the virtual hopelessness of the cause. The party was badly split, and progressive third party nominee Robert La Follette was certain to drain the Democratic vote. The choice of Bryan shocked many supporters, as the Nebraska governor was sympathetic to the Klan, was seen by conservatives as unstable, and was an affront to liberals who perceived the choice as a base political one. The campaign was poorly run from the beginning, including Davis's mistake in choosing a man who had no national campaign experience to be national chairman. One high point was when Davis finally, reluctantly, decided to take a position strongly against the Klan even though it could cost him crucial votes in the South and border states. His campaign speeches were flat and left his listeners uninspired. President Coolidge, the Republican nominee, was popular and honest. The country seemed firmly gripped by prosperity, though farmers were an obvious exception. Davis's total vote was about half of President Coolidge's, and less than twice La Follette's. There were some Western states in which Davis received less than ten percent of the vote. The rejection was total.

Davis returned to Wall Street practice after an extended European vacation. His income continued to grow, and his interest in politics seemed correspondingly to wane. In 1928, he was a partisan for Governor Al Smith, reject-ing any suggestion that Davis himself might run. He neither wanted not expected renomination. In 1932, he campaigned for Franklin Roosevelt, but he distrusted him. Roosevelt seemed a weak, easily manipulated man who could ruin the country. Davis soon became disenchanted with Roosevelt for entirely opposite reasons, that the New Deal was forcefully reshaping America for the worse. Along with several other well-known conservatives, including another defeated Democratic presidential nominee, Al Smith, Davis became active in the anti–New Deal Liberty League. He opposed federal government involvement in relief efforts during the Depression, and seemed unmoved by the suffering. To Davis the protection, even the sanctity of private property was the prerequisite for freedom in America. His belief in the righteousness of his anti–New Deal cause increased as Roosevelt's presidency continued. It was only with the start of World War II that Davis began to speak favorably of the president. His support of the war effort was total, but he continued to support Republican presidential nominees, including Willkie and Dewey, just as he had favored Landon in 1936.

For 30 years after his overwhelming election defeat, Davis practiced corporate law, defending U.S. Steel and other clients in countless pieces of profitable litigation. His reputation as the preeminent trial and appellate attorney in America grew. His major cases included the defense of the Morgans in an intensive Congressional investigation in 1933, defense of selective conscientious objector status of draftees, and representation of Robert Oppenheimer in his effort to regain his security clearance. His two most famous cases came late in his life, first when he successfully thwarted President Truman's effort to take over the steel industry in 1952, and his losing effort to defend segregation in the South. Many commented on the impressiveness and near persuasiveness of his segregation arguments. Davis believed his argument could not be rejected. However, in *Brown vs. Board of Education* in 1954, the Supreme Court unanimously disagreed with Davis. He was shocked and for a time deeply distressed.

His life had been full, his victories far outnumbering his defeats. His 81 years of vigorous activity ended with his death on March 24, 1955.

Analysis of Qualifications

His public offices were few, but in each he excelled. As a one-term state legislator he became a power in the drafting of bills, being looked to by veteran lawmakers for his legal acumen. As a congressman he soon came to the eye of powerful senior Democrats who placed him on the Judiciary Committee. He made his mark in Congress as a speechmaker, a prosecutor in the impeachment of a federal judge, and as the ablest lawyer in the House. His achievements earned him appointment as solicitor general. One justice called him a treat to hear; others lined up behind him in urging the president to appoint him to any vacancy that opened on the court. As ambassador to England he was so tactful as to improve relations between the two countries despite the growing insensitivities of President Wilson to English interests. King George called him a friend. It is hard to rival such almost unblemished success in public life. Davis's great failure was when he sought the ultimate prize, and there he did not shine. His campaign was disorganized and dispirited. The certainty of defeat probably affected his efforts, but still it is of concern that the man who sought the most difficult executive post in the country was such a poor administrator of his own campaign.

As a lawyer he was unequaled. He had grace and sensitivity, with unfailing concern for the people with whom he worked, superiors and subordinates. His presence in a group made him the center of it. His prominence made him president of the American Bar Association at the age of 50; he continued to be a sought-after attorney in the great cases of the 1950s, when he was 80.

His conservatism is the one great political attribute of his politics. For one brief period, when he was a congressman and then a Woodrow Wilson appointee, he began to adopt some progressive attitudes, but this was short-lived. Always opposed to equal rights for Negroes, he was a committed advocate for school segregation. Opposed also to female suffrage, he argued against the equal rights amendment for women in the 1920s. His corporate clients made him identify and be identified with their interests. In the 1924 campaign he spoke volumes about his policies with one phrase: "There is nothing in the purpose of the party I represent that holds for any legitimate business in this country any threat of menace whatever." He abhorred federal power and was an advocate of states' rights.

What manner of president would these qualities have made? Another defeated nominee, James M. Cox, stated that Davis "would have balanced well the equities as between classes and no man would have met his responsibilities with better understanding." The basis for the judgement is difficult to perceive, as balancing class interests was hardly Davis's forte. He was far from heartless, and gave generously to friends if only modestly to charities. But he did not identify or sympathize during the Depression with the poor, and found nothing in that great national tragedy to require the federal government to expand from the limited powers he envisioned it should have. He had *laissez-faire* economic views that could not be shaken. A Davis presidency may not have been markedly different from the Coolidge presidency. Davis had no interest in imposing additional federal controls over wild speculation on the stock market that contributed to the crash in 1929. He would not have backed governmental support for the farmers who suffered even while most of the remainder of the country prospered during the "Roaring Twenties." His talents were too great for him to be described as anything less than an acceptable choice for president, but he might well have been ranked, as was Coolidge, as a caretaker businessman who did nothing while the country, imperceptibly to most, slid into the Depression.

DAVIS BIBLIOGRAPHY

Davis, Julia. *The Embassy Girls.* Morgantown, W. Va. (1992).

———. *Legacy of Love: A Memoir of Two American Families.* New York City (1961).

Harbaugh, William H. *Lawyer's Lawyer: The Life of John W. Davis.* New York City (1973).

Huntley, Theodore A. *The Life of John W. Davis.* New York City (1924).

JOHN W. DAVIS and CHARLES W. BRYAN
(From the collection of David J. and Janice L. Frent)

Kluger, Richard. *Simple Justice.* New York City (1976).
Murray, Robert K. *The One Hundred and Third Ballot: The Democrats and the Disaster in Madison Square Garden.* New York City (1976).

---

*1924 vice presidential nominee —
Democratic Party*

Charles W. Bryan

Full name: Charles Wayland Bryan.
State represented: Nebraska.
Birth: February 10, 1867, Salem, Illinois.
Age on Inauguration Day (March 4, 1925): 58 years, 1 month.
Education: Taught at home by his mother until he was ten years old; Salem public schools, 1877–1881; Whipple Academy, 1882–1884; University of Chicago, 1885, but dropped out.

Religion: Rarely attended church; little personal interest in religion.
Ancestry/prominent relatives: Scotch-Irish ancestors; William Smith Bryan arrived in American around 1650 and settled in Virginia; William Jennings Bryan (brother), three-time presidential nominee.
Occupation: Aide to his brother William Jennings Bryan (see election of 1896); public official; newspaper publisher.
Public office: Mayor of Lincoln, Nebraska, May 1915–1917; defeated for Democratic nomination for Nebraska governor, 1916 and 1918; city council of Lincoln, 1921–1923; governor of Nebraska, 1923–1925; unsuccessful Democratic nominee for vice president, 1924; defeated for governor, 1926 and 1928; governor, 1931–1935; defeated for Democratic nomination to U.S. Senate, 1934; mayor of Lincoln, 1935–1937; lost Democratic nomination and then defeated as independent for governor, 1938; defeated for U.S. House seat, 1940;

received Democratic nomination for governor, 1942, but defeated.

Home: Lincoln, Nebraska.

Death: March 4, 1945, Lincoln, Nebraska, at age 78 years, 1 month.

Burial: Wyuka Cemetery, Lincoln, Nebraska.

Personal characteristics: 6'2" tall, 200 pounds, thick mustache; shiny bald head; constantly wore skull cap to alleviate his sensitivity to light shining on his head.

Father: Silas L. Bryan (November 4, 1822–1880); successful Illinois farmer, attorney, judge, and in 1872, unsuccessful nominee for U.S. House of Representatives.

Mother: Maria Elizabeth Jennings (May 24, 1832–June 27, 1896); married November 4, 1852; daughter of prosperous farmer.

Siblings: Virginia Ann (September 8, 1853–December 26, 1857). John Henshen (June 4, 1856–December 31, 1857). Frances Maria (March 18, 1858–December 6, 1934), married (1) Alfred C. Millson, March 6, 1877, and (2) James W. Baird on June 8, 1893. William Jennings (March 19, 1860–July 26, 1925), married Mary Elizabeth Baird on October 1, 1884. Hiram Lillard (October 4, 1862–July 19, 1863). Russell Jones (June 12, 1864–August 11, 1881). Nancy Lillard (November 4, 1869–January 30, 1904). Mary Elizabeth (May 14, 1872–April 25, 1962), married Thomas Stinson Allen on June 28, 1898.

Wife: Elizabeth Louise Brokaw (1872–October 7, 1952); married on November 29, 1892.

Children: Silas Millard (October 23, 1893–July 9, 1957), married Frances Marie Schibsby, May 5, 1918. Virginia (1898–August 13, 1899). Mary Louise (March 2, 1902–October 5, 1947), married William Ernest Harnsberger on June 19, 1924.

In 1912, a newspaperman who had observed the relationship between Charley Bryan and his much more famous brother William Jennings Bryan, described the brothers' interdependence:

> During all the years that W.J. has been battling for political reforms and Bryan ideals, his brother Charles has stuck loyally by his side and been the one man that William Jennings Bryan has most trusted—and depended upon—to personally direct and carry into exe-

cution many things in relation to his work along moral lines. One who has not visited his office and has not been in touch with the part delegated to Charles Bryan can have no adequate idea of the part he has and is playing in the political arena with his brother.

In 1915, with William Jennings Bryan's career in elective politics closed, Charley Bryan started to campaign for his own election. They were one of only two brother acts among the defeated major party nominees for America's two top elective offices (the other was the Pinckneys). Their symbiotic relationship explains much of the success and failure of each.

The Bryan brothers grew up in a prosperous, though not affluent family in Salem, Illinois. Their father was a farmer, lawyer and judge. He had also been an unsuccessful candidate for the U.S. House of Representatives in 1872, starting a tradition of ambition and losses for national office. It was a close, happy, devout home, in which thrice-daily Bible reading and prayers were mandatory. Religion was central to their lives, but only William Jennings among the brothers carried that religious fervor into adult life. Charley, though believing in the value of the church as a moral guide for society, was apparently close to being an agnostic and rarely attended church once he left home. Education was not nearly as central as religion in the Bryan household. Studies were at home until Charley reached his tenth birthday, and then he started at the Salem public schools. Never attentive as a student, the younger Bryan brother was more enamored with athletics and the outdoors. Baseball and boxing were his most successful sports, and in his age group as a teenager Charley won the southern Illinois boxing championship. Silas Bryan, the boys' father, died in 1880, leaving some money for a college education for his sons, but it would be tight financially. William Jennings took advantage of the funds that were available, but Charley, after a few disinterested years at Whipple Academy in preparation for college, attended the University of Chicago for less than a year.

It was not as a scholar that Charley made a name at Whipple, but as a precocious baseball player and, somewhat related to the first, as what the student paper called "undoubtedly the lady's man at the college." Though not an intellectual, Bryan displayed an awesome memory for facts that he thought important. He was well-read in current affairs and could recite names, dates, and statistical information to shore up first his brother's political arguments and subsequently his own. Particularly critical for his chosen profession was an uncanny memory for names and faces, a talent in constant use on the campaign trail.

After leaving the University of Chicago in 1885, Charley returned to the family's Salem farm. William Jennings was little in evidence after their father's death, since he was away at school and then trying to establish his legal and political career. The brothers were not close as children, since there was a seven-year age difference, but after Silas Bryan's death Charley turned to his older brother frequently for advice. With William Jennings becoming well-established in Nebraska and raving to Charley about the opportunities there, the younger brother joined him in 1891. His first job was with a company selling soap, tobacco, gum, candy, and a variety of other products. William was elected to the United States Congress in 1890, but Charley at first played little role in the political field. When William Jennings made his move for the presidency, Charley finally got involved. On June 30, 1896, the brothers met in Salem for their mother's funeral. The Democratic National Convention was just days away, and Charley asked his politician brother, who was not an announced presidential candidate, who would win the nomination. The stunning response was that if events broke favorably, Bryan would win. He was right.

Though the campaign for president was headquartered in Nebraska, Charley continued in his business pursuits in Omaha until October. Then the candidate turned to him for help in handling the massive correspondence pouring into the office. Imaginatively, Charley turned the tedious task of answering the mail into a critical part of his brother's future presidential campaigns. The name and address of each correspondent was catalogued, along with whatever relevant data could be found, such as religious preference, occupation, family, and other details that could prove significant in later contacts. By the end of the

year following the election, Charley had developed a card file of over 200,000 names. That list would grow to close to half a million by the end of William Jennings' electoral contests. The file was never allowed to get dusty. Mail was sent frequently, and between cataloguing new names and contacting existing ones, Charley's time for years was dominated with work on the file.

Though defeated in 1896, the Democrat's presidential nominee was hardly ready to give up the fight. In 1900, he again gained the nomination. Brother Charley was in the background, performing the same chores as earlier. With another defeat for his efforts, William Jennings Bryan and his brother decided to continue the battle through a newspaper. Charley's organizational work gave an initial subscribers list for the paper, while his older brother was the heart and soul. The *Commoner*, so named for its audience of middle and lower class readers, was a tremendous success. The first year the articles seemed to lack much fire, but after complaints reached the paper's office, changes were made. The content was mainly political news and editorials, with some personal interest stories. No advertisements from big business or alcohol interests were allowed, as both brothers were agrarian populists who waged war against corporations and liquor their entire political lives. The *Commoner* was the vehicle for W.J. Bryan's political propaganda for over 20 years, and even when he was not a candidate for office, the paper tried to weigh in on the side of the candidates he did support. At first Charley's title was business manager, and later he became publisher and assistant editor. Regardless of title, Charley ran the paper while his brother tended to other affairs. The only financial troubles through the years were fears that the paper would make too much money and become a focus of political attack on the brothers. Subscription prices were kept low to encourage circulation as well as keep profits down. Though the potential was there, the paper never did make the Bryans millionaires.

William Jennings did not run for president in 1904, but he energetically and vainly tried to halt the naming of a conservative candidate. Alton B. Parker's nomination caused the

Bryans to sit the general election out. Overwhelming defeat for Parker helped put the Bryan team back in position for 1908, and this time Charley was firmly in control of his brother's nomination drive. "The List" was effectively used to organize the progressive Democrats throughout the country. By convention time Charley could confidently and accurately forecast a first-ballot victory. He also achieved adoption of the platform he wanted. John Worth Kern was suggested by Charley as a running mate, and that too was accepted. The boss of Tammany Hall, Charles Murphy, recognized political machine success when he saw it and commended the political manager in the Bryan family:

> Mr. Bryan [Charley], you had the delegates and you had them organized. I have been attending the conventions for twenty-eight years, but this is the first time they ever dealt the cards on top of the table and told me in advance what I was going to draw. I confess, it beats me.

The nominee was grateful as well, and thereafter never failed to credit his brother's political skills and instincts.

That was the last success enjoyed by the Bryan brothers in 1908, as William Howard Taft proved unbeatable. Until the next presidential election, Charley returned to his newspaper chores for the *Commoner*. In 1912, Charley sent a questionnaire to each Democratic presidential candidate, asking them where they stood on critical issues. The perceived Bryan favorite and friend, Champ Clark, found the idea of the questions insulting and gave an unsatisfactory response. Woodrow Wilson, however, realized the political benefits of stroking the Bryan brothers and answered thoughtfully and respectfully. At the convention, Charles Bryan played a role in preventing Clark's nomination when he suggested to his brother, once it appeared that Clark had made a deal with New York Democrats, that a resolution be introduced denouncing any candidate who was under any obligations to Wall Street. The resolution caused a furor on the floor, was adopted by a wide margin (who could vote in favor of Big Business?) and helped slow a switch of New York votes to Clark. On balance, however, it does not appear the Bryans were leading players at the 1912 convention. Charley met with Wilson after the convention to assist in planning strategy for the campaign, and continued on in an advisory capacity.

After 1912, the brothers went their separate ways in the development of their careers. With William Jennings Bryan appointed as secretary of state, Charles Bryan began to concentrate more on Nebraska politics and his own advancement. In Lincoln, Charley headed a movement to get a reform charter for the city adopted. When a charter he disliked was presented to the voters instead, Bryan worked against it and was credited with its overwhelming defeat. He demonstrated after this election, and throughout his subsequent career, an unattractive tendency to take credit loudly and glowingly for the success of any venture in which he was involved. Humility was a word never used to describe the younger Bryan.

One issue that turned Bryan against the charter was its rejection of municipal ownership of utilities. In 1913, Bryan had headed the Municipal Ownership League, and backed a slate of city council candidates who would work for municipal control of all utilities. They lost, but Bryan's start in Lincoln politics was made. In 1915, Charley took a more direct approach and announced as a candidate for mayor. The mayor was chosen by the five city council members from their own ranks, and thus Bryan had first to be elected to the council. He was the highest vote getter of any of the five winning candidates, and at the first meeting of the new council he was elected mayor. He had again made the utilities the key issue, this time focusing on the price of natural gas. During the campaign, Bryan met with company officials and convinced them to lower the price. It was a clear triumph for the candidate, one achieved through not-at-all veiled threats of what would happen once he was elected if the price were not lowered.

As mayor, Bryan started slowly with fulfilling campaign promises, but after two months in office the mayor called a special meeting of the council. An elaborate, detailed plan for city government reorganization was the purpose, and he was defeated on a 3–2 vote. During the remainder of his term he continued the fight. Businessmen and a majority of the city council opposed him, but Bryan was building a reputation as a defender of the people. The mayor felt cocky when his term was completed, and offered a five hundred dollar prize to anyone who could find a 20-year period in city government that had accomplished what he had in two.

Bryan had not run for another term as mayor because on February 16, 1916, he announced for governor of Nebraska. His only issue at first was prohibition. Bryan had become chairman of a statewide organization favoring prohibition. Bryan's opponents included the leaders in the Democratic Party who allied themselves with Nebraska United States Senator Gilbert Hitchcock, who was up for reelection in 1916. Senator Hitchcock and the Bryan brothers had been bitter opponents in Nebraska politics for years, and would remain so. A complete slate of Bryan candidates was entered against a slate of Hitchcock opponents in the primary, and Hitchcock's forces won convincingly. Bryan went down to defeat, gaining 33,000 votes to the Hitchcock candidate's 46,000. The Democratic nominee went on to win in November. For the next two years fellow Democrat Bryan was his most vocal critic. In 1918, brother Charley ran again for governor, making government ownership of a broad range of businesses his campaign platform. These included slaughter houses, gas stations, all public utilities, grain elevators, and other critical businesses. Prohibition was another issue. Success evaded Bryan on his second try, and the margin of defeat was somewhat larger than in 1916.

In 1920, Bryan would not make another try for governor, but instead concentrated on taking control of the state's Democratic Party. Senator Hitchcock was attempting to become the state's favorite son candidate for president. It was a hard-fought campaign, with Hitchcock being attacked for failure to support prohibition and female suffrage. The election was considered a Bryan victory, with each faction sharing delegates to the national convention. At the convention the Bryans refused to support the nominee, James M. Cox, and his running mate Franklin D. Roosevelt.

With another try for governor imminent, Bryan first ran for and was elected to another term on the Lincoln city council in 1921. Businessmen warned that Bryan wanted to end free enterprise in the city. He was the top vote getter for city council, but when it met another man was chosen mayor. Bryan was outraged, and was even more chagrined when he received appointment as commissioner for streets. For a time street-cleaner Bryan was made the butt of jokes, but the last laugh was on them. Using his personal popularity in the city, he obtained petitions signed by a large number of Lincoln's voters, demanding the changes he desired. The council saw the futility of opposing him, as refusal would lead to Bryan's using the petitions to require a recall election. Bryan had already demonstrated whom the people of the city supported. Thus from his position as street commissioner, Bryan was in control of the council. A municipal coal yard was established that sold coal at a far lower price than commercial yards. The threat of establishing a municipal ice plant forced the price of ice to fall. Businessmen were aghast and brought suit. The state Supreme Court held that there was nothing unconstitutional about a city owning a coal yard, but that the Lincoln city charter did not authorize it. In short order Bryan secured voter approval of charter revision, and the issue was settled.

For two years Bryan battled the major businesses of Lincoln. A municipal gas station was established that sold gasoline at 16 cents a gallon, where before commercial stations had sold it for 22 cents. A nationwide reputation was spreading for the dynamic, unconventional Nebraska politician. Descriptions of him usually included such adjectives as "radical," or "socialist." With farmers suffering from collapsing commodity prices, many in the state were ready for some socialism. In order to gain maximum advantage from his skyrocketing popularity, Bryan refused to commit on which office he would seek in the 1922 election. In return for supporting Hitchcock, Bryan received assurances that the senator would help Bryan's gubernatorial campaign. His announcement for governor came on June 18, with a call for drastically lower taxes, reorganization of state government, and a lower state budget. Victory came, 214,000 to 164,000 for his Republican opponent. Hitchcock was thrown out of the Senate by almost the same margin by *his* Republican opponent. Most state officials, including a majority of the legislature, were Republican. With a radical Democrat as governor, there was sure to be controversy.

Governor Bryan immediately reduced the employees of his office, and where possible, in other branches of government. His proposal to discard the present six departments of the state executive branch, each with its own secretary and staff, was defeated in the legislature. Bryan refused to appoint department secretaries anyway, and took over many department functions himself. The university budget was slashed, as were many other items. Eight million dollars of the outgoing Republican governor's thirty million dollar budget were dropped, and the legislature could not get the three-fifths majority necessary to increase the budget. When he labeled any legislature brash enough to oppose him as a "tool of the special interests," a short-lived impeachment move started in the legislature.

Besides controversy with the legislature, Bryan's first term as governor was marked by rabid calls for government ownership of a vast range of businesses. He felt oil companies were charging too much. He demanded that Standard Oil be dissolved, with the government taking over the business. When he tried to set up a state oil company, he found the industry conspiring against him and, discreetly but monopolistically, refusing to sell to the state. The governor called for a federal investigation, and finally a supply was found. The coal industry was next and after condemning the private companies for exorbitant profits, Bryan called for the purchase of coal at the mines and distribution by a non-profit citizens' group. Bryan achieved this innovation. Throughout his administration, this and similar proposals of government ownership of coal and oil companies, of utilities and other vital industries, made him an ogre to business and a white knight to the economically disadvantaged. Few in the country had not heard of the crusading Nebraska governor.

In 1924, brother Charley wanted William Jennings Bryan to run for president, but the old warrior refused. Rumors circulated in 1923 that the Nebraska governor would instead be on the ticket with Al Smith. A favorite son candidacy was started for the governor. Bryan declined to run for reelection in 1924 and focused on national politics. At the convention he was among a total of 60 candidates nominated for president. When John Davis finally won on the hundred and third ballot, a decision had to be made on a running mate. At midnight after the convention selected its candidate for president, a meeting was held in which Davis stated no preference. Senator Thomas Walsh of Montana was suggested, but he refused. Josephus Daniels, newspaper editor, former secretary of the navy in the Wilson administration, and friend of both Bryans suggested the Nebraskan. No one objected, Davis assented, and Bryan enthusiastically agreed.

Many felt Bryan could help among populist Midwest and Western voters who were not attracted to the conservative West Virginian and New York attorney John Davis. But Bryan seemed disinterested in Davis's success, and gave a lackluster performance. Rarely straying far from home base in Lincoln, Bryan was summoned to the Chicago party headquarters and given a tongue-lashing for his passivity. Newspaper speculation began that Bryan wanted Progressive Party candidate Robert M. La Follette to gain sufficient electoral votes to throw the election into the House, where a deadlock might occur. If that happened, the Senate would choose from among the vice presidential candidates, and Bryan seemed likely to win that contest. The vice president would serve as president until, and unless, the House finally broke a stalemate. That Machiavellian scenario gained impetus when Bryan praised La Follette in a speech at Wichita on October 8. It was not to be, however, and President Calvin Coolidge won a full term in a landslide. Coolidge and the Republicans had made charges of socialism against the radical Nebraska governor a principal issue in the campaign, and it probably helped increase their margin of victory.

After the election, the Bryan brothers hoped to drive Eastern conservative Democrats who had nominated Davis for president out of the party. William Jennings Bryan's death in 1926 helped end that scheme. In 1926 and 1928, brother Charley was defeated for governor, but he remained optimistic. With the Depression, reason for Democratic optimism was obvious. Elected easily in 1930 on a lower budget and austerity campaign, the new governor proceeded to try that approach to soften the effects of the depression. Bryan was a nineteenth-century Jeffersonian when it came to government involvement with relief problems, and to him the less direct government help the better. Though he attacked big business relentlessly and demanded government takeover of industries, he turned not to government for assistance for the unemployed and hungry, but instead to businesses and the neighbors of the suffering to help out voluntarily. The national administration started to complain about the governor, saying he was hindering the operation of their programs in the state. Bryan was reelected in 1932. Immediately after the election, Bryan suffered a serious heart attack, but the details were kept secret to avoid the lame-duck Republican lieutenant governor from trying to take over, or after the inauguration to prevent the new Democratic one from doing so. Close friends ran the government for months.

Roosevelt's adviser Harry Hopkins publicly called on Bryan to "do his part" in relief efforts. Other public statements criticizing Bryan followed. In 1934, the governor tried to move up to the United States Senate. Roosevelt was pleased when the 67-year-old veteran of political wars went down to defeat in the primary. Bryan was restless for office thereafter, but except for a term as Lincoln mayor, his subsequent electoral tries were failures. Growing weak and blind, but mentally still alert, Bryan died of cancer in 1945.

Analysis of Qualifications

His reputation was first as a highly effective, tireless organizer for his brother, William Jennings Bryan. Brother Charley on his own built a reputation as a Midwestern populist. His battle as Nebraska governor seemed a radical and ultimately hopeless effort to preserve a way of life that was slipping away. He felt the sim-

ple answers were best; the complex society that developed inexorably had to have populist reforms imposed, such as municipal ownership of many burgeoning businesses, to keep the simple values intact.

Though a reformer, Charley Bryan was first a political infighter. He seemed to revel in combat, with city council members in Lincoln, with the state legislature once he became governor, or with fellow Democrats who did not agree with him. Extroverted and energetic, Bryan was also arrogant, self-assured, and abrasive. A poor speaker in public and an equally poor listener, Bryan knew it all and told others boastfully of the fact. Opponents were called instruments of predatory businesses. Though Bryan could be pompous and egotistical, he had the redeeming virtues of being a hard worker and of always avoiding financial improprieties. He also liked rough language and sports, was "one of the boys" except when it came to drinking. While his brother conducted his fundamentalist crusade that ended in the embarrassing Scopes Monkey Trial, Charley Bryan was one who watched religion from the sidelines. At a Billy Sunday revival, partially arranged by the younger Bryan because he believed it was good for society to have moral values, Sunday called for Bryan to come forward with the others and commit his life. Bryan declined, saying, "I have a few scores to settle with some people first." Will Rogers, in typical prosaic fashion, called him a "regular guy who said hell and damn like the rest of us."

As mayor and then as governor, Bryan insisted on being in control. He did not share his power with others. That was also true of his function as organizer for his older brother. Leadership was by appeal to the people, not by compromise or bargain. As a consummate political operator, the governor did use political bargaining to advance his own career, such as in 1922 when he forced Senator Hitchcock's forces to support him in return for Bryan's endorsement of the senator. To many, Bryan was a dictator in his elective positions. Threats to have opponents recalled on the council, or blustering criticisms of opponents once he became governor, demonstrated a complete lack of an essential ingredient of presidential success: realizing what is politically possible and working with friends as well as adversaries to attain it.

A President Charles Bryan would have been a confrontational leader. Like his brother William Jennings, the younger Bryan's perspective was from rural and small-town America, and adjustment to modern society never was achieved. His answer to the Depression was that neighbors should help neighbors, certainly a laudable sentiment but one that could hardly succeed when so few neighbors were in a position to help anyone. Business leaders were constant foes. As a result, major political powers would have been aligned against a President Bryan. He would have attempted to regulate every business of any size in the country, or else take it over.

As a political leader, Bryan revealed deficiencies in personality that forecast an eccentric, bitter presidency. The small, inexpensive, efficient government that Bryan wanted was a creature of a smaller, simpler age. It was well a Bryan presidency is left to the "what might have been."

BRYAN BIBLIOGRAPHY

"Bryan Family Genealogy," typescript in Nebraska State Historical Society Library, Lincoln.

Osnes, Larry G. "Charles W. Bryan: 'His Brother's Keeper.'" *Nebraska History* XLVIII (1967), pp. 45–67.

_____. "Charles W. Bryan: Latter-Day Populist and Rural Progressive." Unpublished doctoral dissertation, University of Cincinnati (1970).

1924 presidential nominee—
Progressive Party

Robert La Follette

Full name: Robert Marion La Follette, Sr.

State represented: Wisconsin.

Birth: June 14, 1855, Primrose, Wisconsin.

Age on Inauguration Day (March 4, 1925) 69 years, 8½ months.

Education: Local Primrose schools, 1859–1866; private school in Fayette, Wisconsin, 1866–1867; Argyle, Wisconsin, school, 1867–1870; Wisconsin Classical and Commercial Academy, 1870–1873; University of Wisconsin, 1874–1879; University of Wisconsin law school, 1879–1880; admitted to bar in 1880.

Religion: Unitarian.

Ancestry/prominent relatives: Huguenot and Scotch-Irish forebears; Robert M. La Follette, Jr. (son), U.S. senator from Wisconsin, 1925–1947; Philip Fox La Follette (son), Wisconsin governor; Bronson La Follette (grandson), Wisconsin attorney general, defeated for U.S. Senate.

Occupation: Attorney.

Public offices: Dane County, Wisconsin, district attorney, 1880–1884; U.S. representative, March 4, 1885–March 3, 1891, defeated; defeated for Republican gubernatorial nomination in 1896 and 1898; Wisconsin governor, January 1, 1901–January 1, 1906, resigned; U.S. senator, January 2, 1906, until his death, June 18, 1925; defeated for Republican presidential nomination in 1912, 1916, 1920, and 1924; unsuccessful independent candidate for president in 1924.

Home: Maple Bluff Farm, outside of Madison, Wisconsin.

Death: June 18, 1925, in Washington, D.C., at age 70 years.

Burial: Forest Hill Cemetery, Madison, Wisconsin.

Personal characteristics: Short (5'4" tall) and wiry; black, later gray hair, piled atop his head in a pompadour; solidly built, square jaw, lion-like head, flashing eyes.

Father: Josiah La Follette (July 4, 1817–1856); farmer, local Wisconsin politician.

Mother: Mary (Ferguson) Buchanan (November 22, 1817–April 21, 1894); first husband died; married in 1845; died of pneumonia.

Stepfather: John Z. Saxton (1792–November 1872), married 1862; Baptist deacon; store-owner.

Siblings: Ellen Buchanan (half-sister) (1841–?). William (c. 1847–April 30, 1913), newspaperman, politician. Josephine (1853–?); married Robert G. Siebecker. Marion, died as an infant.

Wife: Belle Case (April 21, 1859–August 18, 1931); married December 31, 1881; an attorney, woman suffrage speaker on Chautauqua circuit, also spoke publicly for other causes, teacher, author.

Children: Fola (September 10, 1882–February 17, 1970), married George Middleton on October 29, 1911; actress, woman suffrage speaker on Chautauqua circuit, teacher, author. Robert M. La Follette, Jr. (February 6, 1895–February 24, 1953); married Rachel Wilson Young in 1930; U.S. senator, editor, economic research consultant. Philip Fox La Follette (May 8, 1897–August 18, 1965); married Isabel Bacon in 1923; attorney, served three terms as governor of Wisconsin, colonel U.S. Army, served under General MacArthur in World War II, author. Mary (August 16, 1899–), married Ralph G. Sucher, June 15, 1921, divorced; artist, researcher, editor.

Historic sites/memorials: La Follette's statue is in Statuary Hall in the national capitol, one of two from Wisconsin. "Maple Bluffs," 733 Lakewood Boulevard, La Follette's home, outside of Madison, still stands.

For 20 years this Wisconsin governor and senator was one of the premier leaders of the progressive movement in America. He was intelligent, dynamic, resourceful, and untiringly dedicated to the public good as he saw it. He was a symbol of a new kind of politics for millions of Americans, but he would never gain the electoral prize he valued most.

Though in his campaign autobiography for the 1912 presidential nomination, La Follette would write of an Abraham Lincoln–like poverty-to-power background, in fact the La Follette family was relatively prosperous. There was much tragedy, however. His mother's first husband had died, leaving a widow and two children, and La Follette's own father died when Bob was only eight months old. Seventy-year-old storekeeper John Saxton then became his stepfather. The family moved from its sizeable farm to Saxton's Argyle, Wisconsin, store, where a strict, almost frightening religion was practiced and preached by the new stepfather. Bob became embittered toward religion, especially after Saxton told Bob his father had gone to hell because the elder La Follette apparently was an agnostic. Bob's religious growth was stunted permanently.

After local schools had poorly prepared him for an advanced education, Bob found it necessary to get remedial help at Madison Academy. Then at the age of 20 he entered the University of Wisconsin. Though the direction may have already been established, Bob's liberal political views received dramatically stronger impetus from a speech given by Wisconsin chief justice Edward G. Ryan. Ryan's speech at the university called the accumulation of wealth the handmaiden of disaster for all countries, from ancient Rome to the America of his day. This concept helped shape La Follette's career-long disdain of capitalists.

Bob's college career was hardly all academic reflections, because the costs of education required him constantly to search for additional income. With borrowed money he purchased the *University Press* newspaper, and made it and himself a financial success. His money worries solved, La Follette achieved a different kind of success with his speaking skills. La Follette's forte was not in reasoning, but in oratory. Many victories were achieved in interscholastic contests, but the greatest was his triumph at the Interstate Oratorical Contest of May 1879, in Iowa City. Preliminary rounds in other cities had culled most speakers out, and only the best collegiate talent in the Midwest was present. His topic was Iago, the villain in Shakespeare's *Othello*. Both his analysis and especially his delivery were exceptional. In the days before intercollegiate athletics, La Follette's victory at this contest gained him fame throughout his state.

The young orator then attended the Wisconsin law school, but at the same time studied in the office of a local Madison attorney. He passed the bar examination in February 1880 and began private practice in the capital. By June he was running for Dane County district attorney, opposing the Republican political boss who, though friendly towards La Follette, had selected another for the race. The party convention named La Follette after an energetic campaign for the nomination. He then defeated a respected Democratic opponent. The inexperienced young attorney tried all cases himself. It was trials with many errors. Still, he gained a reputation as a skillful advocate, and in 1882 was the only Republican elected in his county when he ran for a second term. His margin, though, was only 93 votes.

La Follette's sights were higher than district

attorney, and again over the objection of the local Republican boss he ran for Congress in 1884. He was viewed by many as a rising star who could rid the party of its unsavory image. With the help of former President Grant's good friend, George Bryant, and some other influential politicians, La Follette gained the Republican nomination after a spirited campaign. His Democratic opponent was the incumbent, and to defeat him the Republican campaigned so actively as to become ill in late October. His efforts proved sufficient, and he won by 491 votes.

La Follette, a future independent Republican, was at first a mainstream party man in Congress. His speech opposing the Democratic tariff proposal soon after his arrival in Congress was extremely well received. When his party took control of Congress in the 1886 elections he became at 31 the youngest member of the prestigious Ways and Means Committee since William McKinley. Serving three terms, La Follette's most direct contribution to legislation in Congress was probably his work with McKinley on the tariff of 1890. This high protective tariff made far more enemies than friends. La Follette was surprisingly caught up in the Democratic landslide of 1890 that buried him and many other proponents of that measure. A few local issues also doomed the three-term congressman.

Opening his law practice back up in Madison, La Follette stayed active in politics. In the fall of 1891, La Follette's brother-in-law was the judge in a case that could cost Republican senator Philetus Sawyer hundreds of thousands of dollars if he lost. Judge Siebecker withdrew from the case. No satisfactory explanation was given, but the rumors immediately started that a bribe must have been paid. Senator Sawyer went public to counteract the rumors, saying that he had only offered La Follette a retainer for legal services. La Follette then announced that Senator Sawyer had offered him a large sum to use his influence on the judge. La Follette became an outcast in party circles, and many felt, unjustly, that he had fabricated the story in an effort to construct a reformer reputation. He called this the turning point in his career as thereafter he felt driven to root out corruption and boss influence in politics.

The shunned ex-congressman was not without his friends in high places, including William McKinley. In 1892, La Follette forced his way into the Wisconsin campaign by giving speeches on behalf of his party's candidates. In 1894, he worked for Congressman Nils Haugen's selection as the nominee for governor, but the party organization easily stopped the reformers' efforts and named their own man. In 1896, La Follette sought the gubernatorial nomination for himself and believed he had enough delegates. When he lost at the convention, La Follette blamed bribery by the conservatives. In 1898, he tried and failed again.

The issues dividing the party were the growing progressive concerns of direct primaries to nominate candidates, equalization of taxes whereby the wealthy and corporations paid their fair share, and regulation of railroads and other large corporations. The Wisconsin reformers saw their own Republican Party as suspect on these issues as the Democrats. With defeats suffered by the progressives in three successive elections, La Follette's cause and career seemed finished. After the 1898 debacle, he collapsed from exhaustion and took six months to recuperate. But in fact the tide had turned. La Follette was hesitant to try yet a third time for the governor's chair in 1900, but with a few additional and wealthy backers, with a supportive newspaper established in Milwaukee, with the legislature feeling the public pressure and adopting much of the progressive platform, the cause was far from lost. The business community and La Follette patched up many of their differences and some of his old antagonists were dead. A well-organized campaign frightened off his lone opponent and gained him easy nomination at the convention. The Democrats fielded a weak opponent and La Follette finally had the governorship.

In his inaugural address the "Wisconsin Idea" of government was eloquently expressed. National attention was directed at this progressive platform, especially of direct primaries and increased taxes on the wealthy. La Follette was not a trusting man, and his erstwhile businesses and old-line Republican supporters were cut out of participation in his administration.

He was secretive; he thought those who opposed him could only do so for base motives, including bribery. Still, much opposition to his programs did exist and his first administration was not productive. A severe party split developed, in large part because the governor was so savage in his denunciation of those who agreed within or outside the party. La Follette stumped the state for his policies, appearing at county fairs and wherever else he could find a crowd. In 1902, he wanted more than reelection; he wanted to throw the entrenched rascals out. The election resulted in a smashing progressive victory, with La Follette's allies taking control of the assembly. In the next legislative session the direct primary law was enacted, subject to a popular referendum on the issue. In 1904, La Follette and his Republican adversaries again did battle, this time over selection of delegates to the national convention. A heated fight for delegates to the state convention was the first battleground, with La Follette winning because of efficient, iron-fisted rule of the convention that gave most contested seats to his forces. The rival delegations then established a rump convention that drew up its own slate for the national convention. At the Chicago gathering the anti-La Follette delegation was seated, and rather than continue the controversy, La Follette took his supporters home. Theodore Roosevelt's failure to side with his supposed fellow progressives angered the Wisconsin governor and would lead to future animosities.

With another solid La Follette victory at the polls in 1904, the progressives were safely in control in Wisconsin. He took advantage of his power by being elected by the legislature to the United States Senate in 1905. He delayed taking his Washington seat until January 1906, because of unfinished gubernatorial plans. In the Senate, La Follette was no regular party man. He was denied membership on the Interstate Commerce Committee where his attacks on the railroads would have had a proper forum. His maiden Senate speech concerned new legislation to regulate railroad rates. La Follette was also a defender of the Indians, and argued forcefully for withdrawal of many Indian lands from commercial exploitation. With national recognition given him as a pro-gressive leader, La Follette needed little encouragement to run for the presidency in 1908. President Roosevelt had anointed William Howard Taft as the next president, however, and La Follette then set his sights on 1912.

Taft's progressive credentials never satisfied the Wisconsin senator. That he would oppose Taft's renomination became clear early. In January 1909, La Follette founded his own newspaper, *La Follette's Weekly*, meant to be a forum for progressive ideas but particularly for his own presidential candidacy. Publicly his relations with Theodore Roosevelt were cordial, but in fact the two men had little respect for each other. La Follette intentionally and incredibly ignored Roosevelt in his *Weekly* as a contender for progressive support in 1912, trying to dampen any move to the ex-president. Those dissatisfied with Taft were torn between supporting La Follette in what appeared to be a gallant but lost cause, or wait for Roosevelt to jump into the race. When a national league of progressives was established in January 1911, sponsored mainly by Republicans dissatisfied with Taft, La Follette drafted the declaration of principles. He remained constantly in the public eye through his attacks from the Senate on the Taft administration. Roosevelt's supporters were working behind the scenes to undercut La Follette's chances. When it appeared the progressives had a chance to beat Taft, Roosevelt made the decision to enter the race. Getting La Follette out of the campaign was the first priority.

The climax of La Follette's campaign came in the disastrous speech he gave before the Periodical Publishers Association on February 2, 1912. He was ill, preoccupied with the serious illness of his daughter, and poorly prepared. He harangued, repeated himself, and droned on for two hours after another speaker had already exhausted the audience for three hours. This performance gave many people torn between the two progressives the excuse they needed to break to Roosevelt. Roosevelt and La Follette both continued to vie for the nomination; their failure to join forces helped ensure Taft's renomination. Roosevelt was then selected by a third party convention, which in turn guaranteed the Democrat's victory.

President Woodrow Wilson impressed La Follette. The Wisconsin senator called the former college professor's efforts "the best public record any President has made on progressive policies." Many of the president's programs seemed not quite sweeping enough, and several appointments seemed to La Follette to be a throwback to old-style politics. But it was not until Wilson began to break away from neutrality concerning the growing conflict in Europe that the Wisconsin progressive broke with him completely. La Follette's Wisconsin background, with support coming there from many Germans and other eastern Europeans, had helped create in him an anti–English bias. Great Britain represented imperialism, and La Follette's sympathies were with the people colonized, not the colonizers. Clamor for war also indicated to La Follette the self-interest of munition manufacturers and other capitalists who hoped to profit from American involvement. La Follette tried again for the presidential nomination in 1916, and then supported Hughes over Wilson in the fall campaign. Though he sympathized with the Wilson slogan, "he kept us out of the war," La Follette feared that it would have little continuing validity.

In 1917, La Follette received the greatest public abuse this controversial man ever suffered. The cause was his filibuster in the Senate against the arming of American merchant ships. Though still a neutral in the war, America was having its merchant ships threatened by full-scale German submarine warfare. To La Follette, Germany should not be criticized for sending ships to the sea bottom that were carrying munitions to aid its enemies. Private citizens should not travel on such vessels, and if they did so then they were accepting the risks involved. Woodrow Wilson condemned La Follette and his handful of supporters in the Senate as a "little group of willful men, representing no opinion but their own, [who] have rendered the great government of the United States helpless and contemptible." After war was declared over his opposition, La Follette continued to oppose many measures, including the draft, the espionage bill, and some regulations on food. At most four other senators would join him in his

objections. Basically, however, he supported measures he thought necessary for the successful prosecution of the war since American soldiers could not be abandoned in the field.

One final blow to his prestige occurred when a speech he delivered in September 1917 was misquoted in public reports. It was a dramatic anti-war speech, which included a line, "I don't mean to say that we hadn't suffered grievances ... at the hands of Germany. We had." He was erroneously quoted as saying, "We had no grievances against Germany." Many called for his expulsion from the Senate. There was a national revolt against the anti-war senator that did not die down until the war was over. When Wilson proposed participation in the League of Nations, La Follette was again boldly in dissent. Unlike fellow Republicans such as Henry Cabot Lodge, the Wisconsin senator did not merely desire to amend the Versailles Treaty; he wished for its complete rejection. Subsequently when the issue of joinder of the World Court arose, he opposed America's participation there.

La Follette's arguments against the League were that it was a coalition of victors in the war, especially England, against the vanquished, whose purpose was to divide the spoils of war. La Follette accused Wilson of abandoning his earlier aim of a completely open discussion of the war, and instead the president was participating in secret consultations with other countries on how to decide the world's future.

For a time Progressives found it difficult to champion La Follette as their leader. His opposition to the war was a severe political liability. He pushed for greater regulation of railroads, and eventually argued for government operation of railroads, telephone and telegraph companies, and other essential operations. He continued to champion as few others would the more radical causes. Never seriously in the running for the 1920 Republican presidential nomination, he was offered an independent candidacy but refused it. In 1922, his Senate seat was to be contested, but by that time the people desired to forget the war. The continuing controversy over the League made La Follette's previously unpopular stands seem much more acceptable. From an outcast, La Follette had turned into a prophet. His reelection was by better than a three-to-one margin. Once again he stood at the fore of the Progressive movement for 1924.

In advance of that election, La Follette led the call for an investigation of the Harding administration's Teapot Dome scandal. He sought the election of fellow progressives regardless of party nationwide. Everywhere La Follette saw the ugly hand of greedy capitalists, from foreign policy decisions, to the debates over the handling of public lands, water power, radio technology, and electricity. Frequently La Follette's solution was government ownership. The constant threat to democracy he thought was powerful monopolies. Wherever there was accumulated wealth, La Follette attacked it.

Knowing he might be a candidate for president in 1924, La Follette toured Europe to establish better foreign policy credentials. He spoke highly of Lenin and of Russia generally, and of great improvements in the country since the 1917 Revolution. His health was weakening, and in truth he was in no condition to be making a strenuous campaign. In January 1924, a definite decision to run was made. The nomination of John Davis by the Democrats to run against President Calvin Coolidge seemed a good omen, since it permitted La Follette to be the only progressive in a race against two conservatives. The collection of liberals and progressives that nominated La Follette were united in their support for "Fighting Bob" but showed few other similarities. Social workers, Wilson supporters, unionists, socialists and every other brand of liberalism were present. They did not try to agree on a running mate for La Follette, but left the choice to him. La Follette wanted Louis Brandeis, but the Supreme Court justice was not interested. Finally Burton Wheeler, a Montana Democrat who had endorsed La Follette, received the nod.

Polls showed Davis to have little support, and for a time some thought the race was between the Republicans and the Progressives. The Republican slogan took advantage of La Follette's radical image, particularly his anti-war extremism, by crying "Coolidge or chaos." Coolidge won in a rout, with La Follette com-

ing in second in many Western states, though he carried only Wisconsin. The senator made plans for a new party to carry on the fight. He was ousted from the Republican Party in the Senate, thereby losing his seniority. He argued he had lost because the wealthy had coerced or inveigled their workers into voting against him.

There would not be another campaign, as La Follette remained sick after the election, and finally died in June 1925.

Analysis of Qualifications

Bob La Follette started his political career as a relatively orthodox Republican. He opposed the machine-backed candidate, not for the reasons of principle, just for reasons of ambition. In Congress he remained essentially within the party mold. Yet after ten years in political battles, after being rebuffed repeatedly by the Wisconsin machine in his quest for the governorship, La Follette became a committed progressive. The "Wisconsin Idea" of constantly enlarging the opportunities for citizen impact upon government spread throughout the Midwest — direct primaries, the initiative and referendum, and state regulatory authority over railroads. His third-party campaigns were failures, but he dominated his state's politics for decades. His influence and popularity were so great that his 30-year-old son and namesake could step into his Senate vacancy with ease after La Follette's death. This was, quite obviously, no standard politician.

"Fighting Bob" was his nickname, and it was apt. Political opponents, regardless of past friendship or support were personal enemies. To oppose La Follette was to incur his wrath. Many saw La Follette as an atavism of eighteenth-century Jeffersonian principles, of agrarian idealism which saw industrial growth as an evil. Every device possible must be given to the people to permit them to control government and keep it out of the hands of the rich and privileged. The rich and privileged saw La Follette, properly saw him, as a bitter enemy who thought they were the cause of all of the world's problems. His faith in democracy was unlimited. Even after his final defeat for the presidency in 1924, he still saw hope for progressivism: "I believe in democracy— It is a religion with me. I don't say we can win the next election on these principles. But I do say that it will win in the end."

Throughout his career, La Follette refused to compromise. On several occasions, most notably in his opposition to World War I, he blithely ignored the damage to his political career that his stands inevitably would cause. There was a moral courage, a self-righteousness that caused him to view those who trimmed their sails as traitors. The most notable enemy made in this way was Theodore Roosevelt, who La Follette never believed was a true progressive because Roosevelt too often compromised. La Follette was so committed, his politics so much of a religion, that he was distrustful. His governorship demonstrated the secrecy with which he operated. He was austere, demanding, constantly in motion for the cause. His speeches were masterpieces, carefully crafted, meticulously organized, stocked with countless statistics which he could make sing. For three hours he once enthralled a meeting of farmers by reciting figures on railroad freight rates. His skills at debate, and his ruthless use of those skills, made him a feared adversary. Fighting Bob's uncompromising spirit made him a great senator, because whether right or wrong, he stood up for what he believed.

Would such characteristics have made a great president? The 1920s were America's greatest age of complacency. La Follette would not have let the people rest. He wanted dramatic new measures of democratic government; he wanted regulation or government ownership of numerous essential industries; he argued for increased inheritance taxes and corporate levies to fund new programs. His confrontational style, his hatred of opponents, his lack of a party would have made working with Congress almost impossible. His first gubernatorial term had been unproductive, but he was able to elect a sympathetic legislature after one term of stalemate. Whether such success could have been repeated on the national level is certainly to be doubted. No political leader who had made as many powerful enemies as he did among the entrenched political and economic forces in the country would have had easy success in the White House.

La Follette's great role in American political history was as a catalyst, a valuable element in the political mix that forced both parties and the government into needed changes. He identified problems if not always workable solutions. His rightful place was in the Senate; he would have been miscast as president.

LA FOLLETTE BIBLIOGRAPHY

Barton, A.O. *La Follette's Winning in Wisconsin*. Madison, Wisc. (1922).

Doan, Edward. *The La Follettes and the Wisconsin Idea*. New York City (1947).

Greenbaum, Fred. *Robert Marion La Follette*. Boston (1975).

Holmes, F.L. *Badger Saints and Sinners*. Milwaukee (1939).

La Follette, Belle C., and Fola La Follette. *Robert La Follette*. 2 vols. New York City (1953).

La Follette, Robert M. *Autobiography*. Madison, Wisc. (1913), reprinted in 1960, Madison.

Lovejoy, A.F. *La Follette and the Establishment of the Direct Primary in Wisconsin, 1890–1904*. New Haven (1941).

Madison, Charles A. "Robert M. La Follette: The Radical in Politics," in Harvey Goldberg, ed., *American Radicals, Some Problems and Personalities*. New York City and London (1969), pp. 91–110, reprint of 1957 edition.

Maney, Patrick J. *"Young Bob" La Follette: A Biography of Robert M. La Follette, Jr., 1895–1953*. Columbia, Mo. (1978).

Manning, Eugene. "Old Bob La Follette: Champion of the People." Unpublished doctoral dissertation, University of Wisconsin (1966).

Maxwell, Robert S., ed. *La Follette*. Englewood Cliffs, N.J. (1969), "Great Lives Observed" series.

_____. *La Follette and the Rise of Progressives in Wisconsin*. Madison, Wisc. (1956).

Thelen, David. *The Early Life of Robert M. La Follette, 1855–1884*. Chicago (1966).

Young, Donald, ed. *Adventures in Politics: The Memoirs of Philip La Follette*. New York City (1970).

Some genealogical information provided by Mary La Follette, Washington, D.C., and by Bronson La Follette, Madison, Wisconsin.

ROBERT M. LA FOLLETTE and BURTON K. WHEELER
(From the collection of David J. and Janice L. Frent)

1924 vice presidential nominee—
Progressive Party

Burton K. Wheeler

Full name: Burton Kendall Wheeler.
State represented: Montana.
Birth: February 27, 1882, in Hudson, Massachusetts.
Age on Inauguration Day (March 4, 1925): 43 years.
Education: Hudson, Massachusetts, public schools, graduated, 1900; then University of Michigan law school, graduated 1905, admitted to bar in 1905.
Religion: Methodist.
Ancestry/prominent relatives: Great-great-great-great-grandfather, Obadiah Wheeler, was a Quaker who fled from England in 1635; another ancestor had been a passenger on the *Mayflower*.
Occupation: Attorney.
Public offices: Montana house of representatives, 1910–1912; defeated for Democratic attorney general nomination, 1912; U.S. attorney for Montana, 1913–1918; defeated 1920 as Democratic nominee for governor; U.S.

senator, March 4, 1923–January 3, 1947, defeated; unsuccessful nominee of Progressive Party for vice president, 1924; unsuccessful candidate for Democratic presidential nomination, 1940.

Home: Hunting lodge on shores of Lake McDonald in Glacier National Forest, during summers; rest of year in Washington, D.C.

Death: January 6, 1975, Washington, D.C., at age 92 years, 10½ months.

Burial: Rock Creek Cemetery, Washington, D.C.

Personal characteristics: Nearly six feet tall, broad shoulders, large head, rumpled suits; talked rapidly, wore octagonal glasses, always a cigar in his mouth.

Father: Asa Leonard Wheeler (February 1, 1832–September 10, 1921); a poor shoemaker, farmer.

Mother: Mary Elizabeth Tyler (1837–April 30, 1898); married in 1852.

Siblings: George (died in infancy). Cora (died in infancy). Nellie (c. 1857–March 24, 1938), married George Hinds. Jennie, married Eugene Converse. Emma, married Augustus Russel. Oscar (c. 1863–November 27, 1937), shoemaker, married Linda Bell Underwood. Charles, married Lil Inman. Ernest (c. 1875–August 29, 1950), government employee; married (1) Florence Randall, and (2) Grace Snow. Maude, married Richard Mitchell.

Wife: Lulu M. White (November 26, 1884–September 5, 1962); married September 7, 1907.

Children: John Leonard (May 15, 1909–), married Helene Albright. Elizabeth Hale (April 17, 1911–), married Edwin Colman on February 15, 1936. Edward Kendall (October 23, 1913–), married Charlotte S. Sharp on April 15, 1939; attorney. Frances (1916–May 1957), married Allen Sayler in August 1940. Richard Burton (December 8, 1918–), married (1) Gladys Carter in 1942 and (2) Elizabeth Nicolson on June 14, 1958. Marion Montana (April 23, 1925–), married Robert M. Scott on February 26, 1949.

Historic sites: Wheeler home, 1232 E. 2nd Street, Butte (private).

Burton K. Wheeler was the tenth child in a poor Massachusetts family. After completing his education in public schools, Burton took a business course and began work in Boston as a bookkeeper. Using money he saved in about three years of work, he was able to enter the University of Michigan law school in Ann Arbor where several relatives lived. There he supported himself through parttime jobs, including in the summer selling *Old Dr. Chase's Recipe* book. Trying to sell one to a farmer in Albany, Illinois, he met the daughter, Lulu White, and later married her.

After graduation from law school, Wheeler first sought a job in Telluride, Colorado, where Lulu's uncle was located, and then also inquired in Salt Lake City; Portland, Oregon; San Francisco; Los Angeles, and Tucson. Prospects seemed poor in each of these places, and he finally landed in Butte, Montana. He was broke and had no good leads on employment. Apparently he would have left Butte except that he lost his last fifty dollars in a poker game, and had to accept a bill-collecting job that he had earlier refused. His office was located next to the City Prosecutor's office, and through that proximity, Wheeler was appointed in several criminal cases.

The Anaconda Copper Company controlled politics in Montana. Friendliness towards Anaconda determined many politicians' success. Anaconda was headquartered in Butte, and it was extremely difficult to be its opponent. The company little understood Burton Wheeler, and in 1910 it supported him for election to the state house of representatives. For a time he was satisfactory to the company, but then he began to champion better working conditions in the copper mines. Fighting for those principles brought him to the attention of Thomas J. Walsh, a candidate for the United States Senate. For 52 days the legislature was locked in balloting for the Senate, and finally both Walsh and his company-backed opponent withdrew. Anaconda was outraged that "their" representative, Wheeler, had been backing Walsh. The possibility for such legislative deadlocks ended in 1912 when nomination of Senate candidates became a matter for party primaries. That year Walsh was elected to the United States Senate. Walsh's election, together with the gaining of the presidency by Woodrow Wilson, placed the new senator in a position of being able to control patronage for his state. Wheeler was named United States attorney for Montana in recognition of his support of Walsh.

Wheeler has been called a "born prosecutor," and indeed during his entire career he seemed to be on the attack. As United States attorney he won his share of convictions, not by careful preparation but instead by emotional and effective courtroom oratory. Many Montanans did not appreciate his refusal to prosecute opponents of World War I, or labor organizers. A violent strike in the copper mines found Wheeler supporting the miners and blaming the mine owners. When Senator Walsh was running for reelection in 1918, Wheeler's liberal record as a prosecutor and his opposition to the war, were too much of a burden to carry. In October, Walsh accepted Wheeler's longstanding offer to resign if it would help the senator's campaign.

Wheeler was angry over this turn of events, and his political statements became even more extreme. The absence of strong Democratic allegiance was already becoming clear, as earlier in the year he had urged voters to work for any party that attacked the copper companies. In 1920, he sought and received the endorsement of the Nonpartisan League for governor. Interestingly, a black and a Blackfoot Indian were also on the nonpartisan ticket. Wheeler's strong anti-company views were reluctantly accepted by the Democrats at their convention, and the nonpartisan league ticket became the Democratic one as well. Wheeler's campaign was dramatic and colorful, primarily directed towards ending Anaconda's control of politics. Democrats deserted him in droves. The greatest defeat ever suffered by a Montana Democrat running for statewide office was inflicted on Wheeler in the general election. The image of Wheeler as a radical, with many accepting the charge that he was a "Bolshevik," was well implanted in the public mind.

Wheeler decided he had to become more conservative in his public image. Economic times for the farmers were worsening. In 1922, this ambitious politician made his peace with Anaconda, and in return for not interfering with the company's effort to control the legislature, he received Anaconda's acquiescence in his United States Senate campaign. In 1922,

Wheeler won the primary easily over three opponents, and then beat a Republican challenger in the general election who had been weakened by the Harding scandals. Though his election in Montana depended on his Democratic party support, almost immediately Wheeler ignored his party. In December 1922, just a month after his election, Wheeler attended a conference of progressives that had been called by Wisconsin senator Robert La Follette. He toured Minnesota and spoke against the Democratic Senate candidate there who seemed too conservative for Wheeler's taste. The new senator from Montana sided with the Senate progressives, many of whom were Republicans. The first great fame earned by Wheeler was his call for investigation of United States attorney general Harry M. Daugherty. Daugherty had been implicated in the Teapot Dome scandal. After he refused Wheeler's call for his resignation, a select committee was appointed to investigate the charges. Wheeler was the chief interrogator, and from March until June 1924, he led the investigation. All except the first few weeks received little public attention, because President Coolidge asked Daugherty to resign in late March. Wheeler felt that it was in retaliation for this effort that in April 1924, a Montana grand jury indicted Wheeler for accepting a fee to practice before the Department of the Interior. He was exonerated both in Montana and in a Senate investigation.

From obscurity in 1923 when he took his Senate seat, Wheeler had within a year soared in public recognition. Thus when La Follette was nominated in 1924 for president by the Progressives, Wheeler was an attractive choice for running mate. After being named, Wheeler denounced both established parties and campaigned on a liberal platform against conservatives Coolidge and Davis. The campaign got nowhere in Montana and the Progressives only carried La Follette's Wisconsin in the general election.

This treason earned him the opposition of many Democrats. In 1928, he received serious competition for reelection from a former conservative Democrat governor. Nonetheless, Wheeler won the primary easily, continued to refrain from attacking Anaconda directly, and gained a 12,000-vote majority while Herbert Hoover was carrying the state by 44,000 votes.

Most of Wheeler's time in the Senate was spent on farm problems. In foreign policy he was isolationist. He voted against most measures to strengthen the American military. In April 1930, he became the first nationally renowned Democrat to endorse Franklin Roosevelt for president. In the campaign leading up to Roosevelt's nomination, Wheeler was one of the inner circle of supporters. Wheeler was also a significant factor in getting Joseph Kennedy's support for the New York governor. Wheeler convinced Huey Long to join on the Roosevelt bandwagon. Rumors circulated for a time that Roosevelt had asked Wheeler to be his running mate, but Roosevelt denied them.

With Roosevelt's election, Wheeler hoped to exert strong influence on the new administration. He devoted his energy for two years to require a return to the free coinage of silver at a sixteen-to-one ratio. Wheeler saw the coinage of silver as a panacea for the international economic crisis. He remarked, "We will have bimetallism or we will have bolshevism." The Roosevelt administration never endorsed his plan, and finally a much weakened proposal to purchase silver was adopted. The Montana senator promised the measure would cause the price of wheat to triple in the year; the purchasing power of half the world's population would quadruple within the same period. The rise in the price of silver, a slow improvement in the economy, and the attention of Congress turning to other matters meant that Wheeler's nostrum never received much support. Wheeler saw economics as a fight between creditors and debtors, between East and West, between the haves and the have-nots. Few economists could be found to agree with Wheeler that the free coinage of silver was the answer to any of the international economic problems.

Though Wheeler could not convince Roosevelt on monetary policy, the two men worked more in harmony on the question of public utilities. Wheeler became the president's leader in the Senate on legislation ending public power holding companies. Wheeler in the Senate and Speaker Sam Rayburn in the House were the floor leaders. With vigorous yet even-handed conducting of hearings on the measure, Wheeler secured a strong Senate bill and eventual passage in that chamber. Wheeler attacked far more industries than just utilities, however, and throughout his career saw big business as the people's enemy. He suggested national ownership of all railroads and introduced a bill to accomplish that. He also wanted national ownership of all natural resources.

That Wheeler could not be counted on as a consistent New Deal advocate was confirmed again in 1935 in the support Wheeler gave to United States Supreme Court decisions striking down the National Recovery Act, the Railroad Retirement Act, and other measures. Yet as Supreme Court invalidations increased, Wheeler became apprehensive. A Roosevelt aide approached Wheeler to introduce legislation increasing the size of the Supreme Court so that the president could appoint sympathetic judges. Wheeler curtly refused. In February of 1937, Roosevelt's infamous court-packing plan was introduced. Wheeler's opposition was immediate and forceful. He called the bill a prelude to dictatorship. The court's actions may have been wrong, Wheeler said, but even more dangerous was the presidential counteraction. Wheeler's suspicions of Roosevelt's appetite for power increased. Wheeler led the opposition to the court-packing plan, and relations between the president and the Montana senator became bitter. Wheeler's words were at times caustic, calling the plan a demonstration of "crisis, power, haste, and hate." The court was the last bastion of liberty to Wheeler, and the president the vanguard of tyranny.

The president tried to cause political trouble for Wheeler in Montana. Wheeler was just one of many Democratic adversaries of the president to feel the heat. The senator retaliated by saying Roosevelt was following a "tortured road to despotism." Hitler and Mussolini were given as examples of where Roosevelt was leading the country. Wheeler refused to compromise, and Roosevelt matched him in obstinacy. Wheeler's statement, "We must teach that man in the White House a lesson" was indicative of his frame of mind. The defeat of the court-packing plan, aided greatly by the audacity of the proposal as well as Wheeler's determination, was a tremendous achievement for the Montana senator. His warnings of an executive dictatorship were intensified throughout the remainder of Roosevelt's presidency.

In October 1937, shortly after the court-packing plan was killed, Roosevelt visited Montana, praised that state's Congressional delegation, but quite obviously ignored Wheeler in his statement. Roosevelt was supporting first-term Congressman Jerry O'Connell to run against Wheeler in 1940. O'Connell was a strong liberal labor supporter. He would become the leading Montana New Deal Democrat. Rumors of reprisals by the Roosevelt administration against opposition Democratic senators were rampant, and Wheeler at first publicly refused to credit them. Wheeler would not soften his criticism of the president's proposals. He denounced what seemed to him a rush towards war. Under no circumstances, Wheeler said, did he see the United States as being justified in entering the war in Europe. Roosevelt described Wheeler as a New England conservative in the mold of Calvin Coolidge. The president also stated that he believed Wheeler's wife was actually controlling him. Lulu White Wheeler was an ambitious, talented woman, who had her own outspoken political behavior. She started a one-woman crusade against Roosevelt and, like her husband, became a member of the America First movement to keep the United States out of war.

Fearing O'Connell's possible 1940 Senate candidacy, Wheeler sought to defeat him in 1938 when O'Connell ran for Congress. Wheeler first campaigned for a Democratic opponent in the primary, but O'Connell won narrowly. Wheeler then worked behind the scenes for O'Connell's Republican opponent. That candidate, Jacob Thorkelson, defeated O'Connell in the November election in a tremendous upset. Wheeler's power in the state was clear. So was his willingness to ignore party labels in the furtherance of his own ambitions.

Roosevelt would not announce whether he would run for reelection in 1940. Wheeler's name circulated in most politicians' discussion of possible challengers. Wheeler was disconsolate in 1939 when war erupted in Europe, because it seemed to insure Roosevelt's renomination. Rumors circulated that Wheeler might be given the vice presidential nomination, but Wheeler refused to be considered. He continued as an opponent of measures to prepare the country for war, including the lifting of the arms embargo in October 1939. He would later oppose the Lend-Lease plan of sending destroyers to England. Finally on July 2, 1940, with Roosevelt still not saying whether he would run for another term, Wheeler announced for the presidency. Two weeks later at the national convention Roosevelt's "draft," which the president had carefully orchestrated, caused Wheeler to renounce his candidacy and support the president. He informed the Roosevelt campaign that previous protests notwithstanding, he would accept the vice presidential nomination. The offer never came. Even before the November election Wheeler was back on the attack against Roosevelt. The administration was accused of being infected with war fever. He said a great military buildup was unnecessary because America could defend its own shores from invasion with the small force already in place. In the 1940 election, Wheeler's allegiance to Roosevelt was so weak that he voted for Norman Thomas, the Socialist presidential candidate.

Wheeler had been renominated in Montana in 1940 without much trouble. He also secured the defeat of O'Connell when he again tried to be elected to the House, when Wheeler backed the Republican nominee. His opposition to Roosevelt did not slacken. The administration's peacetime draft bill would, Wheeler warned, "slit the throat of the last democracy still living; [passage would] accord Hitler his greatest and cheapest victory to date." The Lend-Lease Act was bitterly attacked as showing Roosevelt's dictatorial ambitions. In one of his most caustic and unreasonable remarks, Wheeler called Lend-Lease "the New Deal's triple-A foreign policy" that was designed to "plow under every fourth American boy." Roosevelt retorted in kind, saying Wheeler had said "the most untruthful, the most dastardly, unpatriotic thing that has been said in public life in my generation." That Wheeler refused to admit that war was coming, and equally refused to help America prepare for it, is shown by the fact that on December 5, 1941, two days before Pearl Harbor, he predicted to reporters that "the Japanese are bluffing, and don't want war with the United States." When war erupted nonetheless, he publicly supported measures to gain America's victory while privately saying that American big business as well as Roosevelt had wanted war and had made it inevitable.

Wasteful wartime spending, huge profits by war industries, and overwhelming wartime bureaucracy became his new targets during World War II. In 1942, Wheeler struck out at fellow Democrat, but bitter rival, Senator James Murray of Montana. Wheeler's desire to see Murray's Democratic primary opponent win failed, with Murray's winning by a razor-thin margin. That the two men were not best of friends was shown by Murray's telegram to President Roosevelt:

> I have defeated and discredited Senator Wheeler and restored the good name of Montana.... Wheeler came here with the conceit and arrogance of a dictator attempting to discredit you and the established policies of our country.... He will leave Montana and sneak into Washington a discredited and disgruntled politician....

The primary lost, Wheeler then turned to the general election and supported the Republican candidate. Murray won by only 1,212 votes. The two senators exchanged public unpleasantries; Wheeler perhaps got the last word by saying, "If I were Senator Murray and had lost my hometown, a Democratic stronghold, and only won by such a small margin, I wouldn't do any boasting. I would realize that the people of my state expected me to get back to Washington and do a much better job in the future than I did in the past."

Wheeler could not continue to ignore the party organization in the state and expect to retain his own position. The Democratic organization deserted him because of his antics against Roosevelt, Senator Murray, and O'Connell. Wheeler condemned Roosevelt's campaign for a fourth term. The United Nations was called a cruel hoax. Only reluctantly did Wheeler vote for the charter of the United

Nations, and then spent four hours in the Senate criticizing the new organization.

Wheeler's unconventional, abrasive political style finally caught up with him in the July 1946, Democratic Senate primary. Leif Erickson was the Democratic opponent with the backing of the countless Democrats that Wheeler had antagonized over the years. A vicious campaign resulted, with a libelous book being published against him by a former secretary of O'Connell's. Wheeler was called a Nazi; the book was full of lies, pornographic allusions, and an idealization of Communism. It circulated little in the state of Montana and had probably nothing to do with Wheeler's defeat. Wheeler called for an investigation of the campaign against him, which he said was led by New York and Hollywood communists. In an overwhelming upset, Erickson defeated Wheeler, much to the relief of the Democratic establishment.

After the defeat, Wheeler retired from active politics and practiced law in Washington. He died on January 6, 1975, having almost reached his ninety-third birthday.

Analysis of Qualifications

The Wheeler record from his first splash on the national scene as a brash and ambitious upstart who had served in the United States Senate only a few weeks, was as a militant liberal. His reputation for radicalism was largely deserved. He proposed government ownership of all natural resources and government corporations to take over the railroads and utilities; Wheeler opposed war measures during both World War I and World War II, defended organized labor against all comers, and otherwise felt himself the protector of the common man against malevolent forces of big business and big government. Franklin D. Roosevelt was probably considered by Wheeler the biggest evil he ever encountered. Constant warnings that Roosevelt was leading the country into despotism and tyranny akin to that of Hitler and Mussolini were voiced. Yet for all his aggressive anti-business statements, Wheeler was politically mute in Montana about the Anaconda Copper Company from the moment he sought the Senate nomination in 1922. Coexistence with the giant political force was too important for his own advancement to have done otherwise.

This emotional, non-reflective, intuitive man was called by Drew Pearson during the 1930s "the laziest politician in Washington." Others commented on his reliance on his sharp tongue instead of careful preparation, whether on the floor of the Senate or in committee work. Yet this does not mean he was ineffective. In stopping the Roosevelt court-packing scheme, in pushing through that same president's utility holding company bill, and in conducting an investigation into the Daugherty involvement in the Harding scandals of the 1920s, Wheeler performed important services.

On the stump, Wheeler was a dramatic and entertaining speaker, even if his delivery was far from polished. He was self-assured, folksy, a friendly man who attracted support easily. Yet he was also vindictive and conspiratorial. Working against Jerry O'Connell in 1938 and 1940 because he feared the young congressman might someday pose a threat to his own career, trying to defeat fellow Democrat Montana senator Jim Murray in 1942 because of their rivalry, Wheeler never let the niceties of party loyalty interfere with personal vendettas. His machine in Montana was for a time an awesome creation, electing in an overwhelmingly Democratic district a Republican unknown in order to defeat O'Connell in 1938. yet it all unraveled by 1946. Another, far more consistent Democrat ousted him from what, until that time, had been the longest tenure by any statewide Montana official. Wheeler's opposition to World War II was a major factor in his 1946 defeat. During two world wars, Wheeler had been a carping critic of defense measures; in preparing for World War II, the Montana senator was one of the most extreme isolationists. A self-righteous man, he could even so demean the motives of opponents as to call Roosevelt's Lend-Lease measure a policy designed to "plow under every fourth American boy."

The world was black and white to Wheeler: it was the rich and powerful against the poor, business against labor, Eastern industrialists against Western farmers. Most of all, it was us against them, though the "us" and "them" were shifting collections of politicians, voters, and specific interest groups that were either with Wheeler or against him. He split his own state party into shards of opponents, and tried to rebuilt a coalition of Wheeler adherents from both parties. The split was not along ideological lines (no firmer progressive existed than the hated Jerry O'Connell) but on a personal basis. He was simplistic, doctrinaire, incapable of compromise and little inclined toward leadership. Instead he was someone who antagonized friend and foe for 24 years on the national stage. Burton Wheeler never indicated an ability to have performed in the difficult, complex role of the presidency.

WHEELER BIBLIOGRAPHY

Anderson, John Thomas. "Senator Burton K. Wheeler and United States Foreign Relations." Unpublished doctoral dissertation, University of Virginia (1982).

Colman, Elizabeth Wheeler. *Mrs. Wheeler Goes to Washington: Mrs. Burton Kendall Wheeler, Wife of the Senator from Montana.* Helena (1989).

Gilbert, Clinton W. *"You Takes Your Choice."* New York City and London (1924), pp. 159–172.

Howard, Joseph Kinsey. "The Decline and Fall of Burton K. Wheeler." *Harper's Magazine* CXCIV (March 1947), pp. 226–36.

Kelly, Joseph P. "A Study of the Defeat of Senator Burton K. Wheeler in the 1946 Democratic Primary Election." Unpublished master's thesis, Montana State University (1959).

Kin, David George (David G. Plotkin). *The Plot Against America: Senator Wheeler and the Forces Behind Him.* Missoula, Mont. (1946).

Ruetten, Richard T. "Burton K. Wheeler: A Progressive Between the Wars." Unpublished doctoral dissertation, University of Oregon (1961).

_____. "Showdown in Montana, 1938: Burton Wheeler's Role in the Defeat of Jerry O'Connell." *Pacific Northwest Quarterly* LIV (1963), pp. 19–29.

Spritzer, Donald E. "Burton K. Wheeler and Jim Murray, Senators in Conflict." *Montana Magazine of Western History* XXIII (1973), pp. 16–33.

Wheeler, Burton K., and Paul F. Healy. *Yankee from the West.* New York City (1962).

"Wheeler of Montana." *The New Republic* (September 20, 1943), pp. 390–392.

Family data were provided by Leslie Wheeler, Southfield, Massachusetts, with assistance also rendered by David Walters, Montana Historical Society, Helena.

1924 vice presidential nominee—
Republican Party

Frank Lowden

Full name: Frank Orren Lowden.

State represented: Illinois.

Birth: January 26, 1861, near Sunrise City, Minnesota.

Age on Inauguration Day (March 4, 1925): 64 years, 1½ months.

Education: Local Iowa schools; University of Iowa, 1881–1885, graduated as valedictorian; attended evening classes at Union College of Law, 1886–1887, graduated valedictorian; admitted to bar, 1887.

Religion: Presbyterian.

Ancestry/prominent relatives: English and Scottish ancestors on father's side arrived in America in 1638, settling in Massachusetts; his mother traced her ancestry to Holland, France, and England. Directly descended from Pilgrim Captain Miles Standish; father-in-law was George M. Pullman, railroad car builder.

Occupation: Attorney, businessman, farmer.

Public offices: Declined to be appointed first assistant U.S. postmaster general, 1900; defeated for Republican nomination for governor of Illinois, 1904; member of Republican National Committee, 1904–1912; declined to be appointed U.S. district judge, 1905; U.S. representative, November 6, 1906–March 3, 1911; governor of Illinois, 1917–1921; unsuccessful candidate for Republican presidential nomination, 1920 and 1928; declined to be appointed either secretary of navy or an ambassador, 1921; rejected appointment as ambassador to Great Britain, 1923 and 1932; rejected Republican vice presidential nomination, 1924; declined to be appointed U.S. secretary of agriculture, 1929.

Home: "Sinnissippi," a 4,000-acre estate on Rock River near Oregon, Ogle County, Illinois.

Death: March 20, 1943, of cancer, in Tucson, Arizona, at age 82 years, 2 months.

Burial: Graceland Cemetery, Chicago.

Personal characteristics: Handsome, short, stocky, gray, full hair, blond earlier in life; blue eyes; always well dressed and groomed; pleasing if forceful voice, short arms, small hands.

Father: Lorenzo Orren Lowden (1833–January 15, 1899), a blacksmith and farmer.

Mother: Nancy Elizabeth Bregg (October 8, 1836–May 16, 1908), married March 16, 1856.

Siblings: May A. (February 5, 1857–?), married a Mr. Hammer. Eugene W. (June 25,

FRANK LOWDEN
(From the Chicago Historical Society, Prints and Photographs Division)

1858–January 25, 1862). Eva D. (June 29, 1862–?), married a Mr. Sheldon. Caroline E. (October 3, 1863–October 29, 1865). Alice L. (October 14, 1865–?). Arthur B. (November 8, 1870–August 9, 1871). Walter (April 24–May 4, 1873). Ina Isabel (July 24, 1875–November 5, 1957), music career. Bertha Eleanor (November 5, 1877–June 26, 1956), English professor. Edie (April 5–15, 1883).

Wife: Florence Pullman (c. 1869–July 5, 1937), daughter of George M. Pullman, railroad car magnate, married April 29, 1896.

Children: George Mortimer Pullman (January 20, 1897–?). Florence (May 4, 1898–?), married Philip Miller. Harriett Elizabeth (August 7, 1900–?), married Albert F. Madlener, Jr., in 1925. Frances Orren (December 16, 1903–?), married (1) John B. Drake, Jr., in 1925, and (2) Frederick Willem Wierdsma.

Historic sites/memorials: Lowden State Park and Lowden Miller State Forest, both named in his honor. Sinnissippi Farm is still owned by Lowden descendants.

Frank Lowden's father was a blacksmith. The boy's education was gained in rural schools to which he had to walk miles each day. His family was so rootless that he was born in Minnesota, moved to Iowa at age seven and lived in a cabin, and then taught school in order to earn money to attend college. Yet this poor farm boy rose by his own tenacity and intelligence, and not merely incidentally by help from a wealthy wife, to the peak of political power and financial largesse in America. It would have made a good rags-to-riches novel, except that Frank Lowden's life was, of course, a true story.

Despite financial and other disadvantages, Frank's parents tried to provide a superior education for their children. They were members of a literary society, and his father helped build a one-room schoolhouse in their Minnesota village. Lorenzo Lowden was also independent. At church one day he rose and condemned all religious creeds, and for the rest of their lives both parents refused to belong to an organized church. Money was scarce. The blacksmith business was competitive in the community, and the large Lowden family — eleven children in all — had considerable expenses. In 1868, when Frank was seven, hard

times forced the family to move to Iowa. Central Iowa was primitive, but it was a haven for many other disadvantaged people looking for a new start. Local schools provided what education was attainable, which was not much. In 1874, Frank and a sister began studies at an academy in nearby New Providence, run by Quakers. Once having conquered the education challenges of the community, Frank succeeded in having age limitations waived and was given a certificate, at age 14, to teach in local district schools. Additional money was gained by simultaneously serving as a janitor. For five years Frank continued to teach, saving his money assiduously so that he could attend college. In September 1881, Lowden passed the necessary examinations for admission to the University of Iowa. There he was popular, successful academically, and participated in athletics. He was class valedictorian when he graduated in 1885. With the law as his ultimate career goal, Frank was uncertain exactly where to turn. The first stop was Burlington (Iowa) High School, Frank serving as principal and instructor. The salary was good, the comradeship congenial with the other instructors, and the decision difficult at year's end whether to continue. A college friend had introduced Frank to a Chicago attorney, and in August 1884, Frank entered the offices of that lawyer's firm as a clerk. Two years later he began studies at Union College of Law at night. Union College had a two-year curriculum, but Frank's years at the law firm permitted him to complete the course of study by June 1887, when he graduated. Again, he was valedictorian.

Lowden's law practice was strongly business-oriented. His mentor in the firm died in 1890, and Frank moved into a partnership with another attorney. His reputation as a good trial attorney was widespread. By 1894, income was sufficient to permit the previously unthinkable, a foreign cruise. With a friend he sailed for France in August. That first morning on the ship his friend pointed out the daughter of railroad car tycoon George M. Pullman, and Lowden seemed awestruck. During the rest of the voyage and for a few days in Paris, the two Chicago attorneys and Florence Pullman, the young heiress, were companions. When Frank and Florence parted in Paris, Frank wrote her a short, melodramatic love letter. Her reply was not quite in kind, yet encouraging. Through the coming months they wrote, and when Florence returned to Chicago they began to see each other regularly. Florence's parents were displeased with the budding romance, and requested she desist. The father became increasingly obstructionist and cold. Once Mr. Pullman learned that they had become secretly engaged, he required his daughter to write to Lowden and request "release" from the pledge. Yet Pullman finally relented, and the couple was married in 1896.

Mr. Pullman died the following year, and control of much of the family business was assumed by Lowden. In 1902, this newfound wealth permitted Lowden, son of a poor Iowa farmer, to purchase and gradually enlarge an estate in north central Illinois, which he named "Sinnissippi." In time it would grow to a four-thousand-acre showplace, rarely profitable for its farm products but a source of relaxation and enjoyment for the Lowdens.

Frank's political involvement had been increasing along with his law practice in Chicago. During the 1896 McKinley campaign, Frank was a speaker for the Republicans. Four years later he attended the national convention that renominated McKinley. Lowden was also active in local party affairs. McKinley offered him the post of assistant postmaster general, but Chicago legal work was more promising and the offer was refused. Prominence as the son-in-law of the late George Pullman, the fortune that brought, as well as his own skills soon earned Frank mention for high state office. Early in 1903, Lowden's sights turned to the governorship. Never a candidate for any office, Lowden decided to start with the state's highest. Charles S. Deneen was state's attorney for Cook County (Chicago); he had for 15 years been in elective or appointive office, and he wanted the nomination too. Lowden's ambitions became public as he moved around the state trying to gain support for the nominating convention. Many saw him as a presumptuous, wealthy upstart, with no claim to high office. His principal political alliance was with the U.S. Congressman William Lorimer, who disliked Deneen. The cam-

paign lasted for over a year, until the summer of 1904 at the state party convention. Lowden's campaign style, not surprisingly, was to leave unmentioned his present status as Pullman's son-in-law, and emphasize his own humble beginnings as a farm boy. The convention opened in early May, and the contest was fiercely fought for over 70 ballots. It continued into June. On the seventy-third ballot, Lowden got 631 votes, 120 short of the nomination. On the seventy-ninth, Deneen was nominated. Lowden took the defeat gracefully and campaigned for his former adversary. Lowden was subsequently selected Republican National Committeeman, an important position of influence for the novice politician. The good fight he had just waged would stand him in good stead in the future. The party swept to imposing victories in November, which helped heal the wounds of the previous summer.

Republican Congressman Robert Hitt had served for over 20 years in Washington. In 1906, many thought it was time he retired. Sinnissippi lay in Hitt's district, and Lowden's supporters encouraged their hero to run for the seat. Hitt finally agreed to step down and wrote Lowden to give him the news first. After a tough primary battle, in which Lowden's wealth and connections to the Pullman empire were used against him, Lowden won with about 11,000 votes to his opponent's 8,000. The same tack was taken by the Democratic nominee in November, and it caused an even closer result. Yet the Republican won and Lowden was off to Washington. Hitt died in September, and thus Lowden started his term immediately after the election.

After only two years as a resident of his county, never having been elected to any office, and burdened as well as advantaged with his wealth, Lowden was now being sent to Congress. For three terms he remained there, serving competently if not spectacularly as a supporter of presidents Roosevelt and Taft. His interests were in agriculture, not in finance nor foreign affairs. He remained out of party battles in Illinois, even refusing to run for governor. The growing split in the party between the Progressives and the Old Guard spilled over into the selection of a United States senator in 1909. Lowden had considerable support for the post, but during the months of balloting in the state legislature Lowden refused to have his name used as a candidate. Lowden wanted the post, but so long as the man he had promised to support remained in the contest, Lowden refused to be considered. The deadlock was broken, however, not with Lowden's selection but with his mentor's, William Lorimer. A state senate investigation reached the conclusion that Lorimer's election was due to bribery, but the evidence was conflicting. Lowden's identification with Lorimer meant that he too was tainted by the scandal. The United States Senate in 1912 voted to deny Lorimer the seat.

Ill health plagued Lowden, in part brought on by excessive drinking and smoking, and by pressure from the political grind. In September 1910, he went to Europe to seek rest and recuperation, but when he returned his maladies continued. The following year was an intense one in the House, with the assault on "Uncle Joe" Cannon's dictatorial authority as speaker taking place. Lowden usually voted with the Old Guard Republicans to preserve the speaker's authority. His reasoning was that corruption would be even easier if the entire House had the power to name the members of committees. This latest drain on his strength helped lead Lowden's doctors to prescribe a complete rest. He soon announced that he would not be a candidate for reelection in 1910, and would retire to Sinnissippi.

Business worries replaced political ones for the next few years. One of his least profitable investments was in the *Springfield Evening News*, which he had bought in 1904. Over the next few years its operations were unprofitable but interesting to Lowden, and he refused to sell on several occasions until finally, in 1914, he did so at considerable loss. Mining ventures interested Lowden, some in Latin America and others in the American Southwest. Purchase of farm and timber lands in this country also took much of his idle cash. The farm boy in Lowden made him interested in several agricultural investments, and he purchased large acreage in Arkansas which he called "South Bend" plantation. It totaled 15,000 acres by 1915, with substantial numbers of tenant farm-

ers, and a mansion house which had been built by a relative of Henry Clay in 1848. It would become a haven for the often weary Lowden who needed seclusion to gain rest from his bad health and business and political worries. Another plantation in northeast Arkansas was purchased by the Lowdens, named Florendon, which required drainage and other improvements to turn it from little more than a swamp into productive acreage. Despite these expensive and exciting ventures, Lowden's true home remained at Sinnissippi. The nickname "Squire of Sinnissippi" was soon gained, much to his enjoyment. The image of a wealthy squire, tending his crops and his livestock, was politically and personally attractive for Lowden.

Nineteen hundred and twelve found the Republican Party self-destructing over the competing ambitions and views of Theodore Roosevelt and William Howard Taft. Lowden revealed his party regularity and his conservatism, by siding with President Taft both during the pre-convention squabbles, and then after the nominations when Roosevelt went his separate, Bull Moose way. In 1916, this loyalty paid off when Lowden ran for governor. An expensive, well-organized campaign that was well under way by the summer of 1915 led to Lowden's nomination in the party primary, more than doubling the total of his closest competitor. Lowden kept up an energetic, exhausting campaign right through the November 8 election, and gained a 150,000-vote plurality out of 1,260,000 cast. A note of congratulations soon found its way to Lowden's desk from Theodore Roosevelt, whom Lowden had opposed four years before more out of party consistency than ideology. Roosevelt said:

> Let me heartily congratulate you. I earnestly hope you will now assume a position of leadership. We need leadership! What I most desire is that you shall help bring the Republicans far enough forward to enable us to hold the progressives far enough back to keep a substantial alignment.

Lowden determined to serve as governor and then give up political life. The sincerity of that decision probably should not be doubted, but his ability to abide by it became increasingly doubtful. The Lowden administration was not spectacular, because Lowden did not have the personality to perform in dramatic ways. It was successful, however. As World War I erupted soon after Lowden took office, his quick support of President Wilson in the prosecution of that war made news, and gained respect for the Republican governor. The major domestic issue the governor faced was governmental reorganization. One hundred and twenty-five state agencies and bureaus were consolidated into nine departments. Some state agencies were streamlined. What became known as the "Illinois Plan" was pushed by the new governor, and became a model of efficiency for the whole country. By the 1920s, the Illinois Plan had been followed in 14 states in one form or another.

Four good years as Illinois governor placed Lowden in the midst of speculation over the 1920 Republican presidential nomination. As a multimillionaire, tied by family to one of the great American fortunes, Lowden definitely had political liabilities as a candidate. Still, his relations with organized labor were acceptable, because he was open and accessible to the Illinois Federation of Labor. He was handsome, forceful, almost presidential in appearance, and had the image of a successful businessman who would apply the same techniques to American government. The entire Illinois delegation was not behind him, as intraparty squabbles particularly with the party machine in Cook County made unanimity impossible. Issues were far less important than personalities. Lowden used the "Red Scare" issue and said, "All good Americans should instantly resist every sign of disloyalty and disorder." In foreign affairs Lowden accepted the Republican position in the Senate on the League of Nations, saying the League was a good idea that needed amending. On no issue was Lowden strident, and such observers as Walter Lippman thought the Illinoisian was a logical choice for the party:

> The people are tired, tired of noise, tired of politics, ... and longing for a place where the world is quiet and where all trouble seems dead leaves, and spent waves riot in doubtful dreams of dreams....
> Lowden is the noiseless candidate in the campaign. I have watched his appeal to the voters. He tells them that he will talk only of prosaic things and he does. He assures them he will not bother them much and he will not.

Two other leading candidates vied for the honor, Hiram Johnson and General Leonard Wood. Both had formidable claims on the support of large segments of the electorate. Lowden's main hope was as a compromise candidate. Some of the hope for compromise was lost when a Senate committee investigating campaign expenditures examined why many Missouri Wood delegates were switching to Lowden. Lowden's Missouri manager was called to testify, and reported that $38,000 had been spent in the state. Two minor state politicians, it was discovered, had been given $2,500 each without a good explanation for the transaction. The whole episode tainted the Lowden campaign, even though no complicity by Lowden in the matter ever was suggested. The other candidates attacked Lowden and struck their own innocent, outraged pose. Lowden would later state that the Missouri matter was the most important cause of his defeat.

After the first ballot, Lowden trailed the leader Wood by a small margin, with Senator Johnson third. Warren Harding followed far behind. After a deadlock developed, the archetypical "smoke-filled room" meeting occurred, in which party leaders anxious to have a president they could control finally decided on Harding. A Lowden supporter informed his candidate of the meeting, but the governor refused to release his delegates. Lowden and General Wood then met, but they could not agree on a common strategy. Lowden finally just gave up, and released his delegates. Harding was easily named a few ballots later.

The governor refused to seek another term. When Harding was elected, most expected a senior cabinet post for this important Midwest politician, but the new president only offered the position of secretary of the navy or a high ambassadorial post. Lowden declined. Harding did not immediately take "no" for an answer, but Lowden repeated his refusal. What the former governor instead devoted himself to were his business interests, especially the improvement of agriculture. Though business in general was booming, Lowden presciently warned that the depression among farmers would in time doom the entire economy. He endorsed what many saw as a radical measure, the McNary-Haugen price support bill that twice was vetoed by Republican presidents. Lowden also became a central figure in several organizations dealing with agriculture and rural America, including the Farm Foundation, International Livestock Board, and was president of the Holstein-Friesian Association from 1921 to 1930.

Politics could not entirely escape Lowden, but when Harding died and Coolidge succeeded him, there was no chance that the 1920 Illinois candidate would try again in 1924. Some, including President Coolidge, believed Lowden was advancing his political interests with his active participation in farm organizations, especially Lowden's leadership of the Wheat Growers Advisory Committee. Cooperative marketing of farm commodities was the goal of the committee, a popular idea throughout the Midwest. The organization proved short-lived, however, and in 1924 Lowden and the committee parted ways. In 1924, Lowden faced conflicting demands from supporters that he should run for the Senate or run for the Illinois governor again. He did neither. Most presented their demands in the form of which office would be the better stepping-stone to the presidency, but Lowden stated, "any man who runs for one office in order to get another, hasn't sense enough to fill either." After flirting with the idea of challenging Coolidge, he rejected it. Friendship with the president's supporters had not been injured by Lowden's discreet consideration of his own presidential race, and speculation surfaced that Coolidge would select the Sage of Sinnissippi for vice president. Lowden immediately and at every subsequent mention of the possibility declined to be considered. Being in the honorary, subordinate role of vice president had no appeal to him, and his sincerity in the rejection of the office was clear. Lowden's principal pre-convention activity was to stop the movement to name him to the second spot on the ticket. Despite his insistent protests, Lowden was named on the second ballot. His irrevocable refusal of the nomination was then read to the convention, but the delegates recessed

for 90 minutes in order that further inquiries could be made. A new telegram was sent by the reluctant nominee, and this time it was taken as the final word. Lowden's public comment was colorful, saying that he would not want the presidency by "walking slowly behind the hearse of some other man." President Coolidge, who had gained his office exactly that way, probably was not amused. Charles G. Dawes was then nominated for vice president. Dawes was a friend of Lowden's, and when Secretary of Agriculture Henry Wallace died during the campaign, Davis suggested to Coolidge that Lowden be named his successor. It was advice that was not accepted.

Four years later, Lowden's concern that the national administration was uninterested in reforming the crumbling American system of agriculture, led him somewhat unwillingly to enter the 1928 contest for president. The national convention endorsed Coolidge's farm policies, which led to Lowden's withdrawal from the contest for the nomination. He had few delegates and was not a serious contender. Herbert Hoover was named, and Lowden took no part in the campaign. Despite such rebelliousness, Hoover offered his former rival appointment as secretary of agriculture and later, ambassador to Great Britain. Both offers were refused.

Lowden lived for another 15 years, but those years were occupied with far more business than politics. One of his longest projects were serving as one of the court-appointed trustees for the bankrupt Rock Island Railroad. Political candidates sought his advice and support, and probably some of his money. When President Frank Roosevelt took office, Lowden had hopes that firmer measures would be taken to deal with farm problems. Yet he split with the president over the 1937 court-packing scheme. When Roosevelt broke the tradition of serving no more than two terms, Lowden condemned the decision. He believed the Republicans would win in 1940, but Roosevelt surprised him.

Florence Lowden died in 1937, and it was a difficult blow from which Lowden never quite recovered. In the late autumn of 1936 she had visited Hot Springs, Arkansas, for surcease from her rheumatism, but returned to Sinnissippi little improved. Her health remained poor all through the following winter and spring, and she died in her sleep on July 4. Lowden was diagnosed in 1938 as having cancer, but it is unclear whether Lowden was told. When he traveled to a winter home in Tucson, Arizona, in January 1943, he was weak and in pain. He could not eat, his hands were swollen, and in fact he seemed ready to die. In March, he did.

Analysis of Qualifications

Political life for Frank Lowden began in the rough and tumble of Chicago. For ten years he was a Republican workhorse, not closely allied with reform, but more with party regularity. As a rich, physically attractive, intelligent man without previous experience in office, Lowden took what appeared to be a presumptuous leap into the governor's race in 1904, and almost won. With that defeat, his connection with Chicago was broken. He moved to his estate 100 miles west of the city, and slowly his focus returned to the difficult problems of rural life that he had known so well as a boy. By the 1920s, the growing disaster of agriculture, which he experienced firsthand even if not painfully, became his all-consuming interest.

Lowden was a gifted speaker and made an excellent attorney. He was a man of wildly fluctuating moods, with long bouts of depression and nervous tension that led to physical problems, followed by much gayer periods. This multimillionaire businessman had as governor a reformer streak, seeking "blue sky" legislation, collective marketing for farmers, and governmental reorganization. Some legislation favorable to labor and a constitutional amendment establishing an income tax were measures he backed on the national level.

Lowden's best chance for the presidency came in 1920, but the bargains made at the convention left the country with Warren Harding. There is no doubt that Lowden's vastly sharper mind, political skills, and moral backbone would have made him far superior to the Ohio senator. In 1924, when he refused the vice presidency, Lowden was already exhibiting his dislike for the conservative farm policies of the national administration that made him sit out Hoover's presidential campaign four years later. Lowden's interests were not in foreign afairs, and his presidency would have focused on domestic issues. Cooperative marketing and commodity price supports would have been a key of his farm policy, and regardless of the effectiveness of these measures at least it can be said that Lowden was intent on action, not complacency.

It is difficult to say how well prepared Lowden was for the presidency. His interests were parochial, but he had a good mind and revealed a good grasp of his responsibilities and possibilities while serving ably as Illinois governor. Corruption would not have ravaged his administration, but whether he would have chosen good and able individuals for his government is not clearly indicated by his service as governor. The Republican Party in 1924, however, clearly chose for vice president a man of national stature. Frank Lowden was a satisfactory if unspectacular selection.

LOWDEN BIBLIOGRAPHY

Hutchinson, William T. *Lowden of Illinois: The Life of Governor Frank O. Lowden*. 2 vols. Chicago (1975), reprint of 1957 edition.

Judah, Charles, and George Winston Smith. *The Unchosen*. New York City (1962), pp. 155–190.

Russell, Francis. *The Shadow of Blooming Grove: Warren G. Harding in His Times*. New York City and Toronto (1968).

Election of 1928

NOMINATIONS

Republican Party Convention (19th): June 12–15, 1928, at the Civil Auditorium, Kansas City, Mo. *President*— Herbert Hoover, nominated on the first ballot with 837 votes out of 1,089 cast. *Vice president*— Charles Curtis, nominated on the first ballot with 1,052 votes out of the 1,089 cast.

Democratic Party Convention (25th): June 26–29, 1928, at Sam Houston Hall, Houston, Texas. *President*— Alfred E. Smith, nominated on the first ballot with 849⅙ votes out of 1100 cast. Before votes were switched on this ballot, he had received 724⅔. *Vice president*— Joseph T. Robinson, nominated on the first ballot with 1035⅙ out of 1100 votes. Before shift he had 914⅙.

GENERAL ELECTION, November 6, 1928

Popular Vote

Hoover	21,411,991
Smith	15,000,185
Others	378,188

Electoral Vote

Hoover–Curtis — 444 (40 states)
Smith–Robinson — 87 (8 states)

Winners

Herbert Hoover, 31st president
Charles Curtis, 31st vice president

Losers

Alfred E. Smith
Joseph T. Robinson

---

*1928 presidential nominee—
Democratic Party*

Al Smith

Full name: Alfred Emanuel Smith, Jr.
State represented: New York.
Birth: December 30, 1873, New York City.
Age on Inauguration Day (March 4, 1929): 55 years, 2 months.

Education: Attended New York parochial schools until forced to drop out in 1887, at age 14.

Religion: Roman Catholic.

Ancestry: Grandparents were Irish immigrants.

Occupation: Several blue collar jobs after dropped out of school; at age 21 became subpoena server and remained government worker or public official thereafter.

Public offices: New York State Assemblyman, 1904–1915 (Democratic majority leader, 1911; elected speaker of House, 1913); delegate to New York Constitutional Convention, 1915; sheriff of New York County, 1916–1917; president of New York City Board of Aldermen, 1918; governor of New York, 1919–1921, defeated in 1920, 1923–1929; unsuccessful candidate for Democratic presidential nomination in 1920, 1924, and 1932; unsuccessful Democratic nominee for president, 1928.

Death: October 4, 1944, New York City, of lung congestion and an acute heart condition; age 70 years, 9 months.

Burial: Calvary Cemetery, Long Island City, New York.

Home: Fifth Avenue apartment, New York City.

Personal characteristics: Tall and slender as young man; became stocky in middle age; open, ruddy, smiling face; light gray eyes, large nose; strong voice with New York east side accent; fastidious dresser, always wore brown derby; a great wit, and considerable acting ability.

Father: Alfred E. Smith, Sr. (c. 1840–November, 1886); truck driver in New York.

Mother: Catherine Mulvehill (1850–May 18, 1924); married September, 1872; daughter of Thomas and Maria Mulvehill, who came to the United States from Ireland in 1841.

Siblings: Mary (December 30, 1875–?); married John J. Glynn, a New York policeman in 1895.

Wife: Catherine Dunn (c. 1879–May 4, 1944); married May 6, 1900, daughter of Christopher and Emily Dunn.

Children: Alfred E., Jr. (January 26, 1901–November 15, 1968); lawyer; married Bertha Mary Gott on October 16, 1924, separated in 1932. Emily Josephine (December 23, 1901–March 13, 1980); married John A. Warner on June 5, 1926. Catherine Alice (April 15, 1904–January 14, 1982); married Frances J. Quillinan. Arthur Williams (August 20, 1907–September 7, 1955); businessman; married Anne Hess on February 1, 1925. Walter Joseph (December 28, 1909–).

Historic sites/memorials: Alfred E. Smith house, 25 Oliver St., New York (private).

Presidential candidates had come from humble backgrounds before. Lincoln's log cabin poverty is merely the best remembered example, but hardly the only one. Alfred E. Smith came from a new type of poverty, the first son of poor immigrants. He was raised in the squalor of tenement living in New York City's Lower East Side. Smith was Irish and Catholic, a Tammany Hall machine politician, and he was nominated for president of the United States. The reason for Al Smith's conquering of his political and personal handicaps is deeply rooted in luck, intelligence, and personality.

Al Smith's father was a son of Irish immigrants who escaped with so many others from the famine and poverty of their native land in the decades prior to the American Civil War. His family was deeply religious; for seven years Al was an altar boy at St. James Catholic Church. Church clubs provided most of the organized recreation for Al and his peers, a necessary diversion from the other temptations readily available in the streets, alleys, and wharves of this overcrowded and impoverished section of New York. At the age of 11, Al began his first job selling newspapers. After his father died when Al was only 13, he took on a series of jobs including being a chaser for a trucker, an oil factory worker, and then for three years, 12 hours a day, a worker at the Fulton Fish Market. His days there began at 4:00 A.M., some days at 3:00 A.M., unloading, cleaning and selling the fish. When later his absence of a college degree was noted, he protested that

he had a "F.F.M.," a degree earned at the Fulton Fish Market. As a release for his desire to perform, Smith became an inveterate theatergoer. He also acted in amateur plays in the neighborhood. It was only when confronted by his wife-to-be's parents with a choice between acting and their daughter that he foreswore the stage as a career.

Politics was more than an abstraction to the Fourth Ward, the area of New York City including the East Side tenements. Politics was concrete; it meant jobs, social acceptability, and, for some, power. Smith became a regular at Tom Foley's saloon, a center of political discussion as well as drinking. Foley was a real power broker in the community. He and another influential politician, Henry Campbell, took an interest in Smith. When a split with the entrenched Tammany Congressional candidate arose, Al sided with those favoring another candidate. This marked him in Foley and Campbell's minds as someone with a future. Smith's immediate future was secured when Campbell procured a job for him as a subpoena server starting in 1895, a position that paid him the satisfactory sum of over a thousand dollars a year. After eight years, Smith was given the opportunity to move up.

In 1901, the old-line Tammany organization was successfully challenged by men such as Campbell and Foley. Young Smith found himself on the inside of the machine's reformed operations. In 1903, he was the Tammany, and therefore Democratic, nominee for the state assembly. With the nomination came automatic election in this part of the city. Smith was to serve until 1915, but his early years in Albany as a legislator were confused and frustrating. He did not understand the legislation that daily buried his desk; he felt lonely and without friends in the new surroundings. He roomed with future New York mayor and senator Robert Wagner, who helped explain some of the more intricate workings of both the legislature and the specific legislation. Within a few years, with Smith being reelected annually with ease, he began to feel more confident. Indeed, by the time his tenure in the assembly had ended, he was one of the most knowledgeable authorities on state government to be found in Albany.

In the legislature, Smith imagined himself a voice for the people against the entrenched special interests. He initiated bills to lower utility rates and to control banks and insurance companies. He argued for better representation for New York City, which decades before the one-man/one-vote concept became established, was grossly underrepresented in the legislature. In sum, he represented the people who put him where he was. His vision was not much broader than necessary to fulfill that function.

In 1910, the Democrats for the first time in 20 years took control of all branches of New York government. The younger Democrats found themselves in positions of power. Smith was designated majority leader in the lower house of the legislature; his old roommate Robert Wagner took the same position in the state senate. Four years of internal Democratic bickering occurred between a new group of reformers within the party, including Franklin D. Roosevelt, a Dutchess County assemblyman, and the old-guard. Smith more often than not placed himself against the reformers. Few of the Young Turks knew as much about government and the legislature as did Smith. Many reformers were seeking change with no real idea of what that change would be. Such bickering caused the Democrats to lose their assembly majority in 1911, but they were returned to power in 1912, at which time Smith became speaker.

In 1913, Smith took part in the Democrats' successful impeachment of their own governor whom they had elected only months before. Bill Sulzer had been elected with full Tammany support, but upon taking office Sulzer joined the so-called reformers and attacked the Tammany machine. He was also corrupt, which was a convenient basis for impeachment. Sulzer was removed by the senate after his impeachment by the house, and Smith again showed his allegiance to Tammany. In this and other battles in the assembly, Smith's ties with the machine made him appear to many as nothing more than a party hack. Indeed, guiding principles in his efforts were few, other than an open-minded pragmatism that permitted him to support much progressive legislation that did not conflict —

indeed it at times melded with — Tammany's aims. Al Smith's involvement with the machine had not tainted him with any hint of corruption. His politics was the always-practiced policy of assisting one's constituents and, where this did not conflict, abetting the general welfare of the state. Perhaps as a result of a tragic fire in 1911, however, Smith became more of a social reformer than his early in the assembly would have forecast.

On March 25, 1911, a fire broke out on the eighth floor of a New York ten-story building. The injuries would have been few except that the employers had locked the doors to the room where the work occurred in order to prevent the workers from leaving before the workday was over, to prevent labor organizing, and to halt pilfering. The one exit became blocked by the fire, and one hundred forty-three men and women were killed, many in jumping out of windows to their deaths. Smith became a member of the committee that investigated not only this fire but industrial conditions generally.

Al Smith became one of the leaders in the movement to improve the workers' condition through legislation. Smith's committee visited every manufacturing town in the state, examined the factories, and interviewed both management and labor. The result of this investigation was both newfelt concern as well as action. The Tammany assemblyman did not lose faith in business; he did not turn radical or socialist, but he did become a champion of minimal legislation to set health and safety standards in all industries. Child and female labor were particular concerns of his. He wanted guidelines for the employment of both the young and women. Fire codes were an immediate concern after the 1911 disaster, as well as ventilation for factories. Smith's reputation began to have a dual image, both as industrial reformer and as machine politician. Both roles were important for his later success.

In 1915, Smith was a delegate to the state constitutional convention, a convention dominated by Republicans. Smith, the poorly educated but vastly experienced legislator, was widely praised for his understanding of the needs of the state and the workings of the existing government. No less a blue blood and a Republican than Elihu Root, also a delegate, said that "of all men in the convention Mr. Smith is the best informed on the business of the state of New York." Smith was ready for bigger things.

Tammany also believed Smith was prepared for a larger stage. Prior to any statewide campaign, it was thought that Smith should run for a citywide post. In 1915, he received the nomination for sheriff of New York County. His victory in the primary was narrow, primarily achieved by his loyal support by the machine. The general election went much more smoothly. The position was largely honorific, but the recompense was staggering for the day, allowing Smith to receive as much as $50,000 a year through the antiquated fee system that was the sheriff's compensation. The post enabled him to give countless speeches, have his name prominently displayed in the newspapers, and placed him in prime position for another promotion. That promotion was to the presidency of the city Board of Aldermen, a four-year term that Smith gladly did not complete.

Smith became governor of New York mainly because the head of Tammany Hall, Smith's long-time benefactor Charles Murphy, had groomed him for the race. Smith was not perfect governor material for the machine, because he was incorruptible. But Tammany had changed just as New York politics was changing. The honest immigrant son, who was one of them if not completely beholden to them, was as good a candidate as was likely to be elected. His victory over the incumbent Republican governor was only by 15,000 votes, and two years later he was ousted from office in the Harding and Republican landslide that followed the First World War. Following his 1922 election, Smith was to gain a lockhold on the affections of New York's voters. His victory margins thereafter were staggering. In 1924, he even defeated the son and namesake of former president Theodore Roosevelt, an accomplishment of considerable impact.

As governor, Smith was constantly opposed by the Republicans and conservative Democrats who did not like his brand of politics. Many saw Smith as the banner carrier for a new liberalism that was practical and not

visionary, that looked to the problems of the city and tried to use government to ameliorate them.

One postwar problem was housing, both the cost of it and its availability. Smith favored continuing war rent controls to prevent the ever-escalating building costs from putting rents out of reach. He backed various stimulus programs to get the building industry booming. Subsidies were encouraged for medical care. His concern for industrial work conditions had not waned, and he pushed legislation in that field. His frequent battles with the legislature and with various departments of state government made him an advocate of sweeping reform in government administration. After several legislative rebuffs, constitutional amendments were approved overwhelmingly by the people in 1925, permitting the consolidation of state agencies and boards into 16 departments. The number of statewide elected officials was reduced to just four, the governor, lieutenant governor, attorney general and comptroller. This enabled the governor to appoint his own people to the top administrative posts, and control them.

In 1920, Smith had received a few token and complimentary votes for president at the Democratic national convention, but there was nothing token about his support in 1924. His initial approach was cautious, as early avowal of candidacy would subject him to attacks by every other aspirant. He was also concerned about the religious issue that would so quickly be raised, if only by rumor, once he announced. Smith was a devout Roman Catholic. There had never been a presidential nominee who was Catholic. Recent events in America should have given him concern that the time was not ripe for that to change. The Ku Klux Klan had become a powerful influence after World War I. Its thrust in those years was not against the Negro, who was still being kept in effective bondage but was rather against immigrants, Catholics, Jews, and all other representatives of non–Anglo Saxon, Protestant society. Even in the North there was strong support for the Klan and similar groups that espoused a "pure" society. The 1924 Democratic convention became a battleground between those who wished squarely to face the bigotry issue and denounce the Klan, and those who desired that the question be ignored in hopes of gaining votes from all sides. The fence-straddlers won the platform debate. Smith saw that his chance for the nomination, which required a two-thirds majority, was nonexistent. The other leading candidate represented appeasement of the Klan and similar organizations. Smith would not yield since that would mean far more than the nomination would be lost. For one hundred ballots neither Smith nor his opponent, former president Woodrow Wilson's son-in-law, William Gibbs McAdoo of California, received the necessary two-thirds vote. Finally Smith relented, but only if all candidates similarly released their delegates and permitted an open choice. Three ballots later John W. Davis was nominated. A weary and already defeated Democratic Party headed for home. The election disaster that followed did not drag Smith down with it, and his impressive margin over Col. Theodore Roosevelt, Jr., in the face of the Republican landslide elsewhere, made him an even more attractive candidate for the party's 1928 nomination.

After 1924, the Klan and related organizations began to decline. Their hatred and prejudice did not have a long life. Smith's nomination began to appear less divisive than it did in 1924. Smith's landslide New York victories seemed to make the all-important New York electoral votes safe for the Democrats. There was little real competition for Smith over the 1928 nomination.

Much of the support that Smith figured he could count on in the general election never appeared. The once and later solid South was not so for him; five states from the old Confederacy left their Democratic moorings for the first time since Reconstruction. Many Catholics preferred just to be left alone and did not support one of their own, fearing increased agitation over their religion. The Republican nominee, Herbert Hoover, attacked Smith as a socialist who desired the end of the American free-enterprise system. Smith's campaign style did not help remove these obstacles. He was not a compromiser when it came to firmly held beliefs, and his religion was certainly firmly held. He wrote in 1927 a thoughtful and definitive article for a popular magazine that attempted to diffuse the fears of those reasonable men who held doubts concerning whether a Catholic president would be loyal to his country or to the Pope. The weakness of the article is that the problem Smith and other Catholics faced was far less prevalent among thoughtful voters as among emotional, prejudiced ones who could not be swayed by reason.

Perhaps the biggest public issue of the day, though perhaps not as influential as the subsurface issue of religion, was prohibition. The great experiment of the 18th Amendment ban on alcohol was as controversial in its day as abortion would be to a later generation. Smith was not in a position to waffle on this issue. He was not the kind of politician who found convenient evasions very attractive, but he also was publicly identified with the repeal of prohibition. His work in the Tammany trenches, that center city machine that could hardly be imagined except within the context of the saloons and bars that were its meeting houses, made him clearly identified as a "Wet." He had fought as governor for the repeal of the enforcement legislation for prohibition, as well as for the repeal of prohibition altogether. Rumors that he was frequently drunk expectedly came, though there was no foundation for the charge.

The final and totally overwhelming burden that Governor Smith had to carry was, thankfully, that the country appeared to be in the midst of great general prosperity. The few pockets of people who did not share in the bounty, most notably the farmers, were not the concern of the majority of Americans who had never known life to be more comfortable. A chicken in every pot was already the norm, and a car in every garage did not seem far off. Smith lost badly, even though he increased the Democrats' share of the vote over what Davis had received four years before.

As Smith was losing the national election, Franklin D. Roosevelt was surprisingly winning the governorship back home in New York. Even Roosevelt apparently did not at first believe he would win, and his timetable called for another race for the governorship in 1932 with his eye on the presidency in 1936.

Victory in 1928 meant advancing the timetable, and also meant dealing with the potential obstacle of Al Smith. Roosevelt completely cut Smith out of New York political power. This former friend and political ally, who even gave the dramatic 1924 nominating speech that coined the name "Happy Warrior" that Smith joyously wore thereafter, had now decided that Smith had to be cast out into the political wilderness in order that he not interfere with Roosevelt's own ambitions. It was a serious blot on the Roosevelt record, but it is an undeniable one.

Out of government and out of favor, Smith turned to business. The crash was still months away. Smith saw great profits and personal financial security in the offer to become head of the company planning the Empire State Building. He became president of the company and would remain so until his death, but the money he put into it was severely jeopardized when the Depression began. The building's foundation had only recently been laid when the stock market crash occurred. Prospects for finishing construction, much less occupying the building with paying renters, darkened. Smith's energies were devoted to the project, which never was to show him much personal profit.

Relations with Roosevelt remained cool. By 1932, both men were candidates for the presidential nomination, Smith announcing in February of that year. The words became bitter, as when Smith accused Roosevelt publicly, if not by name, of being a demagogue who was trying to pit class against class, rich against poor.

Smith's 1932 platform, a fair progenitor of the New Deal programs Roosevelt was to adopt, called for federal takeover of relief efforts that could not be funded by the states. Private business could not pull the people out of starvation, homelessness, and despair. Only the federal government could, through legislation similar to that started in New York under his leadership. The shock of the 1911 fire that awakened Smith not only to new ideas but the new people who espoused them was continuing to have its effect on his proposals. After Roosevelt defeated him at the 1932 convention, Smith gave grudging support and did campaign in the Northeast for the ticket.

The Smith-Roosevelt relationship worsened after the election victory. Roosevelt again ignored Smith in the formation of his government, even though Smith apparently expected to be called for some post. Smith's bitterness and disappointment intensified. In both 1936 and 1940, Smith supported Roosevelt's Republican opponents. He called Roosevelt's policies little more than communism, and walked out of the 1936 Democratic national convention. Once World War II erupted, Smith did favor vigorous prosecution of the war and carefully differentiated his disdain for Roosevelt's domestic policies from his support of the president's war measures.

Smith's political influence was minimal after 1932. He continued to serve as president of the Empire State Building organization. He also involved himself more closely with church activities and charities, including Catholic Charities, the Red Cross, and the USO. He declined to be a candidate for the United States Senate, saying his financial obligations were too great to enable him to live on a Senator's salary. He withdrew to a close circle of family and intimate friends and stayed out of politics. When his wife died in May of 1944, the absence of his strong support in his life seemed to sap his own strength. His health immediately began to fail and he died only five months later.

Analysis of Qualifications

What would Al Smith have been able to contribute to the country during those dark Depression days? Would his presidency have made a difference, or would he have suffered the same fate as Hoover — present at the creation, blamed, and then discarded by his countrymen?

First of all, Smith was no Hoover. As inspiring as Hoover's life and character was, he had an entirely different view from Smith's of the role and capacity of government. Hoover never could shake his ingrained beliefs that free enterprise would recover its bearings and would bring the country out of what was at worst just a severe dip in the normal economic cycles. Hoover was not unconcerned; he must have grieved daily for the plight of his countrymen. He did not, however, think it was the federal government's place to correct those conditions. Al Smith was a totally different man. His views as governor of New York had even been called socialistic by Hoover during the 1928 campaign, but they seemed peculiarly proper for the country as a whole in 1929. What he attempted in New York is almost certainly what he would have attempted in Washington, to bring the government directly into battle to better citizens' lives. There was a new liberalism to Al Smith, one that was not based on radical theory but on practical politics and experience. He was a believer in compromise; he was no ideologue who went to the mat on every issue. Yet he could be indefatigable when it came to issues that he thought could not be compromised.

Smith's shortcomings in the presidency would probably have arisen from his inexperience in Washington. He knew nothing of foreign affairs. He did not know Congress, and what worked on the provincial legislators in Albany may not have convinced the more independent congressmen in Washington. His staff was not familiar with national affairs either, and he would have had to broaden his base of advisers. He rose incredibly far for a man of very narrow experiences and education, but in the White House some of those deficiencies may have become more significant.

It seems fair to suppose that nothing Al Smith could have done in his first months as president would have averted the Depression. The Depression was not of Hoover's making nor would it have been for Smith to halt. Hoover's rejection in 1932 was total, and that rejection arguably would have encompassed Smith just as easily had he been president. The more likely result of four years of a Smith presidency, however, would have been that the voters would have shown understanding and patience towards Smith that was similar to that later given to Franklin Roosevelt. Roosevelt did little more to alleviate the suffering of the impoverished during his presidency prior to World War II than had Hoover during his shorter term of office. The Depression simply was not cured until the war ended it dramatically in 1941. The people did not demand an instant cure, but they did find Hoover lacking in compassion and hope. Smith likely would have risen to that demand of the Depression better than did Hoover. Smith strongly criticized Roosevelt for many of the same types of relief measures utilized by Smith in New York. That attack can partly be blamed on his bitterness and disappointment, not only his loss to Hoover and then Roosevelt four years later, but also at the manner in which Roosevelt treated him after his election. It is also true that Smith had a higher regard for capitalism than did Roosevelt. One writer even called Smith a liberal with a conservative heart.

What the country needed was a sense that Washington was doing everything possible to respond to the needs of the people. Smith had been given an opportunity as governor to act upon similar demands from his constituents, and he had responded brilliantly. There is every reason to believe that he would have done so again as president. It seems probable that Smith would have been remembered as an excellent president, whose talents and personality ably matched the needs of his time.

SMITH BIBLIOGRAPHY

Eldot, Paula. *Governor Alfred E. Smith: The Politician as Reformer*. New York City (1982).

Farley, James A., and James C.G. Coniff. *Governor Al Smith*. New York City (1959).

Feldman, M.I. *The Political Thought of Alfred E. Smith*. New York City (1963).

Finan, Christopher Michael. "Fallen Hero: Alfred E. Smith in the Thirties." Unpublished doctoral dissertation, Columbia University (1992).

Graham, Frank. *Al Smith, American*. New York City (1945).

Handlin, Oscar. *Al Smith and His America*. Boston (1958).

Josephson, Matthew, and Hanna Josephson. *Al Smith: Hero of the Cities*. Boston (1969).

Moore, Edmund. *A Catholic Runs for President*. New York City (1956).

Moscowitz, Henry, and Norman Hapgood. *Up from the City Streets: Alfred E. Smith*. New York City (1927).

O'Connor, Richard. *The First Hurrah: A Biography of Alfred E. Smith*. New York City (1970).

Smith, Alfred E. *Up to Now*. New York City (1928).

Warner, Emith Smith (Smith's daughter). *The Happy Warrior*. New York City (1956).

AL SMITH and JOSEPH ROBINSON
(From the collection of David J. and Janice L. Frent)

1928 vice presidential nominee —
Democratic Party

Joseph Robinson

Full name: Joseph Taylor Robinson.

State represented: Arkansas.

Birth: August 26, 1872, in a log house on a farm near Lonoke, Arkansas.

Age on Inauguration Day (March 4, 1929): 56 years, 6½ months.

Education: Little formal education, a few months spent at each of several county schools and academies; University of Arkansas, 1891–1893; a summer session at University of Virginia Law School, 1895; studied law in office of Judge Thomas Trimble, 1893–1895; admitted to bar in 1895.

Religion: Methodist.

Ancestry: Family tradition is that Joe's mother was one-half Cherokee.

Occupation: Attorney.

Public offices: Arkansas state assembly, 1894–1896; U.S. representative, March 4, 1903–January 14, 1913, resigned; governor of Arkansas, January 16–March 10, 1913, resigned; U.S. senator, March 10, 1913–July 14, 1937; unsuccessful Democratic nominee for vice president, 1928; Senate Democratic leader, 1923–1937.

Home: Little Rock, Arkansas, 2122 Broadway.

Death: July 14, 1937, Washington, D.C., at age 64 years, 10½ months.

Burial: Roselawn Memorial Park, Little Rock, Arkansas.

Personal characteristics: Strong, broad-shouldered man; hawklike nose; portly, with found, freckled face; quick temper, almost violent at times, but other times, so dignified almost seemed arrogant; well-liked; usually seen with cigar.

Father: Dr. James Madison Robinson (1816–1892); doctor, farmer, New York native.

Mother: Matilda Jane Swaim (1832–1899); was part Cherokee; married December 22, 1852.

Siblings: Joe was the fourth son and ninth of eleven children. Sarah Catherine (1864–1957), married Davis F. Scott. Margaret (1856–1944), married H.N. Thomason. Edward R. (1868–1958), married Unity Barnes. William Thomas (1860–1952), married T. Cumi Martin. Martha (died 1853 as infant). James Madison, Jr. (?–?), married Rosie Craft. Julie (died as a child of ten). Mollie (?–?), married Andrew J. Walls. Elizabeth (?–?), married Francis N. Brewer. Marsena (?–?), married Andrew Martineau. The Robinsons also adopted six orphans.

Wife: Ewilda Gertrude Miller (1876–August 7, 1958); married December 15, 1896; daughter of Jesse Miller and Sarah Evelyn Grady.

Children: None.

Historic sites/memorials: The Robinson home, 2122 Broadway, Little Rock, Arkansas, was the last residence of Joseph Robinson.

"Scrappy Joe" Robinson was his nickname as a child. The description applied throughout his life. He always loved to fight, was a tenacious adversary of the Republicans when they were in power, and an indefatigable proponent of the two Democratic presidents, Wilson and Franklin Roosevelt, under whom he also served.

Robinson's story is not quite rags to riches, but there was a consistent surmounting of considerable obstacles in his life. Though his father was a country doctor, there was little income from that profession to support the Robinson family. As one of 17 children, Joe received little formal education in rural Arkansas. His family provided strong religious indoctrination, and the sizeable Robinson library provided the classics, books on history, and perhaps most of all, the Bible to instruct the children. It was a loving, close-knit family as is indicated by the presence of eleven children, together with six orphans who were adopted. The Robinsons were loath to refuse assistance to anyone, and transients were often invited into the home, given a meal, a place to sleep, and perhaps some inspiration when they were sent off the next day.

Joe felt the absence of a good education keenly. When he was only 17, he was issued a teacher's license for the first grade, and taught for two years in local schools. He earned enough money to enter the University of Arkansas in March of 1891, but only remained two years. He then entered the office of Judge Thomas Trimble to begin his study of law. He received no degree from a college or university, but was admitted to practice in the local courts in September of 1895. A few years later he formed a partnership with his legal tutor, Trimble, and soon established himself as a resourceful, intelligent and dynamic trial attorney.

Robinson was not long satisfied just with the legal profession. In 1893, he had his first taste of politics by being elected to the state democratic convention. The following year he ran successfully for state representative, presenting himself as a supporter of President Cleveland. Without Republican opposition, Robinson won by almost fifteen to one over his Populist opponent. At the age of 22, he was the youngest member of the Arkansas assembly. Statewide acclaim was given him for fathering a bill for railroad regulation, which though defeated in the legislature, became the basis of a state constitutional amendment passed by the voters. He retired after one term in order to devote himself to his legal and business interests. He also had to devote himself to his new wife, Ewilda, the daughter of a prominent Lonoke businessman.

For the next 16 years, Joe and his wife lived with her parents. They moved only after Joe was elected governor in 1912. As a popular political speaker, Joe was in demand throughout the state. His law practice was excellent, and soon he gained a reputation as one of the state's best criminal attorneys.

A return to politics was clearly in Joe's mind. In 1900, the new census for the state gave him the opportunity. Since Arkansas had grown substantially in population, it was entitled to a new United States representative. The new district included his home territory, and Joe began campaigning for the seat in July of 1901. He campaigned for regulation of trusts and federal involvement in the construction and maintenance of levees (a substantial concern to flood-prone areas of Arkansas along the Mississippi River). In general, however, issues were not important to his contest against a strong Democratic opponent. Robinson won the nomination easily. Robinson's selection as the Democratic nominee was tantamount to election in turn-of-the-century Arkansas. As a member of the House, he established a generally progressive image, followed through on his antitrust stands as a candidate, advocated child labor legislation, supported the creation of the income tax, and endorsed a women's suffrage amendment to the Constitution. In the House, Robinson revealed his acceptance of his region's views on civil rights. When President Theodore Roosevelt wanted to force California to admit Japanese children to public schools, Robinson angrily denounced the concept. He thought he had thoroughly demolished Roosevelt's position when he compared it to the obviously radical idea of forcing black and white children to attend the same schools in Arkansas.

After ten years as a United States representative, Robinson had a good reputation throughout his state. He had looked after the home folks well, working for flood control projects, new federal buildings, hospitals, and military facilities. Congressional peers also appreciated his work. Future presidential candidate James Cox called him "a man who grew with every year and every responsibility." Speaker Champ Clark called him "one of the ablest of the young members ... and one of the most promising." The hard work Robinson had put in was leading to a run for statewide office, but the potential candidate worried over when and for what. In 1905, he refused to run for governor because the timing did not look right. In 1910, he decided to oppose Senator Jeff Davis when he came up for renomination in 1912, but there was little enthusiasm in the state to greet his decision. Robinson withdrew from the Senate contest when it appeared that the incumbent governor George Donaghey would not run for reelection. In July 1911, he opened the gubernatorial campaign. The governor did not follow through on his earlier indications of retire-

ment, and in October of that year surprised some, and just irritated others, by deciding to run after all. Again, issues were not significant in this one-party state. Robinson supported prohibition, a four-year term for governor, and some progressive legislation. Basically, however, Robinson stooped to a personal attack on Donaghey, saying that he had acted in bad faith in changing his mind in running for reelection. Though heavily outspent by his opponent, Robinson won easily in the primary.

As the time for inauguration drew near in 1913, a new opportunity presented itself. Senator Jeff Davis, who would have been reelected effortlessly by the legislature a few weeks later, died unexpectedly of a heart attack on January 2, 1913. Robinson immediately huddled with his advisers, but was fearful that the voters would react angrily to so sudden rejection of the office just given him. Even so, it was decided that Robinson should get into the Senate campaign. Fresh from his statewide election victory, with many important friends in high places, Robinson was the odds-on choice for the Senate. Many opponents were bitter over Robinson's entry into the race, yet he won in the legislature with 71 votes, to 62 for a scattering of other candidates. He was one of the last United States senators to be elected by a state legislature, for the Seventeenth Amendment to the federal constitution was ratified in 1913, and thereafter senators were elected by the people. Therefore, within the two month period between January 14 to his swearing in as senator on March 10, 1913, Robinson had served as congressman, governor, and now United States senator.

In the Senate, Robinson was identified as a staunch supporter of the new president, Woodrow Wilson. A new child labor law was written by Robinson and another senator. Antitrust legislation was again a central part of his agenda. Most of all, he was the champion of the farmer. Robinson was not long in the Senate until foreign policy began to dominate debate. During the early stages of the war in Europe, the Arkansas Senator supported American neutrality. Even after the *Lusitania* was sunk, Robinson supported Wilson's restraint. When Wilson finally resigned himself to the war, Robinson, was with him. A bill to permit arming of merchant ships became the issue in March of 1917. Though Robert La Follette and a few other senators blocked the bill through a filibuster, Robinson circulated a "round-robin" resolution which indicated 76 senators would vote for the bill if they could only get a chance. That battle led for the first time to the adoption of the cloture rule that could cut off a filibuster with a two-thirds vote. When an American merchant ship was sunk in April 1917, Wilson asked for a declaration of war, and Robinson wholeheartedly supported him.

The "small band of willful men" who wanted to block American entrance into the war continued to haunt Wilson's efforts. Robinson accused La Follette of treason, and said he should be in the German parliament rather than the American Congress. Once war was declared, Robinson charged in an angry speech that no "half-hearted supporter of the flag" could be accepted. It was a biting, inflammatory, bitterly personal attack on La Follette that Robinson gave on the Senate floor, many times ignoring normal Senate decorum.

After one term in the Senate, Robinson let it be known in 1918 that he was considering retiring and accepting a position as an editorial writer for a Chicago newspaper. Wilson sent him a letter strongly urging him to remain and continue the fight for Wilson's programs. The letter was made public. Robinson decided to run again, and soundly defeated the same opponent he had faced six years earlier. With World War I now over, the principal battles on the Senate floor turned to creating a lasting peace. No stronger champion of the League of Nations than Robinson could be found. On almost all issues dealing with the Versailles Treaty, Robinson stood by the president. Years later, Robinson continued to believe that had the Senate followed Wilson's views, permanent peace would have been established.

Robinson was a growing force in the Democratic Party. In the 1920 National Convention he was chosen permanent chairman. In his keynote speech, Robinson strongly defended the president. The senator was a strong internationalist who wanted America to remain a factor in foreign affairs. In the coming years he was a delegate to several international meetings. For the rest of his life, he fought for American membership in the World Court, the judicial arm of the League of Nations. He did find some of the arms reduction treaties, such as the Four-Power treaty in 1921-1922, to be naive.

The Democrats were in a depressing minority during the period beginning in 1920. Robinson never gave up his partisanship, and was a tireless promoter of the Democratic viewpoint. When Oscar Underwood announced his retirement as Democratic Senate leader in 1922, Robinson and North Carolina Senator F.M. Simmons both declared for the position. Robinson got the early commitments from a sufficient number of senators, and Simmons withdrew. From the opening of Congress in December 1923, until his death, Robinson remained the Senate Democratic leader. During these years he was rarely the initiator of programs. He was an organizer, a fighter, a leader for causes that others presented. One of the causes was a bonus for all veterans of World War I. He opposed widespread use of injunctions against labor strikes. Strong foreign relief measures were favored. Not until the New Deal in 1933 would Robinson support federal power projects, and during the 1920s he led the fight against the Muscle Shoals project.

In 1924, the Arkansas legislature urged the party state central committee to instruct that year's delegates to the national convention to vote for Robinson for president. He was nominated at the convention, retained the 18 Arkansas votes for all 103 ballots, but never got more than 46 votes. Many at the convention thought he was close to the nomination as a compromise candidate, but the decision finally went to John Davis.

The bitter party split that had occurred in 1924 caused Robinson, as one of the highest Democratic elected officials in the country, to take a peacemaker role during the next few years. In March of 1927, he held a Democratic Senate caucus to try to resolve party difference on prohibition and religion. The senator did not at first support any Democratic presidential contender in 1928, but he did speak out forcefully against the prejudice aroused by Al Smith's Catholicism. Robinson spoke courageously on the Senate floor. When Alabama Senator Tom Heflin gave a caustic anti-Catholic speech in the Senate, Robinson rose to rebuke him. That speech is suggested by some as the start of the boom for Robinson as Smith's running mate. He was again permanent chairman of the convention in 1928. Smith won the nomination on the first ballot, and Robinson seemed the natural running mate. He was a prohibitionist, which balanced Smith's candid support for repeal of the Eighteenth Amendment. He was a Protestant and a Southerner, which again offset Smith's northeast Catholic, big-city image. Smith did not publicly anoint Robinson as his running mate, but apparently the word passed to Smith's delegates to support the Arkansas leader. He became the first Southerner on a national ticket since the Civil War. Robinson conducted an active, defiant and colorful campaign. The sharpest attacks on the Republicans were on foreign problems. He forthrightly addressed the religious issue, but much less candidly discussed prohibition, since his differences with Smith had to be straddled.

After the disastrous defeat in November, Robinson returned to the Senate to continue his fight against the Republicans. President Hoover named him a delegate to the Naval Conference in London that opened on January 21, 1930, and there he played a central role. Robinson was not an early Roosevelt supporter for the 1932 nomination. Some of Robinson's advisers even tried to push him into the presidential race, but he saw no prospect for success and remained on the sidelines. When Roosevelt won, Robinson was considered for secretary of state, but the president finally decided he would be more helpful as Senate majority leader.

Roosevelt's election to the presidency also gave the Democrats a majority in the Senate. Therefore, Robinson was a central figure in passing New Deal legislation. Though more conservative than the people immediately around Roosevelt, Robinson consistently supported Roosevelt's policies. Only in 1936 did the Senator vote against the president on an important issue, and that only because of Rob-

inson's long-term support for a veteran's bonus bill. Despite such loyalty, Robinson was lukewarm about many of the New Deal programs. The only statute to bear his name was passed in 1936. This was the Robinson-Patman Act, which added price discrimination among purchasers to the list of antitrust violations. The high spending in government severely troubled Robinson. The national deficit disturbed him, and by 1937 he was calling for retrenchment in government. He said, "unquestionably the continued indiscriminate spending by the government must cease." Still, when his old presidential running mate, Al Smith, deserted Roosevelt and became a critic of the president in 1936, Robinson stood by the New Deal. The two former comrades on the 1928 Democratic ticket engaged in an ugly public dispute, which resulted in Robinson calling Smith the "unhappy warrior," the opposite of Smith's 1928 nickname.

Robinson's final battle in the Senate was over Roosevelt's court-packing plan in 1937. Roosevelt did not consult with Robinson or other Senate leaders before presenting the plan, but Robinson was a good soldier in battling for it in an increasingly reluctant Congress. The majority leader's normal Senate floor leadership rebelled against the proposal, and Robinson had to reorganize. He urged Roosevelt to compromise, but the president refused. The scheme to give the president one new appointment to the court for every justice who refused to retire after reaching the age of 70, was seen as a power grab. Many condemned it as the start of a dictatorship. Roosevelt responded that it was merely an effort to create a more liberal, useful court sympathetic to the New Deal. Arch-conservative Justice Willis Van Devanter announced his resignation in 1937 during the height of the battle. Speculation was rife that Robinson would be named to the vacancy. The senator became irate when Roosevelt's closest advisers initially rejected Robinson, considering him too conservative and, for that matter, too old. He avoided the president for two weeks, angry over these objections, but finally in a lengthy conference with the president got both permission to compromise with the opposition as well as a promise of an appointment. Presidential adviser Jim Farley even called Robinson "Mr. Justice," which elated the senator. The promised appointment never came, as during debate on the Senate floor, Robinson was taken ill. He started to reply to a series of questions on the court-packing plan, but suddenly gasped for air and had to call off debate. Slightly more than a week later he was found dead in his apartment.

Analysis of Qualifications

Few people considered Joe Robinson a great man. His contribution to government during his almost 25 years in the Senate was as a party leader. He led the attack on the Republicans when they were in power, and promoted his party's presidents when they were in office. He was a moderate, conservative on some issues, progressive on others, yet basically in the middle of the road. Never an obstructionist, he was also never an innovator. He was, in sum, a most useful and important politician in his role as Senate party leader. What capacity did he have for success in a still larger role?

The man who was serving as vice president in 1928 while Robinson campaigned to replace him was Republican Charles Dawes. Dawes's opinion of his would-be successor was quite favorable: "He is a man of great ability, of high character, of industry and of exceptional qualities as a leader of men. His courage is that of a lion. He never deceives and his decisions are quick but sound. His ideals are high, and he deserves to be rewarded with the best his party can give.... I regard him as a statesman of high rank" (Dawes, *Notes as Vice-President*, p. 5). The Senator was superb in debate, resourceful, articulate, and dogged. Though partisan, he was not blindly so, and could be counted with supporters of several Republican presidents' programs. No surprisingly, since he was from a rural, agricultural state, Robinson was a strong friend of the farmers. Somewhat more surprising, he could usually be counted as a friend of labor and a supporter of populist programs, such as regulation of utilities and railroads, control of trusts, a strong interstate commerce commission, and child labor laws. An internationalist in foreign affairs, Robinson supported the concept of international cooperation through the League of Nations or similar organizations.

Reporters loved Robinson for his color, as well as his candor. His honesty and accuracy made him reliable. He showed common sense and ability as Senate leader, and was praised highly for similar qualities in leadership of the American delegation to the 1930 Naval Conference in London.

Robinson had built a solid career of public service by the time of his nomination for vice president. He continued that service for the remaining nine years of his life. He had not revealed greatness, but he was an able leader. He seemed well prepared for adequate but uninspired service had he been called to the nation's highest office.

ROBINSON BIBLIOGRAPHY

Dawes, Charles G. *Notes as Vice-President, 1928–1929.* Boston (1935).

Chiles, John E. "The Early Public Career of Joseph Taylor Robinson." Unpublished master's thesis, Vanderbilt University (1950).

Grant, Gilbert Richard. "Joseph Taylor Robinson in Foreign Affairs." Unpublished master's thesis, University of Arkansas (1946).

Kincaid, Diane D., ed. *Silent Hattie Speaks: The Personal Journal of Senator Hattie Caraway.* Westport, Conn. (1979).

McNutt, Walter Scott. *Great Statesmen of Arkansas.* Jefferson, Tex. (1954), pp. 107–133.

Neal, Nevin E. "A Biography of Joseph T. Robinson." Unpublished doctoral dissertation, University of Oklahoma (1958).

Newsom, Gene, and Karl Kastner. *Our Joe.* North Little Rock (1937).

Pettus, Beryl Erwin. "The Senatorial Career of Joseph Taylor Robinson." Unpublished master's thesis, University of Illinois (1952).

Ross, Betsy. "Joseph T. Robinson and the Court Fight of 1937." Unpublished master's thesis, University of Maryland (1950).

Skarda, Charles M., *The Late Senator: Notes on the Life of Joe T. Robinson of Arkansas 1872–1937,* Little Rock (1959).

_____. "A Short Pedigree of the Late Senator from Arkansas." Manuscript at the Library of Congress, and at Arkansas History Commission, Little Rock.

Towns, Stuart. "Joseph T. Robinson and Arkansas Politics: 1912–1913." *Arkansas Historical Quarterly* 24 (1965), pp. 291–307.

_____. "A Louisiana Medicine Show: The Kingfish Elects An Arkansas Senator." *Arkansas Historical Quarterly* 25 (1966), pp. 117–127.

Vervack, Jerry J. "Joseph Taylor Robinson," in Timothy P. Donovan and Willard B. Gatewood, Jr.,

eds. *The Governors of Arkansas: Essays in Political Biography.* Fayetteville (1981).
_____. "The Making of a Politician: Joe T. Robinson, 1872–1921." Unpublished doctoral dissertation, University of Arkansas (1990).
Weller, Cecil Edwards. "Always a Loyal Democrat: The Life of Senate Majority Leader Joseph Taylor Robinson." Unpublished doctoral dissertation, Texas Christian University (1993).

Election of 1932

NOMINATIONS

Socialist Party Convention: May 20–24, 1932, at the Municipal Auditorium, Milwaukee, Wisconsin. *President—* Norman Thomas, nominated without opposition. *Vice president—* James Hudson Maurer, nominated without opposition.

Republican Party Convention (20th): June 14–16, 1932, at the Chicago Stadium, Chicago, Illinois. *President—*Herbert Hoover, nominated on the first ballot with 1126½ votes out of 1154 cast. *Vice president—*Charles Curtis, nominated on the first ballot with 634¼ out of 1154 votes. James G. Harbord (N.Y.) and Hanford MacNider (Iowa) were his principal rivals.

Democratic Party Convention (26th): June 27–30, July 1–2, 1932, at the Chicago Stadium, Chicago, Illinois. *President—*Franklin D. Roosevelt, nominated on the fourth ballot with 945 votes out of 1148½ cast. He had received 666 on the first ballot. Al Smith and John Nance Garner were other contenders. *Vice president—*John Nance Garner, nominated unanimously on the first ballot.

GENERAL ELECTION, November 8, 1932

Popular Vote

Roosevelt 22,825,016
Hoover 15,758,397
Thomas   881,951
Others   278,664

Electoral Vote

Roosevelt-Garner — 472 (42 states)
Hoover-Curtis — 59 (6 states)

Winners
Franklin D. Roosevelt, 32nd president
John Nance Garner, 32nd vice president
Losers
Herbert Hoover, Charles Curtis, Norman Thomas, James Maurer

---

*1932 presidential nominee —
Republican Party*

Herbert Hoover

No biographical sketch of Hoover is included since he served as president from March 4, 1929, until March 4, 1933 (31st president).
State represented: California.
Birth: August 10, 1874.
Age on Inauguration Day (March 4, 1933): 58 years, 7 months.
Death: October 20, 1964.

---

*1932 vice presidential nominee —
Republican Party*

Charles Curtis

No biographical sketch of Curtis is included since he served as vice president from March 4, 1929, until March 4, 1933 (31st vice president).
State represented: Kansas.

HERBERT HOOVER and CHARLES CURTIS
(From the author's collection)

Birth: January 25, 1860.
Age on Inauguration Day (March 4, 1933):
73 years, 1½ months.
Death: February 8, 1936.

1932 presidential nominee—
Socialist Party

Norman Thomas

Born November 20, 1884, in Marion, Ohio; died December 19, 1968, in Huntington, New York. Married Frances Violet Stewart on September 1, 1910; they had six children.

Norman Mattoon Thomas was the son of Presbyterian minister Welling Evan Thomas and his wife Emma Mattoon. Norman's grandfather had arrived in America from Wales in 1824. As a boy Norman delivered the local

newspaper, owned by Warren Harding. The future socialist had a quiet, orthodox upbringing. Thomas attended Bucknell University as a freshman. The next year an uncle paid for his education at Princeton University. He graduated from Princeton in 1905 as valedictorian.

Thomas accepted a position as a social worker in lower Manhattan, trying to determine whether he wanted to go to seminary or do something else with his life. He worked with some of the poorest of New York's inhabitants, the Irish immigrants. After a year in New York, he took a leisurely trip around the world, then settled down as an assistant pastor in a tenement neighborhood church in New York. Thomas also began studies at the Union Theological Seminary where he was exposed to the Social Gospel movement. That theology was less concerned with saving souls as it was with nonviolent social revolution. Thomas would later credit the Social Gospel writings of Walter Rauschenbusch for being instrumental in making him a socialist. He was ordained a Presbyterian minister in 1911, and became pastor at a Harlem church. Thomas remained for seven years, involved as much in a social ministry as in a religious one.

The Reverend Thomas strenuously opposed America's entry into World War I. His pacifism accelerated his movement into the socialist camp, but he was already headed that direction because of his belief that capitalism was inherently unjust and exploitive of its workers. In time Thomas would sever all ties with organized religion. In 1917 Thomas and Roger Baldwin established the Civil Liberties Bureau of the American Union Against Militarism. That Bureau became the American Civil Liberties Union, a group in which Thomas was active until his death. In 1918 Thomas officially became a member of the Socialist Party, and also gave up his position as pastor. His wife's wealth enabled him to work full-time on the socialist cause. When Thomas became active in the party, socialism was in a dramatic decline in membership and support. Postwar prosperity sapped socialism of its strength among the disaffected. The smaller the movement got, the more splintered it became as internal bickering became magnified. Thomas's pacifism and anti-government rhetoric made him a member of various lists of "subversives."

Thomas went to work for the Fellowships of Reconciliation, a group of religious pacifists and reformers. Thomas started the group's monthly magazine and was its editor until 1921. From 1921 until 1922 he was an editor of the radical *Nation* magazine. From 1922 until 1937 Thomas was codirector of an educational arm of the Socialist Party called the League for Industrial Democracy. Under the League's auspices, Thomas gave thousands of speeches through the years. He was not a believer in the Marxist class struggle theory, but he did favor public ownership of the means of production and distribution of products and services. He was a union activist, spoke often and approvingly about the upheavals caused by the Bolsheviks in Russia, and also embraced civil rights issues in the United States. His notoriety from all these activities made him, after

Eugene Debs's death in 1926, the leader of the main branch of American socialism.

In 1924 Thomas was the socialist candidate for governor of New York. Over the next seven years he ran for New York mayor twice, Congress, the state senate, and alderman. Starting in 1928, he ran for president every election through 1948. The Great Depression temporarily increased socialism's appeal. As the presidential nominee in 1932, Thomas got almost 900,000 votes, three times what he received four years earlier. It was a fleeting gain, as the party never got more than one percent of the vote after that.

Thomas opposed the New Deal, seeing it as solely concerned with material well-being and ignoring moral issues. He visited Moscow in 1937, just when the show trials were commencing. The obvious brutality and fraud of the regime made him opposed to communism in general and Stalin in particular. As World War II loomed, Thomas argued that America should remain out of the war — he knew fascism was evil, but he feared America's becoming involved in a global war would end true democracy in this country. After Pearl Harbor, Thomas resigned himself to American involvement, but he tried to bring attention to alleged violations of civil liberties. He opposed the internment of Japanese Americans, and was quick to denounce the dropping of the atomic bombs that ended the war in Japan in 1945. He frequently attacked Franklin Roosevelt as having abandoned the New Deal in the cause of pursuing the war.

After Thomas's 1948 defeat for president, his sixth in a row, he urged that the Socialist Party abandon its political party function and just focus on education. His wing of socialism did that. For decades Norman Thomas defended unpopular causes and people. He was charming, humorous, and genuinely interested in the welfare of the common man. He wrote numerous books and countless articles, spoke tirelessly, always spreading his message of a socialist economy.

THOMAS BIBLIOGRAPHY

Fleischman, Harry. *Norman Thomas, a Biography: 1884–1968.* New York (1964).

Gorham, Charles. *Leader at Large, the Long and*

NORMAN THOMAS and JAMES H. MAURER
(From the collection of David J. and Janice L. Frent)

Fighting Life of Norman Thomas. New York (1970).

Johnpoll, Bernard K. *Pacifist's Progress: Norman Thomas and the Decline of American Socialism.* Chicago (1970).

Seidel, Murray B. *Norman Thomas: Respectable Rebel.* Syracuse (1967).

Swanberg, W.A. *Norman Thomas, the Last Idealist.* New York (1976).

1932 vice presidential nominee— Socialist Party

James H. Maurer

Born April 15, 1864, in Reading, Pennsylvania; died March 16, 1944, in Reading. Married Mary Missimer on April 15, 1886; they had two children.

James Hudson Maurer was one of four sons (one died as an infant) of James D. and Sarah Lorah Maurer. The father of the future socialist was a shoemaker, policeman, and railroad worker, who died in a smallpox epidemic when James was eight years old. His mother could not care for all three boys, and thus James spent time with different relatives. He rarely attended school. Instead, at age ten he started work at a hardware plant and earned two cents an hour, 50 hours a week, for two and a half years. After other jobs, James took up the machinist trade.

When James was 16, a fellow machinist and labor organizer named Tom King took an interest in him. King learned that James could not read, and spent several nights a week teaching him. King also helped make him a labor and political activist. James joined the Knights of Labor, one of the earliest and a secret labor organizations in the country, and worked in dissident political movements, including the Populists. After having jobs as a machinist, steam fitter, and plumber, in 1891 James went into business in Reading with his brother Harry. Over the next few years, his labor and political activism caused him to be blacklisted for employment, may have led to his business going bankrupt, and caused him to move to other towns. In 1897, he joined the Socialist Labor Party. He was fired as a foreman at a Coatesville plant after leading a carpenter's strike. Blacklisted again, he moved back to Reading in 1901. There unionization had progressed enough that he could find work.

In Maurer's first year back in Reading he ran as a Socialist for city controller, and in 1902 he ran for the Pennsylvania General Assembly. The Knights of Labor died out and Maurer joined the American Federation of Labor. Beginning in 1904 Maurer represented Pennsylvania on the AFL's national executive committee. In 1906 he was the Socialist Party gubernatorial candidate. In 1910 he was elected from Reading as the only Socialist in the state General Assembly, was defeated in 1912, but again elected in 1914 and 1916. In the legislature Maurer introduced bills on labor issues, such as creating a workers' compensation program, providing widow, orphan, old age and blind pensions, protections for mine and tunnel workers, and providing protections for strikes and other labor actions. Maurer's union activism propelled him to the presidency of the Pennsylvania State Federation of Labor in 1912, a post he would hold until 1928.

Maurer was a national leader in opposing American involvement in World War I in Europe. It is the "laboring man," Maurer argued, who "will be called upon to fight the capitalists' battles for them." After a debate in New York he was quoted as having said "to hell with the American flag," which was a misrepresentation of his remarks. In the state General Assembly Maurer was the only member not to vote to support President Woodrow Wilson's breaking off of diplomatic relations with Germany and the arming of merchant ships. His explanation was shouted down by other legislators.

Maurer's outspoken war opposition gave him substantial Socialist support for president in 1916, but he finished second in a national party referendum to choose a nominee. A historian of labor political parties wrote that had "a convention selected the standard bearers, it is quite possible that [Maurer] would have been the candidate" (Fine, p. 306). His war opposition helped defeat him for another term in the General Assembly in 1918. He was a target of the local press as a German subversive. In the 1920s the most explosive issue dividing Socialists was their attitude towards the Soviet Union. Maurer remained strongly pro-Soviet. He was harassed by governmental officials, and on three occasions was denied a passport to attend international conferences. He became a symbol of radicalism during the red scare at the end of the decade, and a target of newspaper and other public attacks.

Despite setbacks in most of the country, by 1927 socialism was in the ascendancy in Reading. According to a leading historian of American socialism, the success "was due largely to the remarkable personality of James Hudson Maurer ... conservative in his Socialism, traditional in his unionism, pleasant, steady, and good-natured, Maurer was a figure popular in both labor and Socialist circles" (Shannon, p. 188). In 1927 Socialists took control of the Reading city government, electing a mayor and two city councilman, one of whom was

Maurer. Maurer was called the "real leader" of the Socialist government.

In 1928 Maurer retired from the presidency of the state AFL. That same year he was nominated for vice president with Norman Thomas as the presidential nominee. They were nominated again in 1932. The party at its 1934 national convention called for mass resistance to preparations for the war that threatened in Europe, a general strike by all workers, and for taking control of the government should capitalism and democracy fall during the war crisis...." Maurer stood against such militancy, and said that Norman Thomas was among the "betrayers of democracy." Maurer was defeated for the U.S. Senate from Pennsylvania in 1934. He stayed with the party for another two years, but publicly resigned on July 7, 1936, denouncing a "trend towards communism."

Maurer had become seriously ill with a heart ailment after the 1932 election, and became partially paralyzed in 1933. He continued to write, including completing his memoirs in 1938 and writing for socialist periodicals. His wife of over 57 years died five months before he did in 1944.

MAURER BIBLIOGRAPHY

The Norman Thomas biographies listed in his bibliography contain useful material on Maurer.

Fine, Nathan. *Labor and Farmer Parties in the United States, 1828–1928*. New York (1961, reprint of 1928 edition).

Goroff, Daniel Jesse. "James Hudson Maurer: Socialist Labor Leader." Unpublished master's thesis, University of North Carolina, Chapel Hill (1969).

Hendrickson, Kenneth E., Jr. "The Socialists of Reading, Pennsylvania and World War I — A Question of Loyalty." *Pennsylvania History* 36 (1969), pp. 430–450.

Kane, Sylvia K. "James Hudson Maurer: Socialist Legislator." Unpublished master's thesis, Kutztown State College (1980).

Maurer, James Hudson. *It Can Be Done: The Autobiography of James Hudson Maurer*. New York, (1938).

Phillips, Raymond J., Jr. "The Socialist Party in Reading, Pennsylvania." Unpublished master's thesis, University of North Carolina (1964).

Shannon, David. *The Socialist Party of America: A History*. Chicago (1967, reprint of 1955 ed.).

Stetler, Henry G. *The Socialist Movement in Reading, Pennsylvania*. Storrs, Conn. (1943).

Election of 1936

NOMINATION

Republican Party Convention (21st): June 9–12, 1936, at the Municipal Auditorium, Cleveland, Ohio. *President*—Alfred Landon, nominated on the first ballot with 984 votes out of 1,003 cast. *Vice president*—Frank Knox, nominated unanimously on the first ballot.

Democratic Party Convention (27th): June 23–27, 1936, at Convention Hall, Philadelphia, Pa. *President*—Franklin D. Roosevelt, nominated by acclamation. *Vice president*—John Nance Garner, nominated by acclamation.

National Union Party. The party did not have a convention, but on August 13, 1936, the National Union for Social Justice, an organization spearheaded by radio preacher Father Charles Coughlin, began its convention in Cleveland. It endorsed on an 8,152 to 1 vote, the ticket announced on June 19. The platform was written by the two candidates and the priest at Father Coughlin's home *President*—William Lemke. *Vice president*— Thomas C. O'Brien.

GENERAL ELECTION, November 3, 1936

Popular Vote

Roosevelt	27,747,636
Landon	16,679,543
Lemke	892,793
Others	325,000

Electoral Vote

Roosevelt-Garner — 523 (46 states)

Landon-Knox — 8 (2 states)

Winners

Franklin D. Roosevelt, 32nd president

John Nance Garner, 32nd vice president

Losers

Alfred Landon, Frank Knox, William Lemke, Thomas O'Brien

---

*1936 presidential nominee —
Republican Party*

Alf Landon

Full name: Alfred Mossman Landon.

State represented: Kansas.

Birth: September 9, 1887, in West Middlesex, Pennsylvania.

Age on Inauguration Day (January 20, 1937): 49 years, 4½ months.

Education: Marietta (Ohio) Academy; University of Kansas, 1904–8 (LL.B.).

Religion: Methodist.

Ancestry/prominent relatives: First Landons arrived in Massachusetts in 1640s from England; his mother's family (Mossman) arrived from Scotland in 1781; Nancy Landon Kassebaum (daughter), U.S. senator from Kansas. Howard Baker (married Nancy Kassebaum in 1996), U.S. senator from Tennessee.

Occupation: Oil business.

Public office: Governor of Kansas, January 9, 1933–January 11, 1937; unsuccessful Republican nominee for president, 1936.

Death: October 12, 1987, in Topeka, at age 100 years, 1 month.

Burial: Mount Hope Cemetery, Topeka, Kansas.

Home: Farm outside of Topeka; home resembles Monticello.

Personal Characteristics: 5'8" tall, wire-rimmed glasses, reddish-brown eyes, thinning hair.

Father: John Manuel Landon (April 23, 1857–April 27, 1938); a businessman.

Mother: Anne Mossman (1856–1914); married May 12, 1886; daughter of Reverend William H. Mossman and Susanna (Houston) Mossman.

Siblings: Helen (1889–1896); died in a diphtheria epidemic.

First wife: Margaret Fleming (?–June 29, 1918); married January 9, 1915.

Children: Alfred M., Jr., died in infancy. Margaret Anne (Peggy) (April 8, 1917–); married William M. Mills, Jr., in October, 1941.

Second wife: Theo Cobb (September 2, 1897–July 21, 1996); married January 15, 1930.

Children: Nancy Josephine (July 29, 1932–); married John Philip Kassebaum, divorced. She served as a U.S. senator from 1979–1997. Married former Senator Howard Baker on December 7, 1996. John Cobb (Jack) (December 28, 1934–).

Historic sites/memorials: Kansas State University conducts the Alfred M. Landon Lectures on Public Issues. Landon's Monticello-like home still stands outside of Topeka (private).

It is Alf Landon's lot to be remembered as one of the greatest losers of presidential election history. Though the most widely accepted poll of the electorate, which was conducted by the *Literary Digest,* stated that Landon would retire Franklin Roosevelt after one term, instead Landon himself was retired from elective politics after winning only two states. For 50 years thereafter this symbol of defeat would occasionally emerge from political retirement, but his moment on the national stage was fleeting indeed.

There was nothing resembling rags to riches in this candidate's background. Alfred's father was a prosperous oil company superintendent, his mother the educated daughter of a minister. Though the family was then living in Elba, Ohio, Alfred was born in his grandparents' house in West Middlesex, Pennsylvania. The father brought the family back to Ohio soon thereafter. Four years later the Landons moved to Marietta, Ohio, and there Alfred spent the remainder of his childhood. Never excelling in school, Alfred nonetheless was a bright lad who enjoyed reading, but apparently only on subjects that were not schoolwork. Politics were a family staple. The senior Landon, John, was county Republican chairman for a time but changed parties because he opposed GOP stalwarts Mark Hanna and Joseph Foraker. Sports also interested young Alfred, but a dislocated shoulder suffered while playing football when he was 14 ended that budding career.

Ohio held John Landon until 1904, when Kansas Natural Gas Company enticed Alfred's father to the Sunflower State. During the summer that year the family moved to Independence, and in the fall Alfred began studies at the University of Kansas. After only a year he transferred to the school of law at the university. He finally was a serious student, but still sociable and popular. As a fraternity leader he kept an almost paternal eye on the morals of his "brothers" by trying to prohibit gambling, encourage Bible study, outlaw visits in the private rooms after 8:30 on week nights, and otherwise maintain strict discipline and attention to studies. This did not prevent the future governor from being a member of the campus drinking society. It was at campus politics, however, that Landon found his particular success. His skills earned him the nickname of "the Fox."

Though he received his law degree in 1908, that profession held him only long enough for admission to the state bar. He then accepted a job as a bookkeeper at an Independence bank. By 1911, with a few prudent investments from his savings from the bank salary, and with some borrowed money and investments of three other men, he formed an oil company called A.M. Landon & Co. The company proved a great success. It remained an independent, operating in southern Kansas and northern Oklahoma. Landon acquired a small fortune as reward for his labor and business acumen.

While making a mark in the business world, Landon was also cutting a swath through the political one. As a Bull Moose progressive in 1912, Landon organized his county for Theodore Roosevelt. It was with the progressive Republicans that Landon would remain throughout his career. In 1914, he was elected county chairman for the splinter party, and two years later the group returned home to the Republicans. Married in 1915, he was widowed three years later when his wife died of meningitis. Leaving their infant daughter in the care of her grandparents, Alfred enlisted in the army in 1918 and served

with a chemical warfare division. He was still in the United States when the armistice was signed. Landon returned to Kansas and his oil company. Ten years later he would be a millionaire.

Landon was a close adviser of the new governor, Harry Allen. Allen represented the progressive wing of the party and his tenure placed him, and Landon, at odds with the conservative wing of the party. In June 1922, Landon became Allen's private secretary, but three months later he resigned due to boredom.

Republican conservatives took control of the state in 1922. Two years later, Landon's gubernatorial candidate was defeated in the Republican primary. The Ku Klux Klan was struggling with some success for a foothold in Kansas. Landon backed the independent candidacy of Emporia newspaperman William Allen White for governor because the nominees of the two major parties were straddling the Klan issue. White lost badly, but the Klan soon disappeared anyway.

Despite this brief defection, Landon remained a major force in state Republican politics. From 1924 until 1928, Landon concentrated on the oil business. In 1928, he reemerged not only to manage the successful gubernatorial campaign of Republican progressive Clyde Reed, but he was also named chairman of his party's state central committee. Reed won with the highest popular vote ever received by a Kansas governor, while Herbert Hoover received the highest percentage of the vote in state history for president. Landon became a major cog in the Reed machinery. As party chairman and gubernatorial confidant, Landon tried to influence the governor to balance appointments between the conservative old guard faction and the progressives. The effort was in vain, as Governor Reed was not conciliatory towards the conservatives. In the 1930 primary Reed was beaten, and Landon and his lieutenants lost their party positions.

While sitting in the political wilderness, Landon turned full-time to his faltering business. A decline in oil prices had been accelerated by the discovery of the spectacular East Texas Oil Field. Landon and Company was in jeopardy. In 1929, along with other independents, the Kansas oilman organized the Independent Petroleum Association of America. As a director of the Association, he fought in 1930 against a major pipeline company that wished to abandon its longstanding commitments to take the oil of the small independents. When efforts by the federal government to resolve the dispute failed, Landon joined a nationwide boycott by the small producers. He saw the need for increased regulation of the industry, and said "the time has come about for return of the [Theodore] Roosevelt policies in dealing with huge combinations and mergers that tend to produce monopolies...." A temporary truce, with resumed purchases for a short time, was achieved in February 1931. Landon then shifted the battle to the state legislature to gain regulation of the intrastate pipelines. He organized a lobbying effort for the desired legislation. The pressure won the changes Landon had sought, including regulation of production and also pipeline distribution.

The Kansas independent oilman not only was involved in the lobbying effort on the state level but was frequently in Washington to apply pressure for congressional action. This continuing fight over three years led Landon inexorably into greater involvement with the government. Without the petroleum industry conflict, he probably would not have become a candidate for governor in 1932. The announcement was officially made on January 20, 1932. Trying to run a harmony campaign in the midst of bitter party differences was not easy, but it worked. A strenuous personal effort, strong organization, and sizeable newspaper support carried the primary for Landon, with 160,000 votes to his conservative opponent's 59,000. Democratic Governor Harry Woodring was the next test, and the hurdle seemed severe. With the "Hoover" Depression deepening nationwide, but nowhere more painfully than in Kansas, any Republican's chances seemed minuscule. Particularly dangerous to Landon was the entry of maverick Republican Dr. John R. Brinkley. Even so, Landon won with 278,500 to 273,000 for Governor Woodring and 244,600 for Brinkley. Debate was frequent as to whether Brinkley's entry as a candidate helped Landon or the Democrat more, but it is significant that the Republicans not only won the governorship but all other statewide races.

Inaugurated on January 9, 1933, Landon plunged into the task with fervor. During the first two-year term the governor lowered taxes, fought successfully for reorganization of state government and worked to lower utility rates. Efficiency in government was mandated by the harsh economic times. Freedom from special interest lobbyists was sought by creation of a permanent legislative committee to advise the governor and legislature on tax matters. A crisis developed when withdrawals from Kansas banks by out-of-state depositors threatened to degenerate into a bank run. Calling together state bank leaders, the governor received their agreement to a limit on withdrawals. The necessary legislation was rammed through in the span of two years to avert the accelerating danger of bank collapse.

Landon was not loath to use his appointive power to encourage individual legislators to move on his proposals. Frequent arm twisting in private meetings also cajoled those not convinced of the political desirability of his measures. After one legislative session, direct appropriations had been reduced by 25 percent. Taxes had been lowered by over ten million dollars. Restrictions on the weights of motor vehicles on the state's highways were imposed. Lower car-tag fees were set. The poll tax was eliminated. In these and many other ways Landon sought to streamline government, make it cheaper, its tax burden lighter, and its aid to the Depression-scarred Kansan larger.

Relief from unemployment and the poverty it caused was the greatest demand of government. Landon asked Harry Hopkins, President Roosevelt's administrator of Federal Emergency Relief, to allocate aid not only on the basis of physical need but also with consideration for the educational needs of the youth. A loan-program for indigent students was proposed by Landon when the national government seemed slow to respond. Kansas's agricultural industry was reeling under the blows of the Depression as much if not more than other businesses. The governor asked that all railroads serving the state reduce the shipping rates for agricultural products during the emergency.

While significant, even frightening affairs of state government were being faced, Landon also was beset with a political crisis. On August 7, 1933, a federal bank examiner disclosed that the state treasury books were not in order. The son of one of the state's leading business figures, Warren Finney, was implicated. The scandal involved sale of school fund bonds and it appeared to involve politicians throughout state government. The governor himself was not above the public suspicion. His ethics were drawn into question on the state's newspapers' front pages when it was revealed that his 1932 campaign had received a contribution from Warren Finney. Another check, in the amount of $10,000 had been made out to Mrs. Landon in March 1933. It was revealed that this check was return of money, with interest, that she had invested in a Finney business. Finney's son, Ronald, was convicted and served 11 years in the penitentiary.

With his first term an imperfect but nonetheless clear record of achievement, Landon prepared to run for a second two years in office. He prided himself on cooperating with the federal government during these first two Depression years. It was not all harmony, however, as Landon called parts of the New Deal a danger to personal liberty. The only issue used by the Democrats was the Finney scandal, but there was never evidence that could be used persuasively on that score. The final margin was no landslide, but any victory in this greatest of nationwide Democratic sweeps was sweet indeed. He won with 422,000 votes to the Democrat's 360,000. In 1932, when elected to his first term, Landon had been the only Republican governor elected west of the Mississippi. In 1934, he was the only Republican governor elected, period.

The second term continued the direction set during the first: economy, progressive relief legislation, and postponing of some desperately needed reforms, such as upgrading the prisons, until the money could be found. The claim was frequently made, and was well-founded, that Landon was a tax-reducing, yet budget-balancing chief executive.

With Roosevelt's popularity seemingly unassailable, and with very few Republican horses in the stable for 1936, speculation centered on Landon as a presidential candidate. Landon was aware of the vocal Republican faction of conservatives who rejected everything that the New Deal represented. Such men could rally around Herbert Hoover and undoubtedly go down to defeat again. Landon accepted the premise of the New Deal, that government must act imaginatively and directly to handle the economic disaster. He needed support from all party factions, and to some extent as the 1936 convention approached he curried favor in his public statements with both sides. By December of 1934, Landon for President clubs were organizing nationwide. The seriousness of his chances was not deemed great during this period, but Landon was willing to see how far it would go.

Waste and inefficiency in the New Deal became his campaign theme, even before he was a candidate. Other active candidates included Hoover, William Borah, and Frank Knox. Momentum within the party was building for Landon. "Frugal Alf" he was called, the wizard governor whose fiscal wonders had saved Kansas. He endorsed federal relief payments, but then declared his conservatism by saying, "There is no future on the relief roll," and that welfare should only be given to the neediest. The Gallup Poll showed him the clear party favorite. Trying not to antagonize, Landon occupied the important political middle ground and would not be budged from it. Landon's march was unstoppable, as he alone represented to countless Republicans the possibility, however slim, of victory. At the national convention in June, Borah, Knox, and some lesser candidates withdrew before the nomination for president had been made.

The vice presidency proved a ticklish problem. Landon finally agreed to accept Senator Arthur Vandenberg. The senator refused, and Frank Knox was then selected. The infamous *Literary Digest* pronouncements on the coming election began with a poll "revealing" that a majority of Americans opposed the New Deal. Republicans began to be optimistic. "Life, Liberty and Landon" was both the slogan, and to many conservatives, the true issue in the campaign, *i.e.*, life and liberty with Landon or communism and dictatorship with Roosevelt. For a few months Landon was alternately plagued by illness, indecisiveness, and preoccupation with Kansas problems.

Regardless of the tack taken, Landon's prospects seemed to be on the upswing in September. Not only the *Literary Digest*, but every other national sounding of opinion showed Landon the winner except for the Gallup Poll (George Gallup's reputation would deservedly soar after the election). The early fall elections held in Maine, the first state in the Union to vote, showed an impressive Landon-Knox victory. The omens were good that the old maxim, "As Maine goes, so goes the nation," would be fulfilled again. The tide definitely began to shift in late September, however, when Franklin Roosevelt finally took to the stump. Four tiring national tours by Landon were not enough to dispel the Roosevelt magic, the aura of confidence and hope that surrounded the president and made him invincible. Landon's poor speaking style contrasted embarrassingly with the Roosevelt magic tongue. The charges thrown by the Kansan became harsher: The president must answer "whether he intends to change the form of our government — whether labor, agriculture, and business are to be directed and managed by government." This was carefully planned strategy agreed to by Landon and Knox, and it was felt that even if Roosevelt won, the question would help restrain his radicalism during a second term.

During the last weeks of the campaign, Landon's reception had been growing increasingly strong, emotional, and positive. Years later he would say that while leaving St. Louis during this final week, with the cheers of his audience still ringing in his ears, he for the only time during the campaign felt he might win. By morning, and a quick night's sleep, the political realities had reasserted themselves and the delusion was gone. A last entry by the *Literary Digest* pollsters continued to show the Republican with a sizeable lead. The inevitable occurred on election day, and when defeat was clear Landon telegraphed the president, "The nation has spoken. Every American will accept the victory and work for the common cause of the good of our country. That is the spirit of Democracy. You have my sincere congratulations."

Defeated for president, out of office in Kansas, Landon returned to the Kansas oil business. His criticisms of the New Deal did not end. In a nationwide radio address in late 1937, he listed Social Security and the National Labor Relations Act as clear failures. Though remaining vocal, Landon had no illusions about the propriety of another presidential race. He declared in September 1937, that he would in no event be a candidate in 1940. This did not mean he would be disinterested in party affairs. Landon actively campaigned for forward-looking Republicans who would neither be reactionary on the New Deal nor blind supporters of its more radical aspects.

The fox in the White House had a trick to upset the Republicans as they headed into their 1940 national convention. Rumors began circulating that either Landon or his 1936 running mate, Frank Knox, would be lured into the cabinet to establish a coalition government during this period of intense international problems. The president invited Landon to lunch during May. Landon was wary. He expected the invitation to be withdrawn after he continued to criticize the Administration. The two adversaries met on May 22, 1940. No mention of a cabinet appointment was made. Knox was later appointed secretary of the navy.

Over the next 20 years, Landon remained politically active, but never again ran for office. He supported Tom Dewey and then Joe Martin for president in 1940, but backed Willkie in the general election. In 1944 he was with Dewey from the beginning. Landon spoke out forcefully about his fears that Roosevelt was becoming a near-dictator. Generally during World War II Landon was supportive of Roosevelt's foreign and military policies.

With Harry Truman's ascension to the presidency and the war over, Landon's and the country's chief concern was maintaining the peace. Formation of the United Nations was warmly endorsed by the former Kansas governor. Peace gestures towards the Democrats and the new president were made and noticed, causing Landon to be praised in many quarters for his conciliatory motives.

Politics was hardly Landon's only concern.

Profits from his oil business permitted him to diversify his interests. After the war he acquired considerable radio broadcast facilities in Kansas and Colorado. He early saw the future of television, not only commercially but politically. Presciently, he said that the day would come when a candidate would have to be "telegenic" to be elected.

Landon's 15-year control of the state Republican Party was broken in 1947 and 1948, many feeling that Landon was a continuing symbol, and even a cause, of party defeat. He finally lost control of the party organization. Resigning himself to a lesser role, Landon turned to national politics and the 1948 nomination. He hoped for a Robert Taft–Harold Stassen ticket, but saw both desires thwarted by his former favorite, Tom Dewey.

Rejected by his own state party, Landon withdrew from the hectic political pace and turned increasingly to his farm outside of Topeka. Landon could be counted on for support of Truman; he attacked Joe McCarthy's red-baiting; he supported intervention in Korea. Taft was his candidate in 1952, but continuing his string of defeats, Landon saw his favorite rejected and Dwight Eisenhower named instead.

Occasional brief returns to the national stage punctuated what was otherwise retirement. Landon became a fixture at national Republican conventions. Occasional comments on national affairs were offered. The "elder statesman" mantle settled securely around his shoulders as he remained strong and alert well into his nineties. In 1978, his name still worked magic in the Sunflower State. That year his daughter, Nancy Kassebaum, was elected a U.S. senator from Kansas.

Analysis of Qualifications

Alf Landon is remembered for two things — losing as badly as any candidate for president in history, and living interminably thereafter. There is much more to this former Kansas governor than that.

When his state reeled from the blows of economic disaster, Governor Landon rejected traditional conservative Republican dogma and pushed through an enlightened program of relief measures. The budget was balanced,

revenues brought in line with expenditures while taxes were being lowered. The New Deal was no bogeyman to this progressive Midwest politician, and he endorsed far more than he rejected in the programs that streamed out of Washington during the Depression. Still, there was always an independent streak in Landon, even a testiness at times. No man could count on Landon's unwavering, uncritical support on crucial national issues.

Landon was an intelligent, forceful man who unfortunately had no appeal as a public speaker. Folksy and plainspoken on the order of Harry Truman, Landon had no personal magnetism. Instead, he achieved fame as a doer, an accomplisher of fiscal miracles on the state level who could apply the same principles to the federal government. These were not miracles, but merely the careful blending of increased federal assistance with belt-tightening on the state. His business skills were honed in one of the fastest tracks imaginable, that of an independent oil man. He excelled at that high-risk, bold endeavor and would have been equally aggressive in the White House.

In foreign affairs, Landon early joined with those who rightly saw the dangers to America inherent in the mad schemes of European and Asian dictators who would control the world if permitted to do so. A Landon presidency during the late 1930s would not have had its head in the sand, but would have been preparing the country for an increasingly inevitable conflict. As a political leader he was a conciliator, wanting to bring factions together and reason with them. As president he would have cajoled, twisted, bribed and badgered with his appointive and other powers; he would have fought hard for his programs. He was innovative, and presented to his state's legislature schemes that predated some similar New Deal programs. He wanted government to help, but he did not want people to see the government as a permanent support. The crisis must be met sharply, but attention must be given not to let government become monolithic and immovable once the programs were in place. With the emergency past, the government would retrench. Whether he could have accomplished his call for an efficient, less dictatorial New Deal is certainly problematic, yet

Landon should be credited with the foresight not only in commending the sweeping national programs that were enacted, but also in recognizing early the dangers inherent in them.

For two terms Landon gave his state forceful and effective leadership. His ideas were in tune with the general concept of the national administration, one which most historians have credited with superior achievement. As governor, Landon revealed not only ingenuity, but also the legislative skills to see his measures passed. The responsibilities of the presidency are singularly awesome, and no preparation can be seen as truly adequate for that tremendous responsibility. Yet to the degree achievable, Alfred M. Landon seemed worthy of the presidency.

LANDON BIBLIOGRAPHY

"Alfred M. Landon Died at 100; Trounced by Roosevelt in '36." *New York Times* (October 13, 1987), pp. 1, 17.

Fadely, James Philip. "The Making of a Landslide: The Presidential Election of 1936." Unpublished doctoral dissertation, Indiana University (1990).

McCoy, Donald R. *Landon of Kansas.* Lincoln, Nebr. (1966).

Family information was provided by Judy Markley, personal secretary to Mr. Landon, and by the Kansas State Historical Society Library, with assistance also rendered by Senator Nancy Landon Kassebaum.

---

*1936 vice presidential nominee —
Republican Party*

Frank Knox

Full name: William Franklin Knox.

State represented: Illinois.

Birth: January 1, 1874, Boston, Massachusetts.

Age on Inauguration Day (January 20, 1937): 63 years, ½ month.

Education: Jefferson Grade School, Grand Rapids, Michigan; quit Grand Rapids High School as a junior to go to work; Alma College in Alma, Michigan, 1893–1898; completed high school curriculum but attended only three years of college; awarded degree from Alma in 1912, after "specified readings" completed.

Religion: Congregational.

Ancestry: Of Scotch ancestry on father's side; English on mother's.

Occupation: Newspaper publisher.

Public offices: Unsuccessful candidate for Republican nomination, governor of New Hampshire, 1924; unsuccessful candidate for Republican presidential nomination, 1936; unsuccessful Republican nominee for vice president, 1936; U.S. Secretary of the Navy, July 11, 1940–April 28, 1944.

Home: Large red brick colonial house at city edge of Manchester, New Hampshire, where wife remained even when Knox moved to Chicago.

Death: April 28, 1944, Washington, D.C., at age 70 years, 4 months.

Burial: Arlington National Cemetery.

Personal characteristics: 5'9½" tall, gray eyes, red hair, stocky.

Father: William Edwin Knox (April 24, 1847–August 30, 1933); born in St. John's, New Brunswick; businessman, oyster-market owner.

Mother: Sarah Collins Barnard (1849–September 6, 1918).

Siblings: A sister died in infancy. Emma (c. 1875–January 18, 1951); married Herbert Fairfield. Edith (November 13, 1880 (?)–November 13, 1909); married Jay Malette. Sarah (January 18, 1883–August 30, 1967), on May 4, 1902 married Fred Reed. Elizabeth (February 5, 1885–August, 1951); married Earl Cassada.

Wife: Annie Reid (October 13, 1875–September 22, 1958); married December 29, 1898, daughter of Darius Reid of Alma, Michigan.

Children: None.

Newspaper publisher, "Rough Rider" under Teddy Roosevelt, Republican nominee for vice president, secretary of the navy in the cabinet of Democrat Franklin Roosevelt — these are just a few of the high points of the life of Frank Knox. He was an open-minded, vigorous, restless American who in business earned a fortune but never seemed satisfied, in politics commenced his career as a Progressive but concluded it as a much more conservative

ALF LANDON (left) and FRANK KNOX
(From the collection of David J. and Janice L. Frent)

Republican, in the military volunteered for two wars as a soldier and fought even more significantly in a third as civilian head of the Navy. Action, not reflection, characterized Frank Knox.

Both parents had been Canadian natives who entered the United States as children. Frank's father had been trained as a plumber and steamfitter but became a businessman. He would have little success to show for it. Both sides of Frank's family were pious, stern Presbyterians, whose legacy of religious morals and discipline helped direct their descendants.

From the first, William Franklin Knox was simply called "Frank," perhaps to distinguish him from his father whose name also was William. After years of struggle, the family experienced considerable good fortune in the devastating fire in Boston during 1879. Their oyster market escaped the blaze, making the elder Knox's lease on the property extremely valuable. Selling out to another, he used the substantial profit to purchase a lobster canning business in Nova Scotia and moved there in 1880. The Knox luck returned to normal and with little to show for a year of effort the Knoxes returned to the United States and moved to Grand Rapids, Michigan. There they opened a grocery.

In 1885, having turned 11, young Frank wanted to help the struggling family's finances. He stayed in school, but got his first experience in the newspaper world by delivering both a morning and evening newspaper. At age 15, Frank dropped out of school and got a job as a salesman with a wholesale book and stationery company. He was an excellent salesman, but the Panic of 1893 severely cut into the company's business and Frank, the youngest of the salesmen and without a family to support, seemed the proper one to be laid off. His minister advised him to attend college and get a new start on a career. A Michigan Presbyterian school which took its name from the town in which it was located, Alma, would give him the education he needed to get a high school diploma. He could then get a college degree there as well. Knox excelled in athletics and social organizations more than in academics, mainly because he was too busy with outside activities to study hard. Still he maintained a "B" average, starred in football, played baseball, was a member of the YMCA, and worked at sign painting and other odd jobs to pay his way. At the start of his senior year in college, he was forced to drop out to work full time at a business venture that had soured. The spring semester commenced in January 1898, and at the same time the prospects of war against Spain were soaring. When war seemed inevitable, Frank dropped out of school again, rode his bicycle almost one hundred miles with a friend to a military camp and there tried to enlist. He never would return to Alma College, but got his degree in 1912 after completing certain reading requirements.

Knox was not able to enlist immediately in the militia, so back by bicycle he went to Alma to recruit other students. The company he organized signed up, but Knox was absent because he was attending the funeral of his girlfriend's father. Annie Reid would later that same year become Frank's wife. By the time he rejoined his comrades, it was not possible to enlist. He persuaded the authorities to permit him to accompany the others to Tampa, Florida, where training was to occur. The Rough Riders were also being organized. Countless thousands of adventurous young, and some not so young, men were clamoring to get on the regiment with the colorful Theodore Roosevelt. Once at Tampa, Knox visited the Rough Rider camp, talked to another Michigan recruit who promised he would mention Knox to "the colonel." An interview with Roosevelt was arranged, and on June 4, Knox was personally sworn into the Rough Riders by the future president. It was a unique regiment, initially consisting only of men from four southwestern American territories, but soon supplemented by college men from the rest of the country. There were full-blooded Indians alongside Yale and Harvard men. There was also at least one Alma man. The association with the Rough Riders would prove an invaluable boost to Knox's career.

Once in Cuba, Knox fought with the Rough Riders in each of the major engagements, including the charge up San Juan Hill. No battle wound was inflicted, but he did suffer from an equally debilitating bout with malaria and dysentery. He was placed on a hospital ship and returned to the mainland. For a time he was quarantined aboard for fear he had yellow fever, but that proved a false concern. On September 15, 1898, he was discharged and returned to Michigan.

While with Roosevelt's regiment, Knox had sent detailed letters of his exploits to his mother. At least two of these were printed in the Grand Rapids paper, and the publisher became interested in the young man. Knox was offered a reporter's position on the paper, and was also encouraged to assist another part owner of the paper in his campaign for the United States Congress. Knox's appeal as one of the Rough Riders was tapped to draw large crowds to rallies for the candidate. Soon Knox was giving short introductory speeches. Sometimes he told of his days in Cuba with "Teddy," but as he warmed to the task he was giving pure campaign pleas for the candidate. The campaign was a success for the candidate and his young campaign worker.

Beginning on the Grand Rapids *Herald* the same time as Knox was another prominent national Republican-in-the-making, future United States Senator Arthur Vandenberg. Knox was promoted quickly and added within a year to his reporter duties the responsibility of being city editor. In another year, December 1900, Knox was made circulation manager. Soon he felt that he had learned enough from his work on the *Herald* that he was ready to start his own paper. With the investment of John Adams Muehling, a printer and bookbinder he had met, and with the considerable help of another newspaper man, Chase Osborn, Knox bought the Sault Ste. Marie Lake *Superior Journal*. The Grand Rapids paper offered him a sizeable raise to stay, but Knox was much more attracted to the adventure of being his own employer than the security of a salaried position. Knox's responsibilities besides being the publisher focused on soliciting advertisers and subscribers, the financial lifeblood of a newspaper. When the inaugural issue appeared on April 7, 1902, Knox declared that the new paper would be Republican in spirit, but not blind to political ills within that party. He soon established a reputation as a crusader, against the machine-dominated politics of the city and the lawlessness attendant in the presence of rowdy lumberjacks. At least one bullet hole was put through the paper's window. Only one fistfight occurred, however, and that ended with Knox throwing the first and only punch that sent an irate but thereafter cowed saloonkeeper sprawling.

Chase Osborn proved to be a financial angel for the paper, making timely infusions when bills had to be paid and no money was available. Within a year, the rocky course had been traversed and the paper had clearly established itself. Its competitor threw in the towel and sold out to Knox. The triumphant publisher declared gleefully, "I've got the *News-Record*." That initial victory, and the techniques of hard work, efficient management, and crusading editorial policy used to attain it, would become the hallmark of Knox's business career.

The Sault Ste. Marie publisher identified his paper strongly with the progressive policies of his old commander, President Theodore Roosevelt. Those reform views were applied to Knox's attempt to rid the city of boss rule. Backing some upset winners for the United States Congress and Senate helped establish Knox as an important political force in the state. Two years after starting his paper, Knox editorialized that Chase Osborn, fellow newspaperman and close friend, should be the Republican's candidate for governor. Osborn did not run that year, and the successful Republican candidate in 1904 remained in office until 1910. Osborn waited until the vacancy opened, and when it did he had Knox as his campaign manager. After Osborn gained the nomination with ease over two conservative rivals, Knox was tapped as chairman of the party's State Central Committee. Victory was theirs in November, but elected with Osborn was a conservative, old-guard Republican legislature that had little use for Osborn or his campaign manager. Within two years Knox's progressivism would leave him on the outside of the Michigan party, defeated and looking for a different arena to carry on the fight.

What split Knox and the regulars was the 1912 battle for president. Not surprisingly, Knox was as rabid a supporter of Theodore Roosevelt as could be found. President William Howard Taft had asked Knox to head his

Michigan campaign, and when the offer was made in 1911 it did not appear Roosevelt would be a candidate. However, Knox continued to encourage his former commander to enter the field, and even accused Roosevelt of cowardice when he refused to do so. Knox finally got his wish, but the Republican nomination went to Taft. Thus Knox was faced with the difficult decision of bolting the party. When Roosevelt committed to a third party Bull Moose campaign, Knox was with him. Surprisingly, in October Knox pulled up roots in Michigan and moved to Manchester, New Hampshire, where he had just bought an established newspaper. He had become disgusted with Michigan Republican politics, bored with the steady progress of his paper which seemed to have no more foes to conquer, and longed for the excitement of a new challenge.

On October 9, 1912, the first issue of Knox's Manchester *Leader* appeared on the streets. As he had in Michigan, Knox soon drove the competition out because he established his paper as the superior news source in the community. This time it only took nine months for his rival, the Manchester *Union*, to realize it could not compete. Knox also soon was involved in New Hampshire Republican politics. By 1915, he was firmly back in the Republican Party, his transgression into Progressive third party efforts now behind him.

When World War I erupted, Knox enlisted quickly. Because he was 43 years old, he feared he would not see any combat. He had criticized President Woodrow Wilson as being too proud to fight, and thus was pleased when the United States finally declared war in 1917. Knox decided to join the New Hampshire National Guard, and with help from his business and political contacts was selected for officer candidate school despite his age. After three strenuous months, Knox survived all the culling out of recruits who could not measure up to the tough physical, mental, and leadership standards and proudly received congratulations even from Theodore Roosevelt for his appointment as a captain. After being commissioned, he was made personnel officer at Camp Dix, New Jersey. After being promoted to major, he was placed in command of an ammunition train in an artillery brigade, leaving for Europe in the spring of 1918. He remained until February 1919, seeing action at St. Mihiel, Verdun, and Meuse-Argonne. After his return to the United States, he was actively involved in the American Legion, becoming state commander of the organization.

The following year, 1920, was a presidential election year. There was an easy choice for Knox to make, and that was to back General Leonard Wood for the nomination. Wood had also been a Rough Rider, was one of Roosevelt's closest advisers, and fell heir to the former president's support when Roosevelt died in 1919. Knox became Wood's floor manager at the national convention, with Frank Lowden and Hiram Johnson as the principal competition. A deadlock ensued, with the nominee being chosen in the archetypical smoke-filled room by a few kingmakers. Warren G. Harding emerged, but received only a lukewarm endorsement from Knox's paper.

Harding scandals helped lead to a Democrat's winning the New Hampshire governorship in 1922. A conservative Republican majority in the legislature was playing into the governor's hand by their obstructionist tactics. Knox feared for the future of his party. He announced in late 1923 that he would be a candidate for governor. His only opponent was John Winant, a 35-year-old political novice, who had the considerable advantage of being the scion of a long-established New Hampshire family, with millions of family dollars behind him. Knox blamed his narrow defeat in the party primary on the lavish spending by his opponent. That would be his only try for elective office, until 12 years later when he ran for president.

Just as had occurred in Michigan, Knox's victory over all business competitors took some of the excitement out of his work. Much time was spent on civic affairs. Besides the American Legion, other activities demanding Knox's time were the New England Council, a chamber of commerce-type organization, and the New Hampshire Co-Operative Association, which marketed farmers' goods. He took over as president of the co-op after a scandal involving other officers, but it soon failed due to pressure from other agricultural marketing businesses.

William Randolph Hearst, the owner of a

nationwide chain of highly successful news-papers, took notice of this inveterately suc-cessful New Hampshire publisher, and in Jan-uary of 1927 invited Knox to meet with him. Knox was aware that a job offer had to be the purpose of the invitation, and set what he thought were impossibly high requirements of salary and independence before he would con-sider the possibility. To his amazement, Hearst agreed with every demand. Soon Knox was in control of the three Boston newspapers. The next year, 1928, the skills Knox exhibited in Boston so impressed his employer that he was made general manager of all Hearst papers, 27 in all in 17 cities. His salary was rumored to be $100,000 per year, an incredible sum for his day. When towards the end of his tenure with Hearst the owner seemed to be interfer-ing too much in Knox's decisions, Knox resigned. Earlier difficulties with Hearst had also led to resignation, but each time Hearst refused to accept Knox's decision to quit. This time, to make sure there would be no repeti-tion of that result, Knox released his letter of resignation to the press. Both men publicly acted graciously towards the other, but Knox's decision to quit, effective January 1931, indi-cated he could not accept Hearst's interfer-ence.

Two months later the publisher of the Chi-cago *Daily News* died quite unexpectedly. The paper was therefore up for sale, and Knox con-tacted former vice president and Chicago banker Charles Gates Dawes to be an inter-mediary for him in the negotiations. The *Daily News* was an institution in Chicago, had the respect of newspapermen across the country, and it would be a rare honor to be the pub-lisher of so esteemed a paper. Knox won the bidding, and soon announced that he would not "Hearstify" the paper. The "sin, crime, and corruption" which were staples of the news for Hearst, would not become the focus of the dignified *Daily News*. President Hoover and former President Coolidge sent their congrat-ulations — Knox's victory was big news.

When Knox moved to Chicago his army reserve rank of colonel became his new title, and as "Colonel Knox" he would be known the rest of his life. The Colonel applied the efficiency and economy methods so effectively

employed elsewhere in his newspaper career. This meant, in the height of the Depression, considerable pruning of the staff. Over five hundred people were let go of the 1,775-per-son work force for the *Daily News*, hurting morale but greatly increasing the profitability of the paper.

Knox fit in well with other Chicago busi-nessmen. He cultivated their support and esteem. Soon he was admitted to the most prestigious clubs and joined the inner circle of business movers and shakers. After less than a year in Chicago, Knox was called upon by President Hoover to head a task force to reduce the hoarding of currency that was one result of the Depression bank failures. Knox orga-nized the country into districts, appointed state chairmen of the effort, but was largely unsuccessful in getting the American people to return their money to banks.

Unfortunately, one result of the move to Chicago was that Mrs. Knox had to remain behind in Manchester. An asthma condition made life in the already polluted air of Chicago too painful. She remained in their beautiful, spacious home in New Hampshire. Thus it was almost as a bachelor that Knox got in-volved in Illinois business and political life. His first substantial input into the politics of the state was to oppose the machine-backed Republican nominees for governor and Cook County (Chicago) state's attorney. For that disloyalty, Knox would not be forgiven by many of the regulars in the party. At least Knox did support Herbert Hoover over Frank-lin Roosevelt in the 1932 election.

For a few months, Knox remained hopeful and rather quiet editorially about the New Deal. Within a year, however, the *Daily News* began to rail against the danger of dictator-ship that seemed to Knox inherent in the New Deal's growing centralization of authority in Washington. In 1934, Knox was one of the most prominent speakers for Republicans across the country. A nationwide radio hookup on behalf of the Republican National Com-mittee made Knox well-known throughout the country. In his radio speech, Knox unfavorably compared the new Roosevelt to his old one. After the devastating defeat for the Republicans in 1934, at least Knox had established himself as a national spokesman for the party. Since he was one of the few Republicans who did not lose an election that year, if only because he did not run, he seemed somewhat available for the 1936 presidential race.

At first Knox refused to take speculation about the presidency seriously. In mid–1935, Hoover said he definitely would not be a candidate the following year, and encouraged Knox. This began to make the idea plausible. Knox was foresighted enough to realize that the choice was between himself and Alfred Landon, another survivor of the 1934 Republican debacle. Unlike Landon, who attempted to straddle the issues and appear as a Republican New Dealer, Knox was foursquare opposed to the management of the economy that the president was attempting. It seemed to strike at the very foundation of Knox's belief in free competitive business. Yet even in Illinois Knox was not the clear favorite, as the regulars continued to oppose him for his 1932 treachery when he supported Democratic candidates. Though he won the state primary in April, the margin was narrow and indeed he lost most of the state to Idaho Senator William Borah. Fortunately his margin in Chicago was so strong as to gain him a statewide majority. He remained optimistic almost up to the convention balloting, but finally conceded the race and even seconded Landon's nomination.

Arthur Vandenberg was first offered the vice presidential nomination, but Vandenberg refused and argued for Knox. The decision for the Illinois publisher came as a surprise to him, and he heard of his nomination over the radio while in a hotel restaurant. The campaign was strenuous and fruitless. One slip bothered him throughout the campaign, which solely consisted of saying that life insurance and bank accounts throughout the country were insecure. That bit of excess made bankers and businessmen nervous, and Knox was forced constantly to try to explain the remark. Harold Ickes, an old Knox friend, but now a close Roosevelt adviser, said after the campaign, "Frank Knox lost votes, in my judgment. He talked too much and talked too recklessly." Regardless of the validity of the remark, Knox seemed pleased to return to his newspaper business instead of becoming vice president.

During the next four years, Knox's papers were unrepentantly anti–Roosevelt. The various New Deal agencies that attempted to control the economy were anathema to Knox. He toured Europe and wrote articles for his paper, later published in a pamphlet, that compared the New Deal to the worst of the European dictatorships. Knox sincerely felt that the future of America was in jeopardy because of Roosevelt's domestic policies.

These attacks, however, never included criticism of the country's foreign policy. As the war in Europe grew increasingly likely to involve the United States, there was strong public sentiment for a coalition cabinet. Harold Ickes encouraged Roosevelt to appoint Knox to his cabinet. Both Landon and Knox were in strong consideration for a cabinet post, but Landon publicly rejected the idea even before an offer was made. In December 1939, Roosevelt offered the position of secretary of navy to the former Republican vice presidential nominee. Knox thought that unless at least one other Republican was offered a position as well, it would appear Knox was abandoning his party, and not participating in a coalition. Six months later the offer was renewed, with a concomitant offer to Henry Stimson, former Hoover cabinet official, to become secretary of war. Both men were written out of the Republican Party by an overreacting Republican national committee. To many, the appointments seemed to signal that the interventionists, and Knox was one of those, had taken control of foreign policy.

Knox applied his ideas of economy and efficiency to a huge Department of the Navy. He plunged into familiarizing himself with his work, and visited bases throughout the world. Preparedness was the key, and a large navy was needed. Knox was beginning to feel that the country was prepared, and thus it was with great shock on the infamous December 7, 1941, that he heard of the Japanese attack. His reaction was that the message was garbled and it must be the Philippines. "No, sir," was the reply. "This is Pearl." It was Knox who informed the president of the attack. Four days later, Knox was at Pearl Harbor for a personal inspection. His recommendation that the navy commanders involved be replaced was accepted.

For the next three years, Knox was tirelessly involved in war operations. He maintained a considerable degree of civilian control over the navy even in wartime, and kept teamwork at the forefront, not individual honors. In April 1944, with the war in Europe of questionable outcome, but with the Pacific front seemingly under control, Knox suffered a heart attack while attending the funeral of his first partner in the newspaper business. A few days later the secretary suffered a far more serious seizure. He died four days later.

Analysis of Qualifications

A few men stand out in the list of defeated candidates whose nomination for one of these two great national offices came before they had ever served in any public office. In 1940, Wendell Willkie would receive that distinction. Four years earlier, a vigorous, outspoken publisher of one of the country's great newspapers also achieved that honor. Frank Knox had for 34 years aggressively managed a series of outstandingly successful newspapers, had dabbled in political campaigns to various degrees of involvement, and had one abortive attempt at elective office, the governorship of New Hampshire. He had been born in Massachusetts, grew up in Michigan, moved to New Hampshire and later to Boston, and for five years before his 1936 nomination for vice president lived in Chicago. Perhaps the most nomadic of the national nominees, and also among the least experienced in public office, "the Colonel" was also an intriguing study in what-might-have-been.

A few salient features of the Knox personality were his restless energy and his drive to achieve. His frequent moves were a history of taking the risk of moving into unfamiliar territory, and quickly succeeding. Hard work and honesty were trademarks. During the early part of his career he was a Theodore Roosevelt progressive; during his last ten years he was a conservative opponent of Franklin Roosevelt. During those intervening decades he grew in his understanding of the American free enterprise system, and never failed to capitalize on its possibilities for financial success. Among the other great newspapermen who have been nominated at a national convention, he shares little with Horace Greeley, whose fame came from his crusading zeal, at times eccentrically expressed, for countless causes. Knox was a hard-headed businessman. He believed in and worked for good government, but such interests never dominated his paper. The profit motive was not unimportant to Knox's moving from place to place, but more significant was his feeling that he had achieved all that was possible with a particular paper and wanted new challenges.

As secretary of the navy, Knox soon learned the mysteries of a department about which he had little prior knowledge. He worked well with others, and was particularly credited with having selected a superior staff to assist him. He presided over a tremendous navy build-up, applying his hard-won skills at business to the burgeoning demands of the military.

As president, Knox would have been able to apply considerable business acumen, but little political experience. He had never had to work with a legislature, and was used to being an unchallenged boss. There were few negotiations or compromises in Knox's background, and political leadership would have been quite a change. But vigor, quick learning of a new task, and intelligence were Knox's trademarks. If he came to office during the period between 1936 and 1940, he would have encouraged a strong military build-up in anticipation of a conflict in Europe. His foreign policy agreed completely with that of the president, but he would have backed away from much of the New Deal domestic programs. He was a satisfactory choice for vice president who might have performed quite well.

KNOX BIBLIOGRAPHY

Beasley, Norman. *Frank Knox, American.* New York City (1936).

Cash, Kevin. *Who the Hell Is William Loeb?* Manchester (1975).

Hlava, Milton Edward. "Frank Knox, Public Servant: A Biography." Unpublished thesis for the degree of Bachelor of Science in Journalism, University of Illinois, Urbana (1933).

Knox, Frank. *We Planned It That Way.* New York City (1938).

Lobdell, George Henry, Jr. "A Biography of Frank Knox." Unpublished doctoral dissertation, University of Illinois, Urbana (1954).

Lobdell, George H. "Frank Knox," in Paolo

Coletta, ed. *American Secretaries of the Navy.* Naval Institute Press (1980), vol. 2.

Some family information provided by Sally Reed Hayden Fisher, Fort Myers, Florida, with valuable assistance who rendered by Professor George Lobdell, Ohio University, and Adaline Lowe and Helen Hayden, Cassopolis, Michigan.

1936 presidential nominee —
Union Party

William Lemke

Born August 13, 1878, in Albany, Minnesota; died May 30, 1950, in Fargo, North Dakota. Married Isabelle McIntyre on April 16, 1910; they had three children.

William Frederick Lemke was the fourth of ten children of William and Julia Anna Klier Lemke. His father was a farmer who emigrated from Prussia in 1850. In 1881 the family moved to the Dakota Territory and settled by 1883 on a homestead near Cando in Towner County. The family thrived. Within ten years the elder Lemke owned 2,700 acres of land. He died in 1901. Young William lost sight in an eye due to an accident, but was not significantly handicapped from it. He attended the University of North Dakota, receiving a B.A. in 1902. Lemke studied law at North Dakota, then Georgetown, and finally Yale University, from which he graduated in 1905. He began practice in Fargo.

Lemke founded and invested substantial money in a company that purchased 550,000 acres in Mexico for colonization. The Mexican Revolution of 1911 left the country in turmoil for years. Lemke and many of his friends personally lost all their savings. Lemke's biographer believes this financial disaster turned Lemke from a potentially wealthy businessman and establishment attorney with a progressive political bent, into an agrarian radical. He became an attorney for the Society of Equity, an activist group for grain farmers. Those involved with the Society helped found in 1915 the Nonpartisan League. The League started in western North Dakota, but grew to

be a short-lived regional power. Lemke became a salaried employee, and designed the N.P.L. programs for a state-owned bank and a grain elevator, with plans for much greater state ownership.

Lemke at this time was chairman of the North Dakota Republican Party, serving from 1916 to 1920. He was a member of the N.P.L.'s national committee from 1917 to 1921, and helped get N.P.L. endorsements for Republican candidates. The League had surged to control of the North Dakota legislature, the governorship, and many other offices, but by 1920 was faltering badly. During World War I the N.P.L. lost favor because it was isolationist and dominated by socialists. Lemke was elected the state's attorney general in 1920 with N.P.L. help. He was criticized as being a political dictator, controlling through the N.P.L. not only politicians, but also many newspapers. A legislative audit led to allegations that Lemke financially benefited from actions taken by the state bank that he helped create. That and other controversies caused Lemke to be recalled by the voters in 1921. He was indicted, but the charges were later dropped. In 1922 Lemke was defeated for governor as a Republican, and in 1926 for the Senate as a member of the Farmer-Labor Party.

In 1932 Lemke was elected to Congress as a Republican. Lemke wanted the federal government to subsidize crop prices to match costs of production. The Frazier-Lemke Farm Bankruptcy Act of 1934 gave debt relief to farmers, but it was declared unconstitutional. Lemke helped structure and pass a successor bill that did pass constitutional muster. For most of the proposals, Lemke had to overcome President Roosevelt's active opposition.

In 1936 an anti–New Deal coalition formed, consisting of Father Charles Coughlin (his weekly radio program attacked Jews, communists, international bankers, and, eventually, the "dictator" Roosevelt), the Reverend Gerald L.K. Smith (a backer of the recently assassinated Huey Long), and Dr. Francis E. Townsend (a proponent of $200 monthly old-age pensions). In mid–May 1936, Father Coughlin privately contacted Lemke. Over the next four weeks the groundwork for a new party was laid. On June 19 Lemke announced that he was a candidate for president under the new Union Party banner. Six hours later Father Coughlin announced on a nationwide radio broadcast that Lemke was "eligible" for support from his National Union for Social Justice. In fact, Lemke already was the choice. A well-known joke ridiculed Lemke's attempt at a folksy nickname. "Lemke calls himself 'Liberty Bell Bill' because they're both cracked." Father Coughlin's organization spent a substantial sum on the campaign, but Lemke got just under 2 percent of the national vote and carried no state.

Lemke had continued his separate 1936 race for Congress. He won then and again in 1938. After being renominated in 1940, he withdrew and ran an independent and losing campaign for the U.S. Senate. He was a pre-war isolationist, and joined the America First movement. In 1942 he was again elected to Congress and served until his death in 1950.

LEMKE BIBLIOGRAPHY

Bennett, David H. *Demagogues in the Depression: American Radicals and the Union Party, 1932–1936.* New Brunswick, N.J. (1969)

Blackorby, Edward. *Prairie Rebel: The Public Life of William Lemke.* Lincoln, Nebr. (1963).

Coleman, Patrick K., and Charles R. Lamb. *The Nonpartisan League, 1915–22: An Annotated Bibliography.* St. Paul (1985).

Marcus, Sheldon. *Father Coughlin: The Tumultuous Life of the Priest of the Little Flower.* Boston (1973).

Tull, Charles J. *Father Coughlin and the New Deal.* Syracuse (1965).

Warren, Donald. *Radio Priest: Charles Coughlin, the Father of Hate Radio.* New York (1996).

Whitman, Alden, ed. *American Reformers.* New York (1985).

1936 vice presidential nominee—
Union Party

Thomas C. O'Brien

Born June 19, 1887, in Brighton, Massachusetts; died November 22, 1951, in Boston. Married Julia Madeline Hartigan on September 3, 1913; they had four children.

Thomas Charles O'Brien was the son of Michael and Mary Connors O'Brien. Michael O'Brien was born in Ireland. Thomas attended Boston Latin School, then got a degree from Harvard University in 1908. He studied law at Harvard for the next three years. O'Brien worked his way through school as a ticket agent and brakeman for the Boston and Albany Railroad. For two years he practiced in Boston with another lawyer, and then started a solo practice in 1913. That latter year he ran as a Democrat for the General Court, and lost by 19 votes in a GOP district. He was a member of the Massachusetts Advisory Board of Parole and Pardons from 1913 until 1916, then first deputy director of prisons of the state Commission of Institutions for 1916 until 1919. His interest and expertise in prisons then led to appointment as Boston's penal commissioner from 1919 until 1920, and city commissioner of institutions in 1920 until 1922. After first being appointed by the governor to fill a vacancy, O'Brien was elected as a Republican as district attorney for the Suffolk district, serving from 1922 until 1927. O'Brien later wrote that he was a registered Democrat at the time. While continuing to serve in that office, he ran for Boston mayor in 1925 against four other candidates. He explained the defeat as being "lost in the shuffle" of so many contenders. In 1926 he ran for both parties' nomination as district attorney. He lost the Democratic, won the Republican nomination only after appealing to the state supreme court, and then narrowly lost the general election. He returned to the private practice of law in 1927 for the first time since 1913.

When U.S. Senator Frederick H. Gillett retired in 1930, O'Brien ran as a Democrat to replace him. He lost the nomination to Marcus Coolidge, who won in November. In 1934 O'Brien became the attorney for the Brotherhood of Railroad Trainmen and for the Brotherhood of Locomotive Engineers. He handled significant litigation for them and other unions through the years.

O'Brien became a follower of Charles Coughlin, the Detroit Catholic priest. Coughlin's radio program, vilifying Jews, communists, President Roosevelt, and an assortment of other targets, had made him detested by many and extraordinarily popular to others.

WILLIAM LEMKE (left) and THOMAS C. O'BRIEN
(From the Elwyn B. Robinson Department of Special Collections,
William Lemke Papers, Chester Fritz Library, University of
North Dakota; also pictured [top to bottom] are Charles Coughlin,
Francis Townsend and Gerald L.K. Smith)

In November 1934, Coughlin announced the forming of the National Union for Social Justice. O'Brien became an ardent supporter of the Union and its "Sixteen Principles of Social Justice," which were to limit the profits of capitalism, to provide a living wage for every worker, and in other ways for government to force industry to work for social justice, not profits. In 1936 Coughlin decided to present his own national ticket in opposition to President Roosevelt. Behind the scenes he encouraged William Lemke to run. Lemke agreed, and on June 16 he wrote O'Brien to say, "I am happy that you have consented, at my request, to seek the office of vice-president on the Union Party Ballot. We will stand and fall together on the principles which are so dear to both of us." The letter appears to have been more for later public use, as Coughlin had apparently put forth O'Brien's name and arranged for both men to be supported by his organization. Father Coughlin on his radio program on June 19 (O'Brien's forty-ninth birthday) all but anointed them. "Lemke and Yale, Agriculture and Republican," Coughlin summarized for the people. "O'Brien and Harvard, Labor and Democrat. East and West, Protestant and Catholic!" O'Brien met with Lemke, Father Coughlin, and others on June 21 in Massachusetts. A short time later the two candidates and Coughlin met at Coughlin's Detroit rectory. There a platform was prepared that was similar to Coughlin's Social Justice principles.

O'Brien and Lemke spoke at the large Cleveland convention of Coughlin's organization in August. O'Brien accused both established parties of "treason to the masses." He attacked the AFL president William Green for opposing Lemke's farm mortgage bill, and predicted most of labor would support Lemke-O'Brien. O'Brien was simultaneously running for the U.S. Senate in Massachusetts. Senator Coolidge was retiring, and O'Brien appeared on the ballot as the Union Party candidate. Father Coughlin visited Massachusetts and promoted a write-in campaign for O'Brien in the September Democratic Senate primary. Long-time Boston boss James Curley won with 246,000 votes, and the other candidate on the ballot got 104,000. O'Brien received 37,000 write-in votes, and even got 6,000 on the GOP primary ballot.

What more concerned Democrats than the Union Party winning the presidency, was that O'Brien would take enough votes from Governor Curley in the Senate race to cause the Republican, Henry Cabot Lodge, Jr., to win. Curley says that he called O'Brien and offered him $10,000 to withdraw. Curley also called Father Coughlin, but handled the appeal so poorly that Coughlin became more adamant that O'Brien stay in. The Democratic Party tried to keep O'Brien off the ballot, but O'Brien won in court. In the Senate election he got about 132,000 votes. Lodge defeated Curley by 142,000, thanks to the help, as Curley wrote, of "the stalking horse candidate." O'Brien was not the difference in the presidential race, which Roosevelt won in a landslide.

From 1939 until 1946, O'Brien was a member of the Special Massachusetts Railroad Commission. He remained an active practicing attorney, and presented at least one significant case before the U.S. Supreme Court. He was also a delegate to several international conferences on labor issues. In 1951 he again was a minor candidate against James Curley, this time for Boston mayor in the September Democratic primary. Curley argued that he was a better friend of the new Boston-Irish hero, Senator Joseph McCarthy, than was O'Brien. O'Brien got only 1,500 votes out of more than 200,000 cast. O'Brien died two months later. He was a life-long, active Catholic, and a volunteer in many church organizations. He was a big man, 225-pounds, and bespectacled.

Mayor Curley's 1951 campaign, in which O'Brien and others challenged him, is the basis for a novel written by Edwin O'Connor, *The Last Hurrah* (Boston, 1956). It was made into a movie in 1958, with Spencer Tracy as the Curley-like mayor Frank Skeffington. If there is a character with some O'Brien attributes, it most likely is perennial candidate Charlie Hennessey.

O'BRIEN BIBLIOGRAPHY

Beatty, Jack. *The Rascal King: The Life and Times of James Michael Curley, 1874–1958.* Reading, Mass. (1992).

Bennett, David H. *Demagogues in the Depression: American Radicals and the Union Party, 1932–1936.* New Brunswick, N.J. (1969)

Blackorby, Edward. *Prairie Rebel: The Public Life of William Lemke.* Lincoln, Nebr. (1963).

Curley, James Michael. *I'd Do It Again: A Record of All My Uproarious Years.* Englewood Cliffs, N.J. (1957).

"Democrats: No Man's Land." *Time* (June 29, 1936), pp. 10–11.

Marcus, Sheldon. *Father Coughlin: The Tumultuous Life of the Priest of the Little Flower.* Boston (1973).

O'Brien, Thomas C. "Thomas Charles O'Brien," in *Harvard Class Reports*, Boston (6th Report, 1933), pp. 527–529; (1938), pp. 101–102; (1948), pp. 208–209)

"Republicans Count Bay State Winnings." *The New York Times* (November 5, 1936), p. 14.

"Third Party: Lemke Throws Hat into the Ring…." *Newsweek* (June 27, 1936), p. 7.

"Thomas C. O'Brien, Ex-District Attorney of Suffolk, Dies at 64." *Boston Daily Globe* (November 23, 1951), p. 1.

Tull, Charles J. *Father Coughlin and the New Deal.* Syracuse (1965).

Warren, Donald. *Radio Priest: Charles Coughlin, the Father of Hate Radio.* New York (1996).

Appreciation is expressed to Mary Frances O'Brien, curator of Social Sciences, Boston Public Library, for her exceedingly generous efforts that uncovered information on the candidate.

Election of 1940

NOMINATIONS

Republican Party Convention (22nd): June 24–28, 1940, at the Convention Hall, Philadelphia, Pa. *President*— Wendell Willkie, nominated on the sixth ballot, after votes were changed, with 998 out of 1,000 votes, the other two votes cast as "absent." He had 655 votes before shifts. He had received 105 on the first ballot. Thomas Dewey (N.Y.) and Robert Taft (Ohio) were his chief rivals. *Vice president*— Charles McNary, nominated on the first ballot with 890 votes out of 1,000 cast.

Democratic Party Convention (28th): July 15–18, 1940, at Chicago Stadium, Chicago, Ill. *President*— Franklin D. Roosevelt, nominated on the first ballot with 946¹³⁄₃₀ out of 1,100½ cast. *Vice president*— Henry Wallace, nominated on the first ballot with 626¹¹⁄₃₀ out of 1,100 cast. William Bankhead (Ala.) was Wallace's major rival.

GENERAL ELECTION, November 5, 1940

Popular Vote

Roosevelt 27,263,448
Willkie 22,336,260
Others 240,735

Electoral Vote

Roosevelt–Wallace — 449 (38 states)
Willkie–McNary — 82 (10 states)

Winners

Franklin D. Roosevelt, 32nd president
Henry Wallace, 33rd vice president

Losers

Wendell Willkie, Charles McNary

---

*1940 presidential nominee —
Republican Party*

Wendell Willkie

Full name: Wendell Lewis Willkie. He was born Lewis Wendell Willkie, but his name was erroneously changed when he enlisted in the army; he decided he liked the new arrangement. His grandfather had spelled his name Friedrick Willcke, but the registrar at Valparaiso College mistakenly altered the spelling.

State represented: Indiana.

Birth: February 18, 1892, Elwood, Indiana.

Age on Inauguration Day (January 20, 1941): 48 years, 11 months.

Education: Elwood, Indiana public schools; Culver Military Academy; Indiana University (B.A. June 1913) (LL.D. June 1916).

Religion: Born in Methodist family, became Episcopalian as teenager.

Ancestry: Both his mother's and his father's parents were German immigrants.

Occupation: Attorney; utility company executive.

Public offices: Declined to run for Congress as Democrat, 1920; unsuccessful Republican nominee for president, 1940; declined to run for Congress, 1941, and for New York governor, 1942; unsuccessful candidate for Republican presidential nomination, 1944.

Death: October 8, 1944, New York City, 52 years, 7½ months.

Burial: East Hill Cemetery, Rushville, Indiana.

Home: Owned and operated five farms near Rushville, Indiana; lived in New York City.

Personal characteristics: 6'1" tall, 200 pounds, rumpled appearance, wilted suits, disheveled; black hair; blue eyes; in constant motion.

Father: Herman Francis Willkie (July 2, 1857–November 27, 1930); teacher and attorney; born in Germany.

Mother: Henrietta Trisch (April 5, 1858–March 10, 1940); lawyer, teacher.

Siblings: Julia (December 25, 1885–October 7, 1943), linguist and bacteriologist. Robert Trisch (October 9, 1887–?); lawyer, executive with Seagrams. Herman Frederick (September 30, 1890–December 28, 1959); executive with Seagrams, business consultant. Edward Everett (December 25, 1896–October 15, 1956); foods executive. Charlotte (October 24, 1899–); married Paul E. Pihl in 1920, career Naval officer.

Wife: Edith Wilk (August 6, 1890–April 14, 1978); married January 14, 1918.

Child: Philip Herman Willkie (December 7, 1919–April 10, 1974); attorney, banker.

Movies: *The State of the Union* (1948), a fictional account of Willkie's 1940 campaign; Spencer Tracy portrayed the Willkie character.

Historic sites/memorials: The school in Elwood that Willkie attended for 12 years was renamed for him.

Indiana, especially smalltown Indiana, has hardly ever been a hot-bed of liberalism. Yet Wendell Willkie's father was the attorney for the local labor union; his mother was also a lawyer. Discussions in the household inculcated in young Wendell a concern for the working man. His father had even joined the Socialist Party at one point, though in the main he was a liberal Democrat who found, as did Wendell, Woodrow Wilson the ideal public official. Wendell's life was not pampered. The family alternated between a reasonably comfortable existence, when the parents' legal practice was going well, and relatively hard times when it was not. His mother was eccentric in the extreme. By Wendell's adolescent years she had alienated most of the town with her gruff manner and unusual views. yet she was probably the head of the Willkie household. Wendell's father was not prone to coddle his children either. His technique of teaching independence was to give his children enough money at the beginning of summer vacation from college to take them by bus to some faraway place. There they would have to work to make the funds for the trip home. Such travels took Wendell to North Dakota wheatfields and the Texas oil fields.

After graduation from Indiana University, Wendell taught at Coffeyville, Kansas, in order to get enough money to attend law school. A brother had gone to Puerto Rico and enticed Wendell to follow. The promised riches in the sugar cane business were exaggerated, and Wendell returned home with more wisdom than wealth.

Wendell had been a good debater as an undergraduate and a campus politician of some success. At law school these achievements multiplied. He was class orator at the graduation ceremonies for the budding attorneys. With the encouragement of many of his classmates, his already revealed penchant for liberalism caused him to give a slightly radical speech that, unknown to him until just moments before its delivery, was to be heard by the president of the university and the Chief Justice of the state supreme court. Neither luminary was humored by the spectacle and Willkie was verbally put in his place by his irate elders.

Returning to Elwood after getting his law degree, Willkie was rebuffed by his mother in his desire to join the existing Willkie law firm. She told him the town was only large enough for two Willkie lawyers, Wendell's parents. Before these opinions drove him from town, he did become active in the local Democratic Party organization. He also had occasion to meet his future wife at a wedding in which he was the best man and she the maid of honor. The future Mrs. Willkie, Edith Wilk, left town when Wendell's mother refused to be civil to her. Willkie enlisted in the army once World War I began. He married Edith before leaving for Europe, his mother notwithstanding. Action in Europe for Willkie consisted of marching towards the front as the armistice was announced. His legal talents were put to use as a defense counsel for court-martialed soldiers. He was discharged as a captain in the infantry.

His mother's suggestion that he look elsewhere led to the legal department of Firestone Tire and Rubber Company in Akron, Ohio. He did not like the limited experience he was getting as corporate counsel and he decided to join a private law firm in Akron. Firestone matched the salary offer in order to keep him, but Willkie left anyway. His most memorable case in Akron was against Firestone. Though the issues are not important, it is significant that he won alone against a battery of ten Firestone attorneys. But then, juries do tend to sympathize with the outgunned local attorney against the giant corporation. Willkie's disloyalty to the company was not appreciated by Harvey Firestone, however, and Firestone became his bitter opponent.

Willkie's political involvement increased with his growing legal business. He was a delegate to the 1924 Democratic national convention and joined in the unrelenting opposition of many to nominating William Gibbs McAdoo. McAdoo was Willkie's old hero Woodrow Wilson's son-in-law, but more importantly a fence-straddler on the Ku Klux Klan and other bigotry, whether against the foreign born or racial minorities. Willkie was frequently sought after for speeches to civic groups and on the political campaign circuit. His personality neatly complemented his am-

bitions — he was affable, outgoing, easy to get to know and interested in people. He was obviously a "comer," both in his personal relationships but also in his legal skills. He was a good lawyer and a dominant personality, and people took notice.

Considerable notice had been taken of Willkie immediately after he had returned from military service in Europe. Friends and political leaders urged him to run for Congress from his hometown district. The offer was exceedingly enticing, but he was convinced to defer to others when he was told that he could not hope to remain a Democratic congressman in this Republican district for long. All that being elected would do would be to postpone real progress on his legal career. Deflated but convinced, Willkie remained a practicing attorney. Politics continued to interest him and he spoke widely on his favorite subjects of the League of Nations, the Klan and racial prejudice. In 1924, he supported Democratic presidential hopeful Newton Baker of Ohio and campaigned actively for him. His legal skills and his public recognition gained him election as president of the Akron Bar Association in 1926. He also became counsel for a large Ohio utility; in 1928 he was selected to its board of directors. By 1929 Willkie was "on his way."

Bernard Capen Cobb was another who was taking notice of young Willkie. As owner of the Ohio utility on whose board Willkie served, Cobb needed men with legal talents. He needed men even more with drive and ambition to make his company grow in the days when electricity was used for little more than lights in homes, and not in that many homes. In 1929, Cobb joined three utility holding companies together and formed Commonwealth and Southern, with Cobb as chairman of the board. He asked Willkie to assist this giant, multi-state corporation by becoming a partner in the New York City law firm that was to handle its representation. Willkie and Cobb worked closely together; when Cobb's health forced his retirement in January 1933, he had Willkie appointed president of the corporation.

The public utility business in the depths of the Depression had perhaps as low a public image as any large corporation. The worst of the robber barons was Samuel Insull. Holding companies had been stacked on top of holding companies. The sole reason for existence of each layer was to act as a legal entity to own the stock of the next holding company. This greatly watered the stock and inflated its price. Each new holding company could also issue securities, but the whole pyramid of companies, with incredible debt, rested on the base utility. Insull's corporate machinations created a maze of interlocking organizations that the most experienced businessman could not fathom. Insull's empire collapsed in 1932, the year before Willkie took on the mantle of utility executive.

Willkie immediately presented a different image. Far from defending the excesses of his fellow executives, Willkie decided to carve out a progressive role for Commonwealth and Southern. The holding company shenanigans were not repeated in his company. Just at the time Willkie took office, another presidency — of the United States — was being assumed by perhaps the greatest enemy of privately-owned utilities and business, Franklin D. Roosevelt. Willkie's rise to national prominence is directly tied to his differences, and the public airing of them, with President Roosevelt. As Roosevelt attempted to create a new social order, including the effective nationalization of public utilities, so Willkie rose to defeat that ambition.

The most direct threat to Commonwealth and Southern posed by the New Deal was that FDR wished to put the federal government in direct competition with the private utility. In the South, in which a large segment of Commonwealth and Southern's subsidiary companies operated, the New Deal proposed to create the largest utility in America, the Tennessee Valley Authority. With government subsidized rate schedules for TVA, the private utility could not hope to compete. Yet TVA was enormously popular. It promised service in areas that had not been served by private utilities; the rates that would be charged would be drastically lower than those of Commonwealth's subsidiaries. For six years Willkie fought against the creation of TVA; losing that battle, he then attempted to ensure that his

subsidiary lines were purchased at a fair price once TVA entered an area they served.

The words used by all sides in the dispute were hot. To Willkie the TVA was socialism that was merely the first step in government domination of all business. To TVA supporters, Willkie and all utility executives were lumped together as cutthroat enemies of the poor whose only motives were profits. Willkie was the most attractive spokesman for the utilities. He was frequently called upon in public magazines and other forums to present his side of the issues. The TVA fight drove Willkie increasingly into the hardline camp of businessmen opposed to the entire New Deal. Fine distinctions over which social programs were satisfactory and which were not were soon lost in the heat of the dispute. Though both Willkie and the New Deal spokesmen may have been drawn into extreme statements, Willkie continued to exhibit moderation as an executive. He reduced rates charged by the company in hopes of increasing sales. He agreed with the administration that unrestrained use of holding companies should be outlawed, but he did not favor an outright ban. C&S grew under Willkie's leadership and he made the company profitable.

Willkie's unrelenting public relations battle for the industry made him a major public figure. Though his arguments may not always have had immediate public appeal, he insisted he only wanted basic fairness in the way the new public utilities treated private companies such as his own. The New Deal's favorite expression concerning TVA was that it merely created a yardstick by which the performance and rates charged by the private companies could be measured. Willkie showed the sophistry of this argument by hammering on the fact that public-sponsored utilities did not operate under any of the same conditions as did private companies. The whole accounting scheme used to set TVA's rates was preposterous as a "yardstick," with an allocation of many of the initial and maintenance costs of the huge hydroelectric dams being made not for electric power but instead for flood control. Costs allocated to flood control, a public function, were paid out of the federal treasury. Regardless of the desirability of TVA, private companies who charged that public power had unfair advantages were presenting only what was fact. Finally, the administration began to realize that perhaps the courts would not ignore the confiscatory ramifications of such public companies.

Indeed, the confused forecasts of what the United States Supreme Court would do with TVA and similar New Deal ventures were a major impediment to each side compromising. Early rulings by the Supreme Court were uniformly negative to the New Deal.

The Court began to give ground grudgingly, however, as public opinion insisted that the New Deal be implemented. Willkie's position on TVA had been upheld in lower federal courts. On the impetus of that defeat, TVA had finally begun seriously to negotiate with him on a fair price for his company's properties in the TVA region, instead of making a distress sale offer. The Supreme Court reversed the lower courts, but not with a ruling that finally settled the constitutionality of the utility. Despite the setback the nearly consummated settlement with TVA proceeded and a price of $78,000,000 was agreed upon. This was $23,000,000 more than TVA had earlier offered, a tribute to Willkie's persistence and the success of his public relations campaign.

Willkie's emergence as the spokesman for the utility industry shook his moorings in the Democratic Party. The TVA settlement was reached in 1939; earlier that year his name was first mentioned in a serious national column concerning the 1940 presidential nomination. His drive for the nomination began in the newspapers, with many friendly reporters suggesting him as a possibility. Willkie's relations with the press were always good. Not only was Willkie personable with newspapermen, he was also good copy. Willkie's response to these suggestions of a presidential nomination was invariably in the form of jokes, one of which caught the public fancy. Commenting on the suggestion by General Hugh Johnson that he run for president, Willkie replied: "If the government continues to take over my business, I may be looking shortly for some kind of a new job. General Johnson's is the best offer I have had so far." The movement took hold even without his active participation. An army of

volunteers was organized, recruited largely by Oren Root, grand-nephew of former Secretary of State Elihu Root. In the spring of 1940, Root was a 28-year-old lawyer with a big idea and little money. He borrowed $150, and set up a Willkie organization in his mother's apartment. He placed ads in the personal columns of newspapers promoting the idea of Willkie Clubs. This brought in enough money for him to spread his low budget petition drive into a nationwide phenomenon that produced 4.5 million signatures for Willkie. More experienced politicians, though not many, came to his aid. In April 1940, *Fortune* magazine printed his article "We the People," an attack on the alleged socialism of the New Deal. In this article, Willkie encouraged a new freedom for individuals and business to govern themselves.

As powerful as the emotional appeal of Willkie was, the Republican politicians did not join in. By convention time in Philadelphia, Willkie had enlisted the services as his floor manager of Minnesota's popular and youthful (age 33) governor, Harold E. Stassen, whose own frequent presidential campaigns were still in the future. Willkie dates May 11, or just six weeks before the convention opened on June 24, as when he first seriously considered the possibility of his own nomination. As late as that was, he was six weeks in advance of when most Republican leaders believed he had a chance.

The convention campaign was still largely amateurish. Indiana congressman Charles Halleck, *Fortune* editor Russell Davenport, and a few other congressmen along with Governor Stassen were his supporters among those with some claim to political experience. It was not until the week before the convention that other more influential officials began to react to the growing possibility of Willkie's nomination. A few governors, senators and mayors dropped their favorite son roles and endorsed Willkie. Willkie himself arrived at the convention a few days before it opened, a break with tradition that the candidate did not appear and engage in campaigning. It was this final ingredient in the mix that was perhaps the most important. Willkie's tireless, gregarious courting of the delegates convinced enough of them that he was credible and electable to give him at least a fighting chance for the nomination. The early ballots had him in third place behind New York City district attorney Thomas Dewey and Ohio senator Robert Taft. On the fourth ballot he took the lead and on the sixth he won. The selection of Charles McNary, isolationist senator from Oregon whom Willkie had never met, was a balancing act by the old guard politicians who had taken only a reluctant step towards the liberal, internationalist Willkie. They returned to more familiar ground with McNary.

The public opinion polls never showed Willkie with a real prospect of catching Roosevelt. The war that had already begun in Europe probably sealed Willkie's fate. With Willkie having no experience in foreign affairs and with the world crumbling, it did not seem time for a change. Willkie continued his attack on the New Deal as socialistic and undemocratic. He charged that Roosevelt's discarding of the tradition of serving only two terms was an attempt to create a dictatorship. The people were unconvinced, or were scared. Willkie received the largest vote total to that date of any Republican nominee. He cut into some of the normal Democratic support; but it was not nearly enough.

After his defeat, Willkie found himself increasingly under attack by his own, recently adopted party, which had never really accepted him and which was fairly pleased to be done with him. As the world was exploding into war, most prominent Republicans seemed bent on burying their heads in the sands of isolationism. Lend-Lease, the exchange of old American warships with Britain for military bases overseas, was strongly endorsed by Willkie and just as strongly condemned by most of the Republican establishment. Willkie continued to speak out for a strong civil rights policy and opposed lynching and the Jim Crow laws so prevalent in the South. He was ostracized by the Republican Party; his voice became less directed to his party leaders and more to the masses of independents and progressive Republicans. Opposing Willkie included the pinnacle of Republican leadership, Herbert Hoover, Alfred Landon, and Robert Taft. Smear tactics were used against Willkie

by the more extreme isolationists, and it was not a pleasant or easy task for Willkie to continue to speak out.

Willkie returned to his legal practice in New York City, but his law firm there was little more than an office from which he could arrange his public speaking schedule and write the articles necessary to spread his news. The Republicans in Congress continued to oppose every war measure, including selective service and repeal of the Neutrality Act. The latter prohibited the United States from giving direct aid to the allies against Nazi Germany. Just as consistently, Willkie attacked his fellow Republicans for their shortsightedness and self-destruction. Roosevelt spoke approvingly of what Willkie was doing to unify the country behind the war.

One of Willkie's most public services during the period after his defeat was in making a multi-nation tour of the war zones from August through October 1942. He visited South America, Africa, and Asia, including Russia and China. He became increasingly convinced that planning for the postwar world could not wait until peace had arrived. All allied countries must join in developing a lasting peace. He spoke in China for the end of all colonial empires, demanding that after the war no empire of nations must rule over any other nation. The outline of these ideas became so well known but incompletely explained that some of his supporters called on him to write a book to detail his positions. The work, *One World*, was a dramatic bestseller, being until that time one of only three nonfiction books since 1900 to sell a million copies. *One World* performed the feat in seven weeks. Overseas sales, even in postwar Germany, were extremely favorable. The central thesis was that peace must be a global peace. The world must be free economically and politically from rule of one nation over another. A corollary of the thesis was that America must engage directly in ensuring the formation of this new order. It was hardly traditional Republican doctrine.

Willkie's belief in freedom and civil rights was dangerously exemplified, dangerous for a politician with hopes for the presidency, in his legal defense of a Communist who had become a naturalized citizen in 1927, but who was now being threatened with deportation on the ground that as a Communist he was subversive. Willkie argued the case before the United States Supreme Court and won. His belief in free speech and the right of every man to live free from oppression was almost reverential.

The 1944 presidential election approached with no strong Republican candidate in the field other than Willkie. Perhaps the most popular Republican, New York Governor Thomas Dewey, had promised when he ran for governor in 1942 not to run for the presidency in 1944. Distaste for Willkie was so pervasive within the party that Willkie had the ballot requirements of every state examined to determine the feasibility of running as an independent. The difficulties of that scheme caused him to drop it. Willkie announced for the presidency on February 14, 1944, and selected the Wisconsin primary as the place he would stand and fight his opponents in the party. Isolationist Wisconsin was a bad choice, but the alternatives in the limited number of primaries made any electoral stand a risk. He was badly defeated by Dewey in Wisconsin and immediately dropped out of the race. He would not declare for Dewey against Roosevelt once Dewey was nominated, hoping to use his silence as leverage to get one of the major parties to adopt his views.

The Democrats held out the prospect of nominating Willkie as Roosevelt's vice presidential running mate, but the seriousness of Roosevelt's interest in such a unity ticket is difficult to weigh. Harry Truman was the eventual selection.

In the height of the presidential race, with neither candidate yet having been endorsed by Willkie, the 1940 Republican standard-bearer suffered the first of what would become by his death over 15 separate heart attacks. He had never been careful about his health. His eating and smoking habits would have taxed the constitution of any man. The seriousness of his illness was kept secret, Willkie being fearful that what little influence he had would be lost if he could be dismissed as a feeble, hopelessly ill invalid. On October 8, 1944, he died.

It was only five years since he had exploded onto the national stage as a presidential contender.

Analysis of Qualifications

Criticized as an opportunist, Willkie responded that his political lodestar was not rock-hard allegiance to any philosophy, but a pragmatic reaction to problems that confronted him. He started adult life as a Woodrow Wilson Democrat, and he closed his life soon after becoming a Republican presidential nominee. He was an eloquent advocate of free enterprise, but he did not prostitute himself to the cause. Regardless of the different positions in which Willkie found himself, there is a consistency to his adult life that allegations of opportunism cannot obscure.

As a businessman, he railed against unfair and destructive competition from the government. His 1940 campaign for the presidency developed his basic philosophy that the government imposed too many ill-defined and constantly changing regulations, that direct government competition was ruining private industry, and that the tax system as well as production controls were stifling new enterprise. He constantly used and believed the phrase "only the productive can be strong, and only the strong can be free." It was at this point, but only at this point, that Willkie separated himself from the direction of the New Deal. Whether as a Wilson Democrat, a utility executive, or as a presidential candidate, he believed in government involvement with the needs of private individuals. His father had been a labor lawyer, and Willkie himself supported such New Deal legislation as the National Labor Relations Act and the collective bargaining that this law insured. He supported social security and other measures that helped ease the plight of the unemployed, the aged, and the poor. But private enterprise was the answer for Willkie — increasing production and thereby increasing employment was his focus.

Willkie's most substantial contribution in public life was as an internationalist at a time when almost the entire Republican Party wished to shut America's doors and forget what was occurring in Europe and Asia. He did take the politically expedient, but eventually unsuccessful, tack of accusing Roosevelt of being a warmonger during the campaign, but despite such charges it was evident that Willkie strongly endorsed a policy of aiding the allies in the months leading up to America's involvement in war. After his defeat in 1940, Willkie attempted to draft the Republican Party into supporting measures necessary for England's survival.

Willkie also saw the need to plan for the peace that would follow the successful conclusion of the war. His *One World* concepts would have placed America directly into the business of insuring the economic and political freedom of every country. Though the details of Willkie's plans were probably impractical, his basic concern that America play a dominant role in postwar reconstruction was sound.

Willkie had no political experience, but he did have considerable political knowledge based on his seven years of lobbying in Washington. His knowledge of government was a special and significant knowledge, one that informed him how the game was played. Though he was no match for Roosevelt's ability to inspire and lead, Willkie had considerable talents in that area as well. His sudden rise in the capturing of the Republican nomination was based on his inspiration to millions of previously apolitical Americans. His own party may have been his greatest handicap, and particularly before a Pearl Harbor–type incident he would have been forced to rely on the Democratic Party to pass his measures preparing the country for war.

It is hard to argue with success, and Roosevelt had dramatic success in helping win this most awful of wars. Yet the country was presented with another candidate in 1940 whose skills seemed particularly appropriate for the crisis. Perhaps the country chose correctly. Perhaps instead the country missed another inspirational, intelligent, forceful leader who could have been an exceptional president.

WILLKIE BIBLIOGRAPHY

Barnard, Ellsworth. *Wendell Willkie: Fighter for Freedom*. Amherst, Mass. (1971).
Barnes, Joseph. *Wendell Willkie*. New York City (1954).
Bathe, David Allen. "Wendell L. Willkie: A Political Odyssey from Realism to Idealism." Unpublished doctoral dissertation, Illinois State University (1991).
Dillon, Mary Earhart. *Wendell Willkie*. New York City (1952).
Johnson, Donald B. *The Republican Party and Wendell Willkie*. Urbana, Ill. (1960).
Madison, James H., ed. *Wendell Willkie: Hoosier Internationalist*. Bloomington (1992).
Moscow, Warren. *Roosevelt and Willkie*. Englewood Cliffs, N.J. (1968).
Neal, Steve. *Dark Horse: A Biography of Wendell Willkie*. Garden City (1984).
Stahl, Edward M. *We Want Willkie: A Pictorial Guide to the Campaign Memorabilia of Wendell L. Willkie*. Trenton (1972).
Thompson, Sarah. "Wendell Willkie: A Hoosier Liberal." Unpublished doctoral dissertation, Ball State University (1980).
Willkie, Wendell. *One World*. New York City (1943).
Genealogical information provided by Saundra Taylor, curator of the Manuscript Division, Indiana University, Bloomington, and by Wendell Willkie II, Washington, D.C.

---

*1940 vice presidential nominee—
Republican Party*

Charles L. McNary

Full name: Charles Linza McNary.

State represented: Oregon.

Birth: June 12, 1874, on farm near Salem, Oregon.

Age on Inauguration Day (January 20, 1941): 66 years, 7½ months.

Education: Public schools of Salem, Oregon, then business college; Stanford University, 1896–1898; studied law in his brother John's office, 1898; admitted to bar, 1898.

Religion: Baptist.

Ancestry/prominent relatives: Scotch–Irish; first McNary arrived in America in mid–1730s; brother John H. McNary an Oregon politician, and U.S. district judge.

Occupation: Attorney.

Public offices: Deputy county recorder, Marion County (Oregon), 1892–1896; deputy

WENDELL WILLKIE (left) and CHARLES L. McNARY
(From Jonathan Binkley)

district attorney, 1906–1913; appointed as justice of Oregon supreme court, June 1913– January 1915, defeated for election by one vote; Republican state central committee chairman, 1915–1917; appointed U.S. senator, May 29, 1917–November 5, 1918, December 18, 1918– February 25, 1944; became Senate Republican leader, 1933–1944; unsuccessful Republican candidate for president and defeated Republican nominee for vice president, 1940; rejected offer to be nominated to U.S. Supreme Court, 1942.

Home: "Fircone," his family's farm five miles north of Salem, Oregon.

Death: February 25, 1944, at Ft. Lauderdale, Florida, age 69 years, 8½ months.

Burial: Odd Fellows Cemetery, Salem, Oregon.

Personal characteristics: Nearly 6' tall; slender, sandy-haired, blue eyes; poor speaker, genial, companionable.

Father: Hugh Linza McNary (August 30, 1829–July 18, 1883); farmer, schoolteacher, and sometimes bricklayer.

Mother: Mary Margaret Claggett (November 16, 1835–March 5, 1878); married in 1853; daughter of Charles Claggett.

Siblings: Mary Elizabeth (October 5, 1855–

January 23, 1953), married Hentry T. Bruce in 1877. Sarah ("Nina") (August 8, 1857–February 27, 1932). Mattie (January, 1860–February 22, 1898). Nancy Eliza (August, 1862–August 4, 1887). Hattie (September, 1864–June 7, 1879). John (January 31, 1867–October 25, 1936), married Esther Hall on January 29, 1894. Ella (August, 1869–December 26, 1952), married Walter T. Stoltz in 1898. James (April 3–April 23, 1872). Julia M. (1876–December 7, 1880).

First wife: Jessie Breyman (1876–July 4, 1918); married November 19, 1902. Daughter of Eugene Breyman, a Salem merchant; died in car accident.

Children: None.

Second wife: Cornelia W. Morton (?–August 23, 1966), married on December 29, 1923.

Children: Charlotte (?–?), was adopted in 1935.

Charles L. McNary was one of the least partisan men ever to rise to a position of major importance in the United States Senate. He was a conciliator between warring factions in his own party and with the Democrats. He withdrew from conflict and at times from power. To presidents, fellow senators, and the public, he was Charlie McNary, not nearly as respected as he was loved.

The first McNarys migrated to the Oregon Territory in 1845. They escaped death despite the ignorance of their guide, who led them, lost, into desert country in central Oregon. Charlie's father settled near Salem, Oregon, ten years later and married the daughter of a prosperous farmer. Ten children followed; the future senator and would-be vice president was the last of the brood who survived infancy. By the time Charlie was nine, both parents had died. An older sister raised the younger children in Salem. There the baby of the family attended public school and added, marginally, to the family income by delivering newspapers and taking other small jobs. Graduation from high school enabled Charlie to assume greater responsibility, this time through the nepotism of brother John McNary, then recorder for Marion County, Oregon. From 1892 until 1896, Charlie was an assistant, but trying to better himself by taking courses at a local business college. Restless, getting nowhere in school or his job, young McNary left for California with 28 dollars in his pocket. His transportation was free, courtesy of a lumber boat. Two years at Stanford University, waiting on tables in order to meet expenses, got him no degree or fortune. Apparently in 1898 he served in the military long enough to be shipped to the Philippines, but little record of that episode remains.

McNary returned to Salem in 1898, studied law in his brother's office for a few months, and then was admitted to the bar in October. Poorly trained, but likeable and diligent, Charlie soon found financial and professional success in partnership with brother John McNary. For a time the younger brother's career was directly dependent upon the older's, as Charlie became deputy district attorney in 1904 after John was elected as district attorney. These were good times for Charlie McNary and his new wife, Jessie Breyman, whom he married in 1902. McNary was active in civic affairs, president of the Board of Trade for Salem, and dabbled happily at his farm, growing nuts, prunes, cherries, apples and other northwestern crops. McNary also wrote a few articles on horticulture, and seemed to find his

greatest pleasure in being on his farm. Somehow McNary also found time to be dean of the Willamette College of Law. In 1911, he was appointed special counsel for the state Railroad Commission. At 37, McNary was prominent on a small scale, financially secure even though not wealthy, and seemed contented.

Politics was not important to Charlie McNary, at least not nearly as much as it was to John McNary. The older brother had been assistant secretary for the Oregon delegation to the 1912 Republican national convention and played a significant role in Oregon politics. When the state Supreme Court was increased from five to seven members in 1913, Democratic governor Oswald West offered one of the judgeships to John. "Oh, don't do that," he responded. "Appoint Charlie." Again Charles owed his brother for an important career advancement. He would look after himself capably thereafter.

As Supreme Court justice, McNary did not have time to leave much of a mark on the state's jurisprudence, but he did gain some political pluses by his votes to uphold wage and hour statutes against constitutional attack. In 1914, after only a year as a judge, McNary had to face challenge in the primary for election to his first term. First returns showed McNary winning by 13 votes, but a recount indicated he had lost by one vote, 34,609 to 34,608. When asked whether he would ask for a recount, the defeated judge replied, "To Hell with it," and took his loss quietly. A respite in private law practice followed, but not for long.

In 1915, McNary's political standing was evident when he was selected as state party chairman. His familiarity with Republican leaders grew accordingly, a significant factor two years later when the incumbent United States senator died. On May 29, 1917, McNary was named by Republican governor James Withycombe to the vacancy. It was an awesome opportunity for a man who had never even traveled to the East before. In many respects, his provincialism would never leave him, despite serving in the Senate for the rest of his life.

The new senator became known as a moderate progressive, supporting women's suffrage, Wilson's policies on the war, and prohibition. With little record to run on, McNary faced election in 1918 for a full six-year term. The Republican primary pitted against him a former speaker of the Oregon house of representatives, who had immense sums to spend on his campaign. McNary decided to stay in Washington and let the publicity he could generate as a senator working at his job be his campaign. The "Too busy to campaign" campaign, dictated by the fact McNary did not have the war chest to compete with his opponent was effective. McNary won in a landslide, turning back the challenge by 52,500 votes to 31,000. The victory celebration lasted only until July 4 when his wife was killed in an automobile crash. It was a restrained general election campaign, again conducted from Washington with few personal appearances back home in Oregon. The former Democratic governor, Oswald West, who had appointed McNary to the Supreme Court in 1913, was his opponent. Again, the senator was victorious, this time winning with 83,000 votes to West's 64,000.

Both the election campaign and the war in Europe ended in November. The question of support for the Treaty of Versailles would dominate national politics for the next several years. Unlike many Republican senators who would become known as the "irreconcilables," McNary said he would vote for the treaty and wanted the United States to join the League of Nations. When GOP opposition to the treaty intensified, McNary also began expressing some reservations. The Oregonian tried to mediate between the warring factions, a hallmark of his entire career. The chasm was too large to bridge; President Wilson was as irreconcilable on his position as were the hardline Republicans. McNary favored the adoption of resolutions explaining Senate interpretation of the treaty, but without the treaty itself being amended. With Wilson refusing to compromise, the moderates had a difficult decision to make. The junior senator from Oregon sided with the opponents of the treaty, but he was not pleased to see the League of Nations defeated as a result of stubbornness on all sides. McNary's decision to vote against the treaty

was a retraction of his earlier stand. McNary had felt the political heat and responded. The League episode made him retreat from controversy throughout the remainder of his career.

The Democrats were doomed in 1920. The only question was which Republican presidential hopeful would retire them from power. McNary supported fellow Westerner, Senator Hiram Johnson of California. It was a revealing endorsement, because few men represented a more contrasting viewpoint on the treaty fight than these two. What McNary saw appealing in Johnson was his personality — his friendliness and honesty — and his dedication to the needs of the Far West. Those were McNary's most prominent attributes as well. Warren G. Harding's election was accepted with equanimity; as always McNary looked at the positive even in defeat. With the new administration, the Oregon senator found new influence. In 1921, a farm bloc of agriculture state congressmen and senators was organized in Washington, and McNary was a founding member. Farm issues dominated McNary's senatorial career, and he prided himself on understanding the arcane world of the agriculture appropriation bill.

Besides agriculture, anything else of special interest to Oregon was McNary's concern as well. Development of the arid lands of his state for agriculture was pushed even during the 1920s period of agriculture surpluses that were driving farm prices down. His work on forest conservation earned him accolades among conservationists. A survey of forest resources was accomplished in 1923 under his direction. Reforestation of clear-cut or burned areas was the thrust of the 1924 McNary-Clarke Act. The McNary-Woodruff Act of 1928 increased federal purchases of land for forests. From 1919 until 1926 McNary was chairman of the Senate Committee on Irrigation and Reclamation, overseeing the development of the Tennessee, Colorado and Columbia rivers.

In order to continue these efforts, the freshman Oregon senator had to win reelection in 1924. Two principal opponents jumped into the race, the mayor of Portland and the speaker of the Oregon house. The Ku Klux Klan was the overriding, if sometimes silent, issue in the campaign, and both Republican primary opponents curried favor with Klan supporters. McNary did not want to be sullied with the issue, and tried to keep his campaign focus solely on national problems. Again McNary did not return to Oregon to campaign, and again the technique worked. McNary's vote was twice the combined support of his adversaries, and he went on to win the general election with similar ease. It had been a family affair, as his Democratic victim was his cousin. Nineteen hundred and twenty-four had also been a presidential election year. McNary did not deviate from previous habits of avoiding strong identification with any candidate for president. Though he supported President Coolidge, McNary attempted to avoid antagonizing the supporters of a rival candidate, Hiram Johnson.

The single greatest problem facing Oregon in the 1920s was agricultural depression. That crisis caused McNary to present a bill that brought him fame during the period. The McNary-Haugen bill, actually drafted by others outside of Congress, would subsidize farm prices by the sale of the surplus overseas. A ratio price was established, whereby the price of certain farm commodities, principally wheat, would be compared to the average price of all commodities from 1905 through 1914. Since farm prices had not kept pace with the rise in prices elsewhere, this formula would give a substantial subsidy to wheat growers. A government corporation would buy all surplus wheat at that support price, then sell it to foreign markets at whatever price could be obtained. Domestic purchasers would buy at one price, but all surplus that farmers could produce would earn an appreciably higher price. An "equalization fee" would be charged each producer to help offset the losses that the government corporation would suffer when it sold the wheat, but the fee was much less than the increased price the farmers received. McNary-Haugen was call unconstitutional and socialistic; Republican presidents denounced it. It was also a poor answer to the low farm prices that had been caused by oversupply. The bill would have encouraged even greater production, driving domestic prices still lower and increasing the surplus that would be sold at a

loss by the government. Several defeats greeted the McNary-Haugen bill and its several amended versions. Finally in 1927 it passed, but President Coolidge vetoed it.

Throughout what would prove to be a seven-year fight, McNary sponsored the legislation but expressed private reservations and lack of enthusiasm for it. What he was certain of was the need for some answer to disastrously low farm prices. In 1927, his efforts took on new force when McNary became chairman of the Senate Committee on Agriculture and Forestry. Frequent letters home revealed that he was becoming exasperated with the fight over farm relief and just wished for a resolution of the issue, favorable or not. One factor diminishing his zeal for the relief bill was speculation that he might be Coolidge's running mate in 1928. When Coolidge withdrew from the 1928 contest, McNary's opportunity for the vice presidency ended for that year. Typically, McNary endorsed none of the Republican contenders. When Herbert Hoover, an opponent of the McNary-Haugen proposal, was nominated, McNary helped hold many advocates of farm relief in line for the ticket.

President Hoover was no more sympathetic to McNary's farm bill than had been Coolidge, so the senator dropped several of the features that had prompted two Coolidge vetoes. In greatly watered-down form, the bill finally was passed and signed by the president. McNary was short-sighted when he stated that the issue had finally been put to rest. The measure proved ineffective and additional plans were soon being submitted. McNary found himself also at odds with the administration over public power. The senator wanted such projects as Muscle Shoals in Alabama to proceed with government ownership, while Hoover wanted the facilities to be leased to private industry.

Though basically a conservative, McNary was an open-minded, at times progressive politician who could be persuaded by men of greatly varying philosophies. Public power and farm relief were two of the major controversies that found McNary siding with liberals and progressives, much to the dismay of his conservative Republican brethren. Yet so popular was the Oregonian that policy differences rarely made him enemies. Correspondents polled in 1930 ranked him as the most popular senator. McNary was unemotional regardless of the issue, and seemingly unconcerned whether his point of view was victorious or defeated. These characteristics were necessary for him to play the role that fell to him in the 1930s. The Great Depression and Hoover's inability to cope with it badly split the already divided Republican ranks. McNary tried to bridge this gap in his party. When the Republicans were ousted from power in 1932, McNary was elected leader of the greatly reduced Republican ranks in the Senate. The incumbent Republican Senate leader had been defeated in the 1932 general election, one of thirteen Republican seats that fell to the Democrats that year. The newly installed Senate Republican leader was philosophical, finding benefit in the Roosevelt sweep. The new president needed a free hand to work, and McNary realized the election had given him that.

For a year McNary led his party away from conflict with the president. Supporting more of the New Deal proposals than he opposed, McNary irritated many Republicans who thought Roosevelt was threatening the foundation of the Republic with his dynamic new approach to the role of the federal government. McNary found such critics to be moss-backed reactionaries that were the Republicans' albatross. Hoover was one of the more vociferous critics, and McNary just wished the former president would disappear. Senator McNary voted for the Agriculture Adjustment Act, the National Recovery Act, and several other controversial Roosevelt proposals. One favorable result of this comradeship with the president was success in getting a water project approved for the Columbia River in Oregon, the Bonneville Dam. When the initial approval seemed to be unraveling, McNary flew from Oregon to the Capitol and met personally with Roosevelt. The publicity over his successful efforts to save Bonneville greatly inured to his political benefit in Oregon.

The Republicans were getting restless under McNary's low-key, non-combative leadership. It was not until May 1934, that McNary made any serious break with the administration, and

then on a little-understood bill giving the president authority to alter American tariffs when negotiating with foreign governments concerning trade relations. Still McNary remained relatively supportive of the New Deal.

Republicans suffered even sharper setbacks in the 1934 midterm elections, reducing their Senate numbers to only 16. McNary blamed the negativism of the party, with Republicans such as Herbert Hoover sharply attacking the constitutionality of New Deal programs. McNary believed that the relief programs were needed, and more often than not he voted for them. His own reelection would be a problem in 1936, for the disgust many felt towards his party could easily smear him. In 1930, McNary had encountered no difficulty in being reelected, and he felt there was no cause for concern in 1936 either. He even momentarily entertained ambitions for the presidency, but there was little chance of success and McNary knew it. Two opponents appeared in the Republican Senate primary and were dispatched with ease. Republicans were disappointed that their Senate leader was completely neutral in the presidential race. Again the senator campaigned from his desk at the Capitol, and he felt secure. It proved to be a long election evening in November, however. With Roosevelt defeating Alfred Landon in the state by better than two to one, McNary was almost swallowed up in the nationwide rejection of his party. Instead, he was one of the few survivors, winning with 199,000 votes to his Democratic opponent's 193,000.

Back in Washington, McNary's political blood finally started to get a little heated. A cocky President Roosevelt, tired of the Supreme Court's voiding of New Deal legislation and feeling supreme himself after the 1936 election mandate, submitted a court-packing bill to Congress. It would have given him one appointment to the Supreme Court (and every other federal court) for every judge on that court who was over 70 years of age. Six new Supreme Court members could have been named, giving the president a clear majority of supporters on the Court. McNary helped devise, but more importantly helped sell, the strategy of letting opposition to the plan be spearheaded by outraged Democrats who were aghast at so audacious a proposal. Otherwise, a Republican-led rejection of the plan would have made it difficult for angry Democrats to vote against Roosevelt. At all costs, McNary felt the court-packing bill must not become a partisan issue. With only 16 GOP senators, such a battle would be lost before it had hardly begun. Even Hoover had to be muzzled, not altogether effectively. The strategy, and the repulsiveness of the scheme proposed by Roosevelt, spelled victory for the opponents. McNary, feeling victory close at hand, allowed himself a few strong words when he characterized the proposal as one that "never should have been presented to a civilized legislature."

The court-packing debacle for Roosevelt led to greater opposition to the New Deal by McNary. The 1938 elections had also dealt Roosevelt a blow, with eight new Republican senators. In 1939, the Republican Senate leader suggested that the Works Progress Administration be abolished and that relief programs be turned over to the states. Foreign affairs were not ignored. McNary declared that the Neutrality Act should not be amended or repealed, nor should the arms embargo be lifted. After predicting that America would not get involved in the European troubles, McNary was surprised when the conflict escalated into war in September 1939. A quiet isolationist, McNary could remark with the Second World War already raging in Europe, "We have no business in becoming involved in the European mess...."

In 1940, McNary looked upon himself as a real presidential contender. No active campaign was ever commenced, but he hoped for a deadlock in the convention that might lead to his nomination. For that reason his policy of remaining neutral in presidential nomination battles was even more critical than usual. In the shadow of the world conflict, McNary's platform ignored international issues and continued to emphasize farm problems. Other candidates failed to catch the party's imagination, leaving a vacuum for Wendell Willkie to fill. Willkie became the only contender for a Republican nomination that McNary would ever publicly call unacceptable. He was quoted as saying Willkie would be the "ruin" of the party. On three major issues, Willkie and Mc-

Nary were opposed — Willkie favored involvement in the European conflict, McNary opposed; McNary wanted public ownership of power in some areas, and Willkie opposed; reciprocal trade agreements were supported by Willkie and not by McNary. When Willkie received the presidential nomination, political logic, which ignores charges of hypocrisy, required an offer to McNary to run with him and therefore balance the ticket. McNary refused, saying, "Hell, no, I wouldn't run with Willkie." Party loyalty finally persuaded McNary to accept, but relations between the running mates never became cordial. McNary never was optimistic about victory, and kept his campaign low-key. Defeat upset him little, and one imagines that victory would not have been momentous either.

World War II brought McNary more sharply into opposition to Roosevelt's policies. McNary criticized Lend-Lease and other war measures until after Pearl Harbor was attacked. As amended, the Lend-Lease bill finally got McNary's vote. He was not in favor of intervention in the war nor of total isolation. The Republican leader felt America's involvement in the war was an outgrowth of poor negotiations by Roosevelt. The president seemed entirely too bellicose to McNary, and war was the result. Regardless of his personal views, generally McNary kept his remarks restrained in public. His standing in Oregon had never been higher. A Republican primary opponent in the 1942 election got less than 20 percent of the vote, and his Democratic rival less than 25 percent. It was another Republican resurgence, with nine new senators added to the party.

It would be his last campaign. Ill and dizzy from headaches, McNary was discovered to have a brain tumor. After an operation, he went to Florida to recuperate. Initially hopeful statements about his prognosis proved erroneous, and on February 25, 1943, he died, the day after he had been unanimously reelected Senate Republican leader.

Analysis of Qualifications

Few men who have gained the political heights reached by McNary have been as unconcerned about a presidential bid as he was. In 1936, when initial and ultimately inconsequential speculation appeared about McNary's chances for the nomination, he turned down a supporter's offer to raise money for him. He wrote on a Senate restaurant menu and handed it across the table to the would-be fundraiser:

> The presidential bee is a deadly bug
> I've seen it work on others.
> Oh Lord protect me from its hug
> And let it sting my brothers.

When nominated for vice president in 1940, his first response was, "Hell, no." After being convinced to accept, he responded with somewhat less colorful words, "I am grateful for the confidence reposed in me by the convention, but I wished they had imposed the chore on someone else. However, I am a good soldier and will do the best I can."

A good soldier is not quite the right description. McNary was never a battler; he was a conciliator. No cause was ever worth acrimony; few causes were even worth worry, and McNary with equanimity accepted defeat and victory, whether with legislation or with elections. Once voted the most popular man in the Senate, McNary was cheerful, never lost his temper, was always considerate and friendly. Disagreements never became personal with McNary. No principle was so sacred that compromise was impossible. Friendships were made with virtually all senators. As a conciliator this Senate Republican leader was an extremely useful man. He was never the true leader of the Republicans, such men as Robert Taft and Arthur Vandenberg filled that role. Charlie McNary was the friendly, low-key liaison between the factions that helped bring unity to a fractious party.

McNary was indifferent to many issues. If no direct impact on Oregon could be definitely discovered, McNary was unconcerned. Foreign policy was his blindest side. As president at any time during World War II, McNary would have been operating entirely in the dark, having to learn all he could with almost no background or interest in the area. He had no executive experience, and though he had demonstrated skill as a negotiator, never had he revealed the capacity to lead.

Letters home indicated he felt the people did not appreciate him, that on occasion even the presence of an opponent seemed an insult. McNary was unconcerned with all of Oregon politics, except for his own reelection. What motivated McNary was a desire to be liked, not to be controversial, to be useful in some vague way without having fixed goals. Charlie McNary was the most popular senator in part because he just did not ever take that forceful stand that can lead to animosities. There was no emotional commitment in the Oregon senator. In many ways he was admirable, for no position was ever taken until he had listened to all possible positions on the point. He could be swayed from a progressive to an extremely conservative stance, all depending on the persuasiveness of the advocate. More likely, however, McNary would be found in that location he deemed safest, right in the middle.

A poor speaker, awkward at the podium, at times clumsy and unintelligible in syntax, Senator McNary made his mark not at the rostrum, but in private negotiations. Original ideas never came from this basically provincial Westerner. Perhaps there have been quiet, peaceful times in American history when a Charles McNary could have been president with little difficulty, when consolidation and even some retrenchment from momentous change were required. During World War II, when not just America but all the Allies demanded leadership, Charles McNary was the wrong man.

McNARY BIBLIOGRAPHY

Chambers, Edith Kerns. *Genealogical Narrative: A History of the Claggett-Irvine Clans.* Eugene, Ore. (1940).

DeWitt, Howard. "Charles L. McNary and the 1918 Congressional Election." *Oregon Historical Quarterly* LXVIII (1967), pp. 125–140.

Heater, Lyle D. "Family History of McNary's, Claggett's, Irwin's." Unpublished genealogy in possession of the Oregon Society Library, Portland.

Hoffman, George Charles, Jr. "The Early Political Career of Charles McNary, 1917–1924." Unpublished doctoral dissertation, University of Southern California (1951).

_____. "Political Arithmetic, Charles L. McNary and the 1914 Primary." *Oregon Historical Quarterly* LXVI (1965), pp. 363–378.

Johnson, Roger T. "Charles L. McNary and the Republican Party During Prosperity and Depression." Unpublished doctoral dissertation, University of Wisconsin (1967).

Neal, Steve. *McNary of Oregon: A Political Biography.* Portland, Ore. (1985).

Roberts, Walter Keith. "The Political Career of Charles Linza McNary, 1924–1944." Unpublished doctoral dissertation, University of North Carolina (1953).

Shaw, H.R., comp. "Synopsis of Known Events and Reasonably Proven Surmises as to the 'Kentucky–Oregon Clan McNary'." Unpublished genealogy in possession of the Oregon Historical Society Library, Portland.

Smith, Hugh L. "The Oregon McNary Family: Genealogy and Historical Sketches." Unpublished manuscript (1936).

West, Oswald. "Reminiscences and Anecdotes: McNarys and Lanes." *Oregon Historical Quarterly* LII (1951), pp. 145–153.

Election of 1944

NOMINATIONS

Republican Party Convention (23rd): June 26–28, 1944, at Chicago Stadium, Chicago, Illinois. *President—* Thomas Dewey, nominated on the first ballot with 1,056 votes out of 1,057 cast. *Vice president—* John Bricker, nominated unanimously on the first ballot.

Democratic Party Convention (29th): July 19–21, 1944, at Chicago Stadium, Chicago, Illinois. *President—* Franklin D. Roosevelt, nominated on the first ballot with 1,086 votes out of 1,176 cast. *Vice president—* Harry Truman, nominated on the second ballot with 1,031 votes out of 1,173 cast, after vote changes. Before this, he had received 477½ votes; on the first ballot, he garnered 319½. Henry Wallace was his main rival.

GENERAL ELECTION, November 7, 1944
Popular Vote

Roosevelt. 25,611,936
Dewey. 22,013,372
Others.   349,511

Electoral Vote

Roosevelt-Truman — 432 (36 states)
Dewey-Bricker — 99 (12 states)

Winners

Franklin D. Roosevelt, 32nd president
Harry Truman, 34th vice president

Losers

Thomas Dewey, John Bricker

---

*1944 presidential nominee—
Republican Party*

Thomas E. Dewey

Full name: Thomas Edmund Dewey.

State represented: New York.

Birth: March 24, 1902, at Owosso, Michigan.

Age on Inauguration Day (January 20, 1945): 42 years, 10 months.

Education: Owosso, Michigan schools; University of Michigan (B.A., 1923), Columbia University Law School (LL.B., 1925).

Religion: Episcopalian.

Ancestry: French Huguenot ancestor, Thomas Duee, arrived in America around 1630.

Occupation: Attorney.

Public offices: Chief assistant U.S. attorney, 1931–1935; for five weeks was acting U.S. attorney in 1935; special prosecutor in New York City, 1935–1937; New York City district attorney, December 31, 1937–December 31,

1941; defeated for governor of New York, 1938; unsuccessful candidate for Republican presidential nomination, 1940; governor of New York, January, 1943–January, 1955; unsuccessful Republican nominee for president, 1944 and 1948; refused to be appointed chief justice of Supreme Court, 1953 and 1969.

Home: Dapplemere Farm, 65 miles outside New York City, at Pawling, New York.

Death: March 16, 1971, Miami, Florida, at age 69 years.

Burial: Pawling, New York.

Personal characteristics: 5'8" tall; high cheekbones, jutting jaw; dark brown hair, prominent ears; a Charlie Chaplin mustache that perhaps was his best-known feature.

Father: George M. Dewey, Jr. (1870–June 19, 1927); a newspaper editor, GOP activist.

Mother: Annie Louise Thomas (July, 1877–November 23, 1954); married January 25, 1899.

Siblings: None.

Wife: Frances Eileen Hutt (February 7, 1903–July 17, 1970); married on June 28, 1928; daughter of railroad brakeman Orla Thomas and Audie (Lee) Hutt.

Children: Thomas E. Dewey, Jr. (October 2, 1932–); married Ann Reynolds Lawler in September, 1959; financial career. John Martin Dewey (October 16, 1935–); attorney.

Movies: The investigation and prosecution of mobsters like Lucky Luciano, Waxey Gordon, and others that were handled by Dewey were the subject of the *Untouchables* television series and movie, but the prosecutor was not the focus, Elliot Ness was.

It is easy to admire Tom Dewey, to respect him for a brilliant prosecutorial, political and finally legal career in which he excelled at almost every turn. His one notable failure to excel, the surprising defeat in the 1948 presidential race, has with great irony become the accepted image of what was otherwise a startlingly successful series of careers. Perhaps his few defeats, as well as bitter feelings caused by his victories, are best explained by his cold, prickly, perfectionist personality. From childhood to the edge of the presidency, Dewey left supporters, opponents, and everyone in between aghast at just how hard it was to like him.

For 12 years, in the small town of Owosso, Michigan, Tom Dewey's mother made certain that her son never missed a day of school. It was a unique achievement, one classmates and teachers alike probably regretted. Tom's high school principal almost broke that perfect attendance record by expelling this exceptionally bright student, since Tom was so aware of his brilliance that he antagonized his classmates. Never a straight-A student because he ignored the subjects that did not interest him, the future political leader particularly loved music. His rich baritone voice presented real promise of a musical career. He finished third in a nationwide singing contest in 1922, his senior year in college. Hoping to study law while also continuing his musical training, Tom graduated from the University of Michigan in 1923 and then entered that university's law school.

His future wife Frances Hutt had also been a singer, winning her own contests on the state level in Oklahoma. She had become a secretary and aide to a New York singing coach, and traveled with him to a Chicago audition that Tom, on the spur of the moment, decided to enter. Tom won the contest and was offered a scholarship to go to New York City to study. There he continued his voice lessons, continued his legal education at Columbia University, and began a courtship. Five years later, Tom and Frances were married. By then he had abandoned singing as a possible career. His first solo recital had gone pitifully after he contracted laryngitis the morning of the event. The bad reviews caused Tom to turn to the law as his future.

After graduation, Tom made an extended tour of Europe with several friends. On a dare and a bet, Dewey grew a mustache. It would remain for the rest of his life. For one year the young attorney toiled in an unhappy, unrecognized existence as a researcher for a New York firm, occasionally getting a mundane suit to try. An argument with one of the partners led to his firing, but Dewey almost immediately joined another firm. There Dewey found the legal practice much more rewarding, and soon his prestige and income were growing. George Medalie was his legal mentor in the firm. In 1931, Medalie was appointed United

States attorney for the Southern District of New York, perhaps the most prestigious U.S. attorney's office in the nation. Medalie asked his youthful protégée to join him as an assistant. After Dewey held out for the chief assistant position, he was awarded that by the respectful Medalie.

Beginning his duties in March 1931, the chief assistant soon made a reputation as a domineering, tireless, arrogant perfectionist. Long hours were expected of all. Dewey's own workload was supposed to be administrative, but he soon became involved in the trial of some minor cases and proved effective. His success turned not only on his carefully trained voice, but even more so on his careful, methodical preparation. The best prepared case by a subordinate would be shredded by Dewey, who would demand more information, more loose ends tied. During one four-month stretch, he was home for dinner three times. It was a pace that earned him respect, but also enmity. Medalie ran unsuccessfully for United States senator, losing overwhelmingly in the Franklin Roosevelt landslide of 1932. Two days before the trial of mobster and bootlegger Waxey Gordon, Medalie resigned. Dewey had been so involved in the preparation on the trial that there was no alternative but to appoint him acting United States attorney, which was Medalie's purpose in scheduling his resignation so close to the Gordon trial. At 31, Dewey was the youngest U.S. attorney in the nation. The trial over and a conviction obtained, Democratic President Roosevelt replaced Dewey with a Democrat. Eleven years later, Dewey would try to return the favor and make Roosevelt unemployed.

Dewey's short career as a prosecutor had given him brief fame. He earned a reputation as a skilled trial attorney able to present the most complicated case persuasively, and as a man dedicated to the cause of justice and willing to work to attain it. For 18 months Dewey left that reputation behind him as he labored in private practice. Dewey's ambitions were mixed, as he confided to friends that he desired to make money as the head of a prestigious New York law firm, yet he also clearly had some vision of a political career. The corrupt politics of Democrat-controlled New York

City, dominated by the Tammany Hall machine, ignored by a machine-picked district attorney who would not prosecute the corruption and mobster rule around him, were a national disgrace. The New York grand jury in July 1935, ran amuck, rebelled against the Tammany district attorney, and called for investigations by a special prosecutor. The press picked up the call. Among the six names submitted by a special bar committee for consideration was Dewey's. Someone else was chosen who seemed likely to conduct a whitewash. The protests continued. Eventually the first choice and several subsequent ones refused their appointments. The Democratic governor, Herbert Lehman, continually refused to appoint Dewey despite the public clamor for the former acting U.S. attorney, because he feared that a strong political rival would be created. Eventually Dewey got the job anyway. The public's demand for an independent, dedicated prosecutor seemed answered.

Dewey at first moved cautiously. Nothing seemed more important than securing a good staff of attorneys, investigators, and other professionals. Dewey had demanded and received assurances of complete independence from the district attorney's office as well as an adequate staff. Fulfillment of each promise took additional pains by Dewey, but he achieved them. Several young lawyers were hired right out of law school at a dollar a year, as a way of getting energetic and bright lawyers who wanted to establish their credentials. It was the Depression, and over three thousand lawyers lined up for the 20 positions. As he started his work, Dewey gave a half-hour radio appeal to the city, beseeching those with information about the rackets to contact him. Thousands volunteered.

At first, little progress appeared to be made. Months were spent gathering information; leads were followed, witnesses questioned, records carefully sifted. It was a disheartening process, for small bits of relevant information required untold hours of examining the irrelevant. Dutch Schultz became one of his first targets. One farcical trial had already been held in which Schultz's money had bought the affections of the small town to which his tax evasion trial had been moved, affection that moved the jury to acquittal. Dewey pledged to put Schultz away yet. Schultz decided to put the new prosecutor away first. Schultz hired a hit man to end Dewey's threat, but the hired gun informed mobster kingpin Lucky Luciano first. For six hours the heads of the mob debated what to do, and the decision was finally made to prevent Schultz from carrying out his plans. On October 23, 1935, Schultz was murdered, two days before Dewey's planned death. Gang warfare broke out in the city and raged for some time.

Dewey needed some success to keep public approval for his slow-moving administration. Prosecution of loan sharks provided the mechanism. The rackets' involvement in prostitution was weakened by a massive roundup of whores, pimps, and their mob sponsors. An unexpected break came when some of the criminals began to implicate supposedly untouchable Lucky Luciano. Dewey and many others on his staff were incredulous that so suave and careful a gangster as Luciano had stooped to prostitution profits. Luciano was picked up in Arkansas, returned to New York, and held for trial. Forty prostitutes in all testified, a series of witnesses whose credibility had constantly to be shored up by the prosecutor. Hour by hour coverage of the dramatic trial appeared in the media. Defense lawyers accused Dewey of running for governor on the publicity of the trial, of fabricating testimony, and of other assorted sins. The defense allegations did not sway the jury, and a conviction of the head of the New York mob was gained.

The charges against Dewey were partly accurate. The chief prosecutor was at least thinking of a political career. In the summer of 1936, Dewey met discreetly with a few statewide Republican leaders to discuss possibilities. No decisions were reached, but contact had been made. Money was also no small consideration. As satisfying as his prosecution victories must have been, as rewarding politically as the special prosecutor position proved to be, there was little financial incentive to remain. John Foster Dulles offered him a tremendous income to join the prestigious New York firm of Sullivan and Cromwell. Dewey accepted in May 1937.

Dulles and money were not the only pressures. The Republicans in 1937 were trying to get Dewey to agree to run for district attorney. The Sullivan and Cromwell offer and ambitions to run for governor in 1938 caused him to hesitate, and then caused him to make unreasonable demands. Dewey wanted complete independence from the rest of the ticket, a three hundred thousand dollar war chest, control of the police department if elected, and even asked for fabricated news stories demanding that he run. His strongest supporters became fed up, and essentially ignored his demands as the filing deadline approached. Finally Dewey agreed to run without many of the concessions having been made. After a frantic, energetic campaign filled with charges leveled by Dewey against the entrenched Democrat, Dewey was overwhelmingly elected.

Dewey's tenure as district attorney started fast and then accelerated. Politics was expelled from the office; political friends were more often infuriated than satisfied when they suggested appointments. A program was established for providing attorneys to the poor. Backed-up cases were cleared from the docket. Dewey was abrasive, tough, and effective. The public loved him, and his nationwide reputation was growing. More big-name criminals were prosecuted. In 1938, the Republicans began to push the youthful district attorney into a race for governor. Movies were being made of his exploits, from Lucky Luciano's prosecution to others of lesser renown. One Hollywood studio complained of being deluged with unsolicited scripts using Dewey's story as the plot. One more thrust towards the national spotlight came in the highly publicized trial of Jimmy Hines, a Tammany boss, a former political adviser to Franklin Roosevelt, and a man whose control of the "policy" racket was immensely profitable. It was called the "battle of the century," one of several such epochal trials Dewey had during his seven years as a prosecutor. The first trial ended in a mistrial, but on the second Hines was found guilty.

In between the two Hines trials was a race for governor. Dewey had met pollster George Gallup, prominent member of an ill-reputed profession not yet accepted in politics. Gallup helped convince Dewey that the governorship

was obtainable in 1938, despite the popularity of the Democrat incumbent, Herbert
Lehman. Calling himself a "New Deal Republican," Dewey went on the attack against Lehman's administration and tried to tie him to
Tammany. Dewey was to lose narrowly, but he
reshaped the New York Republican Party in
his progressive image.

Dewey next added even more mob and
political scalps to his pelt, starting with Hines.
Pollster Gallup reported to Dewey that half of
the nation's Republicans made him their first
choice for president; even more startling,
Gallup found that Dewey would defeat Roosevelt 58 percent to 42 percent. Dewey was
becoming overwhelmed by the rush of events,
with supporters clamoring for action. Senator
Arthur Vandenberg was his most prominent
backer. He would later be a rival for the presidency. Early in 1940, Dewey began his restrained campaign for the White House. A
tour of the country led to countless speeches
as he preached his message of progressive Republicanism, a New Deal without its excesses.
Handshaking and other requirements of the
campaigning were torture. Yet grinning and
bearing paid off, for in the April Wisconsin
primary Dewey won with 62 percent of the
vote. Robert Taft and Wendell Willkie were
his nominal competitors. The more formidable opponent was the growing threat of war
overseas, and the nation's desire to stick with
the proven incumbent. The Depression still
existed; it would not end until war production
needs restarted the industrial engines. At the
1940 convention, Dewey was stalled by the
more efficient maneuvering of the Willkie
forces. On the fifth ballot the 37-year-old district attorney threw his support to Taft, but
Willkie won anyway.

War had come at last to Europe. Dewey
strongly endorsed the president's growing
alignment with Britain and the Allies. The isolationist majority in the GOP was offended by
Dewey's stands in favor of Lend-Lease and the
complete repeal of the Neutrality Act. Dewey's
early contribution to the war effort was
fundraising help for the USO; in five weeks he
helped raise five million dollars.

In 1941, Dewey decided not to run for
another term as district attorney. So com-

pletely did he dominate the political picture
that Tammany offered to back him. Instead,
he suggested four of his top assistants as possibilities, and both Tammany and the Republicans chose his successor from that list. There
was little doubt that his eyes were again on the
governorship. Willkie was embittered as a
result of the 1940 campaign and threatened to
run for governor. Instead, Willkie listed ten
men he found acceptable for the office, and
Dewey was not among them. It hardly mattered. Dewey won the nomination with ease,
and went on to rout Democrat governor
Lehman. During the campaign the governor-
to-be established even more clearly his international views. It would not be foreign policy
that confronted him when he moved into the
monstrous, foreboding governor's mansion in
Albany in January 1943. It was a bloated, at
times corrupt, always inefficient state government. It took a year for him to fill all his cabinet positions, so important did he consider
the caliber of the men who would assist him.
Administrative reform was an early effort.
Modernizing and humanizing the state's mental hospitals also became a central concern.
Reapportionment of the state legislature and
the creation of a TVA-like Niagara Power
Authority were also hallmarks of his administration. Ill feelings were generated everywhere
he turned, as often among fellow Republicans
as with the Democrats. Yet he passed his programs almost without exception. He was a
strong governor, described frequently by those
he conquered as a dictator. His political appeal
was tested in late 1943 when the lieutenant
governor died. Anxious to have a Republican
in the number two spot should be succeed in
moving to higher office, Dewey backed and
saw the voters accept the 67-year-old Republican state senate leader. In the process he
honed the Republican organization, weak from
decades of failure, into a formidable machine.

When nominated for governor, Dewey had
promised four years of tending to New York's
affairs. Apparently he meant to keep that
promise, not totally for idealistic reasons since
he felt that "that man Roosevelt" might well
be unbeatable. Willkie and Taft were again in
the presidential race for 1944. Youthful former
Minnesota Governor Harold Stassen was men-

tioned as a possibility. Gallup showed Dewey beating "that man" handily if the war was over by November, but losing just as decisively if it still was being waged. Dewey refused to commit himself as a candidate, and maintained his refusal until the national convention nominated him. The nomination was all but unanimous.

No Republican ever found the trick against Franklin Roosevelt. For a time Dewey's chances appeared real. He hit the president hard for "one-man" government, saying that no one was indispensable, regardless of what the president himself might think. The Republican nominee pledged a nonpartisan foreign policy and support for the war. One of the most remembered episodes of the campaign was Roosevelt's charge that the Republicans were even picking on "my dog Fala." The allegation was that Roosevelt had ordered a navy ship back to port to pick the dog up after it was discovered he had been left behind. Roosevelt's speech almost backfired, as Dewey counterattacked with a slashing, effective, partisan attack on Roosevelt and his administration. Dewey's dynamic step away from his cold, cautious, dull style in this speech given in Oklahoma City had the potential of turning the campaign his way, but Dewey himself was so disgusted with the effort, which was so out of character, that he called it "the worst damned speech I ever made in my life." No prodding from associates could put him back on track. Dewey was bitter towards Roosevelt as a result of information Dewey received that indicated Roosevelt had known in advance of the attack on Pearl Harbor and either negligently or deliberately permitted the attack to occur. Almost 40 years later those charges would be renewed with some documentary support. Dewey was reported to have said, privately, that rather than be reelected Roosevelt should be impeached. But Secretary of State George C. Marshall convinced Dewey that the basis of those stories — that the Americans had broken the Japanese codes and therefore knew of the attack in advance — could not safely be revealed without greatly damaging the war effort, since those same codes were still in use by Tokyo. Dewey was incredulous that these same codes could possibly still be used, and

thought the whole Marshall plea was Roosevelt's cover-up. Reluctantly, Dewey acceded to Marshall's entreaties, in part because there was such potential for the issue backfiring. Dewey never did change his mind that Roosevelt was responsible for Pearl Harbor. Some historians agree, but the evidence is circumstantial.

The American people had no serious complaint, however, and returned Franklin D. Roosevelt to yet another term. In defeat, Dewey could be happy that he had run the best race of any of Roosevelt's opponents. Prospects for another try, however, did not seem good. The Taft wing hated him, and no defeated candidate had come back to win election as president since Grover Cleveland in 1892 and before him William Henry Harrison in 1840.

Dewey settled back to running New York. His postwar leadership established his state, as well as himself, as a leader in anti-discrimination legislation. Labor strikes were settled forcefully. A large budget surplus was created, being husbanded for the day when Dewey expected unemployment to soar after the soldiers returned and the wartime factories were shut down. The surplus became one of the few issues in Dewey's 1946 reelection campaign, as his Democratic opponent, Senator Jim Mead, charged that it was a "slush fund." It was an ineffective charge, and Dewey won with the largest percentage in New York history.

In 1948 Republican presidential politics, Stassen and Taft again made up the principal competition for Dewey, with Vandenberg a lesser force. A carefully constructed network of supporters throughout the country was established. Eisenhower was seen as a threat, and Dewey met with the general to set out the reasons that Ike should not run. It was surreal to Eisenhower, but Dewey was covering all the bases. Dewey won the New Hampshire primary, but not convincingly. Then in Wisconsin Stassen won handily, and followed that up in Nebraska. Dewey was reeling, and he decided to place all his chips on the line in Oregon. For three weeks he campaigned, performing all the publicity stunts he had previously refused to do — wearing headdresses, kissing babies, gnawing on a bone presented him by "cavemen." The clincher was a nationally broadcast radio debate with Stassen, in which Dewey argued that the Communist Party should not be outlawed, while Stassen argued the opposite. The civil liberties position staked out by Dewey was appealing: "I am unalterably ... against any scheme to write laws outlawing people because of their religion, political, social, or economic ideas." Oregonians agreed, narrowly, and Stassen was no longer much of a factor. The Dewey organization was unstoppable at the convention, and the New York governor won on the third ballot. Dewey's choice of Earl Warren as a running mate would later be regretted, as he referred to Warren as the "dumb Swede."

The Republicans had a seemingly unassailable margin in the polls after the convention. Harry Truman knew the odds against him, and therefore had little to lose as he embarked on a divisive, angry, aggressive campaign. Truman accused Dewey of being a tool of the conservative, even reactionary elements, a charge Taft must have found humorous. He accused the Republicans of being friends of the communists, and the next breath that they were friends of the fascists that only paid "lip service" to democracy. Comparing the GOP to Hitler, Mussolini, and Stalin, Truman said that Dewey's election would cause the loss of basic freedoms.

Dewey had been carrying on a careful, calm campaign, afraid to lose his margin in the polls. But by mid–October he realized he was in trouble. After a particularly bitter and false series of allegations by Truman, Dewey decided to change his tactics. There were only a few weeks to go before the election, and his advisers insisted he not change his style. Dewey polled the reporters as well as his advisers on the campaign train, and all but a handful argued against slashing back at Truman. Thus Dewey stayed his careful course. The narrow election defeat for Dewey was a surprise, but probably much less of one to Dewey than to the vast majority in the country. He always believed that he lost because he could not hold the farm vote. Farmers had recently suffered a severe drop in prices, an omen to many that another Depression might be in the making. Truman had skillfully, if unfairly,

played on that fear by charging the Republican candidate with being merely another Hoover ready heartlessly to plunge the country back into ruin.

In many ways Dewey's greatest political contributions were still in front of him. Six more years as New York governor were to be served, with successes in cleaning up additional areas of mob rule particularly in the Longshoreman's Union, in establishing a university system and in creating a New York Transit Authority. In national politics Dewey was a critical factor in urging Eisenhower to run for president in 1952, and then in getting Richard Nixon as his running mate. Nixon and Dewey became good friends and each seemed respectful of the other. Dewey wanted no part in either Republican president's administration and, after 1955, was content to practice law. He joined a New York firm that became known as Dewey, Ballantine. He refused cabinet and Supreme Court nominations, and established himself instead as the leader of one of New York's most prominent firms. Frequently an adviser to Eisenhower and then Nixon, he remained interested but not greatly involved in politics. In March 1971, nine months after his wife of 42 years succumbed to a lengthy fight with cancer, Dewey himself died from a quick, massive heart attack.

Analysis of Qualifications

He was an excellent governor. Mental health hospitals, state highways, public transportation, housing, public power systems, and countless other problems received his attention. He was completely honest, requiring all campaign contributions of any substantial sums to be carefully investigated to discover just what they were expecting. There was no end to the work he would perform, a matter of no small irritation to his staff. While greatly improving the quality of governmental services in New York, he also created a budgetary surplus that was guarded passionately. When a later governor, Nelson Rockefeller, multiplied manyfold the expenditures of government in the state, Dewey told him that he liked him, "but I don't think I can afford you."

Dewey's theory of government required

order, system, concern for the needs of the people but not ignoring the costs of programs. He was also critical of growing federal controls, and believed that state governments must be invigorated. Big Brother in Washington seemed to be strangling the American personality, creating an image of cradle to grave security that enervated the drive, the ambition of the country. Though a liberal by any standards, and particularly those of such opponents as Robert Taft and Everett Dirksen, Tom Dewey was nonetheless a devout believer in free enterprise. He wanted a balanced budget; he accepted the right of states to control vast areas of government that were being arrogated by the national government.

Through his life Dewey had a passion for music. It was one of the few things that demonstrated emotion in the Dewey character. His campaign manager thought that perhaps he was never happy. He could be satisfied with his successes, but that satisfaction was completely goal-oriented. An adviser called him "cold as a February icicle." Supporters could be treated with disdain; political friends were soon repelled by his arrogance, his feeling that he was above demands forced on other politicians. He would not stoop, not often at least, to showing compassion or warmth. It was an orderly life, one that demanded few interruptions in the routine. When an important politician unexpectedly appeared on Dewey's 1948 campaign train, he was asked by Dewey to leave while the candidate ate his usual solitary lunch.

Dewey's skills were manifest. As a prosecutor he had been enormously effective. A stickler for detail, an impassioned believer in total preparation of a case, Dewey was almost invincible even against the high-priced defense lawyers hired by mobster money. He was tireless, diligent, precise. He had considerable administrative skills, clearly revealed in his governorship. There were few men who could claim the legislative successes enjoyed during his 12-year tenure as the Empire State's chief executive. He persuaded, badgered, or just forced legislators in line on his programs. At times Dewey played political hardball, most noticeably in coercing many reluctant New York delegates to the 1952 national conven-

tion to vote for Eisenhower, or else face retribution at home.

President Dewey would have served his country efficiently, meticulously, logically. Few programs would have been proposed that were not scrupulously prepared and budgeted; grandiose plans that could not be afforded would have been opposed, but efforts to spread the money that was available as effectively as possible would have been made. Thomas E. Dewey was a brilliant, imaginative man, but one fairly described as the man you had to get to know to really dislike, or in Clare Boothe Luce's words, he "looks like the bridegroom on the wedding cake." Such an image would have hurt his presidency, but little else would have interfered with the efforts of one of the most remarkable men ever to run for president. He could well have been one of the most effective, and least-loved, presidents this country ever had.

DEWEY BIBLIOGRAPHY

Beyer, Barry K. *Thomas E. Dewey, 1937 to 1945: A Study in Political Leadership.* New York City (1979).

Dewey, Thomas E. *Twenty Against the Underworld.* New York City (1975).

Dewey, Walter E. *Family Genealogy* (1912).

Hughes, Rupert. *Thomas E. Dewey: Attorney for the People.* New York City (1940).

Ray, Robert. "A Comparison of the Speaking Styles of Franklin D. Roosevelt and Thomas E. Dewey in the 1944 Presidential Election." Unpublished doctoral dissertation, University of Iowa (1947).

Smith, Richard Norton. *Thomas E. Dewey and His Times.* New York City (1982).

Stolberg, Mary M. *Fighting Organized Crime: Politics, Justice, and the Legacy of Thomas E. Dewey.* Boston (1995).

Walker, Stanley. *Thomas E. Dewey: An American of This Country.* New York City (1944).

1944 vice presidential nominee —
Republican Party

John Bricker

Full name: John William Bricker.
State represented: Ohio.
Birth: Pleasant Township, Madison County, Ohio, on September 6, 1893.

THOMAS E. DEWEY and JOHN BRICKER
(From the collection of David J. and Janice L. Frent)

Age on Inauguration Day (January 20, 1945): 51 years, 4½ months.

Education: Local schools, graduated from high school, 1911; Ohio State University, 1912–1916, B.A.; J.D., 1920; admitted to bar in 1920.

Religion: Mother was a Methodist; he often attended Congregational or Christian Church.

Ancestry: German ancestors left for America to escape religious persecution.

Occupation: Attorney.

Public offices: Solicitor for Grandview Village Council, Ohio, 1920–1928; appointed assistant attorney general and counsel for Public Utilities Commission, 1923–1927; defeated for state attorney general nomination, 1928; appointed to Public Utilities Commission, 1929–1932; Ohio attorney general, January 1933–1937; defeated for governor, 1936; governor, January 9, 1939–January, 1945; unsuccessful candidate for Republican nomination for president, 1944; defeated Republican nominee for vice president, 1944; U.S. Senate, January 3, 1947–January 3, 1959, defeated.

Home: Columbus, Ohio.

Death: March 22, 1986, at age 92 years, 6½ months.

Burial: Greenlawn Cemetery, Columbus, Ohio.

Personal characteristics: 6'2½" tall; silver, wavy hair, with unruly patch on top; at times pudgy; sonorous voice.

Father: Lemuel Spencer Bricker (April, 1859–June 22, 1916), farmer.

Mother: Laura King (August 15, 1863–January 23, 1942); married on December 31, 1885.

Siblings: Mary Ellen (twin) (September 6, 1893–April 3, 1969); married P. Freeman Mooney on October 5, 1912.

Wife: Harriet A. Day (April 13, 1896–June 1, 1985); married September 4, 1920.

Children: Harriet Ellen (June, 1921–March 1922). John Day Bricker (1930–); adopted.

John Bricker was born on a farm about 25 miles southwest of Columbus, Ohio. He almost certainly will be the last candidate who can claim he was born in a log cabin. His parents' home incorporated the smaller log house built on the farm by his great-grandfather. Bricker would emotionally and philosophically remain a part of this simple, agrarian way of life throughout his career.

Though his parents were not wealthy, their one-hundred-acre farm enabled them at least to escape poverty. His ancestors had been farmers for several generations. Until his family moved closer to a school, John and his twin sister Mary Ellen walked two miles to the area's one-room schoolhouse. As the only son in the family, there were endless chores both before his long trek each morning, and then after he returned at night. At 14, John began attending high school in Mount Sterling, Ohio, making the six miles to school by horse and buggy. Perhaps the only noteworthy feature of his boyhood is the fact that he became a skilled baseball player, being paid to play from an early age. When he graduated there was little money for college, and with his father unable to provide much financial assistance, the younger Bricker taught school for a year to raise money. Then he was able to begin studies at Ohio State University.

Again Bricker found glory playing baseball. His debate skills continued to be honed on the college level. He was also active in the campus YMCA, eventually becoming president. Bricker was president of his class his senior year. It was at Ohio State that his abnormally slow heart beat, only 55 beats per minute rather than the normal 72, first became a problem. It kept him from participating in any sports except baseball, and also kept him out of physical education classes. While a freshman, Bricker commuted from the family's farm in order to help with chores.

When Bricker graduated in 1916, offers came to teach high school; the university offered him an instructorship in English; and the family's farm also beckoned. But his sights were on law school. When Bricker's father died two weeks after John received his college diploma, the need seemed evident for him to forego his education and help his mother. Mrs. Bricker knew that her son did not want to spend the rest of his life on the farm, and insisted that he continue with his plans to become a lawyer. She could move into town and operate the farm using hired men. It was through that arrangement that Bricker was able to continue on the path that would lead him to political prominence.

For a year he commuted to law school at

Columbus, continuing to help out on the farm in the early mornings and then at night when he returned. Studying was performed on the commuter train he caught to Columbus. America entered World War I before the young law student had completed his first year, and he immediately tried to enlist. The abnormal heart beat again interfered and none of the services would accept him. Severely disappointed, Bricker continued his studies while also attempting to perform some sort of alternative service. He became the athletic director for an infantry unit. The commander suggested he might be able to go overseas with the troops if he applied as a chaplain. Bricker followed through on the suggestion immediately, even becoming ordained as a minister by his helpful local pastor. His ordination came on February 28, 1918, would end after one year, and did not entitle him to preach. It did however entitle him to be admitted into the army. Europe would not be his destination, but instead Bricker made it only as far as Virginia. His sad but useful service was as a chaplain in a military hospital during an influenza epidemic that killed many soldiers. A few weeks before the Armistice was signed, the chaplain was accepted for overseas duty, but the war ended even before he began his training. Frustrated by his inability to fight in the war, Bricker nonetheless enjoyed one benefit from his tour of duty. He met his future wife during a brief stop while his troop train traveled to his training camp.

After the war Bricker resumed law school and graduated in 1920. He began practice in Columbus and became active in civic and political affairs. His first political work had been as a student, organizing for Charles Evans Hughes and the Republican Senate candidate in 1916. His family had long suspected Bricker's interest in politics would one day make him governor, and just as inevitably he would become president. That road began when Bricker accepted his first public position in 1920, solicitor for a suburban Columbus town, Grandview Heights. An additional public duty came in 1923 when the successful Republican candidate for state attorney general appointed his loyal campaign worker as an assistant. Bricker's special duties involved work for the state Public Utilities Commission. His experience trying cases improved his legal skills, but more importantly for Bricker's career it gave him contacts throughout Ohio. He resigned in 1927 after a new attorney general was elected.

Bricker was restless in private practice and thought it time to make his first run for office. The office he chose was attorney general, but Bricker lost in the primary, coming in a close second in a six-man field. The governor then appointed him to the Public Utilities Commission. His most famous case concerned the rate that could be charged for natural gas in Columbus, a matter long pending before the Commission. Bricker favored a 48 cents per thousand cubic feet (mcf) rate, but the other two Commission members thought more should be charged. The gas company wanted 65 cents. No decision could be reached, and Bricker resigned in protest over the procrastination. The Democratic governor refused to accept the resignation, perhaps in an attempt to embarrass the Republican commissioner. Bricker agreed to go back to work only if the governor instructed the chairman of the Commission to resolve the case. Soon thereafter the Commission ruled for a 55 cents per mcf rate, with Bricker continuing to insist upon 48. The state Supreme Court agreed with Bricker, but the United States Supreme Court held even 55 cents had been too low.

Swimming upstream against a Franklin Roosevelt torrent, Bricker parlayed his moderately liberal Public Utilities Commission record into a narrow victory as Republican nominee for attorney general in 1932. He won by ten thousand votes at the same time as Franklin D. Roosevelt was carrying the state by 75,000, and the Democratic nominee for governor was winning by 200,000. He was the lone bright spot in a dismal year for the Ohio GOP.

As attorney general, Bricker became noted for his assaults on federal encroachment in what he saw as state prerogatives. The Depression meant that much of the attorney general's work involved acting as counsel for the liquidators and conservators of failed banks. In 1934, pressure was brought on Bricker to run for governor, but he decided to try again for attorney general. Again he won against the tide of Democratic successes in Ohio. The governor who was elected, Martin L. Davey, was an inept man who brought much financial and political distress to the state. That image of corruption had not yet taken hold in the public eye when in 1936 Bricker failed as the Republican nominee for governor against Davey.

There were so many charges of graft and other forms of corruption against Governor Davey and his aides by 1938 that there was no doubt somebody was going to beat him. That somebody was, first, Democrat Charles Sawyer, who beat Davey in the primary. Somebody else was John Bricker, who as the Republican nominee that year swept to victory as a consequence of revulsion against Davey and general reaction to six years of Democratic rule. The entire Republican state ticket won.

Bricker's reputation as governor was set by his budget and payroll slashing. Davey had left him a forty million dollar deficit. Thanks to a sales tax and the boom of productivity during World War II, this was turned into a twenty-five million dollar surplus. He cut government employment by two thousand, or ten percent, during his first month in office. While cleaning up state government, Bricker accused the New Deal of extravagance. Bricker complained that the Democrats' programs, state and federal, were governmental paternalism that destroyed the work ethic. The governor's positions seem overly austere, especially his role in the Cleveland relief crisis of 1939. National press stories trumpeted that there was starvation in Ohio. The media charged Bricker with being more concerned with a budget surplus than he was with the poor. Some local newspapers picked up on the characterization of Bricker as cold and unconcerned. Bricker refused to call a special session to deal with the problems, saying both that the problems were exaggerated and that the local officials could use their taxing and other financial tools to remedy the situation. President Roosevelt, among others, stated that Ohio and its governor were not tending to relief needs.

Most of the problems had been caused by cutbacks in the local Work Progress Administration. Bricker criticized the WPA, Civilian Conservation Corps, and other New Deal relief agencies. Ohio towns besides Cleveland were facing similar crises. Both sides in the controversy accused the other of political manipulation of relief programs. Bricker's supporters stated that the problems in Ohio were no different than anywhere else in the country; the real difference was Democratic concern for Bricker as a national candidate. In the midst of the crisis Bricker delivered a speech charging that the whole matter was Democratic sponsored smear tactics against him, but that he was resisting federal takeover in the state.

By February of 1940 passions had cooled, and local relief efforts, such as a bond issue in Cleveland, had partially rectified the problems. The governor then called a special legislative session, something he had refused to do earlier, in order to provide supplemental assistance. The whole matter had made the Ohio governor a nationally known figure, though hardly a noncontroversial one. In November 1939, a group of Chicago businessmen and politicians formed a committee to draft Bricker for the 1940 presidential nomination. Bricker disavowed the effort and they soon disbanded. Earlier in 1939, Bricker had renounced all presidential aspirations for 1940. Many saw the move as a settlement with his fellow Ohioan, Senator Robert A. Taft, whereby Taft would be the candidate for 1940 and if he lost, Bricker would receive Taft's support for 1944. Whether true or not, and there is no direct evidence to support it, that scenario eventuated. With Taft's announcement of his own candidacy on August 3, 1939, Bricker wrote, "If you get the slightest rumor of anything [that indicates my friends are working against Taft] ... I will see that it is stopped." Taft was never particularly respectful of Bricker, though he respected the governor's political clout. When Bricker first ran for governor in 1936, Taft wrote his wife after meeting Bricker, "I received an unfavorable impression. ... He seems to have become very conceited ... I hope I may be wrong." The two would view each other warily for their entire careers.

Rather than the presidency in 1940, Bricker was running for reelection as governor. Though World War II had already begun in Europe,

Bricker refused comment on what American response was appropriate, saying that international issues were beyond his responsibility and knowledge. He would repeat the statements in 1942 and again in 1944, even while a candidate for vice president. Clearly Bricker was avoiding controversy, but he also appeared sincerely to believe the matters were too complex to discuss from his limited vantage point as a governor. In 1940, his reelection total over a weak opponent was a record 364,000 plurality. Two more prosperous years in Ohio, in which Bricker continued to nurture a budget surplus, resulted in a still larger plurality in 1942 — 375,000 votes.

Bricker had made a modestly liberal record as Public Utilities Commissioner, opposing rate increases requested by utilities. As governor he at times showed streaks of the same philosophy, appointing a black to a judgeship, favoring broader eligibility for old-age pensions, and supporting relief measures in the 1940 special session. He was well-poised for 1944.

Though immensely popular in Ohio, some of Bricker's ease in reelection can be traced to weak opponents. His budgetary record of ending a deficit and gaining a surplus can be explained by higher taxes and a booming wartime economy. His budgets were the largest in Ohio history until that time, larger than in New York, which had twice the population. He avoided comment on all national issues, even after announcing as a presidential candidate on November 10, 1943. Republican newspaper editor William Allen White said that Bricker hoped to gain the 1944 nomination:

> ...without saying anything, without getting on either side of the momentous questions of the hour — domestic and foreign.
> Surely the Republican Party ... cannot be so craven that it would conspire to sneak into victory with no issue but Bricker and a belly-ache.
> Bricker is an honest Harding. Thumbs down.

Bricker was not totally silent on foreign affairs, but his views were hazy. Bricker's response, perhaps missing the point, was exasperation. "I'm a governor; Harding was a senator." White's point was that Bricker was a handsome, empty shell. But there were no political bosses behind Bricker pushing him on as there were for Harding. Bricker admittedly was not brilliant, but he had common sense and was good-natured, outgoing, and tremendously popular. Probably no man was more popular with the party leaders as the 1944 national convention approached than was Bricker.

Wendell Willkie and Tom Dewey were Bricker's main opponents for the nomination; an attractive dark horse, available in case of a deadlock, was youthful former Minnesota governor Harold E. Stassen. Bricker's reputation as an isolationist, as an "honest Harding," and as the party bosses' candidate did him no political good. The isolationist image was not totally earned, for he had on several occasions refused to lend his support to isolationist leaders. Bricker stated that America's postwar role could not be to ignore foreign affairs, but neither should there be definite "commitments." By the time of the national convention, with Bricker never having caught fire and polls showing that Dewey was the only candidate with a chance to defeat "that man" Roosevelt, Bricker knew his chances were doomed. One important politician who had not abandoned him was Senator Robert Taft, who had endorsed Bricker at the end of 1942. Bricker remained a candidate until the day after the convention opened. Dewey forces then let the Ohio governor know he was wanted on the ticket. On the third day of the convention, after Dewey's nominating speech, Bricker went to the podium graciously to withdraw his own name as a candidate and to urge Dewey's nomination. Calls from several delegates were "no, no" as Bricker's intentions became clear. He said, "I am more interested in defeating the New Deal philosophy of absolutism than I am in personally being president." His reward of the vice presidential nomination came the next night.

Bricker's campaign was a low-road attack on the New Deal, angrily denouncing the drift towards federal control of matters properly for the states and localities. He and Dewey lost in still another Roosevelt landslide, and he had to retire to Columbus to reopen his law practice.

The former governor stayed on the sidelines only a year, and then jumped into the battle for Ohio's other Senate seat, the one not occupied by Robert Taft. Again he campaigned on the platform of less federal government, control of unions, and other standard Republican planks. The GOP landslide helped, with Bricker's winning by over 300,000 votes. He was a staunch anti-communist, favored the Taft-Hartley Act, was against many federal subsidy programs for housing and urban development. His isolationist proclivities became pronounced now that he had to reach decisions on foreign issues. In 1947, Bricker opposed aid for Greece and Turkey and in 1949 for NATO countries. The fabulously successful Marshall Plan to rebuild Europe was no favorite, and Bricker voted for a cut in appropriations for the program. Accurately, perhaps, as history now records, Bricker denounced the Yalta agreement entered into by Truman with Stalin and Churchill as a sellout of democracy and a guarantee of Soviet conquest of eastern Europe. These stands were popular in Ohio and another easy election victory was gained in 1952.

Elected with Bricker was a Republican-controlled Congress and a Republican president, General Dwight Eisenhower. Bricker had supported Senator Taft for the GOP nomination. Eisenhower would find Bricker a continuing thorn on foreign policy. In March 1953, Bricker opposed Eisenhower's appointment of an ambassador to Russia, and wanted cuts in Eisenhower's foreign aid requests. He even supported Joe McCarthy in his failed effort to avoid censure by the Senate. Bricker told McCarthy: "Joe, you're a son of a bitch, but there are times when you have to have a son of a bitch around and this is one of them." Yet nothing was as significant in Bricker's opposition to the president as his battle for a constitutional amendment to restrict presidential treaty-making functions.

The Bricker amendment was reported out of Senate Committee in June 1953. The central provision held that no treaty would become effective until Congress passed specific legislation enacting it. A corollary premise was that no executive agreement with a foreign government would be effective until approved by the Senate. Another provision barred such organizations as the United Nations from affecting domestic policy without appropriate federal or state enabling laws. Congress had the authority to override state laws if a treaty was involved, and the Bricker amendment would have repealed that right. many of the same concerns would be voiced by the exact opposite of the political spectrum, Democratic liberals, during the Vietnam war.

Bricker's amendment was a burning political issue for years. The American Bar Association endorsed the amendment as a needed clarification of foreign policy procedures. Southern states' rights advocates saw benefits to be gained. Critics included internationalists in general, and President Eisenhower in particular. To them the amendment was an unwieldy yoke on the conduct of foreign affairs. One biographer of Eisenhower stated that the Bricker amendment and its debate upset the president more than any other issue. The president in January 1954 called it a signal, if passed, that America was withdrawing from world affairs. That was Bricker's purpose. Several votes to pass failed, the closest coming on February 26, 1954. After Bricker's version failed decisively, a milder proposal fell one vote short of the two-thirds majority needed. Bricker than dropped the issue, perhaps feeling enough political prestige had already been squandered. The issue remains alive. As recently as 1997 an amendment identical in intent to Bricker's was introduced by Representative Helen Chenoweth (R–Id.).

Bricker's actions were not universally accepted back home, but still he was strongly favored for reelection in 1958. To Bricker's dismay, businessmen who hated union involvement in Ohio had sponsored a state constitutional "right to work" amendment. Nineteen hundred and fifty-eight was a depressing year for Republicans nationwide, but particularly in Ohio, for all but one statewide GOP candidate was defeated. The right to work provision was rejected by a two-to-one margin. Senator John Bricker was defeated by Democrat Stephen Young. Young's statewide election losses had been numerous prior to 1958; he would survive six years later against Robert Taft's namesake son only because of the Johnson landslide; Taft would defeat him in 1970. Bricker lost by only 160,000 out of 3,200,000 votes, on the issue he did not want to make — right to work — but he never tried for office again.

Following the upset, Bricker retired to private law practice in Columbus. His influence in local Ohio politics reappeared occasionally. He campaigned for Republican state and presidential candidates, and attended several national conventions after his defeat. In 1963, speculation arose that he might be a candidate against Senator Young in 1964, but on November 27, 1963, he rejected the suggestion.

Analysis of Qualifications

John Bricker was a splendid example of middle America. Genial, charming, a believer in individualism, a handshaker and backslapper who was liked by all, Bricker exuded the virtues of his smalltown, agrarian upbringing. He was religious, moderate in drink, respected the Sabbath and would not even attend a baseball game on Sunday. His nickname was "Honest John," and that is accurate in all its connotations. He was honest personally, a guardian of the public purse, who weeded out the graft that had grown up in two corrupt terms of his predecessor as governor. Bricker was neither brilliant nor stupid; he was basically serene in who he was and what he was doing.

Until Bricker reached the United States Senate, his reputation included that he would not take a stand on issues. While leading Ohio during World War II, Bricker believed that questions about foreign policy were unfair because he had no responsibilities in the area. His tentative introductory steps onto the foreign policy stage were stumbling, including a statement that America was not, never had been, and never would be isolationist. His point was to dramatize his commitment to America's continuing as an international force after the war was over; the medium for the message was a gross misstatement of American (and his own) political history. Bricker's avoidance of international issues ended when he joined the Senate. No stronger isolationist record can be found among senators during his first term. Starting his second, the Ohio

senator sponsored an amendment designed to curtail adventures by American presidents into international affairs by having the constant restraint of the United States Congress alongside them. A majority of the Senate joined him in the effort, partly out of envious interest in gaining a greater voice over foreign policy, partly out of philosophical agreement, and partially also because John Bricker was an extremely well-liked peer among his fellow senators. In this confrontation with the executive branch, "Honest John" became a symbol to those who wanted to pull back from the bold foreign involvement by the United States following the war. It was not until the battle over the Bricker Amendment that its sponsor at long last emerged from the shadow of Robert Taft, "Mr. Republican," and established himself in the public mind as a man of opinions, influence, and significance. In much the same way as his senatorial brother Taft, Bricker achieved this recognition in a losing effort.

Another facet of the philosophy that created the Bricker Amendment was the Ohioan's strong states' rights viewpoint. Opposition to the New Deal was constantly, bitterly expressed by the Ohioan. Federal encroachment scared Bricker and made him worry about the future of federalism's concept of shared responsibilities between national and state governments.

Primarily because of his obstructionist, negative role in the Senate, in 1949 Bricker was elected by a poll of 211 newspapermen in Washington as the "worst" senator. Walter Lippman called him the "politicians' candidate." Historically he had been remembered, if at all, as an honest man of moderate abilities, a kind and sincere man who made many friends and few enemies, but a man of few accomplishments. He demonstrated no ability in gaining acceptance of his views, not even during the protracted, bitter, and ultimately failed attempt on the Bricker Amendment. John Bricker had not indicated the capacity to perform the awesome tasks of the presidency. His nomination for the vice presidency presented the country with a man who would have had to grow dramatically in office, revealing talents he had not earlier shown, before his administration could have succeeded.

BRICKER BIBLIOGRAPHY

"Bricker, Attorney." *Newsweek* (February 12, 1945), p. 46.

"Bricker of Ohio." *The New Republic* (June 28, 1943), pp. 860–861.

David, Forrest. "The Log Cabin Candidate." *The Saturday Evening Post* (July 10, 1943), pp. 9–11.

Davies, Richard. *Defender of the Old Guard: John Bricker and American Politics.* Columbus, Ohio (1993).

———. "In the Shadow of Warren G. Harding: John Bricker and the Presidential Election of 1944." *Timeline* (Jan./Feb. 1997), pp. 2–19.

"The Education of John Bricker." *The New Republic* (October 30, 1944), pp. 556–557.

Egan, Charles E. "Bricker Nominated for Second Place." *New York Times* (June 29, 1944), pp. 1, 13.

"Four Leading Contenders for Top of Republican Ticket in 1948." *United States News and World Report* (November 1, 1946), p. 58.

Gunther, John. *Inside U.S.A.* New York City (1951).

"Highlights in the Careers of Republican Nominees." *New York Times* (June 29, 1944), p. 15.

Janeway, Eliot. "Ohio's Governor Is Republican Party's Link with Some of Its Best and Oldest Traditions." *Life* (November 6, 1944), pp. 1–2 ff.

Pauley, Karl B. *Bricker of Ohio: The Man and His Record.* New York (1944).

Phillips, Wayne. "Labor Is Dazzled by Ohio Victory." *New York Times* (November 5, 1958), p. 24.

Reston, James. "The Destiny of Bricker." *New York Times* (February 5, 1954), p. 3.

Seasongood, Murray. "John W. Bricker," in J.T. Salter, ed. *Public Men in and out of Office.* Chapel Hill (1946), pp. 395–414.

Tannebaum, Duane Arden. "The Bricker Amendment Controversy." Unpublished doctoral dissertation, Columbia University (1980).

Thatcher, Terence L. "The Bricker Amendment 1952–1954." *Northwest Ohio Quarterly* XLIX (1977), pp. 107–120.

Walker, William O. "John W. Bricker and Joseph R. McCarthy: The Cold War at Home and Abroad, 1950–1954." Unpublished master's thesis, Ohio State University (1968).

Some family information provided by Senator Bricker, Columbus, Ohio.

Election of 1948

NOMINATIONS

Republican Party Convention (24th): June 21–25, 1948, at Convention Hall, Philadelphia, Pa. *President*— Thomas Dewey, nominated unanimously on the third ballot. He had received 434 votes out of 1,094 cast on the first ballot. Robert Taft (Ohio) and Harold Stassen (Minn.) were other major contenders. *Vice president*— Earl Warren, nominated by acclamation.

Democratic Party Convention (30th): July 12–14, 1948, at Convention Hall, Philadelphia, Pa. *President*— Harry Truman, nominated on the first ballot with 926 votes out of 1,234 cast, before vote switches. After changes, he received 947½. Richard Russell (Ga.) received most of the remainder. *Vice president*— Alben Barkley, nominated without a vote. After a motion from the chair, Barkley was declared to have two-thirds of the votes because there were no other nominations.

States' Rights Democratic Party Convention (1st): July 17, 1948, municipal auditorium, Birmingham, Alabama. Delegates from ten southern states attended. *President*— Strom Thurmond, nominated by acclamation on the first ballot. *Vice president*— Fielding Wright.

Progressive Party Convention (1st): July 23–25, 1948, Convention Hall, Philadelphia. *President*— Henry A. Wallace. *Vice president*— Glen H. Taylor. The party was Wallace's vehicle to campaign for president; he had selected Taylor in February.

GENERAL ELECTION, November 2, 1948

Popular Vote

Truman 24,105,587
Dewey 21,970,017
Thurmond 1,169,134
Wallace 1,167,057
Others   290,647

Electoral Vote

Truman-Barkley — 303 (28 states)
Dewey-Warren —189 (16 states)
Thurmond-Wright — 39 (4 states)

Winners

Harry S Truman, 33rd president
Alben Barkley, 35th vice president

Losers

Thomas E. Dewey, Earl Warren, Strom
Thurmond, Fielding Wright, Henry Wallace, Glen Taylor

---

*1948 presidential nominee —
Republican Party*

Thomas E. Dewey

The biographical sketch for Dewey is included in the section on the 1944 election, pages 594–601.

State represented: New York.
Birth: March 24, 1902.
Age on Inauguration Day (January 20, 1949): 46 years, 10 months,
Death: March 16, 1971.

---

*1948 vice presidential nominee —
Republican Party*

Earl Warren

Full name: Earl Warren.
State represented: California.
Birth: March 19, 1891, Los Angeles, California.
Age on Inauguration Day (January 20, 1949): 57 years, 10 months.
Education: Bakersfield (California) public schools; University of California (Berkeley), 1908–1912, B.L.; Berkeley law school (first class), 1912–1914, J.D.

Religion: Baptist.
Ancestry: Scandinavian.
Occupation: Attorney.
Public office: Assistant city attorney for Oakland, June, 1919–April, 1920; assistant district attorney for Alameda County, May 1, 1920–1925; district attorney, 1925–1939; California attorney general, January, 1939–December, 1942; governor of California, January 2, 1943–October 4, 1953; chief justice U.S. Supreme Court, October 5, 1953–June 23, 1969.
Death: July 9, 1974, Washington, D.C., 83 years, 3½ months.
Burial: Arlington National Cemetery.
Home: Lived in Oakland and Sacramento; while chief justice, stayed in Sheraton Park Hotel in Washington.
Personal characteristics: 6'1", 215 pounds, blue eyes, full, white hair by time he was chief justice; booming laugh; outgoing, gregarious.
Father: Methias H. (called "Matt") Varren (December 12, 1864–May 14, 1938), born near Stavenger, Norway; murdered; was a railroad car repairman or car inspector.
Mother: Christine (called "Chrystal") Hernlund (January 1, 1867–May 1, 1940); married February 14, 1886; born in Halsingland, Sweden.
Siblings: Ethel (November 15, 1887–June 18, 1966), married Vernon Plank.
Wife: Nina Elisabeth Palmquist Meyers (March 9, 1893–April 24, 1993), born in Visby, Gotland, an island off the coast of Sweden in the Baltic Sea; father was a Baptist minister and osteopath; married Grover Cleveland Meyers in 1915 and he died in 1919, leaving a three-month-old son; she married Warren on October 14, 1925.
Children: James Cleveland Warren (March 26, 1919–January 14, 1991), son of Mrs. Warren and her first husband; adopted by Warren in 1925; married Margaret Jessee on May 10, 1943; realtor. Virginia (September 13, 1928–), married John Charles Daly, Jr., on December 22, 1960, a radio and television consultant. Earl, Jr. (January 31, 1930–), married Patricia Kent on September 4, 1953, divorced; married Alfretta Safholm on March 4, 1983; lawyer and judge. Dorothy (June 12, 1931–November 24, 1986), married Harry V. Knight, Jr., on November 27, 1968; he is an

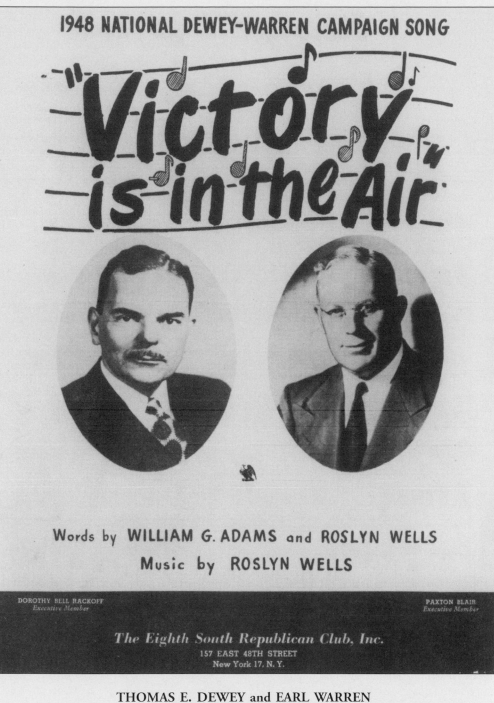

THOMAS E. DEWEY and EARL WARREN
(From the collection of Sy Seidman)
(Roslyn Wells a New York singer and theatrical performer [see page x], wrote the
Dewey campaign in July seeking to have *Victory* or another of her songs [*Tom Dewey for President*]
chosen as the official campaign song. She expressed shock that *Date in '48* by "New Deal favorite"
Meyer Davis had already been selected [Dewey Papers, University of Rochester].)

architect. Nina Elisabeth (called "Honey Bear") (October 13, 1933–), married Dr. Stuart Brien, an obstetrician and gynecologist in Beverly Hills, California on November 1, 1955. Robert (January 9, 1935–), married Carolyn Macklin in December, 1957; divorced; a realtor.

Few candidates elected president or vice president had the impact on American life that Earl Warren did. His defeat for vice president was the only election he ever lost; it was a stunning upset besides. Yet the defeat made him available for the most important task of his life, chief justice of the United States.

Both of Warren's parents had been born in Scandinavia and had been brought to the United States as children. His father became a skilled craftsman for the Southern Pacific Railroad in California. Both parents knew the value of assimilating their two children into American society, and only English was spoken at home. When Earl was four his father was fired by the railroad and blacklisted for participating in a strike, but a few years later the scarcity of workers with the elder Warren's skills got him rehired. The family moved to Bakersfield, California, a rough, bawdy town overflowing with gamblers, prostitutes, and saloons. Neither parent drank liquor, smoked, or gambled. It was a strict home in which telling a lie was unthinkable.

Earl attended public schools, and later got odd jobs to help supplement the family's never-secure finances. At 12 he attended a well-publicized trial of a local criminal. He became mildly interested in the law and returned frequently to observe the courtroom proceedings. When he was 17, Earl spent his summer as a brakeman on Southern Pacific trains. Though his mild interest in the law gave him some direction, his life was without meaningful goals. One biographer credits as a turning point in his life a speech given by Wisconsin senator Robert M. La Follette. Few men had the impact on Warren as did La Follette, and he seemed more attentive to his studies and more directed to public service after being inspired by the Wisconsin progressive.

Though never a scholar, Warren applied himself more diligently once he entered law school. Over the protest of the dean he secured permission to work part-time while registered

as a student. After graduation he became successively an attorney with an oil company, an associate in an Oakland law firm, then a partner with two other recent law graduates. Before their office could fairly be opened, World War I intervened. Warren was patriotically supportive of the war, and tried to enlist. He was too thin and tried to build himself up physically. Once accepted into the army, he was hospitalized after serious complications from minor surgery. Finally, he joined the army as a private in August 1917, and after a month was a sergeant. Warren became a second lieutenant in May 1918, after going through officers' training school. The Armistice was signed while Warren was training soldiers in Waco, Texas, and thus he never saw combat duty.

Prospects for private practice back in Oakland were not inviting, but Warren secured a position as a legislative assistant to an old friend. That placed him in position to become clerk for the judiciary committee. This exposure to the legislature convinced Warren that he loved politics. His political benefactors were aghast, however, when he removed himself from consideration for a job with the Alameda County district attorney. Warren acted after learning his legislator friends were making additional funds for the office contingent on the D.A. hiring Warren. Warren soon became deputy city attorney for Oakland and thereby gained his first meaningful trial experience. After a year another slot on the district attorney's staff opened and Warren was given the job. Three years later Warren became chief deputy, and after another two years was appointed district attorney when the incumbent resigned. Until his election as California governor 14 years later, Warren would remain in his post, foregoing much more lucrative private practice.

Fame came swiftly to the new district attorney. Warren secured indictments of the abusive racketeers who dominated through intimidation and kickbacks the bail bond business. His crime-busting image secured him easy election to a full term in November 1926. He got indictments and convictions of major white-collar criminals, from oil stock crooks, to fraudulent insurance promoters, to embezzlers of the local school board. His reputation was growing, though some thought his motive was publicity-seeking. The charge would frequently be made throughout Warren's career as district attorney, with some justification.

His staff was worked hard, but no harder than "the Chief" (an ironic nickname, a portent of his position as chief justice) worked himself. Unlike some ambitious and zealous prosecutors, however, Warren made it clear with his staff he was not seeking convictions as much as he wanted justice. He even made an extraordinary agreement that if the public defender remained convinced that a client was innocent, even after Warren had shown the defense counsel all the prosecution evidence, he would dismiss the charges. Though over a thousand convictions were secured by his office, none were ever reversed by an appellate court. Perhaps many who should have been convicted were never indicted, but Warren wanted to be certain that his office did not participate in the prosecution of innocent men.

Warren gained the respect of his peers and was elected president of the California District Attorney's Association in 1931. He also became chairman of the State Board of Criminal Investigation. In 1934, he received the United States Flag Association's award for his success as a prosecutor. He was also high-handed and much less concerned with criminals' rights than he would be years later as chief justice. In order to secure indictments against the Alameda County Sheriff and his minions for bootlegging, gambling, and payoffs to protect these "businesses," Warren leaked grand jury testimony — especially the names of those who refused to testify and who claimed the Fifth Amendment privilege. Public pressure for these witnesses to talk became intense. Indictments were finally won, but not until after Warren and his family received death threats. Convictions were also gained against the mayor of Oakland and all but one city commissioner for theft of city funds. His crusading, crime-busting efforts won him smashing reelection victories in 1930 and 1934. No great public controversy over his efforts arose, despite the variety and quantity of his prosecutions, until 1936. That year he conducted a three-month trial that led to the conviction of union members charged with murdering a

rabid union-baiter aboard a merchant ship. Thousands of pickets marched in front of the courthouse. Threats were again made against his family.

As early as 1933, Warren made the state attorney general's office a goal. He told the incumbent that as soon as he decided to step aside, Warren would try for the post. In preparation for that campaign, he secured passage of legislation that gave the attorney general's office much broader prosecutorial powers and, importantly for a family man with six children, raising its salary. That the district attorney was preparing the office for himself was obvious, but the public need for such reforms was also clear. On February 17, 1938, Warren announced as a candidate. Under California law it was possible to file as a candidate in both party primaries. This tactic won the well-known and highly popular crusader the nomination of both Democrats and Republicans for attorney general. Warren was yet to run as a Republican, since no party designation had appeared in his three races for district attorney. On his first day in office, Warren upset some of his own party's plans when he blocked the outgoing Republican governor's appointment of a suspected seller of pardons whom the governor had named to a judgeship.

As attorney general, Warren continued his publicity-filled battles against crime. Perhaps most well-known was his running battle with casino boats that anchored just outside of American territorial waters to run their enterprise. Through a careful reading of various legal authorities, Warren's office determined that there was jurisdiction to raid the boats. One boat refused to surrender, but after a week-long blockade the casino owner finally was taken into custody. Such energetic prosecution of gamblers reflected his father's anti-gambling influence. The publicity also began to make him a national figure, and gained his election as president of the National Association of Attorneys General in 1940.

As Warren was completing his first term as attorney general, his sights were firmly on the governor's chair. The liberal Democratic governor Culbert Olson, and conservative Republican attorney general were frequently in public disagreement. The advent of World War II made the military defense of California from feared Japanese invasion a burning concern. The attorney general and the governor vied over getting authority to control the state's defenses. At times both men became petty. Warren was outraged about Olson's suggestion that the union defendants in the ship murder case were convicted on flimsy evidence. These and other disagreements finally put Warren officially in the 1942 governor's race. Though initially an underdog, he almost again won both parties' nomination. The campaign was bitter, with Warren's supposed anti-labor, publicity-seeking, arch-conservative record being savagely attacked. Many union members did not follow the party line. Though the more radical CIO endorsed Olson, the more moderate AFL supported Warren. Warren's election was overwhelming, winning a majority in all but one county.

One of his first acts as governor was to remove a recording device system he had discovered in the governor's office. His appointments were nonpartisan. Warren stressed his hope to be a governor outside of normal party bickering. Patronage-hungry party workers were outraged by his failure to recognize past services. California was booming. The war helped the state's economy. Warren was able to lower taxes, increase welfare benefits, and provide additional unemployment benefits and pensions. A public works program built many new highways and hospitals. In all, Warren was successfully managing a progressive program of increased government services. One exceedingly nonprogressive stand was his vocal support for internment of Japanese-Americans as a safety measure. He would years later be distraught over this stand.

Warren thought that President Roosevelt would be reelected in 1944. He also did not personally like GOP nominee Tom Dewey, though he admired Dewey's abilities. Warren therefore twice rejected Dewey's offers to be his 1944 running mate. Years later Dewey would call Warren "that big dumb Swede."

The legislature did not meekly accept all of Governor Warren's programs. They rejected major proposals of a comprehensive prepaid medical and hospital care program to be paid for by a payroll tax, and a fair employment,

antidiscrimination bill. Warren did achieve most of his legislative goals. Increased spending for highways was permitted through higher gasoline taxes. He racially integrated the California National Guard at the same time as Truman was trying to integrate the military. In 1946, Warren became the nominee of both parties for governor.

Warren gained his state's endorsement as a favorite son candidate for the 1948 presidential nomination. His Republicanism, long-subdued in his "non-partisan" administration, became much more pronounced. Warren never really got his campaign started. This time Warren did not refuse the vice presidential nomination, but he accepted reluctantly. Dewey promised him a major role in the administration, but even before the campaign was over that promise appeared increasingly fleeting. Dewey cut Warren out of active involvement in campaign decisions. From the start, Warren was extremely cautious about victory, though he was reasonably optimistic. He was surprised and disappointed by the upset win by Truman but did not feel either emotion strongly. He even told the press that the defeat "feels like a one hundred pound sack has been taken off my back."

For a few months, politics lost its zest for Warren, but well before the 1950 election he was again enthusiastic about his job. Conservatives were digusted when he announced for a third term. This time he defeated the late President Franklin D. Roosevelt's son, James, in a landslide. Now 60 years old, Warren felt his last opportunity for the presidency would be in 1952. On November 24, 1951, he announced that he would actively seek the nomination. The following month, a malignant tumor was removed as well as a good part of his intestines. Rumors circulated that he was dying. Warren felt that such amateur prognoses by reporters and politicians were political venom of the worst sort. At the national convention the real battle was between Ohio Senator Robert Taft, Sr., and General Dwight Eisenhower. Eisenhower won.

There was no lack of enthusiasm this time in Warren's aid to the Republican ticket. Part of the energy may have been inspired by what Warren took to be Ike's promise that the first

Supreme Court vacancy would be the California governor's. On September 3, 1953, Warren said he would not run for reelection for governor. Five days later Chief Justice Fred Vinson died unexpectedly. This was the first vacancy, but Eisenhower was not as certain as Warren that a promise had earlier been made, particularly since this was not just a vacancy, but was the chief justice's position. John Foster Dulles was offered the appointment. After his refusal, Governor Dewey was offered the post but he rejected it. Twice rebuffed, the president found ready acceptance from Warren.

Chief Justice Earl Warren's years on the Supreme Court are the stuff of entire volumes. Only the briefest overview can be given here. Three critical conflicts form the peaks of his service. The first was the 1954 decision outlawing segregation in public schools. *Brown v. Board of Education* was argued before the court by former presidential candidate John W. Davis, but former vice presidential loser Earl Warren through methodical prodding and cajoling of a few reluctant justices, secured a unanimous decision against Davis and in favor of desegregation. Less renowned was Warren's participation in the one-man, one-vote cases of *Baker v. Carr* and *Reynolds v. Sims*. These reapportionment decisions reshaped state government by destroying the grip of malapportionment that caused urban centers, though far outnumbering rural voters, to have less of a voice in state legislatures. Equally controversial were the chief justice's decisions in cases dramatically enlarging criminal defendants' rights. The *Miranda* warning rules, restrictions on searches and seizures of suspects and evidence, limitations on use of confessions, and mushrooming requirements about the presence and availability of counsel made the Warren court a symbol of justice to many, and of ivory-towered insanity to others.

The Warren court started a new era in race relations in America. New eras were also mandated in the fields of criminal justice, voting rights, and freedom of speech. These astonishingly rapid and far-reaching series of revolutions cannot be credited solely to Chief Justice Warren. No decision becomes law without at least a plurality supporting it. Yet even

before he became a judge, Warren had revealed considerable abilities as an administrator, as a finder of the compromise that could cause the agreement of the most passionate of antagonists. It is because of these qualities that the court during most of his term on it really was a "Warren court."

In 1964, Justice Warren served as head of the commission appointed to investigate the assassination of President John F. Kennedy. The Warren Commission report has been attacked for supposed omissions and errors, but has yet to be disproved convincingly.

In 1968, Warren announced his retirement, effective upon the confirming of his successor. Republicans did not want to permit the selection of so important a judge by a president whom they hoped shortly to replace with one from their own party. A filibuster blocked President Lyndon Johnson's appointment of Abe Fortas. Warren remained until the end of the already commenced court term. He died five years later.

Analysis of Qualifications

Legal historians rate Earl Warren as one of the greatest chief justices of the Supreme Court, ranked with John Marshall and Charles Evans Hughes as leaders of that great court. Critics have blamed Warren for unleashing a revolution of liberal political change, ignoring his role as only an interpreter of law. If greatness is to be judged by impact alone, then Warren without controversy deserves this high ranking.

For over 25 years Earl Warren starred on the California political scene. His success first as district attorney and then as the state attorney general propelled him into position to run for governor. In all three positions he was courageous, personally so in his ignoring of death threats, professionally so in attacking corruption regardless of where he found it. The fine line between zeal and illegality was at times crossed, or nearly so, in his efforts to combat crime. This is ironic considering his later Supreme Court opinions that greatly enlarged defendants' rights. The prosecutor's energetic pursuit of criminals and his desire to receive political benefit for his efforts were at times inseparable. Warren reaped tremendous publicity and popularity from crime-busting, and that suited his ambitions just fine.

As California governor, Warren established a liberal record that a Democratic president, Truman, and a later California Democratic governor, Pat Brown, would point to approvingly. Brown thought Warren was California's greatest governor. Members of Warren's party were frequently less approving, though Thomas E. Dewey twice recognized Warren's political importance by offering him the vice presidential nomination. Republican presidents Eisenhower and Nixon were no favorites of Warren's. On the other hand, Warren once remarked about Adlai Stevenson, "Why on earth should I want to run [for president] and save the country from my friend...." President Truman several times stated that Warren was a Democrat, but just did not know it. There were many Republicans who agreed.

A President Warren would have brought to bear the same administrative skills, courage, and compassion that so marked his career in other positions. The basic thread running through the controversy surrounding Warren's years on the court is that he was making legislative and political decisions from the judicial branch of government. A President Warren would have been exceptionally well qualified by experience and personality to be seeking similar changes as president. There would have been far greater limits on a President Warren than on Chief Justice Warren. On the court, Warren could not be thwarted as he reshaped America so long as four other justices accepted his view. In the White House, Warren would have been forced to compromise and bargain with Congress. That Chief Justice Warren was pushing the right direction is generally conceded, though serious differences exist concerning whether he pushed too far. Governmental checks and balances on a President Warren would have slowed such changes and resulted in helpful political compromises.

Warren was a warm, genial, intelligent man who worked indefatigably at every position he held. He was concerned and fair-minded; he had old-fashioned ideas about morality, public service and honesty. Earl Warren was an excellent choice for vice president.

WARREN BIBLIOGRAPHY

Harvey, Richard B. *Earl Warren, Governor of California*. New York City (1969).

Katcher, Leo. *Earl Warren: A Political Biography*. New York City (1967).

Lewis, Anthony. "Earl Warren," in Leon Friedman and Fred L. Israel, eds., *The Justices of the United States Supreme Court 1789–1969*. 4 vols. New York City, IV, pp. 2721–2746.

Pollack, Jack Harrison. *Earl Warren, the Judge Who Changed America*. Englewood Cliffs, N.J. (1979).

Rice, Arnold S. *The Warren Court, 1953–1969*. Millwood, N.Y. (1987).

Schwartz, Bernard. *Super Chief: Earl Warren and His Supreme Court*. New York City (1983).

Severn, Bill. *Mr. Chief Justice Earl Warren*. New York City (1968).

Warren, Earl. *The Memoirs of Chief Justice Earl Warren*. Garden City, New York (1977).

Weaver, John D. *Warren: The Man, the Court, the Era*. Boston and Toronto (1967).

White, G. Edward. *Earl Warren: A Public Life*. New York City and Oxford (1982).

Some genealogical information provided by Mrs. Earl Warren, Washington, D.C. Additional assistance was provided by Judge Earl Warren, Jr., in Sacramento, California.

1948 presidential nominee—
States' Rights Party

Strom Thurmond

Born December 5, 1902, in Edgefield, South Carolina. Married Jean Crouch, his secretary, on November 7, 1947. They were married in the governor's mansion at the end of Thurmond's first year as governor. She died on January 6, 1960. They had no children. On December 22, 1968, he married Nancy Moore, the 22-year-old Miss South Carolina of 1966; they have four children. The couple has been separated since March 1991.

James Strom Thurmond was the second of six children born to John William and Eleanor Gertrude Strom Thurmond. John Thurmond was a prosperous lawyer, who served as a legislator, political aide to Senator "Pitchfork Ben" Tillman, and United States attorney for western South Carolina. Strom graduated from Clemson University in 1923 and then taught agriculture and coached at various high schools. He was appointed superintendent of county schools in 1928, and moved his office to his father's building so he could study law under John's tutelage. Strom was admitted to the bar in 1930 after just 18 months of study. Thurmond would later say he had tied with a Harvard graduate for best bar exam score.

This young man in a hurry was elected to the state senate in 1933, then chosen by the legislature in 1938 to be the youngest circuit (trial) judge in South Carolina. The day America declared war on Japan, December 11, 1941, Judge Thurmond took a leave of absence. He was commissioned a lieutenant in an Airborne Division, and on D-Day in 1944 was on a glider that crashed in Normandy. Thurmond also served in the Pacific, and was discharged in 1946 as a lieutenant colonel, with five battle stars and several medals. He stayed in the reserves until 1960, when he retired as a major general.

In 1946, Thurmond was elected over ten other candidates to be South Carolina governor. He had what for the times was considered to be a progressive administration, succeeding in banning poll taxes, and providing significant funding for education even in black schools. A new focus on civil rights occurred nationally, due to President Truman's initiatives such as integrating the military and advocating anti-lynching laws and a ban on the poll tax. This caused Thurmond to take a hard line in favor of segregation and states' rights. In February 1948, Thurmond led a delegation of Southern governors to meet with the national Democratic chairman. They requested a plank in the 1948 national platform in favor of states' rights and urged the withdrawal of various civil rights proposals. Without any concessions from Truman, the Southern dissidents met in July 1948 and unanimously named Thurmond for president. They called themselves the States' Rights Party, but the media dubbed them the Dixiecrats. Favoring segregation, opposing creeping "totalitarianism," Thurmond carried on an active campaign. He carried four Southern states, but Truman won.

As his first term as governor drew to an end in 1950, Thurmond ran for the United States Senate against the incumbent, Olin D. Johnston. Thurmond lost narrowly in the primary,

the second and last time he would lose in his political career. He established a law practice in Aiken. In 1952 he supported the Republican, Dwight Eisenhower, for president. The other senator, Burnet Maybank, died in 1954. Blocked by the state party from getting on the ballot because of his support for Dixiecrats and Republicans, Thurmond waged a write-in campaign against the Democratic nominee Edgar Brown. His crusade against the bosses who thought they had thwarted him proved popular. With 63 percent of the vote, Thurmond became the only U.S. senator ever elected as a write-in candidate.

Thurmond has generally won without difficulty ever since, eight re-elections through 1996. Occasionally "conventional wisdom" would declare him in trouble, especially in 1978 and again in 1996, but the voters did not make the election close either time. For the first 15 years of his service he was among the most vocal and aggressive opponents of civil rights measures. He has the record for the longest filibuster, 24 hours and 18 minutes, set in battling the Civil Rights Bill of 1957. Opposed to the national Democrat Party in various ways since 1948, he officially became a Republican in 1964 and that year supported Barry Goldwater for president. He was a vital part of Richard Nixon's Southern support base in 1968, particularly when Nixon's delegates were being courted by the more conservative Ronald Reagan in a last-minute bid for the nomination.

Senator Thurmond never wavered in his support for strong measures in Vietnam, favored tough criminal statutes including a renewed federal death penalty law, and vigorously has supported the military. Despite Thurmond's earlier record opposing civil rights laws, he became in 1971 the first Southern senator to hire a black staff member. He recommended blacks for the service academies, for federal judgeships, and for other positions that, if nothing else, indicated he realized that Southern politics was changing. When the Republicans have had a Senate majority, from 1981 through 1987 and then again beginning in 1995, Thurmond has been president pro tempore, a position placing him third in line to the presidency.

GOV. J. STROM THURMOND
FOR PRESIDENT

STATES' RIGHTS

SHIELD OF YOUR LIBERTY

GOV. FIELDING L. WRIGHT
FOR VICE-PRESIDENT

STATES' RIGHTS DEMOCRATS

STROM THURMOND and FIELDING WRIGHT
(From the Strom Thurmond Collection, Special Collections Unit, Clemson University Libraries)

Thurmond does not drink or smoke, and at least until the mid–1990s would demonstrate that he could still stand on his head when his vigor was questioned. He has maintained a strenuous exercise regimen well into his nineties. In November 1996, he became at nearly 94 the oldest person ever to serve in the Senate. Another milestone was reached May 25, 1997, when after 41 years and 10 months he passed Arizona Senator Carl Hayden's record as the longest serving senator in the nation's history. The week that he set this record, Thurmond announced that he planned to serve out his term through 2002, when he would be 100 years old, but would not run again.

The Strom Thurmond Institute is at Clemson. A Thurmond statue is in Edgefield, S.C.

THURMOND BIBLIOGRAPHY

Baker, Russell. *Our Next President: The Incredible Story of What Happened in the 1968 Elections.* New York (1968); this is a light, short novel written before the Robert Kennedy assassination,in which Strom Thurmond plays a prominent role in the 1968 campaign.

Banks, James G. "Strom Thurmond and the Revolt against Modernity." Unpublished Ph.D. dissertation, Kent State University (1970).

Cohodas, Nadine. *Strom Thurmond and the Politics of Southern Change.* New York (1993).

Ellers, Joseph C. *Strom Thurmond: The Public Man.* Orangeburg, S.C. (1993).

Garson, Robert A. *The Democratic Party and the Politics of Sectionalism, 1941–1948.* Baton Rouge (1974).

Lachicotte, Alberta. *Rebel Senator: Strom Thurmond of South Carolina.* New York (1966).

McLaurin, Ann Mathison. "The Role of the Dixiecrats in the 1948 Election." Unpublished Ph.D. dissertation, University of Oklahoma (1972).

Ness, Clifford. "The States' Rights Democratic Movement of 1948." Unpublished Ph.D. dissertation, Duke University (1972).

Raum, Tom. "Senate 'Energizer Bunny' to Shatter Longevity Mark. *Washington Times* (May 25, 1997), p. 1.

---

*1948 vice presidential nominee —
States' Rights Party*

Fielding Wright

Born May 16, 1895, in Rolling Fork, Mississippi; died May 4, 1956, in Jackson.

Married Nan Kelly on July 16, 1917; they had two children.

Fielding Lewis Wright was the son of Henry and Fannie Clements Wright. Wright's father was sheriff, and when not in public office operated plantations for wealthy landowners. Fielding attended a local elementary school, but occasionally had a tutor because the family was living on one of the more distant plantations. In 1911 Fielding attended a preparatory academy in Bellbuckle, Tennessee, and in 1912 started at the University of Alabama. Finishing in 1914, Fielding returned to Rolling Fork and studied law with his uncle Will Clements. After being admitted to the bar, he started practice with his uncle.

Wright enlisted as a private in the army in 1918 and went to Europe. He remained in France for a year after the November armistice. For the first three years back home, Wright played semi-professional baseball. He organized and was captain of a National Guard unit in Rolling Fork from 1925 to 1928, These guardsmen were especially critical during the Mississippi Delta's tragic 1927 flood. Wright was elected to the state senate in 1927 where he was an adversary of Governor Theodore Bilbo. Because of a political understanding that the two counties in his senate district would alternate holders of his senate seat, Wright did not run for re-election, but instead ran for the House in 1931. He won, was close to the speaker Thomas L. Bailey, and then was reelected in 1935. A new speaker, Horace Stansel, was elected in January 1936 but became incapacitated with illness in February. Wright was unanimously elected speaker pro tempore. After the session ended Stansel died, and Wright was chosen at the next session to replace him. Wright was a sponsor of the state's first paved road program, and favored Governor Hugh White's Balance Agriculture with Industry Act.

Speaker Wright decided not to run for re-election to the House in 1939. He had in 1938 opened a Rolling Fork law office in partnership with a lawyer and his two sons who continued practicing in Vicksburg. For the next two years the firm was known as Brunini, Wright and Brunini. The firm had an amicable parting in 1940 and remained allies. In 1943, Wright ran for lieutenant governor. He led after the first primary, and carried the runoff with 60 percent of the vote.

Governor Thomas Bailey died from cancer on November 2, 1946, and Wright became governor. Wright first gained national attention by calling a special legislative session for March 1947 to limit the U.S. Supreme Court's ruling that blacks could vote in primary elections. Wright had a Democratic primary that year and beat four opponents without a runoff to win a full term as governor. Less than three weeks after the primary, Mississippi Senator Theodore Bilbo died. Wright considered running in the special November election but agreed with advisers that the timing was atrocious. Many Wright allies helped John C. Stennis win.

Wright again earned national headlines by using his 1948 inaugural address to attack President Truman's civil rights initiatives. These policies "would eventually destroy this nation and all of the freedoms" that it enjoyed. Wright and others with these fears held a states' rights conference in Jackson in May 1948. The delegates reconvened in Birmingham in July after Democrats nominated Truman. Strom Thurmond was named for president with Wright as his running mate. The party won 2 percent of the vote nationwide, but 86 percent of the vote in Mississippi. Though popular, Wright was not a colossus astride the state political scene. Just a week after Wright's nomination in Birmingham, the state's chief justice died; he had earlier in the year announced his retirement. Though the judge died only a month before the primary that would name his successor, Wright appointed one of the two candidates to the vacancy. The other candidate then won the primary on the issue that Wright should have waited for the voters to choose.

Wright served five-plus years as governor. Among his accomplishments was construction of the state's medical school. Leaving office in 1952 he remained in Jackson and practiced law. He ran again for governor in 1955 and was considered the favorite. The candidates all supported segregation and made proposals to limit the Supreme Court's school desegregation rulings. Wright surprisingly came in third. The winner was James P. Coleman, who had been serving as attorney general since being appointed by Governor Wright in 1950.

Wright was stung by the defeat. He continued practicing law, and died less than a year later while watching television in his northeast Jackson home.

WRIGHT BIBLIOGRAPHY

Ader, Emile. *The Dixiecrat Movement: Its Role in Third Party Politics.* Washington (1955).

Brunini, Edmund L., Sr. 1990 interview with author.

Chesteen, Richard Dallas. "The 1948 States' Rights Movement in Mississippi." Unpublished master's thesis, University of Mississippi (1964).

Etheridge, Richard. "Mississippi's Role in the Dixiecratic Movement." Unpublished master's thesis, University of Mississippi (1971).

Hilliard, Elbert R. "A Biography of Fielding Wright: Mississippi's Mr. State Rights." Unpublished master's thesis, Mississippi State University (1959).

Southwick, Leslie H. "Mississippi Supreme Court Elections: An Historical Perspective, 1916–1996." *Mississippi College Law Review* 18, issue 1 (1997).

Sumners, Cecil L. *The Governors of Mississippi.* Gretna, La. (1980), pp. 122–125.

1948 presidential nominee —
Progressive Party

Henry A. Wallace

Born October 7, 1888, near Orient, Iowa; died November 18, 1965, in Danbury, Connecticut.

Married Ilo Browne on May 20, 1914; they had three children.

Henry Agard Wallace's parents were Henry C. Wallace and his wife Carrie May Brodhead. His grandfather was also Henry, nicknamed "Uncle Henry." The newspaper *Wallace's Farmer*, published by the family beginning in 1895, was a profitable and powerful voice for agricultural interests. It dispensed wisdom, morality, and Christian virtue — "Uncle Henry" had been a preacher before becoming a farmer and publisher. He had an immense influence on the idealism of his famous grandson. The future vice president attended Iowa State College and graduated in 1910 with a degree in animal husbandry. Wallace became an independent agriculture researcher for a time, particularly on the economic issues. He developed an experimental hybrid corn that was placed on the market.

After "Uncle Henry" died in 1916, the youngest Henry Wallace became an associate editor of *Wallace's Farmer*. When the middle Wallace, Henry C., became U.S. secretary of agriculture in 1921, the paper was left under the full control of his son. The biggest agriculture problem of the 1920s was overproduction. Both the secretary of agriculture and his son endorsed a bill to permit the federal government to purchase surplus crops at one price and then sell overseas at a lower price. The Coolidge administration opposed the measure. Secretary Wallace died in 1924. This may have made it easier for his son to abandon the party in 1928 and support Al Smith for president. He was so disgusted with what he thought were misguided Hoover policies that after meeting with Governor Franklin D. Roosevelt during the 1932 campaign, he became a public supporter.

In March 1933, Wallace was named by the new president as secretary of agriculture, succeeding to the cabinet post his father had held eight and a half years earlier. During the Depression, overproduction continued to be a serious problem. Wallace wanted production controls, with attendant payments compensating farmers for the limitations. He also aggressively pursued easing foreign trade barriers.

John Nance Garner, President Roosevelt's vice president during his first two terms, had become a bitter Roosevelt foe. To replace him on the 1940 ticket, Roosevelt chose Wallace. Wallace was perceived as radical by many Democrats, and the convention split its vote among 13 candidates. Wallace got a narrow majority on the first ballot. Wallace became a prototype of the activist, public vice president. He made a series of South American goodwill tours, traveled to China and Asian Russia in 1944, and headed a board that was supposed to coordinate economic policies during the war. The board was abolished when the "turf" problems with other officials got too extreme.

Wallace became an independent voice for greater postwar cooperation among nations, including closer relations with Stalin's Soviet Union. Wallace's vision was for an activist United States, working to eradicate hunger and maintain peace, establishing a union of nations to further these goals. His views were denounced by many who did not see realism or sufficient protection of American national interests. Wallace became too controversial for an ailing President Roosevelt. As the 1944 Democratic national convention neared, the most Roosevelt would say publicly is that Wallace was his personal choice for another term. The president's private message to the party's national chairman said he would be happy to run either with Harry Truman or Supreme Court Justice William O. Douglas. The incumbent led on the first ballot, and then lost on the second to Truman.

Wallace was angry, but far preferred Roosevelt to the Republicans. Truman became president in 1945 after Roosevelt died. Wallace favored international, not American, control of nuclear energy, and spoke supportively about Soviet security needs. Truman's hardline views towards the Soviet Union led Wallace to go public with his approach in a speech on September 12, 1946. Truman fired him. Over the next two years Wallace engaged in what he called a "fight for peace." Wallace was in a lonely battle, as few Americans supported his cries for greater understanding of world communism. At the end of December 1947, Wallace announced his independent campaign for president. After an endorsement of his candidacy by the American Communist Party, Wallace came across as at best an unwitting tool of the Soviets. He carried no states in November.

He left politics, lived on a farm in New York, and rarely spoke out on issues.

"Catalpa," the home of Henry C. Wallace, and birthplace of Henry A. Wallace, stands near Greenfield, Iowa.

WALLACE BIBLIOGRAPHY

Blum, John Morton, ed. *The Price of Vision.* (1973).
Kleinman, Mark L. "Approaching Opposition: Henry A. Wallace, Reinhold Niebuhr and the Emergence of American Liberal Internationalism, 1920–1942." Unpublished Ph.D. dissertation, U.C.L.A. (1991).
Lader, Lawrence. "The Wallace Campaign of 1948." *American Heritage* (December 1976), pp. 42–51.
Lord, Russell. *The Wallaces of Iowa.* Boston (1947).
MacDougall, Curtis D. *Gideon's Army.* New York (3 vols., 1965).
Morrison, Dennis L. *Up, Down, and Out: Henry A. Wallace in the Democratic Party.* Waterbury, Conn. (1995).
Schapsmeier, Edward L., and Frederick H. Schapsmeier. *Henry A. Wallace of Iowa: The Agrarian Years, 1910–1940.* Ames, Iowa (1968).
_____, and _____. *Prophet in Politics: Henry A. Wallace and the War Years, 1940–1965.* Ames, Iowa (1970).
Schmidt, Karl M. *Henry A. Wallace: Quixotic Crusade, 1948.* Syracuse (1960)
Sirevag, Torbjorn. *The Eclipse of the New Deal and the Fall of Vice-President Wallace.* New York (1985).
Walton, Richard J. *Henry Wallace, Harry Truman, and the Cold War.* New York (1976).
Webster, Lindsley Elliott. "Thirteen Ventures in Political Guidance: The Books of Henry A. Wallace, 1934–1946." Unpublished master's thesis, Clark University (1955).
White, Graham J., and John Maze. *Henry A. Wallace: His Search for a New World Order.* Chapel Hill (1995).
Young, Allan C. "A Modern Isaiah: Henry A. Wallace and the 1948 Presidential Campaign." Unpublished D.A. dissertation, University of North Dakota (1992).

1948 vice presidential nominee—
Progressive Party

Glen H. Taylor

Born April 12, 1904, in Portland, Oregon; died April 28, 1984, in Burlingame, California. Married Pearl (later Pearl Nitkowskie) in 1922, separated in 1926 and divorced in 1929; one daughter. Married Dora Marie Pike in March, 1931; they had three sons.

Glen Hearst Taylor was the twelfth of thirteen children of Pleasant John Taylor and Olive Higgins Taylor. Pleasant John Taylor was, according to his most famous son, a "hellfire and brimstone" preacher, ministering to the mining camps and other scattered groups of western pioneers. Glen left school at age 12, herded sheep, and worked at moving picture theaters. In 1921 and 1922 Glen was in a traveling vaudeville act with others in the family, and continued with other groups even

GLEN H. TAYLOR (left) and HENRY A. WALLACE
(From the collection of David J. and Janice L. Frent)

after the Taylor Players disbanded. He met Dora Pike, an usherette at one of the theaters. They formed their own business in 1930, the Glendora Players, and were married in 1931.

The Players did not prosper. His own economic distress caused him to study writings on economics, especially theories that capitalism had to change, with direct relief for those in need, a planned economy and more public works spending. Taylor took his Players in a new direction — as the Glendora Ranch Gang, with Taylor as "the Crooning Cowboy." The Gang moved to Pocatello, Idaho, in part because Taylor would have a daily half-hour radio show. Six months after moving to Pocatello, Taylor announced his candidacy for the 1938 Democratic congressional nomination. He finished fourth in the primary. In 1940 he won the Democratic primary for a U.S. Senate seat, but many party leaders considered the singing cowboy a joke and he lost in the general election.

Many of the Ranch Gang were now in the military. Taylor went to California and worked as a sheet metal worker in a munitions factory. In the spring of 1942 he was back in Idaho running for the full term for the U.S. Senate seat he had lost two years earlier. He rode a horse across much of the state to gain attention, and won the nomination. He again lost the general election, but it was a closer vote

than in 1940. Running again in 1944, Taylor projected a more dignified image, acquired a toupee to cover his bald head, and defeated the incumbent Democratic senator, D. Worth Clark, in the primary. His margin of victory was 216 votes. Hanging on tightly to Franklin D. Roosevelt's coattails, Taylor won in November by 5,000 votes out of 210,000 cast.

In the Senate Taylor was a strong defender of labor's interests, energetically pursued completion of the Columbia Valley Authority, supported civil rights measures, and in 1946 called on the Senate to investigate the racist re-election campaign of Mississippi senator Theodore Bilbo. When that failed, he tried to block Bilbo's being seated in 1947. Glen Taylor urged that every effort be made to work with Communists to ensure world peace. On the day the United Nations came into official existence, he introduced a resolution urging the creation of a "World Republic." He annually reintroduced the resolution, which never passed. In December 1947 he called Truman's foreign policy "one of the most magnificent fiascoes the world has ever seen." Taylor filibustered in June 1948 Truman's plan for a peacetime military draft.

Henry Wallace's Progressive Party campaign for president needed a running mate. On February 23 Taylor announced on nationwide radio, with Wallace at his side, that he was running. So strongly identified had Taylor become with pro–Soviet views that his public appearances often included his swearing, with right hand raised, that he was not a Communist. The party carried no states.

The Democrat whom Taylor had ousted from the Senate in 1944, D. Worth Clark, ran against him in 1950. Near the day of the primary, three prominent Idaho Democrats called Taylor a Communist. The newspapers were against him, and Democratic officials generally supported former Senator Clark. Taylor lost the primary by fewer than 1,000 votes, but he lost. He went to work as a carpenter in Idaho and then joined three of his brothers in a construction business in California. He lost two more bids for the Senate, one in 1954 when his chances for victory looked good until accusations during the last two weeks that he had hired Communists to work on his Senate staff. He also lost the 1956 Democratic primary, and then failed in a write-in effort for the general election. Glen Taylor was out of politics for good. He founded Taylor Topper, Inc., a wig manufacturing company.

HAROLD E. STASSEN
(From the author's collection)

*1948 presidential candidate—
Special Lifetime Effort*

Harold E. Stassen

Harold Stassen does not qualify for inclusion under the criteria set out in the Introduction. However, for more than forty years he has reveled in being in the category that this book honors — presidential loser. There are other perennial candidates, but Stassen is unique among them since he once had a legitimate prospect of being elected. For assuming the mantle of quintessential presidential also-ran, Harold Stassen is here given what the Republican Party never gave, the equivalent of a nomination. Stassen is thus alone among two centuries' worth of election losers, in receiving this distinction. The election of 1948 was his best

TAYLOR BIBLIOGRAPHY

Bladholm, Helen Ann. "Glen Hearst Taylor: Principles, Politics, and the Cold War." Unpublished master's thesis, Northeastern Illinois University (1972).

Peterson, F. Ross. *Prophet Without Honor: Glen H. Taylor and the Fight for American Liberalism.* Lexington, Ky. (1974).

Taylor, Glen H. *The Way It Was with Me.* Secaucus, N.J. (1979).

opportunity to win, so he is listed with the also-rans for this campaign.

Born April 13, 1907, in Dakota County, Minnesota, outside of the Twin Cities. Married Esther Glewwe on November 14, 1929. They have two children.

Harold Edward Stassen's parents were William A. and Elsie Mueller Stassen. Harold was the third of four sons, and there was one daughter. All of Harold's grandparents were born in Europe, the Stassens in Norway. Harold grew up on a truck farm, and went through six elementary school grades in four years in a rural school. He started high school in St. Paul, worked hard in several odd jobs, but still graduated at age 15. He had finished too quickly. The minimum age for the University of Minnesota was 16, so he had to wait. His father's illness caused him to take over operation of the truck farm for the year, then he enrolled at the university.

Between semesters Stassen worked as a Pullman conductor, a grocery clerk, and a pan greaser in a bakery. Debate, intercollegiate oratory, and rifle shooting were among his extracurricular interests, and he excelled in all. The rifle team that he captained won three straight national titles. Cadet Lt. Colonel Stassen was the outstanding cadet in the Reserve Officer Training Corps. He was a campus politico, and was elected all-university class president. Even with all these activities, he was an honor student.

While in college Stassen organized and became the first chairman of the Young Republican League. After graduating in 1927, then sweeping through Minnesota law school in two years, Stassen was admitted to the bar in 1929. He started a firm in South St. Paul with an old friend. Stassen ran in 1930 for county attorney and was elected despite spending four months in a sanitarium recovering from tuberculosis. He was reelected in 1934. Stassen gained publicity by threatening to prosecute any farmer who caused violence in a dispute over milk prices, but simultaneously offering to represent the farmers in order to get justice for them. They agreed to employ him, and Stassen got them a price increase.

The conservative old guard in the Republican Party was Stassen's next target. He wrested control by gaining the gubernatorial nomination in 1938. He then beat the incumbent Farmer-Labor (Democratic) Governor Elmer Benson by 678,839 to 387,263 votes. At age 31 he was America's youngest governor ever, and labeled by the national press the "Boy Wonder of the Republican Party." The next youngest governor would be Arkansas' Bill Clinton, elected at age 32 in 1978. One reporter still marveled at him 30 years later. "Every move he made, every speech, was news…. He was bold and unpredictable and courageous and marvelous newspaper copy" (Kirby, "Major Contender," p. 153, footnote 7).

His administration was progressive, honest, and energetic. He ran against the "labor-front reign of terror," but in time got significant union votes because he was seen as fair. He got the legislature to pass labor statutes similar to what Congress in 1947 would adopt as the Taft-Hartley Act. The new statute among other things banned strikes until a cooling-off period. Democratic scandals had helped elect him, and his tenure had a much more honest image. Leftover scandals were investigated; corrupt officials were removed. The governor began weekly radio talks to the state, and maintained a high popularity. In 1940 the rising GOP star gave the keynote address at the national convention, was convention floor manager for the nominee Wendell Willkie, and was reelected governor in November. He was elected to a third two-year term in 1942, but resigned on April 27, 1943, to go on active duty as a lieutenant commander in the U.S. Naval Reserve. In August he became an aide to Admiral Bull Halsey, commander in the South Pacific. He was assistant chief of staff and flag secretary when Halsey became commander of the Third Fleet. While serving in the Navy, Stassen had an unofficial presidential campaign in 1944. He won delegates in some primaries, but was not much of a factor.

Stassen was promoted to Navy captain. He returned home and was placed on leave because President Roosevelt named him one of the American delegates to the San Francisco conference that started the United Nations. Stassen opposed allowing the major nations to have a veto power, but lost the debate within the American delegation. He returned to active duty when the fleet moved into Tokyo Bay, and was in charge of evacuating American POWs.

On December 17, 1946, Stassen announced for president. He was an internationalist, which antagonized the Robert Taft wing of the party, and had staked out progressive positions on domestic programs. He met with Soviet leader Josef Stalin during an European visit in April 1947. By early 1948, after more than a year of campaigning, Stassen had traveled over 160,000 miles, was well-funded and well-known. Stassen lost in the New Hampshire primary, but surprisingly won in Wisconsin where General Douglas MacArthur was the perceived favorite. The next week Stassen took the Nebraska primary, and won a write-in poll in Pennsylvania. Many now saw Stassen as the front-runner, but he made a bad tactical mistake by vigorously challenging Robert Taft in Taft's home state of Ohio. Stassen lost, and as quickly as he had taken the perception lead, he just as quickly faced a make-or-break contest in Oregon. An Oregon radio debate was held between Stassen and Tom Dewey, broadcast nationwide on 900 stations to one of the largest radio audiences in history. Stassen prepared with his friend, Senator Joe McCarthy. This was not a joint press conference like modern, televised debate. It was a one-issue debate, with the proposition being "The Communist Party should be outlawed." Stassen took the affirmative, and Dewey the negative. Stassen had the flu, was worn out from campaigning, and had little of his normal energy. Dewey's persuasive opposition to "laws outlawing people because of their religion, political, social, or economic ideas" was credited with helping him win the primary with 117,000 votes to Stassen's 108,000. The *Oregonian*'s story on the election was, "Dewey appears to have stopped Stassen in Oregon."

Stassen plowed forward, but many Republicans thought Stassen no longer had a chance. Senator Robert Taft urged Stassen to withdraw, and offered him the vice presidential nomination. At the convention, Stassen's support was clearly dropping on the second ballot. Taft again beseeched him to quit, but Stassen would not. Taft decided to concede

and released his delegates. Dewey won on the third ballot. Word circulated that the Arizona delegation was going to put Stassen in nomination for vice president despite Dewey's selection of Earl Warren. The Dewey team stopped that. Stassen was generally credited with having run an appealing if flawed campaign in 1948 that positioned him well for the future. He had by announcing early and forthrightly contending for delegates in the primaries, been responsible for propelling the primaries to a critical role in choosing future nominees. A few days after Dewey's November defeat, Stassen's campaign manager announced that Stassen would seek the 1952 presidential nomination. Much as Dwight Eisenhower spent 1948 to the end of 1950 as president of Columbia University, Stassen became president of the University of Pennsylvania and served from 1948 to 1953.

Stassen ran in 1952, but told Eisenhower that he supported the general and would deliver his delegates at the appropriate time. Stassen even flew to visit Ike, who was then commander of the NATO forces in Europe, to plead with him to come home and campaign. Stassen came in third with only 7 percent of the vote in the New Hampshire primary, then the next week won his home state of Minnesota's primary with 129,000 votes to Ike's 108,000 *write-in* votes. Stassen helped the general at the convention on key procedural votes. At the end of the first ballot, Stassen's 20 delegates were switched to Eisenhower. Stassen was not of critical help, but he had been supportive. When Eisenhower became president, he made Stassen the chairman of the Foreign Operations Administration from 1953 until 1955. In that post Stassen directed foreign aid programs. In 1955 Eisenhower tried to slow down the nuclear arms race by creating the post of assistant to the president on disarmament. The position was given Cabinet rank, and Stassen was appointed to fill it in March 1955. He helped develop the "Open Sky" proposal that would allow both super powers to maintain complete aerial surveillance of the other.

In July 1956, Stassen went to Eisenhower to convince him that Vice President Richard Nixon was too divisive to leave on the ticket that would be chosen a month later at the national convention. Eisenhower in his memoirs said he told Stassen that "You are an American citizen, Harold, and free to follow your own judgment." Just how much the president supported Stassen's "dump Nixon" efforts is unclear, but he was apparently attracted to the idea of not having Nixon on the ticket. Stassen publicly suggested former Massachusetts governor Christian Herter, who was old and ill. Whether Stassen meant Herter as a serious alternative, or whether he was really promoting his own vice presidential candidacy is difficult to fathom. After the convention opened, Eisenhower ordered Stassen to give one of the seconding speeches for Nixon's nomination, and he did.

Disarmament adviser Stassen was considered too accommodating to the Soviets by hard-liners like Secretary of State John Foster Dulles. At a London conference in 1957, Stassen was aggressive and initially highly praised for advancing the seemingly hopeless cause of disarmament. Stassen advanced a proposal too far, though, when he suggested that nuclear testing could be halted if extensive on-site inspection were allowed. He also suggested that future production of fissionable material be only for peaceful uses. This had not been cleared with Britain, who was trying to develop its own nuclear weapons. British outrage at Stassen caused Dulles to fly to London to take charge. Eisenhower rebuked Stassen for causing "acute embarrassment." Senator Hubert Humphrey called for an investigation into Stassen's role in disarmament. One close Stassen adviser felt that had Stassen not been thwarted by Dulles and had achieved an agreement, he would have been well-positioned for the presidential nomination in 1960. Stassen made a detailed presentation of his disarmament views at a cabinet meeting in January 1958. United Nations ambassador Henry Cabot Lodge was the only cabinet member supporting him. Dulles, presidential Chief of Staff Sherman Adams, and some other advisers never could stand Stassen. A month after the cabinet meeting, the president asked Stassen to resign and take another administration position.

Instead, Stassen resigned altogether on February 15, 1958, and announced a bid for Pennsylvania governor. The state GOP chairman said there was "downright opposition" to Stassen in the party. He lost 2-1 in the May 1958, primary, to Arthur T. McGonigle. During the campaign Stassen had been labeled a "carpetbagger." He was accused of just looking for a springboard to another race for president. The day after the election Stassen said that he was not finished in politics. "When God ends my life," he said, "that's when my career will end."

In July 1958, Stassen opened a law office in Philadelphia. On November 12, 1958, after meeting with Eisenhower in the White House, Stassen talked to reporters and said that it was time to dump Nixon for the 1960 nomination and choose New York Governor Nelson Rockefeller. Reporters wondered if he was speaking for the president, but he was not. Stassen was the Republican nominee for Philadelphia mayor in 1959, but got only half as many votes in the November election as did incumbent Mayor Richardson Dilworth. He was never given much of a chance, but one rational explanation for Stassen's effort was that by accepting the thankless task of being a token candidate he was paying his dues as a Pennsylvania Republican.

Stassen now made Philadelphia his home. In March he had started a firm with three other lawyers. In time Stassen would have offices in four cities, including St. Paul, and specialized in international corporate law. He was considered an excellent attorney and made a substantial amount of money as a lawyer in between campaigns. He listed his assets in 1978 as between $500,000 and $1.25 million.

Stassen is often "credited" with having lost a race for Pennsylvania governor in 1962, but in fact he did not run. On January 20, 1964, Stassen held a Washington press conference. On that day he crossed his credibility Rubicon by announcing that he would run for president. His recent previous races had been explicable, arguably eccentric, and certainly long odds contests. Being a presidential candidate in the 1964 GOP primaries, however, meant that he no longer was running for reasons that traditionally are considered those of a serious, mainstream candidate. He said that he was doing it to "enlarge the Republican debate on the critical issues of the day." Those are the reasons of someone who knows he cannot win. Stassen campaigned in several primaries, but won no delegates. On February 10, 1966, he announced his second campaign for Pennsylvania governor. The incumbent, Bill Scranton, was retiring and GOP Lieutenant Governor Ray Shafer was the clear favorite. In the May primary Shafer trounced Stassen and another fringe candidate. In 1968 Stassen again was a presidential candidate. He spent $90,000 and won two delegates. He did not run in 1972 and announced his support for President Nixon's reelection. In 1975, then living in Valley Forge, Pennsylvania, Stassen said that he would run for the U.S. Senate from Pennsylvania in 1976 if Hugh Scott retired. Scott did, but Stassen ran for president instead. He got no delegates, and was not even allowed to put his campaign trailer on the grounds of the national convention in Kansas City as did more serious candidates.

In 1978 Stassen moved back to Dakota County, Minnesota, where he had grown up, and ran for U.S. Senate. He got only 13 percent of the vote in the Republican Senate primary. He issued a press release calling this his eleventh consecutive loss. He now measured news by the record he was creating of defeats. Stassen remained in the St. Paul area and practiced law. On December 7, 1979, he announced that he was a candidate for the 1980 presidential nomination. He got no delegates, but had a victory over one prominent opponent. Bob Dole's disastrous campaign had come apart by the time of the 1980 New Hampshire primary where he won only 597 votes. Stassen got 16,000 more votes than Dole. In 1982 Stassen ran for governor of Minnesota, and came in third in the GOP primary with just 17,000 votes to almost 300,000 split among the other two. In 1984 he ran for president again, got 2 percent of the New Hampshire primary and a few votes elsewhere. In 1986, for the first time since 1942, Stassen actually received the Republican nomination for office. He was unopposed in the GOP primary for Congress. Stassen made a campaign pledge to make the district the most drug-free in the country. He took a drug test, and challenged the incumbent Bruce Vento to do the same. Without a drug test, Vento beat Stassen by better than three to one. Stassen ran again in a few 1988 presidential primaries.

Stassen got nationwide publicity in 1990 by suggesting that President Bush send him to negotiate with Saddam Hussein on a peaceful solution to the crisis over Kuwait. Bush did not take him up on the offer. In Stassen's 1992 presidential campaign he used the slogan of "Seven Mighty Moves" that he would take if elected, and had a list of big public works projects, health care reforms, and other points that no one listened to. He won enough votes in Minnesota to be entitled to one delegate. He tried to become that delegate, but was denied the privilege. In 1994 Stassen ran for the U.S. Senate from Minnesota and lost in the primary. In 1996 there was finally a presidential election without Stassen's filing as a candidate. "I'm walking, not running" Stassen said. Still he made a late bid for a role. After Bob Dole had wrapped up the 1996 Republican nomination, Stassen made him an offer in July. The 73-year-old Dole would look much more vigorous, Stassen said, if he chose the 89-year-old Stassen as his running mate. It did not happen.

Stassen has lost ten presidential races from 1944 through 1992, skipping only 1956, 1960, and 1972. He was defeated for governor three times in Minnesota or Pennsylvania, and lost one race each for Congress, mayor, and the U.S. Senate. It is easy to forget, but Stassen also won two races for county attorney and three for Minnesota governor. He stands, as of 1996, at five wins, sixteen losses.

Stassen explained his continuous running by saying "that you can't be in the bleachers and have any impact." He focused on issues of war and peace. From disarmament to opposition to the Vietnam and Persian Gulf wars, Stassen constantly tried to bring attention to issues of world peace. In Minnesota, Stassen has a certain cachet as a tireless advocate of global unity and peace. A Harold Stassen Chair in International Peace was established at the Hubert H. Humphrey Institute of Public Affairs, at the University of Minnesota. Stassen was invited to join a group of current state leaders who met with Premier Mikhail Gorbachev when the Soviet leader visited Min-

HAROLD E. STASSEN
(From the Collection of the Minnesota Historical Society)

nesota in 1990. By 1994 he was the last living signer of the 1945 United Nations Charter, an occasion for a Minneapolis newspaper to praise Stassen's contribution. The paper also commended a 17-minute video about Stassen and the United Nations that was given to every Minnesota library and school. In March 1997 all 18 members of the Senate Foreign Relations Committee wrote the president to urge that Stassen be awarded the Presidential Medal of Freedom for his work in helping found the United Nations. In late 1997 Stassen announced that he was considering a race for Minnesota governor in 1998 in order to influence the debate on children ("Inside Politics, *Washington Times*, August 25, 1997, p. A7). He thus remains true to his vow in 1958 that he would be finished in politics only "when God ends my life."

Stassen in his prime stood 6 feet, 3 inches tall, blond hair and blue eyes, weighed over 200 pounds, and was athletic in build. He was balding even as a youthful governor, and started wearing a toupee in his later years. He and his wife of almost 70 years live in Sunfish Lake outside of St. Paul.

STASSEN BIBLIOGRAPHY

Ackerman, Donald H. "The Write-in Vote for Dwight Eisenhower in the 1952 Minnesota Primary." Unpublished thesis, Syracuse University (1954).

Ambrose, Stephen E. *Eisenhower: The President.* New York (1984).

_____. *Nixon: The Education of a Politician, 1913–1962.* New York (1987).

Gilbert, Wayne F. "The Rise of Harold E. Stassen." Unpublished history paper (1970), copy at Minnesota Historical Society.

"Harold Stassen: A Tribute to This Visionary Minnesotan." *Star Tribune* (September 17, 1994), p. 18A.

Helm, Hunt. "Resilient Harold Stassen Looks to U.N.'s Past, Future." *Courier-Journal* (October 29, 1988), p. 11A.

Henderaker, Ivan Henrik. "Harold Stassen and Developments in the Republican Party in Minnesota, 1937–1943." Unpublished doctoral dissertation, University of Minnesota (1949).

Hendrickson, Paul. "Stassen: The Once and Future Candidate." *Washington Post* (December 8, 1978), p. D1.

Kirby, Alec. "Childe Harold's Pilgrimage: A Political Biography of Harold Stassen." Unpublished doctoral dissertation, George Washington University (1992).

_____. "A Major Contender: Harold Stassen and the Politics of American Presidential Nominations." *Minnesota History* winter 1996-97, pp. 150–165.

"The Man from Minnesota." *Time* (August 25, 1947), pp. 18–21.

Matteson, Robert E. *Harold Stassen: His Career, the Man, and the 1957 London Arms Control Negotiations.* Inver Grove Heights, Minn. (1993).

_____. *A Search for Adventure and Service:* (Part III), *The Post-War Years, 1946–1952* (1981); (Part IV), *The Eisenhower Years, 1952–1960* (1985). Park Falls, Wisc.

_____. *Stassen versus Stalin: The 1947 Conversation Between Harold Stassen and Joseph Stalin.* Inver Grove Heights, Minn. (1993).

Parson, Jim. "McCarthy, Stassen Are Fed Up with Running." *Star Tribune* (February 23, 1992), p. 1B.

Smith, Richard Norton. *Thomas E. Dewey and His Times.* New York (1982).

Stassen, Harold E. *Eisenhower: Turning the World Toward Peace.* St. Paul (1990).

_____. *Man Was Meant to Be Free.* New York (1951 edition).

_____. Oral history transcript (99 pages), Minnesota Historical Society (1991).

_____. *Where I Stand.* Garden City, N.Y. (1947).

Stuhler, Barbara. *Ten Men of Minnesota and American Foreign Policy, 1898–1968.* St. Paul (1973), pp. 145–168.

Swafford, Tom. "The Last Real Presidential Debate," *American Heritage* 37 (1986), pp. 66–71.

News stories from the *New York Times* fill in the gaps on campaign details.

Election of 1952

NOMINATIONS

Republican Party Convention (25th): July 7–11, 1952, at the International Amphitheatre, Chicago, Illinois. *President*— Dwight Eisenhower, nominated on the first ballot, after vote switches, with 845 votes out of 1,206 cast. Before these changes, he had been given 595 votes. Robert Taft (Ohio) was his major opponent. *Vice president*— Richard Nixon, nominated by acclamation.

Democratic Party Convention (31st): July 21–26, 1952, at the International Amphitheatre, Chicago, Illinois. *President*— Adlai Stevenson, nominated on the third ballot with 617½ votes out of 1,230 cast. He had received 273 on the first ballot. Estes Kefauver and Richard Russell (Georgia) were other leading contenders. *Vice president*— John Sparkman, nominated by acclamation.

GENERAL ELECTION, November 4, 1952

Popular Vote

Eisenhower 33,936,137
Stevenson. 27,314,649
Others. 300,332

Electoral Vote

Eisenhower–Nixon — 442 (39 states)
Stevenson–Sparkman — 89 (9 states)

Winners

Dwight Eisenhower, 34th president
Richard Nixon, 36th vice president

Losers

Adlai Stevenson, John Sparkman

*1952 presidential nominee—
Democratic Party*

Adlai E. Stevenson

Full name: Adlai Ewing Stevenson II.
State represented: Illinois.
Birth: February 5, 1900, Los Angeles, California.
Age on Inauguration Day (January 20, 1953): 52 years, 11½ months.
Education: Public schools in Bloomington, Illinois; Choate School in Wallingford, Connecticut; Princeton University, graduated 1922 (B.A.); Harvard Law School, 1922–1924; Northwestern University Law School, 1924–1926 (J.D.).
Religion: Unitarian.
Ancestry/prominent relatives: Grandfather Adlai E. Stevenson, vice president, 1893–1897, congressman, assistant postmaster general; Adlai E. Stevenson III (son), U.S. senator from Illinois.
Occupation: Attorney.
Public offices: Special assistant to general counsel of Agricultural Adjustment Administration, July 1933–January 1934; chief attorney, Federal Alcohol Control Administration, January–October 1934; administrative assistant to secretary of the navy, June 1941–June 1944; special assistant to U.S. secretary of state, February 1945–1946; alternate delegate to United Nations, 1946 and 1947; governor of Illinois, January 10, 1949–January 8, 1953; unsuccessful Democratic presidential nominee, 1952 and 1956; defeated for presidential nomination, 1960; ambassador to United Nations, January 23, 1961–death, July 14, 1965.
Death: July 14, 1965, London, England, 65 years, 5½ months.
Burial: Evergreen Cemetery, Bloomington, Illinois.
Home: 71–acre farm near Libertyville, 40 miles from Chicago.
Personal characteristics: 5'10" tall; blue eyes and brown hair; bald across top of head.
Father: Lewis Green Stevenson (August 15, 1868–April 5, 1929).
Mother: Helen Davis (1869–November, 1935).

Siblings: Elizabeth ("Buffie") (July 16, 1897–June 27, 1994); married Ernest Ives on February 4, 1927.
Wife: Ellen Borden (December 7, 1909–July 28, 1972); married December 1, 1928, divorced in 1949.
Children: Adlai E. Stevenson III (October 10, 1930–); married Nancy Anderson on June 25, 1955; U.S. senator, attorney. Borden (July 7, 1932–). John Fell (February 7, 1936–).

His forebears were prominent. Among them was a vice president of the United States. Another was a confidant of President Abraham Lincoln; Adlai's father was secretary of state for Illinois. Born in Los Angeles while his father was assistant general manager of the *Examiner* newspaper, Adlai moved with his family back to Illinois. There his father operated several farms owned by an aunt. Adlai's childhood was not precocious; there was little in his educational progress to mark him for future greatness. There was tragedy in the youth's life that intensified an already noticeable reserve. When Adlai was 12 he and some friends were playing with a rifle. As Adlai took the gun to return it to the attic where it had been stored, he accidentally dropped it. The gun discharged upon hitting the floor, killing a young girl. This disaster was not spoken of in the family for years and remained a secret until a reporter brought it up 40 years later.

Stevenson's father wanted him to go to a prestigious school in the East, but his grades were abysmal. After failing entrance examinations three times, Adlai was finally admitted to Choate School in Connecticut for better preparations. Scholastic mediocrity continued to be his station. At Princeton, which he entered in 1919, his grades were again average. He did at least enjoy three-and-one-half years working for the campus paper, the *Daily Princetonian*. He studied law at Harvard and Northwestern, graduating in 1926. Following graduation he took an extended tour of Europe and Russia. Upon his return, he began work at the Chicago law firm of Cutting, Moore, and Sidley. The carefree time of youth was terminated emphatically by his marriage. The bride was Ellen Borden, the daughter of a wealthy Chicago businessman whose fortune would shrink considerably during the Depression. While Adlai was enjoying the approach of his wedding in 1928, his father was enjoying a shortlived boomlet as a possible vice presidential nominee for the Democrats. The convention in Houston finally turned elsewhere.

Adlai involved himself actively in Chicago civic affairs. His wealthy, vivacious and witty bride significantly enhanced his acceptance by Chicago society. The young attorney in spare moments worked for the Lower North Side Community Council, Hull House, and the Illinois Children's Home and Aid Society. His political activities concentrated on the Council on Foreign Relations, rising to president of that organization in 1935. Speeches to civic groups and other audiences on charitable and political issues made him well known and popular.

Legal work rarely intrigued Stevenson. Though he applied himself diligently, his real love was his outside activities. He received a leave of absence from the firm in July 1933, just after the New Deal had been inaugurated, to become a special assistant to the general counsel for the Agricultural Adjustment Administration. In January 1934, Stevenson shifted his governmental service and became chief attorney for the Alcohol Control Administration. After ten months there he returned to the Chicago law firm and became a partner in 1935.

The next six years Stevenson remained in private life, but his participation in political affairs increased. He was finance director of the Democratic national committee for the 1936 reelection campaign of President Roosevelt. His work on the Council on Foreign Relations placed him in the public eye. This work, particularly as war in Europe erupted, seemed harmful to the law firm, not only because he had to divide his time with these other interests, but also because some isolationist clients became irate over his interventionist positions. The tension could not last, and Stevenson's real ambition of public service won out. In 1941 he became personal assistant to Secretary of the Navy Frank Knox. For three years Stevenson was the secretary's speechwriter and administrative assistant. During his first year with Knox, speculation spread in Illinois that this fast-rising scion of a prominent Illinois political family would return home in

1942 and run for the United States Senate. Pearl Harbor made Stevenson drop those ambitions, for a time. A secretary of the navy in wartime was constantly on the move, and his administrative assistant moved with him, both in this country and overseas. In 1943 and early 1944, Roosevelt sent Stevenson on a special mission to Italy to assist relief efforts in the areas liberated by the Allies. Stevenson returned to Knox's office in 1944, and soon thereafter suffered a crushing personal loss when the secretary died on April 28, 1944.

Stevenson returned to Chicago in June and attempted to purchase the *Daily News* paper, which Knox had owned prior to his death. The bidding exceeded what the syndicate headed by Stevenson could justify, and control went to others. Stevenson seemed genuinely excited about a newspaper career and might have been sidetracked significantly from his future course had he not been outbid.

His stay in Illinois was not prolonged, and in February 1945 he was back as a special assistant to the secretary of state, working on educating the public on the value of the soon to be created United Nations. His involvement with that organization continued when he became press spokesman for the American delegation. He had also served at a London conference to draft proposals for the structure of the new organization. His whole family except for the youngest child accompanied him to England, and it was a delightful experience for all. Though the marriage would soon break up, there seemed a momentary brightening of the Stevensons' domestic life as a result of their "vacation" to England.

Ellen Borden Stevenson had gradually become estranged from her husband and from his life. She did not like Washington nor did she find politics nearly as stimulating as did he. Neither spouse worked hard at meeting the other halfway. Ellen's aspirations to be a poet were encouraged by friends, and her interests generally were in the arts, not politics. Partly in response to his wife's desire to remain in Illinois, Stevenson turned down several posts offered him, though he did accept appointment as one of the alternate delegates to the September-December 1946 session of the United Nations.

Politics would now clearly be his life. Stevenson wanted badly to run for the United States Senate seat then held by a Republican, but his aspirations clashed with those of Paul H. Douglas, a University of Chicago professor who was also positioning for the race. On November 6, 1947, a Stevenson for Senate committee was announced. Strong pressures to shift to the governor's race then were put on Stevenson. Finally on December 26, 1947, Stevenson was told that the Democratic state committee had decided to back Douglas for the Senate, and if Stevenson would consent he would be named for the gubernatorial nomination. Stevenson was crestfallen, and he considered fighting the decision. At the last minute, after days of indecision, Stevenson relented.

The odds against Stevenson were long but he was an indefatigable campaigner. The long-entrenched Republicans had grown fat, and some were corrupt. A hard-driving, intellectual campaign that promised to end the corruption caught fire. Stevenson was given an overwhelming victory in November, winning by the largest margin of any gubernatorial candidate in Illinois at that time.

Stevenson's popularity with the press during the campaign continued when he became governor. When he presented his legislative program, it was generally well-received by the media. His review of his record as governor four years later listed as his major accomplishments improvements in unemployment compensation, mine safety, pensions for the aged and blind, state highways, and education. He removed the state highway patrol from political control. A model system of mental hospitals was established. More public perhaps than these were his failures. Much prestige was invested in getting a new constitution adopted in the state, but Stevenson was defeated when the legislature refused to issue the call for a convention. A Fair Employment Practices Commission to correct discrimination on the basis of race, color, or creed was not created despite his support. Still, Stevenson had faced Republican control of one legislative chamber for two years and of both for the remaining two of his term. Governor Stevenson tried to work with the legislative branch in a spirit of compromise, not confrontation. Meetings with

individual legislators were frequent. Stevenson even once met with proponents and opponents of his highway program in an all-night negotiation session after defeat for his program seemed imminent. He managed to hammer out a program acceptable, if grudgingly, by all.

While political fortunes were soaring, the governor's marriage was disintegrating. Mrs. Stevenson had refused to join Adlai at the governor's mansion. In January, soon after the 1949 inauguration, the excuse was that their youngest son should not be removed from his school in Libertyville, outside of Chicago, where the family was living prior to Adlai's election. As summer came and went, the excuse was seen by more and more as a cloak for a domestic crisis. The crisis was resolved, if painfully, at the end of September 1949. Governor Stevenson announced that the couple was getting a divorce. The announcement stated incompatibility as the reason, but that they had separated "with the highest mutual regard." As time passed, any pretense of mutual regard did as well. Mrs. Stevenson was frequently quoted in the press with some disparaging remark about Stevenson. During Adlai's campaign against Eisenhower in 1952, Ellen announced she would vote Republican. Stevenson considered the divorce a great personal failure. He worked all the more arduously at his public duties as a result.

The domestic troubles did not prevent Stevenson from being considered among the frontrunners for the 1952 presidential nomination. Frequent speeches on national issues, including attacks on Senator Joe McCarthy, gave him a nationwide constituency. In June 1951, when McCarthyism was rampant and popular, the governor vetoed a bill that would have created an anti-subversive squad in the state. Stevenson courageously charged that the law would have intimidated innocent citizens without providing greater internal security. Though the presidency beckoned, Governor Stevenson announced in January 1952 that he would run for reelection. President Truman called him to the White House to attempt to change his mind. Stevenson's continued refusal to run infuriated the feisty Truman, and the breach between the two would never be healed. Stevenson's expressed reasons for declining all suggestions of a presidential candidacy were that he had committed to Illinois that he would run for governor, that there were programs he wanted to finish, and that he refused to have his three sons grow up in a fishbowl of publicity should he become president. In April, Stevenson said he could not accept the nomination for any office other than governor.

Not everyone was just waiting for Stevenson. Senator Kefauver of Tennessee, Vice President Barkley, Averell Harriman of New York, and others jumped into the race. A draft Stevenson committee was started without his permission, primarily by some prominent Chicagoans. No other candidate could generate enthusiasm, and even as the Chicago convention opened in July, with Stevenson still refusing to say he was a candidate, most observers predicted his nomination. As governor of the host state, Stevenson gave a welcoming speech which, intentionally on his part or not, roused the delegates to new levels of enthusiasm for his candidacy. On the third ballot he was nominated, even though he had yet to say whether he would accept. He did.

President Truman's disagreeable attitude towards Stevenson worsened as the campaign progressed. Speeches that suggested Stevenson agreed with the general characterization that there was a "mess in Washington" infuriated the president. Much more than the incumbent's personality was debated, however. Stevenson desired peaceful coexistence with Russia and argued for a stronger United Nations. More pointedly, the war in Korea was an issue in the campaign. Stevenson made no real proposals on the war other than to promise his best efforts, but then no politician seemed able to figure a way out of the morass. The Tidelands dispute regarding whether the federal or state government owned offshore oil lands also was inflamed. Stevenson wanted to retain federal control of these lands, and particularly in Texas he hurt himself by his position.

More memorable today than these issues was the question of Stevenson's speaking style. Presidential candidates were not expected to be as witty or as intellectual as the Illinois governor. Stevenson's reputation as an "egghead" probably on balance helped as much as it hurt,

but intelligence was nonetheless a strange, recurring sub-issue in the campaign. Humor in Stevenson's speeches also was jolting to many, leading the criticism that he was undignified.

The real decision was made on the basis of Eisenhower's tremendously attractive personality, which Stevenson could no more counter than any other Democrat could have. The personality of the Republican running mate, Richard Nixon, was much easier to discuss for Stevenson, and he did so with a vengeance. There developed a genuine hatred, a rare emotion for Stevenson, not only as a result of the campaign but also because of Nixon's earlier McCarthy-like tactics as senator and congressman from California. Stevenson's contempt for the future president would never abate.

No issue could dissuade enough voters from the delightful choice of making that grandfather figure, hero of World War II, the president of the country. The defeat was not embarrassingly severe, but it was large enough. Shortly thereafter, Stevenson went on a tour of Asia and the Middle East, writing for a national magazine a record of his observations and working on a book. He reopened his law office, kept up his speechmaking, and generally kept his options open for 1956.

Even if Stevenson was not ready to commit to the next presidential race, he did work hard and successfully in 1954 for the election of Democrats to Congress. As 1956 arrived, there was no draft Stevenson movement. Instead there were hungry competitors for the nomination in the form of Kefauver and Harriman, among others, and there was an incumbent president who had just suffered a heart attack and was not thought a candidate for reelection. Into that mix Stevenson placed his candidacy on November 15, 1955. A month later his son, John Fell Stevenson, was in a serious automobile accident in which two passengers in the car he was driving were killed. Fortunately for the boy's peace of mind the tragedy was not his fault, but nonetheless the parallels with the presidential candidate's own youth were striking.

The campaign took on a more frenzied air after Stevenson was badly defeated by Kefauver in the March 20 Minnesota primary. Stevenson had hoped to stay above the hectic, rubber-chicken, stump-speaking circuit but Kefauver's popular and gregarious style seemed to be catching on. Stevenson became much less the professor and "egghead" and more a standard politician during this race. He later came to believe the change injured his campaign. Still early in the desegregation crisis, even a Democratic candidate felt forced to say and was probably convinced that federal troops should not be used to enforce integration in southern schools. He proposed somewhat more courageously a ban on nuclear testing. He was excoriated as a naive, soft-on-communism weakling who was not fit for the presidency, but after the election the same kind of ban would be proposed by the Eisenhower administration.

The nomination was his again, and this time on the first ballot. Much to the surprise and dismay of some of his advisers, Stevenson announced he would not select his running mate but would leave that crucial decision open to the convention. Stevenson felt the principle of an open convention choice was important. He also must have hoped for political mileage out of emphasizing the importance of the selection not only because of Eisenhower's recent illness, but also because many Democrats felt the Republican vice president was unfit.

Stevenson gave further ammunition to the Republicans in their soft-on-communism charge when he proposed the ending of the draft. Tensions with Russia must be reduced. Most of all, the drift he saw in the country's direction and values must be halted. He wished to shake America's complacency. The people were not ready to be shaken; they were perhaps complacent but they were also pleased with relative prosperity and a peaceful international outlook. Later historians would give much more credit to the opinion of those voters who reelected Eisenhower than did most intellectuals at the time. The people even more overwhelmingly voted for Ike in 1956 than they had four years before. In December, Stevenson announced he would not run again.

His law practice, though not exactly exciting to Stevenson, did seem the place to retreat.

He made a substantial income even though he continued his political activities and international traveling. Europe, Africa, Russia, and Latin America all were visited during the next few years. His prominence, the unavoidable troubles of an incumbent administration, and the absence of a dominant Democratic alternative all led to speculation as early as the year following his landslide defeat that he might be the 1960 nominee.

During these intervening years, Stevenson developed more fully his concept of an international order. World government of a much stronger nature than the United Nations was required before peace could be achieved. All his foreign policy proposals were based on this almost utopian concept, which particularly with the perspective of intervening decades has proven to be visionary. Stevenson felt each nation must be made to see that pursuing its own welfare would only clash with other nations who were doing the same self-centered thing. What was needed was a "world-wide human community." Such concepts attracted many idealists, and some hard-headed politicians came too. Eleanor Roosevelt among others strongly supported him as the 1960 convention approached. The clear frontrunner was youthful Senator John Kennedy from Massachusetts. His money, his energy, his family, and his penchant for hard-ball politics had all been employed in Kennedy's single-minded drive for the nomination. Many in the party were not sure Kennedy was properly seasoned for so awesome a challenge as the presidency. It seems ironic today that what many once saw as the great success of the Kennedy administration, the Cuban missile crisis, would later be seen by some historians as confirmation of the doubts expressed when he was a presidential candidate. He was young, aggressive, and inexperienced as an administrator and those failings could put this country in grave danger.

Stevenson was entreated to announce that he would accept the nomination if offered. At no time, until the day before the balloting, did Stevenson give any support to his own nomination. Many an opportunity slipped away, but perhaps that is what Stevenson desired. He had made a promise not to run, and he was sticking to it. After the convention had started, however, Stevenson put a call in to Mayor Richard Daley of Chicago to see if any delegates could be shaken from Kennedy in Illinois. Daley denied that they could. It was far too little, far too late.

Stevenson wanted to be appointed secretary of state by the new president, but that prize was not to be offered. He hesitated but did finally accept appointment as ambassador to the United Nations. Relations with President Kennedy were never good. Stevenson once referred to the president-elect as "that arrogant young man." Kennedy was equally cold. Stevenson did not gain the influence at the United Nations he had hoped for. Little if any policy was made there, but only public posturing over policy made elsewhere. For four-and-a-half years Stevenson labored to thaw the frigidly cold war with Russia, and to cool the intensifying real war in Vietnam. During the Bay of Pigs debacle in April 1961, Stevenson had not been informed of American involvement and made a statement of American innocence that almost immediately was shown to be false. During the Cuban missile crisis the following year, Stevenson argued that the settlement of the issue should be made politically, not militarily. During his service under President Lyndon Johnson, Stevenson attempted to open peace talks with the North Vietnamese, but the president and Secretary of State Rusk did not trust the Communists. Subsequent events would suggest neither North or South Vietnam could be trusted with peace proposals. As United Nations Ambassador, he was frustrated and impotent.

While in London on United Nations business in 1965, Stevenson dropped dead on a public street from a heart attack.

Analysis of Qualifications

During the 1950s, Adlai Stevenson was the conscience of America. His idealism and intelligence shown brightly, if not popularly. While a majority of America was content in that decade, Stevenson was imploring them to give up their complacency, to realize the international crisis that existed in the continuation of the Cold War, to realize an international responsibility for the poor and hungry, to accept that the real danger from "subversives" in this country was the hysteria to root them out, and in many other respects to understand that America was at a crossroads in its moral leadership. That Stevenson could not convince a majority of his countrymen of his views eventually is probably of less importance than that he helped shape the debate on many critical issues. By degrees he pushed other government leaders towards his point of view.

The one-time Illinois governor loved public service, in part because of his family history of governmental achievement. He was a good administrator as governor, working well with its own staff and with the legislature. He could be tough, but usually he was conciliatory and noncombative, giving each side something to gain by agreement. His staff loved him. His style was not to create formal areas of responsibility for many of his key aides, but to let them use their experience and insights in a free-floating, shifting reaction to new problems that arose. Such a style lost much in efficiency and could also create staff jealousies, as there were constant incursions by one side into what another was doing. Apparently such discord did arise while he was governor, but the respect and affection for him held by his staff helped to minimize the problem. The contrast with his immediate predecessor as a twice-defeated presidential nominee, Thomas E. Dewey, is striking, even though Stevenson at times stated he admired the rigid organization and efficiency of the New York governor's administration.

Stevenson was criticized as unfit for the presidency. The charges were that he was not tough enough; he was indecisive; he was too idealistic and impractical. The indecision charge is documented by several career choices that Stevenson had continually put off making. Stevenson refused in 1952 and 1960 to jump into the presidential nomination battle even though wanting the presidency. He was unable to decide in 1947 whether to accept the gubernatorial nomination once party leaders selected another for the post he really wanted, the Senate. Yet there are few examples outside of this reluctance to promote his own candidacy for high office where such irresolution is apparent. Stevenson constitutionally just could not "beat his own drum." He was self-depre-cating, humorously so; he was famous for his witty and exaggerated descriptions of setbacks in his life and public career. He was strong and determined on the public issues he faced as gov-ernor, and there is every reason to believe that would have been continued in the presidency.

The description of Stevenson as an "egg-head" and the fact he spoke in moralistic terms are two different but related criticisms of his ability to approach problems pragmatically. Richard Nixon was but one of many who called Stevenson naive, too trusting of the Rus-sians, and too idealistic. As speculative as would-be presidents rating is in most aspects, it is even more hazardous when considering a candidate's positions on substantive issues. The proper approach towards the Soviet Union is an area of continuing political disagreement. That Stevenson was intelligent and dynamic in the expression of his positions is to his credit, and that is the extent to which this fac-tor in his make-up can appropriately be weighed for purposes here.

Stevenson's thoughtful, witty presentation of his sensitive approach to world and domes-tic problems made him a force in the Demo-cratic Party. He had performed well as an administrator and political leader while gov-ernor. His subsequent career as Kennedy's United Nations Ambassador further enhanced his reputation as a man who understood world problems. Stevenson was well qualified by experience, intelligence, and character to be president. The man who defeated him has also been ranked by historians as extremely quali-fied, with an entirely different set of back-ground and personality characteristics, and with quite different views. It was a rare pair of elections. The United States deserves more such choices.

STEVENSON BIBLIOGRAPHY

Broadwater, Jeff. *Adlai Stevenson and American Pol-itics: The Odyssey of a Cold War Liberal.* New York (1994).
Cochran, Bert. *Adlai Stevenson, Patrician Among the Politicians.* New York City (1969).
David, Kenneth S. *The Politics of Honor: A Biogra-phy of Adlai E. Stevenson.* New York City (1967).
Ives, Elizabeth Stevenson, and Hildegarde Dolson. *My Brother Adlai.* New York City (1956).
Johnson, Walter, ed. *The Papers of Adlai E. Steven-son.* 8 vols. Boston (1972–1979).
McKeever, Porter. *Adlai Stevenson: His Life and Legacy.* New York City (1989).
Martin, John Bartlow. *Adlai Stevenson and the World.* Garden City, N.Y. (1977).
_____. *Adlai Stevenson of Illinois.* Garden City, N.Y. (1976).
Sievers, Rodney M. *The Last Puritan? Adlai E. Stevenson.* Millwood, N.Y. (1983).
Stevenson, The Rev. Samuel Harris. "A History and Genealogical Record of the Stevenson Family from 1748 to 1926," n.p., n.d.
Some genealogical information was provided by Adlai E. Stevenson, III.

---

*1952 vice presidential nominee—
Democratic Party*

John Sparkman

Full name: John Jackson Sparkman.

State represented: Alabama.

Birth: December 20, 1899, near Hartselle, Alabama.

Age on Inauguration Day (January 20, 1953): 53 years, 1 month.

Education: Attended one-room country school; Morgan County (Alabama) High School; University of Alabama, 1917–1921 (B.A.), graduated Phi Beta Kappa; LL.B. in 1923, M.A. in 1924; admitted to bar in 1925.

Religion: Methodist.

Occupation: Attorney.

Public offices: U.S. commissioner, North-ern District of Alabama, 1930–1931; U.S. House of Representatives, January 3, 1937–November 5, 1946; Majority whip in 1946, resigned; U.S. senator, November 6, 1946–January 3, 1979; unsuccessful Democratic nominee for vice president, 1952.

Home: 150-acre farm outside of Huntsville, Alabama.

Death: November 16, 1985, at age 85 years, 11 months.

Burial: Maple Hill Cemetery, Huntsville, Alabama.

Personal characteristics: 6'1", 200 pounds, ruddy face, blue-gray eyes, curly black hair; shambling gait, rumpled appearance.

JOHN J. SPARKMAN and ADLAI E. STEVENSON
(From the collection of David J. and Janice L. Frent)

Father: Joseph Whitten Sparkman (April, 1868–?); farmer.

Mother: Julia Mitchell Kent (January, 1865–?); married around 1890.

Siblings: Herman C. (July, 1887–?). Mattie Lou (April, 1889–?). Marvin G. (March, 1894–?). Pennie Agnes (December, 1895–?). Flossie Grace (January, 1898–?). Gladys (c. 1902–?). Thelma (c.1907–?). There were also three other children in the family.

Wife: Ivo Hall (October 6, 1899–); married June 2, 1923, daughter of Dr. and Mrs. William P. Hall.

Child: Julia Ann (1924–), married Tazewell T. Shepard, Jr., a Navy pilot.

He was called a "Southern liberal" when he was nominated for vice president in 1952. Fourteen years later George Wallace supporters were calling him far worse. They hoped that their hero would challenge Sparkman for the Senate seat he had held since 1946. In fact, John Sparkman never indicated liberality in the ultimate Southern issue, civil rights. His style was just less strident than that of arch segregationists. However, on almost every other public issue he faced, Sparkman made his Alabaman constituency a shade uneasy. It was that contrast in positions, strongly publicized to the occasional discomfort of the national Democrats in 1952, which made Sparkman a force in national politics.

One of 11 children in a poor farming family, young John Sparkman attended a one-room country school house until he was of high school age. He grew up in the poverty of the Tennessee Valley section of northern Alabama, helping his father with chores on their tract of farm land. The senior Sparkman revealed an interest in politics and held a few minor offices, such as deputy sheriff. Morgan County High School provided John's final preparatory education; then in 1917 he was off for the University of Alabama. Sparkman early demonstrated thrift and business sense, acquiring a bank loan secured on his cotton crop to pay his tuition. He had to keep working in order to stay in school. This poor farmer's son was more than willing to take, at $4.20 per week, a job wheelbarrowing coal for the university, and then cleaning out the spent ashes.

Coincidentally, another student who joined in the labor was future liberal senator Claude Pepper of Florida.

While attending the university, Sparkman enlisted in the army after the war broke out. He served from October 7, 1918, until December 12, 1919. Then back at school he joined the Reserve Officer's Training Corps and was commissioned a second lieutenant upon graduation in 1921. Sparkman became an important figure on campus, earning a teacher's fellowship his junior year and editing the school newspaper in his senior year. He also served as class president. Social activities were hardly ignored, and during a party with other youths from the local Methodist church, one of the games played was "spin the pan." John lost the game, and his penalty was to ask out a girl he did not know. That girl, Ivo Hall, would within a few years become his wife.

After John received his bachelor's degree in 1921, he first tried to obtain a job with a newspaper. That proved hopeless and the disappointed journalist returned to the University of Alabama to attend law school. Two years later he graduated, married Ivo, and went to work as secretary for the Tuscaloosa student YMCA. This salaried position, together with teaching, permitted him to continue his education and get a master's degree in 1924. He was admitted to the bar in 1925 and finally started practicing law, forming a partnership in Huntsville where he would remain until elected to Congress ten years later. He had saved his money, earned Phi Beta Kappa honors in college, had a wife, soon a baby and a mortgage on both a house and a farm of 160 acres outside of Huntsville. The law practice did not quite provide the comfortable living the Sparkmans sought, and Mrs. Sparkman within a few years began teaching school. She would continue until after her husband's election to the Senate. John also taught at Huntsville College.

While the young family strived to obtain a measure of financial and professional success, John's early interests in politics took clearer form. In 1926 and 1932, he campaigned for Hugo Black's election to the U.S. Senate. For 1930 and 1931, he was U.S. commissioner for northern Alabama. Watching and working for others gave way in 1936 to his first personal

political race. U.S. Representative A.H. Carmichael of the Eighth Congressional District decided to retire, and five candidates announced to replace him. A spirited campaign resulted in Sparkman's victory in a runoff in the Democratic primary. Without a meaningful Republican Party in the state, the Democratic nomination was tantamount to election. It was said that Sparkman ran such an appealing campaign that a band hired by one of his opponents dumped their employer after hearing Sparkman and began playing at his rallies for free.

Sparkman's reelection was never seriously contested during the following years, and the congressman established a reputation in Washington as a loyal New Deal Democrat. The Tennessee Valley Authority directly affected his district. Sparkman could be counted among its steadiest and most vocal proponents. He sponsored and saw passed a bill bearing his name to dam the Tennessee River in Kentucky, and cosponsored in the House the Norris bill that authorized TVA to purchase the private utility companies in the area. During the approach to World War II, Sparkman was counted with the internationalists. He voted for Lend-Lease, enlargement of the Army Air Corps, the draft, and other measures to prepare the country for war.

Sparkman's early years in Washington were greatly benefitted by his fellow Alabaman, Speaker William Bankhead. Much as a later Texas Speaker would promote his home state protégé— Speaker Sam Rayburn and a youthful Lyndon B. Johnson — Bankhead took Sparkman under his wing and promoted him. When many Southerners were abandoning President Roosevelt over issues such as the Supreme Court packing, increased centralization of power in Washington, and other intrusions into long-held states' rights principles, Sparkman followed his mentor in remaining loyal to the president. He was called by Drew Pearson in 1941 "one of the ablest young members" of the House. Two years later he organized other young Democratic congressmen into a group whose support of the president could be counted upon. When Sparkman encouraged Roosevelt in 1944 to seek a fourth term, there was no doubt of the Alabaman's continued loyalty. His leadership in the House was given formal recognition in 1946 when he was selected as party whip.

Though rising to considerable influence in the lower house, Sparkman was not content to remain a congressman. In June 1946, incumbent Alabama Senator John Bankhead, the speaker's brother, died. On July 30 a special primary was held to replace Bankhead. With the support of the CIO political action committee, together with his contacts built up after ten years in the House, Sparkman won with a clear majority of the vote over four opponents. He was already on the November ballot as a congressional candidate, and in order to prevent that seat from falling to the Republicans by default, Sparkman remained a candidate for both offices. On November 4 he was simultaneously elected to the House and to the Senate, the only time in American history that has occurred. Not surprisingly, he chose the Senate seat and resigned from the House.

During Harry Truman's presidency, Sparkman was known as perhaps the South's most liberal senator. He supported the controversial nomination of former TVA chairman David Lilienthal as head of the Atomic Energy Commission, while many voted against him because of fears he was a security risk. Housing legislation was a major interest of Sparkman's. As a member of the Joint Committee on Housing and other related committees he worked for passage of low-income housing subsidies. Slum clearance, construction of housing for both poor and middle-income families, and rent controls were key parts of bills he sponsored or endorsed. The Taft-Hartley Act was supported by the Alabaman when first presented to the Senate, but he became convinced by President Truman's veto message and voted to sustain the veto.

Though a consistent administration man in other areas, a split with the president came over civil rights measures. He condemned efforts to prohibit poll taxes or pass anti-lynching laws. A detailed program was presented by Truman in 1948 to deal with civil rights problems; it caused Sparkman's complete break from the president. Sparkman called the following month for the party to nominate Dwight Eisenhower for president and dump Truman.

That having failed, he joined the walkout by Strom Thurmond from the national convention and voted for Thurmond's 1948 Dixiecrat ticket. This apostasy hardly caused him trouble back home. Truman was not even listed on the state's ballot, the only state to exclude the president, and Alabama voters overwhelmingly voted for Thurmond. Another political gamble was Sparkman's failure to be loyal to Governor "Big Jim" Folsom. This caused Folsom to handpick Phil Hamm as Sparkman's opponent in the primary. The governor's dissatisfaction with the senator apparently was not mirrored in the electorate, and Sparkman won handily.

In 1949, one of Sparkman's most significant legislative proposals was introduced. It was the Housing Act of 1949, a comprehensive program to provide low-income housing. In 1950, he was behind that year's housing act that provided relief to middle-income home purchasers. It extended Federal Housing Authority and Veterans Administration programs to the middle class. The *New York Times* called the latter bill "economically irresponsible," but a majority of both houses and the president favored its adoption.

Friendly towards labor, opposed to civil rights laws, considered a liberal on most domestic programs such as housing, an internationalist backer of the Marshall Plan and aid to other foreign countries, Senator Sparkman was a blend of liberalism and Southern political pragmatism. In 1950, he declared, "We Southern Democrat Senators — 21 of us — are banded together and pledged to use every parliamentary device possible to defeat civil rights legislation." Balancing that image was his yeoman work as one of five American delegates to the General Assembly of the United Nations, beginning in 1950. He was effective and liked in the Senate, a good speaker, and by and large an administration supporter. Therefore, when liberal midwestern Democrat Adlai Stevenson received his party's presidential nomination, Sparkman seemed the best Southerner available that could simultaneously hold his region without antagonizing the rest of the country. Many black groups were vocal in opposing his nomination. New York Democratic congressman Adam Clayton Powell, one of the leading national black spokesmen, said that Spark-man's nomination made it impossible for him to support the national ticket. Powell called the selection one of the "great tragedies of our time." Slightly less extreme objections came from many other civil rights circles. The Re-publicans did not let the issue die. Previous presidential loser Tom Dewey pointed out late in the campaign that Sparkman's home state used a ballot that pictured a rooster as the emblem of the Democratic Party, together with the words "white supremacy." Sparkman could only weakly respond that the emblem and slogan had been used since the 1890s. Clearly Sparkman had never done anything to change the practice.

The Alabaman endorsed the anemic civil rights plank in the platform as being the most reasonable compromise of the divergent North-ern and Southern views on the issue. Though running alongside a clear advocate of such leg-islation, the vice presidential nominee had refused to support a fair employment practice commission or limits on Senate filibusters. As is typical with candidates for the number two spot, Sparkman was given the task of attack-ing the opposition. With Joe McCarthy hold-ing forth in the Senate, and the revelations about Republican running mate Richard Nixon's secret expense fund, there was mate-rial for Sparkman to use. One of the issues in the campaign that Nixon gave considerable play was the fact that Ivo Sparkman had a salaried job in the senator's office. Sparkman angrily responded that she earned every cent, and worked longer hours than he dared de-mand of nonrelative employees.

It was a vigorous campaign run by the Deep South senator; he may have averaged nine or ten speeches a day. Sparkman met his running mate only three times during the campaign, and mainly worked separately in the South and West. He later called the campaign a "gruel-ing experience," having made over 400 speeches and traveled 36,000 miles. Defeat left him with few regrets.

With Eisenhower's election and the Repub-lican takeover of Congress, Sparkman found himself in the minority in the Senate for only the second time. Yet he had gained prestige from the presidential campaign and was lis-tened to as never before. Foreign affairs be-came his focus, as housing had been a few years earlier. Service on the Senate Foreign Relations Committee gave him a platform. The division of Vietnam that resulted from the 1954 Geneva Convention was termed a sell-out to the Com-munists. The short-lived but intense contro-versy over Quemoy and Matsu, two islands off the Chinese coast, led Sparkman to charge that administration efforts to prevent an invasion by the Red Chinese could precipitate war. When the British and their allies invaded the Suez in 1956, Sparkman called Eisenhower's handling of that crisis "the worse diplomatic disaster in memory."

In addition to foreign affairs, Sparkman kept a keen eye on small business matters. After 1954, he was chairman of the Senate Small Business Committee, and from that van-tage point shepherded bills through Congress increasing federal aid to small business. An emergency housing bill was introduced by him in 1958 to encourage residential construction during that recession year. Urban renewal was again his concern in 1960 but his ambitious proposals were scaled down on the Senate floor by that pennypincher, Senate majority leader Lyndon Johnson.

The most dramatic civil rights decision by the Supreme Court since the Civil War was handed down in 1954, when in *Brown v. Board of Education of Topeka*, school segregation was outlawed. In response, Sparkman and other senators signed the "Southern Manifesto" call-ing for the voiding of the *Brown* decision, using "lawful means." The first major civil rights bills since Reconstruction were passed during Eisenhower's second term, and Spark-man opposed both of them. Protection of the filibuster, successfully used for decades by the Southern bloc to prevent such legislation, be-came the South's pet issue. Sparkman was as vocal as any Southerner on the sanctity of the filibuster. He warned: while the right to debate is now necessary to protect the South, the time may come when this might be essential for the protection of some other minority interest. The epochal civil rights acts of 1964 and 1965 were similarly denounced by the senator.

When John Kennedy became president, Sparkman renewed his record of consistent support for Democratic administration measures that had been evident during Truman's presidency. Again civil rights was a significant exception. Arms limitations were warmly endorsed, support for mass transportation vigorously given, but medicare opposed by the Alabama senator.

While a national reputation was being built, political fences in Alabama had to be kept repaired. George Wallace dominated the state scene. Unfortunately for Wallace, state law prohibited him from running for a second term as governor. Speculation was rampant that he would challenge Sparkman in the 1966 primary. As the election approached, Sparkman seemed to be trimming his sails in Washington and being less willing to support liberal domestic programs. President Johnson knew a friendly vote when he had one, and offered to do whatever Sparkman wanted to help his reelection. "Just tell me what you want," the president said. "I'll talk for you, or *agin* you, whichever will do the most good." Probably being "agin" Sparkman was the most helpful, and the senator sought no public endorsement. Wallace was prevented by the state constitution from running for the Senate until he had been out of the governor's office for one year, but most observers considered that to violate the federal constitution which was the sole guide for qualifications for the Senate. The business community found Sparkman's gentlemanly soft-pedaling of his stands against civil rights far preferable to the strident attacks of Wallace. They also understood how important Sparkman's seniority was. Major governmental installations dotted the state, with the senator's hometown of Huntsville being a particularly fortunate beneficiary of federal largesse. Wallace never got into the fray, instead deciding to remain as governor through the legerdemain of running his wife for the post. Sparkman won both the primary and general election with ease.

With a fresh six years of protection from the whims of the Wallace constituency, Sparkman reverted to form. As newly installed chairman of the Banking and Currency Committee, Sparkman ended the roadblock to truth-in-lending legislation in 1967 and saw adoption of that far-reaching Act by the Senate. President Johnson's Great Society programs were usually supported, especially sizeable increases in spending on housing. On every conceivable front, Sparkman worked to improve housing in this country, denouncing tight money policies that restricted mortgage credit, sponsoring efforts to dislodge housing funds impounded by President Nixon, and otherwise making housing better, cheaper and more readily available. Vietnam found Sparkman as one of the administration's most hawkish advocates. When Oregon Senator Wayne Morse tried to make drastic cuts in Vietnam aid, Sparkman opposed him. In 1972, he was pressed hard in the Democratic Senate primary and barely avoided a runoff. The issue was more Sparkman's close ties with banking interests than his "liberal" record. Postmaster general in the Nixon Administration, Winton Blount, resigned from the cabinet and opposed Sparkman in the November 1972 general election. The well-financed Blount campaign was unable to dislodge Sparkman despite Nixon's strong support for the Republican. Even more of a burden in Alabama was the presence of Democratic presidential nominee George McGovern on the ballot. Sparkman condemned McGovern's views, and won easily over Blount.

When Senator J. William Fulbright was defeated for reelection in 1974, Sparkman became chairman of the Senate Foreign Relations Committee. He was one of the great powers of the Senate, but was tiring of office. He announced he would retire at the end of his term in 1979. He entered a law firm in Huntsville, tended to his farm, and generally avoided politics.

Analysis of Qualifications

Sparkman's political troubles in Alabama resulted from the perception that he was not a true Southerner. His votes in favor of national administration programs left him open to the charge that he had forgotten his roots and had become, of all things, a national Democrat. Despite threats every six years that his record would defeat him, in fact Sparkman almost always won easily and escaped the rumored danger. Just how justified were the complaints about his votes? During Franklin

Roosevelt's administration Sparkman supported the president on just about every measure, except civil rights. He was a warm advocate of Truman's policies until February 1948, when Truman announced a comprehensive program on racial problems. Partisan, if not viciously so, the senator was a frequent critic of Eisenhower policies. He returned to support of presidential initiatives when the presidency returned to the Democrats in 1961, and throughout the eight Kennedy-Johnson years endorsed the New Frontier, Great Society policies, including support for the Vietnam War. Finally, with Nixon and then Ford in the White House, Sparkman was a critic in the Senate, following his national party's positions.

Throughout this consistent identification with most of the broad aims of the northern wing of the party, Sparkman remained loyal to his region on the most emotional issue of all, race. When George Wallace's opposition to the march of blacks from Selma to Montgomery in 1965 led to violence in "Bloody Lowndes" County, Sparkman did not criticize the governor's motives, but instead took issue with the tactics. That same year, it was estimated that during the preceding almost 30 years Sparkman served in the House and Senate he had opposed nearly one hundred civil rights bills. Somehow, someway, through all this consistency, the voters in Alabama kept being told by Sparkman's opponents that the senator was only half-hearted in his racial views, and could not be trusted. True, he never descended to demagoguery in an attempt to inflame passions. Still, he could always be counted on for the "right" vote.

Fellow congressmen and the press seemed constantly to credit him for dignity, efficiency, and hard work. His rating in 1941 as one of the ablest young House members, his "adoption" by Speaker Bankhead and his easy reelection victories in Alabama made his powerbase strong in the South and his influence significant in the Capitol. Since he was a loyal president's senator, when the president was a Democrat, he also had the chief executive's ear when he wanted it. He frequently wanted it on pork barrel items for Alabama, and few states received greater federal largesse than did Sparkman's Alabama. Huntsville was frequently

called the "town John rebuilt," and the name was appropriate. Substantial federal employee payrolls existed at several installations in the state, and defense contracts were awarded to Alabama companies with regularity.

John Sparkman was a national Democrat on most measures because his poor state needed the economic benefits of federal aid. Few housing bills passed Congress since World War II without Sparkman's direct involvement either as the originator, a sponsor, or shepherd of the legislation. Yet he was also a practical and hard-nosed politician who understood, and probably agreed with, the emotional views held in the South concerning race. With a national constituency rather than a parochial one, a President Sparkman might have in the early 1950s shown much more liberality in civil rights. A diehard segregationist as president during the start of the second American Reconstruction, that period commencing with the 1954 *Brown* Supreme Court opinion on school desegregation, would have been disastrous. Sparkman had been an able, progressive, well-liked congressman and senator. After the 1952 election he continued to grow in prestige and influence in Washington. If, as president, he had rejected what as an Alabama Senator had been the necessity of espousing segregation, he most likely would have performed admirably as president. If he had remained rigid, then the Southern Manifesto that in actuality was only the delaying but ultimately vain effort of one region to deny the implications of the *Brown* decision, could have taken on the shape of presidential policy. Whether that would have been sufficient to imperil the totality of a Sparkman presidency is indeed speculative, but no doubt it would have forever affected the historical record.

SPARKMAN BIBLIOGRAPHY

Douth, George. "John Sparkman," in *Leaders in Profile: The United States Senate.* New York City (1972), pp. 3–7, and (1975), pp. 5–11.
Egan, Leo. "Sparkman Warned on Rights Plank." *New York Times* (July 27, 1952), pp. 1, 20.
"The Men: How Stevenson and Sparkman Came Up." *Newsweek* (August 4, 1952), p. 26.
"The Percentage." *Time* (August 11, 1952), pp. 18–19.

"Poor John." *Time* (May 28, 1965), pp. 24–25.

Sherrill, Robert. "Portrait of a 'Southern Liberal' in Trouble." *New York Times Magazine* (November 7, 1965), pp. 46 ff.

Sparkman, Ivo Hall. *Journeys with the Senator.* Huntsville, Ala. (1977).

"Sparkman, Backer of New, Fair Deals." *New York Times* (July 27, 1952), p. 31.

"Sparkman, Man of the South." *Newsweek* (October 20, 1952), pp. 36–37.

"Sparkman's Role: Soothe South, Hold the 'Liberals.'" *U.S. News & World Report* (August 1, 1952), p. 16.

"Two Men Who Are Expected to Move into Top Spots in Congress." *U.S. News & World Report* (July 25, 1966), p. 19.

Walker, Henry James. "A Political History of a Public Man: John Sparkman of Alabama." Unpublished master's thesis, University of Alabama (1990).

Family information provided partly by Mrs. John Sparkman, Huntsville, Alabama, and from census microfilm for Morgan County, Alabama, for 1900 and 1910.

Election of 1956

NOMINATIONS

Democratic Party Convention (32nd): August 13–17, 1956, at the International Amphitheatre, Chicago, Illinois. *President*— Adlai E. Stevenson, nominated on the first ballot with 905½ votes out of 1,372 cast. Averell Harriman (N.Y.) was his major rival. *Vice president*— Estes Kefauver, nominated on the second ballot with 755½ votes out of 1,372 cast, after vote changes. Before these switches he had received 551½; on the first ballot he received 466½. John F. Kennedy was his chief rival.

Republican Party Convention (26th): August 20–23, 1956, at the Cow Palace, San Francisco, California. *President*— Dwight Eisenhower, nominated unanimously on the first ballot. *Vice president*— Richard Nixon, nominated unanimously on the first ballot.

GENERAL ELECTION, November 6, 1956

Popular Vote

Eisenhower 35,585,245
Stevenson. 26,030,172
Others.   409,955

Electoral Vote

PRESIDENT

Eisenhower — 457 (41 states)

Stevenson — 73 (7 states)
Walter B. Jones —1

VICE PRESIDENT

Nixon, 457
Kefauver, 73
Herman Talmadge, 1

Winners

Dwight Eisenhower, 34th president
Richard Nixon, 36th vice president

Losers

Adlai Stevenson, Estes Kefauver

---

*1956 presidential nominee —
Democratic Party*

Adlai E. Stevenson

The biographical sketch for Stevenson is included in the section on the 1952 election, pages 630–636.

State represented: Illinois.
Birth: February 5, 1900.
Age on Inauguration Day (January 20, 1957): 56 years, 11½ months.
Death: July 14, 1965.

**ADLAI E. STEVENSON and
ESTES KEFAUVER**
(From the collection of David J. and Janice L. Frent)

*1956 vice presidential nominee—
Democratic Party*

Estes Kefauver

Full name: Carey Estes Kefauver.
State represented: Tennessee.
Birth: July 26, 1903, near Madison-ville, Tennessee.
Age on Inauguration Day (January 20, 1957): 53 years, 6 months.
Education: Madisonville public schools, graduated 1920; University of Tennessee, graduated 1924; Yale Law School, graduated with honors, 1927.
Religion: Baptist.
Ancestry/prominent relatives: Huguenot ancestors, came to America from Alsace-Lorraine; name was a French spelling of the German "Kefober"; earliest ancestor in Jamestown by 1624; every direct family line had arrived in America before Revolutionary War; Joe Folk (governor of Missouri) was his mother's cousin.
Occupation: Attorney.
Public office: Appointed Tennessee Commissioner of Finance and Taxation, January–May, 1939, resigned; elected U.S. representative, September 13, 1939–January 3, 1949; U.S. senator, January 3, 1949–August 10, 1963; unsuccessful candidate for Democratic presidential nomination, 1952 and 1956; unsuccessful nominee for vice president, 1956.
Death: August 10, 1963, Bethesda, Maryland; age 60 years, ½ month.
Burial: Madisonville, Tennessee, family graveyard.
Home: Chattanooga, Tennessee.
Personal characteristics: 6'3" tall, heavy-set; long nose; glasses; large ears; huge hands.
Father: Robert Cooke Kefauver (August 25, 1870–February 19, 1958); hardware business, farmer, served as Mayor of Madisonville for five terms; dairyman.
Mother: Phredonia Estes (August 26, 1873–April 30, 1948); married January 14, 1897.

Siblings: Elizabeth (December 1, 1897–October 8, 1901). Robert Fielding (April 19, 1901–August 9, 1914). Nancy Rieves (January 10, 1906–). Nora Mann (April 9, 1911–).

Wife: Nancy Peterson Pigott (c. 1911–November 20, 1967), married August 8, 1935; born in Scotland.

Children: Lyndsay. David Estes (January 27, 1946–); adopted; married Mary Beth Dalness on August 29, 1968; veterinarian. Diane Carey. Gail Estes.

It was an illustrious marriage, that of the parents of Estes Kefauver. The mother, Phredonia Estes, descended from eleventh century Italian Albert Azo, II, Marquis of Liquira. The Estes name came from the House D'Este founded by Albert. Three Esteses fought well in the American Revolution, and another defeated Davy Crockett in a Tennessee election, causing Crockett to leave for Texas. Robert Cooke Kefauver, Estes Kefauver's father, was a dairy farmer, hardware store owner, and five-term mayor of Madisonville, a small east Tennessee town at the foot of the Great Smoky Mountains. Estes was a gangling, gawky youth whose appearance nonetheless posed no problem that his gregarious, fun-loving personality could not overcome. His older brother Robert's death was a crushing loss for Estes, who was then only 11 years old. The tragedy made Estes more introspective; he brooded in his room, read books, and became far more serious than before. In time he worked out of the depression, but the pain perhaps never completely left him.

An early introduction to politics came in the Woodrow Wilson campaign of 1916, when he helped his father nail up posters declaring, somewhat prematurely, "He kept us out of war." Favorable impressions were also left by courtroom drama. Madisonville was the county seat, and Estes found his future calling as a prosecutor from observing the best legal talent in the area.

Graduation from his smalltown high school, with scholastic and church honors, poorly prepared Estes for the big city of Knoxville. Beginning college in the fall of 1920 at the University of Tennessee, Estes left school for home after only a few weeks. He was ridiculed pitilessly because of his gangling appearance,

his church school attendance ribbons he had worn his first day on campus, and his overall lack of sophistication. Finally, he could not take the catcalls of "rube" and "hick" any longer. A lengthy talk with his mother led to a quick return to school. In time, Kefauver outgrew his awkward mannerisms and became a campus celebrity, being selected editor of the student paper, president of the junior class, and president of the Southern Federation of College Students. His athletic ability was not outstanding, but he did make the varsity football team as a substitute. Law school was still the goal, but graduation from college was followed instead by a trip to Hot Springs, Arkansas, to tend to his ill mother. After a year teaching at a high school there (a successful year that caused the principal vainly to invite him back with a sizeable salary offer), Kefauver was off for Yale Law School. He worked hard, both at his studies and at odd jobs to pay his way. These included tutoring students, waiting on tables, clerking in a bookstore, and similar ventures. Both Kefauver and a fellow student, Brien McMahon of Connecticut, indicated political ambitions. The two similarly minded new lawyers parted from Yale after graduation, with Kefauver saying, "I'll see you in Washington." He did, as both became United States senators.

Plans for a job with his relative Joe Folk's Washington law firm went aglimmering with Folk's death. No salaried position could be found, but only a place in the library from which to work at a Knoxville firm. The cases were mundane and financially profitless. However, Kefauver found satisfaction in the nature of the work, helping poor clients, many of whom were Negroes, find redress for their many sufferings. An article he wrote for the *Tennessee Law Review* in 1927 caught the eye of the senior partner with one of the best Knoxville firms, Sizer, Chambliss and Sizer, but no openings were then available. With that prospect of advancement palpable, Kefauver discovered one of his clients had a matter that would bring him into conflict with Sizer. Indications from correspondence on the matter were that Sizer did not approve of Kefauver's client or his cause. Feeling obligated, Kefauver swallowed hard and proceeded diligently and competently. Winning the case, Kefauver found himself summoned to the other attorney's office. An offer of a junior partnership accompanied the congratulations. In the new firm, which beginning in 1930 was known as Sizer, Chambliss, and Kefauver, the young attorney soon accumulated a reputation as well as clients. His social life was also active. A blind date with a girl from Glasgow, Scotland, in the summer of 1934 led to a long-distance letter-writing courtship after her return home. The following summer a starstruck Kefauver sailed for Glasgow to continue the courtship. The future mother-in-law threw her arms around the friend Kefauver had traveled with to Glasgow, and said, "I always hoped my daughter would marry someone just like you." The shade of crimson to which her face subsequently turned was not recorded. Marriage did follow, with a trip to Loch Ness as a honeymoon.

Leadership of a group of young men called The Volunteers, concerned about county government, gave Kefauver his political start. From that good government citizens group base, Kefauver ran for the state senate against the county machine candidate. He lost, by a few hundred stolen votes. His senate campaign had been dogged, ringing doorbells and shaking hands until he could not think, or remember, straight. Kefauver's forgetfulness with names led to a famous, much-quoted and perhaps much-repeated episode when he met a teenager after a speech. Among other pleasantries, the candidate asked the boy how his father was. The boy replied that the father was deceased. Continuing his handshaking rounds, in time Kefauver ended up shaking the same boy's hand again and, unfortunately, asking the same question. The boy's response: "He's still dead." Every politician can probably sympathize.

The new Tennessee governor took this just-defeated candidate and appointed him as state commissioner for Finance and Taxation. The governor wanted a battler for reform legislation, and got him in Kefauver. After four months on the job, with the approval of voters and the press for his performance, Kefauver announced his candidacy for a vacancy in the local United States congressional seat,

caused by the death of an eight-term incumbent. The momentum from his recent favorable publicity, as well as from his own campaign style, propelled him easily to victory in the special election.

Once in Washington, the Tennessee congressman aligned himself completely with the New Deal and with such local concerns as the Tennessee Valley Authority. Appointed to the Judiciary Committee and the Select Committee on Small Business, Kefauver established a reputation as a watchdog for small business against predatory, big business excesses. Also prominent in his congressional career were efforts to reform Congress. More detailed proposals would come later, but in 1943 Kefauver suggested that cabinet members be required to appear periodically before Congress for questioning. Such proposals had been made through the years by several congressmen, including one with whom Kefauver shared the disappointment of having been defeated a a Democratic vice presidential nominee — George H. Pendleton.

Reelection never proved difficult from 1940 through 1946. In his early congressional career, Kefauver played the part of the earnest but deferential new member, not stepping on toes or attempting to advance too quickly. One power to whom he did not defer, however, was Tennessee Senator Kenneth McKellar. McKellar wanted to reduce the Tennessee Valley Authority's independence and tried to require that it be funded each year, thereby placing its existence up for a vote each year. The Senate passed the measure, but Kefauver prevailed in the House in killing the proposal. Subsequent moves by McKellar to bring the headquarters of TVA to Washington were also thwarted by the effective two-term congressman. McKellar and Kefauver would remain foes for the remainder of their joint political careers.

The congressman's record was a liberal one, so much so as to endanger his future advancement in Tennessee. Civil rights bills were supported; labor legislation was championed and laws unions did not like, such as Taft-Hartley, were rejected; poll tax elimination was proposed. Laws that seemed to interfere with civil liberties were opposed, such as the creation in 1945 of a House Committee on Un-American

Activities. In 1946, Kefauver earned fame for proposing a detailed plan for reorganizing Congress. It included limiting the powers of committee chairmen, larger staffs for congressmen, increasing terms for representatives to four years, limiting filibusters, giving both houses a vote on treaties and other proposals. A best-selling book, *A Twentieth Century Congress*, was coauthored with Jack Levin in 1947.

It was with a solid record of achievement behind him that Kefauver announced for the United States Senate in 1947. The incumbent Senator, Tom Stewart, had been abandoned by Boss Crump of Memphis. Crump was mayor of the city and political boss for much of the state. He was not a man to trifle with, but Senator Stewart refused to give up his seat without a fight. Crump supported John Mitchell, and thus a three-way race developed. For a time, Kefauver considered dropping out of the race, as early polls showed him far behind. The charges against him as pro-labor, pro-Communist, and, worst of all, a "nigger-lover" were made orally as well as in print. One scurrilous attack came on June 10, 1948, in every daily newspaper in Tennessee. "Estes Kefauver assumes the role of a pet coon," the advertisement said, and went on to explain that coon-Kefauver had his foot in the drawer, but kept his head turned looking around the room in hopes of deceiving others as to what he was doing. Soon thereafter Kefauver was in the midst of giving a speech in the Peabody Hotel in Memphis, Crump's den. Kefauver reached down and picked up from behind the podium a coonskin cap and put it on. The audience howled, and the laugh was on Crump. Kefauver's line "I may be a coon, but I will never be Mr. Crump's pet coon," perfectly symbolized the issue Kefauver wanted the voters to have in mind on election day. Forty percent of the electorate chose Kefauver on primary day, and the nomination was his. The Republican Party put up no serious opponent and in November Kefauver won in a landslide. From there on, sometimes foolishly, Kefauver would wear the coonskip cap during campaign appearances, even when running for president.

The first speech by this new senator from the South was an attack on the methods used to kill civil rights legislation. Then Kefauver took on monopolies. In 1950, the Kefauver-Celler bill was enacted to outlaw the merger of companies if competition was thereby reduced. Big business would be a constant Kefauver foe. Kefauver then chose an issue that seemed certain to gain him wide publicity. He introduced a resolution to create a committee to investigate the impact of organized crime on society. Kefauver was at first thwarted by other senators who wanted a piece of the publicity that was sure to follow. A compromise was struck, and a special subcommittee of the judiciary committee was organized. In time it would be known by the public as the Kefauver Crime Committee. It took a tie-breaking vote by the vice president, Alben Barkley, to put the committee into being.

Publicity would have been sure to follow the efforts of the Kefauver Crime Committee, but a dramatically broader impact was made possible by the decision of television to broadcast the committee's work. With his own investigation and with help from federal agencies, Kefauver tracked down underworld figures. Called before his committee, criminals squirmed in front of the television lights as they tried to explain away evidence of payoffs, of high living off minuscule public salaries, of greed and graft at many levels of business and government. The exposures gouged many big-city Democratic machines, and the party leadership became disgruntled with this crusading investigator's zeal. Harry Truman fumed in the White House when the New York district attorney's office was exposed. The Senate majority leader, a Democrat from Illinois, was defeated in large part because of spill-over from revelations about the Illinois Democratic machine. After an 11-month orgy of revelations and publicity, the investigation was over and Kefauver had a reputation as a fearless defender of the public. Nineteen bills were introduced to correct problems exposed by the investigation, but only one became law.

It was a perfect springboard for a try at higher office. Twelve years earlier Tom Dewey had used his racket-busting efforts as New York district attorney to run for president; Kefauver's achievements were not nearly as great—convictions growing out of his work were not numerous — but the impact of television merged with Kefauver's own determination as prosecutor established the senator as a political force. In the spring of 1951, with the investigation just completed, Kefauver said he might run for president. Truman was still a factor, and the Tennessean stated he would stay out of the contest if the president sought another term. Truman was most unhappy with Kefauver, partly because the president felt Kefauver had given the Republicans the issue they needed in the fall campaign — corruption by the Democrats. Kefauver jumped into the New Hampshire primary, which had only been established that year. A resounding victory over Truman was won, though the president had not announced for another term. An additional victory came in Illinois, where he defeated Adlai Stevenson. Stevenson backers had run a strenuous write-in campaign for their favorite, the state's governor. In 16 primaries entered by the Tennessee senator, he won 14. Many of the victories were meaningless, as no other candidate seriously campaigned. Kefauver was trying to use the rarely attempted primary route to propel him to the nomination, but the choice of delegates for most states was still tightly in the control of party leaders. Kefauver did not have the support of party leadership; he particularly did not have the president's support.

Perhaps Kefauver nonetheless could have won, despite Truman, despite other Democratic leaders, since the polls showed him the strong plurality favorite of his party. One issue where Kefauver would not compromise, however, was the question of whether tidelands, offshore oil-bearing lands, should be under the control of the federal government or the states. Texas governor Allen Shivers offered Kefauver a deal on the nomination — support for state control over the tidelands in return for Texas's convention votes. Kefauver refused. With the Tennessee senator leading on the second ballot but with Stevenson close, the offer was made again and again refused. Stevenson won, Kefauver lost, and his best chance for the presidency was gone. Shivers ended up supporting Dwight Eisenhower. Stevenson wanted Kefauver as his running mate, but too many Democrats, including Truman, would not

bury the hatchet. Thus the choice went to another Southerner, John Sparkman.

For the next four years the senator was a frequent but not extreme critic of the Eisenhower administration. Again the TVA was defended, this time from efforts by the business-oriented Republicans to weaken its public character. One administration official suggested selling TVA to private utilities, and Kefauver was quick in counterattack. The most serious assault against TVA led to the so-called Dixon-Yates scandal. Dixon and Yates were two private utility executives. Rather than permit additional TVA plants to be built to handle power needs in the Memphis area, the Administration wanted to enter contracts with private companies to provide the power. The Dixon-Yates contract was entered with many details of the negotiations kept secret. As head of a subcommittee investigating antitrust violations, Kefauver conducted his defense of TVA. Kefauver thought outrageous prices were charged under the contract. He alleged the whole scheme was corrupt, with business lobbyists deeply imbedded in the negotiation over the contract. The Eisenhower administration began to have second-thoughts, and withdrew the contract. Kefauver kept after the issue and exposed questionable influence exerted by the utilities. His tenacious investigation wrung every ounce of political benefit out of the issue and again he stood poised for a presidential race.

Worries over reelection had confronted this first-term senator before the Dixon-Yates controversy. A Democratic congressman was his opponent in the party primary. Not surprisingly, Kefauver's liberal voting record was the issue. Despite the issues and the sizeable campaign fund raised by his opponent, Kefauver won the primary by a wide margin and swamped his Republican opponent in the general election.

The victory was followed by a tour of Europe. Seventeen countries were visited, including Russia where he had a conference with Nikita Khrushchev. Upon his return, the Tennessee liberal threw his coonskin cap in the ring one more time for president. An issue was soon made of his refusal to sign the "Southern Manifesto," a repudiation by Southern senators of the Supreme Court 1954 civil rights decision. With Southerners now even more opposed to Kefauver, the senator decided to wage his battle for the nomination again along the lines fought in 1952 — the primaries. Adlai Stevenson was far more visible a figure in the campaign trail in 1956 then he had been four years earlier, and this time Kefauver lost badly to the Illinois governor in many states. By the time of the convention Kefauver abandoned his quest and urged support for Governor Stevenson. In return, the presidential nominee wanted Kefauver for vice president. Opposition was strong, and Stevenson backed away from imposing a choice for running mate. Instead he threw the convention open to make any selection desired. John F. Kennedy and Kefauver were the main contestants, with the Massachusetts senator gaining a majority on the second ballot but not the two-thirds needed to win. Many delegations then changed their votes, giving Kefauver the necessary two-thirds majority. That was the last victory for Kefauver that year, as Eisenhower's popularity was too great for any combination of Democrats to overcome.

For the next few years, from his position as chairman of the Antitrust and Monopoly subcommittee, Kefauver enlarged upon his reputation as the defender of the people's interest against big business. Long hearings were conducted. Once a segment of business power was investigated, Kefauver would announce the next industry to be put in the dock. In 1959, TVA again was the focus, this time over the costs charged by manufacturers of electrical equipment that TVA and other utilities had to purchase. Substantial price-gouging was exposed. In 1959 and 1960, the subcommittee looked at the bakery business. The most public, and perhaps the most important investigation came when the spotlight turned on the drug industry beginning in December of 1959. Kefauver exposed gigantic profit margins by drug companies. Each time the defense was that the 1000 percent markups were necessary for research, but only a small percentage of the profits seemed to be going to that end. Not just prices, but the manner in which new drugs were promoted, without proper safeguards on the effectiveness and safety of the product, was

investigated. The Eisenhower administration and most senators were apathetic about the drug issue. The Kennedy administration was equally reluctant when it took power in 1961 to take on the industry with new laws. President Kennedy first tried to bury the bill, and then to water it down. It appeared no new drug legislation could be passed by Kefauver until the tragic thalidomide episode. A drug used extensively in Europe as a sleeping pill for pregnant women was not yet approved for use in the United States, but its manufacturer was pressuring the Food and Drug Administration for authority. Though the drug had by diligent and almost extra-legal efforts been kept from sale in the United States by the FDA medical officer, Dr. Frances O. Kelsey, some of it still was being used in this country. Grotesquely deformed babies were the result. With this new impetus, finally strong drug regulatory reform was achieved by Kefauver. Probably no greater public service was rendered in Kefauver's 14 years in the Senate than during this fight. And even then, an angry Kennedy administration, which had not wanted the bill in the first place, tried to ignore Kefauver in its ceremonies concerning the new legislation.

Kefauver had in 1960 decided not to make another try for the presidency. Instead, in typical fashion he faced a hard reelection campaign with wild charges thrown at him, and won with ease. Whether he would have remained in the Senate is problematic because the senator was getting tired and even frustrated. His investigations were wearying and frequently thwarted. While speaking in 1963 against another of the dangers he perceived to the public interest, the privately-owned but governmentally funded communication satellite corporation, Kefauver was stricken with a heart attack on the Senate floor. After only a short pause, he went on and completed his speech. Thirty-six hours later he was dead.

Analysis of Qualifications

This long-boned, spectacled blend in appearance of Abraham Lincoln and Alfred E. Newman, was an inveterate nonconformist. A maverick in politics, almost naive in his willingness to take liberal civil rights and consumer interest stands in conservative Tennessee, Estes Kefauver won the affection and admiration of his constituents. Kefauver believed in himself and his causes. After only one year as chairman of a special and highly publicized committee investigating crime and after only two years in the Senate, he was running for president and coming close to winning. Always denied that supreme position, Kefauver left a mark far more indelible than many who gained the White House.

Independence made Kefauver unacceptable to many of his fellow politicians. For that reason he had to go the route of presidential primaries in order to gain even a chance of the presidential nomination. Somehow, on the stump, in that special chemistry that a few politicians are able to achieve with the voters, Kefauver made people feel they had a stake in his future. With an image as a champion of the people, and a record of tireless efforts in that role, Kefauver appealed to the masses. Though polls in 1952 showed him supported by more people for the nomination than was any other Democrat, he was turned back because he could not command enough support among the power brokers. His confidence bordered on self-righteousness, yet his gregarious public appearance masked a loner personality that made it difficult for him to go beyond the superficial friendliness of campaigning and really reveal himself. Few if any of his fellow senators had the feeling they were intimates. Even his wife once remarked she was not certain if Kefauver really was interested in individuals.

There is no doubt, though, that the senator at least had a commitment to the people in the abstract. No more tireless and selfless worker for what he perceived to be the public interest ever burst onto the national scene. Fourteen years in the Senate were filled with investigations and legislation directed towards protecting the public from crime, big business, and other "malefactors." He was a populist from the day he first stepped in the Senate, and as a defender of the underdog he himself was perceived as one. Though his coonskin cap made him an embarrassment to many sophisticates, Kefauver was intelligent and thoughtful. He was a well-educated (Yale graduate)

attorney who wrote persuasively on reform in Congress. The investigations that dotted his career were the forerunner for Ralph Nader and other consumer action lobbyists. His was a high morality, one that made many other senators uncomfortable. Hardly perfect, with his own political ambitions and a willingness to let his career be advanced by the investigations, Kefauver nonetheless always kept the public interest first and his own advancement secondary.

Whether he would have made a successful president depends in large part on whether he could have displayed the executive skills to manage an administration. Considerable difficulties had confronted his reforms in Congress, and a President Kefauver would have had to develop a better working relationship with his fellow politicians. The price of the independence Kefauver had always revealed would have been a Congress that felt it owed the White House nothing. Perhaps Kefauver would have been a frustrated idealist as president, a man of principle who foundered on the rocks of expediency in Congress. But on the other hand, Kefauver had never been an ideologue; he could bargain and compromise. On balance, Estes Kefauver's capacity for the presidency should be measured by what he had achieved. He was a doer, a driving force in the Senate, not a back-bencher willing just to have the office without the responsibility. Greatness had been shown as a muck-raking populist senator. That these talents have not been the ones most used in successful presidencies keeps him from being rated here among the most qualified losing candidates. Still, he merited his party's decision that he try to apply his considerable talents to higher office.

KEFAUVER BIBLIOGRAPHY

Anderson, Jack, and Fred Blumenthal. *The Kefauver Story*. New York City (1956).

Brogan, Hugh. *All Honorable Men: Huey Long, Robert Moses, Estes Kefauver, Richard J. Daley*. New York (1993).

Gorman, Joseph Bruce. *Kefauver: A Political Biography*. New York City (1971).

Kefauver, Estes. *Crime in America*. Garden City, N.Y. (1951).

_____. *In a Few Hands*. New York City (1965).

Moore, William H. "The Kefauver Committee and

the Politics of Crime." Unpublished doctoral dissertation, University of Texas (1971).

Swados, Harvey. *Standing Up for the People: The Life and Work of Estes Kefauver*. New York City (1972).

Some genealogical information provided by Dr.

David Kefauver, Madisonville, Tennessee; additional data obtained from obituaries in the *New York Times* for the relevant dates.

Election of 1960

NOMINATIONS

Democratic Party Convention (33rd): July 11–15, 1960, at the Los Angeles Memorial Sports Arena and Coliseum, Los Angeles, California. *President*— John F. Kennedy, nominated on the first ballot with 806 votes out of 1,521 votes. Lyndon Johnson was his chief rival. *Vice president*— Lyndon Johnson, nominated by acclamation.

Republican Party Convention (27th): July 25–28, 1960, at the International Amphitheatre, Chicago, Illinois. *President*— Richard Nixon, nominated on the first ballot with 1,321 votes out of 1,331 cast. *Vice president*— Henry Cabot Lodge, nominated on the first ballot unanimously.

GENERAL ELECTION, November 8, 1960
Popular Vote

Kennedy 34,221,344
Nixon 34,106,671
Others.   500,945

Electoral Vote

Kennedy-Johnson — 303 (22 states)
Nixon-Lodge — 219 (26 states)
Harry F. Byrd–J. Strom Thurmond —14 (2 states)
Harry F. Byrd–Barry Goldwater —1

Winners

John F. Kennedy, 35th president
Lyndon Johnson, 37th vice president

Losers

Richard Nixon, Henry Cabot Lodge

*1960 presidential nominee —
Republican Party*

Richard M. Nixon

No sketch of Nixon is included since he served as President from January 20, 1969, to August 9, 1974 (37th president).

State represented: California.
Birth: January 9, 1913.
Age on Inauguration Day (January 20, 1961): 48 years, ½ month.
Death: April 22, 1994.

*1960 vice presidential nominee —
Republican Party*

Henry Cabot Lodge

Full name: Henry Cabot Lodge, Jr.
State represented: Massachusetts.
Birth: July 5, 1902, at Nahant, Essex County, Massachusetts.
Age on Inauguration Day (January 20, 1961): 58 years, 6½ months.
Education: St. Alban's School for Boys, Washington, D.C., 1911; then spent two years in Paris and attended French schools; then St. Alban's, 1914–1915; Middlesex Academy (near Boston), 1915–1920; Harvard University, 1920–1923, finished in three years, but graduated *cum laude* with class in 1924.
Ancestry/prominent relatives: Henry Cabot

RICHARD M. NIXON and HENRY CABOT LODGE
(From the collection of David J. and Janice L. Frent)

Lodge (grandfather), U.S. senator from Massachusetts; George Cabot (great-great-great-grandfather), U.S. senator from Massachusetts; Augustus Peabody Gardner (uncle), U.S. representative from Massachusetts; John Davis Lodge (brother), governor of Connecticut; George Cabot Lodge (son), defeated as Republican nominee for U.S. Senate in 1962 against Ted Kennedy; Theodore Frelinghuysen (great-great-grandfather), U.S. Senate, defeated vice presidential nominee in 1844 (see Frelinghuysen for other relatives).

Occupation: Journalist.

Public offices: Massachusetts state legislator, January, 1933–January, 1937; U.S. senator, January 3, 1937–February 3, 1944, resigned, January 3, 1947–January 3, 1953, defeated by John F. Kennedy; U.N. ambassador, February-

ary, 1953–September 3, 1960; unsuccessful Republican nominee for vice president, 1960; ambassador to Vietnam, June, 1963–June, 1964, August, 1965–March, 1967; ambassador to West Germany, February, 1968–January, 1969; head of American delegation for Vietnam War peace talks in Paris, January, 1969–December, 1969; special envoy to Vatican, 1970–1977.

Home: French provincial mansion in Beverly, overlooking Massachusetts Bay; summer home in Nahant.

Death: February 27, 1985, at age 82 years, 8 months.

Burial: Mount Auburn Cemetery, Cambridge, Massachusetts.

Personal characteristics: 6'2½", light blue eyes, trim.

Father: George Cabot Lodge (called "Bay") (October 10, 1873–August 21, 1909); poet.

Mother: Mathilda Frelinghuysen Davis (called "Bessie") (1877–July 1, 1960); daughter of Judge John Davis.

Siblings: John Davis (October 20, 1903–October 29, 1985), married Francesca Braggiotti on July 6, 1929; politician and lawyer. Helena (July 8, 1905–), married Edouard de Streel, a Belgian diplomat.

Wife: Emily Sears (c. 1906–June 6, 1992), married on July 1, 1926; daughter of Dr. Henry Sears of Boston. Married Forrester A. Clark in 1987, a retired investment banker.

Children: George Cabot (July 7, 1927–), married Nancy Kunhardt; professor at Harvard Business School. Henry Sears (1930–), married Elanita Ziegler; a businessman.

Historic sites/memorials: Home of Henry Cabot Lodge, Sr., in Nahant, Massachusetts, located on South Clifford Street (private). It was where Lodge, Jr., was born, and spent much time.

Henry Cabot Lodge, scion of an old New England family, probably never had the capacity to become anything other than just what he was — a Blueblood, progressive, Republican public servant. His family tree is filled with other senators and public officials; his grandfather, for whom he was named, was perhaps the most influential man in Washington immediately after World War I. Young Lodge grew up listening to his grandfather's sermons about public life and the role that Cabot Lodge could play in it. There was never any doubt that Lodge would at least try and probably would succeed in following in his forebear's path.

Cabot Lodge was one of three children growing up in secluded, rich Nahant, a peninsula thrusting out from the Massachusetts shore about 14 miles from Boston. It was a comfortable existence, but one rocked early by tragedy when Lodge's father died when Cabot was only seven. His grandfather, Senator Henry Cabot Lodge, and his uncle John Ellerton Lodge, attempted with varying ability to fill that void. The pain was too immediate in the Nahant surroundings for his mother, and after three years of widowhood, Mrs. Lodge packed up the family for refuge in Paris, leaving in November 1912. At first Cabot and his brother were taught in a boarding school, but the combination of a new country and separation from their mother made them miserable. After a few months they were back with their mother and attending a day school in Paris in which all instruction was in French. After some months French became as natural a language as English. Senator Lodge, seeing his namesake and political heir becoming Europeanized, wrote plaintive letters to mother and son telling them of their heritage and the need to return to America. It took World War I, and a panic flight from Paris, before the mother consented to the return. One biographer credits the war for making Lodge's career possible, because too many more years in Paris would have so alienated, figuratively and literally, young Cabot from his American contemporaries that he might never have comfortably returned to American society. As it was, when the family returned in October 1915, Cabot and his younger brother John were

taunted for apparent arrogance when they slipped, so naturally for them, into speaking French. They had other mundane peculiarities from that different culture, which in time diminished. For years, though, Cabot was criticized for being haughty and for "putting on airs."

Senator Lodge began trying to have a greater influence in the direction of Cabot's upbringing. Thinking that Cabot's schooling should be improved in discipline, the senator diplomatically directed Cabot's mother to send him to a private school in Middlesex, outside of Boston. He also saw to Cabot's political development. Cabot accepted the senator's views on such historically controversial issues as the League of Nations and isolationism. Senator Lodge would treat Cabot as an equal, with few exceptions, and Cabot revered him for it.

When college approached, Cabot followed the family tradition of attending Harvard. His grandfather promised a European tour if he would graduate in three years instead of four. The bargain was made, and both parties fulfilled their commitment. After the European tour, Cabot received a job at the Boston *Transcript* newspaper. Strong political ties and instincts earned him assignments to the two national party conventions in 1924. The Republican convention demonstrated that Senator Lodge had fallen from influence within his own state. He was denied any leadership role within the state delegation. His loyal grandson was livid, but the senator had seen enough of glories. An insignificant insult would not humiliate him. In November, Senator Lodge died, leaving Cabot without his political mentor and his surrogate father. It may have been an even more devastating blow than his father's equally unexpected death 15 years before.

Lodge's financial security was ensured by the senator in his will. Lodge was not raised to be indolent even if work was unnecessary. He continued in journalism, but moved to the New York *Tribune*. In 1926, he married Emily Sears and honeymooned in Italy and France. Upon his return he was faced with the distasteful choice of whether to campaign for William Butler's election to grandfather Lodge's old Senate seat, to which Butler had been appointed after the senator's death. Butler was not the kind of Republican Lodge liked under the best of circumstances, but even less as the inheritor of his grandfather's office. Loyalty to the party conquered reluctance and campaign he did. Butler's defeat was no disappointment, and Lodge returned to the *Tribune*. His duties soon included writing editorials. They were idealistic, enthusiastic, and on foreign policy, isolationist.

Lodge's isolationist philosophy did not prevent him from supporting a strong defense, a support he showed not only through editorials but also by joining the active reserve in 1924. He would continue in the reserves until long after he last left elective office.

Lodge's thoughts had not strayed long from a public career. In 1928, he was urged to run for the United States Congress, but he did not feel the timing was right. In 1930, Congressman Fiorello LaGuardia, later New York City mayor, thought Lodge should try for the United States Senate. Lodge was not even the constitutionally required age of 30 and he declined. With his sights set a little lower, in 1932 he ran for the Massachusetts General Court. He had begun his involvement in local Republican politics some years before and had become well-known by the local, not very democratic committee that hand-picked candidates. One of the leaders of that group took a real interest in Lodge. This leader, John Trowt, decided that Lodge was just the man in 1932. Lodge worked tirelessly in door-to-door campaigning that his wife seemed to enjoy much more than he. He won easily, and was reelected overwhelmingly in 1934. In 1935, Trowt came with another offer, this time proposing that Lodge jump into the United States Senate race. The incumbent had died, and the early favorite was the Democratic governor. Governor James Michael Curley was an imposing political figure, though also generally thought to be dishonest. He was the quintessential lovable crook; most advisers discouraged Lodge from entering the race.

The initial hurdle was getting the nomination. Massachusetts nominations were by state convention, and Mayor Sinclair Weeks of Newton was well-positioned to control the delegates. But Lodge again campaigned hard.

By the time of the convention he had spoken with most of the 700 delegates. Even so, Lodge was in an incredibly close race. When Week's candidate for governor was nominated over the younger candidate more closely identified with Lodge, the omen was not good. Lodge had the good fortune, the kind of fortune that makes or breaks political careers, to have a folksy, sincere nominating speaker who probably gave the speech of his life in favor of Lodge. Abe Glovsky is a little-known figure even within his own state, who threw away a written speech and spoke instead from the heart on behalf of Lodge. Lodge won by 37 votes. The race against Governor Curley was a little easier, and Lodge won by 135,000 votes, the only Republican to capture a Democratic seat in that year of a great Franklin D. Roosevelt landslide (see O'Brien sketch, 1936 election).

In Washington, Lodge found himself one of only 17 Republican senators, fighting an overwhelmingly popular president as well as 79 Democratic senators. He was fortunate in becoming close almost immediately with Republican leader Charles L. McNary, who would in 1940 precede Lodge by 20 years as a defeated Republican vice presidential nominee. Lodge challenged his own party to rise out of its negativism and become more progressive. His main accomplishment of the early Senate years was in being a gadfly in attacks on the Democratic programs, sometimes in ingenious ways. He also became known as a fervent Republican isolationist. The Massachusetts senator even voted against Roosevelt's plan to remove Neutrality Act restrictions on sending aid to Great Britain, saying that if England could not defend itself then it would just have to perish by itself. It was an extreme position that grandfather Lodge probably would have found repugnant. The recriminations from political friends and opponents alike made the opinionated, but not dogmatic, Lodge reconsider. A family friend carefully and persuasively explained his objections to Lodge's stand. The senator credited this discussion with reversing his thinking on the issue.

In 1940, Lodge endorsed Wendell Willkie for the Republican presidential nomination, thinking that Willkie represented a break from the reactionary policies of old-guard Republicans. Willkie of course could no better cope with the FDR magic than could any other Republican challenger, and he lost.

Lend-Lease was an American program of giving destroyers to England in return for military bases. This issue was the turning point for Lodge in his isolationism. He agonized fitfully over Lend-Lease and finally, after explanations from old friends, including General George C. Marshall, he voted for the program. He would thereafter turn his back on the isolationist, "Fortress America," positions he had so long espoused.

Lodge's army reserve activities took on a more urgent pace. He maneuvered with his unit on several occasions, rushing to a military base for training and then returning to the Senate for his duties there. His heart seemed with the military phase of his life almost from the start. His initial desire after Pearl Harbor was to leave the Senate and go into active duty, but Lodge's specialized knowledge of the military was emphasized by friends in urging that his duty was to remain in the Senate. He did remain but nonetheless went on active duty in May 1942. Within a short period the senator was in Africa with a tank unit. While there, German General Erwin Rommel sprung a surprise attack on the American and Allied Army. Lodge found himself in the middle of the first engagement between Nazi and American soldiers in the war. A fierce battle waged, but Lodge was unharmed. After the fight he returned to America, and was involved in training more tank crews.

Nineteen hundred forty-two was reelection year for Senator Lodge. The fierce though brief engagement in Africa was a real political boon. He defeated his Democratic opponent, Joseph E. Casey, by 80,000 votes. His desire still was to resign and fight in Europe, but again friends urged him to look to a higher if not quite so exciting calling and remain in the Senate.

In 1943, he was one of five senators to go on a fact-finding tour of all battlefronts. The information was invaluable. Upon Lodge's return to Washington he gave some candid, perhaps too-candid, explanations of difficulties the war effort was facing. General Crittenberger, with whom Lodge had become friends,

stayed overnight with him in Lodge's Washington home. Lodge again discussed how he truly preferred to resign the Senate. General Crittenberger at first presented the usual arguments for remaining in the Senate, but then changed his mind and even offered to place Lodge on his staff. To make certain that he would not be sent to a stateside post and sit out the war, Lodge went up the chain of command, even to the secretary of war and at last the president. Roosevelt gave him his promise and his blessing, even sending a note the next day saying, truthfully or perhaps only dramatically, that he wished he could go with Lodge.

Lodge left for Europe that day. His work was as a staff aide to top officers, first with General Crittenberger in Italy, and then when a southern attack on German positions in France was ordered, with General Devers. Lodge's fluent French and his political skills were thought perfect for the job of working with Devers as a liaison with the French Resistance who were to help in the liberation. Lodge emerged from the war with American and French battle medals, including six battle stars, the Bronze Star, the Legion of Merit, the Legion d'Honneur, and the Croix de Guerre.

For two weeks upon his return to the United States, Lodge considered with his family the idea of not returning to public life, but then he announced for the Senate. His old Senate seat was now in friendly Republican hands and Lodge took on the unappetizing chore of defeating well-respected Democratic senator David I. Walsh. Nineteen hundred forty-six was a national Republican sweep and Walsh, despite being the initial favorite, lost by 325,000 to Lodge, to his war record, and to the Republican tide. When the Senate opened he was a freshman with no seniority or power, but ironically had he not resigned to join the Army in 1944, just three years before, he would have been the second-ranking Republican. One friend at the Republican Senate caucus suggested that Lodge be returned his seniority he had sacrificed by resigning, but the deathly silence that followed caused Lodge, probably greatly disappointed, to decline the offer chivalrously.

In 1948, the Republicans again lost the presidential race; the hard-earned majorities from 1946 slipped away in both houses of

Congress. Since Governor Thomas E. Dewey of New York represented the Republican progressives, his defeat gave the old guard in the party the reasonable argument that they should be given a chance four years later to name their own candidate, conservative Senator Robert Taft of Ohio. Lodge immediately became concerned that the party would regress to the positions that he felt had already been discredited. Certain defeat and perhaps even disappearance of the Republican Party would result. He cast about for an alternative candidate, but the moderate-liberal wing had little to offer — Dewey already was twice-defeated; Harold Stassen, though still youthful, had already been stamped with the later even more deeply-etched image of perennial also-ran; there were not many others available. Even in 1948 war-hero Dwight Eisenhower had been touted as presidential timber by both parties, and Harry Truman offered to support him for president. Yet Eisenhower was a reluctant candidate. Truman after 1948 had removed Eisenhower from the political scene by making him NATO commander and sending him to Europe. The treks made to NATO headquarters by politicians of both parties must have worn a deep path, but it was Lodge's entreaties that seemed to have the most impact. Lodge argued that the two-party system would disintegrate unless the Republican Party could be saved from the conservative elements in 1952 that almost certainly, in his view, would bring defeat. Eisenhower was backed into the defensive, and Lodge saw more than a glimmer of hope that Ike would acquiesce.

Lodge returned to the United States. Along with Dewey and Stassen, he began a draft Ike campaign. Whatever progress was made was over the continued refusal of Eisenhower to announce his candidacy, or even his party. This latter, almost insuperable hurdle, had to be overcome before Lodge could enter Eisenhower in the New Hampshire primary. This primary Lodge saw as indispensable in establishing Eisenhower's credibility and momentum against Taft. Lodge was forced to a power play, announcing on January 4 that Eisenhower was a Republican, and if the reporters did not believe him they should ask Ike. Lodge sweated through anxious hours until the next

morning when, after Eisenhower initially refused any comment, Ike said that Lodge's statement "substantially" conformed to his political identification. Lodge was off and running, even though not yet with a candidate in tow. Eisenhower easily won the New Hampshire primary in March. Taft continued to roll up the delegates in non-primary states, but Lodge, as successful and resourceful a delegate shaker as ever managed a presidential campaign, worked arduously. It was not until June 1 that Eisenhower resigned the NATO command and returned to announce his candidacy. At the convention Eisenhower won the early skirmishing over several disputed delegations. The Taft forces opened their convention battle on unfavorable terrain. The delegation from Texas was conceded by all to have been stolen at the last minute by Taft supporters. Taft's case was indefensible and he suffered a terrific psychological blow when his Texas delegation was replaced by Eisenhower's. Lodge decided to postpone the first ballot of the nomination until the next day. It was a good decision, because it gave him time to work on the Minnesotans who were still holding to favorite son candidate Harold Stassen. By the next day a few Minnesota delegates had broken loose, and the first tally after all states had voted left Eisenhower just a handful short, 595 for him, 500 for Taft, and 100 scattered. Post-balloting switches made the final result an Eisenhower nomination. No thought had yet been given to the vice presidential nomination, and Lodge and the other advisers almost unanimously agreed that the political pluses were strongly in favor of Senator Richard M. Nixon of California. He was nominated.

By this time Lodge had been on the Eisenhower election team for a year and his fences in Massachusetts, where he was up for reelection, were in great disrepair. The Democrats had decided upon young Congressman Jack Kennedy, and the fight, though not initially looking that tough, soon came to be. Probably the greatest obstacle for Lodge was the bitter feelings engendered by the Eisenhower-Taft fight. Many old-line Taft supporters within the Massachusetts Party never forgave Lodge his role, his primary role, in the defeat of their favorite. Lodge also could not even begin to match the money Kennedy had to put into the race, being outspent $350,000 to $58,000. The final vote was extremely close, and considering the difficulties Lodge faced after his Eisenhower effort had so successfully been concluded, his campaign was a good one. It was not enough, however, and Lodge lost with 1,141,247 votes to Kennedy's 1,211,984. A Lodge dynasty stretching back to the 1790s had come to at least a temporary end, and a Kennedy dynasty was just beginning.

Lodge did not dwell on his defeat, seeing Eisenhower's victory as easy consolation for his own loss. Lodge was definitely in line for some position, including secretary of the still new Defense Department. He was offered the United Nations ambassadorship and promised independence in a newly defined position. He would become as important a spokesman for American foreign policy as the secretary of state. Lodge was credited with refurbishing the image of the United States in debates in the United Nations. He never left until another day, as had his less forceful predecessors, the American response to Soviet charges of aggression or other misdeeds. He became a fixture on the television news reports that more and more Americans were beginning to view every night. After eight years at the United Nations, he was a well-known and liked public figure. He played a major role in presenting and defending the American position in the Suez crisis of 1956 when American allies — Israel, France, and England — invaded Egypt. Russia's invasion of Hungary the same year again put Lodge in the spotlight as he discredited Soviet intentions. His fame, as well as his position, caused him to be the official escort for Russian Premier Nikita Khrushchev when he toured the United States in 1959. Lodge and Khrushchev had several well-publicized adventures with American citizens, press, and with Russian guards. It was a memorable affair.

In 1960 when Richard Nixon received the presidential nomination, the not-very-surprising choice of Lodge was made for vice president. Apparently Lodge anticipated the possibility of the request and even had prepared an acceptance speech several days before the nomination. As Theodore White re-

counted, Nixon had tentatively decided upon Lodge months before but met with his high command at the convention to go over possibilities. The battle lines were between taking a running mate who would appeal to the Midwestern farmers who were upset over farm policy, and taking Lodge. The Midwest was an area of normal and necessary Republican strength that was in danger of slipping away. The decision was for the foreign policy expert Lodge, who might help keep the focus from being on domestic policy where Nixon thought the Republican record was vulnerable.

Lodge was criticized for a lackluster campaign. He was not the tireless campaigner of previous years. As he said, he was asked to campaign morning, noon and night and he could only see fit to give two out of the three. Every afternoon he took an hour nap that enraged Nixon campaigners, but Lodge defended on the basis that a fresh candidate was far more effective than a haggard one. Lodge's heart just did not seem in it, and part of the reluctance may have been a less than enthusiastic attraction to Nixon. In addition, his mother had died that July, and his own United Nations efforts had been recently quite taxing in a battle over the Congo. Yet more damning in the Republican eyes was not something Lodge failed to do, but rather something Lodge consciously decided. In a speech in Harlem, he pledged that Nixon would appoint a Negro to his cabinet. No black had ever served as a cabinet officer. Nixon had no warning and certainly had not decided on this possibility. Nixon eventually retracted the statement for Lodge. Whether Lodge was trying another power play such as when he forced Eisenhower's hand on declaring himself a Republican, or whether Lodge genuinely misunderstood Nixon on the point, is unknown. It left a bad impression for Nixon to overcome both among blacks, because the supposed cabinet commitment had been instantly retracted, and among conservatives in the South, who could not imagine that pledge ever having been made in the first place. It did not likely cause the narrow election defeat, however. Nixon could largely accept that responsibility. Thus Lodge was kept from Washington office twice by John Kennedy. There is reason to think that he probably liked Kennedy more, at least personally, than he ever would Nixon.

After two years in retirement, Lodge was invited back by his old adversary Jack Kennedy. Kennedy needed a strong-willed, nononsense ambassador to Vietnam who could both decipher the military and political conditions there, and deal with them firmly. Lodge almost immediately became opposed to the incumbent Vietnamese leadership. Ngo Dinh Diem and his family were impeding the South Vietnam war effort. President Diem, a member of the extreme minority Catholic faith, had executed many of the large majority Buddhist population. Frequent self-immolations by Buddhist priests and followers scarred the American view of the Diem regime. Diem's policies were alienating whatever anti–Communist factions there were in South Vietnam. Lodge thought, as did most others, that since Diem refused to moderate his policies, he had to be ousted. A coup was planned with American knowledge and moral support, with assurances being given that Diem and his family would be permitted to go into exile. Instead, after the coup Diem was almost immediately killed. Lodge was infuriated, both at the act itself and at the deception. He felt responsible since, based on the assurances of safety given Lodge from the coup leader, he had urged Diem to surrender.

Lodge was the indispensable man for the Americans in Vietnam. He often did not agree with the information being sent by military and civilian leaders and was quick to say so. He was often wrong, but he was almost never self-deceived and certainly not consciously misleading as so many others were. His image was solid back in America. When the 1964 elections approached, Lodge was seen as an attractive alternative for president against the conservative Goldwater and the just-divorced liberal, Nelson Rockefeller. A write-in campaign was begun for him in New Hampshire. Assisted by Lodge's son, George, the volunteer campaigners won a solid Lodge victory strictly on write-in votes and almost no money, 33,000 votes to 20,000 for Goldwater and about the same for Rockefeller. Lodge would not come home to fight for the nomination, as strongly as he feared for the Republican

Party if Goldwater captured its nomination because he even more strongly feared for the situation in Vietnam if he left. When Lodge lost to Rockefeller in the Oregon primary in May, his chances were over. Goldwater won the California primary and for all appearances the nomination. Lodge decided, somewhat quixotically, to return then to fight Goldwater, this time backing Governor William Scranton of Pennsylvania. The task was hopeless and Goldwater easily won. Lodge's hope had been to convince former President Eisenhower to endorse Scranton or some other moderate, but Eisenhower rightly perceived the cause as lost.

President Lyndon Johnson offered to reappoint Lodge to the Vietnam post. To most of his friends' surprise, Lodge accepted. He again found himself fighting not only the Viet Cong but also those Americans he perceived as being naive or deceptive about the war. After two more frustrating years he resigned, and was then appointed by President Johnson and later President Nixon to other diplomatic posts. The most frustrating of all was probably Johnson's sending him to Paris to lead the American effort in opening the peace talks in January 1969, with the North Vietnamese. Lodge felt the North was never interested in negotiating and was only trying to wait out American public opinion. The North Vietnamese believed, rightly as it turned out, that America would in time tire of the struggle and abandon further aid to the South Vietnamese. He left disgusted and discouraged in December 1969.

Lodge returned to his native Massachusetts, and came out of retirement occasionally for short-term political or governmental involvement. He remained committed to the public service, as well as the progressivism, that characterized his entire political life.

Analysis of Qualifications

Lodge was a man of old-fashioned and completely laudatory values — honor, courage, commitment, and as intense as any, devotion to the success of the country and the Republican Party. Yet in 1960, Lodge was found unenthusiastic. His well-publicized and effective efforts at the United Nations probably gave some extra support to the Nixon campaign;

the lackluster campaigning and the unfortunate, though commendable, pledge to appoint a black when no such decision had in fact been made, lost votes.

Lodge gave too much of himself in campaign after campaign, political, military, and diplomatic, for the errors in 1960 to be a strong mark against him. Lodge was the incarnation of noblesse oblige. He was wealthy and knew that to those to whom much was given, much was asked. He had supreme self-assurance and was never humble. This characteristic frequently came across as arrogance. During World War II he sought the physical involvement possible only from active service in the military. His equally important duties in the Senate were secondary to him for reasons that are probably best summarized as "honor." He believed that politics was perhaps the most honorable profession, for politics was to him not the sweating for power and prestige, and at times money, that others have made it, but politics was public service in the most commendable meaning of the phrase.

The great foreign policy issue during the Kennedy-Johnson administration was the Vietnam War. Lodge as ambassador was part of that war. He was an objective, intelligent participant. The light to him was never quite so in view at the end of the tunnel as many in the Johnson administration said. Once the Vietnamese conflict had begun, Lodge was strongly in favor of continuing. He would not as president have cut his losses and withdrawn, and it is unlikely that he would have seen the quagmire soon enough to avoid getting swallowed by it. He subscribed to the domino theory of Communist domination of Indo-China if Vietnam was abandoned. Though in war strategy he may have differed from Kennedy and Johnson's approach, the central aim of strengthening and perpetuating the South Vietnam government would have been his goal as well.

On domestic policy he would not have been quite as profligate a spender as Lyndon Johnson, but then few men were. Lodge was intensely concerned about civil rights. His domestic policy would have been a continuation of the Eisenhower programs with some new initiatives, but perhaps not many. The long

hot summers of racial unrest, had they also occurred under Lodge as they did under Johnson, would have been agonizing and soul-searching for a President Lodge.

Lodge was not the prototypical hail-fellow-well-met. He may have slapped a few backs and even kissed a baby, in addition to his own, a few times, but public record of such occurrences is scarce. He could be cold to those who did not know him, but the coldness was less personal disinterest than it was just reserve. His demeanor was typical patrician restraint. He could also be tough and single-minded, as demonstrated in his amazingly successful fight for Eisenhower's nomination in 1952, and in his diplomatic assignments to the United Nations and to Vietnam.

Henry Cabot Lodge failed to gain either of the nation's two highest offices, but did make important contributions in several areas. Perhaps none was quite as important as his indispensable role in sponsoring Dwight Eisenhower for the presidency. Ike was a man who may have indeed saved the two-party system in this country and also made, not just incidentally, an outstanding president. Lodge also qualified, in background, character, personality and intelligence, as one who likely also would have been found suited to the difficult tasks of that office.

LODGE BIBLIOGRAPHY

Braggiotti, Gloria. *Born in a Crowd.* New York (1957).
Hatch, Alden. *The Lodges of Massachusetts.* New York (1973).
Hess, Stephen. *America's Political Dynasties, from Adams to Kennedy.* Garden City (1965).
Lancer, Elsie Lee. *Henry Cabot Lodge: Man and Statesman.* New York (1964).
Lodge, Henry Cabot. *As It Was: An Inside View of Politics and Power in the '50s and '60s.* New York City (1976).
———. *The Cult of Weakness.* Boston (1932).
———. *The Storm Has Many Eyes: A Personal Narrative.* New York (1973).
Miller, William J. *Henry Cabot Lodge: A Biography.* New York (1967).
Ziegler, Henry A. *The Remarkable Henry Cabot Lodge, Jr.* New York (1964).
Some genealogical information provided by Henry Cabot Lodge, Beverly, Massachusetts.

Election of 1964

NOMINATIONS

Republican Party Convention (28th): July 13–16, 1964, at the Cow Palace, San Francisco, California. *President*— Barry Goldwater, nominated on the first ballot with 883 votes out of the 1,308 cast. William Scranton (Penn.) and Nelson Rockefeller (N.Y.) were his main opponents. *Vice president*—William Miller, nominated unanimously on the first ballot.

Democratic Party Convention (34th): August 24–27, 1964, at Atlantic City, New Jersey. *President*—Lyndon Johnson, nominated by acclamation. *Vice president*—Hubert Humphrey, nominated unanimously on the first ballot.

GENERAL ELECTION, November 3, 1964

Popular Vote

Johnson 43,126,584
Goldwater 27,177,838
Others   336,682

Electoral Vote

Johnson-Humphrey — 486 (44 states)
Goldwater-Miller — 52 (6 states)

Winners

Lyndon Johnson, 36th president
Hubert Humphrey, 38th vice president

Losers

Barry Goldwater, William Miller

1964 presidential nominee—
Republican Party

Barry Goldwater

Full name: Barry Morris Goldwater.

State represented: Arizona.

Birth: January 1, 1909, Phoenix, Arizona.

Age on Inauguration Day (January 20, 1965): 56 years, ½ month.

Education: Phoenix schools; Staunton Military Academy, graduated as top military cadet in 1928; University of Arizona, 1928–1929, dropped out when father died.

Religion: Episcopalian.

Ancestry/prominent relatives: Grandfather Michael Goldwasser was a Polish Jewish refugee, came to California from England in 1852; Barry M. Goldwater, Jr. (son), a U.S. representative from California.

Occupation: Businessman.

Public offices: Appointed to Arizona Colorado River Commission, 1946–1949; Phoenix city councilman, 1950–1952; U.S. senator, January 3, 1953–January 3, 1965; unsuccessful Republican nominee for president, 1964; U.S. senator, January 3, 1969–January 3, 1987.

Home: Ultra-modern home on bluff, outside Phoenix, named Be-Nun-I-Kin ("House on the Hill").

Personal characteristics: 6' tall, blue eyes, curly, silver hair; athletic; in his seventies began to have serious problems with hips and had to use walker and leg braces.

Father: Baron M. Goldwater, called "Barry" (1866–March 6, 1929); Phoenix mercantile businessman.

Mother: Josephine Williams (March 19, 1875–December 27, 1966); married January 1, 1907, daughter of Robert Royal Williams.

Siblings: Robert (July 4, 1910–), married twice. Carolyn (April 15, 1912–), married three times.

Wife: Margaret (Peggy) Johnson (July 8, 1909–December 11, 1985); married September 22, 1934.

Children: Joanne (January 1, 1936–), married twice. Barry Goldwater, Jr. (July 15, 1938–), U.S. Representative, married Susan Lee Sherman, divorced. Michael (March 15, 1940–). Margaret (Peggy) (July 27, 1944–), married twice.

Barry Goldwater is remembered as one of the greatest political losers of all times. The campaign that was run against him was reminiscent of the scandalous, truth-be-damned contests of the 1870s and 1880s. The only difference was that the technology for spreading such information had vastly changed. Goldwater lost the election because he was depicted as a trigger-happy, irresponsible war-monger, while the incumbent president was seen as a sane, peaceloving alternative. Four years of Lyndon Johnson's Vietnam policies would make many people feel duped.

Goldwater's roots hardly presaged a career in politics. His grandfather and several great-uncles helped found a thriving mercantile business, first in southern California and then in the part of the New Mexico territory that would subsequently become the state of Arizona. By the time of Barry's birth in 1909, his father Baron had established a profitable, high quality (and high-priced) women's clothing store in Phoenix. That store was not opened until Baron won an argument against two of his brothers who were partners in the Goldwaters' stores in Prescott, Arizona. The brothers decided upon a game of casino to decide whether to open a branch in Phoenix. Baron won that gamble. Barry's mother was from Chicago, but moved to Arizona because the dry climate would help her lung ailment. His parents met at the Goldwater store. Forty-one-year-old bachelor Baron's idea of propriety differed considerably from Barry's mother's, and she scoffed at the proposal from Baron that she move in with him. Marriage subsequently was agreed to as a desirable precondition for boarding together. Barry was their first child.

Goldwater later related that he had been a poor student, excelling mainly in high spirits, practical jokes, and athletics. Though school-work little interested him, Barry did become fascinated with Arizona history and geography. A lifelong interest in the rugged expanses of his state, and with Indian culture, resulted. After the high school principal suggested to Barry's father that the discipline of a military school would benefit the boy, he was sent off to Staunton Military Academy in Virginia. Barry subsequently called it "the best thing that ever happened to me." His life took on a new direction and discipline; he gained an interest in the military that only increased as he grew older. A military career seemed a definite possibility, but since Barry's father was ill he decided to return home and enroll at the University of Arizona. The death of his father in March 1929 ended Barry's formal education, as he dropped out of school to help at the family store.

Only 20 years old, Barry hardly started at the top in the business. Instead, he began as a junior clerk and worked his way through almost every department. By 1946, he had become general manager, and the following year he became president. Goldwater's Inc. was the top department store in Phoenix. Goldwater gained a reputation as an exceptional businessman with real talents for promotion and sales. His employees knew him as an outstanding employer, who paid higher wages than other department stores in the city, who had the first five-day work week, and who created hospitalization, insurance, and profit-sharing plans for his employees.

While making his mark in the business world, Goldwater was finding outlet for his energy in many other ways. Flying airplanes was one of his most exciting pastimes, but in 1930 when he began taking his pilot lessons, he kept the whole matter secret from his mother. She finally read about it in the local newspaper when he received his pilot's license. The same year Barry also met his future wife, Margaret ("Peggy") Johnson. She was from Muncie, Indiana, and was visiting Phoenix during the winter of 1930-31. Ironically, her family leased the home of Democratic U.S. senator Carl Hayden, whom Goldwater would replace almost 40 years later. The casual acquaintance developed over a two-year period into more serious interest, on Barry's part at least. A proposal came soon thereafter, but Peggy was uncertain both about living in Arizona and about Barry. A subsequent, successful proposal occurred, and in September of 1934, they were married.

Besides airplanes and romance, Goldwater also had a fascination with gadgets of every kind. As a youngster he tinkered with mechanical and electrical equipment. In later life, he packed his ultramodern Phoenix home with an amazing array of gadgetry, including an elaborate ham radio system.

This business and pleasure were ended by the outbreak of World War II. Even before Pearl Harbor, Goldwater volunteered for active duty in the Army Air Force. Already past 30, Barry was not considered prime pilot material. Poor vision also was a handicap. Through persistence and the help of Arizona's two U.S.

senators, Goldwater was able to get increasingly satisfactory assignments. He began as an aerial gunnery instructor, progressed to ferrying aircraft to war zones, and helped train Chinese pilots in Burma. At the end of the war, Goldwater was a colonel, but was reduced in rank to a captain in order that he could serve in the Air National Guard unit in Arizona.

Goldwater was active in the Air National Guard for many years, and became a brigadier general. He insisted that his unit be racially integrated long before that was common. Because of his rank, and perhaps also because of his subsequent political influence, Goldwater has had through the years what to him was the extreme pleasure of flying just about every type of high technology American aircraft.

Back in Arizona now at the age of 36, Goldwater was no longer content to remain on the political sidelines. In 1946, the Democratic Governor appointed him to serve on the Arizona–Colorado River Commission, which placed him in the middle of a heated political war for the most precious of Western resources, water. In 1947, his sights narrowed just to Phoenix, where he helped pass a new, more democratic charter for the city. The charter proved ineffective without new people in office. Goldwater was active in recruiting candidates for the new city council, but when one slot remained unfilled Goldwater himself finally agreed to run. Fortunately there was no party label on the ballot, since Goldwater had already sided with the Republicans and they were badly outnumbered in Arizona. Instead, he was elected on a reform slate with other candidates. In office, he applied the same zeal as he had to every other endeavor.

In 1950, Goldwater and the new Republican state chairman tried to find a candidate for governor. A Phoenix radio personality, Howard Pyle, who had been a war correspondent overseas and was well known throughout the state, agreed to run. Goldwater became his campaign manager. No Republican had won the governorship since 1928, but dissatisfaction with the Korean War, coupled with the weakness of the Democratic gubernatorial nominee allowed Pyle to win a narrow victory.

Two years later Goldwater himself was running for office. The majority leader of the United States Senate was Ernest McFarland. This young Republican Goldwater seemed slightly presumptuous to take him on in 1952. With the unpopularity of the incumbent Democratic president, a hard-hitting and well-organized campaign by Goldwater, and last, but hardly least, with an Eisenhower landslide in the state, Goldwater eked out victory by 7,000 votes. He had done what many thought impossible.

One of the reasons Goldwater wanted to become a senator was to help expose the misdeeds of the Truman administration. He found a fellow believer in Senator Joseph McCarthy of Wisconsin. In Goldwater's 1979 memoirs, he never condemned McCarthy, but only said that he was "the most controversial man I ever served with in the Senate." When the time for McCarthy's censure came, Goldwater was one of twenty-two Republicans who opposed the measure. Fervent anti-communism was from the beginning a hallmark of Goldwater's political philosophy. Viewing McCarthy from that perspective, Goldwater found himself in agreement.

This tough-talking, candid senator took on big labor, and suggested that antitrust laws be applied to unions as well as to business. State right-to-work laws were sacrosanct to him. In his first year in the Senate, Goldwater had been involved in killing proposed amendments to the Taft-Hartley Act, amendments backed initially by President Eisenhower and his secretary of labor, the former president of the AFL Plumbers Union. In 1959, he would be more influential in killing a labor bill backed by Senator John Kennedy and Senator Sam Ervin that the Eisenhower administration supported. Goldwater was the only senator to vote against the bill, and was summoned to the White House to explain his actions. His explanation was so convincing that Eisenhower withdrew his support and a substitute act, the Landrum-Griffin Act, was passed.

Though his reputation nationwide was fairly minimal, Goldwater's popularity at home was growing and solidifying. In 1958, what had promised to be a tough reelection campaign against the man he had defeated six years earlier, Ernest McFarland, ended in a fairly easy victory. Nationwide 1958 had been a dismal Republican year, with dramatic losses in the House and Senate. Goldwater's election put him on center stage. For a while he was considered for president by many conservative Republicans who were disappointed with Richard Nixon as their choice. The South Carolina Republican convention in March 1960, nominated Goldwater for president. This was not a serious attempt to substitute Goldwater for the certain choice of Richard Nixon, but instead was a warning to Nixon that his conservative credentials needed polishing. Nixon and liberal New York governor Nelson Rockefeller met to go over planks for the platform. This gave conservatives the impression that Nixon sold out to the liberals. Goldwater became a more serious candidate. Goldwater probably never believed that he had much of a chance. By the day that nominations were made at the convention, Goldwater agreed only to have his name placed in nomination, and he would then immediately give a speech withdrawing and urging his supporters to vote for Nixon. His plea to his supporters was:

> Let's grow up, conservatives. If we want to take this party back, and I think we can someday, let's go to work.

Goldwater was not pleased with the choice of liberal Henry Cabot Lodge for vice president, nor was he satisfied with the direction that the campaign took in the fall. The Arizonan was a good Republican, however, and he campaigned hard for the ticket. The effort fell just short, and John Kennedy was inaugurated president instead.

Kennedy and Goldwater were, if not good friends, at least on friendly terms despite their philosophical differences. Many conservatives felt they had been cheated out of a real choice in 1960, and Goldwater soon was the accepted candidate of Republican conservatives to run against Kennedy in 1964. The potential future rivals were at odds over the handling of the Cuba crises of 1961 and 1962. Goldwater encouraged the president to use more force during the Bay of Pigs invasion, but his counsel was rejected. In 1962, Goldwater was aghast that Kennedy permitted an agreement to be entered that in return for removal of Russian

missiles from Cuba, the United States would guarantee the security of communist Cuba. The United States also agreed to remove certain missiles from Turkey and Italy. To Goldwater, the whole episode was a retreat by the United States. As the world seemed slowly to be drifting into communism from Goldwater's perspective, the issues seemed clearly drawn between him and President Kennedy. With Kennedy's assassination and the elevation of Lyndon Johnson to the presidency, Goldwater realized immediately that any chance for election had been lost. Nevertheless, after Goldwater had initially told his advisers he wanted to drop out, he agreed to continue the fight. Goldwater had a tendency to fight for principle alone.

The chances were slim, particularly because of the bitter war fought within the Republican party. An "anybody but Goldwater" movement was joined by almost all the other Republican candidates. Goldwater's rhetoric was frequently poorly thought out. His habit of giving extemporaneous speeches caused him irreparable harm. Frequently quoted were his remarks that could be interpreted to mean that he would use nuclear weapons in Vietnam, that he would make Social Security voluntary, or that he was a racist. With a hard fought victory in the California primary to close out the preconvention season, Goldwater clearly had sufficient delegates for nomination. Even so, at the convention William Scranton and other of the more moderate Republican candidates savaged Goldwater with this "Dr. Strangelove" image. It would prove invaluable ammunition for the Democrats in the fall election. The convention turned bitter, as the majority of the delegates who were for Goldwater booed mercilessly the appearance of any moderate Republicans, particularly Nelson Rockefeller.

Disaster followed disaster in the general election campaign. Goldwater became the most alarming politician in America, as many voters believed him likely to start nuclear war if elected. The Johnson campaign ran a commercial showing a child playing, with a voice counting backwards until, when it reached zero, a mushroom cloud obliterated everything else on the screen. In print and on television, Goldwater was made to pay for every slip of the tongue as well as every sincere but unpopular position he had ever taken. It was a lost cause, and the defeat was one of the worst ever suffered in American presidential election history.

For four years Goldwater was in retirement in Arizona. He found it relaxing from the bitterness he had just undergone. Yet, vindication, as well as a platform to continue his conservative fight, were compelling reasons to run again in 1968. The dean of the Senate, longterm Arizona senator Carl Hayden, decided not to run for reelection in 1968, and Goldwater replaced him easily in the November election. Vietnam was the issue during his first term back in the Senate. Goldwater was always for stronger measures, greater military pressure, and found both the Kennedy-Johnson administration and the Nixon effort to conduct a war with limited force to be sacrilegious. It seemed inhumane to be asking American soldiers to fight a war that its leaders had decided we would not attempt to win. When the North Vietnamese finally were forced to sign a peace treaty after 12 intensive weeks of bombing of the North, Goldwater had an "I told you so" feeling that had only this been done eight years earlier, the war would have ended that much sooner.

Goldwater was a consistent defender of President Nixon on Watergate, and found it impossible to believe that such a political professional as Nixon could have been involved in such a slipshod and senseless bit of skullduggery as the Watergate cover-up. When the Watergate tapes made it clear that Goldwater had erred, the Arizonan was outraged that his trust in the president had been so abused. As one approaching elder statesman status in the Republican Party, Goldwater joined several other prominent senators who met with Nixon a few days before his resignation and told him of the need to resign. A few months later, Goldwater was reelected with his largest margin ever. Goldwater's comments on Nixon in later years would be brutal: "I wouldn't trust Nixon from here to that phone.... Anybody that would lie to his wife and lie to his children and then lie to his country, I have no use for" (*Newsweek*, September 29, 1986, p. 27).

During this fourth term in the Senate,

Goldwater's reputation as an unbending conservative began to weaken. Goldwater had always been known as an independent thinker, and a man who said what he was thinking. These attributes placed Goldwater, in his fourth term in the Senate, close to curmudgeon status. It was not such lapses from strict conservative doctrine, however, that made his try for a fifth term in 1980 almost in vain. Instead, the 71-year-old Goldwater almost lost to 49-year-old Bill Schulz, a wealthy Phoenix apartment developer, on the basis that Goldwater had gotten too old, was missing too many votes, and did not have the energy Arizona needed for the future. Goldwater had during 1980 undergone operations on his hips and was in frail health. It was two days after the election before all the votes were counted. What had appeared to be a Schulz victory on election night had been turned into a narrow Goldwater margin.

President Ronald Reagan's election brought the heir to Goldwater conservatism into the White House, and delivered a majority for Republicans to the Senate. The two men were never close. One Goldwater biographer ascribes the reason as Goldwater's jealousy of Reagan's success. Being out of the Senate for four years after the 1964 defeat meant that Goldwater was not senior enough to have a major committee chairmanship. He was chairman of the Select Committee on Intelligence. His focus remained largely on military issues. One of the most significant military reforms measures of recent decades was the Goldwater-Nichols Act of 1986. The bill restructured the joint chiefs of staff and made the chairman, generals such as Colin Powell, the president's chief military adviser. Before, all five joint chiefs, even when they could not agree, were the advisers and therefore sometimes gave conflicting advice. The freeing of the chairman from being bound just to pass through everyone's views was a reform that had been discussed for 25 years. The Nichols part of the bill, named for Representative Bill Nichols of Alabama, reformed other aspects of command.

In early 1984 Goldwater announced that he would not run for reelection in 1986. Margaret Goldwater's death in late 1985 was said to have taken much of the zest out of life for the senator. He walked with a cane, but remained mentally sharp. He could appear even crustier than before, with blunt comments for various opponents, many of them fellow conservatives. When Christian Coalition leader Jerry Falwell criticized Goldwater's fellow Arizonan and Supreme Court appointee Sandra Day O'Conner for being pro-abortion, Goldwater said, "I think that every good Christian ought to kick Falwell right in the" backside. Later he campaigned against an Arizona measure that would have outlawed most abortions. In 1992 he testified in favor of a Phoenix, Arizona, homosexual rights ordinance. Goldwater publicly said that George Bush had run the worst presidential campaign that he had ever seen. He did not seem to think too much of Bob Dole four years later, either. His guiding star was that the "Republican Party should stand for freedom and only freedom." Abortion, homosexual rights, and other issues were analyzed with that libertarian philosophy.

Goldwater even spoke favorably of Bill Clinton. In 1994 he argued that Republicans should stop complaining about President Bill Clinton and just let him govern. He repeated that in the 1996 election year, even saying that Bill Clinton was "a good president, and he has a very good wife."

As the years passed, the always candid Barry Goldwater stayed in character. With his place in the hearts and history of Republicans secure, his straying from conservative orthodoxy hardly mattered. He would remain the person who started the conservative revolution in America. Barry Goldwater was perhaps the most influential presidential also-ran of modern times.

Analysis of Qualifications

"I've often said that if I hadn't known Barry Goldwater in 1964 and I had to depend on the press and the cartoons, I'd have voted against the son of a bitch." Those words were from Goldwater himself, spoken almost ten years after the election. It is a poignant statement. So savage had the Democrats and the press been in 1964 in characterizing Goldwater, that many people viewed him as little short of a monster. When the Republican nominee expressed concern that Social Security was in-

sanely run and actuarially unsound, matters that are accepted as facts 30 years later, one newspaper immediately fabricated a story that he favored ending the program. The story always seemed to stay a step ahead of the truth.

Unfortunately, however, the Arizona Republican was an easy target. For every opposition exaggeration, there was at least a plausible basis. His speeches were extemporaneous. He was accessible and colorful; his shoot-from-the-hip style made good press material. He did not ponder political ramifications. The general election was anticlimactic, for in the primaries and at the convention his fellow Republicans, using ammunition he supplied, had so crippled the Goldwater image that there was little he could do to salvage his campaign. He suggested as a possibility during the primaries that low-yield atomic bombs be dropped in Vietnam to defoliate the trees and reveal the Communist infiltration routes. He argued that Americans were unduly concerned with nuclear weapons. Goldwater thought that recognition of the Soviet Union should be withdrawn and came close to suggesting the sale of the Tennessee Valley Authority. Goldwater spoke his mind, and his mind was obviously of a strong conservative bent. He was easy prey for all who wished him ill, and there were many.

Goldwater's ideology was simple, if revolutionary in 1964. Government should not interfere with private economic decisions, and a strong national defense was the government's over-riding obligation. Fitting the issues of the 1960s into that structure made him come across as extreme, as men of principle often appear. Opposition to the Civil Rights Act of 1964 was one result of this philosophy, as was his lack of zeal for universal, mandatory Social Security participation. There was no compromise in Goldwater's personality. That no-compromise stance led to the selection of William Miller over politically sounder choices as a running mate. That zeal found perfect expression, and embarrassment, in his well-known acceptance speech phrasing: "Extremism in the defense of liberty is no vice! Moderation in the pursuit of justice is no virtue!" He had narrow ideological blinders, making the John Birch Society just a well-intentioned and acceptable organization; McCarthyism a slightly overzealous reaction to very real and continuing dangers of Communists in government; all foreign aid other than for military uses, a senseless, self-defeating bribe.

Communism had no greater foe than Goldwater, and few were more willing to use all-out force in Vietnam to end its menace there. He advised presidents Johnson and Nixon that either total and declared war or a complete withdrawal were the only options in Vietnam. Presidents Johnson and Nixon were fearful of the international repercussions, including drawing Russia and China more directly into the conflict. Goldwater's belief that half-measures in Vietnam were wrong are actually part of the lessons learned from Vietnam by the next generation of military commanders. Perhaps Senator Goldwater had the right answer to end the too long, too costly war, but it is unsettling to realize that few issues were ever other than black and white to the senator.

Barry Goldwater found his perfect political office as a United States senator. As he once described himself, he was a salesman for the conservative movement. As a senator, he had the platform from which to sell. Goldwater was intense, a conservative ideologue, aggressively militaristic, and during the 1964 campaign, he was indignant. In overwhelming numbers the American people decided these attributes were not those they wanted in a president. They were probably right in their decision. Equally justified were the feelings of the people of Arizona that these characteristics were just what they wanted in their senator.

GOLDWATER BIBLIOGRAPHY

Bell, Jack. *Mr. Conservative, Barry Goldwater.* Garden City, N.Y. (1962).

Craven, Michael J. "A Conservative Enigma: Barry Goldwater and the Republican Party, 1953–1974." Unpublished master's thesis, College of William and Mary (1994).

Edwards, Lee. *Goldwater: The Man Who Made a Revolution.* Washington, D.C. (1995).

Goldberg, Robert Alan. *Barry Goldwater.* New Haven (1995).

Goldwater, Barry M. *With No Apologies: The Personal and Political Memoirs of United States Senator Barry M. Goldwater.* New York (1979).

_____, with Casserly, Jack. *Goldwater.* New York (1988).

McDowell, Edwin. *Barry Goldwater: Portrait of an Arizonan.* Chicago (1964)

Reed, Roy. "In 1964 He Was Bela Lugosi, but the Liberals Love Barry Goldwater Now." *The New York Times Magazine* (April 7, 1974), pp. 23 ff.

Rusher, William A. *The Rise of the Right.* New York (1993).

Schapsmeier, Edward L., and Frederick H. Schapsmeier. *Dirksen of Illinois, Senatorial Statesman.* Urbana (1985).

Shadegg, Stephen C. *Barry Goldwater: Freedom Is His Flightplan.* New York (1962).

Smith, Dean. *The Goldwaters of Arizona.* Flagstaff (1986)

Wolf, George D. *William Warren Scranton: Pennsylvania Statesman.* University Park, Penn. (1981).

Some family information provided by Sen. Barry Goldwater, Washington, D.C.

1964 vice presidential nominee—
Republican Party

William E. Miller

Full name: William Edward Miller.

State represented: New York.

Birth: March 22, 1914, Lockport, New York.

Age on Inauguration Day (January 20, 1965): 50 years, 10 months.

Education: Parochial schools; Lockport High School, graduated, 1931, Notre Dame University (B.A. 1935); Union University Law School, LL.B 1938.

Religion: Roman Catholic.

Ancestry: His father was a factory janitor; his mother ran a millinery shop.

Occupation: Attorney.

Public offices: U.S. commissioner for western district of New York, January 1940–July 1942; assistant prosecutor, Nuremberg war criminal trials, 1945–1946; appointed assistant and then deputy district attorney for Niagara County, New York, March 1946–1948; appointed district attorney, January 1, 1948, elected November 1948–1950; U.S. representative, January 3, 1951–January 3, 1965; chairman, Republican national committee, June 2, 1961–1964; unsuccessful Republican nominee for vice president, 1964.

Death: June 24, 1983, in Buffalo, New York, at age 69 years, 3 months.

BARRY GOLDWATER (left) and WILLIAM E. MILLER
(From the collection of David J. and Janice L. Frent)

Burial: Arlington National Cemetery, Virginia.

Home: Lockport, New York.

Personal characteristics: 5'7" tall, 140 pounds; one hazel eye and one dark brown eye; dapper dresser, loved Chesterfield suits and homburg hats; brisk, aggressive; biting humor; jutting nose, pugnacious chin.

Father: Edward J. Miller (1881–August 15, 1958).

Mother: Elizabeth Hinch (1879–March 25, 1963); married around 1910; daughter of Julia Mahar and Edward Hinch.

Siblings: None.

Wife: Stephanie Wagner (January 22, 1923–), married February 26, 1943: daughter of Stephen Wagner and Mary Nowak.

Children: Elizabeth Ann (January 10, 1944–); married Paul F. Fitzgerald on April 15, 1967; a doctor. Mary Karen (May 24, 1947–). William E., Jr. (January 12, 1959–), Army officer. Stephanie (September 29, 1961–).

In twentieth-century America few candidates for either of the nation's two highest offices have risen from such humble beginnings. Perhaps such a rise, and the view of both poverty and success seen firsthand, made Bill Miller the aggressive, acerbic politician that he was.

His father was a janitor at the Harrison Radiator Division of General Motors in Lockport, a small New York community north of Buffalo. His family's modest frame home was torn down two years before Miller's vice presidential nomination, but he had long previously moved into far more comfortable accommodations. The real income for the family came from his mother and her sisters' millinery shop. Bill Miller's contemporaries remembered him, even as a youth, as "a scrappy little son-of-a-gun" who excelled in debate. His memory and combativeness brought him debating success more than did intellectual brilliance. In the seventh grade, as these skills first became evident, Miller decided he wanted to be a trial lawyer. At the age of 17 he matriculated at Notre Dame, where he starred on the varsity debate team. The family was still far from financially comfortable and Miller had to work during the summer

and part-time during the school year to pay his way. An early try at elective office was triumphant as he became head of the student government.

Albany Law School at Union University prepared him for his long-planned legal career. Again he excelled as an advocate and won the top prize for achievement in mock trial work. In 1938, he opened practice in Lockport with an older attorney, an arrangement that lasted until Miller's enlistment during World War II. He was also selected by two federal judges for the western district of New York to be U.S. commissioner. He would later describe that post as a glorified justice of the peace, but more to the point his duties involved handling minor and routine aspects of cases filed before these judges. His first political involvement came as a member of a speaker's bureau for Wendell Willkie in 1940.

During his first year out of law school he handled a routine automobile accident case. The principal witness was his client's daughter, Stephanie Wagner. Only recently graduated from high school, she was a stunning beauty who instantly captivated Miller, who was nine years older. Miller recalled that she was a good witness, though it would be assumed his assessment was more than a professional one. When a favorable decision in the case was announced, the happy attorney personally delivered the message to his client, via her daughter. He drove out to the Wagner lakeside cottage and found Stephanie alone. It was only after several hours of friendly conversation that Miller recalled the message he had come to deliver. Shortly before Miller joined the Army in 1942, the couple became engaged. The following year they were married while the young soldier was home, as Stephanie recalls, on a three-day pass.

During the war Miller was assigned to the Military Intelligence Branch and lived with his wife in Richmond, Virginia. In January 1945, he was selected for Officer Candidate School in the Judge Advocate General Branch at Ann Arbor, Michigan. After four months he was commissioned a first lieutenant. He served as an assistant under chief prosecutor and Supreme Court Justice Robert Jackson at the Nuremberg, Germany, war criminal trials. His experience with Nazis at Nuremberg made a lifelong impression. While fellow arch-conservatives would later use Communism as the symbol of ultimate governmental evil, the Nazis were that incarnation to Miller. He personally interrogated such Nazi leaders as Goering and Keitel.

His war record made him a celebrity in Lockport. Soon after his return his political future began to unfold. Frequent invitations to speak at civic groups established important contacts. Important legal business from businessmen, usually Republicans, was sent this war hero. Additional income came from his appointment as an assistant district attorney for Niagara County. In January 1948, Governor Thomas Dewey appointed him district attorney. The appointment was ratified by a substantial margin in the November elections, the same election in which Dewey was surprised in his race for the presidency. The district attorney post was part-time, but Miller gained political advantage from it by announcing that he was probing municipal officials. Indictments were sought but not gained against the mayor and two city councilmen of Niagara Falls, but two zoning board members were indicted, convicted and imprisoned. The common practice of seeking plea bargains had helped achieve the convictions. Political foes later used this fact as the basis for a charge he was only using the probe for political mileage. One of the less significant defendants later alleged that Miller offered him immunity from prosecution if he would give evidence against the Democratic mayor of Niagara Falls, but the man refused. There is no doubt Miller was always extremely partisan, and probably at this stage in his career he was extremely ambitious. It seems too much to charge, however, that he was attempting to manufacture evidence.

Far more important to Miller's political advancement was an eighteen-week strike at a Bell Aircraft plant in 1949. A UAW official and friend of Miller stated that the district attorney had initially been cooperative with the union, but then Miller changed his mind. Much violence by both sides marred the dispute. Miller charged that the union was Communist dominated. He had over a hundred union members and supporters arrested for conspiracy, assault, and inciting to riot. Invariably he argued for extremely high bail to keep these strikers behind bars, but usually his requested amount was greatly reduced by the judge who set bail. Miller vowed to smash the union and told the workers to walk through the union picket lines. When violence erupted inside the plant after strikers went in for an "inspection," apparently actually to intimidate the non-strikers, Miller ordered the sheriff to drop tear gas and flew into the factory himself in a Bell helicopter. There he made a controversial speech that was permeated with hostility towards the union. Non-strikers were encouraged to continue ignoring the pickets; strikers were warned that they would be jailed as long as possible. Union hostility to Miller in each of his future political campaigns was extreme.

These publicity opportunities thrust Miller into the 1950 congressional race to fill the seat of a retiring Republican congressman. Newspaper support for his strong anti-strike stand was good, and apparently so was the support from the voters. His margin of victory was 23,000 votes. It would increase to a solid 30,000 to 40,000 for the next four elections. Miller at first had been reluctant to run. He was just establishing himself as a trial lawyer and did not feel financially secure enough to get into politics. His wife liked the idea of Miller in Congress, and later called her encouragement "the only time I've ever interfered."

The new congressman was slow to make himself known. Indeed, in 1964 the Democrats argued and several Republicans conceded that he never did make his mark. He would list only two bills as achievements during his 14 years in the House, one a compromise over development of power by private utilities at Niagara Falls, the other the approval of a new canal in his district. The first bill would embroil Miller throughout his public career in controversy over his integrity.

In 1950, Canada and the United States entered a treaty to develop additional hydroelectric power at Niagara Falls. Congress had to determine whether private or public sources would handle the development on the American side. A battle lasted in Congress until

1957, with Miller representing the cause of private company development. His stand led to allegations that he was effectively on the payroll of various utility companies, a charge vehemently denied. Frank E. Smith, then a Mississippi congressman and later Tennessee Valley Authority director, charged that Miller offered him a then lucrative $350–$500 a month position with Lockport Felt Company in return for a favorable vote. Smith was a member of the congressional subcommittee considering Miller's bill for private utility development. Miller denied the charge.

While the debate over the bills continued, yet another allegation against Miller was leveled. The New York congressman was a strong supporter of Dwight Eisenhower, first for the 1952 presidential nomination and, once Ike was in the White House, of his legislative program. In committee, Miller co-sponsored an administration civil rights bill that was then reported out to the House floor, with Miller signing the committee's favorable report. When the bill was debated, however, Miller moved that it be recommitted. If the motion was adopted, the bill would effectively be killed. His motion was defeated, but Republican sponsors of the bill condemned Miller's actions as treachery and a major source of erosion of support for the measure. This change of heart was explained by Miller as a recognition of serious problems with the measure that he had not at first seen. Opponents charged "deal." The "deal" allegation developed from the following events. A bill sponsored by Senator Herbert Lehman was approved in the Senate. It would have given control over Niagara power to the New York State Power Authority, and left private companies out of the lucrative opportunity. The Senate bill was assigned to the House Rules Committee, then chaired by Howard W. Smith of Virginia. A senior member of the committee who wielded great influence was William Colmer of Mississippi. Though hard evidence is lacking, circumstances suggest that Miller exchanged his long-standing and public support for the civil rights bill, which Smith and Colmer found repugnant, for the Rules Committee's agreement to block the Lehman Niagara public developmental measure. Whether the deal was struck, the results were

exactly as the Southerners wanted on civil rights and Miller desired on the Niagara legislation. Miller's response always was that he made his recommitment motion sincerely, that he found the bill a "legal monstrosity" and unconstitutional. However, he would admit the next year to a Buffalo newspaper that as a "political realist" he found it "useless to explain that no 'deal' was involved."

Though his record was made curious by his 1956 vote, Miller consistently supported other major civil rights bills, voting in support in 1957, 1960, and 1964. Barry Goldwater, Miller's 1964 running mate, opposed most of this legislation. On other key votes, the New York congressman voted for Alaska and Hawaii statehood in 1958 and 1959; he favored an increased minimum wage in 1960; he wanted a freeze in farm supports in 1958. In 1959 and 1960, he invariably voted with the Republican-Southern Democratic coalition. The liberal Americans for Democratic Action found him favoring their position 10 percent of the time, while the conservative Americans for Constitutional Action gave him a 92 percent rating.

Miller was much less interested in issues than in politics, which explains the lack of substantive legislative achievements. He was constantly at odds with the liberal Republican leadership in New York, especially governors Dewey and Nelson Rockefeller. In 1959, he endorsed Vice President Richard Nixon over Rockefeller in the race for the 1960 presidential nomination. Rockefeller partisans would complain that Miller likewise worked against the New York governor in advance of the 1964 nomination, though that is less clear. Miller was also a backer of Charles Halleck, the Indiana congressman, in his winning effort to unseat elderly Joe Martin as House Republican leader. In return, Halleck in January 1960 was instrumental in gaining Miller the chairmanship of the Republican Congressional Campaign Committee. Though the 1960 elections were generally a severe disappointment for his party, Miller's Congressional Committee won a stunning 21 seats away from the Democrats. This success propelled him into the chairmanship of the Republican National Committee, the GOP's highest party position in the country.

As RNC chairman, Miller streamlined the operations, reducing staff but increasing research and publicity. He held regional meetings with local party leaders, and he encouraged recruitment of brighter and more articulate candidates for the Republicans. Miller's aggressiveness and keen party spirit found its perfect outlet as chairman. Finding his duties to include constant attack on national Democrats, the witty Miller referred to President John Kennedy as the "foundering father of the New Frontier." Averell Harriman was attacked as having "loused up Laos." Presidential press secretary Pierre Salinger was called "the thinking man's filter." White House staff in general was gibed with "if President Kennedy turns around in his rocking chair, he'll find more extremists in the White House than any place else." Bobby Baker, President Johnson's onetime intimate, later abandoned because of scandal, was said to have written a book entitled *Somebody Up There Likes Me — or at Least I Thought He Did*. Miller's electoral success was less impressive than his humor, as the Republicans lost ground at almost every level in the 1962 campaign.

Near failure came in his own reelection campaign in 1962. His former 30,000 to 40,000 vote margin was reduced in 1960 to 19,800, which was a warning. The message became clearer two years later when he won by a margin of 5,702 out of 139,710 votes cast. The reasons were several. National party involvement had made him seem uninterested in his district. Economic problems in western New York made an attentive congressman seem even more necessary than usual, and Miller was increasingly disinterested. His district was also heavily Catholic, and though Miller was Catholic his frequent attacks on President Kennedy, who was popular with many of his constituents, were harmful. The charge seemed fair that the congressman was more interested towards the end of his tenure in Congress in his political work as chairman, his recreations of golf and bridge (he was an excellent player at both), and job perquisites than in constituent matters. Consequently, with his popularity waning as well as his enthusiasm, Miller announced he would not run for another term in 1964.

Though as party chairman Miller was required to remain neutral in the 1964 presidential nomination battle, many Rockefeller supporters thought he was favoring Goldwater. What little evidence there is consists of Rockefeller aides' belief that confidential information provided the party chairman about their campaign as a courtesy, always seemed to end up in the Goldwater camp. Other charges were more general. What is clear is that the nomination campaign, usually a battle, was this year a bitter philosophical war. After Goldwater's nomination, he was in no mood to give the second spot to a moderate such as William Scranton, his final and belated opponent. Ronald Reagan 16 years later would frequently be compared to Goldwater as an archconservative ideologue, but among the striking differences is that Reagan selected a running mate with a moderate image, George Bush, while Goldwater did not make that move for political unity. In late June, before the July 13–16 convention opened, Goldwater aides had approached Miller as to his availability and found the New York congressman most receptive. On July 15, the formal offer was made as Goldwater asked:

> Bill, I'm going to be walking down a long, lonely road. I wondered if you'd like to come along?

The answer was immediately affirmative.

At a meeting of state party chairmen at the convention, Goldwater would explain his choice of Miller in part because "he drives Johnson nuts." Getting under the president's skin and trying to prompt outbursts of famous LBJ temper was an important campaign tactic. Just as Nixon three elections before, Miller was to be the "hatchet man," to make the charges that would get publicity without blemishing the presidential candidate's image. He was glib, quick on his feet, a great debater with a keen, biting wit. These talents would be put to frequent use.

Miller would later lament that he spent more time correcting Goldwater's *bon mots* than in giving his own attacks. The famous acceptance speech line, "Extremism in the defense of liberty is no vice," was explained the following day by Miller:

you first have to understand what the Senator means by extremism. That's the crux of it. Extremism is significant and praiseworthy in things for which we feel deeply. I hope my wife loves me. I hope she loves me extremely.

Such humor and quick instincts would at times take a much more negative tack. He accused Johnson's campaign of Gestapo-like tactics in dredging up charges against Miller and Goldwater. During the campaign, allegations were made that Miller gave special favors to businessmen in Lockport, particularly at the Lockport Felt Company. Miller charged LBJ with delivering such "dirt" to pet columnists. After Miller had attacked the president for placing a racially restrictive covenant in a deed of property he owned in Austin, Texas, it was revealed that Miller had owned some property in Maryland that had similar restrictions. After Johnson had spoken about "raving, ranting demagogues," without actually naming the Republican ticket, Miller countercharged that Johnson had succumbed to political hysteria and could not be trusted with the cool nerve needed to control our nuclear weapons.

After the campaign ended, Miller said he had realized from the outset that he had no chance for victory. He did admit to being surprised by the severity of the defeat. He announced at the end of the year that he was retiring from politics and would never try for elective office again.

Miller kept his promise. In 1965, he became vice president and general counsel for Lockport Felt Company, the business to which he had been accused of giving unethical favors while in Congress. The long-abandoned law practice was reopened in Lockport and nearby Buffalo. In 1968, he avidly supported his former adversary Nelson Rockefeller for president, joining "Rocky's" national campaign organization in an important post. In return, Rockefeller appointed Miller in 1970 to the $30,000-per-year post of chairman of the Niagara Frontier Transportation Authority.

One other revelation about his career surfaced during the Nelson Rockefeller confirmation hearings in 1974 for vice president. Rockefeller's brother Laurence testified that in 1961 he had made a loan to Miller in the amount of $30,000 at five percent interest. As he then (1974) recalled, the loan was made at Nelson's request.

Miller stayed out of the limelight, other than to become something of a television personality by being shown on advertisements for American Express credit card company in which he asks, "Do you know me?" The obvious implication was that few remembered. After a short illness, Miller died in 1983.

Analysis of Qualifications

William Miller gained the vice presidential nod because he was a gut-level puncher with acerbic wit. He does not stand as one of the most statesmanlike of choices. Some pretense for normal ticket balancing was also stated as a reason for selecting Miller, since he was a northeastern Catholic. If that was part of the reason, it was ineffective in November 1964.

Miller was known at the time of his selection as a dapper, partisan politician. He was once described as having a long rhetorical needle and loving to use it. Politics, as opposed to government, was his forte and he seemed to love his position as chairman of the Republican National Committee from 1961 until 1964. These interests were not supplemented with an abiding concern for his district, since the longer he was in Washington the more removed he appeared to become. Miller's reputation as something of a dandy, wearing Chesterfield coats, homburg hats, and being constantly concerned about his sartorial elegance did not sit well with his constituents either. His career was built on developing friendships in Washington, from Charlie Halleck, to Richard Nixon, and finally to Goldwater, while making enemies at home in the form of Dewey and Rockefeller. One biased enemy, but then enemies usually are, was his 1962 opponent for Congress who described Miller as the "little Joe McCarthy of Niagara County." That was unfair, but a slightly more subdued charge that he had little philosophy other than his partisanship is accurate. Miller summed it best when he said, "As a Congressman I have consistently served the interests of job-producing industries in my district, including the Niagara Mohawk Power Company, the Wurlitzer Company, the Lockport Felt Company and Bell Aircraft...." Indeed these were his chief interests, not only because they produced jobs in his district but because they helped keep his job secure.

At first meeting Miller was memorable for his fast pace and intensity — he talked, thought, and learned fast. Some even described him as too smart, and as a result lazy. His deadly tongue injured him at times as much as it did his adversaries, making him almost equally capable of making enemies as friends.

Reviewing Miller's career, one is struck by the predominance of politics over substance. He was not an obstructionist; he was not counterproductive in Congress. Yet he also did not achieve or lend his support to achievements in any crucial way. Perhaps the cynical candor of presidential nominee Barry Goldwater that he chose Miller "because he drives Johnson nuts" is only fitting. As president, Miller would not have been able to avoid taking stands, trying to lead, attempting to solve problems. There was little in his preparation for that office, however, to permit a prediction that he could break out of a lifetime mold of witty, clever partisanship, and finally begin to be a statesman. He was not, based on past performance, a good choice for vice president.

MILLER BIBLIOGRAPHY

"The Bill Millers Rev Up for November." *Life* (August 7, 1964), pp. 35–36.

Carter, Barbara. "Who Was Bill Miller?" *The Reporter* (November 5, 1964), pp. 21–24.

Finney, John W. "Miller Pledges Republican Help to the President and Humphrey." *New York Times* (November 5, 1964), p. 20.

"Goldwater's Running Mate, William Edward Miller." *New York Times* (July 17, 1964), p. 11.

Kahn, Roger. "Bill Miller: The G.O.P.'s Tough, Shrewd Pro." *Saturday Evening Post* (August 8, 1964), pp. 81–83.

McGill, Douglas C. "Ex-Rep. Miller, 69, Died; Goldwater's 1964 Running Mate." *New York Times* (June 25, 1983), p. 14.

Moley, Raymond. "Two Indispensable Men." *Newsweek* (February 11, 1963), p. 96.

Morris, Joe Alex. "The Party Chairman, Republican Miller." *Saturday Evening Post* (September 29, 1962), pp. 32 ff.

"The Needle Man." *Time* (December 8, 1961), p. 21.

New York Times, various news stories during 1964 campaign: September 17, 1964, p. 39; September 23, 1964, p. 1; September 25, 1964, p. 1; October 29, 1964, p. 20; December 27, 1964, p. 48; January 16, 1965, p. 17.

"Running Mate." *Time* (July 24, 1964), p. 28.

Schaap, Dick. "Where Is Bill Miller?" *Harper's Magazine* (December, 1967), pp. 68–72.

Viorst, Milton. "Who's Bill Miller? The Man Who Thought of Leaving Politics." *The New Republic* (August 8, 1964), pp. 8–9.

Weaver, Warren, Jr. "After 10 Years, a Forgotten Politician Looks Back on a Forgotten Campaign." *New York Times* (June 3, 1974), p. 23.

_____. "Miller Spurned the Usual Road to Political Arena, Bypassed Chiefs of the State G.O.P." *New York Times* (September 6, 1964), p. 44.

_____. "Record of Miller in Congress Is Orthodox G.O.P." *New York Times* (July 18, 1964), p. 6.

White, Theodore. *The Making of the President, 1964.* New York City (1965).

"William E. Miller." *Newsweek* (July 27, 1964), pp. 22–27.

Genealogical information provided by Mrs. Stephanie Miller, Lockport, New York.

Election of 1968

NOMINATIONS

Republican National Convention (29th): August 5–8, 1968, at Convention Hall, Miami Beach, Florida. *President*— Richard M. Nixon, nominated on the first ballot with 692 votes out of 1,333 cast. Nelson Rockefeller (N.Y.)

and Ronald Reagan were the principal alternatives. *Vice president*— Spiro T. Agnew, nominated on the first ballot with 1,119 out of 1,333 cast.

Democratic National Convention (35th): August 26–29, at the International Amphitheatre, Chicago, Illinois. *President*— Hubert H. Humphrey, nominated on the first ballot with 1759¼ out of 2,622 cast. Eugene McCarthy (Minn.) was his main opponent. Robert Kennedy (N.Y.) had been a prime contender until he was assassinated in June. *Vice president*— Edmund Muskie, nominated on the first ballot with 1942½ votes out of 2,622 eligible. Most of the remainder did not vote.

American Independent Party. This party did not hold a convention. *President*— George Wallace. The party was a vehicle for Wallace to get on the ballot of each state. *Vice president*— S. Marvin Griffin, named by Wallace as his temporary running mate on February 14, 1968. Many states required that a presidential candidate have a running mate in order to qualify for inclusion on the election ballot, and Griffin agreed to serve as a stand-in until a final candidate was selected later. Curtis E. LeMay, named by Wallace on October 3, 1968, after several other individuals refused to accept Wallace's request to become his official, final running mate. One of the men who publicly refused was former Kentucky governor A.B. "Happy" Chandler.

GENERAL ELECTION, November 5, 1968
Popular Vote
>   Nixon 31,785,148
>   Humphrey 31,274,503
>   Wallace 9,901,151
>   Others   242,568

Electoral Vote
>   Nixon-Agnew — 301 (32 states)
>   Humphrey-Muskie — 191 (13+ states)
>   Wallace-LeMay — 46 (5 states)

Winners
>   Richard M. Nixon, 37th president
>   Spiro T. Agnew, 39th vice president

Losers
>   Hubert Humphrey, Edmund Muskie, George Wallace, Curtis LeMay

---

*1968 presidential nominee—
Democratic Party*

Hubert Humphrey

Full name: Hubert Horatio Humphrey, Jr.
State represented: Minnesota.
Birth: May 27, 1911, at Wallace, South Dakota, above his father's drugstore.
Age on Inauguration Day (January 20, 1969): 57 years, 8 months.
Education: Public schools in Doland, South Dakota, high school valedictorian in 1929; University of Minnesota, 1929–1930, then returned to help father in Huron, South Dakota drugstore; Denver School of Pharmacy accelerated course, 1932–1933, and became registered pharmacist; University of Minnesota, 1937–1939, Phi Beta Kappa, magna cum laude; M.A. 1940 at Louisiana State University; began Ph.D. at University of Minnesota, 1940–1941, but had to withdraw for financial reasons.
Religion: United Church of Christ (Congregational).
Ancestry: Welsh and Norwegian descent.
Occupation: Pharmacist; teacher.
Public offices: State director of war production training and reemployment, 1942; assistant director, War Manpower Commission, 1943; unsuccessful candidate for Minneapolis mayor, 1943; Minnesota campaign director for Franklin D. Roosevelt, 1944; mayor of Minneapolis, 1945–1949; United States Senate, January 3, 1949–1965; unsuccessful aspirant for Democratic vice presidential nomination, 1956, and for presidential nomination, 1960; Senate Democratic Whip, 1961– 1964; vice president, January 20, 1965–January 20, 1969; unsuccessful Democratic nominee for president, 1968; United States senator, January 3, 1971–January 13, 1978; unsuccessful candidate for Democrat presidential nomination, 1972; declined vice presidential nomination after Tom Eagleton resigned from ticket, 1972.
Death: January 13, 1978, at Waverly, Minnesota, 66 years, 7½ months.
Burial: Lakewood Cemetery, Minneapolis.
Home: Waverly, Minnesota.

Personal characteristics: 5'11" tall, balding, compulsive talker, energetic, constantly in motion, ebullient.

Father: Hubert H. Humphrey, Sr. (March 23, 1882–November, 1949); drugstore owner and local politician.

Mother: Christine Sannes (August 24, 1883–May 2, 1973); married April 16, 1906; born in Norway.

Siblings: Ralph (February 26, 1907–August 27, 1967); married Harriet Burton. Frances (February 18, 1915–); married Dr. William R. Howard. Fern (January 12, 1917–); married William Baynes.

Wife: Muriel Fay Buck (February 20, 1912–); married September 3, 1936; after Humphrey's death, she was appointed to his U.S. Senate seat, serving January 25, 1978–January 3, 1979; on February 8, 1981, she married Nebraska businessman Max Brown.

Children: Nancy Faye (February 27, 1939–); married C. Bruce Solomonson, an insurance broker, on May 14, 1960. Hubert H., III (June 26, 1942–); legislator, lawyer, Minnesota state attorney general; married Nancy Lee Jeffrey on August 14, 1963. Robert Andrew (March 26, 1944–); businessman; married Cheri Rogers on November 2, 1974. Douglas Sannes (February 3, 1948–); married Jan I. Thompson on August 2, 1969.

Historic sites/memorials: Six story Department of Human Services Building in Washington, D.C., named for Humphrey. Bust in lobby. A bust also appears in the Capitol on the Senate side. A mall next to the Martin Luther King Library in Washington is named for Humphrey. At the University of Minnesota the Hubert H. Humphrey Institute of Public Affairs has been established.

Al Smith, another defeated presidential nominee of the Democratic Party, was given the tag "the happy warrior." Hubert Humphrey was probably an even happier warrior. Ebullient, gregarious, one of the first of the modern-day liberal Democratic politicians, he was variously termed compassionate or a "bleeding heart" depending on one's point of view. Yet never was there a more genuinely concerned and loving leader for the underprivileged. What Lyndon Johnson tried to fulfill in his Great Society is what Hubert Humphrey, believed in his very marrow — that government was both of and by the people, but it should primarily be for the people who were in need.

Humphrey's background gave him experiences of poverty and hunger, as so many of his generation suffered during the Great Depression. His father was a druggist and smalltown politician who revered the Democratic Party. His state, South Dakota, was staunchly Republican. Humphrey's family was comfortable enough, but frequently moved during attempts to find better opportunities. Christine Humphrey, Hubert's mother, was born of Norwegian parents who brought her to America when she was a teenager. Humphrey in his memoirs recalls his childhood as a happy time. His contemporaries remembered him as a natural leader even as a child, from sandlot athletics to high school and college honors in debate and academics. One of the remembrances that clearly was painful, however, is when father Hubert, Sr., had to inform the family that the home they lived in had to be sold to help pay off the debts that the Depression made otherwise impossible to pay. The family stayed on in Doland, South Dakota, in a rented home, but the stigma of their veritable bankruptcy was a heavy burden. They were hardly alone.

Humphrey initially attended the University of Minnesota after high school graduation in 1929, but the failing drugstore business back home in Doland required his help. Hubert therefore dropped out in his sophomore year. He became a registered pharmacist in 1933 and ran the drugstore business by himself for a time. Hubert, Sr., had long wanted to run for office, and with the younger Hubert literally minding the store, he was able to win a seat in the South Dakota legislature. Yet Hubert, Jr., had no desire to remain a druggist. His father could blame himself for young Hubert's idealism and affection for Franklin Roosevelt, and the son longed to get involved in government.

In 1937, Hubert was able to return to the University of Minnesota and get his degree in political science. He was an outstanding student and received a Phi Beta Kappa key, was a debate champion, and also graduated magna cum laude in 1939. One year at Louisiana State

University enabled him to receive his master's degree, writing a thesis about the New Deal. Apparently Humphrey chose LSU despite other offers because he received a fellowship there; in those pre-inflation days it amounted to $450. The chairman of the political science department also was a friend of one of his Minnesota professors.

Louisiana widened Humphrey's experiences immeasurably. He saw at close range an entirely new, personal, vindictive style of politics that dominated Louisiana after the Huey Long years, Long himself having been assassinated only four years before. He also saw racial discrimination, probably for the first time, with "separate but equal" facilities being ever-present. He called this a period when his abstract liberalism put on some flesh and blood. Humphrey did manage to get his master's degree, but not before a shock from a mischievous examining professor. During the oral examinations for the degree, the professor told Humphrey that he would have to be failed on the exam. The distraught degree candidate was barely able to get the question "why" enunciated. The professor replied: "Well, if we give you the degree, you'll just as likely as not end up a college professor, and if we flunk you right now, you are more likely to go back to Minnesota and run for the United States Senate, and you'll amount to something" (Humphrey, *The Education of a Public Man*, p. 66). Humphrey's New Deal fervor must have been obvious, and apparently Humphrey had one professor who was at least as good a prognosticator as he was a historian.

Humphrey received his master's degree in 1940 and made a brief attempt at a Ph.D. that was cut short by monetary woes. His first summer back in Minnesota was spent teaching other schoolteachers a course in political science. He then went to the Works Progress Administration teaching program in the Twin Cities, Minnesota, where he primarily worked with trade unions. During World War II, Humphrey remained with various similar programs because he was disqualified for military service due to color-blindness and a double hernia. Finishing his pre–public office career by teaching at Macalester College in St. Paul, Humphrey would return there 25 years later

to work during his next, short period out of public office.

In 1943 Humphrey, aided by the labor union contacts he made through WPA as well as by his professors and peers at the University of Minnesota, ran for mayor of Minneapolis. Incumbent mayor Marvin Kline won in a close contest, and Humphrey paid off his debts by working as a newsman for a local radio station. Heading the Roosevelt reelection campaign in 1944 next occupied his time, and after that success he again ran for mayor in 1945 and won. He made a considerable reputation as an innovator and reformer, and also established a public image as the hardest working mayor the city had ever had. His 1947 reelection victory was by the largest margin in history, two to one over his opponent.

Humphrey's involvement with the state Democratic Party was critical in turning Minnesota from a one-party, Republican state into, within 15 years, close to a one-party, Democratic state. In 1944 he had helped found the historic joining of two state organizations, the populist, Farmer-Labor Party and the traditional Democratic Party. The coalition was central to the decline of Republican fortunes in the state. Humphrey was also a founding member of the Americans for Democratic Action, a national liberal Democratic organization that influenced politics at every level. Humphrey's labor relationships also continued to blossom, and in 1947 he cemented a friendship with William Green, then head of the American Federation of Labor.

Humphrey became the Democratic nominee in 1948 to oppose Senator Joseph Ball, a labor nemesis who had helped sponsor the Taft-Hartley Act whose "right-to-work" provision was anathema to organized labor. At the 1948 Democratic national convention Humphrey's forceful and courageous stand in behalf of a strong civil rights plant in the platform, thrust him onto the national stage. Humphrey crushed Senator Ball in the general election and went to Washington with a ready-made reputation as a champion of civil rights, but also as a windy, aggressive, sanctimonious liberal. Humphrey's first forays in the arcane world of the Senate were as a doctrinaire liberal and by and large he was unsuccessful. His brashness and righteousness were not part of the "good ol' boy" club that would have made him attractive to the Senate powers. Humphrey was later to refer to his first few years in the Senate as the most miserable period in his life, because of his ineffectiveness and ostracism. Not only during this period but throughout his career Humphrey was accused of being undignified, impulsive, and rigid in his political beliefs, ill-suited for the give-and-take compromises of the legislative process. Humphrey was intelligent enough to realize his ineffectiveness and began to master the necessary detail, not only of the legislation he sponsored but also of the process itself.

Humphrey's first and probably most embarrassing and damaging lesson in Senate protocol was his attempt to take on Senator Harry Byrd, Sr., of Virginia. Byrd's pet committee was something ponderously titled "The Joint Committee on the Reduction of Nonessential Federal Expenditures," with Byrd as chairman. On February 24, 1950, Humphrey took on Byrd, his committee, and most importantly, the entire way that Senators conduct themselves. Humphrey attacked the committee in Byrd's absence, which was probably an unintentional slight. The assault interrupted a politically important debate over cotton and peanut acreage allotments being conducted by two Mississippi senators and a Florida one. Humphrey indirectly called Byrd and his committee hypocrites: the committee to remove nonessential expenses was actually itself a waste of taxpayers' money. The speech was given with intensity and righteous indignation. Dignified Harry Byrd rose to respond a few days later, and in quiet and restrained phrases, he humbled Humphrey by showing inaccuracies in the charges made even though perhaps the general thrust of Humphrey's attack had been proper. Byrd dramatically offered to resign from the committee if the Senate agreed with the brash young Minnesota senator. The other Senate powers hardly needed a cue, and they rose to defend Byrd. Humphrey's response was to stiffen the attack on the committee and he became more unwelcome among his fellow senators. Humphrey's chances for influence were given a severe setback. He was later to admit that despite his continued belief in the merit of his charges, the whole episode had been his worst mistake in the Senate. Yet the mistake was indicative of the at-times glib, always emotional and headstrong senator who attacked where he saw villains and thought about the consequences later, if ever.

Humphrey's relationship with Lyndon Johnson was obviously an example of his growing awareness of the way to get things done in the Senate. He did not support Johnson when he first ran for Senate majority leader in 1953, but Johnson was apparently impressed enough by Humphrey's integrity that he began to see him as a force worth having on his side. Humphrey was a key national figure among the traditional liberal forces — civil rights groups, labor, and organizations such as the ADA — and Lyndon Johnson needed his support. In turn, the majority leader gave Humphrey access and influence to the inner-circle in the Senate. Many liberals did not like Johnson, a fact that was painfully evident ten years later during Johnson's presidency, but Humphrey was more than willing to work with him.

Humphrey also began to forge alliances in the Senate because of his innate fondness for people, a fondness that showed. People liked Humphrey because he liked them. The initial negative feeling that many senators had about Humphrey began to crumble in the face of the personal relationships that were being formed.

Humphrey's prominence among the liberal ranks naturally propelled him into speculation about the presidency. The number of liberals was greatly increasing in the Senate. Humphrey was definitely becoming a power to be reckoned with. In June of 1959, Humphrey met with his closest advisers. After an inconclusive meeting, they announced their own draft Humphrey committee. Humphrey stepped up his public appearance schedule and traveled the country as an unannounced candidate. He ran a pure, no-compromise liberal campaign, saying that no Democrat should be selected who was not "right" on all liberal issues. He also tried to keep up his Senate responsibilities, which frequently took him off the campaign trail. Finally in January of 1960 he made his formal announcement. Unfortunately for him the liberal enthusiasm that might at other times have aided him attached instead to a new hero, John Kennedy. Kennedy had not taken any time away from campaigning in order to tend to his Senate responsibilities, but that was only a small part of the explanation. Humphrey just did not seem to have the capacity to excite his forces — lovable, bubbly Hubert could not compete with the glitter of the Kennedys. The first formal battlefield was in Wisconsin. Humphrey's home state, neighboring Minnesota, seemed to give Humphrey a great initial advantage. Perhaps that on balance hurt him, because the very familiarity with Humphrey made him seem stale, while the exciting Kennedy campaign was fresh and invigorating. Image — Kennedy had it, and Humphrey did not. Kennedy received 56 percent of the Wisconsin primary vote and Humphrey was effectively out of the race. The Minnesotan did make a last stand in West Virginia, but some of the same factors defeated him there. He was beaten and broke, having dug into his personal and family funds rather heavily after the contributions started drying up. On May 10 he announced his withdrawal from the race, but made no endorsement of Kennedy. At the July convention he had almost no influence. His true favorite was Adlai Stevenson, but Humphrey realized that Kennedy would be the victor. At the convention itself, a boorish comment from Bobby Kennedy — we want your support "or else" — caused Humphrey the next day to endorse Stevenson's hopeless cause.

Humphrey returned to Minnesota and his Senate reelection campaign. His Republican opponent was a mirror image, in superficial respects anyway, to Humphrey himself 12 years earlier. Kenneth Peterson was mayor of Minneapolis, young, and banking on the refusal of Minnesota voters ever to send a senator back to Washington for a third term. Nonetheless, Humphrey apparently was never concerned. He was right, winning by a landslide even though much of the remainder of the ticket was defeated. With Lyndon Johnson now vice president, the Democratic leadership in the Senate had to change. Mike Mansfield was assured of moving from majority whip to majority leader, but the replacement for Mansfield as whip was uncertain. Mansfield, Bobby Kennedy and Johnson all agreed that

Humphrey should get the vacancy, and that assured the result.

Humphrey's influence in the Senate, despite his opposition to Kennedy during the 1960 nomination campaign, continued to grow. During the next four years he was influential in getting past the Senate the Peace Corps legislation, a nuclear test ban treaty, and the Civil Rights Act of 1964. These were hard-fought battles. Particularly in the case of the civil rights legislation, Humphrey's organizational skills in the Senate were crucial for passage.

With John Kennedy's assassination and Lyndon Johnson's ascension to the presidency, there became a key question for the 1964 presidential campaign — who would be Johnson's running mate? Humphrey was in the speculation from the beginning, but Johnson for political and publicity reasons would not narrow the field and announce his decision. Humphrey received some early indications that he was the choice, but Johnson kept him apprehensive by seeming to be testing his loyalty on key issues. Finally Humphrey was summoned to the White House for the supposed offering of the nomination, but he was asked to travel with Senator Thomas Dodd of Connecticut. This was a diversion to keep the press from guessing the decision. Johnson spoke of the difficulties he had suffered as vice president and how Humphrey must expect the same sort of background role. Johnson pointedly asked whether he could remain loyal and not speak out against the administration regardless of the issue. Humphrey said that he could. He received Johnson's blessing for the nomination. The Johnson-Humphrey ticket went on to win one of the great landslide victories in presidential election history.

Humphrey's vice presidency was indeed a restraining one. Johnson was not an easy man to work under, and Humphrey was gradually isolated from all decision-making functions, especially after, at least as Humphrey recalled in his memoirs, he began to question Johnson's Vietnam policies. He was also apparently held responsible for leaks to the press on various matters. In early 1966, perhaps temporarily out of the doghouse, Humphrey was sent on a world-wide tour that started in Vietnam.

The vice president felt, however, that his isolation from policy-making made him ill-equipped to speak substantively with many of the leaders he met. Humphrey's position on the war took a more pro-administration tone after the trip, and his private attempts to question the direction of the effort diminished. In November 1967, he took another Vietnam fact-finding tour and returned with many of his old doubts about the war. He believed and argued for a gradual policy of disengagement, but continued to keep his comments private and within the inner circle of the White House.

On March 31, 1968, as Humphrey was packing to leave for Mexico City on a scheduled trip, President Johnson stopped at his house and asked for a private conference. The president showed him two endings to a speech he was going to deliver on Vietnam on television that evening. One ending included his withdrawal from the presidential campaign. Humphrey was dumbfounded. He asked the president not to do it. Johnson was noncommittal, but did say that withdrawal might be the only way to get the peace process engaged without charges of political grandstanding. The speech was given, and Johnson withdrew. Humphrey was caught off guard by the day's events, and he had to think about what his own moves would be. Within a few days, though, his commitment to a race for the presidency was made.

Bobby Kennedy seemed to capture the excitement and enthusiasm, as had brother John Kennedy eight years earlier against Humphrey, but the vice president was in a good position to win the nomination. Then came the second Kennedy assassination. Whatever else it did, and the results, personal and political, were far-reaching, Kennedy's death assured Humphrey's nomination. It also added to the frenzy, bitterness and outright hatred that exploded at the Democratic national convention that year in Chicago. The convention in late August, after Richard Nixon had been chosen the Republican nominee, was a disaster. Though Humphrey had the nomination locked up, the violence that exploded in the streets around the convention center as well as in the arena itself set Humphrey so far behind in his quest

for the presidency as to make the cause almost hopeless.

Humphrey painstakingly negotiated with several different factions in the party over a plank for the platform dealing with Vietnam, even getting it approved by Secretary of State Dean Rusk. Then Humphrey was suddenly faced with President Johnson's unalterable opposition. The draft backed away from some of the Johnson stands on the war, including calling for troop withdrawals and reduction in the bombing. The language was hardly criticism of Johnson policies, but the president would brook no half-hearted statement. Humphrey gave in before Johnson's enraged opposition, and a plank completely supportive of the president was adopted. For a vice presidential choice, Humphrey ignored conventional feelings about trying to balance the ticket geographically or philosophically, and chose apparently on the basis of who he thought was most qualified to be president should that eventuality occur. Ed Muskie was his choice. President Johnson did not agree with the decision, but conceded Humphrey's prerogative.

The initial need of the campaign was to put some distance between Humphrey and President Johnson on Vietnam. The campaign was lethargic, disorganized, and pessimistic. The polls showed a tremendous lead by the Republican nominee, Richard Nixon, and the albatrosses of Vietnam, Lyndon Johnson, and the Chicago debacle were strangling him. Only at the end of September did Humphrey, irritated at Johnson's angry reaction to any hint of an independent position on Vietnam, decide to give a televised speech that would indicate his own position on the war. Though the actual speech was only a slight retreat from the president's position, it was touted as a major declaration of independence. The speech, and Nixon and Agnew's own stumbling, caused the campaign to turn around. As the election got closer, it appeared Humphrey might be able to succeed. Unfortunately for him, however, he fell just short.

After leaving the vice presidency on January 20, 1969, Humphrey took a position with Macalester College in St. Paul, Minnesota, where he had taught 25 years earlier. It did not take long for him to realize that being out of public life was no life at all, and he jumped into the Senate race in Minnesota in 1970. Eugene McCarthy was retiring as senator, and the vacancy was tailor-made for him. He won an overwhelming victory over a substantial Republican opponent, Clark MacGregor.

Back in the Senate, Humphrey was caught again by presidential ambition. He initially believed Ed Muskie would be the 1972 nominee and was prepared to support him. However, when Muskie's campaign faltered in 1972, Humphrey decided to enter the presidential primaries. He won some important victories in Pennsylvania, Ohio, Indiana, and West Virginia, but the crucial California primary was lost to George McGovern, and so was Humphrey's chances for the nomination.

In 1976, the senator again considered running for president. During the first few months of the year he was constantly in the speculation. Finally, in April 1976, he announced that he would not be a candidate, Jimmy Carter having already acquired an almost insurmountable lead for the nomination.

In August 1976, Humphrey had a physical checkup. It was determined that he had an advanced malignancy in his bladder and prostate, and even though radical surgery was performed, temporary optimism gave way to the truth that the cancer had spread irretrievably. His health varied for the remaining year and a half of his life. Testimonials by many of his friends, both the powerful and prominent as well as the humble and unknown, probably helped ease the torment.

Analysis of Qualifications

Hubert Humphrey is easily depicted with a few images — endlessly talking, shaking hands, smiling and laughing. Successful politicians almost by definition have to be extroverts, but few could match Humphrey's openness and humanity. Though these images are accurate as far as they go, much more about Hubert Humphrey must be recognized in order to fathom his depth for the presidency.

Compassion was an almost never-ending emotion in the man: compassion for the masses, the hungry, the ill that were in America. No more ardent supporter existed for the various Great Society programs. The needy throughout the world received his attention as a sponsor of the far-reaching Food for Peace program and other proposals. He also had compassion for the individual; strangers and friends alike received financial help from the never-wealthy Humphrey. His heart definitely was in the right place. He is to be honored as a great man in that respect. But a Humphrey presidency, one fears, would have seen almost haphazard enlargement of every program ever devised to attack some of the very real social ills of the country. Humphrey was a never-reconstructed New Dealer. Some policies never grow old, perhaps, but the funding for the programs would have been difficult to find.

Besides being a compulsive talker, Humphrey was also a compulsive worker. His workdays would stretch for 20 hours or more for days on end, and then he would become almost too weary to move. He loved motion and large volumes of work almost as an end unto themselves, a vestige of his Depression upbringing. He was frequently criticized for being involved in too many things and thereby wasting energy and influence. He bombarded Congress with legislation on every conceivable subject, and he indeed could not be master of them all. His speaking method was similar — wordy, bombastic and energetic, but not known for its style or organization. This is not to say he was an ineffective speaker, because his very enthusiasm could propel an audience along with him.

Humphrey's seeming capacity for endless work put him on an incredible schedule, one he never kept. His reputation for being late, hours late, to scheduled events drove his staff crazy. The explanation for his tardy behavior is tied to his compulsive talking as well as his ebullient friendliness — he could not reject a well-wisher or acquaintance who wanted to talk. The demands of the presidency would have had to change that. Humphrey was almost incapable of saying "no," which in a sense explains his liberalism — no man should hunger, or be without shelter, or wanting for anything if it is in the capacity of government to say "yes" to the need.

Much like Jimmy Carter, who did acquire

the office Humphrey coveted, Humphrey immersed himself in much of the minutiae of his work and was not as much of a big-picture man as he would have had to be. His ability to delegate authority and responsibility was limited.

The innate goodness, the inability to be vindictive or unforgiving, would have contrasted markedly with the man who beat him, Richard Nixon. He would not have had the "enemies list" that marred the presidencies of Nixon, Franklin Roosevelt, John Kennedy, and probably others whose lists never became public. In many ways he reflected simple but lost virtues that were genuine: a concern for others that transcended what they could do for him; an optimistic outlook on life; a counting of his blessings in the worst of times, such as during his two-year bout with obviously terminal cancer.

As most candidates who can only be spoken of in the "what might have been" category, Hubert Humphrey has both pluses and minuses that must be weighed in evaluating what his performance in office would have been. Humphrey had experience that qualified him for the position; his liberal views on social issues and his support, though slipping, of the Vietnam War are political reference points that can be measured only within the framework of one's own political opinions. His personality, warm, compassionate, and gregarious, certainly contrasted him with the victor in the election, and would have been a plus. He had the characteristics that parties should look to when nominating a candidate, and he should be ranked as a competent, if not outstanding, choice for the office.

HUMPHREY BIBLIOGRAPHY

Berman, Edgar. *Hubert: The Triumph and Tragedy of the Humphrey I Knew.* New York City (1979).

Cohen, Dan. *Undefeated: The Life of Hubert H. Humphrey.* Minneapolis (1978).

Eisele, Albert. *Almost to the Presidency: A Biography of Two American Politicians* (Eugene McCarthy and Hubert Humphrey). Blue Earth, Minn. (1972).

Engelmayer, Sheldon D., and Robert J. Wagman. *Hubert Humphrey, the Man and His Dream 1911–1978.* New York City (1978).

Garrettson, Charles L., III. *Hubert H. Humphrey and the Politics of Joy: A Case Study in Religious-Political Ethics.* New Brunswick, N.J. (1993)

Griffith, Winthrop. *Humphrey: A Candid Biography.* New York City (1965).

Humphrey, Hubert H. *The Education of a Public Man: My Life and Politics.* Garden City, N.Y. (1976).

Ryskind, Allan. *Hubert: An Unauthorized Biography of the Vice President.* New Rochelle, N.Y. (1968).

Sherrill, Robert, and Harry W. Ernst. *The Drugstore Liberal.* New York City (1968).

Solberg, Carl. *Hubert Humphrey: A Biography.* New York City (1984).

Some genealogical information provided by Mrs. Muriel Humphrey Brown, and by the Minnesota Historical Society, St. Paul.

---

*1968 vice presidential nominee —
Democratic Party*

Edmund Muskie

Full name: Edmund Sixtus Muskie.

State represented: Maine.

Birth: March 28, 1914, at Rumford, Maine.

Age on Inauguration Day (January 20, 1969): 54 years, 10 months.

Education: Rumford Public Schools: Bates College (Lewiston, Maine), graduated *cum laude* 1936, Phi Beta Kappa; Cornell Law School, LL.B. 1939; admitted to bar in 1940.

Religion: Roman Catholic.

Ancestry: Father was Polish immigrant who arrived in United States in 1903.

Profession: Attorney.

Public offices: Maine house of representatives, 1947–1951, Democratic floor leader, 1949–1951; unsuccessful candidate for mayor of Waterville, Maine, 1947; district director, Office of Price Stabilization, 1951–1952; Maine Democratic National Committeeman, 1952–1957; governor of Maine, 1955–1959; United States senator, January 3, 1959–May 8, 1980, resigned; unsuccessful nominee for vice president, 1968; unsuccessful candidate for 1972 Democratic presidential nomination; United States secretary of state, May 4, 1980–January 20, 1981.

Death: March 26, 1996, two days shy of his 82nd birthday.

The first team

VOTE

HUMPHREY-MUSKIE

AFL-CIO COPE, Washington, D.C. 20006

EDMUND MUSKIE (left) and HUBERT HUMPHREY
(From the collection of David J. and Janice L. Frent)

Burial: Arlington National Cemetery.

Home: Vacation home in Kennebunk, Maine; at time of his vice presidential nomination, Muskie and his family lived in a large colonial style home in Westwood, Maryland.

Personal characteristics: 6'4" tall, gangling, craggy-faced; large ears and nose; brown hair and blue eyes.

Father: Stephen Marciszewski (September 21, 1882–January 25, 1956); born in Bialystock, northeast Poland; a tailor; changed his name to Muskie after arrived in America in 1903.

Mother: Josephine Czarnecka (March 19, 1892–May 30, 1973); married February, 1911.

Siblings: Irene (January, 1912–); married Arthur Chaisson in November, 1933. Eugene (October 31, 1919–). Lucy (April 5, 1916–); married Henry Paradis in September, 1945. Frances (April 12, 1921–January 24, 1997); married Fernand Chauinard. Betty (March 1, 1923–February 24, 1983); married Ben Breau in August, 1951.

Wife: Jane Frances Gray (February 12, 1927–); married May 29, 1948.

Children: Stephen (March 18, 1949–); married Alexis Droggittis on June 20, 1970. Ellen (September 22, 1950–); married Ernest Allen on January 3, 1970. Melinda (December 27, 1956–); married Edward Stanton on August 25, 1979. Martha (December 17, 1958–). Edmund, Jr. (July 4, 1961–).

Three recent Democratic also-rans share a remarkable kinship: McGovern, Muskie and Humphrey all were Democrats who grew up in solidly Republican states. It fell to each of them to reshape the moribund Democratic Party within their states, and each succeeded so remarkably that for a time the Democrats were the dominant party, at least in the major offices. Their success also propelled all three to the United States Senate where, equally in common and similarly unsuccessfully, all three were nominated by their party for one of the two highest offices in the country.

Edmund Muskie was the son of an immigrant tailor, who had shortened his Polish name of Marciszewski after his arrival in America in 1903. Marciszewski's ethnic background probably had much to do with his insistence on being a Democrat in almost completely Republican Rumford, Maine, where he and his wife Josephine Czarnecka settled in 1911. The family never knew real financial comfort, but they managed a little better than mere survival. Something of the younger Muskie's own temper and testiness were exhibited in the father, who was wont to express his strong and usually unpopular opinions to his largely Republican customers. The family was close, and a sense of family loyalty and affection grew with Muskie as he developed. Religion was also stressed in this Catholic family. Throughout his life Muskie has kept faithful to his religious

obligations. For a time when Muskie was in high school he seriously considered becoming a priest. As one of few Eastern Europeans in Rumford, he suffered ridicule from his playmates for his heritage. He was painfully shy and made few friends, but in high school began to become more outgoing, particularly when he participated in high school debate activities. At these he excelled.

Money was constantly a problem for Muskie when he left for college. Though his academic successes in high school had earned him scholarship assistance, he still had to work to make up the difference. Odd jobs included working summers as a bellhop and at other tasks in a Maine seaside resort hotel. The hotel was in Kennebunk, Maine, near the same location that a more successful nominee for the vice presidency, George Bush, later would have a summer home. Muskie was an excellent student despite the time he had to devote just to earning enough money to stay in school. Phi Beta Kappa and *cum laude* honors were his upon graduation from Bates College in Lewiston, Maine, in 1936. He was also elected president of his senior class, some indication both that his earlier shyness was being overcome and also that he had some political skills that would aid him later.

At Cornell Law School, Muskie again faced severe financial difficulties. As his second year was about to start, he was on the verge of being unable to continue. A wealthy Maine philanthropist who aided students in just such circumstances gave him the money he needed for that year and the following one. The money was initially a ten-year interest-free loan, but it became a gift after Muskie enlisted in the Navy during World War II. Again Muskie excelled, graduating *cum laude* and passing the Massachusetts and Maine bar exams.

Muskie returned to Maine and purchased the law practice of a deceased attorney in Waterville, Maine. The practice was not particularly interesting, being mainly collections work, but it held out the promise of enough income to establish Muskie in his new career. When World War II erupted, Muskie enlisted and left the practice in charge of his secretary. Another attorney looked in occasionally. After the war, Muskie would return to Waterville and find that there was not much practice to pick up again.

Muskie was an officer aboard a destroyer escort, the USS *Brackett*. Little remarkable, other than survival, occurred during his three years of service. Lieutenant Muskie was discharged in late 1945.

Since Muskie's law practice had not prospered in his absence, he was in dire financial straits. One avenue of relief was running for the legislature. The Maine Democratic National committeeman suggested the race to Muskie. With a somewhat "what's to lose" attitude he jumped into the contest. The fortunes of Maine Democrats were at a low ebb. Even though Muskie won, he was one of only 24 Democrats in a 151-member House. Muskie had campaigned industriously but still seemed surprised at his victory.

Muskie followed his first victory in Maine politics a year later with his first and only defeat. He attempted to oust the incumbent Mayor of Waterville, Russell H. Squires, and lost. One wonders whether financial woes had again set the stage for an attempt at this new office.

In 1948, Muskie was married to Jane Gray, a 19-year-old daughter of a Baptist and Republican papermill worker. Her father had died when she was only 12 and her mother took in boarders in order to keep the family afloat. A brother, Howard Gray, became business manager for the newspaper in Waterville which was owned by a strongly Republican chain. Ironically, it opposed Muskie in his first race for Governor. Jane's marriage caused at least two conversions to occur, one to Catholicism and the other to the Democratic Party. Which was the more dramatic is hard to say.

Muskie was reelected to the state legislature in 1948 and in 1950, but he tired of the relative unimportance of the post and resigned in 1951 to become state director of the Office of Price Stabilization, a federal position established in the states to help control the inflationary wage-price spiral. The position was relatively unpopular in most states since it involved telling both management and labor that they could not do what they wanted to do, but Muskie appeared to avoid the worst of the opprobrium by keeping his contacts frequent

with all sides in the inflation problem. The job was frustrating, however, and Muskie resigned in 1952. A hiatus in his political career developed, at least insofar as holding public office was concerned. Muskie was elected Democratic National Committeeman for Maine in 1952, but he had to try to reestablish a legal career in order to enjoy any income. While engaged in a renovation project on his home, he fell down a flight of stairs and broke his back. His family despaired for his life during the first two weeks following the accident, but he recovered. He would from time to time thereafter have recurring back problems, and as late as 1982 was hospitalized for removal of a vertebra.

In 1954, Muskie almost ran for Congress. The difficulty in that plan was his inability to find any other Democrat rash enough to run for governor. His attempts to convince a broad range of people to run resulted in their convincing him to run instead. The race was against incumbent Governor Burton M. Cross, who was considered to be in a strong position for reelection. The Democrats as well as Cross's fellow Republicans thought Muskie's race little more than a warm-up for more serious competition that might be thrown at Cross two years later. A funny thing happened on Cross's way to the 1956 election, however, and that was his defeat by Muskie in the 1954 contest. Muskie had run at first an uninspired campaign, but by mid-summer it began to have impact. Through the recently popularized medium of television the unknown Democrat was able to project himself to almost all of Maine. The Republicans were much less skillful with television than Muskie, probably because of complacence, and Muskie won a comfortable victory.

Being governor came as such a surprise that the Muskie campaign team had to scramble in order to adjust to being the governor's staff. Muskie was slow in feeling his way around with his new authority. The legislature was still overwhelmingly Republican, and Muskie had to adjust his strong partisanship to adapt to the necessity of coexistence. His first term was built around plans for economic revitalization for Maine through attracting new industry. He wanted an industrial development agency, greater support for public education, and a modernization of state government. The governor was easily reelected in 1956. His gentle treatment of the legislature then turned more assertive. He continued to push industrial expansion in the state, at this stage in his career being far less concerned than he would be later as a United States senator in the environmental impact caused by some types of industry. Muskie also secured a sales tax increase to pay for some of the new programs that he was pushing.

When Muskie managed to have his proposal for a four-year term for governor adopted by the Maine legislature, he had implied that he would not attempt to fill that first, longer term. Therefore, he did not desire to run for reelection as governor in 1958. His sights rose to U.S. senator. The incumbent Republican, Frederick G. Payne, had been rocked by scandal a few years earlier, and Muskie was given a good chance of defeating him. Payne was desperate and attacked Muskie bitterly, including alleging Muskie was an agent of creeping socialism in the country. These attacks put Muskie in a rage, and his public explosions of anger were attractive to the public. Muskie had angry exchanges with many of Payne's supporters and with the senator himself. Muskie's defeat of Payne made him the first Democrat to be popularly elected a senator in Maine.

On arriving in Washington, Muskie almost immediately antagonized the Senate majority leader, Lyndon B. Johnson. Johnson was looking for Muskie's support on a cloture motion in the Senate. Muskie would not commit himself immediately. Johnson apparently wrote him off, at least for a while, as undependable. From the first, Muskie established a strong liberal and pro-labor voting record. When John F. Kennedy began his race for the presidency, Muskie in January of 1960 became one of Kennedy's earliest public supporters. Kennedy's election helped Muskie get better Senate assignments, since the antagonistic Majority Leader Johnson was now elevated to the vice presidency. Muskie's support for President Kennedy, and later President Johnson, was far more consistent than that of almost any other senator. In 1964, Muskie was briefly in the speculation as a running mate for Lyndon Johnson, though finally the president chose Hubert Humphrey instead. Nineteen hundred sixty-four was also the year that Muskie had to run for reelection. It was no contest. He won overwhelmingly with 67 percent of the vote over Clifford G. McIntire.

Now that Hubert Humphrey had become vice president and was no longer majority whip in the Senate, Muskie considered making the race to succeed him. He eventually decided not to run. Muskie would again defer to other candidates when a similar opening arose in 1969. The whip that was elected, Senator Edward Long, became so undependable that majority leader Mike Mansfield appointed Muskie and others in January of 1966 as assistant whips, and they essentially replaced Long.

Muskie in the Senate became an expert on urban and environmental affairs. His civil rights voting record was strongly liberal, though he was not particularly public in his expressions of support. Indeed, it was not until after he began to be in serious speculation as a presidential candidate for 1972 that he began to engage in some of the public posturing on civil rights and other issues that are required in order to attract attention. Muskie's whole Senate style was low-key, which some interpreted as being a sign that Muskie had neither assertiveness nor ambition.

In 1968, Hubert Humphrey became the Democratic presidential nominee. Muskie had long been thought a likely running mate. Humphrey himself had dropped hints to Muskie that he was high on the list of possibilities. Humphrey later was to say that his final choice came down to Muskie and Senator Fred R. Harris of Oklahoma, and that Muskie was chosen because Harris's ebullient demeanor was too much like Humphrey's own. The country probably could not take two Humphreys. Muskie's campaign style was one of the few positive signs in a negative 1968 campaign. The Maine senator seemed to represent the simple but rockhard virtues of New England — calm, strength and intelligence. The tall, craggy Muskie was frequently compared to Abraham Lincoln in appearance. Muskie's placement on the ticket was probably a net plus for the Democrats.

Muskie was so highly commended for his efforts that even his defeat in 1968 was not too disappointing for him, saying he found himself strangely upbeat after the election. His prospects for 1972 looked good. Immediately testing the waters for his own presidential effort, Muskie began a heavy speaking campaign. He joined most Democrats in opposing some of President Nixon's controversial appointments, such as Walter Hickel for Department of Interior, and Judges Clement Haynsworth and Harrold Carswell for the United States Supreme Court. Yet by February 1969, national polls showed that Senator Ted Kennedy of Massachusetts was the favorite among Democrats for the presidency; Muskie came in a weak second. This discouraged Muskie considerably but he decided to continue in order that he would have no regrets later for not having given the race a chance to develop. The tragedy involving Kennedy at Chappaquiddick, in which a passenger in Kennedy's car, Mary Jo Kopechne, was killed in July 1969, put Kennedy out of the 1972 presidential picture. Muskie was vigorously back in the race and the leading candidate by the end of 1969.

Besides his presidential campaign, Muskie's energies were directed towards his growing reputation as one of the Senate's principal backers of environmental legislation. His earlier support as governor of Maine for industry at all costs was almost completely reversed. Also showing considerable change were Muskie's feelings concerning the Vietnam War. As most public leaders, he was an early supporter of America's effort in Vietnam. From 1962 through 1968, his support gradually declined, though as an Administration spokesman in the 1968 campaign, Muskie vigorously argued in behalf of the Johnson war policies. Almost immediately after the campaign, his public and private support for Vietnam plummeted.

In 1970, Muskie had to run for reelection as well as continue his presidential campaign. He almost ignored his Republican opponent, Neil S. Bishop, who had 16 years earlier been one of Muskie's gubernatorial campaign leaders. Muskie dispatched Bishop with little trouble, but his presidential race was not having such luck. Though he was receiving frequent endorsements by influential leaders, he had not achieved the kind of campaign organization that he would need.

Thousands of letters began pouring into Muskie's office, but he did not have the staff to respond to them. Muskie would not get down to the nitty-gritty of conducting the arduous campaign required for a presidential candidate. He inspired no one. Trying to run as the representative of the center of the Democratic party, Muskie was squeezed by the bitterly-opposed and extreme wings of the party, represented by Governor George Wallace of Alabama on the one hand and George McGovern of South Dakota on the other. Some "dirty tricks" provided courtesy of the Nixon campaign also played a small but public role in Muskie's collapse. A story planted by someone from the Nixon campaign in the only statewide New Hampshire newspaper prior to the primary there infuriated Muskie. The story attacked his wife, Jane, and Muskie's typical, angry response finally backfired on him. He made a tearful, bitter, and impromptu speech in front of the newspaper office in the snows of Manchester, New Hampshire. Though he may have looked quite human, he looked anything but presidential in his tirade. Regardless of the legitimacy of his anger, his inability to handle it in this circumstance affected his support. Muskie admitted his campaign's collapse, and withdrew on July 11.

After the Democratic convention chose George McGovern and Tom Eagleton, Muskie could see the inevitability of Nixon's victory. Eagleton's own personal problems whisked him off the ticket two weeks later, but Muskie refused, as did several other leading Democrats, to accept McGovern's offer to replace Eagleton.

In Nixon's second term, Muskie became the first, and until his resignation in 1980 the only, chairman of the Senate Budget Committee. This committee was to rationalize the budget process and to set budget, revenue and spending amounts each year.

In 1980, Muskie agreed to join the floundering administration of President Jimmy Carter as secretary of state. It was rumored that he was tired and bored with the Senate, having served there for 21 years. Even though

Carter's defeat looked quite possible in the November election, the State Department was a new challenge. Muskie finished out the Carter term, wrestling with the question of American hostages in Iran, the aftermath of the bungled attempt to rescue them, and other crises. When Ronald Reagan became president in January of 1981, Muskie was for the first time since 1954 no longer in public office.

Muskie joined a Washington, D.C., law firm in 1981.

Analysis of Qualifications

The campaign in 1968 established Edmund Muskie as one of the bright lights among the defeated vice presidential candidates. Few running mates, especially defeated ones, have ever contributed as much to the level of debate in presidential campaigns as did Muskie that year. As his counterpart on the Republican ticket, Spiro Agnew, was lowering the quality of discussion of major issues, Muskie presented an image of quiet, strong integrity that made a vivid contrast. Muskie emerged from the 1968 campaign as one of the leading contenders for the presidential nomination in 1972. After the Mary Jo Kopechne tragedy took Kennedy out of the race in the summer of 1969, there seemed few who could challenge Muskie for the nomination. But Muskie's decline and fall says much about his capabilities for the presidency. His restrained, dispassionate image masked a volatile temper that could explode at any time. The granite-like strength that his very appearance evoked disguised a lack of ambition, or at least the necessary drive behind that ambition that would make success possible in such a strenuous effort as a presidential campaign.

Muskie's leadership aspirations, at least in the Senate, also deferred to the interests of other candidates. In both 1965 and 1969, he permitted other men to run for Democratic leadership in the Senate even though he was early mentioned at least as prominently in the speculation as were the successful candidates. Muskie defended this lack of apparent willingness to fight by saying that the battles were unimportant, that being an assistant leader in the U.S. Senate was not a sufficient goal in order to engage in the strenuous campaign required. Perhaps his presidential race showed

an equal absence of a willingness to endure the heat of a campaign. Yet for this sometimes passivity, Muskie could still display burning flashes of temper, directed against opponents or his own staff. He was an emotional man who, at least on the snows of Manchester, let his feelings get the best of him.

In all this, Muskie emerges as an extremely private person. He had few enemies, but also few fast friends. He was a thoughtful, intelligent man whose deliberations verged on procrastination. He was cautious, as governor, as senator, and as presidential candidate. He brooded over every detail. He wanted as much information as possible before reaching a conclusion, but even then at times fell into the habit of reciting all the various alternatives without expressing his own opinion. As governor of Maine, he presented his first address to the legislature essentially in that form, without expressing himself on certain issues, but merely presenting the various possibilities the legislature might consider in dealing with problems in that state.

Muskie was always noted for his honesty. Regardless of the financial opportunities available to a U.S. senator, Muskie never took advantage of them, dishonest or honest ones. His sole income outside of his Senate salary was generally fees for giving speeches. As a boy he had not known financial security. Perhaps this helped inculcate thriftiness as well as conservative investment habits.

Had there been a Muskie presidency, it would have been characterized by intelligence and integrity. It would not have been noted for its bold new approaches, as it has never been Muskie's character to be bold. Social programs would have continued to receive a strong push from the White House. Muskie's volatile temper would probably have erupted daily, but by and large it would not have injured the presidency. On balance, Muskie would have been a successful if unspectacular president.

MUSKIE BIBLIOGRAPHY

Alsop, Stewart. "Muskie: No Foundation All the Way Down the Line." *Newsweek* (May 8, 1972), p. 118.

Asbell, Bernard. *The Senate Nobody Knows.* Garden City (1978).

Lippman, Theo, Jr., and Donald C. Hansen. *Muskie*. New York City (1971).

Muskie, Edmund S. *Journeys*. New York City (1972).

"Muskie: The Longest Journey Begins." *Time* (September 13, 1971), pp. 14–19.

Nevin, David. *Muskie of Maine*. New York City (1972).

Radcliffe, Donnie. "Muskie at 80, Still Kicking." *Washington Post* (March 16, 1994), C1–C2.

"What Happened to Muskie?" *Newsweek* (May 8, 1972), pp. 35–37.

Some family information provided by Sen. Muskie.

*1968 presidential nominee —
American Independent Party*

George C. Wallace

Full name: George Corley Wallace, Jr.

State represented: Alabama.

Birth: August 25, 1919, Clio, Alabama.

Age on Inauguration Day (January 20, 1969): 49 years, 5 months.

Education: Clio, Alabama public schools, graduated from high school in 1937; University of Alabama, 1937–1942; received his law degree in 1942 and admitted to bar.

Religion: Methodist.

Ancestry/prominent relatives: Father was a farmer; wife Lurleen was governor of Alabama (1967–1968); brother Jack Wallace succeeded him as an Alabama circuit judge. George Wallace, Jr. (son), was Alabama state treasurer 1987–1995; defeated for Congress in November 1992, and in the 1994 Democratic primary for lieutenant governor.

Occupation: Attorney.

Public offices: Alabama assistant attorney general, 1946; state house of representatives, 1947–1953; state circuit judge, 1953–1959; defeated for Democratic nomination for governor, 1958; governor, 1963–1967, 1971–1979, 1983–1987, retired; defeated for Democratic presidential nomination, 1964, 1972, 1976; defeated as American Independent Party nominee for president, 1968.

Home: Montgomery, Alabama.

Personal characteristics: 5'7" tall; black hair, brown eyes; has jutting, dimpled jaw.

Since 1972 assassination attempt, has been a paraplegic confined to a wheelchair, with many ailments including near deafness.

Father: George C. Wallace, Sr. (September 23, 1897–November 8, 1937); farmer; also held various odd jobs.

Mother: Mozelle Smith (January 5, 1898–October 27, 1988); daughter of Howard and Kate Frink Smith. Married 1918.

Siblings: Gerald (June 11, 1921–1993), attorney. Jack (December 22, 1922–), circuit judge, married Betty Evans on July 10, 1951. Marianne (June 24, 1933–), married Alton Dauphin on July 12, 1953.

First wife: Lurleen Burns (September 19, 1926–May 7, 1968); daughter of Henry and Estelle Burroughs Burns; married May 22, 1943; served as governor of Alabama, 1967–1968.

Children: Bobbie Jo (1944–), married Jim Parsons. Peggy Sue (1950–), married Mark Kennedy. George Corley, Jr. (October 17, 1951–); married and divorced three times. Janie Lee (April, 1961–).

Second wife: Cornelia Ellis (1939–); daughter of Charles and Ruby Lee Folsom Ellis; niece of ex-governor "Big Jim" Folsom–married John Snively III, in 1962 and had two children; divorced in 1969; married Wallace on January 4, 1971; divorced him January 4, 1978.

Children: None.

Third wife: Lisa Taylor (1948–), previously married and had one child, divorced; married Wallace on September 9, 1981. They divorced January 29, 1987.

Children: None.

Movies: In 1997, TNT television network broadcast a movie based on Wallace's life, with Gary Sinise playing Wallace. The George and Lurleen Wallace Foundation called the movie a distortion of the truth.

Historic sites: George and Lurleen Wallace Center for the Study of Southern Politics, a museum and study center being planned in 1995. Two community colleges in Alabama are named for Wallace, in Selma and in Dothan.

On a cold January in 1963, a defiant George Wallace stood on the capitol steps in Montgomery. The new governor warned of a trend towards a "mongrel" nation, which threatened freedom of all races. "Let us rise to the call of freedom-loving blood that is in us and send our answer to the tyranny that clanks its chains upon the South. In the name of the greatest people that ever trod this earth, I draw the line in the dust and toss the gauntlet before the feet of tyranny. And I say: Segregation now! Segregation tomorrow! Segregation forever!" Thus was Wallace inaugurated governor of Alabama and his career thrust upon the national consciousness. Twenty years later, after four presidential campaigns, a paralyzing set of gunshot wounds that reduced him to paraplegia, and, most of all, a New South created by years of turmoil and bloodshed, this one-time race-baiting demagogue said during his fourth inaugural as governor:

> I will always take pride in the broad cross-section of our population who supported me in my campaign ... persons of all races, creeds, color, and religious persuasions.

He then added:

> We are not here to deny the mistakes of the past. We have come to renew our faith in the future.

George Wallace and the state he represented had changed dramatically in 20 years.

There were few luxuries in the Wallace household when George and his three siblings were growing up, but neither was there the abject poverty that an image-conscious Wallace, appealing to poor voters, tried to depict in his later political campaigns. George Wallace, Sr., was a frail man whose lifelong battle with sickness was lost when he reached age 40. He had lost a lung and part of his chest caved in; part of his skull was removed above his eyes and a frightening hole was left. When angry he could get violent and as a teenager he stabbed a (former) close friend in a dispute over a girl. George, Sr., had little aptitude or strength for farming. For young George a closer relative was his grandfather, Dr. George O. Wallace. Both older men exposed the boy to politics at an early age, and almost from the cradle he seemed taken by this fascinating hobby of his two forebears. When George, Jr., was only 11, his father died from Brill's fever,

a kind of typhus. From that point on, the courage and determination of his mother supported the family of four children.

From the start George seemed to have a career in politics as his goal. He sometimes objected to household chores with the statement, "there ain't no future in that stuff." An adequate student, George's prime interests were sports and campus politics. Though he was too small for varsity sports in college, in high school he played quarterback and was known as a scrapper. In both 1936 and 1937 he won the state bantamweight boxing titles. His boxing record was 25 victories, only four defeats and a draw. Future political opponents discovered that he never lost his fighter's disposition. His first political race occurred when he was 15, campaigning among the state legislators for a position as a summer page at the capitol in Montgomery. He won that battle easily, showing the non-stop, single-minded campaigning habits that were honed during the next decades.

When he entered the University of Alabama in 1937, there was little money to support him. He worked scrubbing floors and busing tables for a boarding house, drove a taxi at one stage, and otherwise kept himself constantly busy. From the first day on the Tuscaloosa campus, George was running for freshman class president, and by election day few were the freshmen who had not received a personal plea for support. It worked. His hard work both politically and at odd jobs made him a popular, sympathetic figure. Wallace was an outgoing, friendly character who had ingratiating political instincts. At law school he was an indifferent student, but a skilled politician. People started calling him "governor," because his ambition for the office was candid. George shunned the fraternities because he thought that association would look bad to voters in the future. One friendship that George probably did later decide looked bad was with fellow law student Frank M. Johnson, Jr. As a federal judge years later, the liberal Johnson rendered decisions in civil rights cases that would outrage Wallace. In several campaigns Wallace ran more against Johnson than against his actual election opponent.

Graduation from law school came in 1942.

World War II was his next stop. In October, he volunteered for pilot training in the Army Air Corps, but soon contracted spinal meningitis. For six days he was in a coma and his mother was told he might not live. After recovering he found himself medically disqualified for pilot duty, but saw service as a flight engineer on B-29s in the Pacific. The noise so affected his hearing that it became progressively more impaired as he grew older. By the late 1970s he was almost deaf. When discharged, he received a 10 percent nervous disability that later became a political issue. Wallace retorted by saying at least he was certified as being 90 percent all right, which was more than he felt his opponent could achieve.

While in the service, Wallace began a then-mystifying practice of sending Christmas cards to many friends and even bare acquaintances back home. The mystery ended when he returned to Alabama and almost immediately began running for the legislature. Elected in 1946, he won again four years later. Wallace decided that his future would be advanced by a progressive image. The state chamber of commerce called him a radical; others thought him the state's number one "do-gooder." His proposals included the construction of new trade schools and junior colleges, college tuition to widows and children of war casualties, better mental and tuberculosis hospitals, and higher old-age pensions. The Wallace Industrial Act attracted new industries by guaranteeing relief from property taxes for forty years, and by providing municipal bonds to finance housing for the new industry. During this period he was a political ally of populist, folksy, erratic Governor "Big Jim" Folsom. Folsom's niece Cornelia would in 1971 become Wallace's second wife. A break with Folsom finally came in 1956 over patronage in Wallace's home county. The public reason given for the political separation is illustrative, however, as Wallace blamed Folsom's entertaining of black congressman Adam Clayton Powell in the governor's mansion.

Wallace was reelected to the legislature in 1950. The new governor got a description from his aides on all the legislators. Wallace was described as follows: "energetic, ambitious, smart, probably will be hostile. Liquor habits: moderate. Women: Yes. Interested in legislation re veterans, TB hospitals, Welfare, Education." Within short order some of the summary would be badly outdated. The energy, ambition, intelligence and hostility, as well as rumors of occasional affairs with other women, did remain current information through much of the rest of his career.

Tiring of the legislature and seeing greater publicity and prestige in a judgeship, Wallace ran for circuit judge for his home and surrounding counties in 1952. Elected at age 33, he was thought the youngest circuit judge in the country. From that new pulpit he began to preach on racial issues. He was the first Southern judge to block the removal of segregation signs from railroad stations. Frequent trips were made to Washington to testify against civil rights legislation. From these battles Wallace gained the name the "Fightin' Judge." For six years as a judge, his every move seemed calculated to assist in a 1958 campaign for his career goal, the governorship. He gained useful publicity in 1956 as Alabama's representative on the national party's platform committee, where he fought for a weak civil rights plank. He had provided the same "assistance" at the 1948 convention when many other Southern delegates joined the "Dixiecrat" revolt. At least during the 1940s and '50s, Wallace was remaining within the Democratic Party.

The Fightin' Judge's 1958 campaign for governor was poorly organized and financed. Fourteen candidates crowded the field; from the first Wallace was considered among the top three. The front-runner after the first primary was John Patterson, the state attorney general who had been elected in 1954 to succeed his father. The elder Patterson had been killed mobster-style because of his promise to clean up crime-ridden Phenix City, Alabama. Young Patterson had earned the sympathies of many voters, and in the 1958 gubernatorial contest against Wallace he added to his following by being the hard-line racist candidate. Wallace was no moderate, but the KKK and similar groups endorsed Patterson. When Wallace lost by 314,000 votes to 250,000 he promised some of his aides that he would not be "out-niggered" next time. He wasn't.

For the next four years, Wallace continued to run for governor. The first blow in the fight was struck early in 1959. Wallace refused as circuit judge of Barbour County to turn over voting registration records to the United States Civil Rights Commission. The judge's old law school friend, now federal judge Frank Johnson, issued an order that would have held Wallace in contempt and subject to imprisonment if he did not turn over the records. A late-night meeting at Johnson's home was arranged at Wallace's request. There Wallace asked if Johnson would accept a face-saving maneuver of turning the records over to the state grand jury, who in turn would give them to the Civil Rights Commission. Saving face by compromising with federal authorities would be a recurring Wallace tactic. Johnson agreed. The next day he criticized Wallace, however, saying from the bench that though he would not hold Wallace in contempt of court, if the ploy of using the grand jury was merely for political reasons, he found it distasteful. Wallace's private reaction, later slightly cleaned up for publication, was to call Johnson a "no-good goddamn lying son-of-a-bitching race-mixing bastard."

The 1962 primary was almost anti-climactic. Wallace had positioned himself well, and after leading in the first primary he won with 56 percent of the vote in the runoff. For a time during the campaign he had become depressed and was admitted to a hospital. Marshall Frady, in his book *Wallace*, stated that his depression was brought on by fear he did not have nearly sufficient campaign funds for victory. Friends got twenty thousand dollars in cash together, barged into his hospital room and threw it on the bed. The previously listless Wallace was within moments out of bed and putting on his clothes, ready to go to work.

A few days before his inauguration in 1963, some of the leading Southern segregationists met with Wallace in Montgomery to plan strategy against President Kennedy for the 1964 presidential nomination. Ross Barnett of Mississippi, Leander Perez of Plaquemines Parish, Louisiana, and two Georgians, Ray Harris and James Gray, decided that Kennedy needed competition in their states in 1964. In time it became clear that Wallace would be that man. Exactly when Wallace set his sights

on the presidency is unclear. His 1962 election as governor had secured one ambition, and almost immediately Wallace was off on the next. Recognition as the symbol of a rebellious South was the route to victory Wallace mapped. His inaugural address struck enough sparks to get nationwide attention, at least for a few weeks. Soon additional opportunities came. Shortly before a compromise was worked out between Martin Luther King and Birmingham city officials on desegregation, Wallace blocked it by saying he would not participate in any compromise. Bombings and rioting resulted in Birmingham, and President Kennedy filled the city with federal troops. One tack taken next by Wallace was to appeal to the Supreme Court to hold the Fourteenth Amendment of the Constitution, which guaranteed equal protection, *un*constitutional. It was a novel approach, meant solely for publicity.

During the 1962 election campaign, Wallace had promised to resist any "illegal court orders" requiring desegregation of schools, even if he had to stand in the schoolhouse door. He got his chance. In June 1963, two qualified black youths applied for admission to the University of Alabama. Wallace ordered investigators to find something disqualifying — morally or otherwise — about them, but that effort failed. Next he demanded that something about their parents be uncovered that could cause their rejection, but that failed also. A confrontation with Attorney General Robert Kennedy resulted, where Wallace agreed to admit the students and Kennedy agreed to permit some grandstanding first. On June 11, 1963, at the schoolhouse door in Tuscaloosa, Wallace refused to admit the youths and gave a long statement concerning states' rights and federal tyranny. Shortly thereafter, the federalized National Guard showed up in force. The governor said that in order to avoid violence, he would yield to the inevitable. That day's events received nationwide publicity. Twelve hours later in Jackson, Mississippi, Medgar Evers, that state's NAACP field director, was assassinated outside his home.

At every stage, Wallace interfered with court orders on school desegregation in his state. In September 1963, he temporarily closed Tuskegee schools to avoid a court order.

He campaigned nationwide for his beliefs, and cultivated favor, which hardly needed much seeding, with the Ku Klux Klan, the John Birch Society, and other radical-right groups. In the spring of 1964, the governor announced for president. Big government and federal bureaucrats were the stated issue. He charged nameless government workers in Washington "who could not park their bicycles straight" with setting policy from schoolroom to church for the whole country. He was amazingly successful in the North, winning 34 percent of the vote in the Wisconsin primary, 30 percent in Indiana, and almost 43 percent in Maryland. Working-class voters were his core group of supporters, but his appeal spread to all who felt oppressed, especially the lower middle class struggling to survive and seeing what seemed to them to be handouts from their taxes to blacks and other minorities. The anger which Wallace gave voice to was real throughout the country, but it was not a majority. After Barry Goldwater's nomination by the Republicans, pressure on Wallace to withdraw became intense. On July 19, only four days after Goldwater's nomination, Wallace withdrew and claimed both parties had embraced his conservative cause.

In March 1965, Martin Luther King called for a march from Selma to Montgomery to highlight the drive for black voter registration. Wallace said no march could take place, and privately said, "I am not going to have a bunch of niggers walking along a highway" in his state (Greenhaw, *Watch Out for Wallace*). The march took place anyway. State troopers blocked their path. A melee resulted with billyclubs swinging and tear gas firing. Nationwide revulsion over the act was immediate. President Johnson called on Wallace to permit the peaceful demonstration. The march finally was completed under court order and with federalized national guard protection.

Race was the main issue, but not Wallace's only concern during his first term. Federally funded highway construction was a major achievement. Fourteen new junior colleges and 15 trade schools were built. A regressive tax system was worsened by raising the sales tax and other use taxes, such as on beer, gasoline, cigarettes, and on sporting events. Perhaps most importantly to him, Wallace sought from the legislature a constitutional amendment permitting a governor to succeed himself. What opponents described as Wallace's strong-arm tactics proved unsuccessful.

Wallace was an imaginative, scrappy adversary, and his response to defeat on this issue was to run his quiet, deferential wife Lurleen for the position. Stories that the Wallace marriage was rocky and close to divorce surfaced many times, mainly because of Wallace's preoccupation with politics and his near-ignoring of his family. Lurleen had been diagnosed as potentially having a malignancy as early as 1961, but Wallace had not told her. In mid-January 1966, Mrs. Wallace underwent a hysterectomy and a malignancy was discovered. Despite these medical problems, she agreed to run as George's stand-in. There was no secrecy that she would be the governor in name only. She won with 52 percent of the vote in the first primary, defeating nine candidates. The governorship was hers, or rather, theirs. George Wallace was her one-dollar-a-year-assistant.

As soon as Lurleen was safely ensconced in the governor's office, Wallace was off on his second quest for the presidency. His formal announcement came on February 8, 1968. He said he would run as an independent. Big, impersonal, uncaring national government was the issue, and race was injected only indirectly. Federal civil rights legislation was attacked because the laws trampled on states' rights and individual freedoms, not because of race. Crime was a popular war cry for the Alabaman as well. He said that federal laws and judges protected the criminal instead of the victim. While the presidential race was still heating up, on May 7, 1968, Lurleen Wallace died. A month's lull in the campaign occurred, but then this consummate political animal was back on the road. It was a first for a third party candidate when Wallace secured a place on each of the 50 states' ballots. There can be little doubt that he was a factor that year, as Nixon in particular began focusing his campaign on Wallace's conservative supporters. Public opinion polls showed Wallace getting as much as 21 percent of the vote in September. With his selection of the impolitic Curtis LeMay as a running mate, with strong attacks on his civil rights and racial record, and with fears he might be too militaristic in foreign affairs, Wallace's support began to sag. The final result showed him with 13.6 percent of the vote and with a plurality in five states. He came close to throwing the election into the House of Representatives. Had he done so, it is doubtful he would have been in a position to bargain with the other two candidates to see whom he could support. The Democrats, with a strong majority of the House delegations, would almost certainly have named Hubert Humphrey president.

Governor Lurleen's death meant Lieutenant Governor Albert Brewer succeeded to the office. Wallace assured Brewer he would not try for the office in 1970, but he did anyway. President Nixon feared Wallace's strength. Perhaps $400,000 of Nixon-sponsored money appeared to assist Brewer. The governor led Wallace in the first primary. That lead ended the fairly even-tempered campaign. Smear leaflets against Brewer started appearing, including doctored photographs of Brewer and his family socializing with blacks, a still-dangerous image in Alabama in 1970. A heavy registration drive by Wallace supporters got tens of thousands of additional voters qualified, and he won with less than a one-percent majority. With that victory, he started running for president.

During 1971, Wallace spent much of his time counseling local school districts to ignore court desegregation orders. Wallace announced for president on January 13, 1972, this time as a Democrat and not an independent. Opposition to busing for school desegregation was a central part of the campaign. Wallace started rolling up primary victories. He won the Florida primary with 42 percent of the vote, twice as much as the second place finisher in a crowded field. In Indiana he got 40 percent. Other victories followed in North Carolina, Tennessee, and naturally, in Alabama. On May 15, the day before twin primaries in Michigan and Maryland, he had won more votes than any other contender.

A publicity-seeking drifter named Arthur Bremer put an end to the assault on the nomination. In a Laurel, Maryland, shopping center, Bremer shot the candidate several times before being subdued by Wallace supporters.

Wallace was paralyzed from the waist down, could not walk, lost control of lower body functions, and would remain thereafter in constant pain. Liberals and conservatives in the party visited the wounded candidate in his hospital room. Injured, finally with a trace of sympathy possible, Wallace became a less dangerous and more acceptable politician.

Though he remained in the race for the nomination, the battle had ended in Laurel. Poor organization had already severely damaged his position. In many states his supporters had not properly filed to convert primary votes into delegates; many state contests he did not even enter. He would have fallen far short of his goal of having a strong voice at the convention, equivalent to the size of his nationwide support, even had he not been shot. His sights returned to Alabama. This time he got a gubernatorial succession bill passed. Wallace ran for a second consecutive term in 1974, and there was no contest. The Republicans did not even put up their usual token candidate, and Wallace breezed to victory.

The governor's health was not good. He had remarried in 1971 to Cornelia Snively, "Big Jim" Folsom's niece. She was a glamorous woman 20 years his junior. His incapacity and her beauty made their marriage the subject of many rumors. Wallace himself seemed to worry, as perhaps was natural. Despite his problems, the Fightin' Judge in 1976 tried one more time for the presidency. He had more appeal perhaps as a wounded veteran of previous political wars; he seemed mellower and less threatening. He could not compete with the image of the New South, exemplified by Jimmy Carter, whose smile, vague generalities, and new-face appeal soon made him the Southern favorite, and in time the nation's. Wallace's domestic problems became public when it was revealed that each suspicious spouse had the other's telephone bugged. The marriage finally unraveled completely in January 1978, when they were divorced.

Wallace's third term had a year to go when he announced in June 1977 that he would run for John Sparkman's Senate seat in 1978. He later changed his mind, and that election passed without Wallace's name on the ballot for any office. Nineteen hundred eighty did as well, and instead Wallace was spending his time at a $69,000 per year salary as a fund-raiser for the University of Alabama at Birmingham. Marriage to a country western singer occurred in 1981. She was pretty, thirty years younger than the 62-year-old former governor, and had sung at campaign rallies for him during earlier elections. Retirement was given up in 1982 when the old campaign warrior could not stay off the battleground any longer. Wallace announced for governor. He renounced his segregation past, called on all races to work together, and also stated he had become a born-again Christian. This new image attracted blacks as well as whites, held his old coalition together, and won for him a narrow runoff victory over moderate, youthful lieutenant governor George McMillan. His victory included sweeps of large numbers of the black majority counties, even "bloody Lowndes," where in 1965 his opposition to the Selma to Montgomery march of demonstration led to the bloody encounter between marchers and state police. Some thought the Republicans had put up their strongest candidate since Reconstruction, tough-talking, conservative Montgomery mayor Emory Folmar. Good candidate or not, Folmar soon wore much of the mantle of right-wing extremism formerly shouldered by Wallace. The old warrior won going away, capturing 60 percent of the vote. He became the first man ever elected to four terms as Alabama governor.

Wallace had too many physical ailments to accomplish much in his fourth term. In 1985 he had spinal surgery in Colorado, necessitated by excruciating "phantom pains." In January 1986 he was hospitalized for a urinary tract infection, 16 months after being hospitalized for the same thing. On April 2, 1986, with public opinion polls showing him trailing several other contenders, Wallace announced that his health would prevent his running for another term that November. "I have climbed my last political mountain," he said. "I must pass the rope to another climber." It was a tearful announcement.

In Wallace's last term as governor, and then continuing in retirement, he said that he had been wrong to be such a strong segregationist. He also denied that race was really an issue in his earlier campaigns. Wallace seemed adamant that he would alter the place otherwise reserved for him in history. He sought, it would appear, political redemption. A biographer, Dan Carter, wrote in 1995 that he did not know if Wallace had really changed. He then quoted a former Wallace aide, John Kohn, who said, "If George had parachuted into the Albanian countryside in the spring of 1962 [the year he was actually sworn in as the segregationist Alabama governor], he would have been head of a collective farm by the fall, a member of the Communist Party by midwinter, on his way to the district party meeting as a delegate by the following year, and a member of the Comintern in two or three years." In essence, that aide thought Wallace could be whatever he needed to be (Carter, *Politics of Rage*, p. 15).

Two weeks after he left office in January 1987, his third wife divorced him. They had been living separately for about a year. The divorce papers named "incompatibility" as the grounds.

Wallace took a consulting job at $60,000 per year job at Troy State University. He continued to suffer physically, and apparently almost died in 1992 when he was hospitalized with septic shock. In January 1987 he began working with an ex-state newspaperman, Stephan Leshar, to provide the information Leshar needed for a biography of his life. Wallace also helped on a foundation that was to fund a museum in Montgomery honoring both him and his first wife, the two Governors Wallace.

In 1996 he seemed enthusiastic about the pro–Southern campaign of Republican presidential candidate Patrick Buchanan. He also indicated that he could, and probably did, vote for Bob Dole.

Analysis of Qualifications

George Wallace has come almost full circle. Starting political life as a progressive Alabama state legislator, he soon decided upon race as the dominant issue for his political advancement. For 20 years he lived off the fear and hate that could be engendered by race-baiting, at first on a small level but for 12 years with the whole country as his stage. At the end of his political career, with another term in the governorship, Wallace preached racial moderation, love of neighbor, and rejection of his own past. The common thread in all of this is George Wallace himself, the lover of the limelight, the man possessed by politics who cares little about the details of governing but principally wants to run. He has continually adjusted to his perception of political necessity.

Yet for all his faults, Wallace struck a responsive chord about the evils of government. He could articulate the anger, disgust, and outright rejection of government and make it sound justifiable. He did not have answers to problems, but he could strike home with explanations of what was wrong. With an iron will and audacity, and as an emotional speaker who could fire the spirit of his listeners who agreed with him, Wallace operated at a gut level. His following at its core was almost a religious one, and that core was sizeable. To stand with Wallace was for millions to be standing with America; to be against him was to be against all this country should be.

The world was a stage for Wallace. When cornered, he would as governor bargain for a face-saving exit. In refusing to hand over voter registration records in 1959, in opposing the march in 1965 that led to the bloody Lowndes County attack, Wallace was posturing for public effect while secretly negotiating with the federal government to let him have his show before he gave in. Hardly the most unbiased source, but Cornelia Wallace said a few years after their divorce that Wallace had no principles; he was purely, simply, only a political animal. That seems too pat, and doubtless Wallace did have some very strong opinions. Living through 20 years of turmoil mollified some of the bitterness he felt, so that by 1982 he could sincerely be asking for forgiveness. It is also likely that Wallace could see the changes in Alabama as well as anyone, and he was too good a politician to refuse to react to that change.

Surrounding Wallace had been a large coterie of long-time aides and supporters. Many said during the 1982 campaign that it was the desire of these men, far more than of Wallace himself, that caused him to try one more time for office. Rumors of corruption permeated each of his first three administrations — kickbacks in highway construction, illegal ignoring of competitive bidding requirements in some departments, contractgors with the state who also had close ties with Wallace, and a myriad of other changes. Either as an independent candidate in 1968, or as a Democrat at some other time when he ran for president, Wallace had been so ostracized from established routes to power that he would not have had the normal list of experienced officials to call upon to fill a Wallace administration. Just who would have populated the high-level positions of government would have been a concern had Wallace been elected.

George Wallace hungered for office, for being at the center of the public eye. He could articulate concerns, but he never showed a capacity to govern. Projecting an image of hate during a period when America was exploding — racially, over the Vietnam War, over every kind of social problem in the country — George Wallace was exactly what the country did not need in 1968, or at any other time.

WALLACE BIBLIOGRAPHY

Carlson, Jody. *George C. Wallace and the Politics of Powerlessness, the Wallace Campaigns for the Presidency, 1964–1976.* New Brunswick, N.J. (1981).

Carter, Dan T. *From George Wallace to Newt Gingrich: Race in the Conservative Counterrevolution, 1963–1994.* Baton Rouge (1996).

_____. *The Politics of Rage: George Wallace, the Origins of the New Conservatism, and the Transformation of American Politics.* New York (1995).

Cross, Philip. *The Wallace Factor.* New York City (1976).

"Divorce Trial Is Set for the Wallaces." *New York Times* (January 1, 1978), p. 11.

Duvall, Sam. "Big Man of Alabama Politics Takes Governor's Office Again." *The Alabama Journal and Advertiser* (Montgomery) (January 16, 1983), p. 4B.

Frady, Marshall. *Wallace.* New York City and Cleveland (1968).

Gage, Joan. "The Wallace Women." *The Ladies' Home Journal* (October 1972), pp. 98–105.

Greenhaw, Wayne. *Watch Out for Wallace.* Englewood Cliffs, N.J. (1976).

House, Jack. *Lady of Courage: The Story of Lurleen Burns Wallace.* Montgomery (1969).

Impson, Alvin John. "George Wallace and the Politics of Race." Unpublished doctoral dissertation, Texas A&M University (1994).

Inaugural Address, printed in *The Advertiser* (Montgomery) (January 18, 1983), p. 3A.

Lee, McDowell. *George Corley Wallace: A Legislative Legacy, 1946–1986.* Troy, Ala. (1989).

Leshar, Stephan. *George Wallace: American Populist.* New York, et al. (1994) (an authorized biography that received substantial assistance from Wallace).

MacDonald, Michele, and Sam Duvall. "Wallace's Political Image, Style Leave Mixed Legacy for State." *Birmingham News* (January 11, 1987), pp. 1A, 9A.

"The Messy Wallace Divorce." *Newsweek* (January 9, 1978), p. 23.

Reed, Roy. "George Wallace's Bid for the *New South*." *New York Times Magazine* (September 5, 1982), pp. 15–17, 44–45.

Sewell, Dan. "George Wallace's Final Campaign." *The Roanoke Times* (January 28, 1996), p. F-1.

Sherman, Mike. "Wallace Getting Opportunity to Rewrite History." *Alabama Journal and Advertiser* (Montgomery) (January 16, 1983), pp. 1B & 5B.

Sherrill, Robert. *Gothic Politics in the Deep South.* New York City (1976).

Wallace, Cornelia. *C'Nelia.* Philadelphia and New York City (1976).

Wallace, George. *Stand Up for America.* Garden City, N.Y. (1976).

Wallace, George, Jr. *The Wallaces of Alabama, My Family.* Chicago (1975).

"Wallaces Divorced After 7 Years; Suit Settled Before Trial Starts." *New York Times* (January 5, 1978), p. B10.

Wooten, James T. "Wallace's Last Hurrah?" *New York Times Magazine* (January 11, 1976), pp. 14, 41–56.

Some family information provided by Gerald Wallace, Montgomery, Alabama.

---

*1968 interim vice presidential candidate—
American Independent Party*

S. Marvin Griffin

Griffin was technically, if only temporarily, George Wallace's running mate. His selection was tentative and made solely for state election law procedural reasons.

Samuel Marvin Griffin was born September 4, 1907, in Bainbridge, Georgia, the son of a local newspaper publisher. He attended The Citadel, graduating in 1929. His early career was in journalism, becoming the editor of his father's newspaper in Bainbridge after the elder Griffin suffered a stroke. His first political success was election in 1934 to the Georgia General Assembly. Two years later he failed in a race for a United States House seat. After stints in some appointed positions, and a three-year period in the Army during World War II, he failed in 1946 in a race for Georgia lieutenant governor. In 1948 and 1950, he reversed that result and won the lieutenant governorship.

Griffin's national reputa-

S. MARVIN GRIFFIN and GEORGE C. WALLACE (left)
(Courtesy Samuel M. Griffin, Jr.)

tion was earned after he was elected governor in 1954. He was a segregationist and fought bitterly against the United States Supreme Court's integration rulings. On December 2, 1955, he condemned a Sugar Bowl matchup of the Georgia Tech football team and the University of Pittsburgh squad, which had one black player. Griffin said, "the South stands at Armageddon. The battle is joined. We cannot make the slightest concession to the enemy in this dark and lamentable hour of struggle. There is no more difference in compromising integrity of race on the playing field than in doing so in the classrooms. One break in the dike and the relentless enemy will rush in and destroy us." The Sugar Bowl was held as scheduled. A major scandal rocked Griffin's administration as governor, with charges of corruption in the Highway Department and the State Purchasing Department. Nine state officials and employees were convicted. A grand jury said Griffin's administration was permeated with "perfidious conduct of state officials heretofore inconceivable in the minds of citizens." No charges were ever brought in court against Griffin on these matters, however.

Since a Georgia governor could not succeed himself, Griffin retired in 1958 to the newspaper in Bainbridge. Four years later he was handily defeated for governor by a moderate Democratic candidate in the primary, Carl Sanders. His stated desire to preserve segregation "come hell or high water" had lost some of its impact in Georgia.

His only return to the political wars occurred in 1968 when he was announced on February 14 to be the interim running mate for George Wallace. Many states required that a vice presidential candidate be selected before Wallace could qualify to have his name listed on the general election ballot. Griffin agreed to be the stand-in. It was a considerable surprise that Wallace would name the 60-year-old fellow Southerner, whose governorship had received such unfavorable national attention. During the announcement ceremony, Wallace said Griffin was "a fine American, and certainly I am glad to have him on the ticket, procedurally at least to begin with." Wallace said Griffin "may well be" his final candidate, but

on October 3 Curtis LeMay was substituted. Griffin's name was already on the ballot in most states and LeMay could not be officially substituted so close to the election. With some exceptions, however, electoral college members have freedom under state law to vote for candidates other than those to whom they are pledged. Therefore except perhaps in Florida (which Wallace did not win anyway), an elector could legally vote for Wallace and a running mate other than Griffin.

On June 13, 1982, Griffin died of cancer at a Tallahassee, Florida, hospital. In 1963, he had turned over control of the Bainbridge *Post-Searchlight* to his son, Samuel M. Griffin, Jr., but continued to speak up on political issues, both in speeches and in a twice-weekly column in the newspaper.

GRIFFIN BIBLIOGRAPHY

"LeMay to Appear on Few Ballots." *New York Times*, October 5, 1968, p. 21.
"Marvin Griffin, 74, Former Governor" (obituary). *New York Times*, June 14, 1982, p. D–11.
Sobel, Robert, and John Raimo, eds. *Biographical Directory of the Governors of the United States*. 4 vols. Westport, Conn. (1978), vol. I, p. 322.
"Wallace Names Griffin a Possible Running Mate." *New York Times*, February 15, 1968, p. 24.

1968 vice presidential nominee —
American Independent Party

Curtis LeMay

Full name: Curtis Emerson LeMay.

State represented: Ohio.

Birth: November 15, 1906, in Columbus, Ohio.

Age on Inauguration Day (January 20, 1969): 62 years, 2 months.

Education: Public schools in Columbus, Ohio; Ohio State University, 1924–1928, 1931–1932, B.S. degree.

Religion: Methodist.

Ancestry: Father was French-Canadian.

Occupation: Military man.

Public offices: Refused appointment to U.S. Senate, offered by Ohio governor Frank

A second call to freedom

Elect

WALLACE

LeMAY

GEORGE C. WALLACE and CURTIS LeMAY
(From the author's collection)

Lausche in 1945; unsuccessful vice presidential nominee of American Independent Party in 1968.

Home: Columbus, Ohio; almost all of adult life was spent at various military bases around the world; retired to Southern California in 1965.

Death: October 1, 1990, at March Air Force Base, Riverside, California, at age 83 years, 10½ months.

Burial: U.S. Air Force Academy, Colorado Springs.

Personal characteristics: 5'8" tall, 180 pounds during World War II, became stockier later; black hair turned gray.

Father: Erving LeMay (c. 1884–July 18, 1966); railroad worker, structural iron worker.

Mother: Arizona Dove Carpenter (c. 1887–September 23/24, 1967).

Siblings: Lloyd. Velma. Methyl. Leonard. Patricia. Child who died at birth.

Wife: Helen Estelle Maitland (?–1992); married June 19, 1934; daughter of lawyer Jesse Maitland.

Child: Patricia Jane LeMay (February 8, 1939–), married Dr. James Lodge.

Movie: *Strategic Air Command* (1955) star-

ring Jimmy Stewart. Frank Lovejoy portrays a Curtis LeMay–like general named Ennis C. Hawkes who is in command of the SAC.

Several generals have been nominated for president as a result of glory earned at war. Several have even been nominated decades after their exploits, such as was William Henry Harrison. Yet Curtis LeMay alone among the generals who never held public office was nominated for the vice presidency, having been selected by a presidential candidate who desperately wanted credibility for his campaign. The public, and George Wallace, were to discover that a blunt, aggressive military leader can seem awkwardly out of place in politics.

There were few if any comforts in the LeMay household as Curt was growing up. The oldest of seven children in a poor Ohio family, Curt LeMay moved frequently as his father sought employment at various odd jobs, always low-paying. They lived in Montana, in California, and in Pennsylvania. Returning to his native Columbus, Ohio in 1919, Curt entered high school there in 1920. While others participated in typical social activities, sports, and other high school pleasures, LeMay had to work to help his family. Two summers he was a union structural ironworks employee, and other jobs were equally strenuous.

There was one long-standing ambition in young LeMay's life, throughout the moves and the drudgery. At the age of four or five he saw his first airplane, and it was love at first sight: "its wonderful sound and force ... a thing of wood and metal piercing the air ... something unique and in a way divine." The military seemed the best entrance into flying, but a hoped-for commission to West Point did not materialize. Instead he enrolled in the School of Engineering at Ohio State University. The military still was the goal as Curt joined ROTC. Four years later, not yet having earned his degree, LeMay was commissioned a second lieutenant, Field Artillery Reserve. Active duty began almost immediately in Kentucky. Taking his training at Air Corps Primary Flying School in California, LeMay graduated with his wings in June 1929. Airplanes became an obsession. While other cadets caroused in Los Angeles during time off, Lieutenant Le-May worked on airplane engines and in other ways became even more knowledgeable about his lifelong passion — airplanes.

LeMay was stationed at Selfridge Field, Michigan, after flight school, but in September 1931, went temporarily to Columbus, Ohio's Norton Field. At the end of 1933, he was briefly stationed at Langley Field, Virginia, as a student in advanced navigation. Finally completing his duty at Selfridge, Le-May was transferred to Schofield Barracks, Hawaii, in October 1934. His first promotion came on June 1, 1935, when he was made a first lieutenant. He returned to Langley Field in January 1937 to become operations and intelligence officer of the 49th Bombardment Squadron. That year he participated in a good-will flight of B-17s to South America, and in 1938 made a second such flight, earning the Mackay Trophy for achievement in aviation. In 1939, LeMay entered the Air Corps Tactical School at Maxwell Field, Alabama. Returning to Langley, he served as a commander of a B-17, then served as operations and intelligence officer at Langley for the 41st Reconnaissance Squadron.

As World War II loomed, now Captain LeMay was assigned to the 7th Bombardment Squadron, 34th Bombardment Group, and was Squadron Commander. He was a co-pilot on a B-24 used to survey airports in Africa and Asia Minor for use in ferrying aircraft on transoceanic flights. LeMay earned the Distinguished Flying Cross for "outstanding initiative, resourcefulness, and a high degree of skill...." The accolades were for landing in 14 airports "too small" for his B-24. By March 1942, LeMay was a colonel, and the following month was placed in command of the 305th Bombardment Group in Muroc, California. His Group left for England in September of that year. In 25 missions bombarding targets in Europe, LeMay established his reputation as a strict disciplinarian who earned far more respect than affection from his men. Drilling his group incessantly in the skills needed for successful bombing raids, the commander established an enviable record for bombing effectiveness.

LeMay was awarded many medals. As a result of five missions over Europe in late 1942, he received the Air Medal. One of the missions established new bombing tactics. Because evasive action was taken during bombing runs, many bombs were missing their targets as the planes zigzagged to avoid the flak. LeMay led a raid on the French port of Saint-Nazaire and held a straight course through the fire. The success of that effort caused him to order the next day that all bombing runs would thereafter avoid the zig-zag course used previously. Many saw the order as suicidal, but soon it proved its value. LeMay also developed a new combat formation for the bombers that proved more effective in warding off the attacks of enemy fighter planes and came to be used throughout the Air Corps. He led his bomber group in the first shuttle bombing raid over Germany, attacking the Messerschmitt plant at Regensburg, and then continuing on to Northern Africa. LeMay was awarded the Distinguished Service Cross for his heroism in this mission, having volunteered even though he was not under any obligation to participate.

Temporary rank of brigadier general was awarded LeMay in September 1943, and he was advanced to major general in March 1944. The latter rank, gained when he was only 37, made him one of the youngest men in the service to hold such a commission. Through June 1944, LeMay served as commanding officer of the 3d Bombardment Division, and then in August was moved to Asia to head the 20th Bomber Command. This bomber force had been organized especially to use the new B-29 Superfortresses. Operating out of bases in China and India, the new bombers, more sophisticated but also more unforgiving than the smaller B-17, would require new tactics for effective use. In September, raids on Japan stepped up, beginning with a daylight attack on industrial targets in Anshan. Over 100 planes were used in another attack on Anshan a short time later. The experimental phase of use of the new bombers was just about completed, and more bombers, flying more frequently, became the rule. Losses were light; on some missions all planes returned safely to base. Longer distances were being flown than had ever been attempted before.

Encouraging news hit the United States in November 1944, announcing that Tokyo itself had been attacked by LeMay's forces. Daylight raids on the Japanese capital were soon followed by LeMay's recommendation that low-level, nighttime incendiary raids be made on Tokyo. Gunnery was removed to make space for additional bombs, and in January 1945, 300 planes demolished a ten-square-mile area in the Japanese city. By that time LeMay had become commander of the 21st Bomber Command, which later became the 20th Air Force. On July 31, 1945, LeMay was awarded the Oak Leaf Cluster to his Distinguished Service Medal. Effective August 1, LeMay transferred command of the 20th Air Force to another general and became chief of staff to General Carl Spaatz of the Strategic Air Command. In that position he played a major role in planning the use of atomic bombs on Hiroshima and Nagasaki. When those attacks brought the surrender of Japan, the general returned to the United States as pilot of a B-29 on a non-stop flight from Japan to Chicago.

His first political opportunity was soon offered him by Ohio Governor Frank Lausche, but LeMay declined the chance to be appointed to a vacancy in the United States Senate. The honor was presented because of LeMay's fame during World War II. LeMay was not interested in politics, though, and decided to stay in the Air Force.

LeMay was named special deputy to the AAF Air Matériel Command, Wright Field, Ohio in October 1945, and in December went to Washington, D.C., to become deputy chief of air staff for research and development. Until 1947, the Air Corps had been in the Department of the Army, but in 1947, it became a separate branch of the military. After that change, LeMay was made commander of the United States Air Force in Europe, based at Wiesbaden, Germany. He rendered no greater service in that position than when he organized the Berlin airlift to transport an average of 8,000 tons of supplies per day to West Berlin from June to September 30, 1948. LeMay would himself occasionally fly one of the cargo planes. The Medal for Humane Action was given him for his role in this airlift.

Beginning in October 1948, General LeMay became head of the Strategic Air Command, based in Omaha, Nebraska. LeMay took over a poorly organized command that had to rely on left-over equipment from World War II. Morale was low. LeMay stated that there was not one crew who could do its job in the whole SAC. The move to Omaha had just occurred, and LeMay was questioned as to whether he thought SAC would be a good thing for the city. He was reported to have said, in characteristically blunt fashion, "It doesn't mean a damn thing to Omaha, and it doesn't mean a damn thing to me." LeMay was appalled at what he found, and he immediately set out to change things.

The first change was to clean out the staff and to bring in battle-scarred veterans of his command in World War II. LeMay found poor training techniques, with little effort being made to build SAC into a unit that could actually fight if the need arose. LeMay instituted simulated bombing raids across the country. He later recounted that by the time he retired from SAC, every town of more than 25,000 had been "bombed" at least once, while some, like San Francisco, hundreds of times. When the new commander conducted a test to see how his planes would perform, using a mock bombing raid on Wright Field in Dayton, Ohio, as the site, every plane failed to complete the test according to the requirements. It was a scandal within the Air Force, and information concerning the abysmal failure remained classified for years because of fears enemies might be tempted by such a show of ineptitude.

The cigar-chomping, no-nonsense new commander was outraged and demanded that everyone begin to train as if the country were already at war. Constant flying, high altitude bombing practice, rejection of simulators in reliance upon actual flight time for his pilots, were LeMay's answers. Specific Russian targets were given to each crew, so that if war came they were already prepared for their missions. In essence, the General started from scratch and revolutionized the entire concept of preparations that should be made even during peacetime. Fundamentals of every aspect of bombers were written into manuals, from checklists to follow before takeoff, to actual procedures to follow when approaching for a bombing run. Rating schemes were derived to determine just how effectively different parts of SAC were performing, a means of comparison that irritated many of the individual commanders who felt threatened.

From 1948 until 1957, LeMay ran the Strategic Air Command with a single purpose — preparing for war, should it ever come. His airbases were no vacation spots. Every man carried a weapon, fearing saboteurs or other dangers. Bombers were airborne 24 hours a day. This reduced reaction time to an attack and got planes away from surprise attacks on bases. There was no doubt who was in charge of SAC.

While the general was revamping military procedures, he was also fighting the civilians who controlled the purse strings. Nuclear weapons should be the principal deterrent to the Russians, LeMay declared, not conventional forces. The SAC would play a prominent role in that strategy, as a strong force of bombers would be required to deliver the atomic bombs to their targets. Increased bomber production, not only in numbers but also in quality was necessary. To LeMay, there was a developing "bomber gap" between the United States and Russia, with the Soviets racing ahead in many areas of weaponry. LeMay proved a persuasive advocate on Capitol Hill, winning money for

his command that many doubted could be rationally spent. A large increase in the B-52 bomber force was obtained, when the weapon was already growing obsolete. In 1956, he warned that though America could still win a war against Russia, its superiority was slipping badly. Strength in the air would be needed to thwart Russian designs.

The general was never a strong proponent of missiles. It would have been hard to find a man so emotionally and professionally committed to airplanes who accepted that missiles were the weapon of the future. LeMay cautioned against too much reliance on this new technology. Unless all parts of the American arsenal were strengthened, but particularly the bomber force, LeMay argued that the country was inviting a first strike by the Soviet Union. The Air Force was in competition with other branches of the military, and LeMay fought for his service. The type of war developing in Vietnam made some question how massive bomber forces could be effective there. LeMay's response was that what worked in a big war should also prove effective, either as a deterrent or in actual combat, in a small one.

In 1957, LeMay became Air Force vice chief of staff, serving until 1961, when he became chief of staff. The Eisenhower administration worried LeMay for its lack of enthusiasm over certain weapon proposals, but that was nothing compared to the controversies he became embroiled in during the Kennedy years. In July 1961, LeMay convinced Congress to appropriate far more money than the Pentagon had requested for bomber development, especially on the more modern B-58 and on the experimental B-70. His victory was to be empty, as Secretary of Defense McNamara soon diverted much of the funding to other military projects. McNamara believed that missiles would be far more effective at much less cost, and that aircraft would play purely a subordinate role. These were fighting words for the general who was known as "Old Ironpants," and a running feud developed. The Navy Polaris submarine missile and the F-111 fighter-bomber were questioned by LeMay, especially Pentagon selection of General Dynamics as the contractor for the F-111. McNamara's concept that one airplane ought to be developed for all the services, Navy, Marines, and Air Force, struck LeMay as foolish, and he fought the idea vigorously. In the end LeMay's position proved right, at least in the specific case of the F-111 which never was accepted by the Navy.

In 1963, LeMay only grudgingly accepted the Nuclear Test Ban Treaty signed with Russia and publicly stated that the Soviets would gain tremendous military advantage as a result. The frequent publicity given to the blunt, critical general made him a possible political foe of the administration. Though retirement from his high position might have been timely, and certainly the public differences between him and the White House suggested the need for a change, LeMay was retained in his post partly to avoid giving him an opportunity to get into politics. Such conservative politicians as Senator Barry Goldwater praised the Air Force leader, saying he was far more suited to running the military than McNamara. In 1968, LeMay would agree with that point of view. "It never ceases to amaze me that so many intelligent people believe they can become expert in a field where they have so little training or experience" (*America Is in Danger*, Funk & Wagnalls, 1968). This stirring cry for reduction of civilian influence over the military would cause many people to fear LeMay as a politician.

Retirement from the Air Force finally was accepted in 1965. Retirement from involvement with the military was not. A high-paying position with Network Electronics Corporation became available. LeMay kept attacking the Defense Department and President Lyndon Johnson. The Vietnam War, he charged, was being fought in such a way that America could not win. He would be proven correct, but his answer of increased military pressure was not so clearly accurate. The language that would return to haunt the American Independent Party when LeMay became its vice presidential nominee, was this statement in 1965:

> My solution to the problem would be to tell [the North Vietnamese] frankly, that they've got to draw in their horns and stop their aggression, or we're going to bomb them into the Stone Age. And we would shove them back into the Stone Age with air power or naval power — not with ground forces.

Massive bombing in North Vietnam seemed to LeMay the only answer to the problem. That answer certainly had worked for LeMay during World War II.

In 1967, with increased air attacks being ordered by President Johnson, LeMay continued to be pessimistic. "If we had done what we are doing five years ago, as I recommended, the shock effect would have stopped them, but it's too late for this now." John Kennedy had once remarked that LeMay was just the man for combat, but never the man to be asked whether there should be combat or not. George Wallace disagreed, and in 1968 presented LeMay to the country as his running mate on the American Independent Party ticket. Wallace passed over an assortment of names, from conservative commentator Paul Harvey, to former Kentucky governor Happy Chandler, or Arkansas ex-governor Orval Faubus. There was even a rumor that Wallace might name fried chicken king, or colonel, Harland Sanders. Instead, Wallace wanted Curtis LeMay. The reasons were several. Wallace had his voters, the poor and middle class who were frightened, angry, and bitter people. They despaired over crime, race riots, and the other crises then besetting the country. Wallace, however, frightened far more people than he attracted, and he needed respectability. The tough, decorated, 25 years a general, native of Ohio seemed the best available route to that acceptance.

Almost immediately LeMay squandered some of the advantages Wallace had hoped to gain. At the press conference at which he was introduced, LeMay said that though he did not want to fight in Vietnam, now that we were there it was time to fight as if we wanted to win.

> We seem to have a phobia about nuclear weapons. I think to most military men that a nuclear weapon is just another weapon in our arsenal.... I think there are many occasions when it would be most effective to use nuclear weapons.

LeMay maintained that such weapons were not needed in the jungles of Southeast Asia, but that he would not hesitate to recommend them should that change.

LeMay may not have had any "phobia" about atom bombs, but most private citizens did. Wallace tried during the press conference to get LeMay to back down, when some of the reporters asked the former Alabama governor whether he agreed with his running mate. Wallace told LeMay, "They said you agreed to use nuclear weapons. You didn't say that." LeMay unperceptively answered by reiterating that he did not want to use any weapons, but that he would "use anything we could dream up — including nuclear weapons." Wallace finally broke off the news conference saying, "General, we got to go."

Where LeMay eventually went was Vietnam. In the interim he had continually gotten entangled with the press, which delighted in setting the inexperienced candidate up with questions likely to elicit his strong military opinions. By the time he was hustled off to Vietnam and away from the press by the Wallace campaign, he was ignoring reporters altogether and refusing comment. It was a strange political campaign. The publicity caused him to lose his lucrative position as chairman of the board of the electronics firm. The president stated that the company's stock had plummeted on Wall Street, and the only reason was the adverse publicity engendered by LeMay's connection with Wallace. LeMay's response was that he expected to have to make some sacrifice.

Wallace and LeMay received the largest vote for a third party ticket since the La Follette campaign of 1924, but it was not nearly enough. There were no subsequent forays into politics by LeMay. He retired with his military pension, his memories, and his worries about the future of the country.

Analysis of Qualifications

Few running mates have been quite so hand-picked as was General Curt LeMay. Named and nominated by George Wallace and a few advisers, LeMay initially had only that small constituency to impress. His record did that. When he then was turned loose on the public at large, there was dismay. LeMay had performed brilliantly in the military for almost 40 years, 20 of them as a general. When he attempted to move into politics, he was miscast. In 1945, he had refused an offer to be named a United States senator, saying he preferred the military. The decision was the right one in 1945; he made the wrong one in 1968.

Stern, tough, hard-driving, LeMay made few close friends but many respectful subordinates during his years of service. Iron discipline made his military responsibilities successful. He could be gruff and unforgiving, but he also rewarded effectiveness. Old Ironpants loved to fly, and joined in the most dangerous of missions flown by his men during World War II. That earned respect, as did his turning a disorganized, low-morale Strategic Air Command into a tight fighting unit in the 1950s. LeMay knew what he was about — preparing men to fight and die for their country, or more to the point, trying to help them make other nations' men die for theirs. There was no rest to be had in this effort. He said his men must consider themselves at all times to be at war. In remaking SAC, LeMay demonstrated not only single-mindedness, but also considerable administrative skills. He analyzed the problems and made common sense solutions. The general knew his rank, and expected other people to realize theirs. No "one of the boys" image ever surrounded LeMay, but then his style of leadership hardly needed that.

LeMay reflected a narrow military vision. When he rose to high levels of responsibility, his single-mindedness, his parochial concern for the Air Force, became less admirable. He fought first for the Air Force, and particularly bombers, in competition with other branches of the armed services. He also believed in unlimited use of military power. The damage done to the Wallace campaign by LeMay's statements that nuclear bombs were just "another weapon," probably was not great. Wallace's supporters perhaps were not likely to be violently opposed to a strong military stand. But LeMay probably did help assure that Wallace would be unable to reach out further from his narrow constituency. For ten years he fought with secretaries of defense and with Congress for more military expenditures, getting more money for bombers than even the Defense Department thought could be used. As a political candidate, he was still carrying on that fight.

LeMay was not all military. He liked to tinker with cars, drive a go-cart, play an electric organ. He enjoyed a good family life, having been married over 30 years at the time of his nomination. But the military always came first.

In his career LeMay demonstrated imagination and initiative. He was a doer, a commanding presence that inspired respect. His words on the campaign trail were the same words he spoke for 20 years as a general. They were harsh, militaristic, and scary. There was nothing subtle about the general, and nothing false. He was simply an excellent soldier, one to whom the country owed a great debt. He was not, however, good presidential material. Never having learned to deal with civilians, unused to commands being given that were not followed, unfamiliar with the give and take of Congress, little gifted in public speaking, LeMay would have been a president who either would have turned his administration over to more experienced politicians, which was unlikely, or else become stubborn but frustrated as the new world of politics trapped him. It was good he lost, but it was great that he was a general.

LeMAY BIBLIOGRAPHY

"Bomber on the Stump." *Time* (Oct. 18, 1968), p.21.

Coffey, Thomas M. *Iron Eagle: The Turbulent Life of General Curtis E. LeMay.* New York (1986).

"George's General." *Time* (Oct. 11, 1968), p. 21.

LeMay, Curtis E., with McKinley Kantor. *Mission with LeMay: My Story.* New York City (1965).

"LeMay Loses His $50,000 Job Because He Runs with Wallace." *New York Times* (Nov. 2, 1968), p. 1.

Narvaez, Alfonso A. "Gen. Curtis E. LeMay Dies at 83; Architect of Strategic Air Power." *New York Times* (October 2, 1990), p. B6.

"Old Ironpants." *Newsweek* (Oct. 14, 1968), p. 30.

"Wallace Running Mate: Curtis Emerson LeMay." *New York Times* (Oct. 4, 1968), p. 50.

Zimmerman,Carroll L. *Insider at SAC: Operations Analysis Under General LeMay.* Manhatten, Kans. (1988).

Election of 1972

NOMINATIONS

Democratic Party Convention (36th): July 10–13, 1972, at the Convention Hall, Miami Beach, Florida. *President*— George McGovern, nominated on the first ballot with 1,728.35 out of 3,016 cast. Henry Jackson (Wash.) and George Wallace (Ala.) were his main competitors. *Vice president*—Thomas Eagleton, nominated on the first ballot with 1,741.81 votes out of 3,016 cast. The main alternatives were Frances (Sissy) Farenthold (Texas), Mike Gravel (Alaska) and Endicott Peabody (Mass.). Over 80 people received votes. Eagleton withdrew on July 31, and the Democratic National Committee selected Sargent Shriver.

Republican Party Convention (30th): August 21–23, 1972, at the Convention Hall, Miami Beach, Florida. *President*—Richard Nixon, nominated on the first ballot with 1,347 out of 1,348 votes cast. *Vice president*—Spiro T. Agnew, nominated on the first ballot with 1,345 out of 1,346 votes cast.

GENERAL ELECTION, November 7, 1972

Popular Vote

Nixon 47,170,179
McGovern 29,171,791
Others. 1,385,620

Electoral Vote

Nixon-Agnew — 520 (49 states)
McGovern-Shriver —17 (1+ states)
John Hospers–Theodora Nathan —1

Winners

Richard Nixon, 37th president
Spiro T. Agnew, 39th vice president

Losers

George McGovern, Thomas Eagleton, Sargent Shriver

*1972 presidential pominee —
Democratic Party*

George McGovern

Full name: George Stanley McGovern.

State represented: South Dakota.

Birth: July 19, 1922, at Avon, South Dakota.

Age on Inauguration Day (January 20, 1973): 50 years, 6 months,

Education: Public schools of Mitchell, South Dakota; Dakota Wesleyan College in Mitchell, 1940–42, left to enter Army; returned and graduated, 1946; Northwestern University (M.A.), 1949, (Ph.D.), 1953.

Religion: Methodist.

Ancestry: Grandfather had been alcoholic, died when father was only eight, and his mother died when he was 13.

Occupation: History professor.

Public offices: Executive secretary, South Dakota Democratic Party, 1953–56; United States representative, January 3, 1957–January 3, 1961; defeated for U.S. Senate, 1960; Food for Peace director, 1961–62; U.S. senator, January 3, 1963–January 3, 1981, defeated; unsuccessful candidate for Democratic presidential nomination, 1968, 1984; unsuccessful Democratic presidential nominee, 1972.

Home: Mitchell, South Dakota; in Washington acquired an estate on Chesapeake Bay.

Personal characteristics: 6'1" tall; balding, brown hair; 175 pounds; blue eyes.

Father: Joseph C. McGovern (April 11, 1871–December 4, 1944), minister.

Father's first wife: Anna Faulds (?–1917).

Mother: Frances McLean (February 3, 1891–November 27, 1966); married January 8, 1920; daughter of Justice H. McLean, wealthy Canadian rancher and real estate broker.

Siblings: Olive (November 3, 1920–); married Philip Briles on December 28, 1945; he works for Bureau of Indian Affairs in South Dakota. Mildred (February 7, 1925–); married Harold Brady on August 31, 1947; he is a Methodist minister. Lawrence (Larry) (June 11, 1927–); married Mary Katherine Radeke in 1983 (third wife).

Wife: Eleanor Faye Stegeberg (November 25, 1921–), married October 31, 1943; daughter of Earl Stegeberg and Marian Payne.

Children: Ann Marian (March 10, 1945–); married Wilbur Mead in 1968; divorced; married Frank Wilson on December 27, 1983. Susan (March 27, 1946–); married James Rowen on August 27, 1967. Teresa (June 10, 1949–December 12, 1994). Steven (July 27, 1952–); married Marcelle Jezequel; divorced. Mary Kay (July 9, 1955–)

George McGovern was defeated by one of the largest landslides in American political history. This senator from South Dakota, the "Prairie Populist" as he was sometimes called, was nonetheless a talented politician who managed to acquire and then retain a Senate seat as a liberal Democrat in the midst of rock-ribbed conservative and Republican South Dakota. His undoing as a presidential candidate was that his righteous indignation over the Vietnam War, the very characteristic that enabled him to capture the Democratic nomination, cast him in the mold of an unstable radical who could not be trusted with America's leadership.

McGovern was raised in a religious, relatively poor family in Avon, South Dakota, a small farming community in the southwest part of the state. His father was a minister in a fundamentalist Methodist sect. At the age of six, George moved with his family to Mitchell, South Dakota, where he was to remain until he graduated from high school in 1940. In many respects George was the archetypal minister's son: studious, serious, quiet, not prone to let his emotions be revealed. In later life he retained these qualities.

McGovern became one of the best high school debaters in the state, winning many contests both as a high school student and in college. Scholastic debating in South Dakota was an important activity, receiving the acclaim for its participants that rivaled the athletic endeavors of students in other states. It was through debate that McGovern met the identical twin Stegeberg sisters, who debated for the Woonsocket, South Dakota team. Ila and Eleanor Stegeberg's first encounter with McGovern's team resulted in a rout in favor of the Stegebergs. McGovern's romantic interest in these debate opponents first focused on Ila, but his discovery that she was already spoken for led him to begin a courtship of Eleanor. They were married in 1943, immediately before George left for Europe and World War II as a pilot.

McGovern enlisted in the Army Air Corps, having already learned to fly early in his college years. After being stationed at several bases while being trained, McGovern in February 1944, was sent overseas. He flew B-24 bombers in 35 missions over Europe, being based in Northern Africa. During his thirtieth mission, his plane was badly crippled and his navigator was killed. He managed to nurse the plane to an emergency base, barely avoiding a crash in the Mediterranean. He earned several medals for his valor and skill, including the Distinguished Flying Cross.

The war made McGovern a pacifist. Upon his return to the states, he reentered Dakota Wesleyan College in Mitchell and studied history and politics. He graduated in June 1946, and enrolled in Garrett Theological Seminary in Evanston, Illinois. Part of his seminary training was an assignment to a rural church as pastor, where two dozen parishioners for a service was a major turnout. McGovern enjoyed the preparation and delivery of the sermons, the "teaching" part of a minister's life, but was unhappy with other aspects of the ministry. Late in 1947 he decided to leave religious life. His sights were slowly changing towards politics and government.

McGovern entered the graduate history program at Northwestern University, across the street from the seminary that he had just left. Radical, even Communist-tinged politics had engulfed the students and some of the faculty. The Cold War infuriated and depressed McGovern and his peers. Many of those who had just finished fighting one war had no desire to fight another against Russia, a country that had been an ally. Henry Wallace, the Iowa populist and Franklin Roosevelt's vice president, was in 1948 the Progressive Party candidate for president. Wallace wanted to work with, not be adversaries against, the Soviet Union. He became McGovern's political hero. McGovern's enthusiasm was destroyed when he attended the 1948 Progressive Party convention in Philadelphia as a delegate from Illi-

nois. He was overwhelmed by the radicalism, perhaps even Communism, of many of his fellow delegates. McGovern's support for Wallace evaporated. He later said that he ultimately voted for Truman, or perhaps, did not vote at all.

McGovern received his master's degree in 1949 and then joined the faculty at Dakota Wesleyan in his hometown of Mitchell as a professor of history and political science. McGovern's professorial career almost detoured him from his political prominence, as an opening on the faculty of the University of Iowa appeared in 1952. McGovern's application for the position was runner-up among 80 applications. In considering what to do next, McGovern received an offer from the South Dakota state Democratic Party chairman, Ward Clark, to serve as a full-time executive secretary to organize the almost defunct party.

The Democrats in South Dakota, though never particularly robust, had in 1952 about withered to complete extinction. They were outnumbered at least three-to-one in party registration in every county in the state, and they had elected only two state legislators the previous November. There was no money or organization, and McGovern was expected to provide both if he took the position. After agonizing over the decision, McGovern followed his instincts and agreed to the task. He traveled the state tirelessly, raising money, talking to the "little people" as well as the newspaper editors and other leaders, even some Republicans. He compiled a massive voter/supporter card file for the state, a file that would be invaluable in his own campaigns. McGovern in many cases avoided the old-line Democratic leaders. He wanted party leaders who owed him loyalty. McGovern was fairly open about his dual purpose in the executive secretary position, and Ward Clark was expressly informed that being permitted to develop a personal organization was a precondition to his taking the otherwise thankless job.

By the spring of 1956, real signs of party health were evident. He considered a race against Republican Senator Francis Case, but passed it up to run for Congress in the First District against a four-term incumbent, Harold Lovre. McGovern threw himself into this race with his characteristic energy and personal campaign style, visiting as many of the towns throughout the district as he could, giving speeches and walking the streets almost non-stop. The Republicans took him lightly and did not campaign until after Labor Day, when polls showed a tight contest. It was too late, despite Lovre's scare campaign of painting McGovern as a Wallace radical. McGovern's first attempt at elective office resulted in a 12,000-vote victory. He was the first Democrat from South Dakota in Congress since 1936. McGovern was reelected in 1958 over even greater odds. The incumbent governor, who could not under state law run for another term, decided Congress was a good place to turn. The voters decided otherwise and McGovern beat Joe Foss by 15,000 votes.

In Washington, McGovern focused on farm issues. McGovern also became friends with Robert Kennedy. It was a friendship that developed slowly, but strongly until Robert Kennedy's assassination. McGovern carved out a liberal record. In 1960 he decided to run against United States Senator Karl Mundt. It was a difficult decision, as McGovern's congressional seat, after two hard-fought victories, was relatively secure. Perhaps more important than any other factor was that McGovern pictured Mundt as little more than a South Dakota Joe McCarthy. Good versus evil was the picture McGovern had of the contest. McGovern later told his biographer: "I don't know how he [Mundt] felt about me, but I knew I hated his guts." McGovern's campaign was perhaps the most negative of his career, and in some respects mirrored the obsession that characterized his campaign against Richard Nixon in 1972. He lost his perspective and it showed. John F. Kennedy, campaigning for the presidency, visited South Dakota. Many Democrats, fearful of a Kennedy backlash against them, refused to appear on the platform with him. McGovern's friendship and loyalty with the Kennedys made him an enthusiastic booster of the presidential nominee. That support added to McGovern's election woes. When the election was over, Kennedy had lost to Nixon by 50,999 votes in the state. McGovern did 35,000 votes better, but it was not enough.

That McGovern would be rewarded by the new Democratic president was obvious. Kennedy put him in charge of the Food for Peace program. McGovern traveled the world in an attempt to boost participation in the program. A considerable expansion in the country's effort to feed the world's starving and malnourished population resulted. Many credited McGovern with making real contributions to a major, but not well-publicized, success of the Kennedy administration. In 1962, Senator Francis Case, Republican, was up for reelection. He was a formidable opponent. Nonetheless, McGovern announced his resignation as director of the Food for Peace program in April 1962, to run against Case.

McGovern's prospects changed dramatically when Senator Case suffered a heart attack in late June and died. McGovern secured the Democratic nomination, and the Republicans turned to a state convention to name Case's successor. A lackluster former governor, Joe Bottum, was named. He was perhaps the candidate most likely to be beaten by McGovern. McGovern spent much of the fall campaign in a hospital bed after he contracted hepatitis, probably from an inoculation before one of his overseas trips as Food for Peace director. He won by what initially was a 100-vote margin. After a recount it grew to 597 votes. He was the first Democratic senator from the state in 26 years.

Regardless of the issues, McGovern voted according to the liberal Americans for Democratic Action organization as one of the most consistent liberals in the Senate. His one exceptional year was 1968, when he trimmed his sails in anticipation of his reelection campaign, a not-uncommon tactic among conservative and liberal politicians whose views are out-of-step with the general philosophies of their constituents. Some of the more strident opponents of Kennedy and then Johnson's Vietnam policies, such as Wayne Morse of Oregon, criticized McGovern's early inconsistency on the war. His defense was that he was trying to work quietly to end the war and not make speeches. The more likely explanation is that not only was he personally torn over what to do concerning the war, but an anti-war posture would not appeal to his South Dakota voters. When McGovern finally joined the "doves," he was perhaps the most extreme. As his biographer called it, Vietnam was McGovern's "magnificent obsession." He did not just disagree with, but became angry at many of those supporting the war. An early friendship with Hubert Humphrey was irretrievably strained by Humphrey's support of President Johnson's Vietnam policies. Johnson himself, after several personal attempts to dissuade McGovern from his attacks, became a bitter opponent. President Nixon did not seem to be removing the United States from the war fast enough, so McGovern joined an anti-war march called the Mobilization. He became permanently allied in many voters' minds with the most radical, and at times violent, elements of the peace movement.

McGovern was up for reelection in 1968. That also was a presidential election year. In 1967, McGovern began to consider running against President Johnson. McGovern's first choice was Bobby Kennedy, but Kennedy refused to run. McGovern eventually concluded that he would be throwing away his Senate seat with no prospect of winning the presidency. Eugene McCarthy had some early success, causing Kennedy to get into the race. McGovern was one of Kennedy's strongest supporters. On June 5, 1968, Kennedy won the Democratic presidential primary in South Dakota by a wide margin over Humphrey and McCarthy. McGovern phoned the results in to Kennedy, who was in Los Angeles waiting out the results of the California primary held the same day. After a short phone conversation with Kennedy, McGovern went to bed. A little later that evening, Kennedy was assassinated by Sirhan Sirhan.

Some Kennedy advisers immediately turned to McGovern as a substitute candidate. McGovern wanted Ted Kennedy to fill that role, but the remaining Kennedy brother was adamantly against it. On July 13, the South Dakota delegation to the national convention, which had been elected for Robert Kennedy, voted to remain uncommitted, but secretly were for McGovern if he would announce. McGovern withdrew to a mountain resort in the Black Hills of western South Dakota to consider what to do. Deciding that there was

a chance to win, particularly if the Kennedy delegation from California would stand with him, McGovern announced that he was a candidate on August 10. The national reaction to his candidacy was incredulity and even ridicule. Teddy Kennedy's name reappeared, hampering McGovern's efforts. The California delegation ignored him. Hubert Humphrey's first-ballot victory was secured with 1,760 votes, trailed by McCarthy with 601 and McGovern's 146.

McGovern returned to South Dakota to reignite his Senate campaign. Archie Gubbrud, a former governor, was the Republican nominee. McGovern was fortunate in the choice of his opponent, a hulking, six foot, four-inch farmer whose excitement quotient was in negative numbers. McGovern demonstrated his political acumen and appeal, at least in South Dakota, by winning reelection with 57 percent of the vote.

The Vietnam War continued to be McGovern's main concern, but he also focused on world hunger. In 1969 he headed a select committee to examine hunger in the United States, and made much-publicized trips to slums in the South in order to demonstrate the severity of the problem. The committee's work led to passage of an improved food stamp and welfare reform package.

McGovern accepted an exceedingly thankless task, or so many thought, when he took the chairmanship of a reform committee to revise the rules for selecting delegates to the Democratic National Convention. Much as he had done as executive secretary of the South Dakota party, McGovern used this party position to benefit his own ambitions, this time his presidential ambitions. The nomination rules were rewritten, with much greater emphasis on primaries, on minority and female participation, and on the removal of control by party leaders. An insurgent's opportunities were greatly enhanced by the new rules. No one understood their operation better than McGovern.

In early 1969, McGovern made his commitment to run for the presidency in 1972. He hired additional staff to run the campaign, and he traveled the country extensively if haphazardly. After typical organizational and strategy problems, he hired some new campaign staff. Gary Hart, himself a future presidential candidate, but at this time a lawyer in Colorado, took charge of overall campaign management. Intensive campaigning in early key states made McGovern a media surprise after the Iowa caucuses in January 1972, and in other early contests. His stridence about the Vietnam War had increased. He was to the vast majority of the electorate a one-issue candidate. Committed volunteers, particularly college-age youth, dominated his campaign. He also tried to develop a new welfare program that would scrap the entire present system and give $1,000 to every person in the country. Taxation would then result in those above the poverty income level having to repay the money in a graduated schedule. McGovern was lambasted as a simpleton in the economic area. He spent the early part of the campaign explaining the proposal and the latter part abandoning it.

By May 1, despite some stumbles, McGovern was the clear favorite to win the nomination. The party leadership in many instances was aghast at this "prairie populist" taking over the party. An "Anybody but McGovern" effort began, but it was to no avail. The delegates being sent to the convention in Miami were his delegates, young, minority groups, not previously involved in politics and owing no allegiance to anyone but McGovern and his peace platform. McGovern won easily on the first ballot. His selection of first-term Missouri Senator Tom Eagleton was initially well received. Within days, however, revelations about Eagleton's past history of mental troubles surfaced. McGovern's initial announcement that he was behind his running mate "1000 percent" haunted him after he asked Eagleton to resign from the ticket. McGovern was embarrassed further by being rejected by the following would-be replacements: Ted Kennedy, Hubert Humphrey, Abraham Ribicoff, Edmund Muskie, and Reubin Askew. Finally Kennedy-in-law Sargent Shriver accepted McGovern's offer, and the choice was ratified by the Democratic National Committee.

The campaign rocked from one disaster to another. The peace issue that had won the primaries for McGovern had already garnered all the support possible. Against Nixon, who had just made politically and historically dramatic visits to Red China and Russia, the issue seemed naive and almost treasonous. The war seemed to be winding down. McGovern's promise to end the war immediately, even by "crawling" to the enemy, the North Vietnamese, was disastrous. The Watergate scandal that was to drag Nixon out of office after it exploded in March of 1973 was the weapon that vice presidential candidate Shriver's tried to use, with no effect. The populace was not ready to abandon Nixon over that issue, poorly supported by hard evidence as yet.

McGovern won only 38 percent of the vote, one state plus the District of Columbia, to Nixon's 61 percent and 49 states. States that had never voted for Republicans did this time, and even that bastion of Democratic liberalism, New York City, almost went Republican. South Dakota voted for Nixon 163,000 to 137,000. The rejection was total.

McGovern returned to the Senate a defeated but unchastened man. A former Vietnam prisoner of war, Leo Thorsness, was his opponent when McGovern ran for reelection in 1974. The campaign was bitter. Thorsness told South Dakotans of the vow he made while a prisoner, that McGovern, who the Republican felt had prolonged the war by aid and comfort to the enemy, would not be retained in this position of honor. Thorsness was not a good campaigner, however. Nixon's resignation in August and McGovern's own campaign skills were too much for Thorsness. McGovern's luck also helped, as a potentially more formidable challenger, Al Schock, had lost in the Republican Primary. The Democrats had a great year nationwide in 1974. The factors that made that occur also helped McGovern win a 53–47 percent victory.

McGovern briefly considered getting into the 1976 presidential race, but never did. There were some public opinion polls taken after Nixon's resignation that showed even in his humiliation, Nixon would defeat McGovern in a rerun of the 1972 election. McGovern did remain an active, outspoken, liberal Senator. In 1980, the irony of conservative, Republican South Dakota sending McGovern to the Senate came to an end. In his race for a fourth term, McGovern was defeated by James Abdnor, a four-term congressman who in some respects fit the mold of McGovern's earlier opponents: personally unexciting, a poor stump speaker, even having a minor speech impediment. But folksy, conservative Jim Abdnor beat McGovern by 55 percent to 45 percent. McGovern blamed his defeat on the negativism of a far-right national organization whose acronym, NCPAC, the National Conservative Political Action Committee, was seen on literature and commercials against several liberal Democratic senators in 1980, most of whom lost.

McGovern vowed to create a counterweight to conservative negativism and form his own liberal organization to try to elect liberal Democrats in the 1982 elections and beyond. This group, Americans for Common Sense, raised a million dollars for Democrats in the 1982 elections, but was not an important factor. As the 1984 presidential election approached, McGovern said that the lack of vigorously liberal Democratic contenders made it feasible for him to run again. On September 13, 1983, with few of his old supporters still with him, the still-intensely liberal South Dakotan announced again for president. His wife Eleanor said she would not campaign. It was a sad event for old friends and a point for ridicule by his more numerous foes, as McGovern's presidential aspirations were now compared to those of perennial loser, but always candidate, Harold Stassen. Though he brushed aside claims that he had no realistic chance of winning, at other times the former Democratic presidential nominee seemed to admit that his only purpose was to pressure the other contenders into more liberal positions. On March 13, after a disappointing finish in the Massachusetts primary, McGovern withdrew from the race. He had finished no higher than fourth place in previous primaries.

McGovern stayed a spokesman for liberal politics, writing and speaking on foreign policy and other issues. He became president of the Middle East Policy Council. He also involved himself in a at least one business venture. The business was the Stratford Motor Inn in Connecticut, which McGovern bought in late 1988. It was 30 years old and unprofitable. McGovern tried for two years to make it a success, but ended up filing for bankruptcy.

In 1991 George Bush appeared after the Persian Gulf War to be nearly unbeatable. Most significant national Democratic leaders declined to run. McGovern said in December 1990 that he might run. By March 1991 he was campaigning in Iowa, still saying that he wished younger, "less battle-scarred" candidates would emerge. He said that George Bush was formidable, but presciently noted that six months after Churchill helped win World War II, the British electorate threw him out of office. Finally on May 23, 1991, McGovern announced that he would not be a candidate. His 1972 Arkansas chairman, Bill Clinton, was evaluating whether to be a candidate, but only former Massachusetts senator Paul Tsongas had yet announced.

The worst tragedy of his life was still ahead. McGovern's daughter Terry had struggled with alcoholism since she was a teenager, taking her first drink at 13. On December 12, 1994, at age 45, Terry slipped out of the Madison, Wisconsin, detoxification center where she was being treated. It was bitterly cold the night she left the center. She froze to death, and was found the next morning in an alley, covered with snow. McGovern wrote a book to tell Terry's story and perhaps to help deal with the pain.

Analysis of Qualifications

Richard Nixon got just what he wanted from the Democratic national convention in 1972 — a candidate that the American voter almost certainly could not buy. In the midst of a war against North Vietnam, McGovern said North Vietnam was fighting a war for independence. In the midst of widespread concern for the declining morals and increasing permissiveness in America, McGovern could easily be attacked by using the code phrase of the anti–McGovern campaign — acid, amnesty and abortion. The "acid" was actually an alliterative compromise meant to refer to marijuana, and McGovern was supposedly in favor of legalizing its use. Actually, he backed off any support of legalization but did say he opposed jail sentences for possession. Abortion he did favor, saying that the decision was solely one for the woman and her doctor. And finally, on amnesty, McGovern supported amnesty from prosecution for draft evaders and conscientious objectors, but not deserters. Postwar forgiveness of those unwilling to fight has been a tradition in America, and indeed after Vietnam was concluded President Gerald Ford and Congress did approve a form of amnesty. Yet McGovern's vowing that such amnesty would occur even while the war persisted invited severe criticism from those concerned about morale and discipline within the armed services.

Several aspects of the McGovern character reveal themselves in his political life. His campaign biographer noted the extreme confidence and egotism that evidenced itself. When no one else saw the effort as credible, McGovern ran for the 1968 presidential nomination. Even during the depths of the 1972 general election campaign debacle, McGovern seemed oblivious to the unavoidability of his overwhelming defeat. McGovern's confidence was wrapped up in his devotion to his cause, the cause of peace, the cause of virtue against venality. Such self-righteousness can cause political defeat, and could destroy a presidency.

McGovern also exhibited gracelessness under pressure in the extremely difficult Eagleton situation. Much of the fault for the matter must lie at Eagleton's doorstep, as more candor by the vice presidential nominee would have saved McGovern the entire embarrassment. Yet McGovern fails too, for he offered "1000 per cent" support to Eagleton simultaneously with deciding to dump him from the ticket. Once the decision was made to select a new running mate, Eagleton was not immediately told. Eagleton heard news stories that McGovern had briefed reporters that the decision had been made to dump him. McGovern's inability to confront staff or subordinates had surfaced during his Senate career. Such squeamishness would not have well served a president.

The anti–McGovern cast to the vote in 1972 is overwhelming. That Richard Nixon, unloved even if grudgingly respected, could have enjoyed one of the great landslide presidential victories is unfathomable except on the basis of a complete rejection of his opponent. McGovern was seen as rash and irresponsible,

his judgment questionable and his views unacceptable. He represented the moralist and idealist in politics, rigid and incapable of dealing with the different shades between black and white.

McGovern's twin among the defeated presidential candidates is William Jennings Bryan. Both were preachers, moralists, ideologues, whose hearts and compassion were sincere but whose judgments never gained the respect of a majority of their countrymen.

McGOVERN BIBLIOGRAPHY

Anson, Robert Sam. *McGovern: A Biography.* New York City (1972).

Blumenfield, Laura. "The Life and Death of Teresa McGovern." *Newsday* (February 14, 1995), Part II, p. 3.

Bowman, Kevin Eugen. "George McGovern and the Vietnam War." Unpublished master's thesis, Florida State University (1995).

Dougherty, Richard. *Goodbye Mr. Christian: A Personal Account of McGovern's Rise and Fall.* Garden City (1973).

"Front and Center for George McGovern." *Time* (May 8, 1972), pp. 16–23.

Goldman, Peter, and Richard Stout. "McGovern's Politics of Righteousness." *Newsweek* (Nov. 6, 1972), pp. 43–44.

Hart, Gary. *Right from the Start: A Chronicle of the McGovern Campaign.* New York City (1973).

Knight, Jerry. "Innkeeper George McGovern Files for Reorganization." *Washington Post* (November 7, 1990) pp. G1, G12.

"Living Well is the Best Revenge." *Newsweek* (May 23, 1983), p. 12.

Mailer, Norman. *St. George and the Godfather.* New York City (1983).

Max, Nicholas (pseud.). *President McGovern's First Term.* Garden City (1973) (novel).

McGovern, Eleanor. *Uphill: A Personal Story.* Boston (1974).

McGovern, George S. *An American Journey: The Presidential Campaign Speeches of George McGovern.* New York City (1974).

_____. *Grassroots: The Autobiography of George McGovern.* New York (1977).

_____. *Terry: My Daughter's Life-and-Death Struggle with Alcoholism.* Villard (1996).

"McGovern on the Issues." *Time* (Feb. 14, 1972), p. 11.

"McGovern: Who He Is, What He Stands For." *U.S. News & World Report* (June 26, 1972), pp. 21–24.

Michaels, Marguerite, "Why They Can't Leave." *Parade Magazine* (Nov. 28, 1982), p. 16.

THOMAS EAGLETON (left) and GEORGE McGOVERN
(Courtesy of AP/Wide World Photos)

"Now, It's a New Democratic Race." *Newsweek* (May 8, 1972), pp. 22ff.

Span, Paula. "It's Motel McGovern, the Inn Place." *Washington Post* (March 1, 1990), pp. B1, B4.

"Those Other Campaigners, Pat and Eleanor." *Time* (Oct. 9, 1972), pp. 14–20.

Weil, Gordon Lee. *The Long Shot: George McGovern Runs for President.* New York City (1973).

"What McGovern Thinks." *Time* (June 26, 197 2), pp. 15–19.

Witker, Kristi. *How to Lose Everything in Politics Except Massachusetts.* New York City (1974).

Family data provided by Olive McGovern Briles, Sisseton, S.D., and by Susan McGovern, Madison, Wisconsin.

---

*1972 vice presidential nominee—
Democratic Party*

Tom Eagleton

Full name: Thomas Francis Eagleton.

State represented: Missouri.

Birth: September 4, 1929, St. Louis, Missouri.

Age on Inauguration Day (January 20, 1973): 43 years, 4½ months.

Education: St. Louis Country Day School; Amherst College, graduated cum laude, 1950; Harvard Law School, graduated cum laude, 1953; admitted to Missouri Bar in 1953.

Religion: Roman Catholic.

Ancestry: Irish ancestors; Mark Eagleton (father) held office in St. Louis, unsuccessful candidate for mayor.

Occupation: Attorney.

Public offices: St. Louis Circuit Attorney, 1956–1960; Missouri Attorney General, 1960–1964; Missouri lieutnenant governor, 1964–1968; U.S. senator from Missouri, December 27, 1968–January 3, 1987, retired; nominated by Democratic Party for vice president, July 13, 1972, withdrew July 31, 1972.

Home: St. Louis, Missouri; his home while serving in the Senate was a large colonial-style house in Chevy Chase, Maryland.

Personal characteristics: 6' tall; graying hair.

Father: Mark Eagleton (c. 1895–); lawyer, politician.

Mother: Zitta Louise Swanson (?–1948).

Siblings: Mark Eagleton, Jr., (1925–).

Wife: Barbara Ann Smith (1934–) married February 12, 1956.

Children: Terence Francis (1959–) Christin (1963–); she has worked in television news.

After his relinquishment of the 1972 vice presidential nomination, Tom Eagleton was described as someone who had turned "defeat into victory, humiliation into triumph, liability into asset, mental instability into immense political clout" (Shana Alexander in *Newsweek,* November 13, 1972). Though not the only man to give up a vice presidential nomination, Eagleton stands alone in the political benefits that seemed to flow from that decision.

Eagleton was born into an exceedingly political family. His father Mark was elected to several local offices in St. Louis, but would later lose his bid for mayor of that city. Tom was only 11 when he went with his father to the 1940 Republican national convention, where the elder Eagleton voted for Wendell Willkie. This was the last time the Eagletons found themselves allied with the GOP, as shortly thereafter Mark Eagleton's attraction to Franklin D. Roosevelt convinced him to switch parties. Tom's father was a successful attorney in St. Louis, having risen from the poverty of his own father, an immigrant laborer from County Cork, Ireland. Before Mark ran for mayor, he had served stormy terms as president of the board of education. Mark was a reformer on the school board. He denounced the practice of sending black schools the worn-out equipment from white schools, publicly aired charges of nepotism and corruption in the school administration, and otherwise made the established power structure uncomfortable. Mark resigned his position on the police board because he opposed the governor's decision that policemen who had joined a union should be barred from promotion. The senior Eagleton was described as "kind of a Midwestern Joe Kennedy." He instilled by example and persuasion the need to excel, encouraging, even pushing Tom to develop political interests and skills. Mark Eagleton's boy would be no normal Southern politician.

A successful law practice enabled Mark Eagleton to send his children to the best schools St. Louis had to offer, including the exclusive prep academy Country Day School. That a political career was planned for Tom seems evident in the special tutoring he received, including public speaking lessons and instruction on public affairs. "Field trips" in this kind of educational environment included traveling to Fulton, Missouri, in 1946 to hear the historic speech by Winston Churchill, in which he first characterized communist Europe as being behind an "Iron Curtain." The next stop in this political development was Amherst, Massachusetts, where Tom attended the small, private men's college there and took a summer off for additional public speaking coursework at Northwestern University. The summer after graduation in 1950 he spent in Oxford, and then he returned to Massachusetts to start three brilliant years at Harvard Law School. At each school Tom graduated with honors, and at Harvard he was particularly honored by selection as editor of the Law Review. He was admitted to the bar in St. Louis in 1953. Just as significantly, he was returning home to await a political opening.

Eagleton joined his father's St. Louis law firm. He was assistant general counsel for the Anheuser-Busch brewery. In 1956, he wanted to run for St. Louis Prosecuting Attorney. His father did not agree with the choice of offices. Not in agreement either was his wife of three weeks, Barbara. She had asked before their marriage whether he was going to get into politics, and his reply was, "Of course not!" Three weeks after their wedding he announced to her his decision to run. At 27 years of age, Eagleton became the youngest prosecuting attorney in St. Louis history. The office was overwhelmed with a caseload that had been backing up for years, and young circuit attorney Eagleton reduced that burden by two-thirds. His was strongly opposed to wiretapping, which he described as a "dirty business."

The next office in which Eagleton would become the youngest man ever elected was Missouri attorney general. His victory for attorney general in 1960 made him the first Roman Catholic to win statewide Missouri office. He was also the only Democratic statewide candidate that year who actively supported the nomination and election of John Kennedy for president. A seemingly innocuous article appeared in the local papers shortly after his election, but it was a significant portent for his future:

> Circuit Attorney Thomas F. Eagleton is a patient in Barnes Hospital suffering from a virus, his father, Mark Eagleton, said today. He probably will remain ten or more days, his father said. His illness was complicated by hard work in his successful campaign for the office of Attorney General.

This December 17, 1960, announcement did not disclose that Eagleton had checked into the hospital's psychiatric ward for electric shock treatment, the first of two such series of treatments he would receive. The rumor circulating in Missouri about the new Attorney General was that he had a drinking problem.

As Attorney General, Eagleton enlarged upon his liberal credentials. Opposition to capital punishment, support for consumer protection, and increased availability of court-appointed attorneys for indigent criminal defendants were high points of his term. Consumer protection was elusive, as the attorney general was given very little authority in the area. Nonetheless, Eagleton sent letters to firms that were accused by consumers of bad business practices, stating that they would have 15 days to correct the abuses or else they would be listed with the Consumer Protection Division as violators. Even though the attorney general's office could not take any steps beyond the threatening letter, the usually intimidated company would attempt to rectify the offending situation.

The attorney general was a good politician, obviously on the move, but he took unconventional approaches to advancement. Eagleton became a statewide personality by taking highly controversial public stands on issues. Civil rights legislation received his fervent support; he condemned capital punishment and wiretapping. He was attracting attention if not always adoration, and he was definitely in an enviable political position. In 1964, he again succeeded in being elected as the youngest man in Missouri history to a position, this time as lieutenant governor. And again, a minor newspaper footnote concealed a political time bomb:

> Attorney General Thomas F. Eagleton entered Mayo Brothers Clinic in Rochester, Minnesota yesterday for some tests.
>
> The Attorney General, who was elected Lieutenant Governor in November, reported losing about 14 pounds in the last two weeks. He is expected to remain in the clinic about three days.

Eagleton had again been overcome by exhaustion from campaigning.

As lieutenant governor, Eagleton was entrusted by the governor with increasingly important functions. He chaired several study commissions on state problems. In 1966, he returned to the Mayo Clinic after having been involved heavily in preparations for a statewide education conference. The newspapers reported the event, this time with the cover that he was suffering from gastric disturbances. For the second time, however, Eagleton received electric shock treatment for depression and fatigue, and received intensive psychiatric counseling.

Never ceasing in his effort to excel, Eagleton next took on incumbent Democratic senator Edward V. Long. In 1967, the senator had become involved in a Teamsters Union scandal, and Eagleton sought to move up politically. In a three-way primary race in 1968, Eagleton won with 37 percent of the vote. In a series of debates against his Republican opponent, Thomas B. Curtis, a respected, able 18-year veteran of the House, Eagleton attacked Curtis's conservative voting record. The lieutenant governor called for a bombing halt in Vietnam, a draft lottery, and strong gun control legislation. They were courageous, but not terribly popular stands. Eagleton barely escaped becoming the first Democratic nominee for statewide office to lose to a Republican in over 20 years. He squeaked through with 51.5 percent of the vote, winning nearly all the black vote and therefore the election. The new senator had learned to pace himself better, as he would later explain, and there was no recurrence of his need for hospitalization after this strenuous election campaign.

Eagleton established a reputation for hard work and liberal views. In 1971, he said, "I want to be regarded as a great United States senator. I'd like to be reelected three terms, acquire some seniority, get some good committees and hear James Reston or David Brinkley say some day, "He's a pretty good senator. He works hard at it." Mark Eagleton would not have said it better. In late 1969, Eagleton cosponsored a resolution making political reform in South Vietnam a condition for further American support of that government. He believed that American military power was forcing an unpopular government on the South Vietnamese people and that this country should completely and rapidly withdraw. By 1972, Eagleton had decided that the only American goal in Vietnam should be to get out, making certain that the prisoners of war were first rescued. Only on the question of the draft did Eagleton stray from accepted liberal dogma, as he believed that an all-volunteer army would be a poor-person army, attracting the unemployed and poorly educated who could not find good civilian jobs. He argued against many defense department appropriations, including money for a sophisticated tank which he found to be obsolete, and for an anti-ballistic missile system.

On domestic issues, Eagleton was similarly allied with the Democratic liberal wing. He voted against the appointments of Clement Haynsworth and G. Harrold Carswell to the Supreme Court in 1969, but on the slightly less controversial appointment of William Rehnquist voted in favor of President Nixon's nominee. By mid-1972, Eagleton had amassed a 90 percent favorable voting record in the eyes of the liberal Americans for Democratic Action, while the conservative groups found his support to be almost nil.

In the 1972 Democratic battle for the presidency, Eagleton first sided with Ed Muskie, the 1968 vice presidential nominee. Muskie's campaign was soon floundering, and Eagleton at the convention voted with McGovern on crucial procedural issues that sealed McGovern's nomination. McGovern's staff had given little consideration to the vice presidential slot. Part of the reason is that the hectic convention, with a majority of delegates being inexperienced in national politics, was careening from one crisis and uprising to another. Eagleton was on McGovern's list of possibilities, but was a long shot. As the final day of the convention

opened, McGovern still had no idea whom to select. At 9:15 A.M. on nomination day, McGovern's staff sat down to draw up possibilities. The unstructured meeting that McGovern had insisted upon produced at times good suggestions, at others completely fanciful ones, such as a national news commentator, and a consumer activist. This was definitely "new politics." Seven names appeared on the final list, including Eagleton's, but his was near the bottom. McGovern decided on Mayor Kevin White of Boston. The mayor accepted, but strong opposition from inside the Massachusetts delegation reversed McGovern's tentative decision. McGovern then decided on his friend Gaylord Nelson, a Wisconsin senator. Nelson refused, but recommended Eagleton. A 4:00 P.M. deadline had been imposed by the convention for submission of vice presidential nomination petitions, and after Nelson's phone call refusing the offer it was 3:25. Rumors about drinking and mental problems by Eagleton had been conveyed to McGovern, but the quick investigation that had been made did not confirm the stories. McGovern's assistant investigating the matter told the presidential nominee he had no proof to disqualify Eagleton. At 3:40 Eagleton received a phone call from McGovern, making the surprising, last-second offer.

By that time Eagleton had despaired of being nominated. He had been included in the pre-convention speculation as a running mate to the expected presidential candidate, McGovern. He and Barbara Eagleton had even discussed what to do about this hidden history of psychiatric examinations and treatment. The decision had been made that it was a private affair, that he was cured, and he could now pace himself so as to avoid recurrences. No need to reveal the past was perceived. Subsequent accounts from the McGovern and Eagleton camps would differ on whether direct questions to Eagleton on possible problems were posed. What is clear is that Eagleton was astounded and pleased, and told McGovern that he wanted to accept immediately before McGovern changed his mind. The generally published version of the exchange between Eagleton and a McGovern campaign official is that the proposed nominee was asked if he had any skeletons in his closet, and Eagleton replied that he did not. Other versions state that specific, detailed questions were asked about possible background problems. Regardless of the detail, it is evident that Eagleton revealed nothing about the past episodes.

Almost immediately stories about Eagleton's past surfaced. Anonymous tips went to McGovern's headquarters and to the Detroit *Free Press*, that Eagleton had been given shock treatments. The specific St. Louis hospital was named. The stories gradually intensified, and McGovern's staff called Eagleton about the matter. It was decided that Eagleton should meet McGovern at the presidential nominee's vacation lodge at Sylvan Lake, in the South Dakota Black Hills. It was the same vacation spot where four years earlier McGovern had been persuaded that a presidential race was feasible. There on July 25, eleven days after being nominated, Eagleton was explaining why he desired to remain on the ticket. McGovern remained seemingly unconcerned about the impact of Eagleton's past on the public, and accepted his running mate's assurances that the problems were all behind him. The decision was made by McGovern against the arguments of his advisers to have an immediate press conference explaining the situation and giving complete support to the continuation of the ticket. Eagleton met the press at the hastily called conference and revealed the three hospitalizations. In dignified but nervous tones, Eagleton also revealed after questioning that he had received psychiatric counseling and shock treatments. The long conference concluded, Eagleton said, "this is not the most enjoyable moment in my forty-two years on earth [but] it's not the most unenjoyable either." McGovern then responded that he continued to be confident that Eagleton was "the best possible man I could find in this country to run with me," and he said that knowing what he did now about his running mate's past, he would still select him. In response to a question the next day, McGovern chose these unforgettable words: "I am one-thousand percent for Tom Eagleton and have no intention of dropping him from the ticket." In fact, McGovern's staff was already nearing the conclusion that the Missouri senator would have to be abandoned.

Eagleton continued to campaign and was buoyed by his reception. He soon became a favorite of the crowds for his good-humored doggedness in the face of adversity. Yet mounting calls for his resignation were coming from newspaper editorial columns, party leaders, and McGovern staffers. Syndicated columnist Jack Anderson dredged up and published an unsubstantiated story that Eagleton had been arrested for drunk driving, though he later retracted the story. Finally McGovern became convinced that Eagleton would be a continuing political liability regardless of his competence for the presidency, that he dominated the news and kept other issues from being discussed, and that consequently he must withdraw. In Senate chambers at the Capitol on July 31, the two running mates met and agreed, after a two-hour discussion, that Eagleton should resign.

Though a candidate only 17 days, Eagleton was a celebrity. His frequent appearances on behalf of the new Democratic ticket, McGovern-Shriver, were well-received. Even in strong Republican areas Eagleton was warmly cheered by sympathetic crowds. They may not have been disagreeing with the decision to drop Eagleton from the ticket, but the crowds appeared to want him to understand they supported and respected him.

The election would almost certainly have been lost without the Eagleton debacle, and few blamed him for defeat. He returned to his sharp criticisms of the Nixon domestic and foreign policies, and found his political stock in Missouri soaring. His 1974 reelection campaign hardly needed the boost, but the Watergate scandals that had forced Nixon's resignation perhaps were some ironic balancing of the scales for Eagleton. He won overwhelmingly in an overwhelming Democratic year.

In the next six years, Eagleton continued to build on his solidly national Democratic voting record, for organized labor, against many defense projects, for civil rights legislation. In 1980, Eagleton's record and the Republican tide nationally almost defeated him in conservative Missouri. A strong Republican challenger named Gene McNary capitalized on the public's desire for less government generally, but more military spending. Eagleton eked through with 52 percent of the vote, his margin coming almost exclusively from Kansas City. An unsavory issue was injected into the campaign when one of Eagleton's nieces attempted to extort two hundred thousand dollars from the senator by threatening to publicize fictitious moral charges about him. Eagleton ignored the threat and the niece was indicted for extortion. On October 24, 1980, barely a week before the election, the niece and her lawyer were found guilty. She admitted in court that the allegations were "wild, preposterous, and ridiculous."

Eagleton retired from the Senate in 1987. Later in the year he testified before the Senate Judiciary Committee, opposing the nomination of Robert Bork to the Supreme Court. He said Bork's "views are vintage George III."

Analysis of Qualifications

A senator from border-state Missouri took great political risks in embracing liberal Democratic positions, but Tom Eagleton did so and survived. Few firmer opponents of the Vietnam War existed in the United States Senate after he arrived there in 1968, and few could compare with his support for civil rights legislation. If nothing else, Tom Eagleton had courage. He made his political name by taking controversial stands. Many a faceless, principleless nonentity has been selected to fill the need for a vice presidential running mate. Tom Eagleton was not one of these.

Eagleton was driven by ambition, driven to increasingly higher office at record-establishing young ages, and perhaps driven to mental exhaustion and depression. His father helped establish and direct that drive for excellence, and success appeared early as Tom graduated with honors from every school he attended. This senator-to-be received tutoring in the skills required for political success, especially public speaking. Along the way, Eagleton also acquired a witty, self-deprecating manner that enabled him to avoid taking his victories too seriously.

Eagleton's high-strung, nervous intensity to perform was obvious in the offices he won. He worked hard and long, and he remarked that politics was his life. Where others had recreational, escapist hobbies, Eagleton relaxed with political biographies. He called politics in

his life's blood, and it apparently is. He inherited it from his father.

Once Eagleton was nominated for vice president, he was described by one knowledgeable source as more liberal than McGovern. The characterization is wrong if it implies Eagleton was rigid in his reaction to issues. He differed from McGovern by supporting the military draft, since the Missourian believed that besides rights there were also responsibilities in America. One of the obligations was sharing in defending the country. He opposed the nominations to the Supreme Court of Clement Haynsworth, a dignified and competent judge who unfortunately lacked candor in describing possible conflicts of interest, and of G. Harrold Carswell, who had not in his short judicial service established credentials adequate for the high court. However, when another controversial nominee was presented, William Rehnquist, Eagleton swallowed his serious philosophical differences with the nominee, saying that a senator's function was to review a nominee's professional and ethical qualifications; it was for the president to select the judicial philosophy.

Senator Eagleton is well respected by his peers, by the newspapermen who cover him, and apparently by the Missouri voters. He has shown competence in the offices he held. He is gregarious, good-humored, and fond of practical jokes. He has made few enemies in politics, though he has many opponents. Regardless of agreement with his political views, people have found him an able champion of the causes in which he believes. Closely matching if not completely mirroring the views of his running mate, Tom Eagleton had an openmindedness on issues not always revealed by McGovern. Eagleton was removed from the ticket because many Americans wondered whether his medical history might indicate future problems with mental endurance. That mental determination was not conclusively made even by doctors. Even assuming a possibility of further difficulties with stress, Tom Eagleton was an extremely competent public servant. His severe trials in 1972, and hard-fought electoral and congressional contests since then, revealed mental strength. He was a cut above most running mates.

EAGLETON BIBLIOGRAPHY

Apple, R.W., Jr. "Eagleton Is Firm Despite Pressure by 2 Party Chiefs." *New York Times* (July 31, 1972), p. 1.

Barone, Michael, and Grant Ujifusa. *The Almanac of American Politics, 1982.* Washington (1982), pp. 608–609.

Darst, Stephen. "Eagleton's Wake." *Harper's Magazine* (December 1972), pp. 76–80.

Douth, George. *Leaders in Profile: The United States Senate.* New York City (1975), pp. 380–386.

Eagleton, Thomas. *War and Presidential Power: A Chronicle of Congressional Surrender.* New York City (1974).

"The Eagleton Decision." *Commonweal* 96 (August 11, 1972), pp. 419–420.

"Eagleton Niece Convicted in Extortion Conspiracy." *New York Times* (October 25, 1980), p. 11.

"Eagleton Niece Tells Court of a Plan for Deception." *New York Times* (October 24, 1980), p. 14.

"Excerpts from Eagleton News Parley." *New York Times* (July 26, 1972), p. 20.

Hendrickson, Paul. "Eagleton's Return Trip; the Missouri Senator and the Summer of '72." *Washington Post* (June 20, 1984), p. B1.

Kifner, John. "The Rise and Fall of Tom Eagleton." *New York Times* (August 1, 1972), p. 24.

Kneeland, Douglas E. "Eagleton Tells McGovern It Was 'the Only Decision.'" *New York Times* (August 1, 1972), p. 1.

_____. "Eagleton Tells of Shock Therapy on Two Occasions." *New York Times* (July 26, 1972), p. 1.

Lydon, Christopher. "Missouri's Contribution to the Ticket: Thomas Francis Eagleton." *New York Times* (July 14, 1972), p. 10.

McGinniss, J. "I'll Tell You Who's Bitter, My Aunt Hazel." *Life* (August 18, 1972), pp. 30–31.

"McGovern, Eagleton Statements and News Parley." *New York Times* (August 1, 1972), p. 25.

Naughton, James M. "Eagleton Illness Known to Associates." *New York Times* (July 26, 1972), p. 20.

"Sen. Eagleton Denies Niece's Charge." *New York Times* (October 23, 1980), p. B–12.

"Tom Eagleton." *The New Republic* (August 5 & 12, 1972), p. 9.

Viorst, Milton. "Did Tom Eagleton Do Anything Wrong?" *Esquire* (February 1973), pp. 59–63 ff.

*1972 vice presidential nominee —
Democratic Party*

Sargent Shriver

Full name: Robert Sargent Shriver, Jr.

State represented: Maryland.

Birth: November 9, 1915, in Westminster, Maryland.

Age on Inauguration Day (January 20, 1973): 57 years, 2½ months.

Education: Parochial schools in Westminster and Baltimore, Maryland; Browning School in New York City, then Canterbury in New Milford, Connecticut, graduated, 1934; Yale University, 1934–1938 (B.A. *cum laude*), LL.B. 1941.

Religion: Roman Catholic.

Ancestry/prominent relatives: First Shrivers living in Maryland by 1693; wife is Eunice Kennedy, whose brothers included John, Robert, and Edward Kennedy.

Occupation: Attorney, businessman.

Public offices: Appointed to Chicago board of education, 1954–1960, elected president, October 26, 1955; director of Peace Corps, 1961–1966; director of Office of Economic Opportunity, 1964–1968; mentioned as Democratic candidate for governor of Illinois, 1960, and as vice presidential nominee, 1964 and 1968; ambassador to France, 1968–1970; considered running for governor of Maryland, 1970; unsuccessful Democratic nominee for vice president, 1972; unsuccessful candidate for president, 1976.

Home: Timberlawn, Rockville, Maryland.

Personal characteristics: 6' tall, athletic, trim; jet black hair; considered extremely handsome.

Father: Robert S. Shriver, Sr. (January 12, 1878–June 12, 1942); banker.

Mother: Hilda (Shriver) Shriver (November 2, 1882–August 18, 1977); a second cousin of her husband; married June 1, 1910.

Siblings: Herbert (November 18, 1911–); married Willa Marie Sturgis on January 22, 1949.

Wife: Eunice Mary Kennedy (July 10, 1922–); married May 23, 1953.

Children: Robert S. Shriver, III (April 28,

SARGENT SHRIVER (left) and GEORGE McGOVERN
(From the author's collection)

1954–). Maria Owings (November 11, 1955–). Married actor Arnold Schwarzenegger. She has been a television journalist. Timothy Perry (August 29, 1959–). Mark Kennedy (February 17, 1964–). Anthony Paul Kennedy (July 20, 1965–).

Famous as the brother-in-law of the Kennedy clan, Sarge Shriver's American roots are actually deeper, and in some respects more notable, than those of his famous in-laws. Shrivers first appeared in America 290 years ago. A fortune was built in milling, canning and banking in Maryland. Some fought in the French and Indian Wars and the American Revolution; another ancestor participated in the first convention calling for the addition of a Bill of Rights to the Constitution. Shriver's father was an investment banker whose wealth provided a comfortable living until the Great Crash of the stock market in 1929. There was a silver spoon in his mouth at birth, but it was roughly jerked out during the Depression.

Before those painful times, Sarge enjoyed a comfortable childhood, first in Westminster, Maryland, then in Baltimore after his father had been named a vice president with the Baltimore Trust Company. In parochial school his grades were excellent, and by the time of high school the pudgy boy began to thin and become athletic. Shriver went to boarding school in New Milford, Connecticut, to prepare for college. Teachers remembered him as a hard worker, but not bookish. Sarge was only 14 when the financial crash plunged his father into poverty, just as the senior Shriver was starting a new banking venture in New York City. At least some of the new reality must have become evident when Sarge had to pick up odd jobs to work his way through school. Athletics proved an outlet, and he excelled at quarterback for the school football team.

The next education stop was at New Haven, matriculating at Yale in 1934. He was popular and active outside of the classroom, and a good student. His most satisfying endeavor may have been work on the campus newspaper, a five-times-a-week paper for which he was editor-in-chief from January 1937, until January 1938. It was a prestigious position, and he was even paid for his work. Both factors were important to the financially strapped student. After graduating *cum laude* in 1938, he entered Yale Law School. There apparently never was a strong interest in the law as a career, but a legal education was seen as an important credential in involving himself in some other pursuit, just what he could not be certain. While not setting the school afire, Sarge performed adequately. His outside interests took on a more political cast when he organized an America First chapter on campus. This isolationist organization was a nationwide phenomenon, but Shriver later said he had not become a true believer; he was just concerned America was not prepared for war. His views on intervention in a European war had been influenced during summers he spent guiding groups of young people through Europe. While there he realized that an entire generation of European men had been wiped out by previous wars, and he had no desire to see America embroiled in another such conflict.

While organizing America First in 1940, Shriver also enlisted in the Naval Reserve. The seeming inconsistency lends credence to his explanation that he was not really isolationist. After a year he was ready for graduation from law school, admission to the bar, and active duty in the Navy. Commissioned an ensign, Shriver sailed aboard the battleship *South Dakota* (ironically, George McGovern's home state) to the Pacific, seeing service as a gunnery officer at the Battle of Guadalcanal, among other encounters. Ensign Shriver felt insignificant. Throughout life he loved to be at the center of whatever he was doing. Better prospects seemed at hand when he was transferred to submarine duty in October 1943. After a few months' training, Shriver asked for early assignment to a sub. Six other students of his class arrived for assignment shortly before Shriver did, and the tardy sailor was told there had only been six positions. Shriver exploded in rage, demanding that the commanding officer speak to him. Shriver was put in his place when that confrontation occurred, and after a year he did get assigned to the submarine *Sandlance*. Erroneous orders requiring him to return to the States caused another explosion, with the same response that he should learn to follow orders. The mix-up was corrected, however, and before long Shriver had reason to wonder whether he should not have meekly accepted the assignment back to the mainland. Shriver's submarine was to be one of the vessels for the perilous mission of sailing near the Japanese shoreline, rising to the surface and then directing American planes to their targets. Two atomic bomb blasts made these conventional air raids unnecessary. Shriver may have felt those bombs saved his life.

The end of the war brought decorations and inactivity. He was discharged as a lieutenant commander in 1945. For a few unhappy months Shriver was a very junior lawyer in a New York firm. A Yale contemporary helped Shriver become an assistant editor for *Newsweek* magazine. The job paid little, but Shriver displayed the doggedness, good humor, and sartorial elegance that would become trademarks. At a cocktail party in 1946, he met Eunice Mary Kennedy, daughter of wealthy businessman, ambassador, and founder of a political dynasty, Joseph P. Kennedy, Sr. Kennedy heard that Shriver had editing skills, and called him in to discuss the editing of his deceased son's diaries for publication. Joe Kennedy, Jr., had been killed on a mission during the war, and the senior Joseph wanted to perpetuate his memory. Shriver candidly told Kennedy that the papers were not worthy of publication. Apparently appreciating the young man's honesty, Kennedy hired him on anyway. For two years he was a personal aide to Kennedy, but in 1948 Shriver moved to Chicago to become assistant manager of a new venture undertaken by his wealthy employer.

The Chicago Merchandise Mart was then the largest building in the world, built just as the Depression hit. That timing made it a gigantic burden. By the time Kennedy purchased the Mart, it had only slightly improved its balance sheet as a trade center and office complex. Filling it with tenants became Shriver's duty. In subsequent careers Shriver would demonstrate the same ability, first recognized in Chicago, as a "super salesman." He was charming, easy to meet and like, trustworthy.

Shriver was also tremendously effective and made Kennedy never regret his selection.

Simultaneous with Shriver's growing esteem in the Kennedy business operation was his courtship to the boss's daughter. Eunice Kennedy had been appointed in 1947 by President Truman as director of a committee studying juvenile delinquency. Kennedy assigned Shriver to help. Through five years of on and off dating the relationship warmed. In 1953, they were married in an elaborate ceremony officiated by Francis Cardinal Spellman, attended by seventeen hundred people, including leading politicians from throughout the country. In a toast at the reception, Eunice innocently referred to Shriver's future need to "measure up" to his in-laws: "I searched all my life for someone like my father and Sarge came closest." Shriver's mother had a slightly different reaction to the marriage: she opposed it as being beneath him.

Shriver had plunged not only into his job in Chicago, but also political, social, and civic affairs. In 1954, the Chicago mayor appointed Shriver to the Chicago Board of Education. The exact reason for the appointment is unclear, and there was some speculation that Shriver's father-in-law, who was friends with the mayor, played a role. The position put Shriver in the public eye. Some eyebrows had been raised because the incumbent board member that Shriver replaced wanted to keep his job. The following year the newest member was elected president of the board. His interests, outlined to reporters, were to involve parents and the public more, to increase vocational training and other practical programs, to encourage experimenting with programs, and to improve students' analytical abilities. School board president Shriver desired the schools to train students for work in society, but almost more important to him was that a foundation of knowledge in history, literature, and other disciplines be laid. Shriver was given high marks for his drive, his refusal to use the position as a political stepping stone, and his persuasiveness in selling ideas not only to the rest of the board, but also to the state legislature. Again Shriver showed his salesmanship. His Springfield customers in the legislature bought his ideas. There was no scandal of any

sort during his five years on the board, an unusual feat in Chicago. The "Mr. Clean" and "boy scout" image was shined and became publicly recognized.

Outside of his school board involvement, Shriver also found time for chairing the Catholic Interracial Council, which attempted to develop programs within the church to promote racial understanding and harmony. In 1958, Shriver won that organization's award for effective work against bigotry. Shriver was no Sunday-only Catholic, but practiced his faith through his weekday endeavors. Hatred of racial discrimination was founded in his understanding of Christianity. Shriver was well-read in the theology of the Catholic church, and frequently used Biblical references to support his fight against discrimination. Enabling more black youths to enter the Catholic high schools of Chicago became his concern; tuition subsidies were the result. A nationwide conference of Catholic Interracial Councils was initiated by Shriver. Interracial workshops for Chicago students were organized by this tireless advocate, who put his ideas into action.

The publicity from the non-stop Shriver civic involvement placed him as a contender for the 1960 Democratic nomination for Illinois governor. Success with lobbying the legislature on behalf of Chicago schools gave impetus to the speculation. Chicago Mayor Richard J. Daley, a Catholic, and likely Democratic presidential nominee Jack Kennedy, also Catholic, seemed to party professionals sufficient representation for that religion. Shriver as gubernatorial nominee would threaten an imbalance on the ticket. Daley himself seemed the main reason Shriver was pushed aside. But Shriver also helped take himself out of contention. Jack Kennedy was not only Catholic, he was also related. That relationship placed demands upon Shriver that frequently in years to come required him to subordinate his own ambitions. When Shriver started carving out his own place in politics, that family tie became strained. That was later. In 1960, Shriver was candidate for nothing, but was an important but still not top aide in the Kennedy presidential campaign. His main function was to serve as a liaison between the Democratic

National Committee and the field campaign workers. Later he served to unite the Kennedy campaign team with the Lyndon Johnson vice presidential workers.

To work in the campaign, Shriver left Illinois behind and moved to suburban Washington, D.C. For an ambitious Illinois politician, the move would have been unthinkable. It suggests Shriver may not have hungered for office in a typically famished manner. Perhaps his most dramatic involvement in the campaign came after Martin Luther King was jailed in Atlanta and subsequently sentenced to four month's hard labor in Georgia State Prison. For a week the Kennedy camp had gingerly sidestepped the issue because of fears of either losing the South if it supported King or losing black votes if it did not. One of Shriver's aides suggested to him that the Kennedy campaign could be benefitted by the simple gesture of a phone call to Mrs. King. Shriver immediately approved the suggestion and went to see his brother-in-law Jack. Driving out to a Chicago motel in which Kennedy was staying for the night, Shriver waited until all other advisers had left the room, leaving him and the future president alone. He persuaded Kennedy to make the call to Coretta King, assure her of nothing more than Kennedy's concern. The call was made. It was publicized widely not only by the press but also through pamphlets distributed in black neighborhoods. In the incredibly close November election, or so Dwight Eisenhower believed, the phone call made the difference.

Following the victory, Shriver was rumored to be in line for a cabinet post. But before that could happen, Kennedy placed him in charge of the talent hunt for the administration. It was not a new suggestion, but it was an idea that had never been successfully employed. Shriver was to locate and screen personnel for all levels of the executive branch. He believed his biggest coup was luring Robert S. McNamara from the presidency of Ford Motor Company to be secretary of defense. Shriver's job did not end with making suggestions for whom should be appointed, but it was his responsibility in many cases then to convince the individual to accept the post. McNamara, again, exemplified the biggest catch for Shriver

on that score. Insofar as Shriver's own Cabinet post was concerned, the family's claim was satiated when Bobby Kennedy was appointed attorney general. There seemed little possibility that another brother, or in-law, could appropriately be named to the cabinet. Another post was available, one not even outlined in detail but only mentioned in a few throwaway lines in the closing days of the fall campaign. Kennedy had suggested in late October that young men should be sent overseas as "ambassadors of peace" to give technical and educational assistance to underdeveloped nations. With the election won, flesh had to be put on this barebones suggestion. Shriver was charged with developing the concept. His ultimate responsibility would prove much greater.

Most Kennedy advisers wanted the Peace Corps, as the "ambassadors of peace" concept came to be called, to be part of the State Department. Most also wanted it to be lumped together with the rest of foreign aid. Shriver immediately objected that for Peace Corps workers to be governed under the same programs as the provision of weapons and other non-peace materials would compromise their efforts. Nonetheless the decision was made to include it in the overall foreign aid program. Shriver was overseas drumming up support in possible host countries, and he turned to his friend Lyndon Johnson for help in changing the decision. Johnson argued with the new president. Kennedy responded that if the vice president and Shriver felt it was that important, then he would go along. Kennedy had equally sobering words when he told Shriver that since everyone in Congress seemed to feel the Peace Corps would be a fiasco, he wanted Shriver since "it would be easier to fire a relative than a friend."

Turning Shriver loose on the Peace Corps, Kennedy also cut him adrift. Once when Shriver became perturbed about lack of administration backing of the Corps, Eunice inquired with her brother, the president. The response was that since Shriver wanted the Peace Corps to be independent, he would have to bear the burden of that independence by himself. Shriver did brilliantly. For weeks he lobbied on Capitol Hill, showing that super-salesmanship exhibited so many times before. The fear of many was that idealistic, nonconformist American youngsters, "hippies" and assorted other malcontents, would flood the ranks. Embarrassments would multiply daily. Shriver assuaged these and many other fears, got close to the budget he wanted, and began his direction of the Peace Corps with his professional and political reputation very much on the line.

Important to Shriver was that the military, and particularly the CIA, would not have any involvement. Fears that volunteers would be suspected and treated in host countries as spies for the CIA made that requirement significant. The number of volunteers was gratifying. The number rejected in order to preserve the Corps from the embarrassments feared by its opponents, was close to 80 percent. From a base of 1,000 volunteers, it grew to 10,000 in 1964. It was not the "Children's Crusade" or "Kiddie Corps" that many feared, but to the contrary became probably the most popular program initiated by the Kennedy administration. The reason for the success was largely Shriver's. He dominated the Peace Corps in ways that drew his administrative abilities for higher office into question. He drove his staff crazy, with extreme demands upon their time and energy. There was little firm control, and the turnover of bureaucratic personnel working in Washington for the Corps was staggering. He could not unwind, but seemed to be in constant motion. His bubbling enthusiasm for the program approached missionary zeal. Government regulations were not allowed to impede his program suggestions.

In 1964, President Johnson added new responsibilities. Johnson had announced his war on poverty, and Shriver was chosen to head a new agency solely concerned with poverty programs, the Office of Economic Opportunity (OEO). Again Shriver was faced with starting up a program and defining its mission. Many feared a huge, central poverty bureaucracy. Shriver the salesman and politician went to work on Congress to convince them of the practicality. The Job Corps, Community Action Programs, VISTA, and other programs all fell within Shriver's respon-

sibility. As the Vietnam War demanded ever-increasing parts of the federal budget, as "guns and butter" proved a fleeting concept, the antipoverty agencies became competitors — fierce ones — for the shrinking share of the pie. Shriver poorly handled the conflicts, not only within the OEO but also from other, established poverty agencies. In part, this demonstrated the truth in a frequent criticism of the Shriver style, that he revels in initiating programs but is weak on continuing his drive into long-term administration.

Shriver's continuing work for Johnson severely strained his relations with the Kennedys. In 1964, Johnson announced his esteem for Shriver by saying, "I regard Sargent Shriver as one of the most brilliant, most able and most competent officials in the government. I regard him as my real confidant." Many took this as a trial balloon for a possible vice presidential nomination for Shriver on the Johnson ticket that would be named later in the year. Eunice Kennedy Shriver reportedly said that he could not run. "It's Bobby's turn," she said. Bobby (Robert F. Kennedy) had been eliminated by Johnson as a possibility at the same time he was floating Shriver's name, and that was galling. Robert Kennedy apparently became incensed toward his brother-in-law.

Further cause for a rift came in 1968 when Hubert Humphrey, Johnson's vice president and Bobby Kennedy's rival for the presidential nomination until the latter's assassination, suggested Shriver as a possible running mate. Instead, Shriver was named ambassador to France in 1968. After Humphrey lost the election to Richard Nixon, Shriver continued at his post. Nixon respected de Gaulle and wanted good relations which made Shriver's job easier. In March 1970, he returned to the United States to take up law practice in Washington and New York.

Back in the country after a two-year absence, Shriver began to be mentioned as a possible gubernatorial candidate in his native Maryland. The incumbent Democratic governor, Marvin Mandel, proved too strong to dislodge, and Shriver soon retreated even from his unannounced candidacy. A 1970 fall campaign on behalf of Democratic candidates picked up some IOUs. The practice of law had to suffice for another two years. To the surprise of his partners, he put in long hours in the practice, and did not take the role of a senior partner who merely tried to bring in business. But there was little doubt Shriver hoped for something else in politics before he would be willing to quit the public arena.

Something else came in 1972. George McGovern first considered selecting Shriver for vice president at that year's national convention. Shriver was discarded in the hectic, rushed attempt to name a running mate when it was discovered he was in Moscow and could not easily be reached for a conference. Tom Eagleton got the nod instead. But 18 days later a new nominee was required after Eagleton quit the ticket. Another Kennedy, Ted, had been McGovern's first choice, but he refused. Similar responses came from other politicians unwilling to tie their futures to the obviously doomed campaign. Abraham Ribicoff, Lawrence O'Brien, Hubert Humphrey, Reubin Askew and Edmund Muskie all refused. While Muskie was being sounded out, McGovern asked Shriver whether he would be interested should Muskie decline. Lyndon Johnson, Mayor Richard Daley, and the Kennedys were all consulted before Shriver gave his answer. It was yes. To the press he said that he was "very happy and very proud." To himself he must have admitted the likely failure of the campaign, but considered he had nothing to lose and a lot to gain regardless.

Sargent Shriver became the Democrats' Agnew during the campaign. His stridence was softened by his charm, elegance, and compassion, but there was savagery in his attacks nonetheless. As the McGovern point man, he charged Nixon with having squandered real hopes for peace in Vietnam in 1969 while Shriver was French ambassador. "Nixon had peace handed to him literally in his lap — but he blew it." The administration called Shriver's charges political fantasy. His Catholicism, sincere and all-pervasive, showed its effects when he stated America should "harness for God the energies of love." It was the same fervent idealism and optimism brought to bear in a political campaign that he had long revealed in his other work. He seemed to love campaigning, even for a lost cause. Watergate, then a back-burner issue that would not become heated until March 1972, was a frequent line of attack, but few listened to Shriver. Impeccably dressed, always smiling, tireless because of his ability to take quick, refreshing naps anywhere, invigorated by occasional workouts in health cubs while on the campaign trail, Shriver exuded excitement. It was not nearly enough, as the Democratic ticket suffered one of history's most crushing defeats.

Shriver would not be content with such a role again. In late 1975, he announced for the presidential nomination, calling freely upon the glory of the Kennedy image to spur his campaign on. It may have been the wrong tack, as many negative images had creeped into the formerly pure-white Camelot legend. Hoping that his name recognition would give him early success in the primaries, Shriver planned to build on those victories as other candidates were winnowed out. As America was becoming more conservative, Shriver continued to espouse the liberal tenets of a decade earlier. He had the very real burden of being perceived as nothing more than a Kennedy in-law, with no personal attributes worth remembering. His skills were many, but Jimmy Carter's campaign as an outsider who would bring competence to Washington took hold. On March 22, 1976, Shriver dropped out of the race, admitting Carter's growing lock on the nomination.

Among the other post-political activities, Shriver in 1978 was a partner in a group that bought the Baltimore Orioles.

Analysis of Qualifications

In company with a handful of other also-rans, Sargent Shriver has never held elective office. In the few appointed positions he held, Shriver demonstrated ability, but also serious deficiencies. Whether he would have made a good president can be evaluated only on scant evidence, therefore, but several points are apparent.

As director of the Peace Corps, Shriver was imaginative, compassionate, enthusiastic. Yet he was also quickly bored by administrative detail. He ran his office as a one-man show, in part because the president made it clear he was on his own. Staff was in constant turmoil over the demands made, the lack of firm control, the constant motion that at times seemed to substitute for action. At the same time, for all his deficiencies in management, Shriver made the Peace Corps a smashing success. This agency was the epitome of idealistic government, sending volunteers to every primitive pocket of poverty in the world in a selfless attempt to share American money and knowledge. Shriver's religious zeal, his liberal concern for the underprivileged, his abilities as a salesman of himself or programs, and his gung-ho enthusiasm to be at the center of things made him a perfect choice for this office.

Another facet of the Shriver personality was also displayed to advantage in his Peace Corps work. He is frequently described as an instigator, a man enthusiastic over starting up a program but little less driven to excel in the day-to-day management. Ideas streamed from him, and it took a cautious, nonsubservient staff to tell him which were brilliant and which crazy.

Shriver was as likeable and charming a man as ever held the distinction of having lost in a presidential campaign. He seemed to thrive on crowds and campaigning. Good rapport was established with young people, perhaps initially by his Kennedy connection, but then also by his obvious good humor, his liberal ideas, and his movie-star caliber good looks. Shriver was never hesitant to use his Kennedy relations, and laced his speeches with references to his in-laws. That this was a handicap as well as a boon was neatly summarized in the 1976 comment that everybody and his brother-in-law were running for president.

Sargent Shriver is far more than just a relative to some famous people. He is an intelligent, well-read, serious man. He was a masterful lobbyist, a "supersalesman" who started by filling the white elephant Merchandise Mart in Chicago with tenants for Joseph Kennedy. He sold the Peace Corps to a chary Congress, and followed that with congressional success in establishing the Office of Economic Opportunity. There was some of the Hubert Hum-

phrey effervescence in Shriver, with the same dizzying habit of descending into endless chatter. He could mesmerize people; he appeared to some to have, to use 1960s parlance, charisma.

His achievements have solely been in the middle level of government, and he has never been entrusted with a top position. In every office he held he performed with grace and energy. His background in government, however, was not the reason he was selected as a vice presidential nominee. His relationship to the Kennedys was. Perhaps he would have risen to the demands of the presidency. Shriver is one of those poorly revealed, insufficiently tested might-have-beens who was called to high national service mainly for reasons far removed from his capacity for the presidency. He might have made a good president, but there were too many unknowns about Shriver's abilities for his party to have been justified in selecting him to serve so close to the presidency.

SHRIVER BIBLIOGRAPHY

"Brother-in-Law." *Newsweek* (January 26, 1976), p. 21.

"Busting the Boys." *Newsweek* (August 17, 1970), p. 32.

"Democratic Drummer." *Newsweek* (October 12, 1970), p. 43–44.

Finney, John W. "The New Democratic Vice-Presidential Choice." *New York Times* (August 6, 1972), p. 28.

Jenkins, Peter. "Candidate Shriver Is a Supersalesman in a Very Tough Territory." *New York Times Magazine* (October 15, 1972), pp. 36–37 ff.

Liston, Robert A. *Sargent Shriver: A Candid Portrait.* New York City (1964).

Lydon, Christopher. "Shriver's Catholicism Pictured as Something Close to Politics." *New York Times* (September 16, 1972), p. 12.

"The New Nominee: No Longer 'Half a Kennedy.'" *Time* (August 14, 1972), pp. 16–17.

Peer, Elizabeth. "The Shriver Hard Sell." *Newsweek* (October 9, 1972), pp. 33–34 ff.

"Shriver 'Happy and Very Proud' to Be on the McGovern Ticket." *New York Times* (August 6, 1972), p. 28.

"Shriver Is 5th Democrat to Quit Presidential Race." *New York Times* (March 23, 1976), p. 19.

"Shriver Unchained." *Time* (September 18, 1972), pp. 16–17.

"Shriver's Other Running Mate." *Time* (August 21, 1972), p. 13.

"Time for Sargent?" *Time* (April 20, 1970), p. 21.
Viorst, Milton, ed. *Making a Difference: The Peace Corps at Twenty-Five.* New York (1986).

Some family data provided by Mr. Shriver.

1973 Confirmation of a Vice President

Vice President Spiro T. Agnew resigned on October 10, 1973. Under the Twenty-fifth Amendment, President Richard Nixon had the authority to name a new vice president, with Congress having the responsibility of reviewing the nomination. On October 12, Nixon named Gerald Ford. He announced that John Connally (Texas), Nelson Rockefeller, Ronald Reagan, and Elliot Richardson (Mass.) had also been prime candidates.

November 27, 1973, the Senate voted 92 to 3 for Ford.

December 6, 1973, the House voted 387 to 35 for Ford.

Winner

Gerald Ford, 40th vice president

Loser

None

1974 Confirmation of a Vice President

President Richard Nixon resigned on August 9, 1974, and Vice President Ford succeeded him. On August 20, Ford named Nelson Rockefeller as his choice for vice president. George Bush and Donald Rumsfeld (Ill.) were said to be the other serious contenders for the nomination.

December 10, 1974, the Senate voted 90 to 7 for Rockefeller.

December 19, 1974, the House voted 287 to 128 for Rockefeller.

Winner

Nelson Rockefeller, 41st vice president

Loser

None

Election of 1976

NOMINATIONS

Democratic National Convention (37th): July 12–15, 1976, at Madison Square Garden, New York City. *President*— Jimmy Carter, nominated on the first ballot with 2,238½ votes out of 3,008 cast. Rep. Morris Udall (Ariz.) and Gov. Edmund G. Brown, Jr. (Calif.) were his main opponents. *Vice president*— Walter Mondale, nominated on the first ballot with 2,817 out of 3,008 votes.

Republican National Convention (31st): Aug. 16–19, 1976, at Kemper Arena, Kansas City, Missouri. *President*— Gerald Ford, nominated on the first ballot with 1,187 votes, to 1,070 for Ronald Reagan, and one vote to another candidate. *Vice president*— Robert J. Dole, nominated on the first ballot with 1,921 out of 2,259 votes cast.

GENERAL ELECTION, November 2, 1976

Popular Vote

Carter 40,828,587
Ford 39,147,613
Eugene McCarthy.   751,728
Others.   823,731

Electoral Vote

Carter-Mondale — 297 (23 states)
Ford-Dole — 240 (27 states)
Ronald Reagan–Dole —1

Winners

Jimmy Carter, 39th president
Walter Mondale, 42nd vice president

Losers

Gerald Ford, Robert Dole

*1976 presidential nominee—
Republican Party*

Gerald Ford

No biographical sketch of Ford is included since he served as president from August 9, 1974, until January 20, 1977 (38th president).

State represented: Michigan.

Birth: July 14, 1913.

Age on Inauguration Day (January 20, 1977): 63 years, 6 months.

*1976 vice presidential nominee—
Republican Party*

Robert J. Dole

Robert Dole's biography appears on pages 776–783 in the section on the election of 1996, when he was the losing Republican nominee for president.

State represented: Kansas.

Birth: July 22, 1923, in Russell, Kansas.

Age on Inauguration Day (January 20, 1977): 53 years, 6 months.

GERALD FORD (left) and ROBERT DOLE
(From the author's collection)

Election of 1980

NOMINATIONS

Republican National Convention (32nd): July 14–17, 1980, at the Joe Louis Arena, Detroit, Michigan. *President*— Ronald Reagan, nominated on the first ballot with 1,939 of 1,994 votes. *Vice president*— George Bush, nominated on the first ballot with 1,832 out of 1,994 votes.

Democratic National Convention (38th): August 11–14, 1980, at Madison Square Garden, New York City. *President*— Jimmy Carter, nominated on the first ballot with 2,123 votes. Edward Kennedy (Mass.) had 1,150.5 votes, and 54.5 were cast for other candidates. *Vice president*—Walter Mondale, nominated by acclamation.

National Unity Campaign. After being defeated in most early Republican primaries, John Anderson withdrew from the GOP race. On April 24, 1980, he announced his independent campaign. *President*— John Anderson. *Vice president*—Patrick J. Lucey, named by Anderson on August 25.

GENERAL ELECTION, November 4,1980

Popular Vote

Reagan 43,901,812
Carter 35,483,820
John Anderson 5,719,722
Others 1,407,942

Electoral Vote

Reagan-Bush — 489 (45 states)
Carter-Mondale — 49 (5+ states)

Winners

Ronald Reagan, 40th president
George Bush, 43rd vice president

Losers

Jimmy Carter, Walter Mondale, John Anderson, Patrick Lucey

*1980 presidential nominee—
Democratic Party*

Jimmy Carter

No biographical sketch on Carter is included since he served as president from January 20, 1977, to January 20, 1981 (39th president).

State represented: Georgia.
Birth: October 1, 1924.
Age on Inauguration Day (January 20, 1981): 56 years, 3½ months.

---

*1980 vice presidential nominee—
Democratic Party*

Walter Mondale

No biographical sketch on Mondale was included with this election since be served as vice president from January 20, 1977, to January 20, 1981; see however, sketch at election of 1984, pages 734–740.

State Represented: Minnesota.
Birth: January 5, 1928.
Age on Inauguration Day (January 20, 1981): 53 years, ½ month.

---

*1980 presidential candidate—
"National Unity" Independent*

John B. Anderson

Born February 15, 1922, in Rockford, Illinois. Married Keke Machakos on January 4, 1953; they have five children.

John's parents were E. Albin Anderson, a Swedish immigrant, and Martha Edna Ring Anderson. They operated a grocery in Rock-

Re-Elect
CARTER
MONDALE

Keep them
working for you.

JIMMY CARTER (left) and WALTER MONDALE
(From the author's collection)

left for Army service as an artilleryman, including ten months in Europe during which time he was involved in several significant battles.

Anderson returned to the university and received his law degree in 1946. With interruptions for a graduate fellowship at the Harvard Law School (LL.M., 1949), and being a staff adviser to the United States High Command for Germany, based in West Berlin (1952–1955), Anderson practice law in Rockford. Anderson won a contested Republican primary in 1956 to be state's attorney for the county, then easily took the general election. In 1960, he was one of five men who contested the Republican primary for an open congressional seat. Anderson's energetic campaign proved effective and he won a handsome victory in the April GOP primary, and then easily won the November election.

In Congress Anderson initially displayed a strong conservative voting record. Reelection was rarely difficult. In 1964 he was one of Barry Goldwater's staunchest supporters, particularly for a Midwesterner. By 1968 Anderson recognized that his views were evolving. In his autobiography he said that the change had not been overnight, but he termed his transformation as slow growth. He cast the deciding vote in committee that permitted a strong open housing bill to reach the House floor. The vote occurred during a time of rioting. Anderson argued that "I legislate today not out of fear, but out of a deep concern for the America I love."

When a vacancy in the third-ranking GOP leadership position in the House opened up in

ford, in an area where many other Scandinavians lived. There were six children in the family, but three died young. Religion was a dominant part of their lives. As Anderson wrote later, at age nine "I made a public confession of my desire to accept the Lord Jesus Christ as my personal savior." In high school he was a skilled debater and was valedictorian at his 1939 graduation. He graduated in 1942 from the University of Illinois with a degree in political science, and was admitted to Phi Beta Kappa. He enrolled in the law school, but then

1969, Anderson was easily elected. At first he generally backed President Richard Nixon's policies, but found him insufficiently liberal on civil rights issues. Anderson gradually joined those opposed to continuing the war effort in South Vietnam. He was one of the earliest Republican advocates in 1973 of having an independent prosecutor examine the Watergate affair, and in 1974 was ahead of most of his party in calling on the president to resign. Anderson's increasingly liberal voting record and his differences with the majority of Republicans may have led to his toughest election challenge in 1978, when he almost lost to a much more conservative challenger in the primary.

On June 8, 1979, he announced that he was exploring a race for the presidential nomination. The media seemed intrigued by this relatively liberal, iconoclastic Republican. As *Newsweek* (March 17, 1980) termed it, there came to be an "Anderson craze": he fluctuated from a "noble-loser cult hero" favorably featured in the *Doonesbury* cartoon strip, to, after two close losses in New England primaries, "a legitimate if still long-shot contender." He had enjoyed a remarkably favorable press (Germond and Witcover, p. 231), but his Republican fortunes declined by late March. Distaste both for Jimmy Carter and Ronald Reagan caused him to announce a "National Unity" candidacy as an independent. Early after his third-party entry, some national polls showed him with 20 to 25 percent of the vote. There was a rumor that national newscaster Walter Cronkite was going to be his running mate, but the false story died in a few days before Cronkite, who was on a sailing vacation, even heard about it. For a variety of reasons, Anderson's support dwindled and he did not affect the outcome.

In 1981 Anderson announced that he would form a National Unity Party to run congressional candidates in 1982 and 1984, and potentially to be his vehicle for a second presidential campaign. In 1983 he said that he would run "if the party were to ask me to be the standard bearer." None of that came to pass, however, and on April 26, 1984, Anderson announced that he would not be a candidate in 1984 or 1988. Anderson has retired from active political life. He teaches and also practices law in Washington, D.C.

ANDERSON BIBLIOGRAPHY

Anderson, John B. *Between Two Worlds: A Congressman's Choice.* Grand Rapids (1970).

Bennetts, Leslie. "Keke Anderson: A Loyal Wife with Her Own Ideas." *New York Times* (July 9, 1980), page B-8.

Bisnow, Mark. *Diary of a Dark Horse: The 1980 Anderson Presidential Campaign.* Carbondale, Ill. (1983).

Brown, Clifford W., Jr., and Robert J. Walker. *A Campaign of Ideas: The 1980 Anderson/Lucey Platform.* Westport, Conn. (1984).

"Cronkite Scales Down a Dream of Sailing Around the World." *New York Times* (Jan. 18, 1981), Section 5, page 13.

Germond, Jack W., and Jules Witcover. *Blue Smoke and Mirrors: How Reagan Won....* New York (1981).

Goldman, Peter, et al. "John Anderson: The Wild Card." *Newsweek* (June 9, 1980), pp. 28–38.

Golubovskis, Georgs M. *Crazy Dreaming: The Anderson Campaign, 1980.* Flint (1981).

Jones, Clayton. "Anderson — How Different?" *Christian Science Monitor* (October 9, 1980), page 12.

Kotche, James R. *John B. Anderson: Congressman and Presidential Candidate.* Rockford, Ill. (1981).

Magoon, Michael. "Third Party Presidential Candidates in American Politics." Unpublished Ph.D. dissertation, Brown University (1994).

Morganthau, Tom, et al. "The Lonely Liberal." *Newsweek* (December 24, 1979), page 33.

Radcliffe, Donnie. "Greek Spirits of 1980." *Washington Post* (September 4, 1980), p. B1.

Stacks, John F. *Watershed: The Campaign for the Presidency 1980.* New York (1981).

---

*1980 vice presidential candidate —
"National Unity" Independent*

Patrick J. Lucey

Born March 21, 1918, in La Crosse, Wisconsin. Married Jean Vlasis on November 14, 1951; they have three children.

Patrick Joseph Lucey was the son of Gregory, a grocer and president of a bank, and Ella McNamara Lucey. The family was Roman Catholic. Pat's two brothers became priests, and one of his four sisters is a nun. After parochial schools, he attended St. Thomas College, in St.

JOHN ANDERSON (left) and PATRICK J. LUCEY
(From the author's collection)

Paul, Minnesota, from 1936 to 1939. He would not get his degree until after World War II. Pat was drafted in 1941 and served in the Caribbean Theater. He was discharged in 1945 as a captain. His college degree was earned the next year at the University of Wisconsin.

From 1945 Lucey was a manager of 14 farms in the southwestern part of the state. His start in politics came with election to the state assembly in 1948. Lucey lost an election for Congress in 1950. He married Jean Vlasis in 1951, which started a personal, political, and professional partnership. The couple built a successful real estate business in Madison. Pat was instrumental in developing the modern Wisconsin Democratic Party. He served as state party executive director from 1951 to 1953, and as state party chairman from 1957 to 1963. Lucey was active in many Democratic statewide campaigns, including the initial U.S. Senate elections of William Proxmire (1957, to replace Joseph McCarthy) and Gaylord Nelson (1962). Senator Proxmire later credited Lucey with playing a bigger role than anyone else in building the state party. In 1960 he helped John Kennedy win a critical victory in the Wisconsin primary; in 1968 he was a national leader in Robert Kennedy's race. In between those two national campaigns, Lucey was elected Wisconsin lieutenant governor in 1964. He tried to move up to governor in 1966, but lost. He won in 1970.

Lucey gained a reputation as a progressive governor, and one who micro-managed. He tried to revolutionize local school financing, and succeeded in passing a plan to make the administration of the university system more efficient. Similar to President Nixon's revenue sharing program on the federal level, Lucey backed a plan for the state to share tax revenues with municipalities.

The governor's wife, Jean, gained a reputation — to use the word frequently applied to her — as "volatile." Whether that was the word, she certainly exhibited a candor unusual in a politician's spouse. She was often compared to the spouse of another high-profile politician, Attorney General John Mitchell, whose wife Martha was newsworthy for her acid tongue. Jean Lucey blasted a group of welfare mothers who had chained themselves to the gate to the governor's mansion. In a line that may have pleased many taxpayers, she went to the gate and said, "If you're clever enough to agitate, you're clever enough to work." The publicity from an incident in which Governor Lucey locked her out of a room in March 1972 and the police were called, may well have kept the governor from being selected for vice president in 1972. Both may have been drinking, and Jean was kicking at the door from the outside while the governor stayed locked inside. Considering that the presidential nominee George McGovern suffered an historically sweeping defeat, that locked-door incident may have been useful.

Lucey easily won reelection in 1974. When Jimmy Carter became president in 1977, he named Lucey as ambassador to Mexico. He resigned in 1979 and returned to the United States. Lucey was strongly critical of Carter, calling his administration a "disaster." He worked on Ted Kennedy's challenge to President Carter in the 1980 presidential primaries, but Kennedy failed. At the convention Lucey resigned as a delegate, because of a rule stating that delegates must support the party nom-

inee. He admitted that he might support Anderson's independent bid. Lucey publicly said the decision was up to Jean. Two weeks after the Democratic convention Jean Vlasis Lucey and Keke Machakos Anderson, wives with similar Greek heritages, met to discuss their husbands' futures. Keke Anderson convinced the reluctant Jean. The ticket was announced, but in November they did not carry any state.

Lucey revealed that he was considering running for governor again in 1982, but met bitter opposition from Democrats livid with him for abandoning the party in 1980. The chairman of the Milwaukee party said he "wouldn't vote for Pat Lucey if he were running alone." Lucey ended up not running then or since. He became a consultant on government affairs and international economic development.

LUCEY BIBLIOGRAPHY

Conant, James K. "Executive Decision-Making in the State (Wisconsin)." Unpublished doctoral dissertation, University of Wisconsin (1983).

Lyons, Richard D. "Anderson's Running Mate." *New York Times* (August 26, 1980), p. B6.

MacPherson, Myra. *The Power Lovers: An Intimate Look at Politicians and Their Marriages.* New York (1975), pp. 107–110.

Radcliffe, Donnie. "Greek Spirits of 1980: The Other Ticket." *Washington Post* (September 4, 1980), p. B1.

Ryan, Frank. "Wisconsin's New Focus: Patrick Lucey Does Not Appear to Be Catching Fire." UPI wire service story (May 11, 1982).

Election of 1984

NOMINATIONS

Democratic National Convention (39th): July 16–19, 1984, at the Moscone Center, San Francisco, California. *President*— Walter F. Mondale, nominated on the first ballot with 2,191 votes. Gary Hart (Colo.) had 1,200.5

votes, Jesse Jackson (S.C.) had 465.5, 26 votes were scattered among other candidates, and 40 abstained. *Vice president*— Geraldine A. Ferraro, nominated by acclamation.

Republican National Convention (33rd): August 20–23, 1984, at the Dallas Convention

Center, Dallas, Texas. *President*—Ronald Reagan, nominated on the first ballot with 2,233 votes, while two delegates abstained. *Vice president*— George Bush, nominated on the first ballot with 2,231 votes, 2 cast for others, and 2 abstentions. Ballots were cast simultaneously for president and vice president, apparently the first time that has occurred.

GENERAL ELECTION, November 6, 1984
Popular Vote
    Reagan 54,451,521
    Mondale 37,565,334
    Others.   634,187
Electoral Vote
    Reagan-Bush — 525 (49 states)
    Mondale-Ferraro —13 (1+ states)
Winners
    Ronald Reagan, 40th president
    George Bush, 43rd vice president
Losers
    Walter Mondale, Geraldine A. Ferraro

---

*1984 presidential nominee—
Democratic Party*

Walter F. Mondale

Full name: Walter Frederick ("Fritz) Mondale. The name was Americanized from "Mundal" to "Mundale" by his great-grandfather; the government erred in homestead papers and spelled the name "Mondale," and the family adopted the change.

State represented: Minnesota.

Birth: January 5, 1928, in Ceylon, Minnesota.

Age on Inauguration Day (Jan. 20, 1985): 57 years, ½ month

Education: Elmore, Minnesota public schools. Macalester College 1946–48; University of Minnesota 1950–51 (B.A. cum laude); University of Minnesota School of Law 1953–1956 (LL.B.); admitted to bar in 1956.

Religion: Presbyterian

Ancestry: Norwegian father, Scotch mother

Occupation: Attorney

Public offices: Congressional district chairman in 1948 Hubert Humphrey Senate campaign; appointed executive secretary, Students for Democratic Action 1949–1950; managed Orville Freeman's unsuccessful campaign in 1950 for attorney general of Minnesota; worked on Orville Freeman's campaign for Minnesota governor 1956 and 1958; special assistant to Minnesota attorney general 1958–1960; appointed Minnesota attorney general May 4, 1960, elected November 1960, served May 1960–December 1964; appointed U. S. senator November 17, 1964, served December 30, 1964–December 30, 1976; vice president of the United States January 20, 1977–January 20, 1981, defeated for reelection 1980; unsuccessful Democratic presidential nominee 1984; declined to run for U.S. Senate, 1990; ambassador to Japan, August 1993– .

Home: North Oaks, Minnesota (St. Paul suburb)

Personal characteristics: 5' 11" tall, weighs 165 pounds. Brown hair, pale blue eyes. Considered to have sardonic wit, and to be a mischievous prankster, but appears stiffly serious in public.

Father: Theodore Sigvaard Mondale (January 25, 1876–December 1948), farmer, then Methodist minister in Minnesota; his father, Ole Frederickson Mundal, arrived with his parents from Norway in 1856.

Father's first wife: Jessie Larson (January 18, 1886–June 1, 1923), married in 1902, died from encephalitis; daughter of Louis and Julia (Nelson) Larson.

Half brothers/sister: R. Lester (May 28, 1904–), Unitarian minister; married Eldred Klose in June, 1925, then Faye Smead in June 1935, and then Rosemary Delap on May 31, 1961. Clifford T. (August 6, 1906–), manufacturer's representative; married Ruth Bringgold on January 19, 1931. Willard (March–September 1910). Eleanor (March 31, 1910–March 15, 1975), adopted March 20, 1916 after her father committed suicide; married William Archer on August 19, 1945; made custom draperies. Buford F. (July 15, 1916–December 9, 1965), heating and air conditioning representative; married Margaret Eggum on August 10, 1940.

Mother: Claribel Hope Cowan (May 1, 1892–March 5, 1967), married June 19, 1925; was of Scotch ancestry; part-time music teacher. Daughter of Robert and Clara Belle (Morton) Cowan.

Siblings: Clarence "Pete" (July 12, 1926–) professor of American Studies at George Washington University; married Virginia Aceto. William Morton "Mort" (Dec. 14, 1934–), educator, administrator for National Education Association; married Shirley Edwards, and then Elaine Wood.

Wife: Joan Adams (Aug. 8, 1930–), daughter of the Reverend John Maxwell Adams and Eleanor Jane Hall; married Dec. 27, 1955; art activist, historian.

Children: Theodore Adams "Teddy" (October 12, 1957–), a lawyer; married Pamela Ann Burris on June 11, 1988. Eleanor Jane (January 19, 1960–), actress; married Chicago Bears football player Keith Van Horne on April 9, 1988. William Hall (February 27, 1962–), lawyer.

For five of the six national elections from 1964 until 1984, either Walter Mondale or Hubert Humphrey was on the Democratic presidential ticket. Both were Minnesotans; both were senators; both were elected vice president; both carried the liberal, activist banner. One was the political mentor of the other, and each owed at least some of his success to the other's support. Humphrey once told Mondale, "Don't make all the mistakes I made." Walter Mondale did not make many mistakes, but like his fellow Minnesotan, neither did he gain the ultimate American political prize, the presidency.

Theodore Mondale, Walter's father, was a farmer, and a fairly successful one. At age 35, despite a limited education, he became a preacher. His severe Norwegian accent was made even less understandable because of a stutter. The ministry could not provide much income, and neither was it protection against life's ills. Post–World War I farm price declines caused the Mondales to lose their farm to foreclosure. Trials seemed endless, as Theodore contracted lockjaw after an amateurishly conducted tonsillectomy. For a year he jammed a piece of wood into his mouth and gradually pried his jaw open. Rural life of great struggle and poverty is what greeted Walter at his birth. Soon he was called "Fritz." The Reverend Mondale's high standards were rigid, but a tight

bond developed between the father and his most famous son. Despite the setbacks, the family was happy and optimistic. A commitment to social justice was inbred in the children, as was a sense that no failing was as serious as lying, cheating, or stealing.

Fritz met Hubert Humphrey for the first time in 1946. Humphrey was running for election as mayor of Minneapolis, and Mondale was enthralled by Humphrey's style and his philosophy. He immediately went to work on mundane campaign chores and was thrilled with Humphrey's election.

Mondale next organized the traditionally Republican Second Congressional District for Humphrey's 1948 campaign for the U.S. Senate. Though trying to stay in college, Mondale gained the loan of a car, raised funds, brought in student volunteers, and helped lead Humphrey to victory in the second district as part of a smashing statewide margin. Mondale had been industrious, resourceful, and noticed.

The thrill of victory soon turned to depression. Six weeks after the election Fritz's father died. Soon afterwards Mondale agreed to go to Washington as executive secretary of the student arm of the liberal Americans for Democratic Action. He dropped out of Macalester College in 1949, his junior year. In 1950 Mondale returned to Minnesota to manage Orville Freeman's losing race for state attorney general. In 1951 Mondale finally received his bachelor's degree from the University of Minnesota. After a two-year stint in the army, he returned for three years at Minnesota Law School. Being an attorney probably was a means to the end of getting into politics. For 18 months following graduation he worked for Orville Freeman's former law firm in the Twin Cities, then went out on his own. In 1956, with Mondale's help as a key campaign aide, Freeman was elected Minnesota governor. As campaign manager two years later, Mondale helped Freeman to a second term.

That success led to Fritz's election as party finance chairman. The future seemed clear. In 1959 he moved from St. Paul to Minneapolis, moving out of state legislative and congressional districts with Democrat incumbents to ones with Republican officials. A challenge against the Republican state senator seemed imminent, but the first of several bolts of lightning struck Mondale before he could announce. Elected with Freeman had been a colorful, emotional attorney general, Miles Lord. Governor Freeman refused to appoint Lord a Minnesota Supreme Court justice. Lord's disappointment caused him to resign as attorney general on April 30, 1960. There were many aspirants, but Freeman named Mondale attorney general on May 4, 1960. Much favorable publicity was soon generated by an already commenced but theretofore secret investigation by the attorney general's office of fraud at a major Minnesota charity. This helped Mondale sweep to victory over Republican Gaylord Saetre in the election that was held only six months after his appointment.

During the next four years Attorney General Mondale established a consumer protection division within his office, focused on civil rights issues, and was strenuous in prosecuting antitrust cases. Mondale also organized other state attorneys general to support the position of Clarence Earl Gideon, a Florida prison inmate, in his appeal to the United States Supreme Court. The Supreme Court agreed with Mondale and Gideon that legal counsel had to be provided free to indigent criminal defendants. Minnesotans must have liked his initiatives, as they reelected him in 1962.

In 1964 Mondale was placed on the Democratic National Convention's Credentials Committee. This was a place of significance, as black Mississippians under the banner of the Freedom Democratic Party were trying to dislodge the state's lily-white delegation to the convention. Fannie Lou Hamer, a black activist from Mississippi, testified to police harassment, beatings, and jailings she and others endured because of their efforts to register blacks to vote. President Lyndon Johnson was adamant that a deal be struck between the Freedom Democrats and the whites. Johnson ordered Hubert Humphrey to resolve the dispute. Mondale was Humphrey's man on the committee. The compromise that was reached assured Humphrey's nomination for vice president.

The Johnson-Humphrey landslide over Barry Goldwater caused lightning to strike Fritz Mondale again. On November 17, 1964,

Governor Rolvaag named Mondale to the soon-to-be vacant Humphrey Senate seat. From the first Senator Mondale was restrained, dignified, earnest, but cautious. He drove his aides and himself mercilessly, and earned a reputation as aloof and stiff. It was a problem he had exhibited earlier in dealing with staff, but his nervousness in this new, very public office intensified his awkwardness.

Mondale's first Senate election was in 1966. The Democratic-Farmer-Labor Party was in shambles, with infighting weakening its hold on state politics. Mondale was touched by the scandal of having received illegal corporate contributions, but he was guilty of no intentional wrong. Nonetheless, his specific problems and a general nationwide Republican trend caused Mondale to have the smallest margin he ever received in Minnesota, until 1984. He won with 53.9 percent of the vote over Republican Robert A. Forsythe. It was not large, but it was enough.

Since Humphrey was President Johnson's heir apparent, Mondale felt constrained to support the administration's position on the growing war in Vietnam. While other liberals were beginning their dovish flight away from Johnson, Mondale revealed uncertainty and silence. He would later call this reluctance his greatest mistake in public life. Mondale was a vocal proponent of the Great Society. Open housing became a special interest. In 1968 he insisted over the objection of many in the Senate leadership that the omnibus civil rights bill include an open housing guarantee. Through a tremendous display of perseverance and parliamentary skill, Mondale shepherded the bill past a filibuster and into law.

Upon Lyndon Johnson's withdrawal from the 1968 presidential race, Mondale and Oklahoma Senator Fred Harris became cochairmen of Hubert Humphrey's campaign for president. The assassination of Kennedy the night of June 3 confirmed that the nomination battle, tragically, was over. Despite that, the election against former Vice President Richard Nixon got excitingly close in late October, Humphrey lost.

Mondale's voting record in the Senate was consistently among the most liberal. The problems of migrant workers, their poverty, abysmal housing, and hunger became a passionate concern after he personally inspected conditions in Florida and elsewhere. Anti-defense votes were frequent; consumer safety was also a standard issue for his support. Children's rights, expanded health care, day care centers, nutritional supplements, and educational assistance were pushed. The space program little interested Mondale. He set hearings on the problems of migrant workers in North Carolina on the day that Apollo 11 was launched on its way to place Neil Armstrong and Buzz Aldrin on the moon. "Perhaps we belong on the moon," he said, "but we surely belong there, in North Carolina, with all the resources the nation could mobilize."

After Mondale's reelection over Republican Phil Hansen with 56.7 percent of the vote in 1972, he began serious exploration of a run for the 1976 presidential nomination. On November 21, 1974, Mondale held a press conference to announce his plans. Many of his top aides, and even his wife Joan, felt that it would be to run. It was not. He cited the long odds for victory, the terrible strain and effort needed, and the money required. "Basically," he stated, "I found I did not have the overwhelming desire to be president which is essential for the kind of campaign that is required." In a more humorous vein, Mondale remarked that he could not face another year of "sleeping in Holiday Inns." Hubert Humphrey's reaction was that his old comrade seemed to lack "the fire in the belly" required for ultimate political power in America. Ambition had always burned in Humphrey. Mondale sided with no candidate as the presidential nomination battle continued without him.

Mondale would have a role to play in the 1976 national election after all. Jimmy Carter's early lock on victory gave him the opportunity to interview prospective running mates. Summoned to Carter's home in Plains, Georgia, were Mondale, Ohio Senator John Glenn, and Maine Senator Edmund Muskie. Mondale had prepared arduously for the encounter, as he wanted the nomination. According to Carter's memoirs, it was Mondale's suggestions for an activist role for the vice president that separated Mondale from the other finalists, and led to his selection.

Jimmy Carter and Walter Mondale narrowly won election. Mondale helped decide key appointments. He became the first vice president to have an office in the West Wing of the White House, putting him adjacent and with easy access to the president. He wielded power because Carter listened to him. Every document that Carter saw, Mondale saw. He attended any meeting, however sensitive, he wanted. He was a generalist, advising and participating in almost everything. He and his president established a strong bond of friendship and respect. The president estimated he spent more time with Mondale than with all other aides combined.

The decline in President Carter's popularity was apparent to all by 1979. Lengthy sessions with aides, including Mondale, at Camp David had led to the notion that America was suffering from a "crisis of confidence." Mondale felt Carter's reference to a "national malaise," was silly, but could not convince the president. The 1976 ticket was renominated in 1980. Mondale helped hold Minnesota in the Democratic column, but 45 states were in the Republican's.

Mondale almost immediately laid plans to challenge President Reagan in 1984. He took a lucrative partnership with the Washington office of a Chicago-based law firm, but that was only to permit him to campaign, not to practice law. He built what for a time was considered the best as well as the biggest political machine in American political history. He tried to educate himself, even getting from historian Barbara Tuchman a list of important books that he should read. Experts in every field came in to conduct one-on-one seminars on their specialties. Ted Kennedy, who had challenged for the nomination in 1980, in December 1982 declared that he would not run. By February 21, 1983, Fritz Mondale was ready, with a fire in the belly and no further squeamishness about spending a year, or two, in Holiday Inns.

Politically, 1983 mainly belonged to Mondale, as money-raising and political polls all showed a big Fritz lead among Democrats. He had been surprisingly bested in a few straw polls along the way, but after his Iowa caucus victory in February 1984, Mondale had a seeming lock on the nomination. Iowa gave Colorado Senator Gary Hart some momentum because of a weak but still second-place finish. For all the endorsements—the AFL-CIO, the National Education Association, the National Organization for Women—for all the money and impressive organization and talent, that little boost to Hart was all the Mondale campaign needed to be tossed into near-disaster. Hart's additional media attention brought on by his Iowa showing caused those with doubts about Mondale to focus on Hart. The "new ideas" senator from Colorado won in New Hampshire with 39 percent to Mondale's 29 percent.

The secondary Democratic contenders, except for Jesse Jackson, soon dropped out. The rest of the primaries became a competitive, bitterly personal drive by Mondale and Hart. Mondale's organizational lead proved out, even though Hart won about as many votes as did the former vice president. Hart said he had new ideas, but Mondale helped remove the glitter from that image by asking Hart, at a campaign aide's inspiration, "Where's the beef?" Wendy's Hamburgers' popular, soon to be maddeningly repeated, slogan was just the clever hook Mondale needed to convince voters the Colorado senator had more slogan than substance.

Hart continued in the race until the national convention in July, but Mondale had the margin needed by the end of the last primary. He could then indulge in the same magisterial process that Jimmy Carter had eight years earlier, and summon the supplicants for vice president to his native state hideaway. Mondale apparently wanted a black, Hispanic, or a woman. His liberalism compelled him to desire such a choice; he also needed something dramatic to break the perception that President Reagan had too big a lead to be overtaken. Geraldine Ferraro was the choice. At the convention, during a period when national polls were showing the margin between Mondale and Reagan narrowing, Mondale took another risk. He announced during his acceptance speech that he would raise taxes soon upon taking office, in order to reduce the monstrous budget deficit. "Let's tell the truth," he said. "Mr. Reagan will raise taxes, and so will

I. He won't tell you. I just did." It was a bold political gamble.

Regardless of what Mondale did or said, Reagan's regained landslide margin could not be narrowed. He felt Reagan was dissembling by presenting a meaningless picture of American prosperity when economic disaster was awaiting. The voters were not listening. What was left were two make-or-break televised debates with the president. Mondale crammed for the debate during much of September. On October 7, in Louisville, Kentucky, Mondale surprised the president with a respectful, almost regretful approach, calling the president a good man who just did not understand America's future. Reagan performed poorly, and at times looked confused. The overall effect was to give Mondale's campaign a momentary boost. The margin closed slightly, but by the time of the second debate it had returned virtually to where it had been before Louisville. Mondale's chances were ended by an adequate performance by Reagan in the second debate in Kansas City, highlighted by Reagan's humor on the suddenly significant issue of whether he was too old to serve. "I will not make age an issue of this campaign. I am not going to exploit for political purposes my opponent's youth and inexperience." The Democratic nominee suffered one of the worst electoral defeats in American presidential politics. He won only his native Minnesota with a 15,000 vote margin out of two million cast, and the always Democratic District of Columbia.

In a somewhat sour postmortem the next day, Mondale warned President Reagan that he would have to eat a lot of crow soon on the deficit and taxes. He added he would not run again for public office. Instead, he went back to the Washington law firm that he had joined in 1981. In August, 1987 he returned to practice law in Minneapolis.

In June 1989, with polls showing an excellent chance of victory in 1990 over Republican Senator Rudy Boschwitz, Mondale repeated his pledge not again to run for office. He stayed out of government until 1993. President Bill Clinton was reported to have offered the position of ambassador to Russia, but Mondale declined. On June 8, 1993, his appointment as ambassador to Japan was announced. One of the most publicly awkward tasks Mondale had to perform grew out of the rape in 1995 of a 12-year-old Japanese girl by three Marines based in Okinawa. President Clinton, Secretary of Defense Perry, and Mondale all at different times apologized to the Japanese people for the crime. Mondale was the one actually present on a daily basis during the controversy, so bore the worst of the burden. Another recurring issue concerned the return of the base on Okinawa to Japan. About 27,000 of the 47,000 American troops in Japan were based there. No resolution had occurred by late 1997.

Analysis of Qualifications

In 1984 Mondale's campaign came across with three overwhelming negatives. He was viewed as boring, as a big tax and spender, and as bound to special interests. In a less clear but pervasive way, he was also tied to the pessimism of the Jimmy Carter years. The dynamics of the 1984 primary and general election campaign were at times unfair to Walter Mondale. In an age of television, Mondale — as he said himself—"never really warmed up to television, and in fairness to television, it's never really warmed up to me." In private Mondale could be a witty and interesting conversationalist, but in public he lacked excitement. An experienced politician, who many times performed well in critical tasks, Mondale in 1984 was depicted as being part of a long standing problem instead of the leader for the future.

He withdrew throughout his political life from confrontation. Lacking "fire in his belly" was the most gastronomically jolting description given Mondale's personality, but many people agreed with the description. Few doubted his integrity, his intelligence, or the sincerity of his beliefs. He had genuine sympathy for the underdog and hated privilege. As the margin of his 1984 defeat seemed increasingly clear, the candidate stated, "I would rather lose an election about decency than win one about self-interest." He meant, it is assumed, that if decency were to lose he wanted to be the one who carried that banner.

Through 20 years in national office Mon-

dale had exhibited intelligence, honesty, and Eagle Scout earnestness. He was a loyal subordinate, first to Hubert Humphrey and later to Jimmy Carter. As with many career subordinates, a question exists as to whether he could take a leadership role. On balance it is likely Mondale would have been a competent, at times activist, even-tempered president. He lost because his political philosophy was unacceptable in 1984. He lost by a landslide because he ran against Ronald Reagan.

MONDALE BIBLIOGRAPHY

Broder, David, et al. *The Pursuit of the Presidency 1980.* New York City (1980).

Carter, Jimmy. *Keeping Faith: Memoirs of a President.* New York City (1982).

Germond, Jack W., and Jules Witcover. *Blue Smoke and Mirror — How Reagan Won and Why Carter Lost the Election of 1980.* New York City (1981).

_____, and _____. *Wake Us When It Is Over — Presidential Politics of 1984.* New York City (1985).

Gillon, Steven M. *The Democrats' Dilemma: Walter F. Mondale and the Liberal Legacy.* New York (1994).

Goldman, Peter, and Tony Fuller. *The Quest for the Presidency, 1984.* Toronto, New York City, et al. (1985).

Harris, David. "Understanding Mondale." *The New York Times Magazine* (June 19, 1983), pp. 26-56.

Humphrey, Hubert H. *The Education of a Public Man; My Life and Politics.* Garden City, N.Y. (1976).

Lewis, Finlay. *Mondale: Portrait of an American Politician.* New York City (1984).

Mondale, R. Lester, and Maria Mondale. *The Mundale-Mondale Clan.* Cape Giradeau, Mo. (1975).

Perry, James M. "Cautious Candidate: How Walter Mondale Climbed to High Office by Avoiding Crusades." *The Wall Street Journal* (July 17, 1984), pp. 1 & 12.

Shapiro, Walter, et al. "Can Anyone Beat Fritz?" *Newsweek* (January 9, 1984), pp. 26-32.

_____. "Fritz Up Close." *Newsweek* (July 23, 1984), pp. 38-46.

Solberg, Carl. *Hubert Humphrey: A Biography.* New York City and London (1984).

Weinraub, Bernard. "Politician in the Minnesota Tradition: Walter Frederick Mondale." *New York Times* (July 19,1984), pp. 1 & 14.

Witcover, Jules. *Marathon: The Pursuit of the Presidency 1972-1976.* New York City (1977).

The family information was provided by the Reverend R. Lester Mondale and Mrs. Maria Mondale of Fredericktown, Missouri.

---

*1984 vice presidential nominee—
Democratic Party*

Geraldine A. Ferraro

Full name: Geraldine Anne Ferraro Zaccaro.

State represented: New York.

Birth: August 26, 1935, Newburgh, New York.

Age on Inauguration Day (January 20, 1985): 49 years, 5 months.

Education: Tutored at home, then Marymount School (Tarrytown, N.Y.), graduating at age 16; Marymount Manhattan College (B.A. 1956); Fordham University (night) Law School (J.D. 1960), admitted to bar 1960.

Religion:Roman Catholic.

Ancestry: Father immigrated from Italy in 1920; mother's parents also immigrated from Italy.

Occupation: Schoolteacher while attending law school; attorney.

Public offices: Queens assistant district attorney 1974–1978; United States representative January 3, 1979–January 3, 1985; unsuccessful Democratic vice presidential nominee 1984. Defeated for Democratic U.S. Senate nomination, 1986 and 1992.

Home: Forest Hills Gardens community, Queens, New York.

Personal characteristics: short, slim, with frosted blond hair; strong New York accent; known both as warm and gregarious, and as impatient, stern, and tough.

Father: Dominick Ferraro (1899–May 29, 1944), owned a restaurant and department store.

Mother: Antonetta L. Corrieri (1906–), married October 2, 1926; worked crocheting beads after her husband died.

Siblings: Carl (May, 1929–), works with New York City human resources administration. Anthony (born May 1929, died after a few days). Gerard (1930–1933), killed in automobile accident.

Husband: John Zaccaro (1933–), wealthy real estate broker and businessman; married July 16, 1960.

Children: Donna (1962–). John (1964–). Laura (1966–).

"This is an exciting choice," Walter Mondale said in announcing his pick for vice president. Delivered in a typically, for him, unexciting monotone, this line admitted the motivation behind the choice of Geraldine Ferraro to be his running mate. The Democrats knew that Mount Reagan loomed nearly insurmountably before them. If they were to conquer it, they would need to rewrite the laws of elections. Choosing an articulate, aggressive, trailblazing candidate might be their only hope. Perhaps their plight was hopeless, as the first sex-balanced ticket was toppled in a landslide.

Geraldine Anne Ferraro was the fourth child in a tragedy-scarred, upper-middle class family in Newburgh, New York. Dominick Ferraro owned a successful restaurant in this quiet city 60 miles up river from New York City. He also operated a five-and-dime. Dominick had been 21 years old before he left his native Italy. Italian was the more natural language for him, but his bride encouraged him to perfect his English. That bride, Antonetta Corrieri, was the first generation of her family to be born in America. Antonetta and to a lesser degree Dominick had experienced poverty, but soon that was behind them as the Newburgh businesses flourished.

The first children born to the young Italian-Americans were twins. One of the boys was sickly from birth and lived only a few days. The next pregnancy was terminated when a doctor's erroneous prescription caused a miscarriage. Then in 1930 little Gerard was born. Three years of happiness were all that was permitted them, as Gerard was killed in an automobile accident. A few moments before the accident Gerard was handed up to his mother in the front seat so that she could hold him. The baby's toys were literally buried with him, and so was a substantial portion of his mother's will to live. After two years of morbid depression, Mrs. Ferraro agreed with a doctor's advice that another child might help end her sorrow. In 1935, Geraldine was born and named in honor of her deceased brother.

WALTER F. MONDALE and GERALDINE A. FERRARO
(From the author's collection)

For the next eight years the Ferraros seemed to have broken this pattern of tragedy. Gerry's father was so enchanted with her that the first year he celebrated her birthday each month, giving her a seemingly never-ending supply of dolls and frilly clothes. This idyllic family setting was destroyed on May 29, 1944, when Gerry's father suffered a massive heart attack at the age of 44. On May 1 of that same year, both of her parents had been indicted for conducting a policy or numbers game at their store. After Dominick's death, the charges were dropped. The future national party candidate may not have known of the indictment until it became public during the 1984 campaign.

The Ferraros' economic security died with Dominick. The large, comfortable house in Newburgh gave way to an apartment in the Bronx, and later a return to Queens. Antonetta Ferraro started crocheting beads to bring in some money. She discouraged Geraldine's interest in the occupation, as she had far loftier ambitions for her daughter.

Sending Geraldine away from home to prep school was difficult for both. For college, then, the 16 year old moved back in with her mother and attended Marymount Manhattan College. More traditional-minded members of the Ferraro clan doubted the need to send a young woman to college, since she "of course" would soon get married and raise a family. Even her own kin did not quite understand just where it was that these two strong-willed women were going, together almost.

A teaching certificate gained along with her bachelor's degree did not long interest Geraldine. Teaching second-graders during the day, she attended night law school at Fordham University. Many professors and fellow students seemed to begrudge her this place in the school. There were only two women in her class, and Geraldine was told that those slots would have been better utilized by men. She graduated in 1960, took the bar, and in July married John Zaccaro after a five-year courtship.

For the next 14 years Ferraro was an extremely energetic housewife. There were diapers, carpools, and the PTA to be sure, but there were also political and civic meetings that kept her busy. She raised three children, worked actively if not centrally in local Democratic politics, and enjoyed the life of a wife of a prosperous real estate broker. John Zaccaro's initial efforts in real estate were, in his own words, a "flop" but as his firm began to specialize in commercial properties in Greenwich Village, Chinatown, and Soho, financial success was achieved.

This financially comfortable but ambitious Forest Hills Gardens housewife asked her cousin Nick Ferraro for a position on his staff at the Queens district attorney's office. She worked with the Investigations Bureau. She was one of only a few women prosecutors in the city when she began work in 1974. Any concern among the other prosecutors that she had not fairly gained her post was dispelled by the energy and intelligence she put into her work. She first merely helped prepare cases for others to try. After all, she had graduated from law school 14 years before and had little experience. By the next year she had moved on to the Special Victims Bureau. This department handled cases involving rape and the abuse of children and the elderly. Two years later she was selected head of her Bureau.

Ferraro's defense attorney opponents remembered her as a tough, but fair adversary. She handled six trials during her tenure, won all of them, and none was reversed on appeal.

A former assistant district attorney recalled her as one of the hardest working people he had ever been around. She seemed to have a rapport with jurors. During the presentation to a grand jury of one particularly grotesque case of child sexual abuse, she sat down with the distraught child in her lap while she asked the girl questions about the ordeal.

Politics had always interested Ferraro. In 1972 she had been a community activist in blocking a planned high-rise that might have disrupted the serenity of her secluded, exclusive neighborhood. She had worked for her cousin Nick's campaigns. Now it was time for her own campaign. Some thought was given to running for the city council. A prize of considerably loftier proportions became achievable when long-time 9th District Congressman James J. Delaney announced in April 1978 that he was retiring. It was a fairly conservative working class district, but it was also ethnic and well-familiar with the Ferraro name because of state senator/district attorney Nicholas Ferraro's campaigns. With John Zaccaro's encouragement, Ferraro decided to try.

The party establishment, including Mario Cuomo, supported one of her two opponents in the primary. Yet with a substantial expenditure of Zaccaro money, with a tireless personal campaign, and with the advantages earned from years of civic and political involvement, Ferraro won with 53 percent of the vote in the three-way primary. The party leaders did not immediately rally around her for the general election, but among her most prominent benefactors was the president's mother, Lillian Carter. Miss Lillian told an audience, "I don't know anything about her except that my Jimmy likes her." As much as $110,000 in loans were made by John Zaccaro to the campaign. Federal Election Commission rules, however, limited loans even from family members to $1,000. The campaign later claimed that they had been assured by a former attorney with the commission that the loans were legal, but the attorney denied this. The FEC apparently was not overly concerned, and merely imposed a $750 fine. Regardless, the infusion of money helped the Ferraro campaign surge and led to a comfortable 10 percent margin over her Republican opponent.

In the House the new Queens congress-woman established herself as a team player. She became a particular favorite of House Speaker Thomas P. "Tip" O'Neill and it gained her sizable rewards. Ferraro was proud to hear that she was considered "one of the boys," because that meant she was accepted as some-one who knew how to get things done.

The Queens representative was in the high-est rankings of liberal Democrats. Such orga-nizations as the liberal American for Democ-ratic Action and the AFL-CIO gave her 90 percent and some years even 100 percent rat-ings for "correct" votes. Conservatives were correspondingly distraught over her record. Ferraro opposed many major defense weapon systems, including the B-1 bomber, the MX missile, the "Star Wars" system, and chemical weapons. She voted against many of President Ronald Reagan's foreign policy decisions, including the leaving of troops in Beirut, Lebanon in 1983 or the conducting of CIA operations in Central America. In sum Ferraro was an above-average Democratic loyalist and a far-below average Democratic supporter of President Reagan. She voted with a majority of Democrats in 1983 on 92 percent of the votes, and supported Reagan on only 15 per-cent.

With a pro-labor, pro–domestic spending record, Ferraro also ranked as one of the most consistent supporters of the New Deal philos-ophy of large government programs to aid the needy. Increasingly comfortable reelection margins in 1980 and 1982, as well as growing personal clout, gained her a position on the House Budget Committee in 1983. She had preferred the Ways and Means Committee, but that proved too lofty a goal.

Geraldine Ferraro's ambition had never been disguised. Some fellow politicians have been leery, or perhaps jealous, of her rapid suc-cess in gaining increasingly more prestigious positions. She was elected secretary of the Democratic caucus in 1980. That post enabled her to sit on the critically important House Policy and Steering Committee, which among other things makes committee assignments. Tip O'Neill was a key backer in the rise. She wanted a prominent role at the 1984 national convention, and campaigned arduously for it.

She said, "If they're looking for a woman for the platform committee, and they are, they've got to have someone who can handle it and who wants it." Ferraro achieved her coup of being named national convention platform committee chairman. This enabled her to travel the country and gain valuable publicity as she held platform hearings in the spring of 1984.

Ferraro announced no favorite for the pres-idential nomination. Being platform commit-tee head enabled her to avoid choosing sides. All through the spring her name was near the top of the list of potential vice presidents for Democrats who wanted a woman on the na-tional ticket. Ferraro made it clear she felt she should be considered and said, "If I weren't capable I wouldn't be talked about." When the primaries ended in early June, Walter Mondale appeared by all accounts to have sufficient del-egates for the nomination. Mondale deter-mined early he should name a black, Hispanic, or a woman. Though he may have varied in his determination, what is accepted as his final "short list" of contenders suggests this re-mained his plan. Besides Ferraro, also on the list were three mayors: San Francisco's Dianne Feinstein, black Tom Bradley of Los Angeles, and Hispanic Henry Cisneros of San Antonio. White male governor Michael Dukakis rounded out the list.

Mondale went through the same public interview process for a running mate as had Jimmy Carter when Mondale was selected. Early reports after the Mondale-Ferraro meet-ing indicated that Mondale had been put off by Ferraro's aggressiveness for the job, and her too-candid explanation to the press of the political factors that would go into Mondale's decision. Those reports were apparently false, and Mondale had been impressed. Feinstein and Ferraro were the final two contenders. Mondale called Ferraro on the phone and said, "I'd like you to run with me." The answer was immediate, and affirmative.

Almost from the start the Ferraro campaign became embroiled in controversy. A brief speech to the enthusiastic delegates at the Democratic national convention was her last triumph for awhile. The first few weeks after the San Francisco convention were filled with revelations, some true and some not, about financial irregularities in her past campaigns or in her husband's business. The first crisis arose over John Zaccaro's refusal to reveal financial information about himself, after Ferraro had announced that all would be made public. The media presented that refusal as a major issue of integrity, until Zaccaro was forced to succumb to the demand to release his records. Stories about the illegal use of campaign loans in 1978 surfaced, as did disclosures that Ferraro had failed to comply with congressional financial reporting requirements. Ferraro's position on the ticket, to some of the more optimistic Republicans at least, seemed for a time to be in jeopardy. Mondale stayed quiet, as in similar circumstances George McGovern had when revelations about his running mate Tom Eagleton first surfaced, and as Dwight Eisenhower had when Richard Nixon's place on the ticket was at risk. Ferraro had to redeem herself, and did so in an updated version of Nixon's "Checker's speech" that had saved his vice presidential nomination 32 years before. A tremendous package of financial information was prepared and released to the press. Ferraro held an exhaustive press conference to go over the details of the disclosures.

What the disclosures revealed were that the Zaccaros were wealthier than their Republican counterpart family, the George Bushes. This was an awkward revelation after Ferraro had earlier declared themselves "not rich people." More substantive was the growing controversy Ferraro found herself in over the abortion issue. As a Roman Catholic, Ferraro said she was personally opposed to abortion. Yet she also said that a decision as personal as childbearing was one to be made by each individual, and not imposed by a church or a society. Hecklers in increasing numbers plagued her campaign stops. Several significant members of the Catholic clergy, especially in her native New York, advised their parishioners not to vote for pro-abortion candidates.

The most significant single event in the Ferraro campaign was probably her October debate with Vice President Bush. Her main mission was to appear sufficiently competent and serious to be trusted as vice president. She showed an awkward novice status on foreign affairs, and the vice president scored well in comparison. On the other hand, the most memorable line in the debate was delivered in response to Bush's attempt to highlight her amateur status. He took her to task for failing to distinguish between Carter's troubles in Iran and Reagan's in Beirut. The Democrats had prepared a line for just such a moment, and Ferraro delivered splendidly. "I almost resent," she said, "your patronizing attitude that you have to teach me about foreign policy."

Despite the overwhelming electoral defeat in November, Geraldine Ferraro had scored a tremendous personal political victory. Since winning election as vice president had been considered unlikely almost from the start, Ferraro was even before election day in the speculation for a race against Republican New York Senator Alfonse D'Amato in 1986. That opportunity was seriously damaged because of revelations about John Zaccaro that resulted in his criminal conviction shortly after the 1984 election. On January 7, 1985, John Zaccaro pleaded guilty to having submitted a falsely inflated contract of sale for property, to have overstated his net worth by 500 percent, and to have altered a property appraisal, all in order to get financing for a multi-million dollar real estate development. Zaccaro was only sentenced to perform 150 hours of community service. In October 1987 Zaccaro was acquitted of bribery and extortion charges involving a cable television contract.

On December 11, 1985, with polls showing her well behind Senator D'Amato, Ferraro announced that she would not run. Out of politics, she still faced frequent public crises involving her family. In February 1986, allegations that her son John was a cocaine dealer at Middleburg College in Vermont became national news. Two years later he was tried and convicted of selling cocaine to undercover police. The 24 year old was sentenced to four months in a house arrest program in Vermont.

Over the next few years she wrote her memoirs, campaigned for other candidates, and dealt with family matters. In 1992 Ferraro ran for the Democratic nomination to challenge GOP Senator Alfonse D'Amato. She was the clear front-runner until New York City comptroller Elizabeth Holtzman started running strongly negative television ads against her.

Much like the GOP attacks in 1984, the advertisements centered on ethics questions concerning her husband. The harshness of the ads seemed to hurt Holtzman almost as much as Ferraro. The result was that state attorney general Robert Abrams narrowly won the primary, with 37 percent of the vote, to 36 percent for Ferraro and 15 percent for black activist Al Sharpton. The perpetrator of Ferraro's downfall, Holtzman, came in fourth at 15 percent. Ferraro was bitter and refused for several days to concede.

Ferraro became the liberal spokeswoman on CNN's *Crossfire.* In late 1997 she considered once again running against Senator D'Amato.

Analysis of Qualifications

Geraldine Ferraro would not have received her place on the 1984 Democratic ticket had she not been a woman. But does that mean she was undeserving? Just what were her objective qualifications for so lofty a place?

Ferraro is a warm, outgoing, intelligent woman with sincerity and strength. She is articulate and at times, humorous. She is also extremely ambitious, with a reputation from some as more of a superb politician than a skilled statesman. As would be true for most three-term representatives, Ferraro's legislative achievements were scarce. Her main accomplishment for which she was solely responsible was getting a zip code changed for part of her district. She was a sponsor of legislation to give women equal rights in pensions and other retirement benefits. As her service in Congress advanced, by most measures she became more of a feminist, more anti-military, and more pro-labor. She supported most abortion rights bills and the Equal Rights Amendment. Yet to some of the more radical feminists, Ferraro has seemed overly compromising.

Her willingness to compromise for what seem to be achievable goals may be the key element of Ferraro's political personality. Her rise in Congress was meteoric, but her ascent was judged by political accomplishments, not legislative ones. Geraldine Ferraro accomplished a great deal in six years in Washington. She revealed political skills of persuasion and compromise that are valuable in leadership. She had also just begun to be involved in important decision-making tasks in Congress, and had scarcely commenced her education in foreign affairs or national defense issues. She had come a long way. To be president, it would appear she still had a long way to go.

In some respects Ferraro's qualifications are akin to those of Sargent Shriver in 1972. He also had never had major responsibilities. He too had performed well in subordinate positions, but had yet to be tested in any major position. Most pointedly, Shriver had also been chosen for reasons quite apart from his ability to assume the presidency. Each of the two nominees might have risen to the demands of this highest office if called upon. They were both, however, gambles for the American voters. Neither the fact that Shriver was a Kennedy-in-law nor that Ferraro was a woman was the only reason for the selection of either. These were sufficiently influential causes, though, as to point out again just how politics, not past performance, governs the choice for vice president.

FERRARO BIBLIOGRAPHY

Anderson, Kurt, et al. "Show and Tell." *Time* (September 3, 1984), pp. 14–18.

Baske, Kevin Timothy. "The Rhetoric of Character Legitimation: Geraldine A. Ferraro and the 1984 Vice-Presidential Campaign." Unpublished doctoral dissertation, University of Southern California (1989).

Blumenthal, Sidney. "Once Upon a Time in America." *The New Republic* (January 6 and 13, 1986), pp. 28–36.

Borger, Gloria. "The Child Star's New Role." *U.S. News & World Report* (September 14, 1992), pp. 35, 38.

Brenner, Marie. "Gerry Rides It Out." *New York* (September 3, 1984), pp. 23–29.

Breslin, Rosemary, and Joshua Hammer. *Gerry! A Woman Making History.* New York City (1984).

Bumiller, Elisabeth. "The Rise of Geraldine Ferraro." *The Washington Post* (April 29, 1984), pp. Kl and K5.

Ferraro, Geraldine, with Linda Bird Francke. *Ferraro: My Story.* Toronto, New York City, et al. (1985).

Ferraro, Susan. "What Makes Gerry Run?" *The New York Times Magazine* (March 22, 1992), pp. 46–47, 66 ff.

"Ferraro Narrowly Loses New York Senate Race." *Facts on File 1992* (1992), p. 679A2.

Goldner, Diane, and James Lyons. 'The Ferraro File: What Kind of Prosecutor Was She?" *The American Lawyer* (September 1984), pp. 87–91.

Granat, Diane. "Ferraro's Path to Power: Peanut-Butter Sandwiches to Presidential Ticket." *Congressional Quarterly Weekly Report* (July 14, 1984), pp. 1677–1683.

Katz, Lee Michael. *My Name Is Geraldine Ferraro.* New York City (1984).

Kwitny, Jonathan, and Anthony M. De Stefano. "Representative Ferraro and a Painful Legacy." *The Wall Street Journal* (September 13, 1984), p. 26.

MacPherson, Myra. "On the Ferraro Express." *The Washington Post* (October 19, 1984), pp. Bl and B13.

Mathews, Tom, et al. "A Team Player." *Newsweek* (July 23, 1984), pp. 22–28.

Perlez, Jane. "Liberal Democrat from Queens: Geraldine Anne Ferraro Zaccaro." *New York Times* (July 13, 1984), pp. 1 and 9.

Stanley, Alessandra. "The Rising Star from Queens." *Time* (June 4, 1984), pp. 24–25.

Thomas, Evan, et al. "'Just One of the Guys,' and Quite a Bit More." *Time* (July 23, 1984), pp. 18–20 and 33.

Trotta, Liz. "Ferraro Weighing Run Against D'Amato." *Washington Times* (August 10, 1997), p. A1.

Weinraub, Bernard. "Geraldine Ferraro Is Chosen...." *New York Times* (July 13, 1984), pp. 1, 8.

Election of 1988

NOMINATIONS

Democratic Party Convention (40th) July 25–28, 1988, at Omni Coliseum, Atlanta, Georgia. *President*—Michael S. Dukakis, nominated on first ballot with 2,876.25 votes. The Reverend Jesse Jackson (S.C., 111. and D.C.) received 1,218.5 votes, and 23 were scattered or abstained. Other contenders had been Albert Gore, Jr. (Tenn.), Bruce Babbitt (Az.), Paul Simon (111.), Joe Biden (Del.), Gary Hart (Colo.), and Richard Gephardt (Mo.). *Vice president*— Lloyd Bentsen, nominated by acclamation.

Republican Party Convention (34th), August 15–18, 1988, at the Superdome, New Orleans, Louisiana. *President*— George Bush, nominated on the first ballot with all 2,277 votes cast. Other contenders had been Bob Dole (Kan.), the Reverend Pat Robertson (Va.), Jack Kemp (N.Y.), Paul Laxalt (Nev.), Pete duPont (Del.), and Al Haig (Va.). *Vice president*— Dan Quayle, nominated by acclamation.

GENERAL ELECTION, November 8, 1988

Popular Vote

Bush	48,886,097
Dukakis	41,809,074
Other	800,638

Electoral Vote

Bush-Quayle — 426 (40 states)
Dukakis-Bentsen — 111 (10+ states)
Bentsen-Dukakis — 1

Winners

George Bush, 41st president
Dan Quayle, 44th vice president

Losers

Michael Dukakis; Lloyd Bentsen

*1988 presidential nominee —
Democratic Party*

Michael S. Dukakis

Full name: Michael Stanley Dukakis. His father shortened the name from "Doukakis" in college.

State represented: Massachusetts.

Birth: November 3, 1933, in Brookline, Massachusetts.

Age on inauguration Day (January 20, 1989): 55 years, 2½ months.

Education: Brookline public schools. Swarthmore College 1951–55 (B.A., Phi Beta Kappa). Harvard Law School (J.D., 1960, with honors).

Religion: Greek Orthodox.

Ancestry/prominent relatives: Both parents immigrated from Greece as children. Olympia Dukakis, a cousin, is an Oscar-winning actress.

Public offices: Defeated for Brookline Redevelopment Authority 1958. Elected Brookline town meeting representative 1959–1961. Founded Commonwealth Organization of Democrats 1960. Massachusetts state representative 1962–1970. Defeated at state party convention for attorney general nomination 1966. Defeated nominee for lieutenant governor 1970. Governor 1975–1979; defeated in 1978; 1983–1991. Defeated Democratic presidential nominee 1988.

Home: Victorian duplex at 85 Perry Street, Brookline, a few blocks from home where he grew up.

Personal characteristics: 5'8" tall; brown, thick hair; brown eyes. Does not smoke, rarely drinks, known for his honesty and extreme frugality. Self-assured, hard-working, almost cocky.

Father: Panagis "Panos" Dukakis (Jan. 15, 1896–Nov. 6, 1979), born in Pelopi, Greece, arrived in America at age 16. He was first Greek immigrant to be admitted to Harvard Medical School. Obstetrician.

Mother: Euterpe Boukis (Sept. 4, 1903–); she was nine years old when arrived in America. Graduated Phi Beta Kappa from Bates College. Her father was a clerk in Greece. Married September 4, 1929.

Sibling: Stelian Panos (July 11, 1930–July 29, 1973), attempted suicide in 1950; rest of his life an emotional struggle. Struck by hit-and-run driver on March 17, 1973, while bicycling, and never regained consciousness.

Wife: Katherine "Kitty" Dickson (December 26, 1936–), married June 20, 1963, daughter of Harry Ellis Dickson and Jane (Byrnes) Dickson. Father was a violinist with Boston symphony and associate director of Boston Pops. Kitty married John Chaffetz on March 17, 1957, divorced 1960.

Children: John (June 9, 1958–), child of wife and her first husband, adopted by Dukakis; married Lisa Thurmond; he is an actor who has appeared in *Jaws II* and "Family Ties." Andrea (November 10, 1965–). Kara (November 4, 1968–).

Not since Thomas E. Dewey in 1948 had such an intensely disciplined, unemotional man been nominated for president. "Technocrat" seems the label for both. Dewey was likened to the plastic groom on a wedding cake. Dukakis resembled the same stiff figure. Like Dewey, Dukakis also had a huge lead in national polls months before the election and was considered a likely winner. But like Harry Truman, George Bush ran a "give 'em hell" campaign that left the early favorite a groomsman, not a groom — plastic or otherwise.

The parents of the future Massachusetts governor were distinguished examples of the American dream. His father Panos arrived in America from Greece at age 16. Nine years later be was admitted to Harvard Medical School and became an obstetrician. Michael's mother Euterpe similarly arrived from Greece as a child, yet received an honor-filled college education. Dukakis was the first presidential nominee since Andrew Jackson to have two immigrant parents.

Dukakis was always serious. Friends were few, but respect for his achievements was widespread. One school chum remarked, "I read the Hardy Boys. Michael read the Life of Napoleon." Politics was his early focus. He says that at age seven he and his brother spread out a chart with each state and, listening to the radio, kept a tally of the 1940 Republican National Convention.

Michael was born in the Boston suburb of Brookline. There he remained except for college and the army. Though Michael was a model child, his older brother Stelian was more emotional. Stelian had a mental breakdown at college, when Michael was a high school senior. A short time later he tried to kill himself. For 20 years Stelian wandered from relative mental stability to emotional upheaval. In one of Michael's early political races Stelian went through several neighborhoods distributing literature opposing Michael's election. A team of Michael's supporters was able to retrieve most of it. While riding his bicycle in 1973, Stelian was struck by a hit-and-run driver. After being comatose for four months he died at age 43.

Michael's youth was almost uninterrupted

academic success. He usually finished first in his classes. Tennis star and team captain, three-letter athlete, trumpet player, student council president (after being defeated for senior class president), Eagle Scout, he was "what your mother always wanted you to be, but you never were" according to one friend. The school annual was more picturesque: "Big Chief Brain-in-Face." His parents had emphasized his Americanism, but still he learned Greek at home. It was only when he ran for president that his ethnic background became prominent. This caused some local wags to say they had known him since before he was Greek.

Harvard was where Brookline boys with Michael's record "always" went. That may be why Michael did not, as he had a well-developed disdain for class-consciousness. Instead, Swarthmore College in Philadelphia became his next stop. Again involved in cross-country running, music and politics, Michael excelled. Among his causes were the American Civil Liberties Union and the Students for Democratic Action. Black students found the local barbers unwilling to cut their hair. Michael stepped into the breach, making a political point and some money simultaneously. He cut hair for all who came, white and black. A half-hearted foray into a pre-med curriculum terminated with a "D" in physics. It may have just been a self-generated excuse to avoid following in his father's medical footsteps.

In Philadelphia Dukakis got his first taste of politics by working with other students on reformer Joe Clark's race for mayor. Next he organized students for Adlai Stevenson's presidential race in 1952. He spent one summer in Peru on a student fellowship. A useful byproduct was his fluent Spanish, which was much used during the 1988 campaign.

Graduating cum laude in 1955, Dukakis had one other obligation. Rather than go on to law school, Dukakis joined the army and served two boring years. He served in Korea after the war was over, where he was a clerk-typist. He told a friend, "I have to have that [the Army] on my record."

He began at Harvard Law School in 1957. As a first year law student he ran for a position on the Brookline Redevelopment Author-

ity, but was defeated. As a second-year student Dukakis became one of 240 town meeting representatives in Brookline. Then he and some fellow reformers organized the Commonwealth Organization of Democrats, or C.O.D. This became a potent force in Massachusetts with Dukakis as one of the prime movers. These young good government types were derisively called "googoos." In time they would win. Despite all this political activity, Dukakis graduated from law school with honors in 1960.

Dukakis ran for the legislature in 1962 and won from a traditionally Republican area. He would serve four terms. The passage of the country's first no-fault automobile insurance law was his monumental effort, one that earned him a standing ovation from supporters and opponents alike in the legislature when it passed. Yet, ironically, he had become so unyielding on every detail that he had earlier been removed from the conference committee since he was blocking a necessary compromise. It was on such issues that Dukakis was tireless. He eschewed the grandstanding so prevalent on the Vietnam War, civil rights, and other liberal causes. Instead, he was interested in practical government. For his achievements he was in 1967 voted the year's outstanding legislator.

The unemotional, calculating, frugal Dukakis was introduced by his only previous girlfriend, Sandy Cohen, to a young divorcée, Kitty Dickson. They were wed in 1963. She was Jewish and he Greek Orthodox. They allowed their three children to experience both faiths, though in 1987 Mrs. Dukakis said "none of us are very religious."

Dukakis had met defeat along the way. In 1966 he wanted the state Democratic convention nomination for attorney general, but lost. He was his party's nominee for lieutenant governor in 1970, but was beaten in the general election. After the latter defeat he went back to the Boston law firm that he had entered right out of law school. He also became the moderator of the public television issue forum "The Advocates," which originated in Boston. It helped prepare him for future television debates.

By 1974 Dukakis was ready to take on incumbent Republican Governor Francis Sargent. The state was in dire financial straits, but Dukakis gave a "lead-pipe guarantee" that a tax increase would not be his solution to it. Elected with almost 56 percent of the vote, he had to face an awesome deficit immediately. It was not the $100 million forecast by Sargent during the campaign, but grew to $500 million. Among his measures was ostentatious frugality. The state car was garaged and Dukakis rode the subway to work. The former governor's name was crossed out on his left-over stationery and it was used until depleted. Rather than a scalpel, Dukakis said the social program budget needed a meat cleaver. He wielded one, enraging his liberal constituency.

Finally, there was no choice. A tax bill went through the legislature. The governor made a bad situation worse by failing to help even his fellow Democrats with the painful political risks of backing the measure. Indeed, he seemed oblivious to political considerations. His main problem was his rigidity. He angered supporters by bypassing them for appointments. In order not to appear biased towards friends, he in effect disqualified his closest allies. So incensed did fellow politicians become that even nonsmokers lit up around him because he hated the smoke so much.

The result was that friends and foes alike had grievances. Irish machine pol Edward J. King announced against him for the nomination in 1978, but Dukakis sensed no danger. King won with 51 percent to Dukakis's 41 percent. It was humiliating, but totally unexpected only to Dukakis. His wife called it a "public death." His son John captured the analogy just a little more aptly by calling it a divorce. Dukakis refused to endorse King, who had a tough race against Republican moderate Francis Hatch. King won anyway with 53 percent to Hatch's 47 percent. Dukakis's funk had created more enemies.

Slowly he picked up the pieces. He had been an early admirer of the dogged style and the substance of Jimmy Carter. Rumors surfaced that Dukakis might be offered a cabinet post by President Carter. The all Democratic Massachusetts Executive Council urged Carter not to choose him. So instead Dukakis took a teaching position at the John F. Kennedy School of Government. Slow in getting acclimated, after a year he was a success. The "Advocates" television show took him back too. During this period he seemed to remake his public persona. Painful self-examination taught him his problems in dealing with people, including his sense of infallibility and his refusal to listen. As he admitted later, during his first term these attributes caused him to lose control of the political process.

Over a decade in statewide politics gave him a formidable list of contacts, which was massaged into a 60,000-name computer list. In 1982 he was ready for a rematch with King. The campaign was bitter; this time there was no overconfidence. Dukakis won the primary with 53 percent to King's 47 percent, and then went on to a landslide victory in the general election over Republican John Sears.

Again Dukakis came into office with a serious state deficit. A collection of alphabet agencies and programs was the response. The Revenue Enhancement and Protection program (REAP) cracked down on tax evaders after granting temporary amnesty to those who voluntarily paid back taxes. The Employment and Training Choices plan (ET) helped get welfare recipients back to work. Unemployment dropped from the 12.3 percent it had been in 1974 to 3.2 percent in 1987. Per capita income soared over the same period. A better state-private sector partnership was formed. Government boards were dominated by private sector groups. The question became whether a revitalized Massachusetts economy attracted new jobs, or did the reverse happen? Pentagon expenditures in the state had skyrocketed. The vilified Ed King slashed taxes in his four years, which certainly helped attract industry. As researchers at Harvard's Kennedy School said, "State policy probably at most played a marginal role" in the Massachusetts Miracle.

Reelection came easily in 1986. It did not hurt that other governors had voted him the country's best governor that year. Planning for bigger things was well underway. Dukakis had met a tough political pro, John Sasso, in 1978. Impressed, he brought Sasso aboard to run the 1982 campaign. In Dukakis's words, Sasso became like a brother. If so, he was the "evil twin" who did the tough political chores. The pro took leave from Dukakis during the 1984 race to run Geraldine Ferraro's vice presidential campaign, a valuable and perhaps foresighted experience base for 1988. After the 1984 debacle, Sasso argued to Dukakis that his non-traditional liberalism, his record of business success, and for that matter his very stoicism, were just what the battered Democratic Party would want in 1988. The platform would be simple — "I can do for America what I have done in Massachusetts."

An official announcement of candidacy came in the spring of 1987, but by then the strategy was well-formed. An early strong showing in the Iowa caucuses was essential, as was winning the next test in New Hampshire. A few major victories were needed in the Super Tuesday Southern states on March 8, which would keep the money and support growing while other candidates dropped out. That is pretty close to what happened, though Sasso had left long before that. Sasso had secretly prepared what became known as the "attack video" that revealed how another candidate, Senator Joe Biden, had plagiarized a speech and even personal background details from a British politician. Upon learning of Sasso's authorship Dukakis reluctantly agreed he had to go. Dukakis's best political adviser and friend was leaving, but he would be back.

The governor's battle with his own legislature in the spring of 1988 over what was not yet a campaign issue, a prison furlough program, is instructive. This program was the only one in America which furloughed convicts serving life terms without the possibility of parole. The legislature, dominated by Democrats, passed a bill banning furloughs for first degree murderers. Dukakis fought the bill until it became clear in March 1988 that a citizen referendum would place the issue on the November ballot unless the bill was adopted. Dukakis did not want the issue lingering. He promised not to veto this legislation. This quieted the controversy, temporarily.

By mid–April 1988 Dukakis had sewn up the nomination. The Reverend Jesse Jackson was his final opponent. Almost every Wednesday morning there was a new glowing report of a Dukakis primary victory the night before.

That helped propel him by summer to a 17 percentage point lead over Vice President George Bush. The Democratic Party thought they smelled victory. They were singing Franklin Roosevelt's old anthem, "Happy Days Are Here Again," at the convention.

George Bush and his campaign team focused on Dukakis's record. Ten years as governor provided many items of interest. "Comparative campaigning" it was called by the Bush forces. The horrendously polluted Boston Harbor, a vetoed Pledge of Allegiance bill, and most memorably, the first degree murderer who was given a furlough, disappeared, and almost a year later brutally raped a woman and savagely beat her fiancé, caused the Democrat's daunting lead to disappear. Particularly was this evident in the South, the heartland of Bush's strength. Led by national campaign manager Lee Atwater of South Carolina and his savvy Southern coordinator, the young Mississippian Lanny Griffith, Bush had first won all of Dixie on Super Tuesday. The fall campaign would surge the vice president into impressive leads in every Southern state again.

Dukakis knew the importance of the South. He picked a running mate, Bush's old nemesis Lloyd Bentsen of Texas, to make himself competitive. It worked for awhile, but the good poll numbers of mid-summer withered in the August heat generated by the GOP convention, and disappeared by September. The Dukakis inner circle got irate at the way their man was being attacked. In truth, they also despaired at the way Dukakis was handling the attacks. A Dukakis-Bush debate in late September temporarily buoyed Democrat spirits. They were crushed again in October when Bush outpointed Dukakis in their second and last debate. Dukakis did not lose on substance, but on personality. His passionless, lawyer-like demeanor compared poorly to the very human, likable, and solid performance of Bush. The polling numbers soon showed a sharp break to Bush.

The last four weeks of the campaign brought increasingly larger crowds for Dukakis, as often happens in the waning days of a campaign. Geraldine Ferraro observed the same phenomenon in 1984 and hoped then that the dreary polling numbers were belied by the enthusiasm. Not so. The actual balloting was slightly closer than the worst fears after the second debate. Still, on election night the television maps indicated a sea of Republican states surrounding a few islands of traditional Democratic ones. The GOP had just won its fifth presidential election in the six held since 1968.

Post-mortems were not pleasant. Dukakis was liked by fellow Democrats about as much as he had been after losing in 1978. It had appeared an election the Democrats could not lose, but they had. Dukakis's campaign team expressed regret at their efforts. Sasso said there was no unifying theme for the campaign. The country was in relative economic prosperity, with recent foreign policy successes. An equally important factor was the continued underestimating of George Bush. He was not the frazzled bumbler that was for a time his image. In fact the Democrats had a tough uphill race, a matter disguised by many of the fleeting circumstances that had artificially propped up Dukakis's early lead.

The voters in Massachusetts had also lost much of their fervor. The governor's homecoming was to a staggering state budget deficit and plummeting support. On January 3, 1989, he announced he would not run for another term in 1990, but left open the possibility of again running for president. By February 1989 fewer than half of his state's voters approved his performance. Even worse, his wife Kitty entered a treatment center on February 5 for alcohol abuse that had arisen after the November defeat. A month later she returned home with the problem behind her. She had in 1982 overcome a 26-year addiction to amphetamines. On January 3, 1991, Dukakis left the governor's office and closed the door, at least temporarily, on a 30-year political career that had seen far more success than defeat.

Analysis of Qualifications

Much was made in the 18 months of his presidential campaign that there had been a "Duke I," which was the arrogant pre–1978 defeat Dukakis, and there now was a "Duke II," a kinder, gentler, more human Dukakis. Defeat had been his "Great Awakening," giving him compassion and depth. In fact, there

appears to have been only one Dukakis, but after 1978 his iron will merged with his ambition to form what on the surface was a humbler, more out-going man. Only his tactics had really changed. He understood that government required the grease of politics to run, but it was still slimy to Dukakis. He is the righteous reformer and a bureaucratic Puritan, who is at his best dealing with concrete problems with concrete solutions. Smart, aloof, and stubborn, he is so frugal as to be a penny-pincher. When he said the election was about competence, he alerted the American public of the trait that both defines and confines him.

The economy was called the "Massachusetts miracle." Closer inspection raised questions about the significance of the state's contribution to the favorable news. By 1989, the miracle was a mess and Dukakis's support cratered. Though Governor Dukakis certainly grew in office, and was better at his craft in 1989 than in 1975 when he was first sworn in, the most significant difference between Duke I and Duke II seems to be that one was dealt a bad hand of disastrous economic times, which highlighted any leadership shortcomings, while the other got the good cards, for awhile.

Former Boston Mayor Kevin White's description of Dukakis was that if he were put in charge of an alcoholic rehabilitation program, it would be a model of efficiency, but he personally would not pick up a drunk off the street. His politics are liberal and reformist, but cerebral and impersonal. He was competent, but even many Democrats said he had no vision. Dukakis's abilities were as a manager of government, but he always had trouble leading. A frequently quoted analogy was if Dukakis were a car, he would be a Honda — economical, reliable, and unexciting. His religion, said one longtime friend, is government. Harvard Professor Sam Beer, says Dukakis "loves to govern…. That is what he was made for."

For all Dukakis's good qualities, there are disturbing similarities to another recent initially unknown, determined, humorless, technocrat governor whom the Democrats put forth, Jimmy Carter. The similar background experiences and personal characteristics warn that a Dukakis presidency might have been much like that of Carter's. Carter's presidency was a checkerboard of dramatic successes and dismal failures, the failures being both substantive but just as often, public relations disasters. The 1988 campaign confirmed certain suspicions about Governor Dukakis, and moved him from what would likely have been a high "satisfactory" category of presidential prospects, down markedly by the end of the campaign.

DUKAKIS BIBLIOGRAPHY

Bidinotto, Robert James. "Getting Away with Murder." *Reader's Digest* (July, 1988), pp. 57–63.

Black, Christine, and Thomas Oliphant. *All By Myself: The Unmaking of a Presidential Campaign.* Chester, Conn. (1989).

Butterfield, Fox. "Dukakis." *The New York Times Magazine* (May 8, 1988), pp. 22ff.

Carlson, Margaret. "A Tale of Two Childhoods." *Time* (June 20, 1988), pp. 14–16.

Cloud, David S. "Michael Dukakis' Phoenix-Like Political Rebirth." *Congressional Quarterly Weekly Report* (July 2, 1988), pp. 1802–1803.

Cramer, Richard Ben. *What It Takes: The Way to the White House.* New York (1992).

Drogin, Bob. "For Dukakis, Key Is Voter Perception." *Los Angeles Times* (January 17, 1988), pp. 1ff.

Dukakis, Kitty, with Jane Scovell. *Now You Know.* New York (1990).

Dukakis, Michael, and Rosabeth Moss Kanter. *Creating the Future: The Massachusetts Miracle and Its Promise for America.* New York City (1988).

Edsall, Thomas B. "Tough Lessons from the School of Hard Knocks." *The Washington Post National Weekly Edition* (July 18-24, 1988), pp. 8–9; "Out of the Ashes of Defeat" (July 25–31, 1988), pp. 11–12; "The Real Massachusetts Miracle was the Transformation of Dukakis" (August 1–7, 1988), pp. 14–15.

Gaines, Richard, and Michael Segal. *Dukakis and the Reform Impulse.* Boston (1987).

Goldman, Peter, and Tom Mathews. "The Inside Story of Campaign '88." *Newsweek* (November 21, 1988), pp. 32–148.

Kenney, Charles, and Robert L. Turner. *Dukakis: An American Odyssey.* Boston (1988).

Kramer, Michael. "Is Dukakis Tough Enough?" *U.S. News & World Report* (July 25, 1988), pp. 12–20.

Lucas, Peter. *Luke on Duke: Snapshots in Time, Collected Michael Dukakis Columns by the* Boston Herald. Boston (1988).

Martz, Larry. "Dukakis, By the People Who Know Him Best. "*Newsweek* (July 25, 1988), pp. 24–43.

Nyhan, David. *The Duke: The Inside Story of a Political Phenomenon.* New York City (1988).

Rainie, Harrison, and Donald Baer. "A Doer's Profile: The Icy Calm of Mike Dukakis." *U.S. News & World Report* (April 18, 1988), pp. 28–37.

Robbins, Harvey B. *Betrayal: Michael Dukakis and the Battle to Save Historic Prowse Farm.* Ottawa, Ill. (1988).

Shribman, David. "Gov. Dukakis's Role in Economic Turnaround in Massachusetts Draws Questions in Campaign." *The Wall Street Journal* (July 21, 1988), p. 54.

Starr, Mark. "The 'Massachusetts Mess.'" *Newsweek* (January 2, 1989), p. 28.

Wills, Garry. "Born to Bustle." *Time* (July 25, 1988), pp. 24–29.

_____. "Are You Ready, America, for President Dukakis?" *Gentlemen's Quarterly* (February, 1988), pp. 204–209, 251–252.

1988 vice presidential nominee —
Democratic Party

Lloyd Bentsen

Full name: Lloyd Millard Bentsen, Jr.

State represented: Texas.

Birth: February 11, 1921, in Mission, Texas.

Age on Inauguration Day (January 20, 1989): 67 Years, 11½ months.

Education: Sharyland, Texas public schools; graduated McAllen, Texas, High School at age 15; University of Texas (LL.B. 1942).

Religion: Presbyterian.

Ancestry/prominent relatives: Grandparents Peter and Tina Petersen Bentsen were Danish immigrants who went to South Dakota in 1882, and in 1917 moved to south Texas to raise citrus and cotton. Great-great uncle, Henry Wilson (born "Jeremiah Colbaith") was vice president of the United States, 1873–1877. Ken Bentsen (nephew), a U.S. representative, 1997– .

Occupation: Businessman.

Public Offices: Hidalgo County judge (an administrative post) 1947–1948. United States Representative, December 4, 1948–January 3, 1955, retired. Considered running for U.S. Senate 1964, dissuaded by President Lyndon

MICHAEL S. DUKAKIS (left) and LLOYD BENTSEN
(From the author's collection)

Johnson. United States senator, January 3, 1971–January 20, 1993. Unsuccessful candidate for Democratic presidential nomination 1976. Defeated vice presidential nominee, 1988. Secretary of the treasury, January 20, 1993–December 31, 1994.

Home: Washington townhouse; 130-acre farm near Middleburg, Virginia; Houston condominium; 10,000 acre ranch in south Texas.

Personal Characteristics: 6'2" tall, silver-haired, athletically trim. Reserved, dignified, smooth but unexciting speaker, almost patrician. Very private person, said to have many acquaintances, but few close friends.

Father: Lloyd M. Bentsen, Sr. (Nov. 24, 1893–Jan. 17, 1989), born in South Dakota, became wealthy in south Texas land promotion, cattle ranching, and farming. Died in car accident.

Mother: Edna Ruth Colbath (Dolly) (Sept. 6, 1898–June 23, 1977), married on March 18, 1920; daughter of Edward and Ascha Colbath.

Siblings: Kenneth (Nov. 21, 1926–), mar-ried Mary Bates; Houston architect. Don (March 18, 1924–), married Nell McCarter; a south Texas businessman. Betty (Nov. 21, 1931–), married R. Dan Winn, a south Texas businessman.

Wife: Beryl Ann (B.A.) Longino (Feb. 22, 1922–), daughter of Burl and Ann Longino, married on November 27,1943.

Children: Lloyd Millard, III (Sept. 29, 1944–) businessman. Lan Chase (May 21, 1947–), businessman. Tina Ann (Sept. 19, 1951–), married Rick Smith; Norwegian native adopted as infant.

The "Magic Rio Grande Valley" it is called. Not really a valley, it is a strip of flat, arid land made fertile by what used to be frequent silt-depositing floods of the Rio Grande, before dams and levees were built. In the early twentieth century the land was made arable through irrigation canals. Buried in deepest south Texas, the valley extends north from the Rio Grande and inland from the Gulf of Mexico 50 miles at its maximum. A narrow band continues up-river less than one hundred miles. In that majority Mexican ancestry region, a few huge fortunes were made and sometimes lost in land promotion that brought settlers there in the 1920s from the equally fertile, but much colder Midwest. Some of the biggest fortunes were those of Lloyd Bentsen, Sr., and his brother Elmer.

The future United States senator's father first went to the region in 1917. Twenty-four years old at the time, he and an army buddy named Ray Landry were on a weekend of revelry from a military base in San Antonio, 200 miles to the north. Ray Landry's family gained Texas-sized fame as well — his son would be the Dallas Cowboy football coach, Tom Landry. Lloyd, Sr. ("Mr. Lloyd" he would be called), met "Dolly" Colbath on his first trip, and returned in 1920 after the war to marry her. Bentsen got into land promotion, driving Midwesterners around and showing them how their dreams could be realized in the temperate climate and fertile soil of south Texas.

As with many developers, with profits came lawsuits. Mr. Lloyd estimated there were 15 to 17 in all. Some claims were made that the land sold was not irrigated as promised, and occasionally the plaintiffs were successful. The Bentsen operation continues, managed effectively by Mr. Lloyd until his death at a still-vigorous age of 95 in a car accident on January 17, 1989. Mr. Lloyd and his brother Elmer were said to be worth $50 million each through their many ventures. It had all started with the $1.50 in Mr. Lloyd's pocket when he arrived in Mission, Texas, in 1920.

Lloyd, Jr., was born in the valley, attended public schools, became an Eagle Scout, and graduated from high school at age 15. He learned to speak Spanish fluently. As a schoolboy he placed first in his district's declamation contest for eight straight years. He then went to the University of Texas, was president of his fraternity, and in five years had a law degree. By then World War II had erupted. In 1942 Bentsen enlisted in the Army Air Corps as a private and trained as a bomber pilot. Before going overseas he married New York model Beryl Ann Longino, a Texas native.

In Europe Bentsen became a major, was squadron commander at age 24, was shot down twice, and finished with 50 combat missions. Once his B-24 bomber had two engines crippled over Vienna, but he managed to fly over the Alps to crash on the Yugoslavian Isle of Viz controlled by resistance forces. That gained him the Distinguished Flying Cross.

After being discharged in July 1945, Bentsen went back to the Valley. He was elected county judge in 1946 at age 25, the youngest in the state. The brash young candidate's platform was "Beat the Machine." The position had no judicial duties, but was the chief executive for the county. In 1948 he decided to run for Congress. This time the machine he denounced was that of George Parr, whose stuffing of a Duval County ballot box would that same year elect Lyndon Johnson a U.S. senator. Bentsen borrowed the campaign theme of someone who had been elected to Congress two years earlier as a young war hero, John F. Kennedy. Bentsen used one of the same campaign handouts, replacing the pictures of Kennedy and his PT boat with himself and his B-24 bomber, and had thousands printed. As Bentsen later said, "the rhetoric was great." Bentsen led an intense four-man first primary by 3,000 votes, then won the runoff by 10,000.

The freshman congressman gained the sponsorship of fellow Texan and House Speaker, Sam Rayburn. He joined the frequent, invitation-only bull sessions in Rayburn's office. Bentsen hosted others at his hilltop, seven-bedroom retreat in Spring Brook, Maryland. Guests would sip bourbon and more importantly, rub elbows with the powers in Washington, including Supreme Court justices, congressional leaders, and some rising stars who had not yet shown brightly.

As a good Texas politician, Bentsen was known for his poker-playing skills. A persistent story is that Bentsen won a house from another congressman in one late-night poker game. Bentsen's response to questions is, "There are some who have alleged it." Other passionate recreations in the years ahead would be tennis, skeet shooting and quail hunting, and he excelled in all.

Bentsen usually voted as other Texas Democrats, supporting irrigation and land reclamation projects important to his region, and in favor of the *bracero* program that allowed farmers to use low-wage Mexican aliens. Frequently mentioned during future campaigns for national office was his being one of only two Texans and seven Southerners to vote to kill the poll tax in 1949. His most memorable position was to favor the use of atomic weapons against North Korea in 1950. It was what he felt necessary to end the war, instead of fighting with "one hand tied behind us." He later called that a youthful indiscretion of a bomber pilot.

The young congressman was a rising star himself by 1954. He was part of the national Texas political establishment led by Rayburn and Lyndon Johnson. A different and at times rival faction was headed by Governor Allan Shivers. Disputed years later is whether Bentsen joined the Texas Democratic revolt led by Shivers that in 1952 urged Texans to support Republican presidential nominee Dwight Eisenhower instead of liberal Democrat Adlai Stevenson. A 1952 south Texas newspaper report quoted Bentsen as saying he could not personally support Stevenson, though he would "not attempt to tell the rest of the people how to vote." Running for the Senate in 1970, Bentsen said this was incorrect and that he had supported Stevenson. Bentsen was forced to choose sides more clearly in 1956. He helped Rayburn and Lyndon Johnson take control of the Texas state convention and thereby block Governor Shivers' attempt to lead the party to Ike again. One price of the bitter intraparty divisions was the defeat of Bentsen's wife B.A. for Democratic National Committeewoman.

Sam Rayburn told Bentsen that he was "Doing good. Keep your nose clean and in 30 years you're going to be a big man around here." In fact, one Texan who entered the House the year Bentsen left became speaker 30 years later — Jim Wright. Thirty years at a $12,500 salary was too long for Bentsen. Instead, financial independence was his goal. Bentsen told Mr. Lloyd that "if I stay there, I won't have anything except what you give me.... I want to make money just like you

did." He decided not to run for reelection in 1954, and was replaced by his good friend Joe Kilgore. Even so, there was serious, but ultimately false speculation that he would run for governor.

The ex-congressman used $7 million in family loans to launch an insurance company, Consolidated American Life. It was a larger initial capitalization than for any Texas insurance company incorporated prior to that time. The company then bought a well-established Nebraska company, Lincoln Liberty Life. Bentsen moved to Houston and took personal control. Accompanying his salesman in order to learn the business, he was no absentee owner. A former agent said, "We all used to wonder why, if he was so wealthy, how come he worked so hard?" Insurance profits allowed Bentsen to diversify into oil, banking, shopping centers, a funeral home and other ventures. He was shrewd and innovative, including in the area of data processing technology. Bentsen was considered a wizard money manager, and indefatigable.

Success in business did not divert him totally from politics. In 1960 he was the Houston finance chairman for the Kennedy-Johnson ticket, and raised more money than did all the rest of the Texas finance chairmen combined. Two years later he was a key participant, and first contributor, in John Connally's successful race for Texas governor.

His full-time re-entry into politics was only a question of time. Liberal Democratic Senator Ralph Yarborough, first elected in 1957, was running again in 1964. President Lyndon Johnson did not want a bloody intraparty fight going on at home while he was running for a full term as president. LBJ cajoled Bentsen and badgered Joe Kilgore out of challenging Yarborough, even after Kilgore had relinquished his House seat in order to run. This hardly meant, though, that Johnson, Connally, and other Democratic conservatives wished Yarborough any longer of a career than absolutely necessary. Bentsen in 1968 was encouraged by Connally insiders to run for governor, but he had no interest. "The next time a Senate race comes along," Bentsen said, "I might be interested in that." Bentsen meant it, and announced against Yarborough on January 6, 1970.

Also entering national government about this time was John Connally, who was named by President Nixon as secretary of the treasury. Bentsen advised him not to get into government again because he had not made $2 million yet, the standard Bentsen established to judge whether a political career was affordable. Bentsen had made his "two," and was ready. His long absence from office meant that he was little remembered by a rapidly growing Texas electorate. Yarborough became the target of a tough, high-budget media campaign. The senator was said to be too liberal on social issues and too dovish on Vietnam. Television commercials focused simplistically and angrily on gut-level issues. Ironically, the Dukakis-Bentsen team accused their adversaries in 1988 of the same thing. Yarborough was not exactly using kid gloves. He accused one Bentsen company of being a big "tax dodger," and others of being war-profiteers. Though the events preceded his opponent's adulthood, Yarborough also hit hard on the land fraud claims brought against Mr. Lloyd.

When the mud stopped flying, Bentsen was the nominee with 53 percent to the incumbent's 47 percent. The day after the primary, liberal Democrat Maury Maverick said Bentsen's support had been "anti-nigger, anti–Mexican, anti-young people and sock-it-to-'em in Vietnam." Liberal Democrats in Texas despised Bentsen for years as a result. An obstacle remained, a Republican nominee, though with one exception it had never been much problem in Texas. Only John Tower in 1960 and again in 1966 had won Texas statewide office as a Republican. Bentsen's adversary: George Bush. Bush was gravely disappointed by Bentsen's primary victory. His campaign had been premised on doing to Yarborough in November what Bentsen just finished doing in May — paint him as a liberal extremist out-of-touch with Texans. It would be difficult to use that strategy on Bentsen.

The fall campaign was tame compared to the Democratic primary. Bentsen was the early favorite. For the primary Bentsen had tried to be the clear conservative alternative. For the general, he moved to the left. President Nixon and Vice President Agnew both campaigned for Bush. A puzzlingly inept story was given

national columnist David Broder by GOP strategists in Washington, that if Bush won he would replace Agnew on the 1972 national ticket. The story was unfounded and was intended to boost Bush's prestige. Instead, it outraged Agnew's conservative hard-core and peeled no votes away from Bentsen. Other than a few differences over the economy, the candidates agreed on issues. A big rural turnout driven by constitutional amendments regarding liquor and tax breaks was too much for Bush to overcome. Bentsen again won with 53 percent, to his opponent's 47 percent.

Though losing must have been a bitter disappointment for George Bush, election to the Senate would have put him on a significantly different political road, one that may well not have led him to the White House in 1988. So in 1970, perhaps both candidates won.

Following Bentsen's November victory, he was named as part of the ideological majority President Nixon claimed in the Senate. Bentsen demurred, and said he was not part of the "Nixon team." In a speech to a Democratic group in January 1971, he pledged allegiance to his party. His votes showed an independent streak. The first vote one he cast was to limit filibusters. The supersonic transport was a favorite conservative, Nixon-backed measure, and Bentsen opposed it in 1971. The Trident submarine's accelerated development program was single-handedly almost blocked by Bentsen in 1972, a battle that gained the freshman senator respect with few scars. After a trip to Vietnam, the new senator became part of the anti-war faction. He was not completely a national Democrat, and supported Nixon on some controversial measures, such as the appointment of William Rehnquist to the Supreme Court. Fifteen years later he opposed another controversial nominee, Robert Bork.

There were those who thought Bentsen's eye had been on a presidential race since his arrival in 1971. Certainly his centrist votes were more appealing to national Democrats than would have been a more traditionally conservative Texan voting record. Senate Majority Leader Mike Mansfield encouraged his ambition by listing him in mid–1973 as one of three "new faces" who were prime 1976 presidential candidates. During 1974 he traveled to more than 30 states in a pre-campaign warm-up. On February 17, 1975, the freshman senator announced for president. Under Texas law, he would be able simultaneously to run for re-election to the Senate. *Newsweek* in covering his announcement called him a "distant second" to front-runner Henry Jackson of Washington, but "measurably ahead" of Morris Udall, Fred Harris, and little-known ex–Governor Jimmy Carter. The little-known Georgian felt Bentsen would be his principal challenger, but later decided the Texan "didn't have his heart in it." Bentsen had to fight speculation that he was primarily running for vice president.

Support and money did not grow, so in October 1975 he scaled back from a national strategy and concentrated just on eight to ten states. Winning some of those would give him a bloc of delegates that might be useful if the convention deadlocked. This new strategy caused his campaign manager to quit. His main targets were Southern states. Despite the tacit support of both of the states' U.S. senators, in the January 24, 1976, Mississippi caucuses Bentsen only got 1.6 percent of the vote. On February 7, after an all-out effort and even with the support of the old Robert Kerr machine, Bentsen received only 12 percent in Oklahoma. Three days later Bentsen withdrew, but remained as a Texas favorite-son candidate. Jimmy Carter embarrassed him even there, as on May 1 Carter won 92 of the 98 Texas delegate votes.

Re-election to the Senate began with his rout of future GOP senator Phil Gramm in the Democratic primary. The growing Texas Republican Party put up an attractive candidate in Dallas congressman Alan Steelman. Bentsen's senate vote to eliminate the oil depletion allowance for major oil companies may have been intended for northern voters during his presidential quest. Texas oilmen were angry. Still, Bentsen coasted to a 57 percent victory in November.

The now electorally secure senator focused on his congressional power. He was described as "well-organized, thorough and very fair." He is respected for unusual acumen regarding the economy and finance, and especially knowledgeable regarding the intricacies of the tax code. Gaining a seat on the Senate Finance Committee, he would become its chairman when the Democrats regained a majority in 1987. That role helped make him one of the most successful Democrat fundraisers, as businesses eager for his ear gladly contributed to his campaigns. He has been called the "King of PACs" in honor of this prowess. Shortly after becoming Finance Committee chairman in 1987, Bentsen stumbled badly, which is rare, by creating a breakfast club. For $10,000, lobbyists could have monthly breakfasts with him. The public outcry, which dubbed the episode "Eggs McBentsen," led him to drop the plan.

Re-election in 1982 was untroubled, winning 60 percent over another Dallas congressman, Jim Collins. Bentsen had methodically developed a powerful statewide organization, beginning with his 1970 election. In 1982 it was credited with increasing Democratic turnout so ably that the incumbent Republican Governor Bill Clements was defeated. In 1984 several reports named Bentsen as a likely running mate either to Walter Mondale or Gary Hart, but it did not happen that year.

Election to a fourth term was initially the senator's sole 1988 focus. A second mission was added on July 12, 1988, when Democratic nominee-to-be Michael Dukakis named Bentsen his running mate, to be confirmed by the national convention two weeks later. The other finalists were John Glenn, Indiana congressman Lee Hamilton, and Al Gore. Reaction was generally positive that a man of his stature had been chosen. A few remarked, however, that Bentsen was one of the few Democrats blander than Dukakis.

Bentsen was to keep the Republican nominee, George Bush, busy trying to win their mutual home state of Texas while also making the Democrats more competitive in other southern states. It worked for awhile. The first polls taken after the national convention showed the Democrats surging into a modest 48 percent to 44 percent Texas lead. Then news stories soon began highlighting the issue differences between Dukakis and Bentsen. Dukakis opposed a 600-ship navy, the MX missile, the B-1 bomber, the 1981 Reagan tax cuts, prayer in public schools, and aid to the Nicaraguan Contra rebels. Bentsen supported each.

The Democrats' campaign peak was Bentsen's October 5 debate in Omaha against Dan Quayle. "Senator, you're no Jack Kennedy" was Bentsen's, and the Democrats', most memorable message in the fall. For them, the remainder of the election season was downhill. Bentsen campaigned hard throughout the country, and closed with an outdoor rally with Dukakis on the courthouse grounds in Edinburg, Texas, a few miles from Bentsen's home. Bentsen must have known by then that victory was unlikely. Yet in defeat he triumphed personally. Bentsen was now a nationally known, even more respected senator. He led some lists of potential 1992 presidential candidates. The same day he lost for vice president, Bentsen was re-elected to the Senate over his fourth consecutive Republican congressman opponent, this time Beau Boulter, who had called Bentsen's dual race for senate and vice president "unethical" and "arrogant." Texas voters disagreed.

Bentsen did not run for president in 1992. He remained in the Senate until President Bill Clinton named him his first secretary of the treasury. Business leaders were pleased to see the centrist, business-oriented Bentsen be named to so critical a post. During Bentsen's tenure, the Whitewater scandal touched the Treasury Department. Details of the investigation into the failed savings and loan that is central to the scandal were leaked to the White House. Deputy Treasury Secretary Robert Altman ended up resigning over that and other incidents. There were reports that Bentsen was privately expressing frustration at having his counsel, which was pro–free trade, pro-business, and anti-deficit, ignored in the Clinton administration. He resigned at the end of his second year in the cabinet.

Analysis of Qualifications

Two things are central to understanding Lloyd Bentsen. The first is his intense competitive drive. The other, almost antagonistic feature, is that he is one of the most private people in national politics. These features took him almost to the top in government, but left him a shadowy figure.

A long-time Texas Democratic official, Bob Bullock, who became lieutenant governor in 1995 (with George Bush's son as governor), said "Hell, I don't know Bentsen…. I don't even know anybody else who does." His career has been in business boardrooms and political cloakrooms, not as a high-profile spokesman on any issue. When he announced for president in 1975, 2 percent of the people had heard of him. When he was nominated for vice president in 1988, his fame had not spread much further.

Though publicly obscure, Bentsen was called one of the four of five most powerful and influential senators. Partly this was because of his obvious intelligence and his willingness to work harder and learn more than most politicians about legislation. The stellar achievement of his first term was a complex pension reform bill. He was successful because he understood more about it than other senators. He was known for his almost unique enthusiasm and talent for organization. His business background caused him to develop skills at which career politicians can only marvel. Bentsen is a rational, competent man, enthusiastically dedicated to efficiency in government, and with some idea of how to do it.

He was also a master legislative deal-maker. Unlike Lyndon Johnson, Bentsen was no arm-twisting, back-slapping cajoler, but instead won allies to an issue through thoughtful persuasion. Former Majority Leader Mike Mansfield called him, even as a first-term senator, "two heads taller" than any other senator who was being mentioned as a potential presidential candidate. His competitive drive means, in Bentsen's own words, that he "always needs something to do."

Bentsen clearly was a man who valued his independence. He left Congress in 1955 so he could make his own money, even though his family already was wealthy. His senate voting record from the first was centrist, neither reliably Southern nor national Democrat. He was obviously offended when Nixon tried in 1971 to claim him as part of his effective Senate majority. The senator declared independence immediately and forcibly. His ideology, whenever it seems to come into view at all, often proves a mirage. Definitely he was pro-business, pro–Texan interests, but even there he surprised by voting against issues dear to both groups. In fact, he had a pragmatic streak that allowed him to evaluate issues with fewer ideological filters than do most.

Few vice presidential nominees have had the stature in Congress or their party as did Bentsen. He was the oldest nominee since Alben Barkley, and only five this century have been older. As president he probably would have been bland — fittingly, the name Lloyd means "gray" in Welsh. Yet Lloyd Bentsen must rank as one of the superior choices for vice president. With his intelligence, experience, and pragmatism had he become president the country would have been in good hands.

BENTSEN BIBLIOGRAPHY

Banks, Jimmy. *Money, Marbles and Chalk: The Wonderful World of Texas Politics.* Austin (1971), pp. 199–212.

Baskin, Robert E., et al. "Bentsen in '76?" An eight article biographical series, *Dallas Morning News* (September 29–October 6, 1974), pp. IA, et al.

Benenson, Bob. "Texas Sen. Lloyd Bentsen: A Solid Establishment Man Able and Willing to Maneuver." *Congressional Quarterly Weekly Report* (July 16, 1988), pp. 1958–1960.

Bentsen, Lloyd M. "A Flyboy's Story." *Houston Chronicle* (May 7, 1985).

Carlson, Margaret B. "Patrician Power Player." *Time* (July 25, 1988), pp. 22–23.

Clark, Champ. "A Rich, Cool Texan Sets Out to Become President Lloyd Bentsen." *People Weekly* (February 24, 1975), pp. 25–29.

Cochran, Mike. "Elder Bentsen Built Financial Empire." Edinburg (Texas) *Daily Review* (January 18, 1989), p.2.

Edsall, Thomas B., and David Maraniss. "For Business, Defense and Oil: Tory Texan Bentsen Cut from Mold of LBJ." *The Washington Post* (July 13, 1988), pp. Al and A4.

Foscue, Edwin J. "Historical Geography of the Lower Rio Grande Valley of Texas." *The Texas Geographic Magazine* III (Spring, 1939), pp. 1–15.

Fritz, Sara. "Senator's Style Provides Ticket a Rare Symmetry." *Los Angeles Times* (July 13, 1988), pp. 1 and 11.

Goulden, Joseph C. "Bentsen: Money Man from Texas," *The Nation* (March 8, 1975), pp. 267–272.

Ivins, Molly. "Corporation Man." *The Nation* (July 30/August 6, 1988), p. 81.

Johnson, Joan R. Sloan. *The Bentsen Family from Denmark to Texas.* Austin (1985).

Kaus, Mickey, et al. "The Ayes of Texas." *Newsweek* (July 25, 1988), pp. 20–22.

King, Wayne. "Bentsen: A Private Man in Public Life." *New York Times* (July 22, 1988), pp. Al and A13.

Kondracke, Morton M. "Is Bentsen a Democrat?" *The New Republic* (September 26, 1988), pp. 19–22.

MacPherson, Myra. *The Power Lovers: An Intimate Look at Politicians and Their Marriages.* New York (1975), pp. 396–408.

Nelson, Mark. "Quiet Contender." *Houston City Magazine* (July, 1982), pp. 34–37, 83 ff.

Reinert, Al. "The Unveiling of Lloyd Bentsen." *Texas Monthly* (December, 1974), pp. 66–75, 104–124.

Rosenbaum, David E. "A Candidate Who Is More Like Bush: Lloyd Millard Bentsen, Jr." *New York Times* (July 13, 1988), pp. Al and A15.

Saunders, Freddie Milam. "The Bentsen Brothers, Empire Builders," in *Roots by the River.* Mission, Tex. (1978), pp. 258–262.

Wieck, Paul R. "Lloyd Bentsen, Progressive Capitalist." *The New Republic* (November 22, 1975), pp. 15–17.

Election of 1992

NOMINATIONS

Democratic Party Convention (41st) July 13–16, 1992, at Madison Square Garden, New York City. *President*— Bill Clinton, nominated on the first ballot with 3,372 votes. Former Governor Jerry Brown (Cal.) received 579 votes, and former Senator Paul Tsongas (Mass.) had 209 votes. Other contenders

GEORGE BUSH (left) and DAN QUAYLE
(From the George Bush Presidential Library)

during the primaries had been the Reverend Jesse Jackson (D.C.), Senator Robert Kerrey (Neb.), former Senator Tom Harkin (Iowa), and Governor Doug Wilder (Va.). *Vice president*— Albert Gore, nominated by acclamation.

Republican Party Convention (35th), August 17–20, 1992, at the Astrodome, Houston, Texas. *President*— George Bush, chosen on the first ballot with 2,166 votes; Pat Buchanan had 18. Three were scattered, while New Hampshire's 23 votes were not cast. *Vice president*— Dan Quayle.

United We Stand movement. This was the vehicle for Ross Perot's unofficial candidacy for president. His openness to running became public on February 20, 1992, when Perot stated on the television interview program, "Larry King Live," that he would run if volunteers got him on the ballot in all 50 states. After campaigning as an unofficial candidate for five months, Perot declared on July 16 that he would not run. However, on October 1, Perot announced he was formally entering the race. *President*— Ross Perot, without a convention or other meeting. *Vice president*— James B. Stockdale, named by Perot on March 30 as an interim candidate who would satisfy the legal requirement of many states that a presidential candidate had to have a running mate to appear on the ballot. On October 1, he was named by Perot as his official ticket mate.

GENERAL ELECTION, November 3, 1992

Popular Vote

Clinton	44,909,326
Bush	39,103,882
Perot	19,741,657
Others	670,149

Electoral Vote

Clinton — 370 (32+ states)
Bush — 168 (18 states)

Winners

Bill Clinton, 42nd president
Al Gore, 45th vice president

Losers

George Bush, Dan Quayle, Ross Perot, James Stockdale

1992 presidential nominee—
Republican Party

George Bush

No biographical sketch on Bush is included since he served as president from January 20, 1989–January 20, 1993.

State represented: Texas.
Birth June 12, 1924.
Age on Inauguration Day (January 20, 1993): 68 years, 7 months.

1992 vice presidential nominee—
Republican Party

Dan Quayle

No biographical sketch is included on Quayle since he served as vice president from January 20, 1989–January 20, 1993.

State represented: Indiana.
Birth: February 4, 1947.
Age on Inauguration Day (January 20, 1993) 45 years, 11½ months.

1992 presidential nominee—
United We Stand

Ross Perot

Full name: Given the name Henry Ray Perot at birth, but after his brother Ross died in 1936, he was renamed Henry Ross Perot.

State represented: Texas.
Birth: June 27, 1930, in Texarkana, Texas.
Age on Inauguration Day (January 20, 1993): 62 years, 7 months.
Education: Texarkana public schools. Texarkana Junior College, graduated 1949. U.S. Naval Academy, Annapolis, graduated 1953.
Religion: Presbyterian.
Ancestry: Descended from French traders; great-grandfather arrived in Texas from Louisiana before the Civil War.
Occupation: Billionaire businessman— electronic, computer industry.
Public offices: None.

Home: 22-acre estate in Dallas, Texas; vacation homes in Vail, Colorado; Bermuda; and Lake Texoma.

Father: (Gabriel) Ross Perot, Sr. (1899–1955); son of merchant and cotton buyer, and was a businessman himself.

Mother: Lulu May Ray (1897–1979), born near Texarkana.

Siblings: Gabriel Ross Perot, Jr., (1924–1927); Bette (1929–).

Wife: Margot Birmingham (1934–), grew up in Greensburg, Pennsylvania, one of five daughters of Donald and Gertrude Birmingham. Her father was a Pittsburgh bank president until he suddenly went blind, then started career selling home products. She attended Goucher College; married 1956.

Children: Ross, Jr. (1958–), a Dallas real estate developer; married Sarah Fullenwider. Nancy (1960–), married Ross Clayton Mulford, a Dallas attorney. Suzanne (1964–), married a Dallas investment broker. Carolyn (1968–) married Carl Rathjen, an orthopedic surgeon. Katherine (1971–).

Memorial: Perot has purchased and maintained his birthplace in Texarkana, at 2901 Olive Street. After another family bought the house in 1958, they painted the bricks. Perot bought it back in 1969, and since sandblasting would destroy the bricks, they were removed and then placed back with the painted side facing in. The house at times is lived in by tenants, rent-free.

Movie: The Perot-sponsored 1979 rescue of his company employees in Iran was made into *On Wings of Eagles* (TV movie 1986); Richard Crenna played Perot.

Perot's father was barely five feet tall, portly, and with a sense of humor. His business was horse-trading, cattle selling, and cotton brokering. He made a comfortable living in Texarkana, a city lying on the Arkansas border in northeast Texas. The sign outside his business said "G.R. Perot, Cotton Buyer. Sell It. You Can't Eat It." Ross by the age of eight was helping in the horse trading business. He broke horses at his father's corral across the street from the stockyard. The broken nose that is still evident today came from a lost battle in those boy-horse wars, and there were many less permanent injuries as well.

Gabriel Ross and Lulu's first child was named Gabriel Ross, Jr., but he died in 1927 from illness. The future billionaire was born three years after that tragedy and given the name Henry Ray. When Henry Ray became 12 in 1942, his name was legally changed to Henry Ross. He has since been called Ross, like his father.

In June 1942, Ross joined the Boy Scouts. In the incredible period of 16 to 18 months (instead of five years), he had gone through all the projects necessary to rise through the ranks to Eagle Scout. In 1942 Ross also got a paper route. There is a story that Perot tells about being refused a job because no routes were available. However, since no papers were being delivered in a particularly rough black part of town, Perot at age 12 bargained for the job of getting subscribers there. In return he wanted a 70 percent commission instead of the usual 30 percent. The bargain was struck, Perot was immensely successful, riding on horseback as he recalled to deliver papers to prostitutes and flophouses. Then management tried to renege on its end of the bargain. Perot took his complaint to the publisher and won. "Since then," Perot says, "whenever I have a problem I go straight to the top." These lessons learned from life's events are a staple of Perot's speeches and conversations. Some biographers have found the story rather strongly challenged in its details, such as there already being deliveries in the part of town in question, and to Perot's riding a bike and not a horse. There is no one else alive to comment on details of the financial bargain.

Perot's mother was a religious woman. Her discipline was by setting high expectations for her children. Much of her teaching was by example, such as always being open to transients who needed a hand-out. These people are "down on their luck," she would explain to Ross. On Mother's Day 1929, she got a Dodge touring car, a hearse-size vehicle that remained the family car until 1947. Religion, charity, and frugality are all hallmarks of the adult Ross Perot.

After high school Ross attended the junior college in Texarkana. His plan was then to enroll at the University of Texas and become a lawyer. Another Perot story challenged as myth is that he had an application pending with Texas Senator Pappy Lee O'Daniel to be appointed to Annapolis. O'Daniel was leaving office in early 1949, and an aide told him that he still had one Annapolis appointment to make. "Does anyone want it?" the senator asked. He was told that a young man from Texarkana did. "Give it to him." Perot did not excel at athletics or at his studies—finishing academically in the middle of his class. He did stand out as a leader, a midshipman who took to heart the credo of unswerving devotion to duty. He was elected president of his senior class and formed a student court that tried student misconduct cases.

His first assignment after graduating in 1953 was on the destroyer USS *Sigourney*. The ship sailed around the world. Perot rose fast to become chief engineer in two years. When Perot began to encounter trouble, he tried to resign. He later explained that he was blocking improper use of the ship's recreation fund by the ship's captain, a charge the captain denied when it came up almost 40 years later. Perot wrote a letter to the secretary of the navy, complaining of the Navy being a "fairly Godless organization," where the norm include "drunken tales of moral emptiness, passing out penicillin pills [for venereal disease] and seeing promiscuity on the part of married men...." The letter requested an early discharge, but it was denied. His father wrote Senator Lyndon B. Johnson and other officials, seeking his son's early release. Instead Lieutenant (j.g.) Perot was transferred to the aircraft carrier USS *Leyte*. Though disappointed about having to remain in the Navy, Perot had the good fortune on the *Leyte* to be exposed to electronics and to meet an IBM executive who came on board for a tour. The executive urged the obviously talented and aggressive Perot to apply for a position when he was discharged. He would.

Perot was a civilian again in 1957. With his wife of one year Perot went to Dallas. He interviewed with various companies, but took a job with IBM. Perot became a computer salesman. It was a commission business, one that rewarded hard work, initiative, and dogged pursuit of goals. In short, it demanded the qualities that Perot had in abundance. Before long

Perot was setting records for sales and making more money by far than his supervisors. Perot was as aggressive as salesmen can be. In 1962 he sold the largest and most expensive computer IBM made to a brand new college that did not yet have a campus. The commission on that sale in January caused him to meet his sales quota for the entire year. Two years later when the computer was ready, the school did not need it and downgraded to a computer that cost about the same to purchase as the other had to rent for a month. Perot got to keep his commission.

Perot was chafing under the restraints. He recounts going to a Dallas barbershop and while waiting his turn, reading this quote from Henry David Thoreau in a *Reader's Digest*: "The mass of men lead lives of quiet desperation." That was not going to be him, he vowed, and he left—after his haircut—committed to leave IBM. He knew many of his customers were buying equipment they did not really understand and would not be able fully to use. With $1,000 loaned from his wife's bank account—the amount of capital required under Texas law—Perot formed Electronic Data Systems on his 32nd birthday, June 27, 1962. This computer service company was breaking new ground, but Perot necessarily turned to friends from IBM to help him get it started. Perot was going to make E.D.S. different, like a family with high personal standards. Many of his employees were retired military, including Vietnam veterans that other employers often shunned. He established a strict dress code, banned alcohol from all company meals and meetings, and discharged anyone committing marital infidelity. (His 1996 running mate, Pat Choate, had to defend himself in the press against charges that he had not measured up to this standard.) There are stories that polygraph tests were given to employees suspected of crimes or drug use.

Perot did not rent an office of his own. He hired himself out as a consultant to Blue Cross–Blue Shield of Texas, a health insurer. During the day he worked there as a consultant, and at night used that office for his own company. The first big account was with Frito-Lay, the snack food giant based in Dallas. That company was ordering a large new computer from IBM. An E.D.S. salesman convinced Frito-Lay they did not need a new computer, but just better use of what they had. E.D.S.'s employees moved into Frito-Lay's offices at night to program and input raw data into Frito-Lay's own computers. Excess computer time needs were answered by renting computer time at other companies during off hours. E.D.S.'s overhead was nil. What E.D.S. needed were highly skilled, highly motivated people. Perot got them through hard-nosed raiding of other companies like IBM.

What gave the company its quantum leap into enormous profits was, ironically considering Perot's political persona, the dramatic growth of the federal government due to President Lyndon Johnson's Great Society. With Medicare came the need to process staggering amounts of information, needs that fell on people in government who had no expertise with computers. In Texas Perot's team created the software necessary to keep up with the millions of claims, ending the chaos that had descended on the management of the program, and not incidentally greatly reducing fraud. The contract took E.D.S. from a company with $26,000 in profits in 1965, to one with a $2.4 million profit in 1968. Perot's success in Texas helped him win contracts in many other states.

Loyalty in this fast-growing company came from many attractive concepts, including the compensation plan. Substantial cash and stock incentives fattened the paychecks of many employees. By one report E.D.S. had created one hundred millionaires among the employees. The company's success caused Perot to decide to take the company public. When the first shares of E.D.S. were offered on the New York Stock Exchange on September 12, 1968, the starting price was $16.50. At the end of the day the stock had reached $23.50. *Fortune* called this "perhaps the most spectacular personal coup in the history of American business." Eighteen months later the shares were selling at $162.50 per share, a more complete coup. Perot's personal worth, if only on paper, had become $200 million on the first day of trading and reached $1.5 billion at the stock's peak. It was only paper, and gyrations in the market, especially in the early 1970s, would

cause his stock to plummet in value. During one day in the spring of 1970 his personal holdings dropped $500 million, said to be the largest one-day personal loss in the history of Wall Street. He would come out all right in the end.

The year after Perot's wealth was created, he started to spread it in lavish amounts to charity. He created a foundation that has donated over $100 million. His causes have been large and small, frequently friends and employees with the amounts necessary for personal crises. In 1969 wives of former American prisoners of war in Vietnam approached him asking for help to get to Paris and meet with the North Vietnamese who were negotiating with American officials. Perot took care of that relatively inexpensive matter, and then got much more involved. The first use of the "United We Stand" name was for the organization Perot created to gain support for President Nixon's Vietnam policies and to publicize the plight of the POWs. Within a few weeks Perot's group had collected 26 tons of clothes, food, medicine and mail to send to the prisoners. Two Perot-chartered planes took off in December with the supplies with a flight plan for Hanoi, North Vietnam. They never were allowed to deliver their Christmas bounty. After much wrangling and nonsensical conditions, the North Vietnamese revealed themselves as something other than the simple, oppressed, saintly people that many opponents of American policies may have believed. They were as calculating and cold as the situation required.

In January 1970 Perot offered a one hundred thousand dollar payment to the Vietnamese if they would release the POWs but that was rebuffed. He flew with the wives of some of the prisoners to Paris, but could not meet with officials. Perot also tried another Christmas-time flight in 1971, but again the North Vietnamese would not permit entry.

At this stage Perot was an ally of President Nixon. In 1971 the Nixon White House encouraged E.D.S. to take personal charge of saving a major Wall Street brokerage house, duPont Glore Forgan. E.D.S. already had a contract to update data management at duPont Glore Forgan. Perot says he ultimately invested and lost $60 million. He had gotten an 80 percent stake in the company in return, but after the brokerage continued to lose money, Perot sold out in 1974.

In 1978 the Shah of Iran's government jailed two E.D.S. employees in an effort to force a large E.D.S. team back to work on a computer project. Most of the workers had left the country while a dispute about the contract dragged on, but Paul Chiapparone and Bill Gaylord were imprisoned. In Perot's view the U.S. State Department unconscionably took a neutral stance. So Perot turned to commando Arthur "Bull" Simons to train E.D.S. executives to act as a rescue team. Perot flew into the country and met with the two prisoners, telling them that if the prison was stormed, they should use their freedom to make their way to the Hyatt Crown Regency Hotel. The actual rescue involved Simons stirring up a crowd outside the Tehran prison to start a riot. The two men escaped to a hotel, where they joined up with the commandos and began a dangerous, frequently challenged race overland for the Turkish border. The men arrived safely, and Perot was a hero — not only over Iran, but over the American government that had seemed so ineffectual.

Perot next made national headlines in 1984 when General Motors Corporation bought E.D.S. for $2.5 billion dollars worth of special issue GM stock. The plan was that Perot's company would remake GM by revolutionizing how the huge company handled information. It was not a marriage in corporate heaven. When GM's market share and profitability did not improve, Perot said "revitalizing GM is like teaching an elephant to tap dance. You find the sensitive spots and start poking." Perot did not only tend his data processing role, but assumed the role of spokesman for the workers, shareholders, dealers, and customers. He was a very bothersome thorn in GM's side, and GM removed it by buying him out in December 1986. Perot was paid twice the market price for his GM stock. E.D.S. remained part of GM. The fiercely independent Perot and the huge, bureaucratic General Motors probably never could work together. Perot was paid better than GM for the experience.

Eighteen months later, the exact time he

had contracted not to compete with his old company, Perot Systems was formed. Perot tried to lure away many of his old employees from E.D.S., and there are reports that he took refusals as serious breaches of loyalty, including the refusal of one of the men he helped rescue from Tehran. By 1991 his wealth was estimated at $2.2 to $3 billion.

Ross Perot's high-level involvement with politics and his huge fortune began at nearly the same time. A year after E.D.S. became a public corporation, Perot was trying to become an insider in the Nixon White House. He had frequent meetings and phone calls with high-ranking officials. Charles Colson, who had been Nixon's special counsel, said, "I don't know anybody in the whole four years I was at the White House who was able to muscle himself in quicker into the president's own confidence." Perot met with Nixon personally at least three times, and attended socials another eight.

When Reagan was president, Perot again focused on the Vietnam POW-MIA issue. In 1986 he either asked for or sought — the stories vary — an opportunity to ferret out the truth concerning whether any soldiers were still being imprisoned in Southeast Asia. After a year he began to believe then–Vice President George Bush and even President Reagan were coldly unconcerned about that possibility, that they were more interested in keeping the issue quiet than in possibly rescuing still-captured POWs. His animosity towards George Bush has remained intense.

In June 1991 there were rumblings of a "draft Perot" for president movement. A Florida financier, Jack Gargan, was in charge. President Bush at that stage was so popular from the Persian Gulf War victory that little was made of the Perot stirrings. Lawyer-businessman John Jay Hooker of Nashville pestered Perot, saying he should run. Perot kept saying he was not qualified. In early February 1992, Perot was in Nashville and met with Hooker. The suggestion was made by former Jimmy Carter adviser Bert Lance, a friend of Hooker's, that getting Perot on a television interview show might be a good boost. Bush's ratings were by then declining rapidly, and alternatives were being looked at seriously. On

February 20, 1992, Cable News Network interviewer Larry King asked his guest Ross Perot, "Is there any scenario in which you would run for president?" The answer was that if supporters got his name on all 50 state ballots, he would be a candidate. Other interview programs followed. The campaign had begun.

Getting Perot's name on the ballot was achieved. On June 2, Perot led both the incumbent president and his Democratic challenger Bill Clinton in a national poll. He hired, still only on an exploratory basis, two experienced national campaign managers — Democrat Hamilton Jordan and Republican Ed Rollins. By late June his support in polls was starting to slip, as intense scrutiny of his past began. Reports of private investigators he had hired, even to investigate part of President Bush's past, of tight controls over his employees, of all the large and small eccentricities that made Perot such a forceful personality, were causing an image to grow of Perot as kook. For several days in July, his non-campaign was rocked by dissension. Ed Rollins resigned in mid–July. Polls started to show Bill Clinton as the likely winner. On July 16, without ever having gotten into the race, Perot got out. There were understandable political and personal reasons for declining. Perot added others, such as later alleging that the Republicans were going to try to embarrass him by disrupting his daughter's wedding.

Over the next few months, no longer considered a possible candidate, Perot was no longer rocked by such frequent negative stories. Not quite as sudden as his exit, Perot eased back into the race. On October 1, with his running mate Admiral James Stockdale by his side, Perot says that Bush and Clinton were not addressing the government "mess." He would. Perot participated in the debates, gave folksier answers than usually have been heard from a national candidate, and broadcast countless long "infomercials" that promoted his candidacy. He had a former POW as national volunteers chairman, Orson Swindle. It was not enough. He came in third at 22 percent of the vote. A post-election poll indicated his support would have gone equally to the other two candidates if he had not been on the ballot. There was also a poll that inspired him for the future. Forty percent — a plurality — said they would have voted for him had they thought he could win.

In 1993 Perot took center stage in the debate over the North America Free Trade Agreement. Trade barriers with Mexico would be dramatically reduced by NAFTA. Perot was convinced that a "great sucking sound" would be made by jobs being siphoned away to the cheap labor of Mexico. Perot wrote a book with his 1996 running-mate-to-be, Pat Choate, just on the dangers of NAFTA. Perot agreed to debate Vice President Al Gore on Perot's favorite television show, "Larry King Live," on November 9, 1993. Pre-debate expectations were that the wooden Gore would be no match for the folksy Perot. Instead, Perot came across as testy and unprepared, while Gore was sharp and entertaining. Perot later speculated that Gore was secretly being told either the questions or the answers with a hidden earpiece.

In 1994 Perot's United We Stand organization held a national leadership convention. The group was not especially smooth-running, with dissension between the grass-root organizers and the Dallas-based national office. Well into 1996 Perot kept his decision to himself on whether he would run for president. His poll numbers were dismal, in single digits compared to the giddy first place position he held at times in 1992. He announced that there would be a party convention in the summer. Former Colorado Governor Richard Lamm, a Democrat, announced he would contest for the nomination. At the first stage of the convention on August 11, Perot gave a speech saying he would run if nominated. Over a million ballots were mailed to party members around the country, but only 50,000 were cast. Perot won 2–1 over Lamm. Lamm criticized the process as being rigged, pointing out among other things that he and many of his supporters never got a ballot. "If this is the way Perot runs an election," Lamm said, "the thought of Perot running the country is terrifying." Lamm backed no one for the election.

The Commission on Presidential Debates concluded that Perot had too little support to

justify being included in any national televised debates. Perot sued, but the courts found
they had no authority to intervene. As Perot's
chances of winning appeared nil, there was
public speculation about his withdrawing,
since he said he preferred Bob Dole over President Clinton. On October 23 a meeting was
held on an airplane in a Dallas hanger, between
Perot and Dole campaign manager Scott Reed.
Progress appeared to be made, until Perot got
a report that news of the meeting had been
leaked to the press. Perot left, but discussions
with Reed continued that night. Dole was
reported to have called Perot at 11:30 that night,
and woke Perot up. The answer was "no."

In 1996 Perot got less than half the vote that
he received in 1992.

Analysis of Qualifications

He has been called a "genius" and, by others, "nuts." Views have varied from whether
he is a leader or an agitator, modest or an ego-
maniac, a man of exceptional honesty or a
teller of fables. Perot's undeniable positive
characteristics are significant. He is a driven,
highly successful man, fiercely loyal to his
workers, hugely generous to charities, and a
patriot, an American original who reshaped
presidential campaigns profoundly. Perot
made mistakes in the business world, but they
were far outnumbered by his smashing successes. He is a rare blend of doggedness and
nimbleness, whether pursuing the delivery of
Christmas-time flights of food and presents to
POWs through the ever-changing maze of
Communist interference, or in starting his
own company in the fiercely competitive electronics and computer world. He has a way,
even in losing as he did in the POW flights,
and to a lesser extent in the NAFTA debate,
of making a public relations coup out of defeat.

The problems he has encountered, in his
early life, in business and in politics, are instructive. Perot's strict and commendable
views of morality has made him unwilling to
work with those who do not measure up to
that standard. Perot excelled at the perfectionist environment of the best and brightest
at Annapolis, but quickly rebelled and wanted
a discharge when faced with the immorality of

many sailors at sea. His fierce independence
and refusal to compromise has made him spectacularly successful, but that same approach
has not made him able to last long in arena in
which he was not totally in charge. Besides the
Navy, his experience at IBM and then with
General Motors are examples. It is difficult to
have confidence in his ability to work in the
give-and-take, the half-loaf or none attitudes
of Washington politics.

There is also a recurring theme of Perot's
suspicion that corruption and conspiracy un-
derlie the actions of those who oppose him. He
charged the Republicans with a wide array of
dirty tricks in 1992, some of which may have
been true, but the numbers and unlikely
nature of some of the charges made Perot seem
overly distrusting. Disagreements and setbacks
led to such allegations as that Gore had a hidden earpiece during their NAFTA debate, and
that Reagan and Bush were not just disagreeing regarding POW-MIA issues, but actually
selling out the soldiers. He seemed overly
quick to denigrate the motives, ethics and even
worth of his opponents.

In sum, Perot is a combination of rare gifts
and troubling traits. There is no doubt a Perot
presidency would have been endlessly fascinating. There would be an incredible gamble,
though, to send Perot to the White House,
and have him try the approaches that made
him successful most of the time in the business world. Many people justifiably are disgusted with the ways of politics and compromise, but for Perot to be effective in the
environment that has existed in Washington in
one way or another since our nation began
might require a miracle, and not just good
luck.

PEROT BIBLIOGRAPHY

Behar, Richard. "Ross Perot's Days at Big Blue."
Time (July 20, 1992), pp. 62–63.
Broussard, James Allen. "A Champion for the
Disaffected: Ross Perot's 1992 Presidential Cru-
sade." Unpublished Ph.D. dissertation, Univer-
sity of Arizona (1995).
Carlson, Tucker. "Temperamental Tycoon." *The
Weekly Standard* (April 8, 1996) pp. 19– 23.
Efron, Sonni, and J. Michael Kennedy. "Angry Vot-
ers See Perot Riding in Like Cavalry." *Los Ange-
les Times* (March 22, 1992), pp. A1, A24 ff.

ROSS PEROT (left) and JAMES B. STOCKDALE
(From the author's collection)

Fineman, Howard. "The Man and the Myth."
  Newsweek (June 15, 1992), pp. 20–23.
Follett, Ken. *On Wings of Eagles.* New York (1983).
Gleick, Elizabeth. "Perot's Hidden Assets." *People*
  (June 15, 1992), p. 106.
Goldman, Peter, et al. *Quest for the Presidency, 1992.*
  New York (1994).
Gross, Ken. *Ross Perot: The Man Behind the Myth.*
  New York (1992).
Ingham, John N., and Lynne B. Feldman. *Contemporary American Business Leaders: A Biographical Dictionary.* Greenwood Press: Westport,
  Conn. (1990), pp. 506–515.
Levin, Doron P. *Irreconcilable Differences: Ross Perot Versus General Motors.* Boston (1989).
Mason, Todd. *Perot: An Unauthorized Biography.*
  Homewood, Ill. (1990)
Mintz, John. "Perot-Bush Battle Rooted in Vietnam." *Washington Post* (April 18, 1992), p. A1, A8.
Perot, Ross. *Not for Sale at Any Price: How We Can Save America for Our Children* (1993).
Posner, Gerald. *Citizen Perot: His Life and Times.*
  New York (1996).
Remnick, David. "Our Nation Turns Its Lonely
Eyes to H. Ross Perot." *The Washington Post Magazine* (April 12, 1987), pp. 25, et seq.
Sheehy, Sandy. *Texas BigRich.* New York (1990),
  pp. 387–405.
Simmons, E.R. *No Pass–No Play: Texas Darkest Day, H. Ross Perot Runs Amok* . Simmon (1994).
Solomon, John. "Nixon Administration Documents Show Perot as 'Ultimate Insider.'" *Washington Post* (May 8, 1992), p. A4.
Wills, Garry. "The Rescuer." *The New York Review of Books* (June 25, 1992), pp. 28–34.
Wright, Lawrence. "The Man from Texarkana."
  The New York Times Magazine (June 28, 1992),
  pp. 20–23ff.

*1992 vice presidential candidate —
United We Stand*

James B. Stockdale

Full name: James Bond Stockdale.
State represented: California.

Birth: December 23, 1923, Galesburg, Illinois.

Age on Inauguration Day (January 20, 1993): 69 years, 1 month.

Education: United States Naval Academy, graduated 1946. Stanford University (M.A. 1962.)

Religion: Episcopalian.

Ancestry: Stockdale's grandfather was living in Iowa when he became an invalid, causing Stockdale's father to leave school at age 16 to go to work; the family moved to Illinois three years later to live with the grandmother's side of the family.

Occupation: Navy officer; retired in 1979. Became senior research fellow at the Hoover Institution at Stanford University, where he has written several books.

Public offices: None.

Home: House in Coronado, California, that purchased in 1960s.

Personal characteristics: Strong-willed, intellectual, more a first-class professor than any kind of politician. A short man with military bearing, good physical condition, but walks with limp due to injuries, most intentionally inflicted by his captors, while a prisoner in North Vietnam. Full head of white hair at time of nomination.

Father: Vernon Beard Stockdale (February 14, 1888–September 10, 1964); married in 1919; worked at vitreous china (bathroom fixtures) factory in Illinois for 40 years; became vice president of company.

Mother: Mabel Edith Bond (January 10, 1889–October 29, 1967), daughter of Minda and Jasper Bond, a farming family. Graduated from Hedding College in 1910.

Siblings: None.

Wife: Sybil Elizabeth Bailey (born November 25, 1924–), daughter of Sidney and Lucretia Bailey, who operated a dairy business. Married June 28, 1947.

Children James Bond, Jr. (December 11, 1950–), married Marina Call in 1975. Sidney (August 3, 1954–), married Nancy Kittredge in 1987. Stanford (December 6, 1959–), married Brenda Carlson in 1987. Taylor (April 3, 1962–), married Anne Watson in 1990.

Memorials: He was admitted to the Carrier Aviation Hall of Fame in 1993, which is on the carrier Yorktown in Charleston, S.C. Monmouth College in Illinois, named its student center "Stockdale Center."

Movies: Stockdale's imprisonment in Vietnam was made into an NBC television movie: *In Love and War* (1987). James Woods played Stockdale.

One superlative too frequently applied to others without a doubt applies to Admiral James B. Stockdale. He is a great American hero. As the highest ranking American soldier imprisoned at "Hanoi Hilton" during seven years of the Vietnam War, Stockdale was a leader and an inspiration to men in the most trying of circumstances. To the extent the brutality that these men endured could be made somewhat more bearable, Stockdale more than anyone else was the man who did so. Had he been elected vice president, that office may well have been a far less significant part of his contribution to his country.

Jim Stockdale grew up in Galesburg, a town not far from the Iowa border in west-central Illinois. His father Vernon started as the timekeeper and payroll clerk for a bathroom fixtures factory that an Englishman started in town. When he retired 40 years later he was vice president of the company. He and Mabel Bond could not marry because of the objections of Mabel's father. Two years after the couple started talking of marriage, Mabel's father died. As soon as Vernon returned from Navy service, they were married. Their only child received his first name from the Englishman employer, James Simpson. The baby's middle name was his mother's maiden name. James Bond Stockdale had some heroic adventures ahead, out of which at least one movie would be made.

Jim worked on the family farm, and at age 16 spent a summer working at his dad's factory. In reflecting years later, Stockdale thought that certain factors had shaped his commitment to seek an Annapolis appointment. Jim's father spent two years in the Navy. When Jim was seven he visited the Naval Academy. Admiral Richard Byrd made a strong impression on the boy when he spoke at a college commencement exercise that Jim witnessed at age eleven. Once deciding on the Navy, Jim was helped again by his father. Vernon got to know the local congressmen and the two men agreed that if Jim met the physical and academic standards, he would get an appointment. He did.

Jim entered Annapolis in 1942. For the next 37 years he was on active duty in the Navy. Once Jim rushed home from Annapolis because his father was near death. Fortunately he survived, and lived until 1964. Jim married Sybil Bailey in 1947, the year after he graduated. Stockdale took flight training and received his wings in 1950. His naval career included the normal large number of different assignments. After being in Pensacola, Florida, Stockdale in January 1954 was ordered to Patuxent River Test Pilot School in Maryland. It was an intense, exhilarating life for a young Navy pilot. When he flew a jet for the first time, what he knew came from reading the manual. He mastered it, as he always would flying. He finished third out of 17 pilots in his class. Stockdale was asked to stay on as an instructor at the school. He learned to fly just about everything that the Navy had. After three years, Stockdale left to join a squadron that would be flying the Navy's hottest new carrier fighter, the Crusader. Before being assigned to a carrier, he took a survival course that included prisoner of war training. The fact that the Koreans were not following Geneva Convention rules convinced the American military that for this and future wars, soldiers and sailors needed to be prepared for some rough treatment if they were captured.

In January 1957 Stockdale began his assignment at Moffett Field in California. He would be deployed for nine months on a carrier, then was back in California with his family. After three years, Stockdale was sent to Stanford University to get a master's degree. While there, he took some philosophy courses and began a life-long devotion to the subject. Getting his degree in 1962, Stockdale was assigned to San Diego, then in 1964, was named commanding officer aboard the USS *Ticonderoga*.

In April, 1964 Stockdale left for sea duty. In four months he became a central but generally unknown figure in a turning point in the Vietnam War. He considered the events so significant, and presumably troubling, that he started his 1984 memoir (*In Love and War*) by describing them. Admiral Thomas Moorer,

Commander of the Seventh Fleet in the Pacific, in June 1964 needed eight F-8 fighters and pilots to be sent to the USS *Constellation*. Stockdale's Fighter Squadron Fifty-One (VF 51) was sent. They began flying protection for photo reconnaissance missions over Laos and Vietnam. Stockdale became concerned that the details in the reports he filed of each mission were being changed by the time official reports were sent up the chain of command. He kept his own copies after that.

One Sunday morning, August 2, an unusual intelligence briefing was held concerning the USS *Maddox*, an old destroyer Stockdale had served on in 1946. It was steaming up the Vietnamese coast in the Gulf of Tonkin. That afternoon a report came in that the *Maddox* was being threatened by torpedo boats. Stockdale, Dick Hastings, Robair Mohrhardt, and Ev Southwick took off in their Crusaders. Stockdale later wrote that he was especially pleased Ev was with them, because he was one of the best pilots and had phenomenal visual acuity for the task ahead, which could include spotting fast-approaching black specks that would be MIG fighters. As the four planes approached the *Maddox*, they switched to the ship's radio frequency. A report was being sent of an attack by torpedo boats. By the time the planes arrived, the Vietnamese boats were steaming back to the coast. Stockdale's group fired missiles at and strafed the boats. They destroyed some, damaging the rest. The four pilots flew back, puzzled over the reasons for so brazen an attack by the torpedo boats.

On Tuesday, August 4, another report was sent that the *Maddox* and a second destroyer, the *Joy*, were being harassed. Stockdale was the only Crusader pilot who flew to assist, while other, slower attack aircraft were sent too. As Stockdale approached in the darkness, he heard the same radio voice that he heard from the *Maddox* on Sunday. He was describing numerous radar contacts with boats. The surreal quality of the next 60 minutes was exasperating for Stockdale. Never higher than one thousand feet, Stockdale scanned the waters intently as the destroyers reported torpedoes being fired and attacks by the PT boats. Stockdale never saw a thing. The only boat wakes he ever saw were those of the two destroyers.

He would dive down in the direction of gunfire from the American ships, but that did not uncover the phantom attackers. Stockdale later saw a transcript of the radio broadcasts. Towards the end the operator indicates strong doubts about the reliability of the sonar that was showing PT boats and torpedoes. The radioman also is suspicions because there were no visual sightings by anyone. The next morning Stockdale was awakened because the Americans were launching reprisal attacks against the Vietnamese. Stockdale was stunned. He felt that he was one of the few people who knew that "We were about to launch a war under false pretenses." Two defense department civilians came to see him a week later. He told his tale, but it did not stop the Tonkin Gulf Resolution and the start-up of much more active American involvement. It is obvious that Stockdale was convinced no attack had been made in the Gulf of Tonkin.

Stockdale was home in California from November 1964 to April 1965. In February he became the CAG, a Carrier Air Group Commander. That made him the highest ranking aviator on board his new ship. That ship was the *Oriskany*, on which Stockdale began a nine-month deployment in April. His wife knew that this would be the last sea duty for awhile, and he might then be assigned to Washington. The tour was a dangerous one. Many of the new CAG's pilots were being shot down over Vietnam. On September 8, 1965, Stockdale flew his two hundredth mission in Southeast Asia. It would be the last one for awhile, as the ship was to sail the next day for Hong Kong and a rest. This time Stockdale had a slower-speed Skyhawk. His primary target had to be skipped because of poor visibility. As he lined up for approach to the secondary target, he heard an antiaircraft cannon. He saw it off to his right, and moments later felt the jolt of an impact. His fire-warning light came on and he knew his plane has been badly hit. The plane nosed down. The safety of rescue in the Tonkin Gulf was just three miles in the distance, but Stockdale could not make it. He barely was able to eject. His parachute opened, but he was fired on from the ground. Unfortunately, he landed in the middle of a village. Injured by his ejection and

landing, he was unable to defend himself as some of the civilians start to beat him. He was kicked, bodily twisted, his clothes ripped, and he started to lose consciousness. A policeman broke up the brawl. Before the whistle-blowing authority arrived, Stockdale was stood upright and his clothes cut off. He was naked, with a broken arm, a busted knee, a leg bent 60 degrees from perpendicular, and worst of all perhaps, a broken back because he forgot to brace himself properly when ejecting.

In the evening Stockdale was given some old blue shorts and a work shirt. He was carried by two soldiers. There was no stretcher, despite his serious injuries. They made it to Highway 1, where trucks were hidden under a canopy of trees. He was placed into a truck, and the convoy left under cover of darkness. Stockdale was in and out of consciousness, and dared to hope the CIA or some other group was going to rescue him. In time, he was dimly aware of arriving at a concrete building on the outskirts of a city. After being carried in, he was laid down on a cement slab bed. A person in surgical attire took from his medical kit a large surgical saw. He was about to cut off Stockdale's badly mangled leg. Through gestures Stockdale insisted that he not do so. The man with the saw relented. He gave Stockdale an anesthetic. When he awoke, Stockdale realized he had been unconscious for a day. His entire upper body except for his unbroken right arm was in a cast. He looked as quickly as he could to see if he still had two legs. He did, but one of them was in a cast. There was no time to recuperate, as Stockdale was loaded back on a truck for more travel. Three days later, he arrived at Hanoi and was placed in a military prison.

The injured prisoner lay on his back for a month. There was little medical attention, and little attention to his basic physical needs. After a month he received the first of what he was told would be three surgeries on his leg. Two weeks later, one of the guards presented Stockdale with an aeronautical map so Stockdale could prove he was grateful for their efforts to get him well. Stockdale was to mark the in-flight refueling areas. There were no such consistent locations, but Stockdale refused to cooperate even to tell them that much.

When he refused, he was taken to another prison. Stockdale needed crutches to walk, but the ones he got were much too tall for him. He felt some excitement in the new prison, as he realized that for the first time since he was shot down 47 days before, he was within talking distance of other Americans. Stockdale's cell was tiny and unpleasant, but he was able to sneak a few whispered conversations with other prisoners.

Within days of Stockdale's arrival, the North Vietnamese starting torturing in order to force information beyond that of name, rank, serial number, and date of birth. For six days Lt. (jg) Rodney Knutson was beaten, but still would not relent. A new torturer was brought in, who slid a hemp rope around Knutson's upper arms, pulling it tight and doubling the prisoner over. This cut off circulation and caused incredible pain. As Stockdale recounted, there was no option of death under this torture — just continuing, impossible pain. Knutson did not have much valuable to say, but the tragic new policy was in place. There would be torture until whatever information the North Vietnamese wanted was given. Such conduct was a war crime under international law, but the Vietnamese were not concerned.

Stockdale learned from other prisoners and helped refine a code for tapping messages. Only part of each word was spelled with the code, but the prisoners became proficient with its use. Stockdale said it became "more accurate and almost as fast as talking." Being caught using it meant severe punishment, but it was worth the penalty.

Communications from family back home were infrequent. Letters were kept from prisoners, a few doled out to buy cooperation. Stockdale got his first one on Christmas Day 1965, picked at random by his jailers from all his wife had written. A few days later, having been seen trying to get with one of his crutches a cigarette thrown from another cell, he was taken to another room and strapped by leg irons into a bed. His hands were also bound. What little food he had been getting before was reduced in quantity. This went on for 12 days, and then Stockdale was taken in for "quiz." He was told that he must write a let-ter to the American government, explaining the Vietnamese will to fight and calling the American war effort immoral. Stockdale refused, but he was sent back to his cell with pen and paper. Soon he was subjected to the hemp rope torture, after first being struck in the face and knocked off his crutches. Seated on the floor, with an iron bar holding his feet together, Stockdale had his upper arms tied with ropes. The torturer put his foot in Stockdale's back as he pulled on the rope, jerking the victim's shoulders together and his arms back. Before it was over, Stockdale's head had been pushed all the way to the floor between his legs, while his arms were pulled straight back. He had to submit. In the years to come, he would be put through such torture 14 more times. It was probably best that in these early weeks he had no idea that was ahead.

Stockdale wanted to make sure his superiors knew that whatever he wrote was forced. He convinced the Vietnamese that the letter had to be written to a political office in the military. The letter was filled with double entendres and just plain nonsense. Still he worried the Americans would not realize what was behind it. Another propaganda demand was made a few months later. Stockdale was to appear at a press conference with foreign journalist, to denounce America's war on Vietnam. He refused, and a beating would not have been effective — too many bruises for the press and cameras would have given the lie to Vietnamese insistence on how well the prisoners were treated.

For four years Stockdale remained in solitary confinement, "talking" to fellow prisoners by tapping code and an occasional whispered conversation. Two of those years he was in leg irons most of the time. He was the "Hanoi Hilton's" highest ranking prisoner, and secretly took charge of preparing rules for conduct. The aim was to maintain morale by a prisoner maintaining some control over his own life. "BACKUS" became the acronym governing a prisoner's actions. B — No Bowing to the enemy. A — No giving an address on radio or television. C — No confessing to alleged war crimes. K — Don't kiss the enemy good-bye by expressing gratitude for an early release. U — Unity over S — Self. Old friends from the military kept appearing, like Jeremiah Denton, an Annapolis classmate who would serve one term in the U.S. Senate. New friends would be made, such as Orson Swindle, who would be director of the Perot-Stockdale campaign in its later stages in 1992 and almost be elected to Congress from Hawaii in 1996. Swindle's torture once was to be kept awake for 20 days sitting on a stool. Any dozing was met with a sharp whack from a pole. There were at least two other prisoners who later turned into politicians: Leo Thorsness who ran against George McGovern for the Senate in 1974 and lost narrowly; and John McCain, who would later be elected to the Senate from Arizona.

After four years Stockdale was released from solitary. There were still many painful encounters ahead. Once when he was being ordered to participate in a film, he used the razor he had been given for shaving, to chop at his hair. He then banged his face against a wooden stool, making it too bloody for proper appearance for the camera.

As a peace treaty ending the American phase of the long Vietnamese struggle seemed imminent, the prisoners began to be treated somewhat better. The Vietnamese did not want the effects of their cruelty to be overly obvious. Seven and a half years after that fateful mission over North Vietnam, Stockdale was released along with the other prisoners on September 12, 1973. Their departure was in order of their capture—first in, first out. Stockdale was one of the first. They were driven to an airfield where American C-141 cargo planes awaited. First they went to Clark Air Force Base in the Philippines for medical tests. Three days later he was with his wife and four children.

Years later, during his vice presidential campaign, Stockdale wrote that the secret of survival was "comradeship." That was why a tapping code and all the other little tricks were so vital to maintaining not just order, but sanity. He summed up the necessary attributes this way: "pride, dignity, an enduring sense of self-worth and to that enigmatic mixture of conscience and egoism called personal honor" (*Wall Street Journal*, October 13, 1992).

Adjustment to freedom and family took time. He held the rank of Navy commander (equivalent of a lieutenant colonel) when he was shot down. Within a few weeks of his return, he was promoted to rear admiral. His wife was pleased because it meant no more sea duty. Stockdale was assigned to North Island Naval Air Station. On March 4, 1976, he was awarded the Congressional Medal of Honor for his heroic efforts to organize and maintain morale among the prisoners of war in Hanoi. He also at various times won 26 combat decorations, including two Distinguished Flying Crosses, three Distinguished Service medals, four Silver Stars, and two Purple Hearts. In April 1976 he was transferred to the Pentagon. Promoted to vice admiral, he became president of the Naval War College in Newport, Rhode Island in 1977.

In 1979 the admiral retired because of his continuing disabilities from his many injuries and lack of proper treatment. He became president of the Citadel, the South Carolina military college. He resigned after less than a year, saying that he faced too much resistance to his attempts to liberalize the curriculum and admissions policies, and reduce hazing. Since 1981 Stockdale has been a senior research fellow at the conservative "think tank," the Hoover Institution on War, Revolution, and Peace, located at Stanford University. He has written several books.

When Perot in 1969 was trying to fly mail, food, and medicine to Hanoi at Christmastime, he and Sybil Stockdale met. The ex-POW met Perot within days of being released in 1973. Perot found few more enthusiastic supporters than the Stockdales when in 1992 he began exploring a run for the presidency. Early in the campaign Stockdale agreed to the use of his name as Perot's running mate, whenever the campaign legally needed a vice presidential candidate in order to proceed with getting on the ballot in various states. His "stand-in" status was meant to disappear when a more established public figure was later selected. By July 1992, when Perot temporarily withdrew, no replacement had yet been found. Stockdale said he was surprised, but not upset by the withdrawal. Perot got back in the race on October 1. The two Stockdales stood alongside the two Perots when the reentry announcement was made. This time Stockdale was the final choice as a running mate.

The best-remembered part of Stockdale's campaign was his televised debate on October 13 in Atlanta with Vice President Dan Quayle and Senator Al Gore. He prepared a line that would humorously lighten his serious problem of being unknown. When his anonymity was raised, he responded pleasantly, "Who am I? Why am I here?" The audience laughed. At another point he asked for a question to be repeated, saying with a smile, "I didn't have my hearing aid turned on." At another time he admitted lack of knowledge on a health care question by saying, "I'm out of ammunition." All this, in the sound-bite world of modern communication, caused his rhetorical "Who am I" to get treated by the media as a befuddled cry for help. After the election he said his debate preparation was based on faulty premises. "I was naive in believing that my main task was to be one of parrying gibes and defending my position. In hindsight, I needed a plan of attack."

A key Perot supporter, Nashville lawyer John Jay Hooker, and some others were so concerned about the treatment that Stockdale was getting in the press that they urged Perot to return Stockdale to "stand-in" status. The public would be told that if Perot won, Stockdale would resign and be replaced by an appointment permitted under the constitution whenever there was a vacancy. Perot refused, as he still saw Stockdale as a strong leader who deserved better than dismissal from the ticket. That was academic, as both men lost in November.

In 1996 Stockdale initially supported California GOP governor Pete Wilson for president, and then became a Bob Dole advocate. He was even a delegate to the Republican National Convention in San Diego. He said, "I like Ross, but I want Dole to be president. That doesn't mean there's anything amiss between us." Stockdale had been a lifelong Republican, and called 1992 his "only excursion away and now I'm going back home."

Analysis of Qualifications

Admiral Jim Stockdale was considered in

the 1992 campaign as the man who was forced to perform out of character, a soldier on a political stage. The evidence given is the debate performance. The operative word, though, is "performance." As choices for high position increasingly become a matter of who is the better performer, there will be a greater premium for the talents of a talk-show host, the ability to be engaging, quick with the crisp "sensitive" answer, strong with an agenda that can be captured in a few pithy sentences. Whether Stockdale can excel in such ways, he did not in his most public moment in 1992.

There is no analogous figure to Stockdale among our presidents. Though there certainly have been military men, they have been nominated after leading great armies. A few, like Dwight Eisenhower in forging and maintaining a coalition military force with the Allies, actually had to demonstrate skills directly relevant to the presidency. Most, like Ulysses Grant or James Garfield, were elected because of the glory of battles won. Admiral Stockdale's heroism was on a smaller scale, his organizational talents and drive limited to a few hundred men who needed a way to communicate, a sense of pride, or a reason to keep on living. Being able to provide those things is a valuable presidential quality, but not the total quantum of what is needed.

Stockdale is a scholar, a man who has read, absorbed, and applied the teachings of great philosophers. In an age in which politicians do not seek to challenge the voters, but only to entertain them, Stockdale was out of place. Erudite conversations are not the quality time that candidates seek to have with their constituencies. Political imagery that most think is necessary for election is built with thinner material than the weighty substance that a Hoover Institution scholar normally offers.

All that being said, Stockdale's strongly positive attributes are only a great start for presidential leadership. Where evidence is lacking is that a career in the Navy prepared him for the rest of what a president must do. Having never had to accomplish anything in politics until he was 68 years old, Stockdale never was called upon to exhibit the kind of skills necessary for the give and take of working with other politicians. He had never had to go to a large mass of voters, and certainly not the entire country, and convince them of the merits of his plans. He never had to stock a government with people of his own choosing, so there is no record of his talents at selecting from among the huge stable of contenders for cabinet and lower positions. In sum, nothing in his background disqualified him from making a good president, but doubt remained of whether he was ready for that dramatic a change from all that he had done before.

Admiral Stockdale, contrary to his agreement initially only to be a temporary stand-in, found himself being presented to the American people a month before the election as a contender for an office a heart-beat from the presidency. He might have done well, but he might also have found the whole crazy political system too foreign to his 37 Navy years to adjust to it. He must be considered a man whose prospects for presidential success were at best uncertain.

STOCKDALE BIBLIOGRAPHY

Denton, Jeremiah A., Jr. *When Hell Was in Session.* Mobile (1982).

Goldman, Peter, et al. *Quest for the Presidency, 1992.* New York (1994).

Grogan, David, and Don Sider. "Running with Ross." *People* (October 19, 1992) pp. 85–88.

Images of Excellence: Vice Admiral James Stockdale. Boiling Springs, N.C. (1990).

Keating, Susan Katz. "Who Am I? A Leader in Worst of Times." *Washington Times* (October 18, 1992) pp. A1, A6.

Nissenbaum, Dion. "Stockdale Says He Wasn't Ready to Debate." *San Francisco Chronicle* (January 9, 1993), p. A4.

Rosenbaum, David E. "Eager to Face the Test: James Bond Stockdale." *New York Times* (October 2, 1992), p. A19.

Stockdale, James B. *Courage Under Fire: Testing Epicetus's Doctrines in as Laboratory of Human Behavior.* Stanford (1993).

_____. *Thoughts of a Philosophical Fighter Pilot.* Stanford (1995).

_____. *A Vietnam Experience: Ten Years of Reflection.* Stanford (1985).

_____, and Sybil Stockdale. *In Love and War.* New York (1984).

Yang, John E. "Perot Chooses Unlikely Running Mate." *Washington Post* (October 2, 1992)

Election of 1996

Republican National Convention (36th): August 12–15, 1996, in San Diego Convention Center, San Diego, California. *President—* Robert J. Dole, nominated on the first ballot with 1,928 votes. Pat Buchanan (Va.) got 43, and 19 abstained or voted for others. Other contenders had been Lamar Alexander (Tenn.), Bob Dornan (Calif.), Steve Forbes (N.J.). Phil Gramm (Tex.), Alan Keyes (Mary.), Richard Lugar (Ind.), and Arlen Specter (Penn.). *Vice President—* Jack Kemp, nominated unanimously.

Reform Party Convention (1st): Held in two stages. (1) August 11, 1996, in Convention Center, Long Beach, California. Ross Perot (Tex.) and former Governor Richard Lamm (Colo,), who announced on August 5 that his running mate would be former GOP Rep. Ed Zschau (Calif.), spoke to the convention. Ballots were mailed to 1.3 million people, with voting to occur by return mail, e-mail or fax over the next week. (2) August 18, 1996, in Valley Forge, Pennsylvania, at Convention Center. *President—* Ross Perot, chosen with 32, 145 mail-in votes to Richard Lamm's 17, 121. *Vice president—* Pat Choate, announced by Perot on September 10, 1996. It was reported that former Senator David Boren (D–Okla.), Representative Marcy Kaptur (D–Ohio), and Representative Linda Smith (R–Wash.) all declined Perot's offer to run on the Reform ticket.

Democratic National Convention (42nd): August 26–29, 1996, in United Center, Chicago, Illinois. *President*— Bill Clinton, received all 4,289 votes. *Vice president*— Al Gore, nominated unanimously.

GENERAL ELECTION, November 5, 1996
Popular Vote

Clinton 47,401,054
Dole 39,197,350
Perot 8,085,285
Others................ 1,528,194

Electoral Votes

Clinton-Gore — 379 (31 states)
Dole-Kemp —159 (19 states)

Winners

Bill Clinton, 42nd president
Al Gore, 45th vice president

Losers

Bob Dole, Jack Kemp, Ross Perot, Pat Choate

---

*1996 presidential nominee —
Republican Party*

Robert J. Dole

Full name: Robert Joseph Dole.
State represented: Kansas.
Birth: Russell, Kansas, July 22, 1923.
Age on Inauguration Day (January 20, 1997): 73 years, 6 months.
Education: Russell public schools; University of Kansas, pre-med, 1941–1943, left for service in World War II after two years; University of Arizona; Washburn University (B.A. 1949, J.D. 1952, cum laude); admitted to bar in 1952.
Religion: Methodist.
Ancestry: Dole's father was a grain elevator operator.
Occupation: Attorney.
Public offices: Kansas State legislature, 1951–1953; prosecuting attorney of Russell County, Kansas, 1953–1960; U.S. representative, January 3, 1961–January 3, 1969; United States senator, January 3, 1969–June 11, 1996.

Republican National Chairman, January 1971– December 1972. Unsuccessful Republican nominee for vice president in 1976; unsuccessful candidate for Republican presidential nomination, 1980 and 1988. Senate majority leader 1985–1987, minority leader 1987– 1995; majority leader 1995–1996, resigned. 1996 Republican presidential nominee.

Home: Russell, Kansas.

Personal characteristics: 6'2" tall, 170 pounds, black hair; lost use of right arm and hand in World War II injury; quick, at times biting wit.

Father: Doran Ray Dole (1900–December 9, 1975); grain elevator operator.

Mother: Bina Talbott, daughter of Joseph and Elva Talbott; farmers.

Siblings: Kenneth. Gloria (1922–). Norma Jean.

First wife: Phyllis Holden (1936–); married in 1948; divorced January 12, 1972; she subsequently married Lon Buzick, a Sylvan Grove, Kansas rancher.

Child: Robin (1965–).

Second wife: Mary Elizabeth ("Liddy") Hanford (July 20, 1936–); married December 6, 1975; lawyer, was a Federal Trade Commissioner when married, later became presidential adviser and then secretary of transportation; daughter of John Van and Mary Ella (Cathey) Hanford.

Bob Dole's family was not wealthy; they were not exactly impoverished, either, but daily expenses were a constant struggle. Their two-room frame home in Russell, Kansas, was on the wrong side of the tracks. Hard work was almost sacred. Dole's father managed a cafe, ran an eggs and creamery store, and then was manager of the local grain elevator. Work dominated the elder Dole's existence and the son inherited his attitude. To help with expenses, Bob worked at a soda fountain after school. Money was saved by Mrs. Dole's making many of the kids' clothes.

Dole apparently stayed out of most normal childhood troubles, and was a good student. His real promise was shown in sports. Dole's former high school coach thought him hardworking, never-complaining, always ready to tackle, literally or figuratively, the toughest tasks. Classmates and townspeople still recall when Dole made an incredible catch on the last play of the "big game," and then sloshed down the muddy field to victory. All the opposing coach could do was sling his hat in the mud and jump up and down on it.

World War II erupted while Dole was attending the University of Kansas in Lawrence, in a pre-med program. During his sophomore year, he enlisted in the Army and two years later, as a 21-year-old second lieutenant, he was fighting in Italy. On April 14, 1945, while leading his platoon across the Po River in northern Italy, Dole was struck by fire from a German machine gun. He lay paralyzed for hours, with his hands pinned above his head, his right shoulder shattered, his neck vertebrae fractured, and his life bleeding out of him. In inimitable Dole style, he would later say, "it was sort of a long day." For 39 months he was in Army hospitals, much of the time in a cast from his neck to his hips. Doctors did not think he would walk again. His weight dropped from 194 to 122 pounds. One kidney was removed in 1945 due to infection. When blood clots on the lungs formed, doctors advised the family that he would not live. Only the use of a then experimental drug, streptomycin, saved his life. Dole emerged from the hospital with permanent damage to his spinal cord, leaving his right arm permanently paralyzed and shorter than his left. Much of the arm was rebuilt from bone and tissue from his leg in a special and expensive operation paid for by a fund-raising drive in his hometown.

Also emerging with Dole as a result of this experience was his first wife, Phyllis Holden. She was a physical therapist who had helped him learn to write left-handed, feed himself, and otherwise regain basic living skills. School was paid for by the G.I. Bill and by income from his wife's job. She worked a full day and then took notes on his reading and even wrote examination answers that he dictated to her. Dole's injuries had seemed to rule out a medical career, so he turned to the law and graduated from Washburn University in 1952. Two years before that, as a law student, he had been elected to the Kansas legislature. Dole also served as prosecuting attorney for Russell County. Until his defeat as vice president, he would put together a string of electoral victo-

ries that finally totaled 11. By 1996, he had 14 straight victories in other than nationwide elections.

Dole was a superb campaigner, and a tireless one. Politics was his life and he set a tight schedule for advancement. He was so successful that he even converted the mother of one of his election opponents to his cause. In 1960 Dole encouraged a seven-term Republican congressman to retire, and he was nominated by 987 votes in the Republican primary. His general election victory was much more sweeping.

In Washington, the new congressman established a reputation as a Kennedy opponent, a conservative, but no ideologue. Farming was his constituents' interest, and Dole supported most farm subsidy programs. He gained recognition for exposing details about the Billie Sol Estes grain storage fraud and the Bobby Baker scandal. His reputation at home and in Washington was as a hard-hitting conservative who could at times be ruthless. His sarcastic, painfully biting humor was also becoming a trademark. Americans for Constitutional Action, a conservative organization that rates elected officials, found Dole to have one of the most consistently high conservative voting records in the House. In 1964, when running against Democrat Bill Bork for reelection, his ruthlessness showed when television and radio ads were run stating "Bork is a jerk." Such tactics did not shake his support in Kansas.

Dole was not an unbending conservative. This was revealed in his support for most of the landmark civil rights bills. That Russell and the state of Kansas in general are poor backgrounds for understanding race sensitivities became clear years later when, to a black audience, Dole used the completely innocent phrase that it was time "to call a spade a spade." The uproar from the crowd made Dole aware of a double entendre he had previously overlooked. Dole also came to support food stamp proposals, though early in his Congressional career he opposed them. His record reveals other swings in voting, from being for the Civil Rights Act of 1964 and the Voting Rights Act of 1965, to being against the Civil Rights and Equal Opportunity Acts of 1966. He would later credit Senator George McGovern for his change of heart on food stamps. Dole went to Congressional committee meetings across the country investigating nutrition and hunger in America, and could not believe the seriousness of the problems that he found. The experience made him an advocate of several subsidy programs he might earlier have opposed.

Republican Senator Frank Carlson of Kansas decided to retire in 1968. As a candidate to succeed him, Dole won more than two-thirds of the votes in the primary and swept to victory in November over his Democratic opponent. In the Senate Dole was an outspoken defender of President Nixon, one unafraid of the Democrats' principal spokesmen. Dole's committee responsibilities were minimal his first term. Consequently, he spent much time on the Senate floor. So few Republicans were present during some of the sessions that he quipped, "the Democrats could steal the furniture." His defense work for the administration included attacks on those who opposed the Supreme Court nominations of Clement Haynsworth and G. Harrold Carswell. The most critical issues involved Vietnam, and Dole was a stout supporter of President Nixon there too. His sharp tongue frequently stung Democrats and liberals who fought to reverse Vietnam policy, including such jibes as calling antiwar activist Ramsey Clark a "left-leaning marshmallow," and Ed Muskie a crybaby. The taunts set Dole's image as a hatchet-man, even among some Republicans. Ohio Republican senator William Saxbe, later attorney general, said that Dole was so antagonistic that he "could not sell beer on a troopship." At least one man was appreciative, and that was President Richard Nixon.

In January 1971, Nixon appointed Dole chairman of the Republican National Committee. One enemy Dole had made was Senate minority leader Hugh Scott of Pennsylvania, a Republican moderate. Dole had talked about challenging Scott as Republican leader in 1971, even though the Kansan was still only in his first term. Then Dole had promised to line up with Howard Baker of Tennessee if Baker tried to take the job from Scott. Therefore, it was not surprising that Senator Scott opposed Dole's selection as national chairman. Dole was replacing the smooth and gracious giant, Rogers Morton of Maryland. The comparison made between the two National Chairmen was that "Rog is a big old St. Bernard, while Dole is a hungry Doberman Pinscher," an apt description of both.

The new heights being reached in Dole's political career seemed to correspond to lows in his personal affairs. Phyllis Dole and her husband had been drawing further apart for years. Though Mrs. Dole enjoyed some aspects of politics, the more her husband was away from home and involved in significant national political issues, the less she felt a part of his life. Divorce was avoided for a time because she felt it could ruin his career. The divorce finally occurred in 1972.

Dole scarcely slowed down, as the national campaign to reelect the president was under way. Fortunately for his future career, but infuriating at the time, Dole was left out of most decisions in the Nixon campaign. Theodore White reported in his *Making of the President 1972* that Dole received a call from a Nixon aide, asking whether Dole wanted to see the president. Dole had so long been cut out of affairs that he was surprised by the invitation. The Republican chairman eagerly accepted. The response was that Dole should turn his television on in ten minutes and watch a Nixon interview. Such treatment caused Dole to suggest that the Committee to Reelect the President should be called "CREEP." Dole's bitter comments about treatment from the White House infuriated many on the president's staff. More trouble came from Dole's complaint that the president had not worked hard enough in 1972 for the election of other Republican candidates. Dole was summoned to Camp David in January 1973. Nixon felt too awkward to inform Dole that he was being fired. Dole had been warned of the purpose of the meeting, however, so he ended the embarrassment by saying that he would quit in order better to prepare for his own reelection in 1974. A heated exchange occurred between Dole and some of Nixon's aides. Dole described his adversaries on Nixon's staff as "the faceless, nameless, spineless ones who do it this way."

In 1974, after the Nixon resignation, Dole found himself embroiled in perhaps the most heated election campaign of his career. The problem was Dole's partisan support for President Nixon. Even so, Dole had not been a blind defender during Watergate. As early as May 18, 1973, he had stated, "Nixon appears to be hiding from the people, who really trust and like him very much." Dole's advice was for Nixon to "come clean" and inform the public of the truth. After President Gerald Ford pardoned Nixon for any offenses that he committed, Dole tried to call Ford "to thank him for throwing me an anchor with the Nixon pardon." Fortunately for Dole, his 1974 Democratic opponent went too far in trying to connect Dole with the Watergate scandal. Congressman William Roy had been far in the lead in public opinion polls when Dole started his counterattack. The senator showed television ads of mud being slung against a poster of Dole's face, with a voice reciting the various charges against him. Then glob by glob, the mud was removed as the "truth" about Dole was recounted. Depicting himself as the innocent victim of a smear dramatically turned the election around. Equally important was the charge that Roy, a gynecologist, was an enthusiastic abortion advocate who had killed babies. Dr. Roy had performed some abortions. The state was inundated with antiabortion literature that included pictures of dead babies in garbage cans. Watergate white knight Lowell Weicker of Connecticut, the most outspoken Nixon critic among Republicans, came in to campaign for his friend Dole. The Kansas senator flippantly dismissed any suggestion of personal involvement in the Watergate break-in by stating it had occurred "on my night off." Dole won by a slim but sufficient 13,532 votes out of nearly 800,000 cast.

The bitterness of Watergate was purged to some extent by the catharsis of Dole's acceptance at the polls. The senator was further cheered by his marriage to Federal Trade Commission member Libby Hanford, then 39. Dole was 52. Some wag at the Federal Trade Commission circulated a memo concerning possible merger problems in the upcoming wedding of a senator and a commissioner, and Miss Hanford responded in kind with a memo of her own.

Dole continued to reveal his conservatism,

with occasional dashes of liberality in food stamps and issues involving the handicapped. He opposed the proposal for guaranteed employment called the Humphreys-Hawkins Bill, generally supported defense programs, and opposed busing solely to achieve racial balance in schools. Dole's change of heart on food stamps, and his 11 years of working with South Dakota senator George McGovern on the Agriculture Committee, later caused McGovern to call his Kansas comrade "the most human man I know in the Senate."

In 1976, Dole signed on early as a backer of President Ford against the challenge of former California governor Ronald Reagan. At the convention, Ford was poorly prepared to select a running mate because the battle with Reagan had been so fierce. After Ford was nominated, he met with Reagan and gave him a list of six men Ford was considering for vice president: Treasury Secretary William Simon, former Treasury Secretary and Texas Governor John Connally, Senator Howard Baker, former cabinet officers Elliot Richardson and William Ruckelshaus, and Dole. Reagan's response was that Dole would be an excellent candidate. At 3:15 the next morning a session started with top Ford aides going over nominees, and the list was expanded. Ambassador to Great Britain Anne Armstrong was high on this list. Ruckelshaus was close to getting the nomination. With all political pluses and minuses calculated, Ford finally decided on Dole. Ford had known him for years, believed they were compatible on issues, and knew he was a slashing, hard-ball campaigner who had saved his own Senate seat two years earlier and might show equal skills this time. Barry Goldwater had years earlier characterized Dole in words that seemed appropriate in explaining the Kansan's 1976 nomination: "He's the first man we've had around here in a long time, who will grab the other side by the hair and drag them down the hill."

At first Dole restrained his hair grabbing, but as the polls showed the Ford-Dole ticket closing a huge gap against Jimmy Carter, Dole returned to his slashingly sardonic style. He got into trouble when he charged the Democrats with being the war party since they were in power during the beginning of all the

American conflicts in this century. Ironically, Jimmy Carter would charge Ronald Reagan with being the war candidate four years later and would receive equally harsh reaction. Editorial response to Dole was frequently bad, and the image as a shoot-from-the-hip politician became almost indelible. Dole's description of his role was that Ford was campaigning from the White House Rose Garden, while he was in the brier patch. After the extremely narrow defeat, many Republicans blamed Dole. Dole contended that he had a positive impact. What does seem significant is that to the extent Dole was added to the ticket to keep the Midwest farm belt Republican, that ploy succeeded. The election was lost in the Northeast and South.

Almost immediately the defeated vice presidential nominee began testing the waters for the top position in 1980. Dole employed a campaign staff early, and then on May 14, 1979, announced his candidacy. His hope was that Ronald Reagan would not run and that Dole could pick off supporters and aides from the former California governor. It was not to be. After devastatingly poor finishes in early caucuses and primaries, including getting less than 1 percent in New Hampshire, he dropped out on March 15, 1980. Dole blamed defeat on his inability to campaign full-time, as he could only devote weekends and recesses from his Senate duties. Dole bemoaned this new burden of campaigning that required someone to be out of office before he could run for president. His reasoning appears sound, as the two finalists for the Republican nomination were the only two serious contenders who were then unemployed, Ronald Reagan and George Bush.

Dole's Kansas base was not eroded by his abortive presidential race. Sixty-four percent of the voters that November gave him their support. Another, far more surprising boost to this longtime minority party senator was the election for the first time in 28 years of a Republican majority in the Senate. Out of this party change, Dole gained the chairmanship of the powerful Senate Finance Committee. Friend and foe alike commended Dole for his leadership in that important committee. It was an ideologically diverse group of Republicans he tried to lead, and opposing him was an ideologically liberal group of Democrats. Nonetheless, Dole became a power as chairman by being a pragmatic legislator who was skilled in piecing together compromises.

Elizabeth Dole was making her own mark. She left the FTC in 1981 and became a presidential adviser. On February 7, 1983, she moved past her senatorial husband on the Washington pecking order when she became secretary of transportation in President Reagan's cabinet.

Dole became Senate majority leader in 1984 when Howard Baker retired. Dole was re-elected easily in 1986, but in the Senate the Republicans lost their majority. Dole was again chosen as GOP Senate leader. He tried again for the presidency in 1988. Dole did well in Iowa, and had the early favorite, Vice President George Bush, on the ropes. Future GOP chairman Haley Barbour, then a television political commentator, complimented Dole on his victory, but presciently warned, "when the champ is down, you better finish him off." Dole did not finish Bush off. Bush ran devastating commercials against Dole the last weekend before the New Hampshire primary, attacking Dole mainly on taxes. They became known as the "straddle ads," because they accused Dole of being on both sides of many issues and that he could not be believed. Bush won a strong victory, and also won a nationally televised rebuke from Dole once the result was clear. Anchorman Tom Brokaw of NBC, who was interviewing Bush late on election night, asked Dole if he had anything to say to Bush. "Yes," Dole said. "Tell him to stop lying about my record." It was typical Dole.

After defeats in the South in March, Dole's chances of victory were obviously gone. He withdrew, but still hoped for a vice presidential nomination. Elizabeth Dole also was a frequently mentioned possibility. Neither Dole made it, as Dan Quayle was named.

With George Bush in the White House, the president's principal adversary from the nomination campaign was his leader in the Senate. Bush and Dole worked well together despite their past differences. Bush opened the door to considering tax increases, after having committed not to do so during the campaign.

Dole, whose chance for the presidency in 1988 had been ended by Bush's Straddle Ads that said Dole could not be trusted on the tax question, helped with the tax increase. Dole also was instrumental in passing the Americans with Disabilities Act, a measure backed strongly by the Bush administration. When Bill Clinton was in the White House, Dole was not an obstructionist opposition leader. A Republican majority was elected in both houses of Congress in 1994, the first time that had happened since 1952, and only the third time since 1928. Dole again was chosen Senate majority leader.

Dole announced his third and final bid for the presidency on April 10, 1995. Ever since 1968, Republicans had chosen the early favorite as their nominee — there may have been doubts along the way, but the person whose past experience seemed to have earned the position always won. Dole was that 1996 favorite. Earning that status usually means being around for a long time, and many fresher candidates were considered for a time. A strong contender, retired General Colin Powell, announced in November 1995 that he would not run. Dole was seriously challenged in early primaries. Dole finished first in the Iowa caucus, but barely. Conservative political commentator Pat Buchanan finished a strong second, and Lamar Alexander, a former Tennessee governor and Bush's secretary of education, earned a spot in the first tier of contenders by coming in a close third. Buchanan then won the New Hampshire primary, edging Dole and leaving Alexander in third. Buchanan was now the focus, which helped Dole. It was unlikely that Buchanan, who had an image as being too conservative and a résumé that seemed too thin, could win the nomination in so traditional a party as the GOP. Lamar Alexander may have been a more serious competitor had he managed to win in New Hampshire, but he quickly ran out of money after his third place finish. When Dole won the Southern state primaries in March, it was over. Businessman Steve Forbes and his flat tax ideas created some excitement, but he too seemed to be trying to make too big a leap, from magazine publisher to president.

Once Dole locked up the nomination, he became mired in polling numbers that showed him uncompetitive against Clinton. Partly to reinvigorate his campaign, on May 15 Dole shocked and delighted his supporters by announcing that he would resign from the Senate and concentrate full-time on the campaign. It helped, but only briefly. There was even talk from some conservatives that Dole should drop out "for the good of the party." At the national convention, Dole said that the election would be about character and trust, suggesting that Bill Clinton did not have the former and did not deserve the latter. Dole wanted to be a bridge to a better America, a simpler one, a country that knew its values. Bill Clinton's team would show that they understood the electorate better, and turned the image around. Clinton would be a "bridge to the twenty-first century," while Dole was cementing his connection to the past.

All through the fall, news stories concentrated on how improbable a Dole victory would be. A few polls indicated something less than the huge margins of most polls. It was a little watched, little discussed campaign. Efforts to get Ross Perot to abandon his certain-to-lose campaign and support Dole once almost seemed to be working, but then fell apart. Clinton won, but by far less than some polls had been showing.

Analysis of Qualifications

Robert Dole is a jumble of contradictions. His voting record had always rated high on conservative political groups analysis, but he was never quite trusted by conservatives. He was an extremely successful and ambitious politician, but at times his actions and words seemed oblivious to political impact. Perhaps most contradictory of all, he gained a reputation as a hatchet man on the political stump, but colleagues in the Senate found him a warm, compassionate man.

Dole's wit is at times the weapon most likely to cause a self-inflicted wound. He has a self-mocking style, a fair indication that the Senator does not take himself too seriously. Sometimes the one-liners have a cutting edge that leaves everyone laughing except for the victim; at other times he has been able to offend a much larger range of people.

Robert Dole was a hard-nosed, practical politician who early in his career could be abrasive and antagonistic, but who nonetheless earned the respect even of his political adversaries. Some did not accept Dole's political style, which has led to such descriptions as Dole's being so abrasive in the 1970s that "he could not sell beer on a troopship." Dole is incredibly hard-working and focused. That may be a heritage from his parents. It has remained with him. He drove his staff almost as hard as he drove himself. His dedication to his craft probably broke up his first marriage, but he appears to have mellowed after his second.

Dole has shown many of the characteristics for success in the presidency. In his 1976 race for vice president, the principal concern was a seeming lack of political maturity and stability. The image he projected was one of a hatchet man who was not a leader. Dole reversed that impression when his party was in power in the Senate, and revealed considerable skills that had not earlier been drawn upon. Had Dole succeeded to the presidency as a result of the 1976 election, he likely would have been an example of a man who appeared to grow in office and overcome some of the less attractive aspects of his political past.

By 1996 Dole's public persona was considerably different. He was gracious, thoughtful, the consummate deal-maker. He could build consensus and reach legislative goals. In the age of more ideological national parties, Dole became out of place. He was too accommodating to his opponents, a man without conviction. Dole's campaign was criticized for having no philosophical message. Much like Bush in 1992, Dole was said to need "vision" of what he wanted to do with the presidency. Dole called his campaign one last mission. "Missions" were from a different era; the politics of the 1990s were not much about sacrifice or responsibility.

Dole was an experienced, able conciliator who wanted to handle the crises that a president would face, but without any particular package of programs and changes that he wanted to implement. He would have been solid, not prone to rash mistakes, an average president perhaps in the nature of a Gerald Ford or a Rutherford B. Hayes. Those men served their country well, but usually without excitement, without entertainment, without glitz. It is not what the American people wanted in 1996.

DOLE BIBLIOGRAPHY

Altman, Lawrence K. "Dole Has Physical; Details Not Given." *New York Times* (Sept. 22, 1976), p. 26.

Balz, Dan, and Ronald Brownstein. *Storming the Gates: Protest Politics and the Republican Revival.* Boston, et al. (1996).

Bob Dole: A Pictorial Biography of a Kansan. Wichita (1996).

"Bob Dole Shoots for the Top with a New Image." *U.S. News & World Report* (Sept. 17, 1979), pp. 40–42.

Clymer, Adam. "Senator Dole Joins G.O.P. Race for '80 Presidential Nomination." *New York Times* (May 15, 1979), p. 1, 20.

"Compromise Crafter Dole Is Earning a Reputation as a Power in the Senate." *Congressional Quarterly Guide to Current American Government*, Washington (Spring 1982), pp. 39–42.

Cramer, Richard Ben. *Bob Dole.* New York (1995).

_____. *What It Takes: The Way to the White House.* New York (1992).

Dole, Robert J., and Elizabeth Dole. *The Doles: Unlimited Partners.* New York (1988).

_____ and _____, with Richard Norton Smith and Kerry Tymchuk. *Unlimited Partners.* New York (1996).

"The Dole Decision." *Time* (Aug. 30, 1976), pp. 22–23.

"Dole Keeps His Gloves On." *Newsweek* (Sept. 13, 1976), pp. 17–18.

"Dole Takes Out After Carter." *US. News & World Report* (Aug. 30, 1976), pp. 19–20.

"Dole-ing It Out." *Time* (May 31, 1971), pp. 20–23.

Fineman, Howard. "The Contradictory Character of Bob Dole." *Newsweek* (Nov. 16, 1987) pp. 65–67.

"Has Gun, Will Travel." *Time* (Aug. 30, 1976), pp. 23–30.

Hilton, Stanley. *Bob Dole.* Chicago (1988).

_____. *Senator for Sale: An Unauthorized Biography of Senator Bob Dole.* New York (1995).

Kneeland, Douglas E. "Dole Comes Under Fire in Midwest for President's Embargo of Grain." *New York Times* (Sept. 24, 1976), p. 23.

Lydon, Christopher. "A Tough Infighter, Robert Joseph Dole." *New York Times* (Aug. 20, 1976), pp. 1, 11.

McLeod, Don, et al. "Bob Dole: The Man to Beat." *Washington Times Insight* (June 1, 1987), pp. 8–19.

ROBERT J. DOLE (left) and JACK KEMP
(From the author's collection)

MacPherson, Myra. *The Power Lovers: An Intimate Look at Politicians and Their Marriages.* New York City (1975), pp. 217–231.

Maraniss, David. "A 20-Year Journey Nears its Destination." *Washington Post* (August 11, 1996), pp. A1, A16.

"A New and Hungry Chairman." *Time* (Jan. 18, 1971), pp. 13–14.

Osborne, John. "Why Dole?" *New Republic* (Sept. 4, 1976), pp. 15–18.

"The Point Man." *Newsweek* (Aug. 30, 1976), pp. 38–40.

"Sen. Dole Abandons His Presidential Bid." *New York Times* (March 16, 1980), p. 31.

Thompson, Jake H. *Bob Dole: The Republicans' Man for All Seasons.* New York (1996).

Toichin, Martin, and Jeff Gerth. "The Contradictions of Bob Dole." *New York Times Magazine* (Nov. 8, 1987), pp. 63ff.

Tributes Delivered in Congress: Robert J. Dole.... Washington, D.C. (1996).

*1996 vice presidential nominee —
Republican Party*

Jack Kemp

Full name: Jack French Kemp.

State represented: New York.

Birth: July 13, 1935, in Los Angeles, California.

Age on Inauguration Day (January 20, 1997): 61 years, 6 months.

Education: Los Angeles public schools; Occidental College (B.A. 1957). Graduate studies at Long Beach State University and at California Western University.

Religion: Raised a Christian Scientist; now a Presbyterian.

Occupation: Professional football player 1957–1969; businessman; works on several conservative policy groups.

Public offices: Special assistant to Governor Ronald Reagan, 1967; United States representative, 1971–1989; secretary of housing and urban development, 1989–1992. Apparent runner-up for 1980 Republican vice presidential selection; unsuccessful candidate for Republican presidential nomination, 1988; defeated vice presidential nominee 1996.

Home: Hamburg, New York, and Bethesda, Maryland.

Personal characteristics: Six feet tall, athletic build. Thick, always neat reddish-brown hair that turned gray; known as a non-stop talker. Energetic, optimistic, compassionate.

Father: Paul R. Kemp (1897–1977), son of Oscar Paddock Kemp and Elva French Kemp; Paul operated a small trucking company.

Mother: Frances Pope (1900–1969), daughter of Gershom Barlow Pope and Lucy Catlett Pope, who were sheep ranchers in Montana.

Siblings: Paul Kemp (July 17, 1928–), married Nancy ___; he was an electronics company executive. Tom Kemp (October 8, 1930–), married Betty ___; he was a food company executive. Dick Kemp (August 22, 1939–), married Carolyn ___; he is an executive at a resort.

Wife: Joanne Main (born Sept. 27, 1936), daughter of educators Donovan and Lois Main of Monrovia, California. She taught school during part of the Kemp marriage.

Children: Jeffrey (July 11, 1959–), after a professional football career, headed the Washington Family Council in Seattle area; married Stacy Parker. Jennifer (November 30, 1962–), married Scott Andrews; she has taught school and is a homemaker. Judith (October 27, 1965–), married Chris Nolan; she has been a congressional aide and is a homemaker. James (June 27, 1971–), a professional football player.

One of the most famous descriptions Jack Kemp has made about himself is that he is a "bleeding-heart conservative." In 1996 he was the candidate who went to places that usually do not vote for Republicans, "from the boroughs of New York to the barrios of California," as he said after being selected as Bob Dole's running mate. He did not cause the Bob Dole ticket to win, but he brought it an enthusiasm and lift that helped make the Republicans competitive for awhile.

Jack Kemp's father expanded a motorcycle delivery business into a small trucking company. Jack's mother was a social worker who

spoke Spanish fluently. The parents and four boys were a tight-knit family living in the middle-class Wilshire district in Los Angeles. Jack worked part-time with the trucking company while attending school. At Fairfax High School in Los Angeles Jack's only interest, indeed his obsession, was sports. He excelled in many, but playing professional football was his dream. In high school he once had to write an essay on an important invention. He picked the invention of the forward pass.

Kemp was six feet tall, not large for an aspiring professional football player. Major college football programs did not want him, so he chose Occidental College in Los Angeles. It was an academically prestigious liberal arts school whose football team used professional-style plays and formations. Which aspect attracted Kemp is obvious. He was a mediocre student, but his senior year as quarterback on the football them he was the small college national leader in passing.

Kemp's professional career was slow to start. Drafted in the seventeenth round by the Detroit Lions in 1957, he was dropped before the season started. He played five games for the Pittsburgh Steelers during the season once starting quarterback Earl Morrall was injured. Kemp was cut from the team by the end of the season. Kemp spent part of 1958 on active duty in the Army as a private, then remained in the Army Reserves until 1962. During part of the 1958 season Kemp was on the New York Giants "taxi squad," the group of reserves who were not regular players. He then tried out for the Canadian Football League's Calgary Stampeders, but he did not make the team. Kemp was there long enough, though, to be disqualified for the NFL in 1959. He did get signed by the San Francisco 49ers near the end of the 1959 season.

Kemp's career break was the formation of the American Football League in 1960. He became a starter that season for the Los Angeles Chargers. In his and the league's first year, Kemp led all quarterbacks in passing. He made 211 of 406 attempts for 3,018 yards in a 14-game season. The Chargers lost in the league championship to the Houston Oilers, 24–16.

Kemp was in a San Diego–based Army

Reserves company that was activated in August 1961 by President Kennedy because of the Berlin crisis. A month after the company was activated, but before he was to report for duty, Kemp injured his shoulder playing football. Because of some restriction of motion in his shoulder, swelling and muscle spasms, Army doctors recommended that he be excused from military service. A professional football player has such a high profile that the Army had the surgeon general make the final decision on his physical fitness. After further examinations, Kemp was exempted by the surgeon general. His certified physical unfitness for the Army, but his deserved reputation as a scrambling quarterback, were fodder for many future negative press stories. There has never been any suggestion that Kemp pressed for special treatment. Indeed, it took strong painkilling injections — a teammate said that Kemp would be given ten injections — and constant attention by team doctors to enable him to play.

Kemp's team lost again in the championship game in 1961, but the Chargers now were in San Diego when they lost to the Oilers in the championship, 10–3. In 1962 Kemp injured his finger early in the season and could not play. League rules limited the number of active players on a team, so the Chargers briefly put him on waivers to make a spot on the roster for another player, planning to "reclaim" him soon thereafter. The Buffalo Bills saw his name on the waiver list, and picked up his contract. With Kemp at quarterback, the Bills won three straight division championships starting in 1964. The first two division titles were followed by winning the League championship game, beating Kemp's old team the San Diego Chargers, 20–7 in 1964 and 23–0 in 1965. Kemp was the most valuable player for the season and for the championship game in 1965. The Super Bowl that for four seasons matched the AFL and NFL winners, and then would pair the NFL conference winners after the two leagues merged, was first held after the 1966 season. In 1966 the Bills lost in the championship game, 31–7 to the Kansas City Chiefs, which meant that the Chiefs played in the first Super Bowl. The Bills did not win their division the rest of Kemp's playing career.

Injuries were starting to reduce Kemp's effectiveness: two broken ankles, two broken shoulders, a broken knee, and eleven concussions. Kemp said that the end of his playing career came when 280-pound tackle Ron McDole landed on his knee. Kemp was a founder of the American Football League Player's Association, and its president from 1965 until 1970. In that role he handled negotiations with the team owners for a comprehensive package of health and pension benefits. Kemp had a poor season in 1969, and retired. His jersey number (15) was retired by the Bills. It was quite a career for a small college quarterback who was too short to play in the pros.

Kemp's interest in politics started at least as early as 1958 when he did volunteer work for Nelson Rockefeller's campaign for New York governor. Then he helped in Richard Nixon's 1960 presidential race. In 1961 in San Diego, future Nixon press director Herb Klein got local football star Kemp to write editorials on good citizenship for the San Diego *Union*. The Klein connection also enabled him to meet many of southern California's most prominent Republicans. Kemp worked in Nixon's failed 1962 California governor's race and Barry Goldwater's 1964 presidential race. After helping in the campaign, Kemp then briefly served in 1967 as an adviser on youth to new California governor Ronald Reagan. This broadening set of experiences caused him to take graduate studies in political science and education at Long Beach State University and at California Western University. After the 1969 season Kemp went to work as the public relations officer for the Midland Bank of Buffalo. Republican leaders in Buffalo approached the local team's ex-quarterback in 1970, and encouraged him to run for Congress. After Kemp agreed to do so, one of the leaders told a Buffalo newspaper, "We were looking for an attractive, articulate, forthright aggressive man. Finding Jack Kemp was like finding the Holy Grail."

His district consisted of almost all-white suburbs of Buffalo. The incumbent Democrat Richard McCarthy had tried to move up to the U.S. Senate, but lost. McCarthy then tried to take back the party nomination for his old seat, which caused a bad Democratic Party split. Kemp did not have a free ride to victory, though, and the Democratic nominee, Buffalo District Attorney Thomas P. Flaherty, criticized Kemp's ties to President Nixon and his governmental inexperience. Kemp won with only 51.6 percent of the vote. It was enough. He would not have another close race until his last one in 1986.

Throughout the 1970s Congressman Kemp maintained a strongly conservative House voting record — full support for President Nixon in his conduct of the Vietnam War, voting for most military appropriations, and opposing federal funding of abortions and busing to achieve racial integration of schools. Yet he also was perceived as a friend of labor unions and was in favor of the Equal Rights Amendment for women.

Kemp's star quality did not diminish away from Buffalo. Besides the obvious attraction of his good looks and celebrity background, Kemp was also a serious student of economic theory. He became a policy disciple of economist Arthur Laffer, a University of Southern California professor who theorized that the economy had borne all the federal taxes that it could; taxes higher than the current load would so hamper the economy as to result in less net taxes. This tradeoff between tax rates and economic productivity, when graphed, was dubbed the "Laffer Curve." Kemp became a proponent of a large tax cut to energize the economy. Kemp would be labeled the first "supply-side politician." In September 1977, the Republican National Committee unanimously endorsed Kemp's call for large and immediate tax cuts. In the late 1970s Kemp was an evangelistic speaker to party conventions, business organizations, and an assortment of other interest groups about his proposals. With Delaware Senator William Roth he sponsored the Kemp-Roth Tax Relief Bill, which would phase in over three years a 33 percent tax cut for most Americans. Democratic President Jimmy Carter supported parts of the plan. One of the increasing criticisms of Kemp during this period was that he was a single-issue politician, and that this ex–football player did not fully understood the huge macro-economic forces that he would attempt

to affect by his policies. House Democratic Leader Jim Wright said that Kemp's bill was "blatant hucksterism." The bill was narrowly defeated by the House in 1978.

In 1979 Kemp wrote a book, *An American Renaissance,* which highlighted his tax strategy as well as the early stages of what would be called the "opportunity society." Kemp used the old phrase that "a rising tide raises all boats." That was the image that best captures his proposals. A more prosperous America, free of onerous tax burdens, regulations, and other shackles, would benefit everyone. In 1979 Kemp was considering a run for the presidency, and drawing some support from conservatives to whom Ronald Reagan also was an appealing candidate. Kemp, who knew his chances of winning the nomination were poor, agreed to support Reagan publicly in return for Reagan's endorsement of the Kemp tax cut. That is what happened. Kemp became an adviser on economic issues.

Kemp had been encouraged to run for the U.S. Senate from New York in 1980. The liberal Republican Senator Jacob Javits' term was up. Kemp apparently would have run had Javits retired, but instead Javits ran for reelection. Kemp declined, and another conservative Republican, Alfonse D'Amato, ran against Javits and beat him in the primary. Once Reagan secured enough delegates for the nomination, Kemp — whose ideas figured so prominently in Reagan's message — was a leading contender for vice president. Reports later indicated that eight people were on Reagan's principal list. Kemp was one of them. Reagan was quoted as saying Kemp was a good man, but a "newcomer." More seasoning required, it would appear. Kemp appeared too eager for the position. The Detroit convention hall was decorated with perhaps too many Reagan-Kemp signs and balloons; too many delegates wore Kemp buttons and hats. In the end, Kemp's image may have been too much like Reagan's, a conservative tax-cutter who would not broaden Reagan's appeal. Many considered the running mate position more than usually significant. There was much optimism about Reagan's winning in November, and much speculation that the vice president to the 69-year-old chief executive would have a great chance one way or another of being the next president. George Bush was selected.

The supply-side politics Kemp had championed since 1975 became administration and party policy under President Reagan. There were strong internal disagreements, however. Reagan budget director David Stockman called Kemp-Roth a "Trojan horse" whose purpose was only to bring down the top rate on the wealthiest people. Stockman agreed that it was "trickle-down" economics, a much more disparaging image than "raising all boats." The tax-cuts that were passed by Congress early in President Reagan's term were the culmination of Jack Kemp's six-year effort. However, those 1981 cuts were followed by a large tax increase in 1982. The explosion of the budget deficit was the impetus. Senator Bob Dole proposed the higher taxes, saying it was an economic necessity. Dole's bill was not a tax increase, he argued, but closed loopholes and broadened the tax base. His future running mate denounced Dole's bill, saying the label as "tax increase" or not did not matter, the effect was to take $100 billion out of taxpayers' pockets. Dole' role earned him future House Speaker Newt Gingrich's epithet as the "tax collector of the welfare state." The more conservative Republicans like Kemp wanted significant program cuts, something that moderate Republicans and Democrats never accepted. Kemp again looked at a major statewide race in New York in 1982, for governor, but declined. Lewis E. Lehrman was the nominee instead. Mario Cuomo, who won his first of three terms, defeated Lehrman only by 51 percent to 47 percent. Other Republicans at times criticized Kemp for passing up challenging races in which other, lesser known Republicans did well.

After Reagan's 1984 reelection, Kemp started to look seriously at running for president in 1988. As perhaps an early campaign platform, he collected in 1984 many of his speeches into a new book, *The American Idea: Ending Limits to Growth*. A new proposal entered his economic thinking. He believed that economic stability required that the dollar be pegged to a commodity such as gold. Political arguments about the gold standard were normal fare in the late 1800s, but had long faded from public debate. Future Federal Reserve chairman

Alan Greenspan was another supporter. This iconoclastic proposal added to the image problems for Kemp. He had been safely conservative on most issues, but raised suspicions on a few. For example, he supported sanctions against South Africa, when more conservative Republicans thought such sanctions made resolution of South Africa's problems more difficult. Kemp received support from auto workers, longshoreman, and other labor unions in his Buffalo district. He more than most Republicans has been identified with blue collar workers and then later also with civil rights groups.

Kemp in 1986 faced problems in his Buffalo district for the first time in 15 years. A well-known Buffalo councilman, James P. Keane, was the Democratic nominee. National Democratic money heavily funded Keane's campaign as the party hoped to wound if not defeat Kemp. Kemp won by 57 percent to 42 percent. In 1984 he had won with 75 percent of the vote, so for Kemp 1986 was a close election.

Kemp's presidential campaign in 1987 was going downhill. His campaign manager, Ed Rollins, wrote Kemp a confidential memo that said basically everything was wrong — no strategy, no grass roots organization, not enough money for the high-budget campaign, too big and top-heavy a staff. Rollins also complained that Kemp's message was too diffused, that Kemp used too many words to explain the policies and vision that he would take to the White House. The latter — Kemp's at times numbing verbosity — was a frequent criticism through the years. Rollins later said that Kemp had been impossible to discipline, that he would not listen to advice. Rollins called it the "quarterback mentality." Kemp was considered Bush's main challenger in local Michigan party regional conventions in 1987 that started the delegate selection process for 1988. Bush beat him badly. Some significant players in the coming Republican revolution were helping Kemp, like Newt Gingrich, Jude Wanniski, and Irving Kristol, but the campaign never caught hold. Kemp did worse than expected in Iowa and finished third in New Hampshire, 25 percent behind Bush. Two days after winning nothing in the Super Tuesday, March 8,

Southern primaries, Kemp withdrew. He had already announced that he would not run for re-election to the House.

Kemp hoped to be Bush's running mate. He was considered, but Dan Quayle was chosen. Kemp's problem in part was said to be that Bush feared being overshadowed by the more gregarious Kemp, and perhaps being mentally exhausted by working with so energetic and talkative a man. When Bush won, Kemp may have expected an upper-tier cabinet post. Instead, he was named to the Department of Housing and Urban Development, a vestige of the Great Society that operated programs that many Republicans did not support. His first major crisis was a corruption investigation that started four months after Kemp took over. The investigation focused on the eight-year service of his predecessor, HUD Secretary Samuel Pierce. Kemp tried to evict drug dealers from public housing, supported plans to move public housing into upper class white neighborhoods, and targeted some of the worst areas as enterprise zones entitled to significant government help and tax breaks. His favorite program may have been Home ownership and Opportunity for People Everywhere (H.O.P.E.). This initiative assisted the poor to buy their housing. He built bridges to the black community and some of its leaders, and gained a trust there few Republicans enjoyed.

In Cabinet meetings Kemp would add his views on many other subjects, from foreign policy to the economy. Vice President Quayle later wrote that Kemp "would sometimes squirm in his chair, and cough that nervous cough of his as he signaled that he couldn't wait to speak...." When Bush did call on him, Kemp "would sometimes go off on tangents and not make any discernible point." During the Bush Administration, Kemp more than any other cabinet official would publicly disagree with the president. Sometimes he argued that he was misquoted. He fought for higher HUD spending, and complained when other programs gained at HUD's expense. Kemp was in public disputes with Bush Budget Director Dick Darman, but then many other Republicans were also. One of the defining moments of the Bush presidency, when the president abandoned his "Read my lips, no more taxes" pledge from 1988 as just so much rhetoric, Kemp said, "If no one else will make the case [against a tax increase], I will." Kemp headed an Economic Empowerment Task Force to develop antipoverty plans. Few of his proposals were accepted by other Bush officials.

Bush's defeat in 1992 left Kemp without a high government position for the first time since 1970. He helped form Empower America in 1993. William Bennett, Jeane Kirkpatrick, and Vin Weber started it with Kemp in what was perceived as a precursor to a 1996 Kemp for President organization. The group was a public policy "think tank," a conservative political advocacy organization that studied problems and then communicated conservative solutions. Whatever the initial plans were, by 1994 Kemp was in a weak fifth position in public opinion polls, behind Bob Dole, Colin Powell, Ross Perot, and Dan Quayle. There were reports that Kemp consulted over dinner with close allies from his House days, most of whom had moved on: Senator Trent Lott, Speaker Newt Gingrich, Senator Dan Coats, and former Representative Vin Weber. On January 30, 1995, Kemp removed himself from the 1996 presidential race. He gave as his formal explanation that he did not need to run. His ideas once "were on the margins of the political debate, but now they are at the center." Less formally, he said, to use "the Newt Gingrich word, there are a lot of 'grotesqueries,' not the least of which is the fundraising side of it. I have no passion for that."

Kemp spent a lot of time from 1993 to 1996 on the speech circuit, getting paid up to $25,000 per speech, one or two a week. He served as a director on six corporate boards. At least two of the positions came because boards had connections with former football players he knew — former Dallas quarterback Roger Staubach and Miami Dolphin Nick Buoniconti. One election-year estimate was that he had earned $1 million per year since he left Bush's cabinet.

In 1995 Kemp was named by the Republican congressional leaders, Senate majority leader Bob Dole and Speaker Newt Gingrich, to head a commission to examine the practicality of radical tax reform. The new Republican House Ways and Means Chairman Bill Archer of Houston, who had been elected to succeed George Bush 24 years earlier, was proposing abolishing income taxes altogether and having a 16 percent national sales tax. Others were suggesting removing the graduated tax and having one, flat rate income tax. Kemp was on record as favoring a flat tax, and that is what the commission proposed in 1996.

Kemp was increasingly seen as a party maverick. He opposed the anti-discrimination, California Civil Rights Initiative in 1996, just as he had the anti-immigration initiative 187 in 1994. As attacks on affirmative action grew, Kemp said he still favored such programs. In March 1996, he endorsed the flat tax proposals and candidacy of Steve Forbes just as it was clear, even to Kemp as he was endorsing Forbes, that Dole would be nominated. He could do the impolitic because in 1996 Kemp was out of consideration for office, on no one's short list as Dole's running mate or for a position in a Dole cabinet. Retired General Colin Powell was the first, second, and third choice on Bob Dole's vice presidential list, but the general had been adamant that he would not accept. Kemp was just a bright might-have-been who would never be. That was wrong. In a dramatic move that surprised most observers and excited pessimistic Republicans, Dole the week before the national convention named Kemp as his running mate. They met at Dole's family home in Russell, Kansas, and campaigned frequently together after that.

Kemp's conservative critics remained. He rejected the negative, attack role frequently played by vice presidential candidates. He was accused of only trying to burnish his positive image for the future and avoiding the necessary dirty work if the 1996 ticket was going to catch up. His televised debate with Al Gore was far too pleasant an exchange for these critics. At one point Kemp stated that Bill Clinton and Gore "aren't our enemies; they're our opponents." In the instant snapshot polls now routinely taken of the political effect of events, 50 percent of those polled thought Gore had bested Kemp in the debate, while only 27 percent chose Kemp. There were those who said

that Kemp tried with "enthusiasm and good cheer ... to compensate for his poor preparation." The campaign ended in defeat, and with Kemp's detractors still suspicious of him. In the spring of 1997 Bob Dole was quoted as saying he should have named someone else, such as Florida senator Connie Mack.

Kemp returned to the think tank, Empower America, full of fresh ideas and perhaps plans for the future. Kemp was being quoted in early 1997 as planning to register a new political action committee preparatory to running for president in 2000.

Analysis of Qualifications

Before Bob Dole surprisingly picked him as his running mate, Jack Kemp was in the political wilderness. He was a leader whose time had apparently passed, though he was still energetic and youthful-looking. Dole may have joined Kemp to his team after simple political calculations that Kemp would best help him win. Regardless of the reasons, Kemp was back in the limelight.

Kemp has been an exasperating colleague for many Republicans. Some have seen him as an overgrown, over-achieving kid. His speeches through years have been filled with such words as "neat" and "super." He can exhibit such excesses of emotion, expressing such passion about everything around him, that Kemp is, as some have said, just "hard to take."

Democrats not committed to the party line that any Republican was bad, could applaud the selection of Kemp. So did many in the usually skeptical media. That was almost entirely because, as the *Washington Post* put it, "Jack Kemp stands for some of the best impulses in the Republican Party. We say that even as arch opponents of and disbelievers in the economic doctrine with which Mr. Kemp is most closely identified" (August 11, 1996, p. C6). Kemp wanted to reach out to Hispanics and blacks, to inner city dwellers who were not sharing in the American dream.

Kemp seems a blend of two predecessors who were nominated for the vice presidency. One predecessor was Theodore Roosevelt, elected vice president in 1900. Roosevelt was the ceaselessly talking, full of ideas, progressive Republican of whom "normal" Republicans were fearful. Kemp's eagerness to be seen as an idea man at times comes across as over-eagerness. It is as if he is saying, "I'm not just a football player; I'm an intellectual." Kemp may have less real intellectual depth that Roosevelt, but Roosevelt's contemporary detractors did not consider him a deep thinker. Nor is Kemp as fully a renaissance man as was Roosevelt. Kemp does come to mind when hearing the description Teddy Roosevelt's wife made when he was off romping with his children: "The president, you know, is about six." Kemp can appear either childish or exuberant, imaginative or just a flake. He like Roosevelt has an extremely close family. Kemp for all his public duties has been present in his family's lives. He is motivator, who attended football games and graduations. He has lived the family values some politicians only mouth.

The other Kemp-like vice presidential predecessor was Hubert Humphrey (a comparison the reporter David Broder made during the campaign). "Voluble" is the word that automatically is used in Humphrey descriptions. So is "compassionate," optimistic, and energetic. Humphrey was much more liberal than Kemp, but he was searching for governmental solutions to the same problems as has Kemp.

Another person to whom Kemp seems comparable is Harold Stassen. The Stassen that Kemp resembles is the significant political figure from 1944 to 1958 who had not yet embarked on quixotic runs for president. Stassen was out of step with more conservative Republicans, a man intent on blazing trails on issues such as disarmament while fellow Republicans were aghast. Stassen seemed more a favorite of the media than of the masses, at least within the Republican Party. Kemp shares many of those characteristics.

Kemp also has been a difficult man for others around him. His extreme optimism also can mean that he is a high-spirited man, impatient with any delay in achieving his goals. At HUD he wanted HUD's programs implemented, and did not want a numbers cruncher at the White House budget office telling him to wait for other priorities. Dole reportedly wanted assurances that during the 1996 campaign at least, Kemp would scrupulously follow the policies laid out by the head of the

ticket. He just does not serve well as anything other than the man in charge, the quarterback. Even in his literal quarterbacking roles, there have been questions about Kemp's independence. O.J. Simpson, who as a rookie was on the Kemp-quarterbacked Buffalo Bills team, wrote a memoir of that first season. Simpson said that when he and the veteran players all were "saying that we should run and the quarterback [Kemp] still keeps throwing passes, it doesn't exactly qualify him as a strong leader. Jack was a heck of a nice guy and a pleasure to talk to — but I was beginning to wonder whether he really heard what you said to him. Telling him I had been open on pass patterns had been like talking to a door" (McConagha, "Inside Politics"). That questionable source still captured what political leaders later would say, namely, that Kemp would do what he wanted to do no matter what others, even presidents under whom they served, were saying.

Kemp has his flaws and his rough edges. But he is a smart man with leadership experience, knowledgeable about government and willing to work hard. It is too much to predict that he would make a great president, but he has the credentials to have made a good one.

KEMP BIBLIOGRAPHY

Anderson, Martin. *Revolution*. San Diego (1988).

Balz, Dan, and Ronald Brownstein. *Storming the Gates: Protest Politics and the Republican Revival*. Boston (1996).

Barnes, Fred. "Notes on Kemp." *The New Republic* (May 9, 1994), pp. 18–23.

Boeth, Richard, et al. "Starring for the GOP." *Newsweek* (February 20, 1978), pp. 31–32.

Dowd, Maureen. "Is Jack Kemp Mr. Right?" *The New York Times Magazine* (June 28, 1987), pp. 19–20, ff.

Drew, Elizabeth. *Election Journal: Political Events of 1987–1988*. New York (1989).

Fineman, Howard. "Kemp, New Ideas, Old Questions." *Newsweek* (December 2, 1985), p. 54.

Frantz, Douglas. "Army Allowed Kemp to Skip Army Call-up For an Injury." *New York Times* (August 18, 1996), sec. 1, p. 27.

Goldman, Peter, et al. *Quest for the Presidency: The 1988 Campaign*. New York (1989).

Gugliotta, Guy. "A Republican Who Makes Party Uneasy." *Washington Post* (August 11, 1996), pp. A1, A18.

Hallow, Ralph Z. "Many Republicans See No Defense for Kemp's Lack of Offense." *Washington Times* (October 11, 1996), p. A1.

"Jack the Swamp Fighter." *The Economist* (September 30, 1989), p. 21–22.

"Just the Job for Jack Kemp." *The Economist* (April 8, 1995), p. 32.

Kemp, Jack. *The American Idea: Ending Limits to Growth*. Washington (1984).

_____. *An American Renaissance: A Strategy for the 1980s*. Washington (1979).

Kunen, James S. "Sure, He'd Rather Be President, but Conservative Jack Kemp May Be the Right-Man on the Right for HUD." *People* (June 18, 1990), pp. 53–58.

Langley, Monica. "Kemp Is Still the Positive-Thinking Quarterback Who Believes Optimism Is the Mother of Victory." *The Wall Street Journal* (October 13, 1987), p. 72.

McConagha, Alan. "Inside Politics: Playing with Jack." *Washington Times* (October 14, 1996), p. A7.

Murray, Frank J. "Spot on Presidential Ticket Eluded Kemp for 16 Years." *Washington Times* (August 11, 1996), p. A4.

Pierce, Greg. "Inside Politics: Kemp and Powell." *Washington Times* (January 24, 1997), p. A5.

_____. "Inside Politics: Mack, Not Kemp." *Washington Times* (April 23, 1997), p. A5.

Quayle, Dan. *Standing Firm*. New York (1994).

Roberts, Paul Craig. *The Supply-Side Revolution: An Insider's Account of Policymaking in Washington*. Cambridge, Mass. (1984).

Rollins, Ed, with Thomas DeFrank. *Bare Knuckles and Back Rooms*. New York (1996).

Rosenbaum, David E. "A Passion for Ideas: Jack French Kemp." *Washington Post* (August 11, 1996), Sec. 1, p. 1.

Stockman, David. *The Triumph of Politics: Why the Reagan Revolution Failed*. New York (1986).

Traub, James. "Jack Kemp Faces Reality." *New York Times Magazine* (May 7, 1989), pp. 38–39ff.

Ullmann, Owen. *Stockman: The Man, the Myth, the Future*. New York (1986).

Weisskopf, Michael. "In 'Wilderness,' Kemp Mined Lode Via Speeches, Directorships." *Washington Post* (August 23, 1996), p. A14.

Wetzstein, Cheryl. "Joanne Kemp a 'Family First' Wife Accustomed to Political Spotlight." *Washington Times* (August 14, 1996), p. A10.

Some family information provided by Jack Kemp.

1996 president nominee —
Reform Party

Ross Perot

The biographical sketch on Perot appears on pages 761–768, as he was defeated for the presidency in 1992.

State represented: Texas.

Birth: June 27, 1930, in Texarkana, Texas.

Age on Inauguration Day (January 20, 1997): 66 years, 7 months.

1996 vice presidential nominee —
Reform Party

Pat Choate

Born April 27, 1941, in Maypearl, Texas. Married Diane Camille Tate in 1968, divorced in 1994; they had no children; married Kay Wooden Casey in 1994.

Pat Choate was one of two sons of Franklin William and Betty Lee (Simpson) Choate. His brother Mark was killed by a drunk driver in 1962. Pat grew up on a cotton farm outside Maypearl (named for the wives of two railroad engineers) about 40 miles south of Dallas. His father started as a sharecropper, and eventually owned his own farm. The family was described as "just good, old country people; solid citizens." There was no electricity at his house until 1948, and the Choates rarely went into town except when it was time to gin the cotton. After going to local schools, Pat attended Arlington State College on a ROTC scholarship, graduating in 1963 with a degree in economics and also receiving his Army commission. While in graduate school Choate developed adult diabetes, however, and was medically discharged into the Reserves in 1965.

Oklahoma's first Republican governor, Henry Bellmon, enticed Choate in November 1965 to work in his administration as an economic planner. While there he earned a doctorate in economics from the University of Oklahoma. Next he was a regional administrator for the Economic Development Administration (E.D.A.) of the U.S. Department of Commerce. From May 1973 to January 1975, Choate was head of Tennessee's Department of Economic and Community Development. In 1975 Choate went back to E.D.A. in the office of Economic Research in Washington. Choate said it was "like falling into a pot of gin," at least for someone with Choate's tastes. He had an $11 million budget and a staff of nine econ-

PAT CHOATE (left) and ROSS PEROT
(AP Photo/Ron Heflin)

omists. A reorganization did not justify the pot of gin and the positions were terminated.

Choate has written six books. His first, co-authored with Susan Walter in 1981, was called *America in Ruins*. It brought attention to the substantial investment needed in American infrastructure. His became well-known in the 1980s in public policy circles, as he focused on the travails of American business, and especially its competitiveness in the world economy. He has been non-partisan, writing speeches for Democrats and Republicans on economic issues. His ideas have been incorporated into campaigns and congressional bills. He has been especially interested in job-retraining as a result of the loss of old industrial jobs. Choate has had considerable success in seeing his ideas become the center of debate. Choate describes himself with the word "'policy.' That's what my career is about."

From 1981 until 1990 Choate worked for TRW, an Ohio-based conglomerate. While there he wrote his most controversial book, *Agents of Influence*, published in 1990. That book has been called both insightful and a "kind of 'McCarthyism,'" as it denounces the heavy investment Japan is making in American lobbyists — the "agents of influence." He feared this country becoming "a Japanese economic colony." The simplistic shorthand some used for Choate's book was "Japan-bashing." He lost his $150,000-per-year job with TRW. The company had sales of $400 million in Japan, a country where leaders were outraged at Choate's allegations of influence buying. Choate sued TRW. The case was dismissed in the trial court, but Choate appealed. Choate took some freelance jobs and kept up his contacts on Capitol Hill. He later was chairman of a populist radio network, United Broadcasting Network, and a frequent guest on talk radio shows.

Agents of Influence was a bestseller, and the subject of two segments on the CBS television network's "60 Minutes" program. The book also brought him to Perot's attention. Choate was Perot's tutor on foreign trade issues in the 1992 campaign, and his coach for the 1993 NAFTA debate with Vice President Gore. Choate's choice as Perot's running mate was announced at the end of a taped 30-minute "infomercial" broadcast on September 10. Calling Choate a person of "intellect, courage, and grit," Perot said, "Thomas Jefferson must be looking down from heaven and smiling at you tonight." One news report suggested a different reaction from Jefferson: "Pat Who?" Within a week Choate had to defend himself against charges made in his ex-wife's 1994 divorce papers—that he had been guilty of adultery with the woman who would soon become his second wife. It was an increasingly typical welcome to a national political campaign. His first wife, a psychotherapist, had left the couple's Washington home in 1988 "to study Jungian psychoanalysis" in Switzerland. She was gone for years. Choate denied the adultery and claimed on September 19 that the allegations were just to extract a better divorce settlement. After the divorce he married Kay Casey, a childhood friend.

Following the 1996 election, Choate continued his work as an author and economist. He became director of a Washington institute named the Manufacturing Policy Project. Choate also hosted a daily radio program, "The Pat Choate Show," carried on Talk America Network.

CHOATE BIBLIOGRAPHY

Bachman, Justin. "Perot's Running Mate has Kept a Low Profile in His Own Hometown." *Fort Worth Star-Telegram* (Sept. 11, 1996).

Baker, Donald P. "After Admonishing His Mother, Choate Begins Run." *Washington Post* (September 12, 1996), p. A12.

Corrigan, Richard. "On Industrial Policy Front, TRW's Pat Choate Lobs Ideas to Politicians." *National Journal* (October 15, 1983), p. 2102.

DiGeorge, Gail. "For Pat Choate, Talk Radio Turns to Static." *Business Week* (November 4, 1996), p. 50.

Fisher, Marc. The Economy-class Candidate." *Washington Post* (September 26, 1996), p. C1.

Grove, Lloyd. "Trade Warriors: Author Pat Choate, Teaching Perot the Ropes of Opposition Strategy." *Washington Post* (November 15, 1993), p. B1.

"Perot Picks Running Mate: Anti-Free Trader Pat Choate." (Memphis) *Commercial-Appeal* (September 11, 1996), p. 2A.

Perot, Ross, and Pat Choate. *Save Your Job, Save Our Country: Why NAFTA Must be Stopped—Now!* New York (1993).

Pierce, Greg. "Inside Politics: Talk-show Guy." *Washington Times* (September 12, 1996), p. A6.

Rothenberg, Randall. "The Idea Merchant." *New York Times* (May 3, 1987), Section 6, p. 36.

Sciolino, Elaine. "Washington at Work: Amiable Idea Merchant Who Is Viewed as the Most-Feared Japan-Basher." *New York Times* (February 8, 1990), p. A24.

Stokes, Bruce. "Pat Choate: A Skillful Packager for the Ideas Bazaar." *National Journal* (February 14, 1987).

Family and other information provided by Pat Choate.

Summary of Evaluations

What should a party seek in an individual it nominates for president or vice president? How well in the 53 elections in the country's history have the losing candidates met these requirements? These are the extremely subjective questions which the evaluations that have been given along with each candidate's biographical sketch have attempted to answer. Those answers will be explained and categorized here.

First, a few words about what these evaluations are not. It is at times nearly impossible to separate ideology from capacity for the presidency. A candidate's views on issues have nonetheless largely been ignored in the rating scheme in this study. The "liberal" principles of George McGovern, the "conservative" viewpoint of Barry Goldwater, the "Copperhead" philosophy of George H. Pendleton and Allen G. Thurman, and other such examples of what a majority of a candidate's contemporaries considered to be extremism cannot totally be disregarded. Yet political positions of candidates are subordinated here to the other criteria that will be discussed. It is not the primary intent to judge a nominee's political views, but instead his likely effectiveness in implementing those views.

Secondly, there have been many surprise performances, both pleasant and unpleasant, among the men who have been elected. "Might-have-been" forecasting is not a science. This review carries with it the asasumption that parties should try to reduce risks when they select candidates for high office. They should avoid untried or discredited politicians.

Finally, political factors are discarded here, while at national conventions they are paramount. Therefore a candidate whose selection answered every geographical, philosophical or other criterion, but whose background reveals serious flaws in his capacity for serving as president, will be regarded negatively.

President rating has been a frequent pasttime for historians. The personal prejudices and political viewpoints of the individuals making any evaluation heavily impact on the result. Yet, allowing for that, a few general observations can be made about the attempts to rank the presidents which are helpful in reaching conclusions about the also-rans. The four highest regarded presidents in one of the most recent rankings — Lincoln, Washington, and both Roosevelts — were, except for Teddy Roosevelt, leaders during times of great crisis, either war or, in Washington's case, the very foundation of a nation and a system of government. It is suggestive that the presidencies during the three most devastating wars in which America has participated have been rated as "great," and no president who served during any American war until Vietnam has been rated lower than "average." Such coincidence suggests the considerable influence of events in the presidential rankings. A president during times of domestic and international calm, as in the case of Dwight Eisenhower, may have difficulty receiving the respect of historians or even of his contemporaries. Greatness has, perhaps too narrowly, been equated with strength.

The "near greats" seem to be men of achievement who served during times that did not reach crisis proportions. Teddy Roosevelt was in this category for several rounds of historian evaluations, but lately has moved up. They were men with strong wills and a clear sense of direction in their administrations.

The "average" category should be viewed merely as that grouping of presidents who were not considered to be touched with greatness, but whose administrations were not negative or counterproductive. They are a hodgepodge of those who merited neither great praise nor severe condemnation.

The "below average" consist mainly of those who permitted the country to drift. It is heavily populated with pre–Civil War presidents who failed to stem the tide of sectional division. All the presidents between James K. Polk and Abraham Lincoln are ranked here, as is Polk's predecessor, John Tyler. The only president in this category who did not serve in the 20 years preceding the Civil War was Calvin Coolidge, whose "Silent Cal" image earned him the same criticism of being a figurehead, do-nothing chief executive.

"Failures" include the scandal-plagued presidents. To some extent this is unfair, as recent revelations about a long line of presidents have shown that the same misdeeds that when publicized can wreck one president's administration, have merely been more successfully hidden in other, far more highly regarded presidencies. Yet it cannot be denied, even if equity seems lacking, that a president whose credibility and influence is completely destroyed because he has to fight a series of scandals, is far less effective than a president who is equally sinful but can devote himself to governmental matters. Thus perhaps the rankings should be considered judgments on administrations, not individuals. In the case of Grant or Harding, though, there is far more than just dishonor that has caused their leadership to be disparaged so severely. They are considered failures because they seemed totally lacking in ability. Grant did not seem to understand government, and Harding did not care.

The literature on presidential rankings acknowledges the inherent subjectivity: presidential reputations are affected by historical circumstances, by the political biases of the evaluator, the kinds of standards (if any) applied, the scandals exposed — or not — and other factors. Evaluations of the possible political greatness of losers are even more hazardous. In the analysis here, historical circumstances have had their impact. For example, internationalism and not isolationism was viewed as indispensable in a 1940 nominee. There were other similar exceptions, mandated by exceptional circumstances. The overall desire, though, is to avoid political and philosophical biases. The rating is not of a defeated nominee's goals, but rather his capacity to achieve them. Only when the goals seem blatantly inappropriate or demonstrably desirable did they impact on the evaluation. Within broad parameters, representatives of every political philosophy start even. The factors listed below can be difficult to measure; giving each appropriate weight in the overall analysis further complicates the effort. Still, any study of the also-rans seems incomplete without evaluating what might have been.

A candidate's previous governmental record can be most instructive. Taking an individual from a minor political office or short tenure in a major one, and thrusting him into the nation's highest executive office is risky to say the least. Besides mere length or variety of service, also to be considered is what an individual has done in that previous service. Warren G. Harding had been a U.S. senator and Ohio lieutenant governor, but clearly was a time-server with no interest in government. Abraham Lincoln was mainly a loser in his political races; his highest political office prior to the presidency was in Congress. Whether Abe Lincoln was "prepared" for the presidency is a matter that can seriously, if fruitlessly, be disputed, but the fact that he rose above any deficiencies is evident. Experience in government is obviously a consideration in whether an individual should be nominated, but equally apparent is that it cannot be the only factor. What it permits is a judgment by voters of whether the candidate has ably managed his responsibilities.

Experience can be meaningful even if it is not in public office. A president is both an executive who can make and implement decisions, and a partner in a three branch government. Several of the also-rans and running mates had been businessmen with little governmental service. Their background is not automatically discredited, but instead the similarity of talents needed in whatever capacity they performed as private citizens to those demanded of a president is considered. Success in any kind of background is regarded as suggestive of performance in the presidency. Did the candidate have a widely acclaimed record as governor of a state; was he a leading figure in building or maintaining a dynamic, profitable business? What negatives can be seen in his performance in the other positions?

Personality should also be considered. Someone of strong but not unbending will, someone with principles but not an ideologue, would seem best able to perform in the compromise spirit that working with Congress requires. A confrontational government is rarely a successful one. Though both John Adams and Andrew Jackson are considered quality presidents, their leadership was made more difficult by self-righteous or vindictive behavior. Andrew Johnson should probably be considered a failure, not because he failed to defend the Constitution, for he did try, but because his stubbornness and lack of political finesse made him ineffective, almost irrelevant to government, and caused his impeachment.

Political skills are related to personality, for they help predict whether a president will control or instead be controlled — will he make a difference or be a figurehead?

Intelligence most certainly is a desirable attribute in any leadership capacity. Genius has never been a requirement, but instead a common sense understanding of what can and cannot be accomplished is the significant skill. Lincoln, Washington, and the other great presidents had that common sense; those at the other end of the rating spectrum did not.

Character cannot be ignored in considering presidential capacity. The moral strength of a candidate, his concern for others or only for political or personal gain, have been factored into these assessments. No candidate has risen to the status of being nominated for national office without at least a modicum of ambition (though Horatio Seymour may be the exception that qualifies the rule), but did that ambition or a drive for money or power become the principal concern? A candidate's religious conviction — his appreciation of a power far greater than his own, his sense that his life has a mission — doubtless affects political leadership. Measurement of that criterion is too prone to error, however, to be of much benefit here. Finally, and basically, character is a measure of honesty and integrity.

Background experience, personality, political skills, intelligence, and character, these are the almost self-evident criteria used to assess the also-rans and their ticket-mates. As self-evident as they may be, they are issues that are too often ignored by parties. The factors are applied here in a free-floating, variously emphasized fashion depending on the individual candidate and the historical circumstances in which he was nominated. This assessment scheme focuses on probabilities. It is considered more likely that an individual will serve as an effective president if he meets these standards than if he does not. Too often a national party has asked the country to roll the dice and vote for its nominee even though he has not previously indicated much capacity for leadership. On occasion the gamble has succeeded. On occasion, had the electoral dice been a little more favorable to some of these losers, some of them would have been more capable presidents than this assessment suggests. The unprovable, modest thesis of the analysis is that on balance far more of the higher ranked also-rans and running mates would have made good presidents, and a higher proportion of the lower ranked ones bad leaders, than those in the opposite category.

The categories used are fairly self-explanatory. A "superior" candidate revealed in his career more than mere adequacy, but through excellence in one or more important ways suggested he had the potential for greatness. At the dreary end of the scale, the "probable failures" are those who were considered unlikely to have been able to serve admirably as chief executive. Some of these no doubt would have made good presidents, but on balance each probable failure had one or more strongly negative characteristics.

The satisfactory nominees are those who demonstrated competence but not brilliance, who were men of sufficient ability to have managed the presidency credibly, but without any indication they would have been superior leaders. The "above average" and the "unsatisfactory" are those who rise above or fall below mere average ranking, but do not seem deserving of the extreme categories.

The obvious focus of these evaluations has not been on what a nominee said he would do if elected, on what his positions were on critical issues, or on where he stood on the liberal-conservative spectrum, but instead on who he was. What a nominee says he believes, and what circumstances might have convinced him to do as president, can often be quite different. That is part of the reason that political philosophy has not been factored in here. Equally important, such considerations would have raised the subjectivity of the evaluations to a fundamentally different level. The historical norm of having two political parties with separate, identifiable philosophies, even if imperfectly so, could not have been maintained if one approach to government is always clearly appropriate and any other definitely wrong. Judging a president is, to this extent, easier. The merits of a president's views on issues as put into practice in office can be measured. Such evidence is one of the luxuries afforded when judging the victors, as opposed to the vanquished. A rather liberal Tom Eagleton in 1972 and a markedly conservative Bob Dole in 1976 are both considered here to be acceptable nominees, even though the nation's difficulties had not appreciably changed in the four years between their nominations.

It is for each reader, should he accept both the standards and their application here, then himself to add the extra criterion of political philosophy and make, if desired, a more complete but more personal judgment.

Presented here are the rankings. First are the also-rans, followed by a separate ranking of the running mates. Finally are polls showing historians' opinions of our presidents. The losers can be compared to the winners. Perhaps equally significant, the changing views of historians even of successful presidential nominees can be better appreciated.

BIBLIOGRAPHY

Amlund, Curtis A. "President-Ranking: A Criticism." *American Journal of Political Science* VIII (1964), pp. 309–15.

Bailey, Thomas A. *Presidential Greatness.* New York City (1966).

Barber, James David. *The Presidential Character: Predicting Performance in the White House.* Englewood Cliffs, N.J. (1977).

Kynerd, Tom. "An Analysis of Presidential Greatness and 'President Rating.'" *Southern Quarterly* IX (1971), pp. 309–29.

Maranell, Gary M. "The Evaluation of Presidents: An Extension of the Schlesinger Polls." *Journal of American History* LVII (1970), pp. 104–113.

Murray, Robert K. *Greatness in the White House: Rating the Presidents*, 2d ed. University Park, Penn. (1997).

Ridings, William J., and Stuart B. McIver. *Rating the Presidents: A Ranking of U.S. Leaders.* Secaucus, N.J. (1997).

Rossiter, Clinton. *The American Presidency.* New York City (1960).

Schlesinger, Arthur M. *Paths to the Present.* New York City (1949).

Prospects for Success as President: The Also-Rans

Superior

1. Charles Evans Hughes (lost to Wilson)
2. Stephen A. Douglas (Lincoln)
3. Henry Clay (J.Q. Adams, Jackson, Polk)

Above Average

4. DeWitt Clinton (Madison)
5. Wendell Willkie (FDR)
6. William Lowndes (J.Q. Adams)
7. Adlai E. Stevenson (Eisenhower)
8. Alton B. Parker (T. Roosevelt)
9. James M. Cox (Harding)
10. Daniel Webster (Van Buren)
11. Alfred E. Smith (Hoover)
12. Thomas E. Dewey (FDR, Truman)

Satisfactory

13. Winfield Scott Hancock (Garfield)

14. William H. Crawford (J.Q. Adams)
15. Hubert H. Humphrey (Nixon)
16. Hugh L. White (Van Buren)
17. John W. Davis (Coolidge)
18. Charles C. Pinckney (Jefferson, Madison)
19. Herschell V. Johnson* (Lincoln)
20. Alfred M. Landon (FDR)
21. John C. Calhoun (J.Q. Adams)
22. Horatio Seymour (Grant)
23. Walter F. Mondale (Reagan)
24. Benjamin Fitzpatrick* (Lincoln)
25. James G. Blaine (Cleveland)
26. Samuel J. Tilden (Hayes)
27. Robert Dole (Clinton)
28. Rufus King (Monroe)
29. Lewis Cass (Taylor)
30. Winfield Scott (Pierce)
31. B. Gratz Brown (Grant)
32. Michael Dukakis (Bush)

Unsatisfactory

33. Barry M. Goldwater (LBJ)
34. John Bell (Lincoln)
35. Ross Perot (Clinton)
36. Charles L. McNary (FDR)
37. Robert M. La Follette (Coolidge)
38. John McLean (Van Buren)
39. George S. McGovern (Nixon)
40. George B. McClellan (Lincoln)
41. John C. Breckinridge (Lincoln)
42. Burton K. Wheeler* (Coolidge)
43. John Charles Frémont (Buchanan)

Probable Failure

44. George C. Wallace (Nixon)
45. William Jennings Bryan (McKinley, Taft)
46. Horace Greeley (Grant)

*H.V. Johnson, Fitzpatrick and Wheeler are the vice presidential running mates of presidential candidates who died prior to the end of the term they would have been serving had they been elected. In one case both candidates died before the end of the term — Wendell Willkie and Charles L. McNary.

Prospects for Success as President: The Running Mates

Vice presidential nominees have frequently been obscure politicians whose abilities are difficult to measure decades or even a century or more later. Consequently, this ranking contains broader categories than for the presidential losers, and the names within each category are in chronological order, by election.

Superior

Thomas Pinckney
Albert Gallatin
Earl Warren
Henry Cabot Lodge
Lloyd Bentsen

Satisfactory

Richard Rush
John Sergeant
Francis Granger
Theodore Frelinghuysen
Charles Francis Adams
William A. Graham
William L. Dayton
Benjamin Fitzpatrick
Herschell V. Johnson
George H. Pendleton
B. Gratz Brown

Henry G. Davis
John W. Kern
Hiram W. Johnson
Nicholas M. Butler
Frank Lowden
Joseph T. Robinson
Frank Knox
John Sparkman
Estes Kefauver
Edmund Muskie
Thomas Eagleton
Jack Kemp

Unsatisfactory or Uncertain

John Langdon
Jared Ingersoll
John E. Howard
Nathan Sanford
Nathaniel Macon

Philip P. Barbour
Silas Wright
William O. Butler
Andrew J. Donelson
Edward Everett
Joseph Lane
Frank Blair
William H. English
John A. Logan
Allen G. Thurman
Whitelaw Reid
Arthur Sewall
Burton K. Wheeler
Charles W. Bryan
Charles L. McNary
John W. Bricker
William E. Miller
Curtis LeMay
Sargent Shriver

The Presidents Ranked (1948)

A poll conducted by Arthur M. Schlesinger of 55 historians, published in Life *magazine on November 1, 1948.*

Great

1. Abraham Lincoln
2. George Washington
3. Franklin D. Roosevelt
4. Woodrow Wilson
5. Thomas Jefferson
6. Andrew Jackson

Near Great

7. Theodore Roosevelt
8. Grover Cleveland
9. John Adams
10. James K. Polk

Average

11. John Quincy Adams
12. James Monroe
13. Rutherford B. Hayes
14. James Madison
15. Martin Van Buren
16. William Howard Taft
17. Chester A. Arthur
18. William McKinley
19. Andrew Johnson
20. Herbert Hoover
21. Benjamin Harrison

Below Average

22. John Tyler
23. Calvin Coolidge
24. Millard Fillmore
25. Zachary Taylor
26. James Buchanan
27. Franklin Pierce

Failure

28. Ulysses Grant
29. Warren G. Harding

The Presidents Ranked (1962)

A poll conducted by Arthur M. Schlesinger, in which 75 historians rated the presidents, published in the New York Times Magazine, *July 29, 1962.*

Great

1. Abraham Lincoln
2. George Washington
3. Franklin D. Roosevelt
4. Woodrow Wilson
5. Thomas Jefferson

Near Great

6. Andrew Jackson
7. Theodore Roosevelt
8. James K. Polk
9. Harry Truman
10. John Adams
11. Grover Cleveland

Average

12. James Madison
13. John Quincy Adams
14. Rutherford B. Hayes
15. William McKinley
16. William Howard Taft
17. Martin Van Buren
18. James Monroe
19. Herbert Hoover
20. Benjamin Harrison
21. Chester Arthur
22. Dwight D. Eisenhower
23. Andrew Johnson

Below Average

24. Zachary Taylor
25. John Tyler
26. Millard Fillmore
27. Calvin Coolidge
28. Franklin Pierce
29. James Buchanan

Failure

30. Ulysses Grant
31. Warren G. Harding

The Presidents Ranked (1982)

A poll of 49 historians, conducted by the Chicago Tribune *and published in the* Chicago Tribune Magazine, *January 10, 1982. (No categories were used, but the presidents were merely ranked.)*

1. Abraham Lincoln
2. Franklin D. Roosevelt
3. George Washington
4. Theodore Roosevelt
5. Thomas Jefferson
6. Andrew Jackson
7. Woodrow Wilson
8. Harry Truman
9. Dwight Eisenhower
10. William McKinley
11. James Polk
12. Lyndon Johnson
13. Grover Cleveland
14. John Kennedy (tie)
14. John Adams (tie)
16. James Monroe
17. James Madison
18. Martin Van Buren
19. John Quincy Adams
20. William Taft
21. Herbert Hoover
22. Rutherford Hayes
23. Gerald Ford
24. Chester Arthur
25. Benjamin Harrison
26. Jimmy Carter
27. Calvin Coolidge
28. Zachary Taylor
29. John Tyler
30. Ulysses Grant
31. Millard Fillmore
32. Andrew Johnson
33. James Garfield
34. Richard Nixon
35. Franklin Pierce
36. James Buchanan
37. Warren Harding
38. William Harrison

The Presidents Ranked (1983)

A poll of 846 historians conducted by Robert K. Murray of Pennsylvania State University, published in the Journal of American History, *vol. 70 (December 1983), pp. 535–55.*

Great

1. Abraham Lincoln
2. Franklin D. Roosevelt
3. George Washington
4. Thomas Jefferson

Near Great

5. Theodore Roosevelt
6. Woodrow Wilson
7. Andrew Jackson
8. Harry S Truman

Above Average

9. John Adams
10. Lyndon B. Johnson
11. Dwight D. Eisenhower

12. James K. Polk
13. John F. Kennedy
14. James Madison
15. James Monroe
16. John Quincy Adams
17. Grover Cleveland

Average

18. William McKinley
19. William Howard Taft
20. Martin Van Buren
21. Herbert Hoover
22. Rutherford B. Hayes
23. Chester A. Arthur
24. Gerald Ford
25. Jimmy Carter
26. Benjamin Harrison

Below Average

27. Zachary Taylor
28. John Tyler
29. Millard Fillmore
30. Calvin Coolidge
31. Franklin Pierce

Failure

32. Andrew Johnson
33. James Buchanan
34. Richard Nixon
35. Ulysses S. Grant
36. Warren G. Harding

The Presidents Ranked (1995)

This poll is the latest of an ongoing survey by the Siena Research Institute, Loudonville, New York. This institute at Siena College has conducted surveys of historians in 1982, 1990, and 1995. Instead of showing all three polls, some interesting differences between the three polls will be highlighted prior to listing the 1995 ratings.

The same five presidents have remained on top—Franklin D. Roosevelt, Lincoln, Jefferson, Washington, and Theodore Roosevelt—but all except FDR have changed relative positions. The bottom five presidents—Pierce, Grant, Buchanan, Andrew Johnson, and Harding—have stayed in the same order in all three polls.

The improvement of Richard Nixon's historical reputation is steady if gradual. Far from the third-worst president ranking he received in the 1983 Murray poll (see above), the Siena College survey had him ranked 28th in 1982, 25th in 1990, and 23rd in 1995.

Jimmy Carter started at 33rd position in 1982, climbed to 24th in 1990, but essentially held his own at 25th in 1995 when the newest president came in ahead of him.

George Bush was ranked 18th in 1990, but only 31st in 1995.

Bill Clinton's first rating is at 16th position in the 1995 poll, better than President Reagan's 20th spot, and 15 places better than President Bush's. Interesting.

The one-month president, William Henry Harrison, has not been ranked in polls other than Siena's. Those surveyed by Siena College do not seem to know quite what to make of him, as he started in 26th position in 1982, went to 35th in 1990, and returned to 28th in 1995.

1995 Siena College Poll of 168 Historians

1. Franklin D. Roosevelt
2. Abraham Lincoln
3. Theodore Roosevelt
4. George Washington
5. Thomas Jefferson
6. Woodrow Wilson
7. Harry S Truman
8. Dwight D. Eisenhower
9. James Madison
10. John F. Kennedy
11. Andrew Jackson
12. John Adams
13. Lyndon B. Johnson
14. James K. Polk
15. James Monroe
16. Bill Clinton
17. John Quincy Adams
18. William McKinley
19. Grover Cleveland
20. Ronald Reagan
21. William Howard Taft
22. Martin Van Buren
23. Richard Nixon
24. Rutherford B. Hayes
25. Jimmy Carter
26. Chester Arthur
27. James Garfield
28. William Henry Harrison
29. Herbert Hoover
30. Benjamin Harrison
31. George Bush
32. Gerald Ford
33. Zachary Taylor
34. John Tyler
35. Millard Fillmore
36. Calvin Coolidge
37. Franklin Pierce
38. Ulysses S. Grant
39. James Buchanan
40. Andrew Johnson
41. Warren G. Harding

1997 McDougall Ranking

Rating by Professor Walter A. McDougall, University of Pennsylvania, 1986 Pulitzer Prize Winner, printed in "Rating the Presidents," National Review (October 27, 1997), pp. 32–36.

His three-part test is (1) Did the president have political success by being widely supported by the people during his administration; (2) did the president deal with the nation's pressing issues and gain general approval; and (3) did the president in retrospect actually promote the best interests of the nation? The presidents are listed within each category in chronological order of their presidencies.

Great

George Washington
Thomas Jefferson
Abraham Lincoln
Theodore Roosevelt
Franklin D. Roosevelt
Dwight D. Eisenhower
Ronald Reagan

Near Great

James Monroe
Andrew Jackson
James K. Polk
Grover Cleveland
Richard M. Nixon*

Average

Calvin Coolidge

Below Average

John Adams
John Quincy Adams
Martin Van Buren
Millard Fillmore
Franklin Pierce
Rutherford B. Hayes
Chester A. Arthur
Benjamin Harrison
William McKinley
William Howard Taft
Warren G. Harding
Harry S Truman
John F. Kennedy
Gerald R. Ford
George Bush
Bill Clinton (tentative)

Failure

James Madison
William Henry Harrison
John Tyler
Zachary Taylor
James Buchanan
Andrew Johnson
Ulysses Grant
James A. Garfield
Woodrow Wilson
Herbert Hoover
Lyndon B. Johnson
Richard M. Nixon*
Jimmy Carter

Richard Nixon is considered to have such a mixed record that he is listed in both the Near Great and the Failure category.

General Bibliography

Each candidate's biographical sketch is followed by a bibliography of the works examined for that nominee. In some cases items are listed that were not actually consulted, but this was done with the intention of presenting as comprehensive a bibliography as possible on the obscure candidates. Where there was no dearth of authorities on a nominee, the bibliographies merely list those works of principal importance.

Not included in the individual bibliographies, however, are those biographical dictionaries, encyclopedias, and other comprehensive sources which contained information about a substantial number of the candidates. These materials are listed in the first section following this bibliographical note.

Certain information about the conventions and the elections themselves was needed, both to prepare the sketches and to write the election summaries. The sources for that information are listed under the second section in the bibliography that follows. Specific elections had at times to be researched fairly exhaustively. There are books and articles available covering almost every individual election, but such authorities were sought out mainly just for those elections in which special care was needed to determine which candidates had been named by state and at times even local nominating meetings. Philip Barbour, for example, has Sister Mary Bartus to thank for his inclusion here as a losing running mate in the 1836 election, as only her work noted that he was nominated by a legislative caucus. Other names surfaced or were discarded depending on what

such investigations uncovered. After 1840, fortunately, there were national nominations by the major parties that greatly limited the candidates under consideration.

Biographical Works

Biographical Directory of the American Congress, 1774–1971. Washington, D.C. (1971).

Current Biography, Maxine Block, et al., eds. New York City (1940–1982).

Dictionary of American Biography. Allen Johnson and Dumas Malone, et al., eds. New York City, 20 volumes and 7 supplements (1943–1981).

Hatch, Louis Clinton, revised and edited by Earl Shoup. *A History of the Vice Presidency of the United States.* Westport, Conn. (1970), reprint of 1934 edition.

Havel, James T. *U.S. Presidential Candidates and the Elections: A Biographical and Historical Guide.* New York (1996).

Kane, Joseph Nathan. *Facts About the Presidents.* New York City (1974).

National Cyclopedia of American Biography, Ainsworth R. Spifford, et al., eds. 61 volumes, New York City and Clifton, N.Y. (1898–1982).

Paul, Karen Dawley. *Guide to Research Collections of Former United States Senators, 1789–1994.* Washington, D.C. (1995).

Political Profiles: The Truman Years. Eleanora Schoenebaum, ed. New York City (1976); The *Eisenhower Years,* Eleanora Schoenebaum, ed. New York City (1977); *The Kennedy Years,* Nelson Lichtenstein, ed. New York City (1976); *The Johnson Years,* Nelson Lichtenstein, ed. New York City (1976); The *Nixon/Ford Years,* Eleanora Schoenebaum, ed. New York City (1979).

Quatannens, Jo Anne McCormick. *Senators of the United States: A Historical Bibliography, a*

Compilation of Works About the Members of the United States Senate, 1789–1995. Washington, D.C. (1995).

Resnick, Mike, ed. *Alternate Presidents*. New York (1992) (short stories by science fiction writers on 28 presidencies that never were: "from Benjamin Franklin to Michael Dukakis").

Stone, Irving. *They Also Ran*. Garden City, N.Y. (1944).

Taylor, Tim. *The Book of Presidents*. New York City (1972).

Electoral Works

Bain, Richard C., and Judith H. Parris. *Convention Decisions and Voting Records*. Washington, D.C. (1973).

Bartus, Mary R. "The Presidential Election of 1836." Unpublished doctoral dissertation, Fordham University (1967).

Brown, E.S. "The Presidential Election of 1824–1825." *Political Science Quarterly* XL (1925), pp. 384–403.

Chase, James S. *Emergence of the Presidential Nominating Convention, 1789–1832*. Urbana, et al. (1973).

Congressional Quarterly. *Guide to U.S. Elections*. Washington, D.C. (1975).

_____. *National Party Conventions, 1831–1972*. Washington, D.C. (1976).

Gage, Elwyn Collins. "National Election of 1824." Unpublished doctoral dissertation, Harvard University (1924).

Gunderson, Robert Cray. *The Log-Cabin Campaign*. Lexington, Ky. (1957).

Livermore, Shaw. *The Twilight of Federalism*. Princeton (1962).

Morgan, William Graham. "The Congressional Nominating Caucus of 1816." *Virginia Magazine of History and Biography* 80 (1972), pp. 461–475.

_____. "The Decline of the National Nominating Caucus," *Tennessee Historical Quarterly* XXIV (1965), pp. 245–255.

_____. "The Origin and Development of the Congressional Nominating Caucus." *Proceedings of the American Philosophical Society* CXIII (1969), pp. 184–196.

_____. "Presidential Nominations in the Federal Era, 1788–1828." Unpublished doctoral dissertation, University of Southern California (1969).

Roseboom, Eugene H. *A History of Presidential Elections*. New York City (1964).

Schlesinger, Arthur M., ed. *A History of American Presidential Elections*. 4 vols. New York City, et al. (1971).

Schlesinger, Arthur M., Jr., David Frent, and Fred L. Israel, eds. *Running for President: The Candidates and Their Images*. New York (1994).

Southwick, Leslie H. "Nominations of Presidential Candidates in the First American Party System: 1788–1824." Unpublished senior political science thesis, Rice University (1972).

Stanwood, Edward. *A History of the Presidency*. 2 vols. Boston and New York City (1928).

Wheaton, James O. "The Genius and the Jurist: A Study of the Presidential Campaign of 1904." Unpublished doctoral dissertation, Stanford University (1964).

Index

*Numbers in **boldface** refer to pages with photographs.*